Pearson Education Limited
Edinburgh Gate
Harlow
Essex CM20 2JE
England

and Associated Companies throughout the world

Visit us on the World Wide Web at:
www.pearson.com/uk

First published 2009
Second edition published 2012

ISBN: 978-0-273-74361-3

British Library Cataloguing-in-Publication Data
A catalogue record for this book is available from the British Library

Library of Congress Cataloging-in-Publication Data
Marketing management / Philip Kotler . . . [et al.]. – 2nd European ed.
     p. cm.
  Includes bibliographical references and index.
  ISBN 978-0-273-74361-3
  1. Marketing--Europe--Management. 2. Marketing--Management. I. Kotler, Philip.
  HF5415.13.M35224 2012
  658.8--dc23

                                                                2012003788

10 9 8 7 6 5 4 3 2 1
16 15 14 13 12

Typeset in 9.5/12 pt ITC Garamond by 73
Printed and bound by Rotolito Lombarda, Italy

Philip
Kotler
Kevin
Lane
Keller
Mairead
Brady
Malcolm
Goodman
Torben
Hansen

MARKETING MANAGEMENT

2nd edition

PEARSON

Harlow, England • London • New York • Boston • San Francisco • Toronto • Sydney
Auckland • Singapore • Hong Kong • Tokyo • Seoul • Taipei • New Delhi
Cape Town • São Paulo • Mexico City • Madrid • Amsterdam • Munich • Paris • Milan

106. 658. 8. 8

PEARSON

At Pearson, we take learning personally. Our courses and resources are available as books, online and via multi-lingual packages, helping people learn whatever, wherever and however they choose.

We work with leading authors to develop the strongest learning experiences, bringing cutting-edge thinking and best learning practice to a global market. We craft our print and digital resources to do more to help learners not only understand their content, but to see it in action and apply what they learn, whether studying or at work.

Pearson is the world's leading learning company. Our portfolio includes Penguin, Dorling Kindersley, the Financial Times and our educational business, Pearson International. We are also a leading provider of electronic learning programmes and of test development, processing and scoring services to educational institutions, corporations and professional bodies around the world.

Every day our work helps learning flourish, and wherever learning flourishes, so do people.

To learn more please visit us at: **www.pearson.com/uk**

MARKETING MANAGEMENT

Visit the Marketing Management, Second European Edition
Companion Website at

www.pearsoned.co.uk/marketingmanagementeurope

to find valuable student learning material including:

- Multiple choice questions to test your understanding
- A range of video case studies to contextualise your
  learning in the real world
- Links to extra international examples and case studies
- An online glossary to explain key terms
- Flashcards to help with your online revision

This book is dedicated to my wife and best friend, Nancy, with love. – PK

This book is dedicated to my wife, Punam, and my two daughters, Carolyn and Allison, with much love and thanks. – KLK

This book is dedicated to Martin and three great girls – Aine, Leah and Isabel – with all my love. – MB

This work is dedicated to my wife, Jill, my daughter Abigail, my son David and to the memory of my father. – MRVG

To Ulla and Emma. – TH

About the authors

Philip Kotler is one of the world's leading authorities on marketing. He is the S. C. Johnson & Son Distinguished Professor of International Marketing at the Kellogg School of Management, Northwestern University. He received his Master's degree at the University of Chicago and his PhD at MIT, both in economics. He did postdoctoral work in mathematics at Harvard University and in behavioural science at the University of Chicago.

Dr Kotler is the co-author of *Principles of Marketing* and *Marketing: An Introduction*. His *Strategic Marketing for Nonprofit Organizations*, now in its seventh edition, is the best seller in that specialised area. Dr Kotler's other books include *Marketing Models; The New Competition; Marketing Professional Services; Strategic Marketing for Educational Institutions; Marketing for Health Care Organizations; Marketing Congregations; High Visibility; Social Marketing; Marketing Places; The Marketing of Nations; Marketing for Hospitality and Tourism; Standing Room Only – Strategies for Marketing the Performing Arts; Museum Strategy and Marketing; Marketing Moves; Kotler on Marketing; Lateral Marketing: Ten Deadly Marketing Sins; and Corporate Social Responsibility.*

In addition, he has published more than one hundred articles in leading journals, including the *Harvard Business Review, Sloan Management Review, Business Horizons, California Management Review,* the *Journal of Marketing,* the *Journal of Marketing Research, Management Science,* the *Journal of Business Strategy* and *Futurist.* He is the only three-time winner of the coveted Alpha Kappa Psi award for the best annual article published in the *Journal of Marketing.*

Professor Kotler was the first recipient of the American Marketing Association's (AMA) Distinguished Marketing Educator Award (1985). The European Association of Marketing Consultants and Sales Trainers awarded him their Prize for Marketing Excellence. He was chosen as the Leader in Marketing Thought by the Academic Members of the AMA in a 1975 survey. He also received the 1978 Paul Converse Award of the AMA, honouring his original contribution to marketing. In 1995, the Sales and Marketing Executives International (SMEI) named him Marketer of the Year. In 2002, Professor Kotler received the Distinguished Educator Award from The Academy of Marketing Science. He has received honorary doctoral degrees from Stockholm University, the University of Zurich, Athens University of Economics and Business, DePaul University, the Cracow School of Business and Economics, Groupe H.E.C. in Paris, the Budapest School of Economic Science and Public Administration, and the University of Economics and Business Administration in Vienna.

Professor Kotler has been a consultant to many major US and foreign companies, including IBM, General Electric, AT&T, Honeywell, Bank of America, Merck, SAS Airlines, Michelin, and others in the areas of marketing strategy and planning, marketing organisation and international marketing. He has been Chairman of the College of Marketing of the Institute of Management Sciences, a Director of the American Marketing Association, a Trustee of the Marketing Science Institute, a Director of the MAC Group, a member of the Yankelovich Advisory Board and a member of the Copernicus Advisory Board. He was a member of the Board of Governors of the School of the Art Institute of Chicago and a member of the Advisory Board of the Drucker Foundation. He has travelled extensively throughout Europe, Asia and South America, advising and lecturing to many companies about global marketing opportunities.

Kevin Lane Keller is the E. B. Osborn Professor of Marketing at the Tuck School of Business at Dartmouth College. Professor Keller has degrees from Cornell, Carnegie-Mellon and Duke universities. At Dartmouth, he teaches MBA courses on marketing management and strategic brand management and lectures in executive programmes on those topics.

Previously, Professor Keller was on the faculty of the Graduate School of Business at Stanford University, where he also served as the head of the marketing group. Additionally, he has been on the marketing faculty at the University of California at Berkeley and the University of North Carolina at Chapel Hill, been a visiting professor at Duke University and the Australian Graduate School of Management, and has two years of industry experience as Marketing Consultant for Bank of America.

Professor Keller's general area of expertise lies in marketing strategy and planning, and branding. His specific research interest is in how understanding theories and concepts related to consumer behaviour can improve marketing strategies. His research has been published in three of the major marketing journals – the *Journal of Marketing*, the *Journal of Marketing Research* and the *Journal of Consumer Research*. He has also served on the Editorial Review Boards of those journals. With over 60 published papers, his research has been widely cited and has received numerous awards. Two of his articles, 'Consumer evaluations of brand extensions' and 'Conceptualizing, measuring, and managing customer-based brand equity' were named by INFORMS Society for Marketing Science in March 2007 on its list of the Top 20 marketing science papers written in the past 25 years that have most affected the practice of marketing science. Professor Keller is acknowledged as one of the international leaders in the study of brands, branding and strategic brand management. Actively involved with industry, he has worked on a host of different types of marketing projects. He has served as a consultant and adviser to marketers for some of the world's most successful brands, including Accenture, American Express, Disney, Ford, Intel, Levi Strauss, Procter & Gamble and SAB Miller. Additional brand consulting activities have been with other top companies such as Allstate, Beiersdorf (Nivea), BlueCross BlueShield, Campbell's, Eli Lilly, ExxonMobil, General Mills, Goodyear, Kodak, Mayo Clinic, Nordstrom, Shell Oil, Starbucks, Unilever and Young & Rubicam. He has also served as an academic trustee for the Marketing Science Institute. A popular speaker, he has conducted marketing seminars to top executives in a variety of forums.

Professor Keller is currently conducting a variety of studies that address strategies to build, measure and manage brand equity. His textbook on those subjects, *Strategic Brand Management*, has been adopted at top business schools and leading firms around the world and has been heralded as the 'bible of branding'.

An avid sports, music and film enthusiast, in his so-called 'spare time', he has served as executive producer for one of Australia's great rock and roll treasures, The Church, as well as American power-pop legends Dwight Twilley and Tommy Keene. He is also on the Board of Directors for The Doug Flutie, Jr Foundation for Autism. Professor Keller lives in Etna, New Hampshire with his wife, Punam (also a Tuck marketing professor), and his two daughters, Carolyn and Allison.

Mairead Brady is an assistant Professor of Marketing at the School of Business, Trinity College Dublin. She holds a PhD from the University of Strathclyde in Scotland, which she completed under the supervision of Professors Michael Saren and Professor Nikolaos Tzokas.

She lectures at undergraduate and Master levels and supervises PhD students. She also lectures to business practitioners, from executive to director level, through her work with the IMI (Irish Management Institute), Failte Ireland and Enterprise Ireland. She provides marketing expertise to innovators and entrepreneurs within universities in Ireland through her work with the Innovation Centre at Trinity College.

As a sought-after consultant, Dr Brady provides consulting and marketing advice to multinational blue-chip companies as well as small start-ups and Irish government agencies. Her clients range from large companies like Vodafone's Global Brand Academy to small start-ups supported by regional Enterprise Boards.

Dr Brady's research focuses on the assimilation and management of digital technologies into marketing practice, along global supply networks (GSN) and at the customer interface. She focuses on analysing the challenges of contemporary marketing practice with papers and work in the area of customer-centric information management; social networking realities and myths; and do marketing metrics drive business?

Dr Brady is the co-founder of the Digital Technology in Marketing Network – with Professor Mark Durkin from the University of Ulster. The aim of the group is to provide thought leadership and journal publications in the digital domain.

With over 70 publications including journal articles and international conference papers and presentations, Dr Brady is a prolific author. She has published in many journals including the *Journal of Marketing Management, Journal of Business and Industrial Marketing, International Journal of Technology Marketing, International Journal of Applied Logistics, Irish Marketing Review, Irish Journal of Management* and *Management Decision*. She has been guest editor of the *Creativity and Innovation Management Journal*, the *Irish Journal of Management* and the *Journal of Business and Industrial Marketing*, which she jointly edited with Professor Rod Brodie of the University of Auckland.

She served as chair of the Irish Academy of Management Conference hosted by Trinity College Dublin, which attracted the highest ever delegate attendance. She was also on the organising committee of the 11th International Product Development Management Conference held at Trinity College. She is also a reviewer and/or track chair for the following conferences: European Marketing Academy Conference (EMAC); IEEE/INFORMS International Conference on Service Operations and Logistics, and Informatics; Academy of Marketing; Irish Academy of Marketing; American Marketing Association; and American Academy of Management.

Additionally, Dr Brady regularly serves as reviewer for journals such as *European Journal of Marketing, Journal of Marketing Management, Qualitative Market Research: An International Journal, Journal of the Irish Academy of Management, Journal of Business and Industrial Marketing* and *Management Research News*. She has contributed book chapters to a selection of books including two chapters to *Marketing Graffiti* written by Professor Michael Saren.

Her many conference publications include the European Academy of Management (EURAM), American Academy of Management (AM), British Academy of Management (BAM), Irish Academy of Management, Academy of Marketing (UK and Ireland), European Academy of Marketing (EMAC), Australian and New Zealand Marketing Academy (ANZMAC), IEEE/Informs, European Group in Organisational Studies (EGOS) and Academy of International Business. She was the communications director for the technology and innovation special interest group of the American Marketing Association.

With a busy work and home life, Mairead still makes the time to enjoy travel and cooking. She particularly likes socialising with friends, though time with her family is her greatest joy.

Malcolm Robert Victor Goodman teaches both undergraduates and postgraduates at the University of Durham in the UK. His specialist subjects are business creativity, organisational change and marketing. He is an external examiner for the Edward de Bono Institute of Creativity at the University of Malta.

He graduated in economics after submitting a practical marketing study on the cricket bat and ball industries of Britain, designed to explore the gap between theoretical knowledge and its application to the real world. This became the springboard for a lifetime interest in the practical application of marketing concepts and techniques. Professor Goodman also holds the Diploma from the UK's Chartered Institute of Marketing.

The paradigm change in many markets, both in Europe and further afield, from sellers' to buyers' markets, sparked his fascination with the problems that many organisations face as they seek to come to terms with the challenges presented by mounting global competition. This has led to him developing a keen interest in business creativity and organisational change. The pursuit of business success now requires a holistic integration of creative management and marketing management skills, and this challenges organisations to pursue and adopt new attitudes and skills.

Publications include original texts on *The Cricket Bat and Ball Industries of Britain* and *Creative Management*. He also contributed a chapter titled 'Managing in times of change: avoiding management myopia' in *Strategy and Performance: Achieving Competitive Advantage in the Global Market* edited by Abby Ghobadian, Nicholas O'Regan, David Gallear and Howard Viney, which has been translated into Chinese. Professor Goodman has produced several papers for academic, trade and industry publications. He has also authored and contributed to distance learning courses in marketing for Durham University Business School and tutored on the UK's Open University Creative Management course.

Before entering the academic profession, Professor Goodman gained experience in the practical application of creative management and marketing skills in executive posts at British Leyland (where he was market planner for British Leyland France); General Motors; Lucas Industries; and the Tube Investments Group. He also served as Marketing Director for Lindley Lodge, a charity charged with the provision of development training programmes for young people, which provided useful experience in getting results with a very small budget. Training courses run for the coal and steel industries were balanced by the pioneering of programmes for national retailers such as Boots and Marks & Spencer.

During his career, management briefs have covered both consumer and business-to-business assignments. These have included product and market planning posts that have provided a wealth of experience in working with outside professional agencies. Professor Goodman has worked on several international assignments and has conducted on-the-spot marketing surveys and management briefs in Europe (particularly France and Germany) and in the Far East (especially Indonesia, Malaysia, Singapore and Thailand).

He has been a consultant to and been involved in creative management and marketing training with many organisations including ICI, Lucas, Marks & Spencer, Price Waterhouse, the Royal Navy, Sunderland Association Football Club and Uniroyal. He has also contributed to the UK government-inspired gifted and talented youth programme (NAGTY) by running two-week summer school programmes in practical business skills at the University of Durham.

In his youth Professor Goodman played football and roamed the pitch for the London-based Crystal Palace FC. A lifetime interest in sport – mainly football and cricket – has convinced him of the importance of taking a holistic and team-based approach to management tasks. His academic career began with an appointment to teach marketing and management skills on the Royal Navy Resettlement Programme and to run UK government-sponsored practical business courses for small businesses (SMEs) at the Portsmouth Management Centre. He also brought and further developed the retail-oriented training programmes that he had pioneered at Lindley Lodge. His current activity is characterised by a strong desire to assist clients and students to apply creative management and marketing skills practically to enable them to make a difference in highly competitive global markets.

Outside of work he cites his main interests – other than sport – to be camping, creative thinking, current affairs and classical music. He is happily married to Jill and has an adult daughter and son.

Torben Hansen is a Professor at the Department of Marketing, Copenhagen Business School (CBS). He received his Bachelor's and Master's degrees from University of Southern Denmark and his PhD from Copenhagen Business School. His main fields of research are consumer behaviour and marketing research methods, and his papers have appeared or are forthcoming in various academic journals, including *Journal of Service Research, Psychology & Marketing, International Journal of Consumer Studies, European Journal of Marketing, Journal of Consumer Behaviour, Journal of Foodservice Business Research, Journal of Product & Brand Management, Journal of International Consumer Marketing, International Journal of Retail & Distribution Management, International Review of Retail Distribution and Consumer Research, Journal of Retailing and Consumer Services* and others, and he has contributed a number of chapters in scholarly books. He has authored or co-authored several books, including *New Perspectives in Retailing: A Study of the Interface between Consumers and Retailers*. He is a frequent speaker at national and international conferences and community forums.

Professor Hansen is Chairman of the Consumer Research Group at CBS, which he took the initiative to establish in 2003. Professor Hansen has served as Chairman of the Danish Money and Pension Panel. The Money and Pension Panel is a board established by the Danish Parliament with the purpose of improving consumers' knowledge of and interest in financial matters. Apart from the chairman the panel comprises eight Danish consumer-oriented and financial organisations. In 2011 he was appointed member of the BEUC (the European Consumers' Organisation) Consumer Strategy Council. Professor Hansen has received several awards for his research, including the Marketing Trends Award, the International Academy of Business & Public Administration Research Award, and the Copenhagen Business School Gold Medal.

Professor Hansen has worked as a consultant for various companies and collaborates with several private organisations and public authorities, including the Danish Chamber of Commerce, the Ministry of Science, Technology and Innovation, the Confederation of Danish Industry and the Danish Consumer Council. He is a VIP member of the Danish Shareholders' Association. As a consumer behaviour expert, he is often called upon by the press, which relies on him for assessments of market trends and comments on consumer behaviour issues.

Professor Hansen has served as a reviewer for several leading marketing journals, including *Journal of Service Research, Journal of the Academy of Marketing Science, International Review of Retail, Distribution and Consumer Research, Journal of Consumer Psychology, Journal of Retailing and Consumer Services, International Journal of Retail and Distribution Management, British Food Journal* and *Journal of Marketing Management*. In 2010 he was appointed Chairman of the Northern European scientific committee for the ESCP-EAP International Congress Marketing Trends, a yearly conference sponsored by the Prime Minister of the French Republic. He has chaired, or been a member of, several assessment committees for various academic positions and has wide teaching experience, which also includes course coordinator and Master's and PhD supervision activities.

Professor Hansen has a passion for food and wine, and often experiments with exotic spices and new recipes, which he with various success serves for people who visit his wife and him in their home. He has appeared on Danish television as a guest chef in a popular comedy cook and talk show. In his spare time he often goes boating in his small but fast boat, which he also uses for fishing expeditions. He enjoys do-it-yourself work on his old country house.

Brief contents

Contents

Supporting resources

Visit **www.pearsoned.co.uk/marketingmanagementeurope** to find valuable online resources

Companion Website for students

- Multiple choice questions to test your understanding
- A range of video case studies to contextualise your learning in the real world
- Links to extra international examples and case studies
- An online glossary to explain key terms
- Flashcards to help with your online revision

For instructors

- Complete, downloadable Instructor's Manual
- PowerPoint slides that can be downloaded and used for presentations
- Testbank of question material

Also: the Companion Website provides the following features:

- Search tool to help locate specific items of content
- E-mail results and profile tools to send results of quizzes to instructors
- Online help and support to assist with website usage and troubleshooting

For more information please contact your local Pearson Education sales representative or visit

www.pearsoned.co.uk/marketingmanagementeurope

Guided tour

Chapter openers introduce an at-a-glance list of **learning outcomes**, a visual representation of the **chapter journey** on which the reader is about to embark and a brief introduction that includes a prelude **company case example** relating to the themes discussed in the chapter.

Video documentaries open each part of the book. They include interviews with top management teams from a variety of European and international organisations who discuss how their products or services are marketed. Access these documentaries online at **www.pearsoned.co.uk/marketingmanagementeurope**

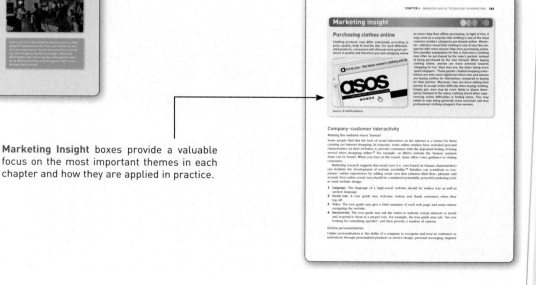

Marketing Insight boxes provide a valuable focus on the most important themes in each chapter and how they are applied in practice.

Throughout the text you will find vivid, brief illustrations of chapter concepts using **real companies and situations.**

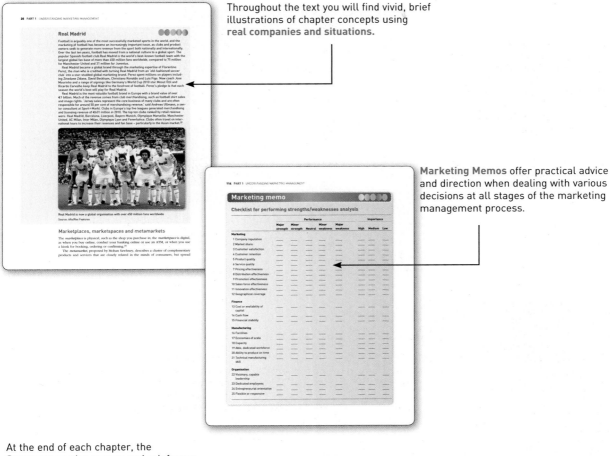

Marketing Memos offer practical advice and direction when dealing with various decisions at all stages of the marketing management process.

At the end of each chapter, the **Summary** section recaps and reinforces the concepts put forth at the start of the chapter.

Applications has two practical exercises to challenge the reader: **Marketing debate** suggests opposing points of view on an important marketing topic from the chapter and asks you to choose a side. **Marketing discussion** identifies provocative marketing issues and allows for a personal point of view.

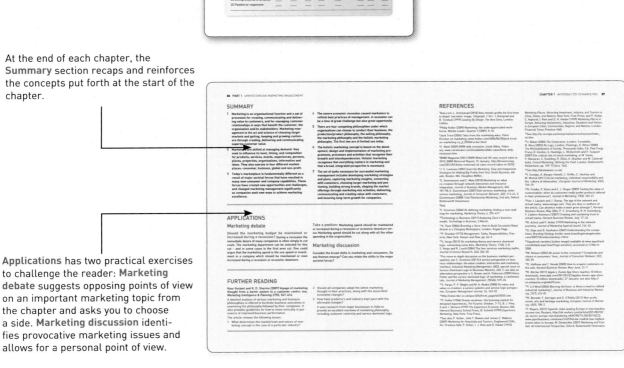

Preface

What is *Marketing Management* all about?

The American edition of *Marketing Management* is the world's leading marketing text because its content and organisation consistently reflect changes in marketing theory and practice. This new European edition of *Marketing Management* has been inspired by the American edition and explores the challenges facing European marketing practitioners. Increased global competition for business in European markets has led to a need for firms to develop market offerings that are especially tailored to meet the requirements of individual countries and customers. In the sellers' markets of yesteryear, competition was less pronounced and many firms concentrated on becoming cost-effective performers. This led to the formation of a mindset known as the *least-cost production paradigm*.

The paradigm change to and towards buyers' markets calls for marketers to provide customers with what they want and has become a challenge for supplying firms. It usually requires additional costs and may also involve substantial changes to their *modus operandi*. Additional costs are entailed as firms seek to meet customer-perceived value requirements. This normally entails offering a carefully tailored package of product and service benefits, and places increased importance on relationship marketing. The task of marketers is to discover accurately what their targeted customers want and then to develop appropriate market offerings by effective applications of the marketing mix. The marketing of services has assumed a great importance in most developed western economies and increasingly across the world as the leading emerging economies gather strength. Service benefits have become of greater importance as a means of increasing the customer-perceived value of offerings made by traditional product marketing firms.

The onward march of digital technology has had a profound effect on the practice of marketing. Firms now sell goods and services through a variety of direct and indirect channels. Mass advertising is increasingly giving way to new forms of communication as information and communication technologies (ICT) gather momentum. Communication has become truly two-way and customers are reporting more and more to other customers what they think of specific companies and market offerings using email, blogs, podcasts and other digital media to do so.

In response, companies are moving from managing product or service portfolios to relationship marketing. They do so by managing customer portfolios, compiling databases on individual customers in order to be able to fine tune their offerings and messages to meet bespoke needs. They are replacing traditional sellers' market product and service standardisation with more sophisticated marketing. The drive toward effectiveness (meeting the individual requirements of customers) is potentially expensive if pursued in an undisciplined fashion. Marketers are paying increased attention to efficiency and developing marketing metrics to measure their performance on key operative functions such as customer profitability and lifetime value. Monitoring payback on specific marketing decisions can be difficult due to the nature of the variables that influence customer buying behaviour and the contextual dynamics and complexities of individual markets. However, it is important for firms to seek improved methods to measure the return on their marketing investment and its impact on shareholder value.

As companies change their thinking in the light of emerging customer demands in buyers' markets, so they give increased attention to changing their marketing organisation. Marketing is increasingly being seen as a company-wide rather than a functional activity. It drives the company's vision, mission and strategic planning. Marketing is about identifying and consistently delivering appropriate customer-perceived value offerings to targeted customers. This involves a host of vital decisions such as who the company wants as its customers; which of their needs to satisfy; what products and services to offer; what process to design; what communications to send and receive; what channels of distribution to use; and what partnerships to develop. Marketing can only succeed when all functions in an organisation work in a holistic way as a team with the single aim of consistently pleasing or delighting their customers by balancing the concepts of effectiveness and efficiency.

Marketing management

In order to achieve this successfully, marketers practise marketing management on a national, international and often global scale. Marketing management is the development, design and implementation of marketing programmes, processes and activities that recognise the breadth and interdependencies of the business environment. Four key dimensions and operating attitudes define the task:

1 **Internal marketing**: ensuring everyone in the organisation consistently embraces appropriate marketing principles, especially senior management.
2 **Integrated marketing**: ensuring that the best possible way of utilising the marketing mix is employed to consistently deliver market offerings that continually delight customers.
3 **Relationship marketing**: developing sound and lasting relationships with all the members of the firm's value chain, customers and other marketing partners.
4 **Performance marketing**: the design and application of marketing metrics to gauge the costs and returns of marketing activities.

Marketing management recognises that 'everything matters' with marketing and that a broad, integrated perspective is often necessary. Therefore, these four dimensions are woven throughout the book.

Organisation

The text specifically addresses the following tasks that constitute the essence of modern marketing management in the 21st century:

1 understanding marketing management;
2 capturing marketing insights;
3 connecting with customers;
4 building strong brands;
5 shaping the market offering;
6 delivering value;
7 communicating value; and
8 managing marketing, implementation and control.

The most significant organisational changes in the European edition as compared to the American edition are:

- All chapters provide a European focus and include illustrations drawn from European companies.
- The text argues the case for marketing management in Europe and explores its practice through the use of the expanded 7P marketing mix.
- Management skills and the core requirements of a successful manager are introduced in this text, which sees management skills as a critical need for marketing managers.
- The aim of marketing management is the provision of customer-perceived value offerings to both consumers and business-to-business customers.
- The growth in digital marketing has provided marketing management with an array of tools including the internet, social networking and viral marketing, self-service technologies, dashboards and databases,

to name but a few. Several digital advances have revolutionised market research, product and service development, supply and communication practice, all highlighted in Chapter 4.
- To complement the use of digital technologies the book provides a window into the increasing use of creative marketing techniques, as companies seek to develop and sustain innovatory products/services and processes.
- As marketing management becomes more crucial in Europe, there is a need to make sure that marketing initiatives are both effective and efficient. The text devotes a whole chapter to exploring marketing metrics.
- A selection of topic templates, including formats to encourage readers to practise drawing up marketing plans, are also included.
- A set of European videos, case studies and exercises are featured to help readers bridge the gap between knowledge and practice.

Chapter by chapter changes

Chapter 1 Introduction to marketing

- emphasis on the importance, scope and philosophy of marketing;
- marketing in a recession and during turbulent times;
- understanding consumer during a recession;
- business cycle forecasting;
- understanding the European marketing environment: company and consumer challenges.

Chapter 2 Understanding marketing management

- understanding the four core functions of management;
- recessionary and other contemporary challenges for marketing managers;
- rethinking the role of marketing management;
- why is marketing management difficult?
- managing networks, managing technologies, and managing innovation and change externally and internally;
- an overview of marketing management using the contemporary marketing practice framework from transactions to relational and network marketing.

Chapter 3 Developing marketing strategies and plans

- importance of the business environmental paradigm change from sellers' to buyers' markets and the challenges that it presents to marketing management;

- the importance of the transformation in the concept of value and the need for firms to develop and deliver value to their customers;
- change today not tomorrow – five key strategies for managing change;
- critique of conventional SWOT analysis;
- moving from know-what to know-how – a sample Euromart marketing plan enables readers to get to grips with the practical application of marketing concepts and reflects the eight major themes featured in the text;
- the appendix contains a more detailed marketing planning example that is linked to key chapter assignments.

Chapter 4 Managing digital technology in marketing

- understanding the role and range of digital technology and digital marketing within marketing practice;
- information management challenges;
- technologist, financial and marketing perspectives;
- managing individual technologies including the internet, social networking, viral, email and mobile marketing, search engines, virtual worlds and self-service technologies;
- how to gain competitive advantage by using the internet;
- comprehensive coverage of digital marketing within distribution and communication practice;
- consumer digital shopping behaviour;

Chapter 5 The changing marketing environment and information management

- European macroenvironment;
- European market population;
- European cultures;
- importance of green marketing in Europe.

Chapter 6 Managing market research and forecasting

- conducting market research in European markets;
- European ethnographic research;
- European market research case study;
- contacting market potential in Europe;
- the market potential in Europe.

Chapter 7 Analysing consumer markets

- three perspectives on the study of European consumer behaviour;
- European lifestyles and social groups;
- consumer emotions;
- consumer planned behaviour;
- means–end chains.

Chapter 8 Analysing business markets

- the internationalisation of European firms;
- uncertainty in business relations;
- transaction cost economics;
- egovernment in Europe.

Chapter 9 Dealing with competition

- gaining competitive advantages in the European marketplace;
- balancing customer and competitive orientations;
- European blue-ocean thinking.

Chapter 10 Indentifying, analysing and creating target market differentiating and positioning strategies

- geodemographic market research agencies that operate in Europe;
- description of key trends in the social and cultural environment – youth and ethnic markets;
- forces shaping social change;
- perceptual or positioning mapping;
- the challenge of repositioning.

Chapter 11 Creating customer value, satisfaction and loyalty

- the pursuit of customer-perceived value;
- customer lifetime value – a conceptual dream or real-time activity?
- the experience economy;
- co-creation;
- the empowered customer;
- emotional turn/mood management.

Chapter 12 Creating and managing brands and brand equity

- what are the key strategic brand management decisions?
- managing and measuring brand equity;
- brand mantra, narratives and storytelling;
- managing service brands.

Chapter 13 Digital and global brand management strategies

- managing brands in a digital world;
- understanding the consumer's digital brand experience;
- understanding social networking branding challenges;
- branding issues in virtual worlds and gaming;
- global consumption issues: brand communities and brand tribes;
- understanding a nation's brand index.

Chapter 14 Designing, developing and managing market offerings

- the development of balanced product portfolios as product life cycles shorten;
- the challenge of high customer churn rates as market evolution gathers pace under the influence of dynamic competition and innovation;
- the ecological issues surrounding packaging in Europe;
- labels – their function and legal regulation in Europe.

Chapter 15 Introducing new market offerings

- many cultures, many markets – the importance of introducing new product offerings in Europe;
- the story told by EU surveys such as Innabarometer;
- examples of good new product development practice at Dyson, Reckitt Benckiser and Unilever.

Chapter 16 Developing and managing pricing strategies

- the power of pricing;
- the changing European pricing environment;
- customer-perceived value pricing;
- everyday low pricing practices in Europe.

Chapter 17 Designing and managing supply networks

- managing multichannel and channel multiplicity;
- digital channels, including online and ecommerce
- mobile commerce including location-based services.

Chapter 18 Managing process, people and physical evidence at the consumer interface

- design and management of service process;
- people management issue at the customer interface;
- managing the physical evidence and the experience environment;
- managing digital technologies at the customer interface.

Chapter 19 Designing and managing marketing communications

- markets can be regarded as conversations – the rising importance of word-of-mouth communication;

- guerrilla marketing – getting noticed;
- generating media 'talkabout' as in the case of the groundbreaking Dove Comedy Tour;
- updating company images – a choice between evolution and revolution.

Chapter 20 Managing mass and personal communications

- the essentials of managing mass and personal communications;
- marketing communications – more a matter of reminding customers than informing them?
- the need to be innovative with press campaigns (Nissan Qashqai launch publicity);
- the increasing use of TV sponsorship for branded products and services.

Chapter 21 Implementing marketing management

- internal marketing critique – a dream or widespread practical activity?
- creative management and marketing practice;
- creativity – a mystical gift for some or something for all?
- the importance of leadership in creative marketing management;
- creative marketing;
- assessing marketing ethical standards;
- ethnic and green marketing;
- key tasks for marketing managers;
- key company marketing cultures (the transactional marketing, relationship marketing, customer relationship marketing and customer perceived-value marketing journey);
- getting started – a template to begin practising marketing.

Chapter 22 Managing marketing metrics

- the need for marketing metrics;
- what marketing metrics should do;
- the chain of marketing productivity;
- accounting-based metrics;
- outcome metrics;
- shareholder value;
- customer lifetime value;
- brand equity and financial performance;
- the Balanced Scorecard.

Acknowledgements

This second European edition of *Marketing Management* contains contributions from many people: in particular, from Phil Kotler, whose work, comments and guiding hand greatly assisted the development of text of the European edition; and from Kevin Lane Keller, whose insights into marketing have also inspired the authors of this European edition.

The text has been co-authored by Malcolm Goodman of Durham University, Torben Hansen of the Copenhagen Business School and Mairead Brady of Trinity College, Dublin. Our thanks are due to many academics in our own and other universities as well as contacts too numerous to detail.

We would like to thank the reviewers who have helped develop the content and perspective of this second European edition. We are very grateful for their insightful comments and recommendations. Our thanks go to:

Dr Ruth Ashford, Manchester Metropolitan University, Head of Marketing and Retail Division and Chartered Institute of Marketing Chief Examiner

Professor Douglas Brownlie, Department of Marketing, University of Stirling

Professor David Carson, Ulster Business School, University of Ulster

Christian Grönroos, Professor of Service and Relationship Marketing, Hanken Swedish School of Economics and Business Administration, Finland

Professor Evert Gummesson, Stockholm University School of Business, Sweden

Dr Paul Hewer, Department of Marketing, University of Strathclyde

Associate Professor Jan Møller Jensen, Department of Marketing and Management, University of Southern Denmark

AC Muir, Department of Management, University of Glasgow

Michael Saren, Professor of Marketing, University of Leicester

Dr Gary Warnaby, Management School, University of Liverpool

No publishing exercise on this scale can reach a satisfactory climax without the hard work and dedication of a host of people who work in support of the project. We wish to record our appreciation of the driving but encouraging and gentle hand of our acquisitions editors, Rachel Gear and Amanda McPartlin, and Najette Hunt, marketing manager. We also wish to acknowledge the professional and creative contributions of Mary Lince, desk editor; Maggie Wells, text and cover designer; Lisa Steer, picture researcher; Lynette Miller, permissions editor; Chris Bessant, copy-editor; Brian Burge, proofreader; and David Barraclough, indexer.

In addition we all owe a lot to our families and close friends who have exercised patience and have supported us during the hectic authoring weeks. We have produced a fresh and modern text that we hope you will enjoy.

Mairead Brady
Malcolm Goodman
Torben Hansen

Publisher's acknowledgements

We are grateful to the following for permission to reproduce copyright material:

Cartoons

Cartoon on page 758 © Mike Baldwin/Cornered, www.cartoonStock.com.

Figures

Figures 1.1, 17.3 from The healthcare network economy: the role of Internet information transfer and implications for pricing, *Industrial Marketing Management*, 34, pp. 147–56 (Schau, H. J., Smith, M. F. and Schau, P. I. 2005), Copyright 2005, with permission from Elsevier; Figure on page 26 from Recession-proofing your organization, *MIT Sloan Management Review*, 50(3), p. 47 (Navarro, P. 2009), © 2009 from MIT Sloan Management Review/Massachusetts Institute of Technology. All rights reserved. Distributed by Tribune Media Services; Figure 1.4 from Reach of Social Networking Sites by Market in Europe, Panel only data, comScore Media Matrix, Dec. 2011, with permission from comScore, Inc; Figures 2.1, 2.3, 2.4 from *Organisational Behaviour and Management*, Cengage Learning (Martin, J. and Fellenz, M. 2009), Copyright © 2009 Cengage Learning. Reproduced by permission of Cengage Learning EMEA Ltd; Figure 2.2 reprinted by permission of *Harvard Business Review*. From Rethinking marketing by Rust, R., Moorman, C. and Bhalla, G., January–February, 2010. Copyright © 2010 by the Harvard Business School Publishing Corporation; all rights reserved; Figure 2.5 originally published in *Global Business Review*, Vol. 6, No. 1. Copyright © International Management Institute, New Delhi. All rights reserved. Reproduced with the permission of the copyright holders and the publishers Sage Publications India Pvt. Ltd., New Delhi; Figure 2.6 from The decline and dispersion of the marketing competence, *MIT Sloan Management Review*, 46(4), pp. 35–43 (Frederick, W., Malter, A., Ganesan, S. 2005), © 2005 from MIT Sloan Management Review/ Massachusetts Institute of Technology. All rights reserved. Distributed by Tribune Media Services; Figure 2.7 from The fall and rise of the CMO, *Strategy+Business*, 37, pp. 3–8 (McGovern, G. and Quelch, J. A. 2004). Reproduced with permission from strategy+business, the award-winning management quarterly published by Booz & Company. www.strategy-business.com; Figures 3.3, 9.1 adapted with the permission of Free Press, a Division of Simon & Schuster, Inc., from *Competitive Advantage: Creating and Sustaining Superior Performance* by Michael E. Porter. Copyright © 1985, 1998 by Michael E. Porter. All rights reserved; Figure 3.4 reprinted by permission of Harvard Business School Press. From *Marketing Moves* by Kotler, P., Jain, D. C. and Maesincee, S. Boston, MA, 2002, p. 29.

Copyright © 2002 by the Harvard Business School Publishing Corporation; all rights reserved; Figure 3.7 reprinted by permission of *Harvard Business Review*. From Strategies for diversification by Ansoff, I., September–October, 1957. Copyright © 1957 by the Harvard Business School Publishing Corporation; all rights reserved; Figure 4.1 from Managing customer-centric information: The challenges of information and communication technology (ICT) deployment in service environments, *International Journal of Applied Logistics*, 1(3), pp. 88–105 (Fellenz, M. R. and Brady, M. 2010), with permission from IGI Global; Figure 4.2 © *Enterprise 2.0*, by Niall Cook, 2008, Gower; Figure 4.3 reprinted by permission of *Harvard Business Review*. From Strategy and the internet by Porter, M. E., March, 2001. Copyright © 2001 by the Harvard Business School Publishing Corporation; all rights reserved; Figure 4.4 adapted from http://www.fredcavazza.net, reprinted by permission of Fred Cavazza; Figures 4.6, 13.1 from Forrester Research, Inc., Global Social Media Adoption in 2011, April 2011, with permission from Forrester Research, Inc; Figure 4.7 from Worldwide mobile music revenues, 2006–2011 (billions), www.eMarketer.com, with permission from eMarketer Inc; Figure 5.1 from Europe in figures, *Eurostat Yearbook 2010* (Eurostat 2010), © European Communities, 1995–2010; Figure 5.3 from 2011 Global R&D Funding Forecast, R&D Magazine, December 2010 p. 4, www.rdmag.com; Figure 5.4 from Building belief, *Marketing Week* (Roberts, J. 2011), http://www.marketingweek.co.uk/disciplines/data-strategy/building-belief/3025135.article, with permission from Centaur Media plc; Figure on page 252 reprinted by permission of *Harvard Business Review*. From What does your logo really tell consumers? by van Qauquebeke, N. and Giessner, S., 88(12), 2010. Copyright © 2010 by the Harvard Business School Publishing Corporation; all rights reserved; Figure 7.2 from Values and Lifestyles in *Consumer Behaviour – a Nordic Perspective*, edited by K. M. Ekstrom, pp. 307–324 (Hansen, T. 2010), with permission from the publisher, Studentlitteratur; Figure 7.4 from Maslow, Abraham H.; Frager, Robert D. (Editor); Fadiman, James (Editor), *Motivation and Personality, 3rd*, © 1987. Printed and Electronically reproduced by permission of Pearson Education, Inc., Upper Saddle River, New Jersey; Figure 7.8 from What about disposition?, *Journal of Marketing*, July, 23 (Jacoby, J., Berning, C. K. and Dietvorst, T. F. 1977), Copyright 1977. Reproduced with permission of American Marketing Association in the format Textbook via Copyright Clearance Center; Figure 7.9 from I. Aizen (2006) TpB diagram. Retrieved from www.people.umass.edu/aizen/tpb.diag.html. Copyright © 2006 Icek Aizen; Figure 8.1 from MarketingSherpa 2011 B2B Marketing Benchmark Report; Lead Author: Jen Doyle, Senior Research Manager, MECLABS, http://www.marketingsherpa.com/article.php?ident=31736; Figure 8.2 adapted from Where are you positioned on the trust dimensions?, *Don't Just Relate – Advocate: A Blueprint for Profit in the Era of Customer Power*, p. 99 (Urban, G. 2005), Indianapolis, Indiana: Wharton School Publishers. Copyright © 2005. Reprinted by permission of Pearson Education, Inc., Upper Saddle River, NJ; Figure 9.2 reprinted by permission of Harvard Business School Press. From *Blue-Ocean Strategy: How to Create Uncontested Market Space and Make the Competition Irrelevant* by Chan Kim, W. and Mauborgne, R. Boston, MA 2005. Copyright © 2005 by the Harvard Business School Publishing Corporation; all rights reserved; Figure 10.5 adapted from *Defining the Business: The Starting Point of Strategic Planning*, Prentice Hall (Abell, D. F. 1980) Chapter 8, pp. 192–6, Copyright © 1980. Reprinted by permission of Pearson Education, Inc., Upper Saddle River, NJ; Figure 11.6 from *Customer Loyalty: How to Earn It, How to Keep It*, Jossey-Bass (Griffin, J. 1995) p. 36, Copyright © 1995. Reproduced with permission of John Wiley & Sons, Inc; Figure on page 456 from Creatives Simon Morris, Patrick McLelland and Clive Pickering for John Lewis plc. Full page advertisement in *The Guardian*, 25 June 2008, p. 38. Reproduced with permission; Figure 11.7 adapted from Selectively pursuing more of your customer's business, *MIT Sloan Management Review*, Spring, 45 (Anderson, J.C. and Narus, J. A.), © 2003 from MIT Sloan Management Review/Massachusetts Institute of Technology. All rights reserved. Distributed by Tribune Media Services; Figure 12.1 from *Corporate Religion*, 1st ed., Financial Times Prentice Hall (Kunde, J. 2002), Copyright © 2002 Pearson Education Ltd and reproduced with permission from Kunde & Co.; Figure on page 474 from *Managing Brands for Value Creation*, Booz & Company (Harter, G., Koster, A. and Peterson, M. 2005) p. 2, Exhibit 1, Exhibit 2, reprinted with permission; Figure 12.3 adapted from *Strategic Brand Management*, 3rd ed., Prentice Hall (Keller, K. L. 2008) Copyright © 2008. Reprinted by permission of Pearson Education, Inc., Upper Saddle River, NJ; Figure 12.4 from Keller, Kevin, *Strategic Brand Management, 3rd*, © 2008. Printed and Electronically reproduced by permission of Pearson Education, Inc., Upper Saddle River, New Jersey; Figures 12.7, 12.8 from BAV Consulting, BrandAsset® Valuator UK, All Adults, 2011, with permission from BrandAsset® Consulting; Figure 12.10 from From goods to service branding: An integrative perspective, *Marketing Theory*, 9(1), pp. 107–111 (Brodie, R. J. 2009), Copyright © 2009, Sage Publications. Reprinted by permission of Sage Publications; Figure 13.2 reprinted by permission of *Harvard Business Review*. From Branding in the digital era by Edelman, D., December 2010. Copyright © 2010 by the Harvard Business School Publishing Corporation; all rights reserved; Figure 13.4 adapted from The wisdom of consumer crowds: collective innovation in the age of networked marketing, *Journal of Macromarketing*, 28(4) (Kozinets, R. V., Hemetsberger, A. and Schau, H. J. 2008), Copyright © 2008, Sage Publications. Reprinted by permission of Sage Publications; Figure 13.5 from Keller, Kevin, *Strategic Brand Management, 3rd*, © 2008. Printed and electronically reproduced by permission of Pearson Education, Inc., Upper Saddle

River, New Jersey; Figure 13.6 Nation Brand Hexagon, with permission from Simon Anholt; Figure 15.7 adapted with the permission of Free Press, a Division of Simon & Schuster, Inc., from *Diffusion of Innovations*, Third Edition, by Everett M. Rogers. Copyright © 1962, 1971, 1983 by The Free Press. All rights reserved; Figure 16.7 reprinted by permission of *Harvard Business Review*. From Strategies to fight low-cost rivals by Kumar, N., December 2006. Copyright © by the Harvard Business School Publishing Corporation; all rights reserved; Figure 17.2 from Hotel networks and social capital in destination marketing, *International Journal of Service Industry Management*, 17(1), pp. 58–75 (von Friedrichs Grängsjö, Y. and Gummesson, E. 2008), © Emerald Group Publishing Limited all rights reserved; Figure 17.5 adapted from One step closer towards e-business - the implementation of a supporting ICT system, *International Journal of Logistics*, 9(3), p. 289 (Iskanius, P. and Kilpala, H. 2006), reprinted by permission of the publisher (Taylor & Francis Ltd, http://www.tandf.co.uk/journals); Figure 17.8 adapted from A new framework for service supply chains, *The Service Industries Journal*, 27(2), pp. 105–24 (Baltacioglu, T., Ada, E., Kaplan, M., Yurt, O. and Kaplan, Y. 2007), reprinted by permission of the publisher (Taylor & Francis Ltd., http://www.tandf.co.uk/journals); Figure 17.13 from Managing marketing channel multiplicity, *Journal of Service Research*, 13(3), pp. 331–340, Figure 1 (Van Bruggen, G. H., Anita, K. D., Jap, S. D., Reinartz, W. J. and Pallas, F. 2010), Copyright © 2010, Sage Publications. Reprinted by permission of Sage Publications; Figure 17.14 adapted from Multi-channel shopping: understanding what drives channel choice, *Journal of Consumer Marketing*, 19(1), pp. 42–53 (Schoenbachler, D. and Gordon, G. 2002), with permission from Emerald Group Publishing Limited; Figure 17.15 from *Introduction to Location Based Services* (Agrawal, Mohit 2009) http://www.telecomcircle.com/2009/06/introduction-to-lbs, with permission from Mohit Agrawal; Figure 18.1 adapted from *Services Marketing Management: A Strategic Perspective*, 2nd ed. (Kasper, H., van Helsdingen, P. and Gabbott, M. 2006), Copyright © 2006 John Wiley & Sons Ltd. Reproduced with permission of John Wiley & Sons Ltd; Figure 18.2 from *Service Operations Management: Improving Service Delivery*, 2nd ed., Prentice Hall (Johnston, R. and Graham, C. 2005), Copyright © 2005 Pearson Education Ltd. Reproduced with permission; Figure 18.3 from Fisk. *Interactive Service Marketing*, 2E © 2004 South-Western, a part of Cengage Learning, Inc. Reproduced by permission. www.cengage.com/permissions; Figure 18.6 from The new frontier of experience innovation, *MIT Sloan Management Review*, 44(4), pp. 12–18 (Prahalad, C. K. and Ramaswamy, V. 2003), © 2003 from MIT Sloan Management Review/Massachusetts Institute of Technology. All rights reserved. Distributed by Tribune Media Services; Figure 18.7 adapted from *North American Self-Service Kiosks Market Study*, IHL Group (Holman, L. and Buzek, G. 2008), Reproduced by permission of IHL Consulting Group; Figure 20.7 reprinted by permission of *Harvard Business Review*. From Match your sales-force structure to your business life cycle by Zolters, A., Sinha, P. and Lorimer, S. E., July-August 2006. Copyright © 2006 by the Harvard Business

School Publishing Corporation; all rights reserved; Figure 22.1 adapted from Measuring marketing productivity: current knowledge and future directions, *Journal of Marketing*, 68, October, p. 77 (Rust, R. T., Ambler, T., Carpenter, G. S., Kumar, V. and Srivastava, R. K. 2004), Copyright © American Marketing Association; Figure 22.2 adapted from Choosing the right metrics to maximize profitability and shareholder value, *Journal of Retailing*, 85(1), pp. 95–111 (Petersen, J.A., McAlister, L., Reibstein, D. J., Winer, R. S., Kumar V. and Atkinson, G. 2009), Copyright © 2009 with permission from Elsevier; Figure 22.3 adapted from Sales modelling carried out by BrandScience copyright © Omnicom Media Group; Figure 22.4 adapted from Calculating the value of customers' referrals, *Managing Service Quality*, 13(2), p. 126 (Helm, S. 2003), with permission from Emerald Group Publishing Limited; Figure 22.5 adapted from How Marketing Affects Shareholders Value, reprinted by permission of The Arrow Group Ltd., in *Value above Cost*, Pearson Education (Sexton, D. E. 2009); Figure 22.6 reprinted by permission of *Harvard Business Review*. From Using the balanced scorecard as a strategic management system by Kaplan, R. S. and Norton, D. P., July-August 2007. Copyright © 2007 by the Harvard Business School Publishing Corporation; all rights reserved; Figure 22.7 reprinted by permission of *Harvard Business Review*. From Using the balanced scorecard as a strategic management system by Kaplan, R. S. and Norton, D. P., July-August 2007. Copyright © 2007 by the Harvard Business School Publishing Corporation; all rights reserved; Figure 22.8 adapted from *Kellogg on Branding: The Marketing Faculty of the Kellogg School of Management* edited by P. Kotler and A. Tybout (Schultz, D. 2005), Chapter 13, Marketing Measurement Pathways, Copyright © 2005 John Wiley & Sons, Inc. Reproduced with permission of John Wiley & Sons, Inc; Figure 22.9 from *Marketing by the Dashboard Light - How to Get More Insight, Foresight, and Accountability from Your Marketing Investments* (LaPointe, P. 2005). Copyright © 2005, Patrick LaPointe. Reproduced with permission.

Logos

Logo on page 510 from with permission from Philips Electronics UK Limited; Logo on page 510 from Inter IKEA Systems BV; Logo on page 510 from with permission from BP; Logo on page 510 from with permission from UBS AG; Logo on page 510 with permission from Siemens AG; Logo on page 510 adidas and the adidas 3-Bars logo are registered trade marks of the adidas group, used with permission; Logo on page 548 with permission from South African Tourism; Logo on page 548 from Polish National Tourist Office; Logo on page 548 from St. Lucia Tourist Board; Logo on page 548 from Turkish Culture and Tourism Office; Logo on page 548 from Singapore Tourism Board.

Screenshots

Screenshots on page 21, page 143, page 164, page 166, page 423 Microsoft screenshot frame reprinted with permission from Microsoft Corporation; Screenshot on page 46 from http://www.eve-online.com, Courtesy of CCP Games; Screenshot on page 154 from http://www.secondlife.com/showcase, available under Creative Commons license: http://creativecomons.org/licenses/by-nc-sa/2.0/deed/en; Screenshots on page 164 from http://www.ikea.com/, with permission from Inter IKEA Systems BV; Screenshot on page 175 courtesy of Google, Inc; Screenshot on page 436 from Yahoo! Music screenshot., Text and artwork copyright © 1998 by Yahoo! Inc. All rights reserved; Screenshot on page 550 from Nation Brands Index http://www.simonanholt.com/Research/research-introduction.aspx, with permission from Simon Anholt.

Tables

Table 2.1 from The decline and dispersion of the marketing competence, *MIT Sloan Management Review*, 46(4), pp.35–43 (Frederick, W., Malter, A., Ganesan, S. 2005), © 2005 from MIT Sloan Management Review/Massachusetts Institute of Technology. All rights reserved. Distributed by Tribune Media Services; Table 2.3 from Beyond global marketing and the globalization of marketing activities, *Management Decision*, 40(6), pp. 574–583 (Svensson, G. 2002), © Emerald Group Publishing Limited all rights reserved; Table 3.1 reprinted by permission of Harvard Business School Press. From *Peripheral Vision: Detecting the Weak Signals That Will Make or Break Your Company* by Day, G. S. and Schoemaker, P. J. H. Boston, MA 2006. Copyright © 2006 by the Harvard Business School Publishing Corporation; all rights reserved; Table 3.2 BP mission statement, reproduced with permission; Table 3.2 Oticon A/S mission statement, reproduced with permission; Table 3.2 Philips mission statement, reproduced with permission; Table 3.4 adapted from The 12 different ways for companies to innovate, *MIT Sloan Management Review*, 47(3), p. 78 (Sawhney, M., Wolcott, R. C., Arroniz, I. 2006), © 2006 from MIT Sloan Management Review/Massachusetts Institute of Technology. All rights reserved. Distributed by Tribune Media Services; Table 3.5 3M Company and 3M Innovative Properties Company mission statement copyright © 3M IPC, reproduced by courtesy of 3M. No further reproduction is permitted without 3M's prior written consent; Table 3.5 Robert Bosch GmbH mission statement, reproduced with permission; Table 3.5 Fiat mission statement, with permission from Fiat SpA; Table 3.5 L'Oréal mission statement, with permission from L'Oréal; Table 3.5 Michelin mission statement, with permission from Michelin Type Public Limited Company; Table 3.5 Nokia mission statement, reproduced with permission; Table 3.5 Siemens AG mission statement, reproduced with permission; Table 3.5 Divine Chocolate Ltd. mission statement, reproduced with permission; Table 4.2 from Internet Usage in the European Union, http://www.internetworldstats.com/stats9.htm, Copyright © 2000–2012, Miniwatts Marketing Group. All rights reserved; Table 4.3 from Users of the world unite! The challenges and opportunities of social media, *Business Horizons*, January-February, 53(1), pp. 59–68 (Kaplan, A. and Haenlein, M. 2010), Copyright © 2010, with permission from Elsevier; Table 7.1 LOHAS Market Segments copyright © LOHAS www.lohas.com; Table on page 297 from Small and medium-sized enterprises (SMEs), http://ec.europa.eu/enterprise/policies/sme/facts-figures-analysis/sme-definition/index_en.htm, © European Communities, 1995–2010; Table 9.3 reprinted by permission of *Harvard Business Review*. From Defensive marketing: how a strong incumbent can protect its position by Roberts, J. H., November, 156, 2005. Copyright © 2005 by the Harvard Business School Publishing Corporation; all rights reserved; Table 10.2 compiled by Peter Sleight and published in F. Brassington and S. Pettit (2003), *Principles of Marketing*, 3rd ed., Chapter 5, p. 187. Copyright © Peter Sleight. Reproduced with permission; Table 10.3 after *Principles of Marketing*, Prentice Hall (Brassington, F. and Pettit, S. 2003), Copyright © 2003 Pearson Education Ltd. Reproduced with permission; Table 10.4 adapted from Monitoring social change, *International Journal of Market Research*, 37(1), pp. 69–80 (Hasson, L. 1995). Reproduced from the *International Journal of Market Research* with permission. Copyright © 1995 Market Research Society. www.ijmr.com; Table 10.6 adapted from *Segmenting the Industrial Market*, Lexington Books (Bonoma, T. V. and Shapiro, B. P. 1983), with permission from The Rowman & Littlefield Publishing Group; Table 10.7 adapted from *Market-based Management*, 4th ed., Prentice Hall (Best, R. J. 2005), Copyright © 2005. Reprinted by permission of Pearson Education, Inc., Upper Saddle River, NJ; Table 11.2 reprinted by permission of *Harvard Business Review*. From Avoid the four perils of CRM by Rigby, D. K., Reichheld, F. F. and Schefter, P., February, 106, 2002. Copyright © 2002 by the Harvard Business School Publishing Corporation; all rights reserved; Table 12.1 adapted from Interbrand 2011, http://www.interbrand.com/en/best-global-brands/Best-Global-Brands-2008/Best-Global-Brands-2008.aspx, with permission from Interbrand; Table 13.1 adapted from How brand community practices create value, *Journal of Marketing*, 73, September, pp. 30–51 (Schau, H. J., Muniz, A. M., Arnould, E. J. 2009), Copyright 2009 reproduced with the permission of American Marketing Association in the format Textbook via Copyright Clearance Center; Table 13.2 from Social media measurement: It's not impossible, *Journal of Interactive Advertising*, 10(1), pp. 1–10 (Murdough, C.), reprinted with permission; Table 13.6 reprinted by permission of *Harvard Business Review*. From Strategies that fit emerging markets by Khanna, T., Palepu, K. G. and Sinha, J. 83(6) 2005. Copyright © 2005 by the Harvard Business School Publishing Corporation; all rights reserved; Table 13.7 adapted from Institute of Practitioners in Advertising (IPA), IPA Effectiveness Awards databank, www.ipaeffectivenessawards.co.uk, email info@ipa.co.uk for further details; Table 15.1 from The World's Fifty Most Innovative Companies (2009), *Special Report, Business Week*, 9 May. Used with permission of Bloomberg L. P. Copyright © 2012. All rights reserved; Table 15.3 adapted from Managing new-product development for strategic competitive advantage, in D. Iacobucci (ed.), *Kellogg on Marketing*, Table 6.1, p. 131 (Jain, D. 2001). Copyright © 2001 John Wiley & Sons, Inc. Reproduced with permission of John Wiley & Sons, Inc; Tables 15.4, 15.5 adapted from *Flash EB No 267– 2009 Innobarometer*, Conducted by The Gallup Organization upon the request of DG Enterprise and Industry, http://ec.europa.eu © European Union, 1995–2012; Table 16.1 adapted from Behavioural perspectives on pricing: buyers' subjective perceptions of price revisited in T. Devinney (ed.), *Issues in Pricing: Theory and Research*, pp. 35–57 (Winer, R. S. 1988), with permission from The Rowman & Littlefield Publishing Group; Table 16.2 adapted from *The Strategy and Tactics of Pricing*, 3rd ed., Prentice Hall (Nagle, T. T. and Holden, R. K. 2001) Chapter 4, copyright © 2001. Reprinted by permission of Pearson Education, Inc., Upper Saddle River, NJ; Table 16.3 from Why the highest price isn't the best price, *MIT Sloan Management Review*, Winter, pp. 69–76 (Anderson, J. C., Wouters, M. and Van Rossum, W. 2010), © 2010 from MIT Sloan Management Review/Massachusetts Institute of Technology. All rights reserved. Distributed by Tribune Media Services; Table 18.1 reprinted by permission of *Harvard Business Review*. From Breaking the trade off between efficiency and service by Frei, F., 84(11) 2006. Copyright © 2006 by the Harvard Business School Publishing Corporation; all rights reserved; Table 22.1 adapted from What does marketing success look like?, *Marketing Management*, Spring, pp. 13–18 (Ambler, T. 2001), with permission from the American Marketing Association.

Text

Extract on pages 25–26 adapted from Recession-proofing your organization, *MIT Sloan Management Review*, 50(3), pp. 45–54 (Navarro, P. 2009), © 2009 from MIT Sloan Management Review/Massachusetts Institute of Technology. All rights reserved. Distributed by Tribune Media Services; Extract on page 30 reproduced by permission of Sage Publications Ltd., London, Los Angeles, New Delhi, Singapore and Washington, DC, from Ellis, N., Fitchett, J., Higgins, M., Gavin, J., Ming, L., Saren, M. and Tadajewski, M. (2011) *Marketing: A Critical Textbook*, modified from Jones, D. G. B. and Richardson, A. J., The myth of the marketing revolution, *Journal of Macromarketing*, 27(1), Copyright © 2011, Sage Publications; Extract on page 32 adapted from *Ten Deadly Marketing Sins*, John Wiley & Sons, Inc. (Kotler, P. 2004) pp.10, 145–148. Copyright © 2004 John Wiley & Sons, Inc. Reproduced with permission of John Wiley & Sons, Inc; Extract on page 79 from Danone expands its pantry to woo the world's poor by Christina Passariello, *The Wall Street Journal, Business*, 30 June 2010, http://online.wsj.com/article/SB10001424052748703615104575328943452892722.html, Wall Street journal [only staff-produced materials may be used] Copyright 2010 by DOW JONES & COMPANY, INC. Reproduced with permission of DOW JONES & COMPANY, INC. in the format Textbook via Copyright Clearance Center; Extract on page 99 Google mission statement and philosophy, with permission from Google; Extract on pages 122–123 adapted from K. Kashani and D. Turpin (1999), *Marketing Management: An International Perspective*, Section 1, published 1999, Macmillan Business, reproduced with permission from Palgrave Macmillan; Extract on pages 299–300 based on a white paper by Bill Lee, Success stories: the top 5 mistakes, 2004 Bill Lee Customer Reference Forum, bill@customerreferenceforum.com; Extract on page 504 reprinted by permission of *Harvard Business Review*. From The brand report card by Keller, K. L., January-February 2000. Copyright © 2000 by the Harvard Business School Publishing Corporation; all rights reserved; Extract on page 514 adapted from Forrester Research, Inc., Global Social Media Adoption in 2011, April 2011, with permission from Forrester Research, Inc; Extract on pages 540–541 adapted from The ten commandments of global branding, *Asian Journal of Marketing*, 8(2), pp. 97–108 (Keller, K. L. and Sood, S. 2001), with permission from the authors; Extract on pages 566–567 adapted from The relevance of brand relevance, *Strategy+Business*, 35, Summer, pp. 1–10 (Aaker, D. A.). Reprinted with permission from Strategy+Business, the award-winning management quarterly published by Booz & Company (www.strategy-business.com); Extract on page 576 adapted from M. Sawhney (1999) Rethinking marketing and mediation in the networked economy, Winning strategies for ecommerce lecture at the Kellogg School of Management, 7-10 April, with permission from Mohanbir Sawhney; Extract on page 621 adapted from *Product Leadership: Creating and Launching Superior New Products*, Basic Books (Cooper, R. 1998). Copyright © 1998 Robert G. Cooper. Reprinted by permission of Basic Books, a member of the Perseus Books Group; Extract on pages 753–754 from The service models of frontline employees, *Journal of Marketing*, 74(4), pp. 63–80 (Mascio, R. 2010). Reproduced with permission of American Marketing Association in the format Textbook via Copyright Clearance Center; Extract on page 803 adapted from Keller, Kevin, *Strategic Brand Management*, 3rd, © 2008. Printed and Electronically reproduced by permission of Pearson Education, Inc., Upper Saddle River, New Jersey.

The Financial Times

Table 1.1 adapted from FT Europe 500 2011, http://media.ft.com/cms/32aafd58-98d4-11e0-bd66-00144feab49a.pdf, © The Financial Times Limited 2011. All Rights Reserved. Pearson is solely responsible for providing this adapted content and the Financial Times Limited does not accept any liability for the accuracy or quality of the adapted version; Extract on pages 445-446 adapted from Case study: Loyalty Management UK, *Financial Times*, 12 February 2004 (Stewart, A.), © The Financial Times Limited 2004. All Rights Reserved. Pearson is solely responsible for providing this adapted version of the original article and the Financial Times Limited does not accept any liability for the accuracy or quality of the adapted version.

Photographs

The publisher would like to thank the following for their kind permission to reproduce their photographs:

(Key: b-bottom; c-centre; l-left; r-right; t-top)

2 IKEA Ltd: (br); 6 ©BMW Group: (cr); 9 Alamy Images: David Pearson (tl). Corbis: Ralph A. Clevenger (b). Image courtesy of The Advertising Archives: (tr); 12 Rex Features: KPA / Zuma; 18 GfK GeoMarketing Purchasing Power Europe: (tr); 20 Rex Features: Aflo (c); 40 Alamy Images: Jochen Tack; 56 PunchStock: Creatas; 62 Getty Images: Odd Andersen (tr); 67 Press Association Images: Jim Mone / AP; 84 Siemens: Agency: Publicis-München; 90 Courtesy of Asda; 93 Courtesy of Kodak Ltd (UK): (tc); 102 Press Association Images: Koji Sasahara / AP; 103 PepsiCo: (b); 107 Alamy Images: Adrian Sherratt; 128 Fotolia.com: (br); 130 Getty Images: Stuart Franklin (br); 153 Alamy Images: John James; 157 Audi UK: (c); 163 Alamy Images: NetPics (tl); 172 Fotolia.com; 187 McDonalds Corporation: courtesy of © havi-logistics.com (b); 208 Sigg UK: Sigg Switzerland AG www.sigg.com (br); 214 Alamy Images: Anna G. Tufvesson / Nordicphotos; 216 Pearson Education Ltd: (t); 228 Photo Disc; 244 Alamy Images: Realimage (br); 247 Courtesy of Fernandes Bottling Co NV; 250 Image courtesy of The Advertising Archives; 251 Bang & Olufsen: (bc); 252 AT&T: (b); 256 Pearson Education; 263 Adidas: (b); 267 Pandora: Pandora 2012 Summer Advertisement (b); 298 Alamy Images: Profimedia International s.r.o.; 312 David Domingo www.daviddomingo.org: (b); 330 Getty Images: Mitchell Funk / Photographer's Choice (br); 334 Bjorn Beheydt: www.photographersdirect.com; 341 www.CartoonStock.com: (tc); 344 Photographers Direct: Stephen F. Faust; 355 AIAIAI: (c). www.eyevine.com: Dave Yoder / Polaris; 366 Alamy Images: Steve Sant; 371 Alamy Images: Richard Levine; 372 Alamy Images: Gregory Wrona; 373 Alamy Images: Justin Kase z03z; 378 Press Association Images: Sandra Campardo / AP; 379 www.eyevine.com: Sara Krulwhich / The New York Times; 399 Nespresso: (cl); 404 Photo Edit Inc: David Young-Wolff; 416 Alamy Images: Simon Belcher; 421 Serif; 424 DK Images: Richard Leeney; 427 Alamy Images: Goddard Automotive; 438 Emmanuel Church Durham; 446 Corbis: John G. Mabanglo / epa; 451 Rex Features: Phillipe Hays; 467 Getty Images: Jacques Demarthon / AFP; 468 www.CartoonStock.com; 476 Image courtesy of The Advertising Archives; 480 Kellogg's Group; 484 Courtesy of Dyson; 488 Corbis: Daniele La Monica / Reuters; 492 Image courtesy of The Advertising Archives: (tr, tl); 539 Tesco Stores Ltd: (c); 546 Rex Features: Most Wanted (tc); David Fisher (tl); Carolyn Contino / BEV (tr); 549 Getty Images: JAVIER SORIANO / AFP (t); 556 AP Wide World Photos: Douglas C. Pizac; 562 Alamy Images: Mark Scheuern; 577 Alamy Images: Jupiter Images / Brand X; 581 Daimler AG; 582 Corbis: John Van Hasselt; 592 AP Wide World Photos: Martin Meissner; 598 Serif; 599 Photo Edit Inc: Bill Aron; 600 Alamy Images: mediablitzimages (UK) Ltd; 608 Rex Features; 616 Courtesy of the Xerox Corporation; 617 PunchStock: Paul Aresu (br). ; 623 Reckitt Benckiser Group plc; 626 Corbis: image 100; 627 The Kobal Collection: Warner Brothers TV / Bright / Crane Pro / The Kobal Collection / Chris Haston; 641 Alamy Images; 648 Æ+Y phone by Æsir: (bl); 651 CCS Healthcare AB, Sweden; 657 Getty Images: Michele Constantini / PhotoAlto Agency RF Collections (tc); 659 Getty Images: A & L Sinibaldi / Stone (bc); 668 Monika Elena Photo; 671 Sainsbury's Supermarket Limited: (bc); 688 Daimler AG; 692 Alamy Images: Ian Canham (b); 703 Reproduced by kind permission of

Eastman Kodak Company, trademark and copyright owner; 707 Stihl: Courtesy of Stihl GB (c); 710 Courtesy of Volvo Car Corporation: (b); 713 Daimler AG; 715 Getty Images: OMAR TORRES / AFP (t); 722 Getty Images: Todd Warshaw (b); 730 Alamy Images; 736 Copyright (c) Swiss International Air Lines; 744 Inter IKEA Systems B.V.; 753 Corbis: Pascal Della Zuana (tl); 767 Rex Features: Phil Yeomans; 769 Alamy Images: Ulrich Baumgarten / vario images GmbH & Co. KG; 774 Reproduced with kind permission of Unilever PLC and group companies; 776 Serif; 780 Charlie Magee Photography; 787 Spectrum Brands (UK) Ltd; 792 Alamy Images: Chris P. Batson; 796 Used by permission of Ocean Spray: Photographer William Huber; 808 Alamy Images: Justin Kase z12z (bc); 813 Image courtesy of The Advertising Archives; 819 Getty Images: Patrik Stollarz / AFP; 830 Red Bull Content Pool: Kevin Yang (tr); 837 Corbis: Shawn Thew / epa; 860 Serif; 873 Serif; 881 Newscom: Ross Haily / Fort Worth Star Telegram / MCT / NewsCom; 891 B&Q plc: ZPR London (l, r); 893 Serif; 906 Serif; 908 Serif; 918 iStockphoto: Curt Pickens; 920 Image courtesy of The Advertising Archives: (bl).

In some instances we have been unable to trace the owners of copyright material, and we would appreciate any information that would enable us to do so.

Understanding marketing management

Video documentary for Part 1

Go to www.pearsoned.co.uk/
marketingmanagementeurope to watch the
video documentary that relates to Part 1 and
consider the issues raised below.

Marketing Management is designed to take both
business practitioners and students on a journey to
explore the marketing manager's world.

Part 1: Understanding marketing management
provides an overview of this journey and addresses
four essential themes:

1   What is marketing?
2   What is marketing management?
3   What are marketing strategies and plans?
4   What are the challenges of managing digital
    technologies in marketing?

It is surprising how few people have a clear understanding of what is meant by the words 'marketing'
and 'management'. Part 1 explores the world of the
marketing manager from the point of view of *what*
they do and the rest of the book provides guidance
as to *how* they do it.

The video documentary for Part 1 greatly assists our
understanding of how real-life marketers, from a
range of European organisations, perceive marketing,
and why it is essential to their success. Marketing is
a business activity that is relevant to all types of business, whether private, public, charity or other not-for-
profit organisations. It is about the identification and
fulfilment of customer needs, and the establishment
and maintenance of brand values.

As you watch the documentary, consider how in a
highly competitive, technology-enabled global market,
companies need to exercise both vision and mission;
need to understand marketing and management and
also to use the range of digital technologies available to
them. They also need to identify what to do and where
to go (*concept of market effectiveness*); and then seek
to establish a suitable brand value image by carefully
using company resources (*concept of efficiency*).

Hear a variety of top marketing executives from a wide
range of organisations offer their own interesting and
varied perspectives on the key themes of Part 1 including:
Ashish Joshi, Director, Royal Enfield Motorcycles Europe
(top); Colin Green, Director of Global Marketing, Land
Rover (centre); and Voluntary Services Overseas, London,
UK (bottom).

Chapter 1

Introduction to marketing

IN THIS CHAPTER, WE WILL ADDRESS THE FOLLOWING QUESTIONS:

1 Why is marketing important?

2 What is the scope of marketing?

3 What are some fundamental marketing concepts?

4 What are the current European marketing realities?

5 What is the marketing philosophy?

6 What is an overview of the tasks for successful marketing management?

Marketing managers need to understand consumer needs and align marketing mix activities to satisfying these at a profit – IKEA understands the consumer need for good-quality, well-designed but low-cost furniture. Source: IKEA Ltd.

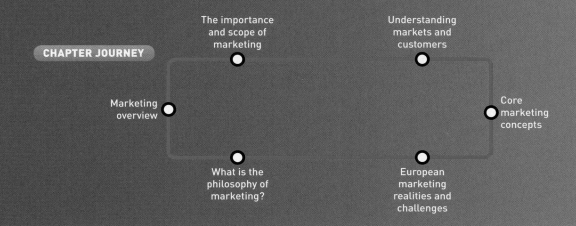

CHAPTER JOURNEY

The importance and scope of marketing

Understanding markets and customers

Marketing overview

Core marketing concepts

What is the philosophy of marketing?

European marketing realities and challenges

Marketing management is a challenging and rewarding career choice because it is a core management function central to all company efforts. Good marketing has become increasingly vital for success. But what constitutes good marketing is constantly evolving and changing, with globalisation, turbulent markets and advances in technology all changing the market. What stays the same is the philosophy of marketing, which puts the customer at the centre of profitable companies.

Take IKEA.

IKEA is the world's most successful furniture retailer, designing and manufacturing ready-to-assemble home furniture and furnishings in a Scandinavian style. The company, which originated in Småland, Sweden, distributes its products through its retail outlets and online. As of April 2011, IKEA had over 320 outlets in 38 countries, most of them in Europe, North America, Asia and Australia. Despite the recession from 2008 onwards, IKEA benefited from customers searching for cheaper furniture. While rivals suffered a sharp decline in sales, IKEA opened 15 new stores which helped boost revenues. IKEA's 500 million-plus customers do more than purchase IKEA products; they identify with the culture and authenticity that IKEA has attached to its products. The warm, welcoming Swedish style has become a model of simplicity, practicality and informality.[1] Each chapter of this text explores the various marketing management challenges for IKEA as outlined below:

- **Introduction to marketing:** IKEA management value the customer and satisfy the customer's need for high-quality design at affordable prices (Chapter 1).
- **Marketing management:** Ingvar Kamprad, the founder of IKEA, recognises the importance of marketing management throughout his global enterprise (Chapter 2).
- **Marketing plans and strategies:** IKEA needs plans and strategies to guide the company. Its strategy to succeed revolves around low costs (Chapter 3).
- **Digital technologies:** IKEA uses a range of digital technology both internally and externally. It has over 470 million annual visitors to its website, which hosts over 12,000 products (Chapter 4).
- **Capturing marketing insights:** IKEA continually researches the market to understand its consumers, markets and competitors (Chapters 5–9).
- **Customer segments and target markets:** IKEA understands consumer segments and chooses to target the price-conscious consumer (Chapter 10).

- **Positioning in the market:** Its brand is positioned within the quality at low prices market space (Chapter 11).
- **Managing the brand:** A strong brand image and identity is created through a coherent branding strategy (Chapter 12).
- **Digital and global branding:** IKEA understands the digital and online brand communities and how to manage a brand globally (Chapter 13).

To position its brand in the eyes of the consumer IKEA manages the 7Ps of the marketing mix activities:

- **Product/service:** IKEA offers a self-assembly furniture product with a commitment to product design, consumer value and clever solutions using inexpensive materials in a novel way and minimising production (Chapter 14).
- **New marketing offerings:** IKEA is a market leader in introducing new products to its range and also in providing new service offerings to its customers (Chapter 15).
- **Pricing:** It keeps prices low, with a focus on good value for the customer (Chapter 16).
- **Place/global supply network and channels:** IKEA operates a major retail and distribution supply and demand network, with over 320 retail stores globally and about 1,500 suppliers in more than 50 countries (Chapter 17).
- **Process:** IKEA uses a maze service process design to route its customers through its retail stores (Chapter 18).
- **Physical evidence:** IKEA uses its store as the primary medium for presenting and communicating the IKEA concept (Chapter 18).
- **People:** The management style is people based and IKEA recruits staff who share the IKEA vision (Chapter 18).
- **Promotion/communicating value:** IKEA has an integrated marketing communication strategy through advertising, direct mail, personal selling, internet, catalogue, PR and publicity (Chapters 19 and 20).

The choosen marketing mix activities, aligned to the target market and positioning, must be implemented throughout the organisation.

- **Implementing marketing:** IKEA implements its plans through the operationalisation of marketing (Chapter 21).
- **Measuring success:** It uses metrics to quantify, compare and interpret its marketing performance (Chapter 22).

IKEA has grown to be one of the most successful and profitable European companies through a marketing focus on providing customers with what they want.

Good marketing is no accident, but a result of careful planning and execution using state-of-the-art tools and techniques. It becomes both an art and a science as marketers strive to find creative new solutions to often-complex challenges amid profound changes in the 21st-century marketing environment. In this book, we describe how top marketers balance discipline and imagination to address these new marketing realities. In the first chapter, we lay the foundation by reviewing important marketing concepts, tools, frameworks and issues.

The importance of marketing

The first decade of the 21st century challenged companies to prosper financially or even to survive in the face of an unforgiving economic environment. Marketing is playing a key role in addressing those challenges. Finance, operations, accounting and other business functions will not really matter without sufficient demand for products and services so the company can make a profit. In other words, there must be a top line for there to be a bottom line. Thus financial success often depends on marketing ability.

Marketing's broader importance extends to society as a whole. Marketing has helped introduce and gain acceptance of new products and services that have eased or enriched people's lives. Successful marketing builds demand for products and services, which, in turn, creates jobs. By contributing to the bottom line, successful marketing also allows firms to engage more fully in socially responsible activities.[2]

Companies of all kinds – from consumer product manufacturers (mobile phones from Nokia or Ericsson, or cars from BMW or Porsche), to service providers like health-care insurers (Bupa) or hotels (Premier Inn or Club Med), from non-profit organisations (Amnesty International) to industrial product manufacturers (Airbus or Siemens) – all use marketing to understand their core customers and grow their businesses.

Marketing is a complex set of tasks as well as a philosophy of business and it has been the Achilles heel of many formerly prosperous companies – like Christian Lacroix, Waterford Wedgewood and Land of Leather. The role of marketing is always to think customer. Peter Drucker confirms the importance of this customer focus:

> **The purpose of business is to create a customer. The business enterprise has two – and only two – basic functions: marketing and innovation. Marketing and innovation produce results; all the rest are costs. Marketing is the distinguishing, unique function of the business.**

Today, when top management are surveyed, their priorities are often: finance, sales, production, management, legal and people. Missing from the list: marketing and innovation. When one considers the trouble that many business icons have run into in recent years, it is easy to surmise that Drucker's advice would have helped managers to avoid the problems they face today.[3]

Marketing during challenging economic times

The economic recession of 2008 onwards brought budget cuts and intense pressure from senior management to make each euro of marketing spend count. It was important for marketing to respond swiftly and decisively. More than ever, marketers need to understand and adapt to the latest marketplace developments. At greatest risk are firms that fail to carefully monitor their customers and competitors, continuously improve their value offerings and marketing strategies, and satisfy their employees, stockholders, suppliers and channel partners in the process.

Marketing managers have to rethink and reorient their marketing efforts to deliver customer satisfaction within competitive markets. Many market leaders, such as Nokia, realise that they cannot afford to relax their marketing effort as their leadership is challenged by fast and agile competitors like Samsung, and changing consumer tastes. The big European brand winners are companies like Zara and BMW, companies that really understand marketing and how to satisfy changing consumer needs. Awareness of changing consumer and business trends and the use of marketing expertise to change before, or react to, these trends is a core requirement.

Skilful marketing is a never-ending pursuit. As Jay Conrad Levinson, author of *Guerrilla Marketing*, noted: 'Marketing is not an event, but a process . . . It has a beginning, a middle, but never an end, for it is a process. You improve it, perfect it, change it, even pause it.

BMW motorbikes defy recession

BMW prides itself on being the world's number-one car and motorbike manufacturer in the luxury niche market, and also on its marketing ability to react to changing consumer lifestyle segments and match these segments with products. During the recession years of doom and gloom in the car and motorbike sector, BMW's star bike, the R1200 GS,[4] celebrated its most successful sales years ever. The 2010 registration data show that BMW UK sold a record-breaking 6,703 new bikes. This was great news in a motorcycle market that fell 16 per cent overall.

BMW UK was the only volume motorcycle manufacturer to show double-digit growth in the UK, with sales up 12 percentage points. Adrian Roderick, General Manager of BMW Motorrad UK,[5] said: '2010 was another fantastic year for BMW Motorrad UK. In a motorcycle market that is sadly continuing to decline, we have increased our sales and share of the market through BMW's focus on understanding customer needs and satisfying them.'

BMW understand their customers and satisfy their needs

Source: © BMW Group

But you never stop it completely.'[6] This is particularly true in recessionary times. The severe economic recession caused marketers to rethink best practices of management. A recession can be a time of great challenge but also great opportunities. See BMW above.

Marketing insight

Marketing in an age of turbulence

The severe economic recession caused marketers to rethink best practices of management. Kotler and Caslione see management entering a new age of turbulence in which chaos, risk and uncertainty characterise many industries, markets and companies. According to them, turbulence is the new normal, punctuated by periodic and intermittent spurts of prosperity and downturn – including extended downturns amounting to recession, or even depression. They see many new challenges in the foreseeable future, and unlike in past recessions, there may be no assurance that a return to past management practices will ever be successful again.

According to Kotler and Caslione, marketers should always be ready to activate automatic responses when turbulence whips up and chaos reigns. They recommend

marketers keep the following eight factors in mind as they create marketing strategies.

1 Secure your market share from core customer segments. This is not a time to get greedy. Ensure your core customer segments are firmly secured, and be prepared to ward off attacks from competitors seeking your most profitable and loyal customers.

2 Push aggressively for greater market share from competitors. All companies fight for market share, and in turbulent and chaotic times, many have been weakened. Slashing marketing budgets and sales travel expenses is a sure sign that a competitor is buckling under pressure. Push aggressively to add to your core customer segments at the expense of your weakened competitors.

3 Research customers more now because their needs and wants are in flux. Everyone is under pressure during times of turbulence and chaos, and

all customers – even those in your core segments whom you know so well – are changing. Stay close to them as never before. Research them more than ever. Don't find yourself using old, tried-and-tested marketing messages that no longer resonate with them.

4 **Minimally maintain, but seek to increase, your marketing budget.** With your competitors aggressively marketing to your core customers, this is the worst time to think about cutting anything in your marketing budget that targets them. In fact, you need to add to it, or take money away from forays into totally new customer segments. It is time to secure the home front.

5 **Focus on all that's safe and emphasise core values.** When turbulence is scaring everyone in the market, most customers flee to higher ground. They need to feel the safety and security of your company and your products and services. Do everything possible to tell them that continuing to do business with you is safe, and to sell them products and services that keep making them feel safe.

6 **Drop programmes and activities *quickly* that are not working for you.** Your marketing budgets will always be scrutinised, in good times and bad times. If anyone is to cut one of your programmes, let it be you, before anyone else spots any ineffective ones. If you are not watching, rest assured someone else is, including your peers whose budgets could not be protected from the axe.

7 **Don't discount your best brands.** Discounting your established and most successful brands tells the market two things: your prices were too high before, and your products or services will not be worth the price in the future once the discounts are gone. If you want to appeal to more frugal customers, create a new brand with lower prices. This lets value-conscious customers stay close to you, without alienating those still willing to pay for your higher-priced brands. Once the turbulence subsides, you may consider discontinuing the value product or service line – or not.

8 **Save the strong; lose the weak.** In turbulent markets, your strongest brands and products or services must become even stronger. There is no time or money to be wasted on marginal brands or offerings that lack strong value propositions and a solid customer base. Appeal to safety and value to reinforce strong brands, and product and service offerings. Remember, your brands can never be strong enough, especially against the waves of a turbulent economy.

Source: Based on Philip Kotler and John A. Caslione (2009) *Chaotics: The Business of Managing and Marketing in the Age of Turbulence*, AMACOM.

The scope of marketing

To prepare to be a marketer, you need to understand what marketing is, how it works, who does it and what is marketed.

What is marketing?

Marketing is about identifying and meeting human and social needs. One of the shortest definitions of marketing is the process of 'meeting needs profitably'. This has been called 'balanced centricity' – which is a focus on the customer (customer centric) but also on the company and its profit or other objectives.[7] When Nokia (the largest company in Finland) realised that phone design was crucial and designed a range of clam shell phones, the company captured part of a growing market. It demonstrated marketing savvy and expertise in turning a private or social need into a profitable business opportunity. Marketing is a revenue-generating function of a business, and the ultimate test of marketing success is a profit level that allows a company to prosper in the long run.[8]

There is much debate about a definition of marketing. A definition must be generic enough to cover a large variety of products and services in both consumer and business-to-business markets. It must be applicable to different marketing contexts and be able to change. Professor Christian Gronroos of the Hanken Swedish School of Economics in Finland proposed a definition that encompasses customer value, relationship marketing, services marketing and the promise concept.[9]

> **Marketing is a customer focus that permeates organizational functions and processes and is geared towards making promises through value propositions, enabling the fulfillment of individual expectations created by such promises and fulfilling such expectations through support to customers' value-generating processes, thereby supporting value creation in the firm's as well as its customers' and other stakeholders' processes.**

Managing exchange processes between companies and consumers and/or business-to-business customers calls for a considerable amount of work and skill. *Marketing management* takes place when at least one party to a potential exchange manages the means of achieving desired responses from other parties – fulfils promises. Thus we see **marketing management** as *the art and science of choosing target markets and getting, keeping, and growing customers through creating, delivering, and communicating superior customer value.*

Some business people who don't understand marketing think of marketing as 'the art of selling products', or simplistically equate it with **advertising**. Both of these are marketing tactics visible to the consumer. Many people are surprised when they hear that selling is *not* the most important part of marketing and that not all companies have large advertising budgets. Selling and advertising are aspects of the tip of the marketing iceberg. Most of what occurs in marketing happens before the customer sees an advertisement or meets a sales representative. These are the representation of the marketing strategy rather than the totality of marketing. Just like an iceberg, over 80 per cent of marketing occurs out of sight of the consumer. Advertising and sales are the final rather than the beginning stages of marketing. Take Benetton and Zara – two companies that view marketing very differently. Zara succeeded through a core understanding of the customer whereas Benetton's over-focus on advertising damaged the business.

Zara and Benetton

Benetton, which for years had focused on provocative advertising, had to rethink its marketing strategy when new fast-fashion competitor Zara entered the young fashion market and started capturing market share and brand loyalty through a comprehensive marketing strategy. Zara understood the new pattern of consumer behaviour of teenagers and young adults – markets that craved new styles quickly and cheaply and were happy with concepts such as 'fast fashion' and 'disposable clothing'. Zara produces around 12,000 styles per year (compared to the average of 3,000), which means that fresh fashion trends reach the stores quickly. A typical Zara's customer visits a Zara shop 17 times a year compared to the average of three times per year for other fashion shops.[10] Zara studied customer needs and saw that global supply network management – getting the fashion into the shops quickly (Chapter 17) was critical to success. It also decided to use its shop and the purchasing process as the company's main image vehicle (Chapter 18), rather than the more traditional focus on advertising (Chapters 19 and 20). Zara's advertising budget is 0.03 per cent of its revenues,[11] which is very different from Benetton, which focused on creative advertising, spending €80 million on advertising alone. Benetton has now seen the errors of its ways, investing over €160 million in modernising its global supply chain. Zara has become the world's largest clothing retailer, by focusing on understanding consumer needs and behaviour and by providing value to the customer.

Marketing means understanding customer and consumer needs and making marketing choices to match these needs. Zara prospered due to its focus on rapid delivery of fashion styles to the market, while Benetton floundered due to its over-focus on advertising. Advertising is not everything; marketers need to use the full range of the marketing mix variables to succeed.
Source: David Pearson/Alamy (left); Image courtesy of The Advertising Archives (right)

Peter Drucker, a leading management theorist, describes the process of marketing this way: 'The aim of marketing is to know and understand the customer so well that the product or service fits him/her and sells itself.' Ideally, marketing should result in a customer who is ready to buy. All that should be needed then is to make the product or service available.[12] When Nintendo designed its Wii game, when Sony designed its PlayStation 3

The main focus of marketing is on what occurs below the waterline rather than above it. These are all the decisions that marketers make before the product or service comes to the market, and afterwards to maintain its position in the market. Non-marketers are inclined to think that marketing is only what occurs above the line.
Source: Ralph A. Clevenger/Corbis.

game system, when Apple launched its iPod, and when Toyota introduced its Prius hybrid car, these companies were swamped with orders because they had designed the 'right' product or service, based on executing and managing carefully designed and complete marketing programmes aimed at a recognised customer need.

Understanding markets

The creation of value is the core purpose and central process of economic exchange. Marketers focus on need satisfaction and creating value for the customer. Charles Revson of Revlon once observed: 'In the factory we make cosmetics; in the chemist we sell hope.' Products and services are platforms for delivering benefit or value. Marketing managers can market seven entities: services, products, events, experiences, people, places and ideas (social marketing). Let's take a quick look at these categories.

Services

Services are moving to centre stage in the global arena. Service is defined as the application of competencies (knowledge and skills) for the benefit of another party.[13] Services include airlines, hotels, car hire, hairdressers and beauticians, maintenance and repair, accountants, bankers, solicitors, engineers, doctors, software programmers and management consultants. The European economy, as a mature economy, consists of a 70–30 services-to-product GDP ratio.

Many market offerings consist of a mix of products and services. Take a physical product like a car, which provides the service of getting from one place to another. But the car comes with its own need for services such as insurance, finance, repairs and petrol. The Swedish car manufacturer Volvo has built a service into its cars that alerts the driver if they are falling asleep. Another example is a mobile phone provider such as Nokia. The company provides a product (mobile phone handsets) but also a service (networks). Nokia sees itself as a service or solutions provider and this is reflected in its slogan: 'Connecting People'.

According to the World Trade Organization (WTO), the services sector accounts globally for €1 trillion of world trade. Over two-thirds of the workforce in Europe are employed in services and between 60 and 70 per cent of the gross value-added figure achieved by European countries can be attributed to services. Table 1.1 shows a mix of service and product companies within the top European companies.

Table 1.1 The top European companies

Europe rank 2011	Europe rank 2010	Company	Country	Sector
1	3	Royal Dutch Shell	UK	Oil & gas producers
2	1	Nestle	Switzerland	Food producers
3	7	Gazprom	Russia	Oil & gas producers
4	4	HSBC	UK	Banks
5	9	Vodafone Group	UK	Mobile telecommunications
6	5	Novartis	Switzerland	Pharmaceuticals & biotechnology
7	8	Total	France	Oil & gas producers
8	2	BP	UK	Oil & gas producers
9	6	Roche	Switzerland	Pharmaceuticals & biotechnology
10	16	Siemens	Germany	General industrials

Historically, business management theory focused on products rather than services, but now there is a blurring of the boundaries between products and services. For example, the iPod made by Apple not only provides an individual music download service through iTunes but also functions as the playing equipment.

All companies can be considered service companies, with service as the fundamental basis of exchange – what is called a service dominant logic – used to denote this shift in thinking from a goods (product) dominant logic. A service logic is multi-dimensional, enabling the mutual creation of value, with service as a mediating factor.[14]

This perspective acknowledges the importance of the customer experience of exchange, whether with a product or service, and thus the full 7 Ps of the marketing mix are used for all companies. A can of soup is not viewed as being a product, but instead as being the appliance to which the user of the can of soup co-creates value with the provider of the soup. It acknowledges that the company alone does not offer value to a consumer; value is in fact created when the company and the customer work together; this is known as **value co-creation**. Value co-creation is the focus on value-in-use and in-context and suggests that service systems within companies should simultaneously access, adapt and integrate resources to create value with their customers.[15]

Products

Marketing has always oriented towards the marketing of products, reflecting its historical development in the agricultural sector. European companies manufacture and market billions of fresh, canned, bagged and frozen food products, and millions of cars, refrigerators, television sets, machines and various other mainstays of a modern economy. In marketing, the term 'product' is often used as a catch-all word to identify solutions that a marketer provides to its target market. Something is considered a **product** if it is a tangible item – often something that can be touched or 'dropped on your foot'.

Events

Music shows such as Take That or U2 tours, the Glastonbury music festival in England or the Hurricane music festival in Germany, the Frankfurt book fair and other major trade fairs or international summits are all global marketing events that take months to plan and market. Event marketing is big business, as evidenced by the battles to host such events as the Olympic Games and the World Cup in football. For example, London won a two-way fight with Paris by 54 votes to 50, to host the 2012 Olympic Games. The British Prime Minister described the win as 'a momentous day for Britain'.[16]

Experiences

By managing several services and products, a firm can create, stage and market experiences. Take Alton Towers – the most popular theme park in Britian – or Disneyland Paris or Legoland in Denmark and Germany. They all represent experiential marketing, allowing customers to experience a fairy kingdom, a pirate ship, a Lego town or fun rides and water park activities complete with hotel accommodation and food. There is also a growing market for customised experiences, such as spending a week at a Samba Soccer camp, on a yoga retreat in Kitzbühel, Austria, or skiing on Mont Blanc in the Alps.[17]

Persons

Artists, musicians, chefs, CEOs, financiers and other professionals can all become celebrities through clever marketing. Some people have done a masterful job of marketing themselves and becoming global celebrities – think of David Beckham, Bono, Penélope Cruz and Carla Bruni. In the United Kingdom, chefs such as Gordon Ramsay, Jamie Oliver

Jamie Oliver has skilfully managed his career as a brand with books, television shows and restaurants
Source: KPA/Zuma/Rex Features

and Nigella Lawson have all become household names, with their own brands of restaurants, cookbooks and kitchen utensils.

Places

Cities, states, regions and nations compete to attract tourists, factories, company headquarters and new residents.[18] Place marketing includes a full marketing programme to attract both tourism and inward economic investment, often called Foreign Direct Investment (FDI). Europe is the most visited region in the world with six European countries in the world's top ten destinations for holiday-makers – France tops the list for top destination and Paris tops the list for most visited city (see Table 1.2).[19]

Table 1.2 Top ten most visited cities by estimated number of international visitors, 2010

City	Country	International visitors (millions)
Paris	France	15.1
London	United Kingdom	14.6
New York City	United States	9.7
Antalya	Turkey	9.2
Kuala Lumpur	Malaysia	8.9
Singapore	Singapore	8.6
Hong Kong	China	8.4
Dubai	United Arab Emirates	8.3
Bangkok	Thailand	7.2
Istanbul	Turkey	6.9

Source: *World Tourism Figures* (2010) United Nations World Tourism Organization; http://en.wikipedia.org/wiki/Tourism#Most_visited_countries_by_international_tourist_arrivals.

Ideas

Every market offering includes a basic idea. **Social marketing** is an umbrella term used to describe how, in different ways, marketing can encourage positive social behaviour.[20] Whether it is concerned with obesity, gambling or drink-driving, to encourage people to drive slowly, think about recycling, stop smoking or eat healthily, marketing can be instrumental in encouraging people to think differently. For example, both Europe's 'Safe and Sober' campaign,[21] and the UK's 'Alcohol: Know your Limits' campaign supported alcohol restraint.[22] The '5 a day' campaign by the UK's Department of Health encourages consumers to think about eating five portions of fruit and vegetables a day. Supermarkets such as Marks & Spencer and Tesco now display a '5 a day' sign on products that contribute to this objective.

Marketing's role in creating demand

Marketers are skilled at stimulating demand. Demand is the willingness and ability of buyers to purchase different quantities of a product or service, at different prices, during a specific time period. Both willingness and ability must be present; if either is missing, there is no demand. Great marketing is when you see an unrecognised need and launch an appropriate offering and the offering matches this need and there is demand and ultimately profitable sales of your offering.

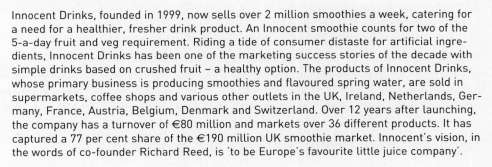

Innocent Drinks

Innocent Drinks, founded in 1999, now sells over 2 million smoothies a week, catering for a need for a healthier, fresher drink product. An Innocent smoothie counts for two of the 5-a-day fruit and veg requirement. Riding a tide of consumer distaste for artificial ingredients, Innocent Drinks has been one of the marketing success stories of the decade with simple drinks based on crushed fruit – a healthy option. The products of Innocent Drinks, whose primary business is producing smoothies and flavoured spring water, are sold in supermarkets, coffee shops and various other outlets in the UK, Ireland, Netherlands, Germany, France, Austria, Belgium, Denmark and Switzerland. Over 12 years after launching, the company has a turnover of €80 million and markets over 36 different products. It has captured a 77 per cent share of the €190 million UK smoothie market. Innocent's vision, in the words of co-founder Richard Reed, is 'to be Europe's favourite little juice company'.

Marketing managers seek to influence the level, timing and composition of demand to meet the organisation's objectives. Eight states of market demand are possible:

1 **Full demand.** Consumers buy all services or products brought to market.
2 **Overfull demand.** There are more consumers demanding the service or product than can be satisfied.
3 **Irregular demand.** Consumer purchases vary on a seasonal, monthly, weekly, daily or even hourly basis.
4 **Declining demand.** Consumers begin to buy the service or product less frequently or not at all.
5 **Negative demand.** Consumers dislike the service or product and may even pay a price to avoid it.
6 **Non-existent demand.** Consumers may be unaware of or uninterested in the product or service.
7 **Latent demand.** Consumers may share a strong need that cannot be satisfied by an existing product or service.
8 **Unwholesome demand.** Consumers may be attracted to services or products that have undesirable social consequences.

In each case, marketers must identify the underlying cause(s) of the demand state and then determine a plan of action to shift the demand to a more desirable state.

Core marketing concepts

Needs are the basic human requirements such as those for air, food, water, clothing and shelter. Humans also have strong needs for recreation, education and entertainment. These needs become *wants* when they are directed to specific objects that might satisfy the need. A German consumer needs food but may want a sandwich, while a consumer in China needs food but may want rice. Wants are shaped by our society.

Demands are wants for specific products or services backed by an ability to pay. Many people want a Mercedes; only a few are able to buy one. Companies must measure not only how many people want their offering, but also how many are willing and able to buy it.

These distinctions shed light on the frequent criticism that 'marketers create needs' or 'marketers get people to buy things they don't want'. Marketers do not create needs: needs pre-exist marketers. Marketers, along with other societal factors, influence wants. They might promote the idea that a Mercedes would satisfy a person's need for social status. They do not, however, create the need for social status.

Some customers have needs of which they are not fully conscious or that they cannot articulate. What does it mean when the customer asks for a 'powerful' lawnmower or a 'peaceful' hotel? The marketer must probe further. We can distinguish five types of needs:

1 Stated needs (the customer wants an inexpensive car).
2 Real needs (the customer wants a car whose operating cost, not initial price, is low).
3 Unstated needs (the customer expects good service from the dealer).
4 Delight needs (the customer would like the dealer to include an onboard GPS navigation system).
5 Secret needs (the customer wants friends to see them as a savvy consumer).

Responding only to the stated need may shortchange the customer.[23] Consumers did not know much about mobile phones when they were first introduced, and Nokia and Ericsson fought to shape consumer perceptions of them in terms of size, shape and usage. To gain an edge, companies must help consumers learn what they want.

Segmentation, target markets and positioning

Not everyone likes the same cereal, restaurant, university or film. Therefore, marketers start by dividing the market into segments. They identify and profile distinct groups of buyers who might prefer or require varying product and service mixes by examining demographic, psychographic and behavioural differences among consumers.

After identifying market segments, the marketer decides which present the greatest opportunities – which are its *target markets*. For each, the firm develops a *market offering* that it *positions* in the minds of the target buyers as delivering some central benefit(s). (See Chapters 10 and 11.) Volvo develops its cars for buyers to whom safety is a major concern, positioning its vehicles as the safest a customer can buy.

Offerings and brands

Companies address customer needs by putting forth a **value proposition** – a set of benefits that satisfy those needs. The intangible value proposition is made physical by an *offering*, which can be a combination of products, services, information and experiences.

A *brand* is an offering from a known source. A brand name such as German-based T-Mobile carries many associations in people's minds that make up its image: mobile phone, network availability, mobile phone accessories, convenience, cost and billing, and customer service along with its distinctive logo. All companies strive to build a brand image with as many strong, favourable and unique brand associations as possible. (See Chapters 12 and 13.)

Value and satisfaction

The buyer chooses the offerings he or she perceives to deliver the most *value*, the sum of the tangible and intangible benefits and costs to them. Value, a central marketing concept, is primarily a combination of quality, service and price ('qsp'), called the **customer value triad**. Value perceptions increase with quality and service but decrease with price.

We can think of marketing as the identification, creation, communication, delivery, and monitoring of customer value. *Satisfaction* reflects a person's judgement of an offering's perceived performance in relation to expectations. If the performance falls short of expectations, the customer is disappointed. If it matches expectations, the customer is satisfied. If it exceeds them, the customer is delighted.

Marketing channels

To reach a target market, the marketer uses three kinds of marketing channels (see Chapter 17). *Communication channels* deliver and receive messages from companies to target buyers and include newspapers, magazines, radio, television, mail, telephone, billboards, posters, fliers, CDs, audiotapes and the internet. Beyond these, companies communicate through the look of their retail stores and websites and other media. Marketers are increasingly adding dialogue channels such as email, **blogs** and free phone numbers to familiar monologue channels such as advertisements.

The marketer uses *distribution channels* to display, sell or deliver the physical product or service(s) to the buyer or user. These channels may be direct to the customer via the internet, mail or mobile phone or telephone, or indirect with distributors, wholesalers, retailers, and agents as intermediaries.

To carry out transactions with potential buyers, the marketer also uses *service channels* that include warehouses, transportation companies, banks and insurance companies. Marketers clearly face a design challenge in choosing the best mix of communication, distribution and service channels for their offerings.

Supply networks

The supply network or value network (traditionally called the *supply chain*) is a longer more complex channel stretching from raw materials to components to finished products carried to final buyers. The supply chain for coffee may start with Ethiopian farmers, who plant, tend and pick the coffee beans, selling their harvest to wholesalers or perhaps a Fair Trade cooperative. If sold through the cooperative, the coffee is washed, dried and packaged for shipment by an ATO (Alternative Trading Organisation) that pays a minimum of €0.90 a pound. The ATO transports the coffee to the market where it can sell it directly or via retail channels. Each company captures only a certain percentage of the total value generated by the supply network's value delivery system. When a company acquires competitors or expands upstream or downstream, its aim is to capture a higher percentage of supply network value.

Businesses operate within a complex interacting set of businesses and markets linked through exchange and other processes, referred to as the *network economy*. A **network organisation** often has a small core organisation and then outsources value activities to key partners. A network is a group of companies that has a minimum of formal structures and relies instead on the formation and dissolution of teams to meet specific objectives. A network organisation utilises information and communications technologies extensively, and makes use of knowledge across and within companies along the value or supply network. Such organisations often link across boundaries and geographical areas, and work together for a common purpose. They have multiple leaders, lots of formal and informal links and interacting levels.[24] Managing a network of companies is a core marketing requirement.

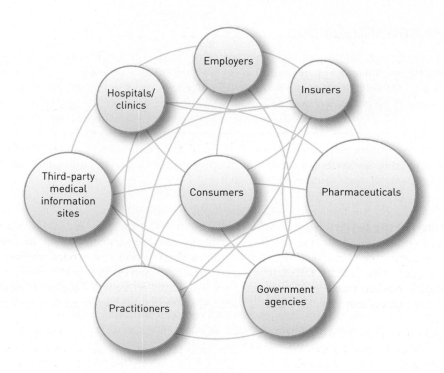

Figure 1.1 The healthcare market: an example of a contemporary network
Source: H. J. Schau, M. F. Smith and P. I. Schau (2005) The healthcare network economy: the role of internet information transfer and implications for pricing, *Industrial Marketing Management*, 34, 147–56. Reproduced with permission.

Take, for example, the healthcare network in Figure 1.1. This reflects not only the linkages between companies within the network, but also the participation by the consumer in these networks. Marketing outcomes are dependent on networks, and these face competition from other networks of companies as well as competition from individual companies.[25]

Competition

Competition includes all the actual and potential rival offerings and substitutes a buyer might consider (see Chapter 9). Many companies have a less than perfect understanding of their competitive environment. The number of businesses in any industry that have no competitors can be counted on the fingers of one hand. To understand competition you need to perform a detailed competitor analysis. **Competitor analysis** is the gathering, organising and interpreting of information about existing and potential competitors. Competitive analysis is an ongoing process that should be an integral part of your overall strategic planning. When a company positions its brand in a customer's mind, it is positioning that brand against other brands. It is critical to understand the strengths, weaknesses, opportunities and threats of each of those competitors along with the industry structure itself. This knowledge about your competition is necessary because you want to uniquely 'own' an important benefit in your customer's mind.[26]

Markets

Traditionally, a 'market' was a physical place where buyers and sellers gathered to buy and sell products and trade services. Economists describe a *market* as a collection of buyers and sellers who transact a particular service or product, or product or service class (such as the housing market, the airline market or the gaming market).

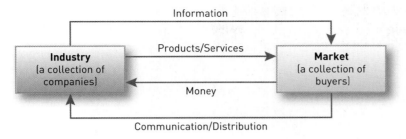

Figure 1.2 A simple marketing system

Marketers use the term **market** to describe various groupings of customers who buy their products or services. They view other companies with similar or substitute products and services as constituting the industry, and groups of buyers as constituting the market. They talk about need markets (the health food market), product or service markets (the shoe market or the holiday travel market), demographic markets (the youth market), and geographic markets (the French market). They extend the concept still further to describe other, not immediately obvious markets, such as voter markets, labour markets and donor markets.

Figure 1.2 shows the relationship between the industry and the market. Companies and buyers are connected by four flows. The company distributes products and services to the market; and in return it receives money or payment and information, such as customer attitudes and sales data. The inner loop shows an exchange of money for products and services; the outer loop shows an exchange of information.

Types of market

Consider the following key markets: consumer, business, global and non-profit.

Consumer markets

Consumer purchases are generally made by individual decision-makers or a decision-making unit, either for themselves or for others with whom they have relationships. The consumer market is made up of companies marketing consumer products and services as diverse as soft drinks (Red Bull), make-up (L'Oréal), air travel (AirFrance), shoes (Clarks) and car insurance (the Automobile Association) (see Chapter 7).

Consumer purchasing power within Europe is larger than in the USA (see Figure 1.3). European consumers had a net household income of approximately €7.9 bn available for consumer purchases in 2010. This corresponds to an average purchasing power of €11,945 per inhabitant of the 42 countries considered by the study. This is an increase of around 2.1 per cent over the previous year's level. The financial crisis has definitely left its mark in some countries. However, there have been no major shifts in the purchasing power levels of the wealthier countries evaluated.

Within the consumer market the level of choice has expanded. Take Tesco – the UK-based retailer – where the average number of product lines has exploded from 5,000 in 1983 to over 50,000 in 2011. Only 20 years ago the average UK consumer could choose between three TV channels; now there are around 300 channels broadcasting to UK subscribers. The café chain Coffee Republic offers 11 different types of coffee, four added toppings, three types of milk and sugar, and three types of cup size – in all, 6,000 different ways to have a cup of coffee. A visit to any chemist will yield 14 different types of dental floss and over 20 different toothpastes.[27] We live in a time of 'choice explosion'.[28]

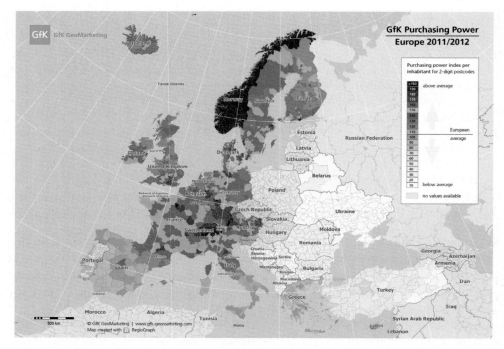

Figure 1.3 European purchasing power in 2010/11
Source: GFK Geomarketing (2011) GfK Purchasing Power Europe study finds Europeans' consumer potential on the rise again in 2010, www.gfk.com/imperia/md/content/presse/pressemeldungen2010/20101117_pr_purchasing-power_europe.pdf

Customers can now log on to the internet and choose from over 100,000 CDs rather than having to travel to a shop that can physically stock perhaps only 25,000 CDs. This changes choice, it changes distribution, it changes the service aspects and it changes the marketing programmes that marketers need to use. Information technology changes space–time–place relations; we have yet to grasp the scope of this disruption.[29]

Apple iTunes

As of 2011 Apple's iTunes had sold over 10 billion music downloads to more than 50 million customers. The Apple's iTunes App Store, launched alongside iPhone 3G, has grown to over 300,000 apps, with roughly 159 million iPhone, iPod touch and iPad devices sold to date. 'With more than 10 billion apps downloaded in just two and a half years – a staggering seven billion apps in the last year alone – the App Store has surpassed our wildest dreams,' said Philip Schiller, Apple's senior vice president of Worldwide Product Marketing. 'The App Store has revolutionised how software is created, distributed, discovered and sold. While others try to copy the App Store, it continues to offer developers and customers the most innovative experience on the planet.'[30]

Business markets

The terms *business*, *business-to-business* or *industrial marketing* focus on understanding business buying centres and on how businesses purchase in different ways to consumers (see Chapter 8). **Business markets** are often networked organisations operating in a complex environment. Nowadays the focus is on neither consumers nor business markets, but on recognising that the lines between the two are blurring in four important ways:[31]

1 A blurring of value networks through outsourcing and other relationships that allow networks of companies and customers to operate (see Chapter 17). When Apple set up its iTunes online music store, it brought together recording companies with music and customers who wanted to download music tracks for €0.99 – a mix of consumer and business-to-business marketing for Apple.

2 A blurring of relationships with customers, as customers are invited to participate with companies in the design and delivery processes. The decline in travel agencies as customers book directly with airlines is an example where the customer is very involved in the business – booking, checking in and seat selection are all carried out by the customer.

3 A blurring of functions within the firm as marketing and other functions are more integrated through technology.

4 A blurring of products, services and customer experience, moving from an 'industrial' base to a knowledge-based society.

Pharmaceutical firms have long focused on business markets such as doctors, hospitals, clinics and insurance providers. In recent years, however, they have recognised the need to combine this approach with extensive campaigns to build consumer awareness and demand for new medicines and treatments. Rather than relying on channels to drive awareness, these companies work from the consumer side and the industrial side simultaneously to create sales in the middle.

Global markets

Globalisation characterises the climate of business and society in the 21st century. This text is oriented towards global companies and each chapter explores both global and local marketing issues. We have more global companies than at any other time in the history of the world. Global companies face unique and additional decisions and challenges (see Chapter 2). They must decide which countries to enter; how to enter each (indirect exporting, direct exporting, licensing, joint ventures or direct investment); whether to adapt their product and service features to each country; how to price their products and services in different countries; how to adapt their communications to fit different cultures; and how to manage their service process, people and technology across the globe and within a network of companies. They make these decisions in the face of different requirements for buying, negotiating, owning and disposing of products and services; different cultures, languages and legal and political systems; and currencies that might fluctuate in value. Yet the pay-off for doing all this additional marketing can be huge.

Non-profit, voluntary and government markets

Companies selling to non-profit organisations such as churches, universities, charities and government agencies need to understand marketing as much as private, profit-making companies. There is no agreed definition of the non-profit sector, which has also been called the third sector, as opposed to the public sector and the business sector. It is variously termed the independent sector in Scandinavian countries; civil society in central and eastern Europe; the charitable sector or voluntary sector in the United Kingdom and Ireland; and the *économie sociale* in France. On average 5 per cent of the annual gross domestic produce of the OECD nations arises from these sectors, and governments throughout the world are increasingly involved in marketing programmes, communications, campaigns and regulations.[32]

Real Madrid

Football is arguably one of the most successfully marketed sports in the world, and the marketing of football has become an increasingly important issue, as clubs and product owners seek to generate more revenue from the sport both nationally and internationally. Over the last ten years, football has moved from a national culture to a global sport. The popular Spanish football club Real Madrid is the world's best-known football team with the largest global fan base of more than 450 million fans worldwide, compared to 75 million for Manchester United and 31 million for Juventus.

Real Madrid became a global brand through the marketing expertise of Florentino Perez, the man who is credited with turning Real Madrid from an 'old-fashioned soccer club' into a star-studded global marketing brand. Perez spent millions on players including Zinedane Zidane, David Beckham, Christiano Ronaldo and Luis Figo. New coach Jose Mourinho and a range of signings like Germany's World Cup 2010 star Mesut Özil and Ricardo Carvalho keep Real Madrid to the forefront of football. Perez's pledge is that each season the world's best will play for Real Madrid.

Real Madrid is the most valuable football brand in Europe with a brand value of over €1 billion. Much of the revenue comes from club merchandising, such as football shirt sales and image rights. 'Jersey sales represent the core business of many clubs and are often responsible for around 50 per cent of merchandising revenue,' said Andreas Ullmann, a senior consultant at Sport+Markt. Clubs in Europe's top five leagues generated merchandising and licensing revenue of €631 million in 2010. The top ten clubs ranked by retail revenue were: Real Madrid, Barcelona, Liverpool, Bayern Munich, Olympique Marseille, Manchester United, AC Milan, Inter Milan, Olympique Lyon and Fenerbahce. Clubs often travel on international tours to increase their revenues and fan base – particularly in the Asian market.[33]

Real Madrid is now a global organisation with over 450 million fans worldwide

Source: Aflo/Rex Features

Marketplaces, marketspaces and metamarkets

The *marketplace* is physical, such as the shop you purchase in; the *marketspace* is digital, as when you buy online, conduct your banking online or use an ATM, or when you use a kiosk for booking, ordering or confirming.[34]

The *metamarket*, proposed by Mohan Sawhney, describes a cluster of complementary products and services that are closely related in the minds of consumers, but spread across a diverse set of industries.[35] The car metamarket consists of car manufacturers, new and used car dealers, financing and insurance companies, mechanics, spare parts dealers, service shops, car magazines, classified car adverts in newspapers, and car websites on the internet. In purchasing a car, a buyer will get involved in many parts of this metamarket, and this creates an opportunity for *metamediaries* to assist buyers in moving seamlessly through these groups, although they are disconnected in physical space. **Metamediaries** are intermediaries that bring together collections of companies or people. One example is Auto Trader, the world's largest car marketplace (www.autotrader.com), which provides a website where car buyers can study the stated features and prices of different cars and easily click to other sites to search for the lowest price or nearest dealer, for financing, accessories and used cars. Metamediaries are also operational in other metamarkets such as the home ownership market, the parenting and baby care market, and the wedding market.

Autotrader.nl is a metamediary website that helps prospective car buyers navigate the car metamarket.
Source: European Auto Trader BV.

The new European marketing realities

We can say with some confidence that the marketplace is not what it used to be. It is dramatically different from what it was even ten years ago. Marketers must attend and respond to a number of significant developments locally, globally and more specifically within the European Union.

The contemporary environment is a world of immense complexity, contradiction and change, including global conglomerates with stunning technological developments; poverty amidst plenty; ongoing financial crises across the globe; the growth in the European Union to 27 member states; conflicts and social unrest around the world and particularly in the Middle East; and unprecedented stock growth and decline.[36]

A feature of Europe is the diversity in European markets, with embedded cultural, political, historical and geographical characteristics – from the powerful large nations at the centre, like Germany and France, to more peripheral nations like Greece, Ireland and Portugal.[37] T. R. Reid, the author of *The United States of Europe: From the Euro to Eurovision – the superpower nobody talks about*, notes that

> **Europe covers just 6 per cent of the Earth's total area and is home to just 12 per cent of the global population; yet Europe has 40 per cent of the world's wealth and accounts for more than half of all global commerce. European countries comprise five of the world's ten richest nations. The continent was the birthplace of 'Western values', the combination of individual rights, democratic governments and free markets that has spread around the world.[38]**

Major societal forces

Today the marketplace is radically different as a result of major, and sometimes interlinking, societal forces that have created new behaviours, new opportunities and new challenges.

Recession, global downturn and economic recovery

A recession is a general slowdown in economic activity over a sustained period of time, or a business cycle contraction. In 2008 a worldwide recession occurred, which fundamentally changed the marketplace. Many companies struggled to survive after almost 15 years of unprecedented growth and prosperity. The previous generation had been nicknamed the McLuxury generation, enjoying increased consumer spending fuelled by easy credit and a property boom in many European countries. This era's consumers are called the McThrift generation, looking for quality and value now that spending has contracted and growth has slowed. A recession can be a time of great challenge but also great opportunity. Some of the most successful companies in the world were founded and flourished during recessions/depressions, such as Wikipedia, IBM, CNN, Burger King, Microsoft and UPS (see marketing memo below).

Marketing memo

Marketing: a winner in a crisis

According to a German study, marketing is more efficient in times of crisis.

In times of recession, companies can win – or lose – market share very rapidly. Companies often respond incorrectly during a recession, with marketing budgets being slashed when the company's management and shareholders call for savings to be made. This study analysed the behaviour of 700 brands during the last recession after the internet bubble burst. The most important results were:

- 54 per cent of companies that recorded growth in sales and market share during the last recession maintained or raised their marketing budgets.

- Market shares shift faster during times of recession than in times of growth.

- The losers are often brands in the mid segment, as they cannot increase their marketing expenditure.

- 63 per cent of winners in the last recession introduced new products and innovations, compared to just 19 per cent of the losers.

The clear winners during the last recession were those companies that did not reduce their marketing budgets but instead invested anti-cyclically. They were able to achieve significantly higher growth than in normal times.[39]

Recessions or economic downturns force marketers to review their focus on their customers and to concentrate their marketing effort where it is most needed, as the case of Burberry shows.

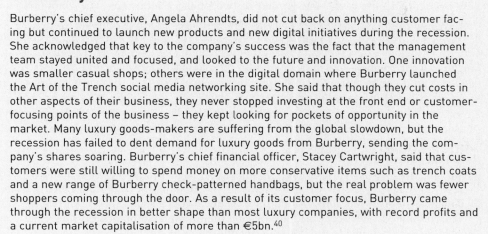

Burberry

Burberry's chief executive, Angela Ahrendts, did not cut back on anything customer facing but continued to launch new products and new digital initiatives during the recession. She acknowledged that key to the company's success was the fact that the management team stayed united and focused, and looked to the future and innovation. One innovation was smaller casual shops; others were in the digital domain where Burberry launched the Art of the Trench social media networking site. She said that though they cut costs in other aspects of their business, they never stopped investing at the front end or customer-focusing points of the business – they kept looking for pockets of opportunity in the market. Many luxury goods-makers are suffering from the global slowdown, but the recession has failed to dent demand for luxury goods from Burberry, sending the company's shares soaring. Burberry's chief financial officer, Stacey Cartwright, said that customers were still willing to spend money on more conservative items such as trench coats and a new range of Burberry check-patterned handbags, but the real problem was fewer shoppers coming through the door. As a result of its customer focus, Burberry came through the recession in better shape than most luxury companies, with record profits and a current market capitalisation of more than €5bn.[40]

Heightened competition

Companies are facing more intense competition from domestic and foreign brands, resulting in rising marketing costs and shrinking profit margins. Many brands are buffeted by powerful retailers that market their own-label brands. Many brands have become megabrands and extended into related or unrelated product or service categories: easyJet now has at least 17 products or services, including easyMobile, easyCinema and easyHotel. Within the mobile phone market the main players, such as Vodaphone, TMobile, Orange and 3, have to compete with unrelated companies like Tesco, the UK retailer – with over 2.5 million customers – along with ASDA, which have both entered the mobile phone market, as has Italian fashion designer Prada. These are entrants into an already competitive market. Another Italian fashion designer, Armani, has expanded into hotels with the Armani Hotel in Dubai.

Globalisation

The increase in world trade, a continuing integration of the world's major economies, and the onward march of globalisation mean that marketing will continue to have a more global orientation. This, coupled with technological advances in transportation, shipping and communications, has made it easier for companies to market and easier for consumers to buy products and services from all over the world. We now consider it normal to ship kiwi fruit from New Zealand and oranges from South Africa, and in the services area we find it normal to access money from ATMs all over the world and to phone home from anywhere without any difficulty.

Increased range of information and digital technologies

The marketplace has more technology than ever before. Companies can communicate and connect globally in minutes and real-time online information is normal. The range of technologies within the marketing domain is extensive – from internets to databases, from kiosks to planning software, from mobile phones to self-service technologies (see Chapter 4). Marketing managers need to understand and embrace the current range of digital technologies both internally and externally and also monitor new and innovative technologies.

The adoption and use of information technology should be customer focused, providing value to the customer and gaining valuable insights for the company, from the information collection aspect of technology.[41]

Industry convergence

Industry boundaries are blurring at an incredible rate as companies are recognising that new opportunities lie at the intersection of two or more industries. The computing and consumer electronics industries are converging as the giants of the computer world release a stream of entertainment devices – from iPods and MP3 players to plasma TVs and camcorders. Google has developed a smart car which can drive without a driver – from a search engine to a car engine – moving Google into car manufacturing. Nike and Apple have succeeded with a sports and music industry convergence. Nike has teamed with Apple iPod to offer a Nike–Apple workout experience. A sensor is placed in the Nike sports shoe and a receiver is attached to an iPod Nano. During training, the iPod will select music, provide statistics, and coach, encourage and provide feedback on running performance.

Retail transformation

Retailing in Europe has been transformed in four ways:

1 **The growth of own brands.** Within the consumer goods sector, powerful retailers now control limited shelf space and are placing their own-label brands on shelves in competition with national brands. By offering their own-brand labels, they can reap higher profit margins and, with the huge quantities they purchase, can bargain hard with their suppliers.

2 **Retail internationalisation.** Although international retailing has a long history, the processes of internationalisation have accelerated dramatically over the last two decades, with the major retailers launching across the globe. European players dominate retail landscapes across world regions; UK-based Tesco is one of the world's biggest retailers along with Carrefour, the French retailer. Tesco aims to generate more than half the group's total sales from international markets, with Tesco's move into South Korea and the USA as part of its international expansion.

3 **The fragmentation of the retail market in Europe.** Traditionally the European market has many small retailers, but most areas are succumbing to the growing power of giant retailers.

4 **Competition forces.** Competition from an explosion of retail outlets, out-of-town shopping centres and the internet has caused many changes in retailing. In response, entrepreneurial retailers are building entertainment into their shops, with bookshop–café combinations, lectures, demonstrations and in-store performances providing an 'experience' rather than a product assortment (see Mac Cosmetics below).

MAC Cosmetics

A division of French cosmetics giant Estée Lauder, MAC (which stands for Make Up Artist and Customer) has 1,000 stores worldwide, which don't simply sell make-up and lipsticks. Instead, they rely on highly paid 'artists' to bond with each customer during a free make-up consultation and application lesson. While this service process strategy (see Chapter 18) is hardly new in the world of retail make-up, what is unique is that MAC's artists are not focused on increasing their commission and loading customers down with more products. Rather, they are trained to collaborate with customers so they will leave the store with €50 or more of MAC products *and* the feeling, 'I can definitely do this at home.' The goal, says Matthew Waitesmith, MAC's head of 'artist training and development', is for each customer to feel she has had an authentically artistic experience 'that hopefully means they'll return to the place that makes them feel like an artist'.[42]

New consumer capabilities

Contemporary consumers and consumption patterns are changing.

Consumers in a recession or economic recovery

The arrival of a recession and economic recovery heralded a change in **consumer behaviour**. Consumers who are fearful for their livelihood may switch segments if their economic situation changes for the worse. All groups prioritise consumption by sorting products and services into the following categories:

- essentials – necessary items;
- treats – something to give pleasure;
- postponables – offerings they can put off but will purchase another time; and
- expendables – purchases they will cancel.

Consumers in a recession can be divided into four groups:

1 **The slam-on-the-brakes segment**: the most vulnerable and hardest-hit group, which has responded by eliminating, postponing and decreasing all types of spending. Some have low incomes, but anxious higher-income consumers fall into this category as well.
2 **Pained but patient**: these consumers tend to be resilient and optimistic about the long-term picture, but less confident about recovery in the near term. This group is also cutting spending in all areas, but less aggressively.
3 **Comfortably well off**: consumers who feel secure about their ability to ride out the recession. Their consumption is relatively unchanged, but they may tend to be more selective and less conspicuous with their spending.
4 **Live-for-today consumers**: consumers who may be in debt but who will continue to spend at pre-recession levels.

As stated in a recent *Harvard Business Review*: 'Marketers typically segment according to demographics or lifestyle. In a recession, such segmentation may be less relevant than a psychological segmentation that takes into consideration consumers' emotional reactions to the economic environment'.[43] Understanding the cyclical nature of markets and the stage of economic development provides marketers with the ability to forecast the spending patterns of their customers. The marketing insight below provides a technique for business cycle forecasting.

Marketing insight

How to become a business cycle forecaster

'Give an executive team a forecast, and guide it for a quarter. Teach an executive team how to forecast, and guide it for a lifetime.' This aptly captures the value of learning how to become your own business cycle forecaster by using a 'GDP forecasting equation'. A nation's gross domestic product (GDP) measures its economic growth, and changes in the GDP growth rate chart movements in the business cycle. GDP refers to the market value of all final goods and services produced within a country in a given period. It is often considered an indicator of a country's standard of living. By following GDP's four components – consumption, business investment, net exports and government spending – any manager can develop a very keen sense of where the business cycle may be heading and quickly spot potential recessionary dangers ahead.

At the right of the diagram on the next page are the economic indicators and reports that managers regularly follow to anticipate movements and key turning points in the business cycle. A tabulation of these will indicate the GDP of the nation. The ISM index is a national manufacturing index based on a survey of purchasing managers (PMI) at roughly 300 industrial companies. The ISM index calculates nine different sub-indices.

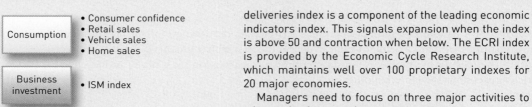

deliveries index is a component of the leading economic indicators index. This signals expansion when the index is above 50 and contraction when below. The ECRI index is provided by the Economic Cycle Research Institute, which maintains well over 100 proprietary indexes for 20 major economies.

Managers need to focus on three major activities to advance business cycle management:

1 Developing and deploying forecasting capabilities to anticipate movements and key turning points in the business cycle;

2 Applying well-timed business-cycle management strategies and tactics across the functional areas of the organization in a synergistic and integrative fashion;

3 Over the longer term, building a recession proof organization with an orientation toward business-cycle management, an executive team with a high degree of economic and financial market literacy, a facilitative organizational structure and a supportive organizational culture.

These comprise new orders, production, employment, supplier deliveries, inventories, prices, new export orders, imports and backlogs of orders. The production index is used to help predict industrial production. The prices index is used to help predict the producer price index. The new orders index is used to help predict factory orders. The employment index is used to help predict manufacturing employment. And the supplier

Source: Peter Navarro (2009) Recession-proofing your organization, *MIT Sloan Management Review*, 50(3), 45–54.

Consumer sophistication

Consumers are more marketing-savvy with many cynical about marketing efforts – inundated with hundreds of pitches a day, and increasingly suspicious of business promises.[44] Professor Stephen Brown from the University of Ulster suggests that 'Today's consumers were trademarked at birth and brought up on branding'.[45] Children as young as three can recognise brand logos, and the average child sees between 20,000 and 40,000 commercials a year.[46] Consumer sophistication is reflected in:

- **Greater ease in interacting**. Today's buyers can place orders from home, office or mobile phone, 24 hours a day, seven days a week, and quickly receive services and products at their home or office. Customers can also track and monitor their orders worldwide. DHL provides a tracking service online so that the customer knows where their parcel is at any time.
- **Technically savvy consumers**. Many customers are now technologically savvy, interactive, mouse clicking, engaged and intelligent. Consumers are using technology in ways that marketers are only beginning to understand. Across Europe, around 60 per cent of Germans and Britons are online. More than seven in ten Dutch, Swedish and Danish households have a personal computer.[47] Europe showed the highest growth in social networking reach among the major global regions during 2010.[48] The iGeneration

(a jocular allusion to the popular iPod boom, experienced by the internet generation) are people who grew up with computer technology as normal. They have no memory of (or nostalgia for) pre-internet history; they take the internet for granted, accept the utility of services such as email, Wikipedia, search engines and social media such as Facebook and YouTube. The term 'Generation Now' has been coined to reflect the urge for instant gratification that technology has imparted. This is the most connected generation ever, with several European countries, including the United Kingdom, having more mobile phones than people.

- **Self-expression and interaction**. Rather than companies providing information to customers – what can be called 'top down' – the internet generation wants to discover new things for themselves and then share their discoveries. The 'me-to-we' generation wants to connect and share, and has created an online world that operates beyond traditional boundaries. User-generated content allows customers to express themselves online. YouTube and social networking sites such as Facebook bring together people with a common interest but also allow consumers to share information. Social networking and the internet in general have had a dramatic impact on the way marketers have to define and interact with their customers. Young adults are moving away from other mediums to social networking. This has been driven by web 2.0 technologies, broadband penetration and also ubiquitous digital cameras and camera phones (see Figure 1.4).

- **A substantial increase in buying power**. With an increased ability to offer advice on products and services, the internet, social networking and other technologies, such as mobile phones, notebooks and iPads, fuel personal connections and user-generated content and increase the power of the consumer.[49] Some 35 per cent of young, first-time car buyers consider the internet their most important shopping tool.[50] In the hotel sector, browsing the internet and checking hotel information on Trip Advisor is now the norm. Trip Advisor is a customer-to-customer advice and discussion forum. In 2010 it became the first travel site to have more than 40 million monthly users providing reviews and opinions, making it the world's largest travel site. With sites like price.com and lastminute.com consumers are only a click away

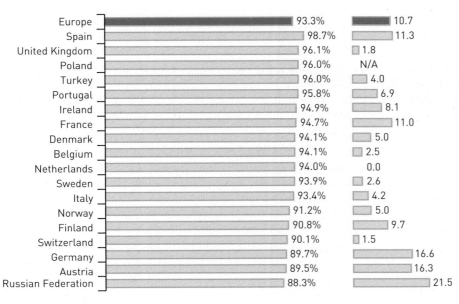

Figure 1.4 Reach of social networking sites by market in Europe
Source: Panel only data, comScore Media Metrix, Dec. 2011 vs Dec. 2009.

from comparing competitor prices and product and service attributes. Business buyers can run a reverse auction in which sellers compete to capture their business. They can readily join with others to aggregate their purchases and achieve deeper volume discounts.

- **An amplified voice to influence peer and public opinion.** The internet can be used as a vehicle to influence companies. Kryptonite, a company that makes high-priced bicycle locks, found itself in an awkward position when several blogs showed how the firm's U-shaped locks could be easily picked using only a Bic pen.[51] With the instructions posted on the internet, many consumers were able to open the iPhone to any network despite the desire of the company to use only one network.

- **Co-creation.** Much of consumer experience with brands and companies now involves co-creation, where the consumer and the company combine to define, create and shape their experience of the product or service. BMW encourages buyers to design their own models from among 500 options, 90 exterior colours and 170 trims. Around 80 per cent of BMW cars are co-created with the customer. This links to **customisation** where customers have an input into the design role, customising the product or service to suit themselves, where traditionally products and services were designed by companies. Companies can produce individually differentiated products or services, whether they are ordered in person, on the phone or online, thanks to advances in factory customisation technology and the increased sophistication of databases, computers and the internet. For a price, customers can customize their M&M sweets by colour and even apply short personalised messages (see www.mymms.com/default.aspx) and the same can be done with Heinz tomato ketchup bottles (www.myheinz.com).[52]

- **Self-service technologies.** More and more companies are choosing to provide self-service technology options for their customers. Self-service checkouts at supermarkets, self-check-ins at airports, cinema ticket collection and online investment trading have all proliferated. Self-service should be a choice for customers rather than a cost-saving exercise by the company. Many self-service technologies have been designed without any marketing input. Take the ATM – what would it look like if it had been designed and managed by marketers rather than technologists?

Understanding the marketing philosophy

The marketing philosophy or concept is one of the simplest ideas, but it is also one of the most important, and one that is often difficult for a company to embrace. At its very core is customer satisfaction. Satisfied customers are more valuable, more likely to purchase more, and more likely to relate positive word of mouth. The **marketing concept or philosophy** states that the organisation should strive to satisfy its customers' wants and needs while meeting the organisation's profit and other goals. In simple terms, 'the customer is king'.

This marketing philosophy needs to be adopted by the whole company, from top management to the lowest levels and across all departments of the organisation. The customers' needs, wants and satisfaction should always be foremost in every manager's and employee's mind.[53]

Many companies have not progressed to a marketing concept but are challenged to move from the old-fashioned product or sales concept.

Amazon

Amazon was one of the first companies to create a tailored and authentic online shopping customer experience. Creating goodwill with the customer is a subtle art. Bill Price, former and first Global VP of Customer Service with Amazon, discusses how they made customers fall in love with the site and the company. He notes that from the beginning, their focus was on offering customers compelling value.

> We set out to offer customers something they simply could not get any other way, and began serving them with books. We brought them much more selection than was possible in a physical store (our store would now occupy 6 football fields), and presented it in a useful, easy-to-search, and easy-to-browse format, in a store open 365 days a year, 24 hours a day. We maintained a dogged focus on improving the shopping experience. We now offer customers gift certificates, 1-Click SM shopping, and vastly more reviews, content, browsing options, and recommendation features. We dramatically lowered prices, further increasing customer value. Word of mouth remains the most powerful customer acquisition tool we have, and we are grateful for the trust our customers have placed in us. Repeat purchases and word of mouth have combined to make Amazon.com the market leader in online bookselling.[54]

Amazon has placed the customer at the heart of their business and every aspect of the operation focuses on the customer and how the company can create value for them.

The production philosophy

The **production concept or philosophy** is one of the oldest concepts in business and is the orientation within the company which focuses on the product or service that the company makes or provides, rather than on a customer need. It is the idea of a product looking for a market. Managers of production-oriented businesses concentrate on achieving high production efficiency, low costs and mass distribution. The thinking is aligned to the product concept, which proposes that consumers prefer products that offer the best quality, highest performance or most innovative features. Managers in these organisations focus on making superior products or services and improving them over time. However, these managers are sometimes caught up in a love affair with their products or services. A new or improved offering will not necessarily be successful unless it is aligned to customer needs and then produced, priced, distributed, communicated and managed throughout its life. With this focus you often have a product looking for customers or a product that is way above what the customer wants.

The selling philosophy

The **selling philosophy** is a focus on making sales rather than really understanding the customers. The selling concept suggests that businesses have to persuade or force customers to buy the organisation's products or services. The organisation must, therefore, undertake an aggressive selling and promotion effort.

Traditionally, the selling concept was practised most aggressively with unsought products or services that buyers normally do not think of buying, such as insurance. Some companies also practise the selling concept when they have overcapacity. Their aim is to sell what they make, rather than make what the market wants. Company success based on hard selling carries high risks. It assumes that customers who are coaxed into buying a product or service will like it, and that if they don't, they will not return it, bad-mouth the company or complain to consumer organisations, but that they might even buy it again. The films *Tin Man* and *Glengarry Glen Ross* – where the sales reps put pressure on customers to order products they do not want or need in order to keep their own jobs – are examples of hard-sell antics and show clearly the dangers of an overfocus on sales.

The marketing philosophy

The marketing concept or philosophy emerged in the mid-1950s.[55] Instead of a product-centred and sales-oriented 'make-and-sell' philosophy, business shifted to a customer-centred, 'sense-and-respond' philosophy. The marketing task is not to find the right customers for your products or services, but to design the right services and products for your customers. Dell Computers does not prepare a perfect computer for its target market. Rather, it provides product platforms on which each person customises the features they desire in their computer. Customising the outside panel of the computer also allows customers to customise the look of the computer.

The marketing concept holds that the key to achieving organisational goals is being more effective than competitors in understanding the target market's needs and in creating, managing, delivering and communicating superior customer value to that chosen target market(s).

Theodore Levitt of Harvard Business School explored the contrast between the selling and marketing philosophy and noted that

Selling focuses on the needs of the seller; marketing on the needs of the buyer. Selling is preoccupied with the seller's need to convert his product into cash; marketing with the idea of satisfying the needs of the customer by means of the product or service and the whole cluster of things associated with creating, delivering and finally consuming it.[56]

The box below highlights the key characteristics from each era which can be used to discover the dominant concept within an organisation.

Breakthrough marketing

The key characteristics of the production, sales and marketing eras

Production era (1870–1930)

P1. Demand exceeds supply. There are shortages and intense hunger for goods.
P2. There is little or no competition within product markets (between firms selling the same goods to the same markets).
P3. The company, not customers, is the centre of focus for a business.
P4. Businesses produce what they can produce and focus on solving production problems.
P5. Businesses produce limited product lines.
P6. Products sell themselves. Wholesalers and retailers are unsophisticated in their selling and marketing.
P7. Profit is a by-product of being good at production.

Sales era (1930–50)

S1. Supply exceeds demand.
S2. There is competition within product markets.
S3. Businesses are conscious of consumers' wants and some market research is done.
S4. Businesses must dispose of the products they produce and therefore focus on selling.
S5. Businesses produce limited product lines.
S6. Hard selling is necessary, backed by advertising.
S7. The primary goal of the firm is sales volume; profit is a by-product.

Marketing era (1950 onwards)

M1. Supply exceeds demand.
M2. There is intense competition within product markets.
M3. The customer is at the centre of a company's business; the purpose is to satisfy customers' needs and wants.
M4. Customers determine what products are made. Businesses focus on marketing problems.
M5. Businesses produce extensive product lines.
M6. A wide range of marketing activities are used and coordinated to satisfy customers' needs.
M7. Businesses focus on profit rather than sales volume.

Source: N. Ellis, J. Fitchett, M. Higgins, J. Gavin, L. Ming, M. Saren and M. Tadajewski (2011) *Marketing: A Critical Textbook*, London: Sage, modified from Jones, D.G.B. and Richardson, A.J., The myth of the marketing revolution, *Journal of Macromarketing*, 27(1), pp. 15–24, p. 18.

The holistic marketing philosophy

Without question, the trends and forces that have defined the first decade of the 21st century are leading business firms to a new set of beliefs and practices.

The **holistic marketing** philosophy is based on the development, design and implementation of marketing programmes, processes and activities that recognise their breadth and interdependencies. Holistic marketing acknowledges that everything matters in marketing – and that a broad, integrated perspective is often necessary. Today's best marketers recognise the need to have a more complete, cohesive approach to marketing, which moves beyond the production or selling approaches to business and really embraces the marketing philosophy.

Successful companies keep their marketing focused on their target customers and the enduring and changing needs in their marketplace – and marketspace – and align them with their marketing mix activities (see Figure 1.5).

The box on the next page suggests where companies go wrong – and how they can get it right – in their marketing.

Holistic marketing recognises and reconciles the scope and complexities of marketing activities. Figure 1.6 provides a schematic overview of four broad components characterising holistic marketing: relationship marketing (see Chapters 2 and 11), integrated marketing (Chapters 2 and 21), internal marketing (Chapter 21) and performance marketing (Chapter 21). We will examine these major themes throughout this book.

Figure 1.5 The 7Ps components of the marketing mix must be aligned to the target market

Marketing memo

Marketing right and wrong

The ten deadly sins of marketing

1 The company is not sufficiently market focused and customer driven.
2 The company does not fully understand its target customers.
3 The company needs to define and monitor its competitors better.
4 The company has not properly managed its relationships with its stakeholders.
5 The company is not good at finding new opportunities.
6 The company's marketing plans and planning process are deficient.
7 The company's product and service policies need tightening.
8 The company's brand building and communications skills are weak.
9 The company is not well organised to carry on effective and efficient marketing.
10 The company has not made maximum use of technology.

The ten commandments of marketing

1 The company segments the market, chooses the best segments, and develops a strong position in each chosen target market.
2 The company maps its customers' needs, perceptions, preferences and behaviour, and motivates its stakeholders to obsess about serving and satisfying the customers.
3 The company knows its major competitors and their strengths and weaknesses.
4 The company builds partners out of its stakeholders and rewards them generously.
5 The company develops systems for identifying opportunities, ranking them and choosing the best ones.
6 The company manages a marketing planning system that leads to insightful long-term and short-term plans.
7 The company exercises strong control over its product and service elements.
8 The company builds strong brands by using the most relevant communication and promotion tools and techniques and other mix elements.
9 The company builds marketing leadership and a team spirit among its various departments.
10 The company constantly adds technology that gives it a competitive advantage in the marketplace.

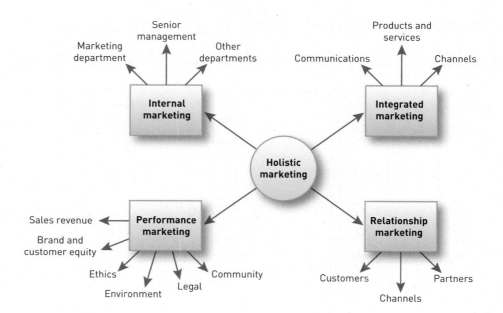

Figure 1.6 Holistic marketing dimensions

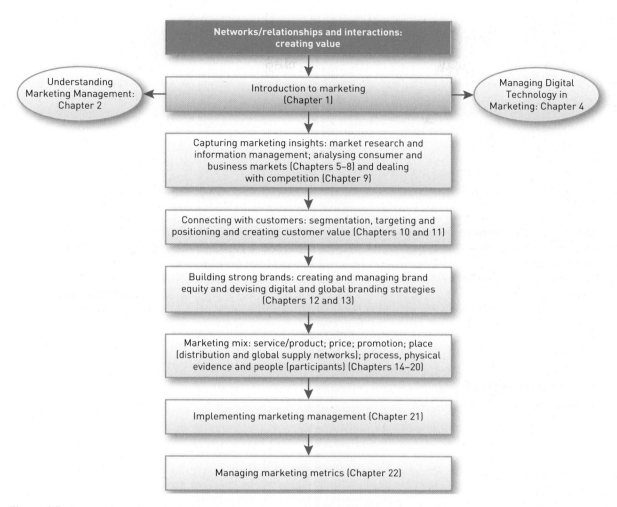

Figure 1.7 An overview of marketing management activities reflecting the main chapters in the text

Overview of marketing management

This section and Figure 1.7 provide an overview of the textbook and of marketing management in practice.

The following case study provides a brief overview of each chapter and the main elements of marketing management.

Zeus, Inc. (name disguised), operates in several industries, including cameras, film and chemicals. Corporate management is considering what to do with its Atlas camera division, which produces a range of 35 mm and digital cameras. Although Zeus has a sizeable market share in the camera market and is producing good revenue, the 35 mm market itself is declining rapidly and Zeus's market share is slipping. In the faster-growing digital camera segment, Zeus faces strong competition and has been slow to gain sales. Zeus's corporate management wants Atlas's marketing management (Chapter 2) to produce a strong turnaround marketing plan for the division (Chapter 3).

Understanding marketing management

The marketing strategy should take into account changing European and global opportunities and challenges, changing customer perspectives and a variety of new challenges and marketing realities (Chapter 1). To understand marketing is to understand management (Chapter 2) and the marketing team must understand the integrated marketing they will need to use throughout the organisation. Marketing management skills will be needed to change the direction of the organisation and to manage both an internally and externally challenging environment.

Developing marketing strategies and plans

The first task facing Atlas is to identify its potential long-run opportunities, given its market experience and core competences (Chapter 3). Atlas must find the customer needs and then it can design its offering to match these needs. It could also look to other customer needs and make a line of video cameras, or it could use its core competency in optics to design a line of binoculars and telescopes. Whichever direction it chooses, it must develop a concrete marketing plan that specifies the marketing strategy and tactics going forward.

Managing digital technology in marketing

Atlas needs to review the digital technologies within its organisation and at the customer interface (Chapter 4). Other camera manufacturers are embracing technology at the customer interface and have a range of self-service devices both in shops and at home, for customers. Depending on the target market, more of the marketing focus could be linked to technologies, social networking, the internet or digital channels, and Atlas needs to understand how to use them innovatively.

Capturing marketing insights

Atlas needs a reliable marketing information system to monitor closely its marketing environment, and it needs to understand its internal database information (Chapter 5). Atlas also needs a dependable marketing research system. To transform marketing strategy into marketing programmes, marketing managers must measure market potential, forecast demand, and make basic decisions about marketing expenditures, marketing activities and marketing allocation (Chapter 6). Atlas must clearly understand its customers and to do so needs to understand consumer markets (Chapter 7). Who buys cameras, and why do they buy? What are they looking for in the way of features and prices, and where do they shop? Atlas also sells cameras to business markets, including large corporations, professional firms, retailers and government agencies (Chapter 8), where purchasing agents or buying committees make the decisions. Atlas needs to gain a full understanding of how organisational buyers buy. Atlas must also pay close attention to competitors (Chapter 9), anticipating its competitors' moves and knowing how to react quickly and decisively. It may want to initiate some surprise moves, in which case it needs to anticipate how its competitors will respond.

Connecting with customers: segmentation, targeting and positioning

Atlas must reconsider the segmentation in the market and how best to create value for its chosen target markets, and it must decide how to position in the market (Chapter 10). Suppose Atlas decides to focus on the consumer market, and to develop a positioning strategy for that market. Should it position itself as the 'Mercedes' brand, offering superior cameras at a premium price with excellent service and strong advertising, such as British Airways in the airline business? Should it build a simple, low-priced camera aimed at more price-conscious consumers, such as those who travel on Ryanair or easyJet? Or something in between? It must look to develop strong, profitable, long-term relationships with customers (Chapter 11).

Building strong brands

Atlas has a range of marketing mix elements that it must integrate and use to create and maintain its brand in the eyes of its consumers. Atlas must understand the strengths and weaknesses of the Zeus brand as customers see it (Chapter 12). A brand is an offering from a known source. A brand name such as Virgin carries many associations in people's minds that make up the brand image: in the case of Virgin, fun and innovation. Atlas will have to build a strong, favourable and unique brand image in the mind of the consumer through the use of the marketing mix variables. Managers need to manage the brand across the global and within digital brand communities (Chapter 13).

Shaping the market offerings

Once the target market and positioning have been selected, the marketing managers now have the full range of the marketing mix techniques to match to consumer needs. Aligned to its positioning and at the heart of the marketing programme is the product and service – the offering to the market, which includes all the unique features of managing services and/or the product quality, design, features and packaging (Chapter 14). They may consider introducing new services and products to align to a target market (Chapter 15).

A critical marketing decision relates to price (Chapter 16). Atlas has to decide on wholesale and retail prices, discounts, allowances and credit terms. Its price should align well with the offer's perceived value or positioning; otherwise, buyers may be confused and turn to competitors' products or services.

Delivering value

Atlas must also determine how to manage all aspects of product and service delivery properly in order to deliver to the target market the value embodied in its products and services. Nowadays companies are part of networks of companies and channel members making the product or service accessible and available to target customers (Chapter 17). Atlas must identify, recruit and link various intermediaries to manage the delivery of its products and services efficiently to the target market. It must understand the various types of retailers, wholesalers and physical distribution firms and how they make their decisions, as well as internet channels and other technology-based self-service or distribution systems (Chapter 17). Atlas needs to understand the service process the customer will go through, any physical evidence that creates or confirms the brand image and also the impact of people during the customer–company encounter (Chapter 18).

Communicating value

Atlas must adequately communicate to the target market the value embodied by its products and services. It will need an integrated marketing communication programme that maximises the individual and collective contributions of all communication activities (Chapter 19). Atlas needs to set up a communication plan that could consist of advertising, sales promotion, publicity and public relations, and personal communications, in the form of direct and interactive marketing, as well as hire, train and motivate salespeople (Chapter 20).

Implementing marketing management

Finally, Atlas must build a marketing organisation that is capable of implementing the marketing plan (Chapter 21). Because surprises and disappointments can occur as marketing plans unfold, Atlas will need feedback and control mechanisms to understand the efficiency and effectiveness of its marketing activities and how it can improve them. Atlas also needs to report back to the corporate board, which will have allocated a budget to this marketing endeavour and will need to see the returns and measure the effectiveness of the marketing strategy and tactics (Chapter 22).

Marketing focuses on understanding the customer and honing in on their current (and more importantly their future) needs so that the total company effort is towards customer satisfaction at a profit. Marketing is all the organised efforts, activities and expenditure designed first to acquire a customer and secondly to maintain and grow a customer at a profit.

SUMMARY

1 Marketing is an organisational function and a set of processes for creating, communicating and delivering value to customers, and for managing customer relationships in ways that benefit the customer, the organisation and its stakeholders. Marketing management is the art and science of choosing target markets and getting, keeping and growing customers through creating, delivering and communicating superior customer value.

2 Marketers are skilled at managing demand: they seek to influence its level, timing, and composition for products, services, events, experiences, persons, places, properties, organisations, information and ideas. They also operate in four different marketplaces: consumer, business, global and non-profit.

3 Today's marketplace is fundamentally different as a result of major societal forces that have resulted in many new consumer and company capabilities. These forces have created new opportunities and challenges, and changed marketing management significantly as companies seek new ways to achieve marketing excellence.

4 The severe economic recession caused marketers to rethink best practices of management. A recession can be a time of great challenge but also great opportunity.

5 There are four competing philosophies under which organisations can choose to conduct their business: the production/product philosophy, the selling philosophy, the marketing philosophy and the holistic marketing philosophy. The first two are of limited use today.

6 The holistic marketing concept is based on the development, design and implementation of marketing programmes, processes and activities that recognise their breadth and interdependencies. Holistic marketing recognises that everything matters in marketing and that a broad, integrated perspective is necessary.

7 The set of tasks necessary for successful marketing management includes developing marketing strategies and plans, capturing marketing insights, connecting with customers, choosing target marketing and positioning, building strong brands, shaping the market offerings through marketing mix activities, delivering, communicating and creating value with customers, and ensuring long-term growth for companies.

APPLICATIONS

Marketing debate

Should the marketing budget be maintained or increased during a recession? During a recession the immediate desire of many companies is often simply to cut costs. The marketing department can be selected for this cut – and in some cases is the first area cut. One could argue that the marketing spend is the one spend or investment in a company which should be maintained or even increased during a recession or economic downturn.

Take a position: Marketing spend should be maintained or increased during a recession or economic downturn *versus* Marketing spend should be cut along with all the other spending in the organisation.

Marketing discussion

Consider the broad shifts in marketing and consumers. Do any themes emerge? Can you relate the shifts to the major societal forces?

FURTHER READING

Kaur Gurjeet and R. D. Sharma (2009) Voyage of marketing thought from a barter system to a customer centric one, *Marketing Intelligence & Planning* 27(5), 567–614.

A detailed analysis of various marketing and business philosophies is offered to facilitate business executives in examining the philosophy followed by their companies. It also provides guidelines for how to move vertically in pursuance of improved business performance.

The article reviews the following issues:

1 What determines the needed level and nature of marketing concept in the case of a particular industry?

2 Should all companies adopt the latest marketing thought in their practices, along with the associated innovative changes?

3 How have academics and industry kept pace with the aforesaid changes?

It uses research from major businesses in India to provide an excellent overview of marketing philosophy, including customer centricity and service dominant logic.

REFERENCES

[1]Ikea.com; L. Armitstead (2010) Ikea reveals profits for first time to dispel 'secretive' image, *Telegraph*, 1 Oct.; I. Kamprad and B. Torekull (1999) *Leading By Design: The Ikea Story*, London: Collins.

[2]Philip Kotler (2009) Marketing: the underappreciated workhorse, *Market Leader*, Quarter 2 (2009), 8–10.

[3]Jack Trout (2006) Tales from the marketing wars: Peter Drucker on marketing, www.forbes.com/2006/06/30/jack-trout-on-marketing-cx_jt_0703drucker.html.

[4]C. Nash (2009) BMW defy recession, *Inside Bikes*, February, www.carolenash.com/insidebikes/bike-news/bmw-defy-recession.htm.

[5]BMW Magazine (2011) BMW Motorrad UK sees record sales in 2010, BMW Motorrad Report, 31 January, http://bmwmcmag.com/2011/01/bmw-motorrad-uk-sees-record-sales-in-2010/.

[6]J. C. Levinson (2007) *Guerrilla Marketing: Easy and Inexpensive Strategies for Making Big Profits from Your Small Business*, 4th edn, Boston, MA: Houghton Mifflin.

[7]E. Gummesson and C. Mele (2010) Marketing as value co-creation through network interaction and resource integration, *Journal of Business Market Management*, 4(4), 181–98; E. Gummesson (2007) Exit services marketing: enter service marketing, *Journal of Consumer Behavior*, 6(2), 113–41; E. Gummesson (2008) *Total Relationship Marketing*, 2nd edn, Oxford: Butterworth Heinemann.

[8]Ibid.

[9]C. Gronroos (2006) On defining marketing: finding a new road-map for marketing, *Marketing Theory*, 6, 395–417.

[10]Technology in Business (2011) Analysing Zara's business model, *Technology in Business*, 3 March.

[11]K. Floor (2006) *Branding a Store: How to Build Successful Retail Brands in a Changing Marketplace*, London: Kogan Page.

[12]P. Drucker (1973) *Management: Tasks, Responsibilities, Practices*, New York: Harper and Row, pp. 64–5.

[13]S. Vargo (2011) On marketing theory and service-dominant logic: connecting some dots, *Marketing Theory*, 11(3), 3–8; S. Vargo and R. Lusch (2004) The four services marketing myths, *Journal of Service Research*, 6(4), 324–35.

[14]For more in-depth discussion on the business markets perspective, see C. Gronroos (2011) A service perspective on business relationships: the value creation, interaction and marketing interface, *Industrial Marketing Management*, 40(2), special issue on Service-Dominant Logic in Business Markets, 240–7; see also an alternative perspective in S. Brown and A. Patterson (2009) Harry Potter and the service-dominant logic of marketing: a cautionary tale, *Journal of Marketing Management*, 25(5/6), 519–33.

[15]S. Vargo, P. P. Maglio and M. A. Akaka (2008) On value and value co-creation: a service systems and service logic perspective, *European Management Journal*, 26, 145–52.

[16]http://news.bbc.co.uk/sport2/hi/front_page/4655555.stm

[17]P. Kotler (1984) Dream vacations: the booming market for designed experiences, *The Futurist*, October, 7–13; B. J. Pine, II and J. Gilmore (1999) *The Experience Economy*, Boston, MA: Harvard Business School Press; B. Schmitt (1999) *Experience Marketing*, New York: Free Press.

[18]See also P. Kotler, John T. Bowen and James C. Makens (2009) *Marketing for Hospitality and Tourism*, Englewood Cliffs, NJ: Prentice Hall; P. Kotler, I. J. Rein and D. Haider (1993) *Marketing Places: Attracting Investment, Industry, and Tourism to Cities, States, and Nations*, New York: Free Press; and P. Kotler, C. Asplund, I. Rein and D. H. Haider (1999) *Marketing Places in Europe: Attracting Investments, Industries, Residents and Visitors to European Cities, Communities, Regions, and Nations*, London: Financial Times Prentice-Hall.

[19]See http://ec.europa.eu/enterprise/services/tourism/index_en.htm.

[20]J. Bakan (2004) *The Corporation*, London: Constable; N. Klein (2001) *No Logo*, London: Flamingo; G. Ritzer (2000) *The McDonaldization of Society*, Thousands Oaks, CA: Pine Forge Press; R. Gordon, G. Hastings, L. McDermott and P. Suiquier (2007) The critical role of social marketing, in M. Saren, P. Maclaran, C. Goulding, R. Elliot, A. Shankar and M. Catterall (eds), *Critical Marketing: Defining the Field*, London: Butterworth-Heinemann, pp. 159–73 (at p. 164).

[21]See http://drinkaware.co.uk/.

[22]I. Szmigin, A. Bengry-Howell, C. Griffin, C. Hackley and W. Mistral (2011) Social marketing, individual responsibility and the 'culture of intoxication', *European Journal of Marketing*, 45(5), 759–79.

[23]N. Franke, P. Keinz and C. J. Steger (2009) Testing the value of customization: when do customers really prefer products tailored to their preferences?, *Journal of Marketing*, 73(5), 103–21.

[24]See J. Lipnack and J. Stamp, The age of the network and virtual teams, www.netage.com. They are also co-authors of the article, Can absence make a team grow stronger?, *Harvard Business Review*, May 2004. P. S. Greenberg, R. H. Greenberg, Y. Lederer Antonucci (2007) Creating and sustaining trust in virtual teams, *Harvard Business Review*, July, 17–26.

[25]R. Achrol and P. Kotler (1999) Marketing in the network economy, *Journal of Marketing* (special issue), 146–63.

[26]D. Daye and B. VanAuken (2007) Understanding the competition, *Branding Strategy Insider*, www.brandingstrategyinsider.com/2007/10/understanding-t.html

[27]Aquafresh varieties (online image) available at www.aquafresh.com/default.aspx?startPage=varieties, accessed on 5 March 2008.

[28]W. Nelson (2002) All power to the consumer? Complexity and choice in consumers' lives, *Journal of Consumer Behavior*, 2(2), 185–95.

[29]D. Hoffman and T. Novak (2000) How to acquire customers on the web, *Harvard Business Review*, May–June, 21–7.

[30]R. Ritchie (2011) Apple's iTunes App Store reaches 10 billion downloads, www.tipb.com/2011/01/22/apples-itunes-app-store-reaches-10-billion-downloads/, 27 January; see also http://en.wikipedia.org/wiki/ITunes.

[31]Y. (J.) Wind (2006) Blurring the lines: is there a need to rethink industrial marketing?, *Journal of Business and Industrial Marketing*, 21(7), 474–81.

[32]R. Bennett, F. Kerrigan and D. O'Reilly (2011) Non-profit, social, arts and heritage marketing, *European Journal of Marketing*, 45(5), 700–2.

[33]I. Rogers, (2011) Spanish clubs leading Europe in merchandise income rise, Reuters, http://uk.reuters.com/article/2011/02/22/uk-soccer-europe-merchandising-idUKTRE71L5Q920110222; www.sportbusiness.com/news/162596/real-madrid-has-highest-brand-value-in-europe; M. Desbordes (2007) *Marketing and Football: An International Perspective*, Oxford: Butterworth Heinmann;

C. Vitzthum (2005) Real Madrid needs a new goal, *BusinessWeek*, 25 June (www.businessweek.com/magazine/content/05_26/b3939423.htm).

[34]Ibid. and W. Chan Kim and R. Mauborgne (1999) Creating new market space, *Harvard Business Review*, January–February, 1–14.

[35]M. Sawhney (2001) *Seven Steps to Nirvana*, New York: McGraw-Hill.

[36]L. Penaloza (2000) Consuming people: from political economy to theaters of consumption – a review, *Journal of Marketing*, 64(1), 106–11; A. Fuat, K. Firat and N. Dholakia (1998) *Consuming People: From Political Economy to Theaters of Consumption*, London and New York: Routledge.

[37]R. Savitt (1998) This thing I call Europe, *International Marketing Review*, 15(6), 444–6.

[38]T. Reid (2004) *The United States of Europe*, London: Penguin, 245.

[39]I. Albrecht (2010) Brand-oriented companies are almost twice as successful as others, www.irisalbrecht.de/en/marke.htm; www.youtube.com/watch?v=yk8crJJzk7A&feature=related

[40]Vanessa Friedma (2011) Woman in the news: Angela Ahrendts, *Financial Times*, 22 April, www.ft.com/cms/s/0/e2f598ea-6d13-11e0-83fe-0144feab49a.html#ixzz1PAORFWLB: A. Wilson (2009) Burberry to cut 540 jobs as recession deepens, *Telegraph*, January, www.telegraph.co.uk/finance/newsbysector/retailandconsumer/4295112/Burberry-to-cut-540-jobs-as-recession-deepens.html; Burberry soars 13% as retailer beats the blues, *Daily Mail* online, www.thisismoney.co.uk/money/article-1172280/Burberry-soars-13-retailer-beats-blues.html#ixzz1PAN1WHMF.

[41]M. R. Fellenz and M. Brady (2010) Managing customer-centric information: the challenges of information and communication technology (ICT) deployment in service environments. In Zongwei Luo (ed.), *Service Science and Logistics Informatics: Innovative Perspectives*, Hershey, PA: IGI Global, pp. 46–64.

[42]D. Sacks (2006) MAC Cosmetics Inc., *Fast Company*, September, p. 62.

[43]J. Quelch and K. Jocz (2009) How to market in a downturn, *Harvard Business Review*, April, 52–62.

[44]M. Moynagh and R. Worsley (2002) Tomorrow's consumer – the shifting balance of power, *Journal of Consumer Behaviour*, 1(3), 293–301.

[45]S. Brown (2003) Marketing to Generation®, Forethought, *Harvard Business Review*, June, 81(6), 2–3.

[46]M. Lindstrom (2010) *Brand Sense: Sensory Secrets Behind the Stuff We Buy*, Philip Kotler (foreword), New York: Free Press; M. Lindstrom (2003) Branding is no longer child's play!, *Journal of Consumer Marketing*, 21(213), 175–82.

[47]See http://russiatoday.ru/business/news/6776.

[48]http://sembassy.com/2011/03/europe-social-networks-reach/.

[49]M. Stelzner (2011) Social Media Marketing Industry Report: *How Marketers Are Using Social Media to Grow Their Businesses*, April, Social Media Examiner, 1–41; A. Kamenetz (2006) The network unbound, *Fast Company*, June, 69–73; see also M. Barrett (2007) The rise of social networking and the lessons for brands, content and all media business, Accenture Global Forum (www.accenture.com/global/services/by_industry/communications/access_newsletter/articles_index/gcf07_barrett.html); see www.bikeforums.net/video/1.mov.

[50]D. Kiley (2006) Advertisers, start your engines, *BusinessWeek*, 6 March, p. 26.

[51]The blogs in the corporate machine, *The Economist*, 11 February 2006, 55–6.

[52]B. Horovitz (2006) In trend toward vanity food: it's getting personal, *USA Today*, 9 August.

[53]See www.enotes.com/management-encyclopedia/marketing-concept-philosophy.

[54]J. Stoddard (2011) *Marketing: A Historical Perspective*, Encyclopedia of Business, 2nd edn.

[55]See also N. Ellis, J. Fitchett, M. Higgins, J. Gavin, L. Ming, M. Saren and M. Tadajewski (2011) *Marketing: A Critical Textbook*, London: Sage, pp. 13–33. J. B. McKitterick (1957) What is the marketing management concept?, in F. M. Bass (ed.), *The Frontiers of Marketing Thought and Action*, Chicago: American Marketing Association, pp. 71–82; F. J. Borch (1957) The marketing philosophy as a way of business life, in *The Marketing Concept: Its Meaning to Management* (Marketing Series, No. 99), New York: American Management Association, pp. 3–5; R. J. Keith (1960) The marketing revolution, *Journal of Marketing*, January, 35–8.

[56]T. Levitt (1960) Marketing myopia, *Harvard Business Review*, July–August, 50–65.

Chapter 2

Understanding marketing management within a global context

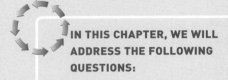

IN THIS CHAPTER, WE WILL ADDRESS THE FOLLOWING QUESTIONS:

1 What is management?
2 What is marketing management?
3 How is global marketing management practised?
4 How is marketing management practised within developing markets?

Zara understands that listening to its customers is a core part of marketing management and provides its customers with fast-fashion clothing.

Source: © Jochen Tack/Alamy.

Marketing management is a challenging and rewarding career. Marketing is at the centre of all business operations and is the voice of the customer in the organisation. It is a major task to manage the fulfilment of customer needs, matched to profit or other objectives of a company and within a changing and complex internal and external environment.

Zara, the Spanish clothing shop, provides very good insights into marketing management challenges.

The global success of Spain's best-known fashion house, Zara, relies on marketing management expertise in understanding the company's target markets' needs and managing its internal operations to supply these needs at a profit. Under the management leadership of its founder Amancio Ortega Gaona, Zara has redefined the rules of retailing and has become a global market leader with over 1,000 stores in 70 countries. Zara management maintains tight control of internal operations aligned to the needs of its target market for fast fashion. The marketing manager ensures that all aspects of the operation are coordinated to serve the customer's need for fast fashion at reasonable prices – from design to just-in-time production and delivery, on to the shop floor and through to the sales counter in the stores and ultimately to the final customer. Zara has built in more flexibility than its rivals to respond quickly to changing fashion trends and to deliver value to its customers. While its rivals focus on outsourcing much of their production to China and India, and creating sophisticated advertising campaigns, Zara's 'fast fashion' strategy manages all operations in-house in its Spanish headquarters at La Coruna, where departments such as design, production and marketing all rub shoulders with each other. This allows the building of relationships between departments and an informal organisation that minimises bureaucracy and allows for speedier reaction times, which is vital for providing customers with the latest fashion trends. Zara can make a new line from start to finish in two weeks, against an industry average of six months. Zara introduces 10,000 new designs a year and therefore delivers value for its customers by offering quality and up-to-date fashion at reasonable prices. A combination of strong marketing management and a marketing team that listens to its customers, together with an ability to plan, organise, lead and control, has changed a small shop located in Spain into a worldwide success. Inditex (valued at €4 billion) – Zara's parent company – is the world's largest clothing retailer by sales and is an industry icon.[1]

What is management?

Management in today's business world is demanding and will continue to be so.[2] Economically the last few years have seen difficult times for many marketing leaders. The world economy went into a steep recession in 2008 and businesses have since been confronted by challenging and turbulent market conditions. The globalisation of business, the financial challenges across Europe and beyond, the massive increase and spread of digital technologies, the development of supply networks spanning the globe, and changing consumer needs and demands are all contemporary challenges for marketing managers.

Many management roles have changed, from managing small to medium-sized national companies to managing global companies spanning continents. Ferrerro Rocher, the chocolate manufacturer, was founded in 1946 in Alba, a small town in Italy. It started as a small pastry shop using local hazelnuts as an alternative to chocolate. It now employs 22,000 people, has 18 factories and enjoys revenues of over €6 billion, and its products are sold in over 100 countries around the globe. What was once a small Italian company now purchases approximately 25 per cent of the world's supply of hazelnuts.[3]

Management is 'a process that involves the major functions of planning, organizing, leading and controlling resources in order to achieve goals.[4] Management centres on trying to achieve objectives using the four major functions. **Managing** is the activity of trying to achieve a goal using resources of whatever kind. Without goals there is no purpose that can guide decisions about planning, organising, leading and controlling. **Managers** are the people within the organisation charged with running the organisation on behalf of the owners.[5]

- Management can be viewed as a process or series of continuing and related activities.
- Management involves the achievement of organisational goals.
- Management reaches organisational goals by working through and with people.
- Managers have the responsibility to combine and use organisational resources to ensure that the organisation achieves it purpose.

The process of management

Management is neither an art nor a science but a process. Management is the ability to use organizational resources to achieve organisational goals through the functions of planning, organising, leading and control.

1 **Planning** establishes the direction of the organisation.
2 **Organising** divides organisational activities among work groups, allocates the people, technological, physical, financial and informational services required to achieve tasks
3 **Leading** motivates employees to achieve organisational goals.
4 Finally, **control** measures and evaluates organisational performances.[6]

Therefore there are four basic pillars in the management process: planning, organising, leading and controlling. These are guided by the goals that the company needs to achieve in order to gain the desired result (see Figure 2.1).

1 Planning

Planning is the process of establishing goals and objectives and selecting a future course of action in order to achieve them. Planning involves figuring out how to achieve the organisation's overall goals. In planning, a manager looks to the future – pointing out

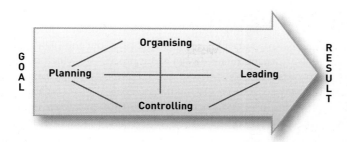

Figure 2.1 The process of management
Source: J. Martin and M. Fellenz, (2010) *Organisational Behaviour and Management*, Cengage Learning, Hampshire.

what management wants to achieve and how they are going to achieve it. Decision making is a central component of planning because choices need to be made in the process of finalising plans. Zara only commenced online sales in September 2010, which could appear slow by industry standards – most retailers started online sales during the 1990s. For example, rival H&M launched its first web-based store in 2006.[7] Pablo Isla, Zara's chief executive, noted 'For us, now is the right time to go online.' The company's plan was first to concentrate on its Asian expansion and to control costs during the economic downturn before venturing into the online sales format. The online rollout then began in Spain, the UK, Portugal, Italy, Germany and France, and has been very successful.

The importance of planning cannot be overstated. As the saying goes: *If you don't have a plan to succeed, you really have a plan to fail.* Although business and marketing plans may overlap in some areas, what sets a marketing plan apart is its focus on the customer. According to Sir George Bull, chairman of Sainsbury, the third largest chain of supermarkets in the United Kingdom: 'the marketing plan starts with the customer and works its way around the business'.[8] The marketing manager must be able to manage the effective design and implementation of a customer-focused marketing plan for the organisation. One of the core marketing concepts is a customer-centric focus: to understand and put the customer into the centre of the company. However, understanding customers has absolutely no value if you don't do something with the insights gained into customer behaviour. Knowing that 52 per cent of customers are concerned about the environment is an interesting though useless piece of data, unless you can do something with it.

Regardless of the industry, a good *marketing plan* has to be clear and convincing and show how the recommendations will actually work. The power of a great marketing plan is that it clearly presents the core ideas, creates consensus and drives execution. In today's fast-moving world, managers cannot hide behind fancy charts and complicated analyses; they have to make smart choices and execute plans. A tight marketing plan, grounded in goals, strategic initiatives and tactics, can help make this happen.[9]

Despite the enthusiasm for planning in textbooks, many companies operate without formal marketing plans, while others write long and detailed plans which are ignored. Evidence suggests that only one-fifth of companies have marketing planning processes.[10] There are many reasons for this. It could be that in today's extremely dynamic business environment, the formal marketing plan becomes obsolete for many companies before it is even printed. Others contend that plans are generated primarily to meet investors' requirements and are seldom used in day-to-day management.[11]

2 Organising

Organising is the process of making sure the necessary human, physical, technological, financial and informational resources are available to carry out the plan which will achieve the organisational goals.[12] **Organisational design** is the process by which managers select and manage aspects of an organisation's structure and culture so that the organisation can control the activities necessary to achieve organisational goals.[13] Most organisations follow the traditional pattern of setting up departments. Most departments work as stand-alone units reporting hierarchically to the top of the organisation. Such an organisational design is called a functional structure and in practice often leads to department silos which can separate rather than join departments. The main responsibility of the *marketing department* is to act as the 'boundary-spanner' between the company and its customers. While there is a need for a separate marketing department, the philosophy of the company should be a marketing philosophy. It is not an either/or but a both/and perspective that is needed. The marketing department is needed to integrate all departments, processes and activities towards the customer.[14]

Owing to the importance of the marketing department as a key driver of business strategy, top management should focus attention on the work of this department above all.[15] There can be three key problems with marketing departments:

1 The marketing department lacks the resources needed to get its primary job done.
2 The marketing staff do not have the management skills or power to unite all the departments in the company towards the customer.
3 There is constant friction between marketing and other departments in the company.

Any combination of these three can spell doom for even the smallest of companies.

Staffing is dividing work into specific jobs and tasks and specifying who has the authority to accomplish certain tasks. Staffing ensures that the necessary human resources are available to achieve organisational goals. The well-documented failure of the British Airways Terminal 5 opening can be attributed to a lack of staff, a lack of staff training and a misunderstanding of how the human, technological, informational and physical resources needed to be organised so that they would all operate together and effectively when opening the terminal. Instead much of the organisation was left to chance, and staff training was poor and not checked properly prior to opening, resulting in cancelled flights and disrupted passengers, as well as confused and angry staff who could not operate the systems.

3 Leading

Leading means influencing others to achieve organisational objectives. It involves energising, directing and persuading others, and creating a vision. Leadership includes many interpersonal processes: motivation, communicating, coaching and showing people and groups how they can achieve their goals. While management is accomplishing work through people, leadership focuses on inspiring people. This aspect of management is often harder to pin down and people who have this skill are often said to be born with it or to have a 'natural' talent for leadership.[16] Many leadership roles in today's organisations centre on change and the management and implementation of change. Recent research suggests that the core leadership skills needed to bring about successful change within organisations are the ability to:

• understand and incorporate the wider change context;
• build leadership teams to think and act for the whole organisation;
• understand the underlying systems that produce the performance outcomes;
• be patient with people as they make the transition;
• display extremely high levels of self-awareness;
• set tangible measures for the achievement of change.[17]

Leadership is the *process of influencing others to understand and agree about what needs to be done and how to do it, and the process of facilitating individual and collective efforts to accomplish shared objectives.*[18] Leaders need to develop a sense of shared purpose within organisations. They also must show that they can execute their visions. Matti Ala-huhta, the CEO of Kone, the Finnish elevator and escalator company, recently won the 'European Manager of the Year Award'. At the presentation of the award, Mr Alahuhta emphasised that he was especially pleased to get the award in the middle of an economic recession. He continued:

> **The key challenge for leaders in difficult times is to see even this phase as an opportunity. Instead of emphasising costs only, such an approach requires the development of a positive spirit and getting people to direct their energy towards a clear common goal. It also requires the continuing active development of people and overall competitiveness of the company. Finally, it requires a high level of activity directed towards customers and a lot of internal communication concerning markets, the company's own actions, targets and business progress.**

The box below reflects how leading-edge companies use technologies and management challenges to recreate environments that will help managers to learn leadership skills under difficult circumstances.

Marketing insight

Web-based simulation for leadership

The dynamic business landscape means that decision making is distributed throughout organisations to enable people to respond rapidly to change. A lot of work is done by global teams, partly composed of people from outside the organisation, over whom a leader has no formal authority – they may be assembled for a single project and then disbanded. Collaboration within these geographically diverse groups is a necessity which can occur through digital or face-to-face interaction. What will leadership look like in such a world – a world whose features have already begun to transform business?

> The answers may be found among the exploding space stations, grotesque monsters, and spiky-armored warriors of games such as Eve Online, EverQuest, and World of Warcraft. Despite their fantasy settings, these online play worlds – sometimes given the moniker MMORPGs (for 'massively multiplayer online role-playing games') – in many ways resemble the coming environment and thus open a window onto the future of real-world business leadership.[19]

Gamers have six key characteristics that are useful in a workforce: they are orientated towards the bottom line; they understand the need for diversity; they understand that one cannot achieve something alone; they are excited by change; they see learning as something enjoyable; and they think laterally.

Leading 25 guild members in a six-hour raid on Illidan the Betrayer's temple fortress is hardly the same as running a complex global organization. For starters, the stakes are just a bit higher in business. But don't dismiss online games as mere play. The best ones differ from traditional video games as much as universities do from one-room schoolhouses. In fact, these enterprises are actually sprawling online communities in which thousands of players collaborate with and compete against one another in real time within a visually three-dimensional virtual world – one that persists and evolves even while a player is away.[20]

Take Everet, a web-based simulation which uses the dramatic context of a Mount Everest expedition to reinforce student learning in group dynamics and leadership. Players are assigned one of five roles on a team attempting to summit the mountain. The simulation lasts six rounds totalling about 1.5 hours of seat time. In each round, team members analyse information on weather, health conditions, supplies, goals or hiking speed, and determine how much of that information to communicate to their team mates. They then collectively discuss whether to attempt to reach the next camp en route to the summit. The team must decide how to distribute effectively the supplies and oxygen bottles needed for the ascent – decisions which affect hiking speed, health and ultimately the team's success in summiting the mountain. Failure to communicate and analyse information accurately as a team has negative consequences on team performance.[21]

MMORPG: massively multiplayer online role-playing game

Source: Courtesy of CCP Games.

Sources: Adapted from B. Reeves, T. W. Malone and T. O'Driscoll (2008) Leadership's online labs, *Harvard Business Review*, July, 59–66; M. A. Roberto and A. C. Edmondson (2007) Leadership and team simulation: Everest, web-based simulation product, *Harvard Business Review*, September, 4; J. McGonigal (2008) Making alternative reality the new business reality, in HBR list 'Breakthrough ideas for 2008', *Harvard Business Review*, February, 13–14; see also J. S. Brown and D. Thomas (2008) The gamer disposition, in HBR list 'Breakthrough ideas for 2008', *Harvard Business Review*, February, 12–13.

4 Controlling

Controlling generally involves comparing actual performance to a predetermined standard (see Chapter 22). Any significant difference between actual and desired performance should prompt a manager to take corrective action. Such corrective action may well involve determining whether the original plan needs revision given the realities of the day. In many cases, financial controls dominate the business landscape but marketing controls should be equally important in terms of using customer information as a driver for change and decision making.[22]

Controlling also monitors that the plan fits the reality and that revisions are made accordingly. The control function is extremely important because it helps managers evaluate whether all the four major management functions have been implemented. Controlling is closely associated with planning because planning establishes goals and the methods for achieving them. Controlling also investigates whether planning was successful. Bill Ogle of Motorola notes that

Measurement is essential. It allows us to see how our message resonates with our target audiences. And with today's digital tools – we can see the ebbs and flows of

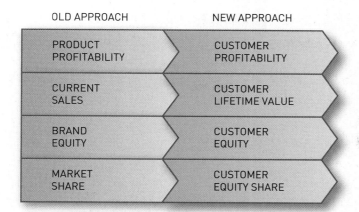

Figure 2.2 New marketing management approaches to controlling and measuring customer satisfaction, value and loyalty
Source: Reprinted by permission of *Harvard Business Review*. From Rethinking Marketing by Rust, R., Moorman, C. and Bhalla, G., January–February 2010. Copyright © 2010 by the Harvard Business School Publishing Corporation; all right reserved.

campaign effectiveness and message resonance in real time. Marketers now have the capability to react as things happen. Tracking campaign effectiveness back to sales is the ultimate goal in every campaign.[23]

Building an effective internal control systems requires three steps. First, the goals must be set; secondly, the performance standards (control measures) must be used for problem solving rather than blaming or punishing; and thirdly, reward should be tied to performance. The control process sets standards, measures actual performance, compares actual performance to standards, and suggests corrective action if necessary.

- **Goals/objectives**. These are the tangible measures of an achieved vision. They are the targets which guide decisions about planning, organising, leading and controlling, and against which performance is measured. Goals should stretch the organisation and be clear and concise. Modern performance appraisals are usually referred to as SMART objectives – specific, measureable, attainable, realistic and time bounded.
- **Results**. These are what have been accomplished, the actual outcomes, the objective(s) attained. Results are often monitored from a financial perspective, but customer satisfaction and loyalty and other customer-focused results increase the long-term viability of the company. A marketing philosophy (new approach) with a move away from a product/production philosophy (old approach) will mean a change in how results are measured (see Figure 2.2).

Why is management difficult?

Management is complex because uncertainty and variety exist within businesses and markets. These are introduced by two main influences: people and organisational context (see Figure 2.3).

People management is the art of giving direction to people. Managing people or employees introduces major challenges. Goals are achieved through people and, more fundamentally, without people there would be no organisations.[24] A manager's most important, and often most difficult, role can be to manage people. Managers must lead, motivate, inspire and

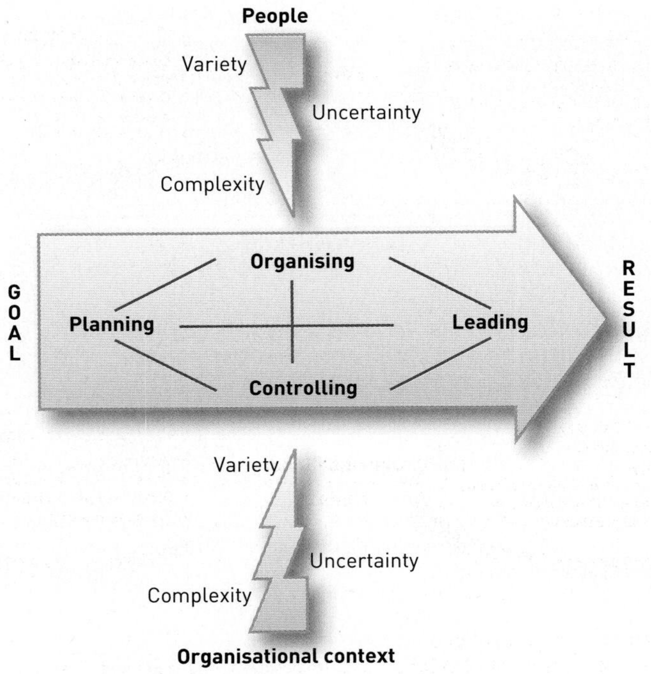

Figure 2.3 Why is management difficult?
Source: J. Martin and M. Fellenz (2010) *Organisational Behaviour and Management*, Cengage Learning, Hampshire.

encourage people. Sometimes they also have to hire, fire, discipline or evaluate employees. Finding the right people and giving them the right skills can be a major challenge, as can retaining staff and motivating them to produce results. Marketing managers often have to manage people outside of their own organisations, including distributors, retailers, agencies and networks of companies.

The **organisational context** includes the way the organisation is structured and how it operates. It focuses on the structures, resources and functions as well as the behaviours and culture within the organisation. The organisational context is different for different companies. As Henry Mintzberg, a leading management strategist noted: 'Organizations differ as do animals, it makes no more sense to prescribe one kind of planning to all organizations than it does to describe one kind of housing for all animals.'[25] People and organisational context as well as external context (Chapter 5) inevitably introduce additional challenges because of their complexity, uncertainty and variety.

- **Complexity.** A large number of potentially relevant factors may have a bearing on the intended outcomes.
- **Uncertainty.** There may be insufficient information about the nature and likelihood of certain events that may have a bearing on the intended outcome.
- **Variety.** Different and potentially unexpected events may be encountered as part of the process.

With the uncertainty of the financial crisis from 2008–11 onwards, many businesses had to change their plans and review spending and development. Many hotels in Greece had to shut down or refocus, after banks stopped lending to tourist ventures and also tourist numbers declined to their country. The financial crisis across Europe

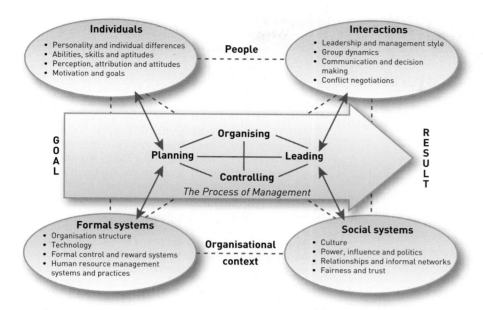

Figure 2.4 Managing in organisations
Source: J. Martin and M. Fellenz (2010) *Organisational Behaviour and Management*, Cengage Learning, Hampshire.

introduced greater uncertainty for both companies and customers, and also increased the complexity and variety of challenges – many of them new – which a manager had to deal with.

There is a reciprocal relationship between management, people and organisations, as Figure 2.4 shows. The diagram highlights the core issues and processes associated with:

- **Individuals**. Individual members of the organisation have different personalities, different styles of thinking and different levels of physical and cognitive ability (e.g. intelligence) and thus will perform at different levels. This also relates to how individuals select and use information and what motivates them to achieve their own and organisational goals.
- **Interactions**. This refers to the interactions among people, whether as individuals, functions or groups. It includes leadership and management styles; group and team dynamics; communication among people; and the use of information for decision making. The elements of conflict and negotiation are also relevant, particularly due to the need to collaborate to achieve results.
- **Formal systems**. This reflects the structure of the organisation and its activities, aligned to the technology used to achieve results. It also includes the formal systems for control, evaluation and reward, and the human resources in relation to recruitment, promotions, training and development. In business it is often felt that what gets measured gets managed – so these formal systems can have a large impact on what occurs within an organisation.
- **Social systems**. This relates to the culture and shared norms and expectations within an organisation, and the use of power and influence. It also reflects the informal networks or social relationships among organisational members. Fairness and trust are important

Breakthrough marketing

Managing Burberry: overcoming the 'chav' challenge and the recession to become a €2 billion brand leader

Burberry, the UK-based fashion empire, is one of the most widely recognised brands in the world. Angela Ahrendts, its chief executive, takes it all in her stride, propelling the company into the digital age without compromising the brand's soul – or her own. She won businessperson of the year in 2010 by increasing revenues by more than 40 per cent and profits by more than 30 per cent. She also led the company into the FTSE 100 – the first British fashion house to be listed. She is credited with transforming the 154-year-old Burberry brand into a technologically savvy international fashion powerhouse. Once little more than a licensing shell built around a sturdy trench coat and its check lining, the company now sells everything from €3,000 duffel bags and silk T-shirts to cashmere hot-water-bottle covers and a recently released cosmetics line. There was a time when the ubiquitous check had been commandeered by the rough-and-tumble working-class youth, or 'chavs', worn head-to-toe by C-list celebrities and widely counterfeited. But since Ahrendts took over in 2006 and removed the iconic pattern from all but about 10 per cent of the items produced, Burberry has reclaimed its identity. She reinvented the Burberry brand and managed it globally with extraordinary focus. Her core management style was to lead from the top. She also understands the benefit of planning and of having a vision of what she wants to create. 'I don't look at Gucci or Chanel or anyone,' she says. 'If I look to any company as a model, it's Apple. They're a brilliant design company working to create a lifestyle, and that's the way I see us.' She leads by working with and through people. A previous colleague noted that

'People want to work for her because she's completely unadorned and she has a life. She's all talent and no pretension.'

Her ability to react to uncertainty, complexity and variety is shown clearly in her reaction to the 2008 recession. Ahrendts can recall the exact moment everything fell apart. It was September 2008, and she was at a two-day board meeting where the management team was euphoric; earnings were up 20 per cent. Then, one by one, all the board members began to excuse themselves to answer their phones: Lehman Brothers was imploding. In a single quarter, revenues would drop by 14 per cent. Ahrendts announced immediately that she would cut €50 million in expenses. Anything that would not be evident to the consumer was slashed. She put on hold plans to overhaul half a dozen flagship stores, froze raises and bonuses, and cut jobs – about 10 per cent of the workforce. The company began shipping some of its products by boat instead of air. She slashed the corporate travel budget and started doing meetings by videoconference. To her, speed was crucial; swift surgery would leave less time to bleed and stop morale from deteriorating. In the end, her management team was galvanised by the catastrophe, says Andy Janowski. 'It's easy', Ahrendts says, 'to run a company while the economy is expanding, and easy to get lazy.' She expects to increase global retail square footage by 10 per cent a year until at least 2013.[26]

She says that she has learned both analytical skills and right-brain creative skills during her management of one of the top fashion brands. The ability to turn a brand around from a chav brand in danger of losing its luxury allure to one which Catherine Middleton – the Duchess of Cambridge – wore weeks before the Royal Wedding in April 2011 is an amazing management success story.[27]

To hear Angela Ahrendts discuss the secret of her management success log on to YouTube: www.youtube.com/watch?v=UbEj0hNW4Eg.

aspects of the social system, aligned to what is expected from people and how they experience the operation of management.

Good management can be the ultimate difference between success and failure, as the above box shows.

What is marketing management?

Marketing management is a business discipline which achieves goals through the practical application of marketing techniques and the management of a firm's marketing resources and activities. It is the planning, organising, leading and control of the business activities required to price, process and design products and services, to manage people, and to promote and distribute satisfying services and products to target markets in order to achieve organisational objectives.

The role of a marketing manager can vary significantly based on the business's size, **corporate culture** and industry context. To create an effective, cost-efficient marketing management strategy, firms must possess a detailed, objective understanding of their own business and the market in which they operate.

> **Marketing will realize its full potential only when viewed simultaneously as an organization-wide commitment to putting the customer first, a strategic management responsibility for shaping the customer value proposition, and a functional responsibility to sense and respond to the market.**[28]

Marketing directors operate in a rapidly changing environment which is putting even greater demands on marketing executives. Research suggests that marketing directors only last about two years, well below the average tenure of 54 months for other senior directors. One explanation is that the role of marketing – and thus management expectations – varies widely among firms. Harvard's John Quelch and Gail McGovern found tremendous variability in the responsibilities and job descriptions for marketing managers. The variance exists because different models are appropriate for different types of company at different stages of development.[29]

Another challenge that marketing directors face is that the success factors for top marketers are many and varied. Marketing directors must have strong quantitative skills but also well-honed qualitative skills; they must have an independent, entrepreneurial attitude but also work in close harmony with other departments such as sales; and they must capture the 'voice' and point-of-view of consumers yet have a keen bottom-line understanding of how marketing creates value within their organisation.[30]

A recent survey asked 200 senior marketing executives which innate and learned qualities were most important. Here are their answers:

Innate:
- risk-taker
- willingness to make decisions
- problem-solving ability
- change agent
- results-oriented

Learned:
- global experience
- multichannel expertise
- cross-industry experience
- digital focus
- operational knowledge

Perhaps the most important role for any marketing director is to infuse a customer perspective and orientation into business decisions, and particularly at **touchpoints** – where a customer directly or indirectly interacts with the company. The marketing director is responsible for directing virtually all customer efforts for the company and ensuring that all company efforts have a customer focus.[31] They also must compete with other companies in challenging environments, as the box shows on the next page.

The practice of management

What do managers actually do in practice and every day? Managers and management styles can differ, and much of how a company is managed results from the type of management style in use in that organisation.

Marketing insight

Management challenges in recessionary environments

A core management skill is the ability to manage customers, staff and the organisation during challenging business cycles. A recession is one such challenge, as are economic recovery, natural disasters and major societal changes either through political situations, economic concerns, societal changes, technological upheavals and/or environmental changes. Marketing managers must be particularly focused on anticipating challenges and have contingency plans in place for each eventuality, and a plan for the unexpected too.

From the point of view of a recession or economic downturn the major challenge is to improve on performance while cutting costs. The following steps provide some guidelines on how to manage when the market changes, particularly during a recession when the role is to ensure that the companies come through the recession intact:

Increase communication. Communicate more than normal and stay in touch with staff. Communicate in an honest and open way, share what you know about the situation and also explain to them what you do not know. Staff meetings and face-to-face discussions are preferred over email in a crisis, as emails can appear cold and distant. People need to be informed, and rumour and gossip will fill the space left by the lack of communication. As Mick Holbrook, Director of Organisation and People Development at PwC, suggested *'the best companies will keep their staff committed by involving them in what's going on . . . people will maintain a high level of engagement if they feel their company is being honest with them, and involving them if they can [in company decisions'.[i]* Give staff an outlet for their views, a method to communicate with senior managers and others rather than a one way release of information. In this era of technology proliferation the dividing line between internal and external communication can be blurred. What is said internally is often repeated externally, so the two messages must be aligned so that customers and staff are communicated to in a united way.

Embrace change and stay positive. Try to stay positive and focused on what is good about the company and the situation. Even in the face of extreme recession it is a good idea to try and boost morale through low cost perks for staff, and innovations, no matter how small, for customers. Recession can bring about positive change and many companies prosper during a recession. As Charles Darwin said 'it is not the strongest of the species that survives, nor the most intelligent, but the one most responsive to change'.

Involve staff in decision making. Try to give staff a voice in decision making–particularly where cutbacks or layoffs are concerned. They may have some great ideas, which can support the company and customers. During recessions, many staff agree to salary cuts and shorter working weeks to avoid layoffs. Staff also like to feel that they are part of the process and have some control over the situation rather than at the mercy of some nameless unseen entity working behind closed doors.

Stay close to the customer. This is the time to become more focused on the customer and their wants and needs. Instead of cutting the market research budget or general marketing spend, you need to know more than ever how consumers are redefining value and responding to the recession. Staying close to the customer aligns the company with their needs and brings them into the decision making within the company.

Marketing is a management arena that is always under pressure to provide results and to manage for the long term. With challenging economic conditions the marketing skills set are needed more than ever as customers are conscious of value, businesses are worried about survival and employees are worried about their jobs.

[i] Holbrook, Mick (2008) cited in 'Talent management special report: Rules of engagement', available from http://www.personneltoday.com/articles/2008/10/17/47993/talent-management-special-report-rules-of-engagement.html

The nature of managerial work often means that managers race around from task to task, with 'brevity, variety and fragmentation' as core characteristics of managerial work.[32] Much of management theory assumes that managers spend their time reading reports and analysing data. Though they do spend time in these areas, studies have revealed that much of management is involved with interpersonal and communication issues. For example, managers spend a lot of time operating as a figurehead, making speeches, interacting with

Marketing memo

Management and leadership styles

What exactly is a management style?

Management and leadership style is the general and consistent approach that a manager uses: for example, how the decision-making process is done or how employees are treated. Each style has its own set of positive and negative characteristics, and reflects the manner in which tasks are managed and completed. There are many management styles in business – the following is a brief discussion of the main ones:

- Democratic. In a democratic management style, the manager usually delegates power to the subordinates and leaves the decision-making process to them. It is of the highest importance that those given the responsibility are those who are efficient in executing the tasks. This business leadership style is most suitable and effective in a situation where the manager wants to teach employees the process of decision making.

- Autocratic. In an autocratic leadership style, the manager is fully responsible for making the decisions. Hence, other employees are left out of the decision-making process. This is most effective in a condition where prompt decisions are required. This leadership style, however, can easily demotivate employees and dampen their productivity level.

- Participative. In participative management style, the manager gives staff and subordinates the chance to be involved in the decision-making process.

Believed to be one of the best methods of boosting the motivation of employees, this style will make employees feel valued by the management. While there is a sense of collective decision making, however, the manager will have the final say.

- Laissez-faire. A laissez-faire manager sets the tasks and gives staff complete freedom to complete it as they see fit. There is minimal involvement from the manager. The manager, however, does not sit idle and watch them work. He or she is there to coach or answer questions, and supply information if required. There are benefits: staff are again developed to take responsibility, which may lead to improved motivation. However, with little direct guidance from the manager, staff may begin to feel lost and not reach the goals originally set within the time frame.

Choosing the best style

Ultimately, the best management style is one that can get the job done effectively. A leader is expected to adopt roles, rules and concepts according to the situation and condition of the company, as well as the skills and mindset of the employees.

Sources: D. Goleman and R. Boyatzis (2008) Social intelligence and the biology of leadership, *Harvard Business Review*, September, 1–8; D. Goleman (2007) *Social Intelligence: The New Science of Human Relationships*, New York: Bantam; Premier Training (2011) *Selecting the Best Management Style for Your Business*, Huntingdon; J. Purcell and B. Ahlstrand (1994) *Human Resource Management in the Multi-divisional Company*, Oxford: Oxford University Press.

people and getting and receiving information from conversations and meetings. Managers also spend a lot of time away from their desk, running day-to-day operations, rather than on the long-term strategic needs of the company.

Managers have to balance the conflicting demands made by the need for short- and long-term results with the needs of various stakeholders, including customers, shareholders, employees and communities. The nature of management means that they need to be able to convey and explain a clear vision. As Jim Kilts, a former CEO at Kraft, Gillette and Nabisco, says: 'I want rigorous analysis and thoughtful assessments, but I don't want complexity. If strategies and plans aren't easily understood by everyone, they will be acted on by no one.'

Managers have a wide array of alternative strategies they can undertake in running a business. These different alternatives yield differing cashflow streams. Effective management requires a long-term focus and choosing strategic alternatives that yield the highest overall expected net present value (i.e. strategies that maximise the return on the investment made in them).

The core marketing management skills

There is no one established set of tasks or clearly defined role for the marketing manager. Marketing is not a 'one size fits all' discipline, and the variety and challenges of each situation are unique. Marketing managers need a range of skills to be able to use the full expanse of techniques available to them in creative and imaginative ways, while always monitoring the financial outlays and returns needed. The marketing insight box explores the core skills needed for marketing practitioners.

Some of the unique marketing management skills required by marketing managers are as follows:

- managing across the organisation;
- managing networks, relationships and interaction;
- information handling and management;
- managing innovation and change;
- analytical and creative skills.

We will now analyse these in more detail.

Managing across the organisation

Although an effective marketing director is crucial, increasingly marketing is *not* done only by the marketing department. Because marketing must affect every aspect of the

Marketing insight

Marketing skills for an MBA

In a recent study of MBA graduates, a number of skills were recognised as being needed by marketing people.[33] The four most important were:

1 Decision making under uncertainty: ability to adapt to new situations; ability to make decisions with imperfect information; ability to integrate information from a wide variety of sources.

2 Communication skills: oral and written communications skills.

3 Data collection and analysis: information-gathering skills; quantitative skills.

4 Strategic/analytical thinking: ability to think strategically; ability to think analytically.

MBA alumni reported greatest usage of their interpersonal skills and oral and written communication skills. Integrating information from a wide variety of sources was also high on the list, as were analytical thinking, creative problem-solving skills and strategic thinking. The skills used least involved financial analysis (conducting cost–benefit analyses of proposed changes and preparing budgets) and direct staff management (recruiting, managing and maintaining staff).

The future

In relation to the skills and abilities needed by marketing in the future, six underlying dimensions were suggested:

1 Information analysis and strategic planning: developing a strategic plan; strategic thinking; developing creative problem-solving skills; integration of information from a wide variety of sources; analytical thinking.

2 Communication skills: oral and written communication skills; interpersonal skills; leadership skills.

3 Statistical and financial analysis: conducting financial analyses and preparing a budget; analysing, organising and interpreting statistical data; conducting cost–benefit analyses of potential changes.

4 Organisation management: recruiting, managing and maintaining staff; stress management; managing change.

5 Career management: managing their career; networking skills.

6 Marketing-specific skills: technical skills for the marketing speciality – for example, developing web-based marketing, and designing and conducting market research.

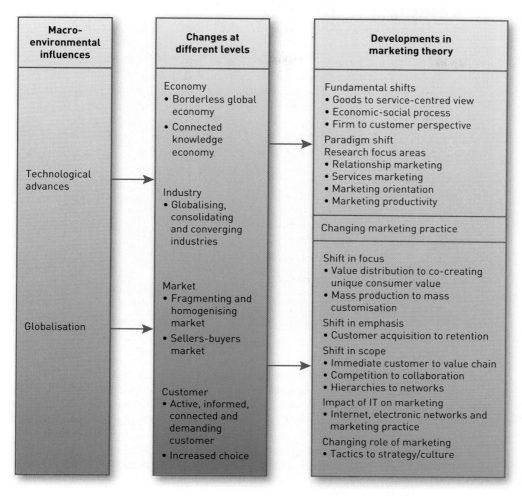

Figure 2.5 Environmental changes and developments in marketing theory and practice
Source: From J. Thomas and R. K. Gupta (2005) Marketing theory and practice: evolving through turbulent times, *Global Business Review*, 6(1), 95–112. Copyright © International Management Institute, New Delhi. All rights reserved. Reproduced with the permission of the copyright holders and the publishers Sage Publications India Pvt. Ltd, New Delhi.

customer experience, marketers must properly manage all possible touchpoints, such as store layouts, package designs, product functions and customer service. Marketing must also be influential in key general management activities, such as product innovation and new business development. To create a strong marketing organisation, marketers must think like executives in other departments, and executives in other departments must think more like marketers.[34]

As David Packard of HP observed, 'Marketing is far too important to leave to the marketing department.' Companies now know that every employee has an impact on the customer and must see the customer as the source of the company's prosperity. Marketing managers manage through and with other departments and functions, and therefore interact and collaborate with other departments and functions in order to achieve objectives.

Organisations are often divided into functions, departments and teams. **Functions** are a distinct group of staff who serve as specialists in achieving a set of given objectives and carrying out corresponding activities, and they are usually permanent within organisations. Examples of functions are the marketing function and the accounting function.

Marketing departments are challenged with bringing other departments together to focus on the customer.
Source: Creatas/PunchStock.

Functional initiatives are activities where an individual or function has minimal or no contact with personnel from other functions; these are often called functional-specific activities. *Multifunctional initiatives* are where employees play a liaison role and represent their respective function's view. *Cross-functional activities* are carried out by individuals from different departments with a preselected team leader from a department responsible for team management. A **team** comprises a group of people linked through a common purpose. Teams are especially appropriate for conducting tasks that are high in complexity and have many interdependent subtasks.

Departments are at a higher level and encompass many functions. The marketing department, for example, contains the market research function and the advertising function.

The ability of marketing to unite with other departments such as sales, production and finance is crucial to gaining the acceptance and enthusiasm of other departments concerning marketing and the marketing mix programme. Take, for example, new product or service development engineers – they must work with marketing from the beginning rather than bringing marketing in after they have developed a new product or designed a new service. Some companies use marketing only for the promotional area and ignore all the rest of marketing. 'Tick-box' marketing is when marketing is brought in *after* the product or service has been developed and for promotions only – ticking off the promotional items such as brochures, point-of-sale displays and advertising without any understanding of the other aspects of marketing. Such a mindset contributes to product and service failure because there is no clear understanding of consumers and marketing needs.

The marketing department must have a strong leader who directs a well-organised team that can work with all the other departments company wide. A constant effort is needed to ensure that the marketing manager is able to provide the marketing skills needed to manage the company offering to the customer, and to identify opportunities and manage product and services to satisfy needs and expand **brand awareness**, loyalty and, ultimately, profitability.[35]

For many companies, marketing is successful; the department is well defined and there is agreement on the scope and contribution of marketing to the business. Alternatively, despite the fact that marketing affects business and financial performance, marketing can have a poor image within some companies.[36] For these companies, marketing is

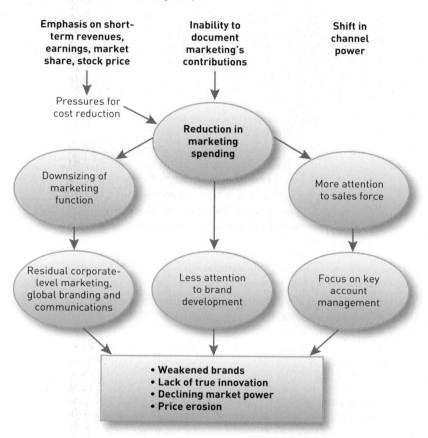

Forces shaping marketing's role

Financial pressures, a shift in channel power and marketing's inability to document its contribution to business results have combined to force reductions in marketing spending and influence – with significant consequences for marketing's impact.

Figure 2.6 Forces shaping marketing's role
Source: F. Webster, A. Malter and S. Ganesan (2005) The decline and dispersion of marketing competence, *MIT Sloan Management Review*, 46(4), 35–43. © 2005 from MIT Sloan Management Review/ Massachusetts Institute of Technology. All rights reserved. Distributed by Tribune Media Services.

underrepresented at board level and a financial, production or sales rather than a marketing philosophy dominates.[37] Some of the reasons for this are highlighted in Figure 2.6, which reflects a range of issues facing marketing managers.

Marketing management in organisations can be at a disadvantage because of organisational and environmental pressures. These can include the following:

- uncertain definition of the term 'marketing' and the lack of understanding of marketing by some people;
- the tyranny of the profit and loss or financial focus of companies, often focusing on short-term gain to the detriment of long-term sustained growth;
- the difficulty in directly measuring marketing returns;
- shifts in channel power and the loss of manufacturing control;
- increased demands of customers;
- the limiting of marketing's role within top management;
- marketing managers not having the same status as managers in other areas, such as finance, engineering and sales;
- moving staff from other areas into marketing without formal marketing training and expecting them to learn while there;

- not providing marketing with ample resources;
- lack of alignment between marketing strategy and business strategy.

There are different characteristics of companies that embrace marketing and companies that do not embrace a marketing philosophy. These are shown in Table 2.1.

For many companies, the Anglo-Saxon model of business with its financial philosophy dominates. A *financial philosophy* is where finance and financial models are used to evaluate business, and as such decisions are made predominantly through financial analysis and with profit maximisation as the main goal. Marketers are perceived to be 'unaccountable' by the rest of the organisation; they are seen as unable to demonstrate a return on investment in the activities over which they have control.[38] Marketing needs to have a match of intuitive and creative ideas that can be tried and tested along with techniques which can be measured and monitored. The failure of many companies, especially during the economic upheavals of 2008 and beyond, can be attributed to an overfocus on profit maximisation during the boom years of 2002–8. Companies like Waterford Crystal and Woolworths forgot about the customer in their rush to expand and grow share value.

McGovern and Quelch suggest eight ways to improve marketing directors' success, as shown in Figure 2.7.

Table 2.1 Characteristics of companies at the two extremes of marketing's influence

Marketing plays an influential role in corporate strategy in most companies – there is both an opportunity and a viable approach for building marketing competence as a source of competitive advantage.

Key dimensions	Characteristics when marketing is *not* influential in corporate decisions	Characteristics when marketing *is* influential in corporate decisions
Definition of marketing	Wide disagreement and ambiguity about the role and importance of marketing and customer orientation	Clear and shared understanding of the role of marketing: strong customer orientation in the corporate culture
Top-management objectives	Focused on current stock price, earnings per share (EPS), cost reduction, market share, sales volume	Focused on long-term growth in revenue, profitability, EPS and cash flow
Orientation and functional background of CEO	Little or no marketing experience; focused on financial community	Deep understanding of marketing; compelling vision of customer value. Advocate for the customer
Top-management priorities	Cost reduction and labour productivity	Customers, resellers and key accounts. Market information and tracking data are key management tools
Growth strategy	Growth achieved through mergers and acquisitions	Growth achieved through serious commitment to research and development, product innovation
Role of brands	Strong brands used as cash cows to fund acquisitions, growth strategy	Substantial investment to build and maintain brand equity
Focus of new product service development	Product service and technology focused	Customer analysis is hard-wired into product service development
Portfolio strategy	Managed for cash flow; pricing used to achieve volume goals	Customer portfolio analysed and managed for loyalty and profitability

Source: F. Webster, A. Malter and S. Ganesan (2005) The decline and dispersion of marketing competence, *MIT Sloan Management Review*, 46(4), 35–43. © 2005 from MIT Sloan Management Review/Massachusetts Institute of Technology. All rights reserved. Distributed by Tribune Media Services.

1 Make the mission and responsibilities clear. Be certain that the case for having a marketing director is strong and the mission is well understood by leaders in the organisation, particularly the CEO, the board and line management. Without a clear need (real or perceived), the role will be rejected by the organisation.

2 Fit the role to the marketing culture and structure. Avoid having a marketing director in a marketing-led company that has many individual brands rather than a single corporate umbrella – unless the person appointed to the position is a well-connected insider.

3 Choose a marketing director who is compatible with the CEO. Beware the CEO who wants to hire a marketing director but doesn't want to relinquish any marketing control. Find a CEO who recognises his or her responsibility to be the cheerleader for marketing and the brand, but realises the need to be guided and coached by a marketing specialist.

4 Remember that showpeople don't succeed. The marketing director should work hard to ensure the CEO is successful at being the principal cheerleader for the brand.

5 Match the personality with the marketing director type. Be certain that the chief marketer has the right skills and personality for whichever of the three marketing director models he or she might fill (marketing director, marketing services; classic marketing director or 'super' marketing director). There is little tolerance for on-the-job training.

6 Make line managers marketing heroes. By stretching their marketing budgets, marketing directors can improve a division's marketing productivity and help business unit leaders increase their top-line revenues.

7 Infiltrate the line organisation. Have the marketing director support the placement of marketing professionals from the corporate marketing department into divisional marketing roles. Provide input from the marketing director into the annual reviews of line managers.

8 Require right-brain and left-brain skills. The most successful marketing director will have strong creative and technical marketing expertise, be politically savvy, and have the interpersonal skills to be a great leader and manager.

Figure 2.7 Improving marketing directors' success
Source: From G. McGovern and J. A. Quelch (2004) The fall and rise of the CMO, *Strategy+Business*, 37, 3–8. Reproduced with permission.

Because of the diversity of operations and situations across companies, the marketing memo on the next page provides a good checklist for the questions marketing managers should ask, to ensure that they have a marketing philosophy and customer focus throughout all departments in the company.

Managing networks, relationships and interactions

Much of marketing management operates with a relational and networked approach, demanding the coordination of networks of suppliers, customers and service providers at a range and level never before witnessed in business history. The network school of management suggests that companies have a multitude of relationships within a web complex. The ultimate outcome of relationship marketing is a unique company asset called a **marketing network**, consisting of the company and its supporting stakeholders – customers, employees, suppliers, distributors, retailers and others – with whom it has built mutually profitable business relationships. The operating principle is simple: build an effective network of relationships with key stakeholders, and profits will follow.[39]

Marketing memo

Marketers' frequently asked questions

1 How can we gather customer information and use the insight to drive the business?

2 How can we spot and choose the right market segment(s)?

3 How can we differentiate our product or service offerings?

4 How should we respond to customers who buy on price?

5 How can we compete against lower-cost, lower-price competitors?

6 How far can we go in customising our offering for each customer?

7 How can we grow our business?

8 How can we build stronger brands?

9 How can we reduce the cost of customer acquisition?

10 How can we keep our customers loyal for longer?

11 How do we lose customers who are not within our target market?

12 How can we tell which customers are more important?

13 How can we measure the payback from advertising, sales promotion, public relations and our online activities?

14 How can we improve sales force productivity?

15 How can we establish multiple channels and yet manage channel conflict?

16 How can we get all company departments to be more customer oriented?

17 How do we manage the service process?

18 How can we manage and improve the customer experience environment or any physical evidence?

19 How can we best manage and motivate the people who provide the service?

20 How can we use our marketing mix activities to support our target market needs and positioning strategy?

21 How can we integrate all elements of the marketing mix, from managing the service process to controlling the supply network?

22 How can we be consistently ahead of consumer needs and really understand the future?

Understanding relationship marketing

Relationship marketing places greater emphasis on customer retention. Attracting a new customer may cost five times as much as retaining an existing one. Companies build customer share by offering a larger variety of products or services to existing customers, and keeping their value offering relevant and worthwhile to the consumer. A bank aims to increase its share of the customer's wallet; a supermarket aims to capture a larger share of the customer's 'stomach' or purse. Companies also target separate offers, services and messages to individual customers based on information about past transactions, demographics, psychographics, media and distribution preferences. By focusing on their most profitable customers, products and channels, these firms hope to achieve profitable growth, capturing a larger share of each customer's expenditures, by building high customer loyalty. They estimate individual customer lifetime value and design their market offerings and prices to make a profit over the customer's lifetime. The lifetime value of a customer to a pizza company, for example, is valued at between €2,000 and €6,000. This concept reflects a move from a 'one-to-many' approach to a 'one-to-one' approach.[40]

Partner relationship management (PRM) is nurturing partnering arrangements with key suppliers and distributors, thinking of these intermediaries not as customers but as partners in delivering value to final customers, so that everybody benefits.

Understanding network marketing

Marketing operates in a networked world and managing a network of people, companies, relationships, technologies and interactions is a core skill of marketing managers. Viewing companies as networks of relationships and interactions called virtual organisations is the suggested model for today's business world. This moves away from hierarchical entities to a more organic, integrative, network-based and process-oriented philosophy, with groups of separate enterprises linked through high-speed technologies. Networks are expected to have an enduring, profound, radical and pervasive effect on marketing.

As network management and interfirm cooperation become crucial, information management between manufacturers, service providers and their suppliers needs to become more efficient and effective using the latest information and communication technologies to interconnect manufacturers, suppliers, retailers and transporters, so that they can easily exchange information with each other. However, the use of information technologies is not all that is necessary – it is even more important to manage the relationships effectively with all companies in the network.[41] Increasingly, a key goal of marketing is to develop deep, enduring relationships with people and organisations that could directly or indirectly affect the success of the company's marketing activities. **Network marketing** aims to build mutually satisfying long-term relationships with key constituents in order to earn and retain their business.[42]

PayPal

Whether you are buying football boots from Chile or a mobile phone from Finland, or selling surfboards in Costa Rica, PayPal works for you. With a network of more than 190 countries and regions, and in multiple currencies, PayPal reaches across the globe to give consumers and businesses a way to pay or get paid. PayPal's success in terms of users and volumes was the product of a three-phase strategy described by eBay CEO Meg Whitman: 'First, PayPal focused on expanding its service among eBay users in the US. Second, we began expanding PayPal to eBay's international sites. And third, we started to build PayPal's business off eBay.' This is an example of building a network through eBay users and then expanding the network to other retailers and wholesalers.

Four key constituents in network marketing are customers, employees, marketing partners (channels, suppliers, distributors, dealers, agencies) and members of the financial community (shareholders, investors, analysts). Marketers must respect the need to create prosperity among all these constituents and develop policies and strategies to balance the returns to all key stakeholders. To develop strong relationships with these constituents requires an understanding of their capabilities and resources, as well as their needs, goals and desires. Working in collaboration with partners is the idea of competent collaboration. Marketing management increasingly focuses on collaboration through close relationships with customers and partners to co-create solutions to complex problems or jointly to pursue marketplace opportunities. Within the network, all need to collaborate together to the mutual benefit of all – take the launch of a Harry Potter book below.

Harry Potter

Bloomsbury, the publishers of the Harry Potter range of books, has always operated a global network for managing the launch of each book, which always creates hype and demand. The success of Harry Potter is enormous – it is the third most popular book in the world, after the Bible and the *Red Book* by Mao, it has been translated into 67 languages, placing its author J. K. Rowling among the most translated authors in history, and it is a best seller in over 120 countries. It is the highest grossing film series of all time and has a brand value of €15 billion. The publishers collaborated with printers, distributors, delivery companies, retailers and the media to ensure that the books went on sale at midnight on the same day across the globe – creating massive queues and a heightened

The Harry Potter marketing success relies on collaboration across a network of suppliers, distributors, publishers, retailers, the media and the consumer.
Source: © Odd Anderson/Getty Images.

sense of demand. Book retailer Waterstone's opened 140 of its stores at midnight and online retailer Amazon received more than 400,000 advance orders in the UK alone. The UK Royal Mail had to employ an extra 150 vans to handle delivery. Bloomsbury networks with Warner Bros, which have made films of all seven books. The films have in turn spawned eight video games and have led to the licensing of more than 400 additional Harry Potter products (including an iPod). Universal and Warner Brothers also announced the creation of 'The Wizarding World of Harry Potter', a new Harry Potter-themed expansion to the Islands of Adventure theme park at Universal Orlando Resort in Florida. A global network of players and a global consumer base has created and maintained Harry Potter as one of the iconic brands of this century.

Being able to collaborate successfully allows a firm to innovate, to respond to change and to achieve strategic marketing objectives. Successful collaboration requires:

- collaborative capability (the skills, capabilities and supporting processes);
- absorptive capability (the ability to learn and apply new knowledge);
- developing project-specific capability;
- selecting the right partner;
- managing the collaboration process;
- developing the right team.[43]

Marketing managers need to ask the following questions:

1 Can the company recognise when collaboration is needed on marketing projects?
2 Does the company have the commitment of senior management to invest the necessary time, resources and effort for marketing collaboration?
3 Can the company improve on whom they select as collaborators in marketing projects?
4 Does the company have the capabilities to learn from the collaboration partners?
5 Is the marketing manager committed to collaborating in ways that improve relationship quality with partners?

Understanding dominant marketing practices

The European market is particularly suited to network models of marketing and business because it has an interdependence view of markets where companies do not operate alone but rather in groups or networks.[44] Before marketers decide which marketing mix elements to use, they must understand relationships, networks and interactions as a fundamental prerequisite to implementing the marketing mix.[45] The contemporary marketing practice (CMP) framework in the marketing insight box highlights the different marketing practices included in relationship marketing and network marketing.

Marketing insight

The contemporary marketing practice framework

The contemporary marketing practice framework (see Table 2.2) offers an interesting perspective on how we could view marketing's move from transactional exchange to relational and networked marketing.[46] This framework suggests that companies often have a dominant focus but that they practise marketing across

the full range of transaction, database, emarketing, interaction and network marketing practices. It shows marketing managers which core skills set they need, depending on the marketing practice they use. Remember that all of the practices can be in operation but that one usually dominates.

In the case of network marketing, if a marketing manager was managing with network marketing as the dominant focus then the orientation would be towards the aspects listed in the final column of Table 2.2.

Table 2.2 The contemporary marketing practice framework

	Transaction marketing	Database marketing	emarketing	Interactive marketing	Network marketing
Purpose of exchange	Economic transaction	Information and economic transaction	Information-generating dialogue between a seller and many identified buyers	Interpersonal relationships between a buyer and seller	Connected relationships between firms
Nature of communication	Firm to mass market	Firm to targeted segment or individuals	Firm using technology to communicate 'with' and 'among' many individuals (who may form groups)	Individuals 'with' individuals (across organisations)	Firms 'with' firms (involving individuals)
Type of contact	Arm's length, impersonal	Personalised (yet distant)	Interactive (via technology)	Face to face, interpersonal	Impersonal – interpersonal (ranging from distant to close)
Duration of exchange	Discrete (yet perhaps over time)	Discrete and over time	Continuous (but interactivity occurs in real time)	Continuous (ongoing and mutually adaptive, short or long term)	Continuous (stable yet dynamic, may be short or long term)

▶ Marketing insight *(continued)*

Table 2.2 *(continued)*

	Transaction marketing	Database marketing	emarketing	Interactive marketing	Network marketing
Formality of exchange	Formal	Formal (yet personalised via technology)	Formal (yet customised and/or personalised via interactive technology	Formal and informal (i.e. at both at business and social level)	Formal and informal (i.e. at both at business and social level)
Managerial intent	Customer attraction	Customer retention	Creation of IT-enabled dialogue	Interaction	Coordination
Managerial focus	Product or brand	Product/brand and customers (in a targeted market)	Managing IT-enabled relationships between the firm and many individuals	Relationships between individuals	Connected relationships between firms (in a network)
Managerial investment	Internal marketing assets	Internal marketing assets (emphasising information technology capabilities)	Internal operational assets (IT, website, logistics); functional systems integration	External market assets (focusing on establishing and developing a relationship with another individual)	External market assets (focusing on developing the firm's position in a network of firms)
Managerial level	Functional marketers (e.g. sales manager, product manager)	Specialist marketers (e.g. customer service manager, loyalty manager)	Marketing specialists (with) technology specialists, senior managers	Employees and managers (from across functions and levels in the firms)	Senior managers

Sources: R. Brodie, N Coviello and H., Winklehofer (2008) Investigating contemporary marketing practices: a review of the first decade of the CMP Research Program, *Journal of Business and Industrial Marketing*, 23(2), 84–94; M. Brady, M. R. Fellenz and R. Brookes (2008) Researching the role of information and communication technologies in contemporary Marketing, *Journal of Business and Industrial Marketing*, 23(2), 108–14; adapted from N. Coviello, R. Brodie and H. Munro (1997) Understanding contemporary marketing: development of a classification scheme, *Journal of Marketing Management*, 13(6), 501–22; N. Coviello, R. Brodie, P. Danaher et al. (2002) How firms relate to their markets: an empirical examination of contemporary marketing practices, *Journal of Marketing*, 66(3), 33–46.

Information handling and management

Information abounds in marketing. There is 'almost limitless amounts of marketing data concerning customer details, buying patterns, channels of distribution and the performance of partners and so on'.[47] In a digital world, the ability to store, process, analyse and transmit information far exceeds the ability to use this information. In many cases it is not a question of too little information, but too much. The real power base in marketing comes from a company's information power and not its sales power. Marketers who can analyse information and react to the knowledge that this information yields, by creating innovative and creative products and services, will be successful – not the company with the best sales force or advertising.

> **Never before have companies had such powerful technologies for interacting directly with customers, collecting and mining information about them and tailoring their offerings accordingly. And never before have customers expected to interact so deeply with companies and each other to shape the products and services they use.[48] (See Chapter 4.)**

In the future, marketing will rely less on experience, intuition and guesswork and much more on the information provided by information technology systems, monitoring every stage of the product/service design, development and delivery through to consumption. The marketing manager will have to manage huge amounts of information from multiple sources, channels and all members of networks, relationships and interactions, along with the internal and external environment (see Chapters 5–9).

Managing innovation and change

To survive and succeed, every business has to become a change agent. Marketing must be able to abandon what is not successful and continuously improve every product, service and process within the company.[49] This requires the exploitation of successes, especially those that are unexpected and unplanned for – and it requires systematic innovation. Change should be normal and expected rather than feared and avoided.

Where is the next innovation going to come from? Marketing managers need to be futurologists. They need to be at least a year or two ahead of the market and tell the company where the market is going. Contemporary companies imitate each other's structures and strategies, resulting in decreased margins for all.[50] A solution to this is to build a capability in strategic innovation and imagination. Take Apple, which rocked the mobile phone world with the iPhone, prompting rivals to imitate the touch-screen design. The challenge is to create a marketing culture that values human capital and innovation, to provide a steady stream of innovation.[51] Innovation is about much more than new products and services. It is about reinventing business processes and building entirely new markets that meet untapped customer needs. The Taka Group, a Mumbai-based conglomerate, developed a €2,000 car for the large untapped market in small cars at an affordable price. The car is inexpensive in part because of the distribution model, which sells the car in kits. Virgin Atlantic, the UK-based airline, is another innovative company.

Virgin Atlantic

Emerging out of the music-centred Virgin Group, Virgin Atlantic Airways has led the journey of the Virgin brand from its counter-culture origins to pioneering and delivering customer-centric, service-led innovation in the airline sector. Its key emphasis is on innovation and differentiation. Sir Richard Branson, the founder and Chief Executive, confirms his vision for the airline as: 'Innovation, value for money, and the simple idea that flying should actually be fun.'[52] Expanding from its original transatlantic base linking London with New York and Miami, Virgin has become a major international global airline, introducing process and service innovations and redefining the economy and business-class travel experience along the way. Resembling a flying luxury hotel, business class innovations have included providing a limousine service, onboard masseurs and unique lounges. In economy class, Virgin introduced the individual multichannel entertainment system and also onboard SMS text messaging. It was also the first airline to launch a podcasting service.[53] Breda Bubear, Virgin Atlantic advertising and communication head, said: 'Podcasting gives us a fantastic opportunity to communicate with our customers in a new and innovative way'[54].

According to Andrew Hargadon, a product designer for Apple, 'the big challenge in managing innovation lies, not in building up two very strong skills in innovation and in operations, but rather in building the bridge between them – developing the people and processes that facilitate the routinisation of novelty. An ability to turn good ideas into practical processes that organisations can value, adopt, implement, and manage.' Having the ideas is not the same as converting them into process improvements, new product designs, supply network innovations, and ultimately added value for the customer. That is execution. The challenge is to ask what new ideas can be implemented to stay ahead of the competition. Many companies, often through success, become complacent and stop focusing on or managing innovation. The marketing insight below highlights the dangers of becoming complacent.

Analytical and creative skills

Marketing managers need to be both analytical and creative. They tend to think with the right side of the brain and forget that they can succeed in formulating the most ingenious marketing plan ever and yet fail due to a lack of monitoring and control.[55] For a discipline that focused on the creative tasks of advertising, promotion, packaging, print and TV advertising, marketing has moved from an emphasis on solely creative activities to analytical ability and activities: towards left-brain number crunchers who can understand modelling of information and analyse findings to produce innovative marketing mix programmes.[56] Much of marketing is now related to analysis: analysing computer models that can optimise everything from shelf space to sales representative allocations. For example, dynamic pricing models and yield management systems in airlines and hotels allow for

Marketing insight

Marketing management: the dangers of complacency

Many firms that are deeply entrenched in their industry, where they have dominated for years, can develop a particular mindset that leaves them vulnerable to aggressive and innovative competition. They forget to carry out marketing with an inside-out perspective and so miss the opportunities to change. They often suffer from the three Cs of:

- Complacency: smugness, self-satisfaction and contentment.

- Conservatism: management which believes that the future will be the same as the past and adheres to tradition rather than market need.

- Conceit: the belief that 'we are the best' and that no other company could be better.

Staying marketing focused can be difficult when you are successful.[57] Take the example of Airbus, which has successfully competed with Boeing in its marketplace. The 800-passenger aircraft Airbus A380 – designed and developed by Airbus – is more than double the capacity of a Boeing 747. For 35 years, Boeing's 747 aircraft set the standard for jumbo commercial aircraft and controlled this market. As far as Boeing was concerned, theirs was as big as an aeroplane should be: 'our 747 jumbo jet is the largest that can be profitably used'.[58]

Airbus, which started as a European consortium from France and Germany, and was later joined by Spain and the UK, decided to try and beat Boeing at their own game. The company, which is now controlled by a Dutch aerospace organisation, thinks its plane will create the blueprint for the next generation of airborne giants. 'It's the plane of the future, a cruise ship in the sky', said John Leahy, Airbus's top executive, who is credited with helping the company surpass Boeing as the world's largest aircraft maker. The A380 'will change the way we fly, just as the 747 did'.[59] A passenger on the inaugural flight congratulated Airbus on its innovation. 'First of all, well done to Airbus for making the biggest flying machine of mankind. It's awesome and unbelievable. Secondly, Airbus has made air travel so comfortable. I dread travelling in a 747 from now on, especially in economy class.'

► Marketing insight *(continued)*

By focusing on innovation and trying harder than the competition, the A380 provides customers with luxury and speed. For Airbus it cements its position as the world's leading manufacturer of passenger airplanes.
Source: Jim Mone/AP/PA Photos.

seat and room allocation at the optimised rate. It is the marketing manager's role to ensure that their business can monitor and utilise this information.

Marketing has long outsourced much of the creative right-brain marketing activities, such as advertising and promotion campaigns, but nowadays marketing departments also outsource many of the critical left-brain marketing activities, such as customer database and database analysis.[60] As marketing has become more scientific and specialised, marketing practitioners are increasingly turning to advanced statistical techniques for dissecting segments, managing services and selecting prices and allocations. For example, Tesco outsourced its database management to a company called DunnHumby, which has been instrumental in the development and operation of Tesco's Clubcard, a loyalty card scheme that has been a major influence for this retail giant over the past decade. When it first started working with DunnHumby, Tesco was the number-two supermarket chain in the United Kingdom and today it is number one. The most commonly outsourced tasks that must be monitored by marketing are call centres, website design and management, direct mail programmes and database management, along with the more traditional advertising agencies and market research.[61]

Contemporary management and especially marketing management faces a number of other fundamental challenges, such as the demands for ethical and corporate responsible behaviour (Chapter 22), ever-increasing performance pressures (Chapter 23) and the increasingly complex environment due to globalisation – discussed in the following section.

Understanding global marketing management

The principal impact of the increasingly complex and globalised world on marketing practices is that all managers, whether they operate nationally, internationally or globally, are impacted by events around the globe. The tsunami in Japan in 2011 disrupted many supply networks and impacted business for many months, while the unrest in the Middle East has affected many global strategies.

Nokia

Nokia, the Finnish multinational, is the world's largest mobile phone maker. As with many companies, the Japanese earthquake and tsunami disrupted the supply of some of its products. However, Nokia said that it did not expect the disruption to have any significant impact on its profits.

Nokia has 132,000 employees in 120 countries, sales in more than 150 countries, global annual revenue of over €42 billion and operating profit of €2 billion. Nokia has an installed base of over 900 million handsets. Olli-Pekka Kallasvuo, the chief executive of Nokia, says:

> We are based in many markets. Our customers are everywhere, our people are everywhere . . . As a manager you have a nationality and you are a patriot, but as a manager you have to look at the totality. We are from many points of view the most global company there is, if you look at our customer base, the investors and where our people are.

Some organisations are national, operating within national borders. Others are international companies operating in more than one country, but are not necessarily global. RyanAir operates across Europe but not outside of European air space, unlike a global company such as Lufthansa which is a worldwide airline flying around the globe.

Marketing managers, when deciding to go international or to go global, must make a series of management decisions, shown in Figure 2.8. We will examine each of these decisions here.

Deciding whether to go abroad

Internationalisation is the process through which a firm moves from operating solely in the domestic or home marketplace to operating in international markets. Many companies now look to the global market rather than simply remaining in their domestic market. Outside the domestic market, marketing managers need to understand different consumers, different languages and different laws, deal with volatile currencies, face political and legal uncertainties, or redesign or modify their products or services to suit different customer needs and expectations.

Globalisation is a business orientation based on the **belief** that the world is becoming more homogeneous and that distinctions between national markets not only are fading but for some offerings will eventually disappear. The underlying principle of globalisation is that consumer preferences and requirements are similar across countries.[62]

Several factors draw companies into the international arena:

- Some international markets present higher profit opportunities than the domestic market.
- The company needs a larger customer base to achieve economies of scale.
- It wants to reduce its dependence on any one market.
- The company decides to counterattack global competitors in their home markets.
- Customers are going abroad and require international service.

Before making a decision to go abroad, the company must be aware of and weigh up several risks:

- The company might not understand foreign preferences and could fail to offer a competitively attractive product or service.
- The company might not understand the foreign country's business culture even if they are geographically close.
- It might underestimate foreign regulations and incur unexpected costs.
- The company might lack managers with international experience.
- The foreign country might change its commercial laws, devalue its currency or undergo a political revolution and expropriate foreign property.

Deciding how to enter the market

Once a company decides to target a particular country, it must determine the best mode of entry. Its broad choices are *indirect exporting, direct exporting, licensing, joint ventures,* and *direct investment,* shown in Figure 2.9. Each succeeding strategy entails more commitment, risk, control, and profit potential.

Figure 2.8 Major decisions in international marketing

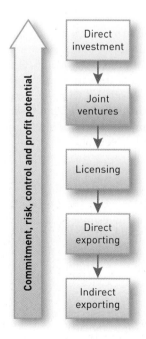

Figure 2.9 Five modes of entry into foreign markets

Indirect and direct exporting

Companies typically start with export, specifically *indirect exporting* – that is, they work through independent intermediaries. *Domestic-based export merchants* buy the manufacturer's products and then sell them abroad. *Domestic-based export agents*, including trading companies, seek and negotiate foreign purchases for a commission. *Export-management companies* agree to manage a company's export activities for a fee. Indirect exporting has two advantages. First, there is less investment: the firm does not have to develop an export department, an overseas sales force or a set of international contacts. Secondly, there is less risk: because international marketing intermediaries bring know-how and services to the relationship, the seller will make fewer mistakes.

Companies may eventually decide to handle their own exports. The investment and risk is somewhat greater, but so is the potential return. *Direct exporting* happens in several ways:

- **Domestic-based export department or division.** A purely service function may evolve into a self-contained export department operating as its own profit centre.
- **Overseas sales branch or subsidiary.** The sales branch handles sales and distribution, and perhaps warehousing and promotion as well. It often serves as a display and customer-service centre.
- **Travelling export sales representatives.** Home-based sales representatives travel abroad to find business.
- **Foreign-based distributors or agents.** These third parties can hold limited or exclusive rights to represent the company in that country. Many companies use direct or indirect exporting to 'test the waters' before building a plant and manufacturing their product overseas.

Licensing

Licensing is a simple way to engage in international marketing. The licensor issues a licence to a foreign company to use a manufacturing process, trademark, patent, trade secret, or other item of value for a fee or royalty. The licensor gains entry at little risk; the licensee gains production expertise or a well-known product or brand name. Licensing arrangements vary. Companies such as Hyatt and Marriott sell *management contracts* to owners of foreign hotels to manage these businesses for a fee. The management firm may have the option to purchase shares in the managed company within a stated period. In *contract manufacturing*, the firm hires local manufacturers to produce the product.

A company can enter a foreign market through *franchising*, a more complete form of licensing. The franchisor offers a complete brand concept and operating system. In return, the franchisee invests in and pays certain fees to the franchisor. McDonald's and Avis have entered scores of countries by franchising their retail concepts and ensuring that their operations are culturally relevant.

Joint ventures

Historically, foreign investors have often joined local investors in a **joint venture** company in which they share ownership and control to reach more geographic and technological markets and to diversify investments and risk. A joint venture may be necessary or desirable for economic or political reasons. The foreign firm might lack the financial, physical or managerial resources to undertake the venture alone, or the foreign government might require joint ownership as a condition for entry.

Joint ownership has drawbacks. The partners might disagree over investment, marketing or other policies. One might want to reinvest earnings for growth, the other to declare more dividends. Joint ownership can also prevent a multinational company from carrying out specific manufacturing and marketing policies on a worldwide basis. However, the value of a partnership can extend far beyond increased sales or access to distribution. Good partners share 'brand values' that help maintain brand consistency across markets.

McDonald's handpicks its global partners one by one to find 'compulsive achievers' who will make the desired effort.

Direct investment

The ultimate form of foreign involvement is direct ownership: the foreign company can buy part or full interest in a local company or build its own manufacturing or service facilities.

If the market is large enough, direct investment offers distinct advantages. First, the firm secures cost economies through cheaper labour or raw materials, government incentives and freight savings. Secondly, the firm strengthens its image in the host country because it creates jobs. Thirdly, the firm deepens its relationship with government, customers, local suppliers and distributors, enabling it better to adapt its products or services to the local environment. Fourthly, the firm retains full control over its investment and therefore can develop manufacturing and marketing policies that serve its long-term international objectives. Fifthly, the firm assures itself of access to the market in case the host country insists that locally purchased goods have domestic content. The main disadvantage of direct investment is that the firm exposes a large investment to risks such as blocked or devalued currencies, worsening markets or expropriation. If the host country requires substantial severance for employees, reducing or closing operations can be expensive.

Top management usually begins to pay more attention to global opportunities when over 15 per cent of revenues come from international markets.[63]

Complex decision making

Network theory suggests that the internationalisation process is far more complex and less structured than the four stages described above. Findings from a recent study of five small Norwegian computer software firms suggest that network relationships affect which foreign entry forms firms choose and, to some extent, which markets they decide to enter.[64] There is also a lack of consistency in companies' method of foreign market choice; companies look for competence, solidity and the ability to generate sales when searching for international partners, rather than a uniform structure for all countries. This study also found that a company may choose one entry form in one market and a different one in another, similar market, very much depending upon the options available in terms of their network relationships. A key challenge is to balance the allocation of resources between expanding the network through current relationships and a focus on establishing new relationships and customers.

The study's results illustrate the increasingly complex relationship between firms across national borders and supports the contention that the internationalisation process is driven by existing network relationships, often with major partners driving foreign market selection and also providing the mechanism for market entry.[65]

Deciding which markets to enter

In deciding to internationalise, the company's marketing objectives and policies need to be defined. What ratio of international to total sales will it seek? Some companies start small when they venture abroad. Some plan to stay small; others have bigger plans.

The marketing manager must decide how many countries to enter and how fast to expand. Typical entry strategies follow the *waterfall* approach: that is, gradually entering countries in sequence; or the *sprinkler* approach, namely entering many countries simultaneously. Increasingly, firms – especially technology-intensive firms – are *born global* and market to the entire world from the outset.[66]

BMW, Benetton and The Body Shop followed the waterfall approach. It allows firms to plan expansion carefully and is less likely to strain human and financial resources. When first-mover advantage is crucial and a high degree of competitive intensity prevails, such as when Microsoft introduces a new version of Windows software, the sprinkler approach is better. The sprinkler effect allows the company to enter all markets quickly, but the main risk is the substantial resources needed and the difficulty of planning entry strategies into many diverse markets at the same time.

The marketing manager must also decide on which countries to consider. Their attractiveness is influenced by the customer base, the product or service itself, and the geography, income, population and political climate of the countries involved.

Evaluating potential markets

Although the world is becoming flatter for globalised organisations, there is still some 'uniqueness' among countries. However much nations and regions integrate their trading policies and standards, each nation still has unique features. A country's readiness for different products and services, and its attractiveness as a market, depend on its economic, political, legal and cultural environments.

Suppose a marketing manager has assembled a list of potential markets to enter. How does it choose among them? Many companies prefer to market to neighbouring countries because they understand these countries better and can control their costs more effectively. It is not surprising that Germany's largest trading partner is France, but it is interesting to note that its second largest trading partner is the United States. Germany's other export partners are the United Kingdom (8.4 per cent), Italy (7.4 per cent), the Netherlands (6.2 per cent), Austria (5.3 per cent), Belgium (5.0 per cent), and Spain (4.9 per cent).[67] The two largest US export markets are Canada and Mexico, while Swedish companies often choose their Scandinavian neighbours – Finland and Norway.

At other times, *psychic proximity* determines choices. Many US firms prefer to sell in Canada, England and Australia – rather than in larger markets such as Germany and France – because they feel more comfortable with the language, laws and culture. Companies should be careful, however, in choosing markets according to cultural similarities. Besides overlooking potentially better markets, firms may perform superficial analysis of some very real differences among countries and adopt predictable marketing actions that put them at a disadvantage.[68] Understanding cultural differences is core for all markets, as the case of Disneyland Paris shows.

Disneyland Paris

How could a company like Disney get it so wrong when it expanded out of its domestic market in Florida, America to open in Paris, France? Disney overlooked European cultural issues when it first introduced EuroDisney – now called Disneyland Paris – to France.

- It did not serve wine at lunch – expected by Europeans.
- Lunch was served at 11.00 or 14.00, but Europeans like to eat at 13.00–13.30.
- It asked staff not to wear jewellery or to have facial hair – both requirements which annoyed their European staff members.
- It overlooked many customer holiday behaviours, preferences and needs. Disney assumed that European customers would plan a week's holiday to Disneyland and organised all its packages and promotion around this type of a visit. Unfortunately this did not align with what its customers wanted, which was a shorter three- or two-day visit which could be added on to their holiday. The company had to learn quickly and has redeveloped most of its marketing, including its service process design, staffing and pricing. Disneyland Paris now has more visitors than the Eiffel Tower.

It often makes sense to operate in fewer countries, with a deeper commitment and penetration in each. In general, a company prefers to enter countries: (1) that rank high on market attractiveness; (2) that are low in market risk; and (3) in which it possesses a

Marketing insight

The challenges of marketing management in Europe

Europe is the world's second-smallest continent by surface area, covering about 10,180,000 square kilometres or 2 per cent of the Earth's surface and about 6.8 per cent of its land area. The economy of Europe is currently the largest on Earth, and it is the richest region as measured by assets under management, with over €26 trillion compared to North America's €19 trillion, representing one-third of the world's wealth.[69]

Marketing managers must know and understand their market and customers. Within Europe, that means understanding 27 countries and over 20 official languages.[70] Europe has a large variation of wealth among its countries. The richer states tend to be in the west, with many of the eastern European economies still emerging from years of stagnation and the collapse of the Soviet Union and Yugoslavia. All countries have been impacted to some extent by the recession and banking crisis of 2008–11 and onwards, with the peripheral nations of Greece, Ireland and Portugal seeming to fare the worse.

The multicultural aspects of contemporary Europe provide challenges for marketers. Marketing managers have to design marketing mix programmes that reflect these issues and address various unique national markets within Europe. Companies marketing in Europe face 2,000 years of historical and cultural differences, and a daunting mass of local rules. Italians eat chocolate for breakfast, the French croissants, the Germans cheese and ham, the Polish *chleb* (bread) and an assortment of *szinki* (cold meats), while the English often enjoy a fry-up with eggs, bacon, sausages and baked beans. A study found that people in Italy – a country where society is based more on personal contacts with consumers – were much less likely to accept self-service and automatic machines for customer contacts than people in northern Europe, where customers were more accepting of distance in the service process and welcome automated channels and self-service technologies.[71]

The EU creates an additional set of legal considerations for marketers. Essentially, firms are regulated by the EU and the member states in which they operate. From a marketing perspective, EU legislation aims to impose uniform quality, safety and operating practices in the marketing process. It is important for marketers to be familiar with the decision-making processes in the EU and the different categories of legislation. EU law can affect marketers in many ways, including market research, planning, product and service strategy, promotion and pricing among others. For example, Sweden and Norway do not permit any television advertising to be directed towards children under 12 and no advertisements at all are allowed during children's programmes. Austria does not permit advertising during children's programmes, and in the Flemish region of Belgium, no advertising is permitted five minutes before or after programmes for children. Sponsorship of children's programmes is not permitted in Denmark, Finland, Norway and Sweden, while in Germany and the Netherlands, although it is legal, it is not used in practice. The UK has the highest level of advertising to children, with no restrictions.[72]

Before engaging in strategic marketing planning, companies must examine the relevant EU policy. The EU has restrictions in relation to competition law, personal data, research and segmentation, product liability and product safety, metric labelling, promotion and communication, including online and web standards, as well as regulations relating to distribution and pricing.[73] Marketers may unintentionally create marketing plans that run counter to legal and ethical standards. The high cost of failing to comply with competition law was evident when Dutch brewers Heineken, Grolsch and Bavaria were fined €273 million by the European Union for operating a beer cartel in Holland.[74]

competitive advantage. Many European companies trade within the European Union, as described in the marketing insight box above.

Deciding on the marketing mix programme

Marketing managers must decide how much to adapt their marketing strategy to local conditions.[75] At one extreme are marketing managers who use a globally *standardised marketing mix* worldwide. Standardisation of all marketing mix activities, including the product/service design, communication and distribution channels, promises the lowest costs. International fashion designers standardise their offering, with brands like Gucci and Chanel available around the globe – luxurious and fashionable to many, but they lack

Table 2.3 The differences between global and glocal marketing

Global marketing	Glocal marketing
Strategic level	Strategic, tactical and operative levels
Wider scope	Wide/narrow scope
Standardisation	Standardisation/adaptation
Homogenisation	Homogenisation/tailoring
Similarities	Similarities/differences
Concentration	Concentration/diffusion
Dependence	Dependence/independence
Synchronisation	Synchronisation/flexibility
Integration	Integration/separation

Source: G. Svensson (2002) Beyond global marketing and the globalization of marketing activities, *Management Decision*, 40(6), 574–83. Copyright © Emerald Publishing Group Ltd. Reproduced with permission.

any connection to community or individual expression. They are found in every high-end shopping centre and airport in the world – manufactured in large, industrial factories.

At the other extreme is an *adapted marketing mix*, where consumer needs are different and therefore the marketing mix activities need to be tailored to each target group. When both forces prevail to some extent, a **glocal strategy** that standardises certain elements and localises others can be the way to go. As this is often the case, many marketers seek a blend of centralised global control from corporate headquarters with input from local and regional marketers. Glocal marketing recognises that there often needs to be a balance between local and global marketing activities – this is the concept of *thinking globally and acting locally*. Glocal marketing understands the conflicting desires of consumers for products and services of a global quality but which reflect local lifestyles – which have a 'local soul'.[76] Table 2.3 summarises some pros and cons of standardising versus glocalisation of the marketing mix programme.

The development of the World Wide Web, the rapid spread of cable and satellite TV around the world, and the global linking of telecommunications networks have led to a convergence of lifestyles. Increasingly, common needs and wants have created global markets for standardised products and services, particularly among the young middle class.

However, although many companies have tried to launch their version of a world product or service, most products or services require at least some adaptation. Toyota's Corolla car model exhibits some differences in styling across its markets. For example, its European models were sold as the Corolla GT with DOHC engines and fixed Levin-style headlights. The Middle East received the same basic model as the North American market, with pop-up headlights and the regulated 5 mph (8 km/h) bumpers. Even Coca-Cola is sweeter or less carbonated in certain countries.

Managing in developing markets

One of the sharpest distinctions in global marketing is between developed and developing or less mature markets such as Brazil, Russia, India and China (BRIC countries) along with Indonesia and South Africa.[77] Many market leaders rely on developing markets to fuel their growth, and must look to these markets for development potential, see marketing insight on the next page.

Marketing insight

Spotlight on key developing markets

Brazil

The vast majority of people in Latin America have little money to spend. According to the World Bank, 25 per cent live on less than €1.40 a day, and many millions more earn only a few hundred euros a month. In Brazil, the region's biggest market and the twelfth largest economy in the world, low-income groups make up 87 per cent of the population, but earn only 53 per cent of the income. Marketers in the region are finding innovative ways to sell products and services to these poor and low-income residents.

Nestlé Brazil saw sales of Bono cookies jump 40 per cent after it shrank the package from 200 grams to 140 grams while lowering the price. Recognising that illiteracy is a problem, Unilever launched a brand of soap in north-east Brazil with the simple name, 'Ala'. Brazilian firms that have succeeded internationally include brewer and beverage producer AmBev, which merged with Interbrew to form InBev; aircraft manufacturer Embraer; national airline Varig and sandal maker Havaianas. The world famous Rio Carnival and world champion football team have helped create an image of fun and physical fitness for Brazil.

Brazil has already experienced some 'go-go' growth years in the 1960s and 1970s, when it was the world's second-fastest-growing large economy. It also differs from other emerging markets in being a full-blown democracy, unlike Russia and China, and it has no serious disputes with neighbours, unlike India. But Brazil's growth in recent years has been slower, and a number of obstacles exist that are popularly called *custo Brasil* (the cost of Brazil). For example, the cost of transporting products eats up nearly 13 per cent of Brazil's GDP, 5 percentage points more than in the United States. Most observers see Brazil's economic, social and political transformation as still a work in progress.

Russia

There has been an increase in western companies setting up in Russia, including Dutch brewer Heineken, Swedish retailer IKEA, US banker Citibank and more than a dozen car manufacturers. Their target is Russia's growing middle class, which now accounts for over one-third of the population.

However, the average Russian earns €208 a month, about 10 per cent of the European average, and only a third own cars. Many elderly Russians feel they have been left behind, as do those who live far from the capital, Moscow. Concerns about the business climate remain. Although the economy has produced 7 per cent annual growth in GDP, the Organisation for Economic Cooperation and Development (OECD) cautions that economic reforms have been stagnant, and ranks Russia as one of the most corrupt countries in the world. Many feel that the government has been unpredictable and sometimes difficult to work with.

Motorola's experience in Russia is instructive. A total of 167,500 Motorola handsets were seized on arrival at Moscow airport, alleged to be smuggled and counterfeit, to violate a Russian patent, and to be a danger to public health. Around 50,000 were supposedly destroyed by the interior ministry, though some were later said to have turned up on the black market. Eventually most of the handsets were returned, but perhaps more telling was Motorola's reaction. With Russia being the company's third-biggest handset market in the world (behind the United States and China), Motorola takes a fairly sanguine attitude to the ups and downs inherent in doing business there and plans to stay the course.

India

Following market-based economic reforms in 1991, India has become one of the fastest-growing major economies, and is considered a newly industrialised country. According to a 2011 PwC report, India's GDP will overtake that of Japan during 2011 and that of the United States by 2045.[78] Moreover, during the next four decades, India's economy is expected to grow at an average of 8 per cent, making the nation potentially the world's fastest-growing major economy until 2050. The report also highlights some of the key factors behind the country's high economic growth – a young and rapidly growing working-age population; the growth of the manufacturing sector due to rising levels of education and engineering skills; and sustained growth of the consumer market due to a rapidly growing middle class.

The Indian economy is the world's tenth largest economy by nominal GDP and fourth largest economy by purchasing power parity. However, it continues to face the challenges of poverty, illiteracy, corruption and inadequate public health. A nuclear weapons state and a regional power, it has the third-largest standing army in the world, and ranks tenth in military expenditure among nations.

India's recent growth rate has been as explosive as its neighbour China's. Reforms in the early 1990s that significantly lowered barriers to trade and liberalised capital markets have brought booming investment and consumption. But it is not all about demand. With its large numbers of low-cost, high-IQ, English-speaking employees, India is snapping up programming and call centre jobs once held by other workers in a wave of outsourcing that shows no signs of stopping. With 467 million workers, India has the world's second largest labour force. The service sector makes up 54 per cent of the country's GDP, the agricultural sector 28 per cent, and the industrial sector 18 per cent.[79]

While India's ascent inevitably means lost jobs for white-collar workers, it also means a larger market for western goods – and pain for traditional Indian families. Along with training in accents and geography, India's legions of call centre employees are absorbing new ideas about family, material possessions and romance, and questioning conservative traditions. They want to watch Hollywood movies, listen to western music, chat on mobile phones, buy on credit rather than save, and eat in restaurants or cafés. They are being targeted relentlessly by companies that have waited to see India develop a western-style consumer class.

India still struggles with poor infrastructure and highly restrictive labour laws. Its retail channel structure, although improving, still lags. The quality of public services – education, health, provision of water – is also often lacking. But all these obstacles have not prevented global firms such as Mittal, Reliance, Tata, WiPro and Infosys from achieving varying degrees of international success.

China

In 2011, China overtook Japan as the world's second-biggest economy.[80] 'It's realistic to say that within ten years China will be roughly the same size as the US economy,' said Tom Miller of GK Dragonomics, a Beijing-based economic consultancy.[81] The reality of life for many Chinese can tell a different story. 'Most people in China are still poor, more people live in the countryside than in cities,' added Mr Miller. 'The average Japanese person is much much richer than the average Chinese person.'

China's 1.3 billion people have marketers scrambling to gain a foothold there, and competition has been heating up between domestic and international firms. However, initial gains in the Chinese market did not necessarily spell long-term success for many international firms. After investing to establish the markets, foreign pioneers in television sets and motorcycles saw domestic Chinese firms emerge as rivals. In the 1990s, virtually all mobile phones in China were made by global giants Nokia, Motorola and Ericsson. Within ten years, their market share had dropped to 60 per cent. China's membership of the World Trade Organization has eased manufacturing and investment rules, and modernised retail and logistics industries. Greater competition in pricing, products and channels has resulted.

Selling in China means going beyond the big cities to the 700 million potential consumers who live in small villages, towns and cities in the rural interior. About half of potential PC buyers live outside major cities; only one-third of overall retail revenues come from China's 24 largest cities. Rural consumers can be challenging, though, as they have lower incomes, are less sophisticated buyers, and often cling to local cultural and buying habits, while China's emerging middle class consists of more active and more discerning consumers who demand higher-quality products.

South Africa

One of the toughest places in the world to do business is Africa. According to the World Bank, of the 35 least business-friendly countries, 27 are in sub-Saharan Africa. Sierra Leone imposes harsh taxes; in the Democratic Republic of Congo, registering a business takes 155 days and costs almost five times the average Congolese's annual income of €75; and in Angola, enforcing a contract takes over 1,000 days. To avoid all the government red tape and restrictions, 42 per cent of the region's economy is informal, the highest proportion in the world. Bad roads – if there are roads at all – a lack of reliable electricity and volatile currency fluctuations add to the logistical and financial challenges. War, famine, AIDS and disaster are even more significant human difficulties.

But some successful businesses are emerging, especially in banking, retailing and mobile telephones, and many are using South Africa as a launch pad. Although many Africans are poor, they will still pay for what they need. Mobile phone operator Celtel invested in rural services by introducing the Me2U service, by which callers could send airtime credit to other mobile phones. Because most Africans don't have bank accounts, it has become a convenient and cheap way to transfer money, even replacing cash in some villages. South Africa's MTN, the largest mobile phone operator in the region, built its own microwave transmission backbone and power supplies in Nigeria, and the first solar payphone in Lake Victoria, Uganda. South Africa's Net 1 has built a customer base of 3.6 million accounts by issuing free smart cards to indigent people who have no bank accounts or credit cards, taking tiny percentages of their transactions for revenue.

The payoff for companies willing to deal with the complications and risk associated with doing business in Africa is often large margins and a lack of competition. SABMiller, the world's second-largest brewer, enjoys its best operating margins (over 42 per cent) in Africa. Local knowledge is key, and South African companies are well placed to take advantage of opportunities. Finding a local partner can help in terms of expertise and contacts. SABMiller's African operations are joint ventures with locals, some of them government.

In 2011, South Africa's jobless rate, the highest of 61 countries tracked by Bloomberg, increased to 25 per cent in the first quarter as Africa's biggest economy

> ▶ **Marketing insight** *(continued)*

failed to create employment for new job-seekers. The number of people in work fell by 14,000 to 13.1m. While economic growth has picked up, reaching an annualised 4.4 per cent, that was not sufficient to create jobs for school-leavers seeking employment for the first time.[82]

Sources: *Brazil:* A. Regalado (2007) Marketers pursue the shallow-pocketed, *Wall Street Journal*, 26 January; Land of promise, *The Economist*, 12 April 2007; M. Campanelli (2006) Marketing to Latin America? Think Brazil, *DMNEWS*, 20 June. *Russia:* J. Bush (2006) Russia: how long can the fun last?, *BusinessWeek*, 18 December, pp. 50–1; Dancing with the bear, *The Economist*, 3 February 2007, pp. 63–4. *India:* M. Kripalani and P. Engardio (2003) The rise of India, *BusinessWeek*, 8 December, pp. 66–76; J. Slater (2004) Call of the west, *Wall Street Journal*, 2 January, A1; India on fire, *The Economist*, 3 February 2007, pp. 69–71. *China:* D. Roberts (2007) Cadillac

floors it in China, *BusinessWeek*, 4 June, p. 52; B. Einhorn (2007) Grudge match in China, *BusinessWeek*, 2 April, pp. 42–3; R. Flannery (2007) Watch your back, *Forbes*, 23 April, pp. 104–5; D. Roberts (2007) Cautious consumers, *BusinessWeek*, 30 April, pp. 32–4; S.-H. Park and W. R. Vanhonacker (2007) The challenge for multinational corporations in China: think local, act global, *MIT Sloan Management Review*, May; D. Roberts (2007) Scrambling to bring crest to the masses, *BusinessWeek*, 25 June, pp. 72–3; BBC (2011) China overtakes Japan as world's second-biggest economy, www.bbc.co.uk/news/business-12427321. *South Africa:* The flicker of a brighter future, *The Economist*, 9 September 2006, pp. 60–2; H. Coster (2006) Great expectations, *Forbes*, 12 February, pp. 56–8; Going global, *The Economist*, 15 July 2006, pp. 59–60; Akanksha Awal (2011) South African jobless rate increases to 25%, *Financial Times*, 4 May, http://blogs.ft.com/beyond-brics/2011/05/04/london-headlines-244/.

The unmet needs of the emerging or developing world represent huge potential markets for food, clothing, shelter, consumer electronics, appliances, and many other products and services. Eight out of ten people in the world now live in developing countries, a number that will increase to nine in less than 20 years. This so-called 'Bottom of the Pyramid' includes more than 4 billion people, or about 60 per cent of the world's population. Many of these people have only about €1.40 a day in disposable income, but their sheer numbers translate into immense purchasing power, especially for the food industry, but also in new markets like health and beauty as the case of Nivea shows.

Nivea

Sales of men's health and beauty merchandise in China were set to overtake those in North America in 2011 and will probably grow about five times faster until 2014. Rising incomes, the growing popularity of magazines such as the Chinese editions of *Esquire* and *GQ*, and the desire to find a competitive edge at work are driving demand for men's skin-care products. Beiersdorf, the Hamburg-based cosmetics company that owns the Nivea brand, routinely undertakes market research in China to tap this and other markets.[83] Peter Kleinschmidt, a member of the executive board of Nivea, is convinced that 'Asia, as well as eastern Europe and South America, are among the most important engines of economic growth.'[84] In 2010, Beiersdorf said that the rapid increase in demand for its beauty products really helped its profits. The company opened a new factory near Shanghai in 2009, producing over 12,500 tons of personal care products. The German company also plans to move into the Asian hair care market and recently spent €270 million to acquire an 85 per cent stake in China's second-largest manufacturer of hair care products. 'It would be a sign of western arrogance to assume that consumers in China or Brazil have been waiting for generations to finally be blessed with our German products,' says Kleinschmidt. He speaks from experience. In Korea, for instance, Beiersdorf's attempt to introduce a face care product based on a western formula was a failure. It contained rice and lotus ingredients, a big seller in Germany, where it is marketed as one of the secrets of Asian beauty, but it was met with derision by Asian focus groups.

Many market-leading firms are relying on developing markets to fuel their future growth. Fiat, for example, sells its Palio car only in developing countries such as India.
Source: Fiat Group.

Developed nations and the prosperous parts of developing nations account for about 20 per cent of the world's population. Can marketers serve the other 80 per cent, which has much less purchasing power, and living conditions ranging from mild deprivation to severe deficiency?[85] This imbalance is likely to get worse, as more than 90 per cent of future population growth is projected to occur in the less developed countries.

Successfully entering developing markets requires a special set of skills and plans – see the marketing insight box. Consider how the following companies pioneered ways to serve these 'invisible' consumers:[86]

- The Fiat Palio is a supermini designed by the Italian car manufacturer Fiat. Fiat developed this 'world' car as a low-cost, low-specification car for consumers in developing nations.
- Colgate-Palmolive tours Indian villages with video vans that show the benefits of teeth brushing.
- In India, German consumer products maker Henkel sells miniature packages of its 'Pril' dishwashing detergent for 1 rupee apiece, or a little less than 2 cents.[87]
- Another innovation is the Nokia C1, a mobile phone that, though lacking complex functions, contains a built-in flashlight – a valuable feature in countries where power outages are a daily occurrence – and a back-up battery that can last six weeks.[88]
- Nokia has developed a mobile phone with a dust-resistant keypad for the Indian market.
- Africa is now generating €3bn of sales for Nestlé. Fritz van Dijk, who is in charge of emerging markets, says that the Swiss group is always adapting to local tastes, such as adding honey and ginger to Nescafé in sub-Saharan countries.[89] In Ghana, Nestlé sells shrimp-flavoured instant soup cubes for 2 cents apiece, while other seasoning cubes have been reformulated to suit African palates. According to Nestlé, the flavour of fermented beans is in great demand in African countries.

These marketers capitalise on the potential of developing markets by changing their conventional marketing practices.[90] Marketing in developing areas cannot be 'business as usual'. Economic and cultural differences abound; a business infrastructure may barely exist; and local competition can be surprisingly stiff.[91] In China, PC maker Lenovo, mobile phone provider TCL and appliance manufacturer Haier have thrived despite strong foreign competition. Besides their detailed understanding of Chinese tastes, these companies have vast distribution networks, especially in rural areas. Competition is also growing from other developing markets. China has exported cars to Africa, south-east Asia and the Middle East. Tata of India, Cemex of Mexico and Petronas of Malaysia have emerged from developing markets to become strong multinationals, selling in many countries.[92]

Marketing insight

Mobile banking in Africa

Millions of Africans are using mobile phones to pay bills, move cash and buy basic everyday items. It has been estimated that there are a billion people around the world who lack a bank account but own a mobile. Africa has the fastest-growing mobile phone market in the world and most of the operators are local firms. In countries like South Africa, for example, mobile phones outnumber fixed lines by eight to one. In Kenya there were just 15,000 handsets in use a decade ago. Now that number tops 15 million, compared to only 500 bank branches. Setting up a phone bank account is straightforward: the customer registers with an approved agent, who provides an ID card, and deposits money into the account. It can be used for everything from beer to cattle – one Masai farmer told the BBC that when he sells cows in Nairobi, he puts the money on his phone to ensure that robbers cannot get his cash. A Kenyan woman said she uses the technology to transfer money from her phone to that of her parents, while a Nairobi businessman found it was handy for settling customer accounts. The BBC has a video clip at http://news.bbc.co.uk/2/hi/8194241.stm.

Source: Based on L. Greenwood (2009) Africa's mobile banking revolution, 19 August, BBC News.

Consumers in emerging markets buy their products from tiny bodegas, stalls, kiosks and small shops not much bigger than a closet, which Procter & Gamble calls 'high-frequency stores'. Smaller packaging and lower sales prices are often critical when incomes and housing space are limited. Unilever's 4-cent sachets of detergent and shampoo have been a big hit in rural India, where 70 per cent of the country's population still lives. When Coca-Cola moved to a smaller, 200 ml bottle in India, selling it for 10–12 cents in small shops, bus stop stalls and roadside eateries, sales jumped.[93] The French food company Danone has had great success in the Chinese market.

Breakthrough marketing

Danone

Twice a week after work, Senegalese webmaster Demba Gueye treats himself to a snack: a 10-cent tube of Dolima drinkable yogurt. It is a splurge considering his €2-a-day food budget, and the 50-gram sachets are 'teeny'. But the 25-year-old says they are delicious. 'I'm crazy about it,' he says. The yogurt is an attempt by French food company Danone SA to fill a worrying gap in its business. Danone has become one of the world's fastest-growing food companies thanks to its high-end healthy products, such as Danone yogurt, Badoit and Evian water and Bledina baby food. But momentum is slowing in the company's traditional, rich-world markets in North America and western Europe. Danone is among a vanguard of western multinationals staking much of their future on the world's poor. Last year, 42 per cent of its sales were from emerging markets – up from just 6 per cent ten years ago. Danone aims to reach one billion customers a month by 2013, up from 700 million today. Digging deeper, the company is now trying to target customers who live on euro-a-day food budgets. Dolima, launched last November, sells at a rate of more than 30,000 tubes per month, with sales rising at an average monthly rate of 10 per cent. In Indonesia, Danone is targeting 10-cent drinkable yogurts at the poor; in Mexico, it has 15-cent cups of water. 'The objective is to do business, not just with the top of the pyramid,' says chief executive Franck Riboud. Other giants of consumer goods, from mobile phones to shampoo, are pursuing variations of this strategy. German sportswear maker Adidas AG is experimenting with a €1 trainer for barefoot Bangladeshis. Paris-based L'Oréal sells sample-sized sachets of shampoo and face cream in India for a few cents. These companies tread on delicate territory. They must grapple with the fact that their potential customers, while numerous, have extremely limited budgets.

Source: Christina Passaviello (2010) Danone expands its pantry to woo the world's poor, *Wall Street Journal*, 30 June.

The challenge is to think creatively about how marketing can fulfil the dreams of most of the world's population for a better standard of living.

SUMMARY

1 Management is a process that involves the major functions of planning, organising, leading and controlling resources in order to achieve goals.

2 Planning establishes the direction of the organisation. Organising divides organisational activities among work groups, allocates the people required to achieve tasks, and coordinates results. Leading motivates employees to achieve organisational goals. Control measures and evaluates organisational performances.

3 Marketing managers need five unique skills: managing across organisations; managing networks, relationships and interaction; information management; understanding and managing change; analytical and creative skills.

4 Marketers need to overview the core network of relationships that the firm has and to manage them for maximum benefit to all.

5 Marketing is not a task undertaken only by the marketing department. Marketing is managed through other functions and needs to affect every aspect of the company's operations and the customer experience.

6 In deciding to go abroad, a company needs to define its global marketing objectives and policies, and decide which markets to enter. Countries should be rated on three criteria: market attractiveness, risk and competitive advantage.

7 Once a company decides on a particular country, it must determine the best mode of entry. Its broad choices are indirect exporting, direct exporting, licensing, joint ventures and direct investment. Each succeeding strategy involves more commitment, risk, control and profit potential.

8 The developing world provides unique opportunities but also challenges for marketing managers, who must be aware of and cater to local needs and low incomes.

APPLICATIONS

Marketing debate

Marketing managers need to have unique skills *versus* Marketing managers need to have the same skills as other managers.

Marketing discussion

Global marketing produces unique management challenges. Critically evaluate the challenges of marketing globally and specifically in the developing world.

FURTHER READING

Peter C. Verhoef and Peter S. H. Leeflang (2009) Understanding the marketing department's influence within the firm, *Journal of Marketing*, 73(2), 14–37.

These authors from the University of Groningen in the Netherlands study the influence of the marketing department within firms. The study investigates such influence and assesses its determinants and consequences. The results show that the accountability and innovativeness of the marketing department represent the two major drivers of its influence. This influence is related positively to market orientation, which in turn is related positively to firm performance. The study suggests that having a market orientation or marketing philosophy means that the firm performs better, is more profitable and the marketing department is more influential. A key implication is that marketers should become more accountable and innovative to gain more influence.

REFERENCES

[1]M. Johnson (2011) Investors relieved as Indetex profits soar, *Financial Times*, 23 March, www.ft.com/cms/s/0/a4744924-5529-11e0-87fe-00144feab49a.html#ixzz1Js9OSblb; M. Mulligan (2010) Inditex puts Zara products online, *Financial Times*, September, www.ft.com/cms/s/0/05b87696-b5e4-11df-a048-0144feabdc0.html#ixzz1Js8aEaUT; The Retail Doctor (2010) Look who's coming to town!, *Inside Retailing*, July, www.insideretailing.com.au/Latest/tabid/53/ID/8737/Look-whos-coming-to-town.aspx; Mark Mulligan (2010) Inditex puts Zara products online, www.ft.com/cms/s/0/05b87696-b5e4-11df-a048-00144feabdc0.html#ixzz1LlLG4PLA.

[2] P. Drucker (2003) Future of management: start seeing change as a golden opportunity, *Executive Excellence*, 20(5), 3–5.

[3] Z. Wood (2009) Family behind Ferrero Rocher linked to deal with Cadbury, *Guardian*, 17 November, www.ferrero.com/products/the-most-famous-products/ferrero-rocher/a-brillant-idea.

[4] J. Martin and M. Fellenz (2010) *Organisational Behaviour and Management*, Hampshire: South Western Cengage Learning.

[5] Ibid

[6] S. Tiernan, M. Morley and E. Foley (2006) *Modern Management*, 3rd edn, Dublin: Gill and McMillan.

[7] Doe Jones Deutschland (2011) Zara to launch online stores on H&M's home turf, www.dowjones.de/site/2011/02/zara-to-launch-online-stores-on-hms-home-turf.html; M. Mulligan (2010) Inditex puts Zara products online, *Financial Times*, September, 1, 10.

[8] M. B. Wood (2011) *The Marketing Plan: A Handbook*, 4th edn, Harlow: Pearson; W. Knight (2011) Behind every successful product is a good marketing plan, www.themarketingsite.com/live/content.php?Item_ID=3849.

[9] T. Calkins (2009) A marketing plan for turbulent times, *Ivey Business Journal Online*, 73(2), 1–2.

[10] A. Greenyer (2006) Back from the grave: the return of modelled consumer information, *International Journal of Retail and Distribution Management*, 34(2/3), 212–19.

[11] B. Allred, K. Boal and W. Holstein (2005) Corporations as stepfamilies: a new metaphor for explaining the fate of merged and acquired companies, *Academy of Management Executive*, 19(3), 23–37. M. McDonald (2007) *Marketing Plans: How to Prepare Them, How to Use Them*, 6th edn, London: Butterworth Heinemann.

[12] A. DuBrin (2012) *Management Essentials*, Hampshire: South Western Cengage.

[13] Martin and Fellenz (2010), op. cit.

[14] F. E. Webster, Jr, A. J. Malter and S. Ganesan (2005) The decline and dispersion of marketing competence, *Sloan Management Review*, 46(4), 35–43.

[15] P. Kotler (2004) A three part plan for upgrading your marketing department for new challenges, *Strategy and Leadership*, 32(5), 5–9.

[16] C. O'Neill and J. Mowll (2010) *Managing*, Harlow: FT Prentice Hall.

[17] Ibid.

[18] G. A. Yuk (2010) *Leadership in Organizations*, 6th edn, London: Prentice Hall.

[19] B. Reeves, T. W. Malone and T. O'Driscoll (2008) Leadership's online labs, *Harvard Business Review*, July, 59–66.

[20] Ibid.

[21] M. A. Roberto and A. C. Edmondson (2007) Leadership and team simulation: Everest, web-based simulation product, *Harvard Business Review*, September, 4–11.

[22] M. R. Fellenz and M. Brady (2010) Managing customer-centric information: the challenges of information and communication technology (ICT) deployment in service environments, *International Journal of Applied Logistics*, 1(3), 88–105; R. Rust, C. Moorman and G. Bhalla (2010) Rethinking marketing, *Harvard Business Review*, January–February, 94–101.

[23] P. Taylor (2011) Q&A with Bill Ogle of Motorola, www.ft.com/cms/s/0/2b1cbb44-651c-11e0-b150-00144feab49a.html#ixzz1JsqLvUGz.

[24] Martin and Fellenz (2010), op. cit.

[25] H. Mintzberg (1994) The fall and rise of strategic planning, *Harvard Business Review*, January, 397–405.

[26] N. Has (2010) Earning her stripes, *Wall Street Journal*, 9 September, http://magazine.wsj.com/features/the-big-interview/earning-her-stripes/tab/print/.

[27] J. Earle-Levine (2011) By royal approval, *Financial Times*, 8 April, www.ft.com/cms/s/2/aeab5bce-6165-11e0-a315-00144feab49a.html#ixzz1Jsi1tNQm.

[28] G. Day (1999) *The Market Driven Organization*, New York: Free Press; G. Day and D. Reibstein (2004) *Wharton on Dynamic Competitive Strategy*, New York: Wiley.

[29] G. McGovern and J. A. Quelch (2004) The fall and rise of the CMO, *Strategy/Business*, 37, 3–8.

[30] Richard Rawlinson (2006) Beyond brand management, *Strategy+Business*, Summer.

[31] Elisabeth Sullivan (2009) Solving the CMO Puzzle, *Marketing News*, 30 March, 12.

[32] S. Crainer and D. Dearlove (2004) *Financial Times Handbook of Management*, 3rd edn, Harlow: Pearson Education; H. Mintzberg (1973) *The Nature of Managerial Work*, New York: HarperCollins College Division. See also H. Mintzberg (2007) *Mintzberg on Management*, New York: Free Press.

[33] G. Bruce and G. Schoenfeld (2006) Marketers with MBAs: bridging the thinking–doing divide, *Marketing Intelligence and Planning*, 24(3), 257.

[34] Constantine von Hoffman (2006) Armed with intelligence, *Brandweek*, 29 May, 17–20.

[35] P. Kotler (2004) A three part plan for upgrading your marketing department for new challenges, *Stategy and Leadership*, 32(5), 4–9.

[36] J. Egan (2006) Sidelined? The future of marketing in the contemporary organisation, *Irish Journal of Management*, 27(2), 99–119 and Webster et al. (2005), op. cit.

[37] McGovern and Quelch (2004), op. cit.

[38] S. Baker and S. Holt (2004) Making marketers accountable: a failure of marketing education?, *Marketing Intelligence and Planning*, 22(5), 557–67.

[39] James C. Anderson, Hakan Hakansson and Jan Johanson (1994) Dyadic business relationships within a business network context, *Journal of Marketing*, 15 October, 1–15.

[40] E. Gummesson (2008) *Total Relationship Marketing*, 2nd edn, Oxford: Butterworth Heinemann.

[41] M. R. Fellenz and M. Brady (2008) Managing the innovative deployment of information and communication technologies (ICTs) for global service organisations, *International Journal of Technology Marketing*, 3(1), 39–55; L. Po-Chien and Bou-Wen Linb (2006) Building global logistics competence with Chinese OEM suppliers, *Technology in Society*, 28(3), 333–48.

[42] E. Gummesson and C. Mele (2010) Marketing as value co-creation through network interaction and resource integration, *Journal of Business Market Management*, 4(4), 181–98; Gummesson (2008), op. cit. E. Gummesson (1999) *Total Relationship Marketing*, Boston, MA: Butterworth-Heinemann; R. McKenna (1991) *Relationship Marketing*, Reading, MA: Addison-Wesley; M. Christopher, A. Payne and D. Ballantyne (1991) *Relationship Marketing: Bringing Quality, Customer Service, and Marketing Together*, Oxford: Butterworth Heinemann.

[43] N. Nic, R. Lusch, Z. Zacharia and W. Bridges (2008) Competent collaborations, *Marketing Management*, March/April, 19–24.

[44]L.-G. Mattsson and J. Johanson (2006) Discovering market networks, *European Journal of Marketing*, 40(3/4), 259–75.

[45]Gummesson (2008), op. cit.

[46]R. J. Brodie, N. E. Coviello and H. Winklhofer (2008) Contemporary marketing practices research program: a review of the first decade, *Journal of Business and Industrial Marketing*, 23(2), 84–94; M. Brady, M. R. Fellenz and R. Brookes (2008) Researching the role of information and communication technologies in contemporary marketing, *Journal of Business and Industrial Marketing*, 23(2), 108–14.

[47]A. Lockett and I. Blackman (2004) Conducting market research using the internet: the case of Xenon Laboratories, *Journal of Business and Industrial Marketing*, 19(3), 178–87.

[48]R. Rust, C. Moorman and B. Gaurav (2010) Rethinking marketing, *Harvard Business Review*, January–February, 96–101.

[49]P. Drucker (2003) The future of management: start seeing change as a golden opportunity, *Executive Excellence*, 20(5), 3.

[50]M. Porter (1996) What is strategy?, *Harvard Business Review*, November–December, 61–78.

[51]L. Berry, V. Shankar, J. Turner Parish, S. Cadwallader and T. Dotzel (2006) Creating new markets through service innovation, *MIT Sloan Management Review*, 47(2), 56–63.

[52]www.virgin-atlantic.com/en/gb/passengerinformation/index. jsp; Virgin Atlantic Airways: leveraging information to keep frequent flyers in their skies, *What Works*, 7, May 2011.

[53]See Innovation Leaders website, Profile: Virgin Atlantic (retrieved from http://fp05-527.web.dircon.net/va_company_ profile.html).

[54]J. Lepper (2005) Virgin Atlantic launches podcast guides to New York, Brandrepublic.com, 28 June, www.brandrepublic. com/news/482167/virgin-atlantic-launches-podcast-guides- new-york/.

[55]In Webster et al. (2005), op. cit.

[56]G. McGovern and J. Quelch (2005) Outsourcing marketing, *Harvard Business Review*, 83(3), 22–6.

[57]R. H. Hartley (2006) *Marketing Mistakes and Successes*, 10th edn, Hoboken, NJ: John Wiley and Sons.

[58]Hartley (2006), op. cit.

[59]P. Pae (2005) A plane as big as the Globle, www.mindfully.org/ Technology/2005/A380-Largest-Airliner17jan05.htm.

[60]Ibid.

[61]Ibid.

[62]C. Sutton-Brady, R. Voola and U. Yukel (2010) Fukuyama's end of history thesis: are western marketing theories the end point of marketing theory evolution? *Journal of Business and Economics Research*, July, 8(7), 37–45.

[63]M. R. Czinkota and I. A. Ronkainen (2005) *International Marketing*, 7th edn, Florence, KY: South-Western College Publishing.

[64]O. Moen, M. Gavlen and I. Endresen (2004) Internationalization of small, computer software firms: entry forms and market selection, *European Journal of Marketing*, 38(9/10), 1236–51.

[65]J. Bell (1997) A comparative study of the export problems of small computer software exporters in Finland, Ireland and Norway, *International Business Review*, 6(6), 585–604; N. Coviello and H. Nunro (1997) Network relationships and the internationalisation process of small software firms, *International Business Review*, 6(4), 361–86.

[66]For a timely and thorough review of academic research on global marketing, see J. K. Johansson (2002) Global marketing: research on foreign entry, local marketing, global management, in B. Weitz and R. Wensley (eds), *Handbook of Marketing*, London: Sage, pp. 457–83. Also see J. K. Johansson (2003) *Global Marketing*, 2nd edn, New York: McGraw-Hill. For some global marketing research issues, see S. Douglas and S. R. Craig (2005) *International Marketing Research*, 3rd edn, Upper Saddle River, NJ: Prentice Hall.

[67]See http://en.wikipedia.org/wiki/Economy_of_Germany.

[68]Johansson (2002), op. cit.

[69]http://en.wikipedia.org/wiki/Europe.

[70]See http://ec.europa.eu/publications/booklets/move/45/en.doc.

[71]A. Lorenzon, P. J. Van Baaten and L. Pilotti (2005) Marketing knowledge management in strategic adoption of CRM solutions: global support of applications in Europe. Department of Economics, University of Milan, Italy, Departmental Working Paper No. 2005-03.

[72]Advertising to children; UK the worst in Europe, *Food Magazine* (UK), January–March 1997 (www.mcspotlight.org/media/press/ food_jan97.html).

[73]D. Thorne LeClair (2000) Marketing planning and the policy environment in the European Union, *International Marketing Review*, 17(3), 193–207.

[74]Ibid.

[75]S. Zou and S. T. Cavusgil (2002) The GMS: a broad conceptualization of global marketing strategy and its effect on firm performance, *Journal of Marketing*, 66, 40–56; T. Levitt (1983) The globalization of markets, *Harvard Business Review*, May–June, 92–102; B. Wysocki, Jr. (1997) The global mall: in developing nations, many youths splurge, mainly on US goods, *Wall Street Journal*, 26 June, A1; What makes a company great?, *Fortune*, 26 October 1998, 218–26; D. M. Szymanski, S. G. Bharadwaj and P. R. Varadarajan (1993) Standardization versus adaptation of international marketing strategy: an empirical investigation, *Journal of Marketing*, October, 1–17; Burgers and fries a la francaise, *The Economist*, 17 April 2004, 60–1; Johansson (2002), op. cit.

[76]T. Khanna and K. G. Palpeu (2006) Emerging giants: building world-class companies in developing countries, *Harvard Business Review*, October, 2–10.

[77]According to the *CIA World Factbook* (https://www.cia.gov/ library/publications/the-world-factbook/index.html), there are 34 developed countries: Andorra, Australia, Austria, Belgium, Bermuda, Canada, Denmark, Faroe Islands, Finland, France, Germany, Greece, Holy See, Iceland, Ireland, Israel, Italy, Japan, Liechtenstein, Luxembourg, Malta, Monaco, Netherlands, New Zealand, Norway, Portugal, San Marino, South Africa, Spain, Sweden, Switzerland, Turkey, United Kingdom and United States. They note that DCs are similar to the new International Monetary Fund (IMF) term 'advanced economies' that adds Hong Kong, Singapore, South Korea and Taiwan but drops Malta, Mexico, South Africa and Turkey.

[78]PricewaterhouseCoopers (2011) The world in 2050 www.pwc. com/gx/en/world-2050; http://en.wikipedia.org/wiki/India.

[79]http://en.wikipedia.org/wiki/India.

[80]BBC (2011) China overtakes Japan as second largest economy (2011) www.bbc.co.uk/news/business-12427321.

[81]Ibid.

[82]Akanksha Awal (2011) South African jobless rate increases to 25%, *Financial Times*, 4 May, http://blogs.ft.com/beyond-brics/2011/05/04/london-headlines-244/.

[83]F. Balfour (2010) Skin care products strike it big in China – for men, Bloomberg – *BusinessWeek,* December, www.business-week.com/magazine/content/11_02/b4210022517035.htm.

[84]J. Bonstein (2008) European firms eye developing world, *BusinessWeek*, 16 January www.businessweek.com/globalbiz/content/jan2008/gb20080116_886509.htm?campaign_id=rss_daily.

[85]See www.populationmedia.org/issues/issues.htm.

[86]Adapted from V. Mahajan, M. V. Pratini De Moraes and J. Wind (2000) The invisible global market, *Marketing Management*, Winter, 31–5. See also Khanna and Palepu (2006), op. cit.

[87]Bonstein (2008), op. cit.

[88]Ibid.

[89]L. Lucas (2011) Emerging markets fuel Nestlé sales growth, *Financial Times*, 7 February, www.ft.com/cms/s/0/420bac2e-3a8e-11e0-9c65-00144feabdc0.html#ixzz1W1hBjo8f.

[90]C. K. Prahalad (2005) *The Fortune at the Bottom of the Pyramid: Eradicating Poverty Through Profits*, Upper Saddle River, NJ: Wharton School Publishing; N. Dawar and A. Chattopadhyay (2002) Rethinking marketing programs for emerging markets, *Long Range Planning*, 35, 457–74.

[91]B. J. Bronnenberg, J.-P. Dubé and S. Dhar (2007) Consumer packaged goods in the United States: national brands, local branding, *Journal of Marketing Research*, 44, February, 4–13; B. J. Bronnenberg, J.-P. Dubé and S. Dhar (2007) National brands, local branding: conclusions and future research opportunities, *Journal of Marketing Research*, 44, February, 26–8; B. J. Bronnenberg, J.-P. Dubé and S. Dhar (2007) Market structure and the geographic distribution of brand shares in consumer package goods industries, Working Paper, UCLA Graduate School of Management.

[92]S. Hamm and D. Roberts (2006) China's first global capitalist, *BusinessWeek*, 11 December, 52–7; B. Einhorn (2007) Grudge match in China, *BusinessWeek*, 2 April, 42–3; R. Flannery (2007) Watch your back, *Forbes*, 23 April, 104–5; The fast and the furious, *The Economist*, 25 November 2006, 63–4.

[93]M. Kripalani (2003) Finally, Coke gets it right, *BusinessWeek*, 10 February, 47; M. Kripalani (2002) Battling for pennies in India's villages, *BusinessWeek*, 10 June, 22-E7.

Chapter 3

Developing marketing strategies and plans

IN THIS CHAPTER, WE WILL ADDRESS THE FOLLOWING QUESTIONS:

1 How does marketing affect customer-perceived value?

2 How is corporate and divisional strategic planning conducted?

3 How is business unit strategic planning carried out?

4 What is involved in developing a marketing plan?

Siemens AG is a leading energy company focused on a growth strategy.

Source: Courtesy of Siemens AG/Agency: Publicis-München.

Marketing and
customer
value

Corporate and
divisional strategic
planning

Business unit
strategic
planning

The nature and
content of a
marketing
plan

arketing strategies and plans that can guide marketing activities are key activities of the management process. Developing the right marketing strategy over time requires a blend of discipline and flexibility. Firms must adopt a strategy and constantly seek new ways to improve it. The main task of marketing is to develop strategies that deliver customer-perceived value.

A highly successful business-to-business marketer, Siemens, for instance, must continually design and implement marketing activities at many levels and for many business units of the organisation.

Siemens AG (Berlin and Munich) is a global powerhouse in electronics and electrical engineering, operating in the industry, energy and healthcare sectors. For over 160 years, Siemens has stood for technological excellence, innovation, quality, reliability and internationality. The company is the world's largest provider of environmental technologies, generating some €28 billion – more than one-third of its total revenue – from green products and solutions. In the tax year ending 30 September 2010, its revenue totalled €76 billion and its net income €4.1 billion. At that time, Siemens had around 405,000 employees worldwide.[1]

This chapter begins by examining the main strategic marketing implications in creating customer-perceived value. This is followed by a review of the relationship between corporate strategy and divisional marketing strategy. Once the divisional marketing strategy has been set, it is up to marketers in the operating parts or business units to develop marketing plans that will be both effective (in that they deliver the right customer-perceived value) and efficient in terms of resources. The chapter ends with some advice on how to draw up a formal marketing plan that is keyed into the architecture of the book.

Marketing and customer-perceived value

Many in the United States, with notable exceptions, have tended to view marketing from a product-oriented and transactional standpoint. In Europe, practitioners have traditionally tended to place a greater emphasis on customer relationship concepts (see Chapter 1). Both viewpoints in basic economics terms emphasise the importance of satisfying customers' needs and wants. The UK's Chartered Institute of Marketing (CIM) defines marketing as 'the management process of anticipating, identifying and satisfying customer requirements profitably'. In the highly competitive European buyers' markets of today, the task of any business is to form lasting relationships with customers by delivering customer-perceived value at a profit (see Chapter 11). In hyper-competitive economies, following the paradigm change from supply-dominated markets (where demand exceeds supply) to buyer-dominated markets (where supply exceeds demand), marketers are challenged with the task of positively differentiating their business activities in the eyes of increasingly rational buyers faced with an abundant choice of providers. Companies succeed by fine tuning the customer-perceived value-delivery process (see Chapter 11).

Business environment paradigm change

The main consequences for organisations of the transition from sellers' to buyers' markets include the following:

- There is competition that really bites.
- Customers usually demand more (perceived-value) for their money.
- Customers have a choice of possible providers.
- A transformation occurs in the concept of value, which is now heavily influenced by buyers who demand that providers meet their perceived-value expectations.
- Customers really do become the true focus of business activities.
- Customer relationship management assumes vital importance;
- Traditional separate 'product' and 'service' approaches to marketing activity need to be replaced by a value-dominant logic that combines 'product' and 'service' attributes/ benefits to develop successful customer-perceived value offerings.
- Markets fragment into segments that appeal to customers who have distinct perceived-value requirements.

In sellers' markets (Figure 3.1) companies strive to increase the volume of goods and services supplied and to reduce costs as much as possible. This has been termed the *least-cost production paradigm* or the pursuit of *efficiency*. This understanding of the business process, however, will not be as successful in buyers' markets. Wise competitors seek to be *effective* by discovering through market research what customers value and then using their resources as efficiently as possible to supply it. Sensible competitors acknowledge the need to deliver customer-perceived value successfully. This realisation inspired a new view of business processes, which places marketing at the *beginning* of corporate

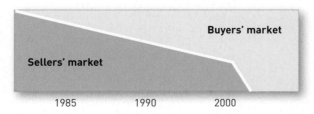

Figure 3.1 Paradigm change from sellers' to buyers' markets
Source: M. R. V. Goodman, Durham University.

planning. Instead of emphasising making and selling, companies now see themselves as part of a process that delivers personalised customer-perceived value market offerings.

The value delivery process

A common view of marketing is that a firm makes something and then sells it. In this view, marketing takes place in the second sequence of the process. Companies that hold this belief have the best chance of succeeding in economies marked by goods shortages (sellers' markets), where consumers are not fussy about quality, features or style.

As Figure 3.2 shows, the value delivery process involves four sequences. The first sequence, discovering the required value (see Parts 1, 2 and 3 of this text), represents the research that marketing must do before any marketable value offering exists. Marketing practitioners segment the market, select the appropriate target market, and develop their offering's *customer-perceived value* positioning (see Chapter 10). Market customisation, i.e. segmentation, targeting and positioning (STP), is the essence of strategic marketing. Once the business unit has discovered the customer-perceived value (see Chapter 11), the second sequence involves developing a suitable customer offering (see Parts 4 and 5 of this text). Marketers put together a package of specific product and service benefits at appropriate price levels. The third sequence concerns successfully delivering the customer-perceived value packages (see Part 6 of this text). The final sequence is about successfully communicating the value offerings to targeted customers (see Part 7 of this text). As buyers' markets are highly competitive, these sequences need to be repeated continuously if a company is to achieve a lasting market advantage. In this sense the sequences resemble the action that occurs in a four-cylinder car engine.

Following nearly two generations of sellers' markets, businesses have suddenly become exposed to buyers' markets. The stable conditions of sellers' markets (unsaturated markets) have given way to the challenging conditions posed by rampant **buyers' markets**.

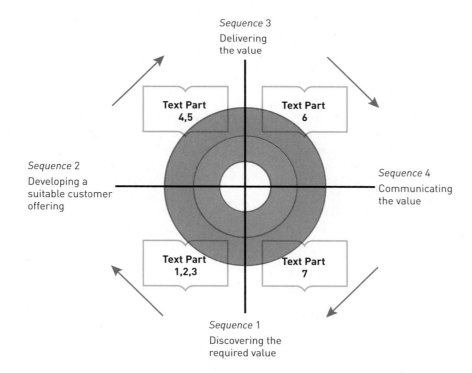

Figure 3.2 Repetitive sequences of the value delivery process
Source: M. R. V. Goodman, Durham University.

Nike

Critics of Nike often complain that its shoes cost almost nothing to make, yet cost the customer so much. True, the raw materials and manufacturing costs of training shoes are relatively cheap, but marketing them to the consumer is expensive. Materials, labour, shipping, equipment, import duties and suppliers' costs are less than €25 a pair. Compensating the sales team, distributors, administration and endorsers, as well as paying for advertising and R & D, adds €15 or so to Nike's total. Nike sells to retailers to make a profit of, say, €7. The retailer therefore pays roughly €47 to put a pair of Nikes on the shelf. When we factor in the retailer's overhead (typically €30, covering human resources, lease and equipment), along with a €10 profit, the shoes cost the customer over €80.

London Business School's Nirmalya Kumar has set forth a '3Vs' approach to marketing:

1 define the value segment or customers (and their needs);
2 define the value proposition; and
3 define the value network that will deliver the promised service.[2]

Webster views marketing in terms of:

1 *value-defining processes* such as market research and company self-analysis;
2 *value-developing processes*, including new product development, sourcing strategy and vendor selection; and
3 *value-delivering processes* such as advertising and managing distribution.[3]

Gale[4] sees marketing as a business process that identifies and delivers high levels of *market-perceived value*, which he defines as *market-perceived quality* relative to *market-perceived price*. Kotler is in agreement with this view but refers to it as *customer-perceived value*. Marketing is ultimately about firms successfully answering the question: why should customers buy from them?

The value chain

Porter has proposed the **value chain** as a tool for identifying ways to create more customer-perceived value (see Figure 3.3).[5] According to this model, every firm is a synthesis of

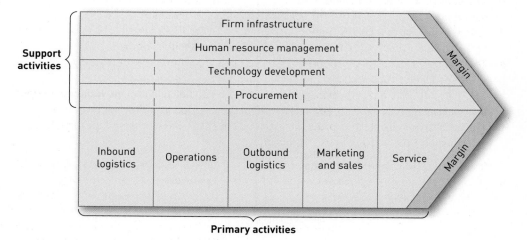

Figure 3.3 The generic value chain
Source: Adapted with the permission of Free Press, a Division of Simon & Schuster, Inc., from *Competitive Advantage: Creating and Sustaining Superior Performance* by Michael E. Porter, Copyright © 1985, 1998 by Michael E. Porter.

activities performed to design, produce, market, deliver and support its final market offering. The value chain identifies nine strategically relevant activities – five primary and four support activities – that create value and cost in a specific business.

The *primary activities* consist of inbound and outbound logistics. Inbound logistics refers to bringing materials into the business's operations and converting them into final saleable products and operations. Outbound logistics include shipping out final products, marketing them, and sales and servicing support activities. The *support activities* – procurement, technology development, human resource management and firm infrastructure – are handled in specialised departments. The firm's infrastructure covers the costs of general management, planning, finance, accounting, legal and government affairs.

The firm's task, whether large or small, is to examine its costs and performance in each value-creating activity and seek ways to make improvements. Managers should estimate their competitors' costs and performances as *benchmarks* against which to compare their own costs and performance. Additionally, they should go further and study the 'best practice' as exhibited by the world's best companies.[6]

Toyota

Having become the leading automotive manufacturer in the world and on the eve of its 70th year, Toyota unveiled its Global Vision 2020 in November 2007. The announced investment plan revealed Toyota's intention to invest heavily in cutting-edge technologies and to continue its policy of making its value chain ever more effective and efficient. Toyota has become an iconic manager of the modern *keiretsu* – a network of mutually supportive companies. The company's *keiretsu*, which comprises group companies, several large component manufacturers and many hundreds of smaller suppliers, sustains a relationship that would be hard to match elsewhere. The *keiretsu* corporate family creates an environment of trust that acts as a dynamic driver for constantly improving the value chain. Toyota continues to enjoy a strong sales performance in Europe.[7]

The firm's success depends not only on how well each functional department performs its work, but also on how well the company coordinates departmental activities to conduct *core business processes*.[8] These core business processes include:

- **The market sensing process**: all the activities in gathering market intelligence, disseminating it within the organisation, and acting on the information.
- **The new market offering realisation process**: all the activities in researching, developing and launching new high-quality offerings quickly and within budget.
- **The customer acquisition process**: all the activities in defining target markets and prospecting for new customers.
- **The customer relationship management process**: all the activities in building deeper understanding, relationships and market offerings targeted at individual customers.
- **The fulfilment management process**: all the activities in receiving and approving orders, shipping on time and collecting payment.

Strong companies are re-engineering their work flows and building cross-functional teams to be responsible for each process.[9] At Xerox, a Customer Operations Group links sales, shipping, installation, service and billing so that these activities flow smoothly into one another. Winning companies are those that excel at managing core business processes through cross-functional teams. 3M's Technical Training organisation[10] has made cross-functional team working a part of its training curriculum for professional/technical employees involved in new product development. In the company's Industrial Specialties Division, the whole business is effectively managed by means of cross-functional team working. Each product family – for example, adhesives, fasteners and urethane films – is

ASDA uses cross-
functional teams
to encourage and
facilitate creativity and
innovation.
Source: Courtesy of ASDA.

run by cross-functional team working that involves people from the laboratories, manufacturing and marketing. Motorola, Nissan and Polaroid provide further examples of well-known companies marketing in Europe that have reorganised their employees into cross-functional teams which are also found in both non-profit and government organisations (see Chapter 21).

To be successful, a firm also needs to look for competitive advantages beyond its own operations, in the value chains of suppliers, distributors and customers. Many companies today have partnered specific suppliers and distributors to create a superior value delivery network (see Chapter 17).

Core competencies

Traditionally, companies owned and controlled most of the factors of production that shaped their businesses – land, labour and capital. Prahalad and Hamel[11] have urged managers to look not only at their physical resources, but also at the unique skills and knowledge embedded in their organisations and to concentrate on what they do best.[12] However, this efficiency argument was open to question soon after it entered the business arena as it failed to take into account fully the entire impact of emerging global buyers' markets and the internet. This has led to a fundamental change in business architecture. Companies and suppliers have increasingly begun to collaborate to form value chains, to deliver researched customer value market offerings (see Chapter 17).

One important key, then, is to own and nurture the resources and competencies that make up the *essence* of the business. Nike, for example, does not manufacture its own shoes, because Asian manufacturers are more cost efficient in this task. Instead, it nurtures its superiority in shoe design and merchandising, which are its two core competencies. A **core competency** has three characteristics:

1 It is a source of competitive advantage and makes a significant contribution to customer-perceived value.
2 It has applications in a wide variety of markets.
3 It is difficult for competitors to imitate.[13]

Competitive advantage also accrues to companies that possess distinctive capabilities, such as Apple's iPhones and iPads, Dyson's vacuum cleaners and Telma's electronic braking retarders. Whereas the term 'core competencies' refers to areas of special technical and production expertise, *distinctive capabilities* describes excellence in broader business processes. The chief executive of Microsoft, speaking at the annual financial analyst meeting in July 2007, stated that in today's fast-paced business environment, Microsoft would have 'to have multiple competencies and multiple business models all living in one body'.[14]

ILVA – venture unfulfilled

When the Danish home store ILVA arrived in the United Kingdom it was billed as a furniture retailer that could potentially compete successfully with IKEA by offering a new purchasing experience. It was going to revolutionise the furniture market with its contemporary ranges and four upmarket shops. The company proudly proclaimed, 'We think that furniture should look good, cost less and last for ages.' It offered a wide range of furniture and accessories at affordable prices, and put its eclecticism down to its being 'inspired by cultures from around the world'. The 10,000-item strong range featured such strange delights as cow-hide floor throws and authentic vine wood tables, with exclusive individual touches such as mosquito bites on the hide of some leather items. The merchandise was more expensive than IKEA but cheaper than that of Habitat.

ILVA was established in 1974 and, like IKEA, has its roots deep in Scandinavia. It now enjoys the popular prestige of being the second largest furniture and homeware retailer in Denmark. Stores in Sweden and Denmark have won civic architectural awards and been hailed as some of the most beautiful modern buildings in northern Europe. However, initially the venture was a failure in the UK as the market was not researched effectively. ILVA's offerings were viewed by inquisitive customers who visited its stores as being too expensive, and much of its furniture was seen as too large to fit into many UK homes. Furthermore, early customers were badly let down by poor customer service.

In many respects it is reminiscent of Marks & Spencer's similar ill-fated venture that cost them more than £30 million. Even before the UK stores opened, ILVA ran up losses of £11.5 million, and in August 2007 the troubled retailer was sold to an Icelandic furniture group that owns rival UK furniture retailer The Pier.

Wise companies research the market, especially foreign ventures, before proceeding to realise a dream. Initially ILVA's dream fell flat in the United Kingdom but the new ownership repositioned the business and launched a new TV advertising campaign in the spring of 2008. However, in June 2008, after running up huge losses, exacerbated by the decline in the UK furniture market – which in turn was caused by a declining housing market and dwindling customer confidence – ILVA announced that it had made a strategic withdrawal from the United Kingdom. The company will continue to operate stores in Denmark and Sweden.[15]

How can companies avoid the disappointment suffered by ILVA? According to Day, market-driven organisations excel in three distinctive capabilities: market sensing, customer linking and channel bonding.[16] In terms of market sensing, he believed that significant opportunities and threats often begin as 'weak signals' from the 'periphery' of a business. He suggested a systematic process for developing peripheral vision, and practical tools and strategies for building 'vigilant organisations' attuned to changes in the environment, by asking questions in three categories[17] (see Table 3.1).

Another important key is the extent to which competitive advantage results from how well the company has fitted its core competencies and distinctive capabilities into customer-perceived value offerings. Competitors have difficulty imitating companies such as

Table 3.1 Becoming a vigilant organisation

Learning from the past

- What have been our past blind spots?
- What instructive analogies do other industries offer?
- Who in the industry is skilled at picking up weak signals and acting on them?

Evaluating the present

- What important signals are we rationalising away?
- What are our mavericks, outliers, complainers and defectors telling us?
- What are our peripheral customers and competitors really thinking?

Envisioning the future

- What future surprises could really hurt or help us?
- What emerging technologies could change the game?
- Is there an unthinkable scenario that might disrupt our business?

Source: Reprinted by permission of Harvard Business School Press. From *Peripheral Vision: Detecting the Weak Signals That Will Make or Break Your Company* by Day, G.S. and Schoemaker, P.J.H Boston, MA 2006. Copyright © 2006 by the Harvard Business School Publishing Corporation; all rights reserved.

Apple, Dell, IKEA, L'Oréal and Red Bull because they are unable to copy their specific activity systems.

Business realignment may be necessary to maximise core competencies. It has three steps:

1 (re)defining the business concept or 'big idea';
2 (re)shaping the business scope; and
3 (re)positioning the company's brand identity.

Consider what Kodak is doing to realign its business.

Kodak

With the advent of the digital era and consumers' new capacity to store, share and print photos using their PCs, Kodak faces more competition than ever, both in-store and online. In 2004, the company started the painful process of transformation. It started off by expanding its line of digital cameras, printers and other equipment, and it also set out to increase market share in the lucrative medical imaging business. Making shifts is not without challenges, however. The company announced in the summer of 2006 that it would outsource the making of its digital cameras. Kodak also eliminated 15,000 jobs in 2006 and spent money acquiring a string of companies for its graphics communications unit. Not only must Kodak convince consumers to buy its digital cameras and home printers, but it must also become known as the most convenient and affordable way to process and print digital images. An important initiative has been the introduction of the company's ink cartridges, which are sourced in China. So far, the company faces steep competition from Sony, Canon and Hewlett-Packard.[18]

Source: Courtesy of Kodak Ltd (UK).

The final key to successfully applying core competencies, in order to develop customer value offerings, is to change corporate attitudes to reflect the importance of customer-perceived value: that is, to move from customisation of offerings to personalisation of customer offerings. As Professor Prahalad says, 'this is not best practice, it is next practice'.[19]

A holistic marketing orientation and customer value

A **holistic marketing** orientation can also help capture customer-perceived value. One view of holistic marketing sees it as 'integrating the value exploration, value creation, and value delivery activities with the purpose of building long-term, mutually satisfying relationships and co-prosperity among key stakeholders'. According to this view, holistic marketers succeed by managing a superior value chain that delivers a high level of product quality, service and speed. Holistic marketers achieve profitable growth by expanding customer share, building customer loyalty and capturing customer lifetime value. Figure 3.4, a holistic marketing framework, shows how the interaction between relevant actors and value-based activities helps to create, maintain and renew customer-perceived value.

The holistic marketing framework is designed to address three key management questions:

1 **Value exploration**: how can a company identify new value opportunities?
2 **Value creation**: how can a company efficiently create more promising new value offerings?
3 **Value delivery**: how can a company use its capabilities and infrastructure to deliver the new value offerings more efficiently?

Marketing practitioners might approach these questions as follows.

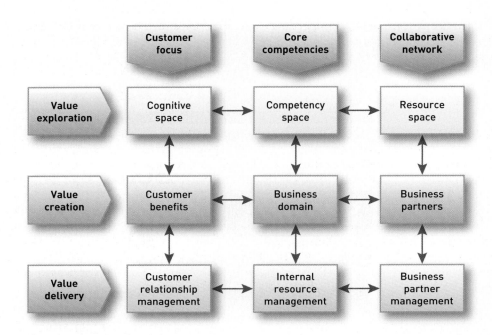

Value exploration

Finding new value opportunities is a matter of understanding the relationships between three spaces:

1 the customer's cognitive space;
2 the company's competence space; and
3 the collaborator's resource space.

The customer's *cognitive space* reflects existing and latent needs and includes dimensions such as the need for participation, stability, freedom and change.[20] A company's *competency space* can be described in terms of breadth – broad versus focused scope of business; and depth – physical versus knowledge-based capabilities. The collaborator's *resource space* includes horizontal partnerships, with partners chosen for their ability to exploit related market opportunities, and vertical partnerships, with partners who can serve the firm's value creation (see Chapter 11).

Value creation

Value-creation skills for marketers include identifying new customer benefits from the customer's viewpoint; utilising core competencies from its business domain; and selecting and managing business partners from its collaborative networks. To create new customer benefits, marketers must understand what customers think about, want, do and worry about, and observe whom they admire and interact with, and who influences them (see Chapters 6–8).

Value delivery

Delivering value often means making substantial investments in infrastructure and capabilities. The company must think about customer relationship management, internal resource management and business partnership management. *Customer relationship management* (CRM) allows the company to discover who its customers are, how they behave, and what they need or want. It also enables the company to respond appropriately, coherently and quickly to different customer opportunities. To respond effectively, the company requires *internal resource management* to integrate major business processes, such as order processing, general ledger, payroll and production, within a single family of software modules.

Finally, *business partnership management* allows the company to handle complex relationships with its trading partners to source, process and deliver customer-perceived value offerings. (see Chapters 11, 17 and 18).

The central role of strategic planning

Successful marketing thus requires companies to have capabilities such as understanding customer-perceived value, creating customer-perceived value, delivering customer-perceived value, capturing customer-perceived value, and sustaining customer-perceived value. Only a select group of companies stand out as master marketers. These include North American companies, such as Procter & Gamble, Nike, Disney, Starbucks, Wal-Mart, Enterprise Rent-A-Car, McDonald's and Ritz-Carlton; Asian companies, such as Canon, Nissan, Samsung, Sony and Toyota; and European companies, such as IKEA, Club Med, Bang & Olufsen, Danone, Electrolux, Nestlé, Nokia, Lego, Tesco and Virgin. The breakthrough marketing box describes how Intel created customer-perceived value and built a brand in a category for which most people thought branding impossible.

Breakthrough marketing

Intel

Intel makes the microprocessors that are found in 80 per cent of the world's personal computers. In the early days, Intel microprocessors were known simply by their engineering numbers, such as '80386' or '80486'. Intel positioned its chips as the most advanced. The trouble was, as Intel soon learned, numbers cannot be trademarked. Competitors came out with their own '486' chips and Intel had no way to distinguish itself from the competition. Worse, Intel's products were hidden from consumers, buried deep inside PCs. With a hidden, untrademarked product, Intel had a hard time convincing consumers to pay more for its high-performance products.

Intel's response was a marketing campaign that created history. The company chose the Pentium trademark and launched the 'Intel Inside' marketing campaign to build awareness of the brand and get its name outside the PC and into the minds of customers.

Intel used an innovative cooperative scheme to extend the reach of the campaign. It would help computer makers who used Intel processors to advertise their PCs if the makers also included the Intel logo in their advertisements. Intel also gave computer manufacturers a rebate on Intel processors if they agreed to place an 'Intel Inside' sticker on the outside of their PCs and laptops.

Intel continues its integrated ingredient campaigns to this day. For example, when launching its Centrino mobile microprocessor platform, Intel began with TV advertisements that aired in the United States and 11 other countries. These advertisements include the animated logo and now familiar five-note brand signature

melody. Print, online and outdoor advertising followed shortly thereafter. Intel created eight-page inserts for major newspapers that urged the wired world only to not 'unwire', but also to 'Untangle. Unburden. Uncompromise. Unstress.'

Intel launched a new brand identity in 2006, supported by a US$2 billion global marketing campaign. The company introduced a new logo with a different font and updated visual look, and also created a new slogan: 'Leap Ahead'. In addition to the new logo and slogan, Intel developed a new microprocessor platform called Viiv (rhymes with 'five') aimed at home entertainment enthusiasts. These moves were designed to create the impression of Intel as a 'warm and fuzzy consumer company', with products that went beyond the PC. Intel remains one of the most valuable brands in the world. The 2010 rankings of the world's 100 most powerful brands published by Millward Brown Optimor showed the company's brand value at number 48.

Sources: C. Edwards (2004) Intel everywhere?, *BusinessWeek*, 8 March, 56–62; S. Van Camp (2004) ReadMe.1st, *Brandweek*, 23 February, 17; How to become a superbrand, *Marketing*, 8 January 2004, 15; R. Slavens (2003) Pam Pollace, VP-Director, Corporate Marketing Group, Intel Corp, *B to B*, 8 December, 19; K. Hein (2003) Study: new brand names not making their mark, *Brandweek*, 8 December, 12; H. Clancy (2003) Intel thinking outside the box, *Computer Reseller News*, 24 November, 14; C. L. Webb (2003) A chip off the old recovery?, *Washington Post*, 15 October (www.washingtonpost.com); Intel launches second phase of Centrino ads, *Technology Advertising and Branding Report*, 6 October; D. Kirkpatrick (2004) At Intel, speed isn't everything, *Fortune*, 9 February, 34; D. Clark (2005) Intel to overhaul marketing in bid to go beyond PCs, *Wall Street Journal*, 30 December.

Figure 3.5 The strategic planning, implementation and control processes

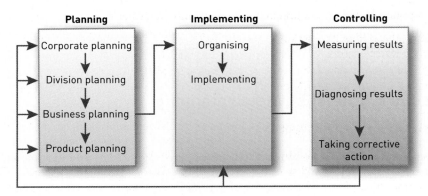

These companies focus on the customer and are organised to respond effectively to changing customer needs. They all have a strong commitment to marketing throughout their companies. However, it is just as important for small companies to contemplate these capabilities. All of them can practise marketing to further their fortunes, for sound marketing management is not the preserve of large corporations.

To ensure that they select and execute the right activities, marketers must give priority to strategic planning in three key areas:

1 managing a company's businesses as an investment portfolio;
2 assessing each business's strength by considering the market's growth rate and the company's position and fit in that market; and
3 establishing a strategy.

For each business, marketers must develop a suitable strategy for achieving the company's long-run objectives.

Most large companies consist of four organisational levels (see Figure 3.5): the corporate level, the division level, the business unit level and the product level. Corporate headquarters is responsible for designing a corporate strategic plan to guide the whole enterprise; it makes decisions on the amount of resources to allocate to each division, as well as on which businesses to acquire or divest. Each division establishes a plan covering the allocation of funds to each of its constituent business units. Each business unit develops a strategic plan to carry that business unit into a profitable future. Finally, each product level (product line, brand) within a business unit develops a marketing plan for achieving its objectives in its own markets.

The **marketing plan** is the central instrument for directing and coordinating the marketing effort. The marketing plan operates at two levels: strategic and tactical. The **strategic marketing plan** lays out the target markets and the customer-perceived value offerings that the firm will offer, based on an analysis of the best market opportunities. The **tactical marketing plan** specifies the marketing tactics, including product features, promotion, merchandising, pricing, sales channels and service.

Today cross-functional teams develop the marketing plan with inputs from every important business function. Management then implements these plans at the appropriate levels of the organisation, monitors results, and takes any necessary corrective action. The complete planning, implementation and control cycle is shown in the Euromart marketing plan at the end of this chapter.

Planning will now be discussed at each of the four levels of an organisation in turn.

Corporate and divisional strategic planning

Some corporations give their business units a great deal of freedom to set their own sales, profit goals and strategies. Others set goals for their business units but let them develop their own strategies. Still others set the goals and participate in developing individual business unit strategies.[21]

All corporate headquarters undertake four planning activities:

1 defining the corporate mission;
2 defining the business;
3 assigning resources to each **strategic business unit** (SBU);
4 assessing growth opportunities.

Defining the corporate mission

Organisations exist to accomplish their business interests by making cars, lending money, providing a night's lodging and so on. Over time the mission may change, to take advantage of new opportunities or respond to new market conditions. Amazon.com changed its mission from being the world's largest online bookstore to aspiring to become the world's largest online store. eBay changed its mission from running online auctions for collectors to running online auctions of all kinds of goods. In the spring of 2010, France Telecom's Orange brand merged with Deutsche Telekom's T-Mobile to form a new marketing initiative, 'Everything Everywhere', that will change the way the companies' customers access the world, for entertainment, education, information – 'wherever they are and whenever they want'.

To define its mission, a company ought to address Drucker's classic questions:[22] What is our business? Who is the customer? What is of value to the customer? What will our business be? What should our business be? These simple-sounding questions are among the most difficult a company will ever have to answer. Successful companies ask them continuously and answer them thoughtfully and thoroughly.[23] An additional question for business to address in today's highly competitive markets is: why should people bother to buy from them?

Organisations develop **mission statements** to share with managers, employees and (in many cases) customers. A clear, thoughtful mission statement provides employees with a shared sense of purpose, direction and opportunity. Mission statements are at their best when they reflect a vision, an almost 'impossible dream' that provides a direction for the company for the next 10–20 years. Sony's former president, Akio Morita, wanted everyone to have access to 'personal portable sound', so his company created the Walkman and portable CD player. Table 3.2 lists five sample mission statements.

Which of the mission statements in Table 3.2 do you think would best impress their respective customers? Good mission statements have five major characteristics.

1 They focus on a limited number of goals. The statement 'We want to produce the highest-quality products, offer the most service, achieve the widest distribution and sell at the lowest prices' claims too much.
2 Mission statements stress the company's major policies, values and culture. They help employees to focus on the importance of working together to ensure that market offerings satisfy the company's customers.
3 They define the major competitive spheres within which the company will operate:

- **Industry**. Some companies will operate in only one industry; some only in a set of related industries; some only in industrial goods, consumer goods or services; and some in any industry. For example, DuPont prefers to operate in the industrial market, whereas, for example, AkzoNobel and Siemens operate in both industrial and consumer markets.
- **Products and applications**. Firms define the range of products and applications they will supply. The mission of the UK crockery company Churchill is 'to be a leading provider to the tabletop market and deliver value through excellence in design, quality and customer service'.
- **Competence**. The firm identifies the range of technological and other core competencies it will master and leverage. Germany's Bosch cites its vision as 'creating value and sharing values' and its mission, 'as a leading technology and service company, we take advantage of our global opportunities for a strong and meaningful development.

Table 3.2 Sample mission statements

BP

'We are taking action to close the competitive gap through a focused effort on our three priorities of safety, people and performance. We are determined to operate safely and reliably, to develop the capability of our people and to drive performance through restoring operational momentum.'

eBay

'We help people trade practically anything on earth. We will continue to enhance the online trading experiences of all – collectors, dealers, small businesses, unique item seekers, bargain hunters, opportunity sellers and browsers.'

Oticon

'Our mission
The professionals we work with across the globe and the specialists at Oticon share a common goal:

To assure that our hearing solutions provide the highest possible satisfaction.
To accomplish our mission, we continuously:

- Develop innovative and effective solutions
- Establish and build strong partnerships
- Share knowledge with professionals and hearing aid users.'

Philips

'We have a passion to improve the quality of people's lives through the timely introduction of meaningful technological innovations.'

Volvo

'To create the safest and most exciting car experience for modern families.'

Sources: Courtesy of BP, Oticon and Philips. Reproduced with permission.

Our ambition is to enhance the quality of life with solutions that are both innovative and beneficial.'

- **Market segment**. The type of market or customers a company will serve constitutes the market segment. Aston Martin makes only high-performance sports cars. Mothercare serves the baby and toddler market.
- **Vertical**. The vertical sphere is the number of channel levels, from raw material to final product and distribution, in which a company will participate. At one extreme are companies with a large vertical scope; at one time Ford owned its own rubber plantations, sheep farms, glass manufacturing plants and steel foundries. At the other extreme are 'hollow corporations' or 'pure marketing companies', such as some financial brokers who contract out or factor nearly everything.
- **Geographical**. The range of regions, countries or country groups in which a company will operate defines its geographical sphere. Some companies operate in a specific state. Others are multinationals such as Volkswagen and Unilever, which operate in almost every country in the world.

4 Mission statements take a long-term view. They should be enduring; management should change the mission only when it ceases to be relevant.
5 A good mission statement is ideally brief, flexible and distinctive. Good examples are Disney's 'to make people happy', 3M's 'to solve unsolved problems innovatively' and Wal-Mart's 'to give ordinary folk the chance to buy the same things as rich people'.

Compare the rather vague missions statements on the left with Google's mission statement and philosophy on the right.

To build total brand value by innovating. To deliver customer value and customer leadership faster, better and more completely than our competition.
We build brands and make the world a little happier by bringing our best to you

Google mission

To organise the world's information and make it universally accessible and useful.

Google philosophy
Never settle for the best.
Ten things we know to be true
1 Focus on the user and all else will follow
2 It's best to do one thing really well
3 Fast is better than slow
4 Democracy on the Web works
5 You don't need to be at your desk to need an answer
6 You can make money without doing evil
7 There is always more information out there
8 The need for information crosses borders
9 You can be serious without a suit
10 Great just isn't good enough[24]

While few would argue with the prime purpose of a mission statement, it is important for organisations to live up to the promises they declare. Avis's famous mission statement 'We try harder' provides a real challenge.[25]

Defining the business

Companies often define their businesses in terms of products: They are in the 'auto business' or the 'clothing business'. However, market definitions of a business are superior to product definitions. Companies must see their businesses as a customer-satisfying process that delivers expected standards of customer-perceived value and not as a goods-producing process.

Viewing businesses in terms of customer needs can suggest additional growth opportunities. IBM redefined itself from a hardware and software manufacturer to a 'builder of networks'. Table 3.3 gives several examples of companies that have moved from a product to a market definition of their business. The table highlights the difference between a target market definition and a strategic market definition.

A target market definition tends to focus on selling a product or service to a current market. Pepsi could define its target market as everyone who drinks a cola beverage,

Table 3.3 Product-oriented versus market-oriented definitions of a business

Company	Product definition	Market definition
BP	We sell fuels	We supply energy . . . beyond petroleum
Beiersdorf	We sell cosmetics (Nivea)	We sell beauty
EDF	We supply electricity	We supply energy
Renault	We sell automobiles	We supply personal and business transport vehicles
SNCF	We run a rail network	We are a people and goods mover
Xerox	We make copying equipment	We help improve office productivity

and competitors would therefore be other cola companies. A strategic market definition, however, focuses also on the potential market. If Pepsi considered everyone who might drink something to quench their thirst, their competition would also include non-cola soft drinks, bottled water, fruit juices, tea and coffee. To compete effectively, Pepsi markets additional beverages, such as Tropicana.

A business can define itself in terms of three dimensions: customer groups, customer needs and technology.[26] Consider a small company that defines its business as designing incandescent lighting systems for television studios. Its customer group is television studios; the customer's need is lighting; and the technology is incandescent lighting. The company might want to expand. It could make lighting for other customer groups, such as homes, factories and offices; or it could supply other services needed by television studios, such as heating, ventilation or air conditioning. It could design other lighting technologies for television studios, such as infrared or ultraviolet lighting.

Large companies normally manage quite different businesses, each requiring its own strategy. The Virgin Group has classified its businesses into seven strategic parts or strategic business units. An SBU has three characteristics:

1 It is a single business, or a collection of related businesses, that can be planned separately from the rest of the company.
2 It has its own set of competitors.
3 It has a manager responsible for strategic planning and profit performance, who controls most of the factors affecting profit.

The purpose of identifying the company's strategic business units is to develop separate strategies and assign appropriate funding. Senior management knows that its portfolio of businesses usually includes a number of 'yesterday's has-beens' as well as 'tomorrow's breadwinners'.[27]

Assigning resources to each SBU[28]

Once it has defined SBUs, management must decide how to allocate its corporate resources. The 1970s saw several portfolio planning models introduced to provide an analytical means for making investment decisions. The American General Electric/McKinsey Matrix classifies each SBU according to the extent of its competitive advantage and the attractiveness of its industry. Management would want to grow, 'harvest' or draw cash from, or hold on to the business. Another model, the Boston Consulting Group's Growth-Market Share Matrix, uses relative market share and annual rate of market growth as criteria to make investment decisions.

Portfolio planning models such as these have fallen out of favour as many view them as oversimplified and too subjective. More recent methods that firms use to make internal investment decisions are based on shareholder value analysis, and whether the market value of a company is greater with an SBU or without it (whether it is sold or spun off). These value calculations assess the potential of a business based on potential growth opportunities from global expansion, repositioning or retargeting, and strategic outsourcing. In layman's terms each SBU needs to make a positive contribution to the perceived strength of the company. Unilever, for example, has over 100 SBUs and each one, such as Dove, either does or is planned to (if it is a relatively new market offering, such as Ben & Jerry's) contribute positively to the corporate shareholder value.

Assessing growth opportunities

Assessing growth opportunities includes planning new businesses, downsizing and terminating older businesses. If there is a gap between future desired sales and projected sales, corporate management will have to develop or acquire new businesses to fill it.

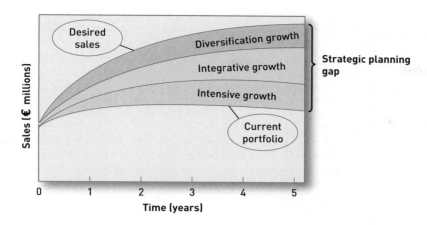

Figure 3.6 The strategic planning gap

Figure 3.6 illustrates this strategic planning gap for a major manufacturer of blank compact disks called Musicale (name disguised). The lowest curve projects the expected sales over the next five years from the current business portfolio. The highest curve describes desired sales over the same period. Evidently, the company wants to grow much faster than its current businesses will permit. How can it fill the strategic planning gap?

The first option is to identify opportunities to achieve further growth within current businesses (intensive opportunities). The second is to identify opportunities to build or acquire businesses that are related to current businesses (integrative opportunities). The third option is to identify opportunities to add attractive businesses unrelated to current businesses (diversification opportunities).

Intensive growth

Corporate management's first course of action should be a review of opportunities for improving existing businesses. One useful framework for detecting new intensive growth opportunities is Ansoff's 'product–market expansion grid' (Figure 3.7).[29]

The company first considers whether it could gain more market share with its current products (i.e. in post-paradigm terms, market offerings) in their current markets. Next it considers whether it can find or develop new markets for its current market offerings, in a market development strategy. Then it considers whether it can develop new products (i.e market offerings) of potential interest to its current markets with a product development strategy. Later the firm will also review opportunities to develop new market offerings for new markets in a diversification strategy.

	Current products	**New products**
Current markets	1 Market penetration strategy	3 Product development strategy
New markets	2 Market development strategy	(Diversification strategy)

Figure 3.7 Three intensive growth strategies: Ansoff's product–market expansion grid
Source: Reprinted by permission of *Harvard Business Review*. From Strategies for diversification by Ansoff, I., September–October 1957. Copyright © 1957 by the Harvard Business School Publishing Corporation; all rights reserved.

Starbucks

When Howard Schultz, Starbucks' CEO until 2000, came to the company in 1982, he recognised an unfilled niche for cafés serving gourmet coffee directly to customers. This became Starbucks' market penetration strategy and helped the company attain a loyal customer base in Seattle. The market development strategy marked the next phase in Starbucks' growth and it applied the same successful formula that had worked wonders in Seattle throughout North America and, finally, across the globe. Once the company had established itself as a presence in thousands of cities internationally, Starbucks sought to increase the number of purchases by existing customers with a product development strategy that led to new in-store merchandise, including compilation CDs, a Starbucks Duetto Visa card that allows customers to receive points towards Starbucks purchases whenever they use it, and high-speed wireless internet access at thousands of Starbucks 'HotSpots' through a deal with T-Mobile. Aware of the rising appeal of Fairtrade, the company adopted it enthusiastically in its sourcing of materials. Finally, Starbucks pursued diversification into grocery store aisles with Frappuccino® bottled drinks, Starbucks brand ice cream and the purchase of tea retailer Tazo® Tea. Even a famous brand such as Starbucks cannot rest on its laurels in today's competitive buyers' markets. In February 2007 Howard Schultz was moved to accuse the company of losing its creativity. A survey in *Consumer Reports* magazine that February judged McDonald's coffee to be better than Starbucks'.[30]

Howard Schultz of Starbucks waves after opening the company's first store outside North America in 1996. Today Starbucks has stores across the globe.
Source: Koji Sasahara/AP/ PA Photos

So how might Musicale use these three major intensive growth strategies to increase its sales? It could try to encourage its current customers to buy more by demonstrating the benefits of using compact disks for data storage in addition to music storage. Musicale could also try to attract competitors' customers if it noticed major weaknesses in competitors' marketing programmes. Finally, Musicale could try to convince non-users of compact disks to start using them.

How can Musicale use a market development strategy? First, it might try to identify potential user groups in the current sales areas. If Musicale has been marketing compact disks only to consumer markets, it might go after office and factory markets. Secondly, it might seek additional distribution channels in its present locations. If it has been supplying its disks only through stereo equipment dealers, it might add mass merchandising or online channels. Thirdly the company might consider marketing in new locations in its home country or abroad. If Musicale sold only in Europe, it could consider entering the Asian and Middle Eastern markets.

Management should also consider new customer-perceived value market offering possibilities. Musicale could develop new features, such as additional data storage capabilities or greater durability. It could offer the CD at two or more quality levels, or it could research an alternative technology such as flash drives.

By examining these intensive growth strategies, managers may discover several ways to grow. Still, that growth may not be enough. In that case, management must also look for integrative growth opportunities.

Integrative growth

A business can increase sales and profits through backward, forward or horizontal integration within its industry. For example, Louis Vuitton has expanded from being a provider of luxury leather goods and fashions to forge a broad luxury portfolio that includes perfumes (Dior and Givenchy), champagne (Moet) and the prestigious Paris-based department store Le Bon Marché.

PepsiCo, the US-owned company, manufactures and markets a variety of carbonated and non-carbonated drinks, as well as salty or sweet grain-based snacks and other foods. The company has pursued a strategy of integral growth since its foundation in 1965. In Europe the company markets several well-known beverage brands including Pepsi Cola, 7 Up and Fiesta, and in 1998 Tropicana was acquired. The company also has its own Bottling Group. Many consumers snack while refreshing themselves and the company

Pepsi look after producing and delivering their drinks to customer purchase points
Source: PepsiCo

has a wide portfolio of famous snack brands including Doritos, Quavers, The Smith's Snackfood Company, Walkers and Wotsits. In 2001 PepsiCo purchased Quaker Oats. The company has also formed partnerships with several brands to distribute these or to market them with their own brands.[31]

How might Musicale achieve integrative growth? The company might acquire one or more of its suppliers, such as plastic material producers, to gain more control or generate more profit through backward integration down the value chain. It might acquire some wholesalers or retailers, especially if they are highly profitable, in forward integration. Finally, Musicale might acquire one or more competitors, provided that the government does not bar this horizontal integration as part of its anti-monopoly policy. However, these new sources may still not deliver the desired sales volume. In that case, the company must consider diversification.

To understand how Group Danone has used internalisation to focus its growth strategy in the food products sector, visit www.pearsoned.co.uk/marketingmanagementeurope.

Diversification growth

Diversification growth makes sense when good opportunities exist outside the present businesses – the industry is highly attractive and the company has the right mix of business strengths to be successful. For example, from its origins as an animated film producer, Walt Disney Company has moved into licensing characters for merchandised goods, entering the broadcast industry with its own Disney Channel as well as ABC and ESPN acquisitions, and developing theme parks and vacation and resort properties.

Diversification growth

Cisco Systems, Inc.
Known for years as a mass producer of rooters and switches, Cisco is attempting to diversify beyond these nuts and bolts products into the business of changing how consumers communicate and view television in both the United States and Europe. With its recent US$6.9 billion acquisition of Scientific-Atlanta, Inc., widely recognised for its expertise in video delivery, Cisco hopes to enter consumers' living rooms with items such as home-networking equipment, wirelessly networked DVD players, and services such as video on demand. The diversification move is already paying off: Scientific-Atlanta produced 7 per cent of Cisco's US$8 billion in revenue.[32]

Saltzgitter
Saltzgitter, the German steel group, is planning to diversify into a new area of business to be less dependent on the economic cycles of the steel industry. The company is particularly keen to add to its current operations in steel pipelines.[33]

PZ Cussons
PZ Cussons, the soap and detergents group, is transforming itself from a paternalistic Greek family-owned business into an international meritocracy. Rather than target global markets, the company tailors its products to local markets. It operates a completely different model to its main rivals such as Procter & Gamble and Unilever. It has a strong interest in the electrical goods market.[34] See also www.pzcussons.com/pzc/about/ourcompany/ourstrategy/

Microsoft
Microsoft announced in July 2007 that it intended to diversify into new businesses such as advertising and consumer electronics, as it believes that these will eventually grow to rival desktop and server software.[35]

Several types of diversification are possible for Musicale. First the company could choose a *concentric strategy*. This occurs when a company seeks to develop new market offerings that have technological or marketing synergies with existing product lines, though the new market offerings themselves may appeal to a different group of customers. Musicale might start a laser disk manufacturing operation, as it knows how to make compact disks. Secondly, the company might use a *horizontal strategy* to search for new products that could appeal to current customers, even though the new market offerings are technically unrelated to its current product line. For example, the company could produce compact disk cases, though they require a different manufacturing process. Finally, Musicale might decide to spread its risks by seeking new business opportunities that have no relationship to its current technology or activities (*a conglomerate strategy*) and review opportunities that may lie in markets such as, for example, application software or personal organisers.

Downsizing and divesting older businesses

Weak businesses require a disproportionate amount of managerial attention. Companies must carefully prune, harvest or divest tired old businesses in order to release needed resources to other uses and reduce costs. In the face of serious difficulties, Deutsche Telecom spun off its media and broadcast services business to a private equity-based European competitor in a deal worth €850 million. The German group has lost millions of fixed-line customers in recent years as rivals offered internet-based telephone services and mobile phone services at prices Deutsche Telecom could not match. Telefonica, Spain's largest telecommunications group, after three years of energetic activity, during which it paid €27 billion for O2 of the United Kingdom, has decided to consolidate its interests and develop its core business. Several of its non-core activities, such as the television production business Endemol, have been divested.[36]

Downsizing and divesting

Danone

Paris-based Groupe Danone has grown by a series of acquisitions to become a leading player in the European food products sector. For some years the company's growth was the result of horizontal (market) and vertical (supply/value chain) acquisitions that did not seem to reflect a well-fashioned strategy. It embarked on a programme of internalisation. In the 1990s the incoming CEO sharpened the strategy and focused on the dairy, beverages and cereals sectors.

The group's turnover came to €14.982 billion in 2009. Turnover growth increased 3.2 per cent in 2009 on a like-for-like basis, enabling the group to reach its growth targets and providing proof positive of the effectiveness of the strategy established in late 2008 to address the world economic crisis. The current operating margin of the group is up for the fifteenth consecutive year, firmly anchoring its global market positions: today, in volume, Danone is the world number 1 in fresh dairy products, number 2 in bottled waters, number 2 in baby nutrition and the European leader in medical nutrition.

This performance was made possible by the use of three major levers to confront the crisis. The first is the priority given to growth in volumes and market share through three initiatives: a market-by-market rebalancing of the product portfolio, increased promotion and a readjustment of publicity. This prioritising meant a 5.2 per cent increase in volumes sold in 2009, with the added benefit of protecting jobs within the group as well as at Danone's industrial partners. The second lever is the staff's adaptability, facilitated by efficient and committed operating structures in every country where Danone is present. The establishment of the Danone Ecosystem Fund is the third lever, supporting operations at the group's direct and often local partners. Moreover, Danone continues to invest in research and development despite the economic climate – €206 million in 2009, or 1.4 per cent of the company's turnover.

Three centuries after the benefits of Evian mineral water were discovered, over a century after Blédine was first marketed, and nearly a century after the first Danone yoghurt was retailed in a pharmacy, health innovation remains more than ever a driver of the group's business growth. The baby nutrition and medical nutrition businesses, which Danone undertook in 2007 in buying up Numico, account respectively for 20 per cent and 6 per cent of the group's 2009 turnover and increased significantly over 2008 (+7.9 and +11.4 per cent). These two lines naturally round off the group's brand portfolio and are perfectly aligned with its mission of bringing health through food to as many people as possible. Today, Danone is the only food group to focus totally on health.

PepsiCo

Over the last five decades PepsiCo has sold off several famous brands in both the United States and Europe, such as the fast-food restaurants Kentucky Fried Chicken, Pizza Hut and Taco Bell.[37]

Relationship between missions and visions

While missions are essentially concerned with what the company is about and how it behaves, visions are more associated with future corporate goals. Visions may be vague or precise but give the organisation a sense of purpose. Good business leaders create a vision for an organisation, articulate the vision, and motivate personnel to seek and achieve it (see also Chapter 6).

A vision and a mission can be one and the same, but the concepts, though related, are not necessarily the same. Broadly speaking, *visions* refer to future intentions and *missions* to delivering present ones. Both visions and missions are inspirational. Visions once achieved need to be restated. Missions, on the other hand, are continuous in that they encapsulate an organisation's purpose. A paradigm change from sellers' to buyers' markets challenges everything an organisation stands for and may require a complete and challenging evaluation of both vision and mission statements.

Organisation and organisational culture

(See also Chapters 15 and 21.)

Strategic planning happens within the context of the organisation. A company's organisation consists of its structures, policies and corporate culture, all of which can become dysfunctional in a rapidly changing business environment. Whereas managers can change structures and policies (with difficulty), the company's culture is very hard to change. Yet adapting the culture is often the key to successfully implementing a new strategy.

What exactly is a corporate culture? Most businesspeople would be hard pressed to describe this elusive concept, which some define as 'the shared experiences, stories, beliefs and norms that characterise an organisation'. Yet, walk into any company and the first thing that strikes you is the corporate culture – the way people dress, talk to one another and greet customers.

A customer-centric culture can affect all aspects of an organisation. As one expert says:

To me, being consumer centric is more a principle – the driving value of a company – than a process. It's in a company's DNA, top to bottom. It means you recognize the diversity across the face of consumers, and that you are open to observations and opinions other than your own; this allows you to be an advocate for the consumer – whether you are a leading innovator or packing boxes in the warehouse . . . The question is, do you see consumers as the driving life force of your company for as long as it exists, or do you see them as simply a hungry group of people that needs to be satisfied so your business will grow in the short term?[38]

Sometimes corporate culture develops organically and is transmitted directly from the CEO's personality and habits to the company employees. Sir James Dyson, the inventor of the Dual Cyclone bagless vacuum cleaner, and CEO of the company that carries his name, inspires his staff as he is a designer and an innovator in his own right[39] (see also Chapter 21).

Marketing innovation

Innovation in marketing is critical. The traditional view is that senior management hammers out the strategy and hands it down. Hamel offers the contrasting view that imaginative ideas on strategy exist in many places within a company.[40] Senior management should identify and encourage fresh ideas from three groups that tend to be underrepresented in strategy making: employees with youthful perspectives; employees who are far removed from company headquarters; and employees who are new to the industry. Each group is capable of challenging company orthodoxy and stimulating new ideas. Jump Associates, a US innovative strategy firm, offers five key strategies for managing change in an organisation:[41]

1 **Avoid the innovation title.** Pick a name for the innovation team that will not alienate co-workers.
2 **Use the buddy system.** Find a like-minded collaborator within the organisation.
3 **Set the metrics in advance.** Establish different sets of funding, testing and performance criteria for incremental, experimental and potentially disruptive innovations.
4 **Aim for quick hits first.** Start with easily implemented ideas that will work to demonstrate that things can get done, before quickly switching to bigger initiatives.
5 **Get data to back up your gut feelings.** Use testing to get feedback and improve an idea. The marketing insight box describes how some leading companies approach innovation.

For further discussion see Chapter 15.

Research in Motion, the company that developed the Dyson Dual Cyclone bagless vacuum cleaner, fosters a culture of innovation that CEO Sir James Dyson carefully cultivates and values highly.
Source: ©Adrian Sherratt/Alamy

Table 3.4 The 12 dimensions of business innovation

Dimension	Definition	Examples
Offerings (what)	Develop innovative new products or services	• Gillette Mach3Turbo razor • Apple iPod music player and iTunes music service and iPad
Platform	Use common components or building blocks to create derivative offerings	• Danone and Nestlé's yogurts • Disney animated movies
Solutions	Create integrated and customised offerings that solve end-to-end customer problems	• DHL logistics services Supply Chain Solutions • IKEA Building Innovations for construction
Customers (who)	Discover unmet customer needs or identify underserved customer segments	• Eurocar Rent-A-Car focuses on replacement car renters • Fairtrade coffee and tea providers
Customer experience	Redesign customer interactions across all touchpoints and all moments of contact	• NatWest customer service improvement programme • AA extended range of breakdown services, e.g. gas and plumbing rescue services
Value capture	Redefine how company gets paid or create innovative new revenue streams	• Google paid search • Blockbuster revenue sharing with movie distributors
Processes (how)	Redesign core operating processes to improve efficiency and effectiveness	• Toyota Production System for operations • Siemens Design for Six Sigma quality control
Organisation	Change form, function or activity scope of the firm	• Cisco partner-centric networked virtual organisation • Procter & Gamble front–back hybrid organisation for customer focus
Supply chain	Think differently about sourcing and fulfilment	• Moen ProjectNet for collaborative design with suppliers • General Motors Celta use of integrated supply and online sales
Presence (where)	Create new distribution channels or innovative points of presence, including the places where offerings can be bought or used by customers	• Starbucks music CD and coffee sales in coffee stores • Diebold RemoteTeller System for banking
Networking	Create network-centric intelligent and integrated offerings	• Otis Remote Elevator Monitoring service
Brand	Leverage a brand into new domains	• Virgin Group 'branded venture capital' • Yahoo! as a lifestyle brand

Source: Adapted from M. Sawhney, R. C. Wolcott and I. Arroniz (2006) The 12 different ways for companies to innovate, *MIT Sloan Management Review*, 47(3), 78. © 2006 from MIT Sloan Management Review/Massachusetts Institute of Technology. All rights reserved. Distributed by Tribune Media Services.

Marketing insight

Different approaches to innovative marketing

In most markets there is too much sameness: too much safe differentiation between competitors. Go-ahead companies are constantly seeking ways to gain and sustain a strong market identity. This can be achieved by a commitment to the importance of new product development and by novel use of the tools of the marketing mix.

When IBM surveyed top CEOs and government leaders about their agenda priorities, their answers about innovation were revealing. Business-model innovation and coming up with unique ways of doing things scored high. IBM's own drive for business-model innovation led to much collaboration, both within IBM itself and externally with companies, governments and educational institutions. CEO Samuel Palmisano noted how the breakthrough Cell processor, based on the company's Power architecture, would not have happened without collaboration with Sony and Nintendo, as well as competitors Toshiba and Microsoft.

Procter & Gamble similarly has made it a goal for 50 per cent of the company's new products to come from outside the company's laboratories – from inventors, scientists and suppliers whose new product ideas can be developed in-house.

Similarly 3M, the US-based industrial and technology group whose products include Scotch tape and optical film, has been giving people 'tinkering time' for as long as anyone can remember. The reasoning is that 'exploring different areas is a very good way of keeping people inventive and keeping their imaginations fired up,' says the company's senior technical manager. One of 3M's most famous products, the Post-it note, was a result of tinkering.[42]

JCB

JCB has for several years developed an innovative marketing approach in a business-to-business industry that many would consider staid. It is famous for the use of events and stunts such as JCB dancing diggers. The tradition of innovative marketing continues today and the company promoted the launch of its JCB Dieselmax engine in August 2006 by using two high-performance versions of its new engine in a world record attempt for a diesel-powered vehicle in the United States. The JCB Dieselmax car reached 350.092 mph on the Bonneville Salt Flats in Utah. The company's marketing director, Chris Wright, says that supporting challenges such as the Dieselmax record not only raises the brand's profile but also helps to attract top engineers and puts a spotlight on British engineering.[43]

BMW

To reach customers across the globe, the marketing department of BMW has decided to put less money and effort into traditional media such as television and newspapers. It is pioneering new ways of reaching customers,

such as offering them the chance to download audio books and other material from the internet.[44]

Facebook

In the fickle world of advertising trends, Facebook is enjoying the free marketing that comes from displacing MySpace and YouTube as the hippest online social network. However, many people are starting to think that the program is starting to lose its appeal and in all likelihood will be replaced by a new online social network before long.[45]

Business writer C. K. Prahalad believes much innovation in industries, from financial and telecom services to healthcare and automobiles, can come from developments in emerging markets such as India. Forced to do more with less, Indian companies and foreign competitors are finding new ways to maximise minimal resources and offer quality products and services at low prices. Consider the money transfer company Western Union. On a visit to rural districts in Uttar Pradesh, India's most populous state, it discovered that many people were in receipt of remittances sent by relatives working in the oilfields of Saudi Arabia. This prompted Western Union to open branches in rural areas where people had huge difficulties in receiving money as most of the 65,000 bank branches in India are in urban areas, and about 80 per cent of India's population of 1.1 billion lack access to financial services. Significantly, India is the world's largest recipient of remittances, according to the World Bank. Inward remittances from Indians working overseas surged from circa US$2 billion in 1990–1 to US$53.9 in 2009–10.[46]

Finally, to find breakthrough ideas, some companies find ways to immerse a range of employees in solving marketing problems. Samsung's Value Innovation Programme (VIP) isolates product development teams of engineers, designers and planners with a timetable and end date in the company's centre just south of Seoul, while 50 specialists help guide their activities. To help make tough trade-offs, team members draw 'value curves' that rank attributes such as a product's sound or picture quality on a scale from 1 to 5. To develop a new car, BMW similarly mobilises specialists in engineering, design, production, marketing, purchasing and finance at its Research and Innovation Centre or Project House.

Sources: S. Hamm (2006) Innovation: the view from the top, *BusinessWeek*, 3 April, 52–3; J. McGregor (2006) The world's most innovative companies, *BusinessWeek*, 24 April, 63–74; R. Karlgard (2006) Digital rules, *Forbes*, 13 March, 31; J. Rooney and J. Collins (2006) Being great is not just a matter of big ideas, *Point*, June, 20; M. Ihlwan (2006) Camp Samsung, *BusinessWeek*, 3 July, 46–7; M. Sawhney, R. C. Wolcott and I. Arroniz (2006) The 12 different ways for companies to innovate, *MIT Sloan Management Review*, 47(3), 75–85; P. Engardio (2006) Business prophet: how C.K. Prahalad is changing the way CEOs think, *BusinessWeek*, 23 January, 68–73.

Firms develop strategy by identifying and selecting from different views of the future. The Royal Dutch/Shell Group has pioneered scenario analysis, which consists of developing plausible representations of a firm's possible future that make different assumptions about forces driving the market and that include different uncertainties. Managers need to think through each scenario with the question: 'What will we do if this happens?' They need to adopt one scenario as the most probable and watch for signposts that might confirm or disconfirm it.[47]

Table 3.5 More sample mission statements

3M

'Our mission is to be innovative through product generations.'

Bosch

'Creating value – sharing values . . . Our ambition is to enhance the quality of life with solutions that are both innovative and beneficial.'

British Gas

'We are committed to providing the best value energy and the highest quality services expertise in the country. Our vision is clear and embedded to our management team to help us meet the challenges ahead.'

Fiat

'We don't just want to get you from A to B. We want to get you there with a smile on your face.'

L'Oréal

'For more than a century L'Oréal has been pushing back the boundaries of science to **invent beauty** and meet the aspirations of millions of women and men. Its vocation is universal: to offer everyone, all over the world, **the best of cosmetics** in terms of quality, efficacy and safety, **to give everyone access to beauty** by offering products in harmony with their needs, culture and expectations.'

Michelin

'To make a sustainable contribution to progress in the mobility of people and goods by constantly enhancing freedom of movement, safety, efficiency and pleasure when on the move.'

Nokia

'Nokia is about enhancing communication and exploring new ways to exchange information. Everyone has a need to communicate and share. Nokia helps people to fulfil this need and we help people feel close to what matters to them. We focus on providing consumers with very human technology – technology that is intuitive, a joy to use, and beautiful.'

Siemens

'Our knowledge and our solutions are helping to create a better world. We have a responsibility to the wider community and we are committed to environmental protection.'

Divine Chocolate Ltd

'To improve the livelihood of smallholder cocoa producers in West Africa by establishing their own dynamic branded proposition in the UK chocolate market, thus putting them higher up the value chain.'

Sources: Courtesy of 3M, Bosch, Fiat, L'Oréal, Nokia, Siemens and Divine Chocolate Ltd.

Business unit strategic planning

The business unit strategic planning process consists of the eight steps shown in Figure 3.8. Each step is examined in the sections that follow.

The business mission

Each business unit needs to define its specific mission within the broader company mission. Thus, a television studio-lighting-equipment company might define its mission as 'To target major television studios and become their vendor of choice for lighting technologies that represent the most advanced and reliable studio lighting arrangements.' Notice that this mission does not attempt to win business from smaller television studios, win business by being lowest in price, or venture into non-lighting products.

SWOT analysis

The overall evaluation of a company's strengths, weaknesses, opportunities and threats is called SWOT analysis. It is a way of monitoring the external and internal marketing environment.

A business unit has to monitor key *macroenvironment forces* and significant *microenvironment actors* that affect its ability to earn profits. The business unit should set up a marketing intelligence system to track trends, important developments and any related opportunities and threats.

Good marketing is the art of finding, developing and profiting from these opportunities.[48] A **marketing opportunity** is an area of buyer need and interest that a company has a high probability of profitably satisfying. There are three main sources of market opportunities. The first is to supply something that is in short supply. This requires little marketing talent, as the need is obvious. The second is to supply an existing market offering in a new or superior way. There are several ways to uncover possible customer-perceived value improvements: the *problem detection method* asks consumers for their suggestions; the *ideal method* has them imagine an ideal version of the product or service; and the *consumption chain method* asks consumers to chart their steps in acquiring, using and disposing of a market offering that meets their customer-perceived value expectations. This last method often leads to a very new market offering.

Opportunities can take many forms, and marketers have to be good at spotting them. Consider the following:

- A company may benefit from converging industry trends and introduce a hybrid market offering that is new to the market. For example, several major mobile phone manufacturers released phones with digital photo capabilities.

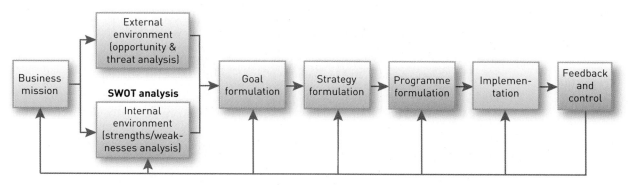

Figure 3.8 The business unit strategic-planning process

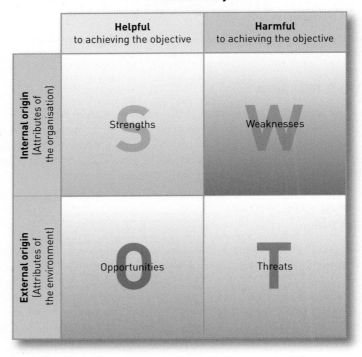

Figure 3.9 Using SWOT analysis to monitor the internal and external position of an organisation

- A company may make a buying process more convenient or efficient. Consumers can now use the internet to find more books than ever before and search for the lowest price with a few clicks.
- A company can meet the need for more information and advice. For example, Guru. com facilitates finding professional experts in a wide range of fields.
- A company can customise a market offering that was formerly offered only in a standard form. Timberland allows customers to choose colours for different sections of their boots, add initials or numbers to their boots, and choose different stitching and embroidery.
- A company can introduce a new capability. Dell offers both standard and coloured laptops at an extra charge. Consumers can now create and edit digital 'iMovies' with the new iMac and upload them to an Apple Web server or website such as YouTube to share with friends around the world.
- A company may be able to deliver a market offering faster than the competition. DHL, for example, has discovered a way to deliver mail and packages much more quickly than the UK Post Office.
- A company may be able to offer a market offering at a much lower price. Pharmaceutical firms have created generic versions of brand-name drugs.

To evaluate opportunities, companies can use **market opportunity analysis** (MOA) to determine their attractiveness and probability of success by asking questions such as:

1 Can we articulate the benefits convincingly to a defined target market(s)?
2 Can we locate the target market(s) and reach them with cost-effective media and trade channels?
3 Does our company possess or have access to the critical capabilities and resources we need to deliver the customer benefits?
4 Can we deliver the benefits better than any actual or potential competitors?
5 Will the financial rate of return meet or exceed our required threshold for investment?

(a) Opportunity matrix

Success probability

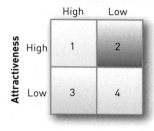

1 Company develops more powerful lighting system
2 Company develops device to measure energy efficiency of any lighting system
3 Company develops device to measure illumination level
4 Company develops software program to teach lighting fundamentals to TV studio personnel

(b) Threat matrix

Probability of occurrence

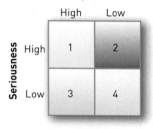

1 Competitor develops superior lighting system
2 Major prolonged economic depression
3 Higher costs
4 Legislation to reduce number of TV studio licences

Figure 3.10 Opportunity and threat matrices

In the opportunity matrix in Figure 3.10(a), the best marketing opportunities facing the TV-lighting-equipment company are listed in the upper-left cell (no. 1). The opportunities in the lower-right cell (no. 4) are too minor to consider. The opportunities in the upper-right cell (no. 2) and lower-left cell (no. 3) are worth monitoring in the event that any improve in attractiveness and success probability.

An **environmental threat** is a challenge posed by an unfavourable trend or development that would lead, in the absence of defensive marketing action, to lower sales or profit. Figure 3.10(b) illustrates the threat matrix facing the TV-lighting-equipment company. The threats in the upper-left cell are major, because they can seriously hurt the company and they have a high probability of occurrence. To deal with them, the company needs contingency plans. The threats in the lower-right cell are minor and can be ignored. The firm will want to carefully monitor threats in the upper-right and lower-left cells in the event that they might grow more serious.

Internal environment (strengths/weaknesses) analysis

It is one thing to find attractive opportunities, and another to be able to take advantage of them. Each business needs to evaluate its internal strengths and weaknesses.

IBM

In the early 1980s IBM dominated the personal computer industry but its position was vulnerable. Many purchased from IBM at the time as the reliability of the IBM clones was unproven in use and thus risky. As the clones proved to be reliable the sales of IBM suffered when it failed to respond effectively, burdened as it was by a heavy bureaucracy.

Businesses can evaluate their own strengths and weaknesses by using a form such as the one shown in the marketing memo box.

Marketing memo

Checklist for performing strengths/weaknesses analysis

	Performance					Importance		
	Major strength	Minor strength	Neutral	Minor weakness	Major weakness	High	Medium	Low
Marketing								
1 Company reputation	____	____	____	____	____	____	____	____
2 Market share	____	____	____	____	____	____	____	____
3 Customer satisfaction	____	____	____	____	____	____	____	____
4 Customer retention	____	____	____	____	____	____	____	____
5 Product quality	____	____	____	____	____	____	____	____
6 Service quality	____	____	____	____	____	____	____	____
7 Pricing effectiveness	____	____	____	____	____	____	____	____
8 Distribution effectiveness	____	____	____	____	____	____	____	____
9 Promotion effectiveness	____	____	____	____	____	____	____	____
10 Sales force effectiveness	____	____	____	____	____	____	____	____
11 Innovation effectiveness	____	____	____	____	____	____	____	____
12 Geographical coverage	____	____	____	____	____	____	____	____
Finance								
13 Cost or availability of capital	____	____	____	____	____	____	____	____
14 Cash flow	____	____	____	____	____	____	____	____
15 Financial stability	____	____	____	____	____	____	____	____
Manufacturing								
16 Facilities	____	____	____	____	____	____	____	____
17 Economies of scale	____	____	____	____	____	____	____	____
18 Capacity	____	____	____	____	____	____	____	____
19 Able, dedicated workforce	____	____	____	____	____	____	____	____
20 Ability to produce on time	____	____	____	____	____	____	____	____
21 Technical manufacturing skill	____	____	____	____	____	____	____	____
Organisation								
22 Visionary, capable leadership	____	____	____	____	____	____	____	____
23 Dedicated employees	____	____	____	____	____	____	____	____
24 Entrepreneurial orientation	____	____	____	____	____	____	____	____
25 Flexible or responsive	____	____	____	____	____	____	____	____

Critique of conventional SWOT analysis

Over the years, SWOT analysis has been severely criticised as a sole and conventional tool for formulating strategy. While it can provide an indication of which listed items characterise a business and which do not, it can tend to oversimplify critical issues, problems and themes as much as illuminate them. SWOT analyses are essentially descriptions of conditions whereas strategies define actions. Furthermore, they can present findings uncritically and without clear prioritisation so that, for example, weak opportunities may appear to balance strong threats. Consequently, they should be seen only as a basic initial review tool and used with caution.[49]

Clearly the business does not have to correct *all* its weaknesses, nor should it gloat about all its strengths. The big question is whether the firm should limit itself to those opportunities for which it possesses the required strengths, or consider those that might require it to find or develop new strengths. For example, managers at Texas Instruments (TI) were split between those who wanted TI to stick to industrial electronics, where it has clear strength, and those who wanted the company to continue introducing consumer products, where it lacks some required marketing strengths.

Sometimes a business does poorly not because its people lack the required strengths but because they fail to work together as a team. In one major electronics company, engineers look down on the salespeople as 'engineers who couldn't make it', and salespeople look down on the service people as 'salespeople who couldn't make it'. It is crucial to assess interdepartmental working relationships as part of the internal environmental audit.

Goal formulation

Once the company has performed a SWOT analysis it can proceed to develop specific goals for the planning period. This stage of the process is called **goal formulation**. Goals are objectives that are specific with respect to magnitude and time.

Most business units pursue a mix of objectives, including profitability, sales growth, market share improvement, risk containment, innovation and reputation. The business unit sets these objectives and then manages by objectives (MBO). For an MBO system to work, the unit's objectives must meet four criteria:

1 **They must be arranged hierarchically, from the most to the least important.** For example, the business unit's key objective for the period may be to increase the rate of return on investment. Managers can increase profit by increasing revenue and reducing expenses. They can grow revenue, in turn, by increasing market share and prices.
2 **Objectives should be quantitative whenever possible.** The objective 'to increase the return on investment (ROI)' is better stated as the goal 'to increase ROI to 15 per cent within two years'.
3 **Goals should be realistic.** Goals should arise from an analysis of the business unit's opportunities and strengths, not from wishful thinking.
4 **Objectives must be consistent.** It is not always possible to maximise sales and profits simultaneously.

Other important trade-offs include short-term profit versus long-term growth, deep penetration of existing markets versus developing new markets, profit goals versus non-profit goals, and high growth versus low risk. Each choice calls for a different marketing strategy.[50]

Many believe that adopting the goal of strong market share growth may mean forgoing strong short-term profits. Volkswagen has 15 times the annual revenue of Porsche – but Porsche's profit margins are seven times bigger than VW's. Other successful companies such as Google, Microsoft and Samsung have maximised profitability *and* growth. Yet management experts Charan and Tichy believe that most businesses can be growth businesses *and* grow profitably as, for example, BP, Bosch, IKEA, Nestlé and Tesco have done.[51]

Strategic formulation

Goals indicate what a business unit wants to achieve; **strategy** is a game plan for getting there. Every business must design a strategy for achieving its goals, consisting of a *marketing strategy* and a compatible *technology strategy* and *sourcing strategy*.

Porter's generic strategies

Porter has proposed three generic strategies that provide a good starting point for strategic thinking: overall cost leadership, differentiation and focus.[52]

- **Overall cost leadership.** Firms pursuing this strategy work hard to achieve the lowest production and distribution costs so they can price lower than their competitors and win a large market share. The problem with this strategy is that other firms will usually compete with still lower costs and hurt the firm that bases its whole future on cost alone.
- **Differentiation.** The business concentrates on uniquely achieving superior performance in an important customer benefit area valued by a large part of the market. Thus the firm seeking quality leadership, for example, must make items with the best components, put them together expertly, inspect them carefully and communicate their quality effectively.
- **Focus.** The business focuses on one or more narrow market segments. The firm gets to know these segments intimately and pursues either cost leadership or differentiation within the target segment.

Belkin Corporation

For most people, a surge protector is a necessary item to avoid electrical surges damaging a personal computer. Yet one company decided to focus not on the utilitarian aspect of the surge protector but on its aesthetic aspect. An example of both focus and differentiation, Belkin Corporation's surge protectors organise consumers' workspaces and protect their equipment. Its Concealed Surge Protector organises cables and keeps them out of view with a unique closing cover. By differentiating itself from the average surge protector, Belkin can charge premium prices for its product.[53]

The online air travel industry provides a good example of these three strategies. British Airways is pursuing a differentiation strategy by offering the most comprehensive range of additional services to the traveller (executive airport lounges, optional onboard entertainment packs, etc.). On the other hand, Ryanair is pursuing a lowest-cost strategy; and LastMinute is pursuing a niche strategy in focusing on travellers who have the flexibility to travel at very short notice.

According to Porter, firms pursuing the same strategy directed to the same target market constitute a **strategic group**. The firm that carries out that strategy best will make the most profits. International Harvester went out of the farm equipment business because it did not stand out in its industry as lowest in cost, highest in customer-perceived value or best in serving some market segments.[54]

Porter draws a distinction between operational effectiveness and strategy. Competitors can quickly copy the operationally effective company using benchmarking and other tools, thus diminishing the advantage of operational effectiveness. Porter defines strategy as 'the creation of a unique and valuable position involving a different set of activities'.

A company can claim that it has a strategy when it 'performs different activities from rivals or performs similar activities in different ways'.

Strategic alliances

Even giant companies – IBM, Philips, Nokia and Unilever – often cannot achieve leadership, either nationally or globally, without forming alliances with domestic or multinational companies that complement or enhance their capabilities and resources. The Dutch company Philips formed a strategic alliance with Dell to collaborate on the development of a range of electronic items such as computer monitors. The European aircraft manufacturers formed a strategic alliance to create the Airbus to compete successfully with their arch US rival Boeing. The Finnish company Nokia negotiated a strategic alliance with the German fixed-line company Siemens.

Just doing business in another country may require the firm to license its market offerings, form a joint venture with a local firm or buy from local suppliers to meet local 'domestic content' requirements. As a result, many firms are rapidly developing global strategic networks, and success goes to those who build the better global network. The Star Alliance, for example, brings together 18 airlines, including Lufthansa, United Airlines, Singapore Airlines, Air New Zealand and South Africa Airways, into a huge global partnership that allows travellers to make nearly seamless connections to hundreds of destinations.

Many strategic alliances take the form of marketing alliances. These fall into four major categories.

1 **Product or service alliances**. One company licenses another to provide its market offering (customer-perceived value offering), or two companies jointly market their complementary market offerings or combine resources to produce a new market offering. The credit card industry, for example, has a variety of cards jointly marketed by banks such as Royal Bank of Scotland and Crédit Lyonnais; credit card companies such as Visa; and affinity companies such as Virgin.

2 **Promotional alliances**. One company agrees to carry a marketing communication promotion for another company's market offering. McDonald's, for example, teamed up with Disney for ten years to provide offerings related to current Disney films as part of its meals for children strategy.

3 **Logistics alliances**. One company offers logistical services for another company's market offering. For example, BP has formed an alliance with the Russian company TNK to further oil exploration and extraction.

4 **Pricing collaborations**. One or more companies join in a special pricing collaboration. Hotel, car rental and sea ferry companies often offer mutual price discounts.

Companies need to give creative thought to finding partners that might complement their strengths and offset their weaknesses. Well-managed alliances allow companies to obtain a greater sales impact at less cost. To keep their strategic alliances thriving, corporations have begun to develop organisational structures to support them, and many have come to view the ability to form and manage partnerships as core skills called **partner relationship management** (PRM).[55]

Programme formulation and implementation

Even a sound marketing strategy can be sabotaged by poor implementation. If a company has decided to attain technological leadership, it must plan programmes to strengthen its R&D department, gather technological intelligence, develop leading-edge market offerings, train the technical sales force and develop advertisements to communicate its technological leadership.

Once they have formulated marketing programmes, the marketing people must estimate their costs. Is participating in a particular trade show worth it? Will a specific sales contest pay for itself? Will hiring another salesperson contribute to the bottom line? **Activity-based**

cost (ABC) accounting can help determine whether each initiative in a marketing programme is likely to produce sufficient results to justify its costs.[56]

Today's businesses are also increasingly recognising that unless they nurture other stakeholders – customers, employees, suppliers, distributors – they may never earn sufficient profits for the stockholders. For example, a company might aim to delight its customers, perform well for its employees and deliver a threshold level of satisfaction to its suppliers. In setting these levels a company must be careful not to violate any stakeholder group's sense of fairness about the treatment they receive relative to others.[57]

A dynamic relationship connects the stakeholder groups. A smart company creates a high level of employee satisfaction, which requires an increased effort, which leads to higher-quality market offerings. This in turn creates higher customer satisfaction and leads to repeat business. This generates higher growth and profits and higher stockholder satisfaction, which results in more investment. This virtuous circle spells profits and growth. The marketing insight box highlights the increasing importance of the proper bottom-line view to marketing expenditures.

According to McKinsey & Company, strategy is only one of seven elements – all of which start with the letter 's' – in successful business practice.[58] The first three – strategy, structure and systems – are considered the 'hardware' of success. The next four – style, skills, staff and shared values – are the 'software'.

The first 'soft' element, *style*, means that company employees share a common way of thinking and behaving. McDonald's employees smile at the customer, and British Gas employees are very professional in their customer dealings. The second element, *skills*, means that employees have the skills needed to carry out the company's strategy. *Staffing* means that the company has hired able people, trained them well and assigned them to

Marketing insight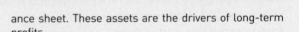

Marketing's contribution to shareholder value

Companies normally focus on maximising profits rather than shareholder value. Doyle argues that profit maximisation leads to short-term planning and under-investment in marketing, promoting a focus on building sales, market share and current profits. It also leads to cost cutting and shedding assets to produce quick improvements in earnings, and erodes a company's long-term competitiveness by eliminating investment in new market opportunities.

Companies normally measure their profit performance using ROI (return on investment), calculated by dividing profits by investment. This method presents two problems:

1 Profits are arbitrarily measured and subject to manipulation. Cash flow is more important. As someone observed: 'Profits are a matter of opinion; cash is a fact.'

2 Investment ignores the real value of the firm. More of a company's value resides in its intangible marketing assets – brands, market knowledge, customer relationships and partner relationships – than in its balance sheet. These assets are the drivers of long-term profits.

Doyle posits that marketing will not mature as a profession until it can demonstrate the impact of marketing on shareholder value, which is defined by the market value of a company minus its debt. The market value is the share price times the number of shares outstanding. The share price reflects what investors estimate is the present value of the future lifetime earnings of a company. When management is choosing a marketing strategy, Doyle wants it to apply shareholder value analysis (SVA) to see which alternative course of action will maximise shareholder value.

If Doyle's argument is accepted, instead of seeing marketing as a specific function concerned only with increasing sales or market share, senior management will see it as an integral part of the whole management process. It will judge marketing by how much it contributes to shareholder value by delivering consistently high levels of customer-perceived value.

Source: Based on P. Doyle (2000) *Value-Based Marketing: Marketing Strategies for Corporate Growth and Shareholder Value*, Chichester: John Wiley & Sons.

the right jobs. The fourth element, *shared values*, means that employees share the same corporate culture values. When these elements are present, companies are usually more successful at strategy implementation.[59]

Another study of management practices found that superior performance over time depended on flawless execution, a company culture based on aiming high, a structure that is flexible and responsive, and a strategy that is clear and focused.[60]

Feedback and control

(See also Chapter 22.)

A company's strategic fit with the environment will inevitably erode, because the market environment changes faster than the company's 7Ss. Thus, a company might remain efficient while it loses effectiveness. Drucker pointed out that it is more important to 'do the right thing' – to be effective – than 'to do things right' – to be efficient. The most successful companies excel at both.

Once an organisation fails to respond to a changed environment, it becomes increasingly hard to recapture its lost position. Consider how the fortunes of the Lotus Development Corporation have waned. Its Lotus 1-2-3 software was once the world's leading software program, and now its market share in desktop software has slipped so low that analysts largely ignore it.

Organisations, especially large ones, are subject to inertia. It is difficult to change one part without adjusting everything else. Yet organisations can be changed through strong leadership, preferably in advance of a crisis. The key to organisational health is willingness to examine the changing environment and adopt new goals and strategies.

Change today, not tomorrow

Here are some words of wisdom from John Whybrow, Chairman, Wolseley.

> **Business leaders need to be alert to the changing landscape and respond swiftly to changing circumstances – today rather than tomorrow.**

> **Managers and directors are generally slow to respond to change. We wait for tomorrow. The truth is, we shouldn't wait. We should do it now.**

> **If only we'd looked at those issues ten or five years earlier, we wouldn't have had such a dramatic state of affairs to contend with.**

> **The world is not going to be recreated in our image; the world will do what it wants to do. We must respond, and respond today, not tomorrow.**[61]

The nature and content of a marketing plan

Working within the plans set by the levels above them, marketing managers develop a marketing plan for individual markets, lines, brands, channels or customer groups. Each level, whether line or brand, must develop a marketing plan for achieving its goals. A marketing plan is a written document that summarises what the marketer has learned about the marketplace and indicates how the firm plans to reach its marketing objectives.[62] It contains tactical guidelines for the marketing programmes and financial allocations over the planning period.[63] It is one of the most important outputs of the marketing process.

Marketing plans are becoming more customer- and competitor-oriented, and better reasoned and more realistic than in the past, as most markets become increasingly competitive. They draw more inputs from all business functions and are team developed. Planning is becoming a continuous process in order to respond to rapidly changing market conditions.

Most marketing plans cover one year in 5–50 pages. The most frequently cited short-comings of current marketing plans, according to marketing executives, are lack of realism, insufficient competitive analysis and a short-run focus. (See the marketing memo box for some guideline questions to ask in developing marketing plans.)

What, then, does a marketing plan look like? What does it contain?

Contents of the marketing plan[64]

The marketing plan should contain the following elements:

1 **Executive summary and table of contents**. The marketing plan should open with a brief summary for senior management of the main goals and recommendations. A table of contents outlines the rest of the plan and all the supporting rationale and operational detail.

2 **Situation analysis (context)**. This section presents relevant background data on sales, costs, the market, competitors, and the various forces in the macro-environment. How do we define the market, how big is it, and how fast is it growing? What are the relevant trends? What is the customer-perceived value of the market offering and what critical issues does the company face? Firms will use all this information to carry out a SWOT (strengths, weaknesses, opportunities, threats) analysis.

3 **Marketing strategy (customer, competition, channel and company strategic approach)**. Here the product marketing manager defines the mission, marketing and financial objectives, and groups and needs that the market offerings are intended to satisfy. The manager then establishes the company's competitive positioning, which will inform the 'game plan' to accomplish the plan's objectives. All this requires inputs from other business functions, such as purchasing, manufacturing, sales, finance and human resources.

4 **Financial projections (cash analysis)**. Financial projections include a sales forecast, an expense forecast and a break-even analysis. On the revenue side, the projections show the forecast sales volume by market portfolio category. On the expense side, they show the expected costs of marketing, broken down into finer categories. The break-even analysis shows how many units the firm must sell monthly to offset its monthly fixed costs and average per-unit variable costs.

5 **Implementation controls**. The last section of the marketing plan outlines the controls for monitoring and adjusting implementation of the plan. Typically, it spells out the

Marketing memo

Marketing plan criteria

Here are some questions to ask in evaluating a marketing plan.

1 Is the plan simple? Is it easy to understand and act on? Does it communicate its content clearly and practically?

2 Is the plan specific? Are its objectives concrete and measurable? Does it include specific actions and activities, each with specific dates of completion, specific persons responsible, and specific budgets?

3 Is the plan realistic? Are the sales goals, expense budgets and milestone dates realistic? Has a frank and honest self-critique been conducted to raise possible concerns and objections?

4 Is the plan complete? Does it include all the necessary elements? Does it have the right breadth and depth?

Source: Based on T. Berry and D. Wilson (2000) *On Target: The Book on Marketing Plans*, Eugene, OR: Palo Alto Software.

goals and budget for each month or quarter, so management can review each period's results and take corrective action as needed. Firms must also take a number of different internal and external measures to assess progress and suggest possible modifications. Some organisations include contingency plans outlining the steps management would take in response to specific environmental developments, such as price wars or strikes.

Sample marketing plan: Euromart

Introduction

The eight themes featured in this book reflect the key interests of marketing managers (see Figure 3.11). In today's competitive business environment, companies need to be constantly aware of the characteristics and developments in both domestic and international markets. This requires a commitment to carrying out both *ad hoc* and continuous market research. Resources are under increasing pressure as companies across the globe seek to find a place in the marketplace, so individual firms need to be able to harness new methods and technology to measure their cost, revenue and profit performances.

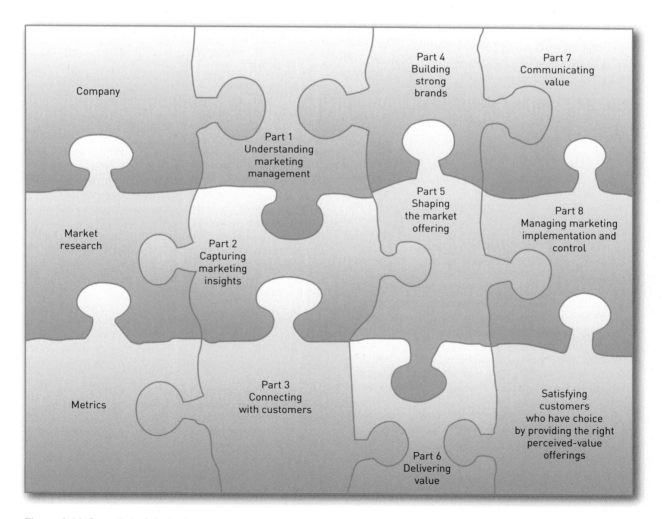

Figure 3.11 Snapshot of the text

The ultimate task of marketers is to guide and assist their companies to secure satisfied or preferably delighted customers. This book explores the tasks facing marketing managers in the pursuit of meeting customers' perceived value requirements, which emerge from a series of inputs from customers, value chain members and other stakeholders. The art/science of the successful company is to incorporate the detail of what customers really want and supply this efficiently and profitably in times of rampant global competition – not an easy task.

The key tasks of marketers are outlined in the marketing memo box 'Getting started'.

Marketing memo

Getting started

The key tasks facing marketers are:

1 to have an understanding of marketing management (Part 1);

2 to capture marketing insights (Part 2);

3 to successfully connect with customers (Part 3);

4 to build strong brands (Part 4);

5 to shape the marketing offering (Part 5);

6 to deliver value (Part 6);

7 to communicate value (Part 7);

8 to successfully manage and control the implementation of marketing activity (Part 8).

Chapter 21 closes with the marketing memo box 'Getting to grips with the practice of marketing', which is designed to assist marketers and students to bridge the sometimes troublesome gap between marketing theory and practice; between knowledge and the ability to put that into practice and thus develop *know-how*.

Wise companies and marketers set out to delight their customers – whether consumer or business-to-business – by successfully researching context (market situation); customer (requirements); competition (relevant competitive offers); cash implications (money in – revenue, and money out – expenditure, e.g. on market research, offer development and supply); and channels (distribution and marketing communications aspects). In addition they need to accept the underpinning marketing philosophy that in buyers' markets the customer needs to be a prime focus for the firm.

The next section presents a sample marketing plan featuring the fictional Euromart Company.

Euromart marketing plan

1 Executive summary

2 Contextual/situational analysis

3 Customer analysis/marketing strategy I

4 Competition analysis/marketing strategy II

5 Company strategic approach/marketing strategy III

6 Channel analysis/marketing strategy IV

7 Cash analysis/financial projections

8 Marketing management implementation and control

1 Executive summary

Euromart is a new company that has recently been founded to provide books, computer hardware and software and electrical appliance offerings for students. The company is based in Copenhagen but rents premises on the mainstream university campuses in Eire, Netherlands, Norway, Sweden and the United Kingdom. Other branches are planned to open in 2009/10 in France, Germany, Russia and Spain. Euromart trades through its campus retail outlets and has developed a sophisticated online business.

Exhaustive market research has been carried out in both the mainstream university campuses where Euromart has shops and among its growing number of online customers. As a result there are ambitious plans under way to broaden the company's appeal by establishing new market offerings in the financial services and travel industries.

Euromart is run by a small, highly motivated management team who have all graduated from mainstream universities in the last five years. The company's mission is to provide quality offerings at prices that are affordable to students. Euromart sees its offerings as being a combination of customer-perceived value product and service attributes.

To maintain the company's initial early successes, net profits grew by 70 per cent in the first three years of operation. Euromart firmly believes in the benefits of sound medium- and long-range planning to prosper the business.

▶ Marketing memo (continued)

2 Contextual analysis
2.1 Market environment
   2.1.1 Euromart currently operates separate businesses in five European countries with plans to expand into four more in the next two years.
   2.1.2 The business environment in each operating country is constantly monitored by means of political, economic, socio-cultural, technological, legal and environ-mental profiling (PESTLE analysis).
   2.1.3 Each market is researched to identify whether it is a sellers' or a buyers' market. Buyers' markets (where supply exceeds demand, giving rise to fierce competition) are managed with a firm resolve to pro-vide customers with the right customer-perceived value offerings.
2.2 Market entry
   2.2.1 All main means of entering new national markets are researched to determine the best method for the company (e.g. own business, partnership, strategic alliance).
   2.2.2 All expansions of the existing business in each country are researched country by country so the range of offerings available in each country varies according to local requirements.

3 Customer analysis
3.1 Customer markets
   3.1.1 Euromart markets to individual student cus-tomers in its portfolio of national markets.
   3.1.2 The company also has a thriving business-to-business interest in its national market portfolios.
3.2 Segmentation, targeting and positioning
   3.2.1 Each national market is carefully seg-mented to reveal attractive target markets by means of demographics, **geodemo-graphics** and behavioural factors.
   3.2.2 Euromart supplies offering portfolios for full-time, part-time, distance learning, executive and mature students.
   3.2.3 Each national market senior executive is responsible for meeting corporate head-quarters' targets but does have some free-dom to calculate the best positioning of resources that are released by the Copen-hagen head office.
3.3 Branding
   3.3.1 Each national company is empowered to 'develop the Euromart brand'.

3.3.2 Each national company is free to research and make a case to the Copenhagen head office for new market offering ventures.

4 Competition analysis
4.1 Identify major competitors.
4.2 Assess major competitors' strengths and weaknesses.
4.3 Select competitors to attack and avoid.

5 Company strategic approach
5.1 Mission
   5.1.1 To treat customers as Euromart's best friends and to deliver the best purchasing experience.
5.2 Marketing strategy
   5.2.1 Build the Euromart brand as the 'student's friend'.
   5.2.2 Grow the company profitably in existing countries and expand into carefully selected countries on the back of a positive overall profit performance.
   5.2.3 Maintain customer purchase standards and continuously monitor customer satisfaction to build Euromart's brand reputation.
   5.2.4 Target markets – students, books, com-puters and electrical appliances.
   5.2.5 Positioning – three market offering ranges – essential (market entry), value plus (mid-market) and premium (niche).
   5.2.6 Develop customer awareness and then expand the target market offering portfolio.
   5.2.7 Seek to maximise use of modern digital and Internet marketing strategies.

6 Channel analysis
6.1 Distribution
   6.1.1 Design appropriate global and local supply networks for both consumer and business-to-business markets.
   6.1.2 Continuously monitor performance of supply networks to secure efficiency and effectiveness of the Euromart customer-perceived value interface
6.2 Marketing communication
   6.2.1 Design and implement suitable corporate marketing communications programme.
   6.2.2 Design and implement suitable consumer (student) marketing communications pro-grammes for all active national markets
   6.2.3 Design and implement suitable business-to-business marketing communications pro-grammes for each active national market
   6.2.4 Seek to maximise use of digital and inter-net marketing communications.

▶ Marketing memo *(continued)*

7 Cash analysis

7.1 Control expenditure (money out)

    7.1.1 Maintain tight but appropriate financial control.

    7.1.2 Set budgets for headquarters activities (e.g. corporate marketing communications, staffing).

    7.1.3 Set budgets for each national branch by market offering categories (i.e. books, computer items and electrical appliances) for both consumer (student) and business-to-business markets.

7.2 Revenue (money in)

    7.2.1 Forecast sales in each national branch

    7.2.2 Segment sales forecast in each national branch by market offering categories and consumer and business-to-business markets.

8 Marketing management implementation and control

8.1 Euromart supports a marketing-oriented culture to provide market offerings that meet customers' expectations by placing a strong emphasis on market research to discover market contextual data, customer requirements, the activities of competitors and the most appropriate way to run their channel operations (distribution and marketing communications). Market research is extended to staff, the supply/value chain and interested stakeholders. Euromart is characterised by a customer relationship approach to running its business.

8.2 Euromart headquarters has a minimal headcount.

8.3 All budget holders will be incentivised to hit and improve both their sales forecast and profit targets.

8.4 Headquarters management foster and encourage creativity and innovation throughout the business.

9 Contingency plans

9.1 This section describes actions to be taken by Euromart if specific threats or opportunities materialise during the planning period.

9.2 Actions to counter sudden changes in the business environment (e.g. the credit crunch, escalating fuel costs).

9.3 Actions to contain any invasive competitor's moves.

Source: Checklist adapted from K. Kashani and D. Turpin (1999) *Marketing Management* (Section 1), IMD: Lausanne, published by Macmillan Business, and reproduced with permission from Palgrave Macmillan.

SUMMARY

1 The customer-perceived value delivery process involves choosing (or identifying), providing (or delivering) and communicating superior customer-perceived value. The value chain is a tool for identifying key activities that create value and costs in a specific business.

2 Strong companies develop superior capabilities in managing core business processes such as new market offering realisation, inventory management, and customer acquisition and retention. Managing these core processes effectively means creating a marketing network in which the company works closely with all parties in the production and distribution chain, from suppliers of raw materials to retail distributors. Companies no longer compete – marketing networks do.

3 According to one view, holistic marketing maximises value exploration by understanding the relationships between the customer's cognitive space, the company's competence space and the collaborator's resource space. It maximises value creation by identifying new customer benefits from the customer's cognitive space, utilising core competencies from its business domain, and selecting and managing business partners from its collaborative networks. It also maximises value delivery by becoming proficient at customer relationship management, internal resource management and business partnership management.

4 Market-oriented strategic planning is the managerial process of developing and maintaining a viable fit between the organisation's objectives, skills and resources and its changing market opportunities. The aim of strategic planning is to shape the company's businesses and market activities so that they yield target profits and growth. Strategic planning takes place at four levels: corporate, division, business unit and

market offering (customer-perceived value product and service mix).

5 The corporate strategy establishes the framework within which the divisions and business units prepare their strategic plans. Setting a corporate strategy entails four activities: defining the corporate mission, establishing strategic business units (SBUs), assigning resources to each SBU based on its market attractiveness and business strength, and planning new businesses and downsizing older businesses.

6 Strategic planning for individual businesses entails the following activities: defining the business mission, analysing external opportunities and threats, analysing internal strengths and weaknesses, formulating goals, formulating strategy, formulating supporting programmes, implementing the programmes, and gathering feedback and exercising control.

7 Each market offering programme within a business unit must develop a marketing plan for achieving its goals. The marketing plan is one of the most important outputs of the marketing management process.

APPLICATIONS
Marketing debate

What good is a mission statement?

Virtually all firms have mission statements to help guide and inspire employees as well as signal what is important to the firm and to those outside the firm. Mission statements are often the result of much deliberation and discussion. At the same time, some critics claim that mission statements sometimes lack 'teeth' and specificity. Moreover, critics also maintain that in many cases mission statements do not vary much from firm to firm, and make the same empty promises.

Take a position: Mission statements are critical to a successful marketing organisation *versus* Mission statements rarely provide useful marketing value.

Marketing discussion

Consider Porter's value chain and the holistic marketing orientation model. What implications do they have for marketing planning? How would you structure a marketing plan to incorporate some of their concepts?

REFERENCES

[1]See www.siemens.com/press/en/materials.php

[2]N. Kumar (2004) *Marketing As Strategy: The CEO's Agenda for Driving Growth and Innovation*, Boston, MA: Harvard Business School Press.

[3]F. E. Webster, Jr (1997) The future role of marketing in the organization, in D. R. Lehmann and K. Jocz (eds), *Reflections on the Futures of Marketing*, Cambridge, MA: Marketing Science Institute, pp. 39–66.

[4]B. T. Gale (1995) *Managing Customer Value*, New York: Free Press.

[5]M. E. Porter (1985) *Competitive Advantage: Creating and Sustaining Superior Performance*, New York: Free Press.

[6]R. Hiebeler, T. B. Kelly and C. Ketteman (1998) *Best Practices: Building Your Business with Customer-Focused Solutions*, New York: Simon and Schuster; J. Pine, D. Peppers and M. Rogers (2009) *Do You Want to Keep Your Customers For Ever?*, Cambridge, MA: Harvard Business School Press; A. S. Bigger and L. B. Bigger (2010) Lessons from the storms of life; measure today to survive tomorrow, *Executive Housekeeping Today*, 32(3), 6–9. See also www.businessdictionary.com/definition/best-practice.html; www.dinesh.com/History_of_Logos/Worlds_Best_Brands_and_Logos.html.

[7]L. Lewis (2007) Toyota sets out vision of greener future, *The Times*, 12 November. See also http://blog.toyota.co.uk/the-toyota-global-vision and for 2011 update of the Toyota Global Vision see www.earthtimes.org/articles/press/toyota-unveils-global-vision,1702203.html.

[8]M. Hammer and J. Champy (1993) *Reengineering the Corporation: A Manifesto for Business Revolution*, New York: Harper Business; M. Maleki, and D. Anand (2008) The critical success factors in customer relationship management (CRM)(ERP) implementation, *Journal of Marketing and Communication*, 4(2), 67–80.

[9]J. R. Katzenbach and D. K. Smith (1993) *The Wisdom of Teams: Creating the High-Performance Organization*, Boston, MA: Harvard Business School Press; Hammer and Champy (1993), op. cit; A. S. Carr, K. Hale and S. Muthusamy (2008) The cross functional coordination between operations, marketing, purchasing and engineering and the impact on performance, *International Journal of Manufacturing Technology and Management*, 13(1), 55–77.

[10] R. Rigby (2007) Trailblazers with tinkering time on their hands, *Financial Times*, 6 November.

[11] C. K. Prahalad and G. Hamel (1990) The core competence of the corporation, *Harvard Business Review*, May–June, 79–91.

[12] C. K. Prahalad and G. Hamel (1994) *Competing for the Future*, Cambridge, MA: Harvard Business School Press.

[13] C. K. Prahalad and V. Ramaswamy (2000) Co-opting customer competency, *Harvard Business Review*, 1 January, 79–90.

[14] R. Waters (2007) Microsoft defends its diversification, *Financial Times*, 27 July.

[15] E. Unsworth (2006) ILVA an IKEA beater?, *Manchester Evening News*, 28 August; R. Fletcher (2007) ILVA sold to Icelandic furniture group, *Daily Telegraph*, 2 August; T. Braithwaite (2008) Backers pull the plug on ILVA UK, *Financial Times*, 26 June.

[16] G. S. Day (1994) The capabilities of market-driven organizations, *Journal of Marketing*, October, 38.

[17] G. S. Day and P. J. H. Schoemaker (2006) *Peripheral Vision: Detecting the Weak Signals That Will Make or Break Your Company*, Cambridge, MA: Harvard Business School Press.

[18] L. Lazaroff (2006) Kodak's big picture focusing on image change, *Chicago Tribune*, 29 January, 5, 9; H. C. Lucas Jr and J. M. Goh (2009) Disruptive technology: how Kodak missed the digital photography revolution, *Journal of Strategic Information Systems*, 18(1), 46–55.

[19] S. London (2002) The future means getting personal, *Financial Times*, 12 December.

[20] K. Ushikubo (1986) A method of structure analysis for developing product concepts and its applications, *European Research*, 14(4), 174–5; W. O. Maznah (2009) The mediating effect of cognitive and emotional satisfaction on customer loyalty, *International Journal of Management Innovation Systems*, 1(2), 1–13.

[21] Y. J. Wind and V. Mahajan with R. E. Gunther (2002) *Convergence Marketing: Strategies for Reaching the New Hybrid Consumer*, Upper Saddle River, NJ: Prentice Hall.

[22] P. Drucker (1973) *Management: Tasks, Responsibilities and Practices*, New York: Harper and Row, Chapter 7.

[23] R. A. Oliva (2001) Nowhere to hide, *Marketing Management*, July/August, 44–6.

[24] *The Economist Miscellany* (2005), London: Profile Books, pp. 32–3. See also www.google.co.uk/corporate.

[25] A. Sangera (2005) Too many mission statements, *Financial Times*, 22 July. See also www.avis.com/car-rental/content/display.ac?navId=T6M21S01.

[26] J. F. Rayport and B. J. Jaworski (2001) *e-commerce*, New York: McGraw-Hill, p. 116.

[27] T. Kemmler, M. Kubicova, R. Musslewhite and R. Prezeau (2001) E-performance II: the good, the bad, and the merely average, *McKinsey Quarterly* (mckinseyquarterly.com).

[28] This section is based on Chapter 16 of R. M. Grant (2005) *Contemporary Strategy Analysis*, 5th edn, Malden, MA: Blackwell Publishing.

[29] The same matrix can be expanded into nine cells by adding modified products and modified markets. See S. J. Johnson and C. Jones (1957) How to organize for new products, *Harvard Business Review*, May–June, 49–62.

[30] See www.starbucks.com; H. Schultz (1997) *Pour Your Heart Into It*, New York: Hyperion; A. Serwer (2004) Hot Starbucks to go, *Fortune*, 26 January, pp. 60–74; A. Ward (2007) Why Schultz has caused a stir at Starbucks, *Guardian*, 26 February.

[31] PepsiCo company website (www.pepsico.com). For small business application see J. Wiklund, H. Patzelt and D. Shepherd (2009) Building an integrative model of small business growth, *Small Business Economics*, 32(4), 351–74.

[32] B. White (2006) Expanding into consumer electronics, Cisco aims to jazz up its stodgy image, *Wall Street Journal*, 6 September, p. B1.

[33] M. Ruch (2006) Saltzgitter aims for diversification, *Financial Times*, 16 August; K. Coyne, (2008) *Plastics News*, 21 January, 19(46), 3.

[34] D. Blackwell (2007) Diversification bolsters Cussons, *Financial Times*, 1 August.

[35] R. Waters (2007) Microsoft defends its diversification, *Financial Times*, 27 July.

[36] M. Mulligan (2007) Alierta spells out Telefonica growth plans, *Financial Times*, 12 October.

[37] PepsiCo company website (www.pepsico.com).

[38] E. J. McCarthy (1996) *Basic Marketing: A Managerial Approach*, 12th edn, Homewood, IL: Irwin.

[39] Dyson company website (www.dyson.co.uk).

[40] C. K. Prahalad and G. Hamel (1990) The core competence of the corporation, *Harvard Business Review*, May–June, 79–91.

[41] Jump Associates.

[42] Rigby (2007), op. cit.

[43] M. Gorman (2007) Icon celebrates its success, *Marketing Week*, 27 September.

[44] K. Jackson (2006) BMW benefits from audio books, *Automotive News Europe*, 11(20), 15.

[45] C. Grande (2007) Advertisers eye hip sites as testing ground, *Financial Times*, 29 June.

[46] A. Yee (2007) A cash lifeline for the rural poor, *Financial Times*, 12 June; Reserve Bank of India, *Annual Report 2009–2010*.

[47] P. J. H. Shoemaker (1995) Scenario planning: a tool for strategic thinking, *Sloan Management Review*, Winter, 25–40. See www.search.shell.com/search?_utma=32229756.1049589686.1303638774.1303638774.1303638774.1&_utmb=32229756.3.10.1303638774&_utmc=32229756&_utmx=-&_utmz=32229756.1303638774.1.1.utmcsr=(direct)|utmccn=(direct)|utmcmd=(none)&_utmv=-&_utmk=13051317 for information on Shell scenario planning activities.

[48] P. Kotler (1999) *Kotler on Marketing*, New York: Free Press.

[49] T. Hill and R. Westbrook (1997) SWOT analysis: it's time for a product recall, *Long Range Planning*, 30 (February), 46–52; E. K. Valentin (2001) SWOT analysis from a resource-based view, *Journal of Marketing Theory and Practice*, 9(2), 54–70.

[50] D. Dodd and K. Favaro (2006) Managing the right tension, *Harvard Business Review*, December, 62–74.

[51] R. Charan and N. M. Tichy (1998) *Every Business Is a Growth Business: How Your Company Can Prosper Year After Year*, New York: Time Business/Random House.

[52] M. E. Porter (1980) *Competitive Strategy: Techniques for Analyzing Industries and Competitors*, New York: Free Press, Chapter 2.

[53] S. C. Miller (2006) It protects electronic devices from power surges and gives dust bunnies no place to hide, *New York Times*, 14 September, p. C10; See also www.belkin.com/pressroom/release/uploads/08_15_06Concealed_CompactSurge.hml.

[54] M. E. Porter (1996) What is strategy?, *Harvard Business Review*, November–December, 61–78.

55For some recent interesting readings on strategic alliances, see R. Agarwal, R. Croson and J. T. Mahoney (2010) The role of incentives and communication in strategic alliances: an experimental investigation, *Strategic Management Journal*, 31(4), 413–37; H. R. Greve, J. A. C. Baum, H. Mitsuhashi and T. J. Rowley (2010) Built to last but falling apart: cohesion, friction and withdrawal from interfirm alliances, *Academy of Management Journal*, 53(2), 302–22; J. Hong and H. Yu (2010) A research on influential factors related to the stability of competition-oriented strategic alliances, *International Journal of Business and Management*, 5(11), 148–51; C. E. Ybarra, E. Candace and T. A. Turk (2011) Strategic alliances with competing firms and shareholder value, *Journal of Management and Marketing Research*, January, Vol. 6, 1–10.

56R. Cooper and R. S. Kaplan (1991) Profit priorities from activity-based costing, *Harvard Business Review*, May–June, 130–5.

57As a tool for monitoring stakeholder satisfaction, see R. S. Kaplan and D. P. Norton (1996) *The Balanced Scorecard: Translating Strategy into Action*, Boston, MA: Harvard Business School Press.

58T. J. Peters and R. H. Waterman, Jr (1982) *In Search of Excellence: Lessons from America's Best-Run Companies*, New York: Harper Row, pp. 9–12. See also 'Enduring ideas' in *McKinsey Quarterly*, 2008, issue 2, following p. 125.

59See www.themanager.org/Models/7S%20Model.htm for explanation of the McKinsey 7S model.

60N. Nohria, W. Joyce and B. Roberson (2003) What really works, *Harvard Business Review*, 81(7), 42–53.

61*Mastering Change* (2005), London: BBC Books.

62M. B. Wood (2003) *The Marketing Plan: A Handbook,* Upper Saddle River, NJ: Prentice Hall.

63D. R. Lehmann and R. S. Winer (2001) *Product Management*, 3rd edn, Boston, MA: McGraw-Hill/Irwin.

64See the Euromart sample marketing plan described in the closing marketing memo to this chapter.

Chapter 4

Managing digital technology in marketing

IN THIS CHAPTER, WE WILL ADDRESS THE FOLLOWING QUESTIONS:

1 What is the range and scope of digital technologies in marketing?

2 How should digital technology be managed?

3 What are the main digital technologies in marketing?

4 How can marketers analyse and understand consumer digital shopping behaviour?

5 What is consumer digital interactivity?

Managing digital technology in marketing can be both challenging and fun
Source: © vanlev/fotolia.com

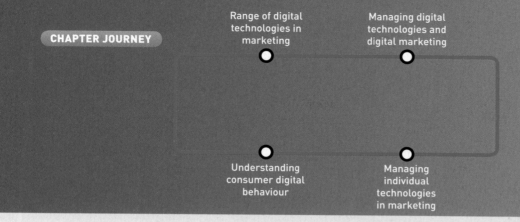

Range of digital
technologies in
marketing

Managing digital
technologies and
digital marketing

Understanding
consumer digital
behaviour

Managing
individual
technologies
in marketing

Technological advances in the last ten years have fundamentally changed how we live, how we practise marketing and how business operates. Digital technologies are challenging the strategies, structures and operations of many businesses and forcing marketers to rethink their understanding of consumer behaviour.[1] Consumers and businesses now operate in a networked technology-based world with internet, mobile phones, constant communications, self-service technologies, online shopping, instant messaging and social networking. Consumers spend almost half their waking hours using a proliferation of technology, including online browsing, purchasing and social networking, mobile phone use and/or watching television.[2] Marketing managers engage with a wide range of technologies, including databases, email, internets, intranets, extranets, computer networks, planning software, CRM systems, social networking and so on. As Chris Anderson, author of *The Long Tail* notes, 'we are in the new era of networked consumers and digital everything'.[3] Technology is so crucial to marketing that the spelling of marketing could include information technology (IT) and be changed to MarkITing.[4] Technology is now embedded in business and consumer life, and the skills needed to manage technology and to understand how customers use it are core requirements for marketing managers. Take Burberry.

Burberry is a company that really embraces technology within marketing and throughout their business. Both Christopher Bailey, the chief creative officer and Angela Ahrendts, the chief executive are core believers in the power of digital technologies to enhance their marketing, from building and supporting their brand image to helping with ongoing engagement and relationship building with their customers. For example the Burberry Spring Fashion show engaged with customers across a range of technologies including social networking sites, their internet site and iPads. Customers could *click to buy* the latest version of the classic Burberry trench or any items from the spring range, in real time on their own or store supplied iPads. A fashion and technology first from Burberry was the linking of both mobile and broadcast technology with a live broadcast of the Burberry fashion show in high definition (HD) and 3D to anyone with a smart phone and to HD theatres set up in Burberry shops in Paris, New York, Dubai, Tokyo, and Los Angeles.

Burberry has also focused on online sales which have increased by over 60 per cent since they launched their social networking site, called Art of the Trench. This site is used by consumers who love Burberry and who take photos of themselves and others in their Burberry trench coats and then share these images on line.

This provides the customer with a forum to discuss with other customers and also provides Burberry with great research and feedback on their products. Bailey says that he looks at the site for ideas. He says that designing fashion and designing a web based business are similar – each creates with the customer in mind. He says that nowadays 'It's about staying connected . . . Brands are more and more multidimensional . . . It's about an *experience* as well as buying a product. And I think what we've found is that the more we entertain, the more we allow people *into* our brand'.

In an era when companies have 'friends', Burberry has made social-networking history: friended by one million people in its first year on Facebook, it then reached two million in the next six months, and in one month more the company was at the three million mark – inspiring Joanna Shields, vice president for Facebook Europe, Middle East, and Africa, to call Burberry 'a thriving media enterprise' and 'the most widely followed fashion brand on Facebook'. Bailey and Burberry are also looking to future digital technologies like location based information. With the use of iPhones and tracking software, location based information can be fed to customers so whether they are in Paris or Milan, if they pass a Burberry window, a message could be sent that would say 'you're at Burberry, and this product is available here and in this size'.[5]

Digital technologies in marketing

Digital technologies are transforming how marketers reach, engage and deliver value to customers. In a digital age, organisations must understand how customer networks behave and how to be innovative with the products, services, communications and relationships that their customers seek. The rise of digital technologies has transformed marketing. Marketers today face a constant proliferation of digital technologies, media channels, the

Nike – Tune your Run
Source: Stuart Franklin/
Getty Images

growing power of the connected customer, powerful databases and dashboard technology to monitor, manage and analyse data and information, and an explosion of new digital challenges. To succeed, marketers must be able to plan, implement and measure digital strategies that are suited to today's customers and integrated with their traditional marketing and business practices. Nike developed a running shoe with iPod technology which provides statistics, music and motivation for runners in its 'Tune your Run' campaign. This engages with customers through technology to form a bond between the customer and the company's product. The management of the bond is the marketing challenge which is supported by technology.

Understanding digital technology and digital marketing

Digital technology is digitised information which is recorded in binary code as combinations of the digits 0 and 1, also called bits, which represent words and images. This enables immense amounts of information to be compressed on small storage devices that can be easily preserved and transported. Digitisation also quickens data transmission speeds. Digital technology is primarily used with new physical communications media, such as satellite and fibre optic transmission. When information, music, voice and video are turned into binary digital form, they can be electronically manipulated, preserved and regenerated perfectly at high speed. For example, music can be downloaded and distributed over and over again, to the concern of the music industry and to the joy of the music lover.

Digital marketing has a similar meaning to electronic marketing: both describe the management and execution of marketing using electronic or digital media such as the web, email, interactive TV, wireless media, mobile technology and self-service technology, in conjunction with digital data from a range of databases and software applications.[6] Digital marketing is an integrated and essential part of marketing efforts. Recent global research by Chartered Marketing Officers (CMO) Council members, seeking to define the new 'DNA of Marketing Directors', indicates that being 'digitally savvy' and 'customer centric' are top characteristics of successful senior marketers. A *Marketing Outlook* 2010 survey found that digital marketing skills were the number-one priority, with sales and marketing alignment and customer data integration and analytics as numbers two and three respectively. Other studies, such as 'Routes to Revenue' and 'Giving Customer Voice More Volume', have consistently shown that improved and more relevant customer communications, data analytics and digital channels are at the forefront of marketers' thinking.[7] This is demonstrated by the example of Zara.

Zara

Zara has excelled in digital marketing, with technology and more importantly customer information as the central component of their business. Its computerised ordering and dispatching system means that managers in its 4,700 stores can provide daily updates on sales and taste trends through hand-held personal digital assistants (PDAs), feeding a constant stream of data to the centre of the organisation. The company also sees the internet and social networking as 'indispensable tools and extraordinary channels for communications'. However, Zara views these digital technologies, particularly the internet, as 'complementary rather than cannibalistic'.[8] Zara has online sites throughout Europe and is 'liked' by more than 4.5 m people on Facebook. The number of searches for Zara.com has more than doubled since online shopping at the site was launched, according to Google Trends. Swedish rival H&M has also begun selling online, as have US rivals Gap and Banana Republic.

Digital technology: an information and interactions perspective

Viewing the range of technologies available to marketing from an information and interactions perspective allows the different management issues to come to the fore.

Information management

Information technologies include all the technologies used to support information gathering, research, analysis, planning and monitoring. These include internet research, dashboards, databases, planning software and analytics. These technologies are mainly used to gather, monitor and manage customer information and to turn that information into timely and usable knowledge. Information technology has revolutionised the data gathering and the processing and management of information, enabling marketers to capture, analyse and distribute information more rapidly, more widely and more economically than ever before.

Due to the abundance of information coming from many sources, marketing has been referred to as an 'information-handling' department.[9] This is a real challenge for marketing. Increasingly, marketers find themselves overwhelmed with an abundance of data from a myriad of sources, such as customer interactions and feedback, market research, social media, loyalty cards, RFID chips and sensor information, among many others. Too often managers believe that *more* information means *better* information. Yet in an age of extreme information-overload, companies cannot afford to be blinded by the assumption that mere data *availability* is the answer to any competitive challenge. The notion that more data means better data is not correct.[10] Companies often try to keep every little bit of information they have on their customers when their information management focus should be on data minimisation and information availability. This involves moving away from the mindless collection of largely meaningless data, by identifying, processing, aggregating and deploying information where needed.[11]

The increasing amount of potentially available data about customers is not only expected to surpass the sheer storage capacity worldwide, but already exceeds the ability of most firms to collect, interpret and use such customer information effectively and efficiently. Retailers like Tesco and Sainsbury have millions of customer transactions every hour stored in giant databases which are estimated to contain more than 2.5 petabytes of information. Facebook contains more than 40 billion photos. This phenomenon is called 'big data'.[12]

Information can be viewed in four ways, moving from an internal product or company orientation to a customer-centric marketing focus (see Figure 4.1).

1 **Descriptive customer information.** Most companies focus on this basic type of information – how many, how much, how often.
2 **Analytic customer information.** This is the first step in developing more customer-centric information management and focuses on customer-relevant information to help select target customers as well as identify the organisational practices that help maximise the value that the company creates for them. This is a focus on selecting the gems that matter in the data.[13] Tesco chooses target markets from database analysis: for example, customer groups who purchase baby products are sent coupons for more baby products.
3 **Predictive customer information.** This includes both the prediction of trends and changes in customer preferences as well as the prediction of customer responses (for example, to particular interactions, or to new service offerings of the company).
4 **Holistic customer information.** This level is characterised by information management that enables customer perspectives to be comprehensively identified and understood. Thus, decision-makers throughout the organisation have the information available that

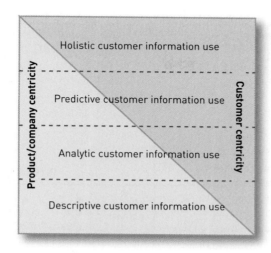

Figure 4.1 A hierarchical model of customer-centric information use.
Source: M. R. Fellenz and M. Brady (2010) Managing customer-centric information: the challenges of information and communication technology (ICT) deployment in service environments, *International Journal of Applied Logistics*, 1(3), 88–105.

enables them to identify, and – more importantly – to identify with, relevant customer views. Such a comprehensive understanding requires tacit as well as explicit knowledge of customer views, preferences and experiences, and by necessity must involve extensive and intensive interactions with customers.

Interaction technologies

Interaction technologies are technologies which support communications, connections and collaborations with customers and businesses across networks. They include internet, email, mobile communications, social networking sites, twitter, interactive products and services, and self-service technologies, to list the main ones in a growing range of technologies. Over the last two decades, marketing has increasingly been shifting towards interactivity, connectivity and ongoing relationships.[14] Digital technology is facilitating this shift and changing the way companies interact with customers as never before. The speed and reach of the interactions has changed with instant communication and worldwide dissemination as core features. For example, contacting customers via the internet or email can be much more cost efficient than a communication medium such as television or a sales force. Traditionally, communication was from company to customer but now more and more communications and connections are initiated and controlled by the customer through **Web 2.0**, **social networking** and user-generated content. The terms 'social networking' and 'Web 2.0' are often used as interchangeable; however, Web 2.0 mainly focuses on online applications and social networking on the social aspects of Web 2.0 applications (participation, openness, conversation, community, connectedness). Web 2.0 is a collection of open-source, interactive and user-controlled online applications expanding the experiences, knowledge and market power of the users as participants in business and social processes. Web 2.0 applications support the creation of informal users' networks, facilitating the flow of ideas and knowledge.[15] The 4C model in Figure 4.2 provides a view of Web 2.0 technologies based on the level of formality and interaction enabled by these tools.[16]

Whether company directed or customer controlled, a mixture of information and interaction technologies dominate marketing practice, as the case of DisneyLand Paris shows.

```
        CONNECTION      FORMALITY      COLLABORATION

          *              *                        *
        Mashups        Social                   Wikis
                     networking
                                          *
          *                           Human-based
        Tagging                        computation


                *                                          INTERACTION
            Syndication

                                  *
                            *   Social   *        *
                         Discussion approach Maria   Social
                           form            sharing cataloguing
                      *
                  *  Virtual
                     words              *
                  Blogs              Social
                                   bookmarking
          *              *
        Social       Instant
       presence      messaging

        COMMUNICATION                  COOPERATION
```

Figure 4.2 Level of formality and interaction through Web 2.0
Source: N. Cook (2008) *Enterprise 2.0: How Social Software Will Change the Future of Work*, Gower, Hampshire.

Disneyland Paris

With 15 million visits in 2011, Disneyland® Paris is the most visited tourist destination in Europe and 91 per cent of its visitors are European. Disneyland Paris use a combination of information and interaction technologies to create and manage the customer experience from the web to the park and throughout the lifetime of the relationship. Disneyland shows how analytics and engagement merge to produce a stunning result. Through the utilisation of data-driven personalisation based on customer analytics, Disney is able to offer its customers a highly relevant, personal and dynamic engagement that extends beyond the website, and across customer service and additional points of engagement. The end goal is to create an experience that takes a user from website to parks to movies (either in the cinema or at home), spanning all points of customer experience contact. 'From your physical experiences to your virtual experiences, we want to make sure we know it's you – the same person who visited Disneyland Paris or Walt Disney World. You're the same person who bought a movie through our movie rewards site . . . marketing is deeply involved and driving that process.'[17] With more than 200 million 'Likes' across all of its Facebook pages, Disney is one of the most powerful brands around, online and off.

The range of technologies in marketing

Given the dynamic nature of technology, a contemporary challenge is to keep up with current technologies and new developments. Technological innovations such as voice over internet, wireless broadband, mobile banking, online media, online publishing, e-learning, life-sciences, genetic engineering, biotechnology, nanotechnology, quantum technologies, artificial brains, robotics and high-performance computing are but a few examples of how our world has changed forever through enormous technological advancement in only a few decades.[18]

A holistic view of the totality of technologies available to marketers provides an overview of both the range of technologies and the skills and resources that are needed to manage them. Though not an exhaustive list and one which needs constant updating, Table 4.1 provides an overview of the main technologies in marketing divided into the information and interaction perspectives.

Table 4.1 Technologies in marketing: an information and interactions perspective

Information (research, analysis and planning)	Interactions (communications, connections and collaborations)
Analysis and planning	**Communications**
Marketing planning systems	Internet
Performance tracking software	• website design software
Executive support systems	• website security
Decision support systems	• interactive website applications
Enterprise resource planning (ERP)	• ecommerce applications
Knowledge management systems	• social networking
Pricing software	Cloud computing
Project management software	Software as a service
Promotion tracking software	Intranets
Media spend analysis packages	Extranets
Logistics systems	Electronic data interchange (EDI)
Geographical information systems	Email
Customer profitability analysis	Video conferencing
PRISM clusters – databases	Call centre
Forecasting software	Automatic call distribution
Marketing modelling	Computer telephony integration
Enterprise information systems (SAP, PeopleSoft/i2)	Mobile communication devices
	Instant messaging
	Tracking devices
Databases	Bluetooth
Centralised customer database	SMS – short messaging service
• integrated with sales	Facsimile communications
• integrated with call centre	Tweeting
• integrated with internet	Helplines
• integrated with point of sale	Voicemail
Data consolidation and display	Spam blocking systems
Data mining	Voice activated/recognition software
Data warehousing	Computer links with suppliers
Data profiling	Computer links with customers
Data visualisation and analysis packages	Web casting
GQL – graphical query language	Web meetings: WebEx
SQL – standard query language	Skype
	Digital imaging software
Research	Blippar augmented reality
Internet	
Marketing information systems	**Self-service technologies**
Data analysis packages	Integrated TV and internet
Geographic information systems	Internet technology
Demographic online systems	ATM
Internet survey – design and application	Automated vending machines

(Continued)

Table 4.1 (*Continued*)

Information (research, analysis and planning)	Interactions (communications, connections and collaborations)
Online mailing lists	Handheld scanners
Nielsen information database	Biometrics
Web analytical technologies	Mobile phones
Website performance and activity tracking	Bluetooth technologies
Monitoring and tracking software	Monitoring devices
Searchable databases	Customisation software
	Personalisation software
Customer relationship management	
CRM software	**Sales related**
Customised front/back office systems	Customer relationship management
Marketing evaluation software	Sales force automation packages
Contact management software	Mobile phones
Personalisation technologies	Laptops
Customisation technologies	Telemarketing
	Customised sales force systems
Retailing system	Customised customer applications
Electronic point of sale	Access databases
Planogram, Spaceman Category Management	Sales reporting software
Personalisation/customisations	
Bar codes – scanning	**Supply chain management**
	Supply chain management software
New product and service development	Automated production
Product development and design software	Internet marketplace
Simulation technologies	emarketplace/ehub
Idea generation tool: Idea Garden	Inventory management software
Imaginatik's Idea Central	Material planning and supply software
Statistical tools	Electronic data interchange
CAD (Computer-aided design)	QR/ECR (efficient customer response software)
	Eprocurement systems
Metrics	Online purchasing transactions
Dashboards	RFID (Radio frequency identification devices)
	Interactive products
Others	Biometric
Training and educational software	Bluetooth technologies

General underlying and platform technologies

Hardware: Personal computers, networked computers, mainframe, laptops, personal palm computers, mobile phones, digital assistants

Office packages: Word, PowerPoint, Excel Smart and iWork

Internal communications: Groupware systems, Lotus Notes, wide/local area networks – WAN/LAN

Source: Based on: Brady, M., Fellenz, M. R. and Brookes, R. (2008) Researching the Role of Information and Communication Technologies in Contemporary Marketing, *Journal of Business and Industrial Marketing*, **23** (2), 108–114; M. Brady (2006) A holistic view of ICT within the marketing domain: challenges and issues, British Academy of Management Conference, Belfast, September.

Each marketing situation demands a different set of digital technologies. Some are similar across companies, such as the internet and databases, while others are unique to certain industries – for example, Planogram software, a shelf-space management software for retailers, or yield management systems which are used to manage hotel rooms. A range of technologies will be used for different needs. Consider the example of Orange.

Orange

Orange, French Telecom's mobile phone brand, uses a range of information and inter-action technologies to increase awareness of its brand among a defined target market. These include text messages, CRM software, cinema commercials, social networking sites and other technologies. For example, the Orange Wednesday cinema campaign was a simple two-for-the-price-of-one offer for cinema tickets on Wednesdays. A short video clip told the story of the Wicked Witch of the West from the *Wizard of Oz*, who enjoys cinema trips with her friend, Vicki. The €7 million campaign harnessed digital technologies to interact with the customer and to communicate the offer (text message reminders), it used information technology to access customer data to target the customers (CRM software), and it used cinema and TV advertising to create interest. All of these technologies were coordinated to drive phone usage and to increase Orange's brand profile.

Managing digital technologies and digital marketing

Due to the explosion in technology both internally in organisations and externally at the customer interface, managing digital technologies means managing the implementation and ongoing operations of these technologies within marketing, across the organisation, along the supply network and at the customer interface. These are not technical challenges but managerial challenges. Often there is a focus on the capital investment in technology, while ignoring the investment of time, energy and talent needed to develop the capabilities required to leverage these investments. Ongoing management of both the implementation and the operation of the technology is crucial. Nike spent over €400 million on supply chain software that caused over €100 million in lost sales, a 20 per cent stock dip and a collection of class-action lawsuits. The main issues were that the technology was too slow, did not integrate well and had some bugs, and that Nike's planners were inadequately trained in how to use the system before it went live.

Technology management is 'concerned with exploring and understanding information technology as a corporate resource that determines both the strategic and operational capabilities of the firm in designing and developing products and services for maximum customer satisfaction, corporate productivity, profitability and competitiveness'.[19] There are four main responsibilities:

1 selection of digital technologies;
2 supporting the adoption of digital technologies;
3 exploitation of digital technologies; and
4 uniting marketing and IT staff.

Selection of digital technologies

Selecting the best technology focuses on the capabilities of the technology and what benefits it brings – matched to the needs of marketing strategy – rather than on the technology itself. This focus on the outcomes from the technology reflects the following questions:

- Will customers benefit from this?
- What is the best technological application to meet requirements (i.e., filling the identified gap)?
- How much is this technology going to cost in terms of the technology itself, but also in terms of human and management skills and time needed?
- Will the benefit be worth the cost to the organisation?

These questions embody many more detailed ones (e.g. should the organisation build or buy? should it upgrade or start from scratch? who will do the work? how long will it take?). Answering these questions should help determine the best technology solution. However, priorities must be established and also considered within the ultimate cost.[20] Questions like the ones below are a helpful starting point for building a shared understanding and commitment to change throughout the organisation:

- What is the total cost of digital marketing across the organisation, who is responsible for managing the content across channels, and is the publishing of content across the digital technology well managed for cost-effectiveness?
- What is the plan – including the people and finance to be invested – for engaging and nurturing a core group of passionate **brand advocates**? How do we plan to tap the feedback value they can provide? How can we react in real time?
- How well does our digital-marketing approach – including the content, the links between different channels, and the investment levels – correspond to the way our customers make purchasing decisions?
- What early-warning signs do we track on an ongoing basis to keep ahead of changes in customer behaviour, the actions of competitors, and attitudes towards our brand? Who is responsible for acting on what we learn about what our customers see, do and say?[21]

The answers can help marketing leaders and their senior colleagues in other functions decide whether a company is investing sufficiently in delivering digital technologies and what it will need to track the quality and impact of its efforts. Marketing may require more resources, which in turn should provide greater accountability for sales, innovation and operational efficiency, better visibility through metrics about the returns from digital technologies and greater clarity about how these technologies will directly improve corporate performance and customer satisfaction.[22]

Supporting the adoption of digital technologies

Marketers must help and guide the implementation process across the company to ensure that digital technology is implemented smoothly. Adoption can be challenging, especially where it crosses departments and changes work practices. Resistance to technologies that change work practices or customer interactions needs to be monitored and managed carefully, as the case of British Airways shows.

British Airways Terminal Five

The new British Airways Terminal 5 at London's Heathrow airport was designed for maximum customer service but on the opening day many staff had problems operating the technologies, which caused massive disruption for customers. British Airways (BA) had to cancel more than 200 flights after computer log-on failures and staff swipe cards issues, resulting in turmoil at the airport.

The opening of T5 has been described as a huge embarrassment to BA and a humiliation for the British Airports Authority (BAA). What should have been an opportunity for BAA to showcase Heathrow as one of the world's great airports and for BA to improve its record on baggage handling instead turned into a nightmare of delays, passenger confusion and chaos.

Among many issues were technical glitches with the sophisticated new baggage set-up, designed to handle 12,000 bags an hour. BAA declared the week before the opening: 'We have a world-class baggage system that is going to work perfectly on day one.' However, although some testing of the technology had occurred, it had not been sufficiently trialled and staff were not comfortable with the technology on the first day. All technologies, particularly those at the customer interface, need to be supported and managed prior to, during and after adoption. According to baggage handlers, the problems had started weeks before, but rather than receiving proper training, handlers say they were simply shown around the terminal. The technology had never been tested in a 'live' terminal. Adoption of technology needs to be properly supported with training, ongoing implementation plans and contingency planning to deal with problems when, or if, they arise.

Preplanning how the key issues that may arise will be handled is crucial. Staff and customers have to be encouraged to change their processes.

Stages theory of IT adoption

To manage digital technology, marketing managers must understand how companies adopt technology. The most common view is that digital technology assimilation into companies occurs in three stages – known as the stages theory of assimilation, moving from automation to information and then to transformation.[23]

1   **Automation stage.** This is where technology is used to replace previously manual tasks. A bank ATM machine is an example of automation. The ATM is used to replace the cashier in the bank. Check-in kiosks at airports also automate a process that previously involved a human dimension of checking in each passenger. Now passengers automatically check in either online at home or at the airport through self-service technology kiosks. These systems are designed to create efficiency – to make the process go faster.

2   **Information stage.** This is when the information from the automation of the operation is used to improve the service provided, so that rather than just going faster, the system is more efficient and more effective. Online check-in or airport self-service kiosks allow passengers to choose their own seating, making their trip more effective. Another example is British food retailer Tesco, which is thriving in large part due to its ability to mine the data generated by its Clubcard loyalty scheme, which monitors purchases and rewards frequent buyers with discounts and coupons. The company, which also solicits customer feedback through phone and written surveys, is considered by analysts to be top of the class at using the information it garners to be more effective.

3   **Transformation stage.** Transformation relates to major change, where the technology transforms the industry or the process. Managers need to know how to manage when technology changes the rules of the game. The music industry is a good example, where the downloading of music has changed how music is distributed. The technological impact on the music industry means that digital music sales are increasing all the time and affecting the sales of the physical CD. Tourism is another area where digital technology has transformed the market. Consumer purchasing behaviour has changed with TripAdvisor and booking sites as dominant sources of customer information prior to purchase. Many customers now check online through booking sites for cheap rates and last-minute offers, and use TripAdvisor to find out ratings from customers. Online booking and mobile bookings have transformed the purchase cycle. Sharing information after purchase now creates a cycle of customer-to-customer information.

Exploitation of digital technologies

While digital technology opens the way to new opportunities (e.g. new modes of communication, new customers and new markets), it also imposes the threat that these opportunities will be exploited just because they are available and not because they are part of a deliberate marketing strategy. Thus, while digital technology has influenced and changed the way marketing is practised, it should not be seen as an instrument that dominates other marketing instruments. Rather, digital marketing *complements* other marketing activities, with which it should be integrated. Successful digital marketers also act differently. They seek to immerse consumers in their content, investing to deliver an experience that goes beyond a straight transaction. To ensure that their digital efforts are as effective as possible, they closely monitor what consumers are seeing, doing and saying.

Marketing must be able to extract the maximum benefit from digital technology through knowledge of a range of current and future digital technologies. Consumers are rushing online and using a myriad of technologies in record numbers, and marketers must go there too. Exploiting new and innovative technologies holds the promise of higher profits and greater accountability, but it requires a sophisticated, strongly aligned blend of marketing savvy and technological expertise. Marketing must work together with technologists to develop a marketing technology architecture that combines the abilities to analyse consumer behaviour, help make marketing decisions and manage customer interactions, content management and publishing processes. While some of this technology is already available, many more challenging and innovative technologies are in the pipeline. Business and technology leaders must distinguish between opportunities and fads, prioritise solutions that engage customers and swiftly apply the truly game-changing technologies that drive business growth. Managing and exploiting individual technologies is explored later in this chapter.

Uniting marketing and IT staff

IT and marketing staff need to engage collectively with each other and work together with a shared understanding of the central role of technology in defining today's customer experience and powering effective market engagement.[24] Recent research indicates that:

- Only one-quarter of marketers say they consult their own in house IT staff, when selecting and deploying marketing solutions.
- 46 per cent of marketing executives do not agree that their company's chief information officers understand marketing objectives and requirements.
- Nearly two-thirds of marketers report challenges in implementing marketing and IT solutions, citing the lack of priority given to marketing by IT as the chief reason for discord.
- Meanwhile, some 48 per cent of IT executives also report problems in implementing marketing solutions and IT projects. One of the top reasons, they say, is that marketing has bypassed IT in implementing projects.[25]

The management challenge of making the most appropriate deployment of digital technology must be integrated into a holistic understanding of at least three fundamentally different orientations. Specifically, the IT staff's drive to use the technologies that suit their operations or are easiest to implement (technologists' perspective) must be checked both by the business logic that requires short-term profitability and longer-term economic viability and sustainability (finance perspective) and by the marketing logic that places customer needs and customer value at the heart of business (marketing perspective).[26] These three different orientations all require attention, but none on its own can deliver the full value required:

- **Technologists' perspective**: IT managers drive towards what is technologically possible.
- **Finance perspective**: finance managers drive towards what is profitable for the company.

- **Marketing (customer-centric) perspective**: marketing managers drive towards increasing the value for the customer.[27]

Recognising the challenge of integrating these three orientations is only the first step towards a more holistic deployment of digital technology. A second step is to recognise and address the challenge of enabling the organisation to coordinate this integration. Marketing should be aware of and able to coordinate the three different perspectives. There are a number of aspects to this, including the potentially politically difficult task of identifying internal champions, equipping them with the relevant skill-set and enabling them through appropriate organisational arrangements. In addition, the power base and business philosophy in many organisations is finance related and thus often singularly focused on creating and maximising short-term shareholder value rather than jointly maximising long-term customer and organisational value.[28] The marketing memo box explores this further.

Marketing memo

Technologists are from Mars and marketers are from Venus – not any more

Marketing and IT staff have been viewed for many years as two functions and roles which could not be more extreme in their differences. But recently, according to Forrester Research, these dramatically different perceptions have started to fade as they both see they have more in common than they imagined.[29] The stereotypes show the marketers as creative, driven by gut instinct and filled with insightful knowledge about customer needs, while the IT person is pragmatic, driven by budgets and compliance and a specialist in operational efficiency and cost control. They are supposed to speak different languages, value different skills and have diametrically opposing views of the world.

But nowadays they both focus on demonstrating their value to customers. They must both be able to measure their results and align these results to business strategy. They both have to deal with a rapidly changing business climate where customers and employees have more readily available and useful technology tools available to them than ever before. And, ultimately, they must both answer to their boards and shareholders for their mistakes. Marketers and technologists both play a vital role in delivering compelling customer experiences. Marketers focus on developing a brand experience that drives growth, while technologists plan and implement effective technology solutions that enable the business strategy.

There are five characteristics which should unite the two perspectives:

1 **Building a solid partnership.** It is essential to have a shared view of the customer, the business goals and common metrics that define success. Marketers realise that technology is a key enabler for any effective marketing programme, but sometimes easy access to technologies that do not require IT support perpetuates poor communication and the stereotype of the dysfunctional IT/marketing relationship. Marketers need to be masters of technology and technologists need to understand the customer. Innovation in the business must be built on a solid partnership between these two with shared goals and metrics, a common business language, and deep collaboration.

2 **Innovation across the customer lifecycle.** Customers are the lifeblood of any business. Empowered customers and employees are finding their voice and amplifying their messages on a worldwide scale. The challenge faced by marketers and technologists is how to orchestrate a diverse set of opportunities and resources – people and technology – from within and beyond the firm, to create and maintain a compelling brand experience that delivers value to the consumer and results in more successful products and services, more loyal customers, and stronger brands.

3 **Tapping disruptive technologies to maximise growth.** Today's explosion in technology innovation and adoption puts IT everywhere. But unlike previous growth cycles, the current surge does not have a single-technology focus. Instead, marketers and technologists must navigate a cornucopia of technologies based on cloud computing, mobile platforms, predictive analytics and online social interaction that all promise to transform the business inside and out.

► **Marketing memo** *(continued)*

4 Redrawing organisational boundaries to promote agility. Digital business leaders must transform the culture, the tactics and the technology of their organisation to become more agile. To lead by example, technologists and marketers will need to accept change, dare to challenge the status quo, act continuously, participate personally and, most importantly, tear down boundaries that exist within the company. Now is the time for marketers and technologists to link arms and redefine the working relationship between their functions. Co-innovation and co-creation of strategy will blur the lines between marketing and IT, and ultimately result in better solutions that are built for ongoing change. These challenges, though difficult to overcome, are not insurmountable. However, they require not only a verbal commitment, but action to support organisational and process redesign and collaboration.[30]

5 Integration rather than outsourcing. Another concern is marketers' use of external agencies, which often leads to fragmented IT and can require costly integration into the corporate IT strategy. The technology spend can be like a black hole and build up islands of information not managed within the corporate IT strategy. One of the issues is that the agencies that marketing hires can develop proprietary technologies that do not match the inhouse technology. Using outsourcing in the digital arena should be aligned to the technology inside the organisation and supported by IT staff.

_____

Sources: Adapted from S. Yates (2011) CIOs are from Mars, CMOs are from Venus? Not any more, *Computer Weekly*, 14 April; C. Saren (2011) Forrester Research: Marketing is an IT spending blackhole, *Computer Weekly*, 14 April. Read more at www.cmo.com/leadership/cios-are-mars-cmos-are-venus-not-anymore#ixzz1Jxqk1V1Q.

Managing individual technologies in marketing

Many of the technologies used in marketing are discussed throughout this book. This section explores seven diverse technologies which provide a flavour of the complexity and challenges in this domain:

- the internet;
- social networking: blogging, seeding and viral marketing;
- email marketing;
- search engine optimisation;
- virtual worlds;
- mobile marketing;
- self-service technologies.

The internet: understanding competitive advantage

The internet has revolutionised the world. Not since the invention of the steam engine has anything had such a profound impact on mankind. With utterly remarkable speed, huge scale and depth, the internet has permeated many aspects of our lives, and the way we do business. It has the capacity to provide users with the power easily and instantaneously to harness limitless sourcing and acquisition of information, and instant, global and cheap interactions.[31]

The internet is ubiquitous, allowing 24/7 communications through a low-cost, open standard available to individuals and companies to establish a website or otherwise make use of the possibilities for exchanging products and services, money and information in an online setting. As of 2011 there were over 1 billion internet users worldwide and over 338 million in the European Union (see Table 4.2).[32]

Table 4.2 Internet user statistics and population for the 27 European Union member states compared to the rest of the world

World region	Population (2011 est.)	% pop. of world	Internet users, latest data	Penetration of (% population)	User growth, 2000–11 (%)	% users of world
European Union	502,748,071	7.3	338,420,555	67.3	258.5	16.2
Rest of world	6,427,307,083	92.7	1,756,585,450	27.3	558.9	83.8
Total world	6,930,055,154	100.0	2,095,006,005	30.2	480.4	100.0

Notes: (1) The European Union internet statistics were updated for 31 March, 2011. (2) Population data are from the US Census Bureau. (3) Usage numbers come from Nielsen Online, ITU, GfK, and other trustworthy sources. Internet usage in the European Union, http://www.internetworldstats.com/stats9.htm © Copyright 2000–2012, Miniwatts Marketing Group. All rights reserved.

The internet does not in itself offer companies competitive advantage; rather, online success depends on companies' abilities to exploit online market opportunities. This is no different from an offline setting. Success depends on other factors, such as its integration into organisational routines and the management skills of the firm, co-specialisation with other organisational resources and the exploitation of networks.[33]

The internet can *reduce transaction costs* by reducing information asymmetries and by facilitating coordination of independent processes such as design and engineering. Transaction costs occur when products or services are transferred from one organisation to another and may include search costs, contracting costs, monitoring costs and enforcement costs (see Chapter 8 for a review of transaction costs). Moreover, the internet allows knowledge sharing within a network.[34] By utilising information and communication technologies for supporting supply network integration, companies are better able to control the flows of material, information and finance.

Search costs (i.e. the time, money and mental resources spent when searching for favourable products and services) are recognised as an important determinant of customers' decision-making processes in the marketplace (see also Chapter 7).[35] Many online retailers have attracted consumers by offering a *reduction in search costs* for products or service and related information.[36] Moreover, several websites are offering consumers

On the website Costameno.it, Italian consumers can compare 800,000 products.
Source: http://www.costamerio.it, Limbarda S.r.L.

easy access to comparison information about various products and services. Covering 11 European countries, Kelkoo is a leading shopping guide, which attracts 30 million unique visitors each month. Other leading comparison sites serving European customers include Shopzilla, Shopping.com, Ciao, Pricerunner, Costameno and Le Guide.

Michael E. Porter has used his 'five forces' framework (see Chapter 9 for a review of this framework) to discuss how the internet may influence industry structure.[37] Porter argues that gaining a competitive advantage through the internet does not require a radically new approach to business. It requires building on the proven principles of effective strategy. In this respect, two underlying profitability drivers are fundamental: (1) *industry structure*, which determines the profitability of the average competitor; and (2) *sustainable competitive advantage*, which allows a company to outperform the average competitor. Since these vary widely across industries and companies, an analysis of potential profitability should be carried out by looking at individual industries and individual companies.

The general attractiveness of an industry is determined by five underlying forces of competition: the intensity of rivalry among existing competitors, the barriers to entry for new competitors, the threat of substitute products or services, the bargaining power of suppliers, and the bargaining power of buyers. Figure 4.3 suggests some implications of the internet for industry attractiveness. Note that these are only general trends and that variations may occur across industries. Some of these trends influence the attractiveness of an industry positively, whereas others influence industry attractiveness negatively.

While the net effect of these trends – as looked upon from the company's perspective – seems negative, this is not true for all industries. Internet auctions provide an example of this. Here, customers and suppliers are fragmented and thus have little power. Substitutes, such as classified ads and flea markets, have less reach and are less convenient to use. Even though entry barriers are relatively modest, companies can build economies of scale by using the internet – in particular, because of many buyers and sellers.

However, since the internet influences industry attractiveness in a way that might put average profitability under pressure, the pressure to reach and maintain competitive advantage also increases. Fundamentally, marketing managers can react to this pressure in two ways. They can seek to increase their operational effectiveness (doing the same things as their competitors but doing them better) and/or they can seek to increase their strategic positioning (doing things differently from their competitors in order to provide additional value to customers). The internet, and other forms of digital technology, can be a powerful tool in increasing operational effectiveness. However, no matter how well digital technology supports the activities within an industry, companies can only build competitive advantage if they are able to improve and sustain operational effectiveness better than their competitors. With the digital revolution this task has become more difficult to accomplish. Because of the openness of the internet, in combination with many companies relying on similar internet applications, improvements in operational effectiveness tend to be broadly shared among companies in an industry.

Understanding social networking

Social networking has revolutionised the way people communicate and share information with one another in today's society and is used by millions of people every day. **Social media** are a group of internet-based applications that build on the ideological and technological foundations of Web 2.0 and that allow the creation and exchange of user-generated content. **Social networking** is the grouping of individuals into specific groups, like small rural communities or a neighbourhood subdivision, mostly carried out, in its most popular form, online. The main types of social networking service are those that contain directories of some categories (such as former classmates), means to connect with friends (usually with self-description pages) like Facebook, or shorter versions like Twitter; and recommender systems linked to trust – like TripAdvisor. Popular sites now combine many of these. There are also more targeted social networking sites, such as

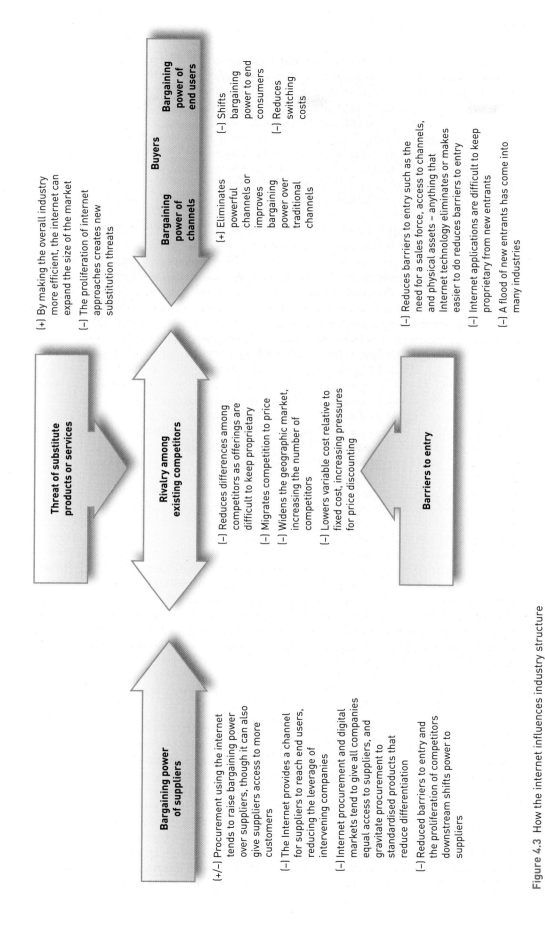

Threat of substitute products or services

(+) By making the overall industry more efficient, the internet can expand the size of the market

(–) The proliferation of internet approaches creates new substitution threats

Buyers

Bargaining power of channels

(+) Eliminates powerful channels or improves bargaining power over traditional channels

Bargaining power of end users

(–) Shifts bargaining power to end consumers

(–) Reduces switching costs

Rivalry among existing competitors

(–) Reduces differences among competitors as offerings are difficult to keep proprietary

(–) Migrates competition to price

(–) Widens the geographic market, increasing the number of competitors

(–) Lowers variable cost relative to fixed cost, increasing pressures for price discounting

Barriers to entry

(–) Reduces barriers to entry such as the need for a sales force, access to channels, and physical assets – anything that Internet technology eliminates or makes easier to do reduces barriers to entry

(–) Internet applications are difficult to keep proprietary from new entrants

(–) A flood of new entrants has come into many industries

Bargaining power of suppliers

(+/–) Procurement using the internet tends to raise bargaining power over suppliers, though it can also give suppliers access to more customers

(–) The Internet provides a channel for suppliers to reach end users, reducing the leverage of intervening companies

(–) Internet procurement and digital markets tend to give all companies equal access to suppliers, and gravitate procurement to standardised products that reduce differentiation

(–) Reduced barriers to entry and the proliferation of competitors downstream shifts power to suppliers

Figure 4.3 How the internet influences industry structure

Source: Reprinted by permission of *Harvard Business Review* from Strategy and the Internet by Porter, M. E., March, 2001. Copyright © 2001 by the Harvard Business School Publishing Corporation; all rights reserved.

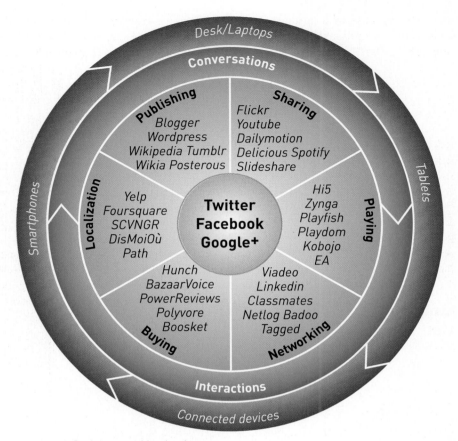

Figure 4.4 Social networking landscape
Source: Reprinted by permission of Fred Cavazza.

Flister for movie reviews, last.fm for radio stations, and LinkedIn – a business-orientated social network. Social networking has become possible through the concept of **user-generated content**, which is any form of content such as video, blogs, discussion forum posts, digital images, audio files, and so on that is created or posted by consumers or end-users and is then publicly available to other consumers and end-users. Social networking sites can be used to publish, to share, to discuss, for commerce (purchasing), for location-based information, for networking and for games, all highlighted in Figure 4.4.

Social networking is now in the fabric of many people's lives. We will now compare offline and online social networks across three dimensions: tie strength, online homophily and source credibility.

1 **Tie strength**. In general, tie strength refers to the strength of the dyadic interpersonal relationships in the context of a social network.[38] Strong ties are characterised by: a sense that the relationship is intimate and special, with a voluntary investment in the tie and a desire for companionship with the partner; an interest in frequent interactions in multiple contexts; and a sense of mutuality of the relationship, with the partner's needs known and supported.[39] Individual-to-individual social ties seem less relevant in an online environment than in an offline environment. Instead, individuals tend to use the websites themselves as proxies for individuals. Like brands, websites can have 'personalities' and therefore they can be treated as people with whom the individual can have personal relations. This notion receives support from social response theory, which states that consumers apply social rules to respond on websites when these

possess human-like attributes, or social cues. That is, consumers may treat websites as social actors even though they are fully aware that websites are not humans.[40]

2 **Homophily.** The likelihood of a tie usually depends on the attributes of the people involved. For example, for most social relations the likelihood of a relationship is a function of the age, gender, geography, lifestyle and status of individuals. Ties are often more likely to occur between those who have similar attributes than between those who do not. This tendency is called *homophily* by attributes.[41] However, in an online setting, homophily can be thought of as the congruence between a user's psychological attributes and website content. That is, dominant dimensions of homophily are not gender or status but shared group interests and mindset.

3 **Source credibility.** Source credibility is always a key concern in communication efforts. Source credibility depends on a message source's perceived ability or motivation to provide accurate and truthful information concerning the issue under consideration. Source credibility is high if the source is perceived to have high expertise and high trustworthiness.[42] In an online social network setting, source credibility refers to the perceived competence of the website and its membership, and source credibility seems especially to be based on site trustworthiness and the expertise of the actors visiting the site. Consumers participating in online communications may influence the opinions of other people and their view of the company. TripAdvisor provides a platform for customer-to-customer communication which is used as the main credible source of hotel information for millions of travellers across the globe. Facebook (see below) taps into the use of peer-to-peer information sources and is a credible source of information for consumers as well as a site for friends and fun.

Facebook

The social networking site Facebook was founded in 2004 by Harvard student Mark Zuckerberg and has since featured in the movie *Social Networking*. Since its inception Facebook has gained more than 500 million users who post photos and comments. Over 50 per cent are called active users, logging on to Facebook daily. Users spend a combined 700 billion minutes on Facebook each month and have an average of 130 friends. From a business perspective, more than 250 million people engage with Facebook monthly through external websites, and there are over 2.5 million websites integrated with Facebook. Since social plugins (which allow people to see what their friends have liked, commented on or shared on sites across the web) called 'like' buttons were launched in April 2010, an average of 10,000 new websites integrate with Facebook every day.

A classification using self-disclosure/self-presentation and social presence/media richness can clarify the different social networking types available.

- **Self-presentation.** In any type of social interaction, people have the desire to control the impression that other people form of them. Social media allow people to present themselves in a certain way on the internet. They do this for many reasons including to influence others, to get a reward and to create an image that is consistent with one's personal identity.
- **Self disclosure.** This is the conscious or unconscious revelation of personal details. Self-disclosure is a critical step and there are different levels of self-disclosure, including breadth of disclosure, depth of disclosure and a combination of both.
- **Social presence.** This is the acoustic, visual and physical content that can be achieved – influenced by the intimacy (interpersonal and mediated) and the immediacy (asynchronous versus synchronous) of the medium. For example, the degree of social presence can be said to be lower for mediated (telephone conversation) than interpersonal (face to face) and for asynchronous (email) than synchronous (live chat) communication. The higher the social presence, the higher the social influence.

Table 4.3 Classification of social media by social presence/media richness and self-presentation/self-disclosure

| | | Social presence/media richness | | |
		Low	Medium	High
Self-presentation/ self-disclosure	**High**	Blogs	Social networking sites (e.g. Facebook)	Virtual social worlds (e.g. Second Life)
	Low	Collaborative projects (e.g. Wikipedia)	Content communities (e.g. YouTube)	Virtual game worlds (e.g. World of Warcraft)

Source: A. M. Kaplan and M. Hantein (2010) Users of the world, unite! The challenges and opportunities of social media, *Business Horizon*, 53(1), 59–68.

- **Media richness.** This is based on the view that the role of any communication is the resolution of ambiguity (doubtfulness or uncertainty of meaning or intention) and the reduction of uncertainty. Richness relates to the amount of information that can be transmitted at any one time. Some media are better at resolving ambiguity and uncertainty than others.

Using these features, social networking can be classified as high, medium or low in terms of social presence and media richness, and high or low in terms of self-presentation and self-disclosure, as seen in Table 4.3.

Blogging

Blogs – a mix of the words 'web' and 'log' – are usually types of personal online diary posted on the web in chronological order. The content of the blog does not have to be personal but can also be professional. There is no defined format for blogs, which range from one-liners to relatively long, well-thought-out arguments for or against a topic of interest. There are over 150 million blogs on the internet.[43] Marketers can monitor blogs and other 'user-generated content' – such as chat groups, message boards and electronic forums – to analyse what is being said online about products and services, as well as to follow the cult status that some blogging communities accord to brands. Blogs can be used to communicate with customers or for research and gathering of customer information. Companies can use web-tracking software to monitor each time their company is mentioned in a blog. Some of the more popular monitoring sites are www.socialmention.com, www.tweetmonitor.com and technocratic.com.

Bloggers can be influential members of their community of interest, in which case marketers might want to engage or influence them. One method of influence is through seeding. **Seeding** describes 'the practice of purposely positioning a product or service within a blog.'[44] It is placing seeds of information around the internet and particularly on social networking sites. Companies can ask successful bloggers to evaluate products or services on their site. Bloggers who agree to seed a product or service often fear being seen as a 'sell-out' – there can be a moral tension, a conflict between ethical perspectives and a legitimacy perception issue. Alternatively, being asked to seed a product or service by a company can be seen as a compliment, as the bloggers perceive themselves to be part of an elite community.[45] It is important that the seeds match the characteristics and interests of the target group. The Aussie hair care product used a lot of seeding to create awareness and became what is known as a 'discovered brand' where customers find out about the brand from other customers rather than from the company.

Viral marketing

Viral marketing is an internet adaptation of marketing using the word-of-mouth effect and is an **advertising message** spread by consumers among other consumers (see also Chapter 7). Viral marketing has been treated by many as an almost coincidental marketing instrument – as a 'funny instrument' that might add a little extra attention and colour to primary marketing efforts – though the reach of these viral clips can be phenomenal. T-Mobile, the German mobile phone company, launched a viral campaign of the British royal wedding which had 5 million hits in five days and within a month of the wedding had received over 25 million views.

The number of new videos that are placed on the internet is gigantic. More than 20 hours of video are uploaded every single minute on YouTube.[46] Breaking through such an overwhelming stream of information is not an easy task. Therefore, the first and most difficult task is to attract online attention among target segments.[47] In a viral marketing campaign, a company may use the influence of its own customers to promote a product or service to prospective customers, but it may also post its campaign material in a diversity of places. Some viral marketing campaigns only manage to get 5 per cent of video recipients to forward the video to other customers, while the share for the more popular ones is usually around 30 per cent.[48] Often the funniest, most memorable and topical ones can really capture the imagination and be forwarded around the world.

Old Spice

Having tried to revive the brand of Old Spice for almost 20 years, Procter & Gamble managed to do it using the fastest-growing online viral campaign ever. On 14 July 2010, the company uploaded a 30-second video spot on YouTube, to promote its Old Spice brand. This video, entitled *The Man Your Man Could Smell Like*, was viewed 23 million times in 36 hours. Mustafa, the star of the viral campaign, asks women: 'Does your man look like me? No. Can he smell like me? Yes.' Old Spice Guy has gone from being the old guy to the hottest guy. To promote the campaign, Procter & Gamble has Mustafa posting real-time video responses to Twitter and Facebook queries, all in character, standing bare-chested in a bathroom with the ad agency's copywriters behind the camera writing the jokes. In two days, the agency produced more than 180 videos, including exchanges with celebrities such as Ellen DeGeneres and Demi Moore. This tongue-in-cheek campaign allowed the brand to be seen as an authoritative, experienced men's brand. Old Spice's marketing manager said, 'We articulate the voice of experience through humour. It's our goal to engage our consumers in a way that's not only entertaining, but also relevant, humorous and in the Old Spice tone.'

Viral marketing is especially suited for social networks as members are connected to each other in a way that increases the trustworthiness of the messages that are transferred among friends.[49] Essentially, the successful viral marketing campaign gives the right message to the right messengers in the right environment.[50] Viral marketing builds upon the notion that word of mouth is no longer just an act of intimate, one-on-one communication, but operates on a one-to-many basis.

Targeting the influentials on social networking

Although social network users typically have numerous online 'friends', only a fraction of those friends may actually influence a member's site usage. Because most of the network links are 'weak', managers should seek to identify the 'strong' links (i.e. the links corresponding to friends who affect a given user's behaviour). To that end, managers may focus on users who have many friends or users with a high number of profile views[51] – see the marketing memo box.

Marketing memo

User participation in social networking

All large-scale, multi-user communities and online social networks rely on users to contribute content to websites, which is called **user-generated content**. The reality is that most users don't participate very much. Often, they simply lurk in the background. In contrast, a tiny minority of users usually accounts for a disproportionately large amount of the content and other system activity. This phenomenon of participation inequality was first studied in depth by Will Hill in the early 1990s.

User participation often more or less follows a *90-9-1 rule* (see Figure 4.5):

- 90 per cent of users are lurkers (i.e. they read or observe, consume, but don't contribute). They could also be termed viewers of content.

- 9 per cent of users contribute from time to time, but other priorities dominate their time.

- 1 per cent of users participate a lot and account for most contributions: it can seem as if they are always connected and commenting with postings, minutes after whatever event they are commenting on occurs.

Virtual communities provide an attractive place for organisations to mine information regarding customer perceptions, needs and demographics, as well as to generate revenue through sales of products, services, information and advertising. However, the community conversation provides information about only one type of community user, the poster. Information about the lurker, who never posts, is conspicuously absent from the postings. Lurkers may be a large portion of the user community and could provide key revenue sources and vital information, or they could potentially turn into posters.[52]

If managed well, social networking allows firms to engage in timely and direct consumer contact at relatively low cost and higher levels of efficiency than can be achieved with more traditional communication tools. Understanding the ladder of engagement (see Figure 4.6) helps marketers to understand the levels of engagement with customers from personal to social and then to advocate.

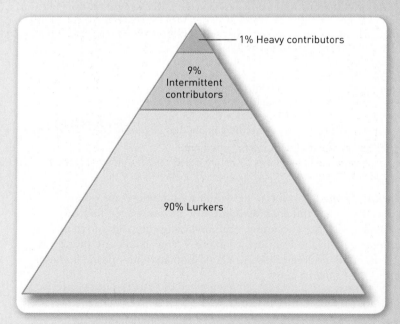

Figure 4.5 User participation in social networking

Source: C. Ridings, D. Gefen and B. Arinze (2006) Psychological barriers: lurker and poster motivation and behaviour in online communities, *Communications of the Association for Information Systems*, 18(1), 329–54.

▶ **Marketing memo** *(continued)*

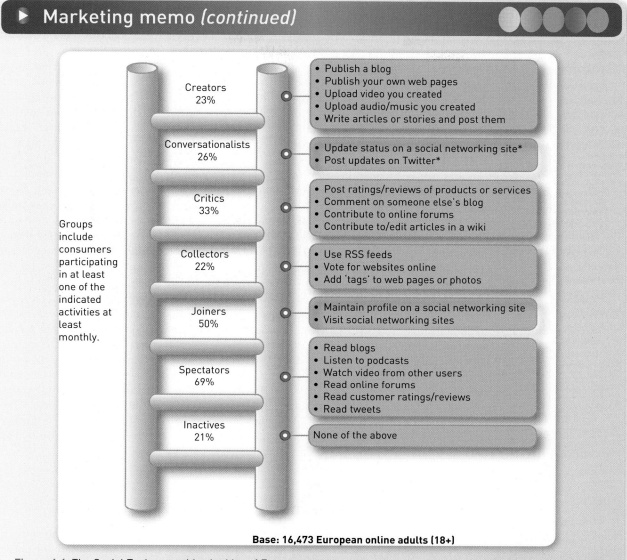

Creators 23%
- Publish a blog
- Publish your own web pages
- Upload video you created
- Upload audio/music you created
- Write articles or stories and post them

Conversationalists 26%
- Update status on a social networking site*
- Post updates on Twitter*

Critics 33%
- Post ratings/reviews of products or services
- Comment on someone else's blog
- Contribute to online forums
- Contribute to/edit articles in a wiki

Collectors 22%
- Use RSS feeds
- Vote for websites online
- Add 'tags' to web pages or photos

Joiners 50%
- Maintain profile on a social networking site
- Visit social networking sites

Spectators 69%
- Read blogs
- Listen to podcasts
- Watch video from other users
- Read online forums
- Read customer ratings/reviews
- Read tweets

Inactives 21%
- None of the above

Groups include consumers participating in at least one of the indicated activities at least monthly.

Base: 16,473 European online adults (18+)

Figure 4.6 The Social Technographics Ladder of Engagement
*'Conversationalists' participation in at least one of the indicated activities at least weekly.
Source: Forrester Research Inc., Global Social Media Adoption in 2011, April 2011.

To find out how Cadbury, a world-leading confectionery company, used an online viral marketing campaign to generate buzz and to defend its dominant market share position in the UK, go to: www.pearsoned.co.uk/marketingmanagementeurope or www.digitalbuzzblog.com/cadbury-eyebrow-dance/ and view their viral 'eyebrow' campaign.

Email marketing

Email communication is characterised by cost effectiveness and time efficiency, making it an attractive direct channel for managers. Consumers are most receptive to emails from companies with which they already have a relationship but are often irritated by irrelevant communication messages. **Spam** is the use of email to send unsolicited bulk messages indiscriminately. While the most widely recognised form of spam is email spam, the term is applied to similar abuses in other media: instant messaging spam, Usenet newsgroup spam, web search engine spam, spam in blogs, wiki spam, online classified ads spam, mobile phone messaging spam, internet forum spam, junk fax transmissions, social networking spam and file-sharing network spam. Spamming remains economically viable because advertisers have no operating costs beyond the management of their mailing lists, and it is difficult to hold senders accountable for their mass mailings. Because the barrier to entry is so low, spammers are numerous, and the volume of unsolicited mail has become very high. In 2011, the estimated figure for spam messages is around seven trillion.[53] Most consumers can recognise the difference between 'spam' and legitimate direct marketing emails. While email marketing may lead to favourable results, such as creating a new relationship or maintaining a past relationship with a customer, it could also cause internet users to unsubscribe and break the relationship.[54]

Managers considering an email marketing campaign must be aware that legal restrictions apply in this area. The EU Directive on privacy and electronic communications (2002/58/EC), often referred to as the 'spam directive' or the 'opt-in directive', states that sending commercial email messages is only allowed if recipients have given their prior consent. However, there are some exceptions to that rule. If there is an existing customer relationship, a seller of a product or a service has the right to market to the customer its own similar products or services. This right only applies if the customer has not initially refused commercial contact via email, and the sender also has to offer the recipient a free-of-charge and easy-to-use mechanism to say no to future emails.[55] Despite the opt-in directive, email marketing rules are not necessarily identical across EU member states. For example, business-to-business (B2B) emails require a mandatory opt-in in Austria, but may be sent to some companies on an opt-out basis in the United Kingdom. Thus, although the EU directive gives companies an overview of the base standard in Europe, each country's local email marketing laws still need to be checked on a case-by-case basis.[56]

Managing search engine optimisation

Search engine optimisation (SEO) is the process of improving the visibility and thus the volume and quality of traffic to a website from search engines, via the 'natural' or unpaid ('organic' or 'algorithmic') search results. Search engine optimisation attempts to discern patterns in search engine listings, and then develop a methodology for improving rankings. SEO considers how search engines work, what people search for, the actual search terms typed into search engines and which search engines are preferred by their targeted audience. Optimising a website may involve editing its content and HTML and associated coding both to increase its relevance to specific keywords and to remove barriers to the indexing activities of search engines. Usually, the earlier a site is presented in the search results or the higher it 'ranks', the more searchers will visit that site. 'Paid searches' is a micromarketing technique unique to the internet. If you type in a few words on a popular search engine, a column of paid advertisements, often called sponsored links, will appear on the right.

Google is by far the most widely used search engine in European countries. Marketers know that consumers use Google for checking online and being on the first page of a Google search can be crucial for many companies; thus many marketers are eager to influence their website's Google rankings. Data about the frequency of use of search terms are available on Google through Google AdWords, Google Trends, and Google Insights for Search.

Google

Though Google is viewed as a search engine, Google is, first and foremost, an advertising company. Though the company mission is 'to organize the world's information and make it universally accessible and useful', 97 per cent of the company's revenue comes from advertising on its various sites through its AdWords programme. So although Google runs over one million servers in data centres around the world, and processes over one billion search requests and about 24 petabytes of user-generated data every day, it gets its revenue from advertising on the site. No company can pay for its ranking, but it can optimise its ranking through words used, tags and links – search engine optimisation.

The Google search engine attracted a loyal following among internet users, who liked its simple design and ease of use.

Source: ©John James/Alamy.

Virtual worlds

Millions of people have joined virtual worlds such as Second Life, Warhammer and There. com. These online games, known as 'massively multiplayer online games' (MMOG), allow people to inhabit alternative virtual worlds as a character of their choosing.

Second Life

Second Life is an online, 3D virtual world imagined and created by its users, called residents. The game has over 20 million residents; of which 5 million users are considered regulars. Sixty per cent of Second Life's users come from the United Kingdom, the United States, Germany and France. There are currently about 500,000 residents who log into Second Life on a weekly basis. These 'residents' can explore, socialise and participate in activities and services using Second Life's currency, the Linden Dollar.

Second Life is one of the biggest virtual worlds in existence and many major brands, including Coca-Cola, Vodafone, IBM, Toyota, Sony and Adidas, already have a presence there. Sweden and Estonia have both opened embassies on Second Life, designed to promote their country's image and culture, rather than providing any real or virtual services.[57] Second Life is becoming part of popular culture, with the Italian singer Irene Grandi using some scenes from Second Life in her music video 'Bruci la città'. The St Patrick's Day parade – to celebrate Ireland's national day – went virtual with 12 million people viewing

The 'residents' of Second Life can explore, socialise and participate in activities and buy products and services using Second Life's currency, the Linden Dollar.

Source: http://www.secondlife.com/showcase.

the parade in Second Life, the largest ever viewing . The availability of virtual classrooms on Second Life has been taken up by many universities including Delft University of Technology in Holland and Edinburgh University in Scotland. At Insead University in France, the MBA class was given on the Second Life campus. Professor Sarvary lectured on the evolution of modern media on Second Life to students who had been invited by email.[58]

Mobile phones

The mobile phone has become an indispensable item with 5.3 billion mobile phone subscribers globally.[59] As Friedrich Joussen, head of Vodafone Germany, notes: 'Today, the mobile phone – next to keys and wallets – is the most important thing people carry with them when they leave the house.' Mobile phones and particularly smartphone sales continue to grow. A **smartphone** is a mobile phone that offers more advanced computing ability and connectivity than a contemporary mobile phone and may be thought of as a handheld computer integrated with a mobile telephone. A smartphone is often combined with a camera phone and a personal digital assistant (PDA), a high-resolution touchable display and a QWERTY keyboard.[60] While Nokia remains number one in both smartphones and mobile phones in Europe, Samsung is the brand leader in the USA, and in Japan it is Sharp.[61]

Mobile phones are now being used for multiple activities, including text messages (SMS), multimedia messaging services (MMS, allowing the sending of images, audio and video), emails and internet browsing and video watching. The introduction of 3G and 4G services offers enhanced broadband wireless data and greater network capacity (see also Chapter 6). In western Europe over 90 per cent of mobile subscribers have an internet-ready phone. Almost one in five global mobile subscribers have access to fast-mobile internet (3G or better) services and the number of smartphones is growing.

Mobile commerce or mobile advertising is a growing and promising potential business area.[62] By using mobile advertising companies can communicate directly with their consumers without location barriers. Top international companies such as Nike, BMW and Virgin are using mobile advertising campaigns to convey commercial content to customers.[63]

BMW

When BMW used text messaging to inform its customers that snow tyres were a necessity not a luxury, it had great success: 30 per cent of those who received the message purchased snow tyres from a BMW dealership. Mark Mielau, Head of Digital Media, BMW Germany, concedes that some of those customers might have come to purchase tyres anyway, but not all of them. He estimated that the campaign increased BMW's revenue by over €120,000, assuming that a set of snow tyres retails for about €340. Nearly 6 per cent of those who received the message responded by either calling a dealership or requesting to be called. According to BMW this was a success as it corresponded to an average response of 2.7 per cent.[64]

There must be an awareness that mobile consumers often regard their mobile phone as a private item and therefore are sensitive to receiving messages from companies if such messages have not been asked for in advance.[65] Mobile advertising researchers Ramin Vatanparast and Mahsa Asil suggest that 'mobile advertisements should be able to provide relevant information and rewards, be delivered by trusted organizations, and also give the viewer control over the message'.[66]

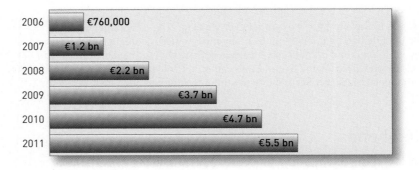

Figure 4.7 Worldwide mobile music revenues, 2006–11
Source: www.emarketer.com

The real winner for the mobile phone is texting. Text messaging or texting is the common term for the sending of SMS (short message service) which are short text messages, normally of about 160 characters. Text messaging is the most widely used data application in the world, with 2.4 billion active users, or 74 per cent of all mobile phone subscribers.

The most common application of the service is person-to-person messaging, but text messages are also often used to interact with automated systems, such as ordering or distributing products and services from mobile phones. Purchasing ringtones and downloading music from iTunes are both good examples. It is expected that sales from mobile music and ringtones will reach almost €5 billion by 2011. Figure 4.7 shows the growth in this one area of mobile distribution.

Mobile communication can also be interactive with the ability to link to print and billboards from QR codes. A **QR code** is a matrix barcode (or two-dimensional code) that is readable by dedicated QR barcode readers, mobile phone cameras and less commonly, computers with webcams. The code consists of black modules arranged in a square pattern on a white background. The information encoded may be text, URL or other data, and when you take a picture of the image you transfer straight to the website.

Audi provides an instructive case of a company using mobile phone communication for marketing purposes.

Audi

Audi, the European luxury car brand, has made extensive use of mobile communications for both communication and integration with their customers. Readers of French magazines were offered an unusual invitation in an advertisement for the Audi Q7. They were asked to point the camera in their mobile phones at a quick response (QR) code in the advertisements which automatically connected them to a website that streamed video of the Audi Q7 in action.[67] Audi also placed QR codes (see the barcode in the image below) on billboards. When viewers used their mobile phone and took pictures of the code, they were logged onto Audi's website and to Audi's Facebook and YouTube pages, where users were invited to tweet about their favourite designs. Audi recently launched a car calendar with no car images; instead viewers had to upload an Audi app on their smartphone to receive the images of the car in what is called augmented reality – the overlaying of digital data on the real world.[68]

Audi Gebrauchtwagen
:plus

Hier ist ein Gebrauchtwagen versteckt.

Machen Sie sich selbst ein Bild!

Kompromisslos Audi.

Unsere besten Gebrauchten haben eine ganze Reihe von Pluspunkten: den zertifizierten *:plus* 110-Punkte-Check, die 12-monatige *:plus* Gebrauchtwagen-Garantie, die flexible *:plus* Finanzierung und, und, und. Denn wer sich für Gebrauchtwagen *:plus* entscheidet, bekommt alles, was einen Audi ausmacht. Wer hingegen noch unentschieden ist, bekommt weitere Informationen und attraktive Fahrzeugangebote unter: **www.audi.de/gebrauchtwagenplus**

A billboard and a print advertisement featuring QR codes which link directly to the Audi website
Sources: Audi UK

Self-service technologies

Digital technologies have revolutionised the interactions between companies and customers. **Self-service technologies** (SSTs) provide customers with a technological interface which allows them to produce services without direct service employee involvement. SSTs include the internet, phone, mobile phone, kiosks and others. Many companies opt to use digital technology to replace interpersonal contacts and face-to-face meetings. Much of self-service technology use is driven by attempts to cut costs and to reduce human contact, which can be fraught with difficulties. The use of digital technology to avoid interpersonal and interactional problems at the consumer interface, and to increase the predictability of and the control over the service interaction for the company, may only superficially increase service quality.

Many customers prefer self-service technologies for a variety of reasons: they may be disappointed with human-based services, or may find SSTs easier and more convenient to use, in which case they add value to the customer experience. However, too often digital deployment is simply guided by the desire to cut cost or as a defensive problem avoidance approach that attempts to make services more programmable and thus easier to control and manage. To the degree that such approaches fail to take consumers' experience of the service adequately into account, they lag behind the full potential of service value co-creation. They can also create an informational wall between the company and the customer. Companies should view the advances in self-service technologies as a complement to traditional and human forms of engagement rather than as a substitute for connecting with customers. Research confirms that customers like to have a range of options available to them and to choose the most suitable for their needs and wants, rather than have the choice dictated to them by the company.

Nespresso

Nespresso, the French subsidiary of the Switzerland-based Nestlé, views self-service technologies as an important part of its customer engagement strategy. It sells individual-serving coffee capsules for use in coffee machines, and the capsules are sold exclusively via Nespresso's catalogues, on the website, by phone and through 200 retail shops. Nespresso has 20 global customer relationship centres employing over 1,100 'coffee specialists'. The centres handle an average of 12 calls a minute, 24 hours a day. When Nespresso realised how much customers wanted to talk about their product, the company trained its call centre staff to engage with customers longer, offering more information about types of coffee. Intentionally extending call times violates accepted practice for running an efficient call centre, but as Deschamps, the President of Nespresso France, notes: 'When people have a problem, they prefer human contact ... they prefer to go to a boutique or call.' After the company launched its website more than half the orders moved to the web, with 30 per cent from the retail outlet and 20 per cent by phone. Even with this move in sales Nespresso continued to invest in the call centre, noting that even if customers are not ordering on the phone, they like to call. Nespresso would save money if it directed customers to search for information on its website or relied on a steady stream of tweets to inform followers of new flavours, but Deschamps believes it is better to offer them a variety of ways to interact with the company. 'It's hard for any company to anticipate how consumer behaviour might change. The same customer who usually orders by phone might decide to use the internet one day because she is in a hurry. A week later that person might go back on the phone to ask advice about the coffee'.[69]

Managing the range and complexity of digital technologies challenges marketers to change how they behave, with an understanding that customer behaviour has changed and will continue to do so. Understanding the techniques needed is highlighted in the breakthrough marketing box.

Breakthrough marketing

Gaining an edge through digital marketing

Recent research by David Edelman in the *McKinsey Quarterly* suggests that companies that make the deep strategic, organisational and operational shifts required to become effective digital marketers can be more agile and productive, while also accelerating revenue growth.[70] Since the dawn of the internet, marketers have regarded it as a vast laboratory, launching experiment after experiment to generate sales and customer loyalty. Not surprisingly, many have failed. Consumers adopt digital technology as they see fit, fundamentally altering the way they make purchasing decisions. Companies that understand this evolution are now carefully moving digital interactivity toward the centre of their marketing strategies, rethinking their priorities and budgets, and substantially reshaping their processes and skills.

Research from dozens of companies navigating this shifting landscape has shown that the most successful digital marketers think differently. They view themselves as publishers of online content, not just marketers, and they recognise the opportunity to inspire consumers, who will in return become advocates for their products, services and brands.

Some marketers have made great progress thinking and acting in these new ways, while others have not. But even marketing professionals still in the starting blocks have been exposed more intensively to the transformation in consumer behaviour than have executives from outside the marketing function.

Edelman and Salsberg suggest how non-marketers and marketers can make sense of the changing consumer landscape and establish their priorities.

- **Think . . . like a publisher, not an advertiser.** Consumers today learn about products and services by reading online reviews, comparing features and prices on websites, and discussing options via social networks. Supporting this process requires a vast and growing range of content well beyond advertisements. While many companies chasing digital opportunities have slowly but steadily begun publishing everything from static content (such as product descriptions) to games and other multimedia, most behave like simple advertisers. If they adopted the mind-set of publishers, they could lower costs and eliminate unnecessary duplication, inconsistent interactions and content quality.
- **Think . . . of your customers as marketers.** Traditional marketers spend about 60 per cent of their advertising budgets on working media (or paid placement), 20 per cent on creating content, and the balance on

employees and agencies. Digital channels, with their social nature, reverse the economics, focusing on a smaller core of engaged people who can share information and positive impressions with a broader audience. Active digital marketers typically devote about 30 per cent of their advertising budgets to paid media and 50 per cent to content. Customers do more of the heavy lifting as they decide what to look at, play with content, and forward it to their online communities. Allowing consumers to make brands their own inevitably raises concerns among companies fearful of losing control over brands. The key is striking a balance between retaining control and creating opportunities for consumers to embrace your content.

- **Act . . . to help the customer.** Few customers today are content merely to watch or read advertisements and then wander into a store for advice from a salesperson. Many customers receive marketing emails, search for products online, or use mobile devices to find retail coupons. They continually interact with brands as they move closer to making purchase decisions, and digital channels can unify that experience and prevent the leakage of opportunity. Television commercials should inspire keywords for consumers to search. Great search positioning should offer easy-to-find web links to specific offers promoted by other media. Links should go deep into specific places to help consumers learn about and buy products or services. Company sites should show exactly the same products or services, with exactly the same images, rich descriptions, and inventory availability.
- **Act . . . as if information is priceless.** When prospective customers actively evaluate their product or service options, the right message, in the right location, is needed immediately. When online conversations start to critique a brand, no response can be fast enough. When you need to optimise your search and other media spending on ever-faster cycles, there is no time to waste. Savvy digital marketers are therefore mastering intelligence-gathering tools and processes. These tools analyse what customers are seeing, by examining positions in search results or coverage on key retail sites; what customers are doing, by analysing their online behaviour; and what customers are saying, by mining online discussions and soliciting ongoing feedback. This intelligence — the lifeblood of digital leadership — disseminates insights throughout an organisation and promotes the personalisation needed to help consumers regard a brand as their own.

Source: D. Edelman (2010) Gaining an edge through digital marketing, *McKinsey Quarterly*, 3, 129–34.

Understanding consumer digital behaviour

Several models and theories can be applied for the purpose of understanding consumer digital behaviour: that is, consumers' decisions on what to buy, in what amount and where – offline or online. We now consider five main perspectives on consumer digital behaviour:

1 the theory of planned behaviour;
2 the technology acceptance model;
3 the theory of adoption of innovations;
4 the trade-off/transaction costs perspective;
5 the perceived risk perspective.

The theory of planned behaviour

A consumer may be prevented from buying online if he or she perceives the purchase process as too complex or if the consumer does not possess the resources necessary to perform the considered behaviour. This may happen even if the consumer has a positive attitude towards online shopping. Such considerations are incorporated into the **theory of planned behaviour** (TPB) as perceived behavioural control (PBC).[71] PBC can be conceptualised as the consumer's subjective belief about how difficult it will be for that consumer to generate the behaviour in question. As an example, a consumer considering buying groceries over the internet may hesitate to do so if he or she perceives the ordering process as too difficult. According to TPB, the same consumer may, however, be persuaded that buying groceries is worth trying if one of the consumer's closest friends has already done so with success (social norm).

The technology acceptance model

The **technology acceptance model** (TAM) was developed to predict 'technology acceptance', which can be conceptualised as an individual's psychological state with regard to his or her voluntary or intended use of a particular technology. TAM proposes that the two most important variables in explaining attitude towards system-using intention are perceived ease of use (i.e. perceived complexity) and perceived usefulness. However, TAM can be modified to predict consumer digital shopping behaviour. For example, perceived usefulness can be conceptualised as the degree to which online shopping will provide the consumer with relative advantages in comparison to offline shopping.[72] Evidence, based on a modification of the TAM approach, suggests that both perceived usefulness and perceived ease of using the internet for shopping purposes have positive effects on consumers' intentions to adopt online shopping. In addition, research suggests that attempts to understand consumer motivations for online shopping behaviour may benefit from taking into account the hedonic aspects (e.g. shopping enjoyment and/or fun) of the shopping experience along with perceived usefulness and perceived ease of use.[73]

The theory of adoption of innovations

Digital shopping could be regarded as an innovation, which like other innovations takes time to spread through the social system. The adoption of an innovation depends on various factors (including perceived compatibility, perceived relative advantage, perceived complexity, triability and observability) that are related to the innovation itself and to the consumer.[74] Communicability is the ease with which the innovation can be observed or communicated among potential adopters. Triability or divisibility refers to the possibility of trying the innovation without huge investments. Complexity refers to the potential adopter's perceived complexity of the innovation or of using the innovation. Compatibility is the degree to which the innovation is consistent with existing values and past behaviour. Relative advantage is the degree to which consumers perceive the innovation as superior to existing alternatives. People in favour of online buying often point to the fact that this way of purchasing saves time and offers quality products at lower prices as compared to traditional shopping outlets.

Channel trade-offs and transaction costs

From the channel trade-offs and **transaction costs** perspective, an understanding of consumer online shopping behaviour needs to include consideration of how consumers will make choices relative to available retail alternatives. Often consumers are faced with trade-offs when deciding which retail alternative to use to make a purchase. When evaluating different shopping channel alternatives (including the internet), the channel trade-offs and transaction costs perspective proposes that consumers are likely to choose the channel that minimises perceived transaction costs. Transaction costs (i.e. time, mental, money and physical costs) include costs of obtaining relevant information, costs of evaluating relevant products, order costs and costs of post-sales services. Consumers' perceived transaction costs may, among other factors, be affected by consumers' perceived uncertainty, which are costs associated with unexpected outcomes of the transaction and asymmetry of information: that is, the seller and buyer may not have the same amount of information.

The perceived risk perspective

The suggestion that a high level of uncertainty implies a higher transaction cost and therefore would be regarded negatively by consumers receives support from the perceived risk perspective. Perceived risk can be considered a multidimensional construct, which in a digital context can be conceptualised as a person's perception of the possibility of having negative outcome or suffering from harm or losses associated with shopping online.[75] Consumers perceive risk because they face uncertainty and potentially undesirable outcomes or consequences as a result of their behavioural decisions.[76] For example, a high perceived risk might follow from not knowing the outcome (e.g. the delivered benefits) or the negative consequences (e.g. will digital shopping violate credit card security?) of carrying out online buying.

Synthesising the perspectives

Based on the five perspectives on consumer digital shopping behaviour that we have reviewed, Figure 4.8 presents an overview of factors that may influence consumer digital shopping behaviour (i.e. what to buy, in what amount and where – offline or online?).

Social norms and PBC have both been shown to affect intended consumer use of mobile advertising (advertising activities supported by mobile devices, which allow companies to directly communicate with their consumers without location or time barriers) and mobile media users' adoption of new services.[77] Other recent research found that in relation to general internet shopping behaviour, PBC influenced consumer adoption of this shopping mode.[78] Research results have also demonstrated that perceived usefulness and perceived ease of use may affect digital shopping behaviour (i.e. the TAM perspective). One study found (along with another variable: perceived risk) that perceived usefulness and perceived ease of use explained more than 50 per cent of the consumers' intention to adopt online shopping of books and banking services. Another study revealed that perceived usefulness has a positive impact on consumers' attitudes

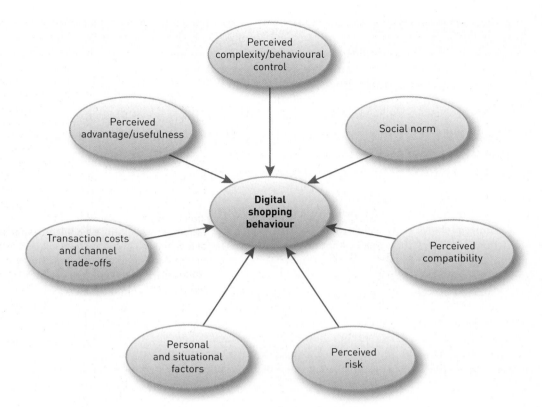

Figure 4.8 Potential determinants of consumer digital shopping behaviour

towards a website and the perceived 'flow' (i.e. whether the experience is enjoyable and involving) of interacting with the website.[79] A study of the attitude of Swiss university students regarding health-related e-service trends found that compatibility has a positive effect on the adoption of online health accounts.[80] Another study has revealed that perceived complexity, perceived compatibility and perceived relative advantage highly influence Danish consumers' adoption of online grocery buying. Perceived transaction cost has been found to influence consumer choice between online and offline shopping channels (i.e. channel trade-offs and the transaction costs perspective). For example, one study reported that time and effort was more important to online purchasers than to inquirers.[81]

While these results concern the inter-channel trade-offs that consumers may carry out when choosing among channels, online intra-channel trade-offs can also be considered. A study of German online consumers suggests that consumers value product-related information (at the expense of product breadth and product depth) and order fulfilment (at the expense of security and simplicity of the transaction process).[82] Research has also revealed that if consumers perceive losses or harm – that is, perceived risk – this may negatively influence their online buying intention. Yet, if consumers perceive high risk, they may also respond by adopting risk reduction strategies such as information search prior to purchase.[83]

Personal and situational factors may moderate consumer online shopping behaviour. For example, in the online search process, the individual shopper is likely to be affected by their vocabulary and understanding of the subject area, as well as their ability to frame a query and to use a search engine.[84] Moreover, factors such as income, education, age, gender and lifestyle can also affect consumer online shopping behaviour,[85] as the marketing insight box demonstrates.[86]

Marketing insight

Purchasing clothes online

Clothing products may differ extensively according to price, quality, body fit and the like. For such differentiated products, consumers will often perceive great variations in quality and therefore perceive shopping online

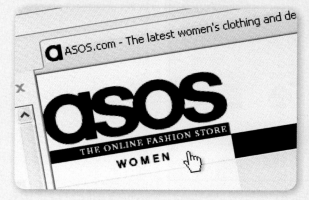

Source: © NetPics/Alamy

as more risky than offline purchasing. In light of this, it may come as a surprise that clothing is one of the most common product categories purchased online. Moreover, statistics reveal that clothing is one of very few categories with more women than men purchasing online. One possible explanation for this is that men's clothing may often be purchased by the man's partner instead of being purchased by the man himself. When buying clothing online, women are more oriented towards 'shopping for fun' than men are, the latter being more 'quick shoppers'. These gender-related shopping orientations are even more significant when men and women are buying clothes for themselves compared to buying for their partner. Moreover, men are more willing than women to accept online difficulty when buying clothing. Simply put, men may be more likely to blame themselves (instead of the online clothing store) when experiencing online difficulties in finding items. This may relate to men being generally more uncertain and less professional clothing shoppers than women.

Company–customer interactivity

Making the website more 'human'

Some people find that the lack of social interaction on the internet is a barrier for them carrying out internet shopping. In response, some online retailers have included personal characteristics on their websites, to provide consumers with the important feeling of being served when shopping online.[87] For example, on IKEA's website the 'human' assistant Anna can be found. When you turn on the sound, Anna offers voice guidance to visiting customers.

Marketing research suggests that social cues (i.e. cues based on human characteristics) can facilitate the development of website sociability.[88] Retailers can contribute to consumers' online experiences by adding social cues that enhance their flow, pleasure and arousal. Four online social cues should be considered potentially powerful marketing tools in retail website design:

1 **Language**. The language of a 'high-social' website should be written text *as well as* spoken language.
2 **Social role**. A tour guide may welcome visitors and thank customers when they log off.
3 **Voice**. The tour guide may give a brief summary of each web page and assist visitors navigating the website.
4 **Interactivity**. The tour guide may ask the visitor to indicate certain interests or needs and respond to them in a proper way. For example, the tour guide may ask, 'Are you looking for something specific?', and then provide a number of options.

Online personalisation

Online personalisation is 'the ability of a company to recognise and treat its customers as individuals through personalised products or service design, personal messaging, targeted

Anna offers online guid-
ance to IKEA customers.
Source: © Inter IKEA
Systems BV 2006.

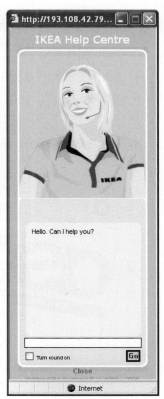

banner ads, special offers on bills, or other personal transactions'.[89] Italian marketing researchers Gaetano 'Nino' Miceli, Francesco Ricotta and Michele Costabile have suggested a 'personalisation continuum', synthesising five different personalisation strategies: product versioning, mass customisation, one-to-one personalisation, customerisation and reverse marketing.[90]

Product or service versioning The purpose of product versioning is to group consumers according to their willingness to pay. Consumers with high willingness to pay choose one version, while consumers with lower willingness to pay choose a different version.[91] Product or service versioning has for a long time been utilised by airlines. When booking a flight, passengers can choose different service versions (first class, tourist class and so on) of the same type of service: transportation. Software products (computer games, programs, etc.) are especially suited for product or service versioning. These offerings, which are capable of being distributed in digital form, are characterised by a distinctive cost structure: producing the first copy is often very expensive but producing subsequent copies is very cheap. The marginal cost of producing one extra unit is almost zero and therefore the price of the units cannot be set according to the price of producing them. Instead, the price should reflect the value that the individual customer attaches to the product or service. But since customers may attach different values, they are also willing to pay different prices for different versions. Moreover, producing many different versions of a certain product requires possible contact with many different customers, a condition that is especially fulfilled when distributing through digital channels.

Mass customisation Mass customisation presents customers with a large amount of product and/or services from which the consumer can choose their 'made-to-order' customised product or service.[92] This approach is well known in, for example, the car (Volkswagen, Fiat) and computer industries (Dell Computers). Mass customisation allows companies to tailor products to customers' individual needs while at the same time maintaining substantial economies of scale (i.e. the reduction in cost per unit that companies obtain when products are produced in high amounts). The negative side of mass customisation is that customers may be confused by the huge variety of offers and thus find it difficult to choose fully satisfying products. Dell is one of the pioneers of mass customisation. In fact, Dell has changed the competitive landscape by doing the following:[93]

- offering customised products directly to online customers on demand without premiums in either price or lead time;
- minimising inventory to unthinkable levels;
- being agile – responding quickly to market/technology changes;
- eliminating the cost and risk of finished goods inventory;
- successfully executing a mass customisation strategy quarter after quarter, year after year.

Although Dell CEO Michael Dell is widely acknowledged as the person who started the 'build-to-order' and 'mass customisation' wave, mass customisation was not planned but was born out of necessity. Michael Dell started his computer assembling business from his college bedroom and did not have the space for mass production. That led to 'build-to-order' computers – where people pay first and get their computers later.[94] Three powerful forces may accelerate the spreading of mass customisation in the future:[95]

- the rate of technological change is accelerating;
- products are becoming more complex; and
- customers empowered by increasing global competition and growing disposable incomes are demanding greater product variety.

One-to-one personalisation When using a one-to-one personalisation approach, marketing provides content or recommendations that are relevant specifically to the individual user based on their individual characteristics and preferences. Web-based one-to-one personalisation is mainly focused on close communication within the company – customer relationship[96] – and involves 'delivering customised content for the individual, through web pages, email, or push technology'.[97] The first time a customer visits a personalised website, they may be asked about their preferences for different kinds of service. By registration of user name and password it is possible later on to offer services that match these preferences. Customers may also be recognised by using cookies (i.e. short pieces of data used by web servers to help identify web users). Personalised websites help customers find the products and services they prefer and have even been compared to a dedicated assistant who knows your tastes well and makes your choice more effective.[98] For example, mycreateabook.com offers 'personalised letters from Santa and the Easter Bunny', while time-frames.com offers 'personalised photo frames, baby's first year picture frames, through time children's frames with unique personalised custom story frame gifts for every occasion'. Consumer research suggests that personalised items lead to more clicks than random suggestions.[99]

Customisation Digital technology allows managers to cater to the needs of individual customers and to meet those needs.[100] Customisation means understanding customers' needs and preferences and other individual characteristics, and then satisfying these needs and preferences by customised products and services. Customisation is different from one-to-one personalisation. Simply put, personalisation is essentially about using the right surname and associating, for example, an email with a recipient in a database. Customisation implies tracking and conditional content – content driven by data associated with the recipient. In other words, customisation implies personalisation – personalisation does not imply customisation.[101]

Reverse marketing Digital media may change the focus of marketing from a supplier perspective to a customer perspective. Traditional marketing has focused on the products and services that firms provide. Although managers for decades have carried out market analyses in order to determine customer needs and wants and thereby to estimate potential

The M&M website allows consumers to customise their M&Ms.
Source: Mars, Inc.

demand, emphasis has subsequently been on manufacturing and seeking orders. Reverse marketing means that manufacturing will only start when the customer orders. While Dell also provides an example of reverse marketing, the offline analogue is McDonald's and its transformation. McDonalds's traditional model was to produce burgers and keep them under heat lamps, serving them when the customer ordered. Due to competition, customer preferences and transformation in technologies, McDonald's later started assembling food only after it has been ordered.[102]

While some customers may find interactions with suppliers enjoyable and valuable, there is also the risk that other customers may become frustrated because they may not possess the necessary competencies and involvement for engaging in such interactions. Such customers may instead end up being dissatisfied. When companies design their personalisation programme it is therefore of utmost importance to realise that considerations concerning segmentation and targeting (see Chapter 10) are also relevant in an online setting.

SUMMARY

1 Digital technology is digitised information which is recorded in binary code as combinations of the digits 0 and 1, also called bits, which represent words and images. Digital marketing refers to the use of digital technology in order to inform, interact with and/or distribute to customers. Digital marketing includes both internet-based marketing activities and other kinds of activity (i.e. mobile phone communication, emails, social media and interactive digital television) that are based on digital technology.

2 Marketing managers can manage digital technology by dividing digital technologies into two categories: information (research, analysis and planning) and interactions (communications,

connections and collaborations), although many can be used for both.

3 Marketing managers can reach, communicate and deliver as well as analyse and monitor customers and marketing programmes like never before. Each marketing situation will demand a different set of digital technologies.

4 Managing the implementation of digital technology within marketing and across the organisation has become a core skill. There are four main responsibilities: (1) selection of digital technologies, (2) supporting the adoption of digital technology, (3) exploitation of digital technology, and (4) uniting marketing and IT staff.

5 Digital technology itself should not be seen as an instrument that dominates other marketing instruments. Rather, digital marketing complements other marketing activities, with which it should be integrated.

6 No matter how well digital technology supports the activities within an industry, companies can only build competitive advantage if they are able to improve and sustain operational effectiveness better than their competitors.

7 Social networking has revolutionised the way people communicate and share information with one another in today's society. Offline and online social networks can be compared across three dimensions: tie strength, online homophily and source credibility.

8 Viral marketing is an internet adaptation of marketing, using word-of-mouth effects. Viral marketing can be understood as an advertising message – usually humorous or innovative – which is spread by consumers to other consumers.

9 Email communication is characterised by cost effectiveness and time efficiency, making email an attractive direct channel for managers.

10 Search engine optimisation (SEO) is the process of improving the visibility and thus the volume and quality of traffic to a website, from search engines.

11 Mobile phones and particularly smartphones have increased the ability of companies and customers to interact. By using mobile advertising, companies can communicate directly with their consumers without location or time barriers.

12 Self-service technologies (SSTs) provide consumers with a technology-supported service without employee involvement. These include the internet, phone, mobile phone, kiosks and others. Many companies opt to use digital technology to replace interpersonal contacts and face-to-face meetings.

13 Five main perspectives on consumer digital behaviour can be considered: the theory of reasoned action and the theory of planned behaviour, the technology acceptance model, the theory of adoption of innovations, the trade-off/transaction costs perspective, and the perceived risk perspective.

14 Factors such as income, education, age, gender and lifestyle can moderate consumer digital behaviour.

15 Social cues (cues based on human characteristics) can facilitate the development of website sociability. Four online social cues should be considered potentially powerful marketing tools in retail website design: (1) language, (2) social role, (3) voice and (4) interactivity.

16 Online personalisation is the ability of a company to recognise and treat its customers as individuals through personal messaging, targeted banner ads, special offers on bills or other personal transactions.

APPLICATIONS

Marketing debate

Ten years from now, digital shopping will be the primary shopping channel used by consumers *versus* Digital shopping will never outperform offline shopping channels as there are simply too many problems associated with digital shopping.

Marketing discussion

Marketing has an extensive range of technologies available for both informational and interactional use. What are the core technology management skills needed for contemporary marketing managers in using these technologies?

REFERENCES

[1] D. Edelman and B. Salsberg (2010) Digital marketing's new vocabulary, *McKinsey Quarterly*, 4, 20–2.

[2] L. Thomas and P. Revoir (2010) Computers and TV take up half our lives as we spend seven hours a day using technology, *Mail Online*, 19 August.

[3] C. Anderson (2006) *The Long Tail: The New Economics of Culture and Communications*, London: Random House.

[4] M. Brady, M. Saren and N. Tzokas (2002) Integrating information technology into marketing practice – the IT reality of contemporary marketing practice, *Journal of Marketing Management*, 18(5–6), 555–78.

[5] R. Sullivan (2011) Techmate, *Vogue*, 1 March www.vogue.com/magazine/article/christopher-bailey-tech-mate/Accessed June 2011.

[6]D. Chaffey, F. Ellis, K. Chadwick and R. Mayer (2008) *Internet Marketing: Strategy, Implementation and Practice,* 4th edn, Harlow Financial Times Prentice Hall, www.davechaffey.com.

[7]CMO Council (2010) Driving revenue through customer relevance, CMO Council, http://resources.cmocouncil.org/reports/cmocio-report-es.pdf,

[8]M. Mulligan Mark (2010) Inditex puts Zara products on line, *Financial Times*, 1 September.

[9]C.P. Holland and P. Naudé (2004) The metamorphosis of marketing into an information-handling problem, *Journal of Business & Industrial Marketing*, 19(3), 167–77.

[10]M. R. Fellenz and M. Brady (2010) Managing customer-centric information: the challenges of information and communication technology (ICT) deployment in service environments, *International Journal of Applied Logistics*, 1(3), 88–105.

[11]D. A. Schweidel, P. S. Fader and E. T. Bradlow (2008) Understanding service retention within and across cohorts using limited information. *Journal of Marketing*, 72(1), 82–94.

[12]The Economist (2010) Data, data everywhere,*The Economist* – Special Report, 25 February.

[13]C. Humby, T. Hunt, and T. Philips (2008) *Scoring Points: How Tesco Continues to Win Customer Loyalty*, 2nd edn, London, Kogan Page.

[14]M. R. Fellenz and M. Brady (2008) Managing the innovative deployment of information and communication technologies (ICTs) for global service organisations, *International Journal of Technology Marketing*, 3(1), 39–55. M. Merisavo (2006) The effects of digital marketing communication on customer loyalty, Working Paper W–400, Helsinki School of Economics. S. L. Vargo and R. F. Lusch (2004) Evolving to a new dominant logic for marketing, *Journal of Marketing*, 68(1), 1–17.

[15]E. Constantinides and S. J. Fountain (2009) Web 2.0: conceptual foundations and marketing issues, *Journal of Direct, Data and Digital Marketing Practice*, 9(3), 231–44.

[16]N. Cook (2008) *Enterprise 2.0: How Social Software Will Change the Future of Work*, Aldershot Gower.

[17]CMO Council (2010), op. cit.

[18]A. Badawy (2009) Technology management simply defined: a tweet plus two characters, *Journal of Engineering and Technology*, 26, 219–24.

[19]Ibid.

[20]http://nces.ed.gov/pubs2005/tech_suite/part_3.asp.

[21]D. Edelman (2010) Gaining an edge through digital marketing, *McKinsey Quarterly*, 3, 129–34.

[22]Ibid.

[23]M. Brady, M. R. Fellenz and R. Brookes (2008) Researching the role of information and communication technologies in contemporary marketing, *Journal of Business and Industrial Marketing*, 23(2), 108–14; R. Nolan, (1973) Computer data bases: the future is now, *Harvard Business Review*, 51(5), 98–114; R. Nolan (1998) Connectivity and control in the year 2000 and beyond, *Harvard Business Review*, July–August, 3–14.

[24]CMO (2010), op. cit.

[25]CMO (2010), op. cit.

[26]M. R. Fellenz and M. Brady (2010) Managing customer-centric information: the challenges of information and communication technology (ICT) deployment in service environments, *International Journal of Applied Logistics*, 1(3), 88–105.

[27]M. R. Fellenz and M. Brady (2008) Managing the innovative deployment of information and communication technologies (ICTs) for global service organisaitons, *International Journal of Technology Marketing*, 3(1), 39–55.

[28]Ibid.

[29]C. Saren (2011) Forrester Research: marketing is an IT spending blackhole, *Computer Weekly*, 14 April.

[30]Simon Yates (2011) CIOs are from Mars, CMOs are from Venus? Not any more, *Computer Weekly*, 14 April.

[31]Badawy (2009), op. cit.

[32]http://royal.pingdom.com/2011/01/12/internet-2010-in-numbers/.

[33]Z. Fernández and M. J. Nieto (2005) The internet: strategy and boundaries of the firm, Working Paper #05-01 (01) *Business Economics Series*, Universidad Carlos III de Madrid, January.

[34]Ibid.

[35]J. B. Kim, P. Albuquerque and B. Bronnenberg (2010) Online demand under limited consumer search, *Marketing Science*, 29(6), 1001–23; P. Rajan Varadarajan and Manjit S. Yadav (2002) Marketing strategy and the internet: an organizing framework, *Journal of the Academy of Marketing Science*, 30(4), 296–312.

[36]R. Garfinkel, R. Gopal, B. Pathak and F. Yin (2008) Shopbot 2.0: integrating recommendations and promotions with comparison shopping, *Decision Support Systems*, 46(1), 61–9; H. Lim and A. J. Dubinsky (2005) The theory of planned behavior in e-commerce: making a case for interdependencies between salient beliefs, *Psychology and Marketing*, 22(10), 833–55.

[37]M. E. Porter (2001) Strategy and the internet, *Harvard Business Review*, March, 62–78. See also M. E. Porter (2008) The five competitive forces that shape strategy, *Harvard Business Review*, January, 79–93.

[38]R. B. Money, M. C. Gilly and J. L. Graham (1998) Explorations of national culture and word-of mouth referral behavior in the purchase of industrial services in the United States and Japan. *Journal of Marketing*, 62, 76–87.

[39]J. Walker, S. Wasserman and B. Wellman (1994) Statistical models for social support networks, in S. Wasserman and J. Galaskiewicz (eds), *Advances in Social Network Analysis*, Thousand Oaks, CA: Sage, 53–78.

[40]L. C. Wang, J. Baker, J. A. Wagner and K. Wakefield (2007) Can a retail web site be social?, *Journal of Marketing*, 71, 143–57.

[41]M. S. Handcock, A. E. Raftery and J. M. Tantrum (2007) Model-based clustering for social networks, *Journal of the Royal Statistical Society: Series A (Statistics in Society)*, 170(2), 301–54.

[42]Z. L. Tormala and R. E. Petty (2004) Source credibility and attitude certainty: a metacognitive analysis of resistance to persuasion, *Journal of Consumer Psychology*, 14(4), 427–42.

[43]http://royal.pingdom.com/2011/01/12/internet-2010-in-numbers/.

[44]M. Trusov, R Bucklin and K. Pauwels (2009) Effects of word of mouth versus traditional marketing: finding from an internet social networking site. *Journal of Marketing*, 73, 90–102.

[45]R. V Kozinets, S. Wilner, A. Wojnicki and K. de Valck (2010) Networks of narrativity: understanding word-of-mouth marketing in online communities, *Journal of Marketing*, 74(2), 71–89.

[46]M. G. Siegler (2009) Every minute, just about a day's worth of video is now uploaded to YouTube, *TechCrunch*, 20 May, http://techcrunch.com/2009/05/20/every-minute-just-about-a-days-worth-of-video-is-uploaded-to-youtube/.

[47]B. Hauge, C. Moseholm and M. D. Svnedsen (2008) Internettet anno 2006, www.marketmagzine.dk.

[48]Viral markedsføring er ved at miste pusten, *Business.dk*, 11 March 2008.

[49]G.-O. Oren (2010) Building consumer demand by using viral marketing within an online social network, *Advances in Management*, 3(7), 7–14.

[50]A. M. Kaplan and M. Haenlein (2011) Two hearts in three-quarter time: how to waltz the social media/viral marketing dance, *Business Horizons*, 54(3), 253–63.

[51]M. Trusov, A. V. Bodapati and R. E. Bucklin (2010) Determining influential users in internet social networks, *Journal of Marketing*, XLVII (August), 643–58.

[52]C. Ridings, D. Gefen and B. Arinze (2006) Psychological barriers: lurker and poster motivation and behaviour in online communities, *Communications of the Association for Information Systems*, 18(1), 329–54. See also W. C. Hill, J. D. Hollan, D. Wroblewski and T. McCandless (1992) Edit wear and read wear, *Proceedings of CHI'92, the SIGCHI Conference on Human Factors in Computing Systems*, 3–7 May, pp. 3–9.

[53]http://en.wikipedia.org/wiki/Spam_%28electronic%29.

[54]A.-S. Cases, C. Fournier, P.-L. Dubois and J. F. Tanner, Jr (2010) Web site spill over to email campaigns: the role of privacy, trust and shoppers' attitudes, *Journal of Business Research*, 63, 993–9.

[55]M. Durnik (2005) New email marketing rules in the European Union: one year later, *MarketingProfs*, 28 June; Directive 2002/58/EC of the European Parliament and of the Council of 12 July 2002 concerning the processing of personal data and the protection of privacy in the electronic communications sector (Directive on privacy and electronic communications).

[56]Email marketing reports: Anti-spam laws and the EU, www.email-marketing-reports.com/canspam/eu/.

[57]See http://en.wikipedia.org/wiki/Second_Life.

[58]M. Sarvary (2008) The metaverse, TV of the future? *Harvard Business Review*, February, 30 – 41.

[59]http://mobithinking.com/stats-corner/global-mobile-statistics-2011-all-quality-mobile-marketing-research-mobile-web-stats-su.

[60]http://en.wikipedia.org/wiki/Smartphone.

[61]http://mobithinking.com/stats-corner/global-mobile-statistics-2011-all-quality-mobile-marketing-research-mobile-web-stats-su.

[62]R. Vatanparast and M. Asil (2007) Factors affecting the use of mobile advertising, *International Journal of Mobile Marketing*, 2(2), 21–34.

[63]Ibid.

[64]Tom Polanski (2010) BMW mobile campaign gets 30% conversion rate eBizine, http://ebizine.com/advertising/bmw-mobile-campaign-gets-30-conversion-rate/

[65]L. Fortunati (2001) The mobile phone: an identity on the move, *Personal and Ubiquitous Computing*, 5, 85–98.

[66]R. Vatanparast and M. Asil (2007) Factors affecting the use of mobile advertising, *International Journal of Mobile Marketing*, 2(2), 58–67.

[67]J. Tawfik and E. Albrecht (2008) *Strategies for e-Business: Creating Value through Electronic and Mobile*, 2nd edn, Harlow: Prentice Hall and Financial Times; R. Waters (2007) Barcode hope for mobile advertising, *Financial Times*, March, www.ft.com/intl/cms/s/0/9axx94f6-cb88-11db-b436-000b5df10621.html#axzz1cRd5IJel.

[68]Audi (2011) Billboard offers wealth of mobile interaction; http://m.obilesites.com/blog/audis-mobile-marketing-prominence/; www.ft.com/cms/s/0/9a4494f6-cb88-11db-b436-000b5df10621.html#ixzz1JxQe5bzd; http://virtualmob.co.uk/BlogWP/2011/05/audi-interactive-calendar-built-on-ar/.

[69]L. Kramer (2010) How French innovators are putting the 'social' back in social networking, *Harvard Business Review*, October, 121–4.

[70]D. Edelman (2010) Gaining an edge through digital marketing, *McKinsey Quarterly*, 3, 129–34.

[71]M. Fishbein and I. Ajzen (1975) *Belief, Attitude, Intention, and Behavior: An Introduction to Theory and Research*, Reading, MA: Addison Wesley.

[72]S. Al-Gahtani (2001) The applicability of TAM outside North America: an empirical test in the United Kingdom, *Information Resources Management Journal*, 14(3), 37–46.

[73]See W. K. Darley, C. Blankson and D. J. Luethge (2010) Toward an integrated framework for online consumer behavior and decision making process: a review, *Psychology and Marketing*, 27(2), 94–116; T. Hansen and J. M. Jensen (2009) Shopping orientation and online clothing purchases: the role of gender and purchase situation, *European Journal of Marketing*, special issue on e-retailing and e-shopping, 43(9/10), 1154–70; T. Hansen (2006) Determinants of consumers' repeat online buying of groceries, *International Review of Retail, Distribution and Consumer Research*, 16(1), 93–114.

[74]E. M. Rogers (1983) *Diffusion of Innovations*, 3rd edn, New York: Free Press.

[75]C. F. X. Liu and K. K. Wie (2003) An empirical study of product differences in consumers, E-commerce adoption behaviour, *Electronic Commerce Research and Applications*, 2(3), 229–39.

[76]C. Boshoff, C. Schlechter and S.-J. Ward (2011) Consumers' perceived risks associated with purchasing on a branded web site: the mediating effect of brand knowledge, *South African Journal of Business Management*, 42(1), 45–54; N. Lim (2003) Consumers' perceived risk: sources versus consequences, *Electronic Commerce Research and Applications*, 2(3), 216–28.

[77]J. H. Lee, J. H. Kim and J. H. Hong (2011) A comparison of adoption models for new mobile media services between high- and low-motive groups, *International Journal of Mobile Communications*, 8(5), 487–506; R. Vatanparast and M. Asil (2007) Factors affecting the use of mobile advertising, *International Journal of Mobile Marketing*, 2(2), 21–34.

[78]See Darley, Blankson and Luethge (2010), op cit. M.-S. Wang, C.-C. Chen, S.-C. Chang and Y.-H. Yang (2007) Effects of online shopping attitudes, subjective norms and control beliefs on online shopping intentions: a test of the theory of planned behaviour, *International Journal of Management*, 24(2), 296–302.

[79]A. V. Hausman and J. S. Siekpe (2009) The effect of web interface features on consumer online purchase intentions, *Journal of Business Research*, 62(1), 5–13.

[80]L. Muhdi and R. Boutellier (2010) Diffusion of potential health-related e-services: an analysis of Swiss health customer perspectives, *Journal of Management and Marketing in Healthcare*, 3(1), 60–72.

[81]T. Broekhuizen and E. K. R. E. Huizingh (2009) Online purchase determinants: is their effect moderated by direct experience?, *Management Research News*, 32(5), 440–57.

[82]G. Odekerken-Schröder and M. Wetzels (2003) Trade-offs in online purchase decisions: two empirical studies in Europe, *European Management Journal*, 21(6), 731–9.

[83]S. S. Martin and C. Camarero (2009) How perceived risk affects online buying, *Online Information Review*, 33(4), 629–54; S. M. Forsythe and B. Shi (2003) Consumer patronage and risk perceptions in internet shopping, *Journal of Business Research*, 56, 867–75.

[84]A. D. Madden, N. J. Ford, D. Miller and P. Levy (2006) Children's use of the internet for information-seeking, *Journal of Documentation*, 62(6), 744–61.

[85]See Darley, Blankson and Luethge (2010), op cit. N. F. Doherty and F. E. Ellis-Chadwick (2006) New perspectives in internet retailing: a review and strategic critique of the field, *International Journal of Retail and Distribution Management*, 34(4/5), 411–28.

[86]Adapted from T. Hansen and J. M. Jensen (2009) Shopping orientation and online clothing purchases: the role of gender and purchase situation, *European Journal of Marketing*, 43(9/10), 1154–70.

[87]C. Dennis, A. Morgan, L. T. Wright and C. Jayawardhena (2010) The influences of social e-shopping in enhancing young women's online shopping behaviour, *Journal of Customer Behaviour*, 9(2), 151–74; Wang et al. (2007), op cit.

[88]Ibid.

[89]C. Imhoff, L. Loftis and J. Geiger (2001) *Building the Customer-Centric Enterprise: Data Warehousing Techniques for Supporting Customer Relationship Management*, New York: Wiley.

[90]G. (N.) Miceli, F. Ricotta and M. Costabile (2007) Customizing customization: a conceptual framework for interactive personalization, *Journal of Interactive Marketing*, 21(2), 6–25.

[91]H. R. Varian (1997) Versioning information goods, Research Paper, University of California, Berkeley, 13 March.

[92]J. Buffington (2011) Comparison of mass customization and generative customization in mass markets, *Industrial Management and Data Systems*, 111(1), 41–62.

[93]D. J. Gardner, Profitability for small manufacturing companies: why 21st century manufacturers can't ignore mass customization, *Business Forum Journal* (www.bizforum.org/Journal/www_journalDG003.htm).

[94]A. Kothari (2005) Mass customization, *Marketing eYe*, 24 January www.biztactics.com/blog/2005/01/mass-customization.php.

[95]T. Jitpaiboon, R. Dangol and J. Walters (2009) The study of cooperative relationships and mass customization, *Management Research News*, 32(9), 804–15.

[96]J. Wind and A. Rangaswamy (2001) Customerization: the next revolution in mass customization, *Journal of Interactive Marketing*, 15(1), 13–32.

[97]D. Chaffey, R. Mayer, K. Johnston and F. Ellis-Chadwick (2000) *Internet Marketing*, Harlow, Financial Times Prentice-Hall, p. 299.

[98]H. Nysveen and P. E. Pedersen (2004) An exploratory study of customers' perception of company web sites offering various interactive applications: moderating effects of customers' internet experience, *Decision Support Systems*, 37, 137– 50; W. Hanson (2000) *Principles of Internet Marketing*, Florence, KY: South-Western College Publishing/Thompson Learning.

[99]P. de Pechpeyrou (2009) How consumers value online personalization: a longitudinal experiment, *Direct Marketing: An International Journal*, 3(1), 35–51.

[100]Ibid. J. Buffington (2011) Comparison of mass customization and generative customization in mass markets, *Industrial Management and Data Systems*, 111(1), 41–62; T. S. Raghu, P. K. Kannan, H. R. Rao and A. B. Whinston (2001) Dynamic profiling of consumers for customized offerings over the internet: a model and analysis, *Decision Support Systems*, 32, 117–34.

[101]T. Barnes (2004) RSS: marketing's next big thing, *Marketing-Profs*, 7 September.

[102]J. Isaksen (2010) Reverse marketing, *OnlyReviews*, http://onlyreviews.com/reversemarketing.html; A. Sharma and J. N. Sheth (2006) Web-based marketing: the coming revolution in marketing thought and strategy, *Journal of Business Research*, 57, 696–702; R. T. Rust and F. Espinoza (2006) How technology advances influence business research and marketing strategy, *Journal of Business Research*, 59, 1072–8.

Capturing marketing insights

Video documentary for Part 2

Go to **www.pearsoned.co.uk/ marketingmanagementeurope** to watch the video documentary that relates to Part 2 and consider the issues raised below.

In any competitive activity, marketing managers need to research the field of play and the strength of the competition carefully. **Part 2: Capturing marketing insights** explores the three broad themes of:

1 identifying and tracking;
2 researching the market; and
3 analysing the competition.

Macro trends, or the broad environmental factors that affect activity in markets, usually lie beyond the sphere of control of marketing managers. However, their influence is considerable and therefore research activity is needed to assess their strength and likely impact on both consumer and business markets. Key business variables such as an economic downturn as well as major market trends that affect purchasing activity need to be identified and tracked. Micro trends that can be managed by practitioners affect customer purchase preferences and include factors such as changing lifestyles, customer needs and purchase activity.

When watching the video documentary that accompanies Part 2, consider the broad macro and detailed micro trends that companies need to evaluate when judging their position in relation to the activities of their competitors. Hard quantitative data such as frequency, level and degree of repeat spend requires continuous monitoring. Soft qualitative data, particularly on perceptions, need to be researched to ensure that companies can develop suitably differentiated market offerings for their customers. These key macro and micro trends can be researched effectively with modern digital marketing techniques.

Hear a variety of top marketing executives from a wide range of organisations offer their own interesting and varied perspectives on the key themes of Part 2 including: Dave Hodgson, Marketing Manager, Marketing Birmingham (top); Simon Topman, Managing Director, Acme Whistles (centre); a newly opened HSBC branch, Mumbai, India (bottom).

Chapter 5

The changing marketing environment and information management

IN THIS CHAPTER, WE WILL ADDRESS THE FOLLOWING QUESTIONS:

1 What are the key methods for tracking and identifying opportunities in the environment?

2 What are the components of a modern marketing information system?

3 What are useful internal records?

4 What is involved in a marketing intelligence system?

5 What are the key methods for tracking and identifying opportunities in the environment?

6 What is database management?

Food and drink industry in sustainability drive

Source: © AirOne/fotolia.com.

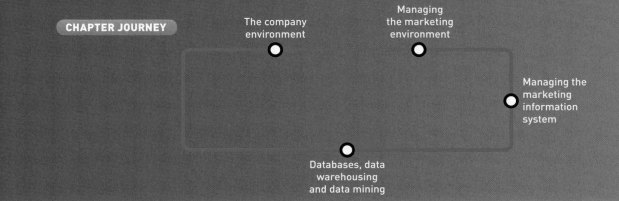

The company
environment

Managing
the marketing
environment

Managing the
marketing
information
system

Databases, data
warehousing
and data mining

Developing and implementing marketing plans requires a number of decisions. Making those decisions is both a creative and an analytical process in which several aspects should be considered. Due to globalisation and technological developments, the marketing environment is changing more rapidly than ever before and it is therefore essential that companies develop and maintain database management systems which provide a structured insight into and inspiration for marketing decision making, together with up-to-date information about macro trends as well as about micro effects particular to their business. A well-designed database management system allows the company to store, modify and extract data when needed. Holistic marketers recognise that the marketing environment is constantly presenting new opportunities and threats, and they understand the importance of continuously monitoring and adapting to that environment.

Take the food and drink industry example below.

Environmentally friendly behaviour is now a major issue for most governments, politicians, citizens, consumers – and companies. Introducing more eco-friendly products, making manufacturing process changes, upgrading outdated practices, reducing waste, minimising energy usage and similar initiatives to reduce energy or resources can now all contribute to the competitiveness of a company. Many industries have recognised this trend, one of them being the food and drink industry. The Food and Drink Federation (FDF) is made up of a wide range of companies and trade associations, from large international food and drink manufacturers with long-established brands to small companies manufacturing organic products, including Ahmad Tea, Border Biscuits, Cadbury/Kraft, Danisco, Kellogg's, Nestlé, and Pinneys of Scotland. FDF has extended its five commitments to improving the sustainability of the industry. It has set new targets across carbon reduction, waste to landfill, packaging reduction, water efficiency and transport miles. FDF's commitments include a 35 per cent reduction in CO_2 emissions by 2020, a 10 per cent reduction in the carbon impact of packaging by 2012 and saving 80 million road miles by 2012. The goal for FDF is to achieve a balance between various demands: the food and drink brands must not only be competitive in function and price, but also safe (during use and after disposal) as well as environmentally friendly. The FDF claims that the new commitments mark the industry's efforts to put sustainability at the core of business strategy and shape the future of the sector.[1]

Like the food and drink industry, virtually every industry is facing up to changes in the natural environment. In this chapter, we consider how firms can develop processes to track trends in the environment. Chapter 6 will review how marketers can conduct more customised research that addresses specific marketing problems or issues.

The company environment

Many companies are facing increasing global competition, faster flows of information and communication, increasing business complexity and rapidly changing customer needs and wants. Such dynamics reduce companies' ability to predict future marketplace changes and therefore add uncertainty to the decisions taken by marketing management. Since the marketing environment is constantly presenting new opportunities and threats, it is highly important that a company continuously monitors and adapts to changes in the marketing environment. In the first part of this chapter we will describe the salient aspects of the current marketing environment. In the second part, we will describe the systems for managing information about the changing marketing environment.

The marketing environment

A company is surrounded by an immediate microenvironment of customers, suppliers, distributors, agencies and competitors that we will describe in later chapters of the book. The company is also surrounded by a macroenvironment of major forces impacting on all companies, such as consumer trends, technological developments, and social, political and legal forces. These forces affect and moderate the behaviour of all the actors in a market including the company's competitors, suppliers, distributors and customers. Marketing scholars often organise the macro forces into five overall forces – political/legal, economic, ecological/physical, social/cultural and demographic, and technological. The acronym PEEST analysis is used to describe an analysis of the company's environment covering these five forces. We will describe and discuss these forces separately, but marketers must pay attention to their interactions, because these will lead to new opportunities and threats. For example, explosive population growth (demographic) leads to more resource depletion and pollution (natural), which leads consumers to call for more laws (political–legal), which stimulate new technological solutions and products (technological), which, if they are affordable (economic), may actually change attitudes and behaviour (social–cultural). The breakthrough marketing box describes how Google has successfully capitalised on the new marketing environment.

Enterprising individuals and companies manage to create new solutions to unmet needs. For example, Interflora was created to meet the need for express delivery of flowers across country borders.[2] However, a new market opportunity does not guarantee success, even if the product is technically feasible. For example, some companies sell portable 'electronic books' or 'ebooks'; but there may not be a sufficient number of people interested in reading a book on a computer screen or willing to pay the required price. This is why market research is necessary to determine an opportunity's profit potential.

To help marketers spot cultural shifts that might bring new opportunities or threats, several firms offer social–cultural forecasts. Euromonitor International, for instance, offers (for a fee) access to internationally comparable statistics, market reports, articles and comments from expert industry and country analysts across the 205 countries researched. It has tracked consumer and market trends since 1972, and in a recent report outlines consumer trends such as 'caring consumption', 'health kick – the goal of wellness', 'home as entertainment venue', 'hunger for happy endings and a slice of the dream', 'luxury in rehab' and 'me as a product'.[3] While reports, articles and other sources may provide valuable background information on the macroenvironment, each company also needs to analyse its macroenvironment to detect needs and trends of particular importance to the company.

Analysing the macroenvironment

Successful companies recognise and respond profitably to unmet needs and trends. We distinguish among fads, trends and megatrends. A **fad** is 'unpredictable, short-lived, and without social, economic, and political significance'. A company can cash in on a fad such

Breakthrough marketing

Google

Founded in 1998 by two Stanford University PhD students, search engine Google's name is a play on the word *googol* – the number represented by a 1 followed by 100 zeros – a reference to the massive quantity of data available online, which the company helps users make sense of. Google's stated corporate mission is 'To organize the world's information and make it universally accessible and useful.'

The company has become the global market leader for search engines through its business focus and constant innovation. As Google grew into a primary destination for web users searching for information online, it attracted a host of online advertisers. These advertisers drove Google's revenue by buying what are called 'search ads', little text-based boxes shown alongside search results that advertisers pay for only when users click on them. Google's search ad program, called AdWords, sells space on its search pages to ads linked with specific keywords. AdWords displays a company's ads on Google and its advertising network. Google auctions off the keyword ads, with the prime key words and prime page locations going to the highest bidder.

In addition to offering prime online 'real estate' for advertisers, Google adds value to advertisers by providing them with a variety of means to better target their ads to users and better understand the effectiveness of their marketing. Google Analytics, which Google provides free to advertisers, provides advertisers with a custom report,

or dashboard, detailing how internet users found the site, what ads they saw and/or clicked on, how they behaved while at the site, and how much traffic was generated. Google client Discount Tire was able to identify where visitors to the site encountered problems that led them to abandon a purchase midstream. After modifying its site and updating its keyword search campaign, Discount Tire measured a 14 per cent increase in sales within a week.

With its ability to deploy data that enable up-to-the-minute improvements of a web marketing program, Google supported a style of marketing where the advertising resources and budget could be constantly

Google has become a business leader in the new marketing environment.

Source: Courtesy of Google, Inc.

▶ Breakthrough marketing *(continued)*

targeted, monitored and optimised. Google called this approach 'marketing asset management', implying that advertising should be managed in the same way as assets in a portfolio, with management marshalling certain resources at one time or place online and others at a different time or place, depending on the market conditions. Rather than follow a marketing plan that had been developed months in advance, companies could use the real-time data collected on their campaigns to optimise the campaign's effectiveness by making it more responsive to the market.

Google has augmented its search capabilities with additional services and features for internet users, including Google Maps, Google Local, Google Finance, Gmail (a Google email service) and Google Video (which was bolstered by the €1.2 billion acquisition of video hosting site YouTube in 2006). These new efforts all offered opportunities for Google to grow by selling the additional targeted advertising space that was created.

In 2011 Google launched Google One Pass, which lets publishers set their own prices and terms for digital content. According to Google's blog: 'With Google One Pass, publishers can maintain direct relationships with their customers and give readers access to digital content across websites and mobile apps. Publishers can customise how and when they charge for content while experimenting with different models to see what works best for them – offering subscriptions, metered access, "freemium" content.'

Sources: www.google.com; G. Lovett (2011) Google launches publisher payments platform, *Marketing Week*, 17 February; C. P. Taylor (2006) Google flex, *Adweek*, 20 March (cover story); R. Karpinski (2006) Keywords, analytics help define user lifetime value, *Advertising Age*, 24 April, p. S2; D. Gorog (2005) Survival guide, *Herald Sun*, 29 March; J. Schlosser (2005) Google, *Fortune*, 31 October, 168–9; J. Graham (2005) Google's profit sails past expectations, *USA Today*, 31 October.

as Tamagotchi, Pokemon, Build-a-Bear or Polly Pocket, but getting it right is more a matter of luck and good timing than anything else.[4]

A **trend** is a direction or sequence of events that has some momentum and durability. Trends are more predictable and durable than fads. A trend reveals the shape of the future and provides many opportunities. For example, the percentage of people who value physical fitness and well-being has risen steadily over the years, especially in the under-30 group and among young women, upscale consumers, and people living in the western world.

Megatrends have been described as 'large social, economic, political, and technological changes [that] are slow to form, and once in place, they influence us for some time – between seven and ten years, or longer'. A current megatrend is 'sustainability', which managers should not ignore as a central factor in the long-term competitiveness of their companies.[5]

Identifying the major forces

Companies and their suppliers, marketing intermediaries, customers, competitors and publics all operate in a macroenvironment of forces and trends, increasingly global, that shape opportunities and pose threats. These forces represent 'non-controllables', which the company must monitor and to which it must respond. Although the forces are non-controllable, they differ in how they may affect a company, as the marketing memo explains.

The early days of the twenty-first century brought a series of new challenges: the steep decline of the stock market, which affected savings, investment and retirement funds; increasing unemployment; corporate scandals; and of course, the rise of terrorism. These dramatic events were accompanied by the continuation of existing trends that have already profoundly influenced the global landscape. At the beginning of the century, more transistors (semiconductor devices used to switch electronic signals) were produced (and at a lower cost) than grains of rice; 24 per cent of European

Marketing memo

Forces in the company environment

The forces in the environment differ in how they may affect a company. Some forces may have a direct and unavoidable impact on a company, while others may just have a slight – and sometimes ignorable – effect. A company should continuously monitor its environment in order to detect possible changes and in order to estimate the possible impacts that such changes might have on the company. Systematising the environmental forces into the four groups described below can assist the company in performing these tasks.

1 **Deterministic forces.** Some environmental forces have a direct and determining influence on a company since the company has no other option than to adapt to these forces. Consider the 2008/9 financial crisis and subsequent recession. Being the first truly global crisis since the word 'globalisation' became widely used,[6] it had a direct and unavoidable influence on market sales for most companies. Another example is the tax that a company pays out of its profit. Tax rates are set by governments, and paying taxes according to tax legislation is unavoidable. Appreciations and depreciations of currencies are another example of a deterministic environmental force.

2 **Moderating forces.** Moderating forces influence the company in several – but not entirely different – ways. As with determining forces, moderating forces often lead to a set of 'known' consequences for a company – but the company does not necessarily have to follow or adapt to changes in moderating forces. Fashion is one example of a moderating force. Fashion companies do not have to moderate their clothing programmes according to various market changes in fashion; nevertheless most fashion companies find it wise to do so in order to stay in business.

3 **Asymmetric forces.** Asymmetric forces lead to a set of 'unknown' consequences for a company. Many political decisions are asymmetric forces; very often the possible outcomes of political decisions are heavily debated in national parliaments, in the press, at workplaces and among citizens. In many countries, an ongoing debate is taking place concerning what environmental restrictions should be put on companies. Many farmers and food companies claim that restrictions have already gone too far since they increase food production costs, which in turn increase product end-price, to a higher level than many consumers regard as a fair price. Others, for example environmental groups, claim that farmers and food companies may even benefit from the restrictions if they change their business according to the new market opportunities – for example, by focusing on increasing the production efficiency of ecological crops.

4 **Indeterministic forces.** These forces are characterised by having only small and negligible – or no – consequences for the company. For example, changes in fashion hardly have noticeable consequences for a producer of steel. However, because business conditions may change rapidly, forces that at present are classified as indeterministic may not necessarily stay as such. The company should therefore continuously monitor its surroundings in order to determine which environmental forces may impose threats and/or opportunities to the company.

---

readers considered blogs their most trusted information source, just behind newspapers with 30 per cent; and insatiable world oil consumption is expected to rise by 50 per cent by 2030.[7]

The sociocultural and demographic environment

There is little excuse for being surprised by demographic developments. The Singer Company should have known for years that its sewing machine business would be hurt by smaller families and more working wives, yet it was slow in responding.

The main demographic force that marketers monitor is *population*, because people make up markets. Marketers are keenly interested in the size and growth rate of the population in cities, regions and nations; age distribution and ethnic mix; educational levels; household patterns; and regional characteristics and movements.

Worldwide population growth

The world population is showing explosive growth: it totalled 6.1 billion in 2000 and will exceed 7.9 billion by the year 2025.[8] Here is an interesting picture:

> **If the world were a village of 1,000 people, it would consist of 520 females and 480 males, 330 children, 60 people over age 65, 10 college graduates and 335 illiterate adults. The village would contain 52 North Americans, 55 Russians, 84 Latin Americans, 95 Eastern and Western Europeans, 124 Africans and 584 Asians. Communication would be difficult because 165 people would speak Mandarin, 86 English, 83 Hindi/Urdu, 64 Spanish, 58 Russian and 37 Arabic, and the rest would speak one of over 200 other languages. There would be 329 Christians, 178 Moslems, 132 Hindus, 62 Buddhists, 3 Jews, 167 nonreligious, 45 atheists, and 84 others.[9]**

The population explosion has been a source of major concern. Moreover, population growth is highest in countries and communities that can least afford it, such as African and Latin American countries. The less developed regions of the world currently account for 76 per cent of the world population and are growing at 2 per cent per year, whereas the population in more developed countries is growing at only 0.6 per cent per year. In developing countries, the death rate has been falling as a result of modern medicine, but the birth rate has remained fairly stable. Feeding, clothing and educating children, although it can also raise the standard of living, is nearly impossible in these countries.

Explosive population growth has major implications for business. A growing population does not mean growing markets, unless these markets have sufficient purchasing power. Nonetheless, companies that analyse their markets carefully can find major opportunities.

Population age mix

National populations vary in their age mix. At one extreme is Mexico, a country with a very young population and rapid population growth. At the other extreme is Japan, a country with one of the world's oldest populations. Milk, nappies, school supplies and toys will be more important products in Mexico than in Japan. In general, there is a global trend towards an ageing population. In 1950 there were 250 million persons aged 60 or over throughout the world. By 2009 the number of persons aged 60 or over had increased three and a half times to 737 million, and by 2050 the number is projected to reach 2 billion.[10]

The structure of the EU population will change in the years to come. Low fertility levels, combined with an extended longevity and the fact that the baby boomers will reach retirement age, will result in a demographic ageing of the EU population. The share of the older generation is increasing, whereas that of working age is decreasing. For example, the share of European persons of 80 years and over is projected to grow from 4.41 per cent in 2008 to 10.99 per cent in 2050.[11] If current trends prevail until 2050, anyone of working age might then have to provide for twice as many retired people as is usual today![12] This might be a threat to the future welfare of European citizens. By 2045, the EU is likely to have a significantly higher proportion of older persons than its main global competitors.[13] In Europe there are ongoing discussions on how these challenges should be met. Possible solutions may include more solidarity between generations (i.e. a more equal distribution of income across generations), increasing the birth rate, and other initiatives.[14]

The changing population has strong implications for marketers. For example, many suppliers may be considering offering special products and services designed for the elderly. Many travel agencies offer specially designed travel packages to senior citizens, including, for example, medical care and special training facilities.

Marketers generally divide the population into six age groups: pre-school children, school-age children, teens, young adults aged 20–40, middle-aged adults aged 40–65, and older adults aged 65 and upwards. Some marketers like to focus on cohorts. **Cohorts** are groups of individuals who are born during the same time period and travel through life together. The 'defining moments' they experience as they become adults can stay with them for a lifetime and influence their values, preferences and buying behaviour. The marketing insight box summarises one breakdown of generational cohorts in the US and UK markets.

Marketing insight

Friends for life

Isenberg School of Management marketing professor Charles D. Schewe and president and founder of consultant firm Lifestage Matrix Marketing, Geoffrey Meredith, have developed a generational cohort segmentation scheme based on the concept that the key defining moments (i.e. moments that define and redefine who a person is) which occur when a person comes of age (roughly between 17 and 24) imprint core values that remain largely intact throughout life. For generational cohorts to form on the basis of certain defining moments, individuals must know of these events. Today, both national and world events tend to be broadcast globally within minutes after they occurred. Thus, while different countries have various generational cohorts embedded within their societies, there are also striking similarities between cohorts on a global scale. The degree of similarity depends on which age group is considered and in which countries. For example, the United Kingdom and the United States share quite a few defining moments and cohort values, while other countries, such as Brazil and Russia, have very different cohort structures and values.

Schewe and Meredith divide the US adult population into seven distinct cohorts, each with its own unique value structure, demographic make-up and markers. In the following, we will look closer at each of these cohorts and the similarities and differences with their UK equivalents. In addition, we will take a look at the latest (i.e. the number eight) cohort: the generation Z cohort.

Depression cohort

Born during 1912–21, aged 91–100 in 2012. This rapidly dwindling group's coming-of-age years were marked by economic strife and elevated unemployment rates. Financial security – what they most lacked when coming of age – rules their thinking. They are no longer in the workforce, but they have had a clear impact on many of today's management practices. Interestingly, the 1930s depression appears a stronger collective memory in the United States than in the United Kingdom.

World War II cohort

Born during 1922–7, aged 85–90 in 2012. In the United States, sacrifice for the common good was widely accepted among members of the World War II cohort. This cohort was focused on defeating a common enemy during their coming-of-age years, and its members are team oriented and patriotic. Here, crucial differences in interpretations between the United States and the United Kingdom exist. Whereas many Americans of this cohort expressed associations with the prosperity that followed the war, of patriotism and a common spirit, the British reflections were more negative, focusing on the meaninglessness and tragedy of the war, and capturing the ever-present fear of destruction and death. According to Schewe and Meredith, these differences can be explained by the fact that the war was actually fought on British soil. The sound of air-raid sirens was often heard, making fear of bombings part of everyday life. Meanwhile, in the United States, except for the 450,000 who actually fought the battles, the war was more of a distant story.

Postwar cohort

Born during 1928–1945, aged 67–84 in 2008. These individuals experienced a time of remarkable economic growth and social tranquillity. In the United Kingdom, the Cold War and the threat of nuclear war set the agenda, and spurred early development towards European unity. At the same time, McCarthyism and the Korean conflict were important developments in the United States. People in this cohort were part of the rise of the middle class, sought a sense of security and stability, and expected prosperous times to continue indefinitely.

Leading-edge baby boomer cohort

Born during 1946–54, aged 58–66 in 2012. The loss of John F. Kennedy and the onset of the Vietnam War had the largest influence on this cohort's values in the United States. Across the continents, the breakthrough in space exploration epitomised by Armstrong taking the first steps on the moon stood out as a very important historic event. Leading-edge boomers championed political, environmental and cultural causes (Greenpeace, civil rights, women's rights), yet were simultaneously hedonistic and self-indulgent (drugs, free love, sensuality).

Trailing-edge baby boomer cohort

Born during 1955–65, aged 47–57 in 2012. This group witnessed the fall of Vietnam, Watergate and Nixon's

▶

resignation. While these events were relatively more important in the United States, the energy crisis was equally severe in the minds of the American and the British. The economic downturn that followed the oil embargo, with its raging inflation rate, stock market decline and rising unemployment, led these individuals to be less optimistic about their financial future than the leading-edge boomers.

Generation X cohort

Born during 1966–1976, aged 36–46 in 2012. Many members of this cohort were latchkey children or have parents who divorced. They have delayed marriage and children, and they don't take those commitments lightly. More than other groups, this cohort accepts cultural diversity and puts personal life ahead of work life. Members show a spirit of entrepreneurship unmatched by any other cohort. Common defining moments were the fall of the Berlin Wall, the dissolution of the Soviet Union and the Gulf War. In the United Kingdom, the Falklands War, the EU common market and the rise of Thatcherism were also epoch events.

Generation N cohort (or Generation Y)

Born during 1977–90, aged 22–35 in 2012. The advent of the internet is a defining and ongoing development for this group, and they will be the engine of growth over the next two decades. A very important historic memory held in common is likely to be the events of 11 September 2001. Although still a work in progress, their core value structure is different from that of Generation X. They are more idealistic and social-cause oriented, without the cynical, what's-in-it-for-me, free-agent mindset of many Xers.

Generation Z cohort

Born from 1991 onwards, aged 21 and under in 2012. Being connected 24/7, members of this cohort often prefer to communicate online – often with friends they have never met. They have never known a world without technology – and without terrorism – and they can not imagine life without mobile phones. They prefer computers to books and want instant results. They are familiar with the consequences of an economic depression. This generation will soon be at the forefront of solving some of the worst environmental, social and economic problems in history. They may be headed for careers that don't even exist today.

Sources: S. Posnick-Goodwin (2010) Meet generation Z, *Educator*, 14(5), 8–18; C. D. Schewe and G. Meredith (2004) Segmenting global markets by generational cohort: determining motivations by age, *Journal of Consumer Behaviour*, 4, 51–63; G. E. Meredith and C. D. Schewe (2002) *Managing by Defining Moments: America's 7 Generational Cohorts, Their Workplace Values, and Why Managers Should Care*, New York: Wiley/Hungry Minds; G. E. Meredith, C. D. Schewe and J. Karlovich (2001) *Defining Markets Defining Moments*, New York: Wiley/Hungry Minds; J. Scott and L. Zac (1993) Collective memories in Britain and the United States, *Public Opinion Quarterly*, 57(3), 315–31.

The diversity of markets

Countries also vary in ethnic and racial make-up. At one extreme is Japan, where almost everyone is Japanese; at the other is the United States, where people come from virtually all nations. European countries lie somewhere between these extremes with large fluctuations between the countries. Ireland is one of the most globalised nations in Europe and, instead of mass emigration, the country now has significant immigration – 167 languages are spoken in Ireland today,[15] similar to multicultural New York. Unlike the United States, the EU consists of independent nations, with different cultures and languages, cooperating in many areas (e.g. economic, legal, monetary) of mutual interest. The EU average of non-nationals in each country is around 6 per cent, with Luxembourg having around 40 per cent and Romania, Slovakia and Bulgaria having less than 1 per cent. Fewer than half of the non-nationals in the EU are ethnic minorities. While the population of ethnic minorities is relatively low on EU average, the group is nevertheless large enough to attract focus from companies, which cannot afford to neglect its purchasing power as well as its possible influence on other citizens.

Several food, clothing and furniture companies have directed their products and promotions to one or more ethnic groups.[16] Yet marketers must be careful not to overgeneralise. Within each ethnic group are consumers who are quite different from each other. For example, each of the Asian consumer groups living in Europe has its own very specific

Phoenix Chinese News and Entertainment Channel

Phoenix Television is a Hong Kong-based Mandarin Chinese television broadcaster providing Infotainment (a combination of the words *info*rmation and enter*tainment*) programmes with popular 'star' anchors and talk show hosts. It is one of the few non-government-related television broadcasters available to the mainland Chinese audience. It operates three domestic channels and two international services – Phoenix North America Chinese Channel and Phoenix Chinese News and Entertainment (PCNE) Channel. Phoenix CNE Channel is a 24-hour, London-based channel, catering to Chinese communities in Europe (encompassing around 1.7 million people) who are eager to stay in touch with what is happening back home. One of Phoenix CNE's key programmes is a weekly TV magazine show entitled *Images of Europe*, which is 30 minutes in length and occupies PCNE's golden time slots at weekends. The channel reaches 50 European and North African countries and regions, and is available on mainstream satellite television networks such as Sky Digital and other cable networks in the United Kingdom, Ireland, France, Germany and the Netherlands. In addition to broadcasting entertaining and informative programmes from Phoenix TV, Phoenix CNE has made great efforts in producing local programmes to meet the particular needs of Chinese viewers as well as mainstream audiences in Europe.

Phoenix CNE Channel is a vivid example of how companies acknowledge the importance of cultural sensitivity and work to refine both their products and their marketing to reach such fast-growing and important consumer groups as the European Chinese.

Source: Phoenix CNE TV

market characteristics, speaks a different language, consumes a different cuisine, practises a different religion, and represents a very distinct national culture. During the years he spent working in advertising abroad, Shane McGonigle, managing director of **advertising agency** Leo Burnett and president of the Institute of Advertising Practitioners in Ireland, picked up a crucial piece of advice as regards multicultural marketing strategies: 'Look for the similarities and respect the differences,' McGonigle says.

This is highly relevant in regard to the European market, in which subsections are beginning to show themselves as divided as much by lifestyle and aspirations as by culture. For instance, a Euromonitor marketing study showed that segmenting consumers by demographic factors, such as age, gender or ethnicity, is becoming less exhaustive. Increasingly, consumers identify with people who lead similar lifestyles to themselves. According to Euromonitor, examples of lifestyles that companies could use as inspiration for new marketing concepts include 'retreat', 'escape' and 'indulge'. 'Retreat' is associated with the followers of the health and wellness trend, and this group is likely to be most receptive to natural and organic products. The 'escape' lifestyle broadly encompasses consumers who are nostalgic for more innocent times past, and who tend to be attracted to vintage and home-grown brands. Finally, 'indulge' lifestylers see themselves as true connoisseurs and demand luxury and exclusivity from their brands.[17]

Diversity goes beyond ethnic, racial and national markets. Around 37 million consumers in the EU and 80 million in Greater Europe have disabilities, and they constitute a market for home delivery companies, such as British companies Ocado and Tesco, as well as for various medical services.[18]

Educational groups

The international standard classification of education (ISCED) is the basic tool for classifying education statistics, describing different levels of education, as well as fields of education and training. It distinguishes seven levels of education: level 0: pre-primary education; level 1: primary education; level 2: lower secondary education; level 3: upper secondary education; level 4: post-secondary non-tertiary education; level 5: tertiary education (first stage); and level 6: tertiary education (second stage). Over two-thirds of the world's 785 million illiterate adults are found in only eight countries (India, China, Bangladesh, Pakistan, Nigeria, Ethiopia, Indonesia and Egypt); of all the illiterate adults in the world, two-thirds are women.[19] In the EU, more than 75 per cent of the population aged 20–24 has completed at least upper secondary education.[20] The large number of educated people in the EU spells a high demand for quality books and magazines, and a high supply of skills.

Household patterns

The 'traditional household' consists of a husband, wife and children (and sometimes grandparents). While the number of households in the countries of the EU is growing, their average size is decreasing. There are, however, great differences between the various regions of the European Union. In the southern member states, larger and more complex households are common, with more generations living together, whereas the tendency for an increasing number of people to live alone is very pronounced in the northern member states.[21]

More people are divorcing or separating, choosing not to marry, marrying later or marrying without the intention of having children. In 2008 there were fewer than five marriages per 1,000 inhabitants in the EU, compared with almost eight marriages per 1,000 inhabitants in 1970. As well as a decrease in the rate of marriages, there was also an increase in the average age at which people got married. Every four out of ten marriages in the EU results in divorce, with relatively few divorces in Greece, Spain, Ireland, Italy, Cyprus and Malta, and more than six divorces for each ten marriages in Belgium, the Czech Republic, Estonia and Lithuania. The number of divorces in the EU has grown steadily over recent decades.[22] Each group has a distinctive set of needs and buying habits. For example, people in the SSWD group (single, separated, widowed, divorced) need smaller apartments; inexpensive and smaller appliances, furniture and furnishings; and smaller-size food packages. Companies such as IKEA, Absolut, Procter & Gamble and Subaru have recognised the potential of this market and the non-traditional household market as a whole.

Yet, in focusing too much on the non-traditional market, companies may miss out on other markets just under their nose. For instance, millions of boomer dads shop a lot more than their fathers or grandfathers did. They married later and are much more involved in raising their children. For instance, many of today's dads push baby buggies, and they don't want to be seen behind some fussy-looking contraption of yesteryear. So the maker of the high-concept Bugaboo stroller designed one with a sleek design and tyres resembling those of a dirt bike.[23]

Geographical shifts in population

This is a period of great migratory movements into and within the European region. Over the past 45 years, the population of today's EU-27 countries has grown from 376 million (1960) to 498 million (2008). Until the end of the 1980s, the 'natural increase' (live births minus deaths) was by far the major component of population growth. Yet, falling birth rates in most EU member states have led to a steady decline of the 'natural increase', and migration has been the major force of population growth since the beginning of the 1990s (as illustrated in Figure 5.1). Thus, recent years have witnessed a significantly growing number of migrants coming into the EU, with net migration increasing from 590,000 persons in 1994 to 1.50 million by 2008. Migrants come from all parts of the world – but in particular from Africa, the Middle East and Asia.[24]

Regional analysis shows that in some European countries more people have left than have arrived. For example, this was the case in Latvia, Lithuania and Poland. Spain and Italy stood out as having by far the highest net inflows of migrants, whereas Scandinavia and the Czech Republic, among others, experienced a positive net migration. These waves of new immigration to Europe have meant that new ethnic groups are beginning to impact the economic, social and political scene – as consumers, workers and investors. Combined with growing numbers of EU residents moving between states, it has offset a gradual erosion of national boundaries and tastes, essentially changing the landscape for marketers, who are increasingly alert to where consumers are gathering, and focusing on the importance of targeting their products and advertising efforts towards specific consumer groups.[25]

In the new EU countries, such as Hungary, Poland, Romania and Bulgaria, this erosion of national tastes is particularly notable, as consumers are developing a strong taste for western lifestyles and brands. According to Euromonitor International, modern Europe's appetite for western lifestyles offers strong growth opportunities for food and drinks companies especially. For example, the introduction of breakfast cereals in Bulgaria has been extremely successful, and the packaged food market in Ukraine has seen double-digit growth over the past six years.[26]

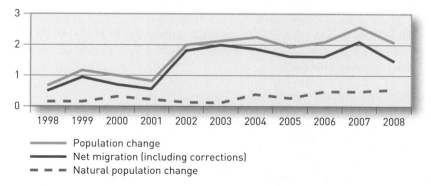

Figure 5.1 Population change, net migration (including corrections) and natural population change, EU-27 (million)
Source: Eurostat (2010) *Eurostat Yearbook 2010*

There are also regional developments in the 'old' EU member states: consumers in the United Kingdom eat more ready meals per capita (citizen) than people elsewhere in the EU, people in Italy prefer frozen soup, whereas the Germans buy more dehydrated soups, and the Spanish eat out more often than any other European nation.[27] Clearly, marketers are learning how to cope with the changes brought about by current population developments in Europe.

The economic environment

The available purchasing power in an economy depends on current income, prices, savings, debt and credit availability. Marketers must pay careful attention to trends affecting purchasing power, because they can have a strong impact on business, especially for companies whose products are geared to high-income and price-sensitive consumers.

Income distribution

There are four types of industrial structure: *subsistence economies* such as Papua New Guinea, with 85 per cent of the population directly deriving their livelihood from farming, leaving few opportunities for marketers; *raw material exporting economies* such as Zaire (copper) and Saudi Arabia (oil), with good markets for equipment, tools, supplies and luxury goods for the rich; *industrialising economies* such as India, Egypt and the Philippines, where a new rich class and a growing middle class demand new types of goods; and *industrial economies* such as countries in western Europe, which are rich markets for all sorts of goods.

Marketers often distinguish countries using five different income-distribution patterns:

1 very low incomes;
2 mostly low incomes;
3 very low, very high incomes;
4 low, medium, high incomes; and
5 mostly medium incomes.

Consider the market for Lamborghinis, an automobile costing more than €100,000. The market would be very small in countries with type 1 or 2 income patterns. One of the largest single markets for Lamborghinis turns out to be Portugal (income pattern 3) – one of the poorer countries in western Europe, but one with enough wealthy families to afford expensive cars.

In EU, the inequality of income distribution (income quintile share ratio), measured as the ratio of total income received by the 20 per cent of the population with the highest income (top quintile) to that received by the 20 per cent of the population with the lowest income (lowest quintile), increased from 4.6 in 1998 to 5.0 in 2007 (EU-27). This ratio varies considerably across EU member states, from 3.3 in Slovenia and 3.4 in Sweden, through 6.0 or more in Greece, Latvia and Portugal, to highs of 6.9 in Bulgaria and 7.8 in Romania.[28] There is a risk that this trend, if it continues, may lead to a two-tier European market, with affluent people able to buy expensive goods and working-class people having to spend more carefully, shopping at discount stores and factory outlet malls, and selecting less expensive store brands.

Savings, debt and credit

Consumer expenditure is affected by savings, debt and credit availability. Consumers are naturally concerned with how much they receive each month in the form of earnings from work, from pensions, from other government transfers such as unemployment benefits, family benefits or sick pay, and from their savings. However, two individuals with the same income can have very different living standards if their income does not measure adequately all the resources that are available to each of them (saving/debts, subsidised public goods and services, etc.) and/or if their needs differ (health, child care, transport). There is significant variation in indebtedness between countries, and between age groups within countries. For instance, the overall mortgage take-up rates range from more than 50 per cent in Sweden, Denmark, Norway, Iceland and the Netherlands to the lows of a few per cent in eastern and southern Europe. Also, the shares of the elderly with mortgage debt are significantly lower than those of other age groups in all European countries.[29]

The social–cultural environment

Society shapes the beliefs, values and norms that largely define consumer tastes and preferences (see Chapter 7). People absorb, almost unconsciously, a worldview that defines their relationship to themselves, to others, to organisations, to society, to nature, and to the universe.

- **Views of themselves**. At the turn of the millennium, a Eurobarometer survey looked into how Europeans viewed themselves and their lives. Overall, more than eight out of ten people felt positive about all things related to their lives, ranging from personal happiness, their health, their family, the economic situation and society in general. In addition, a majority of Europeans felt positive about the legacy passed on in terms of freedom, quality of life, equality, solidarity and welfare. On the other hand, people were most pessimistic when asked about employment, the environment, ethics and personal safety.

    While the question is often asked if a 'European' culture exists at all, this research shows that at least Europeans share a number of fundamental cultural values that guide their way of thinking and living. For instance, more than 90 per cent feel that it is extremely or very important to help others and to value people for who they are. To be involved in creating a better society and putting time and effort into personal development are also considered positive and crucial values by a majority.[30]

- **Views of others**. People are concerned about the homeless, crime and victims, and other social problems. At the same time, they seek out their 'own kind' for serious and long-lasting relationships and avoid strangers. These trends portend a growing market for social support products and services that promote direct relationships between human beings, such as health clubs, cruises and religious activity. They also suggest a growing market for 'social surrogates' such as interactive television, online video games and social media.

- **Views of organisations**. After a wave of company downsizings and corporate accounting and financial scandals, there has been an overall decline in organisational loyalty. Many people today see work not as a source of satisfaction but as a required chore to earn money to enjoy their non-work hours. Companies need to find new ways to win back consumer and employee confidence. They need to make sure they are good corporate citizens and that their consumer messages are honest.[31]

- **Views of society**. Some people defend society (preservers), some run it (makers), some take what they can from it (takers), some want to change it (changers), some are looking for something deeper (seekers), and still others want to leave it (escapers).[32] Consumption patterns often reflect social attitude. Makers tend to be high achievers who eat, dress and live well. Changers usually live more frugally, drive smaller cars and wear simpler clothes. Escapers and seekers are a major market for films, music, surfing and camping.

- **Views of nature**. People have woken up to nature's fragility and the finiteness of its resources. Business has responded to increased interest in being in harmony with and experiencing nature by producing wider varieties of camping, hiking, boating and fishing gear such as boots, tents, backpacks and accessories.

Other cultural characteristics of interest to marketers are the persistence of core cultural values and the existence of subcultures. Let's look at both.

High persistence of core cultural values

Although divorce rates are high in many European countries, most people in Europe still believe in work, in getting married, in giving to charity, and in being honest. *Core beliefs* and values are passed on from parents to children and reinforced by major social institutions – schools, churches, businesses and governments. *Secondary beliefs* and values are more open to change. Believing in the institution of marriage is a core belief; believing that people ought to get married early is a secondary belief.

Marketers have some chance of changing secondary values, but little chance of changing core values. Although core values are fairly persistent, cultural swings do take place. In the 1960s hippies, the Beatles, Elvis Presley and other cultural phenomena had a major impact on young people's hairstyles, clothing, sexual norms and life goals. Today's young people are influenced by new heroes such as Lady Gaga and social network services such as Facebook, Twitter and MySpace.

Existence of subcultures

Each society contains **subcultures**, groups with shared values, beliefs, preferences and behaviours emerging from their special life experiences or circumstances. There are sometimes unexpected rewards in targeting subcultures. Marketers have always loved teenagers because they are society's trendsetters in fashion, music, entertainment, ideas and attitudes. Besides being of similar age, teenagers share on a global scale a youthful lifestyle that values growth and learning with an appreciation of future trends.[33] Marketers also know that if they attract someone as a teen, there is a good chance they will keep the person as a customer later in life. The new online media platforms provide additional opportunities to marketers. The Xbox, which is clearly marketed to young consumers, is taking advantage of social games to target a new audience. Social games are played in social media such as Facebook. 'Social games are a great way of enabling more casual gamers to associate with Xbox and make our brand seem more relevant to them,' says Paul Evans, head of media, Xbox EMEA. 'Typically, these new gaming audiences – broad family and female groups – are either not aware of Xbox, or are ambivalent towards the brand, so this kind of engagement is both beneficial and essential to making a compelling connection. Social games have allowed for interaction and play with Xbox properties without appearing to "try too hard", due to the integral fun component of the games.' Xbox has also stepped outside Facebook to reach a new target audience for Xbox Kinect, young women between 16 and 34, via specialist social network Stardoll.[34]

Having reviewed the sociocultural and demographic environment, we now turn to the ecological and physical component of PEEST analysis.

The ecological and physical environment

The deterioration of the natural environment is a major global problem. There is great concern about 'greenhouse gases' in the atmosphere due to the burning of fossil fuels; about the depletion of the ozone layer due to certain chemicals and global warming; and about growing shortages of water. In western Europe, 'green' parties have vigorously pressed for public action to reduce industrial pollution.

New regulations hit certain industries very hard. Steel companies and public utilities have had to invest billions of euros in pollution-control equipment and more environmentally friendly fuels. The soap industry has increased its products' biodegradability. Great opportunities await companies and marketers who can create solutions that reconcile prosperity with environmental protection. However, consumers often appear confused about product decisions that affect the natural environment. An ACNielsen study shows that Latin American shoppers are the most likely to buy organic food, while the North Americans are the least likely. The Europeans place themselves in between.[35] The Europeans are willing to pay more for healthy and organic food, yet they are not willing to increase their overall food budget. Instead, they conduct a kind of food 'arbitrage': they spend more on fair trade or healthy products, but fund these purchases by buying certain staple products at discount shops. Actually increasing the number of green products they buy requires consumers to break such behavioural habits, overcome scepticism about the motives behind the introduction of the products and their quality level, and change their attitudes about the role such products play in environmental protection.

Marketing insight

Green marketing

Environmental concerns may be manifested in many ways. Environmental marketing agency Terrachoice recently cataloged 5,296 products. In just the two dozen stores it visited in both 2009 and 2010, the number of 'green' products rose from about 2,700 to 4,700, a 73 per cent increase. Given the 2010 economic climate, this increase is particularly impressive. Because greener products are often considered to be (or actually are) more expensive, marketers would be forgiven for avoiding that pitch in a recession. Clearly there is a belief that consumer interest is still rising.[36] In Europe, as well as in the United States, high proportions of consumers are willing to give up baths for showers to help save water, to use public transport, to buy a hybrid car or drive a smaller car as a means of reducing air pollution, to replace incandescent light bulbs with compact fluorescent bulbs or get solar panels installed at their homes to conserve energy. However, even if consumers are ready to change the way they wash themselves, only a small group is willing to shower less frequently or to pay a toll to drive their cars in city centres. Finally, between 16 and 37 per cent of respondents believe that industry and government are primarily responsible for global warming – and only between 7 and 12 per cent suggest that people in general share responsibility for climate change.

A church built in Rome to commemorate the 2000th anniversary of Christianity was designed to take sustainability to new levels. US architect Richard Meier worked with the project's technical sponsor to develop a 'smart', anti-pollution material that essentially cleans itself and simultaneously helps destroy air pollutants found in car exhaust and heating emissions. Or, in more

McDonald's going green

Source: Courtesy of © havi-logistics.com/McDonald's Corporation

popular terms, a compound that not only enhances the sculptural forms of the building but also 'eats' surrounding smog. Several companies are now developing 'smog-eating' products that can be used for the façades of buildings, as well as in paint, plaster and paving materials for roads. The new environment-friendly substances are being tried out in buildings, squares and highways in Europe as well as in Japan.

With Fairtrade Fortnight upon us, the focus on socially and environmentally sustainable business means any claims that brands make are under the spotlight more than ever. A green glow underneath the golden arches logo outside McDonald's European restaurants is supposed to promote the idea that the fast-food chain is an eco-friendly company.[37] From a branding perspective, however, 'green marketing' programmes have not been entirely successful. Two main problems are that, first, consumers may believe the product is of inferior quality as a result of being green; and, secondly, they may feel the product is not really that green to begin with. Sometimes consumers may even feel that the product has been 'greenwashed'. Greenwashing describes a situation in which a company deliberately misleads its customers about the company's environmental practices: that is, greenwashing appears when the company's environmental claims are false or presented in a deceptive manner. Successful green products convincingly overcome both these concerns to persuade consumers they are acting in their own and society's long-run interest at the same time, such as with organic foods that are seen as healthier, tastier and safer, and energy-efficient appliances that cost less to run and last longer. Jacquelyn A. Ottman – founder and president of J. Ottman Consulting – and her colleagues refer to the tendency to overly focus on a product's greenness as 'green marketing myopia'. Figure 5.2 displays their recommendations for avoiding such myopia by following three key

Consumer value positioning

- Design environmental products to perform as well as (or better than) alternatives.
- Promote and deliver the consumer-desired value of environmental products and target relevant consumer market segments (such as market health benefits among health-conscious consumers).
- Broaden mainstream appeal by bundling (or adding) consumer-desired value into environmental products (such as fixed pricing for subscribers of renewable energy).

Calibration of consumer knowledge

- Educate consumers with marketing messages that connect environmental product attributes with desired consumer value (for example, 'pesticide-free produce is healthier'; 'energy-efficiency saves money'; or 'solar power is convenient').
- Frame environmental product attributes as 'solutions' for consumer needs (for example, 'rechargeable batteries offer longer performance').
- Create engaging and educational internet sites about environmental products' desired consumer value (for example, Tide Coldwater's interactive website allows visitors to calculate their likely annual money savings based on their laundry habits, utility source (gas or electricity), and postcode location).

Credibility of product claims

- Employ environmental product and consumer benefit claims that are specific, meaningful, unpretentious and qualified (i.e., compared with comparable alternatives or likely usage scenarios).
- Procure product endorsements or eco certifications from trustworthy third parties, and educate consumers about the meaning behind those endorsements and eco certifications.
- Encourage consumer evangelism via consumers' social and Internet communication networks with compelling, interesting, and/or entertaining information about environmental products (for example, Tide's 'Coldwater Challenge' website included a map of the United States so visitors could track and watch their personal influence spread when their friends requested a free sample).

Figure 5.2 Three keys to avoiding green marketing myopia
Source: J. A. Ottman, E. R. Stafford and C. L. Hartman (2006) Avoiding green marketing myopia, *Environment*, June, 22–36. Reproduced with permission from Helen Dwight Reid Educational Foundation.

▶ Marketing insight *(continued)*

principles: consumer value positioning, calibration of consumer knowledge, and the credibility of product claims.

Many top European companies are embracing sustainability and green marketing. Corporate Knights, Inc., with Innovest Strategic Value Advisors, Inc., a leading research firm specialising in analysing 'non-traditional' drivers of risk and shareholder value, including companies' performance on social, environmental and strategic governance issues, has initiated 'The Global 100 Most Sustainable Corporations in the World'. The list, which covers several European companies such as ABB Ltd (Switzerland), Adidas AG (Germany), Astrazeneca plc (UK), Dexia (Belgium), Hennes & Mauritz (Sweden), Kesko OYJ (Finland), Novo Nordisk (Denmark), Philips Electronics (the Netherlands), Repsol (Spain) and Storebrand ASA (Norway), can be freely downloaded at www.global100. org. The Global 100 companies are sustainable 'in the sense that they have displayed a better ability than most of their industry peers to identify and effectively manage material environmental, social and governance factors impacting the opportunity and risk sides of their business' (www.global100.org).

Questions

1 Green marketing' programmes have not been entirely successful. How can managers improve consumers' perception of the quality of 'green' products?
2 Discuss the pros and cons of McDonald's 'going green' strategy.

Sources: J. Roberts (2010) Voicing your ethical stance, *Marketing Week*, 4 March, www.marketingweek.co.uk/voicing-your-ethical-stance/3010615/article; J. F. Rock (2010) Green building: trend or megatrend? *Dispute Resolution Journal*, 65(2/3), 72–7; J. Adler (2006) Going green, *Newsweek*, 17 July, 43–52; J. A. Ottman, E. R. Stafford and C. L. Hartman (2006) Avoiding green marketing myopia, *Environment*, June, 22–36; J. Meredith Ginsberg and P. N. Bloom (2004) Choosing the right green marketing strategy, *MIT Sloan Management Review*, Fall, 79–84; M. Gunther (2003) Tree huggers, soy lovers, and profits, *Fortune*, 23 June, 98–104; Roper ASW (2002) *Green Gauge Report 2002*, New York: Roper ASW; J. Ottman (1982) *Green Marketing: Opportunity for Innovation*, 2nd edn, Chicago: NTC/Contemporary Publishing Company; www.global100.org; T. Crampton (2007) More in Europe worry about climate than in US, poll shows, *International Herald Tribune*, 4 January, www.iht.com/articles/2007/01/04/news/poll. php?page=1; E. Povoledo (2006) Architecture in Italy goes green, *International Herald Tribune*, 22 November 2006, www.iht.com/articles/2006/11/22/news/smog.php.

Corporate environmentalism is the recognition of the importance of environmental issues facing the firm and the integration of those issues into the firm's strategic plans.[38] Marketers practising corporate environmentalism need to be aware of the threats and opportunities associated with four major trends in the natural environment: the shortage of raw materials, especially water; the increased cost of energy; increased pollution levels; and the changing role of governments.

- The earth's raw materials consist of the infinite, the finite renewable, and the finite non-renewable. *Finite non-renewable resources* – oil, coal, platinum, zinc, silver – pose a particularly serious problem as the point of depletion approaches. Firms making products that require these increasingly scarce minerals face substantial cost increases. Firms engaged in research and development have an excellent opportunity to develop substitute materials.

- One finite non-renewable resource, oil, has created serious problems for the world economy. As oil prices soar to record levels, companies and governments are searching for practical means to harness solar, nuclear, wind and other alternative forms of energy.

- Some industrial activity will inevitably damage the natural environment. A large market has been created for pollution-control solutions, such as scrubbers, recycling centres and landfill systems. Its existence leads to a search for alternative ways to produce and package goods.

- Governments vary in their concern for and efforts to promote a clean environment. Many less developed nations are doing little about pollution, largely because they lack the funds or the political will. It is in the richer nations' interest to help the poorer nations control their pollution, but even the richer nations today lack the necessary funds.

Environmental auditing

Environmental auditing offers a methodology to evaluate the environmental performance of companies and is likely to become increasingly widespread as more and more environmental regulations and codes of practice have to be adhered to in industry. The key objectives of the environmental audit are:[39]

- to determine the extent to which environmental management systems in a company are performing adequately;
- to verify compliance with local, national and European environmental and health and safety legislation;
- to verify compliance with a company's own stated corporate policy;
- to develop and promulgate internal procedures needed to achieve the organisation's environmental objectives;
- to minimise human exposure to risks from the environment and ensure adequate health and safety provision;
- to identify and assess company risk resulting from environmental failure;
- to assess the impact on the local environment of a particular plant or process by means of air, water and soil sampling; and
- to detect the environmental improvements a company can make.

Environmental auditing began in the 1980s. At first, industries and individual businesses created systems that suited their own needs. By the early 1990s there was growing support for the establishment of internationally recognised auditing procedures. In 1993, the European Community issued its Eco-Management and Audit Regulation (1836/93/EC). This regulation was set up as a voluntary management tool for industrial companies, to evaluate, report and improve their environmental performance.[40] An international system – ISO 14001 – was created by the International Standardisation Organisation (ISO) two years later.[41] While specifying a number of environmental management requirements for environmental management systems, ISO 14001 requires an environmental policy to be in existence within the company, fully supported by senior management, and outlining the policies of the company, not only to the staff but to the public. ISO 14001 is implemented voluntarily by the company and consists of six sections: General Requirements; Environmental Policy; Planning; Implementation and Operation; Checking and Corrective Action; Management Review. An increasing number of consultancies undertake environmental audits – examples are UL Europe, Auditeco and Amberley. Being one of the UK's leading energy suppliers and part of E.ON, the world's largest investor-owned power and gas company with headquarters in Germany, E.ON UK runs environmental audits in areas where there is significant environmental risk. These are done by the company's internal audit department and external auditors, as part of the ISO 14001 certification process for E.ON businesses.

The technological environment

One of the most dramatic forces shaping people's lives is technology. Through the years, technology has released such wonders as penicillin, open-heart surgery and the birth control pill, and such horrors as the hydrogen bomb, nerve gas and the submachine gun. It has also given us such mixed blessings as mobile phones and PC games.

Every new technology is a force for 'creative destruction'. Transistors hurt the vacuum-tube industry, xerography hurt the carbon-paper business, cars hurt the railways, and television hurts the newspapers. Instead of moving into the new technologies, many old industries fought or ignored them, and their businesses declined. Yet it is the essence of market capitalism to be dynamic and tolerate the creative destructiveness of technology as the price of progress.

The number of major new technologies we discover affects the economy's growth rate. Unfortunately, technological discoveries do not arise evenly through time – the railway industry created a lot of investment, and then investment petered out until the car industry emerged. In the time between major innovations, an economy can stagnate. In the meantime, minor innovations fill the gap: freeze-dried coffee, combination shampoo and conditioner, anti-perspirants and deodorants, and so on. They require less risk, but they can also divert research effort away from major breakthroughs. New technology also creates major long-run consequences that are not always foreseeable. The contraceptive pill, for example, helped lead to smaller families, more working wives, and larger discretionary incomes – resulting in higher expenditure on holiday travel, durable goods and luxury items. Mobile phones, PC games and the internet are not only reducing attention to traditional media, they are reducing face-to-face social interaction as people listen to music, watch a film on their mobile, and so on. Technologies also compete with each other. For instance, consumers may view video material by a variety of means including mobile phones, TV and the internet.

Marketers should monitor the following four trends in technology: the accelerating pace of change, the unlimited opportunities for innovation, varying R&D budgets, and the increased regulation of technological change.

The accelerating pace of change

Many of today's common products (computers, iPods, mobile phones and so on) were not available 40 years ago. Electronics researchers are building smarter chips to make our cars, homes and offices connected and more responsive to changing conditions. More ideas than ever are in the works, and the time between the appearance of new ideas and their successful implementation is all but disappearing, as is the time between introduction and peak production. Apple quickly ramped up in a little over five years to sell 23.5 million iPods in 2006. In April 2007 the company announced that the 100 millionth iPod had been sold and in September 2010 275 million iPods had been sold, making the iPod the fastest-selling music player in history.[42]

The unlimited opportunities for innovation

Some of the most exciting work today is taking place in biotechnology, computers, micro-electronics, telecommunications, robotics and designer materials. The Human Genome project promises to usher in the Biological Century as biotech workers create new medical cures, new foods and new materials. Researchers are working on AIDS vaccines, totally safe contraceptives and non-fattening foods. They are designing robots for firefighting, underwater exploration and home nursing.

Varying R & D budgets

A large portion of EU R & D expenditure is going into applied and basic research as opposed to experimental development. Hence, basic research is more important in the EU compared to the United States, Japan and China, and accounts for more than one-third of total R & D expenditure in many new member states.[43] To gain sustainable competitive advantage, many companies are no longer content just to put their money into copying competitors' products and making minor feature and style improvements. For instance, EU companies such as AstraZeneca, Roche, GlaxoSmithKline, Bayer and Solvay have increased their R & D investment in areas such as pharmaceuticals, biotechnology and chemicals.[44] However, European R & D spending is expected to slide compared to the rest of the world. According to a recent forecast provided by the *R & D Magazine* in collaboration with Battelle, the relatively low annual rate of increases and the absolute values are inadequate to compete against the large increases seen in China and India and the absolute values seen in the USA. A goal of investing 3.0 per cent of GDP in R & D would help alleviate this technological slide, but this level has not even been close to being achieved; the current European average level of R & D spending is only 1.6 per cent of GDP (2010), as indicated in Figure 5.3.[45]

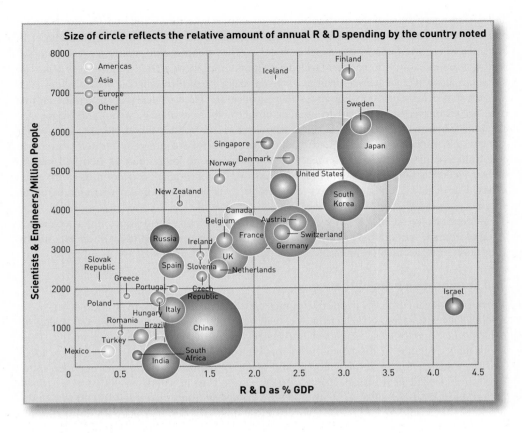

Figure 5.3 World of R & D
Source: 2011 Global R & D Funding Forecast, *R&D Magazine*, December 2010, p. 4, www.rdmag.com

The increased regulation of technological change

Many European governments have expanded their agencies' powers to investigate and ban potentially unsafe products. In the EU either the European Commission or the individual member state must approve all drugs before they can be legally sold. Safety and health regulations have also increased in the areas of food, automobiles, clothing, electrical appliances and construction.

The political–legal environment

The political and legal environment consists of laws, government agencies and pressure groups that influence and limit various organisations and individuals. Sometimes these laws also create new opportunities for business. For example, mandatory recycling laws have given the recycling industry a major boost and spurred the creation of dozens of new companies making new products from recycled materials. Two major trends in the political–legal environment are the increase in business legislation and the growth of special interest groups.

The increase in business legislation

Business legislation has four main purposes: to protect companies from unfair competition, to protect consumers from unfair business practices, to protect the interests of society from unbridled business behaviour, and to charge businesses with the social costs created by their products or production processes. Although each new law may have a legitimate rationale, it may also have the unintended effect of sapping initiative and retarding economic growth.

Legislation affecting business has increased steadily over the years. The European Commission has been active in establishing a new framework of laws covering competitive behaviour, product standards, product liability and commercial transactions for the 27 member nations of the European Union. The recently introduced EU concept of 'Common Commencement Dates' is an innovative solution to improve the life of SMEs (small and medium-sized enterprises). The idea is that business-related legislation comes into force on a limited number of fixed dates, with a view to ensuring a more streamlined flow and early information on new regulation concerning SMEs.[46]

Several countries have passed strong consumer protection legislation. Norway bans several forms of sales promotion – trading stamps, contests, premiums – as inappropriate or 'unfair' instruments for promoting products. Thailand requires food processors selling national brands to market low-price brands also, so that low-income consumers can find economy brands. In India, food companies need special approval to launch brands that duplicate what already exists on the market, such as another cola drink or brand of rice.

Companies generally establish legal review procedures and promulgate ethical standards to guide their marketing managers, and as more business takes place in cyberspace, marketers must establish new parameters for doing electronic business ethically.

The growth of special interest groups

Political action committees (PACs) lobby government officials and pressure business executives to pay more attention to consumers' rights, women's rights, senior citizens' rights, minority rights and gay rights.

Many companies have established public affairs departments to deal with these groups and issues. An important force affecting business is the **consumerist movement** – an organised movement of citizens and government designed to strengthen the rights and powers of buyers in relationship to sellers. Consumerists have advocated and won the right to know the true interest cost of a loan, the true cost per standard unit of competing brands (unit pricing), the basic ingredients in a product, the nutritional quality of food as a percentage of their calorie allowance, the freshness of products and the true benefits of a product.

With consumers increasingly willing to swap personal information for customised products from firms – as long as they can be trusted – privacy issues will continue to be a public policy hot issue.[47] Consumers worry that they will be robbed or cheated; that private information will be used against them; that someone will steal their identity; that they will be bombarded by solicitations; and that children will be targeted.[48] Wise companies establish consumer affairs departments to help formulate policies and resolve and respond to consumer complaints.

Clearly, new laws and growing numbers of pressure groups have put more restraints on marketers. Marketers must clear their plans with the company's legal, public relations, public affairs and consumer affairs departments. Insurance companies directly or indirectly affect the design of smoke detectors; scientific groups affect the design of spray products. In essence, many private marketing transactions have moved into the public domain.

Although every manager in an organisation needs to observe the outside environment, the major responsibility for identifying significant marketplace changes falls to the company's marketers. Assisting with such tasks is the key purpose of the marketing information system.

Managing the marketing information system

Components of a modern marketing information system

Marketers have two advantages: they have disciplined methods for collecting information, and they spend more time than anyone else interacting with customers and observing competition and other outside firms and groups. Marketers may be assisted by companies such as the Nielsen Company, which specialise in delivering marketing information (information concerning buyer behaviour, market trends, brand and corporate image information, and so on) to business managers.

The Nielsen Company

The Nielsen Company is a world-leading demographic, market segmentation research information and media company that includes ACNielsen, Nielsen Media Research, Spectra Marketing Systems and Scarborough Research, among others. Headquartered in both Europe (Haarlem, the Netherlands) and the United States (New York), Nielsen operates in more than 100 countries with a global team dedicated to 'helping clients compete more effectively and discover opportunity with more clarity than ever before'. Nielsen is the official market research services provider to the London 2012 Olympic and Paralympic Games.[49]

Some firms have themselves developed marketing information systems that provide management with rich detail about buyer wants, preferences and behaviour.

DuPont

Operating in more than 70 countries worldwide, including more than 30 European countries, DuPont commissioned marketing studies to uncover personal pillow behaviour for its Dacron Polyester unit, which supplies filling to pillow makers and sells its own Comforel brand. One challenge is that people don't give up their old pillows: 37 per cent of one sample described their relationship with their pillow as being like that of 'an old married couple', and an additional 13 per cent said their pillow was like a 'childhood friend'. Respondents fell into distinct groups in terms of pillow behaviour: stackers (23 per cent), plumpers (20 per cent), rollers or folders (16 per cent), cuddlers (16 per cent) and smashers, who pound their pillows into a more comfy shape (10 per cent). Women were more likely to plump, men to fold. The prevalence of stackers led the company to sell more pillows packaged as pairs, as well as to market different levels of softness or firmness.[50]

Marketers also have extensive information about how consumption patterns vary across countries. On a per capita basis within western Europe, for example, the Swiss consume the most chocolate, the Greeks eat the most cheese, the Irish drink the most tea and the Austrians smoke the most cigarettes.

Nevertheless, many business firms are not sophisticated about gathering information. Many do not have a marketing research department. Others have a department that limits its work to routine forecasting, sales analysis and occasional surveys (see Chapter 6). Some managers complain about not knowing how to get hold of critical information; getting too much information that they cannot use and too little that they really need; and getting important information too late. Companies with superior information enjoy a competitive advantage. They can choose their markets better, develop better offerings and execute better marketing planning.

Every firm must organise and distribute a continuous flow of information to its marketing managers. A **marketing information system** (MIS) consists of people, equipment and procedures to gather, sort, analyse, evaluate and distribute needed, timely and accurate information to marketing decision makers. A marketing information system relies on internal company records, marketing intelligence activities and marketing research. We will discuss the first two topics here, and the third one in the next chapter.

The company's marketing information system should be a cross between what managers think they need, what they really need and what is economically feasible. An internal MIS committee can interview a cross-section of marketing managers to discover their information needs. Table 5.1 displays some useful questions.

Table 5.1 Information needs probes

1 What decisions do you regularly make?

2 What information do you need to make these decisions?

3 What information do you regularly get?

4 What special studies do you periodically request?

5 What information would you want that you are not getting now?

6 What information would you want daily? Weekly? Monthly? Yearly?

7 What magazines and trade reports would you like to see on a regular basis?

8 What topics would you like to be kept informed of?

9 What data analysis programs would you want?

10 What are the four most helpful improvements that could be made in the present marketing information system?

Internal records

Marketing managers rely on internal reports of orders, sales, prices, costs, inventory levels, receivables, payables and so on. By analysing this information they can spot important opportunities and problems.

The order-to-payment cycle

The heart of the internal records system is the order-to-payment cycle. Sales representatives, dealers and customers send orders to the firm. The sales department prepares invoices, transmits copies to various departments, and back orders out-of-stock items. Shipped items generate shipping and billing documents that go to various departments.

Today's companies need to perform these steps quickly and accurately, because customers favour firms that can promise timely delivery. An increasing number of companies are using the internet and extranets to improve the speed, accuracy and efficiency of the order-to-payment cycle.

Sales information systems

Marketing managers need timely and accurate reports on current sales. Tesco is the United Kingdom's national leader in the food sector, and a global player in retailing with outlets in Ireland, central Europe, Asia and the United States (known as 'Fresh & Easy' stores). Tesco uses point-of-sale (POS) data (data available from the electronic cash register) to understand and anticipate customer behaviour, and to manage stock in individual stores, and above all the speedy availability and accuracy of POS data makes a fundamental difference to a retailer's competitiveness and the strength of its supply chain. Simon Alcock, technical specialist, Tesco, says:

> **Managing the supply chain is critical for Tesco in maintaining its leadership in the industry. If customers can't find the product they like on the supermarket shelves, then they can't buy it. The media has highlighted 'out of stocks' as an issue for some of our competitors, this solution will help us tackle the problem.[51]**

Companies that make good use of 'cookies' – records of website usage stored on personal browsers – are smart users of targeted marketing. Although the perception is that most people delete cookies out of concern for their privacy, the numbers tell a different story. Not only do many consumers *not* delete cookies, but they also expect customised marketing appeals and deals once they accept cookies. 'Consumers want and expect to receive information that is relevant and personal, especially when it comes to financial services marketing,' said Michael Penney, EVP of Epsilon's Strategic and Analytic Consulting Group.[52] Technological gadgets are revolutionising sales information systems and allowing representatives to have up-to-the-second information. When visiting a golf shop, sales reps for TaylorMade used to spend up to two hours counting golf clubs in stock before filling new orders by hand. Since the company adopted handheld devices with bar-code readers and internet connections, the reps simply point their handhelds at the bar codes and automatically tally inventory. By using the two hours they save to focus on boosting sales to retail customers, sales reps improved productivity by 20 per cent.[53]

Companies must carefully interpret the sales data so as not to draw the wrong conclusions. Founder of Dell computers Michael Dell gave this illustration:

> **If you have three yellow Mustangs sitting on a dealer's lot and a customer wants a red one, the salesman may be really good at figuring out how to sell the yellow Mustang. So the yellow Mustang gets sold, and a signal gets sent back to the factory that, hey, people want yellow Mustangs.**

The marketing intelligence system

The internal records system supplies *results* data, but the marketing intelligence system supplies *happenings* data. A **marketing intelligence system** is a set of procedures and sources that managers use to obtain everyday information about developments in the marketing environment. Marketing managers collect marketing intelligence by reading books, newspapers and trade publications; talking to customers, suppliers and distributors; monitoring 'social media' on the internet via online discussion groups, emailing lists and blogs; and meeting with other company managers.

A company can take several steps to improve the quality of its marketing intelligence:

- **Train and motivate the sales force to spot and report new developments**. The company must 'sell' its sales force on their importance as intelligence gatherers. The front-line people know and observe customer behaviour first hand, and their knowledge needs to be integrated into marketing strategy and tactics. Using a business intelligence system, a chain of chemists discovered that two of its stores, managed by the same person, had significantly higher sales in chocolate on Valentine's Day. They then discovered that instead of placing the lower-priced chocolates on a lower shelf and the more expensive chocolates higher up, this manager mixed shelf content. He knew that customers came in, reaching for the lower-priced items, but then stopped to revise their decision when they noticed the more expensive products, thinking 'she's worth it'. Communicating such practices and observations is extremely important for generating new business ideas.[54]
- **Motivate distributors, retailers and other intermediaries to pass along important intelligence**. Many companies hire specialists to gather marketing intelligence. Service providers and retailers often send mystery shoppers, also known as 'secret shoppers', to their stores to assess cleanliness of facilities, product quality and the way employees treat customers. Healthcare facilities that use mystery shoppers say the reports have led to a number of changes in the patient experience, including improved estimates of waiting times, better explanations of medical procedures, and even less stressful programming on the television in the waiting room.[55]
- **Network externally**. The firm can purchase competitors' products; attend open houses and trade shows; read competitors' published reports; attend stockholders' meetings; talk to employees, dealers, distributors, suppliers and freight agents; collect competitors' ads; and look up news stories about competitors.

  Competitive intelligence gathering must be legal and ethical, however. Procter & Gamble reportedly paid a multimillion-dollar settlement to Unilever when some external operatives (people from an outside firm) hired as part of a P&G corporate intelligence programme to learn about Unilever's hair care products were found to have engaged in such unethical behaviour as 'dumpster diving' (also known as 'rubbish archaeology') – including rummaging through skips on Unilever's property in search of unshredded documents containing key strategic plans.[56]

- **Set up a customer advisory panel.** Members might include representative customers, the company's largest customers or its most outspoken or sophisticated customers. Many business schools have advisory panels made up of alumni and recruiters who provide valuable feedback on the curriculum.

- **Take advantage of government data resources.** EUROSTAT, the Statistical Office of the EU, provides an in-depth look at the population swings, demographic groups, regional migrations and changing family structure of 498 million people in the 27 EU member states. Acxiom Europe assists companies in maximising the value of information that already exists within the company or from external sources. Having acquired and integrated Claritas Europe (including BPK and Altwood) and Consodata (the United Kingdom, France, Germany, Spain), Acxiom Europe represents one of Europe's leading sources of marketing and information management solutions.[57]

- **Purchase information from outside suppliers.** Well-known data suppliers include the AC Nielsen Company and Information Resources, Inc. These research firms gather consumer panel data at a much lower cost than the company could manage on its own.

- **Use online customer feedback systems to collect competitive intelligence.** Online customer review boards, discussion forums, chatrooms and blogs can distribute one customer's evaluation of a product or a supplier to a large number of other potential buyers and, of course, to marketers seeking information about the competition. Chatrooms allow users to share experiences and impressions, but their unstructured nature makes it difficult for marketers to find relevant messages. Thus some companies have adopted structured systems, such as customer discussion boards or customer reviews. See the marketing memo for a summary of the major categories of structured online feedback systems.

Fat Face

Clothing retailer Fat Face (www.fatface.com) is learning how to use the social media to harness customer input and sales. Garvin Ford, Fat Face data and analytical manager, says: 'Since we gained a Facebook presence with 20,000 fans we have seen our net promoter score [which shows the level of customer satisfaction] go off the scale. We've previously had a presence on social media sites because we felt we should, not because we wanted to do anything specific with it. But now we are trying to tie in our Twitter and Twitter updates with survey responses. It is starting to give some really exciting results.'[58]

Marketing memo

Clicking on the competition

There are five main ways in which marketers can find relevant online information about competitors' product strengths and weaknesses, as well as summary comments and overall performance ratings of a product, service or supplier.

- **Independent customer goods and service review forums.** Independent forums include websites such as Epinions.com, Tripadvisor.com, Consumerreview.com and Bizrate.com. Bizrate.com is a consumer feedback network that collects millions of consumer reviews of stores and products each year from two sources: its more than one million members, who have volunteered to provide ratings and feedback to assist other shoppers; and survey results on service quality from stores that have agreed to allow Bizrate.com to collect feedback directly from their customers as they make purchases. Bizrate Insights is the customer feedback and ratings platform of Bizrate, providing tools and reports to over 6,000

▶ Marketing memo *(continued)*

retailers worldwide and empowering retailers to achieve their end goal of growing sales and customer loyalty. Bizrate is operated by Shopzilla, which operates websites serving consumers and retailers in the UK, French, German and US markets.

- **Distributor or sales agent feedback sites.** Feedback sites offer both positive and negative product or service reviews, but the stores or distributors have built the sites themselves. Amazon.com, for instance, offers an interactive feedback opportunity through which buyers, readers, editors and others may review all products listed on the site, especially books. Aarstiderne.com is a medium-sized online ecology food provider that allows its customers to describe their experience and level of satisfaction with the company.

- **Combo sites.** Combination sites (combo sites) offer both customer reviews and expert opinions. Combo sites are concentrated in financial services and high-tech products that require professional knowledge. Zdnet.com, an online adviser on technology products, offers customer comments and evaluations based on ease of use, features and stability, along with expert reviews. The advantage of this type of review site is

that a product supplier can compare opinions from the experts with those from consumers.

- **Customer complaint sites.** Customer complaint forums are designed mainly for dissatisfied customers. For instance, Planetfeedback.com allows customers to voice unfavourable experiences with specific companies. Another site, Complaints.com, is devoted to customers who want to vent their frustrations with particular firms or their offerings.

- **Public blogs.** Tens of millions of blogs exist online and their numbers continue to grow. Firms such as Jupiter Research and NielsenBuzzMetrics, which operate in global markets, analyse blogs and social networks to provide firms with insights into consumer sentiment: pharmaceuticals want to know what questions are on patients' minds when they hear about problems with a medication; car companies are looking for better ways to spot defects and work out what to do about them.

Source: Aartiderne.com; *The Economist* (2006) The blogs in the corporate machine, 11 February, 55–6; also adapted from R. T. Peterson and Z. Yang (2004) Web product reviews help strategy, *Marketing News,* 7 April, 18.

Some companies circulate marketing intelligence. The staff scan the internet and major publications, abstract relevant news and disseminate a news bulletin to marketing managers. The competitive intelligence function works best when intelligence operations collaborate closely with key users in the decision-making process. In contrast, organisations where intelligence is seen as a distinct, separate function that only produces reports and does not get involved are less effective.[59]

The information gathered from the company's internal records and from the marketing intelligence system must be properly stored and managed in order for the company to take advantage of the information obtained. Databases, **data warehousing** and **data mining** may assist managers in performing these tasks.

Databases, data warehousing and data mining

Today companies organise their information into databases – customer databases, product databases, salesperson databases – and then combine data from the different databases. For example, the customer database will contain every customer's name, address, past transactions, and sometimes even demographics and psychographics (activities, interests and opinions). Instead of sending a mass 'carpet bombing' mailing of a new offer to every customer in its database, a company will rank its customers according to purchase recency, frequency and monetary value (RFM) and send the offer to only the highest-scoring customers. Besides saving on mailing expenses, this manipulation of data can often achieve a double-digit response rate. Companies warehouse these data and make them easily accessible to decision makers. Furthermore, by hiring analysts skilled in sophisticated statistical methods, they can 'mine' the data and garner fresh insights into neglected customer segments, recent customer trends and other useful information. Managers can cross-tabulate customer information with product and salesperson information to yield still deeper insights.

Database marketing

Marketers must know their customers.[60] And in order to know the customer, the company must collect information and store it in a database from which to conduct database marketing. A **customer database** is an organised collection of comprehensive information about individual customers or prospects that is current, accessible and actionable for such marketing purposes as lead generation, lead qualification, sale of a product or service, or maintenance of customer relationships. American Express Business Insights uses spending information from its database of 90 million card members to help businesses better understand their customers. 'Our ability to quickly identify and interpret trends across our global network provides our customers with an unparalleled advantage in understanding their customer base and ultimately helps them make more strategic decisions,' says Sujata Bhatia, vice president of American Express Business Insights for Europe.[61]

Database marketing is the process of building, maintaining and using customer databases and other databases (products, suppliers, resellers) to contact, transact and build customer relationships. The marketing database can assist marketing managers in tasks ranging from daily operation, resource allocation and budget planning to strategic decision processes.[62] Businesses increasingly have the capability to accumulate huge amounts of customer data in large databases. A 2011 survey conducted by *Marketing Week* suggests that most marketers recognise that using data may effectively lead to successful business results (see Figure 5.4).

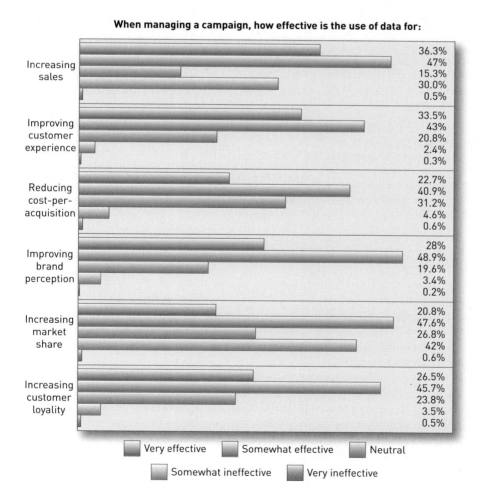

Figure 5.4 Using data may effectively improve business results

Source: J. Roberts (2011) Building belief, *Marketing Week*, 4 April: www.marketingweek.co.uk/disciplines/data-strategy/building-belief/3025135.article.

Marketing insight

The big dig

As companies gather more and more information, their ability to collect and analyse data to generate insights is more critical. Here is what some companies are doing.

Park Resorts entered into database marketing with its 2010 holiday brochure. 'That is when we really started to use data to support our positioning of "creating amazing memories",' says Hayley Jones, database marketing manager at the holiday parks company. 'We're fairly new to using data to drive our marketing and have just built a single customer view. That goes a long way to support this type of activity,' she says. For the annual brochure, Park Resorts started by looking at transactional history, such as which park the customer had visited, their frequency of booking and the time of their visit. This analysis was then used to define the personalised brochure. 'We used images of the park they stayed at to play on notions of memory. People always have memories of holidays – that is the vision we are trying to put forward. That drove the relevance of the brochure,' says Jones. Images were not just linked to the resort, but also to demographics, such as family group. Results from the new, relevant communication were strongly positive and have led the company to go further in looking at what messages and channels it uses with customers.

The need for richer information about customers is also being recognised in marketing and business planning functions. Fiona Sweeney, industry strategist at Acxiom, says scenario planning is becoming a critical tool for clients. 'We have built a fuel price indicator to look at what happens to discretionary income in every household if petrol prices go up,' she says. 'For the very affluent, it has no effect, but there are those in the middle who will be disproportionally affected.' The purpose of this sort of data enhancement is to sense-check marketing plans and the assumptions they make about the affordability of products and services.

Capturing online customer behaviour can yield a wealth of insights. A new customer signing up with a company to get a free weekly online newsletter is often required to give the company his or her name, age, gender and postcode. The company can then combine those facts with information such as observed online behaviour and characteristics of the area in which the customer lives, to better understand how to match the content of the newsletter with the interests of the customer. Although a company must be careful to preserve consumer privacy, it can also help other companies who wish to place an ad in the newsletter with behavioural targeting information. For example, it can help takeaway stores to zero in on working parents aged 30–40 in a given neighbourhood with ads designed to reach them before 10 a.m. when they are most likely to be planning their evening meal.

Questions

1. What are some of the things Park Resorts is doing right to personalise its holiday brochure?
2. What else can be done?

Sources: *Marketing Week* (2011), You can hit bullseye every time; D. Reed (2010) Giving your data a cleaner bill of health, *Marketing Week*, www.marketingweek.co.uk/disciplines/data-strategy/giving-your-data-a-cleaner-bill-of-health/3019359. article; www.park-resorts.com; www.acxiom.com.

Many organisations have realised that the knowledge in these huge databases is key to supporting the various organisational decisions. In particular, the knowledge about customers from these databases is critical for the marketing function. However, many of the useful marketing insights into customer characteristics and their purchase patterns are largely hidden and untapped.

The complexity of business markets is increasing. A shortened life cycle of many products, increasing globalisation as well as the emergence of the internet are all examples of conditions that have contributed to the fact that the environment in which the company must plan and execute its market behaviour has become increasingly complex. Therefore, the transformation process (i.e. the exchange of information, goods and money between buyer and seller) has become still more complicated, and market agents are facing increasing demands on their skills to communicate offerings, needs and expectations in the marketplace.

In response to such challenges, a growing interest in customer relationship management (CRM) can be detected. CRM deals with the identification, attraction and retention of profitable customers by managing relationships with them[63] (an in-depth coverage of CRM is provided in Chapter 11). Also for that reason, customer knowledge is one of a company's most valuable resources. Over the last decade direct channels to the customer, such as ebusiness, call centres and loyalty programmes, have produced huge volumes of data. Many of these data are being channelled into CRM databases for use in targeted relationship management and statistical modelling of consumer behaviour. Such enhanced knowledge should provide improved business results. However, many companies are still at the data storing and explorative stages[64] and have thus not yet benefited from a complete database management system.

Moreover, many companies confuse a customer mailing list with a customer database. A **customer mailing list** is simply a set of names, addresses and telephone numbers. A customer database contains much more information, accumulated through customer transactions, registration information, telephone queries, cookies and every customer contact. Ideally, a customer database also contains the consumer's past purchases, demographics (age, income, family members, birthdays), psychographics (activities, interests and opinions), mediagraphics (preferred media), and other useful information. Ideally, a **business database** would contain business customers' past purchases; past volumes, prices and profits; buyer team member names (and ages, birthdays, hobbies and favourite foods); status of current contracts; an estimate of the supplier's share of the customer's business; competitive suppliers; assessment of competitive strengths and weaknesses in selling and servicing the account; and relevant buying practices, patterns and policies.

Data warehousing and data mining

Savvy companies are capturing information every time a customer comes into contact with any of their departments. Touchpoints include a customer purchase, a customer-requested service call, an online query or a mail-in rebate card. Banks and credit card companies, telephone companies, catalogue marketers and many other companies have a great deal of information about their customers, including not only addresses and phone numbers but also transactions and enhanced data on age, family size, income and other demographic information. Companies with a well-functioning database system are capable of providing answers to the following questions:[65] what data do we potentially have available? what data are needed to achieve our goals? what data are missing that we ought to have? what data will be necessary in the future in order to address the market?

Data are collected by the company's contact centre and organised into a data warehouse where marketers can capture, query and analyse them to draw inferences about an individual customer's needs and responses. Telemarketers can respond to customer enquiries about products and services based on a total picture of the customer relationship. Through data mining, marketing statisticians can extract useful information about individuals, trends and segments from the mass of data. Using sophisticated statistical and mathematical techniques such as cluster analysis, automatic interaction detection, predictive modelling and neural networking,[66] data mining is a process of knowledge discovery and of distilling this knowledge into actionable information.[67] One of the problems data miners are often confronted with is how to present statistics to the general audience. It can be the public, other researchers, decision makers, etc. Consider a simple statement such as 'The probability that it will rain on 31 January is 30 per cent.' What may seem unambiguous is actually interpreted by different people in different ways. A survey of people in five international cities found no agreement on what a 30 per cent chance of rain means. Some thought it means rain on 30 per cent of the day's minutes, others thought rain on 30 per cent of the land area, and so on.[68] There have been attempts to formalise the data-mining process properly into models, procedures and standards. Useful outputs of these attempts are simple diagrams that convey the steps in the process. Perhaps the most widely distributed is CRISP-DM[69] (see the marketing insight box).

Marketing insight

The CRISP-DM project

With funding from the European Commission, the CRISP-DM (CRoss-Industry Standard Process for Data Mining) project developed a data-mining process model. Starting from the knowledge discovery processes used in early data-mining projects and responding directly to user requirements, this project defined and validated a data-mining process that is applicable in diverse industry sectors. CRISP-DM 1.0 (1999) is a methodology that aims to make data-mining and predictive analytics projects more efficient, better organised, more reproducible, more manageable and more likely to yield business success.[70] Partners of the CRISP-DM Consortium include NCR Systems Engineering Copenhagen (the USA and Denmark), DaimlerChrysler AG (Germany), SPSS, Inc. (the USA) and OHRA Verzekeringen en Bank Groep B.V (the Netherlands). However, over 300 organisations have contributed to the process model, and more than 200 organisations worldwide (including, e.g., AirTouch, DeloitteTouche, Capgemini and Lloyds Bank) are members of the CRISP-DM Special Interest Group (SIG). A main purpose for creating a standard data-mining process is to make the process reliable and repeatable even for companies with little data-mining background. While the CRISP-DM 1.0 user guide can be freely downloaded from www.crisp-dm.org, the six-phase data-mining methodology is briefly considered here.[71]

1 Business understanding. This initial phase focuses on understanding the project objectives and requirements from a business perspective, and then converting this knowledge into a data-mining problem definition and a preliminary plan designed to achieve the objectives.

2 Data understanding. The data-understanding phase starts with initial data collection and proceeds with activities in order to get familiar with the data, to identify data quality problems, to discover first insights into the data or to detect interesting subsets to form hypotheses for hidden information.

3 Data preparation. The data preparation phase covers all activities to construct the final dataset (data that will be fed into the modelling tool(s)) from the initial raw data. Data preparation tasks are likely to be performed multiple times, and not in any prescribed order. Tasks include table, record and attribute selection as well as transformation and cleaning of data for modelling tools.

4 Modelling. In this phase, various modelling techniques are selected and applied, and their parameters are calibrated to optimal values. Typically, there are several techniques for the same data-mining problem type. Some techniques have specific requirements on the form of data. Therefore, stepping back to the data preparation phase is often needed.

5 Evaluation. At this stage in the project you have built a model (or models) that appears to have high quality, from a data analysis perspective. Before proceeding to final deployment of the model, it is important to evaluate the model more thoroughly and review the steps executed to construct the model, to be certain it properly achieves the business objectives. A key objective is to determine if there is some important business issue that has not been sufficiently considered. At the end of this phase, a decision on the use of the data-mining results should be reached.

6 Deployment. Creation of the model is generally not the end of the project. Depending on the requirements, the deployment phase can be as simple as generating a report or as complex as implementing a repeatable data-mining process. In many cases it will be the customer, not the data analyst, who will carry out the deployment steps. However, even if the analyst will not carry out the deployment effort, it is important for the customer to understand up front what actions will need to be carried out in order to make use of the created models.

The CRISP-DM consortium is planning to develop a CRISP-DM 2.0. As the role of data mining and predictive analytics continues to evolve, so must the CRISP-DM methodology.

Some observers believe that a proprietary (i.e. company-owned) database can provide a company with a significant competitive advantage. In general, companies can use their databases in five ways:

1 **To identify prospects.** Many companies generate sales leads by advertising their product or service. The ads generally contain a response feature, such as a business reply card or freephone number, and the company builds its database from customer responses. It sorts through the database to identify the best prospects, then contacts them by mail, phone or personal call to try to convert them into customers.

2 To decide which customers should receive a particular offer. Companies are interested in selling, up-selling and cross-selling their products and services. Companies set up criteria describing the ideal target customer for a particular offer. Then they search their customer databases for those who most closely resemble the ideal type. By noting response rates a company can improve its targeting precision over time. Following a sale, it can set up an automatic sequence of activities: one week later, send a thank-you note; five weeks later, send a new offer; ten weeks later (if the customer has not responded), phone the customer and offer a special discount.

3 To deepen customer loyalty. Companies can build interest and enthusiasm by remembering customer preferences and by sending appropriate gifts, discount coupons and interesting reading material.

4 To reactivate customer purchases. Companies can install automatic mailing programs (automatic marketing) that send out birthday or anniversary cards, Christmas shopping reminders or off-season promotions. The database can help the company make attractive or timely offers.

5 To avoid serious customer mistakes. A major bank confessed to a number of mistakes it had made by not using its customer database well. In one case, the bank charged a customer a penalty for late payment on his mortgage, failing to note he headed a company that was a major depositor in the bank. He closed his account. In a second case, two different staff members of the bank phoned the same mortgage customer, offering a home equity loan at different prices. Neither knew that the other had made the call. In a third case, the bank gave a premium customer only standard service in another country.

The downside of database marketing and CRM

Having covered the good news about database marketing, we also need to cover the bad news. Four problems can prevent a firm from using CRM effectively. The first is that building and maintaining a customer database requires a large investment in computer hardware, database software, analytical programs, communication links and skilled personnel. It is difficult to collect the right data, especially to capture all the occasions of company interaction with individual customers. Building a customer database would not be worthwhile in the following cases:

1 when the product is a once-in-a-lifetime purchase (a grand piano);
2 when customers show little loyalty to a brand (there is lots of customer brand switching);
3 when the unit sale is very small (a chocolate bar); and
4 when the cost of gathering information is too high.

The second problem is the difficulty of getting everyone in the company to be customer oriented and to use the available information. Employees find it far easier to carry on traditional transaction marketing than to practise customer relationship marketing. Effective database marketing requires managing and training employees as well as dealers and suppliers.

The third problem is that not all customers want a relationship with the company, and they may resent knowing that the company has collected so much personal information about them. Marketers must be concerned about customer attitudes towards privacy and security. Online companies would be wise to explain their privacy policies and to give consumers the right not to have their information stored in a database.

A fourth problem is that the assumptions behind CRM may not always hold true.[72] For example, it may not cost less to serve more loyal customers. High-volume customers often know their value to a company and can leverage it to extract premium service and/or price discounts. Loyal customers may expect and demand more from the firm and resent any attempt to charge full or higher prices. They may also be jealous of attention lavished on other customers. Loyal customers may not necessarily be the best ambassadors for the brand. One study found that customers who scored high on behavioural loyalty and bought a lot of a company's products were less active word-of-mouth marketers than customers who scored high on attitudinal loyalty and expressed greater commitment to the firm.

Thus, the benefits of database marketing do not come without heavy costs, not only in collecting the original customer data but also in maintaining them and mining them. When it works, a data warehouse yields more than it costs, but the data must be in good condition, and the discovered relationships must be valid.

Database marketing is most frequently used by business marketers and service providers (hotels, banks, airlines; and insurance, credit card and telephone companies) that normally and easily collect a lot of customer data. Other types of company in the best position to invest in CRM are those that do a lot of cross-selling and up-selling (such as Amazon.com) or whose customers have highly differentiated needs and are of highly differentiated value to the company. Packaged goods retailers and consumer packaged goods companies use database marketing less frequently, though some (such as Kraft) have built databases for certain brands. Businesses with low customer lifetime value (CLV), high churn and no direct contact between the seller and ultimate buyer may not benefit as much from CRM. Deloitte Consulting found that 70 per cent of firms found little or no improvement through CRM implementation. The reasons are many: the CRM system was poorly designed, it became too expensive, users did not make much use of it or report much benefit, and collaborators ignored the system. Professor of marketing George Day concludes that one of the reasons many CRM failures occur is that companies concentrate on customer contact processes without making corresponding changes in internal structures and systems.[73] His recommendation? Change the configuration before installing CRM: 'Our findings confirm that a superior (customer-relating) capability is all about how a business builds and manages its organisation, and does not have much to do with CRM tools and technologies.'[74]

SUMMARY

1 Marketers find many opportunities by identifying trends (directions or sequences of events that have some momentum and durability) and megatrends (major social, economic, political and technological changes that have long-lasting influence).

2 Within the rapidly changing global picture, marketers must monitor five major environmental forces: political/legal, economic, ecological/physical, social/cultural and demographic, and technological. The acronym PEEST analysis is used to describe an analysis of the company's environment covering these five forces.

3 In the economic arena, marketers need to focus on income distribution and levels of savings, debt and credit availability.

4 In the social–cultural and demographic arena, marketers must understand people's views of themselves, others, organisations, society, nature and the universe. They must market products that correspond to society's core and secondary values and address the needs of different subcultures within a society. Marketers must also be aware of worldwide population growth; changing mixes of age, ethnic composition and educational levels; the rise of non-traditional families; and large geographic shifts in population.

5 In the ecological/physical environment, marketers need to be aware of the public's increased concern about the health of the environment. Many marketers are now embracing sustainability and green marketing programmes that provide better environmental solutions as a result.

6 In the technological arena, marketers should take account of the accelerating pace of technological change, opportunities for innovation, varying R&D budgets, and the increased governmental regulation brought about by technological change.

7 In the political–legal environment, marketers must work within the many laws regulating business practices and with various special interest groups.

8 To carry out their analysis, planning, implementation and control responsibilities, marketing managers need a marketing information system. The role of the MIS is to assess the managers' information needs, develop the needed information and distribute that information in a timely manner.

9 An MIS has three components: (1) an internal records system, which includes information on the order-to-payment cycle and sales information systems; (2) a marketing intelligence system, a set of procedures and sources used by managers to obtain everyday information about pertinent developments in the marketing environment; and (3) a marketing research system that allows for the systematic design, collection, analysis and reporting of data and findings relevant to a specific marketing situation.

10 Today companies organise their information into databases – customer databases, product databases, salesperson databases – and then combine data from the different databases.

11 A customer database is an organised collection of comprehensive information about individual customers or prospects that is current, accessible and actionable for such marketing purposes as lead generation, lead qualification, sale of a product or service, or maintenance of customer relationships.

12 Database marketing is the process of building, maintaining and using customer databases and other databases (products, suppliers, resellers) to contact, transact and build customer relationships.

13 Data are collected by the company's contact centre and organised into a data warehouse where marketers can capture, query and analyse it to draw inferences about an individual customer's needs and responses.

14 Through data mining, marketing statisticians can extract useful information about individuals, trends and segments from the mass of data.

15 Customer relationship management deals with the identification, attraction and retention of profitable customers by managing relationships with them. Four problems can prevent a firm from effectively using CRM. Building a CRM-related customer database would not be worthwhile in the following cases: (1) when the product is a once-in-a-lifetime purchase (a grand piano); (2) when customers show little loyalty to a brand (there is lots of customer churn); (3) when the unit sale is very small (a chocolate bar); and (4) when the cost of gathering information is too high.

APPLICATIONS

Marketing debate

Is consumer behaviour more a function of a person's age? One of the widely debated issues in developing marketing programmes that target certain age groups is how much consumers change over time. Some marketers maintain that age differences are critical and that the needs and wants of a 25-year-old in 2012 are not that different from those of a 25-year-old in 1982. Others dispute that contention and argue that cohort and generation effects are critical, and that marketing programmes must therefore suit the times.

Take a position: Age differences are fundamentally more important than cohort effects *versus* Cohort effects can dominate age differences.

Marketing discussion

1 What brands and products do you feel successfully 'speak to you' and effectively target your age group? Why? Which ones do not? What could they do better?

2 What are the opportunities from database marketing and CRM? What are the pitfalls? How may the opportunities and pitfalls be moderated by company and market characteristics?

REFERENCES

[1]Based on R. Baker (2010) Food and drink industry in sustainability drive, *Marketing Week*, 8 December, www.marketingweek.co.uk/sectors/food-and-drink/food-and-drink-industry-in-sustainability-drive/3021382.article; R. Baker (2010) Food and drink brands must shout about sustainability, *Marketing Week*, 10 December, www.marketingweek.co.uk/sectors/sustainability/food-and-drink-brands-must-shout-about-sustainability/3021566.article; www.fdf.org.uk; A. Corsano and A. Knitwear (2007) Going green, seeing green, 12 October, www.forbes.com.

[2]Interflora, www.interflora.dk/historie.php.

[3]www.euromonitor.com/TOP_10_CONSUMER_TRENDS_FOR_2010.

[4]See www.badfads.com for examples of fads and collectables through the years.

[5]J. F. Rock (2010) Green building: trend or megatrend? *Dispute Resolution Journal*, 65(2/3) 72–7; J. Naisbitt and P. Aburdene (1990) *Megatrends 2000*, New York: Avon Books.

[6]D. Dapice (2008) Globalization and the markets, *Global Envision*, 24 Janauary, www.globalenvision.org/content/globalization-and-markets.

[7]Indata (2006) *IN*, June 27; B. Craigie (2006) Brits don't buy the brand blog, *Marketing Week*, 29, 47, 38–9.

[8]World POPClock, US Census Bureau, www.census.gov, September 1999.

[9]Although over ten years old, this breakdown provides a useful perspective. See D. H. Meadows, D. L. Meadows and Jorgen Randers (1993) *Beyond Limits*, White River Junction, VT: Chelsea Green, for some commentary.

[10]www.un.org/esa/population/publications/WPA2009/WPA2009-report.pdf.

[11]http://epp.eurostat.ec.europa.eu/cache/ITY_OFFPUB/KS-SF-08-072/EN/KS-SF-08-072-EN.PDF.

[12]Eurostat/European Commission (2007) *Report: Living Conditions in Europe*, Luxembourg: Eurostat Pocketbooks.

[13]Eurostat/European Commission (2007) Report: Europe in figures, *Eurostat Yearbook 2006–07*, Luxembourg: Eurostat – European Commission.

[14]Ibid.

[15]GLEN – Gay and Lesbian Equality Network (2006) Civil marriage for gays should be next reform, *The Irish Times*, 3 April.

[16]E. P. Becerra and P. K. Korgaonkar (2010) The influence of ethnic identification in digital advertising, *Journal of Advertising Research*, September, 279-91; for descriptions of the buying habits of and marketing approaches to African-Americans and Hispanics, see M. I. Valdes (2002) *Marketing to American Latinos: A Guide to the In-Culture Approach, Part II*, Ithaca, NY: Paramount Market Publishing, and A. L. Schreiber (2001) *Multicultural Marketing*, Lincolnwood, IL: NTC Business Books.

[17]D. Dodson (2007) New cosmetics and toiletries global report highlights changes to the segmentation trend, *Euromonitor*, 16 July, www.euromonitor.com/New_Cosmetics_and_Toiletries_Global_Report_highlights_changes_to_the_segmentation_trend.

[18]Council of Europe (2007) Council of Europe hosts blindfolded lunch, café theatre and special film to mark International Day of Disabled Persons, 11 November, www.coe.int/t/dc/press/NoteRedac2006/20061130_handicap_en.asp; European Disability Forum, www.edf-feph.org/Page_Generale.asp?DocID=12534.

[19]The Central Intelligence Agency's World Factbook (www.cia.gov/library/publications/the-world-factbook/geos/xx.html) (accessed 10 September 2008).

[20]Eurostat (2010) Europe in figures, *Eurostat Yearbook 2010*.

[21]*Report: Families in Germany – Facts and Figures, Federal Ministry for Family Affairs*, Senior Citizens, Women and Youth, Berlin, December 2004.

[22]Eurostat (2010) Europe in figures, *Eurostat Yearbook 2010*; Eurostat (2007) Report: Europe in figures, *Eurostat Yearbook 2006–07*, Eurostat/European Commission.

[23]N. Byrnes (2006) Secrets of the male shopper, *BusinessWeek*, 4 September, 44.

[24]Eurostat (2010) Europe in figures, *Eurostat Yearbook 2010*; C. Boswell (2005) *Migration in Europe*, a paper prepared for the Policy Analysis and Research Programme of the Global Commission on International Migration, Global Commission on International Migration, September; available at: www.gcim.org/attachements/RS4.pdf.

[25]Eurostat (2010): Europe in figures, *Eurostat Yearbook 2010*; I. Jakubowski (1995) Marketing in the New Europe, *British Food Journal*, 97, 6, 18–24; F. A. Palumbo and I. Teich (2004) Market segmentation based on the level of acculturation, *Marketing Intelligence and Planning*, 22(4), 472–84.

[26]M. Suggitt (2007) New Europe's hunger for western lifestyles means big business for food and drinks companies, *Euromonitor*, 17 March, www.euromonitor.com.

[27]O. Hofmann (2006) UK consumers eat the most ready meals, *Euromonitor*, 11 October, www.euromonitor.com; O. Hofmann (2007) Spanish manufacturers innovate in health and wellness food, *Euromonitor*, 6 March, www.euromonitor.com.

[28]http://epp.eurostat.ec.europa.eu.

[29]A. B. Atkinson and E. Marlier (eds) (2010) *Income and Living Conditions in Europe*, Eurostat Statistical Books, Luxembourg: Publications Office of the European Union.

[30]European Commission (2001) *How Europeans See Themselves: Looking Through the Mirror with Public Opinion Surveys*, European Documentation Series, Luxembourg: Office for Official Publications of the European Communities.

[31]C. Manescu (2010) Economic implications of corporate social responsibility and responsible investments, PhD thesis, University of Gothenburg, School of Business, Economics and Law; S. Baker (2006) Wiser about the web, *BusinessWeek*, 27 March, 53–7.

[32]Clearing house suits chronology (2001) *Associated Press*, 26 January, and P. Wenske (1999) You too could lose $19,000!, *Kansas City Star*, 31 October.

[33]Cited from S. S. Hassan and L. P. Katsanis (1991) Identification of global consumer segments: a behavioural framework, *Journal of International Consumer Marketing*, 3(2), 11–28; for a good analysis of global youth cultural consumption, see D. Kjeldgaard and S. Askegaard (2006) The globalization of youth culture: the global youth segment as structures of common difference, *Journal of Consumer Research*, 33 (September), 231–47.

[34]M. Nutley (2011) Social media – a new frontier for gaming, *Marketing Week*, January, www.marketingweek.co.uk/disciplines/digital/digital-strategy-supplement/social-media-a-new-frontier-for-gaming/3022558.article.

[35]R. Walzer (2007) At the supermarket, shopping for better health, *International Herald Tribune*, 14 December, www.iht.com/articles/2007/12/14/business/wbspot15.php.

[36]A. Winston (2010) Green marketers are still sinning, October, www.businessweek.com/managing/content/oct2010/ca20101029_631610.htm.

[37]J. Roberts (2010) Voicing your ethical stance, *Marketing Week*, 4 March, www.marketingweek.co.uk/voicing-your-ethical-stance/3010615.article.

[38]S. B. Banerjee, E. S. Iyer and R. K. Kashyap (2003) Corporate enviromentalism: antecedents and influence of industry type, *Journal of Marketing*, 67, April, 106–22.

[39]M. Firoz and A. A. Ansari (2010) Environmental accounting and international financial reporting standards (IFRS), *International Journal of Business and Management*, 5(10), 105–12; R. Welford (1994) Improving corporate environmental performance, *Environmental Management and Health*, 5(2), 6–10.

[40]R. van Gestel (2005) Self-regulation and environmental law, *Electronic Journal of Comparative Law*, 9(1), 1–25.

[41]www.iso.org/iso/iso_14000_essentials; M. Watson and A. R. T. Emery (2004) Environmental management and auditing systems: the reality of environmental self-regulation, *Managerial Auditing Journal*, 19(7), 916–28.

[42]A. Tsotsis (2010), 275 million iPods sold to date, iPod Touch is the most popular, TechCrunch, September 1: http://techcrunch.com/2010/09/01/275-million-ipods/; www.apple.com/pr/library/2007/04/09ipod.html.

[43]S. Frank (2006) R&D expenditure in Europe, *Statistics in Focus*, Luxembourg: Eurostat/European Communities, 6.

[44]The Commission of the European Communities (2007) The 2007 EU industrial R&D investment scoreboard, 5 October, http://iri.jrc.ec.europa.eu/research/scoreboard_2007.htm.

[45]Battelle and R&D Magazine (2010) 2011Global R&D Funding Forecast, December, 1-36.

[46]http://ec.europa.eu/enterprise/policies/sme/business-environment/common-commencement-dates/index_en.htm; see also D. Cohen (1995) *Legal Issues on Marketing Decision Making*, Cincinnati, OH: South-Western.

[47]R. Gardyn (2001) Swap meet, *American Demographics*, July, 51–5.

[48]P. Paul (2001) Mixed signals, *American Demographics*, July, 45–9.

[49]www.nielsen.com.

[50]S. Warren (1998) Pillow talk: stackers outnumber plumpers – don't mention drool, *Wall Street Journal*, 8 January.

[51]http://download.microsoft.com.

[52]www.deleteyourcookies.com/2010/07/report-consumers-prefer-receiving.html

[53]H. Green (2003) TaylorMade, *BusinessWeek*, 24 November, 94.

[54]N. Grossman (2007) How can they get that ability to make more informed decisions?, *Forbes*, 21 September, www.forbes.com/entrepreneurstechnology/2007/09/21/microsoft-oracle-amazon-ent-tech-cx_ng_0921bmightydatamining.html.

[55]S. S. Wang (2006) Health care taps mystery shoppers, *Wall Street Journal*, 10 August.

[56]A. Serwer (2001) P&G's covert operation, *Fortune*, 17 September, 42–4.

[57]www.acxiom.com.

[58]M. Cuddeford-Jones (2010) Data focus can enhance your customer offer, *Marketing Week*, December, www.marketingweek.co.uk/disciplines/data-strategy/data-focus-can-enhance-your-customer-offer/3021555.article.

[59]American Productivity and Quality Center (2002) User-driven competitive intelligence: crafting the value proposition, 3–4 December.

[60]V. Kumar, R. Venkatesan and W. Reinartz (2006) Knowing what to sell, when, and to whom, *Harvard Business Review*, March, 131–7.

[61]R. Baker (2011) American Express launches data analytics tool, *Business Week*, 5 April.

[62]Yu-Hui Tao and Chu-Chen Rosa Yeh (2003) Simple database marketing tools in customer analysis and retention, *International Journal of Information Management*, 23(4), 291–301.

[63]M. Labus and M. Stone (2010) The CRM behaviour theory – managing corporate customer relationships in service industries, *Journal of Database Marketing and Customer Strategy Management*, 17(3/4), 155–73; D. Bradshaw and C. Brash (2001) Managing customer relationships in the e-business world: how to personalise computer relationships for increased profitability, *International Journal of Retail and Distribution Management*, 29(12), 520–30.

[64]D. Crié and A. Micheaux (2006) From customer data to value: what is lacking in the information chain?, *Database Marketing and Customer Strategy Management*, 13(4), 282–99.

[65]Ibid.

[66]C. R. Stephens and R. Sukumar (2006) An introduction to data mining, in R. Grover and R. Vriens (eds), *Handbook of Marketing Research*, Thousand Oaks, CA: Sage, 455–86; Pang-Ning Tan, M. Steinbach and V. Kumar (2005) *Introduction to Data Mining*, Upper Saddle River, NJ: Addison Wesley; M. J. A. Berry and G. S. Linoff, *Data Mining Techniques: For Marketing, Sales, and Customer Relationship Management*, 2nd edn, Hoboken, NJ: Wiley Computer; J. Lattin, D. Carroll and P. Green (2003) *Analyzing Multivariate Data*, Florence, KY: Thomson Brooks/Cole.

[67]C. L. Gunnarsson, M. M. Walker, V. Walatka and K. Swann (2007) Lessons learned: a case study using data mining in the newspaper industry, *Database Marketing and Customer Strategy Management*, 14(4), 271–80.

[68]G. Gigerenzer, R. Hertwig, E. van den Broek, B. Fasolo and K. V. Katsikopoulos (2005). 'A 30% chance of rain tomorrow': How does the public understand probabilistic weather forecast? *Risk Analysis*, 25, 623–9.

[69]Adams, N. M. (2010) Perspectives on data mining, *International Journal of Market Research*, 52(1), 11–19.

[70]Adapted from www.crisp-dm.org no longer functional. CRISP_SM1.0 User Guide now found at ftp://ftp.software.ibm.com/software/analytics/spss/documentation/modeler/14.2/Fr/CRISP-DM.pdf.

[71]Adapted from www.crisp-dm.org no longer functional. CRISP_SM1.0 User Guide now found at ftp://ftp.software.ibm.com/software/analytics/spss/documentation/modeler/14.2/Fr/CRISP-DM.pdf.

[72]W. Reinartz and V. Kumar (2002) The mismanagement of customer loyalty, *Harvard Business Review*, July, 86–94; S. M. Fournier, S. Dobscha and D. G. Mick (1998) Preventing the premature death of relationship marketing, *Harvard Business Review*, January–February, 42–51.

[73]G. S. Day (2003) Creating a superior customer-relating capability, *Sloan Management Review*, 44(3), 77–82; G. S. Day (2003) Creating a superior customer-relating capability, MSI Report No. 03–101, Cambridge, MA: Marketing Science Institute; Why some companies succeed at CRM (and many fail), *Knowledge at Wharton* (http://knowledge.wharton.edu).

[74]This quote is taken from G. Day (2002) Winning the competition for customer relationships, The Wharton School University of Pennsylvania, October, p. 6 (http://mktg-sun.wharton.upenn.edu/ideas/pdf/Day/Winning%20the%20Competition.pdf) (note: parentheses not in original).

Chapter 6

Managing market research and forecasting

IN THIS CHAPTER, WE WILL ADDRESS THE FOLLOWING QUESTIONS:

1 What constitutes good marketing research?
2 What is the marketing research process?
3 How can marketers assess their return on investment of marketing expenditure?
4 How can companies more accurately measure and forecast demand?

Managing digital technology in marketing can be both challenging and fun

Source: Sigg UK/Sigg Switzerland AG www.sigg.com.

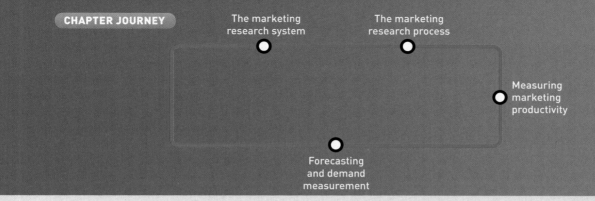

The marketing
research system

The marketing
research process

Measuring
marketing
productivity

Forecasting
and demand
measurement

Good marketers want insights to help them interpret past performance as well as plan future activities. They need timely, accurate and actionable information about consumers, competition and their brands. They also need to make the best possible tactical decisions in the short run and strategic decisions in the long run. Discovering a consumer insight and understanding its marketing implications can often lead to a successful product launch or spur the growth of a brand.

See the SIGG Switzerland example.

For years, Swiss bottle producer SIGG Switzerland had been selling its aluminium water and fuel bottles to the US outdoor market. The company was counting on the Swiss reputation for quality to drive sales of the bottles with an average price twice as high as its closest competitors. However, sales were flat, as US customers did not find the bottles to be worth a price premium. To gain insight into the underlying reasons for the low sales, the Swiss firm decided to conduct market research to uncover customers' perceptions and evaluations of the brand. Some surprising discoveries were made. US customers were worried that their water would taste like the metal container they carried it in, and they did not appreciate the variety of bottle designs. Also, they were worried about whether the bottle would leak. Based on the market research results, SIGG employed a variety of strategies, including an online contest encouraging customers to submit their preferred new bottle design and sponsorship of eco-design blog inhibit.com, where the advantages of using the bottles and the Swiss company's environmentally friendly behaviour were promoted. The market research-based strategy doubled bottle sales in just one year.[1] The beautiful shape of the bottles is one of the reasons that SIGG was incorporated into the collection of the Museum of Modern Art in New-York.

In this chapter, we consider the marketing research system. We also review the steps involved in the marketing research process. Finally, we outline how marketers can develop good sales forecasts.

The marketing research system

Marketing managers often commission formal marketing studies of specific problems and opportunities. They may request a market survey, a product-preference test, a sales forecast by region or an advertising evaluation. It is the job of the marketing researcher to produce insight into the customer's attitudes and buying behaviour. **Marketing insights** provide diagnostic information about how and why we observe certain effects in the marketplace, and what that means to marketers.[2] Gaining marketing insights is crucial for marketing success. If marketers lack consumer insights, they often get in trouble. When Tropicana redesigned its orange juice packaging, dropping the iconic image of an orange skewered by a straw, it failed to test adequately for consumer reactions, with disastrous results. Sales dropped by 20 per cent, and Tropicana reinstated the old package design after only a few months.[3]

We define **marketing research** as the systematic design, collection, analysis and reporting of data and findings relevant to a specific marketing situation facing the company. Spending on marketing research was €21 billion globally in 2009 with Europe accounting for 46 per cent of that amount (the United States accounts for 32 per cent), according to ESOMAR, the World Association of Opinion and Market Research Professionals. The 2009 global spending represents a year-on-year net decline of 4.6 per cent, constituting the first decline since ESOMAR began measuring the industry in 1988.[4] This decline is in line with expectations given the financial and economic downturn in 2008.

Most large companies have their own marketing research departments, which often play crucial roles within the organisation. Telecommunications operator Orange, the key brand of France Telecom serving two-thirds of the company's 203 million customers, has developed a global innovation network called Orange Labs. It is made up of 5,000 employees on three continents, and includes marketers, researchers and other professional groups. The international Orange Labs network reflects Orange's ambition to put innovation at the heart of its strategy, firmly focused on its clients. Thus, it is a main priority of the network to anticipate technological advances and changes in uses worldwide: for instance, by conducting both internal and external survey research, and by designing customer analysis programs to identify where improvements can be made and to suggest appropriate responses.[5] Yet, marketing research is not limited to large companies with big budgets and marketing research departments. Often at much smaller companies everyone carries out marketing research – including the customers.

Companies normally budget marketing research at 1–2 per cent of company sales. A large percentage of that is spent on the services of outside marketing research firms, which fall into three categories:

1 **Syndicated-service research firms.** These firms gather consumer and trade information, which they sell for a fee. Examples: TNS Gallup, Business Monitor (Europe Service), Euromonitor.
2 **Custom marketing research firms.** These firms are hired to carry out specific projects. They design the study and report the findings. Example: TNS Global (www.tnsglobal.com), which is the world's largest custom market research specialist.
3 **Specialty-line marketing research firms.** These firms provide specialised research services. The best example is the field-service firm, which sells field interviewing services to other firms.

Small companies can hire the services of a marketing research firm or conduct research in creative and affordable ways, such as:

- **Engaging students or professors to design and carry out projects.** Companies such as Danske Bank, Carlsberg, IBM, Mars and Price Chopper engage in 'crowdcasting'. Some of them are also sponsors of student competitions such as 'Danske Bank Future Banking Challenge' and the 'Copenhagen Business School (CBS) Case Competition', where top MBA students from countries such as Latvia, the Netherlands, New Zealand, the UK, Thailand, the USA, Pakistan, China and Brazil compete in teams. The payoff to the students is experience and visibility; the payoff to the companies is fresh sets of eyes to solve problems at a fraction of what consultants would charge.[6]

- **Using the internet.** A company can collect considerable information at very little cost by examining competitors' websites, monitoring chat rooms and accessing published data.
- **Checking out rivals.** Many small businesses, such as restaurants, hotels or specialty retailers, routinely visit competitors to learn about changes they have made.
- **Tapping into marketing partner expertise.** Marketing research firms, ad agencies, distributors and other marketing partners may be able to share relevant market knowledge they have accumulated.

Most companies use a combination of marketing research resources to study their industries, competitors, audiences and channel strategies. To take advantage of all these different resources and practices, good marketers adopt a formal marketing research process.

The marketing research process

Effective marketing research follows the six steps shown in Figure 6.1. We illustrate them with the situation shown in the following case:[7]

HWL: 3

Hutchison Whampoa Limited (HWL) is a leading telecommunications and data services provider operating in a number of European countries including Austria, Denmark, Italy, Sweden and the United Kingdom. In 2003, HWL was the first to market an international 3G mobile service under the brand 3 (mobile phone network). 3G means third-generation mobile communication and can be viewed as wireless broadband for mobile phones. As illustrated in Figure 6.2, 3G offers a number of multimedia services.

Since then 3 has been first mover in many fields: in 2006 it was the first to introduce MSN Messenger as a mobile service and the first to launch High-Speed Downlink Packet Access (HSDPA) with a speed of 3.6 megabits per second (Mbps) (100 times as fast as global system for mobile communication [GSM]) in Denmark. In 2010 the speed was increased to 21 Mbps. Also, market research revealed that 3's customers wanted the opportunity to watch TV on their phones, so 3 responded initially by signing an exclusive deal to stream ITV1 to its UK customers. In 2010 Mobile TV was launched, enabling all 3's customers to watch TV on their mobile for €5 per month. The company invested heavily to update and extend its network, as well as to develop new products and services, relying on its major strength in anticipating and meeting customers' needs. 3's market research was directed at investigating which consumer groups found 3G services appealing and which types of benefit were emphasised by these groups.[8]

Step 1: define the problem, the decision alternatives and the research objectives

Marketing managers must be careful not to define the problem too broadly or too narrowly for the marketing researcher. A marketing manager who says, 'Find out everything you can about mobile phone customers' needs' will collect a lot of unnecessary information. One who says, 'Find out whether enough 3G customers would be willing to pay

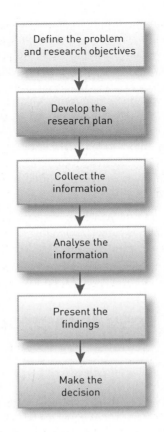

Figure 6.1 The marketing research process.

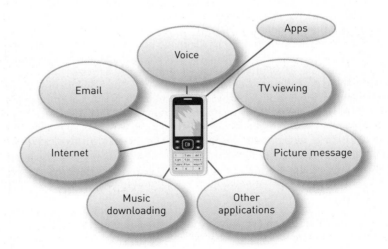

Figure 6.2 In the highly competitive mobile communication industry, marketing research is focusing on which new services customers might be willing to pay extra for, such as television viewing, apps and music downloading.

€5 a month for a mobile TV service for 3 to break even in two years on the cost of offering this service' is taking too narrow a view of the problem. The marketing researcher might respond, 'Why does the mobile broadband connection have to be priced at €5 as opposed to €3, €10 or some other price?' Why does 3 have to break even on the cost of the service, especially if it attracts new customers?' Another relevant question is: How important is it to be first mover in the market, and how long can the company sustain its lead?

Let's say that the marketing manager and marketing researcher agreed to define the problem as follows: 'Will offering a TV service for mobile phones create enough incremental preference and profit for 3 to justify its cost against other possible investments that Hutchison Whampoa might make?' To help in designing the research, management should first spell out the decisions it might face and then work backwards. Suppose management outlines these decisions:

1 Should 3 offer a mobile TV service?
2 If so, should the offer be tailored to a specific consumer segment?
3 What price(s) should be charged?
4 What types of mobile phones, datacards, etc. should complement the service?

Now management and marketing researchers are ready to set specific research objectives:

1 What types of customer would respond positively to a mobile TV service?
2 How many customers are likely to sign up for this service at different price levels?
3 How many additional customers might choose 3 over competitors because of this new service?
4 How much long-term goodwill will this service add to 3's image?
5 How important is a mobile TV service to consumers relative to other services, such as video messaging or game playing?

Not all research projects can be this specific. Some research is *exploratory* – its goal is to shed light on the real nature of the problem and to suggest possible solutions or new ideas. Some research is *descriptive* – it seeks to quantify demand, such as how many customers would purchase a mobile broadband service at €5. Some research is *causal* – its purpose is to test a cause-and-effect relationship.

Step 2: develop the research plan

The second stage of marketing research is where we develop the most efficient plan for gathering the needed information and what that will cost. Suppose the company made a prior estimate that launching a mobile TV service would yield a long-term profit of €500,000. If the manager believes that doing the marketing research will lead to an improved pricing and promotional plan and a long-term profit of €600,000, the company should be willing to spend up to €100,000 on this research. If the research will cost more than €100,000, it is not worth doing.[9]

To design a research plan we need to make decisions about the data sources, research approaches, research instruments, sampling plan and contact methods.

Data sources

The researcher can gather secondary data, primary data, or both. *Secondary data* are data that were collected for another purpose and already exist somewhere, such as in surveys or market reports from research organisations or government agencies. Secondary data may also take the form of internal company information, such as sales records or financial data. *Primary data* are data freshly gathered for a specific purpose or for a specific research project, such as identifying Norwegian consumers' preferences for various supermarket formats.

Researchers usually start their investigation by examining some of the rich variety of low-cost and readily available secondary data, to see whether they can partly or wholly solve the problem without collecting costly primary data. For instance, European cosmetics companies wishing to reach out to consumers groups in Asia might purchase a copy of

Euromonitor's report on 'Beauty and Personal Care in Asia', a survey that provides insights into market trends and pinpoints future growth sectors.[10] Among the helpful findings they would discover in the report are:

- Skin care in China currently grows by over 10 per cent in value per year.
- The 'Gene-repair' concept is currently the hottest trend.
- There is a rising trend for non-traditional companies to enter the cosmetics industry. Examples include Gekkeinan Sake (Moist Moon) and Fuji Film (Astalift).

When the needed data don't exist or are dated, inaccurate, incomplete or unreliable, the researcher will need to collect primary data. Most marketing research projects do include some primary-data collection.

Research approaches

Marketers collect primary data in five main ways: through observation, focus groups, surveys, behavioural data and experiments.

Observational research Researchers can gather fresh data by observing the relevant actors and settings,[11] unobtrusively observing as they shop or as they consume products. Sometimes they equip consumers with pagers and instruct them to write down what they are doing whenever prompted, or they hold informal interview sessions at a café or bar. Photographs can also provide a wealth of detailed information.

Ethnographic research is a particular observational research approach that uses concepts and tools from anthropology and other social science disciplines to provide deep understanding of how people live and work.[12] The goal is to immerse the researcher into consumers' lives to uncover unarticulated desires, meanings or behaviour that might not

A picture is worth a thousand words to skilled marketing researchers, who can glean a number of insights from this photo of a Swedish kitchen.
Source: © Anna G. Tufvesson/Nordicphotos/Alamy.

be captured in other forms of research. Firms such as Lego, IBM, Intel and Microsoft have embraced ethnographic research to design breakthrough products.

Pan-European supermarket chain Lidl, catering to the price-conscious, bottom end of the market, found that data on the brand and its sector was scarce. It asked Ogilvy, an international advertising, marketing and public relations agency, to carry out an extensive audit of the shopping experience by talking to customers in the stores and filming them. The results proved an eye opener for Lidl. It underlined the retailer's strengths – its low prices and quality goods – but also its weaknesses, such as its limited and unfamiliar range – its 'foreignness' in many markets. However, when Ogilvy asked four consumers who usually value well-known, branded products to test shop in a Lidl supermarket, they were all positive in their evaluation of the actual experience. Today, Lidl focuses on simplicity in its brand offer and on its core strength in providing quality products at the lowest possible prices across the EU.[13]

Many other companies have benefited from ethnographic research.

- The global document management company Xerox was one of the first companies to use applied ethnography. In 1979, an anthropologist at Xerox conducted ethnographic fieldwork in the workplace and summarised her findings in a film showing office workers struggling to do a copying job on a Xerox machine. After viewing the film, Xerox engineers began to think about designing Xerox machines differently. This ethnographic work led to the large green button we see on most copiers today that lets us walk up to the machine and easily make a copy.[14]
- At Orange, ethnographic market research is applied to get to know the mindset of its consumers and as input in the product development process. 'For example, it can be difficult to ask consumers what they do in their "dead time", while commuting, between meetings and so on, because it is not in their particular language,' says research analyst Gino Zisa. 'So we thought it would be helpful to observe people in those circumstances in their own environment, rather than in a focus group.'
- Ethnographic research methods are also used by the motor industry in Germany, where – for part of the strategic development for the launch of a luxury sports car – Stephan Tun, managing director at Maritz Research Germany, spent time with owners driving on motorways, going to golf courses, shopping and in their homes. 'It gave us information that was vast and rich, providing a new understanding of a very specialised market,' he says. It fed into final product development, assisted positioning and contributed to the communication strategy.[15]

Ethnographic research can be especially useful in developing markets, especially far-flung rural areas, where companies do not know consumers as well. Also, ethnographic research may assist companies wishing to glean a greater understanding of the population at large and how cultural attitudes affect spending. For example, 'co-creation' specialist Promise has been working with financial services companies and government departments to develop a better understanding of people coming to live in the UK from abroad and how best to communicate with them. Following ethnographic research in targeted branches of a high street bank, Promise conducted focus groups in the respondent's mother tongue, wherever possible. Respondents were also able to bring along a friend, who might have a better level of English. On the back of Promise's research, its financial client was able to develop and tailor its product to individuals who have just moved to the UK. Rather than targeting these people by demographics, it found the common experience of immigration meant customers were looking for greater flexibility as opposed to extensive cover of goods that they may not yet have acquired.[16]

Focus group research A **focus group** is a gathering of six to ten people carefully selected by researchers based on certain demographic, psychographic or other considerations and brought together to discuss various topics of interest at length. Participants are normally

An exploratory research session, with people writing down their motivations and beliefs
Source: OJO Images/Glow Images

paid a small sum for attending. A professional research moderator provides questions and probes based on the marketing managers' discussion guide or agenda.

Moderators try to discern consumers' real motivations and why they say and do certain things. They typically record the sessions, and marketing managers often remain behind two-way mirrors in the next room. Focus-group research is a useful exploratory step, but researchers must avoid generalising from focus-group participants to the whole market, because the sample size is too small and the sample is not drawn randomly.

In fact, an increasing number of marketers are relying on other means of collecting information that they believe are less artificial. 'Focus groups confirm what you already know,' says Eva Steensig, a sociologist at DDB Denmark. DDB, part of the Omnicom Group, introduced a new service called SignBank, which uses the internet and the advertising agency's global office network to collect thousands of snippets of information about cultural change, identify trends within the data and advise clients about what it means to them. Consumers are not experts on their own consumption patterns, says Steensig, and this makes them easily led by focus group moderators. DDB and some other advertisers feel it is better to 'read the signs' of consumption than to ask consumers to comment self-consciously on their own patterns. For instance, DDB's sign spotters in several markets noticed that dinner-party guests were bringing their hosts flowers instead of chocolates, in a nod to current concerns over obesity and health. Anthon Berg, a Danish chocolate company and DDB client, used that information to associate its chocolate more closely with different social occasions. Anthon Berg is now the third most popular brand in Denmark with Lego and Google ranked one and two, respectively.[17]

The marketing insight box offers some practical tips to improve the quality of focus groups. In 3's market research, the moderator might start with a broad question, such as 'How do you feel about mobile phone services?' Questions might then move to how people view the different providers, different existing services, different proposed services and, specifically, a mobile TV service.

Survey research Companies undertake surveys to learn about people's knowledge, beliefs, preferences and satisfaction, and to measure these magnitudes in the general

Marketing insight

Conducting informative focus groups

Focus groups allow marketers to observe how and why consumers accept or reject concepts, ideas or any specific notion. The key to using focus groups successfully is to *listen and observe*. Marketers should eliminate their own biases as much as possible. Although many useful insights can emerge from thoughtfully run focus groups, questions can arise about their validity, especially in today's marketing environment.

Some researchers believe that consumers have been so bombarded with ads that they unconsciously (or perhaps cynically) parrot back what they have already heard instead of what they really think. There is always a concern that participants are just trying to maintain their self-image and public persona or have a need to identify with the other members of the group. Participants also may not be willing to admit in public – or may not even recognise – their behaviour patterns and motivations. And the 'loudmouth' or 'know-it-all' problem often crops up when one highly opinionated person drowns out the rest of the group. It may be expensive to recruit qualified subjects who meet the sampling criteria (€2,000 to €3,500 per group), but getting the right participants is crucial.

Even when marketers use multiple focus groups, it may be difficult to generalise the results to a broader population. For example, within Europe, focus-group findings may vary from region to region because of differences in culture, shopping habits, economic welfare, etc. Also, within individual countries there could be lifestyle differences between people living in major cities and people living in the countryside. Participants must feel as relaxed as possible and strongly motivated to be truthful. Physical surroundings can be crucial to achieving the right atmosphere. As one agency executive noted, 'We wondered why people always seemed grumpy and negative – people were resistant to any idea we showed them.' Finally in one session a fight broke out between participants. The problem was the room itself: cramped, stifling, forbidding: 'It was a cross between a hospital room and a police interrogation room.' To fix the problem, the agency gave the room a make-over. Other firms are adapting the look of the room to fit the theme of the topic, such as designing the room to look like a playroom when speaking to children.

Many firms are substituting observational research for focus groups, but ethnographic observation can be expensive and tricky: researchers must be highly skilled and participants on the level. Then there are the mounds of data to analyse. The beauty of focus groups, as one marketing executive noted, is that 'It's still the most cost-effective, quickest, dirtiest way to get information in rapid time on an idea.' In analysing the pros and cons, Wharton's Americus Reed might have said it best: 'A focus group is like a chain saw. If you know what you're doing, it's very useful and effective. If you don't, you could lose a limb.'

Sources: C. S. Jones (2010) Encouraging healthy eating at restaurants: more themes uncovered through focus group research, *Services Marketing Quarterly*, 31(4), 448–65; N. R. Henderson (2005) Beyond top of mind, *Marketing Research*, 1 September; R. Harris (2005) Do focus groups have a future?, *Marketing*, 6 June, 17; M. Gladwell (2005) *Blink: The Power of Thinking Without Thinking*, New York: Little, Brown; L. Tischler (2004) Every move you make, *Fast Company*, April, 73–5; A. S. Wellner (2003) The new science of focus groups, *American Demographics*, March, 29–33; D. Rook (2003) Out-of-focus groups, *Marketing Research*, 15(2), 11; D. W. Rook (2003) Loss of vision: focus groups fail to connect theory, current practice, *Marketing News*, 15 September, 40; S. J. Kasner (2001) Fistfights and feng shui, *Boston Globe*, 21 July.

population. A company such as 3 might prepare its own survey instrument to gather the information it needs, or it might add questions to an omnibus survey that carries the questions of several companies (at a much lower cost). It can also put the questions to an ongoing consumer panel run by itself or another company. It may do a mall intercept study by having researchers approach people in a shopping mall and ask them questions.

As we will discuss in more detail later in this chapter, many marketers are taking their surveys online, where they can easily develop, administer and collect email and web-based questionnaires. However they conduct their surveys – online, by phone or in person – companies must feel the information they are getting from the mounds of data makes it all worthwhile. Here are two that do:

- **TDC.** This major player on the Danish telecommunications market regularly surveys and interviews its customers on subjects such as needs, motivation and product satisfaction. Customer feedback has resulted in, for example, a low-priced broadband product (TDC Netway) tailored especially to young customers (between 18 and 28 years of age). This 'no nonsense' solution offers broadband internet access and allows customers to call free of charge at all times on fixed-line connections in Denmark, but includes no technical support and can only be ordered online.[18]

- **Star Tour.** Scandinavian travel agency Star Tour continually collects surveys from customers at the end of their holiday (and at www.startour.dk). It uses customers' comments to obtain insights into customer experiences during their holiday and into their feelings about the company and its communications with them.

Of course, by putting out so many surveys, companies may run the risk of creating 'survey burnout' and seeing response rates plummet. Keeping a survey short and simple and avoiding contacting the same customers too often are two keys to drawing people into the data collection effort. Offering incentives is another way companies get consumers to respond. Companies such as UK-based StaTravel offer the chance to win cash prizes, gift certificates or computer equipment in exchange for taking part in their survey. Although a survey is generally accepted as a means of data collection, there is little control over the contextual setting and over the response behaviour of respondents. Thus, consumers may behave differently when engaging in specific choice situations.[19]

Behavioural data Customers leave traces of their purchasing behaviour in store-scanning data, catalogue purchases and customer databases. Marketers can learn much by analysing these data. Actual purchases reflect consumers' preferences and are often more reliable than statements they offer to market researchers. For example, grocery shopping data show that high-income people don't necessarily buy the more expensive brands, contrary to what they might state in interviews; and many low-income people buy some expensive brands. Clearly, companies such as 3 can learn many useful things about their customers by analysing mobile service purchase records and online behaviour.

Experimental research The most scientifically valid research is **experimental research**, designed to capture cause-and-effect relationships by eliminating competing explanations of the observed findings. If the experiment is well designed and executed, research and marketing managers can have confidence in the conclusions.

Experiments call for selecting matched groups of subjects, subjecting them to different treatments, controlling extraneous variables and checking whether observed response differences are statistically significant. If we can eliminate or control extraneous factors, we can relate the observed effects to the variations in the treatments or stimuli. For instance, 3 might introduce a package of mobile internet services in one of its mobile packages and charge €35 one week and €25 the next. If approximately the same number of potential customers visited 3's shops each week and the particular weeks were 'normal' and similar, the company could then relate a significant difference in the number of new customers to the difference in price charged.

Research instruments

In the previous section you learned about the main research *approaches* that marketers use to collect primary data. Depending on the research problem and approach taken, marketing researchers can choose between a number of research *instruments* for collecting primary data. In this section, we will review three commonly used research instruments: questionnaires, qualitative measures and technological devices.

Questionnaire A **questionnaire** consists of a set of questions presented to respondents. Because of its flexibility, it is by far the most common instrument used to collect primary data. Researchers need to carefully develop, test and de-bug questionnaires before administering them on a large scale. The form, wording and sequence of the question can all influence the response. *Closed questions* specify all the possible answers and provide answers that are easier to interpret and tabulate. *Open-ended questions* allow respondents to answer in their own words and often reveal more about how people think. They are especially useful in exploratory research, where the researcher is looking for insight into how people think rather than measuring how many people think a certain way. Table 6.1 provides examples of both types of question; see also the marketing memo box that follows.

Table 6.1 Types of questions

Name	Description	Example
A. Closed questions		
Dichotomous	A question with two possible answers	In considering this service, did you personally contact 3? Yes No
Multiple choice	A question with three or more answers	For whom are you considering purchasing this service? ☐ **Myself** ☐ Entire family ☐ Spouse ☐ Business associates/friends/relatives ☐ Children ☐ An organisation
Likert scale	A statement with which the respondent shows the amount of agreement/ disagreement	Small mobile service providers generally give better service than large ones. Strongly disagree / Disagree / Neither agree nor disagree / Agree / Strongly agree 1 _____ 2 _____ 3 _____ 4 _____ 5 _____
Semantic differential	A scale connecting two bipolar words. The respondent selects the point that represents his or her opinion	3 Large ---------------------------Small Experienced ----------------------Inexperienced Modern ------------------------Old-fashioned
Importance scale	A scale that rates the importance of some attribute	3G mobile service to me is Extremely Important / Very important / Somewhat important / Not very important / Not at all important 1 _____ 2 _____ 3 _____ 4 _____ 5 _____
Intention-to-buy scale	A scale that describes the respondent's intention to buy	If a mobile internet service was available, I would Definitely buy / Probably buy / Not sure / Probably not buy / Definitely not buy 1 _____ 2 _____ 3 _____ 4 _____ 5 _____
B. Open-ended questions		
Completely unstructured	A question that respondents can answer in an almost unlimited number of ways	What is your opinion of 3?
Word association	Words are presented, one at a time, and respondents mention the first word that comes to mind	What is the first word that comes to your mind when you hear the following? Mobile provider _____ 3 _____ Mobile _____
Sentence completion	An incomplete sentence is presented and respondents complete the sentence	When I choose a mobile service provider, the most important consideration in my decision is _____ _____

(Continued)

Table 6.1 (*Continued*)

Name	Description	Example
Story completion	An incomplete story is presented, and respondents are asked to complete it	'I went to a 3 shop a couple of days ago. I noticed that the exterior and interior of the shop had very bright colours. This aroused in me the following thoughts and feelings . . . ' Now complete the story.
Picture	A picture of two characters is presented, with one making a statement. Respondents are asked to identify with the other and fill in the empty balloon	
Thematic apperception test (TAT)	A picture is presented and respondents are asked to make up a story about what they think is happening or may happen in the picture	

Marketing memo

Questionnaire dos and don'ts

1   Ensure that questions are without bias. Don't lead the respondent into an answer.

2   Make the questions as simple as possible. Questions that include multiple ideas or two questions in one will confuse respondents.

3   Make the questions specific. Sometimes it is advisable to add memory cues. For example, be specific with time periods.

4   Avoid jargon or shorthand. Avoid trade jargon, acronyms and initials not in everyday use.

5   Steer clear of sophisticated or uncommon words. Only use words in common speech.

6   Avoid ambiguous words. Words such as 'usually' or 'frequently' have no specific meaning.

7   Avoid questions with a negative in them. It is better to say, 'Do you ever . . .?' than 'Do you never . . .?'

8   Avoid hypothetical questions. It is difficult to answer questions about imaginary situations. Answers are not necessarily reliable.

9   Don't use words that could be misheard. This is especially important when administering the interview over the telephone. 'What is your opinion of sects?' could yield interesting but not necessarily relevant answers.

10   Desensitise questions by using response bands. To ask people their age or ask companies about employee turnover rates, offer a range of response bands instead of precise numbers.

11   Ensure that fixed responses do not overlap. Categories used in fixed-response questions should be distinct and not overlap.

12   Allow for 'other' in fixed-response questions. Precoded answers should always allow for a response other than those listed.

Sources: Based on P. Hague and P. Jackson (1999) *Market Research: A Guide to Planning, Methodology, and Evaluation*, London: Kogan Page; see also H. Baumgartner and J.-B. E. M. Steenkamp (2001) Response styles in marketing research: a cross-national investigation, *Journal of Marketing Research*, May, 143–56.

Qualitative measures Some marketers prefer more qualitative methods for gauging consumer opinion, because consumer actions don't always match their answers to survey questions. *Qualitative research techniques* are relatively unstructured measurement approaches that permit a range of possible responses. Their variety is limited only by the creativity of the marketing researcher.

LEGO

The Danish toy company LEGO, which offers creative and high-quality toys to children across the globe, has an ingenious way of conducting qualitative research on how to tailor its wide product portfolio to the needs of children of all ages. Over the years, LEGO has developed long-lasting relations with, for example, day care centres, which are invited (with parents' permission) to pick out a group of children who match the target group of a specific product or product line to participate in a play session. Usually such sessions are arranged once a year, and it is essential that children play with LEGO toys in their usual surroundings. Video filming is used to capture important insights into how children play with particular products, what they find fun, what catches their interests and spurs their imagination, the functionality of toys and quality of play, etc.

This is just one of the many ways LEGO uses qualitative measures to stay up to date with how children play and how to challenge creative youngsters of particular age groups – an important element of LEGO's vision is to inspire children to explore and challenge their own creative potential.[20]

Because of the freedom afforded both researchers in their probes and consumers in their responses, qualitative research can often be a useful first step in exploring consumers' brand and product perceptions, but it has its drawbacks. Marketers must temper the in-depth insights that emerge with the fact that the samples are often very small and may not necessarily generalise to broader populations. And different researchers examining the same qualitative results may draw very different conclusions. There is increasing interest in using qualitative methods. The marketing insight box describes some popular approaches.

Marketing insight

Getting into consumers' heads with qualitative research

Here are some popular qualitative research approaches to getting inside consumers' minds and finding out what they think or feel about brands and products:

1 Word associations. Ask subjects what words come to mind when they hear the brand's name. 'What does the name Fiat mean to you? Tell me what comes to mind when you think of Fiat cars.' The primary purpose of free-association tasks is to identify the range of possible brand associations in consumers' minds. But they may also provide some rough indication of the relative strengths, favourability and uniqueness of brand associations.

2 Projective techniques. Give people an incomplete stimulus and ask them to complete it, or give them an ambiguous stimulus and ask them to make sense of it. One such approach is 'bubble exercises' in which empty bubbles, such as those found in cartoons, appear in scenes of people buying or using certain products or services. Subjects fill in the bubble, indicating what they believe is happening or being said. Another technique is comparison tasks, in which people compare brands to people, countries, animals, activities, fabrics, occupations, cars, magazines, vegetables, nationalities or even other brands.

3 Visualisation. Visualisation requires people to create a collage from magazine photos or drawings to depict their perceptions of brands, experiences, ideas or other research topics. The ZMET technique asks participants in advance to select a minimum of 12 images from their own sources (magazines, catalogues, family photo albums) to represent their thoughts and feelings about the research topic. In a one-to-one interview, the study administrator uses advanced interview techniques to explore the images with the participant and reveal hidden meanings. Finally, the participants use a computer program to

▶ Marketing insight *(continued)*

create a collage with these images that communicates their subconscious thoughts and feelings about the topic. In one ZMET study about tights, some of the respondents' pictures showed fence posts encased in plastic wrap or steel bands strangling trees, suggesting that tights are close fitting and inconvenient. Another picture showed tall flowers in a vase, suggesting that the product made a woman feel thin, tall and sexy. In this way, the technique seeks to unveil 'hidden knowledge' of underlying beliefs and feelings that influence the behaviour and reactions of consumers.

Drawings or other pictures that express consumers' feelings about products are part of ZMET studies. This vase demonstrated what one woman felt about wearing tights.

Source: Norman H. Olson, Purdue University.

4 Brand personification. Ask subjects what kind of person they think of when the brand is mentioned: 'If the brand were to come alive as a person, what would it be like, what would it do, where would it live, what would it wear, who would it talk to if it went to a party (and what would it talk about)?' For example, the IKEA brand might make someone think of a straightforward Scandinavian female who is reliable and values quality at an affordable cost. The brand personality delivers a picture of the more human qualities of the brand.

5 Laddering. This technique involves asking a series of increasingly more specific 'why' questions that can reveal consumer motivation and consumers' deeper, more abstract goals. Think about how you might answer the following line (or ladder) of questions: 'Why does someone want to buy a Nokia mobile phone?' 'They look well built' (attribute). 'Why is it important that the phone be well built?' 'It suggests that the Nokia is reliable' (a functional benefit). 'Why is reliability important?' 'Because my colleagues or family can be sure to reach me' (an emotional benefit). 'Why must you be available to them at all times?' 'I can help them if they're in trouble' (brand essence). The brand makes this person feel like a Good Samaritan, ready to help others.

Sources: E. Kaciak, C. W. Cullen and A. Sagan (2010) The quality of ladders generated by abbreviated hard laddering, *Journal of Targeting, Measurement and Analysis for Marketing*, 18(3/4), 159–66; C. Marshall and G. B. Rossman (2006) *Designing Qualitative Research*, 4th edn, Thousand Oaks, CA: Sage; B. L. Berg (2006) *Qualitative Research Methods for the Social Sciences*, 6th edn, Boston, MA: Allyn & Bacon; N. K. Denzin and Y. S. Lincoln (eds) (2005) *The Sage Handbook of Qualitative Research*, 3rd edn, Thousand Oaks, CA: Sage; L. Tischler (2004) Every move you make, *Fast Company*, April, 73–5; G. Zaltman (2003) *How Customers Think: Essential Insights into the Mind of the Market*, Boston, MA: Harvard Business School Press.

Marketers don't necessarily have to choose between qualitative and quantitative measures, however, and many marketers use both approaches, recognising that their pros and cons can offset each other. For example, companies can recruit someone from an online panel to participate in an in-home use test in which the subject is sent a product and told to capture his or her reactions and intentions with both a video diary and an online survey.[21]

Technological devices There has been much interest in recent years in various technological devices. Galvanometers can measure the interest or emotions aroused by exposure to a specific ad or picture. The tachistoscope flashes an ad to a subject with an exposure interval that may range from less than one hundredth of a second to several seconds. After each exposure, the respondent describes everything he or she recalls. Eye cameras study respondents' eye movements to see where their eyes land first, how long they linger on a given item, and so on.

Technology has now advanced to such a degree that marketers can use devices such as skin sensors, brainwave scanners and full body scanners to get consumer responses. The following marketing insight box provides a glimpse into some new marketing research frontiers studying the brain.

Technology has replaced the diaries that participants in media surveys used to keep. Audiometers attached to television sets in participating homes now record when the set is on and to which channel it is tuned. Electronic devices can record the number of radio programmes a person is exposed to during the day or, using global positioning system (GPS) technology, how many billboards a person may walk by or drive by during a day. Technology is also used to capture consumer reactions to internet and mobile services.

Marketing insight

Understanding brain science

As an alternative to traditional consumer research, some researchers have begun to develop sophisticated techniques from neuroscience that monitor brain activity to better gauge consumer responses to marketing stimuli.

For example, Oxford-based neuro-marketing research firm Neurosense used functional magnetic resonance imaging (fMRI) to measure how consumers' brains responded to TV programming and ads. This study showed that ads generated activity in eight out of nine brain regions, indicating that consumers indeed register commercial content. Yet programming largely dominated the region of the brain that controls absorption, and hence occupied by far the largest part of consumers' attention. The study also confirmed that ads work best when they are in congruence with the programmes they accompany. Thus, more viewer interest was registered for an ad for the alcopop WKD than for a Red Cross appeal when these were aired during the anarchic cult comedy *South Park*.[22]

Although it can be more effective in uncovering inner emotions than conventional techniques, neurological research is costly, running to as much as €70,000 per project. One major finding to emerge from neurological consumer research is that many purchase decisions are characterised less by the logical weighing of variables than was previously assumed and more 'as a largely unconscious habitual process, as distinct from the rational, conscious, information-processing model of economists and traditional marketing textbooks'. Even basic decisions, such as the purchase of gasoline, are influenced by brain activity at the subrational level.

Neurological research can be used to measure the type of emotional response that consumers exhibit when presented with marketing stimuli. A group of researchers in England used an electroencephalograph (EEG) to monitor cognitive functions related to memory recall and attentiveness for 12 different regions of the brain as subjects were exposed to advertising. Brain-wave activity in different regions indicated different emotional responses. For example, heightened activity in the left prefrontal cortex is characteristic of an 'approach' response to an ad and indicates an attraction to the stimulus. In contrast, a spike in brain activity in the right prefrontal cortex is indicative of a strong revulsion to the stimulus. In yet another part of the brain, the degree of memory formation activity correlates with purchase intent. Other research has shown that people activate different regions of the brain in assessing the personality traits of people versus brands.

The term *neuromarketing* has been used to describe brain research on the effect of marketing stimuli. By adding neurological techniques to their research arsenal, marketers are trying to move towards a more complete picture of what goes on inside consumers' heads. Given the complexity of the human brain, however, many researchers caution that neurological research should not form the sole basis for marketing decisions. These research activities have not been universally applauded, however. The measurement devices to capture brain activity can be highly obtrusive, such as with skull caps studded with electrodes, creating artificial exposure conditions. Others question whether they offer unambiguous implications for marketing strategy. Some critics think that such a development will only lead to more marketing manipulation by companies. Despite all this controversy, marketers' endless pursuit of deeper insights into consumers' response to marketing virtually guarantees continued interest in neuromarketing.

Sources: Brain scans: the advertising tool of the future (2010), *Trend Letter*, 29(7), 12; P. Ciprian-Marcel, R. Lăcrămioara, M. A. Ioana and Z. M. Maria (2009) Neuromarketing – getting inside the customer's mind, *Economic Science Series*, 18(4), 804–7; C. Yoon, A. H. Gutchess, F. Feinberg and T. A. Polk (2006) A functional magnetic resonance imaging study of neural dissociations between brand and person judgments, *Journal of Consumer Research*, 33, 31–40; D. Travis (2006) Tap buyers' emotions for marketing success, *Marketing News*, 1 February, 21–2.

Sampling plan

After deciding on the research approach and instruments, the marketing researcher must design a sampling plan. This calls for three decisions:

1 **Sampling unit: who should we survey?** In the 3 survey, should the sampling unit consist only of mobile broadband customers, 'regular' mobile service customers, or both? Should it include customers under the age of 15? Seniors, parents, children, teenagers? Once they have determined the sampling unit, marketers must develop a sampling frame so that everyone in the target population has an equal or known chance of being sampled.

2 **Sample size: how many people should we survey?** Large samples give more reliable results, but it is not necessary to sample the entire target population to achieve reliable results. Samples of less than 1 per cent of a population can often provide good reliability, with a credible sampling procedure.

3 **Sampling procedure: how should we choose the respondents?** Probability sampling allows us to calculate confidence limits for sampling error and make the sample more representative. Thus we could conclude after choosing the sample that 'the interval five to seven trips per year has 95 chances in 100 of containing the true number of trips taken annually by first-class passengers flying between Stockholm and Rome'. Three types of probability sampling are described in Table 6.2(a). When the cost or time needed to use probability sampling is too great, marketing researchers will take non-probability samples. Table 6.2(b) describes three types.

Contact methods

Now the marketing researcher must decide how to contact the subjects: by mail, by telephone, in person or online.

Mail questionnaire The mail questionnaire is the best way to reach people who would not give personal interviews or whose responses might be biased or distorted by the interviewers. Mail questionnaires require simple and clearly worded questions. Unfortunately, the response rate is usually low or slow.

Telephone interview Telephone interviewing is the best method for gathering information quickly; the interviewer is also able to clarify questions if respondents do not understand them. The response rate is typically higher than for mailed questionnaires, but interviews must be brief and not too personal. Telephone interviewing is getting more difficult because of consumers' growing antipathy toward telemarketers. In Sweden, for example,

Table 6.2 Probability and non-probability samples

(a) Probability sample	
Simple random sample	Every member of the population has an equal chance of selection
Stratified random sample	The population is divided into mutually exclusive groups (such as age groups), and random samples are drawn from each group
Cluster (area) sample	The population is divided into mutually exclusive groups (such as city blocks), and the researcher draws a sample of the groups to interview
(b) Non-probability sample	
Convenience sample	The researcher selects the most accessible population members
Judgement sample	The researcher selects population members who are good prospects for accurate information
Quota sample	The researcher finds and interviews a prescribed number of people in each of several categories

a registry known as 'Nix Telefon', through which consumers can request not to receive telemarketing calls, has experienced high popularity. At the beginning of 2010, 1.9 million Swedish telephone consumers had registered.[23] While telemarketers are obligated by law to check the phone numbers they call against the 'Nix' registry, marketing research firms are so far exempt from this legislation. However, many think it spells the beginning of the end for telephone surveys as a marketing research method. In other parts of the world, such marketing customs and restrictive legislation do not exist. At the beginning of 2011, the number of mobile phone subscribers in Africa exceeded the number of North American subscribers, so mobile phones in Africa are used to convene focus groups in rural areas and to interact with text messages.[24]

Personal interview Personal interviewing is the most versatile method. The interviewer can ask more questions and record additional observations about the respondent, such as dress and body language. At the same time, however, personal interviewing is the most expensive method, is subject to interviewer bias, and requires more administrative planning and supervision. Personal interviewing takes two forms. In *arranged interviews*, marketers contact respondents for an appointment and often offer a small payment or incentive. In *intercept interviews*, researchers stop people at a shopping mall or on a busy street corner and request an interview on the spot. Intercept interviews must be quick, and they run the risk of including non-probability samples.

Online interview An approach of increasing importance, the internet offers many ways to do research. A company can embed a questionnaire on its website in different ways and offer an incentive to answer it, or it can place a banner on a frequently visited site such as Google, inviting people to answer some questions and possibly win a prize. Marketers can also sponsor a chatroom or bulletin board and introduce questions from time to time or host a real-time consumer panel or virtual focus group. The company can learn about individuals who visit its site by tracking how they *clickstream* through the website and move to other sites. It can post different prices, use different headlines, and offer different product features on different websites or at different times to learn the relative effectiveness of its offerings. Online product testing, in which companies float trial 'balloons' for new products, is also growing and providing information much faster than traditional new product marketing research techniques.

Marketers can also host a real-time consumer panel or virtual focus group, or sponsor a chat room, bulletin board or blog and introduce questions from time to time. They can ask customers to brainstorm or have followers of the company on Twitter rate an idea. Online communities and networks of customers serve as a resource for a wide variety of companies. Insights from Kraft-sponsored online communities helped the company develop its popular line of 100-calorie snacks. 'Online is not a solution in and of itself to all of our business challenges,' said Seth Diamond, director of consumer insights and strategy, 'but it does expand our toolkit.'[25]

The marketing memo outlines some of the advantages and disadvantages of online research thus far. Online researchers also use instant messaging in various ways – to conduct a chat with a respondent, to probe more deeply with a member of an online focus group, or to direct respondents to a website.[26] Instant messaging is also a useful way to get teenagers to open up on topics.

Step 3: collect the information

The data collection phase of marketing research is generally the most expensive and the most prone to error. Four major problems arise in surveys. Some respondents will not be at home and must be contacted again or replaced. Other respondents will refuse to cooperate. Still others will give biased or dishonest answers. Finally, some interviewers will be biased or dishonest. Data collection methods are rapidly improving thanks to computers and telecommunications. Some telephone research firms interview from a central location, using professional interviewers to read a set of questions from a monitor and type the respondents' answers into a computer. This procedure eliminates editing and coding, reduces errors, saves time, and produces all the required statistics. Other research firms have set up interactive terminals in shopping centres, where respondents sit at a terminal, read questions from the monitor and type in their answers.

One of the biggest obstacles to collecting information internationally is the need to achieve consistency. Nan Martin, global accounts director for Synovate, Inc., a market research firm with offices in 46 countries, says:

> **In global research, we have to adapt culturally to how, where and with whom we are doing the research . . . A simple research study conducted globally becomes much more complicated as a result of the cultural nuances, and it's necessary for us to be sensitive to those nuances in data collection and interpretation.**

Marketing memo

Pros and cons of online research

Advantages

- **Online research is inexpensive.** A typical email survey can cost only 5–20 per cent of paper surveys, and return rates can be as high as 50 per cent and in some cases even higher.

- **Online research is fast.** Online surveys are fast because the survey can automatically direct respondents to applicable questions and transmit results immediately. One estimate says that 75–80 per cent of a survey's targeted response can be generated in 48 hours using online methods, compared to a telephone survey that can take 70 days to obtain 150 interviews.

- **Survey tracking.** Online surveys can provide researchers with detailed traces about survey response time and pattern, including the exact time when a respondent filled out a survey and the exact page where one abandoned a survey. This information enables survey researchers to better understand response patterns, which in turn allows them to continue refining their methodology.

- **People tend to be honest online.** Britain's online polling company YouGov.com surveyed 250 people via intercom in a booth and the other half online, asking questions such as 'Should there be more aid to Africa?' Online answers were deemed much more honest. People may be more open about their opinions when they can respond privately and not to another person whom they feel might be judging them, especially on sensitive topics.

- **Online research is versatile.** Increased broadband penetration offers online research even more flexibility and capabilities. For instance, virtual reality software lets visitors inspect 3-D models of products such as cameras, cars and medical equipment, and manipulate product characteristics. Even at the basic tactile level, online surveys can make answering a questionnaire easier and more fun than paper-and-pencil versions.

Disadvantages

- **Samples can be small and skewed.** In the 27 EU member states, 69 per cent of households had access to the internet by the end of 2010, compared with 49 per cent during the first quarter of 2006. Household internet access ranged from 36 per cent in Romania to 90 per cent in the Netherlands and Luxembourg. Although it is certain that more and more will go online, online market researchers must find creative ways to reach population segments on the other side of the 'digital divide'. One option is to combine online and offline data collection instruments: for example, by using both online and postal (offline) questionnaires. Providing temporary Internet access at locations such as shopping centres and leisure centres is another strategy. Some research firms use statistical models to fill in the gaps in market research left by offline consumer segments.

- **Online panels and communities can suffer from excessive turnover.** Members may become bored with the company's efforts and flee. Or perhaps even worse, they may stay but only half-heartedly participate. Panel and community organisers are taking steps to address the quality of the panel and the data they provide by raising recruiting standards, downplaying incentives, and carefully monitoring participation and engagement levels. New features, events and other activities must be constantly added to keep members interested and engaged.[27]

▶ Marketing memo *(continued)*

- **Online market research can suffer from technological problems and inconsistencies.** Problems can arise with online surveys because browser software varies. The web designer's final product may look very different on the research subject's screen.

  Online researchers have also begun to use text messaging in various ways – to conduct a chat with a respondent, to probe more deeply with a member of an online focus group, or to direct respondents to a website.[28] Text messaging is also a useful way to get teenagers to open up on topics.

Sources: H. Seybert and A. Lööf (2010) Internet usage in 2010, *Eurostat Data in Focus* 50/2010, 1–8; Internet World Stats (2010) *European Union – Internet Usage Stats and Telecom Reports*, www.internetworldstats.com/eu/eu.htm; survey: internet should remain open to all, 25 January 2006, www.consumeraffairs. com; Highlights from the National Consumers League's survey on consumers and communications technologies: current and future use, www.nclnet.org, 21 July 2005; C. Arnold (2004) Not done net; new opportunities still exist in online research, *Marketing News*, 1 April, 17; L. Miles (2004) Online, on tap, *Marketing*, 16 June, 39–40.

Latin American respondents may be more uncomfortable with the impersonal nature of the internet; they need interactive elements in a survey so they feel as if they are talking to a real person. On the other hand, in Asia, respondents may feel more pressure to conform and may therefore not be as forthcoming in focus groups as online. Sometimes the solution may be as simple as ensuring the right language is used.

Leica Surveying and Engineering

When Leica Surveying and Engineering, a global provider of high-end surveying and measurement equipment, sought to gather competitive intelligence in its industry, it initially deployed surveys only in English because the companys business was typically conducted in English, even across several different European countries. However, the response rate was dismal, even though the sample comprised individuals who had an affinity with the company. Closer review showed that the in-country sales representatives conducted business in their native languages. Consequently, the company redeployed its survey in various languages, such as Spanish and German, and the response rate doubled almost overnight.[29]

Step 4: analyse the information

The penultimate step in the process is to extract findings by tabulating the data and developing frequency distributions. The researchers now compute averages and measures of dispersion for the major variables and apply some advanced statistical techniques and decision models in the hope of discovering additional findings. They may test different hypotheses and theories, applying sensitivity analysis to test assumptions and the strength of the conclusions.

Step 5: present the findings

As the last step, the researcher presents findings relevant to the major marketing decisions facing management. Researchers are increasingly being asked to play a more proactive, consulting role in translating data and information into insights and recommendations.[30] They are also considering ways to present research findings in as understandable and compelling a fashion as possible.

For example, some researchers try to bring data to life for the marketers in their organisation. Marketing research consultancy Arnold 1 Bolingbroke uses a professional film crew and makes feature film presentations of its results: for instance, in its work with European car brands Land-Rover and Jaguar. Bomme Komolafe, market research manager at Jaguar Cars, says:

> **These films are useful because they are accessible at all levels, even to very technically oriented audiences. And when a launch is seven years away, it is so valuable that they can be kept and referred to time and again, whenever we are debating issues as our designs evolve.**[31]

Another way of organising and presenting complex and information-rich research findings, which may be difficult to express in verbal or linear form, is to create visual, artistic collages. The photo below visualises the many aspects of a modern family segment.

'Personas' is another approach that some researchers are using to maximize the impact of their consumer research findings. Personas are detailed profiles of one, or a perhaps a few, hypothetical target market consumers, imagined in terms of demographic, psychographic, geographic or other descriptive attitudinal or behavioural information. Researchers may use photos, images, names or short bios to help convey the particulars of the persona. The rationale behind personas is to provide exemplars or archetypes of how the target customer looks, acts and feels that are as true-to-life as possible, to ensure marketers within the organisation fully understand and appreciate their target market and therefore incorporate a target-customer point of view in all their marketing decision making. Unilever's biggest and most successful hair-care launch, for Sunsilk, was aided by insights into the target consumer whom the company dubbed 'Katie'. The Katie persona outlined the twenty-something female's hair-care needs, but also her perceptions and attitudes and the way she dealt with her everyday life 'dramas'. Although personas provide vivid information to aid marketing decision making, marketers also have to be careful to not over-generalise. Any target market may have a range of consumers who vary along a number of key dimensions. To accommodate these potential differences, researchers sometimes employ two to six personas.

The many aspects of modern families
Source: PhotoDisc

Returning to the 3 case, the main survey findings might indicate that:

1 The chief reasons for having a mobile broadband connection are to browse the web and download data files using your handset, regardless of where the customer is. Also, constant access to information and staying in touch with others are essential consumer motivations.

2 At €35, about five out of ten 3 customers would choose a product package including mobile TV service; about six would choose it at €25. Thus, a fee of €25 would produce less revenue (€150 = 6 × €25) than €30 (€175 = 5 × €35).

3 Offering a mobile TV service would strengthen the public's image of 3 as an innovative and progressive mobile provider. 3 would gain new customers and customer goodwill.

Step 6: make the decision

The managers who commissioned the research need to weigh the evidence. If their confidence in the findings is low, they may decide against introducing the mobile TV service. If they are predisposed to launching the service, the findings support their inclination. They may even decide to study the issues further and do more research. The decision is theirs, but rigorously done research provides them with insight into the problem (see Table 6.3).

A growing number of organisations are using a **marketing decision support system (MDSS)** to help their marketing managers make better decisions. A marketing decision support system is a coordinated collection of data, systems, tools and techniques, with supporting software and hardware, by which an organisation gathers and interprets relevant information from business and the environment and turns it into a basis for marketing action.[32]

Table 6.3 The seven characteristics of good marketing research

1 Scientific method	Effective marketing research uses the principles of the scientific method: careful observation, formulation of hypotheses, prediction and testing.
2 Research creativity	At its best, marketing research develops innovative ways to solve a problem: a clothing company catering to teenagers gave several young men video cameras, then used the videos for focus groups held in restaurants and other places that teens frequent.
3 Multiple methods	Marketing researchers shy away from overreliance on any one method. They also recognise the value of using two or three methods to increase confidence in the results.
4 Interdependence of models and data	Marketing researchers recognise that data are interpreted from underlying models which guide the type of information sought.
5 Value and cost of information	Marketing researchers show concern for estimating the value of information against its cost. Costs are typically easy to determine, but the value of research is harder to quantify. It depends on the reliability and validity of the findings and management's willingness to accept and act on those findings.
6 Healthy scepticism	Marketing researchers show a healthy scepticism towards glib assumptions made by managers about how a market works. They are alert to the problems caused by 'marketing myths'.
7 Ethical marketing	Marketing research benefits both the sponsoring company and its customers. The misuse of marketing research can harm or annoy consumers, increasing resentment at what consumers regard as an invasion of their privacy or a disguised sales pitch.

An example is Dutch-based ABN AMRO bank, which is represented by more than 3,000 branches in more than 60 countries and territories. ABN AMRO uses a decision support system to develop its consumer businesses in Asia. Via this system, regional headquarters in Hong Kong is able to view the region's total business as well as the performance of each individual country's business. The focus for ABN AMRO is on customer relationship management, customer revenue analysis and monitoring credit risk metrics.[33] Once a year, *Marketing News* lists hundreds of current marketing and sales software programs that assist in designing marketing research studies, segmenting markets, setting prices and advertising budgets, analysing media, and planning sales force activity.

Overcoming barriers to the use of marketing research

In spite of the rapid growth of marketing research, many companies still fail to use it sufficiently or correctly, for several reasons:[34]

- **A narrow conception of the research**. Many managers see marketing research as a fact-finding operation. They expect the researcher to design a questionnaire, choose a sample, conduct interviews and report results, often without their providing a careful definition of the problem. When fact finding fails to be useful, management's idea of the limited usefulness of marketing research is reinforced.
- **Uneven calibre of researchers**. Some managers view marketing research as little more than a clerical activity and treat it as such. As a result of this view, they hire less competent, and perhaps less costly, marketing researchers, whose weak training and low creativity lead to unimpressive results. The disappointing results reinforce management's prejudice against marketing research, and low salaries perpetuate the basic problem.
- **Poor framing of the problem**. The famous failure of New Coke was largely due to a failure to set up the research problem correctly, from a marketing perspective. Coca-Cola's market share lead had been slowly declining for 15 consecutive years. And consumer awareness and preference was plummeting too. Against this backdrop, Coca-Cola decided to change the secret formula and adopt a new taste preferred in taste tests of nearly 200,000 consumers. Nevertheless, the real issue turned out to be how consumers felt about Coca-Cola as a brand, not how they felt about its taste in isolation. The consumer upheaval that followed the introduction of New Coke ended with the return of the original formula, now called Coca-Cola Classic.
- **Late and occasionally erroneous findings**. Managers want results that are accurate and conclusive. They may want the results tomorrow. Yet good marketing research takes time and money. Managers are disappointed when marketing research costs too much or takes too much time.
- **Personality and presentational differences**. Differences between the styles of line managers and marketing researchers often get in the way of productive relationships. To a manager who wants concreteness, simplicity and certainty, a marketing researcher's report may seem abstract, complicated and tentative. Yet in the more progressive companies, marketing researchers are being included as members of the product management team, and their influence on marketing strategy is growing.
- **Illusions of seeing**. Most marketing issues usually involve a high level of ambiguity as issues are often laden with doubt and controversy. In spite of this, ambiguity managers may just see what is already lodged in their memories and preferences. This process of perceiving reality as it fits our preconceptions is a natural human process. As psychologist Daniel Gilbert puts it, 'We cook the facts. The brain and the eye have a contractual relationship in which the brain has agreed to believe what the eyes see, but the eye has agreed to look for what the brain wants.'[35]

Failure to use marketing research properly has led to numerous gaffes, including this historic one.

Star Wars

In the 1970s, a successful research executive left General Foods to try a daring gambit: bringing market research to Hollywood, to give film studios access to the same research that had spurred General Foods' success. A major film studio handed him a science fiction film proposal and asked him to research and predict its success or failure. His views would inform the studio's decision about whether to back the film. The executive concluded that the film would fail. For one, he argued, Watergate had made the United States less trusting of institutions and, as a result, its citizens in the 1970s prized realism and authenticity over science fiction. This particular film also had the word 'war' in its title; he reasoned that viewers, suffering from post-Vietnam hangover, would stay away in droves. The film was *Star Wars*. What this researcher delivered was information, not insight. He failed to study the script itself, to see that it was a fundamentally human story – of love, conflict, loss and redemption – that happened to play out against the backdrop of space. Since its release in 1977, *Star Wars* has won seven Academy Awards and influenced a generation of storytellers. It has sold hundreds of millions of dollars of tie-in merchandise, and more than 100 million home video units. Add to this the millions of DVDs recently welcomed into many a home theatre library.[36]

Measuring marketing productivity

An important task of marketing research is to assess the efficiency and effectiveness of marketing activities.[37] Marketers are being held increasingly accountable for their investments and must be able to justify marketing expenditure to senior management.[38] Marketing research can help address this increased need for accountability. Two complementary approaches to measuring marketing productivity are:

1 *marketing metrics* to assess marketing effects; and
2 *marketing-mix modelling* to estimate causal relationships and measure how marketing activity affects outcomes.

Marketing dashboards are a structured way to disseminate the insights gleaned from these two approaches within the organisation. Marketers employ a wide variety of measures to assess marketing effects.[39] **Marketing metrics** is the set of measures that helps them quantify, compare and interpret their marketing performance. Marketing metrics can be used by brand managers to justify and design marketing programmes and by senior management to decide on financial allocations.[40] The marketing-mix modelling approach is reviewed in this chapter, whereas the marketing metrics approach and marketing dashboards are considered in Chapter 22.

Marketing-mix modelling

Marketing accountability also means that marketers must more precisely estimate the effects of different marketing investments. *Marketing-mix models* analyse data from a variety of sources, such as retailer scanner data, company shipment data, pricing, media, and promotion spending data, to understand more precisely the effects of specific marketing activities.[41] To deepen understanding, marketers can conduct multivariate analyses, such as regression analysis, which are statistical procedures aiming at identifying relationships between a set of variables, such as price, quality and demand. These analytical tools will help estimate how each marketing element influences marketing outcomes such as brand sales or market share.[42]

Especially popular with packaged-goods marketers such as Procter & Gamble and Colgate, the findings from marketing-mix modelling help allocate or reallocate expenditure.

Analyses explore which part of ad budgets are wasted, what optimal spending levels are, and what minimum investment levels should be.[43]

Although marketing-mix modelling helps to isolate effects, it is less effective at assessing how different marketing elements work in combination. Wharton's Dave Reibstein also notes three other shortcomings:[44]

1 Marketing-mix modelling focuses on incremental growth instead of baseline sales or long-term effects.
2 Despite their importance, the integration of metrics such as customer satisfaction, awareness and brand equity into marketing-mix modelling is limited, probably due to the difficulty of establishing an explicit connection from investment to metric and to financial outcome.
3 Marketing-mix modelling generally fails to incorporate metrics related to competitors, the trade or the sales force (the average business spends far more on the sales force and trade promotion than on advertising or consumer promotion).

Forecasting and demand measurement

One major reason for undertaking marketing research is to identify market opportunities. Once the research is complete, the company must measure and forecast the size, growth and profit potential of each market opportunity. Sales forecasts are used by finance departments to raise the needed cash for investment and operations; by the manufacturing department to establish capacity and output levels; by purchasing to acquire the right amount of supplies; and by human resources to hire the necessary number of workers. Marketing is responsible for preparing the sales forecasts. If its forecast is far off the mark, the company will face excess or inadequate inventory.

Sales forecasts are based on estimates of demand. Managers need to define what they mean by market demand. For example, Swedish Autoliv is a market leader in state-of-the-art automotive safety systems. However, Autoliv does not see itself as having more than 40 per cent of the world market for side airbags. Rather, the company evaluates the brand much more broadly in terms of the entire €18.5 billion automobile occupant restraint market.[45]

The measures of market demand

Companies can prepare as many as 90 different types of demand estimates for six different product levels, five space levels and three time periods (see Figure 6.3).

Each demand measure serves a specific purpose. A company might forecast short-run demand for a particular product for the purpose of ordering raw materials, planning production and borrowing cash. It might forecast regional demand for its major product line to decide whether to set up regional distribution.

The size of a market hinges on the number of buyers who might exist for a particular market offer. But there are many productive ways to break down the market:

- The **potential market** is the set of consumers who profess a sufficient level of interest in a market offer. However, consumer interest is not enough to define a market for marketers unless they also have sufficient income and access to the product.
- The **available market** is the set of consumers who have interest, income *and* access to a particular offer. For some market offers, the company or government may restrict sales to certain groups. For example, a particular country might ban alcohol sales to anyone under 18 years of age. Eligible adults constitute the *qualified available market* – the set of consumers who have interest, income, access and qualifications for the particular market offer.

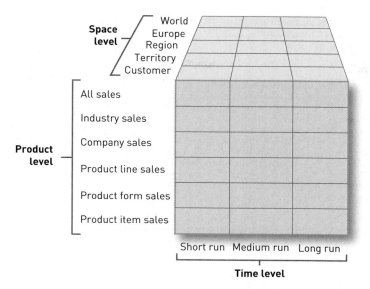

Figure 6.3 Ninety types of demand measurement (6 × 5 × 3)

- The **target market** is the part of the qualified available market the company decides to pursue. The company might decide to concentrate its marketing and distribution effort in southern Europe.
- The **penetrated market** is the set of consumers who are buying the company's product.

These definitions are a useful tool for market planning. If the company is not satisfied with its current sales, it can take a number of actions. It can try to attract a larger percentage of buyers from its target market. It can lower the qualifications for potential buyers. It can expand its available market by opening distribution elsewhere or lowering its price, or it can reposition itself in the minds of its customers.

A vocabulary for demand measurement

The major concepts in demand measurement are market demand and company demand. Within each, we distinguish among a demand function, a sales forecast and a potential.

Market demand

The marketer's first step in evaluating marketing opportunities is to estimate total market demand. **Market demand** for a product is the total volume that would be bought by a defined customer group in a defined geographical area in a defined time period in a defined marketing environment under a defined marketing programme.

Market demand is not a fixed number, but rather a function of the stated conditions. For this reason, we can call it the *market demand function*. The dependence of total market demand on underlying conditions is illustrated in Figure 6.4(a). The horizontal axis shows different possible levels of industry marketing expenditure in a given time period. The vertical axis shows the resulting demand level. The curve represents the estimated market demand associated with varying levels of industry marketing expenditure.

Some base sales – called the *market minimum* and labelled Q_1 in the figure – would take place without any demand-stimulating expenditures. Higher levels of industry marketing expenditures would yield higher levels of demand, first at an increasing rate, then at a decreasing rate. Take fruit juices. Given all the indirect competition they face from other types of beverage, increased marketing expenditures would be expected to help

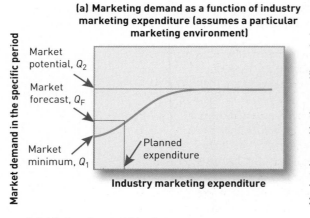

Figure 6.4 Market demand functions.

fruit juice products stand out and increase demand and sales. Marketing expenditures beyond a certain level would not stimulate much further demand, thus suggesting an upper limit to market demand, called the *market potential* and labelled Q_2 in the figure.

The distance between the market minimum and the market potential shows the overall *marketing sensitivity of demand*. We can think of two extreme types of market, the expansible and the non-expansible. An *expansible market*, such as the market for badminton playing, is very much affected in size by the level of industry marketing expenditures. In terms of Figure 6.4(a), the distance between Q_1 and Q_2 is relatively large. A *non-expansible market* – for example, the market for weekly rubbish removal – is not much affected by the level of marketing expenditure; the distance between Q_1 and Q_2 is relatively small. Organisations selling in a non-expansible market must accept the market's size – the level of *primary demand* for the product class – and direct their efforts towards winning a larger **market share** for their product: that is, a higher level of selective demand for their product.

It pays to compare the current and potential levels of market demand. The result is called the **market penetration index**. A low market penetration index indicates substantial growth potential for all the firms. A high market penetration index suggests it will be expensive to attract the few remaining prospects. Generally, price competition increases and margins fall when the market penetration index is already high.

A company should also compare its current and potential market shares. The result is called the company's **share penetration index**. A low share penetration index indicates that the company can greatly expand its share. The factors holding it back could be many: low brand awareness, low availability, benefit deficiencies and high price. A firm should calculate the share penetration increases that would occur if it removed each factor, to see which investments produce the greatest improvement.[46]

Remember that the market demand function is not a picture of market demand over time. Rather, the curve shows alternative current forecasts of market demand associated with possible levels of industry marketing effort.

Market forecast

At a given point in time, there can be only one actual level of industry marketing expenditure. The market demand corresponding to this level of expenditure is called the **market forecast**.

Market potential

The market forecast shows expected market demand, not maximum market demand. For the latter, we need to visualise the level of market demand resulting from a 'very high' level of industry marketing expenditure, where further increases in marketing effort would have little effect in stimulating further demand. **Market potential** is the limit approached by market demand as industry marketing expenditures approach infinity for a given marketing environment.

The phrase 'for a given market environment' is crucial. Consider the market potential for automobiles. This is higher during prosperity than during a recession. The dependence of market potential on the environment is illustrated in Figure 6.4(b). Market analysts distinguish between the position of the market demand function and movement along it. Companies cannot do anything about the position of the market demand function, which is determined by the marketing environment. However, they influence their particular location on the function when they decide how much to spend on marketing.

Companies interested in market potential have a special interest in the **product penetration percentage**, which is the percentage of ownership or use of a product or service in a population. Companies assume that the lower the product penetration percentage, the higher the market potential, although this assumes that everyone will eventually be in the market for every product.

Company demand

Company demand is the company's estimated share of market demand at alternative levels of company marketing effort in a given time period. It depends on how the company's products, services, prices and communications are perceived relative to the competitors'. If other things are equal, the company's market share will depend on the relative scale and effectiveness of its market expenditures. Marketing model builders have developed sales response functions to measure how a company's sales are affected by its marketing expenditure level, marketing mix and marketing effectiveness.[47]

Company sales forecast

Once managers have estimated company demand, their next task is to choose a level of marketing effort. The **company sales forecast** is the expected level of company sales based on a chosen marketing plan and an assumed marketing environment.

We represent the company sales forecast graphically with sales on the vertical axis and marketing effort on the horizontal axis, as in Figure 6.4. We often hear that the company should develop its marketing plan on the basis of its sales forecast. This forecast-to-plan sequence is valid if 'forecast' means an estimate of national economic activity, or if company demand is non-expansible. The sequence is not valid, however, where market demand is expansible or where 'forecast' means an estimate of company sales. The company sales forecast does not establish a basis for deciding what to spend on marketing. On the contrary, the sales forecast is the result of an assumed marketing expenditure plan.

Two other concepts are important here. A **sales quota** is the sales goal set for a product line, company division or sales representative. It is primarily a managerial device for defining and stimulating sales effort. Generally, sales quotas are set slightly higher than estimated sales to stretch the sales force's effort.

A **sales budget** is a conservative estimate of the expected volume of sales, primarily for making current purchasing, production and cash flow decisions. It is based on the sales forecast and the need to avoid excessive risk, and is generally set slightly lower than the sales forecast.

Company sales potential

Company sales potential is the sales limit approached by company demand as company marketing effort increases relative to that of competitors. The absolute limit of company demand is, of course, the market potential. The two would be equal if the company got 100 per cent of the market. In most cases, company sales potential is less than the market potential, even when company marketing expenditures increase considerably. Each competitor has a hard core of loyal buyers who are not very responsive to other companies' efforts to woo them.

Estimating current demand

We are now ready to examine practical methods for estimating current market demand. Marketing executives want to estimate total market potential, area market potential, and total industry sales and market shares.

Total market potential

Total market potential is the maximum amount of sales that might be available to all the firms in an industry during a given period, under a given level of industry marketing effort and environmental conditions. A common way to estimate total market potential is to multiply the potential number of buyers by the average quantity each purchases, times the price. The average quantity of buyer purchases may be estimated based on existing company sales data and/or on primary data collected for this purpose.

If 100 million people buy books each year, and the average book buyer buys three books a year, and the average price of a book is €20, then the total market potential for books is €6 billion (100 million × 3 × €20). The most difficult component to estimate is the number of buyers for the specific product or market. We can always start with the total population in the EU, which was 498 million people in 2010.[48]

Next we eliminate groups that obviously would not buy the product. Assume that illiterate people and children under 12 don't buy books and constitute 20 per cent of the population. This means 80 per cent of the population, or 398 million people, are in the potentials pool. We might do further research and find that people belonging to the 20 per cent of the EU population with the lowest income and/or with lower secondary education (or less) don't read books, and they constitute over 30 per cent of the potentials pool. Eliminating them, we arrive at a prospect pool of approximately 278.6 million book buyers. We use this number of prospective buyers to calculate total market potential.

A variation on this method is the *chain-ratio method*, which multiplies a base number by several adjusting percentages. Suppose a brewery is interested in estimating the market potential for a new light beer. It can make an estimate with the following calculation:

Demand for the new light beer	=	Population	×	Average percentage of personal discretionary income per capita spent on food	×	Average percentage of amount spent on food that is spent on beverages	×	Average percentage of amount spent on beverages that is spent on alcoholic beverages	×	Average percentage of amount spent on alcoholic beverages that is spent on beer	×	Expected percentage of amount spent on beer that will be spent on light beer

Area market potential

Because companies must allocate their marketing budget optimally among their best territories, they need to estimate the market potential of different cities, states and nations. Two major methods of assessing area market potential are the market-buildup method, used primarily by business marketers, and the multiple-factor index method, used primarily by consumer marketers.

Market-buildup method The **market-buildup method** calls for identifying all the potential buyers in each market and estimating their potential purchases. This method produces accurate results if we have a list of all potential buyers and a good estimate of what each will buy. Unfortunately, this information is not always easy to gather.

Consider a machine-tool company that wants to estimate the area market potential for its wood lathe in Greece. Its first step is to identify all potential buyers of wood lathes in the area, primarily manufacturing establishments that shape or ream wood as part of their operations. The company could compile a list from a directory of all manufacturing establishments in Greece. Then it could estimate the number of lathes each industry might purchase, based on the number of lathes per thousand employees or per €1 million of sales in that industry.

An efficient method of estimating area market potentials makes use of the statistical classification of economic activities in the European Union (NACE), consisting of a six-digit code. The first four digits of the code are the same in all European countries. The two last digits might vary from country to country. On 1 January 2008, the classification changed considerably with the implementation of the NACE Regulation 1893/2006 (Rev. 2).[49]

The NACE classifies all manufacturing into 21 major industry sectors and further breaks each sector into a six-digit, hierarchical structure as illustrated.

C	Industry sector (manufacturing)
10	Industry subsector (food)
10.3	Industry group (fruit and vegetables)
10.3.2	Industry (fruit and vegetable juice)
10.3.2.00	(Country specific, the fruit and vegetable juice industry in this country has no sub-industries as illustrated by the last two digits, '00').

To use the NACE, the lathe manufacturer must first determine the NACE codes that represent products whose manufacturers are likely to require lathe machines. To get a full picture of NACE industries that might use lathes, the company can: (1) determine past customers' NACE codes; (2) go through the NACE manual and check off all the six-digit industries that might have an interest in lathes; (3) mail questionnaires to a wide range of companies enquiring about their interest in wood lathes.

The company's next task is to determine an appropriate base for estimating the number of lathes that each industry will use. Suppose customer industry sales are the most appropriate base. Once the company estimates the rate of lathe ownership relative to the customer industry's sales, it can compute the market potential.

Multiple-factor index method Like business marketers, consumer companies also need to estimate area market potentials, but the customers of consumer companies are too numerous to list. The method most commonly used in consumer markets is a straightforward index method. A drug manufacturer, for example, might assume that the market potential for drugs is directly related to population size. If Sweden has 1.83 per cent of the EU population, the company might assume that Sweden would be a market for 1.83 per cent of total drugs sold in the EU.

A single factor, however, is rarely a complete indicator of sales opportunity. Regional drug sales are also influenced by per capita income and the number of physicians per 10,000 people. Thus it makes sense to develop a multiple-factor index, with each factor assigned a specific weight. The numbers are the weights attached to each variable. For example, suppose Sweden has 2.50 per cent of the EU disposable personal income, 2.60 per cent of EU retail sales, and 1.83 per cent of the EU population, and the respective weights are 0.5, 0.3 and 0.2. The buying-power index for Sweden is then 2.40 [0.5(2.50) + 0.3(2.60) + 0.2(1.83)]. Thus 2.40 per cent of the EU drug sales (not 1.83 per cent) might be expected to take place in Sweden.

The weights in the buying-power index are somewhat arbitrary, and companies can assign others if appropriate. A manufacturer might also want to adjust the market potential for additional factors, such as competitors' presence in that market, local promotional costs, seasonal factors and local market idiosyncrasies.

Many companies compute other area indexes as a guide to allocating marketing resources. Suppose the drug company is reviewing the six cities listed in Table 6.4. The first two columns show its percentage of EU brand and category sales in these six cities. Column 3 shows the **brand development index (BDI)**, which is the index of brand sales to category sales. London, for example, has a BDI of 114 because the brand is relatively more developed than the category in that city. Paris has a BDI of 65, which means that the brand in Paris is relatively underdeveloped. Normally, the lower the BDI, the higher

Table 6.4 Calculating the brand development index (BDI)

	(a) **Percentage of EU brand**	(b) **Percentage of EU category**	**BDI**
Territory	*Sales*	*Sales*	$(a \div b) \times 100$
London	3.09	2.71	114
Paris	6.74	10.41	65
Berlin	3.49	3.85	91
Madrid	0.97	0.81	120
Rome	1.13	0.81	140
Amsterdam	3.12	3.00	104

the market opportunity, in that there is room to grow the brand. However, other marketers would argue the opposite – that marketing funds should go into the brand's *strongest* markets, where it might be important to reinforce loyalty or more easily capture additional brand share.

Industry sales and market shares

Besides estimating total potential and area potential, a company needs to know the actual industry sales taking place in its market. This means identifying competitors and estimating their sales.

The industry trade association will often collect and publish total industry sales, although it does not usually list individual company sales separately. With this information, however, each company can evaluate its own performance against the whole industry. If a company's sales are increasing by 5 per cent a year, and industry sales are increasing by 10 per cent, the company is losing its relative standing in the industry.

Another way to estimate sales is to buy reports from a marketing research firm that audits total sales and brand sales. Nielsen Media Research audits retail sales in various product categories in supermarkets and drugstores and sells this information to interested companies. These audits let a company compare its performance to the total industry or to any particular competitor to see whether it is gaining or losing share either overall or on a brand-by-brand basis.

Because distributors typically will not supply information about how much of the competitors' products they are selling, business-goods marketers operate with less knowledge of their market share results.

Estimating future demand

The few products or services that lend themselves to easy forecasting generally enjoy an absolute level or a fairly constant trend and competition that is either non-existent (public utilities) or stable (pure oligopolies). In most markets, in contrast, good forecasting is a key factor to success.

Companies commonly prepare a macroeconomic forecast first, followed by an industry forecast, followed by a company sales forecast. The macroeconomic forecast calls for projecting inflation, unemployment, interest rates, consumer spending, business investment, government expenditures, net exports and other variables. The end result is a forecast of gross national product, which the firm uses (along with other environmental indicators) to forecast industry sales. The company derives its sales forecast by assuming that it will win a certain market share.

How do firms develop their forecasts? They may create their own or buy forecasts from outside sources such as marketing research firms, which interview customers, distributors and other knowledgeable parties. All forecasts are built on one of three information bases: what people say, what people do, or what people have done. Using what people say requires surveying the opinions of buyers or those close to them, such as sales people or outside experts, with surveys of buyers' intentions, composites of sales force opinions and expert opinion. Building a forecast on what people do means putting the product into a test market to measure buyer response. To use the final basis – what people have done – firms analyse records of past buying behaviour or use time-series analysis or statistical demand analysis.

Survey of buyers' intentions

Forecasting is the art of anticipating what buyers are likely to do under a given set of conditions. For major consumer durables such as appliances, several research organisations conduct periodic surveys of consumer buying intentions and ask questions such as: 'Do you intend to buy an automobile within the next six months?' and put the answers on a **purchase probability scale**:

0.00	0.20	0.40	0.60	0.80	1.00
No chance	Slight possibility	Fair possibility	Good possibility	High possibility	Certain

Surveys also inquire into consumers' present and future personal finances and their expectations about the economy. They combine various bits of information into a consumer confidence measure (e.g. European Commission Consumer Surveys, ACNielsen Consumer Confidence Index). The European Commission indicator is based on a monthly survey conducted across the countries of the European Union and those in the euro currency area (EA), with a total sample size of more than 32,000 consumers. It is based on answers to questions about expectations of the financial situation of households, the general economic situation, the unemployment situation and savings. The ACNielsen six-monthly survey is conducted online with 21,000 consumers across Europe.[50]

For business buying, research firms can carry out buyer-intention surveys regarding plant, equipment and materials. Estimates (of demand) are then based on buyers' *intentions*, meaning that some degree of deviance from actual behaviour will necessarily exist. Such estimates tend to fall within a 10 per cent error band around the actual level of demand/sales. Buyer-intention surveys are particularly useful in estimating demand for industrial products, consumer durables, product purchases where advanced planning is required, and new products. The value of a buyer-intention survey increases to the extent that buyers are few, the cost of reaching them is low, and they have clear intentions that they willingly disclose and implement.

Composite of sales force opinions

When buyer interviewing is impractical, the company may ask its sales representatives to estimate their future sales.

Few companies use sales force estimates without making some adjustments. Sales representatives might be pessimistic or optimistic, they might not know how their company's marketing plans will influence future sales in their territory, and they might deliberately underestimate demand so the company will set a low sales quota. To encourage better estimating, the company could offer incentives or assistance, such as information about marketing plans or past forecasts compared to actual sales.

Sales force forecasts bring a number of benefits. Sales reps might have better insight into developing trends than any other group, and forecasting might give them greater confidence in their sales quotas and more incentive to achieve them. Also, a 'grassroots' forecasting procedure provides detailed estimates broken down by product, territory, customer and sales rep.

Expert opinion

Companies can also obtain forecasts from experts, including dealers, distributors, suppliers, marketing consultants and trade associations. Dealer estimates are subject to the same strengths and weaknesses as sales force estimates. Many companies buy economic and industry forecasts from well-known economic-forecasting firms that have more data available and more forecasting expertise.

Occasionally, companies will invite a group of experts to prepare a forecast. The experts exchange views and produce an estimate as a group (*group discussion method*) or individually, in which case another analyst might combine them into a single estimate (*pooling of individual estimates*). Further rounds of estimating and refining follow (this is the Delphi method).[51]

Past sales analysis

Firms can develop sales forecasts on the basis of past sales. *Time-series analysis* breaks past time series into four components (trend, cycle, seasonal and erratic) and projects them into the future. *Exponential smoothing* projects the next period's sales by combining an average of past sales and the most recent sales, giving more weight to the latter. *Statistical demand analysis* measures the impact of a set of causal factors (such as income, marketing expenditure and price) on the sales level. Finally, *econometric analysis* builds sets of equations that describe a system and statistically derives the different parameters that make up the equations.

Market-test method

When buyers don't plan their purchases carefully, or experts are unavailable or unreliable, a direct-market test can help forecast new-product sales or established product sales in a new distribution channel or territory.

SUMMARY

1 Knowing the market and its dynamics is at the heart of a truly market-oriented organisation. In this chapter, you have seen how marketing research spawns an informational foundation that is imperative to a company's efforts to make the best decisions possible, both tactically and strategically. And, since marketing information has come to be regarded as vital to company success, it is also an industry in rapid growth and development.

2 Some of the current trends in marketing research are: neuro-marketing research, online research – including data collection in social networking groups, such as MySpace or Facebook – and observational research. The latter type of research is furthered by technological advances, which make it possible to follow consumers' actual behaviour accurately – in a still stronger focus on what consumers do and how they go about their daily lives.

3 Companies can conduct their own marketing research or hire other companies to do it for them. Good marketing research is characterised by the scientific method, creativity, multiple research methods, accurate model building, cost–benefit analysis, healthy scepticism and an ethical focus.

4 The marketing research process consists of defining the problem, decision alternatives and research objectives, developing the research plan, collecting the information, analysing the information, presenting the findings to management and making the decision.

5 In conducting research, firms must decide whether to collect their own data or use data that already exist. They must also decide which research approach (observational, focus group, survey, behavioural data or experimental) and which research instruments (questionnaire, qualitative measures or technological devices) to use. In addition, they must decide on

a sampling plan and contact methods (by mail, by phone, in person or online).

6 Two complementary approaches to measuring marketing productivity are: (1) marketing metrics to assess marketing effects; and (2) marketing-mix modelling to estimate causal relationships and measure how marketing activity affects outcomes. Marketing dashboards are a structured way to disseminate the insights gleaned from these two approaches within the organisation.

7 There are two types of demand: market demand and company demand. To estimate current demand, companies attempt to determine total market potential, area market potential, industry sales and market share. To estimate future demand, companies survey buyers' intentions, solicit their sales force's input, gather expert opinions, analyse past sales or engage in market testing. Mathematical models, advanced statistical techniques and computerised data collection procedures are essential to all types of demand and sales forecasting

APPLICATIONS

Marketing debate

What is the best type of marketing research? Many market researchers have their favourite research approaches or techniques, although different researchers often have different preferences. Some researchers maintain that the only way to really learn about consumers or brands is through in-depth, qualitative research. Others contend that the only legitimate and defensible form of marketing research involves quantitative measures.

Take a position: The best marketing research is quantitative in nature *versus* qualitative.

Marketing discussion

When was the last time you participated in a survey? How helpful do you think was the information you provided? How could the research have been done differently to make it more effective?

REFERENCES

[1]Based on L. Lande (2007) How a Swiss co. doubled US sales by convincing consumers that its product is hip and worth a premium, *MarketingProfs*, 9 November.

[2]See R. Schieffer (2005) *Ten Key Customer Insights: Unlocking the Mind of the Market*, Mason, OH: Thomson, for a comprehensive, in-depth discussion of how to generate customer insights to drive business results.

[3]Natalie Zmuda (2009) Tropicana line's sales plunge 20% post-rebranding, *Advertising Age*, 2 April.

[4]ESOMAR (2010) *2010 Global Market Research Report*. September, Amsterdam: ESOMAR.

[5]www.orange.com/en_EN/.

[6]www.casecompetition.com/archive/2010; Melanie Haiken (2006) Tuned in to CrowdCasting, *Business 2.0*, November, 66–8.

[7]*The Economist* (2006) Would you fly in chattering class?, 9 September, 63.

[8]www.3g.dk; www.thetimes100.co.uk/index.php; J. Skouboe (2003) Se mig: Videotelefoni i virkeligheden, *Berlingske Tidende*, 7 April, Sektion 3, Business, 15; Messenger to go, press release from 3's website, 31 July, 2006; 3 first med Turbo 3G i Danmark, press release from 3's website, 21 November 2006; K. Stensdal, 3 erklærer internetudbyderne krig, *Computerworld*, 4 April 2007; Mobil-tv nu fra kun 39 kr. om måneden, press release from 3's website, 11 October 2010.

[9]For a discussion of the decision-theory approach to the value of research, see D. R. Lehmann, S. Gupta and J. Steckel (1997) *Market Research*, Reading, MA: Addison-Wesley.

[10]P. Ong (2010) In-cosmetics Asia, *Euromonitor*, available: www.in-cosmeticsasia.com/files/beautyandpersonalcareinasia.pdf.

[11]L. Tischler (2004) Every move you make, *Fast Company*, April, 73–5; A. Stein Wellner (2003) Look who's watching, *Continental*, April, 39–41.

[12]For a detailed review of relevant academic work, see B. Olsen (2011) Reflexive introspection on sharing gifts and shaping stories, *Journal of Business Research*, in press; L. A. Perlow and N. P. Repenning (2009) The dynamics of silencing conflict, *Research in Organizational* Behavior, 29, 195–223; E. J. Arnould and A. Epp (2006) Deep engagement with consumer experience, in R. Grover and M. Vriens (eds), *Handbook of Marketing Research*, Thousand Oaks, CA: Sage, pp. 10–15. For some practical tips, see R. Durante and M. Feehan (2005) Leverage ethnography to improve strategic decision making, *Marketing Research*, Winter.

[13]L. Miles (2003) Market research: living their lives, *BrandRepublic*, 11 December, www.brandrepublic.com/bulletins/marketresearch/article/197919/market-research-living-lives/.

[14]E. Sanders, Special section: ethnography in NPD research – how 'applied ethnography' can improve your NPD process, *PDMA*, www.pdma.org/visions/apr02/applied.html.

[15]www.brandrepublic.com.

[16]Based on L. Fisher (2009) Classification maps draw on group culture, *Marketing Week*, 13 August, www.marketingweek.co.uk/classification-maps-draw-on-group-culture/3003363.article; M. Fielding (2006) Shift the focus, *Marketing News*, 1 September, 18–20.

[17]Markedsføring online (2011) Her er Danmarks mest populære brands, 11 January; E. Pfanner (2006) Agencies look beyond focus groups to spot trends, *New York Times*, 2 January.

[18]http://om.tdc.dk/.

[19]J. C. Kozup, E. H. Creyer and S. Burton (2003) Making healthful food choices: the influence of health claims and nutrition information on consumers' evaluations of packaged food products and restaurant menu items, *Journal of Marketing*, 67 (April), 19–34.

[20]www.lego.com; Erhvervsfremme Styrelsen, BUPL, Samarbejde mellem daginstitutioner og virksomheder – M. Vanderbeeken (2006) Insights from the European market research event, 16 November; MarketingProfs Daily Fix: www.mpdailyfix.com/2006/11/post_14.html.

[21]Paula Andruss (2008) Keeping both eyes on quality, *Marketing News*, 15 September, 22–3.

[22]www.neurosense.com; T. K. Grose (2006) Brain sells, *TIME*, 10 September; www.telegraph.co.uk/motoring/main.jhtml?xml=/motoring/exclusions/supplements/honda/nosplit/honda3switchedon.xml#1.

[23]http://sverigesradio.se/sida/artikel.aspx?programid=109&artikel=4267662; www.mikab.se/index.php3?NodNummer=58&Poe_Session=adb9f75625f1462a6d81ef2ce5373d93.

[24]Danske forskere finder vej til guldskatten (2011) Business.dk, January 24; Fielding (2006), op. cit.

[25]B. Johnson (2006) Forget phone and mail: online's the best place to administer surveys, *Advertising Age*, 17 July, 23.

[26]D. L. Vence (2006) In an instant: more researchers use IM for fast, reliable results, *Marketing News*, 1 March, 53–5.

[27]Elisabeth Sullivan (2008) Qual Research By the Numbers, *Marketing News*, 1 September.

[28]Deborah L. Vence (2006) in an instant: more researchers use IM for fast, reliable results, *Marketing News*, 1 March, 53–5.

[29]Jim Stachura and Meg Murphy (2005) multicultural marketing: why one size doesn't fit all, MarketingProfs.com, published on 25 October.

[30]M. Fielding (2006) Global insights: Synovate's Chedore discusses MR trends, *Marketing News*, 15 May, 41–2.

[31]www.brandrepublic.com; www.arnoldbolingbroke.com.

[32]R. A. Layton (2011) Towards a theory of marketing systems, *European Journal of Marketing*, 45(1/2), 259–76; cf. J. D. C. Little (1979) Decision support systems for marketing managers, *Journal of Marketing*, summer, 11.

[33]D. Power (2006) What are examples of decision support systems in global enterprises?, http://dssresources.com, 26 October.

[34]A. C. Ruótolo (2008) Pitfalls in marketing research, *Research Review*, 15(1), 41–3; R. Grover and M. Vriens (2006) Trusted advisor: how it helps lay the foundation for insight in *Handbook of Marketing Research*, Thousand Oaks, CA: Sage, 3–17;

C. Moorman, G. Zaltman and R. Deshpandé (1992) Relationships between providers and users of market research: the dynamics of trust within and between organizations, *Journal of Marketing Research*, 29, August, 314–28.

[35]Daniel Gilbert, (2007) *Stumbling on Happiness*. New York: Vintage, p. 183.

[36]Adapted from A. Shapiro (2004) Let's redefine market research, *Brandweek*, 21 June, 20; www.fromscripttodvd.com:80/star_wars_a_day_long_remembered.htm.

[37]R. Shaw and D. Merrick (2005) *Marketing Payback: Is Your Marketing Profitable?*, Harlow: FT Prentice Hall.

[38]J. McManus (2004) Stumbling into intelligence, *American Demographics*, April, 22–5.

[39]D. Zahay and A. Griffin (2010) Marketing strategy selection, marketing metrics, and firm performance, *Journal of Business and Industrial Marketing*, 25(2), 84–93; P. Farris, N. T. Bendle, P. E. Pfeifer and D. J. Reibstein (2006) *Marketing Metrics: 50+ Metrics Every Executive Should Master*, Upper Saddle River, NJ: Pearson Education; J. Davis (2005) *Magic Numbers for Consumer Marketing: Key Measures to Evaluate Marketing Success*, Singapore: John Wiley & Sons.

[40]B. Donath (2003) Employ marketing metrics with a track record, *Marketing News*, 15 September, 12.

[41]G. J. Tellis (2006) Modeling marketing mix, in R. Grover and M. Vriens (eds), *Handbook of Marketing Research*, Thousand Oaks, CA: Sage.

[42]J. Neff (2004) P&G, Clorox rediscover modeling, *Advertising Age*, 29 March, 10.

[43]L. Q. Hughes (2002) Econometrics take root, *Advertising Age*, 5 August, S–4.

[44]D. J. Reibstein (2005) Connect the dots, *CMO Magazine*, May.

[45]www.autoliv.com/wps/wcm/connect/autoliv/Home/Who+We+Are/Our%20Market.

[46]For a good discussion and illustration, see R. J. Best, *Market-based Management*, 4th edn, Upper Saddle River, NJ: Prentice Hall.

[47]For further discussion, see G. L. Lilien, P. Kotler and K. S. Moorthy (1992) *Marketing Models*, Upper Saddle River, NJ: Prentice Hall.

[48]http://epp.eurostat.ec.europa.eu/cache/ITY_OFFPUB/KS-EI-10-001/EN/KS-EI-10-001-EN.PDF

[49]http://ec.europa.eu/environment/emas/documents/nace_en.htm.

[50]www.mrweb.com/drno/conf-euro.htm.

[51]For an excellent overview of market forecasting, see G. H. Van Bruggen, M. Spann, G. L. Lilien and B. Skiera (2010) Prediction markets as institutional forecasting support systems, *Decision Support Systems*, 49(4), 404–16; S. Armstrong (2001) (ed.) *Principles of Forecasting: A Handbook for Researchers and Practitioners*, Norwell, MA: Kluwer Academic Publishers and his website: http://fourps.wharton.upenn.edu/ forecast/handbook.html; also see R. J. Best (1974) An experiment in Delphi estimation in marketing decision making, *Journal of Marketing Research*, November, 447–52; N. Dalkey and O. Helmer (1963) An experimental application of the Delphi method to the use of experts, *Management Science*, April, 458–67.

Chapter 7

Analysing consumer markets

IN THIS CHAPTER, WE WILL ADDRESS THE FOLLOWING QUESTIONS:

1 How do consumer and situational characteristics influence buying behaviour?

2 What major psychological and behavioural processes influence consumer responses to the marketing programme?

3 How do consumers make purchasing decisions?

4 How do marketers analyse consumer decision making?

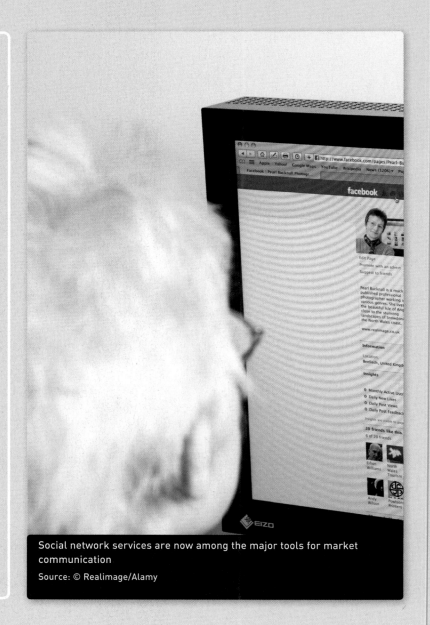

Social network services are now among the major tools for market communication

Source: © Realimage/Alamy

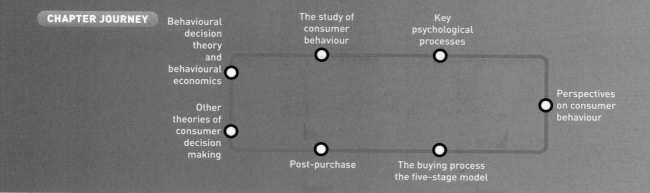

CHAPTER JOURNEY

Behavioural decision theory and behavioural economics

The study of consumer behaviour

Key psychological processes

Perspectives on consumer behaviour

Other theories of consumer decision making

Post-purchase

The buying process the five-stage model

The aim of marketing is to meet and satisfy target customers' needs and wants better than competitors. Marketers are always looking for emerging customer trends that suggest new marketing opportunities.

The emergence of the social web, especially with teens and young adults, has made marketers rethink their practices.

Social network services such as Facebook, MySpace, Twitter, Friendster and Tagged represent a major opportunity for marketers to enter into dialogue with their customers. Essentially, social network services are dedicated to social networking, offering their members an easy and free way of creating personal profiles that may contain all sorts of content, such as photographs, music, blogs and so on. Members can link their profile to those of their friends or can search for new friends who share their interests. In this way the social web takes form – and becomes a sphere for building and maintaining relationships between people.

These popular social networks accumulate a wealth of information about their members that marketers find valuable, and they have paved the way for new forms of communication between marketers and consumers. In fact, worldwide social network spending on advertising is expected to reach €4 billion in 2011, with Facebook attracting 75 per cent of that amount. Facebook has developed an advertising system that invites marketers to present ads to individual Facebook members, based on the details they share with friends on the site. This includes not only the types of data commonly available to marketers, such as demographic data, geographic location and content purchasing habits, but also much more personal information such as interests, preferences, attitudes and relationship status. The system provides a means for businesses to build profiles on Facebook to connect with their audiences; an ad system that facilitates the spread of brand messages virally; and an interface to gather insights into people's activity on Facebook that marketers care about. Examples of organisations and businesses joining Facebook range from small, local firms such as national supermarkets to multinational corporations such as BMW, Novo Nordisk, Unilever and Siemens.[1]

Successful marketing requires that companies fully connect with their customers. Adopting a holistic marketing orientation means understanding customers – gaining a 360-degree view of their daily lives, their plans for the future and the changes that actually occur during their lifetimes so that the right products are marketed to the right customers in the right way. This chapter explores consumer buying dynamics; the next chapter explores the buying dynamics of business buyers.

The study of consumer behaviour

Consumer behaviour is the study of how individuals or groups buy, use and dispose of goods, services, ideas or experiences to satisfy their needs and wants. The needs and wants of consumers often vary across different cultures, situations and individual characteristics. The study of consumer behaviour can be divided into three interdependent dimensions:

1 the study of culture;
2 the study of social groups; and
3 the study of the individual (Figure 7.1).

While it is possible to treat the three dimensions separately, they also have a mutual influence on each other. In the following, each dimension will first be considered separately and then some possible interdependencies between the dimensions are discussed.

Culture

Culture, subculture and social class are particularly important influences on consumer buying behaviour. **Culture** is the fundamental determinant of a person's wants and behaviour. Culture can be conceptualised as the 'meanings that are shared by (most) people in a social group'[2] and can be thought of as the blueprint for human behaviour. In a culture, values and norms are developed that serve as guidelines for human behaviour. Each culture consists of smaller **subcultures** that provide more specific identification and socialisation for their members. Subcultures include nationalities, religions, racial groups and geographic regions. When subcultures grow large and affluent enough, companies often design specialised marketing programmes to serve them. *Multicultural marketing* grew out of careful marketing research, which revealed that different ethnic and demographic niches did not always respond favourably to mass market advertising.

To learn how Quebec's rich and diverse culture has led various multinational companies to adapt their campaigns, visit www.pearsoned.ca/marketingmanagementcanada.

Companies have capitalised on well-thought-out multicultural marketing strategies in recent years, as illustrated in the marketing insight box. As countries become more culturally diverse, however, marketing campaigns aimed at a specific cultural target can spill over and have a positive influence on other cultural groups.[3]

Virtually all human societies exhibit *social stratification*,[4] most often in the form of **social classes**, relatively homogeneous and enduring divisions in a society, hierarchically ordered and with members who share similar values, interests and behaviour. One classic

Figure 7.1 The interaction of the cultural, the social and the individual level

depiction of social classes in the EU is the EGP (Erikson-Goldthorpe-Portocarero) class schema – defined as 11 descending levels, as follows:

1 service class I (comprising higher-grade professionals, administrators and officials; managers in large industrial establishments; large proprietors);
2 service class II (comprising lower-grade professionals, administrators and officials; higher-grade technicians; managers in small industrial establishments; supervisors of non-manual employees);
3 routine non-manual;
4 routine non-manual employees;

Marketing insight

Multicultural marketing in Europe

Marketing targeted at national cultures

Comprising 47 independent countries,[5] Europe has had a tradition of national companies designing marketing programmes for specific national cultures. Many global corporations operating in the European market have followed this practice with success. Coca-Cola in Europe is a characteristic example of a global corporation with a local approach to marketing. During recent years, Coca-Cola has pursued a strategy of moving into niche markets by launching non-traditional soft drinks, such as Avra water in Greece, Cappy juice in Croatia, BURN (energy) in Poland, Fernandes sodas in the Netherlands and Fioravanti in Spain.

Fernandes sodas: a local approach to marketing
Source: Courtesy of Fernandes Bottling Co NV

▶ Marketing insight *(continued)*

As the expansion of the EU has led to increasing numbers of immigrants, the market potential for ethnic drinks has grown. A case in point is Fernandes sodas, produced by Fernandes Concern Beheer NV, one of the oldest corporations in Suriname. Fernandes sodas is a sweet, lemonade-like drink that comes in several brightly coloured flavours such as red cherry bouquet and green punch.

For decades, many Dutch residents with ties to Suriname – a former Dutch colony in South America– had been bringing home cases of Fernandes in their luggage. But in the 1980s Coca-Cola Enterprises Nederland BV began bottling Fernandes under licence and selling the sodas in small ethnic grocery stores in big cities such as Amsterdam.

The South American soda soon became popular. Marte van Esser, spokesperson for Coca-Cola in the Netherlands, commented on its success: 'Every country has its specific needs and Coca-Cola knows how to meet those needs . . . Although originally targeted at the Surinamese, the sodas really are for everyone.' As the roll-out of the no-calorie drink Coke Zero was also highly successful in Europe, Coca-Cola seems to be striking a balance between nurturing its roots and gaining new audiences by respecting the tastes of local consumers. This balance has resulted in steadily increasing profits in Europe (in the third-quarter of 2010, income through European countries rose 4.5 per cent as quantity grew 5 per cent), helping to offset the company's more modest performance in North America.

Marketing targeted at minority groups

In recent years, however, Europe has also witnessed a trend towards multicultural strategies that go across traditional national lines of cultural identity, revolving around ethnic identities. In Ireland, foreign nationals constitute more than 10 per cent of the population, and companies are taking on new challenges in targeting and creating brand awareness among the growing ethnic communities. For instance, local phone company Meteor has tailored advertising campaigns and translated its website into Polish, Latvian, Mandarin and Lithuanian in order to optimise customer experiences.

In the United Kingdom, the need for companies to understand and communicate with ethnic groups has never been greater, as they represent a growing audience of around 5 million consumers with an expected spending power of €420 billion by 2010. Thus, corporations such as British Telecom have increased their investments targeting the ethnic minority market. In one of their campaigns, a black family was portrayed to reach out to ethnic minority customers as well as white customers. The aim of the campaign was to encourage overseas calling, a perfect example of targeting ethnic minority communities. Along similar lines, healthcare chain Boots launched a range of halal baby food. They worked with the Muslim Food Board to develop it and make sure it was properly labelled and within Muslim law. The range featured in the *Muslim Food Guide*, which is distributed throughout the United Kingdom via mosques. Boots ensured its staff were up to speed on the new range to advise customers.

Finally, a number of non-profit and governmental organisations, such as hospitals and law enforcement agencies, have been very successful in developing recruitment campaigns aimed at individuals from under-represented groups, particularly women and those from minority ethnic communities. In both the United Kingdom and Denmark, such strategies have been employed to improve the diversity of the workforce so that it more closely reflects the diversity of the communities it serves. Despite these developments, researchers found that ethnic consumers in the United Kingdom often feel overlooked. At least one in two people from all ethnic groups – including the white population – believed that consumer brands often use ethnic faces in advertising as a token gesture. Also, more than three-quarters of Asian (77 per cent) and black (78 per cent) people and half (50 per cent) of Chinese people in the United Kingdom believed mainstream brands to be of no relevance to them. In addition, 75 per cent of black, 63 per cent of Asian and 50 per cent of Chinese people did not see marketers as knowledgeable of how to market to individuals from ethnically diverse backgrounds. These are important sentiments to bear in mind when designing strategies and campaigns intended for minority communities.

Sources: Based on Coca-Cola Enterprises sales and revenue rise in Europe, *Business Today*, February 2011, www.businesstoday-eg.com/business/europe/coca-cola-enterprises-sales-and-revenue-rise-in-europe.html; S. Emling (2007) Coke goes local to win wider market in Europe, *Cox News Service*, 13 October (www.coxwashington.com/hp/content/reporters/stories/2007/10/13/BC_COKE_EUROPE13_COX.html); Firms target ethnic sector, *TCH Archives, Sunday Business Post*, 5 August 2007 (http://archives.tcm.ie/businesspost/2007/08/05/story25616.asp); L. MacDonald, W. Tanner and C. Wheeler, Advertising and ethnic minority communities: a report by the IPA Information Centre (www.ipa.co.uk/documents/Advertising&ethnic_minority_communities.pdf); Fokusgruppe hjælper politiet med etnisk rekruttering (www.politi.dk/da/aktuelt/nyheder/2006/etniskfokusgruppe_11102006.htm); The recruitment of black and minority ethnic groups to the MPS, Report 8, 1 September 2006 (www.mpa.gov.uk/committees/cop/2006/060901/08.htm); Understanding the multi-cultural market (www.webershand-wick.co.uk/features/understanding-the-multi-cultural-market).

5 self-employed with employees;

6 self-employed with no employees;

7 self-employed, farmers, etc.;

8 manual supervisors;

9 skilled workers;

10 unskilled workers;

11 farm labour.[6]

Social classes have several characteristics. First, those within each tend to be more alike in dress, speech patterns and recreational preferences than persons from two different social classes. Second, persons are perceived as occupying inferior or superior positions according to social class. Third, a *cluster* of variables – for example, occupation, income, wealth, education and value orientation – indicates social class, rather than any single variable. Fourth, individuals can move up or down the social class ladder during their lifetimes. How easily and how far depends on how rigid the social stratification is and on the level of equality in a society.

Social classes show distinct product and brand preferences in many areas, including clothing, home furnishings, leisure activities and automobiles. They also differ in media preferences, with upper-class consumers often preferring magazines and books and lower-class consumers often preferring television. Even within a category such as TV, upper-class consumers tend to prefer news and drama, and lower-class consumers tend to prefer soap operas and sports programmes. There are also language differences – advertising copy and dialogue must ring true to the targeted social class.

Social groups

Social factors such as reference groups, family, and social roles and statuses affect consumers' buying behaviour.

Reference groups

A person's **reference groups** are all the groups that have a direct (face-to-face) or indirect influence on their attitudes or behaviour. Groups having a direct influence are called **membership groups**. Some of these are **primary groups** with which the person interacts fairly continuously and informally, such as family, friends, neighbours and co-workers. People also belong to **secondary groups**, such as religious, professional and trade union groups, which tend to be more formal and require less continuous interaction.

Reference groups influence members in at least three ways. They expose an individual to new behaviours and lifestyles, they influence attitudes and self-concept, and they create pressures for conformity that may affect product and brand choices. For instance, inspired by their friends and colleagues, women may choose to buy high-quality branded products for their child in order to be perceived as a 'good mother'.[7] People are also influenced by groups to which they do *not* belong and by groups to which they do *not want* to belong. **Aspirational groups** are those a person hopes to join; **dissociative groups** are those groups to which a person does not belong and whose values, norms or behaviour an individual rejects; **disclaimant groups** are those groups to which a person belongs but whose values, norms or behaviour an individual seeks to avoid.

Many ads play on the influence of reference groups on product and brand choice. The advertisement for Hugo Boss (page 250), for example, portrays two young, trendy, affluent and relaxed people, implying that choosing the Hugo Boss brand may help the consumer create a similar style or image. In 2011, Nokia launched a global campaign for its E7 smartphone, which encourages people to define their own success. Created by Wieden + Kennedy Amsterdam, the campaign uses a 'success is what you make it' strapline to demonstrate that success is 'no longer about your latest car, your new house, or the amount of money you earn'. With this campaign, Nokia wants to stress that success is more about personal values and human interaction.[8]

Where reference group influence is strong, marketers must determine how to reach and influence the group's opinion leaders or other influential persons of the group. An **opinion leader** is the person who offers informal advice or information about a specific product or product category, such as which of several brands is best or how a particular product may be used.[9] Opinion leaders are often highly confident, socially active and involved with the category, and are often perceived by other consumers as highly credible information sources. **Market mavens** are also perceived by other consumers to offer credible advice, but in contrast to opinion leaders market mavens are not influential because of a specialised product or product category expertise. Instead, they possess a more broad expertise concerning many different products and decisions related to the marketplace.[10] Marketers try to reach opinion leaders and market mavens by identifying

Choosing the Hugo Boss brand helps consumers to create a relaxed style of living.

Source: Image Courtesy of the Advertising Archives.

their demographic and psychographic characteristics, identifying the media they read, and directing messages at them. Today, important inroads into the lives of opinion leaders and market mavens are starting 'friendships' with them in social web forums such as MySpace or Facebook, or offering sponsorships of popular personal blogs or communities based on interests or hobbies.

Family

The family is the most important consumer buying organisation in society, and family members constitute the most influential primary reference group.[11] There are two families in the buyer's life. The **family of orientation** consists of parents and siblings. From parents a person acquires an orientation towards religion, politics and economics, and a sense of personal ambition, self-worth and love.[12] Even if the buyer no longer interacts very much with their parents, their influence on behaviour can be significant. Parents have been found to influence their children's future orientation towards areas as diverse as education, savings, food, smoking, drinking and driving, teen pregnancy, and even the choice of bank or insurance company.[13]

A more direct influence on everyday buying behaviour is the **family of procreation** – namely, one's spouse and children. In Europe, husband–wife involvement in purchases has traditionally varied widely by product category. The wife has usually acted as the family's main purchasing agent, especially for food, sundries and staple clothing items. Now traditional purchasing roles are changing, and marketers would be wise to see both men and women as possible targets. For expensive products and services such as cars, holidays and housing, the vast majority of husbands and wives engage in joint decision making.[14] And marketers are realising that women actually buy more technology than men do, but consumer electronics stores have been slow to catch on to this fact. Some savvy electronics stores are starting to heed women's complaints of being ignored, patronised or offended by salespeople.

Nevertheless, men and women may respond differently to marketing messages. One study showed that women valued connections and relationships with family and friends and placed a high priority on people. Men, on the other hand, related more to competition and placed a high priority on action. Marketers are taking more direct aim at women with products such as Kellogg's Special K Brand or paint manufacturer Jotun's brand 'Lady'.[15] Recently Bang & Olufsen launched the Beolab 11 subwoofer – targeted specifically at gaining acceptance among women.

Another shift in buying patterns is an increase in the number of euros spent and the direct and indirect influence wielded by children and teens. Direct influence describes children's hints, requests and demands – 'I want to go to McDonald's.' Indirect influence means that parents know the brands, product choices and preferences of their children without hints or outright requests ('I think Tommy would want to go to McDonald's'). Research conducted at the University of Vienna, Austria suggests that twice as many purchases in supermarkets are triggered by children than their parents are aware of. A total of 178 parents shopping with their child in Austrian supermarkets were unobtrusively observed while strolling through the aisles, after which they were interviewed. When asked how many products their children had made them buy, on average parents only reported half the number of purchases that had been secretly observed.[16] On a similar note, other studies found that English (UK) and Israeli children exercise quite strong influence on family decision making.[17] Children are highly involved and influential in regard to products of which they are primary users, such as toys, clothing, education and entertainment. Approximately 25 per cent of Israeli children, 40 per cent of English children and a little over two-thirds of US children were reported to be involved in decision making regarding family consumption matters as well. Indeed, research has shown that teenagers are playing a more active role than before in helping parents choose a car, audio/mobile phone equipment or a holiday spot.[18] That is why car manufacturers are upping their marketing programmes for children as young as five. Television can be especially powerful in reaching children, and marketers are using it to target them at younger ages than ever before with product tie-ins for just about everything. By the time children are around 2 years old, they can often recognise characters, logos and specific brands. They can distinguish between advertising and programming by about ages 6 or 7. A year or so later, they can understand the concept of persuasive intent on the part of advertisers. By 9 or 10, they can perceive the discrepancies between message and product.[19] Millions of kids under the age of 17 are also online. Marketers have jumped online with them, offering freebies in exchange for personal information. Many have come under fire for this practice and for not clearly differentiating ads from games or entertainment. Establishing ethical and legal boundaries in marketing to children online and offline continues to be a hot topic as consumer advocates decry the commercialism they believe such marketing engenders.

Roles and status

A person participates in many groups – family, clubs, organisations. Groups are often an important source of information and help to define norms for behaviour. We can define a person's position in each group to which he belongs in terms of role and status. A **role** consists of the activities a person is expected to perform. Each role carries a **status**. A senior vice-president of marketing has more status than a sales manager, and a sales manager

Beolab 11 subwoofer: a new product targeted specifically at gaining acceptance among women.

Source: © Bang & Olufsen

has more status than an office clerk. People choose products that reflect and communicate their role and actual or desired status in society. Thus, marketers must be aware of the symbol potential of products, brands and company logos. Niels van Quaquebeke and Steffen Giessner of the Rotterdam School of Management showed logos of 100 Global 500 companies to two groups of participants. One group rated them on attractiveness and symmetry; the other judged whether the logo suggested that the company behaved ethically. Their finding? Rationally or not, people associate symmetrical logos with more ethical, socially responsible behaviour.

The individual consumer

A buyer's decisions are also influenced by personal characteristics. These include the buyer's age and stage in the life cycle; occupation and economic circumstances; personality and self-concept; and lifestyle and values. Because many of these characteristics have a very direct impact on consumer behaviour, it is important for marketers to follow them closely.

Age and stage in the life cycle

Our taste in food, clothes, furniture and recreation is often related to our age. For example, it is not at all uncommon for parents and teens to have different clothing preferences.[20] Consumption is also shaped by the *family life cycle* and the number, age and gender of people in the household at any point in time. Western households are increasingly fragmented – the traditional family of four with a husband, wife and two kids makes up a much smaller percentage of total households than it once did.[21] In addition, *psychological* life cycle stages may matter. Adults experience certain 'passages' or 'transformations' as they go through life.[22] Yet the behaviour people exhibit as they go through these passages, such as becoming a parent, is not necessarily fixed but changes with the times.

Marketers should also consider *critical life events or transitions* – marriage, childbirth, illness, relocation, divorce, career change, widowhood – as giving rise to new needs. These should alert service providers – banks, lawyers, and marriage, employment and bereavement counsellors – to ways they can help.

Occupation and economic circumstances

Occupation also influences consumption patterns. A blue-collar worker will buy work clothes, work shoes and lunchboxes. A company president will buy lounge suits, air travel and country club membership. Marketers try to identify the occupational groups that have above-average interest in their products and services, and even tailor products for certain occupational groups. Computer software companies, for example, design different products for brand managers, engineers, lawyers and physicians.

Product choice is greatly affected by economic circumstances: spendable income (level, stability and time pattern), savings and assets (including the percentage that is liquid), debts, borrowing power and attitudes towards spending and saving. Luxury goods makers such as Gucci, Prada and Burberry can be vulnerable to an economic downturn. If economic indicators point to a recession, marketers can take steps to redesign, reposition and reprice their products or introduce or increase the emphasis on discount brands so that they can continue to offer value to target customers.

Personality and self-concept

Each person has personality characteristics that influence his or her buying behaviour. By **personality**, we mean a set of distinguishing human psychological traits that lead to relatively consistent and enduring responses to environmental stimuli (including buying behaviour). We often describe it in terms of such traits as self-confidence, dominance, autonomy, deference, sociability, defensiveness and adaptability.[23] Personality can be a useful variable in analysing consumer brand choices. The idea is that brands also have personalities, and consumers are likely to choose brands whose personalities match their own. For example, some people may buy a BMW X5 (a large off-road vehicle) to signal self-confidence and dominance. We define **brand personality** as the specific mix of human traits that we can attribute to a particular brand.

Marketing professor Jennifer Aaker researched brand personalities and identified the following traits:[24]

- sincerity (down to earth, honest, wholesome and cheerful);
- excitement (daring, spirited, imaginative and up to date);
- competence (reliable, intelligent and successful);
- sophistication (upper class and charming); and
- ruggedness (outdoorsy and tough).

She analysed some well-known brands and found that a number of them tended to be strong on one particular trait: Levi's with 'ruggedness'; MTV with 'excitement'; CNN with 'competence'; and Campbell's with 'sincerity'. The implication is that these brands will attract persons who are high on the same personality traits. A brand personality may have several attributes: Levi's suggests a personality that is youthful, rebellious, authentic and American.

A cross-cultural study exploring the generalisability of Aaker's scale found that three of the five factors applied in Japan and Spain, but a 'peacefulness' dimension replaced 'ruggedness' in both countries, and a 'passion' dimension emerged in Spain instead of 'competency'.[25] Research on brand personality in Korea revealed two culture-specific factors – passive likeableness and ascendancy – reflecting the importance of Confucian values (i.e. respect for one's parents, humaneness and ritual) in Korea's social and economic systems.[26]

Consumers often choose and use brands that have a brand personality consistent with their own *actual self-concept* (how we view ourselves), although the match may instead be based on the consumer's *ideal self-concept* (how we would like to view ourselves) or even on *others' self-concept* (how we think others see us).[27] These effects may also be more pronounced for publicly consumed products than for privately consumed goods.[28] On the other hand, consumers who are high 'self-monitors' – that is, sensitive to how others see them – are more likely to choose brands whose personalities fit the consumption situation.[29] Finally, consumers often have multiple aspects of self (serious professional, caring family member, active fun lover) that may be evoked differently in different situations or around different types of people.

Lifestyle and values

People from the same subculture, social class and occupation may lead quite different lifestyles. A **lifestyle** is a person's pattern of living in the world as expressed in activities, interests and opinions. It portrays the 'whole person' interacting with his or her environment. Marketers search for relationships between their products and lifestyle groups. For example, a computer manufacturer might find that most computer buyers are achievement oriented and then aim the brand more clearly at the achiever lifestyle. Here is an example of one of the latest lifestyle trends that businesses are targeting.

LOHAS

Consumers who worry about the environment, want products to be produced in a sustainable way, and spend money to advance their personal health, development and potential have been named 'LOHAS', an acronym standing for *lifestyles of health and sustainability*.

LOHAS consumers ('Lohasians') are interested in products covering a range of market sectors and subsectors, including alternative healthcare, organic clothing and food, energy-efficient appliances and solar panels, as well as socially responsible investing, yoga tapes and ecotourism. While ethical consumerism, eco-consciousness and expectations of positive exchanges among companies and their stakeholders are global phenomena,

Table 7.1 LOHAS market segments

Personal health	**Natural lifestyles**
Natural, organic products	Indoor and outdoor furnishings
Nutritional products	Organic cleaning supplies
Integrative healthcare	Compact fluorescent lights
Dietary supplements	Social change philanthropy
Mind, body, spirit products	Apparel
Green building	**Alternative transportation**
Home certification	Hybrid vehicles
Energy star appliances	Biodiesel fuel
Sustainable flooring	Car-sharing programmes
Renewable energy systems	
Wood alternatives	
Eco-tourism	**Alternative energy**
Eco-tourism travel	Renewable energy credits
Eco-adventure travel	Green pricing

Source: From www.lohas.com. Copyright © LOHAS. Reproduced with permission.

Europeans are 50 per cent more likely than Americans to buy 'green' products, including solar panels, hybrid cars, natural/organic foods, personal care and home products. Moreover, they are 25 per cent more likely to recycle and more than 30 per cent more likely to influence their friends and family about the environment than Americans. Researchers expect that differences in tax structures, subsidies and the longevity of the availability of LOHAS products induce these variations.[30]

Worldwide, this market segment is currently estimated to be worth €395 billion annually.[31] Table 7.1 breaks the LOHAS market into six segments, each with special product and service interests.[32]

Lifestyles are shaped partly by whether consumers are *money constrained* or *time constrained*. Companies aiming to serve money-constrained consumers will create lower-cost products and services. By appealing to thrifty consumers, Wal-Mart has become the largest company in the world. Its 'everyday low prices' have wrung tens of billions of dollars out of the retail supply chain, passing the larger part of savings along to shoppers in the form of rock-bottom bargain prices.[33] Another company focusing on offering low prices to consumers, and aiming to serve money-constrained consumers, is furniture retailer IKEA. IKEA is enjoying global success by appealing to price-conscious shoppers in the furniture market.

While IKEA may offer good value for money, the IKEA concept is not designed to serve time-constrained consumers. When shopping in IKEA consumers often have to queue to receive their chosen products from IKEA's storage and thereafter they must assemble the furniture on their own. Consumers who experience time famine are prone to **multitasking**, doing two or more things at the same time. They will also pay others to perform tasks because time is more important than money. Companies aiming to serve them will create convenient products and services for this group. In some categories, notably food processing, companies targeting time-constrained consumers need to be aware that these very same people want to believe they are *not* operating within time constraints. Marketers call those who seek both convenience and some involvement in the cooking process the 'convenience involvement segment'.[34]

Some marketers – for instance, food retailers and manufactures – may believe that there is still a gender bias in the way that consumers conduct their lifestyle and in the way they perceive and engage with brands, and therefore they may seek to tailor their products and marketing effort to female (or male) lifestyles. The problem is, however, what do women really want?

Marketing insight

What do women really want?

Gender has often been used as a stereotype characteristic. For example, consumers who eat smaller meals and healthy foods are often referred to as 'feminine', whereas those who eat larger meals and unhealthy foods are referred to as 'masculine'. There is some evidence

Are men and women really that different?

that women and men may be socialised to eat differently and that they might view food differently. Compared to men, women generally tend to consider themselves to have a healthier food intake, to be more knowledgeable about healthy food and to read nutritional labels more often. Also, men's eating habits are more likely to be influenced by their spouse, as compared to the other way around. A study of consumers' choice of functional food found that women showed a more positive attitude towards concepts enriched with 'healthy components' like fibre and iron, than men. Other results suggest that women are more concerned than men about reducing salt and fat in their food intake and that women more often prefer to eat fish, fruit and vegetables.

Gender-related lifestyles differences are also found in conjunction with brand preferences and brand behaviour. 'Life has become more complicated in terms of what men and women are expected to do, but brand gender stereotypes still exist,' says chief executive Stephen Cheliotis, of the Centre for Brand Analysis (TCBA). In a gender breakdown of TCBA's Superbrands 2010 data, it was found that, despite an evolution in gender roles and lifestyles, women are still attracted to many stereotypical brands. Also, 'women are more willing to be emotionally engaged with a brand', Cheliotis adds, 'and more willing to reward the brands they are engaged with when it is time to purchase.' Marketing research suggests that when using brands for self-expressive purposes, consumers may draw on masculine and feminine personality traits associated with a brand to enhance their own degree of masculinity or femininity.

Sources: M. Costa (2010) What do women really want?, *Marketing Week*, 17 June; B. Grohmann (2009) Gender dimensions of brand personality, *Journal of Marketing Research*, XLVI (February), 105–19; T. Hansen, H. Boye and T. U. Thomsen (2010) Involvement, competencies, gender and food health information seeking, *British Food Journal*, 112(4), 387–402; L. R. Vartanian, P. C. Herman and J. Polivy (2007) Consumption stereotypes and impression management: how you are what you eat, *Appetite*, 48, 265–77; G. Ares and A. Gámbaro (2007) Influence of gender, age and motives underlying food choice on perceived healthiness and willingness to try functional foods, *Appetite*.

Consumer decisions are also influenced by **core values**, the belief systems that underlie attitudes and behaviours. Core values go much deeper than behaviour or attitude and determine, at a basic level, people's choices and desires over the long term. In that sense, core values are trans-situational goals that serve the interests of individuals or groups and act as guiding principles in consumers' lives.[35] Marketers who target consumers on the basis of their values believe that with appeals to people's inner selves it is possible to influence their outer selves – their purchase behaviour. Marketing researchers have for a long time given prominence to values; consider, for example, Clawson and

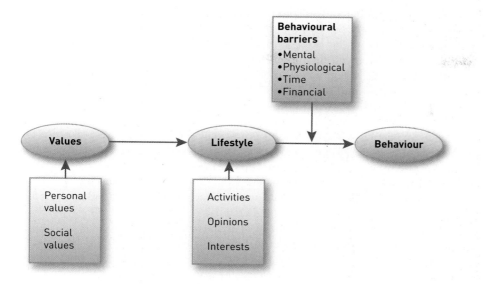

Figure 7.2 Linking values and lifestyles with behaviour.
Source: T. Hansen (2010) Values and lifestyles, in K. M. Ekström (ed.), *Consumer Behaviour – a Nordic perspective*, Lund: Studentlitteratur, 307–24.

Vinson, who in 1978 suggested that 'values may prove to be one of the most powerful explanations of, and influences on consumer behaviour'. The relationships between values, lifestyle and behaviour can be expressed as a hierarchical value–lifestyle–behaviour model (Figure 7.2).

In Figure 7.2 no link has been established between values and behaviour, because consumer research suggests that only a weak relation exists between these two concepts.[36] A distinction is made between social values and personal values. Social values define the desired behaviour or end-state for a society or group, whereas personal values define the desired behaviour or end-state for an individual. Support for the value–lifestyle–behaviour hierarchy has been found in Scandinavian research,[37] which, based on face-to-face survey interviews with 1,000 consumers, found that lifestyle 'intervenes between abstract goal states (personal values) and situation-specific product perceptions and behaviours'. In a similar way, other marketing scholars have pointed out that 'Lifestyles are defined as patterns in which people live and spend their time and money. They are primarily functions of consumers' values.'[38]

Consumers' preferences for certain values are likely to be expressed through their activities, interests and opinions, and ultimately through their consumption. For example, certain activities may be preferred by a person who values excitement (e.g. fast cars, mountain biking, bungee jumping). On the other hand, a person who prioritises security would be likely to have a different set of preferred activities (e.g. going for long walks in the country, attending religious services).[39] Consumer lifestyles are often measured by asking consumers about their activities (work, hobbies and vocations), interests (family, job and community) and opinions (about themselves, others, social issues, politics and business). AIO questions can be of a general nature or may be more specifically related to certain products or services. General types of AIO statements may be more useful for standardised mass consumption products, whereas product/service-related questions may be more useful for differentiated products or services.[40]

The interaction between dimensions

As individuals we are not born with the values and norms that form a culture; we learn them gradually as we grow older. For this learning process to take place the individual does need to be in contact with other individuals. Such contacts can be in the form of either direct social contacts (e.g. communicating with other individuals) or indirect social contacts (e.g. observing the behaviour or communication carried out by other individuals). In this way the social dimension mediates the cultural and individual dimensions. Although the process of learning takes place within a certain cultural context that is saturated with ready-made knowledge of consumption,[41] individuals should not be seen as passive creatures who automatically adopt values and norms from other individuals – they also have independent thoughts and feelings. For example, values of individuality and uncertainty avoidance – dominant values in Sweden and Greece,[42] respectively – are not automatically transferred to new generations in those countries. Individuals' thoughts and feelings can be used for active construction and reconstruction of knowledge. Moreover, some thoughts and feelings may be shared with other individuals who have similar or different thoughts and feelings. Over time such interactions may even influence values and norms in a society; see the marketing insight box.

While the individual interacts with the cultural and social settings, the starting point for understanding consumer behaviour is, however, the consumer her or himself. Reflecting this, the next section reviews the key psychological processes that influence how an individual perceives, evaluates and responds to marketing stimuli.

Marketing insight

Changing cultural norms and values

An example of how values and norms may change over time as people interact in society is found in relation to safe driving. In Denmark, more lives are lost in traffic accidents than in other northern European countries such as the United Kingdom, Sweden and Norway. As a result, the Danish Road Safety Council has as its objective a decrease in the number of serious traffic accidents in Denmark by 40 per cent by 2012. And one of the ways to achieve this goal is to motivate public debate and to influence people's values, norms and behaviour in relation to traffic safety. The council works to stir public debate on subjects such as speeding and drinking and driving, and has been successful with a series of information campaigns renowned for their originality and strong appeals.

As an example, the Danish Road Safety Council launched a campaign called 'Speedbandits' (www.speedbandits.dk) with the purpose of making young drivers aware of how fast they were driving. It had been found that although most young drivers knew the speed limits, many felt that there were 'legitimate' excuses not to remain within these – such as being in a hurry, knowing the road well, believing that they were in control of the situation and only risked their own lives, and so forth. In order to call attention to the notion that we should never speed in traffic, the council embarked upon a viral communication strategy: that is, an advertising message spread by consumers among other consumers (see Chapter 4). The campaign consisted of a single video film that was distributed on the internet, via links and Youtube.com. The video mimics a story on a make-believe TV newscast, and tells how the Danes developed new approaches to increasing safety in traffic. From now on, topless girls would stand by the side of the road holding speed signs, to remind drivers of their speed. The campaign was widely circulated and as such initiated communicative interaction between young people, who forwarded the link to friends, who forwarded to their friends, and so forth.

The video caused some offence in other Nordic countries, where it was interpreted as a negative portrayal of women. In Denmark, however, Speedbandits was interpreted primarily as a humorous and self-ironic campaign. It remains to be seen how the behaviour of young Danish drivers will develop in future years. In another traffic-related area, however, the Danish Road Safety Council has observed a clear positive change over the years. This change relates to drinking and driving – an issue that is also a top priority for the council. Here, campaigns that encourage being a team player (e.g. by sticking to agreements about who should drive), and encourage intervention (e.g. removing a person's car keys if he or she intends to drive after drinking alcohol) have helped alter values and discourse among the Danes, in the sense that drinking and driving generally has come to be considered completely unacceptable.

Source: Based on www.rfsf.dk (homepage of the Danish Road Safety Council); www.trafikklub.dk/db/files/hver_ulykke_er_en_for_meget_3.pdf.

Key psychological processes

The starting point for understanding consumer behaviour is the stimulus–response model shown in Figure 7.3. Marketing and environmental stimuli enter the consumer's consciousness, and a set of psychological processes combine with certain consumer characteristics to result in decision processes and purchase decisions. The marketer's task is to understand what happens in the consumer's consciousness between the arrival of the outside marketing stimuli and the ultimate purchase decisions. Four key psychological processes – motivation, perception, learning and memory – fundamentally influence consumer responses.[43]

Motivation: Freud, Maslow, Herzberg

We all have many needs at any given time. Some needs are *biogenic*; they arise from physiological states of tension such as hunger, thirst or discomfort. Other needs are *psychogenic*; they arise from psychological states of tension such as the need for recognition, esteem or belonging. A need becomes a **motive** when it is aroused to a sufficient level of intensity to drive us to act in order to reach a desired goal. Motivation has both direction – we select one goal over another; intensity – the vigour with which we pursue the goal; and persistency – is the motivation situational or enduring?

Three of the best-known theories of human motivation – those of Sigmund Freud, Abraham Maslow and Frederick Herzberg – carry quite different implications for consumer analysis and marketing strategy.

Freud's theory

Sigmund Freud assumed that the psychological forces shaping people's behaviour are largely unconscious, and that a person cannot fully understand, or may not even be aware of, his or her own motivations. When a person examines specific brands, she or he will react not only to their stated capabilities, but also to other, less conscious cues such as shape, size, weight, material, colour and brand name. A technique called *laddering* lets us trace a person's motivations from the stated instrumental ones to the more terminal ones. Then the marketer can decide at what level to develop the message and appeal.[44]

Motivation researchers often conduct 'in-depth interviews' with a few dozen consumers to uncover deeper motives triggered by a product. They use various *projective techniques* such as word association, sentence completion, picture interpretation and role playing, many pioneered by Ernest Dichter, a Viennese psychologist who settled in the United States.[45]

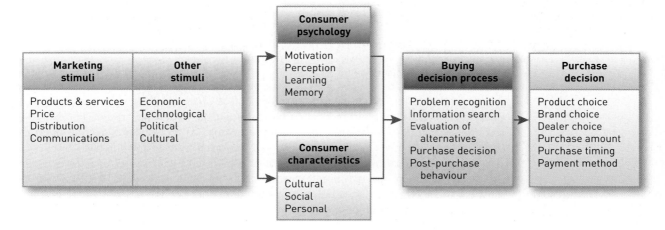

Figure 7.3 Model of consumer behaviour

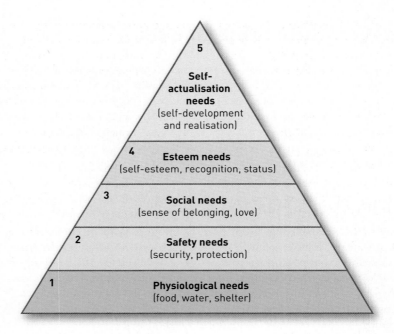

Figure 7.4 Maslow's hierarchy of needs
Source: Maslow, Abraham H.; Frager, Robert D. (Editor); Fadiman, James (Editor), *Motivation and Personality*, *3rd*, © 1987. Printed and electronically reproduced by permission of Pearson Education, Inc., Upper Saddle River, New Jersey.

Today motivational researchers continue the tradition of Freudian interpretation. Jan Callebaut identifies different motives a product can satisfy. For example, whisky can meet the need for social relaxation, status or fun. Different whisky brands need to be motivationally positioned in one of these three appeals.[46] Another motivation researcher, Clotaire Rapaille, works on breaking the 'code' behind a lot of product behaviour.[47]

Maslow's theory

Abraham Maslow sought to explain why people are driven by particular needs at particular times.[48] His answer is that human needs are arranged in a hierarchy from most to least pressing – (1) physiological needs, (2) safety needs, (3) social needs, (4) esteem needs, and (5) self-actualisation needs (see Figure 7.4). People will try to satisfy their most important needs first. When a person succeeds in satisfying an important need, he or she will then try to satisfy the next-most-important need. For example, a starving man (need 1) will not take an interest in the latest happenings in the art world (need 5), or in how he is viewed by others (need 3 or 4), or even in whether he is breathing clean air (need 2); but when he has enough food and water, the next-most-important need will become salient.

Herzberg's theory

Frederick Herzberg developed a two-factor theory that distinguishes *dissatisfiers* (factors that cause dissatisfaction) from *satisfiers* (factors that cause satisfaction).[49] The absence of dissatisfiers is not enough to motivate a purchase; satisfiers must be present. For example, a computer that does not come with a warranty would be a dissatisfier. Yet the presence of a product warranty would not act as a satisfier or motivator of a purchase, because it is not a source of intrinsic satisfaction. Ease of use would be a satisfier.

Herzberg's theory has two implications. First, sellers should do their best to avoid dissatisfiers (for example, a poor training manual or a poor service policy). Although these things will not sell a product, they might easily unsell it. Second, the seller should identify the major satisfiers or motivators of purchase in the market and then supply them. Support for Herzberg's two-factor theory was found in a Danish study investigating the effect of hygiene factors and motivators on visitors' experience and satisfaction with a visit to zoos and aquaria. Bad experiences with hygiene factors such as toilet facilities and eating or refreshment facilities created dissatisfaction with the visit as such, but positive experiences were obviously not capable of creating satisfaction by themselves.[50]

Perception

A motivated person is ready to act. *How* she acts is influenced by her view of the situation. In marketing, perceptions are more important than the reality, because it is perceptions that affect consumers' actual behaviour. **Perception** is the process by which we select, organise and interpret information inputs to create a meaningful picture of the world.[51] The key point is that it depends not only on the physical stimuli, but also on the stimuli's relationship to the surrounding field and on conditions within each of us. One person might perceive a fast-talking salesperson as aggressive and insincere; another, as intelligent and helpful. Each will respond differently to the salesperson. People can emerge with different perceptions of the same object because of three perceptual processes: selective attention, selective distortion and selective retention.

Selective attention

Attention is the allocation of processing capacity to some stimulus. Voluntary attention is something purposeful; involuntary attention is grabbed by someone or something. It is estimated that the average person may be exposed to over 1,500 ads or brand communications a day. Because we have limited mental resources we cannot possibly attend to all these, we screen most stimuli out – a process called **selective attention**. Selective attention means that marketers must work hard to attract consumers' notice. The real challenge is to explain which stimuli people will notice. Here are some findings:

1 **People are more likely to notice stimuli that relate to a current need.** A person who is motivated to buy a computer will notice computer ads; he or she will be less likely to notice mobile telephone ads.
2 **People are more likely to notice stimuli they anticipate.** You are more likely to notice computers than radios in a computer store because you don't expect the store to carry radios.
3 **People are more likely to notice stimuli whose deviations are large in relationship to the normal size of the stimuli.** You are more likely to notice an ad offering €5 off the list price of a bottle of wine than you are likely to notice an ad offering €5 off the list price of a computer. This phenomenon is also known as **Weber's law.**

Though we screen out much, we are influenced by unexpected stimuli, such as sudden offers in the mail, over the phone or from a salesperson. Marketers may attempt to promote their offers intrusively in order to bypass selective attention filters.

Selective distortion

Even noticed stimuli don't always come across in the way the senders intended. **Selective distortion** is the tendency to interpret information in a way that fits our preconceptions. Consumers will often distort information to be consistent with prior brand and product beliefs and expectations.[52]

For a stark demonstration of the power of consumer brand beliefs, consider that in 'blind' taste tests one group of consumers samples a product without knowing which brand it is, while another group knows. Invariably, the groups have different opinions, despite consuming *exactly the same product.*

When consumers report different opinions of branded and unbranded versions of identical products, it must be the case that their brand and product beliefs, created by whatever means (past experiences, marketing activity for the brand, something similar), have somehow changed their product perceptions. We can find examples with virtually every type of product.[53] When Coors changed its label from 'Banquet Beer' to 'Original Draft', consumers claimed the taste had changed even though the formulation had not.

Selective distortion can work to the advantage of marketers with strong brands when consumers distort neutral or ambiguous brand information to make it more positive. In other words, beer may seem to taste better, a car may seem to drive more smoothly, or the wait in a bank queue may seem shorter, depending on the particular brands involved.

Selective retention

Most of us don't remember much of the information to which we are exposed, but we do retain information that supports our attitudes and beliefs. Because of **selective retention**, we are likely to remember good points about a product we like and forget good points about competing products. Selective retention again works to the advantage of strong brands. It also explains why marketers need to use repetition – to make sure their message is not overlooked.

Subliminal perception

The selective perception mechanisms require consumers' active engagement and thought. A topic that has fascinated armchair marketers for ages is **subliminal perception**. They argue that marketers embed covert, subliminal messages on packaging or in ads – for example, saying 'buy it' or 'try it,' or displaying an ambiguous image. Consumers are not consciously aware of them, yet they affect behaviour. Although it is clear that our mental processes include many subtle subconscious effects,[54] no evidence supports the notion that marketers can systematically control consumers at that level, especially in terms of changing moderately important or strongly held beliefs.[55]

Learning

When we act, we learn. **Learning** induces changes in our behaviour arising from experience. Most human behaviour is learned, although much learning is incidental. Learning theorists believe that learning is produced through the interplay of drives, stimuli, cues, responses and reinforcement. Two popular approaches to learning are classical conditioning and operant (instrumental) conditioning.

A **drive** is a strong internal stimulus impelling action. **Cues** are minor stimuli that determine when, where and how a person responds. Suppose you buy an HP computer. If your experience is rewarding, your response to computers and HP will be positively reinforced. Later on, when you want to buy a printer, you may assume that because HP makes good computers, it also makes good printers. In other words, you *generalise* your response to similar stimuli. A countertendency to generalisation is discrimination. **Discrimination** means we have learned to recognise differences in sets of similar stimuli and can adjust our responses accordingly: that is, the ability to notice even small differences in product attributes (e.g. taste, smell, freshness) between brands is learned.

Learning theory teaches marketers that they can build demand for a product by associating it with strong drives, using motivating cues and providing positive reinforcement. A new company can enter the market by appealing to the same drives that competitors use and by providing similar cues, because buyers are more likely to transfer loyalty to similar brands (generalisation); or the company might design its brand to appeal to a different set of drives and offer strong cue inducements to switch (discrimination).

Some researchers prefer more active, cognitive approaches when learning depends upon the inferences or interpretations that consumers make about outcomes (was an unfavourable consumer experience due to a bad product or did the consumer fail to follow instructions properly?). The **hedonic bias** says that people have a general tendency to attribute success to themselves and failure to external causes. Consumers are thus more likely to blame a product than themselves, putting pressure on marketers to carefully explicate product functions in well-designed packaging and labels, instructive ads and websites, and so on.

Memory

All the information and experiences we encounter as we go through life can end up in our long-term memory. Cognitive psychologists distinguish between **short-term memory** (STM) – a temporary and limited repository of information – and **long-term memory** (LTM) – a more permanent, essentially unlimited repository.

Most widely accepted views of long-term memory structure assume we form some kind of associative model.[56] For example, the **associative network memory model** views LTM as a set of nodes and links. *Nodes* are stored information connected by *links* that vary in strength. Any type of information can be stored in the memory network, including verbal, visual, abstract and contextual. A spreading activation process from node to node determines how much we retrieve and what information we can actually recall in any given situation. When a node becomes activated because we are encoding external information (when we read or hear a word or phrase) or retrieving internal information from LTM (when we think about some concept), other nodes are also activated if they are strongly enough associated with that node.

In this model, we can think of consumer brand knowledge as a node in memory with a variety of linked associations. The strength and organisation of these associations will be important determinants of the information we can recall about the brand. **Brand associations** consist of all brand-related thoughts, feelings, perceptions, images, experiences, beliefs, attitudes and so on that become linked to the brand node. In 2011, Adidas launched a global campaign starring Katy Perry, David Beckham and Lionel Messi. The campaign pushes sub-brands Sport Performance, Adidas Originals and Adidas Sport Style, and aims to bring together the diversity of the brand under one strong roof in consumers' mind.[57]

Adidas aims to bring together the diversity of the brand under one strong roof in the consumer's mind

Source: Adidas

We can think of marketing as a way of making sure consumers have the right types of product and service experience to create the right brand knowledge structures and maintain them in memory. Companies such as Procter & Gamble like to create mental maps of consumers (i.e. representations of how consumers' perceive the physical world) that depict their knowledge of a particular brand in terms of the key associations that are likely to be triggered in a marketing setting, and their relative strength, favourability and uniqueness to consumers.

Memory processes

Memory is a very constructive process because we don't remember information and events completely and accurately. Often we remember bits and pieces and fill in the rest based upon whatever else we know.

Memory encoding describes how and where information gets into memory. The strength of the resulting association depends on how much we process the information at encoding (how much we think about it, for instance) and in what way.[58]

In general, the more attention we pay to the meaning of information during encoding, the stronger the resulting associations in memory will be.[59] When a consumer actively thinks about and 'elaborates' on the significance of product or service information, stronger associations are created in memory. It is also easier for consumers to create an association to new information when extensive, relevant knowledge structures already exist in memory. One reason why personal experiences create such strong brand associations is that information about the product is likely to be related to existing knowledge.

The ease with which we can integrate new information into established knowledge structures also clearly depends on its simplicity, vividness and concreteness. Repeated exposures to information, too, provide greater opportunity for processing and thus the potential for stronger associations. Recent advertising research in a field setting, however, suggests that high levels of repetition for an uninvolving, unpersuasive ad are unlikely to have as much sales impact as lower levels of repetition for an involving, persuasive ad.[60]

Memory retrieval

Memory retrieval is the way information gets out of memory. According to the associative network memory model, a strong brand association is both more accessible and more easily recalled by 'spreading activation'. Our successful recall of brand information does not depend only on the initial strength of that information in memory. Three factors are particularly important.

First, the presence of *other* product information in memory can produce interference effects and cause us either to overlook or to confuse new data. One marketing challenge in a category crowded with many competitors – for example, airlines, financial services and insurance companies – is that consumers may mix up brands.

Second, the time between exposure to information and encoding matters – the longer the time delay, the weaker the association. The time elapsed since the last exposure opportunity, however, has been shown generally to produce only gradual decay. Cognitive psychologists believe memory is extremely durable, so that once information becomes stored in memory, its strength of association decays very slowly.[61]

Third, information may be *available* in memory but not be *accessible* (able to be recalled) without the proper retrieval cues or reminders. The particular associations for a brand that come to mind depend on the context in which we consider it. The more cues linked to a piece of information, however, the greater the likelihood that we can recall it. The effectiveness of retrieval cues is one reason why marketing *inside* a supermarket or any retail store is so critical – the actual product packaging, the use of in-store minibillboard displays, and so on. The information they contain and the reminders they provide of advertising or other information already conveyed outside the store will be prime determinants of consumer decision making. Memory can often be reconstructive, however, and consumers may remember an experience with a brand differently after the fact due to intervening factors or other events.[62]

Perspectives on consumer behaviour

Understanding consumer behaviour may often be complicated since many different factors influence the behaviour and since many different forms of behaviour exist. Several perspectives on consumer behaviour can be considered.

The behaviourist perspective

The behaviourist perspective focuses on the impact of external influences on consumer behaviour. In the behaviourist perspective, the consumer is viewed as a 'black box' in the sense that the consumer's behaviour is a conditioned response to marketing stimuli. The complex mental processes that a consumer may undertake in relation to a certain choice situation are not given much attention in the behaviourist perspective and therefore this perspective is also often referred to as an S (stimuli)–R (response) approach. Classical conditioning and operant conditioning are two main theories that have been developed to explain the stimuli–response mechanism.

In classical conditioning, a stimulus with a 'known', or unconditioned, response (for example, lightning is regarded by most people as something powerful, fresh and natural) is paired with a stimulus with a 'neutral' response (for example, a chewing-gum brand). After several exposures to the two stimuli paired together, the consumer gradually learns to associate the chewing gum brand with – for a chewing gum producer – the very favourable characteristics of lightning. Classical conditioning is very often used in advertising – another example is pairing a popular music together with the products presented in TV commercials to generate positive feelings and liking towards the products.[63]

Operant conditioning presupposes that consumers are likely to repeat a behaviour for which they are positively rewarded (reinforced). For example, if a consumer receives a friendly smile when shopping at a retail outlet, she may be more likely to shop there again than if she has been ignored or, even worse, been exposed to a rude employee. While classical and operant conditioning are both part of the behaviourist perspective, they differ on when the learning takes place. In classical conditioning, the learning of associations between stimuli takes place before the response, whereas learning in operant conditioning takes place after the response.

The information-processing perspective

The information-processing perspective emerged in consumer behaviour in the 1960s and 1970s, and considers how consumers mentally process, store, retrieve and use marketing information in the decision process. The information-processing perspective posits that the interaction between the consumer and marketing information is an ongoing cognitive process in which the consumer develops beliefs and attitudes towards the marketing offer. The information-processing perspective presupposes that consumers behave as problem-solving cognitive individuals reaching for a reasoned decision.[64] The 'hierarchy of effects' information-processing model[65] suggests that a stimulus is first processed at its most basic level and then at more abstract levels. Consumers are expected to use their cognitive resources in forming beliefs (cognitive component) about the attributes of a product, which in turn may result in the development of an overall feeling or attitude (affective component) in the sense of liking/disliking a product. Consumers with a positive attitude towards a product are expected to be more willing to consider buying it (conative component) than consumers with a less positive attitude towards the same product.

The direct marketing implication of the information-processing perspective is that in order to sell their products and services, marketers should expose consumers to information about their offers. Consumers are assumed to use the information actively for the purpose of completing five decision-making activities, comprising problem recognition, information search, alternative evaluation, choice and post-purchase evaluation, where problem recognition and information search relate to the cognitive component, alternative evaluation relates to the cognitive and the affective components, choice relates to the conative component, and post-purchase evaluation relates to the cognitive and affective components. The Volvo website photo illustrates how market communication sometimes reflects the information-processing perspective.

The emotional perspective

In contrast to the information-processing perspective, the emotional perspective proposes that consumer affections, like emotional responses, should be included in the explanation of consumer decision making.[66] The consumer looks for new experiences via consumption. In this connection, the primary purpose is not to evaluate relations between attitude, beliefs and the environment, but to fulfil a desire and to obtain pleasure in life. Emotions are caused by consumers' exposure to specific stimuli. Surprise (an emotion), for instance, may be caused by an unexpected gift. The emotional perspective complements the information-processing perspective on consumer behaviour by taking into account consumers' affective responses, like the possible emotional responses to the perception and judgement of products and consumption experiences.

Marketing communication reflecting the information-processing perspective
Source: Courtesy of Volvo Car Corporation.

Breakthrough marketing

PANDORA

Danish jewellery maker PANDORA has taken insights from the emotional bonding experienced in the childhood collecting habit and channelled them towards a target audience of women aged 25 to 49. What really sparked the company's expansion was the creation of the PANDORA charm bracelet, which was introduced in Denmark in 2000. PANDORA offers numerous charms that women can purchase to reflect their personality, or a special occasion. Typically, consumers do not buy the entire 'package' at a time, but one that they can build on into 'infinity'. The charm bracelet concept became such a success that it was launched in the USA only a few years later (in 2003). In 2004, the concept was introduced in Australia and Germany. While the bracelet itself is not that expensive, the charms can be purchased in many different price categories. Because of the price differentiation, some of the charms are highly suitable for birthday or Christmas presents. Made from solid Sterling silver and gold with gemstones, the higher-priced charms may provide the wearer with a more exclusive appearance.

One of the main reasons for consumers' positive engagement with the PANDORA bracelet is probably that each charm may represent something that is important in a woman's life. Also, the idea of collecting charms can

Combine to Create
YOUR OWN STYLE

Become your own jewellery designer and create the combinations that feel just right for you. Design your own favourite combinations on pandora.net.

PANDŌRA
UNFORGETTABLE MOMENTS

PANDORA offers numerous charms that women can purchase to reflect their personality

Source: PANDORA/PANDORA 2012 Summer Advertisement

be seen as a continuation of childhood collecting and subsequently as a reflection of each woman's personal story and individuality. In the childhood, many girls (and boys...) collect all sorts of stuff (erasers, figurines, coins, etc.). According to the PANDORA website, the company mission is 'to offer women across the world a universe of high quality, hand-finished, modern and genuine jewellery products at affordable prices, thereby inspiring women to express their individuality'. According to PANDORA, 'all women have their individual stories to tell – a personal collection of special moments that makes them who they are. That is why we celebrate these moments.'

PANDORA makes other jewellery besides bracelets. Recently, the company introduced its 'new necklace concept', for which there are numerous opportunities to vary the appearance, and especially the style. Moreover, the PANDORA Black Crown Diamond Watch collection, offering consumers the possibility to exchange various parts (bezels and straps), was launched in 2010. At PANDORA's website it is possible to 'design' one's own jewellery. For example, a woman can choose a particular bracelet, equip it with the charms she likes, and immediately see the result. As she goes along, she can instantly see what the price will be. Although PANDORA is positioned as an 'affordable luxury' product, adding just 10–12 charms may quickly push prices up to €2,000, or even more.

PANDORA's products are now sold in more than 65 countries across six continents through over 10,000 points of sale, including more than 550 PANDORA branded concept stores. In 2010, total revenue was €895 million. Accounting for 14.9 per cent of total global sales and with a market growth of 110 per cent in 2010, the UK is the largest European market. As the company has expanded, the jewellery has since 1989 been produced in Thailand, where the company now runs four fully-owned manufacturing facilities. In autumn 2010, PANDORA was introduced at the NASDAQ OMX Copenhagen Stock Exchange.

Like many other popular global brands, PANDORA is faced with the challenge of counterfeiting and unauthorised sellers unlawfully using its brand name. Shoppers buying fakes at a fraction of the price could seriously damage the brand. To prevent this tendency from spreading, PANDORA continues to distinguish itself with the high quality of its products and the aspirational nature of its brand.

Questions

1 What risks does Pandora face? Can it continue with its charm bracelet concept?

2 Discuss the importance of a strong consumer brand to Pandora.

Sources: M. Costa (2011) Pandora has glamourised collecting for grown-ups but needs to protect its brand, *Marketing Week*, 16 February; www.pandora.net; Pandora Annual Report 2010; J. C. Hansen (2011) Hype og spekulation er Pandoras værste fjende, *Berlingske Tidende*, 16 April, 6; P. Tougaard (2011) Lidt kongelig har man da lov at være, *JydskeVestkysten*, 16 April, 14.

Consumer emotions have been shown to have several significant effects. Positive emotions can make one kinder, more generous, more resistant to temptation and more willing to delay self-rewards.[67] Consumers' emotions may also lead to action. As an example, the experience of a rude employee in a service company may lead to some internal reactions, such as 'displeasure'. These internal reactions may lead to complaints by the consumer. Emotions are based on the appraisals (i.e. conscious or unconscious judgement and interpretation of stimuli) that consumers make of stimuli in the environment.[68] A consumer who perceives a product to be of 'good quality' may form an affective response to this appraisal. It is not the product itself that may produce an emotional response, but the consumer's perception and judgement of the product. For example, a consumer may feel differently about a favourite food product after learning that this particular product contains higher levels of salt, sugar or fat than expected.

The cultural perspective

Over recent decades, consumer researchers have been increasingly interested in the cultural aspects of consumer behaviour. In the cultural perspective, marketing is seen as a value transmitter that simultaneously shapes culture and is shaped by it. Marketing is then a channel through which cultural meanings are transferred to consumer goods.[69] In this way, culture is the 'prism' through which consumers view products and try to make sense of their own and other people's consumer behaviour.[70] Products should therefore also be regarded as symbols – objects that represent beliefs, norms and values. While symbols may be used in this way for communication among social groups, marketers can also use symbols when positioning their products. Products are not bought just because they may deliver some wanted functional consequences – they are also bought because of their appearance, colour and name. The popularity of designer bags, sunglasses or shoes from, for example, Marc Jacobs, Dolce & Gabbana or Gucci is an example of this notion. However, the symbolic associations that consumers attach to various appearances, colours and names may vary widely across cultures. To exemplify, the Starbucks brand was found to have very different meanings to local coffee shop patrons in Seattle, who felt a sense of pride in the success Starbucks has experienced in recent years, and to young Japanese coffee shop visitors, who tended to view Starbucks as a symbol of an exciting, fashionable, contemporary lifestyle contrasting restrictive local traditions.[71]

A multiperspective approach

Consumers do not have unlimited mental resources available for receiving, evaluating and using information.[72] Often, therefore, consumers do not undertake comparative evaluations of various brands and associated attributes for the purpose of reaching a reasonable decision, as presupposed in the information processing perspective. Since consumers' processing capacity is limited, consumers cannot process large amounts of cognitive information in relation to all choice situations and may therefore seek to direct their use of mental resources at the information most easily available[73] or at the information offering the greatest relevant knowledge per used resource unit in the eyes of the consumer. Also, research results show that consumers might favour beliefs which are in accordance with a preferred conclusion.[74] Moreover, consumers who have strongly held preferences are likely to counter-argue preference-inconsistent information more than preference-consistent information.[75] These findings suggest that there is a resistance to devoting resources to change already established preferences and that consumers therefore may sometimes look for simple associations between product and expected benefit, which reinforce their established preferences or support their preferred conclusion. In this way, the behaviourist perspective complements the information-processing perspective.

Also, the relationship between emotions and cognition remains an issue in psychology and in consumer behaviour. Most consumer researchers[76] believe that we do not become emotional about unimportant things, but about values, goals, intentions, plans and so on. In other words, we cognitively perceive and evaluate what is happening in the environment and this 'knowledge' needs to be associated with personal relevant issues (e.g. personal well-being, well-being of relevant others, etc.) for an emotion to occur. Consumers' underlying evaluations of a situation combine to elicit specific emotions. For example, someone who has wrecked their car because they were talking on their mobile telephone and was therefore distracted may experience guilt, whereas someone whose car was wrecked by someone to whom they lent their car may be angry.[77] In other words, cognitions and emotions arise as a result of an interaction between consumers, objects and situations – and this interaction may differ across cultures and subcultures. When studying consumer behaviour it is therefore important that none of the different perspectives is excluded beforehand, but that the analyst keeps an open mind to various explanations for consumers' behaviour.

The buying decision process: the five-stage model

Psychological processes play an important role in understanding how consumers actually make their buying decisions.[78] Table 7.2 provides a list of some key consumer behaviour questions in terms of 'who, what, when, where, how and why'.

Smart companies try to fully understand the customers' buying decision process – all their experiences in learning, choosing, using and even disposing of a product.[79] Unilever uses social media, especially Facebook, to investigate consumer buying behaviour. Social media can give you a very quick gauge on things. Our job as marketers is to ask, 'What are the key things that I need to look for?'", says Rachel Bristow, marketing and communications buying director, Unilever.[80]

Marketing scholars have developed a 'stage model' of the buying decision process (see Figure 7.5). The consumer passes through five stages: problem recognition, information search, evaluation of alternatives, purchase decision and post-purchase behaviour. Clearly, the buying process starts long before the actual purchase and has consequences long afterwards.[81]

Consumers don't always pass through all five stages in buying a product. They may skip or reverse some. When you buy your regular brand of toothpaste, you go directly from the need for toothpaste to the purchase decision, skipping information search and evaluation. The model in Figure 7.5 provides a good frame of reference, however, because it captures the full range of considerations that arise when a consumer faces a highly involving new purchase.[82]

Problem recognition

The buying process starts when the buyer recognises a problem or need triggered by internal or external stimuli. With an internal stimulus, one of the person's normal needs – hunger, thirst, sex – rises to a threshold level and becomes a drive; or a need can be aroused by an external stimulus. A person may admire a neighbour's new car or see a television ad for a Madeiran holiday, which triggers thoughts about the possibility of making a purchase.

Marketers need to identify the circumstances that trigger a particular need by gathering information from a number of consumers. They can then develop marketing strategies that trigger consumer interest. Particularly for discretionary purchases such as luxury goods,

Table 7.2 Understanding consumer behaviour

Who buys our product or service?
Who makes the decision to buy the product?
Who influences the decision to buy the product?
How is the purchase decision made? Who assumes what role?
What does the customer buy? What needs must be satisfied?
Why do customers buy a particular brand?
Where do they go or look to buy the product or service?
When do they buy? Any seasonality factors?
How is our product perceived by customers?
What are customers' attitudes towards our product?
What social factors might influence the purchase decision?
Do customers' lifestyles influence their decisions?
How do personal or demographic factors influence the purchase decision?

Source: Based on a list in G. Belch and M. Belch (2004) *Advertising and Promotion*, 6th edn, Homewood, IL: Irwin. Copyright © 2004 McGraw-Hill Companies.

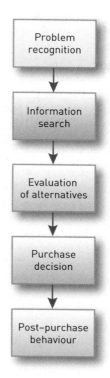

Figure 7.5 Five-stage model of the consumer buying process

holidays and entertainment options, marketers may need to increase consumer motivation so that a potential purchase gets serious consideration.

Information search

Surprisingly, consumers often search for limited amounts of information. Surveys have shown that for durables, half of all consumers look at only one shop, and only 30 per cent look at more than one brand of appliance. We can distinguish between two levels of involvement with search. The milder search state is called *heightened attention*. At this level a person simply becomes more receptive to information about a product. At the next level, the person may enter an *active information search*: looking for reading material, phoning friends, going online and visiting shops to learn about the product.

Information sources

Major information sources to which consumers will turn fall into four groups:

- **Personal**: family, friends, neighbours, acquaintances;
- **Commercial**: advertising, websites, salespeople, dealers, packaging, displays;
- **Public**: mass media, consumer-rating organisations;
- **Experiential**: handling, examining, using the product.

The relative amount and influence of these sources vary with the product category and the buyer's characteristics. Generally speaking, the consumer receives the most information about a product from commercial – that is, marketer-dominated – sources. However, the most effective information often comes from personal sources or public sources that are independent authorities.

Each information source performs a different function in influencing the buying decision. Commercial sources normally perform an information function, whereas personal sources perform a legitimising or evaluation function. For example, doctors often learn of new drugs from commercial sources but turn to other doctors for evaluations.

Search dynamics

Through gathering information, the consumer learns about competing brands and their features. The first box in Figure 7.6 shows the *total set* of brands available to the consumer. The individual consumer will come to know only a subset of these brands, the *awareness set*. Some brands, the *consideration set*, will meet initial buying criteria. As the consumer gathers more information, only a few, the *choice set*, will remain strong contenders. The consumer makes a final choice from this set.[83]

Marketers need to identify the hierarchy of attributes that guide consumer decision making in order to understand different competitive forces and how these various sets get formed. This process of identifying the hierarchy is called **market partitioning**. Years ago, most car buyers first decided on the manufacturer and then on one of its car divisions (*brand-dominant hierarchy*). A buyer might favour General Motors' cars and, within this set, a Saab. Today, many buyers decide first on the nation from which they want to buy a car (*nation-dominant hierarchy*). Buyers may first decide they want to buy a German car, then Audi, and then the A4 model of Audi.

The hierarchy of attributes can also reveal customer segments. Buyers who first decide on price are price dominant; those who first decide on the type of car (sports, passenger, estate car) are type dominant; those who first decide on the car brand are brand dominant. Type/price/brand-dominant consumers make up a segment; quality/service/type buyers make up another. Each segment may have distinct demographics, psychographics and mediagraphics, and different awareness, consideration and choice sets.[84]

Figure 7.6 makes it clear that a company must strategise to get its brand into the prospect's awareness, consideration and choice sets. As another example, if a food shop owner arranges yogurt first by brand (such as Danone and Yoplait) and then by flavour within each brand, consumers will tend to select their flavours from the same brand. However, if all the strawberry yogurts are together, then all the vanilla and so forth, consumers will probably choose which flavours they want first, and then choose the brand name they want for that particular flavour. Australian supermarkets arrange meats by the way they might be cooked, and shops use more descriptive labels, such as 'a 10-minute herbed beef roast'. The result is that Australians buy a greater variety of meats than US shoppers, who choose from meats laid out by animal type – beef, chicken, pork and so on.[85]

The company must also identify the other brands in the consumer's choice set so that it can plan the appropriate competitive appeals. In addition, the company should identify

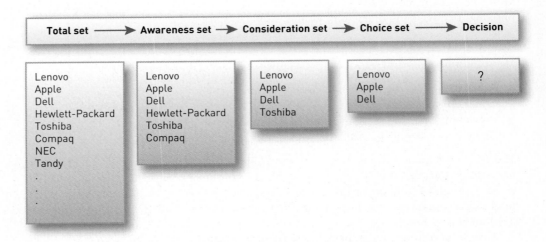

Figure 7.6 Successive sets involved in consumer decision making

the consumer's information sources and evaluate their relative importance. Asking consumers how they first heard about the brand, what information came later, and the relative importance of the different sources will help the company prepare effective communications for the target market.

Evaluation of alternatives

How does the consumer process competitive brand information and make a final value judgement? No single process is used by all consumers, or by one consumer in all buying situations. There are several processes, and the most current models see the consumer forming judgements largely on a conscious and rational basis.

Some basic concepts will help us understand consumer evaluation processes. First, the consumer is trying to satisfy a need. Second, the consumer is looking for certain benefits from the product solution. Third, the consumer sees each product as a bundle of attributes with varying abilities for delivering the benefits sought to satisfy this need. The attributes of interest to buyers vary by product – for example:

- **hotels**: location, cleanliness, atmosphere, price;
- **mouthwash**: colour, effectiveness, germ-killing capacity, taste/flavour, price;
- **tyres**: safety, tread life, ride quality, price.

Consumers will pay the most attention to attributes that deliver the sought-after benefits. We can often segment the market for a product according to attributes important to different consumer groups.

Beliefs and attitudes

Through experience and learning, people acquire beliefs and attitudes. These in turn influence buying behaviour. A **belief** is a descriptive thought that a person holds about something. Just as important are **attitudes**, a person's enduring favourable or unfavourable evaluations, emotional feelings and action tendencies towards some object or idea.[86] People have attitudes towards almost everything: religion, politics, clothes, music, food. Attitudes put us into a frame of mind: liking or disliking an object, moving towards or away from it. They lead us to behave in a fairly consistent way towards similar objects. Because attitudes economise on energy and thought, they can be very difficult to change. A company is often well advised to fit its product into existing attitudes rather than to try to change attitudes. For instance, Arla Foods ran an ad campaign with the slogan 'Good Food Deserves Lurpak' (a butter brand). To many, butter may not be interesting in itself, but because of what it does to the taste experience of a well-prepared meal. Hence, the basic idea was to remind consumers of an existing attitude: namely, that Lurpak tastes better than competing brands and products.[87]

Here's another example of a campaign that reminds consumers of their attitudes.

Six a day

The 'six-a-day' campaign was launched as a research and development project in 1999, based on research findings that eating more fruit and vegetables was preventive to such illnesses as cancer, heart disease, obesity and diabetes. The objective was to persuade Danish consumers to eat more fruit and vegetables – and the recommended amount was 600 g – or roughly six pieces of fruit or vegetables a day. Research had shown that most consumers were well aware of the health benefits of eating fruit and vegetables. However, research also showed that many consumers found previous health campaigns untrustworthy and irrelevant to them. So, the campaign's intention was to to increase relevance and influence behaviour by reminding consumers of their positive attitudes towards eating fruit and vegetables. This was done by:

- providing information on the health benefits of eating fruit and vegetables;

- communicating ideas of how to prepare and serve fruit and vegetables to ensure eating as close as possible to the recommended amount of 600 g each day; and

- working to make it easier to get fruit and vegetables – for instance, in schools.

The campaign was designed by a number of governmental agencies and non-profit organisations, including the Danish Cancer Society, the Danish Veterinary and Food Administration, and the Danish Heart Foundation, among others, which joined forces to broaden knowledge and relevance of the 'six-a-day' recommendation through a number of different channels and strategies, such as the design of a shared logo, the creation of inspiring promotional material and active participation in events, meetings, presentations and so on. As regards media coverage, this campaign employed the internet, newsletters, trade journals and the popular press, but shied away from advertising in 'regular' media such as TV, radio and magazines.

In just five years, the 'six-a-day' campaign helped increase average consumption of fruit and vegetables per day by 100 g (to 379 g) for adults, and by 40 g (to 322 g) for children.[88] However, much still needs to be done in this area. A 2011 GFK survey indicates that 60 per cent of adults consume only half, or less than half, of the recommended amount of fruit and vegetables.[89]

Expectancy-value model

The consumer arrives at attitudes towards various brands through an attribute evaluation procedure.[90] She develops a set of beliefs about where each brand stands on each attribute. The **expectancy-value model** of attitude formation posits that consumers evaluate products and services by combining their brand beliefs – the positives and negatives – according to importance.

Suppose Swedish student Helena Olsson has narrowed her choice set to four laptop computers (A, B, C, D). Assume she's interested in four attributes: memory capacity, graphics capability, size and weight, and price. Table 7.3 shows her beliefs about how each brand rates on the four attributes. If one computer dominated the others on all the criteria, we could predict that Helena would choose it. But, as is often the case, her choice set consists of brands that vary in their appeal. If Helena wants the best memory capacity, she should buy A; if she wants the best graphics capability, she should buy B; and so on.

If we knew the weights Helena attaches to the four attributes, we could more reliably predict her computer choice. Suppose she assigned 40 per cent of the importance to the computer's memory capacity, 30 per cent to graphics capability, 20 per cent to size and weight, and 10 per cent to price. To find Helena's perceived value for each computer,

Table 7.3 A consumer's brand beliefs about laptop computers

Computer	Attribute			
	Memory capacity	**Graphics capability**	**Size and weight**	**Price**
A	10	8	6	4
B	8	9	8	3
C	6	8	10	5
D	4	3	7	8

Note: Each attribute is rated from 0 to 10, where 10 represents the highest level on that attribute. Price, however, is indexed in a reverse manner, with a 10 representing the lowest price because a consumer prefers a low price to a high price.

according to the expectancy-value model, we multiply her weights by her beliefs about each computer's attributes. This computation leads to the following perceived values:

Computer A = 0.4(10) + 0.3(8) + 0.2(6) + 0.1(4) = 8.0
Computer B = 0.4(8) + 0.3(9) + 0.2(8) + 0.1(3) = 7.8
Computer C = 0.4(6) + 0.3(8) + 0.2(10) + 0.1(5) = 7.3
Computer D = 0.4(4) + 0.3(3) + 0.2(7) + 0.1(8) = 4.7

An expectancy-model formulation predicts that Helena will favour computer A, which (at 8.0) has the highest perceived value.[91]

Suppose most computer buyers form their preferences the same way. Knowing this, the marketer of computer B, for example, could apply the following strategies to stimulate greater interest in brand B:

- **Redesign the computer**. This technique is called *real repositioning*.
- **Alter beliefs about the brand**. Attempting to alter beliefs about the brand is called *psychological repositioning*.
- **Alter beliefs about competitors' brands**. This strategy, called *competitive depositioning*, makes sense when buyers mistakenly believe a competitor's brand has more quality than it actually has.
- **Alter the importance weights**. The marketer could try to persuade buyers to attach more importance to the attributes in which the brand excels.
- **Call attention to neglected attributes**. The marketer could draw buyers' attention to neglected attributes, such as styling or processing speed.
- **Shift the buyer's ideals**. The marketer could try to persuade buyers to change their ideal levels for one or more attributes:[92] for example, changing buyers' opinion regarding the ideal size for a computer.

Purchase decision

In the evaluation stage, the consumer forms preferences among the brands in the choice set. The consumer may also form an intention to buy the most preferred brand. In executing a purchase intention, the consumer may make up to five subdecisions: brand (brand A), dealer (dealer 2), quantity (one computer), timing (weekend) and payment method (credit card).

Non-compensatory models of consumer choice

The expectancy-value model is a compensatory model, in that perceived good things for a product can help to overcome perceived bad things. But consumers often take 'mental short cuts' using simplifying choice heuristics. **Heuristics** are rules of thumb or mental short cuts in the decision process.

With **non-compensatory models** of consumer choice, positive and negative attribute considerations don't necessarily net out. Evaluating attributes in isolation makes decision making easier for a consumer, but it also increases the likelihood that he would have made a different choice if he had deliberated in greater detail. We highlight three such choice heuristics here.

1 With the **conjunctive heuristic**, the consumer sets a minimum acceptable cut-off level for each attribute and chooses the first alternative that meets the minimum standard for all attributes. For example, if Helena decided all attributes had to rate at least a 5, she would choose computer C. She would not choose computers A, B or D since computers A and B rate only 4 and 3, respectively, on price, and computer D rates only 4 on memory capacity and 3 on graphics capability.
2 With the **lexicographic heuristic**, the consumer chooses the best brand on the basis of its perceived most important attribute (i.e. memory capacity). With this decision rule, Helena would choose computer A, which has the highest rate on this attribute.

3 With the **elimination-by-aspects heuristic**, the consumer compares brands on an attribute selected probabilistically – where the probability of choosing an attribute is positively related to its importance – and eliminates brands that do not meet minimum acceptable cut-offs.

Our brand or product knowledge, the number and similarity of brand choices and time pressure involved, and the social context (such as the need for justification to a peer or boss) may all affect whether and how we use choice heuristics.[93]

Consumers don't necessarily use only one type of choice rule. Sometimes they adopt a phased decision strategy that combines two or more. For example, they might use a non-compensatory decision rule such as the conjunctive heuristic to reduce the number of brand choices to a more manageable number, and then evaluate the remaining brands. One reason for the runaway success of the Intel Inside campaign in the 1990s was that it made the brand the first cut-off for many consumers – they would only buy a personal computer that had an Intel microprocessor. Personal computer makers such as Lenovo, Dell and Gateway had no choice but to support Intel's marketing efforts.

Intervening factors

Even if consumers form brand evaluations, two general factors can intervene between the purchase intention and the purchase decision (Figure 7.7).[94] The first is the *attitudes of others*. The extent to which another person's attitude reduces our preference for an alternative depends on two things: (1) the intensity of the other person's negative attitude towards our preferred alternative; and (2) our motivation to comply with the other person's wishes.[95] The more intense the other person's negativism and the closer the other person is to us, the more we will adjust our purchase intention. The converse is also true.

Related to the attitudes of others is the role played by suppliers of consumer and market information who publish their evaluations. Examples include *Consumer Reports*, which provides unbiased expert reviews of all types of products and services; J. D. Power, which provides consumer-based ratings of cars, financial services and travel products and services; professional film, book and music reviewers; customer reviews of books and music on Amazon.com; and the increasing number of chatrooms, bulletin boards, blogs and so

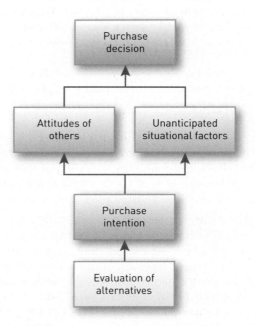

Figure 7.7 Steps between evaluation of alternatives and a purchase decision

on where people discuss products, services and companies. Consumers are undoubtedly influenced by these evaluations, as evidenced by the success of a small-budget film such as *Napoleon Dynamite*, which cost only €270,000 to make but grossed over €30 million at the box office thanks to a slew of favourable reviews by cinemagoers on many websites.

The second factor is *unanticipated situational factors* that may erupt to change the purchase intention. Helena might lose her job, some other purchase might become more urgent, or a store salesperson may turn her off. Preferences and even purchase intentions are not completely reliable predictors of purchase behaviour.

A consumer's decision to modify, postpone or avoid a purchase decision is heavily influenced by *perceived risk*.[96] Consumers may perceive many types of risk in buying and consuming a product:

- **Functional risk**. The product does not perform up to expectations.
- **Physical risk**. The product poses a threat to the physical well-being or health of the user or others.
- **Financial risk**. The product is not worth the price paid.
- **Social risk**. The product results in embarrassment from others.
- **Psychological risk**. The product does not conform to the consumer's perceived self-image.
- **Time risk**. The failure of the product results in an opportunity cost of finding another satisfactory product.

The amount of perceived risk varies with the amount of money at stake, the amount of attribute uncertainty and the amount of consumer self-confidence. Consumers develop routines for reducing the uncertainty and negative consequences of risk, such as decision avoidance, information gathering from friends, and preferences for national brand names and warranties. Marketers must understand the factors that provoke a feeling of risk in consumers and provide information and support to reduce perceived risk.

Post-purchase behaviour

After the purchase, the consumer might experience dissonance that stems from noticing certain disquieting features or hearing favourable things about other brands and will be alert to information that supports his or her decision. Marketing communications should supply beliefs and evaluations that reinforce the consumer's choice and help them feel good about the brand.

The marketer's job does not therefore end with the purchase. Marketers must monitor post-purchase satisfaction, post-purchase actions and post-purchase product uses.

Post-purchase satisfaction

Satisfaction is a function of the closeness between expectations and the product's perceived performance.[97] If performance falls short of expectations, the consumer is *disappointed*; if it meets expectations, the consumer is *satisfied*; if it exceeds expectations, the consumer is *delighted*. The larger the gap between expectations and performance, the greater the dissatisfaction. Here the consumer's coping style comes into play. Some consumers magnify the gap when the product is not perfect and are highly dissatisfied; others minimise it and are less dissatisfied.[98]

Post-purchase actions

If the consumer is satisfied, he or she is more likely to purchase the product again. The satisfied customer will also tend to say good things about the brand to others. On the other hand, dissatisfied consumers may abandon or return the product. They may seek information that confirms its high value. They may take public action by complaining to the company, going to a lawyer or complaining to other groups (such as business, private or government agencies). Private actions include deciding to stop buying the product (*exit option*) or warning friends (*voice option*).[99]

Many companies seek to build long-term brand loyalty through 'loyalty programmes'. Post-purchase communications to buyers have been shown to result in fewer product returns and order cancellations. Computer companies, for example, can send a letter to new owners congratulating them on having selected a fine computer. They can place ads showing satisfied brand owners. They can solicit customer suggestions for improvements and list the location of available services. They can write intelligible instruction booklets. They can send owners a magazine containing articles describing new computer applications. In addition, they can provide good channels for speedy redress of customer grievances. However, there may still be room for improvement. A 2011 Forrester report, which surveyed over 50 global marketing leaders, found that more than a third of chief marketing officers (CMOs) are unhappy with the 'erratic' performance of their loyalty programmes. Even though 79 per cent of CMOs think customer retention is the key metric used by senior management to evaluate loyalty, CMOs admit that loyalty marketing often focuses too much on short-term financial goals and that it may have unclear objectives.[100]

Post-purchase use and disposal

Marketers should also monitor how buyers use and dispose of the product (Figure 7.8). A key driver of sales frequency is product consumption rate – the more quickly buyers consume a product, the sooner they may be back in the market to repurchase it.

One opportunity to increase frequency of product use occurs when consumers' perceptions of their usage differ from reality. Consumers may fail to replace products with relatively short life spans soon enough because they overestimate their product life.[101] One strategy to speed up replacement is to tie the act of replacing the product to a certain holiday, event or time of year.

For example, Duracell has run battery promotions tied in with the springtime switch to daylight-saving time. Another strategy is to provide consumers with better information about either: when they first used the product or need to replace it; or its current level of performance. Batteries have built-in gauges that show how much power they have left; toothbrushes have colour indicators to indicate when the bristles are worn; and so on. Perhaps the simplest way to increase usage is to learn when actual usage is less than recommended and persuade customers of the merits of more regular usage, overcoming potential hurdles.

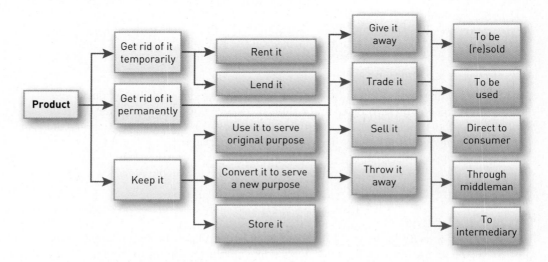

Figure 7.8 How customers use or dispose of products
Source: J. Jacoby, C. K. Berning and T. F. Dietvorst (1977) What about disposition?, *Journal of Marketing*, July, 23. Reprinted with permission of the American Marketing Association.

Blue Indicator bristles fade over time to show that the brush head needs replacing

One way to increase frequency of purchase is to remind consumers when it is time to replace batteries or toothbrushes.
Source: Courtesy of Procter & Gamble UK.

If consumers throw the product away, the marketer needs to know how they dispose of it, especially if – as with batteries, beverage containers, electronic equipment and disposable nappies – it can damage the environment. There is increasing pressure on companies to manage their businesses in an environmentally responsible way. Knowing consumers' disposal behaviour enables companies to be better informed about appropriate disposal behaviour.

Other theories of consumer decision making

The consumer decision process may not always develop in a carefully planned fashion. Here are some other theories and approaches to explain it.

Level of consumer involvement

The expectancy-value model assumes a high level of involvement on the part of the consumer. We can define **consumer involvement** in terms of the level of engagement and active processing the consumer undertakes in responding to a marketing stimulus. A highly involved consumer is more likely to process a large amount of cognitive information. Celsi and Olson (1988: 211) conceptualise involvement as follows: 'like most consumer researchers, we view perceived personal relevance as the essential characteristic of involvement'.[102] Consumers may be involved in buying a product for various reasons, and different consumers may not be involved for the same reason. Consumers may purchase perfume because of its capacity to give pleasure, whereas consumers are more likely to focus on avoiding the negative consequences of a bad choice when buying a vacuum cleaner.[103] In general, factors such as high price, high perceived risk and high product heterogeneity are likely to increase the degree of consumer involvement.

Elaboration likelihood model

Psychologists Richard Petty and John Cacioppo's *elaboration likelihood model*, an influential model of attitude formation and change, describes how consumers make evaluations in both low- and high-involvement circumstances.[104] There are two means of persuasion in their model: the *central route*, where attitude formation or change stimulates much thought and is based on a diligent, rational consideration of the most important product information; and the *peripheral route*, where attitude formation or change provokes much less thought and results from the association of a brand with either positive or negative peripheral cues. *Peripheral cues* for consumers include a celebrity endorsement, a credible source, or any object that generates positive feelings.

Consumers follow the central route only if they possess sufficient motivation, ability and opportunity. In other words, consumers must want to evaluate a brand in detail, have the necessary brand and product or service knowledge in memory, and have sufficient time and the proper setting. If any of those factors is lacking, consumers tend to follow the peripheral route and consider less central, more extrinsic factors in their decisions.

Low-involvement marketing strategies

Many products are bought under conditions of low involvement and the absence of significant brand differences. Consider salt. Consumers have little involvement in this product category. If they keep reaching for the same brand, it is out of habit, not strong brand loyalty. Evidence suggests consumers have low involvement with most low-cost, frequently purchased products.

Marketers use four techniques to try to convert a low-involvement product into one of higher involvement. First, they can link the product to some involving issue, as when Crest linked its toothpaste to avoiding cavities. Second, they can link the product to some involving personal situation – for example, fruit juice makers began to include vitamins such as calcium to fortify their drinks. Third, they might design advertising to trigger strong emotions related to personal values or ego defence, as when cereal makers began to advertise to adults the heart-healthy nature of cereals and the importance of living a long time to enjoy family life. Fourth, they might add an important feature – as for example when Sony PlayStation and Microsoft Xbox launched options for multiplayer online gaming. These strategies at best raise consumer involvement from a low to a moderate level; they do not necessarily propel the consumer into highly involved buying behaviour.

If, regardless of what the marketer can do, consumers will have low involvement with a purchase decision, they are likely to follow the peripheral route. Marketers must pay special attention to giving consumers one or more positive cues to justify their brand choice. For instance, frequent ad repetition, visible sponsorships and vigorous PR are all ways to enhance brand familiarity. Other peripheral cues that can tip the balance in favour of the brand include a beloved celebrity endorser, attractive packaging and an appealing promotion.[105]

Variety-seeking buying behaviour

Some buying situations are characterised by low involvement but significant brand differences. Here consumers often do a lot of brand switching. Think about biscuits. The consumer has some beliefs about biscuits, chooses a brand without much evaluation, and evaluates the product during consumption. Next time, the consumer may reach for another brand out of a desire for a different taste. Brand switching occurs for the sake of variety rather than dissatisfaction.

The market leader and the minor brands in this product category have different marketing strategies. The market leader will try to encourage habitual buying behaviour by dominating the shelf space with a variety of related but different product versions, avoiding out-of-stock conditions, and sponsoring frequent reminder advertising. Challenger firms will encourage variety seeking by offering lower prices, deals, coupons, free samples, and advertising that tries to break the consumer's purchase and consumption cycle and presents reasons for trying something new.

The theory of planned behaviour

In contrast to the low-involvement, variety-seeking situations, the theory of planned behaviour (Figure 7.9) is concerned with situations where consumers are involved and motivated to conduct an in-depth evaluation of the expected outcome of various choices before the purchase is made. TPB is an extension of its precursor, the theory of reasoned action (TRA). TRA regards a consumer's behaviour as determined by the consumer's behavioural intention, where behavioural intention is a function of 'attitude towards the behaviour' (i.e. the general feeling of favourableness or unfavourableness for that behaviour) and 'subjective norm' (i.e. the perceived opinion of other people in relation to the behaviour in question).[106] The theory predicts intention to perform a behaviour by consumer's attitude towards that behaviour rather than by the consumer's attitude towards a product or service. In the model, attitude is based on the consumer's behavioural beliefs – a behavioural belief is the subjective probability that a certain behaviour will produce a given outcome. Also, a consumer's intention to perform a certain behaviour may be influenced by the normative social beliefs held by the consumer. As an example, a consumer might have a very favourable attitude towards having a drink before dinner at

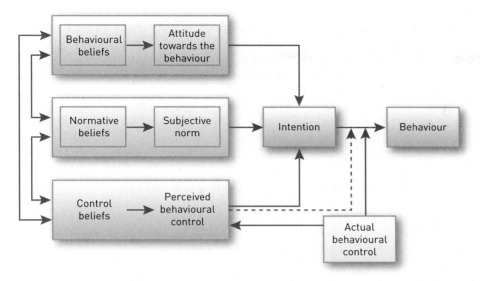

Figure 7.9 The theory of planned behaviour
Source: I. Aizen (2006) TpB diagram Copyright © 2006 Icek Aizen (retrieved from www.people.umass.edu/aizen/tpb.diag.html). Reproduced with permission.

a restaurant. However, the intention to actually order the drink may be influenced by the consumer's beliefs about the appropriateness (i.e. the perceived social norm) of ordering a drink in the current situation (with friends for a fun meal or on a job interview) and her or his motivation to comply with those normative beliefs.[107] TRA is concerned with rational, volitional and systematic behaviour: that is, behaviours over which the individual has control.[108] This assumption has been widely criticised. For example, a consumer may be prevented from buying groceries online if the consumer perceives the purchase process as too complex or if the consumer does not possess the resources necessary to perform the considered behaviour. Such considerations are incorporated into TPB.[109] In comparison with TRA, TPB adds 'perceived behavioural control' as a determinant of behavioural intention. TPB is therefore an extension of TRA. PBC can be conceptualised as the consumer's subjective belief about how difficult it will be for that consumer to generate the behaviour in question. PBC is determined by the total set of accessible control beliefs, that is, beliefs about the presence of factors that may facilitate or impede performance of the behaviour.[110] For instance, a consumer may be keen to go to a very popular concert yet, knowing that it will be difficult to get tickets, she may give up her intention without even trying to realise it.

Means–end chains

In the means–end chain model (MEC model), products are not purchased for themselves or their characteristics, but rather for the meanings they engender in the mind of the consumer (e.g. buying this product would make me happy, would be good for my health, or something similar). The MEC model explores the meanings a consumer attaches to a product through the construction of an associative network, which consists of attributes, functional consequences, psychosocial consequences and values. In this way, the MEC model proposes that consumer knowledge structures are hierarchically organised, referring to different levels of abstraction.[111] While attributes are the distinct characteristics of a product, such as consistency, price, colour, size, ingredients, and so on, functional consequences are the tangible outcomes of using the product. For example, a new toothbrush might brush your teeth gently and effectively. Psychosocial consequences, in contrast, describe the psychological and social outcomes of the product. For example, having clean teeth might make you feel more attractive and comfortable. Values are centrally held cognitive elements that trigger motivation for behaviour, referring to more abstract concepts such as self-esteem, health or happiness. The means–end approach assumes that consumers regard products as means to important ends. That is, the personal consequences produced by a product are more important (more self-relevant) than the characteristics of the product itself. A product is self-relevant to the extent that a consumer sees it as instrumental in achieving important consequences or values.[112] As an example, a large (and growing) proportion of consumers view the internet (and hence internet access) as an indispensable and central component of their lives. To these consumers, internet services have been integrated in daily routines and are seen as helping them to cope with everyday stress and difficulties.[113]

Behavioural decision theory and behavioural economics

As you might guess from low-involvement decision making and variety seeking, consumers don't always process information or make decisions in a deliberate, rational manner. One of the most active academic research areas in marketing over the past three decades has been *behavioural decision theory* (BDT). Behavioural decision theorists have identified many situations in which consumers make seemingly irrational choices. Table 7.4 summarizes some provocative findings from this research.[114]

What all these and other studies reinforce is that consumer behaviour is very constructive and the context of decisions really matters. Understanding how these effects show up in the marketplace can be crucial for marketers.

The work of these and other academics has also challenged predictions from economic theory and assumptions about rationality, leading to the emergence of the field of *behavioural economics*.[115] Here, we review some of the issues in three broad areas – decision heuristics, framing and other contextual effects. The marketing insight box summarises one in-depth treatment of the topic.

Table 7.4 Selected behavioural decision theory findings

- Consumers are more likely to choose an alternative (a home bread maker) after a relatively inferior option (a slightly better, but significantly more expensive home bread maker) is added to the available choice set.

- Consumers are more likely to choose an alternative that appears to be a compromise in the particular choice set under consideration, even if it is not the best alternative on any one dimension.

- The choices consumers make influence their assessment of their own tastes and preferences.

- Getting people to focus their attention more on one of two considered alternatives tends to enhance the perceived attractiveness and choice probability of that alernative.

- The way consumers compare products that vary in price and perceived quality (by features or brand name) and the way those products are displayed in the store (by brand or by model type) both affect their willingness to pay more for additional features or a better-known brand.

- Consumers who think about the possibility that their purchase decisions will turn out to be wrong are more likely to choose better-known brands.

- Consumers for whom possible feelings of regret about missing an opportunity have been made more relevant are more likely to choose a product currently on sale than to wait for a better sale or buy a higher-priced item.

- Consumers' choices are often influenced by subtle (and theoretically inconsequential) changes in the way alternatives are described.

(Continued)

Table 7.4 *(Continued)*

- Consumers who make purchases for later consumption appear to make systematic errors in predicting their future preferences.

- Consumers' predictions of their future tastes are not accurate – they do not really know how they will feel after consuming the same flavour of yogurt or ice cream several times.

- Consumers often overestimate the duration of their overall emotional reactions to future events (movies, financial windfalls, outcomes of sporting events).

- Consumers often overestimate their future consumption, especially if there is limited availability (which may explain why Black Jack and other gums have higher sales when availability is limited to several months per year than when they are offered year round).

- In anticipating future consumption opportunities, consumers often assume they will want or need more variety than they actually do.

- Consumers are less likely to choose alternatives with product features or promotional premiums that have little or no value, even when these features and premiums are optional (like the opportunity to purchase a Collector's Plate) and do not reduce the actual value of the product in any way.

- Consumers are less likely to choose products selected by others for reasons they find irrelevant, even when these other reasons do not suggest anything positive or negative about the product's value.

- Consumers' interpretations and evaluations of past experiences are greatly influenced by the ending and trend of events. A positive event at the end of a service experience can colour later reflections and evaluations of the experience as a whole.

Marketing insight

Predictably irrational

In a recent book, Dan Ariely reviews some of his own research, as well as that of others, which shows that although consumers may think they are making well-reasoned, rational decisions, that is not often the case. As it turns out, a host of mental factors and unconscious cognitive biases conspire to result in seemingly irrational decision making in many different settings. Ariely believes these irrational decisions are not random but are systematic and predictable. As he says, we make the same 'mistake' over and over. Some of the thought-provoking research insights he highlights include:

- When selling a new product, marketers should be sure to compare it with something consumers already know about, even if the new product is literally new-to-the-world with few direct comparisons. Consumers find it difficult to judge products in isolation and feel more comfortable if they base a new decision at least in part on a past decision.

- Consumers find the lure of 'free' almost irresistible. In one experiment, consumers were offered normally high-priced Lindt chocolate truffles for 15 cents and ordinary Hershey kisses for a penny. Customers had to pick one or the other, not both. Seventy-three per cent of the customers went for the truffles. When the prices were cut to 14 cents for the truffles and free for the kisses, however, 69 per cent of customers went for the kisses, even though the truffles were actually a better deal.

- The 'optimism bias' or 'positivity illusion' is a pervasive effect that transcends gender, age, education and nationality. People tend to overestimate their chances of experiencing a good outcome (having a successful marriage, healthy kids or financial security) but underestimate their chances of experiencing a bad outcome (divorce, a heart attack or a parking ticket).

In concluding his analysis, Ariely notes that 'If I were to distil one main lesson from the research described in this book, it is that we are all pawns in a game whose forces we largely fail to comprehend.'

Sources: Dan Ariely (2009) The end of rational economics, *Harvard Business Review*, July–August, 78–84; Dan Ariely (2008) *Predictably Irrational*, New York: HarperCollins; Dan Ariely (2009) The curious paradox of optimism bias, *BusinessWeek*, 24 and 31 August, 48; Dan Ariely (2009) A Manager's guide to human irrationalities, *MIT Sloan Management Review*, winter, 53–9; Russ Juskalian (2008) Not as rational as we think we are, *USA TODAY*, 17 March; Elizabeth Kolbert (2008) What was I thinking?, *The New Yorker*, 25 February; David Mehegan (2008) Experimenting on humans, *Boston Globe*, 18 March.

Decision Heuristics

Above we reviewed some common heuristics that occur with non-compensatory decision making. Other heuristics similarly come into play in everyday decision making when consumers forecast the likelihood of future outcomes or events.[116]

- **Availability heuristic.** Consumers base their predictions on the quickness and ease with which a particular example of an outcome comes to mind. If an example comes to mind too easily, consumers might overestimate the likelihood of its happening. For example, a recent product failure may lead a consumer to inflate the likelihood of a future product failure and make him or her more inclined to purchase a product warranty.
- **Representativeness heuristic.** Consumers base their predictions on how representative or similar the outcome is to other examples. One reason why package appearances may be so similar for different brands in the same product category is that marketers want their products to be seen as representative of the category as a whole.
- **Anchoring and adjustment heuristic.** Consumers arrive at an initial judgement and then adjust it based on additional information. For services marketers, a strong first impression is critical to establish a favourable anchor so that subsequent experiences will be interpreted in a more favourable light.

Note that marketing managers also may use heuristics and be subject to biases in their own decision making.

Framing

Decision framing is the manner in which choices are presented to and seen by a decision-maker. A €200 mobile phone may not seem that expensive in the context of a set of €400 phones but may seem very expensive if those phones cost €50. Framing effects are pervasive and can be powerful.

Marketers can influence consumer decision making through *choice architecture* – the environment in which decisions are structured and buying choices are made. That is, in the right environment, consumers can be given a 'nudge' via some small feature in the environment that attracts attention and alters behaviour. They maintain Nabisco is employing a smart choice architecture by offering 100-calorie snack packs, which have solid profit margins, while nudging consumers to make healthier choices.[117]

Mental accounting

Researchers have found that consumers use **mental accounting** when they handle their money.[118] Mental accounting refers to the way consumers code, categorise and evaluate financial outcomes of choices. Formally, it is 'the tendency to categorize *funds* or items of value even though there is no logical *basis* for the categorization, e.g., individuals often segregate their savings into separate accounts to meet different goals even though funds from any of the accounts can be applied to any of the goals'.[119]

Consider the following two scenarios:

1 Assume you spend €50 to buy a ticket for a concert.[120] As you arrive at the show, you realise you have lost your ticket. You decide to buy a replacement.
2 Assume you decided to buy a ticket to a concert at the door. As you arrive at the show, you realise somehow you lost €50 along the way. You decide to buy the ticket anyway.

Which one would you be more likely to do? Most people choose scenario 2. Although you lost the same amount in each case – €50 – in the first case, you may have mentally allocated €50 for going to a concert. Buying another ticket would exceed your mental concert budget. In the second case, the money you lost did not belong to any account, so you had not yet exceeded your mental concert budget. According to professor of behavioural science and economics Richard H. Thaler, mental accounting is based on a set of core principles:

- Consumers tend to *segregate gains*. When a seller has a product with more than one positive dimension, it is desirable to have the consumer evaluate each dimension separately. Listing multiple benefits of a large industrial product, for example, can make the sum of the parts seem greater than the whole.
- Consumers tend to *integrate losses*. Marketers have a distinct advantage in selling something if its cost can be added to another large purchase. House buyers are more inclined to view additional expenditures favourably given the high price of buying a house.
- Consumers tend to *integrate smaller losses with larger gains*. The 'cancellation' principle might explain why withholding taxes from monthly pay packets is less aversive than large, lump-sum tax payments – the smaller withholdings are more likely to be absorbed by the larger pay amount.
- Consumers tend to *segregate small gains from large losses*. The 'silver lining' principle might explain the popularity of rebates on big-ticket purchases such as cars.

The principles of mental accounting are derived in part from **prospect theory**. Prospect theory maintains that consumers frame their decision alternatives in terms of gains and losses according to a value function. Consumers are generally loss-averse. They tend to over-weight very low probabilities and under-weight very high probabilities.

Profiling consumer product buying and usage behaviour

How can marketers learn about the stages in the buying process for their product? They can think about how they themselves would act, in the *introspective method*. They can interview a small number of recent purchasers, asking them to recall the events leading to their purchase, in the *retrospective method*. They can use the *prospective method* to locate consumers who plan to buy the product and ask them to think out loud about going through the buying process, or they can ask consumers to describe the ideal way to buy or use the product, in the *prescriptive method*. Each method yields a picture of the steps in the process.

Trying to understand the customer's purchase and usage behaviour in connection with a product has been called mapping the customer's **consumption system**,[121] *customer activity cycle*,[122] or *customer scenario*.[123] Marketers can do this for such activity clusters as doing laundry, preparing for a wedding, buying a car or playing with Lego.

LEGO

LEGO of Billund, Denmark, may have been one of the first mass customised brands. To better coordinate new product activities, LEGO revamped its organisational structure into four functional groups managing eight key areas, with one group being responsible for supporting customer communities and tapping into them for product ideas. LEGO also set up what was later renamed Lego Design by ME, which let customers design, share and build their own custom Lego products using LEGO's freely downloadable Digital Designer 3.0 software. The creations that result can exist – and be shared with other enthusiasts – solely online, or, if customers want to build them, the software tabulates the pieces required and sends an order to LEGO's warehouse in Enfield, Connecticut. Customers can request step-by-step building guide instructions and even design their own box to store the pieces.[124]

SUMMARY

1 Consumer behaviour is influenced by three factors: cultural (culture, subculture and social class); social (reference groups, family, and social roles and statuses); and personal (age, stage in the life cycle, occupation, economic circumstances, lifestyle, personality and self-concept). Hence, the study of consumer behaviour can be divided into three interdependent dimensions: (1) the study of culture; (2) the study of social groups; (3) the study of the individual. Research into all these factors can provide marketers with clues to reach and serve consumers more effectively.

2 Virtually all human societies exhibit social stratification, most often in the form of social classes, relatively homogeneous and enduring divisions in a society, hierarchically ordered and with members who share similar values, interests and behaviour.

3 Social factors such as reference groups, family, and social roles and statuses affect consumers' buying behaviour.

4 The family is the most important consumer buying organisation in society, and family members constitute the most influential primary reference group.

5 While the individual interacts with the cultural and social settings, the starting point for understanding consumer behaviour is the consumer him or herself. A consumer's decisions are influenced by several personal characteristics including the buyer's age and stage in the life cycle; occupation and economic circumstances; personality and self-concept; and lifestyle and values.

6 Four main psychological processes affect consumer behaviour: motivation, perception, learning and memory.

7 To understand how consumers actually make buying decisions, marketers must identify who makes and has input into the buying decision; people can be initiators, influencers, deciders, buyers or users.

Different marketing campaigns might be targeted to each type of person.

8 The typical buying process consists of the following sequence of events: problem recognition, information search, evaluation of alternatives, purchase decision and post-purchase behaviour. The marketers' job is to understand the behaviour at each stage. The attitudes of others, unanticipated situational factors and perceived risk may all affect the decision to buy, as will consumers' levels of post-purchase product satisfaction, use and disposal and actions on the part of the company.

9 Consumers are constructive decision-makers and subject to many contextual influences. Consumers often exhibit low involvement in their decisions, using many heuristics as a result.

10 Understanding consumer behaviour may often be complicated, since many different factors influence the behaviour and since many different forms of behaviour exist. Perspectives on consumer behaviour include the behaviourist perspective, the information-processing perspective, the emotional perspective and the cultural perspective. When studying consumer behaviour it is therefore important that none of the different perspectives is excluded beforehand, but that the analyst keeps an open mind to various explanations for consumers' behaviour.

11 Researchers have found that consumers use mental accounting when they handle their money. Mental accounting refers to the way consumers code, categorise and evaluate financial outcomes of choices.

12 Consumers don't always process information or make decisions in a deliberate, rational manner. One of the most active academic research areas in marketing over the past three decades has been *behavioural decision theory* (BDT). Behavioural decision theorists have identified many situations in which consumers make seemingly irrational choices.

APPLICATIONS

Marketing debate

Is target marketing ever bad? As marketers increasingly develop marketing programmes tailored to certain target market segments, some critics have denounced these efforts as exploitive. For example, the preponderance of billboards advertising cigarettes, alcohol and other vices in low-income urban areas is seen as taking advantage of a vulnerable market segment. Critics can be especially harsh in evaluating marketing programmes that target minority groups, claiming they often employ stereotypes and inappropriate depictions. Others counter that targeting and positioning are critical to marketing and that these marketing programmes are an attempt to be relevant to a certain consumer group.

Take a position: Targeting minorities is exploitative *versus* Targeting minorities is sound business practice.

Marketing discussion

What are your mental accounts? What mental accounts do you have in your mind about purchasing products or services? Do you have any rules you employ in spending money? Are they different from what other people do? Do you follow Thaler's four principles in reacting to gains and losses?

Marketing exercises

- In your opinion, what are the ten most important topics/ issues to be learned from this chapter?

- Pick one of the companies mentioned in this chapter. For this company, investigate and discuss: (a) Do you think that any of the ten topics/issues you identified could be related to the problems, or opportunities, that the company – in your opinion – is currently facing or could expect to be facing in the near future? (b) Why?

- In your opinion, what should the company do to deal with the identified problems or to take advantage of the identified opportunities?

REFERENCES

[1]Based on Worldwide Social Network Ad Spending: 2011 Outlook, eMarketer: www.emarketer.com/Results.aspx?dsNav=Ntk:basic%7csocial+network%7c1%7c; C. McCarthy (2007) ComScore's latest numbers: worldwide social-networking growth, 31 July (www.news.com/8301-13577_3-9752857-36.html); C. McCarthy (2007) Facebook ads makes a flashy debut in New York, 6 November (www.news.com/8301-13577_3-9811932-36.html); E. Barsky and M. Purdon (2006) Introducing web 2.0: social networking and social bookmarking for health librarians, *JCHLA/JABSC*, 27; R. Hof (2007) Facebook declares new era for advertising, *BusinessWeek*, 6 November (www.businessweek.com/the_thread/techbeat/archives/2007/11/facebook_declar.html); C. Holahan (2007) Facebook: marketers are your 'friends', *BusinessWeek*, 7 November (www.businessweek.com/technology/content/nov2007/tc2007116_289111.htm?chan=search).

[2]J. P. Peter, J. C. Olson and K. G. Grunert (1999) *Consumer Behaviour and Marketing Strategy*, European edn, Maidenhead: McGraw-Hill, 264.

[3]S. A. Grier, A. Brumbaugh and C. G. Thornton (2006) Crossover dreams: consumer responses to ethnic-oriented products, *Journal of Marketing*, 70 (April), 35–51.

[4]B. Gabriela (2010) Setback of crises: social-economic stratification, *Review of Management & Economic Engineering*, 9(4), 27–36.

[5]www.worldatlas.com/webimage/countrys/eu.htm.

[6]http://ess.nsd.uib.no/files/2003/ESS1SocialClassReport.pdf; www.iser.essex.ac.uk/esec/desc/steps/step4.6.php.

[7]T. U. Thomsen and E. B. Sørensen (2006) The first four-wheeled status symbol: pram consumption as a vehicle for the construction of motherhood identity, *Journal of Marketing Management*, 22(9–10), 907–27.

[8]M. Chapman (2011) Nokia launches global campaign for E7 smartphone, *Marketing Week*, 21 March.

[9]P. S. van Eck, W. Jager and P. S. H. Leeflang (2011) Opinion leaders role in innovation diffusion: a simulation study, *Journal of Product Innovation Management*, 28(2), 187–203; H. S. Nair, P. Manchanda and T. Bhatia (2010) Asymmetric social interactions in physician prescription behavior: the role of opinion leaders, *Journal of Marketing Research*, 47(5), 883–95.

[10]J. D. Laughlin and J. B. MacDonald (2010) Identifying market mavens online by their social behaviors in community-generated media, *Academy of Marketing Studies Journal*, 14(1), 55–70; L. F. Feick and L. L. Price (1987) The market maven: a diffuser of marketplace information, *Journal of Marketing*, 51 (January), 83–97.

[11]S. Yang, Y. Zhao, T. Erdem and Y. Zhao (2010) Modeling the intrahousehold behavioral interaction, *Journal of Marketing Research*, 47(3), 470–84; J. M. Jensen (1991) Family purchase decisions: a buying centre approach, *Proceedings of the 5th Biannual International Conference of The Academy of Marketing Science*, Copenhagen, CBS, 332–7; E. S. Moore, W. L. Wilkie and R. J. Lutz (2002) Passing the torch: intergenerational influences as a source of brand equity, *Journal of Marketing*, April, 17–37; R. Boutilier (1993) Pulling the family's strings, *American Demographics*, August, 44–8; D. J. Burns (1992) Husband–wife innovative consumer decision making: exploring the effect of family power, *Psychology and Marketing*, May–June, 175–89; R. L. Spiro (1983) Persuasion in family decision making, *Journal of Consumer Research*, March, 393–402. For cross-cultural comparisons of husband–wife buying roles, see J. B. Ford, M. S. LaTour and T. L. Henthorne (1995) Perception of marital roles in purchase-decision processes: a cross-cultural study, *Journal of the Academy of Marketing Science*, Spring, 120–31.

[12]K. M. Palan and R. E. Wilkes (1997) Adolescent–parent interaction in family decision making, *Journal of Consumer Research*, 24(2), 159–69; S. E. Beatty and S. Talpade (1994) Adolescent influence in family decision making: a replication with extension, *Journal of Consumer Research*, 21 (September), 332–41.

[13]P. E. Davis-Kean (2005) The influence of parent education and family income on child achievement: the indirect role of parental expectations and the home environment, *Journal of Family Psychology*, 19(2), 294–304; P. Webley and E. K. Nyhus (2006) Parents' influence on children's future orientation and saving, *Journal of Economic Psychology*, 27(1), 140–64; E. R. DeVore and R. B. Ginsburg (2005) The protective effects of good parenting on adolescents: adolescent medicine, *Current Opinion in Pediatrics*, 17(4), 460–5.

[14]K-L. Wu, K. Holmes and J. Tribe (2010) Where do you want to go today? An analysis of family group decisions to visit

museums, *Journal of Marketing Management*, 26(7/8), 706–26; Chenting Su, E. F. Fern and Keying Ye (2003) A temporal dynamic model of spousal family purchase-decision behavior, *Journal of Marketing Research*, 40, August, 268–81; C. Kwai-Choi Lee and B. A. Collins (2000) Family decision making and coalition patterns, *European Journal of Marketing*, 34(9/10), 1181–98; Z. Mottiar and D. Quinn (2004) 'Couple dynamics in household tourism decision making: women as the gatekeepers?', *Journal of Vacation Marketing*, 10(2), 149–60.

15www.kelloggs.dk/spk.aspx; http://www2.kelloggs.com/brand/brand.aspx?brand=215&cat=specialk; www.jotun.dk/www/dk/20030027.nsf!OpenDatabase&mt=&l=no.

16C. Ebster, U. Wagner and D. Neumueller (2009) Children's influences on in-store purchases, *Journal of Retailing and Consumer Services*, 16, 145–54; ScienceDaily (2009) Parents grossly underestimate the influence their children wield over in-store purchases, March 17, www.sciencedaily.com/releases/2009/03/090316075853.htm; R. G. Westergaard (2006) Børnene bestemmer, *FoodCulture*, 28, 6.

17J. Tinson and C. Nancarrow; (2007) GROwing up: tweenagers' involvement in family decision making, *Journal of Consumer Marketing*, 24(3), 160–70; A. Shoham and V. Dalakas (2005) He said, she said . . . they said: parents' and children's assessment of children's influence on family consumption decisions, *Journal of Consumer Marketing*, 3, 152–60.

18A. Fikry and N. A. Jamil (2010) The effect of Malaysian teenagers' ethnicities, influence strategies and family purchase decisions of mobile phones, *Young Consumers*, 11(4), 330–6; J. Bayot (2003) The teenage market; young, hip, and looking for a bargain, *New York Times*, 1 December.

19Deborah Roedder John (1999) Consumer socialization of children: a retrospective look at twenty-five years of research, *Journal of Consumer Research*, 26 (December), 183–213; Lan Nguyen Chaplin and Deborah Roedder John (2005) The development of self–brand connections in children and adolescents, *Journal of Consumer Research*, 32 (June), 119–29; Lan Nguyen Chaplin and Deborah Roedder John (2007) Growing up in a material world: age differences in materialism in children and adolescents, *Journal of Consumer Research*, 34 (December), 480–93.

20www.massgeneral.org/children/adolescenthealth/articles/aa_adolescent_clothing.aspx.

21http://epp.eurostat.ec.europa.eu/portal/page?_pageid=2173,45972494&_dad=portal&_schema=PORTAL&mo=containsall&ms=family&saa=&p_action=SUBMIT&l=dk&co=equal&ci=,&po=matchany&pi=1130671,0&an=product_type&ao=containsall&av=ITY_&as=0&ad=text&na=1&ob=41,0.

22R. Y. Du and W. A. Kamakura (2006) Household life cycles and lifestyles in the United States, *Journal of Marketing Research*, 48 (February), 121–32; L. Lepisto (1985) A life span perspective of consumer behavior, in E. Hirshman and M. Holbrook (eds), *Advances in Consumer Research*, vol. 12, Provo, UT: Association for Consumer Research, 47. Also see G. Sheehy (1995) *New Passages: Mapping Your Life across Time*, New York: Random House.

23K. Siddiqui (2011) Personality influences customer switching interdisciplinary, *Journal of Contemporary Research in Business*, 2(10), 363–72; P. C. M. Govers and J. P. L. Schoormans (2005) Product personality and its influence on consumer preference, *Journal of Consumer Marketing*, 22(4), 189–97; H. H. Kassarjian and M. J. Sheffet (1981) Personality and consumer behavior: an update, in H. H. Kassarjian and T. S. Robertson (eds), *Perspectives in Consumer Behavior*, Glenview, IL: Scott, Foresman, 160–80.

24J. Aaker (1997) Dimensions of measuring brand personality, *Journal of Marketing Research*, 34 (August), 347–56; for a discussion of brand personality and how it can be measured, see also N. Maehle and M. Supphellen (2011) In search of the sources of brand personality, *International Journal of Market Research*, 53(1), 95–114.

25J. L. Aaker, V. Benet-Martinez and J. Garolera (2001) Consumption symbols as carriers of culture: a study of Japanese and Spanish brand personality constructs, *Journal of Personality and Social Psychology*, 81(3), 492–508.

26Yongjun Sung and S. F. Tinkham (2005) Brand personality structures in the United States and Korea: common and culture-specific factors, *Journal of Consumer Psychology*, 15(4), 334–50.

27N. Agrawal and D. Maheswaran (2005) The effects of self-construal and commitment on persuasion, *Journal of Consumer Research*, 31(4), 841–9; M. J. Sirgy (1982) Self concept in consumer behavior: a critical review, *Journal of Consumer Research*, 9 (December), 287–300.

28T. R. Graeff (1997) Consumption situations and the effects of brand image on consumers brand evaluations, *Psychology and Marketing*, 14(1), 49–70; T. R. Graeff (1996) Image congruence effects on product evaluations: the role of self-monitoring and public/private consumption, *Psychology and Marketing*, 13(5), 481–99.

29J. L. Aaker (1999) The malleable self: the role of self-expression in persuasion, *Journal of Marketing Research*, 36(1), 45–57.

30www.porternovelli.com/site/pressrelease.aspx?pressrelease_id=171&pgname=news.

31www.nuovon.com.au/LOHAS/tabid/53/Default.aspx [accessed February 2011].

32A. Cortese (2003) They care about the world (and they shop too), *New York Times*, 20 July.

33D. Reed (2010) Wal-Mart restocks data warehouse, *MarketingWeek*, 21 December; A. Banco and W. Zellner (2003) Is Wal-Mart too powerful?, *BusinessWeek*, 6 October, 100.

34T. Weber (2003) All three? Gee, *Wireless Review*, May, 12–14.

35S. H. Schwartz and L. Sagiv (1995) Identifying culture-specifics in the content and structure of values, *Journal of Cross-Cultural Psychology*, 26, 92–116.

36T. Hansen (2008) Consumer values, the theory of planned behaviour and online grocery shopping, *International Journal of Consumer Studies*, 32, 128–37.

37K. Brunsø, J. Scholderer and K. G. Grunert (2004) Closing the gap between values and behavior: a means–end theory of lifestyle, *Journal of Business Research*, 57, 665–70 at 665.

38B. Gunter and A. Furnham (1992) *Consumer Profiles: An Introduction to Psychographics*. London: Routledge, 70.

39D. A. Laverie, R. E. Kleine III and S. S. Kleine (1993) Linking emotions and values in consumption experiences: an exploratory study, *Advances in Consumer Research*, 20, 70–5.

40T. Harcar and E. Kaynak (2008) Life-style orientation of rural US and Canadian consumers: are regio-centric standardized marketing strategies feasible?, *Asia Pacific Journal of Marketing and Logistics*, 20(4), 433–54.

41F. Cram and Sik Hung Ng (1999) Consumer socialisation, *Applied Psychology: An International Review*, 48(3), 297–312.

42www.geert-hofstede.com/hofstede_greece.shtml; www.geert-hofstede.com/hofstede_sweden.shtml.

43For a review of current academic research on consumer behaviour, see D. J. Macinnis and V. S. Folkes (2010) The disciplinary status of consumer behavior: a sociology of science perspective on key controversies, *Journal of Consumer Research*, 36(6), 899–914; D. J. Macinnis and V. S. Folkes (2006) Consumer psychology: categorization, inferences, affect, and persuasion, *Annual Review of Psychology*, 57, 453–95. To learn more about how consumer behaviour theory can be applied to policy decisions, see Special issue on helping consumers help themselves: improving the quality of judgments and choices, *Journal of Public Policy and Marketing*, 25(1), Spring 2006.

[44]E. Kaciak, C. W. Cullen and A. Sagan (2010) The quality of ladders generated by abbreviated hard laddering, *Journal of Targeting, Measurement and Analysis for Marketing*, 18(3/4), 159–66; T. J. Reynolds and J. Gutman (1988) Laddering theory, method, analysis, and interpretation, *Journal of Advertising Research*, February–March, 11–34.

[45]E. Dichter (1964) *Handbook of Consumer Motivations*, New York: McGraw-Hill.

[46]J. Callebaut, M. Janssens, D. Lorré and H. Hendrick (1994) *The Naked Consumer: The Secret of Motivational Research in Global Marketing*, Antwerp: Censydiam Institute.

[47]M. Wells (2003) Mind games, *Forbes*, 1 September, 70.

[48]A. Maslow (1954) *Motivation and Personality*, New York: Harper and Row, 80–106.

[49]See F. Herzberg (1966) *Work and the Nature of Man*, Cleveland, OH: William Collins; Thierry and Koopman-Iwerna (1984), op. cit.

[50]J. M. Jensen (2007) The relationships between hygiene factors, motivators satisfaction and response among visitors to zoos and aquaria, *Tourism Review International*, special *issue on Zoos, Aquaria and other Captive Wildlife Attractions*, 11(3), 307–16.

[51]B. Berelson and G. A. Steiner (1964) *Human Behavior: An Inventory of Scientific Findings*, New York: Harcourt Brace Jovanovich, 88.

[52]J. E. Russo, M. G. Meloy and V. H. Medvec (1998) The distortion of product information during brand choice, *Journal of Marketing Research*, 35 (November), 438–52.

[53]L. de Chernatony and S. Knox (1990) How an appreciation of consumer behavior can help in product testing, *Journal of Market Research Society*, July, 333. See also C. Janiszewski and S. M. J. Osselar (2000) A connectionist model of brand–quality association, *Journal of Marketing Research*, August, 331–51.

[54]See A. K. Pradeep (2010) *The Buying Brain: Secrets for Selling to the Subconscious Mind*, New York: Wiley; C. Janiszewski (1993) Preattentive mere exposure effects, *Journal of Consumer Research*, 20 (December), 376–92, as well as some of his earlier and subsequent research. For more perspectives, see also J. A. Bargh and T. L. Chartrand (1999) The unbearable automaticity of being, *American Psychologist*, 54, 462–79 and the research programmes of both authors. For lively academic debate, see the Research dialogue section of the July 2005 issue of the *Journal of Consumer Psychology*.

[55]See T. E. Moore (1982) Subliminal advertising: what you see is what you get, *Journal of Marketing*, 46 (Spring), 38–47 for an early classic; and A. B. Aylesworth, R. C. Goodstein and A. Kalra (1999) Effect of archetypal embeds on feelings: an indirect route to affecting attitudes?, *Journal of Advertising*, 28(3), 73–81 for a more current treatment.

[56]R. S. Wyer, Jr and T. K. Srull (1989) Person memory and judgment, *Psychological Review*, 96(1), 58–83; J. R. Anderson (1983) *The Architecture of Cognition*, Cambridge, MA: Harvard University Press.

[57]R. Parsons (2011) Katy Perry stars in 'biggest ever' Adidas campaign, *Marketing Week*, 14 March.

[58]For additional discussion, see J. G. Lynch, Jr and T. K. Srull (1982) Memory and attentional factors in consumer choice: concepts and research methods, *Journal of Consumer Research*, 9 (June), 18–36; and J. W. Alba, J. W. Hutchinson and J. G. Lynch, Jr (1992) Memory and decision making, in H. H. Kassarjian and T. S. Robertson (eds), *Handbook of Consumer Theory and Research*, Englewood Cliffs, NJ: Prentice Hall, 1–49.

[59]D. V. Thompson, V. Debora and R. W. Hamilton (2006) The effects of information processing mode on consumers' responses to comparative advertising, *Journal of Consumer Research*, 32(4), 530–40; T. Hansen (2005) Perspectives on consumer decision making: an integrated approach, *Journal of Consumer Behaviour*, 4(6), 420–37; R. S. Lockhart, F. I. M. Craik and L. Jacoby (1976) Depth of processing, recognition, and recall, in J. Brown (ed.), *Recall and Recognition*, New York: John Wiley & Sons; F. I. M. Craik and E. Tulving (1975) Depth of processing and the retention of words in episodic memory, *Journal of Experimental Psychology*, 104(3), 268–94; F. I. M. Craik and R. S. Lockhart (1972) Levels of processing: a framework for memory research, *Journal of Verbal Learning and Verbal Behavior*, 11, 671–84.

[60]L. M. Lodish, M. Abraham, S. Kalmenson, J. Livelsberger, B. Lubetkin, B. Richardson and M. E. Stevens (1995) How TV advertising works: a meta-analysis of 389 real world split cable TV advertising experiments, *Journal of Marketing Research*, 32 (May), 125–39.

[61]E. F. Loftus and G. R. Loftus (1980) On the permanence of stored information in the human brain, *American Psychologist*, 35 (May), 409–20.

[62]K. A. Braun (1999) Postexperience advertising effects on consumer memory, *Journal of Consumer Research*, 25 (March), 319–32.

[63]R. Batimalai (2011) Top 10 solid examples of pavlov classical conditioning in action, http://ezinearticles.com/?Top-10-Solid-Examples-of-Pavlov-Classical-Conditioning-in-Action&id=2883783.

[64]P. Østergaard and C. Jantzen (2000) Shifting perspectives in consumer research: from buyer behavior to consumption studies, in S. C. Beckmann and R.H. Elliot (eds), *Interpretive Consumer Research: Paradigms, Methodologies and Applications*, Copenhagen: Handelshøjskolens Forlag, 9–23.

[65]R. Lavidge and G. A. Steiner (1961) A model for predictive measurements of advertising, *Journal of Marketing*, October, 59–62.

[66]F. Hansen and S. R. Christensen (2007) *Emotions, Advertising and Consumer Choice*, Copenhagen: Business School Press.

[67]W. R. Swinyard (1993) The effects of mood, involvement, and quality of store experience on shopping intentions, *Journal of Consumer Research*, 20, 271–80.

[68]A. Palmer and N. Koening-Lewis (2010) Primary and secondary effects of emotions on behavioural intention of theatre clients, *Journal of Marketing Management*, 26(13/14), 1201–17; R. P. Bagozzi, M. Gopinath and U. N. Prashanth (1999) The role of emotions in marketing, *Journal of the Academy of Marketing Science*, 27(2), 184–206.

[69]M. P. Pachauri (2002) Consumer behaviour: a literature review, *The Marketing Review*, 2, 319–55; G. McCracken (1988) *Culture and Consumption: New Approaches to the Symbolic Character of Consumer Goods and Activities*, Bloomington, IN: Indiana University Press.

[70]M. Solomon, G. Bamossy and S. Askegaard (2002) *Consumer Behaviour: A European Perspective*, 2nd edn, Harlow: Financial Times Prentice Hall.

[71]C. J. Thompson and Z. Arsel (2004) The starbucks brandscape and consumers (anticorporate) experiences of glocalization, *Journal of Consumer Research*, 31 (December), 631–42.

[72]F. Hansen (1972) *Consumer Choice Behavior: A Cognitive Theory*, New York and London: Free Press/Macmillan; J. R. Bettman, M. F. Luce and J. W. Payne (1998) Constructive consumer choice processes, *Journal of Consumer Research*, 25 (December), 187–217.

[73]I. Simonson (1999) The effect of product assortment on buyer preferences, *Journal of Retailing*, 75(3), 347–70.

[74]Z. Kunda (1990) The case for motivated reasoning, *Psychological Bulletin*, 108(3), 480–98.

[75]S. P. Jain and D. Maheswaran (2000) Motivated reasoning: a depth-of-processing perspective, *Journal of Consumer Research*, 26, 358–71.

[76]See for example R. S. Lazarus (1991) Progress on a cognitive-motivational-relational theory of emotion, *American Psychologist*, 46(8), 819–34; R. P. Bagozzi, M. Gopinath and U. N. Prashanth (1999) The role of emotions in marketing, *Journal of the Academy of Marketing Science*, 27(2), 184–206.

[77]L. Watson and M. T. Spence (2007) Causes and consequences of emotions on consumer behaviour: a review and integrative cognitive appraisal theory, *European Journal of Marketing*, 41(5–6), 487–511.

[78]For a comprehensive review of the academic literature on decision making, see J. E. Russo and K. A. Carlson (2002) Individual decision making, in B. Weitz and R. Wensley (eds), *Handbook of Marketing*, London: Sage, 372–408.

[79]B. Shapiro, V. K. Rangan and J. Sviokla (1992) Staple yourself to an order, *Harvard Business Review*, July–August, 113–22. See also C. M. Heilman, D. Bowman and G. P. Wright (2000) The evolution of brand preferences and choice behaviors of consumers new to a market, *Journal of Marketing Research*, May, 139–55.

[80]L. Fisher (2011) Fools' gold?, *Marketing Week*, 4 April.

[81]Marketing scholars have developed several models of the consumer buying process. See M. F. Luce, J. R. Bettman and J. W. Payne (2001) *Emotional Decisions: Tradeoff Difficulty and Coping in Consumer Choice*, Chicago, IL: University of Chicago Press; J. F. Engel, R. D. Blackwell and P. W. Miniard (1994) *Consumer Behavior*, 8th edn, Fort Worth, TX: Dryden; J. A. Howard and J. N. Sheth (1969) *The Theory of Buyer Behavior*, New York: John Wiley & Sons.

[82]W. P. Putsis, Jr and N. Srinivasan (1994) Buying or just browsing? The duration of purchase deliberation, *Journal of Marketing Research*, August, 393–402.

[83]C. L. Narayana and R. J. Markin (1975) Consumer behavior and product performance: an alternative conceptualization, *Journal of Marketing*, October, 1–6. See also L. G. Cooper and A. Inoue (1996) Building market structures from consumer preferences, *Journal of Marketing Research*, 33(3), 293–306; W. S. DeSarbo and K. Jedidi (1995) The spatial representation of heterogeneous consideration dets, *Marketing Science*, 14(3), pt 2, Summer, 326–42.

[84]For a market-structure study of the hierarchy of atributes in the coffee market, see D. Jain, F. M. Bass and Yu-Min Chen (1990) Estimation of latent class models with heterogeneous choice probabilities: an application to market structuring, *Journal of Marketing Research*, February, 94–101. For an application of means–end chain analysis to global markets, see F. T. Hofstede, J.-B. E. M. Steenkamp and M. Wedel (1999) International market segmentation based on consumer–product relations, *Journal of Marketing Research*, February, 1–17.

[85]V. Postrel (2003) The lessons of the grocery shelf also have something to say about affirmative action, *New York Times*, 30 January.

[86]D. Krech, R. S. Crutchfield and E. L. Ballachey (1962) *Individual in Society*, New York: McGraw-Hill, Ch. 2.

[87]http://ameliatorode.typepad.com/life_moves_pretty_fast/2007/05/index.html.

[88]http://6omdagen.dk/; http://www.foedevarestyrelsen.dk/Ernaering/forside.htm.

[89]L. Dahlager (2011) Næsten ingen klarer seks om dagen, *Politiken*, 6 February, Food section, p. 10.

[90]See L. McAlister (1979) Choosing multiple items from a product class, *Journal of Consumer Research*, December, 213–24; P. E. Green and Y. Wind, *Multiattribute Decisions in Marketing: A Measurement Approach*, Hinsdale, IL: Dryden, Ch. 2; R. J. Lutz (1991) The role of attitude theory in marketing, in H. Kassarjian and T. Robertson (eds), *Perspectives in Consumer Behavior*, 317–39.

[91]This expectancy-value model was originally developed by M. Fishbein (1967) Attitudes and prediction of behavior, in M. Fishbein (ed.), *Readings in Attitude Theory and Measurement*, New York: John Wiley & Sons, 477–92. For a critical review, see P. W. Miniard and J. B. Cohen (1981) An examination of the Fishbein–Ajzen behavioral-intentions model's concepts and measures, *Journal of Experimental Social Psychology*, May, 309–39.

[92]M. R. Solomon (2007) *Consumer Behavior: Buying, Having, and Being*, 7th edn, Upper Saddle River, NJ: Prentice Hall.

[93]J. R. Bettman, E. J. Johnson and J. W. Payne (1991) Consumer decision making, in H. Kassarjian and T. Robertson (eds), *Handbook of Consumer Theory and Research*, NJ: Prentice Hall, 50–84.

[94]J. N. Sheth (1974) An investigation of relationships among evaluative beliefs, affect, behavioral intention, and behavior, in J. U. Farley, J. A. Howard and L. W. Ring (eds), *Consumer Behavior: Theory and Application*, Boston: Allyn & Bacon, 89–114.

[95]Fishbein (1967), op. cit.

[96]M. C. Campbell and R. C. Goodstein (2001) The moderating effect of perceived risk on consumers' evaluations of product incongruity: preference for the norm, *Journal of Consumer Research*, 28 (December), 439–49; G. R. Dowling (1999) Perceived risk, in P. E. Ear and S. Kemp (eds), *The Elgar Companion to Consumer Research and Economic Psychology*, Cheltenham: Edward Elgar, 419–24; G. R. Dowling (1986) Perceived risk: the concept and its measurement, *Psychology and Marketing*, 3 (Fall), 193–210; J. R. Bettman (1973) Perceived risk and its components: a model and empirical test, *Journal of Marketing Research*, 10 (May), 184–90; R. A. Bauer (1967) Consumer behavior as risk taking, in D. F. Cox (ed.) *Risk Taking and Information Handling in Consumer Behavior*, Boston, MA: Division of Research, Harvard Business School.

[97]R. L. Oliver (2006) Customer satisfaction research, in R. Grover and M. Vriens (eds), *Handbook of Marketing Research*, Thousand Oaks, CA: Sage, 569–87.

[98]R. L. Day (1984) Modeling choices among alternative responses to dissatisfaction, *Advances in Consumer Research*, 11, 496–99. Also see P. Kotler and M. K. Mantrala (1985) Flawed products: consumer responses and marketer strategies, *Journal of Consumer Marketing*, Summer, 27–36.

99 A. O. Hirschman (1970) *Exit, Voice, and Loyalty*, Cambridge, MA: Harvard University Press.

100 S. Bearne (2011) CMOs admit brand loyalty schemes underperform, *Marketing Week*, 4 April.

101 J. D. Cripps (1994) Heuristics and biases in timing the replacement of durable products, *Journal of Consumer Research*, 21 (September), 304–18.

102 R. L. Celsi and J. C. Olson (1988) The role of involvement in attention and comprehension processes, *Journal of Consumer Research*, 15, 210–24.

103 G. Laurent and J. N. Kapferer (1985) Measuring consumer involvement profiles, *Journal of Marketing Research*, February, 41–53.

104 R. E. Petty (1986) *Communication and Persuasion: Central and Peripheral Routes to Attitude Change*, New York: Springer-Verlag; R. E. Petty and J. T. Cacioppo (1981) *Attitudes and Persuasion: Classic and Contemporary Approaches*, New York: McGraw-Hill.

105 H. E. Krugman (1965) The impact of television advertising: learning without involvement, *Public Opinion Quarterly*, Fall, 349–56.

106 M. Fishbein and I. Ajzen (1975) *Belief, Attitude, Intention, and Behavior: An Introduction to Theory and Research*, Reading, MA: Addison Wesley.

107 Cf. D. I. Hawkins, R. J. Best and K. A. Coney (2001) *Consumer Behavior: Building Marketing Strategy*, 8th edn, New York: Irwin, McGraw-Hill.

108 Cf. K. E. Thompson, N. Haziris and P. J. Alekos (1994) Attitudes and food choice behaviour, *British Food Journal*, 96(11), 9–17.

109 I. Ajzen (1985) From intention to action: a theory of planned behavior, in J. Kuhl and J. Beckman (eds) *Action Control: From Cognitions to Behaviors*, New York: Springer; I. Ajzen (1991) The theory of planned behavior, *Organizational Behavior and Human Decision Processes*, 50, 179–211.

110 www.people.umass.edu/aizen/, accessed October 2007.

111 T. J. Reynolds, C. E. Gengler and D. J. Howard (1995) A means–end analysis of brand persuasion through advertising, *International Journal of Research in Marketing*, 12(3), 257–66.

112 M. S. Mulvey and J. C. Olson (1994) Exploring the relationships between means–end knowledge and involvement, *Advances in Consumer Research*, 21(1), 51–7.

113 D. L. Hoffman, T. P. Novak and A. Venkatesh (2004) Has the internet become indispensable?, *Communications of the ACM*, 47(7), 37–42.

114 For an overview of some issues involved, see James R. Bettman, Mary Frances Luce and John W. Payne (1998) Constructive consumer choice processes, *Journal of Consumer Research*, 25 (December), 187–217; and Itamar Simonson (1993) Getting closer to your customers by understanding how they make choices, *California Management Review*, 35 (Summer), 68–84. For examples of classic studies in this area, see some of the following: Dan Ariely and Ziv Carmon (2000) Gestalt characteristics of experiences: the defining features of summarized events, *Journal of Behavioral Decision Making*, 13(2), 191–201; Ravi Dhar and Klaus Wertenbroch (2000) Consumer choice between hedonic and utilitarian goods, *Journal of Marketing Research*, 37 (February), 60–71; Itamar Simonson and Amos Tversky (1992) Choice in context: tradeoff contrast and extremeness aversion, *Journal of Marketing Research*, 29 (August), 281–95; Itamar Simonson (1990) The effects of purchase quantity and timing on variety-seeking behavior, *Journal of Marketing Research*, 27 (May), 150–62.

115 Leon Shiffman and Leslie Kanuk (2010) *Consumer Behavior*, 10th edn. Upper Saddle River, NJ: Prentice Hall; Wayne D. Hoyer and Deborah J. MacInnis (2009) *Consumer Behavior*, 5th edn, Cincinnati, OH: South-Western College Publishing.

116 For a detailed review of the practical significance of consumer decision making, see Itamar Simonson (1993) Get close to your customers by understanding how they make their choices, *California Management Review*, 35 (Summer), 78–9.

117 Richard H. Thaler and Cass R. Sunstein (2009) *Nudge: Improviding Decisions About Health, Wealth, and Happiness*, New York: Penguin; Michael Krauss (2009) A nudge in the right direction, *Marketing News*, 30 March, 20.

118 See Richard H. Thaler (1985) Mental accounting and consumer choice, *Marketing Science*, 4(3), 199–214 for a seminal piece; and Richard Thaler (1999) Mental accounting matters, *Journal of Behavioral Decision Making*, 12(3), 183–206 for additional perspectives.

119 Gary L. Gastineau and Mark P. Kritzman (1999) *Dictionary of Financial Risk Management*, 3rd edn, New York: John Wiley & Sons.

120 Example adapted from Daniel Kahneman and Amos Tversky (1979) Prospect theory: an analysis of decision under risk, *Econometrica*, 47 (March), 263–91.

121 H. W. Boyd, Jr and S. Levy (1963) New dimensions in consumer analysis, *Harvard Business Review*, November–December, 129–40.

122 S. Vandermerwe (1999) *Customer Capitalism: Increasing Returns in New Market Spaces*, London: Nicholas Brealey Publishing, Ch. 11.

123 P. B. Seybold (2001) Get inside the lives of your customers, *Harvard Business Review*, May, 81–9.

124 Lego's turnaround: picking up the pieces, *The Economist*, 28 October 2006, 76; Paul Grimaldi (2006) Consumers design products their way, *Knight Ridder Tribune Business News*, 25 November; Michael A. Prospero (2005) *Fast Company*, September, 35; David Robertson and Per Hjuler (2009) Innovating a turnaround at LEGO, *Harvard Business Review*, September, 20–1; Kim Hjelmgaard (2009) Lego, refocusing on bricks, builds on image, *Wall Street Journal*, 24 December.

Chapter 8

Analysing business markets

IN THIS CHAPTER, WE WILL ADDRESS THE FOLLOWING QUESTIONS:

1 What is the business market, and how does it differ from the consumer market?

2 What buying situations do organisational buyers face?

3 Who participates in the business to-business buying process?

4 How do business buyers make their decisions?

5 How can companies build strong relationships with business customers?

6 How do institutional buyers and government agencies do their buying?

Even before the world was ready for it Soitec created an exclusive technological process: Smart Cut™. Now the world has finally caught up with Soitec and the company supplies 80 per cent of the SOI wafers used by chipmakers around the world.

Source: Studio Pons/Soitec SA

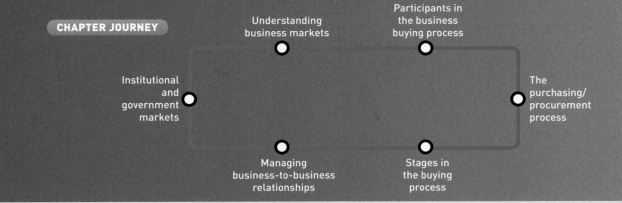

CHAPTER JOURNEY

Understanding
business markets

Participants in
the business
buying process

Institutional
and
government
markets

The
purchasing/
procurement
process

Managing
business-to-business
relationships

Stages in
the buying
process

Business organisations not only sell, they also buy vast quantities of raw materials, manufactured components, plant and equipment, supplies and business services. There are over 19 million businesses in Europe. To create and capture value, sellers in business markets need to understand their organisational customers' needs, resources, policies and buying procedures. In this chapter, you will learn more about the workings of business markets and how companies use this knowledge to market products and build relationships with their business customers.

In 1992 two researchers, André Auberton-Hervé and Jean-Michel Lamure from CEA-Léti (one of Europe's largest microelectronics research institutes) located in Grenoble, France, created Soitec. The name refers to the company's use of silicon-on-insulator technology. Soitec exploits and develops an exclusive technological process, Smart Cut™, which is protected by a portfolio of around 1,000 patents. Smart Cut™ is used today mainly in SOI technology, which offers two major advantages: it considerably increases the speed of microprocessors built on it and cuts by three or four times the power that these microprocessors consume. Soitec's customers were allowed to capitalise (making faster, less energy-consuming chips) on these two advantages without investing in additional process equipment. Back in the early 1990s, Auberton-Hervé and Lamure were sure that the technology they had developed to boost the performance of microchips would be a winner – if only they could get it to work on a mass scale. 'We knew silicon-on-insulator technology could bring real value to the industry,' says Auberton-Hervé. Even though it took almost a decade to work out the kinks, their patience has paid off. In fact, Soitec now supplies 80 per cent of the SOI wafers used by chipmakers around the world and is the global leader in innovative materials for the electronics and energy industries. In late 2009 Soitec acquired German SME Concentrix Solar, a company specialising in concentrated photovoltaics (CPV) technology. This acquisition marked a decisive step in Soitec's development. Soitec now covers the entire value chain, from the development of photovoltaic cells to the installation of solar farms in regions with very high levels of sunlight around the world.[1]

Some of the world's most valuable brands belong to business marketers: ABB, Maersk Line, Siemens and Vestas to name a few. Many principles of basic marketing also apply to business marketers. They need to embrace holistic marketing principles, such as building strong relationships with their customers, just like

any marketer. But they also face some unique considerations in selling to other businesses. In this chapter, we will highlight some of the crucial similarities and differences for marketing in business markets.[2]

What is organisational buying?

A company wanting to sell its products to other companies needs to understand organisational buying behaviour. In their seminal work on organisational buying behaviour, marketing researchers Webster and Wind define **organisational buying** as the decision-making process by which formal organisations establish the need for purchased products and services and identify, evaluate and choose among alternative brands and suppliers.[3]

The business market versus the consumer market

The **business market** consists of all the organisations that acquire goods and services used in the production of other products or services that are sold, rented or supplied to others. The major industries making up the business market are agriculture, forestry and fisheries; mining; manufacturing; construction; transportation; communication; public utilities; banking, finance and insurance; distribution; and services.

More euros and items change hands in sales to business buyers than to consumers. Consider the process of producing and selling a simple pair of shoes. Hide dealers must sell hides to tanners, who sell leather to shoe manufacturers, who sell shoes to wholesalers, who sell shoes to retailers, who finally sell them to consumers. Each party in the supply chain also buys many other goods and services to support their operations. Given the highly competitive nature of business-to-business markets, the biggest enemy to marketers here is commoditisation. Commoditisation eats away margins and weakens customer loyalty. It can be overcome only if target customers are convinced that meaningful differences exist in the marketplace, and that the unique benefits of the firm's offerings are worth the added expense. Thus, a critical step in business-to-business marketing is to create and communicate relevant differentiation from competitors.

Business marketers face many of the same challenges as consumer marketers. In particular, understanding their customers (as this chapter relates to business markets, the term 'customer' is used throughout the chapter) and what they value is of paramount importance to both.[4] Figure 8.1 summarises the business-to-business challenges identified in the MarketingSherpa 2011 B2B Marketing Benchmark Report.[5]

Business marketers, however, have several characteristics that contrast sharply with those of consumer markets:

- **Fewer, larger buyers**. The business marketer normally deals with far fewer, much larger buyers than the consumer marketer does, particularly in such industries as aircraft engines and defence weapons. The fate of Goodyear Tyre Company and other automotive parts suppliers depends on getting contracts from just a handful of major automakers. It is also true, however, that as a slowing economy has put a stranglehold on large corporations' purchasing departments, the small and midsize business market is offering new opportunities for suppliers.

- **Close supplier–customer relationship**. Because of the smaller customer base and the importance and power of the larger customers, suppliers are frequently expected to customise their offerings to individual business customer needs. Business buyers often select suppliers who also buy from them. A paper manufacturer might buy from a chemical company that buys a considerable amount of its paper.

To understand how Dome Coffee worked its business relationships to grow its operations from Australia to an international presence, visit www.pearsoned.com.au/marketingmanagementaustralia.

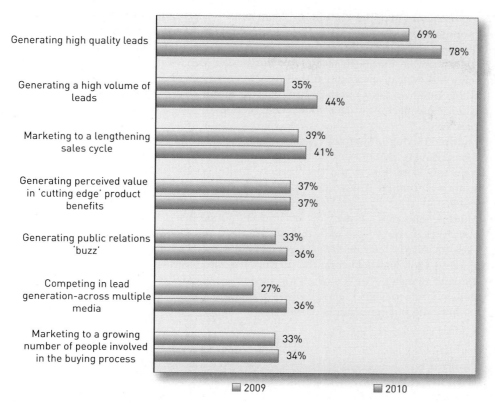

Generating high quality leads — 69% / 78%

Generating a high volume of leads — 35% / 44%

Marketing to a lengthening sales cycle — 39% / 41%

Generating perceived value in 'cutting edge' product benefits — 37% / 37%

Generating public relations 'buzz' — 33% / 36%

Competing in lead generation-across multiple media — 27% / 36%

Marketing to a growing number of people involved in the buying process — 33% / 34%

■ 2009   ■ 2010

Figure 8.1 The top business marketing challenges
Source: MarketingSherpa 2011 B2B Marketing Benchmark Report; Lead Author Jen Doyle, Senior Research
Manager, MECLABS; http://www.marketingsherpa.com/article.php?ident=31736

Midsize businesses present a huge opportunity, and huge challenges. The market is
large and fragmented by industry, size and number of years in operation. Small business
owners are notably averse to long-range planning and have an 'I'll buy it when I need it'
decision-making style. See the marketing insight box on p. 296 for some guidelines on
how to sell to small businesses.

- **Professional purchasing.** Business goods are often purchased by trained purchasing agents, who must follow their organisation's purchasing policies, constraints and

Bluecom

For decades, international business and marketing research has mainly considered established firms and in addition it has been a common belief that companies should first be
established on the domestic market before expanding to international markets. This is no
longer the case. Over the past decades, companies that operate internationally right from
inception – born global firms – have increasingly appeared. Re-established in late 2010,
Bluecom concentrates on distributing fast-moving consumer goods (FMCGs) to retailers,
wholesalers and business market dealers around the world. Bluecom distributes the LG,
Pioneer, Hype and Polti brands.

Source: K. Krabbe (2011) Farverig it-distributør vågner af årelang dvale, *Computerworld*, 18 January;
www.bluecom.com.

requirements. Many of the buying instruments – for example, requests for quotations, proposals and purchase contracts – are not typically found in consumer buying. Professional buyers spend their careers learning how to buy better. Some acquire their skills from the European Institute of Purchasing Management (EIPM), which seeks to train and educate professional business buyers, including buyers from, for example, IKEA, Unilever, LEGO and Electrolux. This means that business marketers must provide greater technical data about their product and its advantages over competitors' products.

- **Multiple buying influences.** More people typically influence business buying decisions. Buying committees consisting of technical experts and even senior management are common in the purchase of major goods. Business marketers need to send well-trained sales representatives and sales teams to deal with well-trained buyers.

- **Multiple sales calls.** A study by McGraw-Hill found that it takes four to four and a half calls to close an average industrial sale. In the case of capital equipment sales for large projects, it may take many attempts to fund a project, and the sales cycle – between quoting a job and delivering the product – is often measured in years.[6]

- **Derived demand.** The demand for business goods is ultimately derived from the demand for consumer goods. For this reason, the business marketer must closely monitor the buying patterns of ultimate consumers. Much of the boom in demand for

Marketing insight

Big sales to small business

- **Don't lump small and midsize businesses together.** There is a big gap between €1 million in revenue and €50 million, or between a start-up with 10 employees and a more mature business with 100. Telecom provider TDC (www.tdc.com) segments business customers into two groups according to whether they have 0–5 employees or more. Here, customers find a 'small Business Resource Center' and a 'Business and Institutional Resource Center', each offering different products and services to these different market segments.

- **Don't waste their time.** That means no cold calls, entertaining sales shows, or sales pitches over long lavish lunches.

- **Do keep it simple.** Simplicity means one point of contact with a supplier for all service problems, or one bill for all services and products.

- **Do use the internet.** Hewlett-Packard found that time-strapped small-business decision-makers prefer to buy, or at least research, products and services online. So it designed a site targeted to small and midsize businesses and pulls visitors through extensive advertising, direct mail, email campaigns, catalogues and events.

- **Don't forget about direct contact.** Even if a small business owner's first point of contact is via the internet, you still need to offer phone or face-to-face time. In major metropolitan areas, global internet carrier Sprint connects with small businesses through its Sprint Experience Centres, where Sprint reps or dealer reps can invite prospects to interact with the technologies.

- **Do provide support after the sale.** Small businesses want partners, not pitchmen. No matter whether you are selling to a retail giant or to a small independent you need to make sure that you are offering the promotional activity and support services necessary to maintain and develop the business relationship.

- **Do your homework.** The realities of small or midsize business management are different from those of a large corporation. Microsoft created a small, fictional executive research firm, Southridge, and football-style trading cards of its key decision-makers in order to help Microsoft employees tie sales strategies to small business realities.

Sources: Based on S. Hemsley (2010) Independents on frontline as brands take to battlefield, *Marketing Week*, 15 July; www.tdc.com; B. J. Feder (2003) When Goliath comes knocking on David's door, *New York Times*, 6 May; J. Greene (2003) Small biz: Microsoft's next big thing?, *BusinessWeek*, 21 April, 72–3; J. Gilbert (2004) Small but mighty, *Sales and Marketing Management*, January, 30–5; V. Kopytoff (2003) Businesses click on eBay, *San Francisco Chronicle*, 28 July; M. Krantz (2004) Firms jump on the eBay wagon, *USA Today*, 3 May.

steel-bar products is derived from the sustained growth in sales of minivans and other light trucks, which consume far more steel than cars. Business buyers must also pay close attention to current and expected economic factors, such as the level of production, investment, consumer spending and interest rate. In a recession, they reduce their investment in plant, equipment and inventories. Business marketers can do little to stimulate total demand in this environment. They can only fight harder to increase or maintain their share of the demand.

- **Inelastic demand.** The total demand for many business goods and services is inelastic – that is, not much affected by price changes. Shoe manufacturers are not going to buy much more leather if the price of leather falls, nor will they buy much less leather if the price rises, unless they can find satisfactory substitutes. Demand is especially inelastic in the short run because producers cannot make quick changes in production methods. Demand is also inelastic for business goods that represent a small percentage of the item's total cost, such as shoelaces.

- **Fluctuating demand.** The demand for business goods and services tends to be more volatile than the demand for consumer goods and services. A given percentage increase in consumer demand can lead to a much larger percentage increase in the demand for plant and equipment necessary to produce the additional output. Economists refer to this as the *acceleration effect*. Sometimes a rise of only 10 per cent in consumer demand can cause as much as a 200 per cent rise in business demand for products in the next period; a 10 per cent fall in consumer demand may cause a complete collapse in business demand.

- **Direct purchasing.** Business buyers often buy directly from manufacturers rather than through intermediaries, especially items that are technically complex or expensive such as mainframes or aircraft.

SMEs

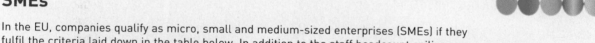

In the EU, companies qualify as micro, small and medium-sized enterprises (SMEs) if they fulfil the criteria laid down in the table below. In addition to the staff headcount ceiling, an enterprise qualifies as an SME if it meets either the turnover ceiling or the balance sheet ceiling, but not necessarily both. In the EU, 99per cent of all businesses are SMEs.

Enterprise category	Headcount	Turnover	or	Balance sheet total
Medium-sized	< 250	≤ €50 million		≤ €43 million
Small	< 50	≤ €10 million		≤ €10 million
Micro	< 10	≤ €2 million		≤ €2 million

Source: EU, Small and medium-sized enterprises (SMEs), http://ec.europa.eu/enterprise/policies/sme/facts-figures-analysis/sme-definition/index_en.htm

Buying situations

The business buyer faces many decisions in making a purchase. The number depends on the buying situation: complexity of the problem being solved, newness of the buying requirement, number of people involved and time required. Three types of buying situation are the straight rebuy, modified rebuy and new task.[7]

- **Straight rebuy.** In a straight rebuy, the purchasing department reorders supplies such as office supplies and bulk chemicals on a routine basis and chooses from suppliers on an approved list. The suppliers make an effort to maintain product and service quality and often propose automatic reordering systems to save time. 'Out suppliers' attempt to offer something new or to exploit dissatisfaction with a current supplier. Their goal is to get a small order and then enlarge their purchase share over time.

- **Modified rebuy.** The buyer wants to modify product specifications, prices, delivery requirements or other terms. The modified rebuy usually involves additional participants on both sides. The 'in suppliers' become nervous and want to protect the account. The 'out suppliers' see an opportunity to propose a better offer to gain some business.

- **New task.** A purchaser buys a product or service for the first time (an office building, a new security system). The greater the cost or risk, the larger the number of participants and the greater their information gathering – and therefore the longer the time to a decision.[8]

The business buyer makes the fewest decisions in the straight rebuy situation and the most in the new-task situation. Over time, new-task situations become straight rebuys and routine purchase behaviour.

New-task buying is the marketer's greatest opportunity and challenge. The process passes through several stages: awareness, interest, evaluation, trial and adoption.[9] Mass media can be most important during the initial awareness stage; salespeople often have

Orica Ltd

Orica Ltd's success grew from its realisation that it could provide more than just explosives to its mining customers. Now it researches the efficiency of different kinds of explosions and manages the entire blast for its clients.

Source: © Profimedia International s.r.o./Alamy.

Orica Ltd, formerly ICI Australia, competes in the cut-throat commercial explosives business. Its customers are quarries that use explosives to blast solid rock face into aggregate of a specified size. Orica is constantly trying to minimise the cost of explosives. The firm realised it could create significant value by improving the efficiency of the blast. To do this, company engineers identified over 20 parameters that influenced the success of the blast, such as the density and shape of the rock, and the chemistry of the explosive charge. Orica then began collecting data from customers on these parameters as well as the outcomes of individual blasts. By collating the data, Orica engineers came to understand the conditions that produced different outcomes. It could then offer customers a contract for 'broken rock' that would almost guarantee the desired outcome. The success of Orica's approach – of managing the entire blast for the quarry rather than simply selling explosives – entrenched the company as the world's leading supplier of commercial explosives.[10]

their greatest impact at the interest stage; and technical sources can be most important during the evaluation stage.

In the new-task situation, the buyer must determine product specifications, price limits, delivery terms and times, service terms, payment terms, order quantities, acceptable suppliers and the selected supplier. Different participants influence each decision, and the order in which these decisions are made varies.

Because of the complicated selling involved, many companies use a *missionary sales force* consisting of their most effective salespeople. The brand promise and the manufacturer's brand name recognition will be important in establishing trust and the customer's willingness to consider change. The marketer also tries to reach as many key participants as possible and provide helpful information and assistance. Once a customer is acquired, suppliers are continually seeking ways to add value to their market offer to facilitate rebuys.

Customers considering dropping six or seven figures on one transaction for high-cost goods and services want all the information they can get. One way to entice new buyers is to create a customer reference programme in which satisfied existing customers act in concert with the company's sales and marketing department by agreeing to serve as

Marketing memo

Maximising customer references

Many firms depend on the opinions and experiences of others in evaluating a new business proposal from a new company. Here is some industry wisdom as to what works and what does not when developing customer information and reference programmes to respond to these demands.

Five common mistakes in developing customer reference stories

1   Failing to state the customer's need and its implications with specificity. Clearly state why customers had a need and how the company's products would resolve it. Such detailed information can better allow salespeople to assess whether a prospect has similar needs and could obtain similar payoffs.

2   Failing to quantify your customer's results. Although outside companies may seem reluctant to share too much hard data, it may just reflect the fact that they don't have the information readily accessible. Assist them in getting it.

3   Failing to describe business benefits of any kind (quantified or not). Don't focus on your expertise in various technologies and industries without saying how it specifically helped customers to enter or grow markets. Make an obvious cause-and-effect link between the solution provided and the claims for your product.

4   Failing to differentiate your offerings from the competition. Make it clear why it was the case that not just any company's products or services could have led to the same solution.

▶ Marketing memo *(continued)*

5 Failing to provide a concise, accessible summary of the story. Make sure you package the customer reference story in a way that a prospect can easily and quickly understand. Here are seven ways to do so.

Seven keys to developing customer reference stories successfully

1 State the customer's needs in compelling terms.

2 Emphasise the barriers in satisfying customer needs.

3 Describe your company's solution in terms of value.

4 List quantified results, especially those that affect ROI.

5 Differentiate your offering from those of competitors.

6 Provide a brief comprehensive summary.

7 Include numerous customer quotes.

Source: Based on a white paper by Bill Lee, Success stories: the top 5 mistakes, 2004 Bill Lee Customer Reference Forum, bill@customerreferenceforum.com

---

references. Technology companies such as HP, Lucent and Unisys have all employed such programmes. The marketing memo provides some tips for developing activities and programmes with impact.

Business marketers are also recognising the importance of their brand and how they must execute well in a number of areas to gain marketplace success. Boeing, which makes everything from commercial aeroplanes to satellites, implemented the 'One Company' brand strategy to unify all its different operations with a one-brand culture. The strategy was based in part on a triple helix representation: (1) enterprising spirit (why Boeing does what it does), (2) precision performance (how Boeing gets things done), and (3) defining the future (what Boeing achieves as a company).[11]

Systems buying and selling

Many business buyers prefer to buy a total solution to a problem from one seller. Called *systems buying*, this practice originated with government purchases of major weapons and communications systems. The government would solicit bids from *prime contractors*, who would enter into a contract with the government – the owner of the project or job – and assume full responsibility for its completion. The contractor who was awarded the contract would be responsible for bidding out and assembling the system's subcomponents from *second-tier contractors*. The prime contractor would thus provide a turnkey solution, so called because the buyer simply had to turn one key to get the job done.

Sellers have increasingly recognised that buyers like to purchase in this way, and many have adopted systems selling as a marketing tool. One variant of systems selling is *systems contracting*, where a single supplier provides the buyer with its entire requirement of MRO (maintenance, repair, operating) supplies. During the contract period, the supplier manages the customer's inventory. For example, Shell Oil manages the oil inventory of many of its business customers and knows when it requires replenishment. The customer benefits from reduced procurement and management costs, and from price protection over the term of the contract. The seller benefits from lower operating costs because of a steady demand and reduced paperwork.

Systems selling is a key industrial marketing strategy in bidding to build large-scale industrial projects, such as dams, steel factories, irrigation systems, sanitation systems, pipelines, utilities and even new towns. Project engineering firms must compete on price, quality, reliability and other attributes to win contracts. With systems selling, customers present potential suppliers with a list of project specifications and requirements. Suppliers, however, are not just at the mercy of these customer demands. Ideally, they are involved with customers early in the process to influence the actual development of the specifications. Or they can go beyond the specifications to offer additional value in various ways, as the following example shows.

Japan and Indonesia

The Indonesian government requested bids to build a cement factory near Jakarta. A western firm made a proposal that included choosing the site, designing the cement factory, hiring the construction crews, assembling the materials and equipment, and turning over the finished factory to the Indonesian government. A Japanese firm, in outlining its proposal, included all these services, plus hiring and training the workers to run the factory, exporting the cement through its trading companies, and using the cement to build roads and new office buildings in Jakarta. Although the Japanese proposal involved more money, it won the contract. Clearly, the Japanese viewed the problem not just as one of building a cement factory (the narrow view of systems selling) but as one of contributing to Indonesia's economic development. They took the broadest view of the customer's needs. This is true systems selling.

Participants in the business buying process

Who buys the trillions of euros' worth of goods and services needed by business organisations? Purchasing agents are influential in straight rebuy and modified rebuy situations, whereas other department personnel are more influential in new buy situations. Engineering personnel usually have a major influence in selecting product components, and purchasing agents dominate in selecting suppliers.[12]

The buying centre

Marketing researchers Webster and Wind call the decision-making unit of a buying organisation *the buying centre*. It consists of 'all those individuals and groups who participate in the purchasing decision-making process, who share some common goals and the risks arising from the decisions'.[13] The buying centre includes all members of the organisation who play any of seven roles in the purchase decision process.

1 **Initiators:** users or others in the organisation who request that something be purchased.
2 **Users:** those who will use the product or service. In many cases, the users initiate the buying proposal and help define the product requirements.
3 **Influencers:** people who influence the buying decision, often by helping define specifications and providing information for evaluating alternatives. Technical personnel are particularly important influencers.
4 **Deciders:** people who decide on product requirements or on suppliers.
5 **Approvers:** people who authorise the proposed actions of deciders or buyers.
6 **Buyers:** people who have formal authority to select the supplier and arrange the purchase terms. Buyers may help shape product specifications, but they play their major role in selecting vendors and negotiating. In more complex purchases, buyers might include high-level managers.

7 Gatekeepers: people who have the power to prevent sellers or information from reaching members of the buying centre. For example, purchasing agents, receptionists and telephone operators may prevent salespersons from contacting users or deciders.

Several people can occupy a given role such as user or influencer, and one person may occupy multiple roles.[14] A purchasing manager, for example, often occupies the roles of buyer, influencer and gatekeeper simultaneously: he or she can determine which sales reps can call on other people in the organisation; what budget and other constraints to place on the purchase; and which firm will actually get the business, even though others (deciders) might select two or more potential vendors that can meet the company's requirements.

The typical buying centre has a minimum of five or six members and often has dozens. Some may be outside the organisation, such as government officials, consultants, technical advisers and other members of the marketing channel. One study found that 3.5 more people on average were involved in making a purchase decision in 2005 than in 2001.[15]

Buying centre influences

Buying centres usually include several participants with differing interests, authority, status and persuasiveness, and sometimes very different decision criteria. For example, engineering personnel may want to maximise the performance of the product; production personnel may want ease of use and reliability of supply; financial personnel focus on the economics of the purchase; purchasing may be concerned with operating and replacement costs; union officials may emphasise safety issues.

Webster cautions that ultimately individuals, not organisations, make purchasing decisions.[16] Individuals are motivated by their own needs and perceptions in attempting to maximise the rewards (pay, advancement, recognition and feelings of achievement) offered by the organisation. Personal needs motivate the behaviour of individuals, but organisational needs legitimate the buying decision process and its outcomes. People are not buying 'products'. They are buying solutions to two problems: the organisation's economic and strategic problem and their own personal need for individual achievement and reward. In this sense, industrial buying decisions are both 'rational' and 'emotional', as they serve both the organisation's and the individual's needs.[17]

For example, research conducted by one industrial component manufacturer found that although top executives at small and medium-sized companies stated that they were comfortable in general with buying from other companies, they appeared to harbour subconscious insecurities about buying the manufacturer's product. Constant changes in technology had left them concerned about the internal effects within the company. Recognising this unease, the manufacturer retooled its selling approach to emphasise more emotional appeals and how its product line actually enabled the customer's employees to improve their performance, relieving management of the complications and stress of component use.[18]

Recognising these extrinsic, interpersonal influences, more industrial firms have put greater emphasis on strengthening their corporate brand. At one time Emerson Electric, global provider of power tools, compressors, electrical equipment and engineering solutions, was a conglomerate of 60 autonomous – and sometimes anonymous – companies. A new chief marketing officer aligned the previously independent brands under a new global brand architecture and identity, allowing Emerson to achieve a broader presence so that it could sell locally while leveraging its global brand name. Record sales and stock price highs soon followed.[19]

Targeting firms and buying centres

Successful business-to-business marketing requires that business marketers know which types of company to focus on in their selling efforts, as well as whom to concentrate on within the buying centres in those organisations. Business marketers may divide the marketplace in many different ways to decide on the types of firm to which they will sell. Finding those business sectors with the greatest growth prospects, most profitable customers and most promising opportunities for the firm is crucial. For instance, as a slowing economy has put a stranglehold on large corporations' purchasing departments, the small and midsize business markets are offering new opportunities for suppliers. In developing selling efforts, business marketers can also consider their customers' customers, or end users, if these are appropriate. Many business-to-business transactions are to firms using the products they purchase as components or ingredients in products they sell to the ultimate end-users. Once it has identified the type of businesses on which to focus marketing efforts, the firm must then decide how best to sell to them. To target their efforts properly, business marketers need to figure out: Who are the major decision participants? What decisions do they influence? What is their level of influence? What evaluation criteria do they use? Consider the following example.

> A company sells non-woven disposable surgical gowns to hospitals. The hospital personnel who participate in this buying decision include the vice-president of purchasing, the operating room administrator and the surgeons. The vice-president of purchasing analyses whether the hospital should buy disposable or reusable gowns. If the findings favour disposable gowns, then the operating room administrator compares various competitors' products and prices and makes a choice. This administrator considers absorbency, antiseptic quality, design and cost, and normally buys the brand that meets the functional requirements at the lowest cost. Surgeons influence the decision retroactively by reporting their satisfaction with the particular brand.

The business marketer is not likely to know exactly what kind of group dynamics takes place during the decision process, although whatever information he or she can obtain about personalities and interpersonal factors is useful.

Small sellers concentrate on reaching the *key buying influencers*. Larger sellers go for *multilevel in-depth selling* to reach as many participants as possible. Their salespeople virtually 'live' with high-volume customers. Companies must rely more heavily on their communications programmes to reach hidden buying influences and keep current customers informed.[20]

Business marketers must periodically review their assumptions about buying centre participants. For years, Kodak sold X-ray film to hospital lab technicians, but research indicated that professional administrators were increasingly making purchasing decisions. As a result, Kodak revised its marketing strategy and developed new advertising to reach out to these decision-makers.

The purchasing/procurement process

In principle, business buyers seek to obtain the highest benefit package (economic, technical, service and social) in relation to a market offering's costs. To make comparisons, they will try to translate all costs and benefits into monetary terms. A business buyer's incentive to purchase will be a function of the difference between perceived benefits and perceived costs.[21] The marketer's task is to construct a profitable offering that delivers superior customer value to the target buyers.

Business marketers must therefore ensure that customers fully appreciate how the firm's offerings are different and better. *Framing* occurs when customers are given a perspective or point of view that allows the firm to 'put its best foot forward'. Framing can be as simple as making sure that customers realise all the benefits or cost savings afforded by the firm's offerings, or becoming more involved and influential in the thought process behind how customers view the economics of purchasing, owning, using and disposing

Pfizer

One of the biggest names in pharmaceuticals, Pfizer views its supplier-diversity pro-gramme as an essential tool in connecting with customers. Pfizer offers strong support for small, minority- and women-owned businesses. The objective of the programme is to develop a supply base that reflects the demographic diversity of the consumer market-place. Gwendolyn Turner, manager of supplier diversity, says: 'Our business touches all kinds of customers, so it only makes sense that our supplier base represents a broad range of people as well.' Pfizer has even developed a mentoring programme that identifies the women and minority suppliers who need help growing, whether it's designing a better website or building a better business plan. Pfizer managers meet with the owners, often on site, to work out what they need. However, one should be aware that the Pfizer supplier-diversity programme is neither a social programme nor a promise that participating com-panies will secure business from Pfizer. It is also not a compromise on the quality, cost or service requirements the company asks of every supplier. Supplier Diversity at Pfizer is an opportunity; it's not a guarantee.

Source: Pfizer (2011), From one small business to another Enhancing Community Through Commerce: www.fizersupplierdiversity.com; S. Caminiti (2006) Drivers of the economy, *Fortune*, 153(7), 17 April, C1–7.

product offerings. Framing requires understanding how business customers currently think of and choose among products and services, and then determing how they *should* ideally think and choose.

Supplier diversity is a benefit that may not have a price tag but that business buyers overlook at their risk. As the CEOs of many large companies see it, a diverse supplier base is a business imperative. Minority suppliers are the fastest-growing segment of today's business landscape.

In the past, purchasing departments occupied a low position in the management hier-archy, in spite of often managing more than half the company's costs. Recent competitive pressures have led many companies to upgrade their purchasing departments and elevate administrators to vice-presidential rank. These new, more strategically oriented purchasing departments have a mission to seek the best value from fewer and better suppliers. Some multinationals have even elevated them to 'strategic supply departments' with responsibil-ity for global sourcing and partnering. At Caterpillar, for example, purchasing, inventory control, production scheduling and traffic have been combined into one department. The upgrading of purchasing means that business marketers must upgrade their sales person-nel to match the higher calibre of the business buyers.

Most purchasing professionals describe their jobs as more strategic, technical and team oriented, and involving more responsibility than ever before. 'Purchasing is doing more cross-functional work than it did in the past,' says David Duprey, a buyer for Anaren Microwave, Inc., which supplies the world's leading Original Equipment Manufacturers with wireless infrastructures, wireless consumer products, satellites and defence electron-ics, among other things. Of buyers surveyed, 61 per cent said the buying group was more involved in new product design and development than it was five years ago; and more than half the buyers participate in cross-functional teams, with suppliers well rep-resented.[22]

Some companies have started to centralise purchasing. Headquarters identifies materials purchased by several divisions and buys them centrally, gaining more purchasing clout. For the business marketer, this development means dealing with fewer and higher-level buyers and using a national account sales group to deal with large corporate buyers. At the same time, companies are decentralising some purchasing operations by empower-ing employees to purchase small-ticket items (such as special binders, coffee makers or Christmas trees) through corporate purchasing cards issued by credit card organisations.

We are now ready to describe the general stages in the business buying decision process.

Stages in the buying process

Robinson and his associates identified eight stages in the business buying decision process and called them *buyphases*.[23] The model in Table 8.1 is the *buygrid* framework.

In modified rebuy or straight rebuy situations, some stages are compressed or bypassed. For example, the buyer normally has a favourite supplier or a ranked list of suppliers and can skip the search and proposal solicitation stages. Here are some important considerations in each of the eight stages.

Problem recognition

The buying process begins when someone in the company recognises a problem or need that can be met by acquiring a good or service. The recognition can be triggered by internal or external stimuli. Internal stimuli might be that the company decides to develop a new product and needs new equipment and materials, or a machine breaks down and requires new parts. Or purchased material turns out to be unsatisfactory and the company searches for another supplier, or lower prices or better quality. Externally, the buyer may get new ideas at a trade show, see an ad or receive a call from a sales representative who offers a better product or a lower price. Business marketers can stimulate problem recognition by direct mail, telemarketing and calling on prospects.

General need description and product specification

Next, the buyer determines the needed item's general characteristics and required quantity. For standard items this is simple. For complex items the buyer will work with others – engineers, users – to define characteristics such as reliability, durability or price. Business marketers can help by describing how their products meet or even exceed the buyer's needs.

Table 8.1 Buygrid framework: major stages (buyphases) of the industrial buying process in relation to major buying situations (buyclasses)

		Buyclasses		
		New task	Modified rebuy	Straight rebuy
Buyphases	1 Problem recognition	Yes	Maybe	No
	2 General need description	Yes	Maybe	No
	3 Product specification	Yes	Maybe	Yes
	4 Supplier search	Yes	Yes	No
	5 Proposal solicitation	Yes	Maybe	No
	6 Supplier selection	Yes	Maybe	No
	7 Order-routine specification	Yes	Maybe	No
	8 Performance review	Yes	Maybe	Yes

The buying organisation now develops the item's technical specifications. Often, the company will assign a product-value-analysis engineering team to the project. *Product value analysis* (PVA) is an approach to cost reduction that studies components to determine whether they can be redesigned, standardised or made by cheaper methods of production. The PVA team will identify overdesigned components, for instance, that last longer than the product itself. Tightly written specifications will allow the buyer to refuse components that are too expensive or that fail to meet specified standards. When HP won ISRI's 1st Design for Recycling Award through an application of PVA methods, it received this accolade.

HP

HP has worked for many years to design products that are easier to recycle. The firm operates several recycling facilities, which allows it to determine the most effective design features to facilitate product recycling. HP has developed standards that integrate clear design guidelines and checklists into every product's design process to assess and improve recyclability. Hewlett Packard's design process includes: using modular design to allow components to be removed, upgraded or replaced; eliminating glues and adhesives by using, for example, snap-in features; marking plastic parts weighing more than 25 g according to ISO 11469 international standards, to speed up materials identification during recycling; reducing the number and types of materials used; using single plastic polymers; using recycled plastic; using moulded-in colours and finishes instead of paint, coatings or plating.[24]

Supplier search

The buyer next tries to identify the most appropriate suppliers through trade directories, contacts with other companies, trade advertisements, trade shows and the internet.[25] The move to internet purchasing has far-reaching implications for suppliers and will change the shape of purchasing for years to come.[26] Companies that purchase over the internet are utilising electronic marketplaces in several forms:

- **Catalogue sites**. Companies can order thousands of items through electronic catalogues distributed by eprocurement software, such as Grainger's.
- **Vertical markets**. Companies buying industrial products such as plastics, steel, chemicals or services such as logistics or media can go to specialised websites (called ehubs). For example, Plastics.com allows plastics buyers to search for the best prices among thousands of plastics sellers.
- **'Pure Play' auction sites**. Online marketplaces such as eBay and Freemarkets.com could not have been realised without the internet. Freemarkets.com provides online auctions for buyers and sellers of industrial parts, raw materials, commodities and services in over 50 product categories and has facilitated over €30 billion worth of commerce since 1995.
- **Spot (or exchange) markets**. A spot market is a market where commodities and cash are bought and sold immediately, with no time between trades. On spot electronic markets prices change by the minute. ChemConnect.com is an exchange for buyers and sellers of bulk chemicals such as natural gas liquids, aromatics, olefins and plastics, and it is a B2B success in an arena littered with failed online exchanges. ChemConnect's international community of members includes more than 9,000 companies from over 150 countries worldwide. First to market, it is now the biggest online exchange for chemical trading, with an average of approximately 1 million barrels traded every day in 2007. FizTrade.com is an instant trading site for physical metals offering both bid and ask, whereas Converge.com is a leading business-to-business

Marketing insight

Alibaba.com in Europe

In October 2007 Alibaba.com opened its first European office in Geneva. Alibaba.com is the world's number-one marketplace dedicated to small and medium-sized enterprises (SMEs), companies employing fewer than 250 people. From Geneva, Alibaba.com assists European SMEs to become more competitive by making their import and export business easier in a growing global market. Alibaba.com provides a platform where SME buyers and suppliers across the globe can connect and exchange raw materials, goods, manufactured products and even services. In just over 11 years, Alibaba.com has built a global community of more than 56 million members from over 250 countries and regions. In April 2010 AliExpress was officially launched on the international marketplace. AliExpress especially assists smaller buyers seeking fast shipment of small quantities of goods. In Europe, SMEs make up more than 99 per cent of the total number of companies and are the principal source of employment and wealth in the European Union. They provide two out of three of the private sector jobs and contribute to more than half of the total value added created by businesses in the EU.

'The large concentration of SMEs is one of the reasons why, in just a few years, Europe has become one of the most important markets forAlibaba.com in terms of active members,' said Kenneth Liu, Alibaba.com vice-president of global operations. The success of Alibaba.com's marketplace is largely down to its efficiency and ease of use, enabling SMEs to save time by making global sourcing available 24/7 and removing barriers of geographies and time zones. Buyers use the site for free and have access to an active global supplier community and easy-to-use sourcing and communication tools. Sellers can also use the site for free, posting products to sell and searching for buyers. Premium fee-based packages are available for sellers who want to increase their exposure to potential buyers. Buyers and sellers meet online at Alibaba.com but transactions are completed offline.

Sources: Based on www.alibaba.com; http://.ec.europa.eu; Alibaba has $82 million password, *Private Equity Week*, 23 February 2004; J. Rossant (2004) Europe's hot growth companies, *BusinessWeek*, 25 October.

global electronics trading exchange. Recognising the cost management advantages that this market can offer, manufacturers have been committing an increasing portion of their procurement budget to the spot market. Today, industry experts estimate that up to one-third of all procurement occurs outside of pre-arranged contracts.[27]

- **Private exchanges.** Hewlett-Packard and IBM operate private exchanges to link with specially invited groups of suppliers and partners over the web.
- **Barter markets.** In barter markets, participants offer to trade goods or services.
- **Buying alliances.** Several companies buying the same goods, such as Transora and Covisint, join together to form purchasing consortia to gain deeper discounts on volume purchases.

Online business buying offers several advantages. It shaves transaction costs for both buyers and suppliers, reduces time between order and delivery, consolidates purchasing systems and forges more intimate relationships between partners and buyers. On the downside, it may help to erode supplier–buyer loyalty and create potential security problems. See the marketing insight box for an example of an online business marketplace.

Eprocurement

Websites are organised around two types of ehub: *vertical hubs* centred on industries (plastics, steel, chemicals, paper) and *functional hubs* (logistics, media buying, advertising, energy management).

In addition to using these websites, companies can use eprocurement in other ways:

- **Set up direct extranet links to major suppliers.** An extranet is a private computer network using internet technology to which access is provided to select groups of vendors, suppliers or customers who need to access selected databases and processes.

For example, a company can set up a direct eprocurement account at Dell or Office Depot, and its employees can make their purchases this way.

- **Form buying alliances.** A number of major retailers and manufacturers such as Ace Hardware, Coca-Cola, Colgate Palmolive, Johnson & Johnson, Kraft, Kroger, Lowe's, Nestlé, Office Depot, PepsiCo, Procter & Gamble, Sara Lee, Staples, Wal-Mart and Wegmans Food Markets are part of a data-sharing alliance called 1SYNC. Several car companies (GM, Ford, DaimlerChrysler) formed Covisint for the same reason. Covisint is the leading provider of services that can integrate crucial business information and processes between partners, customers and suppliers. The company has now also targeted healthcare to provide similar services.

- **Set up company buying sites.** General Electric formed the trading process network (TPN), where it posts *requests for proposals*, negotiates terms and places orders.

Moving into eprocurement means more than acquiring software; it requires changing purchasing strategy and structure. However, the benefits are many: aggregating purchasing across multiple departments yields larger, centrally negotiated volume discounts, a smaller purchasing staff and less buying of substandard goods from outside the approved list of suppliers.

Lead generation

The supplier's task is to ensure it is considered when customers are – or could be – in the market and searching for a supplier. Identifying good leads and converting them to sales requires the whole of the marketing and sales organisations to work in a coordinated, multichannel approach in the role of trusted adviser to prospective customers. Marketing must work together with sales to define what makes a 'sales-ready' prospect and cooperate to send the right messages via sales calls, tradeshows, online activities, PR, events, direct mail and referrals.[28]

Marketing must find the right balance between the quantity and quality of leads. Too many leads, even of high quality, and the sales force may be overwhelmed and allow promising opportunities to fall through the cracks; too few or low-quality leads and the sales force may become frustrated or demoralised.[29] To generate leads proactively, suppliers need to know about their customers. They can obtain background information from vendors such as EUbusiness.com, Business.com, Hoover.com and Dun & Bradstreet, or information-sharing websites such as CSR Europe, Jigsaw and LinkedIn.[30]

Suppliers that lack the required production capacity or suffer from a poor reputation will be rejected. Those who qualify may be visited by the buyer's agents, who will examine the suppliers' manufacturing facilities and meet their personnel. After evaluating each company, the buyer will end up with a shortlist of qualified suppliers. Many professional buyers have forced suppliers to change their marketing to increase their likelihood of making the cut.

Proposal solicitation

The buyer next invites qualified suppliers to submit proposals. If the item is complex or expensive, the buyer will require a detailed written proposal from each qualified supplier. After evaluating the proposals, the buyer will invite a few suppliers to make formal presentations.

Business marketers must be skilled in researching, writing and presenting proposals. Written proposals should be marketing documents that describe value and benefits in customer terms. Oral presentations must inspire confidence and position the company's capabilities and resources so that they stand out from the competition. Proposals and selling are often organised in teams, which may focus on a particular geographic region, industry or market concentration. Salespeople can leverage the knowledge and expertise of co-workers instead of working in isolation.[31]

Table 8.2 An example of vendor analysis

Attributes	Rating scale				
	Importance weights	Poor (1)	Fair (2)	Good (3)	Excellent (4)
Price	0.30				X
Supplier reputation	0.20			X	
Product reliability	0.30				X
Service reliability	0.10		X		
Supplier flexibility	0.10			X	
Total score: 0.30(4) + 0.20(3) + 0.30(4) + 0.10(2) + 0.10(3) = 3.5					

Supplier selection

Before selecting a supplier, the buying centre will specify desired supplier attributes and indicate their relative importance. To rate and identify the most attractive suppliers, buying centres often use a supplier-evaluation model such as the one shown in Table 8.2.

To develop compelling value propositions business marketers need to better understand how business buyers arrive at their valuations.[32] Researchers studying how business marketers assess customer value found eight different *customer value assessment* (CVA) methods. Companies tended to use the simpler methods, although the more sophisticated ones promise to produce a more accurate picture of customer-perceived value (see the marketing memo on p. 310).

The choice and importance of different attributes varies with the type of buying situation. Delivery reliability, price and supplier reputation are important for routine-order products. As regards procedural-problem products, the customer may be uncertain of her or his ability to learn to use the product. Therefore, the three most important attributes are technical service, supplier flexibility and product reliability. For political-problem products that stir rivalries in the organisation (such as the choice of a computer system), the most important attributes are price, supplier reputation, product reliability, service reliability and supplier flexibility.

Overcoming price pressures and improving productivity

The buying centre may attempt to negotiate with preferred suppliers for better prices and terms before making the final selection. Despite moves towards strategic sourcing, partnering and participation in cross-functional teams, buyers still spend a large chunk of their time haggling with suppliers on price. The number of price-oriented buyers can vary by country depending on customer preferences for different service configurations and characteristics of the customer's organisation.[33]

Marketers can counter requests for a lower price in a number of ways. They may be able to show evidence that the 'total cost of ownership' – that is, the 'life-cycle cost' of using their product – is lower than for competitors' products. They can cite the value of the services the buyer now receives, especially if they are superior to those offered by competitors. Research shows that service support and personal interactions, as well as a supplier's know-how and ability to improve customers' time to market, can be useful differentiators in achieving key-supplier status.[34]

While marketers may also improve their productivity to be able to deal with requests for better prices, such improvements may lead to other advantages as well. The Scandinavian metal packaging producer for food products, Glud & Marstrand, has invested in

Marketing memo

Developing compelling customer value propositions

To command price premiums in competitive B2B markets, firms must create compelling customer value propositions. The first step is to research the customer. Here are a number of productive research methods:

- **Internal engineering assessment.** Have company engineers use laboratory tests to estimate the product's performance characteristics. Weakness: ignores the fact that in different applications the product will have different economic value.

- **Field value-in-use assessment.** Interview customers about how costs of using a new product compare to those of using an incumbent. The task is to assess how much each cost element is worth to the buyer.

- **Focus-group value assessment.** Ask customers in a focus group what value they would put on potential market offerings.

- **Direct survey questions.** Ask customers to place a direct monetary value on one or more changes in the market offering.

- **Conjoint analysis.** Ask customers to rank their preferences for alternative market offerings or concepts. Use statistical analysis to estimate the implicit value placed on each attribute.

- **Benchmarks.** Show customers a 'benchmark' offering and then a new market offering. Ask how much more they would pay for the new offering or how much less they would pay if certain features were removed from the benchmark offering.

- **Compositional approach.** Ask customers to attach a monetary value to each of three alternative levels of a given attribute. Repeat for other attributes, then add the values together for any offer configuration.

- **Importance ratings.** Ask customers to rate the importance of different attributes and their suppliers' performance on each.

Having done this research you can specify the customer value proposition, following a number of important principles. First, clearly substantiate value claims by concretely specifying the differences between your offerings and those of competitors on the dimensions that matter most to the customer. For example, Rockwell Automation determined the cost savings customers would realise from purchasing its pump solution instead of a competitor's by using industry-standard metrics of functionality and performance: kilowatt-hours spent, number of operating hours per year and dollars per kilowatt-hour. Also, make the financial implications obvious.

Second, document the value delivered by creating written accounts of costs savings or added value that existing customers have actually captured by using your offerings. Chemical producer Akzo Nobel conducted a two-week pilot study on a production reactor at a prospective customer's facility to document points of parity and points of difference of its high-purity metal organics product.

Finally, make sure the customer value proposition is well implemented within the company, and train and reward employees for developing a compelling one. Quaker Chemical conducts training programmes for its managers that include a competition to develop the best proposals.

Sources: J. C. Anderson, J. A. Narus and W. van Rossum (2006) Customer value propositions in business markets, *Harvard Business Review*, March, 2–10; J. C. Anderson and J. A. Narus, Business marketing: understanding what customers value, *Harvard Business Review*, November, 53–65; J. C. Anderson and J. A. Narus (1995) Capturing the value of supplementary services, *Harvard Business Review*, January, 75–83; J. C. Anderson, D. C. Jain and P. K. Chintagunta (1993) A customer value assessment in business markets: a state-of-practice study, *Journal of Business-to-Business Marketing*, 1(1), 3–29.

a Warehouse Management System (WMS) delivered by Consafe Logistic.[35] The motive behind introduction of the new WMS was fourfold:

1 The system should enable the warehouse to improve its day-to-day operations while improving productivity and thereby reducing costs.
2 The system should provide the management and organisation with a valid system of data analysis for management of operations and capacity of the warehouse and line optimisation of picking work.
3 The system should provide the management board with an effective analysis tool for continuous evaluation of warehouse performance.
4 The system should provide online and real-time information on stock status.

Now, productivity has risen so much that the warehouse can operate to the same level with 22 employees as it did previously with 34. There are also other advantages, such as the fact that today, internal salespeople know exactly what the company holds in stock – important knowledge which they had difficulty in obtaining previously.

Some firms are using technology to devise novel customer solutions. With web technology and tools, VistaPrint printers can offer professional printing to small businesses that previously could not afford it.[36] Some companies handle price-oriented buyers by setting a lower price but establishing restrictive conditions: (1) limited quantities; (2) no refunds; (3) no adjustments; and (4) no services.[37]

Solution selling can also alleviate price pressure and comes in different forms. Here are three examples.[38]

1 **Solutions to enhance customer revenues**. Through a sophisticated data management system, Hendrix Voeders helped farmers to monitor animals' feed consumption and weight gain. Farmers were now able to make microadjustments in nutrients and medicine, resulting in productivity gains such as animal weight gain of 5–10 per cent or increases of 4–5 per cent in live births.
2 **Solutions to decrease customer risks**. ICI Explosives formulated a safer way to ship explosives for quarries.
3 **Solutions to reduce customer costs**. W. W. Grainger employees work at large customer facilities to reduce materials-management costs.

Many companies are seeking solutions that increase benefits and reduce costs enough to overcome any low-price concerns.

Risk and gain sharing can offset requested price reductions from customers. For example, a hospital supplier signs an agreement with a hospital promising €350,000 in savings over the first 18 months in exchange for a tenfold increase in the hospital's share of supplies. If the hospital supplier achieves less than this promised saving, it will make up the difference. If the hospital supplier achieves substantially more than promised, it participates in the extra savings. To make such arrangements work, the supplier must be willing to help the customer to build a historical database, reach an agreement for measuring benefits and costs, and devise a dispute resolution mechanism with directions on how any disagreements between the parties should be resolved.

Number of suppliers

As part of the buyer selection process, buying centres must decide how many suppliers to use. Companies are increasingly reducing the number of suppliers. Ford and Motorola have cut the number of suppliers by 20–80 per cent. These companies want their chosen suppliers to be responsible for a larger component system, they want them to achieve continuous quality and performance improvement, and at the same time they want them to lower prices each year by a given percentage. These companies expect their suppliers to work closely with them during product development, and they value their suggestions. There is even a trend towards single sourcing.

Companies that use multiple sources often cite the threat of a labour strike as the biggest deterrent to single sourcing. Another reason why companies may be reluctant to use a single source is that they fear they will become too comfortable in the relationship and lose their competitive edge. A company that is using only one supplier is Humac, as chronicled in the breakthrough marketing box on page 312.

Order-routine specification

After selecting suppliers, the buyer negotiates the final order, listing the technical specifications, the quantity needed, the expected time of delivery, return policies, warranties and so on. Many industrial buyers lease heavy equipment such as machinery and trucks. The lessee gains a number of advantages: conserving capital, getting the latest products,

Breakthrough marketing

Humac

Humac A/S was founded in 2006 as a result of a merger between Icelandic Öflun ApS and Norwegian Office line. In 2009, Humac was purchased by EEC, which made Humac the largest APR (Apple Premium Reseller) retailer in Scandinavia. Offering both offline and online sales, Humac currently comprises 15 outlets throughout Scandinavia. Just like many other companies Humac has experienced that business can be a tough game, not least because of the 2008 financial crisis and the subsequent recession. It was not until 2011 that the company was able to present a net profit from last year's activities. 'It makes me proud that we have succeeded in bringing the 2010 sales close to the 2007/2008 level. Notably, this has happened even though we have made a cut in expenses and staff,' CEO Denmark Morten Bo Andersen says. Humac receives its largest sales in business markets. According to Morten Bo Andersen, it is often possible to make a higher profit in these markets than in consumer markets. This is because in business markets companies are often more successful in offering value-added products to their customers, such as key-ready total solutions (e.g. solutions including mailserver and storage), which also may include training, support and maintenance to ensure customers' success in *their* markets. Humac has also found that big sales are no guarantee for big profit. One reason is increasing IT market competition. Another reason is that companies comprising strong brands, such as Apple, may use their market power to negotiate low retailer profit margins. However, by focusing on building strong staff competencies, flexibility in their offerings to customers, and customer support, Humac has made it through some tough business years.

Questions

1 Humac is offering only one brand (Apple) to its customers. Discuss the pros and cons of selling products from only one supplier in business markets.
2 How can Humac increase its negotiating power when dealing with Apple?

Sources: H. Rasch (2011) Humac: Vi vokser mest på B2B salg, *CRN*, 23 February, 14; *CRN* online (2011) Stolt af et stærkt team, 15 February; www.humac.dk.

Offering only one brand to its customers, Humac comprises 15 outlets throughout Scandinavia
Source: David Domingo www.daviddomingo.org

receiving better service and gaining some tax advantages. The lessor often ends up with a larger net income and the chance to sell to customers who could not afford outright purchase.

In the case of maintenance, repair and operating items, buyers are moving towards blanket contracts rather than periodic purchase orders. A blanket contract establishes a long-term relationship in which the supplier promises to resupply the buyer as needed, at agreed prices, over a specified period of time. Because the seller holds the stock, blanket contracts are sometimes called *stockless purchase plans*. The buyer's computer automatically sends an order to the seller when stock is needed. This system locks suppliers in tighter with the buyer and makes it difficult for out suppliers to break in unless the buyer becomes dissatisfied with the in supplier's prices, quality or service.

Companies that fear a shortage of key materials are willing to buy and hold large inventories. They will sign long-term contracts with suppliers to ensure a steady flow of materials. Ford and several other major companies regard long-term supply planning as a major responsibility of their purchasing managers. For example, General Motors wants to buy from fewer suppliers, which must be willing to locate close to its plants and produce high-quality components. Business marketers are also setting up extranets with important customers to facilitate and lower the cost of transactions. The customers enter orders directly on the computer that are automatically transmitted to the supplier. Some companies go further and shift the ordering responsibility to their suppliers in systems called *vendor-managed inventory*. These suppliers are privy to the customer's inventory levels and take responsibility for replenishing it automatically through *continuous replenishment programmes*.

Performance review

The buyer periodically reviews the performance of the chosen supplier(s) using one of three methods. The buyer may contact the end users and ask for their evaluations; the buyer may rate the supplier on several criteria using a weighted-score method; or the buyer might aggregate the cost of poor performance to come up with adjusted costs of purchase, including price. The performance review may lead the buyer to continue, modify or end a supplier relationship.

Many companies have set up incentive systems to reward purchasing managers for good buying performance, in much the same way that sales personnel receive bonuses for good selling performance. These systems lead purchasing managers to increase pressure on sellers for the best terms.

Managing business-to-business relationships

The need for managing business-to-business relationships

To improve effectiveness and efficiency, business suppliers and customers are exploring different ways to manage their relationships.[39] Closer relationships are driven in part by supply chain management, early supplier involvement and purchasing alliances.[40] Cultivating the right relationships with business is paramount for any holistic marketing programme. Business-to-business marketers are avoiding 'spray and pray' approaches to attracting and retaining customers in favour of honing in on their targets and developing one-to-one marketing approaches. Also, they are increasingly using online social media in the form of company blogs, online press releases, and forums or discussion groups to communicate with existing as well as prospective customers. Social media are increasingly used as a platform for 'building' strong seller–customer relationships in business markets (see the marketing insight box).

The role of uncertainty in business relationships

Uncertainty refers to situations where the information available for decision making is too vague, or too imprecise, to calculate the probabilities of different outcomes of the decision.[41] Uncertainty can come in many forms and may relate to both institutional aspects (e.g. lack of formal institutional standards, such as professionalisation, industry boundaries and product standards) and transactional aspects (e.g. lack of confidentiality of information and insufficient information).[42] Therefore, uncertainty has also to do with trust among business partners or in an industry.[43] Uncertainty can be highly damaging for the efficiency of business relations and should therefore be reduced. Uncertainty leads to unpredictable outcomes, since it makes it difficult for business negotiators to anticipate the full impact – positive or negative – of a transaction or an agreement.[44] Hence, uncertainty may lead to irrational decisions. Uncertainty may even lead to a collective irrational outcome of a transaction between business partners, although each partner individually performs rational behaviour. The famous example put forward by Akerlof[45] concerning the market for 'lemons' (i.e., used cars of poor quality) illustrates this point. A used car is mainly a 'credence good'[46] since the 'real' quality of a used car cannot usually be determined by the potential buyer until after he or she has purchased it and driven it for a time. Because of a lack of information, the buyer is motivated to pay only a low price for a used car, thereby minimising the potential risk of paying too much for poor quality. If the seller cannot justify a high price, which is difficult because there are no simple means of conveying the quality in a believable way, he will be motivated to sell only lemons. The consequence

Marketing insight

Social media in business markets

Successful business often builds on developing strong relationships with your business partners. Although a large number of conceptualisations of 'relationship marketing' have been proposed, marketing researchers seem to agree that (a) both parties in a relationship must benefit for the relationship to continue; (b) the relationship is often longitudinal in nature; (c) the focus of relationship marketing is to retain customers. In recent years, social media has become an increasingly important platform for developing and maintaining relationships between business partners. Using social media, companies can more easily discuss matters with business partners around the globe, and other relevant parties (e.g. experts, lawyers, politicians and the like) can be invited to take part in the conversations. As stated by social media blogger Niall Harbison, 'social media is cheap and allows you to meet people in a fraction of the amount of time that it would take in "the real world"'. The personalisation that occurs

when using social media may boost the level of trust between parties, which in turn may positively influence customer loyalty. Furthermore, social media may be used in detecting new business partners. For instance, consider a group of engineers discussing the pros and cons of a new construction material for constructing bridges. Engineers from other companies find the open discussion highly interesting and attend the discussion, offering additional viewpoints and ideas. As discussions between parties develop, new possibilities for business collaborations may be detected, and ultimately new business relationships may evolve.

Sources: N. Harbison (2010) How to market your business using social media when you have zero budget, *simplyZesty*, 15 March, www.simplyzesty.com/social-media/market-business-social-media-budget/; B. Gutek, A. D. Bhappu, M. A. Liao-Troth and B. Cherry (1999) Distinguishing between service relationships and encounters, *Journal of Applied Psychology*, 84(2), 218–33; S. D. Hunt, D. B. Arnett and S. Madhavaram (2006) The explanatory foundations of relationship marketing theory, *Journal of Business and Industrial Marketing*, 21(2), 72–87.

is that only low-quality cars will be sold and bought in the marketplace, a situation that hurts both sellers (lack of profit) and buyers (lack of quality). This example – although constructed – points to the need for reducing uncertainty in business relationships. As discussed in the next section, uncertainty is also one of the main concepts considered in the transaction cost economics approach.

Transaction cost economics

Within mainstream economic thinking, all market agents can obtain perfect knowledge about products and prices at no cost. Business agents are fully informed about all products and business terms, and no information asymmetric exists between suppliers and customers. Thus, rationality is assumed for all market agents. In transaction cost economics (TCE), market agents have limits on their ability to make truly rational decisions; they have limited mental resources and thus cannot deal with unlimited amounts of information. *Bounded rationality* can be seen either as the attempt to do as well as possible given the demands of the world – the notion of optimisation under constraints – or as the sub-optimal outcome of the limited cognitive system.[47] The introduction of bounded rationality means that possible information asymmetry may exist between seller and buyer. Thus, a risk arises that market failure will occur due to opportunistic behaviour of the better-informed party. Researchers have noted that establishing a customer–supplier relationship creates tension between safeguarding and adaptation. Vertical coordination can facilitate stronger customer–seller ties but at the same time may increase the risk to the customer's and supplier's specific investments.

Specific investments are those expenditures tailored to a particular company and value chain partner (investments in company-specific training, equipment and operating procedures or systems).[48] They help firms grow profits and achieve their positioning.[49] Specific investments, however, also entail considerable risk to both customer and supplier. TCE maintains that because these investments are partially sunk, they lock firms into a particular relationship. Sensitive cost and process information may need to be exchanged. A buyer may be vulnerable to holdup because of switching costs; a supplier may be more vulnerable because it has dedicated assets and/or technology/knowledge at stake. In terms of the latter risk, consider the following example.[50]

> An automobile component manufacturer wins a contract to supply an under-hood component to an original equipment manufacturer (OEM). A one-year, sole-source contract safeguards the supplier's OEM-specific investments in a dedicated production line. However, the supplier may also be obliged to work (non-contractually) as a partner with the OEM's internal engineering staff, using linked computing facilities to exchange detailed engineering information and coordinate frequent design and manufacturing changes over the term of the contract. These interactions could reduce costs and/or increase quality by improving the firm's responsiveness to marketplace changes. But they could also magnify the threat to the supplier's intellectual property.

When buyers cannot easily monitor supplier performance, the supplier might shirk or cheat and not deliver the expected value. *Opportunism* is 'some form of cheating or undersupply relative to an implicit or explicit contract'.[51] It may entail blatant self-interest and deliberate misrepresentation that violate contractual agreements. In creating the 1996 version of the Ford Taurus, Ford Corporation chose to outsource the whole process to one supplier, Lear Corporation. Lear committed to a contract that, for various reasons, it knew it was unable to fulfil. According to Ford, Lear missed deadlines, failed to meet weight and price objectives, and furnished parts that did not work.[52] A more passive form of opportunism might be a refusal or unwillingness to adapt to changing circumstances.

Opportunism is a concern because firms must devote resources to control and monitoring that they could otherwise allocate to more productive purposes. Contracts may become inadequate to govern supplier transactions when supplier opportunism becomes difficult to detect, when firms make specific investments in assets that they cannot use elsewhere, and when contingencies are harder to anticipate. Customers and suppliers are more likely to form a joint venture (instead of signing a simple contract) when the supplier's degree of asset specificity (asset specificity: whether the assets involved in business transactions are valuable in the context of one or more transactions) is high, monitoring the supplier's behaviour is difficult, and the supplier has a poor reputation.[53] When a supplier has a good reputation, it is more likely to avoid opportunism to protect this valuable intangible asset.

The presence of a significant future time horizon and/or strong solidarity norms typically causes customers and suppliers to strive for joint benefits. As a result, there is a shift in specific investments from expropriation (increased opportunism on the receiver's part) to bonding (reduced opportunism).[54]

According to TCE, companies may act in a self-interested way when possible: that is, they may exploit unforeseen circumstances even though the related actions taken may damage the other party. However, people will only act opportunistically some of the time and not all people are opportunists. The problem is to tell who is an opportunist at what time, which of course is not an easy task. The combination of bounded rationality (which may lead to information asymmetries), with the possibility of people acting opportunistically, therefore introduces uncertainty in business relationships. Along with two other variables (frequency: the frequency of the business transaction and asset specificity), the level of uncertainty explains whether firms will deal with market agents or whether they will seek to integrate their activities vertically (for example, by taking over a supplier). Other things being equal, the higher the frequency, the uncertainty and the asset specificity, the more likely it is that vertical integration will take place, since this solution will result in the lowest transaction costs. *Transaction costs* occur when goods or services are transferred from one organisation to another and may include search costs, contracting costs, monitoring costs and enforcement costs.[55]

A certain amount of uncertainty can always be associated with a transaction, since because of bounded rationality it is difficult and costly to determine all the possible effects a transaction might have.[56] In TCE theory, uncertainty therefore arises because of impenetrable complexity; and since 'objective' uncertainty can be difficult or even impossible to estimate, focus is put on companies' perceived uncertainty. Companies are assumed to take action based on perceived uncertainty. Based on TCE a number of possible such perceived uncertainties can be detected within business relationships. Uncertainties may be related to differences between buyer and seller (e.g. language, culture, technology), trading procedures and contracting procedures, and to the possibility that companies may act in an opportunist way when beneficial for just one of the parties. While TCE is useful in detecting the kinds of uncertainty that may be involved in transactions among business relationships, TCE has been criticised for focusing too much on agent opportunism and thereby neglecting the possibility of inter-firm trust and the evolution of inter-firm relationships.[57] Network theory, however, introduces a view on business relationships that in many aspects deals with this criticism.

Network theory

Whereas TCE is based on analysis of the market behaviour of companies and views the results of that behaviour in terms of 'win–lose' outcomes, network theory emphasises the possibility that both sides can win simultaneously: that is, a win–win outcome. Basically, this possibility arises because of the introduction of 'trust' in network theory. While TCE can be considered an 'anti-trust' approach (people in companies are opportunists), network theory can be considered a 'trust' approach. Networking appears to be among the leading paradigms in the understanding and analysis of partnership between companies. A distinction can be made between strategic (governed) and industrial (non-governed) networks. The governed networks are those strategic networks where members strongly identify with the 'core firm'/network and where there are clear rules for participating in the network's knowledge-sharing activities.

Dyer and Nobeoka[58] have shown that Toyota's ability to create and manage network-level knowledge-sharing processes effectively at least partially explains the relative productivity advantages enjoyed by Toyota and its suppliers. Toyota's network: (1) motivates members to participate and openly share valuable knowledge (while preventing undesirable spillovers to competitors); (2) prevents free riders; and (3) reduces the costs associated with finding and accessing different types of valuable knowledge. Toyota has managed to do this by creating a strong network identity with rules for participation and entry into the network. In 2009 Toyota was the leading automaker in global sales with 6,450,000 units. In 2007, the Volkswagen group began working on a ten-year strategic plan that aimed to narrow the productivity and profit gap with Toyota. 'In the last five, six years, Toyota has pulled ahead of us, and what we plan to do is to reduce the lead they've got,' says CEO Martin Winterkorn. 'If we are approaching Toyota, we are approaching it in terms of productivity goals,' the VW spokesman added. 'The financial side is related. If you are highly productive, you are highly profitable.' In 2009 VW ranked second in global sales with 6,290,000 units, compared to a rank of fourth in 2006 with 5,720,000 units sold.[59]

The strategic networks are managed by the hub, which sends signals to network members as to what actions, activities and structures are considered appropriate. In contrast, industrial networks are sets of interrelated agents performing interconnected activities by employing interdependent resources.[60] In industrial networks the relationships therefore need to be 'coped with' rather than controlled,[61] and in order to be able to manage these relationships a certain level of mutual trust and information sharing is needed. Thus, while emphasis in strategic networks is on coordination and control, emphasis in industrial networks is on trust and on exchange of 'sensitive/confidential' information. Shortcomings in coordination and/or in information sharing could therefore be a significant driver of uncertainty and transaction costs among the parties involved in the network.[62]

In general – covering both types of network – networks can be understood as long-term arrangements among organisations, which allow these organisations to get long-term sustainable advantages.[63] Network theory, developed first in the 1960s and 1970s, is based on the empirical observation that in many industrial markets stability of relations,

SOI Industry Consortium

In November 2007, a group of electronics companies around the world launched the SOI (silicon-on-insulator) Industry Consortium. The consortium aims at accelerating SOI innovations, promoting the benefits of SOI technology and reducing the barriers to adoption. The SOI Consortium's goals are to reduce adoption costs, make SOI best practices available and facilitate design examples across the value chain. The most significant benefits demonstrated by SOI are performance enhancement and power consumption reduction. The founding membership roster includes: AMD, ARM, Cadence Design Systems, CEA-Leti, Chartered Semiconductor Manufacturing, Freescale Semiconductor, IBM, Innovative Silicon, KLA-Tencor, Lam Research, NXP, Samsung, Semico, Soitec, SHE Europe, STMicroelectronics, Synopsys, TSMC and UMC. In 2011, SOI announced the results of an assessment and characterisation of fully depleted silicon-on-insulator (FD-SOI) technology, demonstrating that this advanced CMOS silicon technology is well suited to address the increasing low-power, high-performance requirements for mobile and consumer applications.

Source: Based on www.soiconsortium.org; K. Nargi-Toth (2007) Silicon-on-Insulator Consortium, *Printed Circuit Design and Manufacture*, 24(11), November, 8.

exchange of information, interlacing of technologies and various forms of cooperation and contractual agreement are the rule rather than the exception.[64] In many producer markets, the selling firm has a limited number of highly important customers and the relationships to these customers are often complex, involving several people and functions on both sides. Because of the complexity and uncertainty associated with dealing with new partners, both the selling and the buying company may find it useful to reduce the perceived distance between the companies. As transactions evolve successfully, both parties may believe that the benefits of staying in the relationship outweigh the disadvantages of not operating 'freely' in the marketplace. This reduces opportunism, and increases trust, since both parties share an interest in nursing and maintaining the relationship.

However, building relationships also exposes companies to new uncertainties. In a network relationship, the parties involved are 'selling' their independence for the purpose of attaining lower transaction costs. On the other hand, the closer the relationship, the higher the uncertainty of being stuck and being caught with a single partner.[65] Thus, firms are in need of effective information tools, which not only fulfil intra-network demands for mutual information but also fulfil firms' need for information about alternatives. The higher the collaboration, the higher the dependency, and thus the more difficult it is to change partners. Bringing 'external' market information into the collaboration may motivate each party to maximise short-term transactions in order to maintain long-term network advantages. Hence, because of an increased, collective insight into other market opportunities, costs and the uncertainties associated with not being able to operate 'freely' may decrease.

Much research has advocated greater vertical coordination between members of the distribution chain, or in other words stronger and more organised cooperation between, say, a company and its buyers and/or suppliers.

Vertical coordination

Through vertical coordination both buyers and sellers can transcend merely transacting and instead engage in activities that create more value for both parties.[66] Building trust is one prerequisite to healthy and well-coordinated long-term relationships. The marketing insight box identifies some key dimensions to such trust. Knowledge that is specific and relevant to a relationship partner is also an important factor in the strength of interfirm ties between partners.[67]

Marketing insight

Establishing corporate trust and credibility

Corporate credibility is the extent to which customers believe a firm can design and deliver products and services that satisfy their needs and wants. It reflects the supplier's reputation in the marketplace and is the foundation for a strong relationship.

Corporate credibility depends in turn on three factors:

1 Corporate expertise: the extent to which a company is seen as able to make and sell products or conduct services.

2 Corporate trustworthiness: the extent to which a company is seen as motivated to be honest, dependable and sensitive to customer needs.

3 Corporate likeability: the extent to which a company is seen as likeable, attractive, prestigious, dynamic and so on.

In other words, a credible firm is good at what it does; it keeps its customers' best interests in mind and is enjoyable to work with.

Trust is the willingness of a firm to rely on a business partner. It depends on a number of interpersonal and interorganisational factors, such as the firm's perceived competence, integrity, honesty and benevolence.

Low	High
Transparency Distorted, hidden information	Full, honest information
Product/service quality Low product service quality fails to meet promises	Best product and service to fulfil expectations
Incentive Incentives aligned for company, *not customer gains*	Incentives aligned so employees trust and meet customer need
Partnering with customers Leave customers to work out their own problems	Help customers learn and help themselves
Cooperating design Customers are sold company solutions	Customers help design products individually and through communities
Product comparison and advice No or biased comparison and no advice	Compare to competitive products honestly and comprehensive
Supply chain Customer trust conflict in channel	All supply chain partners aligned to build trust
Pervasive advocacy Marketing pushes services and products	All functions work to build trust

Figure 8.2 Trust dimensions

Source: G. Urban (2005) Where are you positioned on the trust dimensions?, in *Don't Just Relate – Advocate: A Blueprint for Profit in the Era of Customer Power*, Indianapolis, Indiana: Wharton School Publishers, p. 99. Copyright © 2005. Reprinted by permission of Pearson Education, Inc., Upper Saddle River, NJ.

Personal interactions with employees of the firm, opinions about the company as a whole and perceptions of trust will evolve with experience. Figure 8.2 provides a summary of some core dimensions of trust.

Building trust can be especially tricky in online settings, and firms often impose more stringent requirements on their online business partners than on others. Business buyers worry that they will not get products of the right quality delivered to the right place at the right time. Sellers worry about getting paid on time – or at all – and how much credit they should extend. Some firms, such as the global transportation and supply chain management company Ryder System, use automated credit-checking applications and online trust services to determine the creditworthiness of trading partners. At the same time, Ryder System does not neglect that trust is a mutual thing. On the European part of its web-

site (ryder.com) the company provides several reasons why it can be trusted as a business partner, including referring to the fact that, from Bristol to Budapest, over 1,000 companies partner the company.

Sources: B. Violino (2002) Building B2B trust, *Computerworld*, 17 June, 32; R. E. Plank, D. A. Reid and E. Bolman Pullins (1999) Perceived trust in business-to-business sales: a new measure, *Journal of Personal Selling and Sales Management*, 19(3), 61–72; K. L. Keller and D. A. Aaker (1998) Corporate-level marketing: the impact of credibility on a company's brand extensions, *Corporate Reputation Review*, 1 (August), 356–78; R. M. Morgan and S. D. Hunt (1994) The commitment-trust theory of relationship marketing, *Journal of Marketing*, 58(3), 20–38; C. Moorman, R. Deshpande and G. Zaltman (1993) Factors affecting trust in market research relationships, *Journal of Marketing*, 57 (January), 81–101; www.ryder.com.

One historical study of four very different business-to-business relationships found that several factors, by affecting partner interdependence and/or environmental uncertainty, influenced the development of a relationship between business partners.[68] The relationship between advertising agencies and clients illustrates these findings:

- **In the relationship formation stage, one partner experienced substantial market growth.** Manufacturers capitalising on mass-production techniques developed national brands, which increased the importance and amount of mass media advertising.
- **Information asymmetry between partners was such that a partnership would generate more profits than if the partner attempted to invade the other firm's area.** Advertising agencies had specialised knowledge that their clients would have had difficulty obtaining.
- **At least one partner had high barriers to entry that would prevent the other partner from entering the business.** Advertising agencies could not easily become national manufacturers, and for years manufacturers were not eligible to receive media commissions.
- **Dependence asymmetry existed such that one partner was more able to control or influence the other's conduct.** Advertising agencies had control over media access.
- **One partner benefited from economies of scale related to the relationship.** Ad agencies gained by providing the same market information to multiple clients.

Research has found that buyer–supplier relationships differ according to four factors: availability of alternatives; importance of supply; complexity of supply; and supply market dynamism. Based on these four factors, buyer–supplier relationships were classified into eight categories:[69]

1 **Basic buying and selling.** These are simple, routine exchanges with moderate levels of cooperation and information exchange.
2 **Bare bones.** These relationships require more adaptation by the seller and less cooperation and information exchange.
3 **Contractual transaction.** These exchanges are defined by formal contract and generally have low levels of trust, cooperation and interaction.
4 **Customer supply.** In this traditional customer supply situation, competition rather than cooperation is the dominant form of governance.
5 **Cooperative systems.** The partners in cooperative systems are united in operational ways, but neither demonstrates structural commitment through legal means or adaptation.
6 **Collaborative.** In collaborative exchanges, much trust and commitment leads to true partnership.
7 **Mutually adaptive.** Buyers and sellers make many relationship-specific adaptations, but without necessarily achieving strong trust or cooperation.
8 **Customer is king.** In this close, cooperative relationship, the seller adapts to meet the customer's needs without expecting much adaptation or change in exchange.

Over time, however, the roles and nature of a relationship may shift and be activated depending on different circumstances.[70] Some needs can be satisfied with fairly basic supplier performance. Buyers then neither want nor require a close relationship with a supplier. Likewise, some suppliers may not find it worth their while to invest in customers with limited growth potential.

One study found that the closest relationships between customers and suppliers arose when the supply was important to the customer and there were procurement obstacles, such as complex purchase requirements and few alternative suppliers.[71] Another study suggested that greater vertical coordination between buyer and seller through information

Marketing memo

Electronic customer relationship management

Customer relationship management is a business approach or strategy that integrates all business functions which relate to the customer – namely, marketing, sales, customer service and field support – through the integration of people, process and technology.[73] CRM can be considered a fraction of electronic customer relationship management (eCRM) as the latter approach expands CRM by integrating new technologies such as websites, online communities, wireless, voice technologies, email and information appliances into the traditional CRM approach. Moreover, management researchers Pan and Lee argue that a successful eCRM solution requires that all customer-related information is consolidated into a single view. In this way, the eCRM concept facilitates suppliers' understanding of who their customers are and what products are of interest to them – only with such an understanding is it possible to provide customers with the products and services they want. Evidence suggests that businesses are increasingly taking advantage of eCRM to build relationships with customers.[74]

One of the main advantages of eCRM is that information technology makes it possible for a company to interact with a large number of customers, while treating them as individuals. A number of other potential advantages can also be detected:[75] eCRM (a) may reduce the cost of contacting customers; (b) may have the ability of transferring some administrative tasks to customers (e.g. product configuration, order tracking, online customers' details collection) and thereby reducing operational costs; (c) could be integrated with other systems such as production, finance and supply, and thereby improve the work flow of the organisation; and (d) may improve sales by customer profiling and better market segmentation, automated campaign management, email marketing and so on. Hence, eCRM has the potential of offering increased value to both the seller and the buyer by improving mutual understanding, by matching needs and requests and by providing more efficient workflows.

exchange and planning is usually necessary only when high environmental uncertainty exists and specific investments are modest.[72]

Our discussion has concentrated largely on the buying behaviour of profit-seeking companies, but much of what we have said also applies to the buying practices of institutional and government organisations. However, in the following section we want to highlight certain special features of these markets.

Institutional and government markets

The **institutional market** consists of schools, hospitals, nursing homes, prisons and other institutions that must provide goods and services to people in their care. Many of these organisations are characterised by low budgets and captive clienteles: for example, hospitals must decide what quality of food to buy for patients. The buying objective here is not profit, because the food is provided as part of the total service package; nor is cost minimisation the sole objective, because poor food will cause patients to complain and harm the hospital's reputation. The hospital purchasing agent must search for institutional-food vendors whose quality meets or exceeds a certain minimum standard and whose prices are low. In fact, many food vendors set up a separate division to sell to institutional buyers because of these buyers' special needs and characteristics. Heinz produces, packages and prices its Ketchup differently to meet the requirements of hospitals, colleges and prisons.

In most countries, government organisations are a major buyer of goods and services. They typically require suppliers to submit bids and often award the contract to the lowest bidder. In some cases the government unit will make allowance for superior quality or a reputation for completing contracts on time. Governments will also buy on a negotiated contract basis, primarily in the case of complex projects involving major R&D costs and risks, and in cases where there is little competition.

Because their spending decisions are subject to public review, government organisations require considerable paperwork from suppliers, which often complain about bureaucracy, regulations, decision-making delays, and frequent shifts in procurement staff. But the fact remains that public procurement is the process used by public authorities or bodies governed by public law to purchase products and services with tax money. Public procurement is a key sector of the EU economy, accounting for €1,500 billion or about 16 per cent of gross domestic product (meaning the total market value of the goods and services produced by a nation's economy during a specific period of time).[76] A major complaint of multinationals operating in Europe is that each country shows favouritism toward its nationals despite superior offers from foreign firms. Although such practices are fairly entrenched, the European Union is attempting to remove this bias. For example, EU member states' contracting authorities need to wait for at least ten days after deciding who has won the public contract before the contract can actually be signed. The so-called 'standstill period' is designed to give bidders time to examine the decision and to assess whether it is appropriate to initiate a review procedure. If this standstill period has not been respected, the directive requires national courts under certain conditions to set aside a signed contract by annulling it. 'We need effective procedures for seeking review in all EU member states in order to make sure that public contracts ultimately go to the company which has made the best offer,' the EU internal market and services commissioner Charlie McCreevy said.[77]

PublicOpportunity.com

PublicOpportunity.com is a government procurement consulting firm, formed by an American lawyer and a Danish MBA to meet the needs of business in the global marketplace. With offices in the EU and the United States, PublicOpportunity.com provides its subscribers with the latest information and leads necessary for companies wanting to sell to government markets around the world. Once a company has decided which leads to follow up, which governments to target and what contracts to seek, PublicOpportunity.com helps complete the draft. PublicOpportunity.com offers three kinds of service:

1 Subscription service: providing companies with information and leads on current opportunities being offered by various governments that currently need their products or services.

2 Consulting services: offering companies consultation and assistance to understand any requirements that companies must meet.

3 Seminars: conducting an ongoing series of seminars on current issues of interest to the public procurement sector, including designing special seminars and programmes to train companies' employees in dealing with government procurement, the World Trade Organization Agreement, the EU procurement rules and other international treaties and agreements.

Source: www.publicopportunity.com.

Because their spending decisions are subject to public review, government organisations require considerable paperwork from suppliers, which often complain about bureaucracy, regulations, decision-making delays and frequent shifts in procurement personnel. But the fact that the biggest market in the world is the government market makes it also the most potentially attractive customer in the world.

Government decision makers often think technology vendors have not done their homework. In addition, vendors do not pay enough attention to cost justification, which is a major activity for government procurement professionals. Companies hoping to be government contractors need to help government agencies see the bottom-line impact of products. Demonstrating useful experience and successful past performance through case studies, especially with other government organisations, can be influential.[78] The expansion of the EU to 27 countries further increased the opportunities for businesses to win such contracts across the EU and should also bring substantial savings for public bodies through increased competition among contractors. Just as companies provide government agencies with guidelines about how best to purchase and use their products, governments provide would-be suppliers with detailed guidelines describing how to sell to the government. Failure to follow the guidelines or to fill out forms and contracts correctly can create a legal nightmare.[79] Fortunately for businesses of all sizes, the EU has been trying to simplify the contracting procedure and make both bidding and procurement more attractive and effective.

eGovernment in Europe

eGovernment is one of the priorities set by the EU. It comprises a series of initiatives designed to provide more efficient and better-quality public services, reducing waiting times for users and improving transparency and accountability in services. In 2008, the Small Business Act (SBA) was introduced by the European Commission to boost entrepreneurship, promote SMEs' growth and make their life easier according to the 'Think Small First' principle. The 'Think Small First' principle requires that EU legislation takes SMEs' interests into account at the very early stages of policy making in order to make legislation more SME friendly. As one result of the SBA and the 'Think Small First' principle, Italian entrepreneurs can now start up a business in 24 hours. In 2011, the country's authorities introduced a simplified procedure making it possible to set up a company without bureaucratic hassle: all entrepreneurs need to do is send an electronic form to the Companies Register, which resubmits it to the tax and social security offices after registration.

Public procurement is another area where use of ICT can be particularly advantageous. Traditional public procurement operations are complex, time consuming and resource intensive. Use of ICT in public procurement can therefore improve efficiency, quality and value for money in public purchases. Until now the absence of clear EU rules has been an obstacle to the take-up of electronic public procurement in Europe. The adoption of the new package of legislation on public procurement, which includes specific rules on electronic public procurement, should be a turning point for the spread of electronic public procurement in Europe.[80]

European legislation has encouraged competition between firms by means of transparent selection procedures. It also makes provision for redress procedures against awarding authorities that do not fulfil their obligations. European directives are continuously being reviewed with a view to simplifying the existing legal framework and encouraging the use of electronic procedures.[81] Recently the European Commission launched the SIMAP project,[82] which has as its objective the development of the information systems infrastructure needed to support the delivery of an effective public procurement policy in Europe, by providing contracting entities and suppliers with the information they need to manage the procurement process effectively. Initially the project aims to improve the quality of information about the EU procurement opportunities and to ensure that the information is made known to all potentially interested suppliers. In the longer term it will address the whole procurement process, including bids, award of contracts, delivery, invoicing and payment.

EU governments are surely a bundle of customers that are highly attractive to European companies. 'Marketing memo: Selling to EU governments' provides some tips for attacking that multibillion-euro market.

Marketing memo

Selling to EU governments

Public contracts make up a significant share of the EU market, accounting for about 16 per cent of its gross domestic product (2010). Here are three tips for tapping into that market.

1 Getting started. Determining what contracting opportunities are available to you in the European Union – as well as tendering for and securing those contracts – can usually be accomplished for the price of hiring a local employee.

2 Don't miss opportunities. Many small businesses are missing the opportunity to sell their product or service to governments. This is unfortunate since non-economic criteria often play a great role in government buying. Government buyers are often asked to favour depressed business firms and areas, small business firms, and business firms that avoid race, sex or age discrimination.

3 Business plan. To attack this profitable market, winning government contracts should be part of your business plan. Here are some points to consider:

- Keep in mind that governments usually do not pay in advance but expect the deliverables first. So, you need to understand the cash flow issues and plan for them.

- Several EU offices, agencies and institutions have created official accounts on social networks (Facebook, Twitter, and the like) and other sites dedicated to sharing content.

- The European Services Directive obliges EU countries to simplify all procedures involved in starting and carrying out a service activity. Since December 2009, companies and individuals must be able to complete online all necessary formalities, such as authorisations, notifications and environmental licences, through 'points of single contact' (PSCs). On PSCs companies can find out about the rules, regulations and formalities that apply to service activities and complete the administrative procedures online (by submitting the necessary application forms and supporting documents, etc., electronically).

Sources: J. Grimly (2011) Tag Archives: government contracts in the EU, December: International Trade Updates.com; European Union (2012): http://ec.europa.eu/youreurope/business/starting-business/setting-up/index_en.htm; O. Thomas (2003) How to sell tech to the feds, *Business 2.0*, March, 111–12.

Some companies have pursued government business by establishing separate government marketing departments. Companies such as Gateway, Rockwell, Kodak and Goodyear anticipate government needs and projects, participate in the product specification phase, gather competitive intelligence, prepare bids carefully, and produce strong communications to describe and enhance their companies' reputations.

Encouraging entrepreneurship

The Swedish region of Halland has managed to boost young people's interest in entrepreneurship. In 2010 the region received a European Enterprise Award for its work on training tomorrow's entrepreneurs. The region of Halland has invested in developing the business environment of the region by training and motivating young people. In primary and secondary schools, students are now given the chance to participate in business-like projects, and numerous teachers are trained to pass on entrepreneurial skills, with activities from building a town skating ramp to learning mathematics in real-life situations at local companies. Thousands of teachers have taken part in a five-day programme aimed at raising students' interest in entrepreneurship. The result is a boost in the share of young people wanting to become self-employed businesspeople. And already, the number of new businesses in the region has increased significantly.

Source: Based on How entrepreneurs are made – a Swedish success story (2011) February, http://ec.europa.eu/small-business/success-stories/2011/february/index_en.htm.

SUMMARY

1 Organisational buying is the decision-making process by which formal organisations establish the need for purchased products and services, then identify, evaluate and choose among alternative brands and suppliers. The business market consists of all the organisations that acquire goods and services used in the production of other products or services that are sold, rented or supplied to others.

2 Compared to consumer markets, business markets generally have fewer and larger buyers, a closer customer–supplier relationship, and more geographically concentrated buyers. Demand in the business market is derived from demand in the consumer market and fluctuates with the business cycle. Nonetheless, the total demand for many business goods and services is quite price inelastic. Business marketers need to be aware of the role of professional purchasers and their influencers, the need for multiple sales calls, and the importance of direct purchasing, reciprocity and leasing.

3 The buying centre is the decision-making unit of a buying organisation. It consists of initiators, users, influencers, deciders, approvers, buyers and gatekeepers. To influence these parties, marketers must be aware of environmental, organisational, interpersonal and individual factors.

4 The buying process consists of eight stages, called buyphases: (1) problem recognition; (2) general need description; (3) product specification; (4) supplier search; (5) proposal solicitation; (6) supplier selection; (7) order-routine specification; and (8) performance review.

5 Business marketers must form strong bonds and relationships with their customers and provide them with added value. Some customers, however, may prefer more of a transactional relationship.

6 The institutional market consists of schools, hospitals, nursing homes, prisons and other institutions that provide goods and services to people in their care. Buyers for government organisations tend to require a great deal of paperwork from their vendors and to favour open bidding and domestic companies. Suppliers must be prepared to adapt their offers to the special needs and procedures found in institutional and government markets.

APPLICATIONS

Marketing debate

How different is business-to-business marketing?
Many business-to-business marketing executives lament the challenges of business-to-business marketing, maintaining that many traditional marketing concepts and principles do not apply. For a number of reasons, they assert that selling products and services to a company is fundamentally different from selling to individuals. Others disagree, claiming that marketing theory is still valid and only involves some adaptation in the marketing tactics.

Take a position: Business-to-business marketing requires a special, unique set of marketing concepts and principles *versus* Business-to-business marketing is really not that different and the basic marketing concepts and principles apply.

Marketing discussion

Consider some of the consumer behaviour topics in Chapter 7. How might you apply them to business-to-business settings? For example, how might non-compensatory models of choice work? Mental accounting?

Marketing exercises

- In your opinion what are the ten most important topics/issues to be learned from this chapter?
- Pick one of the companies mentioned in this chapter. For this company, investigate and discuss: (a) Do you think that any of the ten topics/issues you identified could be related to the problems, or opportunities, that the company – in your opinion – is currently facing or could expect to be facing in the near future? (b) Why?
- In your opinion, what should the company do to deal with the identified problems or to take advantage of the identified opportunities?

REFERENCES

[1]Based on J. Rossant (2004) Europe's hot growth companies, *BusinessWeek*, 25 October; www.soitec.com.

[2]For a comprehensive review of the topic, see J. C. Anderson and J. A. Narus (2009) *Business Market Management: Understanding, Creating, and Delivering Value*, 3rd edn. Upper Saddle River, NJ: Prentice Hall.

[3]F. E. Webster, Jr and Y. Wind (1972) *Organizational Buying Behavior*, Upper Saddle River, NJ: Prentice Hall, 2. For a review of recent academic literature on the topic, see H. Håkansson and I. Snehota (2002) Marketing in business markets, in B. Weitz and R. Wensley (eds), *Handbook of Marketing*, London: Sage, 513–26.

[4]M. J. Eyring, M. W. Johnson and H. Nair (2011) New business models in emerging markets, *Harvard Business Review*, 89(1/2), 88–95; B. Donath (2005) Customer knowledge takes priority in study, *Marketing News*, 15 (December), 7.

[5]See also *B-to-B Marketing Trends 2010*, Institute for the Study of Business Markets, http://isbm.smeal.psu.edu/.

[6]M. Collins (1996) Breaking into the big leagues, *American Demographics*, January, 24.

[7]P. J. Robinson, C. W. Faris and Y. Wind (1967) *Industrial Buying and Creative Marketing*, Boston, MA: Allyn & Bacon.

[8]M. D. Bunn (1993) Taxonomy of buying decision approaches, *Journal of Marketing*, 57 (January), 38–56; D. H. McQuiston (1989) Novelty, complexity, and importance as causal determinants of industrial buyer behavior, *Journal of Marketing*, April, 66–79; P. Doyle, A. G. Woodside and P. Mitchell (1979) Organizational buying in new task and rebuy situations, *Industrial Marketing Management*, February, 7–11.

[9]U. B. Ozanne and G. A. Churchill, Jr (1971) Five dimensions of the industrial adoption process, *Journal of Marketing Research*, August, 322–8.

[10]N. Dawar and M. Vandenbosch (2004) The seller's hidden advantage, *MIT Sloan Management Review*, Winter, 83–8.

[11]Elisabeth Sullivan (2009) Building a better brand, *Marketing News*, 15 September, 14–17.

[12]J. E. Lewin and N. Donthu (2005) The influence of purchase situation on buying center structure and involvement: a select meta-analysis of organizational buying behavior research, *Journal of Business Research*, 58 (October), 1381–90; R. Venkatesh and A. K. Kohli (1995) Influence strategies in buying centers, *Journal of Marketing*, 59 (October), 71–82. D. W. Jackson, Jr, J. E. Keith and R. K. Burdick (1984) Purchasing agents' perceptions of industrial buying center influence: a situational approach, *Journal of Marketing*, Fall, 75–83.

[13]Webster and Wind (1972) op. cit., 6.

[14]Anderson and Narus (2009) op. cit.; F. E. Webster, Jr and Y. Wind (1972) A general model for understanding organizational buying behavior, *Journal of Marketing*, 36, April, 12–19; Webster and Wind (1972) op. cit.

[15]A. Enright (2006) It takes a committee to buy into B-to-B, *Marketing News*, 15 February, 12–13.

[16]F. E. Webster, Jr and K. L. Keller (2004) A roadmap for branding in industrial markets, *Journal of Brand Management*, II (May), 388–402.

[17]S. Ward and F. E. Webster, Jr (1991) Organizational buying behavior, in T. Robertson and H. Kassarjian (eds), *Handbook of Consumer Behavior*, Upper Saddle River, NJ: Prentice Hall, Ch. 12.

[18]B. Donath (2006) Emotions play key role in biz brand appeal, *Marketing News*, 1 June, 7.

[19]M. Krauss (2006) Warriors of the heart, *Marketing News*, 1 February, 7.

[20]Webster and Wind (1972) op. cit., 6.

[21]J. C. Anderson, J. A. Narus and W. van Rossum (2006) Customer value proposition in business markets, *Harvard Business Review*, March, 2–10; J. C. Anderson (2004) From understanding to managing customer value in business markets, in H. Håkansson, D. Harrison and A. Waluszewski (eds), *Rethinking Marketing: New Marketing Tools*, London: John Wiley & Sons, 137–59.

[22]T. Minahan (1998) OEM buying survey – Part 2: Buyers get new roles but keep old tasks, *Purchasing*, 16 July, 208–9.

[23]Robinson, Faris and Wind (1967) op. cit.

[24]*Institute Of Scrap Recycling Institute*, www.isri.org.

[25]R. Grewal, J. M. Comer and R. Mehta (2001) An investigation into the antecedents of organizational participation in business-to-business electronic markets, *Journal of Marketing*, 65 (July), 17–33.

[26]Knowledge@Wharton (2005) Open sesame? Or could the doors slam shut for Alibaba.com?, 27 July; J. Angwin (2004) Top online chemical exchange is unlikely success story, *Wall Street Journal*, 8 January; O. Kharif (2003) B2B, take 2, *BusinessWeek*, 25 November; G. S. Day, A. J. Fein and G. Ruppersberger (2003) Shakeouts in digital markets: lessons from B2B exchanges, *California Management Review*, 45(2), (Winter), 131–51.

[27]About the spot market, www.converge.com, accessed November 2007; www.chemconnect.com/market_info.html, accessed April 2008.

[28]B. J. Carroll (2006) *Lead Generation for the Complex Sale*, New York: McGraw-Hill.

[29]2009–10 B2B Marketing Benchmark Report, *Marketing Sherpa*. www.SherpaStore.com.

[30]A. Enright (2006) It takes a committee to buy into B-to-B, *Marketing News*, 15 February, 12–13.

[31]For an excellent review on how to motivate salespeople, see F. Q. Fu, K. A. Richards, D. E. Hughes and E. Jones (2010) Motivating salespeople to sell new products: the relative influence of attitudes, subjective norms, and self-efficacy, *Journal of Marketing*, 74(6), 61–76; R. Hiebeler, T. B. Kelly and C. Ketteman (1998) *Best Practices: Building Your Business with Customer-Focused Solutions*, New York: Arthur Andersen/Simon & Schuster, 122–4.

[32]F. Zeng, Z. Yang, Y. Li, and K-S. Fam (2011) Small business industrial buyers' price sensitivity: do service quality dimensions matter in business markets?, *Industrial Marketing Management*, 40(3), 395–404; D. J. Flint, R. B. Woodruff and S. F. Gardial (2002) Exploring the phenomenon of customers' desired value change in a business-to-business context, *Journal of Marketing*, 66 (October), 102–17.

[33]R. N. Bolton and M. B. Myers (2003) Price-based global market segmentation for services, *Journal of Marketing*, 67 (July), 108–28.

[34]W. Ulaga and A. Eggert (2006) Value-based differentiation in business relationships: gaining and sustaining key supplier status, *Journal of Marketing*, 70 (January), 119–36.

[35]Glud & Marstrand improve productivity, quality and overview with new WMS, www.consafelogistics.com, accessed November 2007.

[36]D. Kiley (2006) Small print jobs for peanuts, *BusinessWeek*, 17 July, 58.

[37]N. Kumar (2004) *Marketing as Strategy: Understanding the CEO's Agenda for Driving Growth and Innovation*, Boston, MA: Harvard Business School Press.

[38]Ibid.

[39]For foundational material, see L. M. Rinehart, J. A. Eckert, R. B. Handfield, T. J. Page, Jr and T. Atkin (2004) An assessment of buyer–seller relationships, *Journal of Business Logistics*, 25(1), 25–62; F. R. Dwyer, P. Schurr and S. Oh (1987) Developing buyer–supplier relationships, *Journal of Marketing*, 51 (April), 11–28; and B. B. Jackson (1985) *Winning and Keeping Industrial Customers: The Dynamics of Customer Relations*, Lexington, MA: D. C. Heath.

[40]A. Buvik and G. John (2000) When does vertical coordination improve industrial purchasing relationships?, *Journal of Marketing*, 64 (October), 52–64.

[41]L. G. Epstein (1999) A definition of uncertainty aversion, *Review of Economic Studies*, 66, 579–608.

[42]J. Gluckler and T. Armbruster (2003) Bridging uncertainty in management consulting: the mechanisms of trust and networked reputation, *Organization Studies*, 24(2), 269–97.

[43]S. Ryu, S. Min and N. Zushi (2008) The moderating role of trust in manufacturer–supplier relationships, *Journal of Business and Industrial Marketing*, 23(1), 48–58; A. Giddens (1990) *The Consequences of Modernity*, Stanford, CA: Stanford University Press.

[44]A. Le Flanchec (2004) How to reduce uncertainty in a context of innovation: the case of IBM's negotiation of its European Works Council, *International Negotiation*, 9(2), 271–89.

[45]G. A. Akerlof (1970) The market for 'Lemons': quality uncertainty and the market mechanism, *Quarterly Journal of Economics*, 84(3), 488–500.

[46]M. M. Darby and E. Karni (1973) Free competition and the optimal amount of fraud, *Journal of Law and Economics*, 16(1), 67–88.

[47]Y. Salent (2011), Procedural analysis of choice rules with applications to bounded rationality, *American Economic Review*, 101(2), 724–48; S. Fiori (2009) Hayek's theory on complexity and knowledge: dichotomies, levels of analysis, and bounded rationality, *Journal of Economic Methodology*, 16(3), 265–85; P. M. Todd and G. Gigerenzer (2003) Bounded rationality to the world, *Journal of Economic Psychology*, 24(2), 143–65.

[48]Y. Henry Xie, T. Suh and I-W. Kwon (2010) Do the magnitude and asymmetry of specific asset investments matter in the supplier–buyer relationship? *Journal of Marketing Management*, 26(9/10), 858–77; Akesel I. Rokkan, Jan B. Heide, and Kenneth H. Wathne (2003) Specific investment in marketing relationships: expropriation and bonding effects, *Journal of Marketing Research*, 40 (May), 210–24.

[49]Kenneth H. Wathne and Jan B. Heide (2004) Relationship governance in a supply chain network, *Journal of Marketing*, 68 (January), 73–89; Douglas Bowman and Das Narayandas (2004) Linking customer management effort to customer profitability in business markets, *Journal of Marketing Research*, 61 (November), 433–47; Mrinal Ghosh and George John (1999) Governance

value analysis and marketing strategy, *Journal of Marketing*, 63 (Special Issue), 131–45.

[50]Buvik and John (2000) op. cit.

[51]B. R. Barnes, L. C. Leonidou, N. Y. M. Siu and C. N. Leonidou (2010) Opportunism as the inhibiting trigger for developing long-term-oriented western exporter–Hong Kong importer relationships, *Journal of International Marketing*, 18(2), 35–63; K. H. Wathne and J. B. Heide (2000) Opportunism in interfirm relationships: forms, outcomes, and solutions, *Journal of Marketing*, 64 (October), 36–51.

[52]M. Walton (1997) When your partner fails you, *Fortune*, 26 May, 151–4.

[53]M. B. Houston and S. A. Johnson (2000) Buyer–supplier contracts versus joint ventures: determinants and consequences of transaction structure, *Journal of Marketing Research*, 37 (February), 1–15.

[54]A. I. Rokkan, J. B. Heide and K. W. Wathne (2003) Specific investment in marketing relationships: expropriation and bonding effects, *Journal of Marketing Research*, 40 (May), 210–24.

[55]P. T. Spiller (2010) A tribute to Oliver Williamson: Regulation: a transaction cost perspective, *California Management Review*, 52(2), 147–58; J. H. Dyer (1997) Effective interfirm collaboration: how firms minimize transaction costs and maximize transaction value, *Strategic Management Journal*, 18(5), 535–56.

[56]R. Grewal, A. Chakravarty and A. Saini (2010) Governance mechanisms in business-to–business electronic markets, *Journal of Marketing*, 74(4), 45–62; J. Hallikas, V. M. Virolainen and M. Tuominen (2002) Understanding risk and uncertainty in supplier networks: a transaction cost approach, *International Journal of Production Research*, 40(15), 3519–31; E. Williamson (1987) *Antitrust Economics: Mergers, Contracting, and Strategic Behavior*, Oxford: Basil Blackwell.

[57]Wu, Wei-Ping and W. L. Choi (2004) Transaction cost, social capital and firms' synergy creation in Chinese business networks: an integrative approach, *Asia Pacific Journal of Management*, 21, 325–43; R. Gulati (1995) Does familiarity breed trust?, *Academy of Management Journal*, 38, 85–112.

[58]J. H. Dyer and K. Nobeoka (2000) Creating and managing a high-performance knowledge-sharing network: the Toyota case, *Strategic Management Journal*, 21, 345–67.

[59]http://adrianbalan.wordpress.com/2010/01/19/worldwide-car-sales-by-manufacturer-2009/; T. Armitage (2007) VW chases Toyota productivity, profit with 10-year plan, *Automotive News*, 82, 16.

[60]A. Lundgren (1993) Technological innovation and the emergence and evolution of industrial networks: the case of digital image technology in Sweden, *Advances in International Marketing*, 5, 145–70.

[61]Z. Akbar, R. Gözübüyük and H. Milanov (2010) It's the connections: the network perspective in interorganizational research, *Academy of Management Perspectives*, 24(1), 62–77; T. Ritter (1999) The networking company: antecedents for coping with relationships and networks effectively, *Industrial Marketing Management*, 28(5), 467–79.

[62]Hallikas, Virolainen and Tuominen (2002) op. cit.

[63]M. Z. Yaqub, R. M. S. Yaqub and M. S. Nazar (2010) Dynamics of motivation in strategic networks, *European Journal of Economics, Finance and Administrative Sciences*, 19(April), 28–33; J. C. Jarillo (1988) On strategic networks, *Strategic Management Journal*, 9, 31–41.

[64]S. Laestadius (1995) Can network theory explain technological change?, Working Paper 1995:2, Department of Industrial Economics and Management, Kungliga Tekniska Högskolan, Stockholm, May.

[65]Hallikas, Virolainen and Tuominen (2002) op. cit.

[66]A. Saruliene and M. Vilkas (2010) Vertical integration or outsourcing? Systematization of factors determining the level of integration of supply chain, *Economics and Management*, 740–7; D. Narayandas and V. K. Rangan (2004) Building and sustaining buyer–seller relationships in mature industrial markets, *Journal of Marketing*, 68 (July), 63–77.

[67]R. W. Palmatier, R. P. Dant, D. Grewal and K. R. Evans (2006) Factors influencing the effectiveness of relationship marketing: a meta-analysis, *Journal of Marketing*, 70 (October), 136–53; J. L. Johnson, R. S. Sohli and R. Grewal (2004) The role of relational knowledge stores in interfirm partnering, *Journal of Marketing*, 68 (July), 21–36; F. Selnes and J. Sallis (2003) Promoting relationship learning, *Journal of Marketing*, 67 (July), 80–95; P. M. Doney and J. P. Cannon (1997) An examination of the nature of trust in buyer–seller relationships, *Journal of Marketing*, 61 (April), 35–51; S. Ganesan (1994) Determinants of long-term orientation in buyer–seller relationships, *Journal of Marketing*, 58 (April), 1–19.

[68]W. W. Keep, S. C. Hollander and R. Dickinson (1998) Forces impinging on long-term business-to-business relationships in the United States: an historical perspective, *Journal of Marketing*, 62 (April), 31–45.

[69]J. P. Cannon and W. D. Perreault, Jr (1999) Buyer–seller relationships in business markets, *Journal of Marketing Research*, 36 (November), 439–60.

[70]J. B. Heide and K. H. Wahne (2006) Friends, businesspeople, and relationship roles: a conceptual framework and research agenda, *Journal of Marketing*, 70 (July), 90–103.

[71]Cannon and Perreault (1999) op. cit.

[72]T. G. Noordewier, G. John and J. R. Nevin (1990) Performance outcomes of purchasing arrangements in industrial buyer–vendor arrangements, *Journal of Marketing*, 54 (October), 80–93; Buvik and John (2000) op. cit.

[73]S. L. Pan and J.-N. Lee (2003) Using e-CRM for a unified view of the customer, *Communications of the ACM*, 46(4), 95–9.

[74]S. Alavi, V. Ahuja and Y. Medury (2011) ECRM using online communities, *Journal of Marketing Management*, 10(1), 35–44; J. L. Harrison-Walker and S. E. Neeley (2004) Customer relationship building on the internet in B2B marketing: a proposed typology, *Journal of Marketing Theory and Practice*, Winter, 19–34.

[75]D. Adebanjo (2003) Classifying and selecting e-CRM application: an analysis-based proposal, *Management Decision*, 41(6), 570–7; N. R. Ab Hamid (2005) E-CRM: are we there yet?, *Journal of the American Academy of Business*, Cambridge, March, 51–7.

[76]Public Private Finance (2004) EU public procurement under review, 81, March, 2.

[77]Xinhua News Agency (2007) EU adopts new rules for public procurement, 15 November.

[78]Bill Gormley (2009) The US government can be your lifelong customer, *Washington Business Journal*, 23 January; Chris Warren, How to sell to Uncle Sam, *BNET Crash Course*, www.bnet.com.

[79]M. Swibel and J. Novack (2003) The scariest customer, *Forbes*, 10 November, 96–7.

[80]www.europa.eu; http://ec.europa.eu/small-business/index_en.htm.

[81]www.europa.eu.

[82]www.simap.europe.eu.

Chapter 9

Dealing with competition

IN THIS CHAPTER, WE WILL ADDRESS THE FOLLOWING QUESTIONS:

1 How do marketers identify primary competitors?

2 How should we analyse competitors' strategies, objectives, strengths and weaknesses?

3 How can market leaders expand the total market and defend market share?

4 How should market challengers attack market leaders?

5 How can market followers or nichers compete effectively?

World demand for cars is increasing and competition in the car industry is intense.

Source: Mitchell Funk/Photographer's Choice/Getty Images

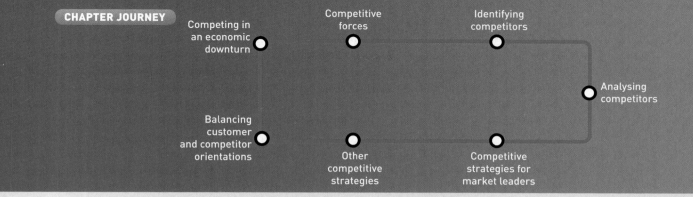

CHAPTER JOURNEY

Competing in an economic downturn

Competitive forces

Identifying competitors

Analysing competitors

Balancing customer and competitor orientations

Other competitive strategies

Competitive strategies for market leaders

To be a long-term market leader is the goal of any marketer. Today's challenging marketing circumstances, however, often dictate that companies reformulate their marketing strategies and offerings several times. Economic conditions change, competitors launch new assaults, and buyer interest and requirements evolve. Different market positions can suggest different market strategies.

Global car competition is changing rapidly. Company takeovers and various forms of company collaborations are seen still more often. Today, even honoured brands such as Ferrari, Bentley and Maserati that used to be autonomous/independent are now part of gigantic conglomerates. One example is Ford, which now holds a broad brand portfolio including Swedish Volvo and Japanese Mazda, among others. Controlling seven different brands, VW constitutes another example. However, due to intense price competition, profit is scarce in the car business. The intense competition in the car business has almost forced car makers to create all kinds of joint ventures, cooperative agreements and so on. Recently, Daimler (maker of Mercedes cars) announced a joint venture with the Renault–Nissan alliance. The car giants have agreed to take stakes in each other and work together to jointly develop new cars. By getting access to Nissan small engine technology, Daimler hopes to crack the small car market. In turn, Nissan will benefit from Daimler engines for its Infiniti premium range. Moreover, by sharing parts and developments costs, mainly in energy-efficient compact cars such as the Mercedes Smart car and the Renault Twingo, the car makers aim to reduce production costs by millions of euros over the coming years. Experts expect that this is just the beginning. Intensified competition will increasingly force car makers to share knowledge and to jointly improve technologies. Car makers are facing a high European demand for small cars. However, developing new technical solutions is often just as expensive for small cars as for larger cars. As a result, selling a Nissan Micra simply does not provide the same kind of profit as selling a Mercedes or a BMW.

As you can tell from the developments in the car market, companies must pay keen attention to their competitors in order to effectively devise and implement the best possible brand-positioning strategies. Markets have become too competitive to focus on the consumer alone. This chapter examines the role that competition plays and how marketers can best compete in the modern business world.[1]

Competitive forces

In his now classic industry competition model, Michael E. Porter, professor at Harvard Business School, has identified five forces that determine the intrinsic long-run attractiveness of a market or market segment: industry competitors, potential entrants, substitutes, buyers and suppliers. His model is shown in Figure 9.1. The threats that these forces pose are as follows:

1   **Threat of intense segment rivalry.** A segment is unattractive if it already contains numerous, strong or aggressive competitors and if these competitors have high stakes in staying in the segment. It is even more unattractive if it is stable or declining, if economics or technology dictates that capacity can be increased only in large increments, or if fixed costs or exit barriers are high. Exit barriers keep companies competing in declining industries even though they are earning subnormal returns on investment. For example, a company may have invested in expensive fixed assets (e.g. specialised machinery) that may be non-transferable to another segment. When exit barriers are high, giving up a specific segment will impose a high cost on the company. These conditions will lead to frequent price wars, advertising battles and new product introductions, and will make it expensive to compete. The mobile phone market has seen fierce competition due to segment rivalry.

2   **Threat of new entrants.** The most attractive segment is one in which entry barriers are high and exit barriers are low.[2] Few new firms can enter the industry, and poorly performing firms can easily exit. When both entry and exit barriers are high, profit potential is high, but firms face more risk because poorer-performing firms stay in and fight it out. When both entry and exit barriers are low, firms easily enter and leave the industry, and the returns are stable and low. The worst case is when entry barriers are low and exit barriers are high: here firms enter during good times but find it hard to leave during bad times. The result is chronic overcapacity and depressed earnings for all. The airline industry has low entry barriers but high exit barriers, leaving all carriers struggling during economic downturns.

3   **Threat of substitute products.** A segment is unattractive when there are actual or potential substitutes for the product. Substitutes place a limit on prices and on profits. If technology advances or competition increases in these substitute industries, prices and profits are likely to fall. Major music labels such as EMI, Warner Music Group and Universal Music Group have seen profitability threatened by the rise of digital music, which has triggered a steep decline in CD sales during recent years.[3]

4   **Threat of buyers' growing bargaining power.** A segment is unattractive if buyers possess strong or growing bargaining power. Buyers' bargaining power grows when they become more concentrated or organised, when the product represents a significant fraction of the buyers' costs, when the product is undifferentiated, when buyers' switching costs are low, when buyers are price sensitive because of low profits, or when they can integrate upstream. To protect themselves, sellers might select buyers that have the least power to negotiate or switch suppliers. A better defence consists of developing superior offers that strong buyers cannot refuse. For example, by building strong consumer brands, by offering exceptional low prices and/or by offering back-up promotion, food producers may successfully find their way onto retailers' shelves.

5   **Threat of suppliers' growing bargaining power.** A segment is unattractive if the company's suppliers are able to raise prices or reduce quantity supplied. Oil companies such as ExxonMobil, Shell, BP and Chevron-Texaco are at the mercy of the limited amount of oil reserves and the actions of oil-supplying cartels such as OPEC. Suppliers tend to be powerful when they are concentrated or organised, when there are few substitutes, when the supplied product is an important input, when the costs of switching suppliers are high, and when the suppliers can integrate downstream: that is, integrate the marketing- and sales-oriented activities directed to customers. The best defences are to build win–win relationships with suppliers or use multiple supply sources.

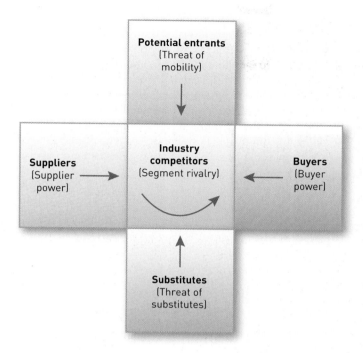

Figure 9.1 Five forces determining segment structural attractiveness
Source: Adapted with the permission of Free Press, a Division of Simon & Schuster, Inc., from *Competitive Advantage: Creating and Sustaining Superior Performance*, Copyright © 1985, 1998 by Michael E. Porter. All right reserved.

Systemising these threats may help managers to become more successful in creating strategies to neutralise them. Although the five forces framework was developed for competitive analysis within specific industries, it has also proven to be a useful analytical tool in other managerial areas such as risk management[4] and public agency analysis.[5]

Identifying competitors

It would seem a simple task for a company to identify its competitors. Vestas and Siemens are major wind power systems competitors; Volkswagen knows that Peugeot is one of its key competitors; and British Airways knows that one of the major competitors in the air travel industry is Lufthansa. However, the range of a company's actual and potential competitors can be much broader than the obvious. And a company is more likely to be hurt by emerging competitors or new technologies than by current competitors, since companies tend to be more alert to known competitors and their market activities.

We can examine competition from both an industry and a market point of view.[6] An **industry** is a group of firms that offer a product or class of products which are close substitutes for one another. Marketers classify industries according to number of sellers; degree of product differentiation; the number of new competitors entering the industry; mobility and exit barriers; cost structure; degree of vertical integration between a company and its suppliers and/or buyers; and degree of globalisation.

Using the market approach, we define *competitors* as companies that satisfy the same customer need. For example, a customer who buys a word-processing package really wants 'writing ability' – a need that can also be satisfied by pencils, pens or typewriters. Marketers must overcome 'marketing myopia', the risk of a company (or even an entire industry) taking a too narrow-minded, product-oriented view of itself and its role in the market. Marketers must define competition on the basis of market needs and opportunities rather than on traditional category and industry terms.[7] An example of such myopia is Coca-Cola, which focused on its soft drink business while failing to see the market for coffee bars and fresh fruit juice bars that eventually impinged on its core business.

The market concept of competition reveals a broader set of actual and potential competitors than competition defined in just product category terms. Rayport and Jaworski, who are influential thinkers in marketing and ecommerce, suggest profiling a company's direct and indirect competitors by mapping the buyer's steps in obtaining and using the product. This type of analysis highlights both the opportunities and the challenges a company faces.[8] The marketing insight box describes how firms can tap into new markets that minimises competition from others.

Marketing insight

High growth through value innovation

INSEAD professors W. Chan Kim and Renée Mauborgne believe that too many firms engage in 'red-ocean thinking' – seeking bloody, head-to-head battles with competitors based largely on incremental improvements in cost or quality, or both. They advocate engaging instead in 'blue-ocean thinking' by creating products and services for which there are no direct competitors. Their belief is that instead of searching within the conventional boundaries of industry competition, managers should look beyond those boundaries to find unoccupied market positions that represent real value innovation.

The authors cite as one example Bert Claeys, a Belgian cinema operator, who was the first to introduce a megaplex cinema in Europe, in the city of Brussels. Despite an industry slump, the 25-screen, 7,600-seat Kinepolis

The Belgian Kinepolis cinema megaplex exemplifies 'blue-ocean thinking' – a competitive strategy that focuses on finding unoccupied market positions instead of battling head to head with established competitors. Here is an exterior shot of the megaplex in Antwerp, Belgium.
Source: Bjorn Beheydt/www.photographersdirect.com.

has thrived on a unique combination of features, such as ample, safe and free parking; large screens and state-of-the-art sound and projection equipment; and roomy, comfortable, oversized seats with unobstructed views. Through smart planning and economies of scale, Bert Claeys creates Kinepolis's unique cinema experience at a lower cost. Despite its success, the concept was not copied in Brussels, since the size of the city did not support a second megaplex cinema.

This is classic blue-ocean thinking – designing creative business ventures to positively affect both a company's cost structure and its value proposition to consumers. Cost savings result from eliminating and reducing the factors affecting traditional industry competition; value to consumers comes from introducing factors the industry has never offered before. Over time, costs drop even more as superior value leads to higher sales volume, and that generates economies of scale.

We can offer other examples of marketers that exhibit unconventional, blue-ocean thinking:

- Novo Nordisk created the world's first insulin pen device, and is a world leader in production and distribution of these insulin delivery systems. Novo Nordisk created a blue ocean by shifting the industry's long-standing focus from doctors to the patients themselves.

- 3M developed 'Post-it' with its unique repositionable adhesive. To take advantage of the brand, 3M now manufactures other products related to the Post-it concept such as Removable Label Pads, Easel Pads, and Shopping Genius.

- Nintendo developed the Wii gaming console that appealed to consumers who were looking for a different console experience. Instead of making a copycat console competing with the likes of Sony PlayStation or Microsoft Xbox, Nintendo created a new style of gaming, employing a wireless controller that worked with motion. In this way, players use the Wii almost as an extension of their own body, and this immersion seems to appeal to a diverse group of players, male and female, young and old.

▶ **Marketing insight** *(continued)*

Formulation principles

a) **Reconstruct market boundaries:**
- Look across alternative industries
- Look across strategic groups within industries
- Look across chain of buyers
- Look across complementary product and service offerings
- Look across functional or emotional appeal to buyers
- Look across time:

b) **Focus on the big picture not the numbers:**

c) **Reach beyond existing demand:**

d) **Get the strategic sequence right:**
- Is there buyer utility (customer value)?
- Is the price acceptable?
- Can we attain target cost?
- What are the adoption challenges?

Execution principles

a) **Overcome key organisational hurdles:**
- Cognitive hurdle (convincing employees of the need of a strategic shift)
- Resource hurdle (it is assumed that resources are needed to execute a strategic shift)
- Motivational hurdle (motivating key players)
- Political hurdle (organisational politics may stand in the way of change).

b) **Build execution into strategy.**

Figure 9.2 Key principles of blue-ocean strategy

Source: Reprinted by permission of Harvard Business School Press. From *Blue-Ocean Strategy: How to Create Uncontested Market Space and Make the Competition Irrelevant* by Chan Kim, W. and Mauborgne, R. Boston, MA 2005. Copyright © 2005 by the Harvard Business School Publishing Corporation. All rights reserved.

- Philips solved the problem of limescale accumulating in kettles as the water was boiled, later finding its way into consumers' freshly brewed tea. The company designed a kettle having a spout filter that effectively captured the limescale as the water was poured. Philips created a blue ocean by inducing people to replace their old kettles with the new filter kettles.

Kim and Mauborgne propose four crucial questions for marketers to ask themselves in guiding blue-ocean thinking and creating value innovation:

1 Which of the factors that our industry takes for granted should we eliminate?

2 Which factors should we reduce well *below* the industry's standard?

3 Which factors should we raise well *above* the industry's standard?

4 Which factors should we create that the industry has never offered?

They maintain that the most successful blue-ocean thinkers took advantage of all three platforms on which value innovation can take place: *physical product*; *service*, including maintenance, customer service, warranties and training for distributors and retailers; and *delivery*, meaning channels and logistics. Figure 9.2 summarises key principles driving the successful formulation and execution of blue-ocean strategy.

Although many blue-ocean success stories relate to consumer markets, research conducted by Cirjevskis, Homenko and Lacinova confirms that blue-ocean thinking can also be viably applied in business markets.

Sources: A. Cirjevskis, G. Homenko and V. Lacinova (2010) New approaches in measuring and assessing viability of blue ocean strategy in B2B sector, *Journal of Business Management*, 3, 162–79; W. Chan Kim and R. Mauborgne (2005) *Blue-Ocean Strategy: How to Create Uncontested Market Space and Make the Competition Irrelevant*, Cambridge, MA: Harvard Business School Press; W. Chan Kim and R. Mauborgne (1999) Creating new market space, *Harvard Business Review*, January–February, 83–93; W. Chan Kim and R. Mauborgne (1997) Value innovation: the strategic logic of high growth, *Harvard Business Review*, January–February, 103–12; www.novonordiskus.com/documents/promotion_page/document/diabetes_care.asp; www.blueoceanstrategy.com/about/lead/novo_nordisk.html; www.marketingweek.co.uk/item/58992/pg_dtl_art_news/pg_hdr_art/pg_ftr_art; www.blueoceanstrategy.com/about/lead/philips.html.

Analysing competitors

Once a company identifies its primary competitors, it must ascertain their strategies, objectives, strengths and weaknesses.[9]

Strategies

A group of firms following the same strategy in a given target market is a **strategic group**.[10] Suppose a company wants to enter the major appliance industry. What is its strategic group?

The company develops the chart shown in Figure 9.3 and discovers four strategic groups based on product quality and level of vertical integration (degree of organisational integration between a company and its suppliers and/or distributors and buyers). Group A has three competitors (Miele, SMEG, LG); group B has four (BSH, Electrolux, Indesit and Whirlpool); group C has three; and group D has three. Important insights emerge from this exercise. First, the height of the entry barriers differs for each group. Second, if the company successfully enters a group, the members of that group become its key competitors.

Objectives

Once a company has identified its main competitors and their strategies, it must ask: what is each competitor seeking in the marketplace? What drives each competitor's behaviour? Many factors shape a competitor's objectives, including size, history, current management

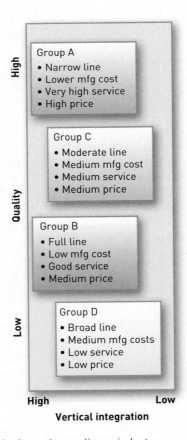

Figure 9.3 Strategic groups in the major appliance industry

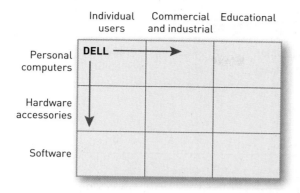

Figure 9.4 A competitor's expansion plans

and financial situation. If the competitor is a division of a larger company, it is important to know whether the parent company is running it for growth or profits, or milking it.

It is useful to assume that competitors strive to maximise profits. However, companies differ in the relative emphasis they put on short-term and long-term profits. Many western firms have been criticised for operating on a short-run model, largely because current performance is judged by stockholders that might lose confidence, sell their stock and cause the company's cost of capital to rise. Japanese firms operate largely on a market-share-maximisation model. They receive much of their funds from banks at a lower interest rate and in the past have readily accepted lower profits. So another reliable assumption is that each competitor pursues some mix of objectives: current profitability, market share growth, cash flow, technological leadership and service leadership.[11]

Finally, a company must monitor competitors' expansion plans. Figure 9.4 shows a product market battlefield map for the personal computer industry. Dell, which started out as a strong force in the sale of personal computers to individual users, is now a major force in the commercial and industrial market. Other incumbents may try to set up mobility barriers to Dell's further expansion.

Strengths and weaknesses

A company needs to gather information about each competitor's strengths and weaknesses. Table 9.1 shows the results of a company survey that asked customers to rate its three competitors, A, B and C, on five attributes. Competitor A turns out to be well known and respected for producing high-quality products sold by a good sales force but is poor at providing product availability and technical assistance. Competitor B is good across the board and excellent in product availability and sales force. Competitor C rates poor to fair on most attributes. This result suggests that the company could attack Competitor A on product availability and technical assistance and Competitor C on almost anything, but should not attack B, which has no glaring weaknesses.

In general, a company should monitor three variables when analysing competitors:

1 Share of market: the competitor's share of the target market.
2 Share of mind: the percentage of customers who named the competitor in responding to the statement, 'Name the first company that comes to mind in this industry.'
3 Share of heart: the percentage of customers who named the competitor in responding to the statement, 'Name the company from which you would prefer to buy the product.'

There is an interesting relationship among these three measures. Table 9.2 shows them as recorded for the three competitors listed in Table 9.1. Competitor A enjoys the highest

Table 9.1 Customers' ratings of competitors on key success factors

	Customer awareness	Product quality	Product availability	Technical assistance	Selling staff
Competitor A	E	E	P	P	G
Competitor B	G	G	E	G	E
Competitor C	F	P	G	F	F

Note: E = excellent, G = good, F = fair, P = poor.

Table 9.2 Market share, mind share and heart share

	Market share (%)			Mind share (%)			Heart share (%)		
	2009	2010	2011	2009	2010	2011	2009	2010	2011
Competitor A	50	47	44	60	58	54	45	42	39
Competitor B	30	34	37	30	31	35	44	47	53
Competitor C	20	19	19	10	11	11	11	11	8

market share but is slipping. Its mind share and heart share are also slipping, probably because it is not providing good product availability and technical assistance. Competitor B is steadily gaining market share, probably due to strategies that are increasing its mind share and heart share. Competitor C seems to be stuck at a low level of market share, mind share and heart share, probably because of its poor product and marketing attributes. We could generalise as follows: *Companies that make steady gains in mind share and heart share will inevitably make gains in market share and profitability.* Firms such as Nokia, IKEA, L'Oréal, Philips and Mercedes (Daimler AG) are all reaping the financial benefits of providing emotional, experiential, social and financial value to satisfy customers and all their constituents.[12]

Marketing memo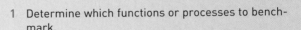

Benchmarking to improve competitive performance

Benchmarking is the art of learning from companies that perform certain tasks better than other companies. There can be as much as a tenfold difference between the quality, speed and cost performance of a world-class company and that of an average company. The aim of benchmarking is to copy or improve on 'best practices', either within an industry or across industries. Benchmarking can be an effective tool in influencing the quality of products and services. Benchmarking has seven steps:

1 Determine which functions or processes to benchmark.

2 Identify the key performance variables (key factors contributing to corporate success) to measure.

3 Identify the best-in-class companies.

4 Measure the performance of best-in-class companies.

5 Measure the company's performance.

6 Specify programmes and actions to close the gap.

7 Implement and monitor results.

▶ Marketing memo *(continued)*

How can companies identify best-practice companies? A good starting point is consulting customers, suppliers, distributors, financial analysts, trade associations and magazines to see who they rate as doing the best job. Even the best companies can benchmark to improve their performance. To pursue its corporate vision to be 'a company that society wants to exist', Honda has even benchmarked its brand and its advertising against rivals from beyond the motor industry, such as Apple. When supermarket chain ASDA in 2011 relaunched its mid-tier private label under the new 'Chosen by You' name, 200,000 UK consumers were taste testing and benchmarking the products. Notably, benchmarking is equally useful for small and medium-sized companies;

its results can be an effective means of developing strategies in a key performance area.

Sources: www.benchmarking.org; D. Shah and B. H. Kleiner (2011) Benchmarking for quality, *Industrial Management*, March/April, 22–5; R. Baker (2010) ASDA own brand is Chosen by You, *Marketing Week*, 21 September; P. O'Connell (2005) Bringing innovation to the home of six sigma, *BusinessWeek*, 1 August; J. E. Prescott, S. H. Miller and the Society of Competitive Intelligence Professionals (2001) *Proven Strategies in Competitive Intelligence: Lessons from the Trenches*, New York: John Wiley & Sons; R. Hiebeler, T. B. Kelly and C. Ketteman (1998) *Best Practices: Building Your Business with Customer-Focused Solutions*, New York: Arthur Andersen/Simon & Schuster; M. Hope (1997) Contrast and compare, *Marketing*, 28 August, 11–13; R. Lester (2006) The possible dream, *Marketing Week*, 26 October, 29(43), 24–5.

To improve market share, many companies benchmark their most successful competitors as well as other world-class performers.[13] The technique and its benefits are described in the marketing memo.

Selecting competitors

After the company has conducted customer value analysis and examined its competitors carefully, it can focus its attack on one of the following classes of competitors: strong versus weak, close versus distant, and 'good' versus 'bad'.

- **Strong versus weak.** Most companies aim their shots at weak competitors because this requires fewer resources per share point gained. Yet the firm should also compete with strong competitors to keep up with the best. Even strong competitors have some weaknesses.
- **Close versus distant.** Most companies compete with the competitors that resemble them the most. Toyota competes with Ford, not with Ferrari. Yet companies should also identify distant competitors. Coca-Cola recognises that its number-one competitor is tap water, not Pepsi; Royal Dutch Shell increasingly worries about the development of more energy-efficient fuels and technologies as well as competitors Exxon and BP; museums now worry about theme parks and malls.[14]
- **'Good' versus 'bad'.** Every industry contains 'good' and 'bad' competitors.[15] Good competitors play by the industry's rules; they set prices in reasonable relationship to costs; and they favour a healthy industry. Bad competitors try to buy share rather than earn it; they take large risks; they invest in overcapacity; and they upset industrial equilibrium. A company may find it necessary to attack its bad competitors to reduce or end their dysfunctional practices.

Selecting customers

As part of the competitive analysis, a firm must evaluate its customer base and think about which customers it is willing to lose and which it wants to retain. One way to divide up

Table 9.3 Customer selection grid

	Vulnerable	**Not vulnerable**
Valuable	These customers are profitable but not completely happy with the company. Find out and address their sources of vulnerability to *retain them*.	These customers are loyal and profitable. Don't take them for granted but *maintain margins* and reap the benefits of their satisfaction.
Not valuable	These customers are likely to defect. Let them go or even *encourage their departure*.	These unprofitable customers are happy. Try to *make them valuable or vulnerable*.

Source: Reprinted by permission of *Harvard Business Review*. From Defensive marketing: how a strong incumbent can protect its position by Roberts, J. H., November, 156, 2005. Copyright © 2005 by the Harvard Business School Publishing Corporation; all rights reserved.

the customer base is in terms of whether a customer is valuable and vulnerable, creating a grid of four segments as a result – see Table 9.3. Each segment suggests different competitive activities.[16]

Faced with formidable competition from its rival Optus (a joint subsidiary of UK-based Cable & Wireless and US company BellSouth), Australian telephone company Telstra conducted this type of segment analysis. Based on this analysis, Telstra developed a series of 'Flex-Plan' products designed to retain the valuable/vulnerables but without losing the margin it realised on the valuable/not vulnerables. The Flex-Plans had a subscription fee but offered significant net savings. Because valuable/vulnerables were highly involved with the category, they were able to see how they could benefit from such plans, but valuable/not vulnerables regarded the plans as unnecessary. As a result, the plans achieved the desired goals.

Terminating customers

The framework displayed in Table 9.3 suggests that companies should 'optimise' their customer portfolios based on customer profitability. When considering terminating relationships with unprofitable customers, four factors need to be taken into account:[17]

1 Are these customers also likely to be unprofitable in the long run (see also Chapter 22)? If unprofitable customers are terminated based on current profitability, companies might lose opportunities to retain potentially profitable customers.

2 Even though some customers are unprofitable by themselves, they can serve as reference clients for the acquisition of other, more profitable customers.

3 Network effects may be present. Network effects apply when the utility that a user derives from the consumption of a good or service increases with the number of other people also using it. For instance, Twitter, Facebook and LinkedIn are more useful the more users join. In the presence of network effects, shrinking the customer base by terminating unprofitable customers can be risky and undesirable.

4 In incidents where terminating customers is deemed unethical by public opinion, termination may backfire and hurt company reputation. When a large bank sought to terminate unprofitable relationships with disabled customers, it was after a short time forced to continue serving these customers due to public debate and pressure.

"Hi. I'm Tiffany and I'll be your waitress tonight — this agreement may be terminated by either party at any time."

Companies may consider terminating relationships with unprofitable customers.
Source: CartoonStock www.CartoonStock.com

Competitive strategies for market leaders

Having identified and analysed its competitors, a company will decide on a competitive strategy. We can gain further insight into competitive behaviour by classifying firms by the roles they play in the target market: leader, challenger, follower or nicher. Suppose a market is occupied by the firms shown in Figure 9.5. Of the total market, 40 per cent is in the hands of a *market leader*; another 30 per cent is in the hands of a *market challenger*; another 20 per cent is in the hands of a *market follower*, a firm that is willing to maintain its market share and not rock the boat. The remaining 10 per cent is in the hands of *market nichers*, firms that serve small market segments not being served by larger firms.

Many industries contain one or two firms that are acknowledged market leaders. These firms have the largest market share in the relevant product market and usually lead the other firms in price changes, new product introductions, distribution coverage and promotional intensity. Some historical market leaders are Microsoft (computer software), Nestlé (food and beverages), Disney (entertainment), Reuters (news and data services), McDonald's (fast food), Sony (home electronics), Visa (credit cards) and Accenture (management consulting).

Although marketers assume that well-known brands are distinctive in consumers' minds, unless a dominant firm enjoys a legal monopoly it must maintain constant vigilance. A product innovation may come along and hurt the leader; a competitor might unexpectedly find a fresh new marketing angle or commit to a major marketing investment; or the leader might find its cost structure spiralling upwards. One well-known brand that lost track of market trends for a while is Bang & Olufsen.

40%	Market leader
30%	Market challenger
20%	Market follower
10%	Market nichers

Figure 9.5 Hypothetical market structure

Bang & Olufsen

Given its status as a renowned luxury hi-fi brand, it may seem unlikely that Bang & Olufsen would be losing out to competitors. However, since 2007 company annual turnover has dropped from €0.6 billion to €0.4 billon (2010). Also, the number of independent Bang & Olufsen sales outlets, the so-called B1 stores, has decreased from well over 800 to fewer than 700. The financial crisis has been tough on Bang & Olufsen as a luxury brand. Hence, in trying to make Bang & Olufsen products financially accessible to more consumers, the company recently launched a 'zero interest and no fees' financing campaign. As another part of its recovery strategy, Bang & Olufsen is trying to penetrate the Chinese market. But the company is still waiting to see a reasonable return from this effort. According to marketing expert Jean-Noël Kapferer: 'To succeed in China, Bang & Olufsen needs to be either the best or most luxurious. But Bang & Olufsen does not match either way.' He adds: 'Technological progress comes primarily from Samsung and Sony. Bang & Olufsen could instead rely on being seen as a luxurious brand that you dream about – but in order to succeed the company needs to build its brand more strongly in this part of the world.' However, in some business areas Bang & Olufsen is increasingly being recognised as a leading luxury brand. Bang & Olufsen has been a part of the market for sound systems for cars since 2005 and today the company is developing sound systems for Audi, Aston Martin, Mercedes-AMG and BMW. In March 2011, readers of the German magazine *auto motor und sport* rated Bang & Olufsen the best car hifi brand. 'The result of this vote shows that car customers appreciate Bang & Olufsen's unique audio systems for cars,' says Johannes Schüler, Head of International Marketing and PR. Perhaps the lesson to be learned from this positive experience is that if Bang & Olufsen can keep its focus on delivering state-of-the-art products in terms of technology, design and brand identity, the brand may well rebound its market share.[18]

In many industries, a discount competitor has entered and undercut the leader's prices. The marketing insight box describes how leaders can respond to an aggressive competitive price discounter.

Marketing insight

When your competitor delivers more for less

Companies offering the powerful combination of low prices and high quality are capturing the hearts and wallets of consumers all over the world. In the United Kingdom, premium retailers such as Boots and Sainsbury's are scrambling to meet intensifying price – and quality – competition from ASDA and Tesco. These and similar value players, such as Aldi, Dell, E*TRADE Financial and Ryanair, are transforming the way consumers of nearly every age and income purchase groceries, apparel, airline tickets, financial services and computers. As value-driven companies in a growing number of industries change the way they compete, traditional players are right to feel threatened. The formula that these upstart firms often rely on includes focusing on one or a few consumer segments; providing better delivery of the basic product or one additional benefit; and matching low prices with highly efficient operations to keep costs down.

To compete with value-based rivals, mainstream companies must reconsider the perennial routes to business success: keeping costs in line, finding sources of differentiation and managing prices effectively. To succeed in value-based markets, companies need to infuse these timeless strategies with greater intensity and focus, and then execute them flawlessly. Differentiation, for example, becomes less about the abstract goal of rising above competitive clutter and more about identifying opportunities left open by the value players' business models. Effective pricing means waging a transaction-by-transaction perception battle to win over those consumers who are predisposed to believe that value-oriented competitors are always cheaper.

Competitive outcomes will be determined, as always, on the ground – in product aisles, merchandising displays, reconfigured processes and pricing stickers. When it comes to value-based competition, traditional players cannot afford to drop a stitch. Value-driven competitors have changed consumer expectations about the trade-off between quality and price. This shift is gathering momentum, placing a new premium on – and adding new twists to – the old imperatives of differentiation and execution.

> ▶ **Marketing Insight** *(continued)*

Differentiation

To counter value-based players, marketers will need to focus on areas where their business models give other companies room to manoeuvre. Successful differentiation calls for marshalling multiple tactics to provide superior delivery of a highly desired consumer benefit. Instead of trying to compete with discounters and other value retailers on price, for example, Danish supermarket chain Irma emphasises high quality across all elements of its business. Embarking on its concept of high-quality products and premium prices, it has been highly successful at targeting customers who appreciate new and special grocery selections, luxury and ecological products, as well as expensive wines. The new management team overhauled Irma's product selections and in-store design to signal a cutting-edge, agenda-setting spirit, aiming both to meet and to inspire consumer demand for high-quality and sustainable everyday lifestyle products. Today, around one-quarter of all products in Irma stores are ecological, and the chain has expanded rapidly in Denmark.[19]

Execution

Value-based markets also place a premium on execution, particularly in prices and costs. Wal-Mart's disastrous experience in trying to compete head-on with the Metro Group and well-established discounters such as Aldi and Lidl in Germany highlights the difficulty of challenging value leaders on their own turf. Matching or even beating a value player's prices – as Wal-Mart did – won't necessarily win the battle of consumer perceptions against companies with already established reputations for the lowest prices.

To compete effectively against value-based players, firms may need to downplay or even abandon some target market segments. To compete with Ryanair and easyJet, British Airways has put more emphasis on its long-haul routes, where value-based players are not evident, and less on the highly competitive short-haul routes where low-cost carriers thrive.

Major airlines have also tried another competitive response, introducing their own low-cost airlines. But KLM Royal Dutch Airline's Buzz and SAS's Snowflake have both been unsuccessful. One school of thought is that companies should set up low-cost operations only if two conditions apply: (1) the firm's existing businesses will be made more competitive as a result; and (2) the new business will derive some advantages it would not have gained by being independent. The success of low-cost operations set up by HSBC, ING, Royal Bank of Scotland and IHG (InterContinental Hotels Group) – First Direct, ING Direct, Direct Line Insurance and Holiday Inn Express, respectively – is due in part to synergies between the old and new lines of business. Thus, success dictates that the low-cost operation must be designed and launched to be a moneymaker in its own right, not just as a defensive ploy.

Sources: Adapted from two insightful articles, N. Kumar (2006) Strategies to fight low-cost rivals, *Harvard Business Review*, December, 104–12; and R. J. Frank, J. P. George and L. Narasimhan (2004) When your competitor delivers more for less, *McKinsey Quarterly*, Winter, 48–59.

Staying the number-one firm calls for action on three fronts. First, the firm must find ways to expand total market demand. Second, the firm must protect its current market share through good defensive and offensive actions. Third, the firm can try to increase its market share, even if market size remains constant. Let's look at each strategy.

Expanding the total market

When the total market expands, the dominant firm usually gains the most. If UK consumers increase their consumption of tomato sauce, Heinz stands to gain the most because it is the top-ranked brand of the sauce sold in this region, with a market share of 80 per cent (2010).[20] If it can convince more people to use tomato sauce, or to use it with more meals, or to use more sauce on each occasion, Heinz will benefit considerably. In general, the market leader should look for new customers or more usage from existing customers.

To learn how retailer Lululemon uses grassroots marketing techniques to position itself in Canada, visit www.pearsoned.ca/marketingmanagementcanada.

New customers

Every product class has the potential to attract buyers who are unaware of the product or who are resisting it because of price or lack of

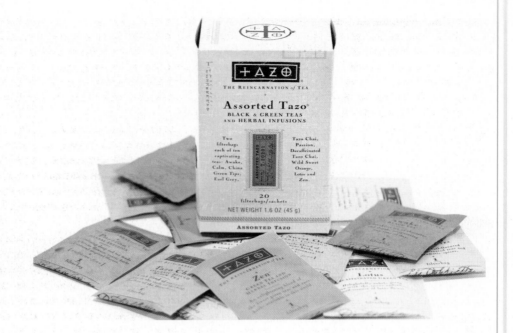

Among Starbucks' expansion efforts have been a new line of premium teas produced by Tazo Tea Company, a Starbucks' subsidiary

Source: Stephen F. Faust/ www.photographersdirect. com

certain features. A company can search for new users among three groups: those who might use it but do not (*market-penetration strategy*), those who have never used it (*new-market segment strategy*), or those who live elsewhere (*geographical-expansion strategy*).

Starbucks Coffee is one of the best-known brands in the world. Starbucks is able to sell a cup of coffee for €2 while the coffee shop next door can only get less than €1. (And if you want the popular café latte, it is €3.) Starbucks has more than 16,800 stores in over 50 countries, and its annual revenue for 2010 topped €7.8 billion. Its corporate website (www.starbucks.com) gives a peek into its multipronged approach to business.[21]

> **To say Starbucks purchases and roasts high-quality whole bean coffees is very true. That's the essence of what we do – but it hardly tells the whole story. Our coffeehouses have become a beacon for coffee lovers everywhere. Why do they insist on Starbucks? Because they know they can count on genuine service, an inviting atmosphere and a superb cup of expertly roasted and richly brewed coffee every time. We're not just passionate purveyors of coffee, but everything else that goes with a full and rewarding coffeehouse experience. We also offer a selection of premium Tazo® teas, fine pastries and other delectable treats to please the taste buds. And the music you hear in store is chosen for its artistry and appeal. It's not unusual to see people coming to Starbucks to chat, meet up or even work. We're a neighborhood gathering place, a part of the daily routine – and we couldn't be happier about it. Get to know us and you'll see: we are so much more than what we brew.**

More usage

Marketers can try to increase the amount, level or frequency of consumption.

The *amount* of consumption can sometimes be increased through packaging or product redesign. Larger package sizes have been shown to increase the amount of product that consumers use at one time.[22] The usage of impulse consumption products such as soft drinks and snacks increases when the product is made more available.

Increasing *frequency* of consumption, on the other hand, requires either: (1) identifying additional opportunities to use the brand in the same basic way; or (2) identifying completely new and different ways to use the brand. Consumers may see the product as useful only in certain places and at certain times, especially if it has strong brand associations to particular usage situations or user types. Naturally, product category usage frequency is often influenced by factors that are not controllable by managers. For instance, mobile usage frequency is affected positively by consumers' attitudes towards the acceptance of mobile phone use in public places.[23]

In the first case – where the marketer focuses on *additional opportunities to use the brand in the same basic way* – a marketing programme may communicate the appropriateness and advantages of using the brand more frequently in new or existing situations, or remind consumers actually to use the brand in those situations. Kellogg's, for example, takes this approach when the company offers its customers inspiration for new ways to eat its cereal for breakfast and brunch. Another opportunity arises when consumers' perceptions of product usage differs from reality. Consumers may fail to replace a short-lived product when they should, because they overestimate how long it stays fresh.[24]

One strategy to speed up product replacement is to tie the act of replacing the product to a holiday, event or time of year. Another might be to provide consumers with better information about either: (1) when they first used the product or need to replace it; or (2) the current level of product performance. Gillette razor cartridges feature coloured stripes that slowly fade with repeated use, signalling the user to move on to the next cartridge.

The second approach to increasing frequency of consumption is to *identify completely new and different applications*. For example, food product companies have long advertised recipes that use their branded products in entirely different ways. Toblerone and Daim (also known as Dime in the United Kingdom) are examples of chocolates that have become main components in delicious ice creams and cakes – Carte d'Or Toblerone and (home-made) Daim Ice Cream Cakes, respectively. On a similar note, sherry brand Tio Pepe has aimed at stretching consumers' associations and uses of the drink by promoting it as a special style of white wine. The brand encourages consumers to drink it just as they would a dry white wine – chilled and in a wine glass – and hence may increase the number of occasions in which Tio Pepe comes into consideration as an appropriate drink.[25]

Product development can also spur new uses. Chewing gum manufacturers such as Cadbury Schweppes, maker of Trident, are producing 'nutraceutical' products to strengthen or whiten teeth. Aquafresh has successfully launched dental chewing gums with health and cosmetic benefits.[26]

Protecting market share

While trying to expand total market size, the dominant firm must continuously and actively defend its current business: AirBus against Boeing, and Google against Yahoo! and Microsoft.[27] The success of online social network sites MySpace and Facebook has brought challenges from upstarts such as LinkedIn personal business network, Dogster for dog owners, Vox for sharing photos and videos, and blog posts for baby boomers and older consumers.[28]

What can the market leader do to defend its terrain? The most constructive response is *continuous innovation*. The leader should lead the industry in developing new products and customer services, distribution effectiveness and cost cutting. It keeps increasing its competitive strength and value to customers by providing comprehensive solutions.

Martelli Lavorazioni Tessili

Consumers who wonder why it costs €140 or more to buy a pair of designer jeans might feel better about the high price tag if they strolled through a Martelli Lavorazioni Tessili factory in Vedelago, Italy. The market leader in the technology of 'distressing' denim, Martelli counts Gucci, Armani, Dolce & Gabbana and Yves Saint Laurent among its clients at the high end and Levi-Strauss, Lee, Wrangler and Gap at the low end. Martelli is uncontested in Europe; its only competitors are in the United States and Japan. The company stays on top by relentlessly innovating – investing at least €3.5 million a year continually to upgrade technology – and by finding cheap but skilled labour to carry out its bizarre but effective techniques. In its main factory with 900 workers, huge washing machines tumble jeans with pumice gravel. Workers wearing face masks put jeans legs over inflated balloons, which then are moved between sets of plastic brushes that scrub the denim. Some workers do painstaking hand work on individual jeans, applying discolouring chemicals with brushes, applying embroidered designs, or using handheld guns to blast jets of quartz sand. After experimenting with hiring workers from Africa and Romania, Martelli found that Chinese, legal immigrants are the most skilled, patient and cost effective for the job of hand-crafting jeans.[29] Not only informal, but also formal garments are treated by Martelli. In fact, there are fewer and fewer differences between formal and informal clothing.

Italy's Martelli Lavorazioni Tessilli is a market leader in the technology of 'distressing' denim.
Source: Dave Yoder/Polaris/www.eyevinearchive.com

In satisfying customer needs, we can draw a distinction between responsive marketing, anticipative marketing and creative marketing. A *responsive* marketer finds a stated need and fills it. An *anticipative* marketer looks ahead into what needs customers may have in the near future. A *creative* marketer discovers and produces solutions that customers did not ask for, but to which they enthusiastically respond. Creative marketers are *market-driving firms*, not just market driven. Many companies assume their job is just to adapt to customer needs. They are reactive mostly because they are overly faithful to the customer-orientation paradigm and fall victim to the 'tyranny of the served market'. Successful companies instead proactively shape the market to their own interests. Instead of trying to be the best player, they change the rules of the game.[30]

A company needs two proactive skills:

1 *responsive anticipation* to see the writing on the wall, as when IBM changed from a hardware producer to a service business; and
2 *creative anticipation* to devise innovative solutions, as when Pepsico introduced H2OH (a soft drink–bottled water hybrid).

Note that *responsive anticipation* is performed before a given change, while *reactive response* happens after the change takes place.

Proactive companies create new offers to serve unmet – and maybe even unknown – consumer needs. In the late 1970s Akio Morita, the Sony founder, was working on a pet project that would revolutionise the way people listened to music: a portable cassette player he called the Walkman. Engineers at the company insisted there was little demand for such a product, but Morita refused to part with his vision. By the 20th anniversary of the Walkman, Sony had sold over 250 million players in nearly 100 different models.[31]

Proactive companies may redesign relationships within an industry, like Toyota and its relationship to its suppliers. Or they may educate customers, as The Body Shop does in stimulating the choice of environmental friendly products.

Companies need to practise *uncertainty management*. Proactive firms:

- are ready to take risks and make mistakes;
- have a vision of the future and of investing in it;
- have the capabilities to innovate;
- are flexible and non-bureaucratic; and
- have many managers who think proactively.

Companies that are *too* risk-averse will not be winners.

Even when it does not launch offensives, the market leader must not leave any major flanks, or vulnerable areas, exposed. It must consider carefully which terrains are important to defend, even at a loss, and which can be surrendered. The aim of defensive strategy is to reduce the probability of attack, divert attacks to less threatening areas, and lessen their intensity. The defender's speed of response can make an important difference in the profit consequences. A dominant firm can use the six defence strategies summarised in Figure 9.6.[32]

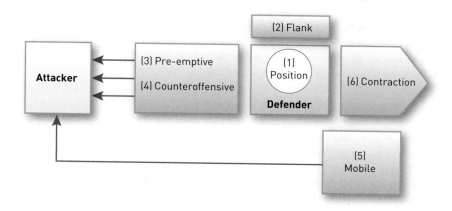

Figure 9.6 Six types of defence strategy

Position defence

Position defence means occupying (and defending) a positive and superior standing in consumers' minds, including for example high-brand equity, customer satisfaction, customer loyalty, or a high repeat-purchase rate. Holding this desirable market position can make the brand seem almost impregnable, as Procter & Gamble has shown with Ariel detergent, Crest toothpaste (marketed as Blend-a-Med in some European countries) for cavity prevention, and Pampers nappies for dryness.

Flank defence

Although position defence is important, the market leader should also erect outposts to protect a weak front or possibly serve as an invasion base for counterattack. Flanking moves tend to occur in the periphery (or on the flanks) of a company's main activities. In marketing terms, this could include introducing new products or brands, repositioning existing products or launching promotional activities. When Europe's number-two car maker, PSA Peugeot Citroën, was attacked by competitors Volkswagen and Renault in its core market of subcompacts, Peugeot's strategic response was a rollout plan of 29 new models, including five entirely new concepts. The company decided to reposition some of its cars in more upscale markets, while steering clear of the race to engineer super-cheap cars for emerging markets. Instead, Peugeot competes in these markets with lower-cost versions of existing models. This strategy protected Peugeot's flanks, although the competition remains fierce in the mature European car market.[33]

Pre-emptive defence

A more aggressive manoeuvre is to attack *before* the enemy starts its offence. A company can launch a pre-emptive defence in several ways. It can wage guerrilla action across the market – hitting one competitor here, another there – and keep everyone off balance; or it can try to achieve a grand market envelopment. Electronic Arts has been experimenting with a radical new business model involving free online access to some of its popular games (FIFA soccer and Battlefield Heroes), while charging customers for so-called microtransactions and carrying in-game ads. In this way Electronic Arts establishes its position as a market leader and sends out market signals to dissuade competitors from attacking.[34]

Marketers can introduce a stream of new products, making sure to precede them with *preannouncements* – deliberate communications regarding future actions.[35] Preannouncements can signal to competitors that they will need to fight to gain market share.[36] If Microsoft announces plans for a new product development, smaller firms may choose to concentrate their development efforts in other directions to avoid head-to-head competition. Some high-tech firms have even been accused of engaging in selling 'vapourware' – preannouncing products that miss delivery dates or are never introduced.[37]

Counteroffensive defence

When attacked, most market leaders will respond with a counterattack. In a *counteroffensive*, the leader can meet the attacker frontally or hit its flank or launch a pincer movement. An effective counterattack is to invade the attacker's main territory so that it will pull back to defend it. Swedish vodka brand Absolut faced an immense challenge as a crop of new 'super premium' brands such as Grey Goose, Chopin and Citadelle came along, questioning Absolut's position as 'coolness in a bottle'. To fight back, Absolut invested heavily in a new high-profile ad campaign, associating the brand with other classics that are 'absolutes' in popular culture, such as the Apollo moon landing and Marilyn Monroe.[38]

Another common form of counteroffensive is the exercise of economic or political clout. The leader may try to crush a competitor by subsidising lower prices for the vulnerable product with revenue from its more profitable products, or the leader may prematurely announce that a product upgrade will be available, to prevent customers from buying the competitor's product. Or the leader may lobby legislators to take political action to inhibit the competition. For instance, a leading pharmaceutical company might attempt to influence legislation regarding testing and marketing of a specific medical product category in order to make it more difficult for potential competitors to enter the market.

Mobile defence

In mobile defence, the leader stretches its domain over new territories that can serve as future centres for defence and offence through market broadening and market diversification. *Market broadening* shifts focus from the current product to the underlying generic need. The company gets involved in R&D across the whole range of technology associated with that need. Thus 'petroleum' companies such as BP sought to recast themselves as 'energy' companies. Implicitly, this change demanded that they dip their research fingers into the oil, coal, nuclear, hydroelectric and chemical industries.

Market diversification shifts into unrelated industries. When Hochtief, the biggest construction firm in Germany, witnessed huge losses in the industry due to increasing costs of raw materials, it was not content with position defence or even with looking for substitute contracts. Instead it moved into the real-estate market where steadier earnings and higher profit margins are expected.[39]

Contraction defence

Large companies must sometimes recognise that they can no longer defend all their territory. The best course of action then appears to be *planned contraction* (also called *strategic withdrawal*): giving up weaker territories and reassigning resources to stronger territories. For instance, Sara Lee phased out products that accounted for almost 40 per cent of the company's revenues, including its strong Hanes hosiery brand, so it could concentrate on its well-known food brands.[40]

Expanding market share

In many markets, one share point is worth tens of millions of euros. No wonder competition has turned fierce in so many markets. Gaining increased share in the served market, however, does not automatically produce higher profits – especially for labour-intensive service companies that may not experience many economies of scale. Much depends on the company's strategy.[41]

Because the cost of buying higher market share may far exceed its revenue value, a company should consider four factors before pursuing increased share:

1 **The possibility of provoking action from competition authorities.** Jealous competitors are likely to cry 'monopoly' if a dominant firm makes further inroads. This rise in risk would diminish the attractiveness of pushing market share gains too far. Microsoft and Intel are examples of companies that have faced great scrutiny for their market leadership and practices.

2 **Economic cost.** Figure 9.7 shows that profitability might *fall* with market share gains after some level. In the illustration, the firm's *optimal market share* is 50 per cent. The cost of gaining further market share might exceed the value if holdout customers dislike the company, are loyal to competitors, have unique needs, or prefer dealing with smaller firms. And the costs of legal work, public relations and lobbying rise with market share. Pushing for higher share is less justified when there are few scale or experience economies, unattractive market segments exist, buyers want multiple sources of supply, and exit barriers are high. Some market leaders have even increased profitability by selectively *decreasing* market share in weaker areas.[42]

Figure 9.7 The concept of optimal market share

3 **Pursuing the wrong marketing activities.** Companies successfully gaining share typically outperform competitors in three areas: new product activity, relative product
quality and marketing expenditures.[43] On the other hand, companies that attempt to
increase market share by cutting prices more deeply than competitors typically don't
achieve significant gains, because enough rivals meet the price cuts and others offer
other values so that buyers don't switch. Competitive rivalry and price cutting have
been shown to be most intense in industries with high fixed costs, high inventory costs
and stagnant primary demand, such as steel, cars, paper and chemicals.[44]

4 **The effect of increased market share on actual and perceived quality.**[45] Too many customers can put a strain on the firm's resources, hurting product value and service
delivery. A slow conversion and significant service problems may lead to customer dissatisfaction, regulator's anger, and eventually bankruptcy.[46] Consumers may also infer
that 'bigger is not better' and assume that growth will lead to deterioration of quality.

Other competitive strategies

The previous section dealt especially with market leaders. However, most firms are not
market leaders. Firms that occupy second, third and lower ranks in an industry are often
called runner-up or trailing firms. Some, such as PepsiCo, Ford and Avis, are quite large
in their own right. These firms can adopt one of two postures. They can attack the leader
and other competitors in an aggressive bid for further market share as *market challengers*,
or they can not 'rock the boat' as *market followers*.

Market-challenger strategies

Many market challengers have gained ground or even overtaken the leader. Toyota today
produces more cars than General Motors and AMD has been chipping away at Intel's market share.[47] Challengers set high aspirations, leveraging their resources while the market
leader often runs the business as usual. Now let's examine the competitive attack strategies
available to market challengers.[48]

Defining the strategic objective and opponent(s)

A market challenger must first define its strategic objective. Most aim to increase market
share. The challenger must decide whom to attack:

- **It can attack the market leader.** This is a high-risk but potentially high-pay-off strategy and makes good sense if the leader is not serving the market well. It often
has the added benefit of distancing the firm from other challengers. When the free

newspaper '*20 Minutes*' attacked *Metro International* in the French and Spanish markets, it focused on qualities such as vivid visuals and local content, and left traditional newspapers out of public debate on the subject.[49] *20 Minutes* is distributed to those travelling on public transport in major cities in, among others, Switzerland, France and Spain, and has rapidly become the most read daily newspaper in France and Spain.[50] An alternative strategy is to out-innovate the leader across the whole segment. Xerox wrested the copier market from 3M by developing a better copying process. Later, Canon grabbed a large chunk of Xerox's market by introducing desk copiers. This strategy often has the added benefit of distancing the firm from other challengers.

- **It can attack firms of its own size that are not doing the job and are underfinanced.** These firms have ageing products, are charging excessive prices or are not satisfying customers in other ways.
- **It can attack small local and regional firms.** Several major banks grew to their present size by gobbling up smaller regional banks, or 'guppies'.

Attack strategies

Given clear opponents and objectives, what attack options are available? We can distinguish among five attack strategies: frontal, flank, encirclement, bypass and guerrilla attacks.

Frontal attack In a pure *frontal attack,* the attacker matches its opponent's product, advertising, price and distribution. The principle of force says that the side with the greater resources will win. A modified frontal attack, such as cutting price, can work if the market leader does not retaliate, and if the competitor convinces the market that its product is equal to the leader's. Max Factor is a master at convincing the market that its products – such as Eye 2000 Calorie Mascara and Lipfinity lipstick – are equal in quality but better value than higher-priced brands.

Flank attack A *flanking* strategy is another name for identifying shifts that are causing gaps to develop, then rushing to fill the gaps. Flanking is in the best tradition of modern marketing, which holds that the purpose of marketing is to discover needs and satisfy them. It is particularly attractive to a challenger with fewer resources and can be more likely to succeed than frontal attacks. In a geographic attack, the challenger spots areas where the opponent is underperforming. The other flanking strategy is to serve uncovered market needs. Ariat International used this type of strategy to attain its position as a leading footwear and apparel brand for equestrian athletes around the world. Ariat discovered an opportunity to design riding boots that were every bit as luxurious and elegant as traditional English riding boots, but ergonomically designed to feel as comfortable as a running shoe – a totally new benefit in the category. Later, Ariat applied the same idea to casual footwear, cowboy boots, work boots and apparel.[51]

Search engines

Given Google's 45 per cent share of the internet search business, it might seem foolhardy for anybody to challenge it. A frontal attack on Google would mean building a better mousetrap – in this case, a better search algorithm. Yet a handful of smaller search companies *are* mounting flank attacks on Google, and they are confident that they will be able to swipe some of the search giant's market share. The flank these small companies are attacking is the one missing element in Google's searches: human intelligence and its ability to reason and contextualise. Recently, Wikia Inc. announced the official launch of Wikiréponses (http://reponses.wikia.com), the French version of Wikia's Question and Answer service. 'The response rate of nearly 80 per cent of the questions answered by the Wikia community demonstrates people's interest in talking about what they know and by doing so, helping others,' said Jimmy Wales, co-founder of Wikia. Wales figures that humans are better at weeding out spam search results. ChaCha, which is a free mobile answers service, employs a similar strategy and has thrived in Korea, where Google has made few inroads. ChaCha, founded by MIT research scientist Scott A. Jones, interacts with over 32 million users per month via mobile text, mobile video, phone apps, online and through social network. In total ChaCha has answered more than 1 billion questions and has become a leading way for brand advertisers to engage with the target audience of their choice.[52]

Encirclement attack The *encirclement* manoeuvre is an attempt to capture a wide slice of the enemy's territory through a blitz. It means launching a grand offensive on several fronts. Encirclement makes sense when the challenger commands superior resources and believes a swift encirclement will break the opponent's will. In making a stand against archrival Microsoft, Sun Microsystems licensed its Java software to hundreds of companies and millions of software developers for all sorts of consumer devices. As consumer electronics products began to go digital, Java started appearing in a wide range of gadgets.

Bypass attack The most indirect assault strategy is *bypassing* the enemy altogether and attacking easier markets to broaden the firm's resource base. This strategy offers three lines of approach: diversifying into unrelated products, diversifying into new geographical markets, and leapfrogging into new technologies to supplant existing products. In the past decade, Pepsi has used a bypass strategy against Coke by: (1) aggressively rolling out Aquafina bottled water before Coke launched its Dasani brand; (2) purchasing orange juice giant Tropicana for €2.3 billion in 1998, which owned almost twice the market share of Coca-Cola's Minute Maid; and (3) purchasing The Quaker Oats Company, owner of the market-leading Gatorade sports drink, for €9.8 billion in 2000.[53]

Technological leapfrogging is a bypass strategy practised in high-tech industries. The challenger patiently researches and develops the next technology and launches an attack, shifting the battleground to its own territory where it has an advantage. Nintendo's successful attack in the video game market was precisely about wresting market share by introducing a superior technology and redefining the 'competitive space'. Google used technological leapfrogging to overtake Yahoo! and become the market leader in search.

Guerrilla warfare Guerrilla warfare consists of waging small, intermittent attacks to harass and demoralise the opponent and eventually secure permanent footholds. The guerrilla challenger uses both conventional and unconventional means of attack. These include selective price cuts, occasional legal action and intense promotional blitzes. For instance, phone operator 3 has used guerrilla advertising around Dublin's Croke Park before a Six Nations rugby union clash between England and Ireland – it used high-pressure hoses to clean three logos into the dirt on the pavements around the stadium.[54]

Choosing a specific attack strategy

The challenger must go beyond the five broad strategies and develop more specific strategies. Any aspect of the marketing programme can serve as the basis for attack, such as lower-priced or discounted products, new or improved products and services, a wider variety of offerings, and innovative distribution strategies. A challenger's success depends

Marketing memo

Making smaller better

Adam Morgan offers eight suggestions on how small brands can better compete:

1 Break with your immediate past. Don't be afraid to ask 'dumb' questions to challenge convention and view your brand differently.

2 Build a 'lighthouse identity'. Establish values and communicate who and why you are. Apple excels at projecting a strong sense of self that makes it relevant and salient to consumers. By wholeheartedly signifying its confidence and fortitude, it becomes a lighthouse brand that consumers can navigate their life by, publicly or privately.[55]

3 Assume thought leadership of the category. Break convention in terms of what you say about yourself, where you say it, and what you do beyond talk.

4 Create symbols of re-evaluation. A rocket uses half its fuel in the first mile to break loose from Earth's gravitational pull – you may need to polarise people to get them to rethink your brand.

5 Sacrifice. Focus your target, message, reach and frequency, distribution and line extensions, and recognise that less can be more.

6 Overcommit. Although you may do fewer things, do 'big' things when you do them.

7 Use publicity and advertising to enter popular culture. Unconventional communications can get people talking.

8 Be idea centred, not consumer centred. Sustain challenger momentum by not losing sight of what the brand is about and can be, and redefine marketing support as the centre of the company to reflect this vision.

Sources: A. Morgan (1999) *Eating the Big Fish: How Challenger Brands Can Compete Against Brand Leaders*, New York: John Wiley & Sons. See also A. Morgan (2004) *The Pirate Inside: Building a Challenger Brand Culture Within Yourself and Your Organisation*, Chichester, England: John Wiley & Sons.

on combining several strategies to improve its position over time. The marketing memo provides some additional tips for challenger brands.

Market-follower strategies

Some years ago, legendary marketing scholar Theodore Levitt wrote an article entitled 'Innovative imitation', in which he argued that a strategy of *product imitation* might be as profitable as a strategy of *product innovation*.[56] The innovator bears the expense of developing the new product, getting it into distribution, and informing and educating the market. The reward for all this work and risk is normally market leadership. However, another firm can come along and copy or improve the new product. Although it will probably not overtake the leader, the follower can achieve high profits because it did not bear any of the innovation expense.

S&S Cycle

S&S Cycle is the biggest supplier of complete engines and major motor parts to more than 15 companies that build several thousand Harley-like cruiser bikes each year. These cloners charge as much as €22,000 for their customised creations. S&S has built its name by improving on Harley-Davidson's handiwork. Its customers are often would-be Harley buyers frustrated by long waiting lines at the dealers. Other customers simply want the incredibly powerful S&S engines. In 2011, S&S Cycle Inc. received the coveted 'Engine of the Year' award for its KN-Kone engine. S&S stays abreast of its evolving market by ordering a new Harley bike every year and taking apart the engine to see what it can improve upon.[57]

Many companies prefer to follow rather than challenge the market leader, a strategy that allows a company to learn more about market needs and reactions or a technology before committing resources to market and product development. Patterns of 'conscious parallelism' are common in capital-intensive, homogeneous-product industries, such as steel, fertilisers and chemicals. The opportunities for product differentiation and image differentiation are low; service quality is often comparable; and price sensitivity runs high. The mood in these industries is against short-run grabs for market share because that strategy only provokes retaliation. Most firms decide against stealing one another's customers. Instead, they present similar offers to buyers, usually by copying the leader. Market shares show high stability.

That is not to say that market followers lack strategies. A market follower must know how to hold current customers and win a fair share of new ones. Each follower tries to bring distinctive advantages to its target market – location, services, financing. Because the follower is often a major target of attack by challengers, it must keep its manufacturing costs low and its product quality and services high. It must also enter new markets as they open up. The follower must define a growth path, but one that does not invite competitive retaliation. We distinguish four broad strategies:

1 **Counterfeiter.** The counterfeiter duplicates the leader's product and packages and sells them on the black market or through disreputable dealers. Music firms Apple and Rolex have been plagued by the counterfeiter problem, especially in Asia.
2 **Cloner.** The cloner emulates the leader's products, name and packaging, with slight variations. For example, Danish Harboes Bryggeri A/S sells imitations of Coca-Cola Zero in look-alike bottles. Its Cola Minus sells for less than half the price of a Coca-Cola Zero.
3 **Imitator.** The imitator copies some things from the leader but maintains differentiation in terms of packaging, advertising, pricing or location. The leader does not mind the imitator as long as the imitator does not attack the leader aggressively. Fernandez Pujals grew up in Fort Lauderdale, Florida, and took Domino's home delivery idea to Spain, where he borrowed €56,000 to open his first store in Madrid. His TelePizza chain now operates almost 1,050 stores in Europe and Latin America.
4 **Adapter.** The adapter takes the leader's products and adapts or improves them. The adapter may choose to sell to different markets, but often it grows into the future challenger, as many Japanese firms have done after improving products developed elsewhere.

What does a follower earn? Normally, less than the leader. For example, a study of food-processing companies showed the largest firm averaging a 16 per cent return on investment; the number-two firm, 6 per cent; the number-three firm, −1 per cent; and the number-four firm, −6 per cent. In this case, only the top two firms have profits. No wonder Jack Welch, former CEO of GE, told his business units that each must reach the number-one or two position in its market, or else! Followership is often not a rewarding path.

Market-nicher strategies

An alternative to being a follower in a large market is to be a leader in a small market, or niche (see also Chapter 10). Smaller firms normally avoid competing with larger firms by targeting small markets of little or no interest to the larger firms. But even large, profitable firms may choose to use niching strategies for some of their business units or companies. Firms with low share of the total market can become highly profitable through smart niching. Such companies tend to offer high value, charge a premium price, achieve lower manufacturing costs, and shape a strong corporate culture and vision, as the breakthrough marketing box shows.

Breakthrough marketing

AIAIAI

AIAIAI was created in 2005 in an old industrial building in Copenhagen. Right from the beginning the building was the setting for a creative environment, comprising more than 200 young people. Besides being a breeding ground for the development of musicians, designers and musicians, the building formed the inspirational background for the development of AIAIAI's collective vision, which still has not changed: the company aims to create headphones and other consumer electronic products that have a clear connection to the creative world, and thus make a heartfelt, different and genuine statement.

offers the Swirl Earphone, which is designed with an emphasis on sturdiness and lasting durability. It has a robust, industrial in-ear housing made to withstand heavy everyday use. In 2011, electronics giant Apple became attracted to a range of AIAIAI headphones and accepted them for sale in European Apple stores. Even though competition is tough, AIAIAI hopes that Apple will also present its products in the US Apple stores. By having its products presented in Apple stores, the company has succeeded in increasing consumers' brand attention, which has subsequently doubled sales. 'The market potential is amazing,' says Jacob Moesgaard, one of the four AIAIAI partners celebrating the success.

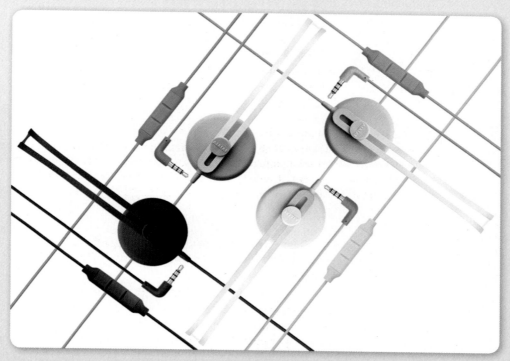

AIAIAI creates headphones for the creative world
Source: AIAIAI

Teaming up with the best possible sound engineers and musicians, the company emphasises an open development process. The design of the company's first headphones, being a tribute to the ones that came with the original 1980s Sony Walkman, makes it easy to hear what is going on in the outside world, which at the same time helps you to avoid getting hit by a car when walking the city streets. A single piece of bent metal holds the ear cups, which slide up or down for size adjustability. It is even possible to pop the ear cups off altogether for on-the-go storage. Among other products, AIAIAI also

Questions

1 Being one of Europe's many SMEs, AIAIAI dreams about expansion. In your opinion: what are the possibilities, what are the pitfalls?
2 Is collaborating with Apple a good idea? Why/why not?

Sources: D. Jensen (2011) Lille dansk firma lander storaftale med Apple, *Computerworld*, 18 March; K. T. Rasmussen (2011) Dansk virksomhed i storaftale med Apple, *Børsen*, 18 March, 20; www.aiaiai.dk; K. T. Rasmussen (2011) Svært at tjene penge hos Apple, *Børsen*, 18 March, 21.

By delivering pre-packed boxes of the season's best ecological vegetables and groceries to customers' doorsteps, the Danish web company Aarstiderne.com (*Aarstiderne* = 'Seasons') offers consumers the chance to spend their time and energy at the cooker and not at the shopping cart. Customers may choose between nine different vegetable and fruit boxes and a wide selection of special boxes, containing for example fish, meat, cheese, bread or processed foods. The boxes include recipes for delicious and easy-to-make everyday meals that are tailor-made to suit each week's box. This solution helps consumers avoid the 'what are we going to eat tonight?' stress of a typical weekday. At the beginning of 2012, 40,000 Danish and 5,000 Swedish families were receiving boxes from Aarstiderne every week.[58]

In a study of hundreds of business units, the Strategic Planning Institute found that the return on investment averaged 27 per cent in smaller markets, but only 11 per cent in larger markets.[59] Why is niching so profitable? The main reason is that the market nicher ends up knowing the target customers so well that it meets their needs better than other firms selling to this niche casually. As a result, the nicher can charge a substantial price over costs. The nicher achieves *high margin*, whereas the mass marketer achieves *high volume*.

Nichers have three tasks: creating niches, expanding niches and protecting niches. Niching carries a major risk in that the market niche might dry up or be attacked. The company is then stuck with highly specialised resources that may not have high-value alternative uses.

Zippo

With smoking on a steady decline, Zippo Manufacturing is finding the market for its iconic metal cigarette lighter drying up. Its marketers need to diversify and broaden their focus to 'selling flame'. Although its goal of reducing reliance on tobacco-related products to 50 per cent of revenue by 2010 was side-tracked by the recession, the company is determined to broaden its brand meaning to encompass 'all flame-related products'. It introduced a long, slender multipurpose lighter for candles, grills and fireplaces in 2001; acquired Case Cutlery, a knifemaker, and D.D.M. Italia, known throughout Europe for fine Italian leather goods; and in 2011 the company launched Men's Watch Line with details such as stainless steel cases, stitched leather straps, and chrome buckles with an etched logo.[60]

Because niches can weaken, the firm must continually create new ones. The marketing memo outlines some options. The firm should 'stick to its niching' but not necessarily to its niche. That is why *multiple niching* is preferable to *single niching*. By developing strength in two or more niches, the company increases its chances of survival.

Marketing memo

Niche specialist roles

The key idea in successful nichemanship is specialisation. Here are some possible niche roles:

- **End-user specialist.** The firm specialises in serving one type of end-use customer. For example, a *value-added reseller* (VAR) customises the computer hardware and software for specific customer segments and earns a price premium in the process.

- **Vertical-level specialist.** The firm specialises at some vertical level of the production–distribution value chain. A copper firm may concentrate on producing raw copper, copper components or finished copper products.

- **Customer-size specialist.** The firm concentrates on selling to small, medium-sized or large customers. Many nichers specialise in serving small customers neglected by the majors.

- **Specific-customer specialist.** The firm limits its selling to one or a few customers. Many firms sell their entire output to a single company, such as Siemens or Peugeot.

- **Geographic specialist.** The firm sells only in a certain locality, region or area of the world.

- **Product or product-line specialist.** The firm carries or produces only one product line or product. A manufacturer may produce only lenses for microscopes. A retailer may carry only ties.

- **Product-feature specialist.** The firm specialises in producing a certain type of product or product feature. Streetcar's car-sharing services target people who live or work in several UK cities – people who need a car from time to time, but wish to save the time and hassle associated with owning a car (parking, insurance and maintenance).[61]

- **Job-shop specialist.** The firm customises its products for individual customers.

- **Quality–price specialist.** The firm operates at the low- or high-quality end of the market. Hewlett-Packard specialises in the high-quality, high-price end of the handheld calculator market.

- **Service specialist.** The firm offers one or more services not available from other firms. A bank might take loan requests over the phone and hand-deliver the money to the customer.

- **Channel specialist.** The firm specialises in serving only one channel of distribution. For example, a soft drinks company decides to make a very large-sized serving available only at petrol stations.

Firms entering a market should initially aim at a niche rather than the whole market. The mobile phone industry has experienced phenomenal growth but is now facing fierce competition as the number of new potential users dwindles. An Irish upstart company, Digicel Group, has successfully tapped into one of the few remaining high-growth segments: poor people without mobiles.

Digicel Group

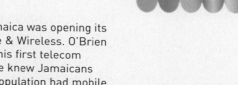

In 2001, Digicel CEO Denis O'Brien heard that the government of Jamaica was opening its local phone market, long monopolised by British telecom giant Cable & Wireless. O'Brien spent nearly $50 million for a licence, using money from the sale of his first telecom venture, Esat Telecom Group plc. O'Brien took the plunge because he knew Jamaicans had to wait over two years for a landline, and only 4 per cent of the population had mobile phones. Within 100 days, Digicel had signed on 100,000 subscribers, luring them with inexpensive rates and phones and improved service. After eight years, Digicel has more than eight million customers across its Caribbean and Central American markets, earning a reputation for competitive rates, comprehensive coverage, superior customer care and a wide variety of products and services. Digicel has also moved into the Pacific in Fiji, Samoa, Papua New Guinea and other markets. Back in Jamaica, it has become an active sponsor of sports and supporter of causes, befitting for its ascendance as a market leader in the region.[62]

Balancing customer and competitor orientations

We have stressed the importance of a company's positioning itself competitively as a market leader, challenger, follower or nicher. Yet a company must not spend *all* its time focusing on competitors.

Competitor-centred companies

A *competitor-centred company* sets its course as follows.

Observed situation

- Competitor W is going all out to crush us in Portugal.
- Competitor X is improving its distribution coverage in Germany and hurting our sales.
- Competitor Y has cut its price in Italy, and we lost three share points.
- Competitor Z has introduced a new service feature in Greece, and we are losing sales.

Reactions

- We will withdraw from the Portuguese market because we cannot afford to fight this battle.
- We will increase our advertising expenditure in Germany.
- We will meet competitor Y's price cut in Italy.
- We will increase our sales promotion budget in Greece.

This kind of planning has some pluses and minuses. On the positive side, the company develops a fighter orientation. It trains its marketers to be on constant alert, to watch for weaknesses in its competitors' and its own position. On the negative side, the company is too reactive. Rather than formulating and executing a consistent, *customer-oriented* strategy, it determines its moves based on its competitors' moves. It does not move towards its own goals. It does not know where it will end up, because so much depends on what its competitors do.

Customer-centred companies

A *customer-centred company* focuses more on customer developments in formulating its strategies.

Observed situation

- The total market is growing at 4 per cent annually.
- The quality-sensitive segment is growing at 8 per cent annually.
- The deal-prone customer segment is also growing fast, but these customers do not stay with any supplier very long.
- A growing number of customers have expressed an interest in a 24-hour hot line, which no one in the industry offers.

Reactions

- We will focus more effort on reaching and satisfying the quality segment of the market. We will buy better components, improve quality control, and shift our advertising theme to quality.
- We will avoid cutting prices and making deals because we do not want the kind of customer that buys this way.
- We will install a 24-hour hot line if it looks promising.

Clearly the customer-centred company is in a better position to identify new opportunities and set a course that promises to deliver long-term profits. By monitoring customer needs it can decide which customer groups and emerging needs are the most important to serve, given its resources and objectives. Jeff Bezos, founder of Amazon.com, strongly favours a customer-centred orientation:

> **Amazon.com's mantra has been that we were going to obsess over our customers and not our competitors. We watch our competitors, learn from them, see the things that they [are doing for customers] and copy those things as much as we can. But we were never going to obsess over them.**[63]

Competing in an economic downturn

Given economic cycles there will always be tough times, like the years 2008–10 were in many parts of the world. Despite reduced funding for marketing programmes and intense pressure to justify them as cost effective, some marketers survived – or even thrived – in the recession. Here are five guidelines to improve the odds for success during an economic downturn.

Explore the upside of increasing investment

Does it pay to invest during a recession? Although the severity of the recent downturn took firms into uncharted territory, 40 years of evidence suggests that those willing to invest during a recession have, on average, improved their fortunes when compared with those that cut back.[64] The amount of investment is not all that matters. Firms that received the most benefit from increasing marketing investments during a recession were often those best able to exploit a marketplace advantage such as an appealing new product, a weakened rival, or development of a neglected target market. With such strong evidence, marketers should consider the potential upside and positive payback of an increased investment that seizes market opportunities. UK supermarket giant Sainsbury launched an advertising and in-store point-of-sale campaign called 'Feed Your Family For a Fiver' that played off its corporate slogan, 'Try Something New Today', to encourage shoppers to try new recipes that would feed families for only €6.

Get closer to customers

In tough times, consumers may change what they want and can afford, where and how they shop, even what they want to see and hear from a firm. A downturn is an opportunity for marketers to learn even more about what consumers are thinking, feeling and doing, especially the loyal customer base that yields so much of a brand's profitability.[65]

Firms should characterise any changes as temporary adjustments, not permanent shifts.[66] With consumer confidence at its lowest in decades, spending shifted in many ways. As one retail analyst commented, 'Moms who used to buy every member of the family their own brand of shampoo are buying one big cheap one.'[67] The potential value and profitability of some target consumers may change. Marketers should evaluate this factor to fine-tune their marketing programme and capitalise on new insights.

Review budget allocations

Budget allocations can be sticky and not change enough to reflect a fluid marketing environment. We have seen repeatedly that the vast penetration of the internet, improved functionality of the mobile phone, and increased importance of events, experiences and emotions as marketing opportunities have dramatically changed the marketing communications and channels environment in just five years.

A recession provides an opportunity for marketers to review closely how much and in what ways they are spending their money. Budget reallocations can open up promising new options and eliminate sacred-cow approaches that no longer provide sufficient revenue benefits. Underperforming distributors can be weeded out and incentives provided to motivate the more effective product sellers.

Marketing communications allow considerable experimentation. In London, T-Mobile created spontaneous, large-scale, interactive 'happenings' to convey its brand positioning that 'Life's for Sharing' and generate massive publicity. Its 'Dance' video, featuring 300 dancers getting the whole Liverpool tube station to dance, was viewed millions of times on YouTube.[68]

Put forth the most compelling value proposition

One mistake in a recession is to be overly focused on price reductions and discounts, which can harm long-term brand equity and price integrity. Marketers should increase – and clearly communicate – the value their brands offer, making sure consumers appreciate all the financial, logistical and psychological benefits compared with the competition.[69]

Marketers should also review pricing to ensure it has not crept up over time and no longer reflects good value. Procter & Gamble adopted a 'surgical' approach to reducing prices in specific categories in which its brands were perceived as costing too much compared with competitive products. At the same time, it launched communications about the innovativeness and value of its many other brands to help ensure consumers would continue to pay their premium prices.[70]

Fine-tune brand and product offerings

Marketers must ensure they have the right products to sell to the right consumers in the right places and times. They can review product portfolios and brand architecture to confirm that brands and sub-brands are clearly differentiated, targeted and supported based on their prospects. Luxury brands can benefit from lower-priced brands or sub-brands in their portfolios. Take Italian Armani as an example.

Armani

Armani differentiates its product line into three tiers distinct in style, luxury, customisation and price. In the most expensive, Tier I, it sells Giorgio Armani and Giorgio Armani Privé, custom-made couture products that sell for thousands of dollars. In Tier II it offers Emporio Armani – young, modern, more affordable styles – and Armani jeans that convey technology and ecology. In lower-priced Tier III are more youthful and street-savvy translations of Armani style, A|X Armani Exchange, sold at retail locations in cities and suburban malls. The brand architecture has been carefully devised so each extension lives up to the core promise of the Armani brand without diluting the parent's image. But clear differentiation also exists, minimising consumer confusion and brand cannibalisation. In tough economic times, the lower end picks up the selling slack and helps maintain profitability.

Because different brands or sub-brands appeal to different economic segments, those that target the lower end of the socioeconomic spectrum may be particularly important during a recession. Value-driven companies such as Aldi, E*TRADE Financial and IKEA are likely to benefit most.

SUMMARY

1 To prepare an effective marketing strategy a company must study competitors as well as actual and potential customers. Marketers need to identify competitors' strategies, objectives, strengths and weaknesses.

2 A company's closest competitors are those seeking to satisfy the same customers and needs and making similar offers. A company should also pay attention to latent competitors, who may offer new or other ways to satisfy the same needs. A company should identify competitors by using both industry- and market-based analyses.

3 A market leader has the largest market share in the relevant product market. To remain dominant, the leader looks for ways to expand total market demand, attempts to protect its current market share, and perhaps tries to increase its market share.

4 A market challenger attacks the market leader and other competitors in an aggressive bid for more market share. Challengers can choose from five types of general attack; challengers must also choose specific attack strategies.

5 A market follower is a runner-up firm willing to maintain its market share and not rock the boat. A follower can play the role of counterfeiter, cloner, imitator or adapter.

6 A market nicher serves small market segments not being served by larger firms. The key to nichemanship is specialisation. Nichers develop offerings to meet fully a certain group of customers' needs, commanding a premium price in the process.

7 As important as a competitive orientation is in today's global markets, companies should not overdo the emphasis on competitors. They should maintain a good balance of consumer and competitor monitoring.

8 Five guidelines improve the odds for success during an economic downturn: (1) explore the upside of increasing investment, (2) get closer to customers, (3) review budget allocations, (4) put forth the most compelling value proposition, and (5) fine-tune brand and product offerings.

APPLICATIONS

Marketing debate

How do you attack a category leader? Attacking a leader is always difficult. Some strategists recommend attacking a leader 'head-on' by targeting its strengths. Other strategists disagree and recommend flanking and attempting to avoid the leader's strengths.

Take a position: The best way to challenge a leader is to attack its strengths *versus* The best way to attack a leader is to avoid a head-on assault and to adopt a flanking strategy.

Marketing discussion

Pick an industry. Classify firms according to the four different roles they might play: leader, challenger, follower and nicher. How would you characterise the nature of competition? Do the firms follow the principles described in this chapter?

REFERENCES

[1]For a detailed academic treatment of a number of issues on competition, see H. Zhang, C. Shu, X. Jiang and A. J. Malter (2010) Managing knowledge for innovation: the role of cooperation, competition, and alliance nationality, *Journal of International Marketing*, 18(4), 74–94; G. J. Kilduff, H. A. Elfenbein and B. M. Staw (2010) The psychology of rivalry: a relationally dependent analysis of competition, *Academy of Management Journal*, 53(5), 943–69; and the Special Issue (2005) on Competitive Responsiveness, *Marketing Science*, 24, Winter.

[2]M. E. Porter (1980) *Competitive Strategy*, New York: Free Press, 22–3.

[3]M. Altberg and P. Cochelin (2007) EMI moves to non-DRM music: what's next?, *S & P Rating News*, 12 April.

[4]J. F. Rice (2010) Adaptation of Porter's five forces model to risk management, *Defense Acquisition Review Journal*, 17(3), 375–88.

[5]A. R. Vining (2011) Public agency external analysis using a modified 'five forces' framework, *International Public Management Journal*, 14(1), 63–105.

[6]A. D. Shocker (2002) Determining the structure of product-markets: practices, issues, and suggestions, in B. A. Weitz and R. Wensley (eds), *Handbook of Marketing*, London: Sage, 106–25. See also B. H. Clark and D. B. Montgomery (1999) Managerial identification of competitors, *Journal of Marketing*, 63 (July), 67–83.

[7]X. Li, L. M. Hitt and J. Z. Zhang (2011) Product reviews and competition in markets for repeat purchase products, *Journal of Management Information Systems*, 27(4), 9–41; What business are you in? Classic advice from Theodore Levitt (2006) *Harvard Business Review*, October, 127–37. See also Theodore Levitt's seminal article Marketing myopia (1960) *Harvard Business Review*, July–August, 45–56.

[8]J. F. Rayport and B. J. Jaworski (2001) *e-Commerce*, New York: McGraw-Hill, 53.

[9]R. A. D'Aveni (2002) Competitive pressure systems: mapping and managing multimarket contact, *MIT Sloan Management Review*, Fall, 39–49.

[10]Porter (1980) op. cit., Ch. 7.

[11]For discussion of some of the long-term implications of marketing activities, see M. B. Ataman, H. J. Van Heerde, and C. F. Mela (2010) The long-term effect of marketing strategy on brand sales, *Journal of Marketing Research*, 47(5), 866–82; K. Pauwels (2004) How dynamic consumer response, competitor response, company support, and company inertia shape long-term marketing effectiveness, *Marketing Science*, 23 (Fall), 596–610; and K. Pauwels, D. M. Hanssens and S. Siddarth (2002) The long-term effects of price promotions on category incidence, brand choice, and purchase quantity, *Journal of Marketing Research*, 34 (November), 421–39.

[12]R. S. Sisodia, D. B. Wolfe and J. N. Sheth (2007) *Firms of Endearment: How World-Class Companies Profit from Passion and Purpose*, Upper Saddle River, NJ: Wharton School Publishing.

[13]For an academic treatment of benchmarking, see D. W. Vorhies and N. A. Morgan (2005) Benchmarking marketing capabilities for sustained competitive advantage, *Journal of Marketing*, 69(1), 80–94.

[14]P. Maidment and D. Bigman (2005) Special report: Energy, *Forbes*, 16 November.

[15]Porter (1980) op. cit., Ch. 7.

[16]This taxonomy and the Telstra example come from the writings of Australian marketing academic John H. Roberts: J. H. Roberts (2005) Defensive marketing: how a strong incumbent can protect its position, *Harvard Business Review*, November, 150–7; J. Roberts, C. Nelson, and P. Morrison (2001) Defending the beachhead: Telstra vs. Optus, *Business Strategy Review*, 12 (Spring), 19–24.

[17]E. Kim and B. Lee (2009) Strategic use of analytical CRM in a market with network effects and switching costs: terminating unprofitable customer relationships, *Journal of Organizational Computing and Electronic Commerce*, 19, 153–72. See also T. Ritter and J. Geersbro (2010) Antecedents of customer relationship termination, paper presented at the 39th EMAC Conference, Copenhagen, Denmark.

[18]O. Hall and K. R. Jensen (2011) Halvhjertet satsning årsag til B & O nedtur, *Dagbladet Struer*, 1 March, 2; *Reuters Finans* (2011)

B & O kåret som bedste brand af tysk bilmagasins læsere, 30 March; *Herning Folkeblad* (2011) Finansieringstilbud fra B & O, 30 March, 18.

[19]C. Lindhardt (1999) FDB skal rettes op, *Politiken*, 11 February; P. F. Gammelby (2001) Irma vokser igen, *Jyllands-Posten*, 24 May; M. Zahle (2007) Bilka vil være billigst: men er det ikke, *Jyllandsposten*, 7 November; A. Bisgaard (2007) Odense får sin Irma tilbage, *Nyhedsavisen*, 27 June; J. Risom and N. Ostrynski (2007) Danmark fører det økologiske kapløb, *Berlingske Tidende*, 4 October; Bedste resultat i Irmas 120-årige historie (2007), *Ritzaus Bureau*, 14 February.

[20]www.ingredientsnetwork.com/processor/full/heinz-a-global-leader-in-sauces.

[21]www.starbucks.com/aboutus/overview.asp; www.scribd.com/doc/49070799/Starbucks.

[22]B. Wansink (1996) Can package size accelerate usage volume?, *Journal of Marketing*, 60 (July), 1–14. See also P. Raghubir and E. A. Greenleaf (2006) Ratios in proportion: what should the shape of the package be?, *Journal of Marketing*, 70 (April), 95–107; and V. Folkes and S. Matta (2004) The effect of package shape on consumers' judgments of product volume: attention as a mental contaminant, *Journal of Consumer Research*, 31 (September), 390–401.

[23]B. Mak, R. C. Nickerson and H. Isaac (2009) A model of attitudes towards the acceptance of mobile phone use in public places, *International Journal of Innovation and Technology Management*, 6(3), 305–26.

[24]J. D. Cripps (1994) Heuristics and biases in timing the replacement of durable products, *Journal of Consumer Research*, 21 (September), 304–18.

[25]R. Gohlar (2007) Not just Granny's tipple, *Marketing Week*, 30 August, 28–9.

[26]Business Bubbles (2002) *The Economist*, 12 October.

[27]G. Stalk, Jr and R. Lachanauer (2004) Hardball: five killer strategies for trouncing the competition, *Harvard Business Review*, 82 (April), 62–71; R. D'Aveni (2002) The empire strikes back: counterrevolutionary strategies for industry leaders, *Harvard Business Review*, November, 66–74.

[28]R. D. Hof (2006) There's not enough 'me' in MySpace, *BusinessWeek*, 4 December, 40; P. Sellers (2006) MySpace cowboys, *Fortune*, 4 September, 66–74; A. Pressman (2006) MySpace for baby boomers, *BusinessWeek*, 16 October, 120–2.

[29]www.martellieurope.com; J. Tagliabue (2006) Yeah, they torture jeans. But it's all for the sake of fashion, *New York Times*, 12 July, C1. Copyright © 2006 *The New York Times*. Reprinted by permission.

[30]Much of the remaining section on proactive marketing is based on a provocative book by Leonardo Araujo and Rogerio Gava, *The Proactive Enterprise: How to Anticipate Market Changes* (in press).

[31]J. Glancey (1999) The private world of the Walkman, *Guardian*, 11 October.

[32]These six defence strategies, as well as the five attack strategies, are taken from P. Kotler and R. Singh (1981) Marketing warfare in the 1980s, *Journal of Business Strategy*, Winter, 30–41.

[33]G. Edmondson (2007) Peugeot Citroën's bold turnaround plan, *BusinessWeek*, 4 September.

[34]Porter (1980) op. cit., Ch. 4; J. Prabhu and D. W. Stewart (2001) Signaling strategies in competitive interaction: building reputations and hiding the truth, *Journal of Marketing Research*,

38 (February), 62–72; J. L. Schenker (2008) EA leaps into free video games, *BusinessWeek*, 22 January.

35R. J. Calantone and K. E. Schatzel (2000) Strategic foretelling: communication-based antecedents of a firm's propensity to preannounce, *Journal of Marketing*, 64 (January), 17–30; J. Eliashberg and T. S. Robertson (1988) New product preannouncing behavior: a market signaling study, *Journal of Marketing Research*, 25 (August), 282–92.

36T. S. Robertson, J. Eliashberg and T. Rymon (1995) New-product announcement signals and incumbent reactions, *Journal of Marketing* 59 (July), 1–15.

37Yuhong Wu, S. Balasubramanian and V. Mahajan (2004) When is a preannounced new product likely to be delayed?, *Journal of Marketing*, 68 (April), 101–13; B. L. Bayus, S. Jain and A. G. Rao (2001) Truth or consequences: an analysis of vaporware and new-product announcements, *Journal of Marketing Research*, 38 (February), 3–13.

38K. Capell (2006) Absolut makeover, *BusinessWeek*, 16 January; K. Kelleher (2003) Why FedEx is gaining ground, *Business 2.0*, October, 56–7; C. Haddad (2002) FedEx: gaining on ground, *BusinessWeek*, 16 December, 126–8.

39S. Haxel (2007) Movers: businesses in the news, *International Herald Tribune*, 6 September.

40Sara Lee cleans out its cupboards (2005) *Fortune*, 7 March, 38; J. Sassen (2006) How Sara Lee left Hanes in its skivvies, *BusinessWeek*, 18 September, 40.

41J. S. Armstrong and K. C. Green (2007) Competitor-oriented objectives: the myth of market share, *International Journal of Business*, 12(1), 115–34; S. E. Jackson, *Where Value Hides: A New Way to Uncover Profitable Growth for Your Business*, New York: John Wiley & Sons.

42N. Kumar (2004) *Marketing as Strategy*, Cambridge, MA: Harvard Business School Press; P. Kotler and P. N. Bloom (1975) Strategies for high-market-share companies, *Harvard Business Review*, November–December, 63–72.

43R. D. Buzzell and F. D. Wiersema (1981) Successful share-building strategies, *Harvard Business Review*, January–February, 135–44.

44R. J. Dolan (1981) Models of competition: a review of theory and empirical evidence, in B. M. Enis and K. J. Roering (eds), *Review of Marketing*, Chicago, IL: American Marketing Association, 224–34.

45L. Hellofs and R. Jacobson (1999) Market share and customers' perceptions of quality: when can firms grow their way to higher versus lower quality?, *Journal of Marketing*, 63 (January), 16–25.

46John Downey (2009) Fairpoint struggles with merger, declining stock, *Charlotte Business Journal*, 19 March; John Downey (2009) Fairpoint faces enduring debt, service headaches, *Charlotte Business Journal*, 15 September.

47J. Birger (2006) Second-mover advantage, *Fortune*, 20 March, 20–1.

48V. Shankar, G. Carpenter and L. Krishnamurthi (1998) Late-mover advantage: how innovative late entrants outsell pioneers, *Journal of Marketing Research*, 35 (February), 54–70; G. S. Carpenter and K. Nakamoto (1996) The impact of consumer preference formation on marketing objectives and competitive second-mover strategies, *Journal of Consumer Psychology*, 5(4), 325–58; G. S. Carpenter and K. Nakamoto (1990) Competitive strategies for late entry into a market with a dominant brand, *Management Science*, October, 1268–78.

49Free papers, costly competition (2007) *BusinessWeek*, 19 November.

50www.schibsted.com/eway/.

51M. V. Copeland (2004) These boots really were made for walking, *Business 2.0*, October, 72–4.

52http://about.chacha.com/about/; A. Klassen (2007) Search Davids take aim at Goliath Google, *Advertising Age*, 8 January, 11; Anonymous (2007) Cha-Cha – CEO interview, *CEO Wire*, 9 January.

53K. Booker (2006) The Pepsi machine, *Fortune*, 6 February, 68–72.

54Team support, sponsorship deals, family – all is fair in love of sport (2007) *Marketing Week*, 19 April, 18.

55A. Morgan (1999) *Eating the Big Fish: How Challenger Brands Can Compete Against Brand Leaders*, New York: John Wiley & Sons.

56T. Levitt (1966) Innovative imitation, *Harvard Business Review*, September–October, 63. See also S. P. Schnaars (1994) *Managing Imitation Strategies: How Later Entrants Seize Markets from Pioneers*, New York: Free Press.

57S. F. Brown (1998) The company that out-Harleys Harley, *Fortune*, 28 September, 56–7; www.sscycle.com.

58www.Aarstiderne.com; J. E. Rasmussen (2007) IndKøbsvaner: Flere køber mad på nettet, *Jyllands-Posten*, 25 September, www.aarstiderne.com/omaarstiderne/English.

59Reported in E. R. Linneman and L. J. Stanton (1991) *Making Niche Marketing Work*, New York: McGraw-Hill.

60Thomas A. Fogarty (2003) Keeping Zippo's flame eternal, *USA Today*, 24 June; Michael Learmonth (2009) Zippo reignites brand with social media, new products, *Advertising Age*, 10 August 12; www.zippo.com

61A. Mitchell (2006) They're talking about a convenience revolution, *Marketing Week*, 28 September, 24–5.

62Kathleen Kingsbury (2006) The cell islands, *Time*, 168, no. 21 (20 November), G20; Traveling made easy with the new BlackBerry Curve 8520, *Digicel-News*, http://digicel-jamaica-news-procomm.blogspot.com.

63R. Spector (2000) *Amazon.com: Get Big Fast*, New York: HarperBusiness, 151.

64R. Srinivasan, A. Rangaswamy and G. L. Lilien (2005) Turning adversity into advantage: does proactive marketing during recession pay off?, *International Journal of Research in Marketing*, 22(2), 109–25.

65P. Lay, T. Hewlin and G. Moore (2009) In a downturn, provoke your customers, *Harvard Business Review*, March, 48–56.

66J. A. Quelch and K. E. Jocz (2009) How to market in a downturn, *Harvard Business Review*, April, 52–62.

67J. Porter and B. Heim (2008) Doing whatever gets them in the door, *BusinessWeek*, 30 June, 60.

68D. Taylor, D. Nichols, D. Kerner and A. Charbonneau (2009) Leading brands out of the recession, *Brandgym Research Paper 2*, www.brandgym.com.

69P. J. Williamson and M. Zeng (2009) Value for money strategies for recessionary times, *Harvard Business Review*, March, 66–74.

70S. Elliott (2009) Trying to pitch products to the savers, *New York Times*, 3 June.

Connecting with customers

Video documentary for Part 3

Go to **www.pearsoned.co.uk/marketingmanagementeurope** to watch the video documentary that relates to Part 3 and consider the issues raised below.

Having gained essential insights into the structure and buying behaviour in both consumer and business markets, marketing managers should then turn to the task of successfully competing in those markets.

Part 3: Connecting with customers explores the key themes of:

1 segmentation;
2 targeting; and
3 positioning.

Segmentation is a matter of dividing markets up into 'bite-sized' chunks so that their specific requirements and potential can be assessed and judged. Once attractive market segments have been identified, companies can apply suitable screening systems to select those that will become their centre of attention – or, their targets. Each targeted market – whether *niche*, *middle* or *entry* – requires separate marketing management attention to ensure that the appropriate mix of customer benefits are blended into suitable market offerings that meet customers' perceived value requirements.

When watching the video documentary that accompanies Part 3, pay close attention to the detailed needs of individual target markets described by the top European marketing managers being interviewed. This attention to detail enables each company to build strong value sets that can be distinctive, but also reflect the overall positive image characteristics of the corporate brand identity. Successful positioning enables companies to efficiently provide the right market offerings to the right target markets in order to secure a sustainable competitive advantage and acceptable degrees of profit.

Sujata Thakur
Regional Director, Incredible India

Hear a variety of top marketing executives from a wide range of organisations offer their own interesting and varied perspectives on the key themes of Part 3 including: Hans Stråberg, President for the Electrolux Group (top); Sujata Thakur, Regional Director, Incredible India (centre); The original IKEA outlet, Älmhult, Sweden (bottom).

Chapter 10

Seeking and developing target marketing differentiation strategies

IN THIS CHAPTER, WE WILL ADDRESS THE FOLLOWING QUESTIONS:

1 What are the different levels of market segmentation?

2 How can a company divide a market into segments?

3 How should a company choose the most attractive target markets?

4 What are the requirements for effective segmentation?

5 How can a firm create, develop and communicate a successful positioning strategy in the market?

6 Why is the concept of positioning so important to marketing practitioners?

7 How can companies seek to differentiate their offerings positively in today's market conditions?

8 When might companies need to reposition their market offerings and what are the main inherent risks of such a strategy?

Morgan Cars: have a long order book and continue to serve a niche market for handbuilt traditional sports cars for baby boomers.

Source: © Steve Sant/Alamy

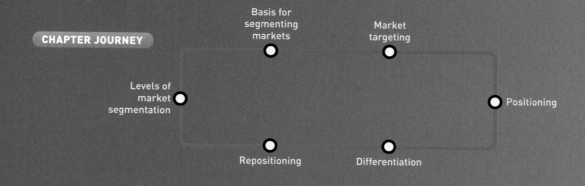

CHAPTER JOURNEY

Basis for
segmenting
markets

Market
targeting

Levels of
market
segmentation

Positioning

Repositioning

Differentiation

Companies cannot connect with all customers in large, broad or diverse markets. However, they can divide such markets into groups of customers or segments with distinct needs and wants. A company then needs to identify which market segments it can serve effectively and efficiently. This decision requires a keen understanding of customer behaviour and careful strategic thinking. To develop the best marketing plans, managers need to understand what makes each segment unique and different. Their next task is to explore specific ways in which companies can effectively position and differentiate their market offerings to achieve a competitive advantage.

One lucrative market segment is that of the people who were born in Europe between 1946 and 1964, who are often referred to as 'baby boomers'. In 2004 baby boomers held 80 per cent of the UK's wealth and bought 80 per cent of all top-of-the-range cars, 80 per cent of cruises and 50 per cent of skin care products.[1] Throughout Europe this market has attracted the attention of marketers as it presents a distinct demographic sector that has provided a variety of marketing opportunities over the years. In the United Kingdom, companies such as Saga and First Choice have tried to make the over-50s market trendy. However, as they approach the evening of their lives, many baby boomers have registered their displeasure at finding themselves on these companies' mailing lists.[2]

To compete more effectively many companies are now adopting target marketing. Instead of scattering their marketing efforts, they are focusing on customers whom they have the greatest chance of satisfying.

Effective target marketing requires that marketers:

- **identify and profile distinct groups of buyers who differ in their needs and preferences (market segmentation);**
- **select one or more market segments to enter (market targeting); and**
- **for each target segment, establish and communicate the distinctive benefit(s) of the company's market offering (market positioning).**

Levels of market segmentation

(See also Chapter 6.)

The starting point for discussing segmentation is **mass marketing**. In mass marketing, the seller engages in the mass production, mass distribution and mass marketing communication of one item for all buyers. Henry Ford epitomised this strategy when he offered the Model-T Ford in one colour – black. Coca-Cola also practised mass marketing when it sold only one kind of cola in a standard bottle.

The argument for mass marketing is that it creates the largest potential market, which leads to the lowest costs, which in turn can lead to lower prices or higher margins. This is the *least cost production paradigm* that has served many firms well for several decades. However, in contemporary buyers' markets in which the number of providers exceeds the likely customer uptake, companies are faced with new challenges. Increasing levels of competition present customers with a wide choice of possible suppliers. This results in them wanting more for their money. There has been a transformation in the concept of value from a factor that was largely determined by suppliers, to one that is now heavily influenced by buyers. Firms now have to provide market offerings that their customers perceive to possess the right value standard. Also many markets display an increasing trend to break up into several segments. Fewer standardised products and services can be offered to customers (standard customer-perceived value offerings). Thus the use of mass marketing is in decline and most companies are turning to *micromarketing* at one of four levels: segments, niches, local areas and individuals.

Segment marketing

A *market segment* consists of a group of customers who share a similar set of needs and wants. Rather than creating the segments, the marketer's task is to identify them and to decide which one(s) to target. Segment marketing offers key benefits over mass marketing. The company can offer a market offering that can be positively differentiated from the competition. If strategy is the art of allocating scarce resources, then segmentation – and the understanding it provides about your customer groups – is part of the science informing that allocation.

However, such a segment is partly a fiction, in that not everyone in the segment wants exactly the same offering. Business-to-business marketing experts Anderson and Narus have urged marketers to present flexible market offerings to all members of a segment.[3] **Flexible market-perceived value offering** consists of two parts: a *naked solution* containing the market offering attributes and benefits that all segment members value and *discretionary value options* that some segment members require. Each customer-perceived option might carry an additional charge: for example, Siemens' Electrical Apparatus Division sells metal-clad boxes to small manufacturers at prices that include free delivery and a warranty. It also offers installation, tests and communication peripherals as extra-cost options. Ryanair offers all economy passengers a seat and soft drinks, and charges extra for alcoholic beverages, snacks and meals.

Market segments can be characterised in different ways. One approach is to identify *preference segments*. **Homogeneous preferences** exist when all customers have roughly the same preferences. At the other extreme, customers with **diffused preferences** vary greatly in their requirements. If several brands are in the market, they are likely to provide market offerings that appeal to identified specific consumer preferences. Finally, **clustered preferences** result when natural market segments emerge from groups of customers with shared preferences. Marketers should divide customers into groups based only on those needs and factors actually driving purchase decisions. A common mistake is to segment customers based on peripheral characteristics that, while interesting, provide no help in achieving the fundamental goal of segmentation: selling more market offerings profitably.

Niche marketing

A niche is a more narrowly defined customer group seeking a distinctive mix of benefits or values. Marketers usually identify niches by dividing a market segment into subsegments. For example, while Hertz, Avis, Eurocar and others specialise in airport rental cars for business and leisure travellers, Enterprise has attacked the low-budget, insurance-replacement market by primarily renting to customers whose cars have been written off or stolen. By creating unique associations with low cost and convenience in an overlooked niche market, Enterprise has been highly profitable.

The objective of a niche competitor, such as Bang & Olufsen, The Body Shop, Cartier or Porsche, is to be a large fish in a small pool. The niche market customers have a distinct set of value requirements and they will pay a premium to the firm that provides the market offering with the best consumer-perceived value. Niche markets are generally fairly small in terms of volume but constitute a sufficiently attractive size, profit and growth potential. Also, they are less likely to attract many other powerful competitors and can benefit from focusing their resources to gain economies through specialisation. Some larger companies, such as IBM, have lost parts of their business to successful niche competitors. This market competitor has been colourfully termed 'guerrillas against gorillas'.[4] The same thing is also happening in the online social networking market, where MySpace has lost ground to Facebook, which in turn is being challenged by Twitter.

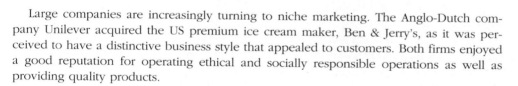

Facebook

Social networking sites such as Facebook show many of the characteristics of fads. They quickly become popular and can be an effective market research medium, but they can just as quickly fall out of favour. These pioneering sites initially enjoy a wide appeal and are crucially reliant on advertising revenue. A sudden drop in traffic numbers can threaten their survival. As competition in current buyers' markets intensifies, social networking sites too will disaggregate. Many upstart social networking nichers hope to capitalise on the tendency of individuals to want to congregate with others who share their own particular passions and values. For instance, there is now 1Up.com, a content-heavy social site where online gaming fanatics can trade tips, stories, opinions and gossip.[5]

Large companies are increasingly turning to niche marketing. The Anglo-Dutch company Unilever acquired the US premium ice cream maker, Ben & Jerry's, as it was perceived to have a distinctive business style that appealed to customers. Both firms enjoyed a good reputation for operating ethical and socially responsible operations as well as providing quality products.

Internet niching

As marketing efficiency increases, niches that were hitherto considered to be too small may become more profitable.[6] The low cost of setting up shop on the internet has led to many small business start-ups aimed at niches. The recipe for internet niching success: choose a hard-to-find market offering that customers don't need to see and touch. After initial losses, Amazon has come of age as an internet shopping centre. Faced by the long-tail product life cycle curve that characterises many of today's businesses, it has restructured its business and is now making profits. The marketing insight box outlines how provocative are the implications of internet niching.

Local marketing

Target marketing is leading to marketing programmes tailored to the needs and wants of local customer groups in trading areas, neighbourhoods, even individual stores. Retail

Marketing insight

Chasing the long tail

The advent of online commerce made possible by technology and epitomised by Amazon.com and iTunes has led to a shift in customer buying patterns, according to Chris Anderson, editor-in-chief of *Wired* magazine and author of *The Long Tail*.

In most markets, the distribution of product sales conforms to a curve weighted heavily to one side – the 'head' – where the bulk of sales is generated by a few products. The curve falls rapidly toward zero and hovers just above it far along the X-axis – the 'long tail' – where the vast majority of products generate very few sales. The mass market traditionally focused on generating 'hit' products that occupy the head, disdaining the low-revenue market niches comprising the tail.

Anderson asserts that as a result of consumers embracing the internet as a shopping medium, the long tail harbours significantly more value than before. In fact, Anderson argues, the internet has directly contributed to the shifting of demand 'down the tail, from hits to niches' in a number of product categories, including music, books, clothing, films and videos.

On his blog, Anderson states his argument as follows:

The Long Tail equation is simple: 1) The lower the cost of distribution, the more you can economically offer without having to predict demand. 2) The more you can offer, the greater the chance that you will be able to tap latent demand for minority tastes that was unreachable through traditional retail. 3) Aggregate enough minority taste, and you'll often get a big new market.

Anderson identifies two aspects of internet shopping that contribute to this shift. First, greater choice is permitted by increased stock and variety. Given a choice between ten hit products, consumers are forced to select one of them. If, however, the choice set is expanded to 1,000, then the top ten hits will be chosen less frequently. Second, the 'search costs' of finding relevant new products are lowered due to the wealth of information sources available online, the filtering of product recommendations based on user preferences that vendors can provide, and the word-of-mouth network of internet users.

Anderson sees the long tail effect as particularly pronounced in media, a category that is historically hit driven but which benefits enormously from these two aspects of online shopping.

The long tail thesis was also supported by researchers Brynjolfsson, Yu 'Jeffrey' Hu and Smith, who conducted two studies to measure the tail in online versus offline book selling and clothing retail. The book-selling study concluded that the increased product variety offered by online bookshops increased customer choice substantially. In the case of online clothing retail, the study found that customers who used both online and catalogue channels purchased a more even distribution of products than would have been the case had they just used catalogue channels.

The same companies that compete in the business of creating hits are beginning to develop ways to evolve niche successes in the long tail. Others have countered that, especially in entertainment, the 'head' where the hits are concentrated is valuable to consumers, not only to the content creators. An article in *The Economist*

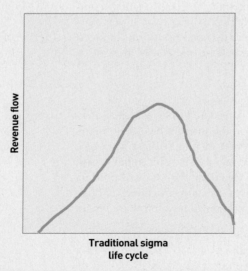

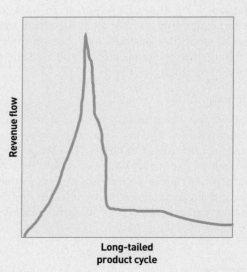

Figure 10.1 Traditional and long-tailed product life cycles
Source: M. R. V. Goodman, Durham University.

Marketing insight *(continued)*

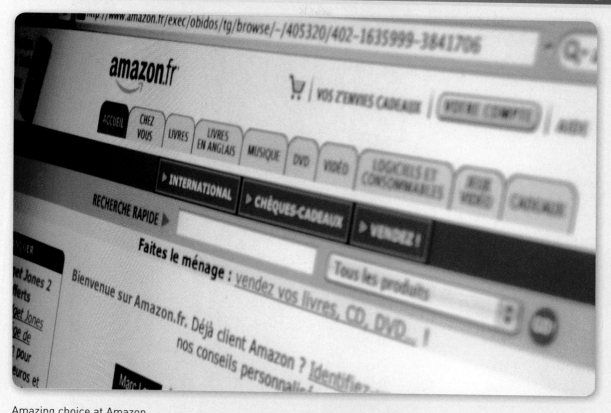

Amazing choice at Amazon.
Source: © Richard Levine/Alamy

argued that 'most hits are popular because they are of high quality' and a critique in the *New Yorker* notes that the majority of products and services making up the long tail originate from a small concentration of 'long-tail aggregators' – sites such as Amazon, eBay and iTunes. This observation challenges the premise that old business paradigms have changed as much as Anderson suggests.

Sources: C. Anderson (2006) *The Long Tail*, New York: Hyperion; 'Reading the Tail' interview with Chris Anderson, *Wired*, 8 July 2006, 30; Wag the dog: what the long tail will do, *The Economist*, 8 July 2006, 77; E. Brynjolfsson, Y. (J.) Hu and M. D. Smith (2006) From niches to riches: anatomy of a long tail, *MIT Sloan Management Review*, Summer, 67; J. Cassidy (2006) Going long, *The New Yorker*, 10 July; www.longtail.com.

firms such as Starbucks have all found great success emphasising local marketing initiatives, but other types of firms are also going local. Supermarkets vary the stock portfolios they carry to suit the locations of their stores. IKEA customises merchandise to match the perceived demand of local areas. The problems experienced in Europe by clothes retailer C&A, which forced them to withdraw from several countries, has been blamed on its Brussels-based central buying policy.

Local marketing reflects a growing trend called *grassroots marketing*. Marketing activities concentrate on getting as close and personally relevant to individual customers as possible. Much of Nike's initial success came from engaging target customers through grassroots marketing, such as sponsorship of local school teams, expert-conducted clinics, and the provision of shoes, clothing and equipment. In similar vein Red Bull has closely engaged students. The breakthrough marketing box on p. 374 profiles another success story.

A Polish food shop opens to provide a taste of home for the large local Polish community in Darlington in the north of England.
Source: © Gregory Wrona/ Alamy

The risks associated with localised marketing include:

- a tendency to drive up manufacturing costs and so reduce economies of scale;
- a tendency to create logistical problems; and
- a possibility that the overall image of the brand may be put at risk.

Those who advocate localised marketing see national advertising as wasteful because it is too remote and fails to address local needs. Those against local marketing argue that it drives up manufacturing and marketing costs by reducing economies of scale and magnifying logistical problems. A brand's overall image might be diluted if the product and message are different in different localities. The advantages are all concerned with the capacity that is granted to firms, to respond to local requirements more effectively than would otherwise be the case. Thus, the customer-perceived value of a firm's offering is enhanced. Overall, this advantage generally outweighs the disadvantages experienced in contemporary buyers' markets.

Individual marketing

The ultimate level of segmentation results in 'segments of one', 'customised marketing' or 'one-to-one marketing'.[7] Today customers are taking a more individual initiative in determining what and how to buy. They log on to the internet; look up information and evaluations of market offers; conduct dialogues with suppliers, users and purchase critics; and, in many cases, design the market offering that they want.

Sainsbury's come to your neighbourhood to offer a convenient but relatively expensive local shopping opportunity.
Source: © Justin Kase z03z/ Alamy

Wind and Rangaswamy see a movement towards 'customerising' the firm.[8] Mass customisation introduces a *new paradigm* whereby companies seek to fragment the market through economies of scope.[9] Customers become integral to the market offering and design processes, with more sophisticated customers undertaking simulations to answer 'what-if' questions. Market offerings are assembled from valued components or attributes to develop unique customer-perceived value to meet individual needs.

Mass customisation, like one-to-one marketing, requires new organisational thinking. Every customer interaction provides an opportunity to learn more about the customer's needs and to adapt existing company offerings to meet changing circumstances. True customer service leads to strong relationships and an enhanced lifetime value experience for customers. Every employee becomes a marketer, as the whole firm networks to provide the right collection of customer-perceived value attributes and benefits for customers.

Customerisation combines operationally driven mass customisation with customised marketing in a way that empowers consumers to design the customer-perceived value offering of their choice. The firm no longer requires prior information about the customer, nor does the firm need to own manufacturing. The firm provides a platform and tools, and 'rents' out to customers the means to design their own market offerings. A company is customerised when it is able to respond to individual customers by customising its market offerings and messages on a one-to-one basis. In the United Kingdom, Towels R Us offers customised towels, roller towels and dressing gowns. Customers can choose from a large range of logos and can add their own messages. Sanford Brands[10] offers to customise pens manufactured by Parker, Sharpie, Waterman, Papermate and Berol. Nike ID enables clients

Breakthrough marketing

HSBC

HSBC wants to be known as the 'world's local bank'. This tagline reflects HSBC's positioning as a globe-spanning financial institution with unique focus on serving local markets. Originally the Hong Kong and Shanghai Banking Corporation Limited, HSBC was established in 1865 to finance the growing trade between China and the United Kingdom. It is now the second-largest bank in the world. Despite serving over 100 million customers through 9,500 branches in 79 countries, the bank works hard to maintain a local presence and local knowledge in each area. Its fundamental operating strategy is to remain close to its customers. As HSBC chairman Sir John Bond said, 'Our position as the world's local bank enables us to approach each country uniquely, blending local knowledge with a worldwide operating platform.' The bank's advertisements in its 'World's Local Bank' campaign depict the way different cultures interpret the same objects or events.

The bank pulls its worldwide businesses together under a single global brand with the 'World's Local Bank' slogan. The aim is to link its international size with close relationships in each of the countries in which it operates. HSBC spends $600 million annually on global marketing, which it consolidated in 2004 under the WPP group of agencies. Going forward, it will be seeking to leverage its position as 'The World's Local Bank' to improve on its $11.6 billion brand value, which placed it 32nd on the 2010 Interbrand Best Global Brands rankings.

Sources: D. Orr (2004) New ledger, *Forbes*, 1 March, 72–3; HSBC's global marketing head explains review decision, *Adweek*, 19 January; Now your customers can afford to take Fido to the vet, *Bank Marketing*, December 2003, 47; K. Hein (2003) HSBC bank rides the coattails of chatty cabbies, *Brandweek*, 1 December, 30; Sir J. Bond and S. Green (2003) HSBC strategic overview, presentation to investors, 27 November; Lafferty Retail Banking Awards 2003, *Retail Banker International*, 27 November 2003, 4–5; Ideas that work, *Bank Marketing*, November 2003, 10; HSBC enters the global branding big league, *Bank Marketing International*, August 2003, 1–2; N. Madden (2003) HSBC rolls out post-SARS effort, *Advertising Age*, 16 June, 12; K. Nicholson (2005) HSBC aims to appear global yet approachable, *Campaign*, 2 December, 15; C. Mollenkamp (2006) HSBC stumbles in bid to become global deal maker, *Wall Street Journal*, 5 October, A1, A12; www.hsbc.com; www.interbrand.com/en/best-global-brands/best-global-brands-2008/best-global-brands.

to design every aspect of a range of five Nike athletic shoes. Designing your own pair of Nike ID Pumas costs from £50 to £150 – about three times the cost of the standard shoes.[11]

Customerisation is particularly important in business-to-business markets. FAG Kugelfischer is a German manufacturer with sales of over €3 billion and Europe's second biggest maker of rolling bearings (devices essential to virtually all kinds of rotary motion) after SKF of Sweden. The company believes that customising bearings to suit individual tastes provides considerable untapped potential and is a key determinant of future earnings growth.[12]

However, customerisation is not for every company. It may be very difficult to implement for some complex purchases but is now breaking through into the car market. Henry Ford launched mass production 99 years ago with his revolutionary assembly line for the Model T car. It proved a brilliant system – at least for as long as there were customers waiting at the end of the line to drive Ford's cars away. However, it lost some of its shine when customers became harder to find, meaning that mass-produced cars remained expensively in car parks and showrooms. Now a new dream is at hand: to turn mass production on its head with the help of flexible systems and internet ordering. Fiat has identified a strong trend in Europe towards customerisation and offers several ways for customers to personalise the latest version of its Punto model. The goal is to deliver precisely the car that a customer wants.

Customerisation can also raise the cost of purchases by more than the customer is willing to pay. Some customers do not know what they want until they see actual items. In spite of this, customerisation has worked well for some market offerings. Mass customerisation harnesses these new technologies to bring customised and personalised market offerings to customers at a mass production price.

One-to-one-marketing or customer-centric marketing was first developed in the late 1980s by the Boston Consulting Group.[13] It seeks to develop long-term relationships with individual customers to tailor responses to their needs.[14]

Bases for segmenting consumer markets

Two broad groups of variables are used to segment consumer markets. Some researchers seek to define segments by looking at descriptive characteristics: geographic, demographic and psychographic. Then they examine whether these customer segments exhibit different needs or company responses. For example, they might examine the differing attitudes of 'professionals', 'blue-collars workers' and other groups towards, say, 'safety' as a customer-perceived benefit when considering purchasing a new car.

To learn how BMW studies changing consumer lifestyles to match product development to segmentation, visit www.pearsoned.co.uk/marketingmanagementeurope.

Other researchers try to define segments by looking at behavioural considerations, such as customer responses to benefits, use occasions or brands. The researcher then sees whether different characteristics are associated with each consumer-response segment. For example, do people who want 'quality' rather than 'low price' in a car purchase differ in their geographic, demographic and psychographic characteristics?

Regardless of which type of segmentation scheme is used, the key is adjusting the marketing programme to recognise customer differences. The major segmentation variables – geographic, demographic, psychographic, and behavioural segmentation for Europe – are summarised in Table 10.1.

Geographic segmentation

Geographic segmentation calls for dividing the market into different geographical units, such as nations, states, regions, counties, cities or neighbourhoods. The company can operate in one or a few areas, or operate in all but pay attention to local variations. White goods manufacturers have to cater for variations in demand across European frontiers. Top-loading washing machines are needed for the French market, front loading for the UK market, slow spin speeds for the Italian market (as they have plenty of sunshine) and ecologically efficient machines for northern European markets. Tesco test marketed the new ultrastrong Dorset Naga chilli pepper in a Newcastle store as customers in the northeast of England have a known preference for stronger flavours. Geographic segmentation can also be used to assist marketers to study 'service' markets. In order to understand the different requirements of European visitors to the tourist attractions on the Danish island of Funen, tourists were segmented by nationality.

More and more, regional marketing means marketing right down to a specific postcode. Many companies use mapping software to show the geographic locations of their customers. The software may show a retailer that most of his customers are within only a 10-mile radius of his shop, and further concentrated within certain postcode areas.

Some approaches combine geographic data with demographic data to yield even richer descriptions of customers and neighbourhoods. This has become known as geodemographic segmentation – 'the analysis of people by where they live'.[15] A number of specialist companies offer a variety of geodemographic databases. Table 10.2 presents some of the leading companies and classification systems that can be accessed in the United Kingdom.

An example of Experian's MOSAIC profile is given in Table 10.3.

All of these databases have numerous sub-segment variations, but they should be used with caution. There are many uncertainties, such as the reliability and validity of the data, and its freshness – CCI makes a selling point out of its claim to update its databases every two years. While this is to be welcomed, these relational databases should be continually updated throughout the year. As strategic marketing planning poses ever stronger challenges, wise companies take out online subscriptions with the database providers.

Geodemographic services are now available in a variety of microsegments for smaller firms because, as database costs decline, PCs proliferate, software becomes easier to use, data integration increases, and use of the internet grows.[16]

Table 10.1 Major segmentation variables for consumer markets

Geographic

Eastern Europe	
Northern Europe	
Southern Europe	
City or metro size	100,000–250,000; 250,000–500,000; 500,000–1,000,000; 1,000,000–4,000,000; over 4,000,000
Location	Urban, suburban, rural

Demographic

Age	Under 5, 5–10, 11–19, 20–34, 35–49, 50–64, over 65
Family unit size	1–2, 3–4, 5 and over
Family life cycle	Young, single; young, married, no children; young, married, youngest child under 5; young, married, youngest child 6 or over; older, married, with children; older, married, no children under 18; older, single; other
Gender	Male, female
Income	Under €10,000; €10,000–20,000; €21,000–29,000; €30,000–39,000; €40,000–49,000; €50,000–59,000; €60,000-69,000; €70,000–79,000; €80,000–89,000; €90,000–99,000; over €100,000.
Occupation	Professional and technical; managers, officials and proprietors; clerical sales; craftspeople; operatives; supervisors; retired; students; homemakers; farmers; unemployed
Education	Primary; secondary; college; university
Religion	Catholic, Protestant, Jewish, Muslim, Hindu, other
Race	White, Black, Asian, Arab
Generation	Baby boomers, Generation Xers
Nationality	E.g. Danish, German, Italian
Social class	Lower, middle, upper middle, aristocrat
Psychographic lifestyle	Culture oriented; outdoor oriented; sports oriented
Personality	Introverted; extroverted

Behavioural

Benefits sought	Quality, service, economy, speed, value
User status	Non-user, ex-user, potential user, first-time user, regular user
Usage rate	Light, medium, heavy
Loyalty status	None, medium, strong, absolute
Readiness stage	Unaware, aware, informed, interested, desirous, intending to buy
Attitude to market offer	Enthusiastic, positive, indifferent, negative, hostile

Demographic segmentation

In demographic segmentation, the market is divided into groups on the basis of variables such as age, family size, family life cycle, gender, income, occupation, education, religion, race, generation, nationality and social class. One reason why demographic variables are so popular with marketers is that they are often associated with customer needs and wants. Another is that they are easy to measure. Even when the target market is described

Table 10.2 Geodemographic companies and classifications

Organisation	Classification system	Examples of data sources used
ABC Ltd/ISL	Residata	Housing types and structure; risk indices; insurance data; PAF; unemployment statistics; Census
CACI	ACORN	Census data
	LifestylesUK	Lifestyle data; ER; Census; Share ownership
	PeopleUK	Lifestyle data; ER; Census; Census share ownership
Claritas Europe	PRIZM	Lifestyle data; Share ownership; Company directors; PAF; Unemployment statistics; Births and deaths
Euro Direct	CAMEO	Census data
Experian	MOSAIC	Census data; Credit card data; CCJs; PAF; ER; Company directors; Access to retail stores

Note: ACORN: A Classification of Residential Neighbourhoods; CCJs: county court judgments: consumers who have been taken to court for debt recovery; ER: electoral register: gives names, addresses and number of adults in 95 per cent of UK households; PAF: postcode address file: the Royal Mail's database of all addresses in the United Kingdom by postcode.

Source: Table compiled by Peter Sleight and published in F. Brassington and S. Pettitt (2003) *Principles of Marketing*, 3rd edn, Harlow: Prentice Hall, Chapter 5, 187. Copyright © Peter Sleight. Reproduced with permission.

Table 10.3 MOSAIC Group H: stylish singles

Nearly 1.3 million households, representing 5.5 per cent of all UK households:

- 2.8 million people in this group
- students and young professionals
- first-time openers of savings and mortgage accounts
- frequent visitors to the cinema, concerts and exhibitions
- like weekend breaks to European capital cities
- prefer the *Guardian*, the *Independent* and the *Observer* newspapers
- television viewing is light: current affairs and late films preferred
- shop for food at convenience stores late in the day
- convenience more important than price
- prefer the city to the outer suburbs
- enjoy living in diverse, cosmopolitan, multicultural environment
- big spenders on mobile phones, music, sports equipment, audio and computer equipment

Source: After F. Brassington and S. Pettitt (2003) *Principles of Marketing*, Harlow: Prentice Hall. Copyright © 2003 Pearson Education Ltd. Reproduced with permission.

in non-demographic terms (say, by personality type) it may be necessary to link back to demographic characteristics in order to estimate the size of the market and the media necessary to reach it efficiently.

Here is how certain demographic variables have been used to segment markets.

Age and life cycle stage

Consumer wants and abilities change with age. Toothpaste brands such as Crest and Colgate offer three main toothpaste lines to target children, adults and older consumers. Age segmentation can be even more refined. Pampers divides its market into pre-natal, new baby (0–5 months), baby (6–12 months), toddler (13–23 months), and pre-schooler (24 months +). LEGO divides its market into Duplo (pre-school), Lego (early mid-school age) and Lego-technic (mid-school to senior school). ClubMed and Club 18–30 are targeted to appeal to single or young couples and the Saga umbrella brand is designed to appeal to the over-50s.

Marketing memo

Gathering geodemographic data

PRIZM (trade name for a geodemographic index marketed by Claritas Europe) is an example of pan-European lifestyle segmentation. This and other similar tools such as ACORN (trade name for A Classification of Residential Neighbourhoods) and MOSAIC (trade name for a geodemographic system that is popular in the UK and owned by the US-based Experian Group, a global services information company) function by assuming that residents of each postal unit form a distinct segment. Claritas, which markets PRIZM, claims that it can be used to:

- assess market potential or demand for a given area;
- develop customer loyalty and value by identifying the most attractive customers;
- reveal emerging niche markets;
- identify and target customers most likely to defect in order to reduce customer turnover (churn).

Source: Based on F. Brassington and S. Pettitt (2003) *Principles of Marketing*, Harlow: Prentice Hall and Claritas Europe.

Nevertheless, age and life cycle can be tricky variables. In some cases the target market may be the psychologically young. For example, the Mini Cooper appeals to enthusiasts in several age groups.

Life stage

People in the same part of the life cycle may differ in their life stage. Life stage defines a person's major concern, such as going through a divorce, going into a second marriage, taking care of an older parent, deciding to cohabit with another person, deciding to buy a new home, and so on. These life stages present opportunities for marketers.

The growing proportion of retired people in the affluent European countries has created new market segments and new requirements in existing markets such as senior citizen banking. The trend towards single-adult households (i.e. the unmarried, divorced,

Memories for baby boomers and a cool car for 20-year-olds.
Source: Sandro Campardo/AP/PA Photos

A marketing bonanza to the bridal industry and marketers targeting newlyweds, the popular Broadway show *The Wedding Singer* entered advertising partnerships with wedding websites and bridal magazines.
Source: Sara Krulwhich/*The New York Times*/www.eyevine.com

widowed or single-parent families) has stimulated the market for foodstuffs that are marketed in small portions. The trend towards more working women has stimulated the market sectors for time-saving items such as microwave ovens, catalogue shopping, easy-to-prepare foods and fast-food restaurants. The wedding industry attracts marketers of a whole host of market offerings who are keen to market to wedding guests, as well as seeking to help newlyweds set up home.

Gender

Men and women have different attitudes and behave differently, based partly on genetic make-up and partly on socialisation.[17] For example, women tend to be more community minded. Men tend to be more self-expressive and goal directed. Women tend to take in more of the data in their immediate environment. Men tend to focus on things that will help them to achieve a goal. A research study examining how men and women shop found that men often need to be invited to touch an item, while women are likely to pick it up without prompting. Men often like to read product information; women may relate to a product on a more personal level.

In many European countries, women are increasingly influencing buying decisions and exercise a considerable influence in the purchase of new homes. Gender differentiation has long been applied in clothing, hairstyling, cosmetics and magazines. Avon has built a successful business selling beauty products to women. Some products have been positioned as more masculine or feminine. Gillette's Venus is the most successful female shaving line ever, with over 70 per cent of the market, and has appropriate design, packaging and advertising cues to reinforce a female image.

However, it is not enough to present a market offering as masculine or feminine. Hyper-segmentation is now occurring within both male and female personal care segments. Nestlé markets its Yorkie chocolate bars in the United Kingdom to attract men and states on the packaging that 'It's not for girls'. Unilever earned kudos by targeting women who may be worried about ageing skin by stressing in their 'Dove Campaign for Real Beauty' that true beauty is timeless.

Dove

Dove's Campaign for Real Beauty features women of all shapes, sizes and colours posing proudly in their underwear. The company claims that the advertising series, developed by Ogilvy & Mather, was not just a vehicle to sell more soap but 'aims to change the status quo and offer in its place a broader, healthier, more democratic view of beauty'. The springboard was a global study sponsored by Dove that researched women's attitudes towards themselves and beauty. Only 2 per cent of women in the study considered themselves beautiful, so not only women, but everyone, took notice when the pictures of beaming full-figured or average-looking women began appearing.[18]

Media have emerged to make gender targeting easier. Marketers can reach women more easily in celebrity, fashion and household women's magazines. Men can be targeted by advertisements on the sporting satellite channels and through popular male magazines.[19]

Some traditionally more male-oriented markets, such as the car industry, are beginning to recognise gender segmentation, and are changing the way they design and sell cars.[20] Women shop differently for cars than men; they are more interested in environmental impact, care more about interior than exterior styling, and view safety in terms of features that help survive an accident rather than handling to avoid an accident.[21] Men are usually more interested in 'go-fast' designs, technical specifications and performance statistics.

Income

Income segmentation is a long-standing practice in such categories as cars, clothing, cosmetics, financial services and travel. However, income does not always predict the best customers. Apparently blue-collar workers were among the first purchasers of colour television sets as it was cheaper for them to buy these sets than to go to the cinema and theatre.

Many marketers are deliberately targeting lower-income groups, in some cases discovering fewer competitive pressures or greater consumer loyalty.[22] In the UK, Matalan and Primark offer a range of cheap clothing lines and TK Maxx offers designer labels at bargain prices.

Yet, at the same time, other marketers are finding success with premium-priced offers, as is the case with Coutts Bank and Moët et Chandon champagne. The growing number of dual-income households commanding high levels of disposable income has boosted the sales of premium goods such as innovative and expensive Dyson multi cyclone vacuum cleaners. Of particular note are the DINKYs (double income no kids yet). The growing number of dual-income households commanding high levels of disposable income have also boosted the sales of premium merchandise and exotic service offers. The 'credit crunch' that erupted in 2008 caused many companies to suffer sales losses and hence profitability declines, as consumer expenditure has been checked by uncertainty, rising credit costs and the threat of higher mortgage interest rates.

Companies are increasingly finding that their markets are becoming 'hourglass shaped', as middle-market consumers migrate towards both discount and premium purchases.[23] Companies that miss out on this new market risk being 'trapped in the middle' and seeing their market share steadily decline. General Motors was caught between highly engineered German imports in the luxury market and high-value Japanese and Korean models in the economy class, and has seen its market share continually slide, bringing the company perilously close to bankruptcy.[24] The marketing insight box describes the factors creating this trend and what it means to marketers.

The new consumer

New consumers defy traditional marketing identification. In reaction to a synthetic, processed and packaged world, their main drive is for an 'authentic experience' used as a means for the individual to define him- or herself. For them, consumption is as much

Marketing insight

Trading up (and down) – the new consumer

While the new consumer growth trends are stronger in the United States than in Europe, European countries are undergoing the same demographic changes.

A new pattern in consumer customer behaviour has emerged in recent years, according to Silverstein and Fiske, the authors of *Trading Up*. In unprecedented numbers, middle-market customers are periodically trading up to what Silverstein and Fiske call 'new luxury' products and services 'that possess higher levels of quality, taste, and aspiration than other goods in the category but are not so expensive as to be out of reach'. Customers might buy an expensive imported French wine, use a premium skin cream or stay in a luxury hotel.

As a result of the trading-up trend, new luxury goods sell at higher volumes than traditional luxury goods, while being priced higher than conventional mid-market items. The authors identify three main types of new luxury product:

1 Accessible super-premium products, such as designer label clothes. Kettle gourmet potato crisps carry a significant premium over middle-market brands, yet consumers can readily trade up to them because they are relatively low-price items in affordable categories.

2 Old luxury brand extensions which extend historically high-priced brands down market while retaining their cachet, such as the Mercedes-Benz C-class and Kenwood audio equipment.

3 Prestige goods, such as fine wines, which are priced between average middle-market brands and super-premium old luxury brands. They are 'always based on emotions, and consumers have a much stronger emotional engagement with them than with other goods'.

The authors note that in order to trade up on the brands that offer these emotional benefits, customers often 'trade down' by shopping at discount stores such as Aldi and Lidl (for staple food items) and at TK Maxx (for goods that confer no emotional benefit but still deliver quality and functionality).

Sources: M. J. Silverstein and N. Fiske (2003) *Trading Up: The New American Luxury*, New York: Portfolio; M. J. Silverstein (2006) *Treasure Hunt: Inside the Mind of the New Consumer*, New York: Portfolio; J. Cioletti (2006) Moving on up, *BeverageWorld*, June, 20.

about services, experiences and citizenship as it is about the acquisition of goods. These new consumers are a potent economic force and increasingly companies are adapting their standard offer lines to meet their requirements.[25] Paradoxically, this aspirational consumption is not always making these new consumers any happier. The paralysing effects of a marketplace that offers a bewildering and ultimately debilitating array of alternatives, results in fuelling not greater satisfaction but greater anxiety.[26]

Generation

Each generation is profoundly influenced by the age in which it is reared – the music, films, politics and defining events of that period. Demographers call these generational groups *cohorts*. Members share the same major cultural, political and economic experiences and have similar outlooks and values. Marketers often advertise to a cohort by using the icons and images prominent in its experiences. Citroën has used Transformer images in its advertising to attract male customers in the United Kingdom who have nostalgic memories of the popular Transformer toys of their childhood. The marketing insight box on p. 382 provides insight into the key age cohort, generation Y.

Although distinctions can be made between the different generational cohorts, they also influence each other. For instance, because so many members of generation Y – echo boomers – are living with their boomer parents, parents are being influenced by what demographers are calling a 'boom-boom effect'. The same products that appeal to 21-year-olds are appealing to youth-obsessed baby boomers. Noxon termed this the 'rejuvenile' mindset. Here are two examples of the rejuvenilisation phenomenon:

1 Adult gadgets, such as mobile phones, cars and even houseware, have been transformed from purely utilitarian to toy-like. Vacuums come in different primary colours; cars in lemon yellow. Mini Coopers look as if they have been designed for the toddler set.

Marketing insight

Marketing to 'generation Y'

They are dubbed 'echo boomers' or 'generation Y'. They grew up amid economic abundance and will probably face years of economic recession. Their world has experienced little economic disturbance. They have been 'wired' almost from birth – playing computer games, navigating the World Wide Web, downloading music, and connecting with friends via instant messaging and mobile phones. They have a sense of entitlement and abundance from growing up during the economic boom and being pampered by their boomer parents. They are selective, confident and impatient. They want what they want when they want it – and they often get it by using credit cards.

The influences that shaped generation Y are incredibly important to marketers because this cohort will shape consumer and business markets for years to come. Born between 1977 and 1994, generation Y vastly outnumbers the post-Second World War baby boomers of generation X. They will command an awesome annual spending power and will probably live (barring any unforeseen catastrophe) well into their eighties.

It is not surprising, then, that market researchers and advertisers are actively seeking to understand generation Y's buying behaviour. As overt branding practices and 'hard sell' marketing are generally not welcomed by this cohort, marketers have tried many different approaches to reach and persuade them.

- **Online buzz.** Nike and Nokia advertise on Internet service providers (ISPs).
- **Student ambassadors.** Red Bull enlists college students as Red Bull student brand managers to distribute samples, research drinking trends, design on-campus marketing initiatives and write stories for student newspapers.
- **Unconventional sports.** Henkel sponsors the Men's European Handball Championships; Red Bull organises gliding races.
- **Cool events.** Toyota sponsored a wheel-changing competition on a road-show truck and TDK has sponsored a dance marathon in Milan.
- **Computer games.** Product placement is not restricted to movies or TV: firms are seeking display opportunities in electronic games from leading companies such as Activision.
- **Videos.** Car companies make sure that their logos appear in film and video productions.
- **Street teams.** Local pizza parlours support Danball, the fun street game in Belgium.

Sources: www.sponsorship.com.news; www.bslworld.com.news.

Marketing memo

Key trends in the social and cultural environment

Grey market

Marketers keep a close eye on the key trends in the social and cultural environment in the countries in which they do business. The changing environment causes a continuous change in social attitudes and perceived values. Improving living standards has a significant effect on the ways in which customers spend their disposable income.

In the developed west, the so-called grey segment of the over-60s makes up over 20 per cent of the population and this figure is expected to rise to around 30 per cent by 2050. The segment constitutes an attractive target market for several perceived-value offerings. Increasingly it will become a significant target for marketing communications activities.

Youth market

As generation X, the *status quo* weary and cynical youth, gives way to generation Y, the European youth market will change as they start to experience relatively declining levels of disposable income in the opening decades of the twenty-first century. This is because most of the developed European economies will experience relatively lower growth levels. The rebellious attitudes of generation X will mutate with the changing fortunes of this market. While fad and fashion will always be attractive to this segment, declining levels of purchasing power will impact on the offerings of the leading clothing companies such as Monsoon, Next and Hugo Boss, whose businesses will become increasingly price dependent.

Ethnic market

Following the rapid expansion of the European Union (which has been a marked feature since 2000), coupled with an increased tendency for ethnic migration, the developed west will be characterised by rising multiethnic societies. As the different cultures have distinct value sets, marketers will develop a strong interest in ethnic marketing programmes. In the United Kingdom, the Halifax Building Society's 'Harvey' character has pioneered the regular use of ethnic actors in TV advertising.

2 Half the adults who visit Disney World every day do so without children. Noxon found that Disney enthusiasts return to the Magic Kingdom to recapture the safety and serenity of childhood.[27]

Social class

Social class can be classified using macro-criteria such as profession, education, family income and property value. In Europe the ESOMAR association, in an attempt to standardise many different national classifications, has developed a model that is based on property, occupation, education and the principal earning power of the main contributor to the household income. Each social class tends to share a mix of common values that has a strong influence on purchasing decisions. Many companies target social class segments and design cars, clothing, home furnishings, leisure activities and so on to suit their preferences. The tastes of these social classes change with the passing of the years. The 1990s were strongly characterised by consumerism and ostentation for the upper classes. Affluent tastes now run more conservatively, although luxury goods makers such as Burberry, Chanel, TAG Heuer and Louis Vuitton still sell successfully to those seeking the good life.

Psychographic segmentation

Psychographics is the science of using psychology and demographics to better understand consumer markets. In *psychographic segmentation*, buyers are divided into different groups on the basis of psychological/personality traits, lifestyle or values. People within the same demographic group can exhibit very different psychographic profiles and thus display different lifestyles. Psychographic profiles are typically developed with reference to three variables, known as the AIO factors, which describe individual lifestyles:

1 activities;
2 interests; and
3 opinions.

Lifestyle studies enhance basic sociodemographic descriptions and aid understanding of customer-perceived value preferences. The main psychographic profiles are general lifestyle studies and product-specific studies. The former classifies the total population into groups according to common characteristics such as 'receptivity to innovation', 'family centred', 'ecologically aware', etc. The latter specifies the importance of such characteristics in consumer purchasing decisions. The French International Research Institute on Social Change (RISC) has identified eight social-cultural variables that greatly influence the development of European society (see Table 10.4).

Table 10.4 The forces shaping social change

1 *Self-development* – affirming oneself as an individual.
2 *Hedonism* – giving priority to pleasure.
3 *Plasticity* – adapting to circumstances.
4 *Vitality* – exploiting one's energy.
5 *Connectivity* – relating to others, mixing cultures.
6 *Ethics* – searching for a sensitive and balanced social life.
7 *Belongings* – defining social links and cultural similarities.
8 *Inertia* – actively, or more often passively, resisting change.

Source: L. Hasson (1995) Monitoring social change, *International Journal of Market Research*, 37(1), 69–80. Copyright © 1995 Market Research Society (www.ijmr.com). Reproduced with permission.

Table 10.5 SINUS typology

1 *Basic orientation:* traditional – to preserve.
2 *Basic orientation:* materialist – to have.
3 *Changing values:* hedonism – to indulge.
4 *Changing values:* post-materialism – to be.
5 *Changing values:* postmodernism – to have, to be and to indulge.

Another European typology has been developed by SINUS GmbH and identifies five social classes and value perspectives as shown in Table 10.5.

One of the most popular commercially available classification systems based on psychographic measurements is the Stanford Research Institute's Consulting Business Intelligence's (SRIC-BI) VALS™ framework. VALS, signifying values and lifestyles, classifies US adults into eight primary groups based on responses to a questionnaire featuring 4 demographic and 35 attitudinal questions. The VALS™ system is continually updated with new data from more than 80,000 surveys per year (see Figure 10.2).[28] Check your VALS™ classification by going to SRIC-BI's website.

The main dimensions of the VALS™ segmentation framework are customer motivation (the horizontal dimension) and customer resources (the vertical dimension). Customers are inspired by one of three primary motivations: ideals, achievement and self-expression. Those primarily motivated by ideals are guided by knowledge and principles. Those

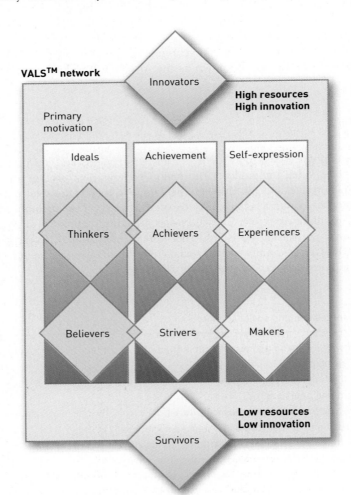

Figure 10.2 The VALS™ segmentation system: an eight-part typology
Source: VALS™. Copyright © SRI Consulting Business Intelligence. Reproduced with permission.

motivated by achievement look for purchases that demonstrate success to their peers. Customers whose motivation is self-expression desire social or physical activity, variety and risk. Personality traits such as energy, self-confidence, intellectualism, novelty seeking, innovativeness, impulsiveness, leadership and vanity – in conjunction with key demographics – determine an individual's resources. Different levels of resources enhance or constrain a person's expression of primary motivation.

The four groups with higher resources are:

1 **Innovators**: successful, sophisticated, active, 'take-charge' people with high self-esteem. Purchases often reflect cultivated tastes for relatively upscale, niche-oriented products and services.
2 **Thinkers**: mature, satisfied and reflective people who are motivated by ideals and who value order, knowledge and responsibility. They seek durability, functionality and value in products.
3 **Achievers**: successful goal-oriented people who focus on career and family. They greatly value products that demonstrate success to their peers.
4 **Experiencers**: young, enthusiastic impulsive people who seek variety and excitement. They spend a comparatively high proportion of income on fashion, entertainment and socialising.

The four groups with lower resources are:

1 **Believers**: conservative, conventional and traditional people with concrete beliefs. They prefer familiar, domestic products and are loyal to established brands.
2 **Strivers**: trendy and fun-loving people who are resource constrained. They like stylish products that emulate the purchases of those with greater material wealth.
3 **Makers**: practical, down-to-earth, self-sufficient people who like to work with their hands. They seek domestic products with a practical or functional purpose.
4 **Survivors**: elderly, passive people who are concerned about change. They are loyal to their favourite brands.

Psychographic segmentation schemes are often customised by culture. The Japanese version of VALS™, Japan VALS™, divides society into ten consumer segments on the basis of two key concepts: life orientation (traditional ways, occupations, innovation and self-expression) and attitudes to social change (sustaining, pragmatic, adapting and innovating).

Marketers can apply their understanding of psychographic profiles to marketing planning. For example, Martini advertising has been targeted at individuals on the basis of what lifestyle they would like to have. It appeals to 'aspirational lifestyle segments'. While psychographic profiles can greatly assist marketers, they do suffer from a number of drawbacks. They are expensive to maintain, update and develop, and they can obscure the relationship between segment characteristics and brand performance.[29]

Behavioural segmentation

In behavioural segmentation, marketers place buyers into groups on the basis of their knowledge of, attitude towards, use of or response to a product/service or market offering package.

Decision roles

It is easy to identify many buyers. In Europe, men normally choose their shaving equipment and women choose their tights, but even here marketers must be careful in making their targeting decisions because buying roles change. For example, in the United Kingdom, Marks & Spencer found that it was women who usually purchased underpants for their men folk. When Dulux discovered that women made 60 per cent of decisions on the brand of household paint, it decided to advertise to women.

People play five roles in a buying decision: *initiator, influencer, decider, buyer* and *user*. For example, assume that a wife initiates a purchase by requesting a modern coffee maker for her birthday. The husband may then seek information from many sources, including his best friend who has a Nespresso and is a key influencer in what models to consider. After presenting the alternative choices to his wife, he then purchases her preferred model which, as it turns out, is a Nespresso that ends up being used by the entire family. Different people are playing different roles, but all are crucial in the buying decision process and ultimate consumer satisfaction.

Behavioural variables

Many marketers believe behavioural variables – occasions, benefits, user status, usage rate, buyer-readiness stage, loyalty status and attitude – are the best starting points for constructing market segments.

Occasions Occasions can be defined in terms of the time of day, week, month or year, or in terms of other well-defined temporal aspects of a consumer's life. Buyers can be distinguished according to the occasions when they develop a need, make a purchase, or use a market offering (product/service) package. For example, cereals have traditionally been marketed as a breakfast-related food item. Kellogg's has always encouraged consumers to eat breakfast cereal on the 'occasion' of getting up. Recently, however, it has tried to extend the consumption of cereals by promoting them as an ideal 'anytime' snack food, whilst Nestlé market cereals as a health food.

Marketers can also extend activities associated with certain holidays to other times of the year. While Christmas, Mother's Day and Valentine's Day are the major gift-giving holidays, these and other events account for just over half of givers' budgets. That leaves the rest available throughout the year for occasions such as birthdays, weddings, anniversaries, house warming and the arrival of new babies.[30]

Benefits Not everyone who buys a product/service market offering wants the same benefits from it. This is recognised by the high street commercial banks that target their finance packages, on the one hand to people who want a high return in the short term, and on the other hand, to those investors who are looking for an attractive return on their money over the longer term. Research in the toothpaste market has found four main 'benefit segments' – economic, medicinal, cosmetic and taste.

User status Every purchase has its non-users, ex-users, potential users, first-time users and regular users. Blood banks cannot rely only on regular donors to supply blood; they must also recruit new first-time donors and contact ex-donors, with a different marketing strategy for each. The key to attracting potential users, or even possibly non-users, is understanding the reasons why they are not buying. Do they have deeply held attitudes, beliefs or behaviours, or just lack knowledge of the product/service offer or brand attributes, benefits and usage?

Included in the potential-user group are consumers who will become users in connection with some life stage or life event. Mothers-to-be are potential users who will turn into heavy users. Producers of child merchandise, such as Danone's Cow & Gate, learn their brand names by maintaining close relationships with clinics and doctors, shower them with free samples and target them with advertisements to capture a share of their future purchases. Market-share leaders tend to focus on attracting potential users because they have the most to gain. Smaller firms focus on trying to attract current users away from the market leader.

Usage rate Markets can be segmented into light, medium and heavy users. Heavy users are often a small percentage of the market but account for a high percentage of total consumption. For example, heavy beer drinkers account for 87 per cent of the beer consumed – almost seven times as much as light drinkers. Marketers would rather attract one heavy user than several light users. A potential problem, however, is that heavy users are often either extremely loyal to one brand, or never loyal to any brand and always looking for the lowest price. They may also have less room to expand their purchase and consumption.

Buyer-readiness stage Some people are unaware of a market offering, some are aware, some are informed, some are interested, some desire it, and some intend to buy. To help characterise how many people are at different stages and how well they have converted people from one stage to another, some marketers employ a marketing funnel. Figure 10.3 displays a funnel for two hypothetical brands, A and B. Brand A performs poorly compared to Brand B at converting one-time triers to more recent triers.

The relative numbers of customers at different stages make a big difference in designing the marketing programme. Suppose a health agency wants to encourage women to have an annual cervical smear to detect cervical cancer. At the beginning, most women may be unaware of the smear test. The marketing effort should go into awareness-building advertising using a simple message. Later, the advertising should dramatise the benefits of the test and the risks of not taking it.

Loyalty status Marketers usually envision four groups based on brand loyalty status:

1 **Hard-core loyals:** consumers who buy only one brand all the time.
2 **Split loyals:** consumers who are loyal to two or three brands.
3 **Shifting loyals:** consumers who shift loyalty from one brand to another.
4 **Switchers:** consumers who show no loyalty to any brand.[31]

A company can learn a great deal by analysing the degrees of brand loyalty. Hard-core loyals can help identify the products' strengths; split loyals can show the firm which brands are most competitive with its own; and by looking at customers who are shifting away from its brand, the company can learn about its marketing weaknesses and attempt to correct them. One caution: what appear to be brand-loyal purchase patterns may reflect habit, indifference, a low price, a high switching cost or the unavailability of other brands.

Attitude Five attitudes about product purchase are: enthusiastic, positive, indifferent, negative and hostile. Door-to-door workers in a political campaign use voter attitude to determine how much time to spend with that voter. They thank enthusiastic voters and remind them to vote; they reinforce those who are positively disposed; they try to win the votes of indifferent voters; they spend no time trying to change the attitudes of negative and hostile voters.

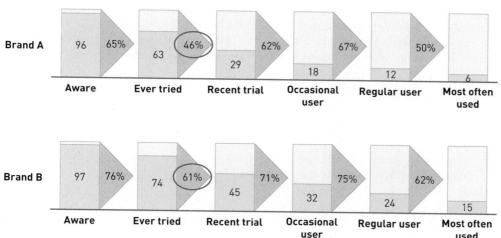

Figure 10.3
Brand funnel

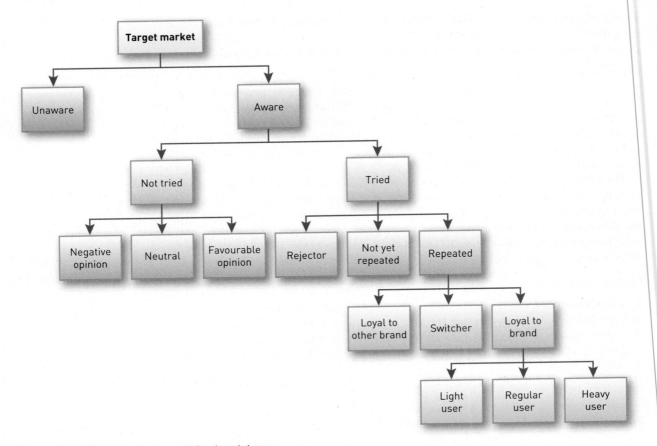

Figure 10.4 Behavioural segmentation breakdown

Combining different behavioural bases can help to provide a more comprehensive and cohesive view of a market and its segments. Figure 10.4 depicts one possible way to break down a target market by various behavioural segmentation bases.

The Conversion Model

The Conversion Model measures the strength of customers' psychological commitment to brands and their openness to change.[32] To determine how easily a customer can be converted to another choice, the model assesses commitment based on factors such as customer attitudes towards, and satisfaction with, current brand choices in a category, and the importance of the decision to select a brand in the category.[33]

The model segments *users* of a brand into four groups based on strength of commitment, from low to high, as follows:

1 **Convertible:** most likely to defect.
2 **Shallow:** uncommitted to the brand and could switch – some are actively considering alternatives.
3 **Average:** also committed to the brand they are using, but not as strongly – they are unlikely to switch brands in the short term.
4 **Entrenched:** strongly committed to the brand they are currently using – they are highly unlikely to switch brands in the foreseeable future.

The model also classifies *non-users* of a brand into four other groups based on their 'balance of disposition' and openness to trying the brand, from low to high, as follows:

1 **Strongly unavailable:** unlikely to switch to the brand – their preference lies strongly with their current brands.

2 **Weakly unavailable:** not available to the brand because their preference lies with their current brand, although not strongly.

3 **Ambivalent:** as attracted to the brand as they are to their current brands.

4 **Available:** most likely to be acquired in the short run.

In an application of the Conversion Model, Lloyds TSB (a UK high street bank) discovered that the profitability of its 'least committed' clients had fallen by 14 per cent in a 12-month period, whereas for the 'most committed' it had increased by 9 per cent. Those who were 'committed' were 20 per cent more likely to increase the number of products they held during the 12-month period. As a result, the bank took action to attract and retain high-value committed customers, which resulted in increased profitability.

Finally, a related method of behavioural segmentation has recently been proposed that looks more at the expectations a customer brings to a particular kind of transaction and locates those expectations on a 'Gravity of decision spectrum'. At the shallow end of the spectrum, consumers seek products and service market offerings that they think will save them time, effort and money, such as toiletries and snacks. Segmentation for these items would tend to measure customers' price sensitivity, habits and impulsiveness. At the other end of the spectrum, the deep end, are those decisions in which customers' emotional investment is greatest and their core values most engaged, such as deciding on a healthcare facility for an ageing relative or buying a new home. Here the marketer would seek to determine the core values and beliefs related to the buying decision. As the model suggests, focusing on customers' relationships and involvement with products and offerings can often be revealing as to where and how the firm should market to customers.[34]

Bases for segmenting business markets

Business-to-business markets (see Chapter 8) can be segmented with variables that are used in consumer markets, such as geography, benefits sought and usage rate, together with some extra ones. As it is common to find a one-to-one relationship between buyer and seller, segmentations are closely fashioned to the needs of individual organisations. Table 10.6 shows one set of variables that can be applied to segment the business market. The demographic variables are the most important, followed by the operating variables – down to the personal characteristics of the buyer.

The table lists major questions that business marketers should ask in determining which segments and customers to serve. A tyre company, for instance, can sell tyres to manufacturers of cars, trucks, farm tractors, forklift trucks or aircraft. Within a chosen target industry, a company can further segment by company size. The company might set up separate operations for selling to large and small customers.

Within a given target industry and customer size, a company can segment further by purchase criteria. For example, government laboratories need low prices and service contracts for scientific equipment; university laboratories need equipment that requires little service; and industrial laboratories need equipment that is highly reliable and accurate.

Business marketers generally identify segments through a sequential process. Consider an aluminium company: the company first undertook macro-segmentation. It looked at which end-use market to serve: automobile, residential or beverage containers. It chose the residential market, and it needed to determine the most attractive product application: semi-finished material, building components or aluminium mobile homes. Deciding to focus on building components, it considered the best customer size and chose large customers. The second stage consisted of micro-segmentation. The company distinguished among customers buying on price, service or quality. Because the aluminium company had a high-service profile, it decided to concentrate on the service-motivated segment of the market.

Table 10.6 Major segmentation variables for business markets

Demographic

1 *Industry*: Which industries should we serve?
2 *Company size*: What size companies should we serve?
3 *Location*: What geographical areas should we serve?

Operating variables

4 *Technology*: What customer technologies should we focus on?
5 *User or non-user status*: Should we serve heavy users, medium users, light users or non-users?
6 *Customer capabilities*: Should we serve customers needing many or few services?

Purchasing approaches

7 *Purchasing-function organisation*: Should we serve companies with highly centralised or decentralised purchasing organisation?
8 *Power structure*: Should we serve companies that are engineering dominated, financially dominated, and so on?
9 *Nature of existing relationship*: Should we serve companies with which we have strong relationships or simply go after the most desirable companies?
10 *General purchasing policies*: Should we serve companies that prefer leasing? Service contract? Systems purchases? Sealed bidding?
11 *Purchasing criteria*: Should we serve companies that are seeking quality? Service? Price?

Situational factors

12 *Urgency*: Should we serve companies that need quick and sudden delivery or service?
13 *Specific application*: Should we focus on a certain application of our product rather than all applications?
14 *Size of order*: Should we focus on large or small orders?

Personal characteristics

15 *Buyer–seller similarity*: Should we serve companies whose people and values are similar to ours?
16 *Attitude towards risk*: Should we serve risk-taking or risk-avoiding customers?
17 *Loyalty*: Should we serve companies that show high loyalty to their suppliers?

Source: Adapted from T. V. Bonoma and B. P. Shapiro (1983) *Segmenting the Industrial Market*, Lexington, MA: Lexington Books. Copyright © 1983 Lexington Books. Reproduced with permission.

Market targeting

There are many statistical techniques for developing market segments and targeting. Talent hits a target no one else can hit; genius hits a target no one else can see.[35] Once the firm has identified its market-segment opportunities, it has to decide how many and which ones to target. Marketers are increasingly combining several variables in an effort to identify smaller, better-defined target groups. Thus a bank may not only identify a group of wealthy retired adults, but within that group distinguish several segments depending on current income, assets, savings and risk preferences. This has led some market researchers to advocate a *needs-based market segmentation approach*. Best proposed the seven-step approach shown in Table 10.7.

Table 10.7 Steps in the segmentation process

	Description
1 *Needs-based segmentation*	Group customers into segments based on similar needs and benefits sought by customer in solving a particular consumption problem.
2 *Segment identification*	For each needs-based segment, determine which demographics, lifestyles and usage behaviours make the segment distinct and identifiable (actionable).
3 *Segment attractiveness*	Using predetermined segment attractiveness criteria (such as market growth, competitive intensity and market access), determine the overall attractiveness of each segment.
4 *Segment profitability*	Determine segment profitability.
5 *Segment positioning*	For each segment, create a 'value proposition' and product-price positioning strategy based on that segment's unique customer needs and characteristics.
6 *Segment 'acid test'*	Create a 'segment storyboard' to test the attractiveness of each segment's positioning strategy.
7 *Marketing-mix strategy*	Expand segment positioning strategy to include all aspects of the marketing mix: product, price, promotion and place.

Source: Adapted from R. J. Best (2005) *Market-Based Management*, 4th edn, Upper Saddle River, NJ: Prentice Hall. Copyright © 2005. Reprinted by permission of Pearson Education, Inc., Upper Saddle River, NJ.

Effective segmentation criteria

Not all segmentation schemes are useful. For example, table salt buyers could be divided into blonde and brunette customers, but hair colour is undoubtedly irrelevant to the purchase of salt. Furthermore, if all salt buyers buy the same amount of salt each month, believe all salt is the same, and would pay only one price for salt, this market would be minimally segmentable from a marketing point of view.

To be useful, market segments must be capable of assessment on five key criteria:

1 **Measurable.** The size, purchasing power and characteristics of the segments can be measured.
2 **Substantial.** The segments are large and profitable enough to serve. A segment should be the largest possible homogeneous group worth pursuing with a tailored marketing programme. It would not pay, for example, for an automobile manufacturer to develop cars for people who are less than four feet tall.
3 **Accessible.** The segments can be effectively reached and served.
4 **Differentiable.** The segments are conceptually distinguishable and respond differently to different marketing-mix elements and programmes. If married and unmarried women respond similarly to a perfume sale, they would not for this purpose constitute separate segments.
5 **Actionable.** Effective programmes can be formulated for attracting and serving the segments.

Evaluating and selecting the market segments

In evaluating different market segments, the firm must look at two factors: the segment's overall attractiveness and the company's objectives and resources. How well does a potential segment score on the five criteria? Does a potential segment have characteristics that

Single-segment concentration

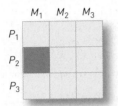

Selective specialisation

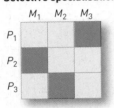

Product specialisation

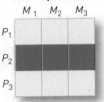

Market specialisation

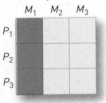

Full market coverage

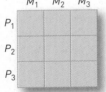

P = Product   *M* = Market

Figure 10.5 Five patterns of target market selection
Source: Adapted from D. F. Abell (1980) *Defining the Business: The Starting Point of Strategic Planning*, Prentice Hall, Chapter 8, pp. 192–6. Copyright © 1980. Reprinted by permission of Pearson Education, Inc., Upper Saddle River, NJ.

make it generally attractive, such as size, growth, profitability, scale economies and low risk? Does investing in the segment make sense given the firm's objectives, competencies and resources? Some attractive segments may not be compatible with the company's long-run objectives, or the company may lack one or more necessary competencies to offer superior value.

After evaluating different segments, the company can consider five patterns of target market selection, shown in Figure 10.5. Each is now described in turn.

Single-segment concentration

Fiat and Volkswagen concentrate on the small-car market – and Porsche on the sports car market. Through concentrated marketing, the firms gain a strong knowledge of the segment's needs and so can achieve a strong market presence. Furthermore, firms are able to enjoy operating economies through specialising their production, distribution and promotion. If firms can capture segment leadership, they can earn a high return on investment.

However, there are risks. A particular market segment can turn sour or a competitor may invade the segment: when digital camera technology took off, the earnings of Kodak (film) and Polaroid fell sharply. For these reasons many companies prefer to spread the risk and choose to operate in more than one segment. If selecting more than one segment to serve, a company should pay close attention to segment interrelationships affecting costs, performance and technology. A company carrying fixed costs (sales force, retail outlets) can add product/service market offerings to absorb and share some costs. The sales force will sell additional items, and a fast-food outlet will offer additional menu offers. Economies of scope can be just as important as economies of scale.

Companies can try to operate in super-segments rather than in isolated segments. A super-segment is a set of segments that share some significant exploitable similarity: for example, many symphony orchestras target people who have broad cultural interests rather than those who regularly attend concerts.

Selective specialisation

A firm selects a number of segments, each objectively attractive and appropriate. There may be little or no synergy among the segments, but each promises to be a moneymaker. This multi-segment strategy has the advantage of diversifying the firm's risk.

Product (market offer) specialisation

The firm makes a certain item that it offers successfully in several different market segments. A microscope manufacturer, for instance, markets to university, government and commercial laboratories. The firm makes different microscopes for the different customer groups and builds a strong reputation in the specific segment market. The downside risk is that the product/service offering may be supplanted by an entirely new technology.

Market specialisation

The firm concentrates on serving many needs of a particular customer group. For instance, a firm can sell an assortment of products/services only to university laboratories. The firm gains a strong reputation in serving this customer group and becomes a channel for additional products/service offerings that the customer group can use. The downside risk is that the customer group may suffer budget cuts or shrink in size.

Full market coverage

The firm attempts to serve all customer groups with all the products/service offers they might need. Only very large firms such as Microsoft (software market), General Motors (vehicle market), and Coca-Cola (non-alcoholic beverage market) can undertake a full market coverage strategy. Large firms can cover a whole market in two broad ways: through undifferentiated marketing or differentiated marketing.

In *undifferentiated marketing* the firm ignores segment differences and trades on the whole market with one offer. It designs a product/service market offering and a marketing programme that will endow it with a superior image and appeal to the broadest number of buyers, and it relies on mass distribution and advertising. Undifferentiated marketing is 'the marketing counterpart to standardisation and mass production in manufacturing.'[36] The narrow product/service offer line keeps down the costs of R & D, production, inventory, transportation, marketing research, advertising and brand management. The undifferentiated advertising programme also reduces advertising costs. The company can turn its lower costs into lower prices to win the price-sensitive segment of the market.

In *differentiated marketing* the firm operates in several market segments and designs different product/service offers for each. Cosmetics firm Estée Lauder markets brands that appeal to women (and men) of different tastes. The flagship brand, the original Estée Lauder, appeals to older consumers; Clinique caters to middle-aged women; Hugo Boss to youthful hipsters; Aveda to aromatherapy enthusiasts; and The Body Shop to eco-conscious consumers who want cosmetics made from natural ingredients.[37]

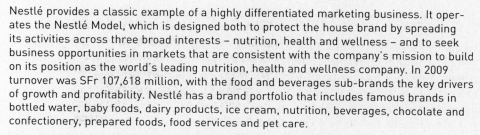

Nestlé

Nestlé provides a classic example of a highly differentiated marketing business. It operates the Nestlé Model, which is designed both to protect the house brand by spreading its activities across three broad interests – nutrition, health and wellness – and to seek business opportunities in markets that are consistent with the company's mission to build on its position as the world's leading nutrition, health and wellness company. In 2009 turnover was SFr 107,618 million, with the food and beverages sub-brands the key drivers of growth and profitability. Nestlé has a brand portfolio that includes famous brands in bottled water, baby foods, dairy products, ice cream, nutrition, beverages, chocolate and confectionery, prepared foods, food services and pet care.

Sources: Nestlé Annual Report 2009; Nestlé website, www.nestlé.com.

Differentiated marketing typically creates more sales than undifferentiated marketing. However, it also increases the costs of doing business. Because differentiated marketing leads to both higher sales and higher costs, nothing general can be said about the profitability of this strategy. Companies should be cautious about over-segmenting their markets. If this happens, they may want to turn to *counter-segmentation* to broaden the customer base. For example, Johnson & Johnson broadened the target market for its baby shampoo to include adults. SmithKline Beecham launched its Aquafresh toothpaste to attract three benefit segments simultaneously: those seeking fresh breath, whiter teeth and cavity protection. Kellogg's markets cereals as an evening snack as well as the traditional breakfast starter.

Additional considerations

Two other considerations in evaluating and selecting segments are segment-by-segment invasion plans and ethical choice of market targets.

Segment-by-segment invasion plans

A company would be wise to enter one segment at a time. Competitors must not know what segment(s) the firm will move to next. Segment-by-segment invasion plans are illustrated in Figure 10.6. Three firms, A, B and C, have specialised in adapting computer systems to the needs of airlines, railroads and trucking companies. Company A meets all the computer needs of airlines. Company B sells large computer systems to all three transportation sectors. Company C sells personal computers to trucking companies.

Where should company C move next? Arrows added to the chart show the planned sequence of segment invasions. Company C will next offer medium-size computers to trucking companies. Then, to allay company B's concern about losing some large

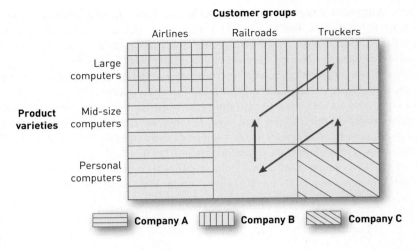

Figure 10.6 Segment-by-segment invasion plan

computer business with trucking companies, C's next move will be to sell personal computers to railway companies. Later, C will offer medium-size computers to railway companies. Finally, it may launch a full-scale attack on company B's large computer position in trucking companies. Of course, C's hidden planned moves are provisional in that much depends on competitors' segment moves and responses.

Unfortunately, too many companies fail to develop a long-term invasion plan. PepsiCo is an exception. It first attacked Coca-Cola in the grocery market, then in the vending-machine market, then in the fast-food market, and so on. Japanese firms also plot their invasion sequence. They first gain a foothold in a market, then enter new segments with products. Toyota began by introducing small cars (Corolla), then expanded into mid-size cars, and finally into luxury cars (Lexus).

A company's invasion plans can be thwarted when it confronts blocked markets. The invader must then find a way to break in, which usually calls for a megamarketing approach. **Megamarketing** is the strategic coordination of economic, psychological, political and public relations skills, to gain the cooperation of a number of parties in order to enter or operate in a given market.

Ethical choice of market targets

Marketers must target segments carefully to avoid consumer backlash. Some consumers may resist being labelled. Single people may reject single-serve food packaging because they don't want to be reminded they are eating alone. Elderly consumers who don't feel their age may not appreciate products that identify them as 'old'.

Market targeting can also generate public controversy.[38] The public is concerned when marketers take unfair advantage of vulnerable groups (such as children)[39] or disadvantaged groups (such as inner-city poor people), or promote potentially harmful products. The cereal industry has been heavily criticised for marketing efforts directed towards children. Critics worry that high-powered appeals presented through the mouths of lovable animated characters will overwhelm children's defences and lead them to want sugared cereals or poorly balanced breakfasts. Parents, consumer associations and the EU are increasingly concerned about the impact of marketing on children, with the Archbishop of Canterbury in the United Kingdom questioning 'a marketing culture that so openly feeds and colludes with obsession'. In the United Kingdom the government has forbidden schools to operate vending machines that offer confectionery and high-salt-content foods. Toy marketers have been similarly criticised. McDonald's and other chains have drawn criticism for pitching high-fat, salt-laden fare to low-income, inner-city residents.

Not all attempts to target children, minorities or other special segments draw criticism. Colgate-Palmolive's Colgate Junior toothpaste has special features such as coloured striped paste designed to get children to brush longer and more often. Other companies are responding to the special needs of minority segments.[40] Thus the issue is not *who* is targeted but rather *how* and *for what*. Socially responsible marketing calls for targeting that serves not only the company's interests but also the interests of those targeted. Many countries also place restrictions on the content and timing of advertising to children. Cadbury's dropped its 'Get Active' promotion that encouraged children to exchange chocolate packaging wrappers for school sports equipment when critics pointed out that 5,440 wrappers would be needed to obtain one football goal.[41]

Creating differentiation and positioning strategies

No company can be successful if its market offerings (product/service packages) resemble every other product and offering. As part of the strategic brand management process, each offering must represent a compelling, distinctive perceived-value offering in the mind of the target market.

A crucial pillar of marketing strategy is market customisation or as it is more generally known STP – *segmentation*, *targeting* and *positioning*. A company discovers different needs and groups in the marketplace (*segmentation*). It selects those *targets* it can satisfy in a competitive way, and then *positions* its offering so the *target* market recognises the company's distinctive offering and image. For market offerings to be successful in current buyers' markets, they need to be developed and differentiated against competitive offerings if a company wants to achieve a sustained competitive advantage (SCA). The creation of a strong brand reputation to generate a lasting SCA involves an active consideration of one or a combination of cost leadership, differentiation and combined cost and brand acceptance opportunities.

Yves Saint Laurent

Founded in 1961, Yves Saint Laurent is one of the greatest fashion names of the late twentieth century. Throughout the years, the ground-breaking designs of the couture house created innovative pieces of clothing. Yves Saint Laurent was the first couture house to launch, in 1966, the modern concept of luxury women's *prêt-à-porter*, in a collection called 'Rive Gauche'. It was followed in 1969 by a Rive Gauche men's ready-to-wear line. The Yves Saint Laurent Rive Gauche boutiques were soon opened throughout the world, allowing fashion-conscious working individuals to wear the Yves Saint Laurent designs. This represented the first step in making luxury labels accessible to a wider public.

In 1999, the Gucci Group (the luxury division of the PPR Group, the official trading name of a French luxury goods company organised around six operating branches: Fnac, Redcats Group, Conforam, CFAO, Puma and Gucci Group),[42] acquired Yves Saint Laurent. Since then the brand has been repositioned at the top segment of the luxury goods market. Under the management of Valérie Hermann, appointed CEO in 2005, and Stefano Pilati, creative director since 2004, the brand has renewed the exceptional legacy of its founder while bringing a contemporary approach to its collections, which combine elegance, top-quality fabrics, refined and discreet but recognisable details.

Today Yves Saint Laurent's collections include women's and men's ready-to-wear, shoes, handbags, small leather goods, jewellery, scarves, ties and eyewear. They are designed for both modern women, who have a keen sense of freedom and follow their instincts with assurance, captivating others with their elegance, and for men who prefer a non-conformist look and assert the different facets of their personality in a modern and sensitive way. The Yves Saint Laurent network currently has 63 directly operated shops, including flagship stores in Paris, New York, London, Milan, Hong Kong and Tokyo. The brand is also present in the most prestigious multibrand boutiques and department stores in the world and is likely to remain so even after the death of the famous designer in 2008, thus providing evidence of its success in developing and communicating an upmarket STP strategy.

Source: http://www.ysl.com

Positioning

Positioning is the act of designing the company's market offering and image to occupy a distinctive place in the minds of the target market.[43] The goal is to establish the brand in the minds of consumers in order to maximise the potential benefit to the firm. Good brand positioning helps guide marketing strategy by clarifying the brand's essence, what goals it helps the consumer achieve (how it addresses their 'genes of meaning') and how it does so in a unique way.[44] Everyone in the organisation should understand the customer-perceived value that underlies the brand positioning and use it as context for making decisions.[45]

The result of positioning is the successful creation of a *customer-focused value proposition*, a cogent reason why the target customer should buy from the provider. Table 10.8 shows how four companies – Dornier, Nivea, Volvo and Wolford – have defined their value proposition given their target customers, benefits and prices.

Positioning is a marketing concept that enables buyers and sellers to gain from being both effective and efficient. In Figure 10.6 an effective buying experience is realised as sellers provide the right market offering at an acceptable price. The seller gains as the right market offering is supplied cost efficiently. It requires that similarities and differences between brands be defined and communicated. Specifically, deciding on positioning requires determining a frame of reference by identifying the target market and the competition, and identifying the ideal points-of-parity and points-of-difference brand associations.

Table 10.8 Examples of value propositions

Company and market offering	Target customers	Benefits	Price premium (%)	Value proposition
Dornier (G)	Commercial weavers	High technology	20	High-quality, sophisticated weaving machines
Nivea (G)	Personal care-oriented people	Life and care	15	Quality skin and beauty care
Volvo (US/SW)	Safety conscious	Durability and safety	20	Safest car in which a family can travel
Wolford (A)	Women	Fashion and technology	30	High-fashion, high-tech seamless tights

Note: (A) Austria; (G) Germany; (US/SW) USA/Sweden

Source: M. R. V. Goodman, Durham University.

Everything Everywhere

The mobile phone industry in the UK, one of the most competitive in the world, awoke on 8 September 2009 to the news that the UK operations of Telecom France (Orange) and Telekom Deutsche (T-Mobile) were planning to merge and to create a new company, Everything Everywhere, designed to exploit the opportunities in the UK market provided by the new generation of mobile phones. The 50/50 merger sets up Everything Everywhere to exploit the emerging technology that allows customers to access entertainment, education and information wherever they were and whenever they wanted. This was approved by the EU authorities on 1 March 2010 and the new venture was officially announced on 1 April 2010. For a period of two years or so, both Orange and T-Mobile will maintain their distinct brand identities but increasingly convert their UK shops to the Everything Everywhere brand. The merger has enabled the combined Orange/T-Mobil brands to become the dominant player in the UK mobile phone market over rivals O2 and Vodafone.

The merger has set up Everything Everywhere to provide an integrated service that will give the new brand a distinct market edge. A strategic partnership with Barclaycard led to the development of the UK's first commercial contactless mobile payments service, which was launched in the summer of 2010.

- The new service will offer consumers greater convenience and control on the high street with over 40,000 stores ready to accept contactless payments.
- An industry-backed secure SIM-based payments approach ensures excellent purchase protection for consumers.
- The latest move builds on Everything Everywhere and Barclaycard's ongoing partnership, which has already produced a co-branded contactless credit card and the forthcoming Orange Cash pre-paid contactless card.

The move will usher in a new era for consumers, offering greater simplicity, convenience and control, and will change the way payments are made on UK high streets. Other new market initiatives include the intention of T-Mobile to pioneer fixed-line services and Orange's proposal to add TV to its existing residential broadband offering.[46]

Competitive frame of reference

A starting point in defining a competitive frame of reference for a brand positioning is to determine **category membership** – the market offerings with which a brand competes and that function as close substitutes. Chapter 9 discussed competitive analysis and considered several factors – including the resources, capabilities and likely intentions of various other firms – in choosing those markets where consumers can be profitably served.

Deciding to target a certain type of consumer, in particular, can define the nature of competition because certain firms have decided to target that segment in the past (or plan to do so in the future), or because consumers in that segment may already look to certain brands in their purchase decisions. To determine the proper competitive frame of reference, marketers need to understand consumer behaviour and the consideration factors that influence consumers' brand choices. In the United Kingdom, for example, the Automobile Association positioned itself as the fourth 'emergency service' – along with police, fire and ambulance – to convey greater credibility and urgency.

Lindauer Dornier GmbH's weaving machines

The privately owned German company Lindauer Dornier GmbH emphasises its drive in technological progress. New developments cover the complete textile machine product line. The new performance generation of air-jet and rapier weaving machines, a new 540 cm wide air-jet weaving machine for technical fabrics and new machine models for specialist weaving complement decisive innovative advances in finishing machines for circular fabrics. Dornier found that its products were too sophisticated for most eastern European markets. Following an earlier initiative in Latin America, it started a second-hand machinery market for those customers, adapting used machines that the company had taken back from customers that had bought new, more technologically advanced machines.

Source: www.lindauer-dornier.com

Points-of-parity and points-of-difference

Once marketers have fixed the competitive frame of reference for positioning by defining the customer target market and the nature of the competition, they can define the appropriate points-of-difference and points-of-parity associations.[47]

Points-of-difference **Points-of-difference** (PODs) are attributes or benefits that consumers associate strongly with a brand, evaluate positively, and believe they could not find to the same extent with a competitive brand. Associations that make up points-of-difference may be based on virtually any type of attribute or benefit. Examples are IKEA (*affordable design*), Michelin (*performance*) and Liebherr (*quality*). Creating associations that are strong, able and unique is a real challenge, but essential in terms of competitive brand positioning.

Points-of-parity **Points-of-parity** (POPs), on the other hand, are associations that are not necessarily unique to the brand but may in fact be shared with other brands.[48] These types of association come in two basic forms: category and competitive.

Category points-of-parity are associations that consumers view as essential to a legitimate and credible offering within a certain product or service category. In other words, they represent necessary – but not sufficient – conditions for brand choice. Consumers might not consider a travel agency truly a travel agency unless it is able to make air and hotel reservations, provide advice about leisure packages and offer various ticket payment and delivery options. Category points-of-parity may change over time due to technological advances, legal developments or consumer trends, but they are the essential factors for marketers.

Competitive points-of-parity are associations designed to negate *competitors'* points-of-difference. If, in the eyes of consumers, a brand can 'break even' in those areas where the competitors are trying to find an advantage *and* achieve advantages in other areas, the brand should be in a strong – and perhaps unbeatable – competitive position. Consider the introduction of Nespresso.

Nespresso

The actress Sharon Stone attended the grand opening in Paris of the Swiss multinational's lavish new coffee shop on the Champs-Elysées on 13 December 2007. Sales of Nespresso coffee machines and capsules have been growing during the past six years by an average of 30 per cent a year. In 2007, they increased by 42 per cent to SFr 1.16 billion and they exceeded the SFr 2 billion mark in 2009. In August 2010, it was reported that Nespresso sales have been growing at an average of 30 per cent per year over the past ten years and more than 20 billion capsules have been sold since 2000 at a current selling price equivalent to about USD 0.43 to USD 0.62 per capsule. The Swiss food group is planning a massive expansion of Nespresso boutiques around the world. The idea is to turn Nespresso into a luxury brand that can sit alongside a Louis Vuitton or Harry Winston store.

Nestlé's star brand risks facing the same dilemma as a pharmaceutical group's block-buster drug. The Swiss company will lose the patent on its precious Nespresso coffee cap-sules in 2012. By then, it hopes to have developed such a cult for its coffee and boutiques that the patent expiry will make little difference to its continued success as a luxury brand. As Nespresso's lead promoter, George Clooney, would say, 'What else?'[49]

Nestlé seek to establish strong points-of-difference
Source: Nespresso

Points-of-parity versus points-of-difference For a market offering to achieve a point-of-parity on a particular attribute or benefit, a sufficient number of consumers must believe the brand is 'good enough' on that dimension. There is a zone or range of tolerance or acceptance with points-of-parity. The brand does not literally have to be seen as equal to competitors, but consumers must feel that the brand does well enough on that particular attribute or benefit. If they do, they may be willing to base their evaluations and decisions on other factors potentially more amenable to the brand: for example, a light beer would presumably never taste as good as a full-strength beer, but it would have to taste close enough to be able to compete effectively.

With points-of-difference, however, the brand must demonstrate clear superiority. Customers must be convinced that Louis Vuitton has the most stylish handbags, Duracell is the longest-lasting battery, and Crédit Lyonnais offers the best financial advice and planning. Often the key to positioning is not so much achieving a point-of-difference as achieving points-of-parity.

Europcar – from car rental company to mobility provider

The company, an integral part of Volkswagen's mobility concept, claims to be the 'world's leading leisure car rental company' and to be highly committed to its customers: 'We promise to deliver the best car rental experience through excellent customer service and high quality vehicles.' Europcar has developed into a global provider of mobility services. This has resulted from the development of partnerships with airlines, railway operators, hotel groups, automobile clubs and roadside assistance services. Europcar thus integrates the business of renting cars within a consistent, global mobility concept.

Europcar offers its customers a wide variety of service solutions to the reservation process. The internet has become an increasingly important tool for booking, alongside the telephone or travel agencies' Global Distribution Systems. As a matter of principle, Europcar does not promote any particular reservation channel, but offers customers the choice of all possible reservation methods to meet their individual needs. In an increasingly complex world, the freedom of each person to set individual priorities – whether in business-to-business or private consumer markets – is becoming more and more important. Europcar's strategy is to provide tailored mobility solutions to offer leading market-perceived value solutions.

Source: www.europcar.com.

Establishing category membership

Target customers are aware that Chanel is a leading brand of cosmetics, Nestlé is a leading brand of cereal and yogurt, Accenture is a leading consulting firm, and so on. Often, however, marketers must inform consumers of a brand's category membership. Perhaps the most obvious situation is the introduction of new product/service offerings, especially when category identification itself is not apparent.

There are also situations where customers know a brand's category membership, but may not be convinced that the brand is a valid member of the category: for example, people may be aware that Swatch produces watches, but they may not be certain whether they are in the same class as Casio, Seiko and Tissot. In this instance, Swatch might find it useful to reinforce category membership. With this approach, however, it is important not to be trapped between categories. Customers should understand what the brand stands for, and not what it does not. The typical approach to positioning is to inform consumers of a brand's membership before stating its point-of-difference. Consumers need to know what a market offering is and what function it serves before deciding whether it dominates the brands against which it competes. For new offerings, initial advertising often concentrates on creating brand awareness, and subsequent advertising attempts to craft the brand image.

Straddle positioning

Occasionally, a company will try to straddle two frames of reference.

BMW

When BMW first made a strong competitive push into the UK market in the early 1980s, it positioned the brand as the only car that offered both luxury *and* performance. At that time, consumers saw luxury cars as lacking performance, and performance cars as lacking luxury. By relying on the design of its cars, its German heritage and other aspects of a well-conceived marketing programme, BMW was able simultaneously to achieve: (1) a point-of-difference on luxury and a point-of-parity on performance with respect to performance cars; and (2) a point-of-difference on performance and a point-of-parity on luxury with respect to luxury cars. The clever slogan 'The Ultimate Driving Machine' effectively captured the newly created umbrella category – luxury performance cars.

While a straddle positioning is often attractive as a means of reconciling potentially conflicting consumer goals and creating a 'best-of-both-worlds' solution, it also carries an extra burden. If the points-of-parity and points-of-difference with respect to both categories are not credible, the brand may not be viewed as a legitimate player in either category, ending up in 'no man's land'. Many early personal digital assistants that unsuccessfully tried to straddle categories ranging from pagers to laptop computers provide a vivid illustration of this risk.

Communicating category membership

There are three main ways to convey a brand's category membership:

1 **Announcing category benefits.** To reassure consumers that a brand will deliver on the fundamental reason for purchasing a category, marketers frequently use attributes and benefits to announce category membership. Thus industrial tools might claim to have durability and antacids might announce their efficacy. A cake mix might attain membership in the baked desserts category by claiming the benefit of great taste, and support this claim by including high-quality ingredients (performance) or by showing users delighting in its consumption (imagery).

2 **Comparing to exemplars.** Well-known, noteworthy brands in a category can also help a brand specify its category membership. When Stella McCartney was an unknown, advertising announced her membership as an up-and-coming UK designer by associating her with famous couturiers – recognised members of that category.

3 **Relying on the product descriptor.** The product descriptor that follows the brand name is often a concise means of conveying category origin. Ford Motor Co., before it sold Jaguar Land Rover to the Indian Tata Steel Group, invested more than US$1 billion on a radical new model called the X-Trainer, to build in its Land Rover plant in the United Kingdom, which combines the attributes of an SUV, a minivan and an estate car. To communicate its unique position – and to avoid association with its Explorer and Country Squire models – the vehicle (later called Freestyle) has been designated a 'sports wagon'.[50]

Choosing POPs and PODs

Points-of-parity are driven by the needs of category membership (to create category POPs) and the necessity of negating competitors' PODs (to create competitive POPs). Two important considerations in choosing points-of-difference are that consumers find the POD desirable and that the firm has the capabilities to deliver on it. As Table 10.9 shows, three criteria can judge both desirability and deliverability.

Table 10.9 Judging desirability and deliverability for points-of-difference

Desirability criteria	Deliverability criteria
Relevance Target consumers must find the POD personally relevant and important. • National Express, a UK train company serving the London to East Coast route, advertised that all its trains had Wi-fi connections in each carriage. While of interest to some business travellers, this was of little interest to most passengers.	*Feasibility* The product design and marketing offering must support the desired association. Does communicating the desired association require real changes to the offering itself, or just perceptual shifts in the way the consumer thinks of the offering or brand? The latter is typically easier. • Volkswagen in Germany has had to work hard to overcome public perceptions that Audi is not a youthful, contemporary brand.
Distinctiveness Target consumers must find the POD distinctive and superior. • Dyson gained a strong early niche market position by differentiating itself on the basis of its unique design and function.	*Communicability* Consumers must be given a compelling reason and understandable rationale as to why the brand can deliver the desired benefit. What factual, verifiable evidence or 'proof points' can ensure consumers will actually believe in the brand and its desired associations? • Substantiators often come in the form of patented, branded ingredients, such as Nivea Wrinkle Control Crème with Q10 co-enzyme or computers that have an Intel processor inside.
Believability Target consumers must find the POD believable and credible. A brand must offer a compelling reason for choosing it over the other options. • Red Bull may argue that it is more energising than other soft drinks and support this claim by noting that it has a higher level of safe stimulants. • Chanel No. 5 perfume may claim to be the quintessential elegant French perfume and support this claim by noting the long association between Chanel and haute couture.	*Sustainability* The firm must be sufficiently committed and willing to devote enough resources to create an enduring positioning. Is the positioning pre-emptive, defensible and difficult to attack? Can a brand association be reinforced and strengthened over time? • It is generally easier for market leaders such as Renault, Visa and Lindt, whose positioning is based in part on demonstrable product or service performance, to sustain their positioning than for market leaders such as H&M and Zara, whose positioning is based on fashion and is thus subject to the whims of a more fickle market.

Marketers must decide at which level(s) to anchor the brand's points-of-difference. At the lowest level are the *brand attributes*, at the next level are the *brand's benefits*, and at the top are the *brand's values*. Thus marketers of Dove soap can talk about its attribute of one-quarter cleansing cream, or its benefit of softer skin, or its value of being more attractive. Attributes are typically the least desirable level to position. First, the buyer is more interested in benefits. Second, competitors can easily copy attributes. Third, current attributes may become less desirable over time.

Brands can sometimes be successfully differentiated on seemingly irrelevant attributes, *if* consumers infer the proper benefit. Kenco differentiates its instant coffee by claiming that it harvests the best mountain-grown beans and then freeze dries them with a unique

Marketing memo

Writing a positioning statement

To communicate a company or brand positioning, marketing plans often include a *positioning statement*. The statement should follow the form: To *(target group and need)*, our *(Brand)* is *(the concept)* that *(what the point-of-difference is or does)*. For example: 'To *busy professionals who need to stay organised*, Palm Pilot is *an electronic organiser* that *allows you to back up files on your PC more easily and reliably than competitive products*.' Sometimes the positioning statement is more detailed:

> *Red Bull*: To young, active soft drink consumers who have little time for sleep, Red Bull is the soft drink that gives you more energy and allows you to push the margins further.

Red Bull

Note that the positioning first states the product's membership in a category (Red Bull is a soft drink) and then shows its point-of-difference from other members of the group (it has more caffeine). The product's membership in the category suggests the points-of-parity that it might have with other products in the category, but the case for the product rests on its points-of-difference. Sometimes the marketer will put the product in a surprisingly different category before indicating the points of difference.

_____

Sources: Red Bull, www.redbull.co.uk; www.cmwinteractive.com/freewheel/RedBull-Consumer/Brochure.pdf; P. Bee (2001) So how safe are these energy drinks?, *Daily Mail*, 17 July; J. Cassey (2001) Enragingly ubiquitous, *Guardian*, 26 June.

process to lock in the freshness. Saying that a brand of coffee is 'mountain grown' is irrelevant because most coffee is mountain grown. The marketing memo outlines how marketers can express positioning formally.

Creating POPs and PODs

One common difficulty in creating a strong, competitive brand positioning is that many of the attributes and benefits that make up the points-of-parity and points-of-difference are negatively correlated. For example, it might be difficult to position a brand as 'inexpensive' and at the same time assert that it is 'of the highest quality'. Lidl, Matalan and Primark need to convince consumers that their merchandise is both cheap and of good quality. Table 10.10 displays some other examples of negatively correlated attributes and benefits. Moreover, individual attributes and benefits often have positive *and* negative aspects.

Burberry Ltd

In recent years the trademark Burberry plaid has become one of the world's most recognisable symbols. From its staid place on Burberry raincoats, the plaid began showing up on dog collars, taffeta dresses and bikinis, on gear worn by British soccer hooligans and, unfortunately, on an increasing number of counterfeit goods. This integral part of Burberry's heritage, called 'the check' by those in the fashion industry, had suddenly become a liability due to overexposure. Consequently, Burberry's sales became sluggish and its CEO, Angela Ahrendt, sought to jump-start sales growth in numerous ways. For one, she has studied Burberry's 150-year history to create new brand symbols, such as an equestrian-knight logo that was trademarked by the company in 1901. Handbags will allude to the brand's tradition as a trench coat maker by featuring leather belt buckles or the quilt pattern that lined Burberry's outerwear. The other tactic Ms Ahrendt is pushing is to invest aggressively in selling Burberry accessories – handbags, shoes, scarves and belts – rather than apparel, which now accounts for 75 per cent of the company's sales. Not only do these accessories have higher profit margins, but they are also less exposed than clothing to changes in fashion.[51]

Table 10.10 Examples of negatively correlated attributes and benefits

Low price vs high quality	Powerful vs safe
Taste vs low calories	Strong vs refined
Nutritious vs good tasting	Ubiquitous vs exclusive
Efficacious vs mild	Varied vs simple

For example, consider a long-lived brand such as Nestlé's KitKat chocolate biscuit finger bar. The brand's heritage could suggest experience, wisdom and expertise. On the other hand, it could also imply being old-fashioned and not up to date.[52]

Unfortunately, consumers typically want to maximise *both* the negatively correlated attributes and benefits. Much of the art and science of marketing is dealing with trade-offs, and positioning is no different. The best approach is clearly to develop a product or service that performs well on both dimensions. BMW was able to establish its 'luxury and performance' straddle positioning due in large part to automotive design, and the fact that the car was in fact seen as both luxurious and high performance. Gore-Tex was able to overcome the seemingly conflicting image of 'breathable' and 'waterproof' through technological advances.

Some marketers have adopted other approaches to address attribute or benefit trade-offs: launching two different marketing campaigns, each one devoted to a different brand attribute or benefit; linking themselves to any kind of entity (person, place or thing) that possesses the right kind of equity as a means to establish an attribute or benefit as a POP or POD; and even attempting to convince consumers that the negative relationship between attributes and benefits, if they consider it differently, is in fact positive.

Perceptual or positioning mapping

Perceptual or positioning mapping is a marketing tool that enables marketers to plot the position of their offering (product or service – but in buyers' markets it is best to see these as customer-perceived *value* offers (see Chapter 11) against those of the competition.

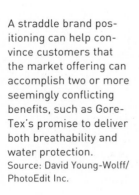

A straddle brand positioning can help convince customers that the market offering can accomplish two or more seemingly conflicting benefits, such as Gore-Tex's promise to deliver both breathability and water protection.
Source: David Young-Wolff/ PhotoEdit Inc.

What can positioning analysis do for a company's business?

To position market offerings/products/services in increasingly crowded markets, companies must understand the dimensions along which target customers perceive products in a category and how they view the firm's offer relative to competitive offers. To understand the competitive structure of their markets, firms need to ask these questions:

- How do customers (current or potential) view their brand?
- Which competitive brands do customers perceive to be their closest competitors?
- What market offering and company attributes are most responsible for these perceived differences?

Once marketers have answers to these questions, they can assess how well or poorly their market offerings are positioned in the market. They can then identify the critical elements of a positioning plan to differentiate their offerings from competitive ones: are the brands in the market strongly or weakly differentiated? Which brand has the central position? What should be done to enable the company's target customer segments to perceive their brand offering as being significantly and positively different? Based on customer perceptions, which target segments are most attractive? How should the firm position new product/service market offerings (see Chapter 13) with respect to the company's existing portfolio? What brand name (the company's or a competitor's) is most closely associated with attributes that the target segment perceives to be desirable?

Positioning maps

When a perceptual or positioning map is plotted, two dimensions are commonly used. Figure 10.7 presents a very basic perceptual map of the UK chocolate block sector market.

The Belgian and Swiss and the UK's Green & Black brands are revealed as high quality and high price. Cadbury's Dairy Milk, Mars' Galaxy and Nestlé's Yorkie are relatively low-quality and relatively high-price brands. Superior-quality chocolate blocks are available from leading supermarket own brands and Fair Trade marked brands. It is clear that the leading mass brands in the United Kingdom need to launch chocolate bars with an improved quality specification as they are becoming increasingly likely to lose market share to the supermarket own brands and branded Fair Trade offerings.

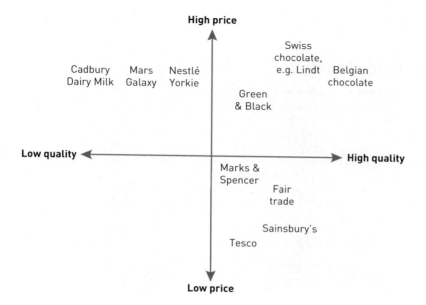

Figure 10.7 Example positioning map of the UK chocolate block sector market
Source: M. R. V. Goodman, Durham University.

Developing a positioning strategy

A company's positioning strategy depends on the existing strength or weakness of their brand and their competitive intent. If the market is undersupplied – a sellers' market – then the volume competitors may be content to pursue the same positioning strategy. In buyers' markets it makes more sense to seek to differentiate their brands positively in the fastest-growing market segments. Ultimately, positioning is about how they want consumers to perceive their market offerings and what strategies they select to achieve this goal.

Repositioning

Today's markets are highly competitive and volatile, so companies need to be prepared to make both proactive and reactive positioning decisions as market conditions dictate. Repositioning can become necessary for the following reasons:

- A competitor launches a market offering that is as good as or better than the existing company's brand: for example, supermarkets now sell new chocolate bar products with superior specifications. Honda and Toyota have a well-earned reputation for continually updating their vehicles by such market-perceived value attributes as design, decor, performance and technological innovation.
- There is a marked consumer change in preference: for example, for quality beers or for better-quality overseas package holidays.
- New market categories appear: for example, the market for energy drinks caused Lucozade marketers to reposition the brand from a drink for people recovering from illness to a high-energy sports drink for young people.
- An initial launch error: for example, EuroDisney miscalculated the number of frugal visitors to the park and made several cultural errors such as not originally serving alcohol in the park or providing appropriate menus in the restaurants.
- There is a need to change the perception of the firm in the eyes of existing and potential customers. Tesco is continuously using integrated marketing communications to emphasise that it is not a low-price retailer. Interestingly enough, it was advised to drop the brand name of Tesco, as it had become too closely associated with low quality and low price, and to replace it with another to boost its strategy of taking the stores up-market. The senior executive refused and achieved a noteworthy success as Tesco now enjoys a better 'quality' image.

Skoda comes of age

Skoda was founded in what is now the Czech Republic in 1895 and started to produce cars in 1905 and trucks in 1924. It was bought by the Volkswagen Group in 1991 after the collapse of the Soviet Union. After being perceived as an unattractive, downmarket marque, Skoda has been steadily repositioning itself in the car market as more of a value brand. Many now regard its vehicles as offering superior market-perceived value than those of its parent company. It is one of the Czech Republic's biggest employers, having more than 27,000 workers in its three factories. Skoda's own production, which includes some output from a factory in China, is set to exceed 640,000 vehicles this year. In 1994 the Czech company, which is more than 100 years old, produced only 173,000 vehicles. The car maker believes it can make one million cars in the foreseeable future. Skoda celebrated its best ever year in 2010. For the first time, total sales are above three-quarters of a million units: 762,600 vehicles were sold and market shares in important markets increased.[53]

See also: www.autoexpress.co.uk/news/autoexpressnews/264577/skoda_to_show_new_design_concept.html#ixzz1F5VrqLVz.

A major repositioning exercise can be an expensive and risky operation, and success cannot be guaranteed. If a company feels the need to change the perceptions of its existing target market, it has to find a way to change entrenched attitudes and views, and this normally requires an immense investment in an integrated marketing communications initiative. It is easier to reposition by seeking to appeal to a different market category, as Lucozade did successfully until Red Bull intensified the competition in the energy drinks category. Overall repositioning is a complex marketing operation but may be the only way to rescue a brand that has faded badly. It may be better in the long run to abandon it and replace it with another which is in tune with the new positioning strategy. This seems to have been the conclusion of Accenture as it appears to be getting ready to commit to the history books long-standing brands that it has acquired which have grown tired, such as Norwich Union.

Developing and communicating a differentiation strategy

Cost leadership

Firms can gain a positive advantage in markets by developing and sustaining cost/efficiency gains. This cost-based approach can prove to be a winning strategy provided that a company offers an acceptable substitute to competitive offers from a reduced cost base. This gives a company the opportunity to benefit from offering a lower price; to offer the same price as its competitors or to improve market-perceived quality by offering additional market-perceived quality attributes for the ruling competitive price. The achievement of cost gains from operating scale economies, experience curve advantages, tight overhead controls and expenditure on R & D, production and marketing costs is a compound strategy practised skilfully by mass-producing firms such as Philips, Siemens and Swatch.

Swatch

Swatch overcomes crisis and leads to the survival of the Swiss watch industry

In the mid-1970s the Swiss watch industry was in the midst of its worst crisis ever. Technologically speaking, the Japanese competition had been outclassed in 1979 with the launch of the 'Delirium', the world's thinnest wristwatch with a limited number of components. But the event that marked the upturn in the industry's fortunes was the founding of SMH, the Swiss Corporation for Microelectronics and Watch Making Industries. And its answer to the crisis was Swatch – a slim plastic watch with only 51 components (instead of the usual 91 parts or more) that combined top quality with a highly affordable price. It first went on sale in 1983. Since then it has gone on to become the most successful wristwatch of all time, and The Swatch Group, the parent company, is the largest and most dynamic watch company in the world.

For many years, new developments have been taking place alongside the standard Swatch watch in plastic – from Irony (the metal Swatch) to the Swatch SKIN Chrono (the world's thinnest chronograph) to Swatch Snowpass (a watch with a built-in access control function that can be used as a ski pass at many ski resorts throughout the world), and Swatch Beat (featuring the revolutionary Internet Time). Outstanding technical capabilities and advances in the fields of science and technology had already been proven by Swatch during its role as the official timekeeper in several Olympic Games and Ski and Snowboard World Cup competitions.

Source: www.swatch.com.

An example of a smaller company successfully focusing on a special market to gain economies of scale is provided by Portugal's Corticeira Amorim, which controls around one-third of the country's cork manufacturing (see www.amorim.pt/mapa_site.php and www.amorimcork.com).

To achieve maximum benefit from this strategy, firms need to generate high market shares to enable them to maximise the benefits of low raw material, labour and overhead costs. The ability to realise high sales volumes at relative high market prices is of crucial importance. If market prices are squeezed downwards by fierce competition, then this strategy can backfire and leave firms with large stocks of unsold market offerings. Ford and General Motors provide examples of two firms that attracted plaudits over the years for cost efficiency, but which came close to bankruptcy as they failed to generate and hold a sufficiently high market share in their target markets.

Distinctive superior quality

Companies can also seek a competitive advantage from successfully creating a strong market-perceived value for their market offerings. Such companies are providing the market with the right quality attributes (performance, reliability, design, novelty, etc.) and the right transactional attributes (price, payment options). Thus a positive registration is made with prospective buyers as the companies meet and more than meet their purchase expectations and so bring about an enjoyable purchasing experience. This allows companies to command higher prices and therefore higher margins than they could achieve wholly by cost reduction activities.[54] Bang & Olufsen and Montblanc are differentiated on the basis of superior design; Duracell on superior durability; and Miele and Liebherr on superior reliability.

Montblanc

The German company Montblanc has been known for generations as a maker of sophisticated, high-quality writing instruments. In the past few years, the product range has been expanded to include exquisite writing accessories, luxury leather goods and belts, jewellery, eyewear and watches. Montblanc has thus become a purveyor of exclusive products that reflect the exacting demands made today for quality design, tradition and master craftsmanship. Montblanc is a truly international brand with operations in more than 70 countries. Montblanc sells its products exclusively through its international network of authorised retailers, jewellers and over 360 Montblanc boutiques worldwide.

Source: www.montblanc.com

Cost leadership and differentiation

The third option is to combine both cost reduction and quality advantages. Fulmer and Goodwin have shown that these strategies are not mutually exclusive, as have Buzzell and Gale.[55] Positive differentiation can be achieved by firms that are determined to offer high levels of market-perceived value (market-perceived quality relative to market-perceived price).

Differentiation strategies

To avoid the commodity trap, marketers must start with the belief that you can differentiate anything (see the marketing memo).

Marketing memo

How to derive fresh consumer insights to differentiate products and services

In 'Discovering new points of differentiation', MacMillan and McGrath argue that if companies examine customers' entire experience with a product or service – the consumption chain – they can uncover opportunities to position their offerings in ways that neither they nor their competitors thought possible. MacMillan and McGrath list a set of questions that marketers can use to help them identify new, consumer-based points of differentiation:

- How do people become aware of their need for your product and service?
- How do consumers find your offering?
- How do consumers make their final selection?
- How do consumers order and purchase your product or service?

- What happens when your product or service is delivered?
- How is your product installed?
- How is your product or service paid for?
- How is your product stored?
- How is your product moved around?
- What is the consumer really using your product for?
- What do consumers need help with when they use your product?
- What about returns or exchanges?
- How is your product repaired or serviced?
- What happens when your product is disposed of or no longer used?

Source: I. C. MacMillan and R. G. McGrath (1997) Discovering new points of differentiation, *Harvard Business Review*, July–August, 133–45.

Competitive advantage is a company's ability to perform in one or more ways that competitors cannot or will not match. Porter urged companies to build a sustainable competitive advantage.[56] But few competitive advantages are sustainable. At best, they may be leverageable. A *leverageable advantage* is one that a company can use as a springboard to new advantages, much as Microsoft has leveraged its operating system to Microsoft Office and then to networking applications. In general, a company that hopes to endure must be in the business of continuously inventing new advantages. According to the American Boston Consultancy Group, in considering differentiation it is important to include all of the conditions of the sale, as well as the tangible product itself. Service, reliability of vendor and delivery times are likely to be as important as inherent tangible characteristics. There are often highly differentiated suppliers in markets for commodity products.

Customers must see any competitive advantage as a *customer advantage*. For example, if a company delivers faster than its competitors, it will not be a customer advantage if customers don't value speed. The Stressless company (www.stressless.com) emphasises that its range of recliner chairs marketed in Europe allows consumers to find just the right comfort position for their body shape. Companies must also focus on building customer advantages.[57] Then they will deliver high customer-perceived value and satisfaction, which leads to high repeat purchases and ultimately to high company profitability. For example, German brewers make much of the purity of their beers, which has resulted from the quality dictated by the historical German beer laws.

Marketers can differentiate brands on the basis of many variables. The obvious means of differentiation, and often the most compelling ones to consumers, relate to the attributes and benefits of the product and service market offerings (reviewed in Chapters 12 and 13). Swatch offers colourful, fashionable watches. Subway differentiates itself in terms of healthy sandwiches as an alternative to fast food. In competitive markets, however, firms may need to go further. Consider these other dimensions, among the many that a company can use to differentiate its market offerings:

- **Personnel differentiation**. Companies can have better-trained employees. Singapore Airlines is well regarded in large part because of its flight attendants. The sales forces of such companies as BMW, Bose, Cisco,[58] de Beers and Shell enjoy an excellent reputation.
- **Channel differentiation**. Companies can more effectively and efficiently design their distribution channels' coverage, expertise and performance. The leading European supermarkets such as Carrefour and Tesco have developed highly effective and highly efficient distribution strategies.
- **Image differentiation**. Designer jewellery (Cartier). Even a seller's physical space, such as international airports' shopping malls and departure lounge shops, can be powerful image generators.

The purpose of positioning

Professional positioning is of benefit to a supplier as it enables a company to invest its resources and skills in the right marketplace. As such, it is both an *effective* and an *efficient* strategy. The right market offering is being placed on the market and professional know-how is applied to achieving this cost effectively. As Figure 10.8 shows, this is also an activity that results in advantages for customers as market offerings are *effective* in satisfying their requirements in dynamic market conditions when they have a choice of suppliers. Additionally, they enjoy an *efficient* buying experience in the marketplace as they select the branded purchase that they perceive as representing the best value.

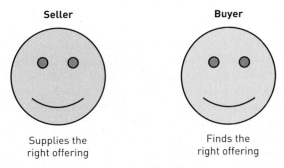

Figure 10.8 Two satisfied and happy people – perfect positioning

SUMMARY

1 Target marketing includes three activities: market segmentation, market targeting and market positioning.

2 Markets can be targeted at four levels: segments, niches, local areas and individuals. Market segments are large, identifiable groups within a market. A niche is a more narrowly defined group. Globalisation and the internet have made niche marketing more feasible to many. Marketers appeal to local markets through grassroots marketing for trading areas, neighbourhoods and even individual stores.

3 More companies now practise individual and mass customisation. The future is likely to see more self-marketing, a form of marketing in which individual consumers take the initiative in designing market offerings and brands.

4 There are two bases for segmenting consumer markets: consumer characteristics and consumer responses. The major segmentation variables for consumer markets are geographic, demographic, psychographic and behavioural. Marketers use them singly or in combination.

5 Business marketers use all these variables along with operating variables, purchasing approaches and situational factors.

6 To be useful, market segments must be measurable, substantial, accessible, differentiable and actionable.

7 A firm has to evaluate the various segments and decide how many and which ones to target: a single segment, several segments, a specific product, a specific market or the full market. If it serves the full market, it must choose between differentiated and undifferentiated marketing. Firms must also monitor segment relationships, and seek economies of scope and the potential for marketing to super segments.

8 Marketers must develop segment-by-segment invasion plans and choose target markets in a socially responsible manner at all times.

9 Deciding on positioning requires the determination of a frame of reference – by identifying the target market and the nature of the competition – and the ideal points-of-parity and points-of-difference brand associations. To determine the proper competitive frame of reference, one must understand consumer behaviour and the considerations that consumers use in making brand choices.

10 Points-of-difference are those attribute and benefit associations unique to the brand that are also strongly held and favourably evaluated by consumers. Points-of-parity are those associations not necessarily unique to the brand but perhaps shared with other brands. Category point-of-parity associations are associations that consumers view as being necessary to a legitimate and credible product offering within a certain category. Competitive point-of-parity associations are those associations designed to negate competitors' points-of-difference.

11 The key to competitive advantage is relevant brand differentiation – consumers must find something unique and meaningful about a market offering. These differences may be based directly on the market offering itself or on other considerations related to factors such as personnel, channels or image.

12 As business conditions change and competitive activity varies, companies may need to reposition some or all of their brands in today's business world.

APPLICATIONS

Marketing debate

Is mass marketing dead? With marketers increasingly adopting more and more refined market segmentation schemes – fuelled by the Internet and other customisation efforts – some critics claim that mass marketing is dead. Others counter that there will always be room for large brands which employ marketing programmes targeting the mass market.

Take a position: Mass marketing is dead *versus* Mass marketing is still a viable way to build a profitable brand.

Marketing discussion

Descriptive versus behavioural market segmentation schemes Think of your need to purchase toothpaste. How would you classify yourself in terms of the various segmentation schemes? How would marketing be more or less effective for you depending on the segment involved? How would you contrast demographic versus behavioural segment schemes? Which ones do you think would be most effective for marketers trying to sell toothpaste to you?

REFERENCES

[1]D. Walker (2004) Live fast, die old, *BBC News Online Magazine*, 16 September (http://news.bbc.co.uk/1/hi/magazine/3659996.stm); J. Ogg (2008) The baby-boomer generation and family support – a European perspective, paper delivered at 33rd Global Conference of ICSW, Tours, France, 30 June.

[2]D. Cowley (2004) Boomers turned off by attempts to make them belong to a group, *Financial Times*, 26 January; J. Ogg (2006) European baby boomer generation – working paper during the ESRC Social Science Week, March; R. Jennings (2009) Interacting via social media isn't the preserve of the young, *New Media Age*, 9 April, 7.

[3]J. C. Anderson and J. A. Narus (1995) Capturing the value of supplementary service, *Harvard Business Review*, January–February, 75–83.

[4]T. Dalgic and M. Leeuw (1994) Niche marketing revisited: concept, applications, and some European cases, *European Journal of Marketing*, 28(4), 39–55; K. Toften and T. Hammervoll (2009) Niche firms and marketing strategy, *European Journal of Marketing*, 43(11/12), 1378–91.

[5]J. Casteleyn, A. Mottart and K. Rutten (2009) How to use Facebook in your market research, *International Journal of Market Research*, 51(4), 439–47.

[6]H. H. Friedman, T. Lopes-Pumarejo and L. W. Friedman (2007) A new kind of marketing: creating micro niches using resonance marketing, *Journal of Internet Commerce*, 6(1), 83–99.

[7]D. Peppers and M. Rogers (2001) One to one B2B, in *Customer Development Strategies for the Business-to-Business World*, New York: Doubleday; M. Rechtin (2005) Aston Martin woos customers one by one, *Automotive News*, 28 March; D. Klabjan and J. Pei (2010) In-store one-to-one marketing, *Journal of Retailing and Consumer Services*, January, 18(1), 64–73; R. Tomei (2010) Doing one-to-one marketing better, *Brandweek*, 51(44), 26.

[8]J. Wind and A. Rangaswamy (1999) Customerization: the second revolution in mass customerization, Wharton School Working Paper, June.

[9]Anderson and Narus (1995) op. cit.

[10]See www.sanfordb2b.co.uk/Customirisation.aspx.

[11]B. Cosgrave (2007) Sneakers for all occasions, *Financial Times*, 9 November.

[12]P. Marsh (2002) Mass customization: make everyone different, *Financial Times*, 21 May; A. Valenzuela, R. Dhar and F. Zettelmeyer (2009) Contingent response to self-customization procedures: implications for decision satisfaction and choice, *Journal of Marketing Research* (JMR), 46(6), 754–63; R. I. McIntosh, J. Matthews, G. Mullineux, and A. J. Medland (2010) Late customisation: issues of mass customisation in the food industry, *International Journal of Production Research*, 48(6), 1557–74; A. Merle (2010) Understanding and managing a mass-customization programme, *Decisions Marketing*, 59 (July–September), 39–48.

[13]R. Winger and D. Edelman (1989) *Segment-of-One Marketing*, Boston MA: Boston Consulting Group (available at: www.bcg.com/publications).

[14]P. Doyle and P. Stern (2006) *Marketing Management and Strategy*, 4th edn, Harlow: Prentice Hall, 418: I. Simonson (2005) Determinants of customer responses to customized offer: conceptual framework and research proposition, *Journal of Marketing*, 69 (January), 32–45; S. Akbar, A. P. M. Som, F. Wadood and N. J. Alzaidiyeen (2010) Revitalization of service quality to gain customer satisfaction and loyalty, *International Journal of Business and Management*, 5(6), 113–22; L. Alrubaiee and N. Al-Nazer (2010) Investigate the impact of relationship marketing orientation on customer loyalty: the customer's perspective. *International Journal of Marketing Studies*, 2(1), 155–74.

[15]P. Sleight (2004) *Targeting Customers: How to Use Geodemographics: Lifestyle Data in Your Business*, 3rd edn, Henley-on-Thames: World Advertising Research Centre.

[16]M. J. Weiss (2000) *The Clustered World*, Boston: Little, Brown & Co.; A. Weinstein (2004) *Handbook of Market Segmentation: Strategic Targeting for Business and Technology Firms*, 3rd edn, Binghampton, NY: Haworth Press.

[17]For a consumer behaviour perspective on gender, see J. Meyers-Levy and D. Maheswaran (1991) Exploring males and females' processing strategies: when and why do differences occur in consumers' processing of ad claims?, *Journal of Consumer Research*, 18 (June), 63–70; J. Meyers-Levy and B. Sternthal (1991) Gender differences in the use of message cues and judgments, *Journal of Marketing Research*, 28 (February), 84–96; R. J. Fisher and L. Dube (2005) Gender differences in responses to emotional advertising: a social desirability perspective, *Journal of Consumer Research*, 31 (March), 850–8; J. Cunningham and P. Roberts (2006) What women want, *Brand Strategy*, December–January, 40–1.

[18]Dove: 'celebrating curves', WARC Case Study, 2005, Henley-on-Thames: World Advertising Centre; E. Wong (2009) P&G, Dial, Unilever target the middle man, *Brandweek*, 50(20), 8; K. Bisseil and A. Rask (2010) Real women on real beauty: self-discrepancy, internalisation of the thin ideal, and perceptions of attractiveness and thinness in Dove's Campaign for Real Beauty. *International Journal of Advertising*, 29(4), 643–68.

[19]T. Lowry (2003) Young man, your couch is calling, *BusinessWeek*, 28 July, 68–9; M. Costa (2010) What men want from a brand relationship, *Marketing Week*, 33(38), 16–20.

[20]D. Klingensmith (2006) Marketing gurus try to read women's minds, *Chicago Tribune*, 19 April; H. Greimel (2010) Nissan: female touch can boost quality, sales, *Automotive News*, 18 January 84(6395), 25.

[21]M. Barletta (2006) Who's really buying that car? Ask her, *Brandweek*, 4 September, 20; R. Craven, K. Maurey and J. Davis (2006) What women really want, *Critical Eye*, 15, 50–3; D. Burrows, Tic Tac targets women with £4m spearmint campaign, *Marketing Week*, 32(38), 6.

[22]C. Van Hoffman (2006) For some marketers, low income is hot, *Brandweek*, 11 September, 6; see Aldi: discounter looks set to challenge major players with new European fuel retailing venture, *Datamonitor, MarketWatch: Energy* (2009) August, 8(8), 8–9; see www.tkmaxx.com/; www.matalan.co.uk; www.primark.co.uk/.

[23]G. L. White and S. Leung (2002) Middle market shrinks as Americans migrate toward the higher end, *Wall Street Journal*, 29 March, A1, A8.

[24]L. Tischler (2003) The price is right, *Fast Company*, November, 83–91.

[25]A. Frean (2007) Not just shopping: insights into the new consumer, *ESCR Society Today*, 21 September (www.escr.ac.uk/ESCRInfoCentre).

[26]K. Kress, N. Ozawa and G. Schmid (2000) The new consumer emerges, *Strategy and Leadership*, 28(5), 4–11; R. Atkinson (2006)

Too much choice is confusing customers, *Mortgage Strategy*, 27 November, 14.

[27]C. Noxon (2006) Toyification nation, *Brandweek*, 9 October; R. O'Connor (2006) Adulthood; are we there yet? – if you're still watching cartoons or playing kickball, then you, kiddo, just might be a 'rejuvenile', *Chicago Tribune*, 6 August, 1.

[28]See www.sric-bi.com.

[29]M. Schoenwald (2001) Psychographic segmentation: used or abused?, *Brandweek*, 22 January, 34–8; J. Barry and A. Weinstein (2009) Business psychographics revisited: from segmentation theory to successful marketing practice, *Journal of Marketing Management*, 25(3/4), 315–40; D. Kovačić, M. Cerjak, J. Markovina and R. Črep (2010) Psychographic segmentation of the Zagreb apple market, *Journal of Food Products Marketing*, 16(3), 293–308.

[30]P. Danziger (2004) Getting more for V-Day, *Brandweek*, 9 February, 19; S. Rahman (2008) Playing Cupid, *Checkout*, 34(1), 52–3.

[31]This classification was adapted from G. H. Brown (1953) Brand loyalty: fact or fiction?, *Advertising Age*, June 1952–January 1953; see also P. E. Rossi, R. McCulloch and G. Allenby (1996) The value of purchase history data in target marketing, *Marketing Science*, 15(4), 321–40; C. Koçaş and J. D. Bohlmann (2008) Segmented switchers and retailer pricing strategies, *Journal of Marketing*, 72(3), 124–42; S. Doherty and R. Nelson (2008) Customer loyalty to food retailers in Northern Ireland: 'devoted loyals' or 'promiscuous switchers'?, *International Journal of Consumer Studies*, 32(4), 349–55.

[32]C. Walker (1995) How strong is your brand?, *Marketing Tools*, January/February, 46–53.

[33]See www.conversionmodel.com.

[34]D. T. Yankelovich and D. Meer (2006) Rediscovering market segmentation, *Harvard Business* Review, February.

[35]For a review of many of the methodological issues in developing segmentation schemes, see W. R. Dillon and S. Mukherjee (2006) A guide to the design and execution of segmentation studies, in R. Grover and M. Vriens (eds), *Handbook of Marketing Research*, Thousand Oaks, CA: Sage; M. Wedel and W. A. Kamakura (1997) *Market Segmentation: Conceptual and Methodological Foundations*, Boston: Kluwe; L. Quinn and S. Dibb, Evaluating market-segmentation research priorities: targeting re-emancipation (2010) *Journal of Marketing Management*, 26(13/14), 1239–55.

[36]W. R. Smith (1956) Product differentiation and market segmentation as alternative marketing strategies, *Journal of Marketing*, 4 July; A. Hampp (2010) Avatar soars on fat ad spending, mass marketing, *Advertising Age*, 81(1), 1–2.

[37]See www.esteelauder.com.

[38]B. Macchietta and R. Abhijit (1994) Sensitive groups and social issues, *Journal of Consumer Marketing*, 11(4), 55–64; J. Angel and D. McCabe (2009) The business ethics of short selling and naked short selling, *Journal of Business* Ethics, 85(1), 239–49.

[39]F. Lawrence (2004) Revealed: how food firms target children, *Guardian*, 27 May; A. Bakir and S. Vitell (2010) The ethics of food advertising targeted toward children: parental viewpoint, *Journal of Business Ethics*, 91(2), 299–311; R. Mules (2010), The ethics of marketing sports drinks to a youth market, *Busidate*, 18(3), 2–5.

[40]O. B. Gonzalez and J-B. Gonzalez (2005) The role of geodemographic segmentation in retail location strategy, *International*

Journal of Market Research, 47(3), 295–316; see also www.colgate.com/app/Kids-World/US/HomePage.cvsp.

[41]F. Lawrence (2003) How much chocolate do you need to eat to get a free netball from Cadbury? *Guardian*, 29 April, www.guardian.co.uk/news/2003/apr/29/uknews; C. Murphy and E. Rogers (2003) Cadbury to scrap Get Active tokens after media criticism, *Campaign*, 3 December.

[42]PPR Group is an official trading name of a French Luxury Group which is organised around six operating branches: Fnac, Redcats Group, Conforam, CFAO, Puma and Gucci Group.

[43]A. Ries and J. Trout (2000) *Positioning: The Battle for Your Mind*, 20th anniversary edition, New York: McGraw-Hill; see also: Evaluating the effectiveness of brand-positioning strategies from a consumer perspective, *European Journal of Marketing*, 2010, 44(11/12), 1763–86.

[44]P. Marsden (2002) Brand positioning: meme's the word, *Marketing Intelligence and Planning*, 20(5), 307–12; Y. Truong, R. McColl and P. J. Kitchen (2009) New luxury brand positioning and the emergence of Masstige brands, *Journal of Brand Management*, 16(5/6), 375–82; B. M. Samuelsen and L. E. Olsen (2010) Promising attributes and experiences, *Journal of Advertising*, 39(2), 65–77.

[45]S. Knox (2004) Positioning and branding your organisation, *Journal of Product and Brand Management*, 13(2), 1105–59; S. Jackson (2007) Market share is not enough: why strategic market positioning works, *Journal of Business Strategy*, 28(1), 18–25; E. Anana and W. Nique (2020) Perception-based analysis: an innovative approach for brand positioning assessment, *Journal of Database Marketing and Customer Strategy Management*, 17(1), 6–18.

[46]R. Wray (2009) Orange and T-Mobile merge, *Guardian*, 8 September; N. Clark (2010) EU approves Orange and T-Mobile merger, *Independent*, 2 March; R. Neate (2011) Orange–T-Mobile tie-up could be copied in Europe, *Daily Telegraph*, 16 February.

[47]K. L. Keller, B. Stenthal and A. Tybout (2002) Three questions you need to ask your brand, *Harvard Business Review*, 80 (September), 80–9; see also: Points of parity and points of difference, *Sales/Marketing Management*, 10 September 2006.

[48]T. A. Brunner and M. Wänke (2006) The reduced and enhanced impact of shared features on individual brand evaluations, *Journal of Consumer Psychology*, 16 (April), 101–11; see also R. G. Brooks, Professor Kevin Lane Keller – A pop idol not just a marketing thought leader, at: www.articlesnatch.com/Article/Professor-Kevin-Lane-Keller---A-Pop-Idol-Not-Just-A-Marketing-Thought-Leader/435394#ixzz1E8ilMrC2.

[49]P. Betts (2007) Nespresso, what else?, *Financial Times*, 13 December.

[50]K. Naughton (2001) Ford's 'perfect storm', *Newsweek*, 17 September, 48–50.

[51]C. Rohwedder (2006) Playing down the plaid, *Wall Street Journal*, 7 July, http://online.wsj.com/article_print/SB115222828906800109.HTML; T. Iezzi (2010) Burberry, *Advertising Age*, 81(41), 22.

[52]G. S. Carpenter, R. Glazer and K. Nakamoto (1994) Meaningful brands from meaningless differentiation: the dependence on irrelevant attributes, *Journal of Market Research*, 31 (August), 339–50; S. M. Broniarczyk and A. D. Gershoff (2003) The reciprocal effects of brand equity and trivial attributes, *Journal of Marketing Research*, 40 (May), 161–75; R. Mortimer (2010) Ruth Mortimer on Fairtrade KitKat, *Marketing Week*, 32(50), 12.

[53]Adapted from C. Buckley (2007) Czech labour shortage forces Skoda to recruit workers from Vietnam, *The Times*, 29 November; P. Neroth (2009) The rise of Skoda automotive, *Engineering and Technology* 4(19), 25–7.

[54]B. Sharp and J. Dawes (2001) What is differentiation and how does it work?, *Journal of Marketing Management*, 17, 739–59; see also; Mastering the fine line between exclusivity and growth, *Black Book: European Luxury Brands at the Cross Roads*, April 2009, 81–6.

[55]W. E. Fulmer and J. Goodwin (1988) Differentiation: begin with the customer, *Business Horizons*, 31(5), 55–63; R. D. Buzzell and B. T. Gale (1987) *The PIMS Principles*, New York: Free Press; A. Chernev (2007) Jack of all trades or master of one? Product differentiation and compensatory reasoning in consumer choice, *Journal of Consumer Research*, 33(4), 430–44; R. Dubey and J. Jayashree (2009) Pharmaceutical product differentiation: a strategy for strengthening product pipeline and life cycle management, *Journal of Medical Marketing*, 9(2), 104–18; V. Shankar, L. L. Berry and T. Dotzel (2009) A practical guide for combining products and services, *Harvard Business Review*, 87(November), 94–9.

[56]M. E. Porter (1980) *Competitive Strategy: Techniques for Analyzing Industries and Competitors*, New York: Free Press.

[57]P. Barwise (2004) *Simply Better: Winning and Keeping Customers by Delivering What Matters Most*, Cambridge, MA: Harvard Business School Press; T. Čater, and B. Čater, (2009) (In)tangible resources as antecedents of a company's competitive advantage and performance, *Journal for East European Management Studies*, 14(2), 186–209; M. Laeequddin and G. D. Sardana (2010) What breaks trust in supplier–customer relationship? *Management Decision*, 48(3), 353–65; A. C. Ott, (2011) Time-value economics: competing for customer time and attention, *Strategy and Leadership*, 39(1), 24–31.

[58]N. Piercy and N. Lane (2003) Transformation of the traditional sales force: imperatives for intelligence, interface and integration, *Journal of Marketing Management*, 19, 563–82; D. A. Kaplan (2009) Sails force, *Fortune International (Europe)*, 160(1), 21; A. Malshe (2010) How is marketers' credibility construed within the sales-marketing interface?, *Journal of Business Research*, 63(1), 13–19.

Chapter 11

Creating customer value, satisfaction and loyalty

IN THIS CHAPTER, WE WILL ADDRESS THE FOLLOWING QUESTIONS:

1 What are customer value, satisfaction and loyalty, and how can companies deliver them?

2 What is the lifetime value of customers and how can marketers maximise it?

3 How can companies cultivate strong customer relationships?

4 How can companies both attract and retain customers?

5 What is the experience economy and how does it relate to customers' perception of value?

Alfa rewrites its service history to gain greater customer satisfaction.
Source: © Simon Belcher/Alamy.

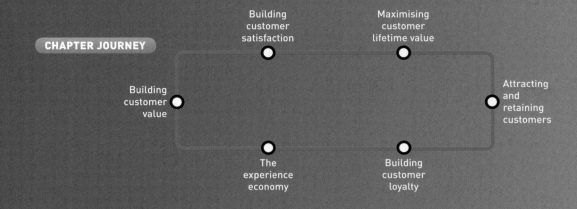

Building
customer
satisfaction

Maximising
customer
lifetime value

Building
customer
value

Attracting
and
retaining
customers

The
experience
economy

Building
customer
loyalty

Today, companies face their toughest competition ever. Moving from a product and sales, least-cost production philosophy, to a holistic marketing philosophy, however, gives them a better chance of outperforming competition (see Chapter 10). The cornerstone of a well-conceived marketing orientation is strong customer relationships. Marketers must connect with customers – informing, engaging and maybe even energising them in the process. Customer-centred companies are adept at building customer relations.

Alfa-Romeo, Fiat Auto's premium brand, delivers high-quality workmanship and distinctive styling but has been plagued by poor service for which the brand has earned notoriety. The company, under the leadership of Sergio Marchionne, Fiat's chief executive since 2004, has decided to reposition Alfa as a luxury brand. This has required paying considerable attention to improving the overall customer-perceived value of this famous marque. Customer service standards had to be improved to provide a firm basis on which customer satisfaction could be improved to build lasting customer loyalty. Since February 2007 Fiat has been working with JDPower, the consumer ratings group, to emulate the best practice of top-end marques such as BMW and Toyota's Lexus. In the United Kingdom, JDPower has presented Alfa's management with its assessment of what was wrong. Car delivery times, spare parts delivery and repair capability emerged as problems. Alfa's 'key performance indicators' were being met, but they had been incorrectly defined. For example, spare parts were deemed in service logs to be available – or even delivered – when they were still at the factory in Italy. Actual delivery and car repairs were not logged at all. Requests for parts from dealers in the United Kingdom were often being filled by other dealers or through an informal parts market. Alfa had also been notching up high warranty costs, with cars just delivered to customers being returned for minor alterations in areas such as finishing, trim and loose screws. Such problems are easily fixable but – as well as costing Alfa – they infuriated customers. Now Alfa is paying for pre-delivery inspections of cars in the UK while it works on improving production quality at factory level.[1]

As Alfa Romeo's experience shows, successful marketers are the ones that fully satisfy their customers profitably. This chapter explores the ways open to companies to win and retain customers and so secure a sustained competitive advantage. The solution lies largely in beating competition by doing a better job of meeting or exceeding customer expectations.

Building customer value

According to Schieffer, creating loyal customers is at the heart of every business.[2] Peppers and Rogers say:[3]

> **The only value your company will ever create is the value that comes from customers – the ones you have now and the ones you will have in the future. Businesses succeed by getting, keeping, and growing customers. Customers are the only reason you build factories, hire employees, schedule meetings, lay fibre-optic lines, or engage in any business activity. Without customers, you don't have a business.**

Dubois et al., Webster and others echo these views and see effective marketing as being about the identification, design and delivery of customer-perceived value.[4] Managers who believe that the customer is the company's only true 'profit centre' consider the traditional organisation chart in Figure 11.1(a) – a pyramid with the CEO at the top, management in the middle, and front-line people and customers at the bottom – obsolete.[5]

Successful marketing companies invert the chart (Figure 11.1(b)). At the top are customers; next in importance are front-line people who meet, serve and satisfy customers; under them are the middle managers, whose job is to support the front-line people so they can serve customers well; and at the base is top management, whose job is to hire and support good middle managers. Customers have been added along the sides of Figure 11.1(b) to indicate that at every level company staff must be personally involved in knowing, meeting and serving customers.

Some companies have been founded with the customer-on-top business model, and customer advocacy has been their strategy – and competitive advantage – all along. With the rise of digital technologies such as the internet, today's increasingly informed consumers expect companies to do more than connect with them, more than satisfy them, and even more than delight them. They expect companies to *listen* to them.[6]

Many companies recognise the importance of satisfying their customers in order to develop brand reputations that can deliver a sustainable competitive advantage. Such communication is particularly important in retailing, where the vast majority of staff are either on the shop floor dealing with customers, or behind the scenes in areas such as the supply/value chain, where they can feel divorced from central operations. Therefore,

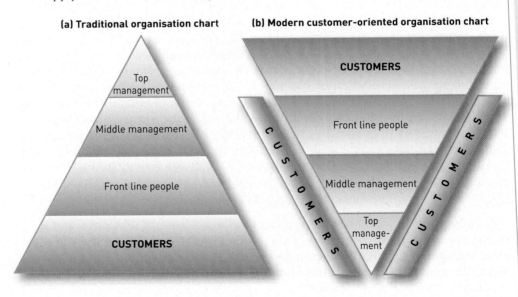

Figure 11.1 Traditional organisation versus modern customer-oriented company organisation

in order to attain this goal companies have developed a commitment to listening to their employees. ASDA, the UK supermarket chain owned by Wal-Mart (see Chapter 3), has become renowned for listening to its staff. According to David Smith, ASDA's director for people, the success enjoyed by the group in repeatedly winning employment plaudits has been hard won. ASDA guards its reputation fiercely – evolving its methods to keep staff happy: 'You have to keep changing. This success that we have around people has not occurred overnight. We have been working on this for ten years,' Smith comments. He believes that ASDA's success with people comes down to a set of 'very simple mechanics' and has little time for companies with grandiose mission statements that fail to live up to their words. The key to ASDA's success is communication. IT involves not only filtering down the right messages from the top of the organisation, but also ensuring that feedback from the stores' staff is treated seriously and communicated back to the top.

It is also vitally important to listen to customers, and many companies are not as effective in this regard as they could be. A well-known UK BBC TV presenter, Jeremy Paxman, complaining about the declining quality of Marks & Spencer's underwear, criticised the company for not effectively listening to its customers. A correspondent to the *Financial Times* also complained about the arrogance and lack of customer service shown by the company to its loyal customer base. His question to Marks & Spencer was: how do you know what your customers feel about your products? It is commonly recognised within businesses that 95 per cent of UK customers with a perceived or genuine complaint will never voice it. If Marks & Spencer does not speak to its customers, it will not know whether or not they are happy with the company's products and service standards.

Following a disappointing set of financial results, DSG International, the UK group that owns consumer electronics and white goods stores such as Curry's and PC World, appointed a new chief executive. The new incumbent told the UK press that he would spend his first few weeks walking the shop floor, listening to customers and staff, rather than adjusting strategy from his desk. 'Value, choice and service' was his mantra.[7]

In today's buyers' markets (see Chapter 10) customers can exercise considerable choice of supplier when they visit the marketplace. Listening to customers makes sense if a firm wishes to be both *effective* (produce what the customer wants) and *efficient* (do this cost efficiently). As the new chief executive at DSG International indicates, 'value, choice and service' are of prime importance. The concept of customer-perceived value (CPV) enables marketers to discover what customers want through the medium of market research.

Customer-perceived value (CPV) is the difference between the prospective customer's evaluation of all the benefits and all the costs of a company's offering and the perceived alternatives. **Total customer benefit** is the perceived monetary value of the bundle of economic, functional and psychological benefits that customers expect from a given market offering because of the products, services, personnel and image involved. **Total customer cost** is the perceived bundle of costs that customers expect to incur in evaluating, obtaining, using and disposing of the given market offering, including monetary, time, energy and psychological costs.

The findings from this activity can be expressed as a customer-perceived value offering that will have both perceived quality and attractive financial attributes. Once they are expressed as a specification, it is the task of firms to translate the *attributes* (components) of such an offering to a value package (consisting of both tangible and intangible attributes) that can be traded in the marketplace. The question is: how? Traditionally, many businesses have assumed that the answer lies in the application of the 4P marketing mix as the primary means of achieving a successful market offering.

As markets become more and more competitive, firms need to pay closer attention to supplying the right market offerings – which have the appropriate customer-perceived value rating. The pursuit of suitable CPV offerings calls into question the established status of the 4P marketing mix, as being an approach of primary importance in many of today's

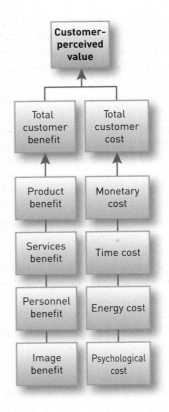

Figure 11.2 Determinants of customer-perceived value

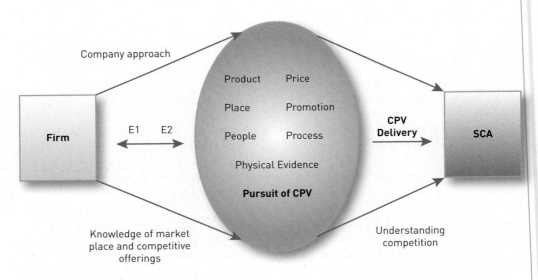

Figure 11.3 The pursuit of customer-perceived value
Source: M. R. V. Goodman, Durham University.

markets. A more useful, practical insight can be gained from consideration of the steps illustrated in Figure 11.3 and discussed below.

Practical, as opposed to many theoretical, marketers begin with a realistic appraisal of their firm's characteristic approach to business. Is this essentially a product/finance-oriented company or a market-oriented company? Many seem to view these positions as being mutually exclusive. However, in the real world, it is best to see these approaches as opposite ends of a continuum. So firms will be at some point between €1 (efficiency/least-cost production orientation) and €2 (effectiveness/CPV market orientation). Firms determined to become truly market oriented (which entails moving closer to €2) will have accepted the need to formulate and adhere to a management of change programme that will transform their organisations. However, depending on the size and complexity of the firm, this transformation may take five to seven years to achieve and requires a consistent and steady hand on the corporate tiller.

The primary concern of firms in buyers' markets should be to face reality and seek to manage a strong and lasting positive differentiation, with the intent of gaining a sustainable competitive advantage. The next concern is to gain the latest intelligence on the marketplace to discover the relative strength of buyers' choice opportunities and to acquire up-to-date information on the relative strength of the competition. The tertiary concern is for the firm then to design, develop and present a suitable set of CPV market offerings to place on the market. This involves consistently listening to customers to deliver a CPV package that meets with customers' approval.

It is rather simplistic to believe that this can be achieved solely by the conventional 4P or 7P marketing mixes. Such CPV offerings usually consist of a mix of tangible and intangible attributes. Conventional products (*tangibles*) usually form only a part of a CPV package, which in buyers' markets normally includes many supportive *services* (*intangibles*). That is why it is more useful to view marketing as being concerned with the provision of customer-perceived value attribute circles that deliver real customer benefits, rather than solely with the traditional products or service marketing mixes.

The emphasis should be placed on the provision of a series of value attributes (see Chapter 10). This is more practically achieved by developing a deep understanding of marketplaces, customers, competition, costs, channels (distribution or place), marketing communications and the company's strategic marketing approach.

Customer-perceived value

An important consequence of the business environmental paradigm change from a sellers' to a buyers' market (see Chapter 3) has been a subtle transformation in the concept of

Value circles that make up CPV offerings can be viewed as a collection of ripple circles. Individual circles may be a tangible product value, an intangible service value or a collection of both.
Source: Serif.

value (see Chapter 10). Value is heavily influenced by buyers as they have a choice of supplier and usually demand more for their money. The concept of *customer-perceived value* has become a matter of increasing concern in the marketing literature. It is imperative for suppliers to offer buyers in competitive markets what they want if they are effectively to generate profitable business. Several empirical studies have sought to explore this in practice. Gounaris et al. researched the relationships between customer value, satisfaction and purchase intentions.[8] Their research suggested that delivering superior customer value enables a firm to achieve favourable ('buy me') behavioural intentions. In contemporary buyers' markets, the concept of CPV has become a vital concern for marketers as it stresses the importance of both the traditional product (tangible) and service (intangible) attribute and benefit components of a market offering.

How then do customers ultimately make choices? They tend to be perceived as value maximisers, within the bounds of search costs and limited knowledge, mobility and income. Customers estimate which market offering will deliver the most perceived value and act on it. A challenging task for market-oriented companies is to define, develop and deliver customer-perceived value when this is often notoriously difficult to define. In many respects, it is a matter of perception and sensitivity.

The truth about beauty creams

On 12 May 2008 a TV programme in the United Kingdom conducted an investigation into the beauty cream market with the intent of discovering whether anti-ageing creams really worked. Such market offerings promise eternal youth to women and the UK market is reputed to be worth €1 billion. As the regulating law stands at present, companies competing in this market do not have to put their creams through accredited scientific tests as they are classed as cosmetics rather than medicines. Nonetheless, they do have to be careful as to the claims they make for their preparations. In 2007 L'Oréal was required by the UK Advertising Standards Authority to withdraw an advertisement campaign that claimed to reduce wrinkles in an hour.

Five creams were selected and given to five women to try for a month. At the start of the test, each of the women was examined by a dermatologist and plastic surgeon to determine the start state of their skin. Table 11.1 summarises the branded creams that were selected for testing.

After a month the women were re-examined by the dermatologist and the plastic surgeon and the performance of the competing cream treatments was evaluated. Despite using pseudo-scientific copy in their marketing efforts ('the science bit'), no real change was observed in the state of the women's skin. While there was evidence of some slight surface improvement, there was no evidence of significant deep skin improvement. There was little to choose between the cheapest and most expensive. The experts advised that the best way to look after skin was to stay out of the sun, use a sunblock, eat healthily, see that sufficient vitamin C was in their diet and avoid anti-wrinkle creams!

Table 11.1 Anti-ageing cream test brands

Brand	Price of total package (£)
Boot's No. 7 Protect and Perfect	70
Dior Capture XP Range	252
Nivea Visage	20
L'Oréal DermGenesis	70
Olay Regenerist Range	80
Simple Protect Moisturising Cream	5

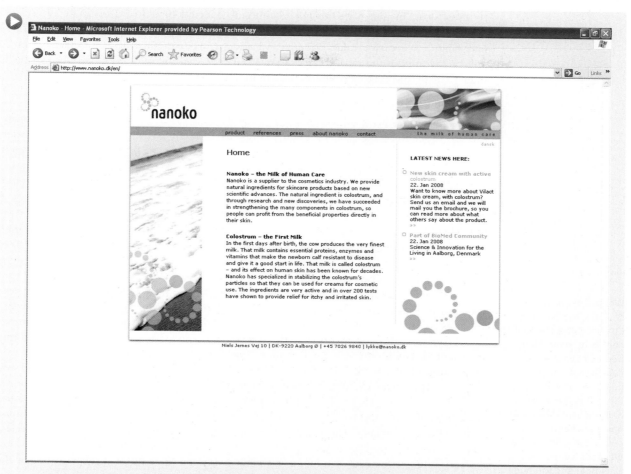

The Danish company Nanoko use cows' milk for its skin lotions.
Source: http://www.nanoko.dk/en.

So customer-perceived value, like beauty, is highly prized and many women buy anti-wrinkle creams in pursuit of a promise and are captivated by slogans such as L'Oréal's 'Because you're worth it'.

There are many skin care products on the market and manufacturers are increasingly seeking to gain a market edge by searching for new ingredients. In Denmark, Nanoko has launched a skin lotion based on milk from cows. In Norway, Bioforskning Skinscience Spermine cream is a crystal extracted from seminal fluid said to be 30 times stronger than vitamin E and able to repair sunburnt skin. Men too are now being targeted by the cosmetics companies in a market that sails close to the wind in terms of the scientifically questionable claims it makes.

Source: UK Channel 4 TV *Dispatches* programme screened on 12 May 2008; staff reporter, *Daily Telegraph*, 30 May 2008.

Whether the offer lives up to expectations affects customer satisfaction and the probability that the customer will become a repeat buyer.

Customer-perceived value (CPV) is thus based on the difference between what the customer gets and what he or she gives up for different possible choices. The customer buys attributes, receives benefits and accepts costs. The marketer can increase the perceived value of the customer offering by some combination of increasing economic, functional or emotional attributes and benefits and/or reducing one or more of the various types of cost. In line with the microeconomic concept of demand elasticity (a concept that measures how the level of customer demand changes as price changes) a customer choosing between two value offerings, V1 and V2, will examine the ratio V1:V2. Offer V1 will be favoured if the ratio is larger than 1. Offer V2 will be selected if the ratio is smaller than 1. Lastly the customer will be totally indifferent if the ratio equals 1.

Applying value concepts

Suppose a buyer for a large construction company wants to buy a backhoe low loader tractor from the UK's JCB or Japan's Komatsu. The competing salespeople carefully describe their company's respective offers. The buyer wants to use the vehicle in residential construction work. The vehicle must deliver certain levels of reliability, durability and performance, and have a good resale value. The buyer evaluates the tractors and decides that the JCB offers greater product performance benefits and also perceives differences in the accompanying services – delivery, training and maintenance – and decides that the JCB offering provides better service as well as more knowledgeable and responsive personnel. He or she gains economic, functional and psychological benefits from these four sources – product, services, personnel and image – and so perceives JCB as delivering the best customer-perceived value offering.

Does this result in a purchase of the JCB low loader tractor? Not necessarily, for the buyer also assesses and compares the total cost of transacting with JCB and Komatsu. This requires a consideration of more than money. As Adam Smith observed over two centuries ago, 'The real price of anything is the toil and trouble of acquiring it.'[9] Total customer cost includes not only the buyer's time, energy and psychological costs expended in acquisition of a JCB, but also the costs incurred by usage, maintenance, ownership and disposal. The buyer evaluates these elements together with the monetary cost to form a total customer cost. He or she then considers whether the JCB's total customer cost is too high in relation to the total customer benefits that Komatsu promises. If it is, the buyer might choose Komatsu. The buyer ultimately chooses the market offering that promises highest customer-perceived value. This is also the case with 'service industries'.[10]

Very often, managers conduct a **customer-perceived value (CPV) analysis** to reveal the company's strengths and weaknesses relative to those of its competitors. The steps in this analysis are:

1 **Identify the major attributes and benefits that customers value.** Customers are asked what attributes and performance levels they look for in choosing a product (market offering) and possible providers.

When most people think of JCBs, the Backhoe Loader is the one that comes to mind. Many people have tried to copy it, but no one has been able to better it. It is the original and the best! With that beefy bucket and arm on the back (that's the bit that's called the Backhoe) and the huge strong shovel on the front, they can do just about any job, anywhere!
Source: Richard Leeney/DK Images.

2 **Assess the quantitative importance of the different attributes and benefits.** Customers are asked to rate the importance of the different attributes and benefits. If their ratings diverge too much, the marketer should cluster them into different segments.

3 **Assess the company's and competitors' performances on the different customer values attributes against their rated importance.** Customers describe where they see the company's and competitors' performances on each attribute and benefit.

4 **Examine how customers in a specific segment rate the company's performance against a specific major competitor on an individual attribute or benefit basis.** If the one company's offer exceeds the competitor's offer on all important attributes and benefits, the company can charge a higher price (thereby earning higher profits), or it can charge the same price and gain more market share.

5 **Monitor customer values over time.** The company must periodically repeat its studies of customer-perceived values and competitors' standings as the economy, technology and features change.

Choices and implications

Some marketers might argue that the process described above is too rational. Suppose the customer chooses the Komatsu tractor. How can this choice be explained? Here are three possibilities.

1 **The company buying team (decision-making unit) might be under orders to buy at the lowest price.** The JCB salesperson's task is to convince the company's buying team that buying on price alone will result in the delivery of lower long-term profits and customer-perceived value.

2 **The buying team will leave before the company realises that the Komatsu tractor is more expensive to operate.** The purchasing team will look good in the short run; they are maximising personal benefits. The JCB's sales team's task is to convince other people in the customer company that JCB delivers greater overall customer-perceived value.

3 **The chief buyer enjoys a long-term friendship with the Komatsu salesperson.** In this case, JCB's salesperson needs to show the chief buyer that the Komatsu tractor will draw complaints from the tractor operators when they discover its high fuel cost and need for frequent repairs.

The point of these examples is clear. Buyers operate under various constraints and in competitive markets make choices that may give more weight to their personal benefit than to the company's benefit. So customer-perceived value is a useful concept and involves the following steps. First, the seller must assess the total customer benefit and total customer cost associated with each competitor's offer in order to know how his or her offer rates in the buyer's mind. Second, the seller who is at a customer-perceived value disadvantage has two alternatives: to increase total customer benefit or to decrease total customer cost.

The former calls for strengthening or augmenting the economical, functional and psychological attributes and benefits of the offering's product, services, personnel and image. The latter calls for reducing the buyer's costs by reducing the price or cost of ownership and maintenance, simplifying the ordering and delivery process, or absorbing some buyer risk, say by offering a warranty.[11]

Delivering high customer value

Consumers have varying degrees of loyalty to specific brands, stores and companies. Oliver defines **loyalty** as 'A deeply held commitment to re-buy or re-patronise a preferred product or service in the future despite situational influences and marketing efforts having the potential to cause switching behaviour.'[12] As most markets have become increasingly competitive, so it has become more difficult for companies to build brand reputations that command sustained customer loyalty. For example, many well-known brands of aspirin are finding it more and more difficult to succeed when generic or supermarket own brands are available at less than half the cost. Another example is provided by Intel, the computer chip market leader, which following its successful 'Intel Inside' promotion became increasingly challenged by rival computer chip companies such as AMD and Cyrix.

Many retailers are seeking to build lasting customer loyalty by offering loyalty card schemes (see the Tesco example in Chapter 5) of varying descriptions. Essentially what they are trying to do is to ensure that brand recognition (awareness) becomes brand preference (first choice if available) and preferably brand insistence (always first choice).

Building customer satisfaction

Customers want loyalty, not perfection

With frustration verging on despair, marketing gurus and brand managers worldwide bemoan the erosion of customer loyalty. The global loyalty power of consumer brands is not what it used to be and marketers resent it. In the dramatic phrase of an advertising agency executive, consumers today are 'brand sluts' who are most loyal to instant gratification. This 'consumer-as-slattern' attitude is a far cry from advertising grand master David Ogilvy's marketing admonition that 'The consumer isn't a moron. She's your wife.'

In reality, the declared demise of brand loyalty is completely misunderstood. A review of the past decade reveals that customers have not been cavalierly unfaithful to established brands; quite the opposite. Established brands have cheated on and betrayed their most loyal customers. They charge more and more for less and less; they chase after the youth market or the hot segment *du jour*; their 'innovations' frequently add more complexity than value; and their willingness to apologise and compensate for errors or mistakes is minimal. The more provocative marketing argument is that 'brand inertia', far more than 'brand loyalty', has kept so many customers for so many companies for so long.

Customers are neither sheep nor fools. They can sense when companies are consistently more loyal to investors, employees and regulators than to the people who buy their products and services. They behave accordingly. Customers are not being disloyal; they are being discriminating. The central marketing question confronting brand leaders, therefore, is not 'How can we radically increase customer loyalty?' but 'How can we radically increase our own loyalty to customers?'

The distinction is enormous. It is analogous to companies that say they promote a culture of 'employee loyalty' even as cutbacks and layoffs surge during economic downturns and mergers. Top management demands loyalty from below while regretfully declining to reciprocate. Yet the moral authority and value of loyalty comes from the courage to hold fast during difficult times. It is the defiant unwillingness of enterprises to be loyal to their best customers that has produced the promiscuous consumer behaviour they deplore. The real sin here is that companies, such as Alfa-Romeo and Marks & Spencer, have wilfully confused 'brand loyalty' with 'customer retention'. Just as with sullen employees, that is the perfunctory loyalty of compliance, not of pride or passion.

This challenge is not complex. Companies demonstrate loyalty to employees by investing in them, fairly compensating them, tapping their expertise and declining to throw them overboard when times get tough. Why should customers deserve any less?

This is where traditional marketing and brand advertising fail. Often it is not the brand attribute of flawless service but the act of rapidly recovering from a mistake that wins customer loyalty and repeat business. There are many examples: airline reservation clerks who waive 'change fees' for inadvertently mis-booked flights or mobile telephone operators who politely and without complaint remove rightly disputed charges from the bill. These are less acts of 'customer service' than demonstrations of loyalty to customers. 'Brand value' comes not from promises of perfection but from gracefully compensating for acknowledged weakness. The global luxury hotel chain Marriott and British Telecom have conducted customer research revealing that their most persuasive 'word-of-mouth' support comes more from individuals who have had an unpleasant problem happily resolved than from those who simply enjoyed 'good' or 'excellent' service. The willingness and ability to see a difficult situation through to success despite cost and risk is what defines loyalty. Many companies already know this and invest accordingly.

To be fair, financial pressures, increasing transparency and the multiple demands of many **corporate social responsibility** movements make it more difficult than ever for companies to balance 'customer loyalty' with 'loyalty to customers'. Consumers are far quicker to see a brand as a mask that the company hides behind.

However, this is where new technology creates new opportunities for reciprocal loyalty. Increasingly, cutting-edge companies such as Google and Apple – strong brands in their own right – create online spaces where customers can collaborate and interact around new features and technical problems. Established brands such as Procter & Gamble and the UK's BBC have used digital media to listen to customer ideas and influence new product (market offering) development. Customers know that these organisations have invested seriously in consultation and greatly value their opinions and views. In this millennium, brand value comes from investing as much in valued customers as in valuable product/service-market offerings.[13]

The **value proposition** consists of the whole cluster of tangible and intangible (product and service) attributes and benefits that the company promises to deliver; it is more than the core positioning of the offering. For example, Volvo's core positioning has been 'safety', but the buyer is promised more than just a safe car; other benefits include a long-lasting car, good service and a long warranty period. The value proposition is a statement

Comfort, safety and speed are key benefits promised in the value proposition of top quality saloons.
Source: © Goddard Automotive/Alamy

about the experience customers will gain from the company's market offering and from their relationship with the supplier. The brand must represent a promise about the total experience customers can expect. Whether the promise is kept depends on the company's ability to manage its value delivery system.[14] The **value delivery system** includes all the experiences that the customer will have on the way to obtaining and using the offering. At the heart of a good value delivery system is a set of core business processes that help to deliver distinctive consumer-perceived value to ensure that the customer has a pleasurable purchasing *experience*. Curiously, Apple does not have a phone number for its iPad and iPod queries but directs customers to a website. Many customers, however, prefer to contact a human voice. As a result some companies – for example, service and insurance businesses – are promoting the 'personal approach' in TV advertisements.

Here's a company that is a master at delivering customer-perceived value.[15]

Superquinn

Superquinn is Ireland's largest supermarket chain and its founder, Feargal Quinn, is Ireland's master marketer. A welcome message is posted at the store entrance to greet and help customers and even offers coffee, as well as providing a carry-out service to customers' cars and umbrellas in case of rain. Department managers post themselves in the aisles to interact with customers and answer questions. There is a high-quality salad bar, fresh bread baked every four hours, and indications of when produce arrived, including the farmers' pictures. Superquinn also operates a child care centre. It offers a loyalty programme that gives points for the amount purchased and for discovering anything wrong within the store, such as dented cans or bad tomatoes. A dozen other firms, including a bank and petrol station that give points for purchases at their establishments, recognise the loyalty card. Because everything is done to exceed normal customer expectations, Superquinn stores enjoy an almost cult-like following. In August 2006 Superquinn was sold to Select Retail Holdings, an Irish property-buying consortium.

Total customer satisfaction

Whether the buyer is satisfied after purchase depends on the offer's performance in relationship to the buyer's expectations, and whether the buyer interprets any deviations between the two.[16] If the performance falls short of expectations, the customer is dissatisfied. If the performance matches the expectations, the customer is satisfied.[17] If the performance exceeds expectations, the customer is highly satisfied or delighted.[18] Customer assessments of purchase experience and expectations depend on many factors, especially the type of loyalty relationship the customer has with the brand.[19]

Although the customer-centred firm seeks to create high customer satisfaction, that is not its ultimate goal. If the company increases customer satisfaction by lowering its price or increasing its customer-perceived value attributes and benefits, the result may be lower profits. The company might be able to increase its profitability by means other than increased satisfaction (for example, by improving manufacturing processes or investing more in R & D). Also, the company has many stakeholders, including employees, dealers, suppliers and stockholders. Spending more to increase customer satisfaction might divert funds from increasing the satisfaction of other 'partners'. Ultimately, the company must operate on the philosophy that it is trying to deliver a high level of customer satisfaction, subject to delivering acceptable levels of satisfaction to the other stakeholders, given its total resources.[20]

How do buyers form their expectations? Expectations result from past buying experience; friends' and associates' advice; and marketers' and competitors' information and promises. If marketers raise expectations too high, the buyer is likely to be disappointed.

However, if the company sets expectations too low, it will not attract enough buyers (although it will satisfy those who do buy).[21] Some of today's most successful companies are raising expectations and delivering performances to match. Korean automaker Kia found success in Europe by launching low-cost, high-quality cars offering six-year warranties – a strategy previously unheard of in the automotive business.

A customer's decision to be loyal or to defect is the sum of many small experiences with the company. Many companies now strive to create a sustainable 'branded customer experience' and, like KVK, place a great emphasis on securing total customer satisfaction.

KVK

KVK is the market leader in the mobile phone market in Turkey. KVK, together with the GSM operating services of Turkcell and its subsidiaries, distributes mobile telecommunication and data products for leading global brands including Nokia, Blackberry, HTC and accessories with the brand name of 'KVK Tools'. KVK also distributes SIM cards of Turkcell, the fifth fastest-growing GSM operator in the world. With 3,500 sales offices, KVK has the widest distribution network in Turkey. The company also provides full after-sales support and technical services to its customers. Customer satisfaction takes precedence over all other issues and KVK has made 'customer satisfaction first' its motto. All KVK marketing strategies are structured according to this principle. The company's mission is to provide leading and creative solutions in line with the changing needs of customers, and its vision is to be a *brand* in mobile life with high-quality products and service.

Source: www.kvk.com/AboutUsEnglish.asp

Monitoring satisfaction

Many companies are systematically measuring how well they treat their customers, identifying the factors shaping satisfaction, and making changes in their operations and marketing as a result.[22] For example IATA, the International Air Transport Association, which represents some 240 airlines comprising 94 per cent of scheduled international air traffic, regularly monitors customer satisfaction in its Global Airport Monitor operation (www.iata.org/index.htm; www.bestransport.org).

Customer satisfaction

Companies should measure customer satisfaction regularly, because an important key to customer retention is customer satisfaction. A highly satisfied customer generally stays loyal longer and buys more as the company introduces new market offerings and upgrades existing ones. They also promote the company by *word of mouth* and pay less attention to competing brands. They tend to be less sensitive to price and can proffer new product/service value-offering ideas to the company. They also cost less to serve than new customers because transactions can become routine.[23] Greater customer satisfaction has also been linked to higher returns and lower risk in the stock market.[24]

The link between customer satisfaction and customer loyalty, however, is not proportional. Suppose customer satisfaction is rated on a scale from one to five. At a very low level of customer satisfaction (level one), customers are likely to abandon the company and even criticise it. At levels two to four, customers are fairly satisfied but still find it easy to switch when a better value offering comes along. At level five, the customer is very likely to repurchase and actively promote the company. High satisfaction or delight creates an emotional bond with the brand or company, not just a rational preference. Xerox's senior management found out that its 'completely satisfied' customers were six times more likely to repurchase Xerox products over the following 18 months than its 'very satisfied' customers.

When customers rate their satisfaction with an element of the company's performance – say, delivery – the company needs to recognise that customers vary in how they define good performance. Good delivery could mean early delivery, on-time delivery, order completeness, and so on. The company must also realise that two customers can report being 'highly satisfied' for different reasons. One may be easily satisfied most of the time and the other might be hard to please but was pleased on this occasion.

Measurement techniques

A number of methods exist to measure customer satisfaction. *Periodic surveys* can track customer satisfaction directly and also ask additional questions to measure repurchase intention and the respondent's likelihood or willingness to recommend the company and brand to others. Theme parks such as Legoland continuously conduct web-based guest surveys of customers who have agreed to be contacted. A key purpose of this is to gather information on customer satisfaction with their theme park experience, including rides, dining, shopping, games and shows.

In the last two decades, it has been suggested that the marketing discipline is undergoing a paradigm shift from a transactional perspective to a relational perspective[25] (see Chapters 1, 3 and 10). At the same time, there has been a call for the discipline to focus on accurate measurement of the outcome of marketing activities[26] (see Chapter 22). Empirical research in this area has predominantly examined the sales and profitability of relationships through customer lifetime analysis, or examined attitudinal measures such as satisfaction and loyalty. Sharma[27] attempted to combine both streams of research by examining the profitability, satisfaction and probability of switching associated with transactional customers, relationship customers (less than five years of relationship) and deep relationship customers (more than five years of relationship) in three business-to-business industries. The results demonstrated that the transactional customers were the most profitable, followed by the relationship and deep relationship customers. The probability of switching was in the reverse direction of profitability and there were no differences in satisfaction measures.

Besides conducting periodic surveys, companies can monitor their *customer loss rate* and contact customers who have stopped buying or who have switched to another supplier to find out why. Finally, companies can hire *mystery shoppers* to pose as potential buyers and report on strong and weak points experienced in buying the company's and competitors' products. Managers themselves can enter company and competitor sales situations where they are unknown and experience at first hand the treatment they receive, or they can phone their own company with questions and complaints to see how employees handle the calls.

In addition to tracking customer value expectations and satisfaction for their own firms, companies need to monitor their competitors' performance in these areas.

Marketing insight

Net promoter and customer satisfaction

Measuring customer satisfaction is a top priority for many companies, but a difference of opinion exists as to how they should go about doing it. Reichheld suggests that perhaps only one customer question really matters: 'How likely is it that you would recommend this product or service to a friend or colleague?' According to Reichheld, a customer's willingness to recommend to a friend results from how well the customer is treated by front-line employees, which in turn is determined by all the functional areas that contribute to a customer's experience.[28]

Keiningham et al.[29] disputed Reichheld's assertions. Their results indicated that recommended intention alone would not suffice as a single predictor of customers' future loyalty behaviour. Use of a multiple indicator instead of a single predictor model performed better in predicting customer recommendations and retention. The practical implications of their research challenge assertions that regard intention as the primary, even sole gauge of customer loyalty.

Influence of customer satisfaction

For customer-centred companies, customer satisfaction is both a goal and a marketing tool. Companies need to be especially concerned today with their customer satisfaction level because the internet provides a tool for consumers quickly to spread dissatisfaction – as well as satisfaction – to the rest of the world. Some customers even set up their own websites to air their grievances and dissatisfaction, targeting high-profile brands such as Mercedes-Benz.[30] Companies that do achieve high customer satisfaction ratings, such as BMW and Skoda, make sure that their target market knows it.

Customer complaints

Some companies think they are getting a sense of customer satisfaction by recording the number of complaints, but studies of customer dissatisfaction show that customers are dissatisfied with their purchases about 25 per cent of the time but that only about 5 per cent complain. The other 95 per cent either feel complaining is not worth the effort, or do not know how or to whom to complain, and they just stop buying.

Of the customers who register a complaint, between half and three-quarters will do business with the organisation again if their complaint is resolved. The figure goes up to almost 100 per cent if the customer feels the complaint was resolved *quickly*. Customers who have complained to an organisation and had their complaints satisfactorily resolved tell an average of 5 people about the good treatment they received. The average dissatisfied customer, however, complains to 11 people. If each of them tells still other people, the number of people exposed to this dissatisfaction may grow exponentially.

The fact is, no matter how perfectly designed and implemented a marketing programme is, mistakes will happen. The best thing a company can do is to make it easy for the customer to complain. Suggestion forms, freephone numbers, websites and email addresses allow for quick, two-way communication. The 3M Company, of Post-it note fame, claims that over two-thirds of its product and service improvement ideas come from listening to customer complaints.

Even companies that think they have done everything possible to ensure customers are happy may still not know what additional market offerings they could be marketing. Their customers may not have told them or may not have thought of them. A spokesperson for Volvo cars comments that companies can get into a rut of measuring the same things repeatedly without considering whether the information is still telling them anything useful.[31] Writing in the *MIT Sloan Management Review*, he says Volvo began to have doubts about its customer strategy; while its measures showed customers were happy with the cars, they appeared to feel less affection for the company. Customer satisfaction was increasing even as loyalty to the Volvo brand was falling.

Having set up ways to gauge customer satisfaction, companies become reluctant to question whether they are measuring the right things. Volvo believes that 'Many factors influence satisfaction and how something is measured can begin to take precedence over *what* is measured.' For example, one Volvo manager insisted the company should concentrate on eliminating quality defects about which customers had complained. But this 'fails to acknowledge that avoiding dissatisfaction might not necessarily generate satisfaction'.

The difference is easy to miss. As Volvo discovered, 'Many companies have fallen into a self-perpetuating pattern in which practices that are not truly customer-oriented are reinforced and those that are customer-centred remain undiscovered and unexplored, all while the company's distance from the customer gradually but inexorably increases.' So what should companies do? They need to find out more about what motivates their customers, about the way they live and use products. Nokia, one of the most successful innovators of recent years, sends researchers to sit at traffic lights, watching how drivers spend their time while they wait. This is a far more expensive and time-consuming way of collecting information. It is also harder to quantify – and makes it difficult to base people's remuneration on the results.

Given the potential disadvantage of having an unhappy customer, it is critical that marketers deal with the negative experience effectively.[32] Beyond that, the following procedures can help to recover customer goodwill:[33]

1 Set up a seven-day, 24-hour freephone 'hot line' (by phone, fax or email) to receive and act on customer complaints.
2 Contact the complaining customer as quickly as possible. The slower the company is to respond, the more dissatisfaction may grow and lead to negative word of mouth.
3 Accept responsibility for the customer's disappointment; never blame the customer.
4 Use customer-service people who are empathetic.
5 Resolve the complaint swiftly and to the customer's satisfaction. Some complaining customers are not looking for compensation so much as a sign that the company cares.

Market offering (product and service) quality

Customer satisfaction has a key quality dimension. Customer-perceived quality (CPQ) relative to customer-perceived price (CPP) defines customer-perceived value (CPV). However, what exactly is quality? Various experts have defined it as 'fitness for use', 'conformance to requirements', 'freedom from variation', 'the purchase attributes that the customer perceives', and so on. In sellers' markets, quality was usually seen to be a production concern, but in the buyers' markets of today, it is a vital concern of marketers. The American Society for Quality Control defines quality as 'the totality of features and characteristics of a product or service that bear on its ability to satisfy stated or implied needs'. This is a customer-centred definition. Thus a seller has delivered quality whenever the product/service offering meets or exceeds customers' expectations. A company that satisfies most of its customers' needs most of the time is called a quality company. However, it is important to distinguish between *conformance* quality and *performance* quality (or grade). A Lexus provides higher performance quality than a Hyundai: the Lexus rides more smoothly, goes faster and lasts longer. Yet we can say that both a Lexus and a Hyundai deliver the same conformance quality if all the units deliver their respective promised quality.

Stockholm's smoothly running and exceptionally clean metro system, the *Tunnelbannen*, found in the late 1990s that cutting costs was not enough. Quality for customers had to be taken into account. It took a new direction and found a better balance between quality and price, adopting a new overall objective – to attract more passengers by offering higher quality.[34]

The drive to produce goods that are superior in world markets has led some countries – and groups of countries – to recognise or award prizes to companies that exemplify the best quality practices, such as the Deming Prize in Japan, the Malcolm Baldrige National Quality Award in the United States, and the European Quality Award.

Impact of quality

Product and service quality, customer satisfaction and company profitability are intimately connected. Higher levels of quality result in higher levels of customer satisfaction, which support higher prices and (often) lower costs as the volume of sales increases. Studies have shown a high correlation between relative product quality and company profitability.[35] Companies that have lowered costs to cut corners have suffered when the quality of the customer experience suffers: for example, a local private dentist who fails to invest in improving patients' experience by regularly updating equipment and the furnishings in the waiting room. Customer-perceived quality is clearly a vital key to customer-perceived value creation and customer satisfaction.

Total quality

Total quality is everyone's job, just as marketing is everyone's job. Marketers play several roles in helping their companies define and deliver high-quality goods and services to target customers:

- They bear the major responsibility for correctly identifying the customers' needs and requirements.
- They must communicate customer expectations properly to product designers.
- They must make sure that customers' orders are fulfilled correctly and on time.
- They must check that customers have received proper instructions, training and technical assistance in the use of the product.
- They must stay in touch with customers after the sale to ensure that they are satisfied and remain satisfied.
- They must gather customer ideas for product and service improvements and convey them to the appropriate departments.

When marketers do all this, they are making substantial contributions to total quality management and customer satisfaction, as well as to customer and company profitability.

Maximising customer lifetime value

Ultimately, marketing is the art of attracting and keeping profitable customers. Yet every company loses money on some of its customers. Pareto's 20–80 rule postulates that the top 20 per cent of customers often generates 80 per cent or more of the company's profits. In some cases the profit distribution may be more extreme – the most profitable 20 per cent of customers (on a per capita basis) may contribute as much as 150–300 per cent of profitability. The least profitable 10–20 per cent of customers, on the other hand, can actually reduce profits from 50–200 per cent per account, with the middle 60–70 per cent breaking even.[36] Figure 11.4 displays one customer profit distribution. The implication is that a company could improve its profits by losing its worst customers.

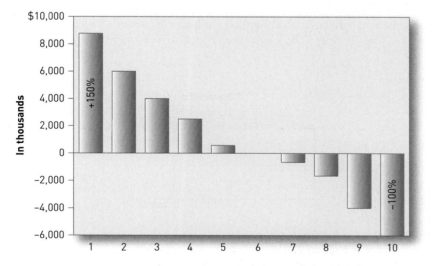

Figure 11.4 The 150–20 rule: 'the 20 per cent most profitable customers generate as much as 150 per cent of the profits of a company; the 20 per cent least profitable lose 100 per cent of the profits'
Source: L. Selden and Y. S. Selden (2006) Profitable customer: the key to great brands, *Advertising Age*, 77(28), 7–9. Copyright © 2006 Crain Communications, Inc.

It is not always the company's largest customers who yield the most profit. The largest customers can demand considerable service and receive the deepest discounts. The smallest customers pay full price and receive minimal service, but the costs of transacting with them can reduce their profitability. The medium-size customers who receive good service and pay nearly full price are often the most profitable.

Customer profitability

What makes a customer profitable? A **profitable customer** is a person, household or company that over time yields a revenue stream that exceeds by an acceptable amount the company's cost stream for attracting, selling and servicing that customer. Note that the emphasis is on the *lifetime* stream of revenue and cost, not on the profit from a particular transaction.[37] Marketers can assess customer profitability individually, by market segment or by channel.

Although many companies measure customer satisfaction, most companies fail to measure individual customer profitability.[38] Banks claim this is a difficult task because each customer uses different banking services and the transactions are logged in different departments. However, the number of unprofitable customers in their customer base has appalled banks that have succeeded in linking customer transactions. Some banks report losing money on over 45 per cent of their retail customers.

Customer profitability analysis

A useful type of profitability analysis is shown in Figure 11.5. Customers are arrayed along the columns and products along the rows. Each cell contains a symbol representing the profitability of selling that product to that customer. Customer 1 is very profitable; he buys two profit-making products (P1 and P2). Customer 2 yields a picture of mixed profitability; he buys one profitable product and one unprofitable product. Customer 3 is a losing customer because he buys one profitable product and two unprofitable products.

What can the company do about customers 2 and 3? (1) It can raise the price of its less profitable products or eliminate them; or (2) it can try to sell customers 2 and 3 its profit-making products. Unprofitable customers who defect should not concern the company. In fact, the company should encourage these customers to switch to competitors.

Customer profitability analysis (CPA) is best conducted with the tools of an accounting technique called activity-based costing. The company estimates all revenue coming from the customer, less all costs. The costs should include not only the cost of making and

		Customers			
		C_1	C_2	C_3	
Products	P_1	+	+	+	Highly profitable product
	P_2	+			Profitable product
	P_3		−	−	Unprofitable product
	P_4			−	Highly unprofitable product
		High-profit customer	Mixed-bag customer	Losing customer	

Figure 11.5 Customer-product profitability analysis

distributing the products and services, but also of taking phone calls from the customer, travelling to visit the customer, paying for entertainment and gifts – all the company's resources that go into serving that customer.

When a company does this for each customer, it can classify customers into different profit tiers: *platinum customers* (most profitable), *gold customers* (profitable), *iron customers* (low profitability but desirable for volume) and *lead customers* (unprofitable and undesirable). The company can then move iron customers into the gold tier and gold customers into the platinum tier, while dropping the lead customers or making them profitable by raising prices or lowering the cost of serving them. More generally, marketers must segment customers into those worth pursuing and those potentially less lucrative customers that should receive little attention, if any at all.

Customer portfolios

Marketers are recognising the need to manage customer portfolios, made up of different groups of customers[39] defined in terms of their loyalty, profitability and other factors. One perspective is that a firm's portfolio consists of a combination of 'acquaintances', 'friends' and 'partners' that are constantly changing.[40] The three types of customer will differ in their product needs, their buying, selling and servicing activities, and their acquisition costs and competitive advantages.

Another perspective compares the individuals who make up the firm's customer portfolio to the stocks that make up an investment portfolio.[41] In marketing, as in investments, it is important to calculate the *beta*, or risk–reward value, for each portfolio item and then diversify accordingly. From this perspective, in order to maximise the portfolio's risk-adjusted lifetime value, firms should assemble portfolios of negatively correlated individuals so that the financial contributions of one offset the deficits of another.

Customer lifetime value – conceptual dream or real-time activity?

As competition in buyers' markets intensifies, it becomes increasingly important for companies to retain their customers as long as they can, and preferably for their lifetime. Winning new customers to replace lost ones is not an easy option. So why do customers defect? In short, because they did not like what was on offer. The customer-perceived value (CPV) package failed to achieve a satisfactory experience. Generally speaking, there are two main reasons why customers defect to a competitor.

The first is a breakdown in trust. Companies should not take their customers for granted but rather should revere them and treat them with respect. While it was Mahatma Ghandi who was the first to coin the phrase 'The customer is king', today most marketers recognise its truth. The concept of customer-perceived value should be interpreted as a task to provide the right customer value package all the time. Mistakes will occur and then they need to be rectified promptly and effectively if customer loyalty is to be retained. Too often the horror stories seem to come from the same sectors: the financial sector, the utilities, satellite TV aerial companies, builders and garages, to name but a few of the cases aired in consumer TV programmes such as the UK BBC's *Watchdog*.

The second reason is a general failure of companies to interface successfully with their customers. The marketing philosophy and culture should be recognised and practised by all in a company. The whole organisation represented by the brand does its job either well or badly. Modern times call for a coordinated team effort to ensure that customers do not experience any problems and are not just satisfied but delighted.[42]

'Chinmusic' is not enough!

Many companies claim to be deeply concerned about customer care. But several do not pay enough attention to delivering customer-perceived value constantly. While the sensitive use of loyalty programmes can prove useful, they are no substitute for failing to recognise constantly the kingship of customers. Companies need to keep their eyes constantly on the alert to avoid becoming myopic in today's highly competitive global markets. Many have found that thinking about the long-term value or lifetime value and hence profitability of loyal customers helps to concentrate their strategy and actions.

The concept of **customer lifetime value** (CLV) and its associated metrics (see Chapter 22) has been developed to express the financial importance of long-term customer retention.[43] Several models have been devised to make a realistic assessment of the profitability of loyal customers, but in reality comparatively few companies actively operate effective CLV metrics. So for many it remains a wonderful ambition but a pipe dream, for in practice too few are held accountable for maximising customers' overall value.[44]

Cultivating customer relationships

Maximising customer-perceived value means cultivating long-term customer relationships. Companies are now moving away from wasteful mass marketing to precision marketing designed to build strong customer relationships[45] (see also Chapter 1). Today's economy is supported by information businesses. Information has the advantage of being easy to differentiate, customise, personalise and dispatch over a variety of networks at incredible speed.

But information flows both ways. For instance, customers now have a quick and easy means of comparison shopping by using specialist internet websites. The internet also facilitates communication between customers. Websites such as Amazon.com enable customers to share information about their experiences with products and services.

Customer empowerment has become a way of life for many companies that have had to adjust to a shift in the importance of their customer relationships. The marketing insight box describes some of the changes that companies have made in their marketing practices as a result.

Marketing insight

Company response to customer empowerment

Often seen as the flag bearer for marketing best practices, Procter & Gamble's chairman, A. G. Lafley, created shock waves for marketers with his Association of National Advertisers' speech in October 2006. 'The power is with the consumer,' proclaimed Lafley, and 'marketers and retailers are scrambling to keep up with her. Consumers are beginning in a very real sense to own our brands and participate in their creation. We need to learn to let go.' In support of his contention, Lafley pointed out how a teenager had created an animated spot for Pringles snacks that was posted on YouTube; how Pantene, the hair care products company, had created a campaign that encouraged women to cut their hair and donate the clippings to make wigs for cancer patients.

Other marketers have begun to advocate a 'bottom-up', grassroots approach to marketing, rather than the

Websites such as Yahoo! Music that empower visitors, allow them to post comments or pictures, or encourage the formation of active communities can benefit companies and customers alike.
Source: Text and artwork copyright © 1998 by Yahoo! Inc. All rights reserved.

► Marketing insight *(continued)*

more traditional 'top-down' approach where the marketers feel they have an advantage. Burger King has launched campaigns on consumer-friendly new media such as YouTube, MySpace, video games and iPods. Allowing the customer to take charge just makes sense for a brand whose slogan is 'Have It Your Way' and whose main rival, McDonald's, already owns the more conservative family market.

To provide a little more control, Yahoo! engages in 'participation marketing' by contacting consumers who already like a particular brand, rather than just casting a wide net. Reflecting the company philosophy, Yahoo! commented that, 'Content is no longer something you push out; content is an invitation to engage with your brand.'

Perhaps the most compelling example of the new brand world comes from master marketer Nike. As part of its *Joga Bonito* (Portuguese for 'play beautiful')

World Cup sponsorship, Nike spent U\$100 million on a multilayered campaign. The centrepiece, however, was Joga.com, a social networking website available in 140 countries. One million members blogged, downloaded videos, created fan communities for their favourite players or teams, and expressed their passions on bulletin-board-type debates. Nike's CEO summed up the new marketing equation well: 'A strong relationship is created when someone joins a Nike community or invites Nike into their community.'

Sources: S. Elliott (2006) Letting consumers control marketing: priceless, *New York Times*, 9 October; L. Story (2006) Super Bowl glory for amateurs with video cameras, *New York Times*, 27 September; T. Wasserman and J. Edwards (2006) Marketers' new world order, *Brandweek*, 9 October, 4–6; H. Green and R. D. Hof (2006) Your attention please, *BusinessWeek*, 24 July, 48–53; B. Sternberg (2006) The marketing maze, *Wall Street Journal*, 10 July.

Customer relationship management

Customer relationship management (CRM) is the process of carefully managing detailed information about individual customers and all customer 'touchpoints' to maximise customer loyalty.[46] A *customer touchpoint* is any occasion on which a customer encounters the brand and product – from actual experience to personal or mass communications to casual observation. For a hotel, the touchpoints include reservations, check-in and check-out, room service, business services, exercise facilities, laundry service, restaurants and bars. For instance, customer-oriented hotels rely on personal touches, such as staff who always address guests by name and high-powered employees who understand the needs of sophisticated business travellers.[47]

Sometimes touchpoints are where you least expect, such as in customer billing. Microsoft's Global CRM product manager, Karen Smith, related what happened when a telecommunications company converted to a unified billing system – one bill for all lines – to cut company costs. One of the customers requested a slightly modified version of unified billing to suit his expense submission purposes, but the service rep replied, 'No, Sir, we can't do that. We use unified billing.' The frustrated customer then switched his two business lines to another telecommunications company but lost his volume discount with the original provider, which still had his personal accounts. Even more frustrated, the customer then moved all his business to the new telecommunications company. Says Smith,

> To find out how the Coles Group handles its customer relations and provides value to its customers with various loyalty programmes and other perks, visit www.pearsoned.com.au/marketingmanagementaustralia.

> **We may think that something will be great to do for our customers, but before we take action we need to really step into their shoes. Companies often focus on CRM functionality and integration, but they forget about some of the most basic touch points.[48]**

Customer relationship management enables companies to provide excellent real-time customer service through the effective use of individual account information. Based on what they know about each valued customer, companies can customise market offerings, services, messages and media. CRM is important because a major driver of company profitability is the aggregate value of the company's customer base.

The Durham Centre

The provision of excellent experiences for private, public and not-for-profit business sectors

Bridging the gap between private, public, business-to-business and not-for-profit market sectors demands a special expertise and attention to detail. The Durham Centre, based on a trading estate two miles out from Durham City centre in the north-east of England, operates during the working week as a fully fledged conference centre and at the weekend as a church and community centre.

Source: Emmanuel Church Durham

The Centre, known as TDC, became fully functional in February 2009. TDC offers the conference trade an exceptional level of customer-perceived value. It is equipped with up-to-date IT (including Wifi) and audiovisual facilities, and provides a cheery, 'nothing is too much trouble' experience for its conference customers, who are seen as honoured guests. The TDC has a suite of rooms containing both plenary and 'break-out' rooms. Coffee, tea and biscuits are available throughout the day and a wide lunch menu is available for customers. The centre has been able to keep its existing customers in post-financial crisis times by paying concerted attention to the special needs of customers and guests. Word-of-mouth recommendation has enabled it to build its order book impressively since its opening in 2009.

TDC is a people-related organisation that seeks to provide the best possible experience for corporate customers, community centre visitors and church members and friends.

Source: Senior management of the TDC centre.

One-to-one marketing

Some of the groundwork for customer relationship management was laid by Peppers and Rogers,[49] who outlined a four-step framework for one-to-one marketing that can be adapted to practising CRM marketing as follows:

1 **Identify your prospects and customers.** Do not go after everyone. Build, maintain and mine a rich customer database with information derived from all the channels and customer touchpoints.

2 **Differentiate customers in terms of (1) their needs and (2) their value to your company.** Spend proportionately more effort on the most valuable customers (MVCs). Apply activity-based costing and calculate customer lifetime value. Estimate net present value of all future profits coming from purchases, margin levels and referrals, less customer-specific servicing costs.

3 **Interact with individual customers to improve your knowledge about their individual needs and to build stronger relationships.** Formulate customised offerings that you can communicate in a personalised way.

4 **Customise products, services and messages to each customer.** Facilitate customer–company interaction through the company contact centre and website.

The practice of one-to-one marketing (see Chapter 5), however, is not for every company: the required investment in information collection, hardware and software may exceed the payout. It works best for companies that normally collect a great deal of individual customer information, carry a wide portfolio of market offerings which can be cross-sold, need periodic replacement or upgrading, and are of high customer perceived value.

Increasing the value of the customer base

A key driver of shareholder value is the aggregate value of the customer base. Winning companies improve the value of their customer base by excelling at strategies such as the following:

- **Reducing the rate of customer defection.** Selecting and training employees to be knowledgeable and friendly increases the likelihood that the inevitable shopping questions from customers will be answered satisfactorily.
- **Increasing the longevity of the customer relationship.** The more involved a customer is with the company, the more likely the customer will remain loyal. Some companies treat their customers as partners – especially in business-to-business markets – soliciting their help in the design of new products or improving their customer service.
- **Enhancing the growth potential of each customer.**[50] This may be done by increasing sales to existing customers with new offerings and opportunities. Football clubs across Europe market a range of merchandise including clothing, scarves, souvenir watches and credit cards.
- **Making low-profit customers more profitable or ceasing to deal with them.** To avoid the direct need for termination, marketers can encourage unprofitable customers to buy more or in larger quantities, forgo certain features or services, or pay higher amounts or fees. Banks, phone companies and travel agencies are all now charging for once-free services to ensure minimum customer revenue levels.
- **Paying additional attention to high-value customers.** The most valuable customers can be treated in a special way. Thoughtful gestures such as birthday greetings, small gifts or invitations to special sports or arts events can send a strong positive signal to the customer. Volvo dealers, for example, have had a long tradition of placing a bouquet of flowers in every new car sold.

Attracting and retaining customers

Companies seeking to expand their profits and sales must spend considerable time and resources searching for new customers. To generate leads they develop advertisements and place them in media that will reach new prospects; send direct mail and make phone calls to possible new prospects; send their salespeople to participate in trade shows where they might find new leads; purchase names from list brokers; and so on.

Reducing defection

It is not enough, however, to attract new customers; the company must keep them and increase their business.[51]

Too many companies suffer from high **customer churn** or defection. Adding customers here is like adding water to a leaking bucket. Mobile phone and cable TV operators, for example, are plagued with 'spinners', customers who switch carriers at least three times a year looking for the best deal. Many lose 25 per cent of their subscribers each year.

To reduce the defection rate, the company must:

- Define and measure its retention rate. For a magazine, subscription renewal rate is a good measure of retention. For a college, it could be the first- to second-year retention rate, or the class graduation rate.
- Distinguish the causes of customer attrition and identify those that can be managed better. Not much can be done about customers who leave the region or go out of business, but much can be done about those who leave because of poor service, badly made products or high prices.
- Compare the lifetime value of a lost customer to the costs incurred to reduce the defection rate. As long as the cost to discourage defection is lower than the lost profit, the company should spend the money to try to retain the customer.

Capturing the heart of the serial switcher

In today's buyers' markets many companies are eagerly trying to build lasting relationships with their customers. However, many companies have been disappointed in the returns from their investment in CRM programmes. The blame for this is usually laid at the door of managers who allowed technology to dominate the corporate strategy, resulting in back office muddle and ill-coordinated approaches to customers. It is crucial that managers believe that customers should be won for life, but many companies failed to organise themselves around the customer. This meant consumer insight was held by individual employees and weakened when they moved on, although, thanks to new tools such as CRM software, many businesses are now building some semblance of corporate memory.

The drive for efficiency and cheaper production costs has led to customers being left out of many businesses' CRM strategies. 'In reality, the customer was never at the heart of CRM,' says Martin Hayward of Dunnhumby, the UK marketing and data analysis consultancy. 'It was simply about making the company machine as efficient as possible.'[52]

Strategies such as farming out customer service to call centres have ended up undermining customer loyalty, which is why brand owners are now struggling to engage with a new generation of 20-something 'serial switchers'. 'These consumers have low brand loyalty and high confidence to move between rival brands at the drop of a hat,' Hayward adds. 'This new mindset is now the major challenge facing brand owners.'

Fast-moving consumer goods brand owners including Procter & Gamble and Unilever, for example, are working more closely with retailers such as Tesco to strengthen their relationship with their customers at point of sale. Meanwhile UK bank NatWest has bucked recent high street banking convention by acknowledging the importance of face-to-face customer relationships and maintaining rather than cutting local branches.

According to José Ferrão, president (Europe, Middle East and Africa) of Carlson Marketing,[53] many companies have been slow to address this challenge because of unwieldy organisational structures that restrict the ability to respond to customer needs and an over-reliance on winning new consumers at the expense of holding on to and deepening their existing client base. Ferrão says:

Telecoms businesses in particular have struggled with customer service levels as many have evolved from land-line business into mobile and cable through acquisitions, after which they continued to operate as separate units. Customers' services expectations from the brand owners they deal with are joined up; what they get from many, however, is anything but consistent.

Mr Hayward, however, concludes that both a customer-centric focus and low prices are viable brand strategies: 'Major brands currently struggling in national and international markets are those with neither a clear customer-service nor price-led market positioning.' The riskiest place to be is somewhere in no man's land between the two.

Retention dynamics

Figure 11.6 shows the main steps in the process of attracting and retaining customers.[54] The starting point is everyone who might conceivably buy the product or service. These *potentials* are people or organisations that might conceivably have an interest in buying the company's product or service, but may not have the means or intention to buy. The next task is to identify which potentials are really good *prospects* – people with the motivation, ability and opportunity to make a purchase – by interviewing them, checking on their financial standing, and so on. Marketing efforts can then concentrate on converting the prospects into *first-time customers*, then into

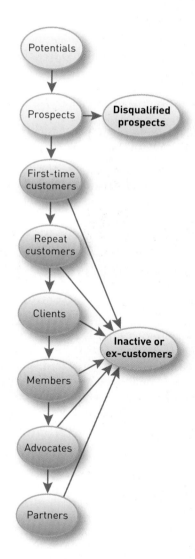

Figure 11.6 The customer-development process

Source: J. Griffin (1995) *Customer Loyalty: How to Earn It, How to Keep It*, New York: Jossey-Bass, 36. See also M. Raphel and N. Raphel (1995) *Up the Loyalty Ladder: Turning Sometime Customers into Full-Time Advocates of Your Business*, New York: HarperBusiness.

repeat customers, and then into *clients* – people to whom the company gives very special and knowledgeable treatment. The next challenge is to turn clients into *members* by starting a membership programme that offers benefits to customers who join, and then turning members into *advocates*, customers who enthusiastically recommend the company and its products and services to others. The ultimate challenge is to turn advocates into *partners*.

Unfortunately, much marketing theory and practice centres on the art of attracting new customers rather than on retaining and cultivating existing ones. The emphasis has traditionally been on making sales rather than on building relationships; on pre-selling and selling rather than on caring for the customer afterwards. More companies now recognise the importance of satisfying and retaining customers.

Satisfied customers constitute the company's *customer relationship capital*. If the company were to be sold, the acquiring company would pay not only for the plant and equipment and the brand name, but also for the delivered *customer base*, the number and value of the customers who would do business with the new firm. Here are some key issues that can influence customer retention:[55]

- Acquiring new customers can cost five times more than satisfying and retaining current customers. It requires a great deal of effort to induce satisfied customers to switch away from their current suppliers.
- The average company loses 10 per cent of its customers each year.
- A 5 per cent reduction in the customer defection rate can increase profits by 25 per cent to 85 per cent, depending on the industry.
- The customer profit rate tends to increase over the life of the retained customer due to increased purchases, referrals and price premiums, and reduced operating costs to service.

For example Enedesa, Spain's largest electricity company, is building and testing a new customer relationship management system to help it to relate to its customers so that it does not lose them to its competitors.[56]

Building customer loyalty

Improving loyalty

Creating a strong, tight connection to customers is the dream of any marketer and often the key to long-term marketing success. The Danish newspaper publishing company Dagbladet Borsen increases customer loyalty through relationship marketing. Companies that want to form strong customer bonds need to attend to a number of different considerations (see Figure 11.7). One set of researchers see retention-building activities as adding financial benefits, social benefits or structural ties.[57] The following sections explain four important types of marketing activity that companies are using to improve loyalty and retention.

Interacting with customers

Listening to customers is crucial to customer relationship management. Some companies have created an ongoing mechanism that keeps senior managers permanently informed of front-line customer feedback.[58]

- MBNA, the credit card giant, asks every executive to listen in on telephone conversations in the customer service area or customer recovery units.
- Deere & Company, which makes John Deere agricultural tractors and has a superb record of customer loyalty – nearly 98 per cent annual retention in some product areas – uses retired employees to interview defectors and customers.

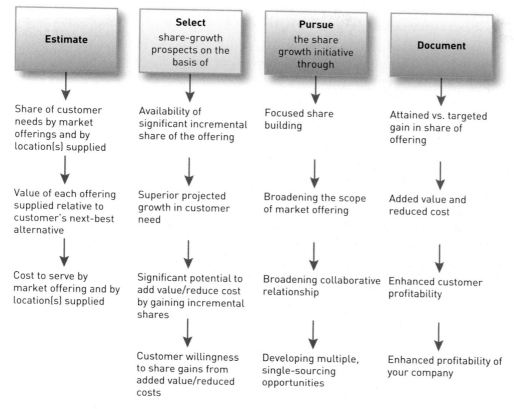

Figure 11.7 Increasing customer share of requirements
Source: J. C. Anderson and J. A. Narus (2003) Selectively pursuing more of your customer's business, *MIT Sloan Management Review*, Spring, 45. Copyright © 2003 from MIT Sloan Management Review/ Massachusetts Institute of Technology. All rights reserved. Distributed by Tribune Media Services.

- Once a quarter, 1.5 million copies of a glossy publication thud through letterboxes across Europe. Silky paper, striking photography and edgy design suggest that the articles about travelling to Oman, Placido Domingo or the Bouroullec brothers – top French designers – could be from an architectural guide, an upmarket travel magazine or the latest lifestyle publication. The Mercedes magazine is all these – and more. Published in a dozen languages and as many distinct editions, the customer magazine for European Mercedes-Benz owners is part of a publishing phenomenon accelerating faster than one of the prestige German car maker's convertibles.

Custom publishing – the business of devising and producing magazines under contract for big companies – has become one of the hottest corners in publishing, an industry not known for breakneck growth. According to the International Customer Publishing Federation, customer magazines are the fastest-growing area of publishing, except the internet, and employ about 20,000 people in Europe alone. Sak van der Boom, an industry consultant, says: 'Four of Sweden's top ten magazines by circulation are now customer products. In the UK, the figure is eight; while in the Netherlands customer magazines constitute the top five.'

Publishing for special interest groups is nothing new: guides and handbooks for clubs and associations have been around for years. But business has mushroomed as consumer-oriented companies, from car makers to retailers, financial services to telecommunications groups, have discovered the appeal of publications delivered directly to customers as a way of marketing brands in a fiercely competitive media environment.

The general manager of Forum, a Munich-based corporate publishing company, who also acts as the federation's spokesman, says:

> **The range of communications channels now available has forced advertisers to become more focused. Television viewers' choice has gone from terrestrial channels to countless alternatives on cable and satellite. Meanwhile, print media have been in decline. Traditional newspapers have suffered falling circulations – not always compensated for by freesheets – and magazines have been volatile.**

Customer publishing is filling the gap. *BMW* – the 108-page customer magazine for that other German luxury car maker – is every bit as glossy as its Mercedes equivalent and has a worldwide circulation of 3.2 million. *Waitrose Food Illustrated*, published monthly by the UK supermarket group, runs to 138 pages per issue.

'Custom publishing is a very effective marketing tool to position a brand among its customers' (Forum). The federation's research demonstrates, it says, declining demand for TV and traditional print media, with only customer magazines and the internet on the ascendant. Julia Hutchinson, chief operating officer of the Association of Publishing Agencies, the UK trade association, says: 'UK customer publishing now accounts for about 5 per cent of companies' total marketing spending, with an annual growth rate of 16 per cent.' That compares with gradually falling rates for traditional print media and sharply declining ones for TV.

'Customer magazines are read on average for 25 minutes. That's a much longer attention span than many other media,' she adds. Such comments may sound odd for anyone recalling early customer publications. Uninspired content, unappealing design and crude photography often made such magazines embarrassing. Articles would be knocked out by company press officers, perhaps 'piggybacking' on a foreign launch to produce an instant travel piece alongside a heavy-handed encomium to the group's latest product.

Today's customer magazines contain a mix of lifestyle, health, sport and travel, explains Wilfred Mons, the Dutchman who publishes nine national editions of *Mercedes* magazine outside the core German market. In an attempt to ensure that the magazine is read, building brand loyalty as a by-product, each edition is tailored to its national audience. In Mercedes' case, the Danish version takes about 75 per cent of its content from the core German edition, which is produced separately by a Munich-based group. By contrast, in the 100-page Italian edition, about 80 per cent of the material is originated locally.

The goal is to make such publications as attractive as paid-for magazines, and many contain genuine advertising, which is a testament to their perceived effectiveness. Julia Hutchinson regards customer magazines as part of the marketing mix, no longer viewed as a sideline of PR. They are now produced as a joint effort between marketing, PR and advertising departments, and include much more sophisticated content.

However, listening is only part of the story. It is also important to be a customer advocate and, as much as possible, to take the customers' side on issues, understanding their point of view.[59] The UK bank Lloyds TSB has established a reputation as being a listening bank. The marketing memo describes six keys to creating customers who feel so strongly about companies and brands that they go way beyond just purchasing and consuming their products and services.

Seeking and retaining customers

Developing loyalty programmes

Two popular customer loyalty programmes that companies can offer are frequency programmes and club marketing programmes. **Frequency programmes** (FPs) are designed to provide rewards to customers who buy frequently and in substantial amounts. They can help build long-term loyalty with high customer lifetime value customers, creating cross-selling opportunities in the process. Originally pioneered by the airlines, hotels and credit card companies, FPs now exist in many other types of business. For example, today most supermarket chains offer price club cards, which provide member customers with discounts on particular items. However, perhaps their real value to the issuer is to provide data on customers' purchasing patterns.

Marketing memo

Creating customer evangelists

McConnell and Huba assert that *customer evangelists* not only buy a company's products or services but believe in them so much that they are compelled to spread the word and voluntarily recruit their friends and colleagues on the company's behalf. On their own 'church of the customer' blog site (www.churchofthecustomer.com) they offer six tips for marketing evangelism:

1 **Customer plus-delta.** Understand what evangelists love by continuously gathering their input.

2 **Publicise your knowledge.** Release your own knowledge, data or intellectual property into a fast-moving distribution network. Sharing knowledge freely makes it more accessible, reducing your biggest threat: obscurity. It is liable to fall into the hands of people who will tell others about it. People talking about your knowledge increases its perceived and actual value.

3 **Build the buzz.** Keep customer evangelists talking by providing them with tools, programmes and features to demonstrate their passion.

4 **Create community.** Give like-minded customers the chance to meet.

5 **Make bite-size chunks.** Bite-size chunks of products and services reduce risk, improve sales cycles and offer upfront value. Even if a customer does not purchase, he or she may spread favourable word of mouth.

6 **Create a cause.** Companies that strive for a higher purpose – such as supporting 'freedom', as Porsche and Air France do – often find that customers, vendors, suppliers and employees naturally root for their success. Customer evangelists crave emotional connection and validation; a well-defined cause generates emotional commitment. When your brand, product or service aspires to change the world, altruism and capitalism converge.

Sources: B. McConnell and J. Huba (2006) Learning to leverage the lunatic fringe, *Point*, July–August; M. Krauss (2006) Work to convert customers into evangelists, *Marketing News*, 15 December, 6; B. McConnell and J. Huba (2003) *Creating Customer Evangelists: How Loyal Customers Become a Volunteer Sales Force*, New York: Kaplan Business.

Loyalty Management UK

On 16 September 2002 Loyalty Management UK (LMUK) launched the Nectar loyalty card. Unlike the majority of such cards, which have only one sponsor, the Nectar scheme now has several sponsors including: Adams, Allsports, Barclaycard, BP, British Gas, Debenhams, e-Energy, Ford, Sainsbury's, Thresher Group, Vodafone and – in Northern Ireland only – Winemark. With more than 13 million Nectar accounts set up since launch, the company deals with a huge volume of customer queries by telephone, email and letter, and through the scheme's website. 'When LMUK launched, we'd already implemented a CRM system [from Siebel Systems] at our multisite contact centres to track and manage customer inquiries,' says Gerard Whelan, LMUK's customer service manager. 'Following the success of the launch, however, customer contact volumes were higher than forecast, and the contact centres struggled to cope,' he adds. The company noticed that a high proportion of enquiries were fairly straightforward and related to the mechanics of the programme (such as questions about where the card could be obtained and used, and where points could be redeemed). It therefore decided that the best approach was to let customers find the answers to such questions themselves on the Nectar website.

The RightNow Loyalty Management Service is one of the new breed of on-demand (i.e. web-hosted) CRM systems. Greg Gianforte, RightNow's founder and chief executive, is emphatic that this is the way the CRM market is heading. 'On-demand CRM is transforming the way corporations consume enterprise software,' he says. 'This model eliminates 80 to 90 per cent of the total cost of ownership associated with traditional CRM software, and also eliminates all the headaches associated with infrastructure.'

Source: From The Financial Times, © The Financial Times Limited 2004. All Rights Reserved. Pearson is solely responsible for providing this adapted version of the original article and the Financial Times Limited does not accept any liability for the accuracy or quality of the adapted version.

Typically, the first company to introduce an FP in an industry gains the most benefit, especially if competitors are slow to respond. After competitors respond, FPs can potentially become a financial burden to all the offering companies, but some companies are more efficient and creative in managing frequency programmes.

Many companies have created **club membership programmes**. Club membership programmes can be open to everyone who purchases a product/service market offering, or can be limited to an affinity group or to those willing to pay a small fee. Although such open clubs are good for building a database or capturing customers from competitors, limited-membership clubs are more powerful long-term loyalty builders. Fees and membership conditions prevent those with only a fleeting interest in a company's offers from joining. These clubs attract and keep those customers who are responsible for the largest portion of business. Some highly successful clubs include the following.

Apple

Apple encourages owners of its computers to form local Apple-user groups. By 2001, there were over 600 such groups, ranging in size from fewer than 25 members to over 1,000 members. The user groups provide Apple owners with opportunities to learn more about their computers, share ideas and get product discounts. They sponsor special activities and events, and perform a community service. A visit to Apple's website will help a customer find a nearby user group.[60]

Local user groups have proliferated among Apple owners, thanks to links on the Apple website that help visitors locate them

Source: John G. Mabanglo/epa/Corbis

Harley-Davidson

The world-famous motorcycle company sponsors the Harley Owners Group (HOG), which now numbers 650,000 members in over 1,200 chapters. The first-time buyer of a Harley-Davidson motorcycle gets a free one-year HOG membership. HOG benefits include a magazine called *Hog Tales*, a touring handbook, emergency road service, a specially designed insurance programme, a theft reward service, discount hotel rates and a Fly & Ride programme enabling members to rent Harley bikes while on vacation. The company also maintains an extensive website devoted to the HOG, which includes information on club chapters and events and a special members-only section.[61]

Personalising marketing

Company personnel can create strong bonds with customers by individualising and personalising relationships. In essence, thoughtful companies turn their customers into clients and then into advocates. One distinction that has been drawn by Kotler is as follows:

Customers may be nameless to the institution; clients cannot be nameless. Customers are served as part of the mass or as part of larger segments; clients are served on an individual basis. Customers are served by anyone who happens to be available; clients are served by the professional assigned to them.

An increasingly essential ingredient for the best relationship marketing today is the right technology. Table 11.2 highlights five imperatives of CRM and shows where technology fits in. Dell Computers could not customise computer ordering for its global corporate customers without advances in web technology. Companies are using email, websites, call centres, databases and database software to foster continuous contact between company and customer.

Ecommerce companies looking to attract and retain customers are discovering that personalisation goes beyond creating customised information. The BBC, the British archetype of a traditional media company, is reaping the benefits of customising its offerings, a practice that is outpacing its commercial rivals in UK broadcasting.

British Broadcasting Corporation

BBC iPlayer, lets British users download current radio and TV programmes up to seven days after broadcast. Not only can viewers download content, they can also build on it and share it. One project, for instance, lets users download footage from BBC news and science shows, remix them, and eventually share them online. Even more radical is http://backstage.bbc.co.uk, which provides data, resources and support for internet developers and designers – inside and outside the BBC – to share in order to build prototypes of new concepts using BBC material. One consumer-created prototype called Sport Map allows people to find the nearest soccer team on the map and get its latest news – a service bound to be popular in a country full of avid soccer fans.

Source: K. Capell (2006) BBC: step right into the telly, *BusinessWeek*, 24 July, 52; http://backstage.bbc.co.uk.

At the same time, online companies need to make sure their attempts to create relationships with customers do not misfire, as when customers are bombarded by computer-generated recommendations that consistently miss the mark. Buy a lot of books or baby gifts on Amazon.com, and your personalised recommendations suddenly don't look so personal! Etailers need to recognise the limitations of online personalisation at the same time as they try harder to find technology and processes that really work.

Table 11.2 Breaking down customer relationship management: what customer relationship really comprises

CRM imperative				
Acquiring the right customer	Crafting the right value proposition	Instituting the best processes	Motivating employees	Learning to retain customers
You get it when . . .				
• You've identified your most valuable customers. • You've calculated your share of their wallet for your goods and services.	• You've studied what products or services your customers need today and will need tomorrow. • You've surveyed what products or services your competitors offer today and will offer tomorrow. • You've spotted what products or services you should be offering.	• You've researched the best way to deliver your products or services to customers, including the alliances you need to strike, the technologies you need to invest in and the service capabilities you need to develop or acquire.	• You know what tools your employees need to foster customer relationships. • You've identified the HR systems you need to institute in order to boost employee loyalty.	• You've learned why customers defect and how to win them back. • You've analysed what your competitors are doing to win your high-value customers. • Your senior management monitors customer defection metrics.
CRM technology can help . . .				
• Analyse customer revenue and cost data to identify current and future high-value customers. • Target your direct-marketing efforts better.	• Capture relevant product and service behaviour data. • Create new distribution channels. • Develop new pricing models. • Build communities.	• Process transactions faster. • Provide better information to the front line. • Manage logistics and the supply chain more efficiently. • Catalyse collaborative commerce.	• Align incentives and metrics. • Deploy knowledge management systems.	• Track customer defection and retention levels. • Track customer service satisfaction levels.

Companies are also recognising the importance of the personal component to CRM and what happens once customers make actual contact. As the US business guru Jeffrey Pfeffer puts it, 'The best companies build cultures in which front line people are empowered to do what's needed to take care of the customer.' He cites examples of firms such as SAS, the Scandinavian airline, which engineered a turnaround based in part on the insight that a customer's impressions of a company are formed through a myriad of small interactions – checking in, boarding the plane, eating a meal etc.[62]

Creating institutional ties

The company may supply customers with special equipment or computer links that help customers manage orders, payroll and inventory. Customers are less inclined to switch to another supplier when this would involve high capital costs, high search costs or the loss of loyal-customer discounts.

Recapturing customers

Regardless of the nature of the category or how hard companies may try, some customers inevitably become inactive or drop out. The challenge is to reactivate dissatisfied customers through *win-back* strategies.[63] It's often easier to win back ex-customers (because the company knows their names and histories) than to find new ones. The key is to analyse the causes of customer defection through exit interviews and lost-customer surveys and recapture only those who have strong profit potential.[64]

Patronise or personalise?

Customer relationship marketing professionals, at the end of the day, have to navigate the narrow channel between earning customer favour and loyalty and irritating them. They may be tempted to seek efficiency (to them) at the cost of becoming ineffective by irritating or patronising the customer. The challenge facing companies is to achieve the right balance between efficiency and effectiveness; between direct human communication and CRM automated systems. With banks in mind, a frustrated customer might respond, 'Press 1 to make an appointment to see me; 2 to query a missing payment; 3 to transfer the call to my living room in case I'm there.' CRM can work, providing the goals are modest and there is some worthwhile benefit for customers. However, its capacity to irritate and repel is massive, so it needs to be carried out sensitively.

The experience economy

The value experience

The term 'experience economy' was first coined in 1999 by Pine and Gilmore[65] when they described an advanced service economy that began to market a 'mass customisation' of service offerings. Using theatre as a metaphor, they argued that business should function in a similar way to a theatre that develops and presents a performance, which it hopes will be appreciated by its audience. To achieve this requires the input of numerous attributes and benefits, some of which are tangible (such as props) and some intangible (such as acting and set expertise). If it all goes well on the night, the audience leaves after having had a pleasurable 'experience'. This, they claimed, will produce repeat business and the 'transformation' that has occurred in their expectations will enhance the customer-perceived value of the company's brand. This in turn will enable it to charge a premium price. In experience terms, the memory itself is now the market offering. Although the concept was originally developed with business-to-business markets in mind, Pine and Gilmore claimed that it could be applied effectively to other markets. Early examples included leisure, hospitality, tourism and urban planning.

The core concept at issue here is that of economic value. The concept of the 'experience economy' claims that customising a product turns it into a service. Customising a service turns it into an experience, which transforms it into a customer-perceived value (CPV) experience. As CPV attributes and benefits can be either tangible or intangible, what ultimately determines an attractive purchase experience is the expertise that a company applies to the development and presentation of the final market offering.

Successful theatrical performances do deliver enjoyable experiences, but for a company or theatre to establish a strong brand appeal, the enjoyable experiences have to be sustained. 'Greatness' lasts only as long as someone fails to imagine something better. Successful companies know that their CPV offerings have to improve consistently. However, recent productivity, technology and transparency developments have placed increasing demands on their value offerings as product/market offering life cycles shorten under the fierce pressure of global competition.

The Pine and Gilmore thesis, although elegantly expressed as a theatrical metaphor, has a serious flaw. Unconstrained customer expectations in rigorous buyers' markets are unrealistic for most suppliers which have to make a profit. Weissman and Mosby[66] believe that the solution to the problem of ever-escalating expectations lies in sustained effective market communications. It is a matter of convincing customers that a good company really does offer a better CPV package. However, what happens when the key distinguishing experience becomes increasingly difficult to discern?

Companies have long realised the necessity of building and sustaining brand reputations by satisfying their customers. However, the experience economy notion implies something a lot more aspirational and personal. Peters[67] refers to this as 'dream fulfilment' – the next rung on the quality–service–experience ladder. Companies seeking to 'get up close and personal' to their customers often experience difficulty in knowing if their brand is sufficiently positively differentiated.

A key question for companies to think through is: just what constitutes a business experience? What do they need to offer to succeed? Neither of these questions was addressed by Pine and Gilmore in their original text. For an experience to be effective it has to engage an individual in its delivery. It is a two-way event. It is an act that implies co-creation between a provider and the customer; the result is a memorable experience that has a high level of CPV. As a result, customers will be prepared to pay a premium price.

According to Prahalad and Ramaswamy,[68] deregulation, emerging markets, new forms of regulation, convergence of technologies and industries, and ubiquitous connectivity have changed many facets of the business world. These factors have changed the nature of consumers. Today they are informed, networked, active and global. These factors have also changed the nature of companies, which are now able to fragment their value chain in ways that were not possible in the past.

These contextual changes in markets are enabling a new form of value creation, *co-creation*, in which value is not created exclusively in the firm and then exchanged with the customer, but is co-created by the firm and the customer. As a result, the world of business is moving away from a company- and product-centric view of value creation towards an experience-centric view of the co-creation of customer-perceived value. High-quality interactions that enable an individual customer to co-create unique experiences with the company are the key to unlocking new sources of competitive advantage. Products or, as this text argues, market offerings are merely artefacts around which compelling individual experiences are created.[69]

Hence companies such as Costa Coffee, Pret A Manger and Starbucks provide a value 'experience' as well as providing their key market offerings.

Marketing memo

Key steps in the co-creation process

1 Define clear objectives for the project.

2 Discover who are the right customers to involve in the process.

3 Work with customers to discover what they really want to include in a market offering.

4 Design market offerings-systems jointly to meet those customers' needs. This includes selecting the partners to be included in a company's network.

5 Decide how to share the customer-perceived value.

6 Overcome internal resistance to change – with seller, buyer and partner organisations.

Sources: www.onedegree.ca/2007/09/co-creation-1s.html; www.promisecorp.com.

Pret A Manger

Pret A Manger, the distinctive sandwich bar operator that creates handmade natural food, avoiding the obscure chemicals, additives and preservatives common to so much of the 'prepared' and 'fast' food on the market today, is being transformed into an international business following its sale to Bridgepoint Capital, the private equity firm in 2008. The acquisition by Bridgepoint bolsters a portfolio of consumer-facing brands that includes Pets at Home, Fat Face, Molton Brown and Virgin Active.

The majority of the Pret A Manger outlets are in London but recent years have seen an expansion into the North American and Chinese markets.

Kotler's concept of CPV, introduced earlier in this chapter, could now be extended to include an additional set of five attributes. Poulsson and Kale argue that a positive experience should include the attributes in the 'experience scorecard' memo below:

1 **personal relevance:** the individual's internal state of arousal, activation and preparedness to engage in a specific experience;

2 **novelty:** an attractive change to regularly experienced stimuli;

3 **surprise:** the emotion generated by the appeal of something that is attractive and new;

4 **learning:** when an experience has been well received, the resultant learning becomes a positive influence on engagement with the provider;

5 **engagement**: the process by which providers seek to co-create CPV offerings with customers.

Source: Based on S. H. G. Poulsson and S. H. Kale (2004) The experience economy and commercial experiences, *Marketing Review*, 4, 267–77.

Pret creates handmade natural foods, avoiding the obscure chemicals, additives and preservatives common to so much of the 'prepared' and 'fast' food on the market today.
Source: Phillipe Hays/Rex Features.

Generally speaking, the best approach is to provide consumers with the opportunity to create their own story, as a successful market offering is part of the larger narrative of customers' lives. Harley-Davidson has achieved this effectively with its HOG website. However, not all purchasing 'experiences' need such a pronounced emphasis on the experiential attributes of a CPV offering. Commodity items such as bread, confectionery and salt are likely to require less perceived value in terms of quality and experiential attributes. Here the main emphasis will usually be on price. However, wise companies should not forget that a too cavalier approach towards commodity customers will result in desertion to the competition. The experience economy is a relationship marketing concept that needs to be interpreted by providers, in an appropriate way for their market activities. It is a matter of fine tuning market offerings in terms of customer effectiveness and provider efficiency and with regard to the wider societal implications of marketing activities, as argued by the 'critical' movement.[70]

The empowered customer

As buyers' markets intensify, so customers increasingly expect more value for their money. Wise companies seek to discover what their customers want and then attempt to deliver more than their customers expect if they intend to develop profitable brands.[71]

European Commission activity

The past US president John F. Kennedy[72] once said, 'Consumers, by definition, include us all … yet they are the only important group … whose views are often not heard.' The European Commission is working hard to change this. Empowered consumers are viewed as good for Europe's economy as they encourage companies to work hard, compete and provide quality offerings in the marketplace. The concept is also seen as a way of breaking down the barriers between Europe's national markets. The internal market in Europe will offer empowered consumers more choice. The Commission has established a new system – the European Consumer Market Watch – to investigate whether various sectors of the economy are delivering the information, choice and value for money consumers deserve.

EU cross-border initiatives

Legislation has been passed to cut charges for roaming – making calls from a mobile phone when abroad – to levels commensurate with the incurred costs. A Single European Payments Area has been set up to facilitate payments and transfers, and the Commission has campaigned to make it easier for consumers to access, assess and compare banking services.

Market paradigm change

Most markets are characterised by an excess of providers, thus empowering consumers through the mechanism of their choice of supplier. Paradoxically, and reflecting the past sellers' market conditions, much of the literature on consumer empowerment focuses on consumers' efforts to regain control of their consumption processes from providers. However, many suppliers now set out to achieve success by seeking to empower consumers. The mechanism by which this takes place consists of researching and providing what consumers want – that is, the right mix of quality, price and experiential attributes and benefits. This provides many 'old school' suppliers with a conundrum, as most traditional marketing techniques are market centric. Gross rating points, for example, define message delivery volume. Even the 4Ps (product, price, place and promotion) speak more to how a company wants to conduct business than to how consumers want to engage with the brand. Integrated marketing requires a deep knowledge of consumers' habits, needs and passions. Regular market research should be viewed by providers as an investment decision that enables them to know what mix of CPV attributes and benefits to include in their offerings, and not as a cost decision to be cut as soon as fortunes falter.

Marketing to the empowered consumer

Until recently there was an observable distinction between traditional brand and direct marketing activity. The former focused on creating awareness and share of mind mainly by means of TV, radio and print advertising. The latter concentrated on inspiring a specific action and share of wallet via mail, telemarketing and email. This distinction is rapidly fading as providers realise that both skill sets need to be integrated and directed to securing customer engagement. However, most marketers are still organised around their traditional product lines, markets or technologies. As consumers take up the new technologies that give them fingertip control of how, when and if they want to be marketed to, marketers should seriously reconsider the traditional 4P mantra, and engage customers on their own terms.

To achieve this requires the adoption by providers of a customer-centric organisational philosophy that really does put the customer at the centre of functional activity.[73] The new mantra should emphasise the question: why should consumers buy from an organisation when they can favour several competitors? It is surprising how many companies allow their agency partners to assume too great an influence over their marketing activity. Marketers need to take a more interactive, cross-disciplinary approach to campaign planning that integrates all the activities necessary to develop the required mix of customer-perceived value attributes.

Interactive marketing

(See also Chapters 4, 17 and 18)

The term 'interactive marketing' was first proposed by Deighton,[74] who described it as 'the ability to address the customer, remember what the customer says and address the customer again in a way that illustrates that we remember what the customer has told us' (see Chapter 18 for more discussion of this channel). It should be noted that interactive marketing is not the same thing as online marketing, although interactivity is facilitated by internet technology. The ability to 'get up close and personal' with customers is boosted when it becomes possible to collect and analyse customer information over the web. Amazon has developed interactive marketing to a fine art and suggests books that fit customers' purchasing profiles.

Cadbury/Schweppes (now demerged as Cadbury was acquired by Kraft in January 2010) used interactive marketing to raise awareness of its use of 100 per cent genuine flavours for its 7Up soft drink in the United States. Visitors to the brand name's website are able to personalise the rabbits who serve as the drink's TV advertising mascots. They can personalise the rabbits with an array of costumes and helpfully provided burps. Text-to-speech technology enables consumers to create custom messages to transmit to others by email. In the United Kingdom, Britvic has held the 7Up franchise since 1987 but has not used sophisticated interactive marketing techniques.

Many companies are now starting to show an interest in how they could extend the benefits of information and communications technology in their marketing activities.[75] As more and more households sign up for broadband in the United Kingdom and TV advertising goes online, providers are starting to show a deep interest in Web 2.0, the second phase of the internet, where consumers can move from information and search to content and user-generated interactivity (see Chapter 4). Problems remain, however, in relation to such issues as payment for the server capacity and bandwidth for commercial and free-to-air broadcasters.

Another interesting development is the use of mobile phones to revive coupon redemption. Procter & Gamble, Del Monte and Kimberly-Clark have joined up to explore the viability of a mobile marketing venture in selected supermarket stores. The companies offer marketing software that consumers can download to their mobile phones, which will present redeemable coupons for discounts on certain products.

Complexity of markets

Complexity has been one of the most frequently used terms for some time now. Managers talk about complex systems, complex interrelationships, complex problems, etc. There is hardly a presentation or discussion among executives without some reference to complexity – for instance, the complexity of markets, market offerings and processes.[76] In many respects management is the art and/or science of handling complexity. In today's fiercely competitive world, companies are finding that complexity is becoming more difficult to manage. On the one hand, it is necessary to bring a system under control but it is wise not to adopt too tight a management *modus operandi* as this can slow down the ability of a company to respond to important market movements. As business becomes an ever more dynamic activity, so wise firms build in some degree of flexibility to respond to market forces. Thus loose/tight approaches hold the promise of getting the right balance between market effectiveness (supplying the right market offering) and provider efficiency.

Market types

Economists describe markets as places where buyers and sellers gather to expedite exchange. As business became a world rather than a local, national or international affair so, in a sense, there is now one global market with many specialist sub-markets.

Communication between the selling and buying parties is a key characteristic of market trading. This has greatly changed in nature as modern technological communication advances have made it possible for this to occur electronically. The global market is highly complex and this is further complicated by the challenging dynamics of modern buyers' markets in the world as a whole, but particularly in the developed nations.

To begin to understand this complexity, five basic markets have traditionally been viewed as a promising start. Figure 11.8 presents this basic structure and shows the flows in a modern exchange economy.

This is, of course, an oversimplification. The complexity of modern markets demands a deep and continuous understanding of the realities evident and emerging in every market of interest to companies. The suppliers' markets evident in most of the developed countries and the export potential that became available in the underdeveloped countries have led to a business approach that has been heavily supply oriented. The added complexity of widespread buyers' choice in most markets has brought many companies to deeply challenging times. So has marketing entered a mid-life crisis? This text has argued that marketing management is also a wide canvas. Theory and practice have their place but how to

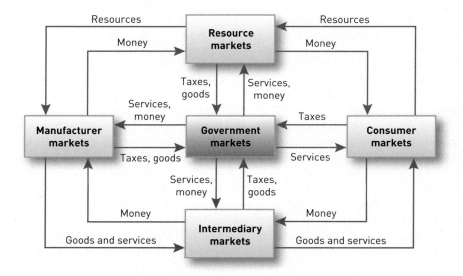

Figure 11.8 Structure of flows in a modern exchange economy

mix knowledge with effective market operations or know-how is a massive challenge for companies as there are no easy answers or quick fixes.

Emotional turn

Emotions matter as they can be fashioned to influence and change attitudes in marketing communications. They affect the way in which an audience can sense their past, present and future: all can seem bright, dull or darkened by emotional outlooks. *Emotional turn*, or as it is sometimes known *affective marketing* (also *affective economics*), emphasises the emotional engagement that marketers seek to gain with their target audiences. Recent advances in the study of neurological and psychological insights – originating from brain scanning and neurological experiments – on basic emotional processes in the brain have led marketers to assess their application potential. Hansen and Christensen and others have brought together much of the theory and understanding of the role that emotion plays in advertising and marketing communications.[77] Their work provides a solid underpinning for all marketers who wish to understand the interactions between feelings, moods and emotionally based reactions to advertising, market offerings, brands and hence consumer choice.

Today marketers influence people differently from in the era of sellers' markets, when companies tended to place the emphasis on rational messages to further their intentions. As consumer choice has increased following the explosion of buyers' markets, marketing practitioners have sought to connect with their targeted audiences by means of emotional communications.[78] As buyers' markets become ever more fiercely competitive, marketers are now seeking to achieve customer engagement. Many might wonder what the practical difference is between engagement and connecting emotionally. The answer lies in the realisation that consumers have a lot more market power today. The concept of engagement recognises this power and seeks to share it between consumers and marketers. As a consequence, consumers are key parties to co-creating their perceived-value offerings. So leading marketers in the experience economy are seeking to engage all five senses in their brand building and are viewing this as the leading edge of their marketing.

Emotion triggers

Emotion lies in the acceptance and perception of many customer-valued brands. It can be expressed in many different forms in advertising. In the United Kingdom, Tesco has used celebrities in soap drama type advertisements to engage with their audience. These have included actresses Prunella Scales and Jane Horrocks in a long-running series. Marks & Spencer has featured the model Twiggy in several of its seasonal clothes videos.

The main appeals designed to elicit emotional responses are as follows:[79]

- **Fear.** This is generally used in one of two ways. First, it is used to demonstrate the negativity and undesirability of certain behaviours that might put the individual and society in danger. Many governments brief marketers to help them with important messages such as the dangers inherent in drinking and driving. Financial firms sponsor TV dramas on the commercial channels and invite viewers to take care of their families in every advertising break. Secondly, fear is used to shame audiences. Examples here would include anti-dandruff shampoos and anti-ageing cream advertisements.
- **Humour.** This draws attention and stimulates interest and is widely used throughout Europe. Marketers, however, should always realise that what is amusing and funny in one culture may not transfer to another. The Walkers' series of TV advertisements featuring Gary Lineker, the ex-international footballer and current TV soccer presenter, in amusing situations did much to boost the company's sales of potato crisps.
- **Animation.** Recent and dramatic advances in animation technology provide the opportunity to register effectively with both child and adult audiences. Children appreciate mini-stories featuring their favourite TV and film characters. Adults laugh at the 'Ask Churchill the dog' screenings.

- **Sex**. The use of sex and sexual innuendo is both powerful and controversial as it usually attracts attention. Recent screenings in the United Kingdom include campaigns for fast-moving consumer goods – such as confectionery and cosmetics – and durables such as cars.
- **Music**. Music is a powerful aid to recall. Old screenings of lawn fertiliser advertisements can easily be reused every season and audiences warm to familiar jingles. Classical music is frequently used to suggest 'quality' in some shape or form.
- **Fantasy and surrealism**. Fantasy is used to provide a distraction from expected or everyday life events and so create 'space' for a market offering message. The advertisements are different and either appeal or distract. Guinness has acquired a quality reputation over the years and car companies such as Citroën, Honda and Toyota are increasingly following suit.

Mood indigo

Literature research has shown that persuasive impact is greater if the target audience is in a happy, benevolent mood. A limitation of many studies concerning mood and advertising effectiveness, however, is that mood is manipulated under experimental, 'laboratory' conditions. As many authors state, these studies require replication under more realistic conditions. Research by Bonner et al. and others[80] has shown that target audiences are often in a better mood on Sundays.

Mood management by John Lewis

COMPUTERS INSTALLED.

SOFAS COVERED.

A LITTLE FAITH IN HUMANITY RESTORED.

We're not about to suggest changing your sofa is going to change your life. But we do like to think the little added touches we do can make all the difference to your day.

It could simply be not feeling pressured into making a purchase. Or having a collection point where you'll find everything you've bought waiting for you. Or some free nursery advice at a time when you're a bit overwhelmed by what lies ahead. Or just simply your new television being guaranteed free for 5 years.

Because in a perfect world, we'd like everyone to leave us with something, even if they buy nothing. So for an unlimited time, an unlimited offer. A little bit of humanity. Free at John Lewis.

johnlewis.com

Source: Creatives Simon Morris, Patrick McLelland and Clive Pickering for John Lewis plc. Full page advertisement in the *Guardian*, 25 June 2008, 38. Reproduced with permission.

Creating customer value, satisfaction and loyalty to develop and sustain long-term advantage in highly competitive markets is the marketer's commission. Such a commission requires vision, mission and a determination to 'delight' customers, for as César Ritz, the famous Swiss hotel proprietor quipped, 'Le client n'a jamais tort' (literally, 'The customer is never wrong').[81]

SUMMARY

1 Customers are value maximisers. They form an expectation of value and act on it. Buyers will buy from the firm that they perceive to offer the highest customer-delivered value, defined as the difference between total customer benefits and total customer cost.

2 A buyer's satisfaction is a function of the product's perceived performance and the buyer's expectations. Recognising that high satisfaction leads to high customer loyalty, many companies today are aiming for TCS – total customer satisfaction. For such companies, customer satisfaction is both a goal and a marketing tool.

3 Losing profitable customers can dramatically affect a firm's profits. The cost of attracting a new customer is estimated to be five times the cost of keeping a current customer happy. The key to retaining customers is relationship marketing.

4 Quality is the totality of features and characteristics of a product or service that bear on its ability to satisfy stated or implied needs. Marketers play a key role in achieving high levels of total quality so that firms remain solvent and profitable.

5 Marketing managers must calculate customer lifetime values of their customer base to understand their profit implications. They must also determine ways to increase the value of the customer base.

6 Companies are also becoming skilled in customer relationship management, which focuses on developing programmes to attract and retain the right customers and meet the individual needs of those valued customers.

7 Future marketing managers should be able competently to develop and maintain customer relations. In this respect, companies not only may be competing against other companies but also may belong to networks that are competing against other networks.

8 The world of business is moving away from a company- and product-centric view of value creation towards an experience-centric view of the co-creation of customer-perceived value.

9 The experience economy is a relationship marketing concept that needs to be interpreted by providers, in an appropriate way for their market activities. It is a matter of fine tuning market offerings in terms of customer effectiveness and provider efficiency, and with regard to the wider societal implications of marketing activities as argued by the 'critical' movement.

10 Most markets are characterised by an excess of providers, thus empowering consumers through the mechanism of their choice of supplier.

11 The added complexity of widespread buyers' choice in most markets has brought many companies to deeply challenging times.

APPLICATIONS

Marketing debate

Online versus offline privacy As more and more firms practise relationship marketing and develop customer databases, privacy issues are emerging as an important topic. Consumers and public interest groups are scrutinising – and sometimes criticising – the privacy policies of firms and raising concerns about potential theft of online credit card information or other potentially sensitive or confidential financial information. Others maintain that the online privacy fears are unfounded and that security issues are every bit as much a concern in the offline world. They argue that the opportunity to steal information exists virtually everywhere and that it is up to the consumer to protect their interests.

Take a position: (1) Privacy is a bigger issue in the online than the offline world *versus* Privacy is no different online than offline. (2) Consumers on the whole receive more benefit than risk from marketers knowing their personal information.

Marketing discussion

Consider the lifetime value of customers (CLV). Choose a business and show how you would go about developing a quantitative formulation that captures the concept. How would that business change if it totally embraced the customer equity concept and maximised CLV?

REFERENCES

[1] A. Michaels and J. Reed (2007) Alfa rewrites its service history, *Financial Times*, 1 January.

[2] R. Schieffer (2005) *Ten Key Consumer Insights*, Mason, OH: Thomson. See also M. Holmlund, A. Hagman and P. Polsa (2011) An exploration of how mature women buy clothing: empirical insights and a model, *Journal of Fashion Marketing and Management*, 15(1) 108–22.

[3] D. Peppers and M. Rogers (2005) Customers don't grow on trees, *Fast Company*, July, 25–6.

[4] P. L. Dubois, A. Jolibert and H. Mühlbacher (2007) *Marketing Management: A Value-Creation Process*, Basingstoke: Macmillan, 1–28; see also G. Hooley, N. F. Piercy and B. Nicoulaud (2008) *Marketing Strategy and Competitive Positioning*, 4th edn, Harlow: Prentice Hall, 3–6; see also A. Payne and S. Holt (2001) Diagnosing customer value: integrating the value process and relationship marketing, *British Journal of Management*, 12, 159–82.

[5] For discussion of some of the issues involved, see G. Urban (2005) *Don't Just Relate: Advocate*, Upper Saddle River, NJ: Pearson Education/Wharton School Publishing.

[6] See G. L. Urban and J. R. Hauser (2004) 'Listening in' to find and explore new combinations of customer needs, *Journal of Marketing*, 68 (April), 72–87; A. M. Pelham and P. Kravitz, (2008) An exploratory study of the influence of sales training content and salesperson evaluation on salesperson adaptive selling, customer orientation, listening, and consulting behaviors, *Journal of Strategic Marketing*,16(5), 413–35; see also: Customer focus: getting to the heart of it, *Velocity*, 2010, 12(2), 30–2.

[7] A. Hill (2008) DSG's new year gift to Browett is a heavy one, *Financial Times*, 3 January.

[8] S. P. Gounaris, N. P. Tzempelikos and K. Chatzpagiotou (2007) The relationships of customer-perceived value, satisfaction and behavioural intentions, *Journal of Relationship Marketing*, 6(1), 63–87.

[9] A. Smith (1970 [1776]) *An Enquiry into the Nature and Causes of the Wealth of Nations*, A. Skinner (ed.), Harmondsworth: Pelican.

[10] J. C. Fandos Roig, J. Sanchez Garcia, M. A. Moliner Tena and J. Liorens Monzonis (2006) Customer perceived value in banking services, *International Journal of Bank Marketing*, 24(5), 266–83.

[11] For more on customer-perceived value, see A. S. Ashton, N. Scott, D. Solnet and N. Breakey (2010) Hotel restaurant dining: the relationship between perceived value and intention to purchase, *Tourism and Hospitality Research*, 10(3), 206–18; L. Mei-Lien and R. D. Green (2011) A mediating influence on customer loyalty: the role of perceived value, *Journal of Management and Marketing Research*, 7(March) 1–12.

[12] G. Hamel (1996) Strategy as revolution, *Harvard Business Review*, July–August, 69–82.

[13] M. Schrage (2007) Customers want loyalty not perfection, *Financial Times*, 2 May.

[14] V. Srivastava and T. Singh (2010) Value creation through relationship closeness, *Journal of Strategic Marketing*, 18(1), 3–17; C. Helm and R. Jones (2010) Extending the value chain – a conceptual framework for managing the governance of co-created brand equity, *Journal of Brand Management*, 17(8), 579–89.

[15] F. Crawford and R. Mathews (2001) *The Myth of Excellence: Why Great Companies Never Try to Be the Best of Everything*, New York: Crown Business, 85–100.

[16] M. Tsiros, V. Mittal and W. T. Ross, Jr (2004) The role of attributions in customer satisfaction: a re-examination, *Journal of Consumer Research*, 31 (September), 476–83; S-K. Rhee and J-Y Rha (2009) Public service quality and customer satisfaction: exploring the attributes of service quality in the public sector, *Service Industries Journal*, 29(11), 1491–512.

[17] For a succinct review, see R. L. Oliver (2006) Customer satisfaction research, in R. Grover and M. Vriens (eds), *Handbook of Marketing Research*, Thousand Oaks, CA: Sage 569–87. M. S. Garver (2009) A maximum difference scaling application for customer satisfaction researchers, *International Journal of Market Research*, 51(4), 481–500; F. Siems (2009) Is customer satisfaction an issue of gender? The market research dilemma, empirical findings, and implications, *Journal of International Business and Economics*, 10(1), 174–81.

[18] For some provocative analysis and discussion, see P. K. Kopalle and D. R. Lehmann (2006) Setting quality expectations when entering a market: what should the promise be?, *Marketing Science*, 25 (January–February), 8–24 ; D. C. Barnes, M. B. Beauchamp and C. Webster, (2010) To delight, or not to delight? This is the question service firms must address, *Journal of Marketing Theory and Practice*, 18(3), 275–83; C-C.Yang (2011) Identification of customer delight for quality attributes and its applications, *Total Quality Management and Business Excellence*, 22(1), 83–98.

[19] J. Aaker, S. Fournier and S. A. Brasel (2004) When good brands do bad, *Journal of Consumer Research*, 31 (June), 1–16; P. Aggrawal (2004) The effects of brand relationship norms on consumer attitudes and behavior, *Journal of Consumer Research*, 31 (June), 87–101; J. Brakus, B. H. Schmitt and L. Zarantonello (2009) Brand experience: what is it? How is it measured? Does it affect loyalty?, *Journal of Marketing*, 73(3), 52–68.

[20] For in-depth discussion see M. D. Johnson and A. Gustafsson (2000) *Improving Customer Satisfaction, Loyalty, and Profit*, San Francisco: Jossey-Bass; see also P. Naidoo, P. Ramseook-Munhurrun and P. Seegoolam (2011) An assessment of visitor satisfaction with nature-based tourism attractions, *International Journal of Management and Marketing Research (IJMMR)* 4(1), 87–98.

[21] For an interesting analysis of the effects of different types of expectation, see W. Boulding, A. Kalra and R. Staelin (1999) The quality double whammy, *Marketing Science*, 18(4), 463–84.

[22] N. A. Morgan, E. W. Anderson and V. Mittal (2005) Understanding firms' customer satisfaction information usage, *Journal of Marketing*, 69 (July), 131–51; S. Marković and S. Raspor (2010) Content analysis of hotel guest comment cards: a case study of Croatian hotel industry, *Our Economy (Nase Gospodarstvo)*, 56(1/2), 65–74.

[23] See, for example, C. Homburg, N. Koschate and W. D. Hoyer (2005) Do satisfied customers really pay more? A study of the relationship between customer satisfaction and willingness to pay, *Journal of Marketing*, 69 (April), 84–96; N. Franke, P. Keinz and C. J. Steger (2009) Testing the value of customization: when do customers really prefer products tailored to their preferences?, *Journal of Marketing*, 73(5), 103–21.

[24] C. Fornell, S. Mithas, F. V. Morgeson III and M. S. Krishnan (2006) Customer satisfaction and stock prices: high returns, low risk, *Journal of Marketing*, 70 (January), 3–14; see also T. S. Gruca and L. L. Rego (2005) Customer satisfaction, cash flow, and shareholder value, *Journal of Marketing*, 69 (July), 115–30;

K. R. Tuli and S. G. Bharadwaj (2009) Customer satisfaction and stock returns risk. *Journal of Marketing*, 73(6), 184–97; C. Fornell, S. Mithas and F. V. Morgeson III (2009) The economic and statistical significance of stock returns on customer satisfaction, *Marketing Science*, 28(5), 820–5.

[25] J. N. Sheth (2001) The future of relationship marketing, *Journal of Services Marketing*, 16(7), 590–2; L. Alrubaiee, Al-N. Nahla (2010) Investigate the impact of relationship marketing orientation on customer loyalty: the customer's perspective, *International Journal of Marketing Studies*, 2(1), 155–74.

[26] R. T. Rust, T. Ambler, G. S. Carpenter, V. Kumar and K. Rajendra (2004) Measuring marketing productivity: current knowledge and future directions, *Journal of Marketing*, 68(4), 76–8; G. Yuhui (2010) Measuring marketing performance: a review and a framework. *Marketing Review*, 10(1), 25–40.

[27] A. Sharma (2007) The metrics of relationships: measuring satisfaction, loyalty and profitability of relational customers, *Journal of Relationship Marketing*, 6(2), 33.

[28] F. K. Reichheld (2003) The one number you need to grow, *Harvard Business Review*, December, 46–54.

[29] T. L. Keiningham, B. Cooil, L. Ahsay, T. W. Andreassen and J. Weiner (2007) The value of different customer retention recommendation and share-of-wallet, *Managing Service Quality*, 17(14), 361–84.

[30] J. C. Ward and A. L. Ostrom (2006) Complaining to the masses: the role of protest framing in customer-created complaint sites, *Journal of Consumer Research*, 33 (September), 220–30; K. Hart (2006) Angry customers use web to shame firms, *Washington Post*, 5 July.

[31] F. Dahlsten (2003) Avoiding the customer satisfaction rut, *MIT Sloan Management Review*, 44(3), 73–7; see also S. Nambisan and P. Nambisan (2008) How to profit from a better virtual customer environment, *MIT Sloan Management Review*, 49(3), 53–61.

[32] C. Homburg and A. Fürst (2005) How organizational complaint handling drives customer loyalty: an analysis of the mechanistic and the organic approach, *Journal of Marketing*, 69 (July), 95–114 ; Y. Ruoh-Nan and S. Lotz (2009) Taxonomy of the influence of other customers in consumer complaint behavior: a social-psychological perspective, *Journal of Consumer Satisfaction, Dissatisfaction and Complaining Behavior*, vol. 22, 107–26.

[33] P. Kotler (1999) *Kotler on Marketing*, New York: 21–2.

[34] R. Anderson (2007) Rail industry: performance targets raise the bar for quality, *Financial Times*, 18 May.

[35] E. Gummeson (1988) Service quality and product quality combined, *Review of Business*, Winter, Issue 3; R. D. Buzzell and B. T. Gale (1987) *The PIMS Principles: Linking Strategy to Performance*, New York: Free Press, Chapter 6. (PIMS stands for Profit Impact of Market Strategy.)

[36] L. Aksoy, T. L. Keiningham and T. G. Vavra (2005) Nearly everything you know about loyalty is wrong, *Marketing News*, 1 October, 20–1; T. L. Keiningham, T. G. Vavra, L. Aksoy and H. Wallard (2005) *Loyalty Myths*, Hoboken, NJ: John Wiley & Sons.

[37] W. J. Reinartz and V. Kumar (2003) The impact of customer relationship characteristics on profitable lifetime duration, *Journal of Marketing*, 67 (January), 77–99; W. J. Reinartz and V. Kumar (2000) On the profitability of long-life customers in a noncontractual setting: an empirical investigation and implications for marketing, *Journal of Marketing*, 64 (October), 17–35.

[38] K. Weir (2008) Examining the theoretical influences of customer valuation metrics, *Journal of Marketing Management*, 24(7/8), 797–824; Ø. Helgesen (2008) Targeting customers: a financial approach based on creditworthiness, *Journal of Targeting, Measurement and Analysis for Marketing*, 16(4), 261–73.

[39] M. D. Johnson and F. Selnes (2005) Diversifying your customer portfolio, *MIT Sloan Management Review*, 46(3), 11–14; C. Homburg, V. Steiner and D. Totzek (2009) Managing dynamics in a customer portfolio, *Journal of Marketing*, 73(5), 70–89.

[40] M. D. Johnson and F. Selnes (2004) Customer portfolio management, *Journal of Marketing*, 68(2), 1–17 ; L. Ta-you Lee (2010) Head or tail? An integrative analysis of customer value and product portfolio, *International Journal of Business and Management*, 5(12), 51–61.

[41] R. Dhar and R. Glazer (2003) Hedging customers, *Harvard Business Review*, May, 86–92.

[42] J. Vanhamme (2008) The surprise–delight relationship revisited in the management of experience, *Recherche et Applications en Marketing (English edition)*, 23(3), 113–38; A. M. Wayne (2010) Customer delight: a review, *Academy of Marketing Studies Journal*, 14(1), 39–53.

[43] H. Bauer and H. Hammerschmidt (2005) Customer-based corporate valuation – integrating the concept of customer equity and shareholder value, *Management Decision*, 43(3), 331–48.

[44] U. Werner (2008) Getting real about CLV, Marakon Associates, www.marakon.com/ideas_pdf/id_031208_werner.pdf; K. Weir (2008) Examining the theoretical influences of customer valuation metrics, *Journal of Marketing Management*, 24(7/8), 797–824.

[45] A. Payne and P. Frow (2006) Customer relationship management: from strategy to implementation, *Journal of Marketing Management*, 22, 135–68; M. Battor and M. Battor (2010) The impact of customer relationship management capability on innovation and performance advantages: testing a mediated model, *Journal of Marketing Management*, 26(9/10), 842–57; H. Ernst, W. D. Hoyer, M. Krafft and K. Krieger (2011) Customer relationship management and company performance – the mediating role of new product performance, *Journal of the Academy of Marketing Science*, 39(2), 290–306.

[46] A. Payne and P. Frow (2006) Customer relationship management: from strategy to implementation, *Journal of Marketing Management*, 22, 135–68; I-Chiang Wang, Chien-Yu Huang, Yen-Chun Chen and Yu-Ru Lin (2010) The influence of customer relationship management process on management performance, *International Journal of Organizational Innovation*, 2(3); D. M. (2010) Customer relationship management as a business process, *Journal of Business and Industrial Marketing*, 25(1), 4–17.

[47] N. A. Aufreiter, D. Elzinga and J. W. Gordon (2003) Better branding, *McKinsey Quarterly*, 4, 29–39.

[48] Ibid.

[49] D. Peppers and M. Rogers (2001) *One-to-One B2B: Customer Development Strategies for the Business-To-Business World*, New York: Doubleday; D. Peppers and M. Rogers (1993) *The One-to-One Future: Building Relationships One Customer at a Time*, New York: Doubleday; D. Peppers, M. Rogers and B. Dorf (1999) *The One-to-One Fieldbook: The Complete Toolkit for Implementing a One-to-One Marketing Program*, New York: Bantam; R. Tomei (2010) Doing one-to-one marketing one bettter, *Brandweek*, 51(44), 26.

[50]K. R. Tuli, S. G. Bharadwaj and A. K. Kohli (2010) Ties that bind: the impact of multiple types of ties with a customer on sales growth and sales volatility, *Journal of Marketing Research*, 47(1), 36–50. C. Fornell, R. T. Rust and M. G. Dekimpe (2010) The effect of customer satisfaction on consumer spending growth, *Journal of Marketing Research*, 47(1), 28–35.

[51]W. Reinartz, J. S. Thomas and V. Kumar (2005) Balancing acquisition and retention resources to maximize customer profitability, *Journal of Marketing*, 69 (January), 63–79; M. Wright and E. Riebe (2010) Double jeopardy in brand defection, *European Journal of Marketing*, 44(6), 560–73; S. Bogomolova (2010) Life after death? Analyzing post-defection consumer brand loyalty, *Journal of Business Research*, 63(11), 1135–41.

[52]See www.dunnhumby.com/reading/customers-for-life.htm.

[53]See www.carlsonmarketing.com.

[54]M. Carter (2006) How to capture the heart of the 'serial switcher', *Financial Times*, 13 February; L. Guo, J. J. Xiao and C. Tang (2009) Understanding the psychological process underlying customer satisfaction and retention in a relational service, *Journal of Business Research*, 62(111), 1152–9.

[55]F. F. Reichheld (2001) *Loyalty Rules*, Boston, MA: Harvard Business School Press; S. Triest, M. Bun, E. Raaif and M. Vernooif (2009) The impact of customer-specific marketing expenses on customer retention and customer profitability, *Marketing Letters*, 20(2), 125–38.

[56]G. Nairn (2006) Customer experience: Enedesa has to learn how to deal with the customer, *Financial Times*, 18 October.

[57]For an academic examination in a business-to-business context, see R. W. Palmatier, S. Gopalakrishna and M. B. Houston (2006) Returns on business-to-business relationship marketing investments: strategies for leveraging profits, *Marketing Science*, 25 (September–October), 477–93; see also for a retail context P-C. Sun and C-M. Lin (2010) Building customer trust and loyalty: an empirical study in a retailing context, *Services Industries Journal*, 30(9), 1439–55; J-F. Coget (2011) The Apple store effect: does organizational identification trickle down to customers? *Academy of Management Perspectives*, 25(1), 94–5.

[58]H. Simonian (2007) The glossy and growing world of customer magazines, *Financial Times*, 11 October; E. A. van Reijmersdal, P. C. Neijens and E. G. Smit (2010) Customer magazines: effects of commerciality on readers' reactions, *Journal of Current Issues and Research in Advertising*, 32(1), 59–67. For top customer magazines in the UK, see Top ten customer publishing magazines, *Marketing Week*, 2010, 33(38), 23.

[59]J. Gallaugher and S. Ramsbotham (2010) Social media and customer dialog management at Starbucks, *MIS Quarterly Executive*, 9(4), 197–212; U. Hakala and U. Nygrén (2010) Customer satisfaction and the strategic role of university libraries, *International Journal of Consumer Studies*, 34(2), 204–11.

[60]See www.apple.com.

[61]See www.hog.com.

[62]J. Pfeffer (2003) The face of your business, *Business 2.0*, December–January, p. 58.

[63]J. S. Thomas, R. C. Blattberg and E. J. Fox (2004) Recapturing lost customers, *Journal of Marketing Research*, 61 (February), 31–45. See video How to recover lost customers, at http://wn.com/How_To_Recover_Lost_Customers. See also C. Homburg, W. D. Hoyer and R. M Stock (2007) How to get lost customers back? A study of antecedents of relationship revival, *Journal of the Academy of Marketing*, 35 461–74.

[64]M. Tokman and L. M. Davis (2007) The WOW factor: creating value through win-back offers to reacquire lost customers, *Journal of Retailing*, 83(1), 47–64; R. Gee, G. Coates and M. Nicholson (2008) Understanding and profitably managing customer loyalty, *Marketing Intelligence and Planning*, 26(4), 359–74.

[65]J. B. Pine II and J. H. Gilmore (1999) *The Experience Economy*, Boston, MA: Harvard Business School Press.

[66]D. Mosby and M. Weissman (2005) *The Paradox of Excellence*, San Francisco: Jossey-Bass.

[67]T. J. Peters and R. H. Waterman (2004) *In Search of Excellence*, London: Profile.

[68]C. K. Prahalad and V. Ramaswamy (2004) *The Future of Competition: Co-Creating Unique Value with Customers*, Boston, MA: Harvard Business School Press.

[69]Other noteworthy contributions to the exploration of the experience economy include: New issues and opportunities in service design research, *Journal of Operations Management*, 20(2), 117–20. In February 2008 the *Journal of Marketing Management*, 24(1/2) devoted a whole issue to creating the service experience. Papers of particular interest include N. Koenig-Lewis, Experiential values over time, 69–85; S. Baron and H. Kim, Consumers as resource integrators, 113–30; T. M. Fernandes and J. F. Procenca, The blind spot of relationships in consumer markets: the consumer proneness to engage in relationships, 153–68; S. Smidt-Jensen, Søren, C. B. Skytt and L. Winther (2009) The geography of the experience economy in Denmark: employment change and location dynamics in attendance-based experience industries, *European Planning Studies*, 17(6), 847–62; S. Askegaard (2010) Experience economy in the making: hedonism, play and coolhunting in automotive song lyrics, *Consumption, Markets and Culture*, 13(4), 351–71.

[70]D. Walsh (2008) Pret A Manger to go global after £345m sale, *The Times*, 22 February.

[71]M. Saren (2007) Marketing is everything: the view from the street, *Marketing Intelligence and Planning*, 25(1), 11–16; M. Saren, P. Maclarun, C. Goulding, R. Elliott, A. Shankar and M. Cateral (2007) *Critical Marketing*, London: Butterworth Heinemann.

[72]C. Lawer and S. Knox (2006) Customer advocacy and brand development, *Journal of Product and Brand Management*, 15(2), 121–9.

[73]In his 1962 speech to the US Congress, President John F. Kennedy outlined four basic consumer rights: (1) the right to be informed, (2) the right to safety, (3) the right to choose and (4) the right to be heard. These were endorsed by the United Nations as basic consumer rights in 1985.

[74]L. Tiu Wright, A. Newman and C. Dennis (2006) Enhancing consumer empowerment, *European Journal of Marketing*, 40(9/10), 925–35; C. Brennan and M. Coppack (2008) Consumer empowerment: global context, UK strategies and vulnerable consumers, *International Journal of Consumer Studies*, 32(4), 306–13; J. Davies, (2009) Entrenchment of new governance in consumer policy formulation: a platform for European consumer citizenship practice?, *Journal of Consumer Policy*, 32(3), 245–67.

[75]J. A. Deighton (1996) The future of interactive marketing, *Harvard Business Review*, November/December, 151–60; R. Varadarajan and M. S. Yadav (2009) Marketing strategy in an

internet-enabled environment: a retrospective on the first ten years of JIM and a prospective on the next ten years, *Journal of Interactive Marketing*, 23(1), 11–22.

[76]M. Brady, M. R. Fellenz and R. Brookes (2008) Researching the role of information and communications technology (ICT) in contemporary marketing practices, *Journal of Business and Industrial Marketing*, 23(2), 108–14.

[77]F. Malik (2004) *Strategy for the Management of Complex Systems*, 8th edn, Berne, Stuttgart, Vienna: Verlaup Paul Haupt; J. Barry and A. Weinstein, (2009) Business psychographics revisited: from segmentation theory to successful marketing practice, *Journal of Marketing Management*, 25(3/4), 315–40.

[78]F. Hansen and S. Riis Christensen (2007) *Emotions: Advertising and Consumer Choice*, Copenhagen: Copenhagen Business School Press.

[79]S. Robinette, C. Brand and V. Lenz (2001) *Emotion Marketing*, New York: McGraw-Hill; B. Kristin (2008) Carrying too heavy a load? The communication and miscommunication of emotion by email, *Academy of Management Review*, 33(2), 309–27; B. Kidwell, D. M. Hardesty, B. R. Murtha and S. Sheng (2011) Emotional intelligence in marketing exchanges, *Journal of Marketing*, 75(1), 78–95.

[80]C. Fill (2009) *Marketing Communication: Engagement, Strategies and Practice*, 5th edn, Harlow: Pearson Education, . 520–4.

[81]F. E. Bonner, J. R. Bonner and J. H. Faasse (2007) In the mood for advertising, *International Journal of Advertising*, 26(3), 333–55.

[82]Slogan coined by C. Ritz and quoted in R. Nevill and C. E. Jerningham (1908) *Piccadilly to Pall Mall*, London: Duckworth & Co.

Building strong brands

video documentary for part 4

Go to **www.pearsoned.co.uk/ marketingmanagementeurope** to watch the video documentary that relates to Part 4 and consider the issues raised below.

Brands are the primary connector between the organisation and its customers. Well-regarded brands acquire strong customer acceptance and value. The word *brand* can be viewed as a mnemonic which summarises marketing activity, encouraging customers to **B**uy **R**egularly **A**nd **N**ever **D**esert (BRAND).

Part 4: Building strong brands explores two important themes:

1 the purpose of branding; and
2 how to create and sustain a strong well-regarded brand.

Successful marketing enhances the value of a brand or family of brands. A brand stands for the vision, mission and success of a company in developing and delivering offerings that have high levels of customer-perceived value. Brands should seek to develop high and lasting confidence ratings with targeted customers. When watching the video documentary that accompanies Part 4, reflect on how Electrolux perfectly captures the role of branding in the purchasing experience in its guiding mantra 'thinking of you'. Brands should fit their customers' needs like well-tailored clothes.

Once established, a brand is a standard that needs to be continually updated in the light of customer requirements. Good brands are well perceived, progressive, responsive to changing customer expectations, respectful and seen to be different by the customer.

Chris Meares
Chief Executive Officer, Group Private Banking, HSBC

Electrolux

Hear a variety of top marketing executives from a wide range of organisations offer their own interesting and varied perspectives on the key themes of Part 4 including: Chris Meares, Chief Executive Officer, Group Private Banking, HSBC (top); Lucy Caldicott, Head of Fundraising, VSO (centre); and an example of Electrolux's high concept household goods (bottom).

Chapter 12

Creating and managing brands and brand equity

IN THIS CHAPTER, WE WILL ADDRESS THE FOLLOWING QUESTIONS:

1 What do we understand by branding?
2 What are the key strategic brand management decisions?
3 How do we create and manage brand equity?
4 How do we manage service brands?

A strong brand aims to command intense customer loyalty. The most successful brands in the world are worth billions to companies. Zara, the Spanish fashion retailer brand, is valued at €3.34 billion. IKEA, the Swedish furniture brand, is another successful European brand, valued at €6.5 billion. How marketers create and manage brands is of the utmost importance. More than one-third of the world's powerful brands are European.

One of the master marketers at creating brands is Procter & Gamble.[1]

Procter & Gamble successfully markets nearly 300 brands in 160 countries by managing the totality of the marketing mix variables and focusing on the brand image of quality and innovation, aligned to excellent brand management and extension strategies.

Source: Courtesy of Procter & Gamble UK.

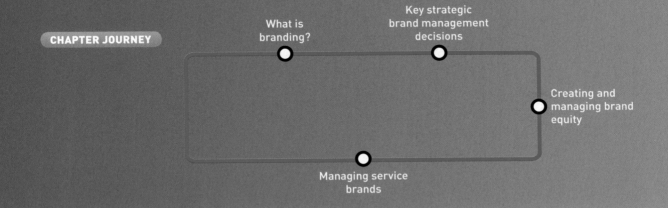
Procter & Gamble (P&G) is one of the most skilful marketers of consumer packaged goods, competing with companies such as Europe's Unilever, Colgate-Palmolive Co., L'Oréal, Henkel and Reckitt Benckiser. It manages many household brands such as Olay, Fairy Liquid, Pringles, Pampers, Braun, Pantene, Oral-B, Ariel, Crest, Wella, Always and Gillette, to name but a few. The company's scope and accomplishments are staggering. It markets nearly 300 brands in more than 160 countries; it is a global leader in 7 of the 12 different product categories in which it competes; 23 of P&G's brands have more than €1 billion in net annual sales, and another 18 have sales between €500 million and €1 billion with total worldwide sales of more than €79 billion a year[2]. Its sustained market leadership rests on a number of different capabilities and philosophies:

- **Customer knowledge.** P&G studies its customers – both end consumers and channel members – through continuous market research and intelligence gathering. It spends more than €100 million annually on more than 10,000 formal consumer research projects and generates more than 3 million consumer contacts via email and call centres. It also puts more emphasis on getting its researchers out into the field, where they can interact with consumers and retailers in their natural environment.
- **Long-term outlook.** P&G takes the time to analyse each opportunity carefully and to prepare the best product. It then commits to making this product a success. It struggled with Pringles potato chips for almost a decade before achieving market success.
- **Product innovation.** P&G is an active product innovator, devoting over €2 billion (3.5 per cent of sales) to innovation research, an impressively high amount for a packaged goods company. It employs more science PhDs than Harvard, Berkeley and MIT combined and applies for roughly 3,000 patents each year. Part of its innovation process is developing brands that offer new consumer benefits. Crest 3D White earned the top non-food spot on the 2010 New Product Pacesetters™ list, and was joined by Olay Professional Pro-X (#7) and Scope Outlast (#8) in the top ten. Five other P&G brands rounded out the top 25 – including Tide Stain Release laundry prewash/additive (#11), Pantene Pro-V Nature Fusion (#13), Secret Scent Expressions (#17), Align (#18) and Febreze Home Collection (#19).[3]
- **Product quality strategy.** P&G designs products of above-average quality and continuously improves them. When P&G says 'new and improved' it means it. Examples include Pantene Ice Shine shampoo, conditioner and styling gel; and Pampers BabyDry with Caterpillar Flex, a nappy designed to prevent leaks when babies' stomachs shrink at night.

- **Brand extension strategy.** P&G produces its brands in several sizes and forms. This strategy gains more shelf space and prevents competitors from moving in to satisfy unmet market needs. P&G also uses its strong brand names to launch new products with instant recognition and much less advertising outlay. The Mr Clean brand has been extended from a household cleaner to a bathroom cleaner, and to a carwash system. Old Spice was successfully extended from men's fragrances to deodorant. Old Spice has toppled Right Guard to become the leading deodorant and antiperspirant for men.[4] Olay has extended into a bodywash called Olay Total Effects.[5]
- **Multibrand strategy.** P&G markets several brands in the same product category, such as Luvs and Pampers nappies and Oral-B and Crest toothbrushes. Each brand meets a different consumer desire and competes against specific competitors' brands. At the same time, P&G prunes carefully to reduce its vast array of products, sizes, flavours and varieties to assemble a stronger brand portfolio focused on the best products.
- **Communication pioneer.** P&G is Britain's biggest advertiser, spending over €200 million on advertising, and it regularly increases its spending on media as it targets growth across the €18 billion worth of brands it manages in the UK.[6] A pioneer in using the power of television to create strong consumer awareness and preference, P&G is now taking a leading role in building its brands on the web and through other digital technologies. P&G's Herbal Essences shampoo sponsored a game on Facebook and Pringles Extreme was launched using advertising on games consoles.[7] It is also infusing stronger emotional appeals into its communications to create deeper consumer connections.
- **Strong sales force.** As part of its communication strategy, P&G's sales force has been named one of the top 25 sales forces by *Sales & Marketing Management* magazine. A key to its success is the close ties its sales force has with retailers.
- **Manufacturing efficiency and cost cutting.** P&G's reputation as a great marketing company is matched by its excellence as a manufacturing company. P&G spends large sums developing and improving production operations to keep its costs among the lowest in the industry, allowing it to reduce the premium prices at which some of its products sell.
- **Brand-management system.** P&G originated the brand-management system, in which one executive is responsible for each brand. The system has been copied by many competitors but not often with P&G's success. Recently P&G modified its general management structure so that each brand category is now run by a category manager with volume and profit responsibility. Although this new organisation does not replace the brand-management system, it helps to sharpen strategic focus on key consumer needs and competition in the category.

It is easy to see that P&G's success is based not on doing one thing well, but on successfully orchestrating the myriad factors that contribute to brand leadership.[8]

The main benefit of a brand is that customers will remember your business. Branding is all about creating value for the customer through all aspects of marketing, which reflects the image that the brand wishes to convey. Managing brands means managing all aspect of the company. In branding, 'everything matters'.

Take the case of Louis Vuitton, the French maker of luxury canvas handbags– the world's most valuable luxury brand in 2011, for the sixth consecutive year.[9]

Rather than ugly scaffolding, the marketing manager of Louis Vuitton chose to use an iconic image of the brand to conceal the building works and to match the brand image.
Source: Jacques Demarthon/AFP/Getty Images

This brand has established a compelling luxury brand distinction over time that is meaningful and connects with its customers, which allows the company to leverage its value and to innovate continuously to stay successful. For Louis Vuitton 'everything matters' and it must and does control every aspect of how its brand is perceived. During the building of the company's fashion museum, its managers realised that the scaffolding and building works would look ugly and would not reflect their brand image. So they covered the scaffold with a designed image of Louis Vuitton luggage which both is iconic and reflects their image of luxury – see the picture above.

Understanding branding

Brands can be extremely valuable assets and an engine for growth within companies. A core management skill of marketers is their ability to create, maintain, enhance and protect brands through their use of all the marketing mix variables. Building a brand is a very expensive and long-term development for companies and must be managed with great expertise.

What is a brand?

A **brand** is a name, symbol, logo, design or image, or any combination of these, which is designed to identify a product or service and distinguish it from those of their competitors. A brand is an entity which offers customers (and other relevant parties) added value over and above its functional performance.[10] A successful brand is an identified product, service, person or place, augmented in such a way that the buyer or user perceives relevant

"No response. We'll have to use the corporate logo flashcards again."

Source: CartoonStock www.CartoonStock.com

unique, sustained added value that matches their needs most closely.[11] A brand basically exists to distinguish a particular product or service from its competitors. A brand is the embodiment of customer goodwill or their feelings and experiences accumulated during the lifetime of use and engagement with the brand. For example, 35 per cent of consumers said 'Mercedes' when asked to name a car that described quality, a reflection of how the brand Mercedes is perceived in the market.

Powerful brands create meaningful images in the mind of the consumer. Nokia, L'Oréal, Gucci and Audi are all European brands that command a strong position in consumers' minds, have a price premium and elicit deep customer loyalty. Newer companies such as Google, Innocent, Red Bull and Zara capture the imagination of consumers and have quickly become major brands. Brands such as Ryanair and easyJet, Aldi and Lidl have all captured market share and brand loyalty in the low price, low service area.

Branding has been around for centuries as a means to distinguish the products or services of one company from those of another.[12] In 2700 BC, Egyptians used such trademarks on farm animals for the avoidance of stealing. One of the earliest signs of branding in Europe was the medieval guilds, which required that craftspeople put trademarks on their products to protect themselves and their customers against inferior quality.[13] In 1266, according to an English law, bakers were obligated to put their specific symbol on every product they sold. In the fine arts, branding began with artists signing their works. The influence of brands in our society is widespread, evidenced by the fact that children as young as three years old can recognise brand logos.[14]

The Chartered Institute of Marketing (UK) defines a brand as a symbol that represents the consumer's experience with an organisation, product or service. A brand is a product or service whose dimensions differentiate it in some way from other products or services, designed to satisfy the same need. It can be viewed as a holistic, emotional and intangible experience. A brand can be strong enough to evoke feelings of belonging, love and affection. Research has continually identified the emotional responses associated with brands, such as sensory pleasure, aesthetic beauty or excitement.[15]

The roles of brands

Brands play many roles. Two of the main roles are functional and emotional roles.

- **Functional role of brands** This relates to the actual performance of the product or service. Did the product work; did the service provide what was needed? This was very prevalent in the early twentieth century as companies stressed how well their offerings worked. Nowadays many of the functional benefits of products and services are similar, so brand management invests in designing an emotional connection. Many marketing experts believe that a good brand should have both functional and emotional components. In other words, they should appeal to the head and the heart.

- **Emotional role of brands** This is concerned with the move away from the functionality of the brand to connecting with the customer emotionally – building emotional ties with the customer rather than focusing on how the product or service works.[16] Nike, for example, does not mention its product or the functional values of its sport shoes or the rational benefits of wearing them, but relates to the emotional connection to great athletics and greatness. Nike is about winning and all the emotions connected with winning. **Emotions** play a powerful role in the customer's selection, satisfaction and loyalty towards brands. Marketers need to understand the emotional dynamics involved when a customer selects and decides to continue to use a product or service brand. Research has confirmed that modern consumers no longer simply buy products and services; instead they buy experiences and dreams.[17] **Emotional branding** is engaging the consumer on the level of senses and emotions; forging a deep, lasting, intimate emotional connection to the brand that transcends material satisfaction; it involves creating a holistic experience that delivers an emotional fulfilment so that the customer develops a special bond with and unique trust in the brand.[18] As Robert Pole, Chief Executive of the Gucci Group, noted: 'We are not in the business of selling handbags. We are in the business of selling dreams!'[19] Marketing is not a battle of products and services, it is a battle of perceptions. The power of a brand lies in what resides in the minds of customers – what they learned, felt, saw, and heard about the brand as a result of their experiences over time.

In our consumer culture, people no longer consume for merely functional satisfaction but consumption becomes meaning based and brands are often used as symbolic resources for the construction and maintenance of identity.[20] People can express themselves – their identities – through their brand choices. Take a look around you; look at how people brand themselves by the clothes they wear, the people they associate with, the places they go, what they consume, what music they listen to, and what they upload on their iPods or to their online social networking site. This is all part of personal branding and shows how the concept of branding is so prevalent within our society that it permeates into the core of life.[21] **Lifestyle branding** can be seen as a way to break free of the cutthroat competition within a category by connecting with consumers on a more personal level.[22] Switching from functional to lifestyle brand positioning, brands might be setting themselves up for a much broader, and often fiercer, competition for a share of consumer identity. Within lifestyle branding Gillette then competes with Dove and Ralph Lauren – all lifestyle brands. The self-expressive function of brands can be related to the notion of *conspicuous consumption*, a term used to describe the acquisition of products and services mainly for the purpose of attaining or maintaining social status.[23]

Let's distinguish between brand identity and image. **Brand identity** is the way a company aims to identify or position itself or its product or service in the minds of the consumer. **Brand image** is the way the consumer actually perceives the visual or verbal expressions of a brand, which leads to the psychological or emotional associations that the brand aspires to maintain in the mind of the consumer.[24] For the right image to be established in the minds of consumers, the marketer must convey brand identity through every available marketing mix variable. Brand identity should be diffused in everything the company does.

The power of the brand lies in what resides in the mind of the consumer. **Brand knowledge** consists of all the thoughts, feelings, images, experiences, beliefs and so on that become associated with the brand. In particular, brands must create strong, favourable and unique brand associations with customers. Think of Volvo (*safety*), Hallmark (*caring*) and Red Bull (*adventure*). Understanding consumer brand knowledge – all the different things that become linked to the brand in the minds of consumers – is thus of paramount importance because it is the foundation of **brand equity** – which is the added value the brand endows a product or service. It is the customer's assessment of the brand above and beyond its objectively perceived value.[25]

The **brand religion model**[26] describes the evolution of the role of brands in consumers' lives as a five-stage process. Figure 12.1 highlights the steps that customers can go through as they move forward in their beliefs about brands. Weak brands play the role of mere *products or services* in people's lives; they have no meaning beyond their functionality. *Concept brands* carry with them emotional values that resonate with consumers and call for increased involvement. *Corporate concepts* are those brands which reflect the corporate strategy, expressing a wider philosophy that extends throughout the company. More valuable still are those brands that become *brand cultures*, seen by consumers as being fully embedded in their social lives. The most coveted place on this evolution is when a product or service achieves a status of a *brand religion*, when consumers view it as a total way of life.

For branding strategies to be successful and brand value to be created, consumers must be convinced there are meaningful differences among brands in the product or service category. Brand differences are often related to attributes or benefits of the product or service itself. Some brands create competitive advantages through intangible image or non-product-related means. Chanel No. 5 perfume has become a leader in its product category by understanding consumer motivations and desires and creating relevant and appealing images around its products. Often these intangible images are the only way to distinguish brands. Customers recognise and relate to images of brands.

Marketers can apply branding virtually anywhere a consumer has a choice. It is possible to brand a physical good (Pantene shampoo, BMW X5 series), a service (France Telecom, Aviva general insurance), a shop (Les Galeries Lafayette, Carrefour), a person (David Beckham, Jamie Oliver), a place (Paris, a region of Spain – the Costa del Sol), an organisation (UNICEF, Automobile Association), a group (U2 or Coldplay), or an idea (free trade, freedom of speech).[27]

The marketing insight box looks at how Toyota through its Lexus brand used emotional branding to create a connection with its customers.

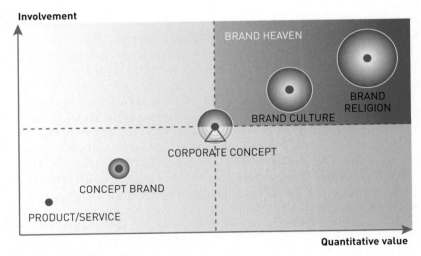

Figure 12.1 Brand religion model
Source: Kunde, J. (2002) *Corporate Religion*, 1st ed., Financial Times Prentice Hall. Copyright © 2002 Pearson Education Ltd. Reproduced with permission. Kunde & Co. (2011) http://kunde-co.com/corporate-religion.aspx.

Marketing insight

Toyota's Lexus creates an emotional brand connection

The idea of Toyota competing in the luxury BMW and Mercedes brand arenas in Europe was something both the market and Toyota did not think was possible. Then came the Lexus, which shows clearly that the luxury market is different and that a different emotional connection was needed. Toyota was not positioned as a premium brand in the minds of consumers, so what it had to do to compete in this market segment was to create a premium brand. Although it shared engineering, chassis and design elements with other Toyota cars, the Lexus went beyond that and into the luxury domain in functionality and also service. According to Toyota, they 'always focused on what matters most to the luxury customer. This is why we build products that are not only admired on the outside but also highly refined on the inside. And why we don't simply produce fine cars but pursue perfection to create the finest luxury vehicles on the road. It's also why we don't merely offer an excellent dealership experience but one that is unequalled in the luxury automotive category. And why we promise to make the most of every moment our customer spends with us.'

This focus on the customer experience gained Lexus the number-one spot in the J. D. Power 2011 Customer Satisfaction Index Study, on the basis of overall dealership experience, service initiation and quality of work.

Lexus has consistently received the highest customer satisfaction rating and over the years has created a brand experience valued by the customer. Almost 96 per cent of Lexus customers said that their cars were perfectly serviced.

The Lexus luxury dealership experience reflects Toyota's understanding that the branding goes beyond the vehicle into every aspect of the product/service offering:

- the way the salesperson approaches customers in the showroom;
- how he or she is dressed (in a suit, compared to Saturn salespeople in polos);
- the layout of the showroom;
- the choice of luxury building materials and interiors – slate floors and leather chairs in the waiting areas;
- the cleanliness of service areas.

Thus the branding of Lexus continues after the sale.

Digital branding (Chapter 13) is also used by Toyota to support the positioning of Lexus, with a Facebook page where customers are encouraged to communicate their queries and concerns on the brand's wall with answers provided by customer service representatives. Toyota offers further service assistance through the Lexus helpline and the brand's website.[28] The brand image of Lexus is highlighted in the image below[29] aligned to the essence, the promises, the benefits and the personality.

LEXUS BRAND

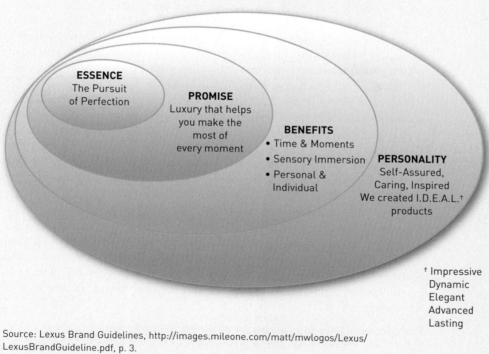

† Impressive
Dynamic
Elegant
Advanced
Lasting

Source: Lexus Brand Guidelines, http://images.mileone.com/matt/mwlogos/Lexus/ LexusBrandGuideline.pdf, p. 3.

Managing brands: consumers and channels

Brands provide many advantages to customers and companies, and valuable functions for companies within their channels of distribution and networks:[30]

- Brands signal a certain level of quality or expected level of satisfaction, so that satisfied buyers can easily choose the product or service again.[31]
- Brands facilitate purchase so that customers do not have high levels of indecision as to what to buy.
- Brands reduce the perceived risk in the purchase situation and reduce the time needed to shop or purchase. As consumers' lives are often complicated, rushed and time starved, the ability of a brand to simplify decision making and reduce risk is invaluable.[32]
- A brand offers legal protection for unique features or aspects of the product or service.[33] The brand name can be protected through registered trademarks. These intellectual property rights ensure that the company can safely invest in the brand and reap the benefits of a valuable asset.
- Brands create greater customer loyalty, which provides predictability and security of demand for the company and creates barriers to entry that make it difficult for other companies to enter the market.
- Brand loyalty also means that companies are less vulnerable to competitive marketing activities or to marketing crises.
- Brand loyalty can also translate into customer willingness to pay a higher price – often 20–25 per cent more than for competing brands.[34] Brand loyalty also ensures that customers are more favourable to price increases.
- Brands are hard to copy. Although competitors may duplicate product or service designs, they cannot easily match lasting impressions left in the minds of individuals and organisations by years of marketing activity and customer experiences. Take the example of bottled water – water is water, yet many companies have created brand images for their water for which they can charge a premium price. The brand names Evian and San Pellegrino, carry the aura of quality, and customers can tell the difference between each brand. Evian, the French brand of mineral water, is portrayed as a luxury and expensive bottled water. San Pelligrino, the Italian mineral water, reflects classic elegance and memorable moments like savouring of food, the enjoyment of friends and family, and the pleasure of sharing. San Pellegrino's Fabio degli Esposti, International Business Unit Director, says that 'In capturing snapshots of life's celebrated moments, our new campaign maintains the brand's classic image while continuing to resonate with today's consumers.'
- Branding can be a powerful means to secure a competitive advantage.[35]
- Brands help companies to differentiate their product or service from others. Think of the perception of the service provision from airlines such as Air France-KLM, British Airways and Lufthansa as opposed to Ryanair and easyJet. All offer the customer air travel, but the brands reflect different levels of service or different segments that have different values – in this case, either service or price – from the high service levels of Air France to the low service levels of easyJet.
- Brands increase marketing communication efficiencies.
- Brands attract higher-quality employees.
- Brands elicit stronger support from channel and supply network partners.
- Brands create growth opportunities through brand extensions and licensing.
- Brands help companies to segment their markets and enable them to have a variety of different products or services within the same market but aimed at different target markets.

Consider how L'Oréal manages its many brands and product ranges.

L'Oréal Paris

L'Oréal is famous for its slogan 'Because you're worth it', and it is this brand and slogan which provide the company with one-third of all the profit made by the L'Oréal group of brands. Let's put that in perspective. L'Oréal owns a large number of the leading cosmetic and beauty brands including:

- L'Oréal Professional hair products
- Maybelline cosmetics
- Garnier hair products
- Vichy skin care
- Biotherm skin care
- Kiehl's speciality skin care, hair care and body care
- Lancome cosmetics
- Shu Uemura cosmetics
- Redken hair products
- Helena Rubenstein
- Elvive hair care
- Plénitude skin care range

Why would L'Oréal want to own so many competing product brands and also keep innovating and bringing out new products? Simple. Each brand is positioned towards a different type of consumer. Lancome, for example, is one of the heavyweights of the cosmetics world, creating pure glamour for those whom money is no object to beauty. Shu Uemura is the work of Mr Shu Uemura, a Japanese make-up artist, and in typical Japanese fashion, offers a high-quality blend of art, technology and style. Maybelline focuses on a larger, younger market with the 'Maybe she's born with it. Maybe it's Maybelline' tagline. The L'Oréal products sit nicely in the mainstream – they are good, consistent products at affordable prices, and have captured the imagination of a select target market with the 'Because you are worth it' slogan.[36]

Strategic brand management

Brand management uses the choice, design and implementation of marketing mix activities to build, measure and manage the brand value.[37] **Strategic brand management** is the long-term effort of consciously providing an offering with an identity that is understood on all levels. This means both internally and externally and includes customers, employees, suppliers and resellers. It is the sustained effort by the company to encourage people to see its brand in the light in which it portrays it.

Strategic brand management can dramatically increase corporate success according to a study by Booz Allen Hamilton, which noted that 80 per cent of European companies that are managed with a strong brand focus have operating profits twice as high as the sector average.[38] The stock values for companies reflect a belief that strong brands result in better earnings and profit performance for companies, which, in turn, create greater value for shareholders.[39] See the marketing insight box on next page.

An important issue is to have a **brand vision** that offers a clear and consistent message about the value of the brand. A brand vision involves recognising the inherent potential of a brand, which is based in part on its customer brand equity – the value of the brand to the company. The brand value is only realised if the right marketing processes, programmes and activities are put in place.

There must be clear value propositions from the consumer perspective. The long-term brand vision is operationalised through both long- and short-term marketing endeavours.

Marketing insight

Europe's brand-oriented companies almost twice as successful

Brand-oriented companies enjoy a high public profile and consumer confidence. Both are painstakingly developed over time as a result of high-quality and innovative products and services, and often resource-intensive communication. Brands created in this way then generate more added value and often constitute the most valuable asset of the company. The consumer confidence that has been built up is extremely important for brand-oriented companies and constitutes a strategic element to competition.

Strategic brand management can dramatically increase corporate success, according to a study by Booz Allen Hamilton and branding experts Wolff Olins. The Booz Allen Hamilton–Wolff Olins study is based on interviews with leading marketing and sales executives at Europe's top 500 companies.

Some 90 per cent of the companies surveyed are convinced that brand orientation is a key factor in their success – a twofold increase compared to five years ago. 'However, only 18 per cent of companies currently place brand management at the heart of their activities and have a clear understanding of the brand across the entire organisation,' said Booz Allen Vice President, Gregor Harter. 'This small group of companies is proving to be exceptionally successful.'

The study places companies into one of three categories:

1 Brand agnostic companies: management assumes that branding only makes a modest contribution to corporate success, focusing instead on factors such as costs and optimising processes.

2 Emerging brand companies: on the threshold of full-brand orientation. These companies recognise the growing importance of brand's contribution to value and have already begun to embed it into their corporate strategy.

3 Brand guided companies: already rigorously implementing brand management to achieve corporate success. The study revealed a clear correlation among brand-guided companies, the application of sophisticated marketing techniques, and corporate success.

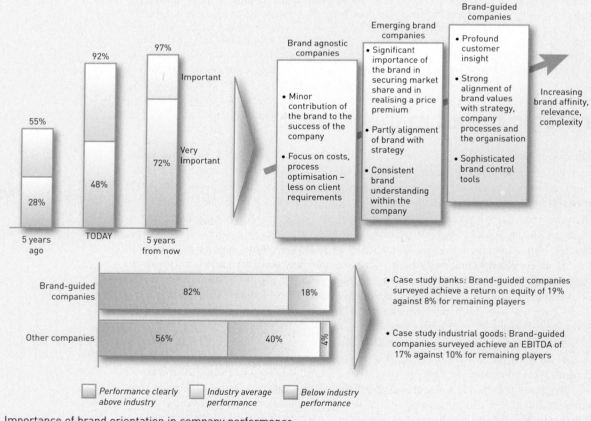

Importance of brand orientation in company performance

*According to the statements of the interviewees

Source: Booz Allen Wolff Olins, European Survey Among Marketing and Sales Officers, 8/2004. In Harter, G., Koster, A. and Peterson, M. (2005) *Managing Brands for Value Creation*, Booz & Co., p. 2, Exhibit 1, Exhibit 2.

▶ Marketing insight *(continued)*

Companies with a strong brand orientation more frequently measure the key ratios that enable them to manage their marketing performance. For example, 45 per cent regularly calculate their share of their customers' total spend, compared to 24 per cent of the other companies surveyed; 64 per cent of brand-guided companies regularly examine whether their brand position allows any degree of price flexibility, compared to only 20 per cent of brand agnostic or emerging brand companies.

The study also revealed another common trait shared by brand guided companies. Brand management is handled at the strategic management level of the organisation and is closely tied to developing strategy and managing the organisation.

Sources: German Brand Association (2009) European Commission Consultation Follow-up to the Green Paper on Consumer Collective Redress: www.c.europa.eu/consumers/redress_cons/responses/CP_GBA_en.pdf; Gregor Harter, Alex Koster, Dr Michael Peterson and Michael Stomberg, *Managing Brands for Value Creation* (2005).

Marketers must provide a clear sense of direction for each employee within the company to appreciate how their role affects brand values. The four core activities are:

1 Ensure identification of the brand with customers and an association of the brand in customers' minds with a specific product or service class or customer need.
2 Firmly establish the brand meaning in the minds of customers (by strategically linking a host of tangible and intangible brand associations).
3 Elicit the proper customer responses to this brand identity and brand meaning.
4 Convert brand response to create an intense, active loyalty relationship between the customer and the brand.

Different marketing activities have different strengths and can accomplish different objectives. Marketers should therefore engage in a range of marketing mix activities, each of which plays a specific role in building or maintaining the brand. Sometimes marketers don't understand the real importance of all aspects of marketing to their brand until they change a crucial element of the brand and over time see the effects. An example is Burberry, the British luxury brand, which had to be repositioned skilfully after it lost control of aspects of its marketing.

Burberry

Burberry found, to its cost, that how the consumer views a company and its products can change. The familiar check pattern, synonymous throughout the world as the Burberry brand of luxury and elitism, began to be worn by more and more people, by C-grade celebrities and even at football matches. The distinctive beige check, once only associated with A-listers, had become the uniform of a rather different social group within the United Kingdom called 'chavs'. 'Chav' is a mainly derogatory slang term for a person fixated on low-quality or counterfeit goods and is often associated with anti-social behaviour. Burberry's appeal to 'chav' fashion sense is a sociological example of prole drift, where an up-market product begins to be consumed *en masse* by a lower socioeconomic group. Burberry argued that the brand's popular association with 'chav' fashion sense was linked to counterfeit versions of the clothing.

Burberry had to react fast to the damage to its brand image. From a product perspective it removed the checked pattern from all but 10 per cent of its product range and discontinued sales of baseball caps from its product line. Burberry also cracked down on fake/counterfeit goods, which allowed what it considered to be the wrong sort of people to look as if they were wearing the brand. It took legal action against high-profile infringements of the brand and invested heavily in protecting against counterfeit. Burberry also changed its supply network, and again became available only in upmarket shops, reflecting its brand image.[40]

The 'chav' phenomenon in Britain damaged the Burberry brand while the image above profiles the brand image that Burberry would like to present.
Source: Image courtesy of The Advertising Archives

Strategic brand management focuses on building the brand after the positioning choices (Chapter 11) have been made. It is the planning and implementing of a brand management programme which consists of the following six main features:

1 creating and managing brand identities: names, logos, slogans and images;
2 managing individual or house brands;
3 managing brand extensions;
4 managing brand portfolios;
5 brand reinforcing and revitalisation; and
6 growing and sustaining brand equity.

We will look at each of these in turn.

Creating and managing brand identities: names, logos, slogans and images

As more and more firms realise that the brand names associated with their products or services are among their most valuable assets, creating, maintaining and enhancing the strength of those brands has become a marketing management imperative.[41] There are three main challenges to creating and managing brand identities:

1 The initial choices need to be made for the brand elements or identities making up the brand. These include the brand names, logos, symbols, characters, slogans, accompanying music, websites, product or service design and features, packaging, and so on.

2 All accompanying marketing activities must support the brand. The Juicy Couture label is one of the fastest-growing fashion labels, whose edgy, contemporary sportswear and accessories have a strong lifestyle appeal to women, men and children. Positioned as a luxury, the brand maintains its exclusive image by limiting distribution, designing cutting-edge fashion and using a somewhat risqué name linked to a rebellious attitude.[42]

3 Other associations need to be transferred indirectly to the brand by linking it to other entities (people, places or things) called secondary brand associations. The brand name Credit Suisse, used as a symbol of reliability in commercial banking, leverages the perceived view of the country as reliable in banking and helps to communicate the positioning of the brand.

Secondary branding

Many brands create brand equity by linking the brand to secondary brand associations. For example, when Nokia introduced a mini laptop it was referred as the Nokia 3G Booklet, thereby creating an association, as consumers are already aware of Nokia mobile phones. Associations can also be made to countries or other geographical regions: for example, Audi's slogan 'Vorsprung durch Technik' solidified its association with Germany – renowned for excellent engineering – and has become one of the best-known slogans in advertising. Brands can be associated with channels of distribution (through channel strategy), as well as to other brands (through ingredient or co-branding), characters (through licensing), spokespeople (through endorsements), sporting or cultural events (through sponsorship), or some other third-party sources (through awards or reviews). Figure 12.2 shows the range of secondary sources of brand knowledge.

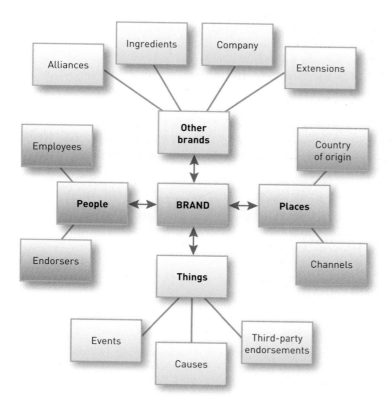

Figure 12.2 Secondary sources of brand knowledge

Choosing brand elements

Brand elements are those trademarkable devices that identify and differentiate the brand. They are often the most tangible representation of the brand. Most strong brands employ multiple brand elements. Nike has the distinctive 'swoosh' logo, the empowering 'Just Do It' slogan, and the 'Nike' name based on the Greek winged goddess of victory. Marketers should choose brand elements to build as much brand equity as possible. The test is how consumers would think or feel about the product or service if the brand elements were all they knew. For example, based on the name alone, what might consumers expect from RightGuard deodorant or the Michelin man cartoon character.

Criteria for choosing brand names

There are six main criteria for choosing brand names, listed below. The first three – memorable, meaningful and likeable – are 'brand building'. The latter three – transferable, adaptable and protectable – are 'defensive' and deal with how to leverage and preserve the equity in a brand element in the face of challenges.

In general, brand names should be short and simple, easy to spell and pronounce, pronounceable in only one way and one language, and easy to recognise and remember. Many, such as BBC, Orange and Mastercard, follow the criteria below, while some very successful names do not. Examples are Birkenstock, Adidas and Stella Artois.

1 **Memorable.** How easily is the brand element recalled and recognised? Short names such as Virgin, Sky, Dove and Zara are memorable brand names.
2 **Meaningful.** Is the brand name credible and suggestive of the product or service? Does it suggest something about a product ingredient or service quality, or the type of person who might use the brand? Consider the inherent meaning in names such as Crisp 'n Dry, Head and Shoulders, Fast Fit Exhausts, RightGuard deodorant, Sure Underarm Protection, Energeriser Batteries and Lean Cuisine low-calorie foods.
3 **Likeable.** How aesthetically appealing is the brand name? Is it likeable visually, verbally and in other ways? A recent trend is playful names like Flickr photo sharing. Concrete brand names such as Mr Muscle, Little Chef, and Shake and Vac are likeable names. Many characters associated with brands are also inherently likeable. Think of Snuggle the Fabric Softener Bear or 'The Snuggle Bear'.[43]
4 **Transferable.** Can the brand element be used to introduce new products or services in the same or different categories? Does it add to brand equity across geographic boundaries and market segments? Though American, Amazon was smart enough not to use an American word so that the brand could be used across the globe. Amazon is the name of the world's largest river and the name suggest the wide variety of goods that can be shipped and is an important descriptor of the diverse range of products the company now sells.
5 **Adaptable.** How adaptable and updatable is the brand name? Take Zara – the brand name is adaptable and timeless across their markets.
6 **Protectable.** How legally protectable is the brand name? Names that become synonymous with product or service categories can be difficult to manage. Brand names such as Kleenex, Hoover, Sellotape, Google, Xerox and Bandaid have all become known as the general title for the product or sevice. You hear people saying 'Did you google that or do you have a bandaid?

See the marketing memo for more discussion of brand names.

Brand elements can play a number of brand-building roles.[44] Brand elements should be easy to recognise and recall, and inherently descriptive and persuasive. The likeability and appeal of brand elements may also play a critical role in awareness and associations,

Marketing memo

Brand names

Brand names come in many styles.

- Acronym: a name made of initials, e.g. BP, UPS and IBM.

- Descriptive: names that describe a product benefit or function, Whole Foods, Volkswagen and Airbus.

- Alliteration and rhyme: names that are fun to say and stick in the mind, Planters Peanuts and Dunkin' Donuts.

- Evocative: names that evoke a relevant vivid image, e.g. Amazon and Crest.

- Neologisms: completely made-up words, e.g. Wii and Kodak.

- Foreign word: adoption of a word from another language, e.g. Volvo and Samsung.

- Founders' names: using the names of real people and founder's name, e.g. Henkel and Adidas. Alfa Romeo combines an acronym from Anonima Lombarda Fabbrica Automobili and an owner's name, as Romeo was added when Nicola Romeo bought ALFA in 1915.

- Geography: many brands are named after regions and landmarks, e.g. Cisco Systems, named after San Francisco, where the company is based.

Source: Merriam Associates (2009) Styles and types of company and product names, http://merriamassociates.com/2009/02/styles-and-types-of-company-and-product-names/.

---

leading to high brand equity.[45] The Snap, Crackle and Pop characters from Kellogg's reinforce the sense of magic and fun for breakfast cereals. The three elf brothers made their debut in 1933 but have since had several makeovers and still maintain their popularity with children all over the world. Bird's Eye also developed an image that remains relevant today – Captain Bird's Eye still sails the Bird's Eye ship. Many UK-based insurance companies have used symbols of strength (the Rock of Gibraltar for Prudential and the stag for Hartford), security (the eagle of Eagle Star), and agility and strength (the horse for Lloyds Bank).

Brand slogans

Brand slogans or tag lines are an extremely efficient means to build and manage brands and are eternally focused. Slogans are part of a persuasive appeal that is intended to convey something good or to remind consumers of a brand's attributes.[46] Brands are attributed humanlike personality traits with whom consumers develop emotional attachments and share commitments. Therefore the **brand slogans** or tag lines can function as useful 'hooks' or 'handles' to help consumers grasp what the brand is and what makes it special – summarising and translating the intent of the total marketing programme. Think of the inherent brand meaning in slogans such as Kit Kat – 'Have a break – have a Kit Kat'; L'Oréal – 'Because you're worth it'; Carlsberg – 'Probably the best lager in the world' or their more recent –'That calls for a Carlsberg'; Boot's – 'Trust Boots', Gillette – 'The best a man can get'; Burger King – 'Have it your way'.

These slogans can be used globally with greater or lesser success. A great example is the 'Snap, Crackle and Pop' slogan, which has been translated across Europe:[47]

- English: 'Snap! Crackle! Pop!'
- French: 'Cric! Crac! Croc!'
- Spanish: 'Pim! Pum! Pam!'
- German: 'Knisper! Knasper! Knusper!'
- Swedish: 'Piff! Paff! Puff!'
- Finnish: 'Riks! Raks! Poks!'
- Dutch: 'Pif! Paf! Pof!'

The Snap, Crackle and Pop slogan has been translated into many European languages.
Source: Courtesy of the Kellogg Group

In a German survey of 1,000 consumers aged 14–49, some slogans did not work so well. When asked to translate 12 popular advertising slogans, almost two-thirds did not properly understand the slogans. For example, Adidas's 'Impossible is nothing' was translated as 'An imposing nothing' and 'Welcome to the Becks experience' was translated as 'Welcome to the Becks experiment'.[48]

Brand mantras

To support the intent of brand positioning and the way firms would like consumers to think about the brand, it is often useful to define a brand mantra which is an internal focus for the brand.[49] A **brand mantra** is an articulation of the heart and soul of the brand and is closely related to other branding concepts like 'brand essence' and 'core brand promise.' Brand mantras are short, three- to five-word phrases that capture the irrefutable essence or spirit of the brand positioning. Their purpose is to ensure that all employees within the organisation and all external marketing partners understand what the brand fundamentally represents with consumers, so they can adjust their actions accordingly. BMW (Bavarian Motor Works) has been known as the 'ultimate driving machine' for over 50 years. This successful mantra applies to all its products, including cars, motorcycles and sport utility vehicles. BMW's communication strategy and brand equity comes with its message about speed, driving and handling.

Brand mantras are powerful devices. They can provide guidance about what products to introduce under the brand, what ad campaigns to run, and where and how to sell the brand. Their influence, however, can extend beyond these tactical concerns. Brand mantras may even guide the most seemingly unrelated or mundane decisions, such as the look of a reception area or the way phones are answered. In effect, they create a mental filter to screen out brand-inappropriate marketing activities or actions of any type that may have a negative bearing on customers' impressions of a brand.

Brand mantras must economically communicate what the brand is and what it is *not*. What makes for a good brand mantra? A high-profile and successful examples is Nike, which shows the power, range and utility of a well-designed brand mantra.

Nike

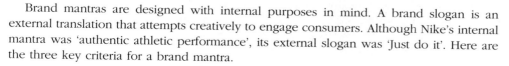

Nike has a rich set of associations with consumers, based on its innovative product designs, its sponsorships of top athletes, its award-winning advertising, its competitive drive and its irreverent attitude. Internally, Nike marketers adopted the three-word brand mantra, 'authentic athletic performance' to guide their efforts. Thus, in Nike's eyes, its entire marketing programme – its products and how they are sold – must reflect those key brand values. Over the years, Nike has expanded its brand meaning from 'running shoes' to 'athletic shoes' to 'athletic shoes and clothing' to 'all things associated with athletics (including equipment)'. Each step of the way, however, it has been guided by its 'authentic athletic performance' brand mantra. For example, as Nike rolled out its successful clothing line, one important hurdle for the products was that they could be made innovative enough through material, cut or design to truly benefit top athletes. At the same time, the company has been careful to avoid using the Nike name to brand products that do not fit with the brand mantra (like casual 'brown' shoes).

Brand mantras are designed with internal purposes in mind. A brand slogan is an external translation that attempts creatively to engage consumers. Although Nike's internal mantra was 'authentic athletic performance', its external slogan was 'Just do it'. Here are the three key criteria for a brand mantra.

1 **Communicate.** A good brand mantra should define the category (or categories) of business for the brand and set the brand boundaries. It should also clarify what is unique about the brand.
2 **Simplify.** An effective brand mantra should be memorable. For that, it should be short, crisp and vivid in meaning.
3 **Inspire.** Ideally, the brand mantra should also stake out ground that is personally meaningful and relevant to as many employees as possible.

Brand mantras are typically designed to capture the brand's points-of-difference: that is, what is unique about the brand. Other aspects of the brand positioning – especially the brand's points-of-parity – may also be important and may need to be reinforced in other ways.

For brands facing rapid growth, it is helpful to define the product, service or benefit space in which the brand would like to compete, as Nike did with 'athletic performance' and Disney does with 'family entertainment.' Words that describe the nature of the product or service, or the type of experiences or benefits the brand provides, can be critical to identifying appropriate categories into which to extend. For brands in more stable categories where extensions into more distinct categories are less likely to occur, the brand mantra may focus more exclusively on points-of-difference.

Brand mantras derive their power and usefulness from their collective meaning. Other brands may be strong on one, or perhaps even a few, of the brand associations making up the brand mantra. But for the brand mantra to be effective, no other brand should singularly excel on all dimensions. Part of the key to both Nike's and Disney's success is that for years no competitor could really deliver on the combined promise suggested by their brand mantras.

Brand narratives and storytelling

Rather than outlining specific attributes or benefits, some marketing experts describe positioning a brand as telling a narrative or story.[50]

Randall Ringer and Michael Thibodeau see *narrative branding* as based on deep metaphors that connect to people's memories, associations and stories.[51] They identify five elements of narrative branding: (1) the brand story in terms of words and metaphors; (2) the consumer journey in terms of how consumers engage with the brand over time and touchpoints where they come into contact with it; (3) the visual language or expression for the brand; (4) the manner in which the narrative is expressed experientially in terms of how the brand engages the senses; and (5) the role/relationship the brand plays in the lives of consumers. Based on literary convention and brand experience, they also offer the following framework for a brand story:

- **Setting**: the time, place and context.
- **Cast**: the brand as a character, including its role in the life of the audience, its relationships and responsibilities, and its history or creation myth.
- **Narrative Arc**: the way the narrative logic unfolds over time, including actions, desired experiences, defining events and the moment of epiphany.
- **Language**: the authenticating voice, metaphors, symbols, themes and leitmotifs.

Patrick Hanlon developed the related concept of 'primal branding', which views brands as complex belief systems. According to Hanlon, diverse brands such as Google, Mini Cooper, Starbucks, Apple, UPS and Aveda all have a 'primal code' or DNA that resonates with their customers and generates their passion and fervour. He outlines seven assets that make up this belief system or primal code: a creation story, creed, icon, rituals, sacred words, a way of dealing with non-believers, and a good leader.[52]

Managing individual or house brands

A branding strategy decision is how to develop a brand name for a product or service category. A brand name should provide a positive contribution to brand equity: for example, it should convey certain value associations or responses. Based on its name alone, a consumer might expect ColorStay lipsticks to be long-lasting and Sunkist Orange Juice to be a healthy, natural orange juice full of vitamin C.

Four general strategies are often used:

1 **Individual names.** The British/Dutch company Unilever has many individually named brands within its company, including many familiar brands such as Hellmann's, Knorr, Bird's Eye, Surf, Dove, Pond's and Calvin Klein fragrances. L'Oréal, the French

cosmetics company, also has many brands including Maybelline New York, the Garnier brand and – more recently – The Body Shop. A major advantage of an individual names strategy is that the company does not tie its reputation to the individual product or service. If a product or service fails or appears to have a brand image contrary to the company's, the other products or service are not damaged. Companies often use different brand names for different quality lines within the same product or service class. Lufthansa owns most of GermanWings but does not share a name with the low-cost airline, in part to protect the brand equity of its Lufthansa brand.

2 **Blanket corporate, family or house names.** Many companies use their corporate, family or house brand across their range of products or services.[53] Development costs are lower with blanket brand names because there is no need to run a 'name' search or spend heavily on advertising to create recognition. An example is Tata – the Indian company probably most famous for the Tata car. It uses the Tata family name across its diverse product categories, such as salt, tea, coffee, cars, and steel. Sales of a new product or service are likely to be strong if the family corporate or house name is good.

3 **Separate family or house names for all products and services.** Inditex, a company most people have probably never heard of, uses separate brand names for its retail shops, from the very familiar Zara and Massimo Dutti to the less familiar Pull & Bear, Stradivarius and Bershka. These are all very different brand names targeted at different segments with various levels of success. If a company produces quite different products, one blanket name is often not desirable. Louis Vuitton and Moët Hennessy manage a whole portfolio of luxury brands under different brand names. They range from wines and spirits (Krug, Belvedere vodka) to jewellery (TAG Heuer, Chaumet) to fashion labels (Marc Jacobs, Donna Karan) and perfume (Gerlain, Parfums Givenchy).

4 **Corporate name combined with individual product names.** Kellogg's combines corporate and individual names in Kellogg's Rice Krispies, Kellogg's Bran Flakes and Kellogg's Corn Flakes, as do Honda, Sony and HP for their products. The company name legitimises, and the individual name individualises, the product or service.

Individual names and blanket family names are sometimes referred to as a 'house of brands' and a 'branded house' respectively, and they represent two ends of a brand relationship continuum. Separate family names come in between the two, and corporate-plus-individual names combine them. Companies rarely adopt a pure example of any of the four strategies.[54]

Two key components of virtually any branding strategy are brand extensions and brand portfolios.

Managing brand extensions

Most new products or services are in fact line extensions – typically 80–90 per cent of new products and services introduced in any one year are brand extensions. Examples include Mars extending its brand to ice cream, Caterpillar to shoes and watches, Michelin to a restaurant guide, Adidas to an aftershave and Apple computers to the iPod music player. Mattel, the owner of the Barbie brand, has had many marketing struggles to extend the Barbie brand from a doll to other products that its customer base will use after they have grown out of playing with their Barbie doll. Mattel has launched a range of Barbie-inspired teenage clothing and also Barbie make-up for teenagers, which it markets through the MAC make-up company. Brand extensions are popular in the industrial market too. Dyson innovated in the vacuum cleaning area with a new improved Dyson cleaner and then moved to hand dryers with the new improved Dyson Airblade hand dryer.

Deciding how to brand new services or products is critical and involves three main choices:

1 The company can develop new brand elements for the new product or service.
2 It can apply some of its existing brand elements.
3 It can use a combination of new and existing brand elements.

The Dyson hand dryer
is a brand extension
from the Dyson vacuum
cleaner, which in itself
was a revolution in
vacuuming.
Source: Courtesy of Dyson.

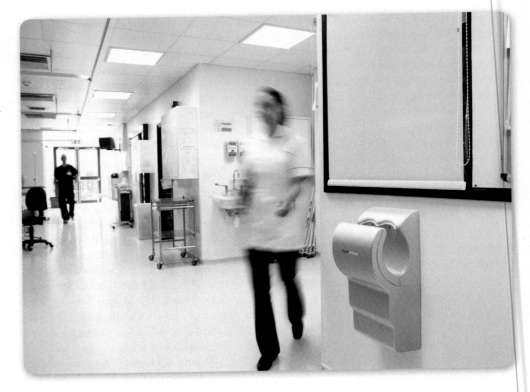

The existing brand is the parent of the brand extension. If the parent brand is already associated with multiple products through brand extensions, it can also be called a **family brand**. The Lucozade brand is now a family brand for the following sports products: Lucozade Sport, Lucozade Hydro Active and Lucozade Sport Nutrition.

Brand extensions fall into two general categories.[55] In a **line extension**, the parent brand covers a new product or service within a product or service category it currently serves, such as with new flavours, forms, colours, ingredients and package sizes. The French food company Danone has introduced several types of Danone yogurt line extension over the years. These include Fruit on the Bottom, All Natural Flavours, and Fruit Blends.

Magnum

Magnum, the Swiss ice cream brand which is now owned by the British/Dutch Unilever company, is marketed as part of the Heartbrand line of products in most countries. The original 1990 Magnum Classic consisted of a thick bar of vanilla ice cream on a stick, covered with white or dark chocolate, with a weight of 86 grams (120 ml). In 1994 the company also started selling Magnum ice cream cones, and in 2002 an ice cream sandwich along with its Magnum Mint, Double Chocolate and other flavours. Also in 2002 Magnum branched into frozen yogurt with its raspberry fruit swirl covered in milk chocolate. Late 2002 saw the launch of 'Magnum Intense' and the limited edition '7 Deadly Sins' series of ice creams. The line extension 'Moments' was introduced in 2003 – these were bite-size ice cream treats with caramel, chocolate or hazelnut centres, followed later in the year by 'mini', 'crunchy' (with almonds) and 'light'. This was followed by another limited edition range in 2005, in which each flavour was named after one of the senses: Magnum Aroma, Magnum Touch, Magnum Sound, Magnum Taste and Magnum Vision. In 2008 Magnum brought out a new variant in the United Kingdom – Mayan Mystica. In 2009 it introduced Magnum Mini Moments and in 2011 Magnum ice cream was launched in the USA and Canada with six varieties: Double Caramel, Double Chocolate, Classic, Almond, White and Dark.

In a **category extension**, the parent brand is used to enter a different product or service category from the one it currently serves. Honda is the fifth largest car manufacturer in the world as well as the largest engine-maker in the world, producing more than 14 million internal combustion engines each year. Honda has used its company name to cover such different products as cars, motorcycles, snowblowers, lawnmowers, marine engines and snowmobiles. This allows Honda to advertise that it can fit 'six Hondas in a two-car garage'. English entrepreneur Richard Branson has used his Virgin brand to enter many different product and service markets, from the airline industry to the music business and soft drinks markets, all with varying degrees of success. His latest project is in the space aviation industry with Virgin Galactic: this will be the world's first spaceline, giving customers the groundbreaking opportunity of being one of the world's first non-professional astronauts.

A **brand line** consists of all products or service – original as well as line and category extensions – sold under a particular brand. A **brand mix** (or brand assortment) is the set of all available brand lines from a company.

Some companies produce **branded variants**, which are specific brand lines supplied exclusively to specific retailers or distribution channels. They result from the pressure retailers put on manufacturers to provide distinctive offerings. A camera company may supply its low-end cameras to large retailers while limiting its higher-priced items to speciality camera shops. Valentino, the Italian designer, designs and supplies different lines of suits and jackets to department stores compared to his own outlets.[56]

A **licensed product or service** is one whose brand name has been licensed to others. Marketers have seized on licensing to push their company name and image across a wide range of products – from bedding to shoes – making licensing a €30 billion plus business.[57] TinTin, the familiar French cartoon character's image, has been licensed to companies manufacturing a range of products from clocks to keyrings. The Harry Potter brand has had phenomenal success with licensing with the books and films spawning eight video games and more than 400 additional Harry Potter products, including an iPod. The Harry Potter brand has been estimated to be worth as much as €15 billion. Hallmark obtained the Harry Potter licence to design Harry Potter greeting cards, wrapping paper and partyware, while Warner Bros own the licence for Harry Potter clothing, ornaments and sweets.

Marketers must judge each potential brand extension by how effectively it leverages existing brand equity from the parent brand, as well as how effectively it contributes to the parent brand's equity.[58] Crest White Strips leveraged the strong reputation of Crest and dental care to provide reassurance in the teeth-whitening arena, while also reinforcing its dental authority image. The most important consideration with extensions is that there should be a 'fit' in the mind of the consumer, based on common attributes, usage situations or user types.

Figure 12.3 lists a number of academic research findings on brand extensions.[59]

One benefit of a successful extension is that it may also serve as the basis for subsequent extensions.[60]

Advantages of brand extensions

As the costs of establishing a new brand name are so high, it is understandable that brand extensions are so popular. Extensions can avoid the difficulty – and expense – of coming up with a new name. They also allow for many efficiencies across all the marketing mix variables, including distribution, inventory, communications, packaging and labelling. Similar or identical packages and labels can result in lower production costs for extensions and, if coordinated properly, more prominence in the retail store via a 'billboard' effect. For example, Bird's Eye offers a variety of frozen foods with similar packaging that increases their visibility when they are stocked together in the freezer. With a portfolio of brand variants within a product category, consumers who need a change – because of boredom, satiation or whatever – can switch to a different product type without having to leave the brand family.

Academics have studied brand extensions closely. Here is a summary of some of their key research findings.

- Successful brand extensions occur when the parent brand is seen as having favourable associations and there is a perception of fit between the parent brand and the extension product.
- There are many bases of fit: product-related attributes and benefits, as well as non-product-related attributes and benefits related to common usage situations or user types.
- Depending on consumer knowledge of the categories, perceptions of fit may be based on technical or manufacturing commonalities or more surface considerations such as necessary or situational complementarity.
- High-quality brands stretch farther than average-quality brands, although both types of brand have boundaries.
- A brand that is seen as prototypical of a product category can be difficult to extend outside the category.
- Concrete attribute associations tend to be more difficult to extend than abstract benefit associations.
- Consumers may transfer associations that are positive in the original product class but become negative in the extension context.
- Consumers may infer negative associations about an extension, perhaps even based on other inferred positive associations.
- It can be difficult to extend into a product class that is seen as easy to make.
- A successful extension can not only contribute to the parent brand image but also enable a brand to be extended even farther.
- An unsuccessful extension hurts the parent brand only when there is a strong basis of fit between the two.
- An unsuccessful extension does not prevent a firm from 'backtracking' and introducing a more similar extension.
- Vertical extensions can be difficult and often require subbranding strategies.
- The most effective advertising strategy for an extension emphasises information about the extension (rather than reminders about the parent brand).

Figure 12.3 Research insights on brand extensions
Source: From K. L. Keller (2008) *Strategic Brand Management*, 3rd edn, Upper Saddle River, NJ: Prentice Hall. Copyright © 2008. Reproduced by permission of Pearson Education, Inc., Upper Saddle River, NJ.

Using brand extensions can ensure positive expectations, as extensions can reduce risk.[61] It may also be easier to convince retailers to stock and promote a brand extension because of increased customer demand. From a marketing communications perspective, an introductory campaign for an extension does not have to create awareness of both the brand *and* the new product or service, but can concentrate instead on the new product or service itself.[62]

Business-to-business companies can use brand extensions as a powerful way to enter consumer markets, as Michelin and Goodyear, both companies with strong brand names discovered.

Disadvantages of brand extensions

On the downside, line extensions may cause the brand name to be less strongly identified with any one product.[65] Ries and Trout call this the 'line-extension trap'.[66] By linking its brand to mainstream food products such as mashed potatoes, powdered milk, soups and beverages, Cadbury ran the risk of losing its more specific meaning as a chocolate brand.[67] **Brand dilution** occurs when consumers no longer associate a brand with a specific or highly similar products or service and start thinking less of the brand.

Michelin and Goodyear

Both French in origin, Michelin and Goodyear were known primarily for their rubber tyres, but have launched a number of brand extensions over the years.[63] Michelin's brand extensions have mainly been in the car accessories area – from inflation and pressure monitoring goods to car floor mats. So far its brand extensions fall into three categories: (1) car and cycle-related products; (2) footwear, clothing, accessories and equipment for work, sports and leisure; and (3) personal accessories – gifts and collectables. Its sports and leisure category now has the potential to overtake the car accessories line.

Like Michelin, Goodyear has a category of products closely aligned to the car industry – such as jack stands and car repair tools – but it, too, has branched out into consumer areas. The company is marketing its own line of cleaning wipes for windows and upholstery, mechanics' gloves and garden hose nozzles, among other products. Interestingly, Goodyear and Adidas partnered to create a series of driving shoes, prominently featuring the Goodyear 'Wingfoot' mark.[64] This was a brand extension for both companies.

If a company launches extensions that consumers deem inappropriate, they may question the integrity of the brand or become confused and perhaps even frustrated: not sure which version of the brand is the 'right one' for them. The company itself may become overwhelmed. When LEGO, the Danish toy manufacturer, decided to become a lifestyle brand and launch its own lines of clothes, watches and video games, as well as design programmes to attract more girls into the brand franchise, it neglected its core market of 5–9-year-old boys. When plunging profits led to layoffs of almost half its employees the company streamlined its brand portfolio to emphasise its core businesses and returned to the core brand values.[68]

The worst possible scenario is for an extension not only to fail, but also to harm the parent brand image in the process. Fortunately, such events are rare. 'Marketing failures', where insufficient consumers were attracted to a brand, are typically much less damaging than 'product or service failures', where the brand fundamentally fails to live up to its promise. New products such as Virgin Cola, Levi's Tailored Classic suits, Fruit of the Loom washing powder, Bic Perfume, Capital Radio restaurant and Pond's toothpaste failed because consumers found them inappropriate extensions for the brand.[69] Even then, product or service failures dilute brand equity only when the extension is seen as very similar to the parent brand.

Virgin

The Virgin brand, which revolves around an authentic and people-orientated brand image, has hundreds of brand extensions – Virgin consists of more than 400 companies around the world. At one stage the brand extension potential of Virgin was widely debated as Virgin entered a range of industries with brand extensions from aeroplanes to trains, from record stores to mobile phones. The UK newspaper, the *Observer* explored a fictitious future world – entitled 'The Virgin Life' – which Virgin controlled if the brand extensions did not stop. 'Every morning you can wake up to Virgin Radio, put on Virgin clothes and make-up, drive to work in a car bought with money transferred from your Virgin bank account' and so on, the article also citing the Virgin gym, Virgin cinema and Virgin hotels.

Virgin has had many successes but also some brand extension failures. Virgin Coke was one such failure and may have been a brand extension too far for the Virgin Group.[70] According to Matt Haig in his book *Brand Failures*, Virgin Cola failed because it did not show the competitor's weakness. In addition, distribution is key in the soft drinks industry and Virgin struggled in this area. Some brand extensions could be seen as brand ego trips and have been costly failures for the group, but others have really engaged with customer needs and brand values, such as Virgin Airways.

Brand switching

Even if sales of a brand extension are high and meet targets, the revenue may be coming from consumers switching to the extension from existing parent-brand offerings – in effect, *cannibalising* the parent brand. Intra-brand shifts in sales may not be a disadvantage if they are a form of *pre-emptive cannibalisation*. In other words, consumers might have switched to a competing brand instead of the line extension if the extension had not been introduced.

One easily overlooked disadvantage of brand extensions is that the company forgoes the chance to create a new brand with its own unique image and equity. Consider the advantages to Disney of having introduced more adult-oriented Touchstone films; to Levi's of creating casual Dockers pants; and to Black and Decker of introducing high-end Dewalt power tools.

Managing brand portfolios

The **brand portfolio** is the set of all brands and brand lines that a particular company offers for sale in a particular category or market segment. Marketers often need multiple brands in order to pursue multiple target markets.

Armani

Armani has set out to create a product line differentiated by style, luxury, customisation and price to compete in three distinct price tiers. In the most expensive, Tier I, it sells Giorgio Armani and Giorgio Armani Privé, which are custom-made runway couture products that sell for thousands of pounds/euro. In the more moderately priced Tier II, it offers Emporio Armani, young and modern, as well as the informal A|X Armani. In the lower-priced Tier III, the company sells the more youthful and street-savvy translation of Armani style, Armani Exchange, at retail locations in cities and shopping centres.

Armani's line of luxury clothing is differentiated to appeal to three distinct price tiers, each with different styles and levels of luxury, using the brand names Georgio Armani, Emporio Armani, A|X Armani and Armani Exchange.
Source: Daniele La Monaca/Reuters/Corbis

The hallmark of an optimal brand portfolio is the ability of each brand in it to maximise equity in combination with all the other brands. If a company can only increase profits by dropping brands, a portfolio is too big; if it can increase profits by *adding* brands, it is not big enough. The basic principle in designing a brand portfolio is to *maximise market coverage*, so that no potential customers are being ignored, but to *minimise brand overlap*, so company brands are not competing for customer approval. Each brand should be clearly differentiated and appealing to a sizeable enough market segment to justify its marketing and production costs.[71]

Brands can also play a number of specific roles as part of a brand portfolio.

Flankers

Flanker or 'fighter' brands are positioned with respect to competitors' brands so that more important (and more profitable) *flagship brands* can retain their desired positioning. Procter & Gamble markets Luvs nappies in a way that flanks its more popular and premium Pampers. Marketers walk a fine line in designing fighter brands, which must not be so attractive that they take sales away from their higher-priced comparison brands.

Cash cows

Some brands may be kept around despite dwindling sales because they still manage to hold on to enough customers and maintain their profitability with virtually no marketing support. Companies can effectively 'milk' these 'cash cow' brands by capitalising on their reservoir of existing brand equity. For example, despite the fact that technological advances have moved much of its market to the newer Mach III brand of razors, Gillette still sells the older Trac II, Atra and Sensor brands. Withdrawing them may not necessarily move customers to another Gillette brand, so it is more profitable for Gillette to keep them in its brand portfolio for razor blades.

Low-end entry level

The role of a relatively low-priced brand in the portfolio may often be to attract customers to the brand franchise. Retailers like to feature these 'traffic builders' because they are able to 'trade up' customers to a higher-priced brand. For example, BMW introduced a 1-series car in part as a means of bringing new customers into the brand franchise, with the hope of later 'moving them up' to higher-priced models.

High-end prestige

The role of a relatively high-priced brand is often to add prestige and credibility to the entire portfolio. Mobile phone companies such as Nokia always have a high-end model in their range. Most Nokia customers will not buy this product but will buy its mid-range, flagship model. Nonetheless, it is often the case that it is the high-end model which attracts the consumers' attention.

Brand reinforcing and revitalisation

As a company's major enduring asset, a brand needs to be carefully managed so that its value does not depreciate.[72]

Brand reinforcement

Marketing reinforces brand equity by marketing actions that consistently convey the meaning of the brand to the consumers with the brand representing the core benefits it supplies and what needs it satisfies. It also conveys what makes the brand superior and what strong favourable and unique brand association should exist in the mind of the consumer. The most important consideration is consistency of support in terms of both the amount and the nature of that support.[73]

Brand equity is reinforced by marketing actions that consistently convey the meaning of the brand in terms of:

- What products and service the brand represents, what core benefits it supplies and what needs it satisfies. Nivea, one of Europe's strongest brands, has expanded its scope from a skin cream brand to a skin care and personal care brand through carefully designed and implemented brand extensions, reinforcing the Nivea brand promise of 'mild', 'gentle' and 'caring' in a broader arena.
- How the brand provides them with the service or products they need and what value added is created.[74] Ryanair has become the largest airline in Europe by focusing on its core brand value – providing cheap airline travel to over 70 million passengers annually,[75] who prefer low cost to high service.

Apple

Apple is the story of a brand that has been managed well throughout its lifespan, which started on April Fool's Day 1976. This €77 billion company has some of the world's best and most innovative consumer products and 82 per cent of the hard drive music market. The company's ability to delight consumers in a bland world of technological equipment and software makes it easy to see why it impacts on so many and across so many segments. From the student who loves their iPod, to the executives who worship their Mac, Apple has brought emotion to their brand and created a brand image and experience that endures and makes us 'Think Differently'.

Apple, Inc. is a master at building a strong brand that resonates with customers across generations and national boundaries. It achieves incredible brand loyalty largely by delivering on its mission, as defined by former CEO Steve Jobs: 'To create great things that change people's lives.' The company has created an army of Apple evangelists, not just because it produces great products that reflect consumer needs, but also because everything it does and all its communcations reflect its brand values. Apple's innovative products combine superior design, functionality and style, and many cite the wildly successful iPod music player as a prime example. Apple has 150 retail stores worldwide to fuel excitement for the brand. The rationale behind the move to retail is that the more people can see and touch Apple products, see what Apple can do for them, the more likely Apple is to increase its market share.

One or even two 'revolutionary' products alone won't keep you at the top of the list of the most successful companies in the world. A major key to Apple's continued success is its ability to keep pushing the boundaries of innovation. Key lessons from Apple are:

- **Don't just focus on building beautiful products.** Build beautiful business models, new ways to create, deliver and capture value. The iPod and iPhone would not have had nearly as much impact if they had not been matched with iTunes and the App Store respectively.

- **Think in terms of platforms and pipelines.** Competitors that chase Apple's latest release find themselves behind when six months later Apple introduces its latest and greatest offering.

- **Take a portfolio approach.** While Apple has been on a phenomenal run, not everything it has introduced has been a success. For example, Apple TV has not had the 'revolutionary' impact that Jobs predicted upon its launch in 2007. But the success of the Apple iPhone and iPad created hype, interest and demand. The sales topped over 125 million iPhones by mid-2011 with Apple set to launch a new phone later in the year, showing how it continually innovates into its brand identity to maintain the image of an innovative company in tune with customer needs.[76]

Reinforcing brand image requires innovation and relevance throughout the marketing programme. The brand must always be moving forward – but moving forward in the right direction, with new and compelling offerings and ways to market them.

Brands that failed to move forwards – such as Benetton and Kodak – find that their market leadership dwindles or even disappears.

Brand revitalisation

Changes in consumer tastes and preferences, the emergence of new competitors or new technology, or any new development in the marketing environment can affect the fortunes of a brand. In virtually every product or service category, once-prominent and admired brands – such as Little Chef, Alitalia and British Airways – have fallen on hard times, struggled with their brand image or even disappeared.[77] A number of brands have managed to make impressive comebacks in recent years, as marketers have breathed new life into them. Volkswagen, Dr Scholl's and Birkenstock are brands that have been revitalised, becoming popular once again but in a different market. For example, Birkenstock – the German sandal – was predominantly used by the medical profession but moved into everyday comfort shoes within the environmentally friendly target market.

Often the first thing to do in revitalising a brand is to understand what the sources of brand equity are to begin with. Are positive associations losing their strength or uniqueness? Have negative associations become linked to the brand? Then it has to be decided whether to retain the same positioning or create a new one and, if so, which new one. Sometimes the marketing programme or marketing mix activities are the source of the problem, because they fail to deliver on the brand promise. In other cases, however, the old positioning is just no longer viable and a 'reinvention' strategy is necessary. Lucozade completely overhauled its brand image to become an energy drink powerhouse.

Brand reinforcement and brand revitalisation strategies

At some point, failure to fortify the brand will diminish brand awareness and weaken brand image. Without these sources of brand equity, the brand itself may not continue to

Lucozade

The European energy drink market continues to grow with Germany and the UK accounting for the largest market share. Energy drinks account for £1 in every £5 spent on soft drinks in the United Kingdom. One of the main players, Lucozade is only in this market due to a successful rebranding or revitalisation of the brand that saw the company move from a child-oriented, health-related tonic to an energy sports drink. The original Lucozade, first manufactured in 1927, was available throughout the United Kingdom for use in hospitals. In 1983, a rebranding of Lucozade into an energy drink started moving the slogan from 'Lucozade aids recovery' to 'Lucozade replaces lost energy', with an advertising campaign featuring the world and Olympic champion decathlete Daley Thompson. The effect of the rebranding was dramatic: the value of UK sales of the drink tripled to almost €95 million. During the 1990s it tapped into the sports market and introduced Lucozade Sport, which is the market leader in sports drinks. Lucozade uses leading sports teams and personalities to keep the sports brand value in front of the consumer. Lucozade is the official drink of the FA and FA Premier League and also sponsors the England Rugby Football Union, the Irish Football Team, the London Marathon, Michael Owen, Steven Gerrard, Damien Duff and Jonny Wilkinson. The brand message is 'Lucozade Sport keeps top athletes going 33% longer', accompanied by the powerful slogan 'Hunger has a thirst'.

These two campaigns show how the Lucozade brand was repositioned from a tonic for sick children to an energy drink for athletes.
Source: Images courtesy of The Advertising Archives

yield valuable benefits. With a fading brand, the depth of brand awareness is often not as much of a problem as the breadth – that is, the consumer has too narrow a view of the brand. Although changing brand awareness is probably the easiest means of creating new sources of brand equity, we often need to create a new marketing mix programme to improve the strength, favourability and uniqueness of brand associations. The challenge in all these efforts to modify the brand image is not to destroy the equity that already exists. *Reinforcing brands* involves ensuring innovation in product design, manufacturing and merchandising, and ensuring relevance in user and usage imagery. *Brand revitalisation*, on the other hand, requires either that lost sources of brand equity are recaptured, or that new sources of brand equity are identified and established. Figure 12.4 summarises the main features of brand revitalisation and brand reinforcment strategies.[78]

Growing, sustaining and managing brand equity

Brand equity is the added value endowed on products and services. It may be reflected in the way consumers think, feel and act with respect to the brand, as well as in the prices, market share and profitability the brand commands.[79]

Brands play a major role in enhancing the **financial value** of companies, and thus the ability to value them or understand their brand value or equity is critical. To companies, brands represent enormously valuable pieces of legal property that can influence consumer behaviour, be bought and sold, and provide the security of sustained future revenues. Companies have paid large sums of money for brands in mergers and acquisitions, often justifying the price premium on the basis of the extra profits to be extracted and sustained from the brands, as well as the tremendous difficulty and expense of creating similar brands from scratch. Although only founded in 1998, Google is one of the most

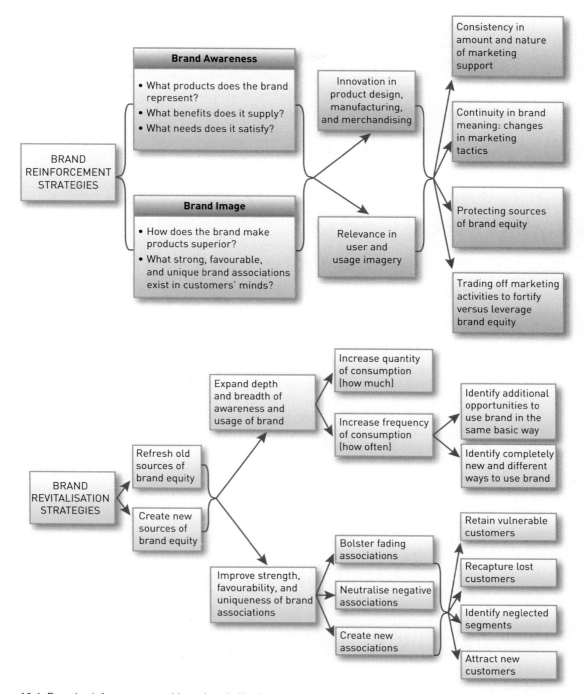

Figure 12.4 Brand reinforcement and brand revitalisation strategies
Source: Keller, Kevin, *Strategic Brand Management*, © 2008. Printed and electronically reproduced by permission of Pearson Education, Inc., Upper Saddle River, NJ.

recognised and valuable brand in the world, valued at €11.51 billion.[80] A strong brand is a valuable asset, as can be seen from Table 12.1, which highlights brand values for the top five brands in Europe.[81]

As Rita Clifton, the author of *Brands and Branding* and the chairperson of Interbrand UK, puts it: 'Well-managed brands have extraordinary economic value and are the most effective and efficient creators of sustainable wealth.'[82] Malcolm Forbes described them as

Table 12.1 The top five European brands

Ranking 2010 (2009)	Brand	Industry	Country of ownership	Brand value (€ m)	(% change)
1(1)	Nokia	Telecommunications	Finland	25,331	−28.1
2(2)	Vodafone	Telcom	U.K.	25,318	6.4
3(4)	Louis Vuitton	Luxury	France	17,186	−10.0
4(3)	Mercedes-Benz	Automotive	Germany	16,940	−12.6
5(5)	BMW	Automotive	Germany	15,267	−9.5

Source: Adapted from Interbrand.com (2011)

'the best marketable investment a company can make'.[83] Brand value is typically over half the total company market capitalisation and so the importance of the brand to the company is clear. Brand value is increasingly included on balance sheets in countries such as the United Kingdom, Hong Kong and Australia. A recent PricewaterhouseCoopers report revealed that 74 per cent of the average purchase prices of acquired companies was made up of intangible assets and goodwill – what is called **brand value**.[84]

Brand valuation

Marketers should distinguish brand equity from brand valuation, which is the job of estimating the total financial value of the brand. The **brand value chain** is a structured approach to assessing the sources and outcomes of brand equity and the manner in which marketing activities create brand value – see the marketing insight box.

For brand equity to perform a useful strategic function and guide marketing decisions, marketers need to understand fully: (1) the sources of brand equity and how they affect outcomes of interest; (2) how these sources and outcomes change, if at all, over time. Brand audits are important for the former; brand tracking for the latter.

A **brand audit** is a consumer-focused procedure to assess the health of the brand, uncover its sources of brand equity and suggest ways to improve and leverage its equity. Conducting brand audits on a regular basis, such as annually, allows marketers to keep their fingers on the pulse of their brands so they can manage them more proactively and responsively. Brand audits are particularly useful background information for marketing managers as they set up their marketing plans and select marketing mix variables, and when they are considering making changes.

Marketing insight

The brand value chain

The brand value chain is a structured approach to assessing the sources and outcomes of brand equity and the manner in which marketing activities create brand value (see Figure 12.5). It is based on several premises.

First, the brand value creation process is assumed to begin when the firm invests in a marketing programme targeting actual or potential customers. Any marketing programme investment that can be attributed to brand value development, intentional or not, falls into this category – for example, product research, development and design; trade or intermediary support; communications and pricing decisions.

Next, customers' mindsets are assumed to change as a result of the marketing programme. The question is how. This change, in turn, is assumed to affect the way the brand performs in the marketplace through the collective impact of individual customers deciding how

much to purchase and when, how much they will pay, and so on. Finally, the investment community considers market performance and other factors such as replacement cost and purchase price in acquisitions to arrive at an assessment of shareholder value in general and the value of a brand in particular.

The model also assumes that a number of linking factors intervene between these stages and determine the extent to which value created at one stage transfers to the next stage. Three sets of multipliers moderate the transfer between the marketing programme and the subsequent three value stages – the programme multiplier, the customer multiplier and the market multiplier.

The *programme multiplier* determines the marketing programme's ability to affect the customer mindset and is a function of the quality of the programme investment. The *customer multiplier* determines the extent to which value created in the minds of customers affects market performance. This result depends on contextual factors external to the customer.

Three such factors are:

1 **Competitive superiority:** how effective the quantity and quality of the marketing investment of other competing brands are.

2 **Channel and other intermediary support:** how much brand reinforcement and selling effort various marketing partners are putting forth.

3 **Customer size and profile:** how many and what types of customer, profitable or not, are attracted to the brand.

The *market multiplier* determines the extent to which the value shown by the market performance of a brand is manifested in shareholder value. It depends, in part, on the actions of financial analysts and investors.

Sources: K. Keller (2009) Brand planning, a Shoulders of Giants publication, http://marksherrington.com/downloads/Brand%20Planning%20eArticle.pdf; K. Keller (2008) *Strategic Brand Management*, New York: Pearson; K. L. Keller and D. Lehmann (2003) How do brands create value?, *Marketing Management,* May–June, 27–31. See also M. J. Epstein and R. A. Westbrook (2001) Linking actions to profits in strategic decision making, *MIT Sloan Management Review*, Spring, 39–49; and R. K. Srivastava, T. A. Shervani and L. Fahey (1998) Market-based assets and shareholder value, *Journal of Marketing*, 62(1), January, 2–18.

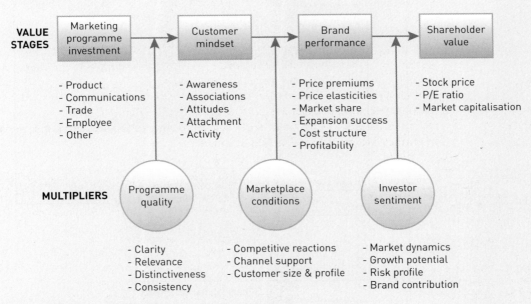

Figure 12.5 The brand value chain
Source: K. L. Keller (2008) *Strategic Brand Management*, Pearson International Edition, New Jersey; K. L. Keller and D. Lehmann (2003) How do brands create value?, *Marketing Management*, May–June, 27–31. See also M. J. Epstein and R. A. Westbrook (2001) Linking actions to profits in strategic decision making, *MIT Sloan Management Review*, Spring, 39–49; and R. K. Srivastava, T. A. Shervani and L. Fahey (1998) Market-based assets and shareholder value, *Journal of Marketing*, 62(1), January, 2–18. K. Keller (2009) Brand Planning, A Shoulders of Giants Publication, http://marksherrington.com/downloads/Brand%20Planning%20eArticle.pdf

Brand tracking studies collect quantitative data from consumers on a routine basis over time to provide marketers with consistent, baseline information about how their brands and marketing programmes are performing on key dimensions. Tracking studies are a means of understanding where, how much, and in what ways brand value is being created, to facilitate day-to-day decision making.

Managing brand equity and brand performance

Marketing managers need a model to link brand equity and brand performance.[85] There are four major stages, as outlined in Figure 12.6.

1 **What companies/marketing managers do.** The full marketing programme and other aspects of the company operations must be managed from both quantitative (factors such as amount of marketing expenditure) and qualitative (clarity and consistency of the marketing programme) perspectives.

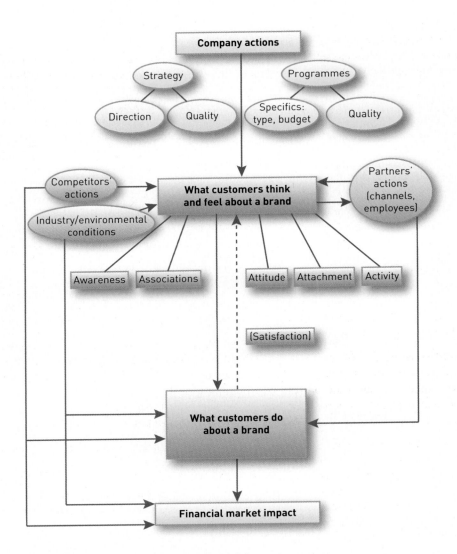

Figure 12.6 A systems model of brand antecedents and consequences
Source: K. L. Keller and D. R. Lehmann (2006) Brand and branding: research findings and future priorities, *Marketing Science*, 25(6), 740–59. Copyright © 2006 The Institute for Operations Research and the Management Sciences (INFORMS).

2 What customers think and feel. Individual customer characteristics as well as competition and other aspects of the environment will influence how customers feel. What they think and feel is not under the sole control of the company. Personal experience and the experience of others will both affect what a customer thinks of a brand.

3 What customers do. The main payoff is when the customer buys the product or service and so affects revenue, share and other metrics commonly used to judge brand success. Of course, other things that customers do (especially word of mouth) impact on the future development of the brand.

4 How financial markets react. Most brands are judged by how they perform financially internally and also in relation to stock prices and market capitalisation (the value of the company if it was sold). This is called the bottom line and is what the chief executive will ask of marketing – that the brand provides a return to the company.[86]

Measuring brand equity

Various models are used to study brand equity[87] (Chapter 22), three of which are customer-based brand equity, the brand asset valuator and the interbrand model, discussed below.

Customer-based brand equity is the differential effect that brand knowledge has on consumer response to the marketing of that brand.[88] Customer-based approaches view the brand from the perspective of the consumer – either an individual or an organisation.[89] The premise of customer-based brand equity models is that the power of a brand lies in what customers have seen, read, heard, learned, thought and felt about the brand over time.[90] Customer-level brand equity can be characterised in terms of awareness, association, attitudes (or attraction) and activity.[91]

A brand has *positive* customer-based brand equity when consumers react more favourably to a product or service and the way it is marketed when the brand is *identified*, than when it is not identified. A brand has *negative* customer-based brand equity if consumers react less favourably to marketing activity for the brand under the same circumstances.

Another model used to measure brand equity is the **BrandAsset Valuator** (BAV), which is based on research with almost 500,000 consumers in 44 countries. The brand asset valuator provides comparative measures of the brand equity of thousands of brands across hundreds of different categories. There are five key pillars of brand equity, according to BAV (see Figure 12.7):

1 Differentiation: measures the degree to which a brand is seen as different from others.
2 Energy: measures the brand's sense of momentum.
3 Relevance: measures the breadth of a brand's appeal.
4 Esteem: measures how well the brand is regarded and respected.
5 Knowledge: measures how familiar and intimate consumers are with the brand.

Differentiation, energy and relevance combine to determine *energised brand strength*. These three pillars point to the brand's future value. Esteem and knowledge together create *brand stature*, which is more of a 'report card' on past performance.

The relationships among these dimensions – a brand's 'pillar pattern' – reveal much about its current and future status. Energised brand strength and brand stature combined form the *PowerGrid*, depicting the stages in the cycle of brand development – each with characteristic pillar patterns – in successive quadrants (see Figure 12.7). Strong new brands show higher levels of differentiation and energy than relevance, while both esteem and knowledge are lower still. Leadership brands show high levels on all pillars. Finally, declining brands show high knowledge – evidence of past performance – a lower level of esteem, and even lower relevance, energy and differentiation.

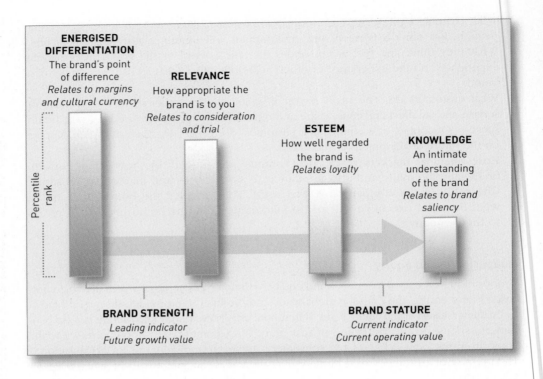

Figure 12.7 BrandAsset® Valuator model
Source: BAV Consulting, Brand Asset® Valuator UK, All Adults, 2011.

Combining these factors, one can create a graphical approach to brand equity, as shown in Figure 12.8.

According to BAV analysis, consumers are concentrating their devotion and purchasing power on an increasingly smaller portfolio of special brands – brands with energised differentiation that keep evolving. These brands connect better with consumers – commanding greater usage loyalty and pricing power, and creating greater shareholder value. A hypothetical €10,000 invested in the top 50 brands grew 12 per cent while the S&P index lost nearly 20 per cent between 31 December 2001 and 30 June 2009. Some of the latest insights from the BAV data are summarised in the marketing insight box.

Top brand valuation company Interbrand defines brand equity or value as the net present value of the earnings a brand is expected to generate in the future. The **Interbrand model** first evaluates the value of the firm from which the value of the brand will be measured. The following is a summary of the Interbrand model for evaluation of brand equity:

1 **Financial analysis**. Interbrand assesses purchase price, volume and frequency to help calculate accurate forecasts of future brand sales and revenues. Specifically, Interbrand performs a detailed review of the brand's equities, industry and customer trends, and historic financial performance across each segment. Once it has established branded revenues, it deducts all associated operating costs to derive earnings before interest and tax (EBIT).

2 **Role of branding**. Interbrand next attributes a proportion of intangible earnings to the brand in each market segment, by first identifying the various drivers of demand, then determining the degree to which the brand directly influences each. The role of branding assessment is based on market research, client workshops

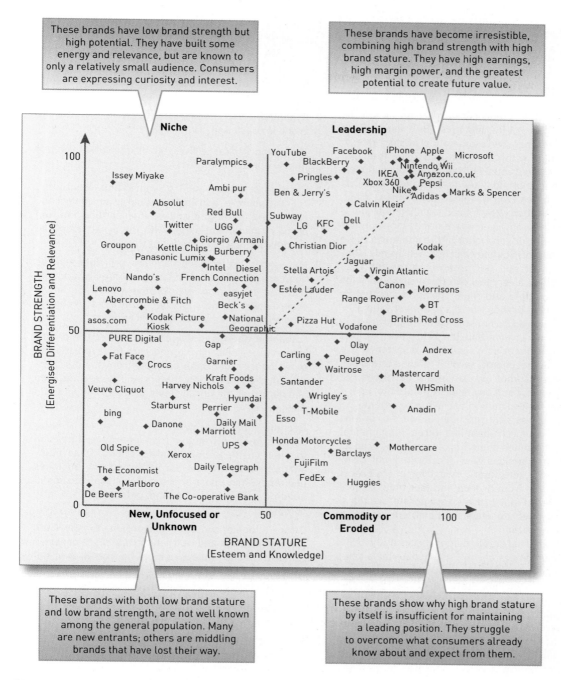

These brands have low brand strength but high potential. They have built some energy and relevance, but are known to only a relatively small audience. Consumers are expressing curiosity and interest.

These brands have become irresistible, combining high brand strength with high brand stature. They have high earnings, high margin power, and the greatest potential to create future value.

These brands with both low brand stature and low brand strength, are not well known among the general population. Many are new entrants; others are middling brands that have lost their way.

These brands show why high brand stature by itself is insufficient for maintaining a leading position. They struggle to overcome what consumers already know about and expect from them.

Figure 12.8 The universe of brand performance
Source: BAV Consulting, Brand Asset® Valuator UK, All Adults, 2011.

and interviews, and represents the percentage of intangible earnings that the brand generates.

3 **Brand strength.** Interbrand then assesses the brand's strength profile to determine the likelihood that the brand will realise forecast earnings. This step relies on competitive benchmarking, and a structured evaluation of the brand's market, stability, leadership position, growth trend, support, geographic footprint and legal protection. For each segment, Interbrand applies industry and brand equity metrics to determine a risk premium for the brand.

Marketing Insight

Brand bubble trouble

In *The Brand Bubble*, brand consultants Ed Lebar and John Gerzema use Y&R's historical BAV database to conduct a comprehensive examination of the state of brands. Beginning with data from mid-2004, they discovered several odd trends. For thousands of consumer goods and services brands, key brand value measures such as consumer 'top-of-mind' awareness, trust, regard and admiration experienced significant drops.

At the same time, however, share prices for a number of years were being driven higher by the intangible value the markets were attributing to consumer brands. Digging deeper, Lebar and Gerzema found the increase was actually due to a very few extremely strong brands such as Google, Apple and Nike. The value created by the vast majority of brands was stagnating or falling.

The authors viewed this mismatch between the value consumers see in brands and the value the markets were ascribing to them as a recipe for disaster in two ways. At the macroeconomic level, it implied that stock prices of most consumer companies are overstated. At the microeconomic, company level, it pointed to a serious and continuing problem in brand management.

Why have consumer attitudes towards brands declined? The research identified three fundamental causes. First, there has been a proliferation of brands. New product introductions have accelerated, but many fail to register with consumers. Two, consumers expect creative 'big ideas' from brands and feel they are just not getting them. Finally, due to corporate scandals, product crises and executive misbehaviour, trust in brands has plummeted.

Yet, vital brands are still being successfully built. Although all four pillars of the BAV model play a role, the strongest brands resonated with consumers in a special way. Amazon.com, Axe, Facebook, Innocent, IKEA, Land Rover, LG, LEGO, Tata, Nano, Twitter, Whole Foods and Zappos exhibited notable energised differentiation by communicating dynamism and creativity in ways most other brands did not.

Formally, the BAV analysis identified three factors that help define energy and the marketplace momentum it creates:

1 Vision: a clear direction and point of view on the world and how it can and should be changed.

2 Invention: an intention for the product or service to change the way people think, feel and behave.

3 Dynamism: excitement and affinity in the way the brand is presented.

The authors offer a five-step framework to infuse brands with more energy.

1 Perform an 'energy audit' on your brand. identify the current sources and level of energy to understand your brand's strengths and weaknesses and how well brand management aligns with the dynamics of the new marketplace.

2 Make your brand an organising principle for the business. Find an essential brand idea or thought that can serve as a lens through which you define every aspect of the customer experience, including products, services and communications.

3 Create an energised value chain. Make the organisation's goals for the brand real for everyone; all participants must think uniquely from the perspective of the brand and understand how their own actions boost the energy level of the brand and fuel the core.

4 Become an energy-driven enterprise. Stakeholders need to transfer their energy and passion to their business units and functions. Once management's aspirations for the brand and business begin becoming part of the culture, the process of building an energised brand enterprise is nearly complete.

5 Create a loop of constant reinvention. Finally, keep the organisation and its brand in a state of constant renewal. Brand managers must be keenly aware of shifts in consumers' perception and values and be ready to reshape themselves again and again.

Sources: Jonn Gerzema and Ed Lebar (2008). *The Brand Bubble: The Looming Crisis in Brand Value and How to Avoid It*, New York: Jossey-Bass; John Gerzema and Ed Lebar (2009). The trouble with brands, *Strategy+Business*, 55 (Summer).

Managing service brands

Though branding has traditionally focused on products, the branding of services is a critical skill for both product and service companies.[92] Customers buy the experience with the brand rather than a product or service, so for example there are a variety of services involved in the purchase of a car: transport, buying the car at a dealer, insurance, tax, petrol, servicing and repairs. All of these are critical along with the actual product – the physical car. With growing recognition of the importance of a service orientation to all brand values, the need to explore the service aspects of the customer experience aligned to the brand value to the customer is highlighted. Brands function both as an entity and a process. A **service branding** approach emphasises the integrative, reciprocal role of the brand, focusing on the value-adding processes and the fact that brand meaning is primarily influenced by brand experience. Competency in customer experience management is aligned to service levels, staff behaviour, brand positioning and environment.[93] The focus is on understanding the nature of value propositions and value creation processes, and how this leads to the creation of customer experiences, and on customer engagement with the brand over time.[94]

Leading services guru Leonard Berry notes:

Branding plays a special role in service companies because strong brands increase customers' trust of the invisible purchase. Strong brands enable customers to better visualise and understand intangible services. Strong service brands are the surrogates when the company offers no fabric to touch, no trousers to try on, no watermelons or apples to scrutinize, no car to test drive.[95]

The best service brands are the ones that:

- align their processes, organisational structures and service processes and environments to deliver a consistently superior brand experience;
- harness the power of customer information to enhance the service experience; and
- leverage that information to expand their offerings into additional categories.[96]

Choosing brand elements for services

Because services are intangible, and because customers often make decisions and arrangements about them away from the actual service location itself (at home or at work), brand recall becomes critically important. So an easy-to-remember brand name is critical. Other brand elements – logos, symbols, characters and slogans – can also help complement the brand name to build brand awareness and brand image. These brand elements often attempt to make the service and some of its key benefits more tangible, concrete and real – for example, Iberia Airlines, 'More than just flying' or KLM, 'The reliable airline' or Air France, 'Making the sky the best place on Earth'. They must also be revitalised and focused to ensure consistency with image and identity.

Because a physical product does not exist, the physical facilities of the service provider – its primary and secondary signage, corporate design and reception area, clothing, collateral material, and so on – are especially important. All aspects of the service delivery process can be branded, which is why UPS is concerned about the appearance of their drivers and why it has developed such strong equity with its brown trucks and brown uniforms.

Given the human nature of services, it is no surprise that brand personality is an important image dimension for services. **Brand personality** is a set of human characteristics that are attributed to a brand name. A brand personality is something to which the consumer can relate, and an effective brand will increase its brand equity by having a consistent set of traits. This is the added value that a brand gains, aside from its functional benefits. There are five main types of brand personality: excitement, sincerity, ruggedness, competence and sophistication. Starwood, which owns the Sheraton, Westin and Four Points brands, trains its hotel employees and call centre operators to convey different experiences for the firm's different hotel brands: Sheraton is positioned as warm, comforting and casual; Westin is positioned in terms of renewal and is a little more formal; Four Points by Sheraton is designed to be all about honest, uncomplicated comfort.[97] Hilton Hotels also has a portfolio of brands that includes Hilton Garden Inns to target budget-conscious business travellers and compete with the popular Courtyard by Marriott chain, as well as DoubleTree, Embassy Suites, Homewood Suites and Hampton Inn.

In a study of four leading banks in the United Kingdom prior to the banking crisis, Professor Leslie de Chernatony, of the University of Birmingham, found that financial services brands that had not achieved 'greatness' tend to be rooted in the past.[98] They place emphasis on financial performance rather than brand success indicators, have inadequate leadership support for the brand, are poorly differentiated, exhibit a lack of understanding and confusion about branding issues, have service quality concerns, demonstrate HR activities that are not focused fully 'on the brand', and possess a culture and values which do not clearly and consistently reinforce the brand.

Aspects of service brand management

Managing a service brand means focusing on four aspects, as portrayed in Figure 12.9.

1 **Service**: how to pamper customers so that they achieve the service levels expected. Many customers accept low service in one aspect of their lives but expect high service in other aspects.

2 **Staff behaviour**: staff are the walking representatives of the brand and their behaviour must be managed at all times. Employee brand commitment is a core feature of successful brands. Service branding and staff are crucial within services, as the perceived brand values can be based on the behaviour of employees. Brands are used symbolically in two different directions: outwardly to communicate to others the kind of brand or company, and inwardly to bolster the sense of *company*.[99] The staff need to understand and live the brand values. To create a collaborative culture, the brand message must be communicated to and understood by all staff so that each individual becomes a brand ambassador.[100] This helps to ensure that every sales call, every client interaction and every conversation delivers the brand as intended – see also Chapter 21 on internal marketing.

   Marketers must ensure that all employees 'walk the walk and talk the talk' to deliver the brand promise. They must adopt an *internal* perspective to ensure employees and supply network partners appreciate and understand the branding values, and how they can help – or hurt – brand equity.[101] It can be a member of the supply network or channels that delivers the brand to the consumer or who is aligned to the brand in the consumer's mind. The purchase experience in a retail outlet or online can impact the brand image, so these partners need to be managed too.

3 **Brand positioning**: this is the initial concept and as discussed in Chapter 10 is crucial for all brands. Where is the brand in the eyes of the consumer and does their experience

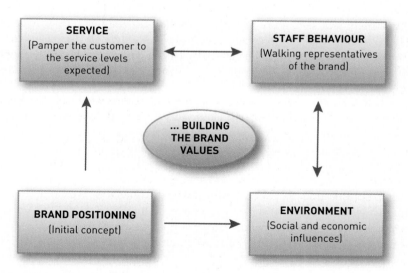

Figure 12.9 Managing service brands

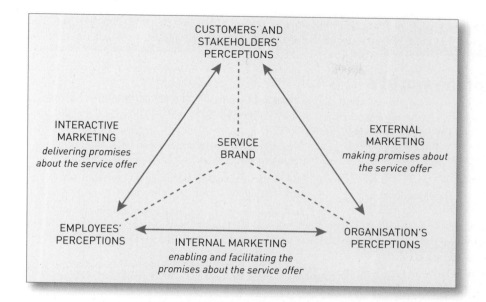

Figure 12.10

Types of marketing and their influence on perceptions of the service brand.
Source: R. J. Brodie (2009) From goods to service branding: an integrative perspective, *Marketing Theory*, 9(1), 107–11.

align to this positioning? Take the Mazda Millenia, a car designed to be part of an upscale luxury brand from Mazda. This incredible car was as good as many cars it competed with and in some ways surpassed them, but car buyers did not relish buying a Mazda when they could buy a Lexus – even if they saved money. Toyota went out and built a new brand because it realised the Toyota name could not successfully apply to both inexpensive and ultra-expensive vehicles. Predictably, Mazda's positioning in the market did not support its amazing car as the consumer did not position Mazda and its service provision or brand in this category.[102]

4 Environment: the social and economic environments are influences that affect the brand. The environment also includes the physical environment in which the service is delivered (Chapter 18).

Service brands can be seen from a variety of perspectives: those of the customer and stakeholder, the organisation and the employee. All these influence the interactive marketing and external marketing programmes (see Figure 12.10).[103]

- **External marketing:** communication between the organisation and customers *making promises* about the service offer.
- **Interactive marketing:** interactions between people working within the organisation/network and end customers that create the service experience associated with *delivering promises* about the service offer.
- **Internal marketing:** the resources and processes *enabling and facilitating promises* about the service offer involving the organisation and people working in the organisation.

Marketing must ensure that the 'making of promises' (brand image with company image) is aligned with the 'delivery of promises' (employee trust and company trust) in creating customer value, customer loyalty and brand value. Great brands must:

- offer and communicate a clear, relevant customer promise;
- build trust by delivering on that promise;
- drive the market by continually improving the promise; and
- seek further advantage by innovating beyond the familiar.

The marketing memo on the next page highlights the top ten traits of the world's strongest brands.

SUMMARY

1 A brand is a name, term, sign, symbol or design, or some combination of these elements, intended to identify the products and services of one company and to differentiate them from those of competitors. The different components of a brand – brand names, logos, symbols, package designs and so on – are brand elements.

2 The key to branding is that consumers perceive differences among brands in a product or service category. Brands offer a number of benefits to customers and companies.

3 A branding strategy for a company identifies which brand elements a company chooses to apply across its various products or service. In a brand extension, the marketing manager uses an established brand name to introduce a new offering. Potential extensions must be judged by how effectively they leverage existing brand equity as well as how effectively the extension, in turn, contributes to the equity of the existing parent brand.

4 Brands can play a number of different roles within the brand portfolio. Brands may expand coverage, provide protection, extend an image or fulfil a variety of other roles for the company. Each brand name must have a well-defined positioning. In that way, brands can maximise coverage, minimise overlap and thus optimise the portfolio.

5 Brand equity should be defined in terms of marketing effects uniquely attributable to a brand. That is, brand equity relates to the fact that different financial outcomes result from the marketing of a branded product or service when compared to the results if that same product or service was not branded.

6 Brand equity needs to be measured in order to be managed well. Brand audits measure 'where the brand has been', and tracking studies measure 'where the brand is now' and whether marketing programmes are having the intended effects.

7 A service branding approach emphasises the integrative, reciprocal role of the brand, which focuses on the value-adding processes. Brand meaning is primarily influenced by brand experience, with competency in customer experience management aligned to service levels, staff behaviour, brand positioning and environment.

APPLICATIONS

Marketing debate

Are brand extensions good or bad? Some critics vigorously denounce the practice of brand extensions, as they feel that too often companies lose focus and consumers become confused. Other experts maintain that brand extensions are a critical growth strategy and source of revenue for the company.

Take a position: Brand extensions can endanger brands *versus* Brand extensions are an important brand-growth strategy.

Marketing discussion

A brand strategy has six main decision components. Discuss the six components, showing how each helps to create the brand identity in the mind of the consumer.

REFERENCES

[1]S. Anthony (2011) Answering your questions about P&G and innovation, *Harvard Business Review Blog*, 23 May; Procter & Gamble (2010) Annual report http://annualreport.pg.com/annualreport2010/downloads/PG_2010_AnnualReport.pdf. Procter & Gamble (2010) Procter & Gamble looks to brand extensions, www.warc.com/LatestNews/News/ArchiveNews.news?ID=26159; Procter & Gamble (2010) P&G's Crest 3D White is tops among 2010 new product pacesetters, www.pg.com/en_US/news_views/blog_posts/2011/apr/crest.shtml; M. Well (2004) Kid nabbing, *Forbes*, 2 February, 84.

[2]Procter & Gamble (2010) Annual report, http://annualreport.pg.com/annualreport2010/downloads/PG_2010_AnnualReport.pdf; Procter & Gamble (2009) Annual report, http://en.wikipedia.org/wiki/Procter_%26_Gamble#cite_note-14.

[3]Procter & Gamble (2010) P&G's Crest 3D White is tops among 2010 new product pacesetters, www.pg.com/en_US/news_views/blog_posts/2011/apr/crest.shtml.

[4]T. Marzilli (2011) Old Spice and RightGuard muscle up some Buzz, BrandIndex, www.brandindex.com/article/old-spice-and-right-guard-muscle-some-buzz.

[5]Procter & Gamble (2010) Procter & Gamble looks to brand extensions, www.warc.com/LatestNews/News/ArchiveNews.news?ID=26159.

[6]J. Neff (2010) P&G hikes ad spending by $1 billion to grow share, sales, *Advertising Age*, 3 August, http://adage.com/article/news/marketing-p-g-hikes-ad-spending-1b-grow-share-sales/145226/; A. Cave (2010) Procter & Gamble to raise ad spend, *Telegraph*, 10 April, www.telegraph.co.uk/finance/newsbysector/retailandconsumer/7575115/Procter-and-Gamble-to-raise-ad-spend.html.

[7]Ibid.

[8]J. Birchal (2009) Value trend tests brand loyalty, *Financial Times*, 31 March, www.ft.com.elib.tcd.ie/cms/s/0/8bf299c8-1d8b-11de-9eb3-00144feabdc0.html#axzz1URB2ErCL; Knowledge@Emory (2006) P&G's A.G. Lafley on leadership, brands, and innovation, 14 September, http://knowledge.emory.edu/article.cfm?articleid=990; *P&G Fact Sheet*, December 2010; J. Galvin (2005) The world on a string, *Point*, February, 13–24; J. Neff (2005) P&G kisses up to the boss: consumers, *Advertising Age*, 2 May, 18; R. Berner (2006) Detergent can be so much more, *BusinessWeek*, 1 May, 66–8; www.pg.com.

[9]A. Roberts (2011) LVMH's Vuitton gains, Gucci declines in brand value, 9 May, Bloomberg, www.bloomberg.com/news/2011-05-08/louis-vuitton-rises-gucci-falls-in-2011-brand-valuation-study.html.

[10]M. McDonald cited in: D. E. Schultz, B. E. Barnes, H. F. Schultz and M. Azzaro (2009) *Building Customer-Brand Relationships*, Armonk, NY: M. E. Sharpe.

[11]K. L. Keller, T. Aperia and M. Georgson (2008) *Strategic Brand Management: A European Perspective*, Harlow: Financial Times/Prentice Hall; L. deChernatony and M. McDonald (2003) *Creating Powerful Brands*, Oxford: Butterworth Heinemann.

[12]Interbrand Group, *World's Greatest Brands: An International Review*, New York: John Wiley & Sons; see also K. Moore and S. E. Reid (2006) The birth of a brand, Working Paper, Desautels Faculty of Management, McGill University.

[13]W. Kingston (2006) Trademark registration is not a right, *Journal of Macromarketing*, 26(1), 17–26.

[14]C. Kopelman, L. Roberts and P. Adab (2007) Advertising of food to children: is brand logo recognition related to their food knowledge, eating behaviours and food preferences? *Journal of Public Health*, 358–67; J. McNeal (1992) *Kids as Consumers: A Handbook for Marketing to Children*, New York: Lexington Books.

[15]D. De Torres (2011) Senses trigger brand recognition, http://dustindetorres.com/uncategorized/senses-trigger-brand-recognition/; Alleres (1990) *Luxe . . . Strategies Marketing*, Paris: Economica.

[16]A. Chernev, R. Hamilton and D. Gal, (2011) Competing for consumer identity: limits to self-expression and the perils of lifestyle branding, *Journal of Marketing*, 75(3), 66–82; S. Morrison and F. G. Crane (2007) Building the service brand by creating and managing an emotional brand experience, *Journal of Brand Management*, 14(5), 410–22.

[17]R. Cesari, R. Lynch and T. Kelly (2011) *Buy Now: Creative Marketing that Gets Customers to Respond to You and Your* Product, New York: Wiley Publishing; Morrison and Crane (2007) op. cit.; H. Brembeck and K. Ekstrom (2004) *Elusive Consumption*, Oxford: Berg; M. Gobe (2001) *Emotional Branding*, New York: Allworth Press; S. Ratneshwar and D. Mick (2005) *Inside Consumption*, London: Routledge.

[18]Morrison and Crane (2007) op. cit.; Gobe (2001) op. cit.

[19]P. Gumbel (2007) Luxury brands: the business of selling dreams, *European Business Review*, 26 October.

[20]Z. Wu, J. Borgerson and J. Schroeder (2011) Fashion systems and symbolic production from historical Chinese culture: creating and managing global Chinese brands, *Advances in Consumer Research*, vol. 37, Available at SSRN: http://ssrn.com/abstract=1800342; R. Elliott and A. Davies (2005) Symbolic brands and authenticity of identity performance, in J. Schroeder and M. Salzer-Morling (eds), *Brand Culture*, London: Routledge.

[21]J. Brakus, B. H. Schmitt and L. Zarantonello (2009) Brand experience: what is it? How is it measured? Does it affect loyalty?, *Journal of Marketing*, 73 (May), 52–68; M. Moynagh and R. Worsley (2002) Tomorrow's consumer: the shifting balance of power, *Journal of Consumer Behaviour*, 1(3), 293–301.

[22]A. Chernev, R. Hamilton and D. Gal (2011) Competing for consumer identity: limits to self-expression and the perils of lifestyle branding, *Journal of Marketing*, 75(3), 66–82.

[23]Ibid.

[24]G. Sonnier (2011) Estimating the value of Brand-image associations: the role of general and specific brand image, *Journal of Marketing Research*, 48 (June), 518–31; W. Coop (2005) A question of identity, *Journal of Marketing*, 11(1), 36–7.

[25]K. Keller (2008) *Strategic Brand Management*, 3rd eds, New York: Pearson.

[26]Jesper Kunde (2002) *Corporate Religion*, Harlow: Financial Times Prentice Hall.

[27]For an academic discussion of how consumers become so strongly attached to people as brands, see M. Thomson (2006) Human brands: investigating antecedents to consumers' stronger attachments to celebrities, *Journal of Marketing*, 70 (July), 104–19; for some practical branding tips from the world of rock and roll, see R. Blackwell and T. Stephan (2004) *Brands That Rock*, Hoboken, NJ: John Wiley & Sons; and from the world of sports, see I. Rein, P. Kotler and B. Shields (2006) *The Elusive Fan: Reinventing Sports in a Crowded Marketplace*, New York: McGraw-Hill.

[28]P. Fennell (2009) Creating the Lexus customer experience, *Executive Issue*, 34, January; Alibaba (2011) Lexus voted no.1 in customer satisfaction, http://www1.albawaba.com/jd-power-lexus-voted-no1-customer-satisfaction.

[29]Lexus Brand Value (2004) http://images.mileone.com/Matt/mwlogos/Lexus/LexusBrandGuideline.pdf.

[30]M. Draganska, D. Klapper, S. B. Villas-Boas (2010) A larger slice or a larger pie? An empirical investigation of bargaining power in the distribution channel, *Journal of Marketing Science*, 29(1), 57–74: R. Clifton and J. Simmons (eds) (2004) *The Economist on Branding*, New York: Bloomberg; R. Riezebos (2003) *Brand Management: A Theoretical and Practical Approach*, Harlow: Pearson Education.

[31]T. Erdem (1998) Brand equity as a signaling phenomenon, *Journal of Consumer Psychology*, 7(2), 131–57.

[32]R. Suri and K. B. Monroe (2003) The effects of time pressure on consumers' judgments of prices and products, *Journal of Consumer Research*, 30 (June), 92–104.

[33]W. Kingston (2006) Trademark registration is not a right, *Journal of Macromarketing*, 26(1), 17–26; C. E. Bagley (2005) *Managers and the Legal Environment: Strategies for the 21st Century*, 3rd edn, Cincinnati, OH: Southwestern College/West Publishing; for a marketing academic point of view on some important legal issues, see J. Zaichkowsky (2006) *The Psychology Behind Trademark Infringement and Counterfeiting*, Philadelphia: LEA Publishing; and M. Morrin and J. Jacoby (2000) Trademark dilution: empirical measures for an elusive concept, *Journal of Public Policy and Marketing*, 19(2), 265–76.

[34]S. Davis (2000) *Brand Asset Management: Driving Profitable Growth Through Your Brands*, San Francisco: Jossey-Bass; M. W. Sullivan (1998) How brand names affect the demand for twin automobiles, *Journal of Marketing Research*, 35, 154–65; A. J. Slywotzky and B. P. Shapiro (1993) Leveraging to beat the odds: the new marketing mindset, *Harvard Business Review*, September–October, 97–107.

[35]The power of branding is not without its critics, however, some of whom reject the commercialism associated with branding activities. See N. Klein (2000) *No Logo: Taking Aim at the Brand Bullies*, New York: Picador.

[36]G. Mulgan (2006) Because you're worth it, *Guardian*, 12 June.

[37]K. L. Keller, T. Aperia and M. Georgson (2008) *Strategic Brand Management: A European Perspective*, Harlow: Financial Times/Prentice Hall.

[38]G. Harter, A. Koster, M. Peterson and M. Stomberg (2005) Europe's brand-oriented companies almost twice as successful, Booz, Allen, Hamilton website (www.boozallen.com/publications/article/659562).

[39]B. Lev (2001) *Intangibles: Management, Measurement, and Reporting*, Washington, DC: Brookings Institution; N. Mizik and R. Jacobson (2005) Talk about brand strategy, *Harvard Business Review*, October, 1.

[40]C. Bothwell (2005) Burberry versus the chavs, *BBC Money Programme*, 28 October (http://news.bbc.co.uk/1/hi/business/4381140.stm).

[41]K. L. Keller and S. Sood (2003) Brand equity dilution, *MIT Sloan Management Review*, 45(1), 12–15.

[42]R. Dodes (2006) From tracksuits to fast track, *Wall Street Journal*, 13 September, B1–2.

[43]A. Baltazar (2007) Silly brand names get serious attention, *Brandweek*, December, 4.

[44]A. Wheeler (2003) *Designing Brand Identity*, Hoboken, NJ: John Wiley & Sons.

[45]P. Fallon and F. Senn (2006) *Juicing the Orange: How to Turn Creativity into a Powerful Business Advantage*, Cambridge, MA: Harvard Business School Press.

[46]J. Larean, A. Dalton and E. Andrade (2011) Why brands produce priming effects and slogans produce reverse priming effects, *Journal of Consumer Research*, 37 (April).

[47]See http://pal2pal.com/BLOGEE/index.php?/site/comments/left_wing_group_turns_cereal_killer/.

[48]Bojan Pancevski (2006) Vorsprung durch Technik slogans break down in reverse, *Telegraph*, www.telegraph.co.uk/news/worldnews/1535893/Vorsprung-durch-Technik-slogans-break-down-in-reverse.html.

[49]Keller, Aperia and Georgson (2008) op. cit.

[50]R. Grover (2009) Selling by storytelling, *BusinessWeek*, 25 May.

[51]R. Ringer and M. Thibodeau (2008) A breakthrough approach to brand creation, www.versegroup.com/downloads/VerseGroup_breakthroughapproach.pdf.

[52]P. Hanlon, *Primal Branding: Create Zealots for Your Brand, Your Company, and Your Future*, New York: Free Press, 2006; Think-Topia, www.thinktopia.com.

[53]For comprehensive corporate branding guidelines, see J. R. Gregory (2004) *The Best of Branding: Best Practices in Corporate Branding*, New York: McGraw-Hill; for some international perspectives, see M. Schultz, M. J. Hatch and M. H. Larsen (eds) (2000) *The Expressive Organization: Linking Identity, Reputation and Corporate Brand*, Oxford: Oxford University Press; and M. Schultz, Y. M. Antorini and F. F. Csaba (eds) (2005) *Corporate Branding: Purpose, People, and Process*, Copenhagen: Copenhagen Business School Press.

[54]J. Balmer (2010) Explicating corporate brands and their management: reflections and directions from 1995, *Journal of Brand Management* 18, 180–96.

[55]P. Farquhar (1989) Managing brand equity, *Marketing Research*, 1 (September), 24–33.

[56]S. M. Shugan (1989) Branded variants, 1989 AMA Educators' Proceedings, Chicago: American Marketing Association, 33–8; see also M. Bergen, S. Dutta and S. M. Shugan (1996) Branded variants: a retail perspective, *Journal of Marketing Research*, 33 (February), 9–21.

[57]A. Bass (2004) Licensed extension: stretching to communicate, *Journal of Brand Management*, 12 (September), 31–8; see also D. Aaker (1995) *Building Strong Brands*, New York: Free Press.

[58]C. Pullig, C. Simmons and R. G. Netemeyer (2006) Brand dilution: when do new brands hurt existing brands?, *Journal of Marketing*, 70 (April), 52–66. B. Loken and D. R. John (1993) Diluting brand beliefs: when do brand extensions have a negative impact?, *Journal of Marketing*, July, 71–84; S. M. Broniarcyzk and J. W. Alba (1994) The importance of the brand in brand extension, *Journal of Marketing Research*, May, 214–28 (note: the entire issue of JMR May 1994 is devoted to brands and brand equity); see also R. Ahluwalia and Z. Gürhan-Canli (2000) The effects of extensions on the family brand name: an accessibility-diagnosticity perspective, *Journal of Consumer Research*, 27 (December), 371–81; Z. Gürhan-Canli and M. Durairaj (1998) The effects of extensions on brand name dilution and enhancement, *Journal of Marketing Research*, 35, 464–73.

[59]F. Völckner and H. Sattler (2006) Drivers of brand extension success, *Journal of Marketing*, 70 (April), 1–17.

[60]K. L. Keller and D. A. Aaker (1992) The effects of sequential introduction of brand extensions, *Journal of Marketing Research*, 29 (February), 35–50; for consumer processing implications, see H. Mao and H. Shanker Krishnan (2006) Effects of prototype and exemplar fit on brand extension evaluations: a two-process contingency model, *Journal of Consumer Research*, 33 (June), 41–9.

[61]Keller and Aaker (1992) op. cit.; J. Milewicz and P. Herbig (1994) Evaluating the brand extension decision using a model of reputation building, *Journal of Product and Brand Management*, 3(1), 39–47.

[62]V. A. Taylor and W. O. Bearden (2003) Ad spending on brand extensions: does similarity matter?, *Journal of Brand Management*, 11 (September), 63–74; S. Bridges, K. L. Keller and S. Sood (2000) Communication strategies for brand extensions: enhancing perceived fit by establishing explanatory links, *Journal of Advertising*, 29 (Winter), 1–11.

[63]B. Meyer (2005) Rubber firms extend brands to gain customers, revenues, *Bnet Business Network*, October.

[64]J. Paisner (2006) Goodyear and Michelin: on your feet, *CoreBrand*, 16 January (www.corebrand.com/index.php?option=com_content&task=view&id=47&Itemid=).

[65]A. Ries and J. Trout (2000) *Positioning: The Battle for Your Mind*, 20th Anniversary Edition, New York: McGraw-Hill; J. A. Quelch and David Kenny (1994) Extend profits, not product lines, *Harvard Business Review*, September–October, 153–60; M. Morrin (1999) The impact of brand extensions on parent brand memory structures and retrieval processes, *Journal of Marketing Research*, 36(4), 517–25.

[66]Ries and Trout (2000) op. cit.

[67]D. A. Aaker (2004) *Brand Portfolio Strategy: Creating Relevance, Differentiation, Energy, Leverage, and Clarity*, New York: Free Press.

[68]Lego's turnaround: picking up the pieces, *The Economist*, 28 October, 76.

[69]M. Haig (2005) *Brand Failures: The Truth About the 100 Biggest Branding Mistakes of All Time*, London: Kogan Page.

[70]J. Doward, J. Arlidge and F. Islam (2000) Branson's big gamble, *Observer*, 27 August (www.guardian.co.uk/society/2000/aug/27/lottery.observerfocus).

[71]J. Trout (2001) *Differentiate or Die: Survival in Our Era of Killer Competition*, New York: John Wiley & Sons.

[72]M. Sherrington (2003) *Added Value: The Alchemy of Brand-Led Growth*, Basingstoke: Palgrave Macmillan.

[73]Keller (2008) op. cit.

[74]For a discussion of what factors determines long-term branding success, see A. P. Adamson (2006) *Brand Simple*, New York: Palgrave Macmillan.

[75]Ryanair (2010) www.ryanair.com/en/news/ryanair-s-traffic-grows-13-percent-in-july-to-a-record-7-6m

[76]S. Anthony (2010) Kindle isn't dead yet, and other reflections on Apple's iPad, *Harvard Business Review* Blog, 3 June; B. Male (2010) 3 innovation lessons from Apple's continued success, *Business Insider*, www.businessinsider.com/3-keys-to-apples-innovation-success-2010-5#ixzz1USPIhBt3; A. Z. Cuneo (2003) Apple transcends as lifestyle brand, *Advertising Age*, 15 June, S2–S6.

[77]M. Speece (2002) Marketer's malady: fear of change, *Brandweek*, 19 August, 34; Haig (2005) op. cit.

[78]Keller (2008) op. cit.

[79]Keller, Aperia and Georgson (2008) op. cit.

[80]Interbrand (2011) http://www.interbrand.com/en/best-global-brands/best-global-brands-2008/best-global-brands-2010.aspx

[81]Ibid.

[82]R. Clifton (2004) The future of brands, *Interbrand*, 23 April (www.brandchannel.com/papers_review.asp?sp_id=356).

[83]See www.brandwave.net/identity.html.

[84]F. N. Dahmash, R. B. Durand and J. Watson (2009) The value relevance and reliability of reported goodwill and identifiable intangible assets, *British Accounting Review*, 41(2), 120–37; T. Hadjiloucas and R. Winter (2005) Reporting the value of acquired intangible assets, PricewaterhouseCoopers Globe White Paper, London: PricewaterhouseCoopers.

[85]K. Keller (2010) Brand equity management in a multichannel, multimedia retail environment, *Journal of Interactive Marketing*, 24(2), 58–70; J. M. Oliveria-Castro, G. R. Foxall, V. K. James, H. B. F. Roberta, M. B. Pohl, B. Dias and S. W. Chang (2008) Consumer-based brand equity and brand performance, *Service Industries Journal*, 28(4), 445–61; K. L. Keller and D. Lehmann (2006) Brand and branding: research findings and future priorities, *Marketing Science*, 25(6), 740–59.

[86]D. O'Sullivan and P. Butler (2010) Marketing accountability and marketing's stature: an examination of senior executives, *Australasian Marketing Journal*, 18(3), 113–20.

[87]Other approaches are based on economic principles of signaling: for example, T. Erdem (1998) Brand equity as a signaling phenomenon, *Journal of Consumer Psychology*, 7(2), 131–57; or for more of a sociological, anthropological or biological perspective, G. McCracken (2005) *Culture and Consumption II: Markets, Meaning, and Brand Management*, Bloomington, IN: Indiana University Press; or S. Fournier (1998) Consumers and their brands: developing relationship theory in consumer research, *Journal of Consumer Research*, 24 (September), 343–73.

[88]K. L. Keller (2007) *Strategic Brand Management: Building, Measuring, and Managing Brand Equity*, 3rd edn, Upper Saddle River, NJ: Prentice Hall.

[89]D. A. Aaker (1991) *Managing Brand Equity*, New York: Free Press; D. A. Aaker (1996) *Building Strong Brands*, New York: Free Press; D. A. Aaker and E. Joachimsthaler (2000) *Brand Leadership*, New York: Free Press; Keller (2008) op. cit.

[90]J. N. Kapferer (1992) *Strategic Brand Management: New Approaches to Creating and Evaluating Brand Equity*, London: Kogan Page, 38; J. L. Aaker (1997) Dimensions of brand personality, *Journal of Marketing Research*, August, 347–56; S. M. Davis (2002) *Brand Asset Management: Driving Profitable Growth Through Your Brands*, San Francisco: Jossey-Bass; for an overview of academic research on branding, see K. L. Keller (2002) Branding and brand equity, in B. Weitz and R. Wensley (eds), *Handbook of Marketing*, London: Sage, 151–78.

[91]Keller and Lehmann (2006) op. cit.

[92]S. Morrison and F. G. Crane (2007) Building the service brand by creating and managing an emotional brand experience, *Journal of Brand Management*, 14(5), 410–21.

[93]L. Sajtos, R. Brodie and J. Whittome (2010) Impact of service failure: the protective layer of customer relationships, *Journal of Service Research*, 13(2), 216–29; see also L. L. Berry (2000)

Cultivating service brand equity, *Journal of the Academy of Marketing Science*, 28(1), 128–37.

[94]R. Brodie (2009) From goods to service branding: an integrative perspective, *Marketing Theory*, 9(1), 107–11

[95]L. Berry, V. Shankar, J. Turner Parish, S. Cadwallader and T. Dotzel (2006) Creating new markets through service innovation, *MIT Sloan Management Review*, 47(2), 56–63.

[96]See www.bcg.com/publications/files/Master_Brands_Apr_01.pdf.

[97]M. Beirne and J. Benito (2006) Starwood uses personnel to personalize marketing, *Brandweek*, 24 April, 9.

[98]L. de Chernatony and S. Cottam (2006) Why are all financial services brands not great?, *Journal of Product and Brand Management*, 15(2), 88–97.

[99]P. Barwise, A. Dunham and M. Ritson (2000) Ties that bind: brands, consumers and business, in J. Pavitt (ed.) *Brand New*, London: V&A, 70–97.

[100]H. Thorbjørnsen and M. Supphellen (2011) Determinants of core value behavior in service brands, *Journal of Services Marketing*, 25(1), 68–76; N. Kimpakorn and G. Tocquer (2010) Service brand equity and employee brand commitment, *Journal of Services Marketing*, 24(5), 378–88.

[101]S. Davis and M. Dunn (2002) *Building the Brand Driven Business*, New York: John Wiley & Sons; M. Dunn and S. Davis (2003) Building brands from the inside, *Marketing Management*, May/June, 32–7.

[102]R. Tehreni (2011) http://blog.tmcnet.com/blog/rich-tehrani/apple/how-poor-branding-and-positioning-have-led-to-tech-and-auto-failure.html.

[103]R. Brodie (2009) From goods to service branding: an integrative perspective, *Marketing Theory*, 9(1), 107–11.

[104]K. L. Keller (2000) The brand report card, *Harvard Business Review*, January–February, 147–57.

Chapter 13

Digital and global brand management strategies

IN THIS CHAPTER, WE WILL ADDRESS THE FOLLOWING QUESTIONS:

1 What is digital branding?
2 What are the social networking branding challenges?
3 What are the challenges for managing global brands?
4 How is branding practised in the developing world?
5 What is celebrity and country/place branding?

A range of European brands
Source: Courtesy of the companies shown.

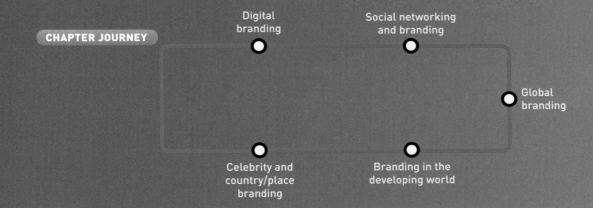

Digital branding

Social networking and branding

Global branding

Celebrity and country/place branding

Branding in the developing world

C ontemporary brand challenges include managing digital branding and global brands. Both demand an understanding of consumer behaviour and what consumers want, whether in the digital arena or off line. Globalisation and digital technology have both transformed how consumers engage with brands and in turn how marketing managers manage brands, nationally, internationally and globally.

Think about your day and you will begin to see how much technology and globalisation are core elements of all you do. Your Nokia mobile phone alarm goes off. You put on a pair of Diesel jeans, a top from Zara, Adidas trainers and not forgetting your Apple iPod which is already in your H&M jacket pocket. For breakfast, you drink your Nespresso and eat a Danone Actimel yogurt before you open your Sony Vaio laptop to check your email on Google. At the bus stop you check the bus timetable online using your smartphone and pay by swiping your RFID card on a scanner. On the bus into college you think about going for a drink of Guinness or a Heineken with friends that evening and you can use Google Latitude to check where they are. You stop at Café Java to surf the net and connect with your friends near and far through Facebook and other sites. These technologies and established global brands hail from countries around the globe including Finland, Switzerland, Japan, Spain, the United States, Italy, France, the United Kingdom, the Netherlands and Ireland.

Global brands are worth billions of euro and many of these are technology brands too, such as no. 1 Nokia (Finland) valued at €25 billion; no. 2 Vodafone (UK) valued at €22 billion; no. 6 Telefonica (Spain) valued at €15 billion; no. 8 Orange (UK) valued at €12 billion; and no. 9 T-Mobile (German) valued at €12 billion.[1] Branding in a globalised world dominated by technology poses challenges of speed, communication and connection.

What is a digital brand?

The digital age has heralded many changes in how marketers manage their brands. Consumers still want brands that have a clear value and brands that deliver on a compelling brand promise, but what they have now is more touchpoints offline and online. **Digital branding** is the creation and management of brands through the use of all forms of digital technologies, many of which are controlled by the consumer. They include television, radio, internet, mobile, social networking sites, virtual games and any other form of digital technology or platform. The core feature of any digital environment is that it is electronic. The concept relates to customer engagement with the brand, which can occur offline or online (digitally).

- **Offline or traditional.** The traditional form of interaction was mainly human, interpersonal, physical engagements between the brand (company) and the customer.
- **Online or digital.** Digital or virtual world interactions take place supported through a variety of technologies. Though often used to refer to the internet, they include any digital technology used.

The human and physical relationships (offline) must be aligned with the digital (online) world. There is also a convergence of the digital and the traditional, such as interactive (digital) billboards (traditional). Honda has an interactive billboard where customers can 'start the car' by texting a code and then the car on the billboard starts with engine noises, flashing headlights and exhaust smoke. Digital branding creates countless new opportunities for brand building. By design or default, every brand has a digital experience. In today's world, a company's digital presence could become the *only* experience that potential customers have with an organisation, particularly prior to and post purchase. The availability of new technologies, the increasing digital savvy of consumers and the success of online-only brands have made it imperative for companies to evolve their corporate websites into 24/7 dynamic brand experiences. Brands like Apple, eBay, Audi and Nike are often praised as best-in-class brands because of their ability to create effective and inspiring experiences.[2] They share a common trait – a strong brand promise that provides meaningful differentiation, creates preference and offers relevance to their audiences in both the digital (online) and offline environments. A brand promise embodies a clear idea and value proposition, and it connects with people on functional *and* emotional levels.[3]

The best companies understand the need to deliver their brand promise in the digital environment, as Nike does.

Nike

Nike partnered with Apple to create Nike+, a digitally driven offering that combines the products and services of Nike with Apple's iPod Nano. Runners can wirelessly connect Nike's sensors, embedded in their running shoes, to their Nanos, which in turn enable them to create personalised workouts and playlists. Performance results can be uploaded to personalised accounts on the Nike+ website, and runners can review their progress, connect with other Nike+ runners around the world, and download workouts created by world famous coaches. The result is a multi-touch digital experience that delivers Nike's brand attributes of performance and innovation to its target customers in a unique, relevant way.[4]

Digital branding as a core management requirement

Sometimes digital branding is just added as an afterthought when it should be a core feature. BMW Films, developed in the early 2000s, was one of the first examples of a company that took digital branding seriously and made an investment in it. BMW designed 'The Hire' series of eight short films (averaging about ten minutes each).[5] As a form of branded content, all eight films featured popular film-makers from across the globe, starred Clive Owen as the 'Driver', and highlighted the performance aspects of various BMW cars. The end results were staggering, with the series viewed over 100 million times and changing the way products were branded. BMW takes online branding seriously and creatively, and invests resources to be successful. Many marketers still treat digital as just one more box to be ticked rather than a core part of marketing.

A compelling digital experience requires that brands and technology are integrated by design. It is not just about using the latest technology or a new media tool, but about creating connections with people in a branded way. With an ever-growing choice of technologies and applications, these innovations can be used to reinforce and optimise a brand in the digital environment, understanding and using the technology to deliver the functional, emotional and experiential promise of a brand. Apple is a powerful example of how an intuitive, human brand idea and game-changing technology come together to evoke tremendous consumer devotion.

Creating a compelling, relevant digital brand in today's climate requires going beyond a corporate website. As old technologies evolve and new ones burst forth, establishing credibility in the digital environment is a lot more challenging. Technologies like Second Life, YouTube, Twitter, Flickr and RSS – can add depth and dimension to a brand. Success in the digital realm hinges on creating the right digital experiences with the right technologies to reinforce the brand strategy.[6]

Digital branding is changing the way brands behave, interact and speak through internet and digital platforms, through creating websites and social networking experiences, designing applications and managing brand assets in real time. Digital branding provides an opportunity for maximising brand potential in effective and innovative ways. This is both an exciting and challenging time for marketing with new digital technologies and the growing ability of consumers to communicate and influence globally. Well-managed digital branding can be even better than the pre-technology or pre-internet days, in that there is the availability of multiple, channel 'touchpoints' with customers, even before they become customers. As the old marketing saying goes: someone needs to see or hear about your product and company several times before they finally convert to a customer. The best part of digital branding is that, managed well and with skill, it is now affordable even for small businesses to connect to a well-defined targeted audience. Brand perception often has less to do with the product or service but relates to everything the customers *perceive*, and much of that perception is now technology and internet based – in the digital realm. Much of what customers learn about brands takes place in the digital world.

A strategic approach is important, involving plans related to how many resources to invest in the technology, aligned to the brand's overall objectives: what does it stand for, what value does it provide and to whom? Once these variables are understood and there is a clear picture of all marketing activity offline, then the strategic engagement online must be invested in. Decisions on how much to invest, in which technologies and platforms, and importantly how to use the technology to engage, enhance and develop the brand with a clear, holistic brand identity, should be made. Staffing and training and, importantly, the monitoring and management of internet chatter and other digital technologies are critical too. The digital space allows companies to experiment with very different opportunities than the traditional world allows. And experimenting with new technologies clearly provides an opportunity to contemporise and personalise the brand. Experiments teach companies what works and should turn into and what should be used in digital brand programmes that maximise return for the company.

Placing the customer at the centre of all digital branding is crucial. Many companies fail to understand the needs and desires of customers and build and maintain websites and a digital presence driven by what they think their customers want or need. The result: a digital experience that neither differentiates the brand nor has relevance to customers or employees. To avoid this, first-hand knowledge about what customers are looking for, what they want and need, and what they dream and worry about is needed. An in-depth, insight-driven look at how a brand touches customers at various stages of interaction – from initial awareness, through trial and purchase, to loyalty and advocacy – is crucial to building an effective digital brand strategy. **Touchpoints** are the many ways in which a customer comes into contact with the business. Every touchpoint that is in any way associated in customers' minds with the brand identity of a business contributes to the customers' experience of that brand. This means every communications, sales contact, service delivery, customer service interaction, website, social networking commentary or self-service experience that the customer comes into contact with can impact on the brand image. The phenomenal reach speed and inter-activity of digital or online touchpoints makes close attention to the brand experience essential and requires an ability to monitor and manage these 24/7 and worldwide.[7] Marketers need to monitor and manage **digital brand health**, which is an assessment of a how the brand is adhering to its strategic direction in the digital world – (see the breakthrough marketing box).

Breakthrough marketing

Brand health in a digital world[8]

A brand's health is more vulnerable in the digital age as consumer opinion travels faster and further, spreading like a communicable disease. Today, brand health is under attack in four ways, through:

1 greater **volume** of data sources;

2 faster **velocity** of consumer data;

3 broader **visibility** of consumer sentiment; and

4 greater **volatility** of consumer behaviour.

To manage these four Vs of digital brand influence, marketing leaders must prescribe a new approach to brand health management by building their:

- brand responsiveness to react quickly to rapidly changing market conditions; and
- brand resilience to counteract unforeseen crises and threats.[9]

A brand's health is strengthened or weakened by every interaction and exposure with a consumer, and the advent of digital technology means that a more vigilant approach to managing brand perception is required. To keep track of the always-on, anytime, anywhere, unfettered-public-opinion-sharing customers, marketers must use a dashboard to augment classic brand metrics.

Marketers need to act and react quickly and intelligently to the collective real-time consumer opinions and behaviours that affect a brand's perception or performance. Brand health can be improved by building the brand's responsiveness and resilience (see Figure 13.1).

- **Sharpen the brand's reflexes by building brand responsiveness.** Like a heart monitor, responsive brand managers manage the real-time performance of the brand's health. This means that marketers must enable the organisation to act quickly on new consumer and marketplace intelligence. A great example is Pizza Hut, who are improving their responsiveness to customer feedback about the restaurant experience and delivery service. It partnered with Radian6 to monitor Facebook and Twitter and put a system in place to classify, prioritise and react to dissatisfied customers.

- **Boost the brand's immune system by building brand resilience.** Marketers must prepare the organisation to weather unpredictable twists and turns of public opinion to protect the long-term value of the brand. How much negative sentiment will cause damage to brand equity? When should the marketing team spring into action? It does not have to be a guessing game. Marketers have tools to capture historical data for share of voice and consumer sentiment in order to create thresholds for when to act.

Source: Adapted from Forrester, Inc., Global Social Media Adoption in 2011, April 2011.

Breakthrough marketing *(continued)*

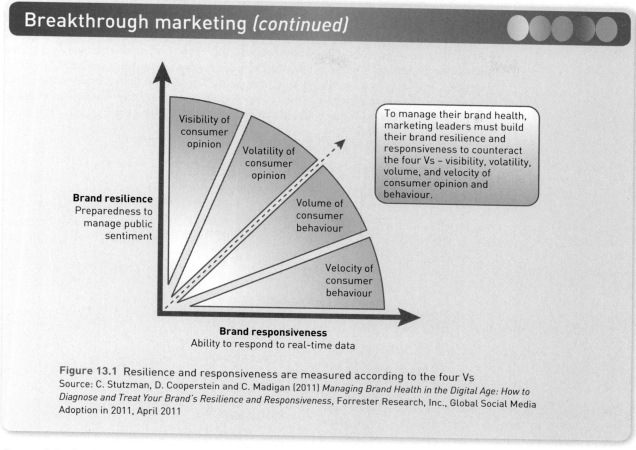

Figure 13.1 Resilience and responsiveness are measured according to the four Vs
Source: C. Stutzman, D. Cooperstein and C. Madigan (2011) *Managing Brand Health in the Digital Age: How to Diagnose and Treat Your Brand's Resilience and Responsiveness*, Forrester Research, Inc., Global Social Media Adoption in 2011, April 2011

Gap and Starbucks both had to deal with all four Vs during the launch of new logos by each company.

Gap and Starbucks

Both Gap and Starbucks received positive and negative consumer sentiment when launching new logos. The backlash against Gap's new logo was intense. Beyond the thousands of tweets and Facebook status updates deriding its design, people found other creative ways to protest the new logo. A fake Twitter account gathered thousands of followers, and Gap logo generators quickly went viral. Gap, without any historical benchmark, appeared to panic over the situation and retracted the new logo in favour of the old one.

Starbucks, on the other hand, was equipped with years of consumer sentiment knowledge built from fostering intimate relationships with consumers through communities like My Starbucks Idea. So Starbucks knew how much criticism to expect and how to handle it. It stuck to its logo and asked consumers to trust it about the decision.

The new Starbucks logo was a departure, but not a radical shift, from the logo that has adorned the coffee chain's cups since 1992. They took the words 'Starbucks' and 'coffee', out of the logo, leaving just the firm's white on green image of a twin-tailed siren. Starbucks said that in the future 'it's possible we'll have other products with our name on it and no coffee in it'.

Wharton marketing professor David Reibstein says retaining the green colour for the logo was critical. 'You can show that colour, and people will recognize it as Starbucks. That colour is really important to them. In a similar way, Apple has taken the most benign colour, white, and owned it'. As Starbucks have confirmed their intention to stay with this logo the social network backlash has abated.

Understanding the new consumer decision journey

The main difference with digital branding is who controls the information and communication – much of this is now outside the control of marketing managers. This means that traditional strategies have to be redesigned to cater for the digital age. Traditionally, customers started with a large number of brands and then arrived at their final choice of one brand to purchase. Once the purchase was made, the relationship with the company usually ended – this is called the funnel metaphor (see Figure 13.2).

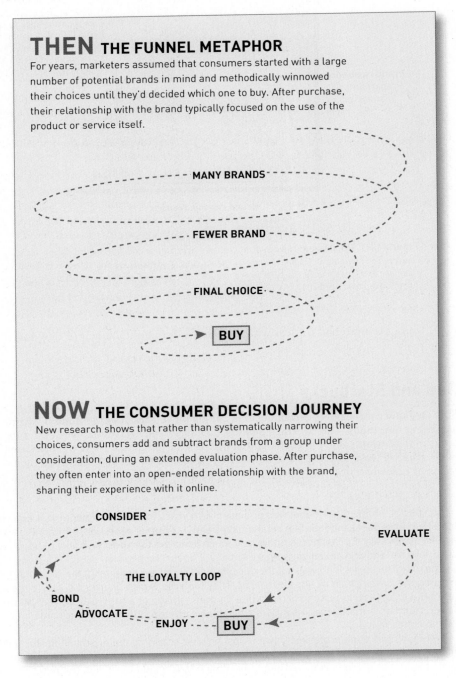

Figure 13.2 The consumer decision journey

Source: Reprinted by permission of *Harvard Business Review*. From Branding in the digital era by Edelman, D., December 2010. Copyright © 2010 by the Harvard Business School Publishing Corporation; all rights reserved.

The new **consumer decision journey** takes into account digital technology and the consumer-to-consumer engagement within a more detailed decision process.[10] At the start the customers adds and subtracts brands from a group and has an extended evaluation period. After purchase they continue to engage with the brand often sharing with other consumers their experience with the brand (see Figure 13.2). Take the purchase of a television. Before purchase the customer searches for information online and after purchase they often continue to interact with other consumers through a variety of sites where they discuss their purchase. The changes from the 'funnel to buy' orientation to a loop which includes consider, evaluate, purchase and advocate is shown in Figure 13.2.

There are four stages to the consumer decision journey:

1 **Consider**. This is the set of brands that the consumer will consider from the range of brands in the product or service category – called the **evoked set**. Due to the amount of choice available, consumers often reduce the number of brands from which they will make a selection. They can also source information on these brands from a variety of sources.

2 **Evaluate**. Consumers start to study the brands and include and exclude brands following some level of information search aligned to their selection criteria.

3 **Buy**. Consumers then purchase either offline or online. Consumers can be dissuaded from their choice at this stage. This can occur offline when they have to wait in a shop for service and decide to leave, or online when the waiting time for the website is too long and they opt out of the purchase. Websites provide bounce rates for companies. The **bounce rate** is the percentage visits in which the person left the website after they arrived on the entrance (landing) page.

4 **Enjoy – advocate – bond**. After purchase a deeper connection can be developed. Many customers go online after purchase. This aspect is missing from the traditional funnel. When customers are pleased they may advocate the brand, adding to the sources for evaluation of others. They can also post negative comments if they are disappointed and they may sever ties. The site www.MyVWLemon.com, has 2,000 members and about 15,000 message board postings from Volkswagen buyers who are unhappy with some aspect of their purchases. Companies have to be aware of and manage these engagements. If the bond is strong, they may skip the evaluate stage and go to the enjoy–advocate–bond stage. Brand advocates are an important aspect of the digital world as they can make or break products and services. A **brand advocate** is a powerful consumer who is willing to recommend a brand to their friends or advocate for the brand.

The two main implications of the consumer decision journey perspective are:

1 Marketers should target stages in the consumer decision journey rather than simply allocate spending to media. Around 70 to 90 per cent of marketing budgets often go to the consider and buy stages, yet marketers would be wiser to allocate communication spend during the evaluation and enjoy–advocate–bond stages. Spending on driving brand advocacy can improve reviews and encourage discussion, which will in turn drive more reviews and discussion.

2 Marketers must study *own media* – that is, the channels a brand controls such as the website – and *earned media* – customer-created channels such as brand communities. They must also study *supportive spend* – which is where staff and technology are used to create and manage content and to monitor the chatter and comments across a variety of channels.[11] Sites like www.socialmention.com give information on online chatter and the sentiment towards a brand online.

Customers need to be reached at the moment that they are going to make their decision. This involves monitoring what customers do, what customers see and what customers say; and then taking action.[12]

Mining the information from digital technology

As consumers connect to the brand in fundamentally different ways, the information aspects have changed (see Chapters 4 and 5). It can be a major task to manage content provision across the digital touchpoints in order to stay online, up to date, relevant and in real time. There is a need for constant research of the digital content proved by the company and also posted by the customer, mining the information and then using the insights from this information to revise brand strategy. To improve a brand's future digital experience, marketers must first understand what it is today. A baseline understanding should include both breadth of experience (i.e. the brand's portfolio of digital properties) and depth of experience (i.e. a drill-down view of specific experiences).

Evaluating the digital presences of your brand means searching for both known and unknown websites that might be lurking under the radar, and also searching for all consumer-generated content across many social networking sites – using search sites linked to a dashboard to alert marketing as to content changes and issues arising. Companies with little or no digital governance structures are fertile environments for site proliferation, which can confuse consumers. All company content across all digital technology should be managed under a unifying digital brand strategy.

Companies should conduct a cross-organisational audit of all online touchpoints with customers or other key audiences. An audit can uncover places where consumers' experience is not aligned with their needs or the brand's promise, and places where there are tremendous opportunities to deliver that promise. The audit may reveal outdated information, creating a potential legal liability and an annoying experience for customers. The explosion in social networking has created the need to explore not just the company's content online but also how others are creating experiences of the brand online. A health care company completed an audit and found a YouTube video of a company sales rep belting out Shania Twain's 'Man, I Feel Like a Woman' at a sales meeting. This is probably not the way the healthcare brand wants to build its credibility, especially in a category where the online environment is critical to its information-hungry consumers.[13]

Understanding the digital brand experience

A brand comes to life in the digital environment through design, content, technology platform, functionality and navigation. Savvy brands use all of these to create a compelling digital experience. Does your website's *functionality* (i.e. checkout, product registration) enhance or detract from your brand's positioning? A defining feature of online versus other branding channels is this functionality. Digital branding enables the customer to self-direct and customise their relationship with a brand. Is *navigation* well designed for the customer? Can the customer navigate around the site easily and quickly? Customers expect speed and ease of use and will leave websites or other technology platforms which do not provide the speed and ease of use required. A brand positioned as easy to use or intuitive is behaving off-brand when its online checkout process is clunky or complicated. It is not enough to promise 'easy to use'; the brand experience has to demonstrate it. For example, Amazon successfully translates its brand promise of great service by using navigation, functionality and content to create a service-driven digital experience that makes it fast and easy to buy books online, and now to read them digitally with the introduction of the Kindle reader – a book and digital shopping device. Net-a-Porter is an online company which took luxury ladies' fashion into the online domain.

Net-a-Porter

The brand strategy of online brand Net-a-Porter netted the owner €50 million when the brand was sold recently. The website design, content, functionality and navigation are excellent. The website is presented in the style of a magazine, allowing customers across the world the chance to see, review and buy the latest look. Shoppers can find a range of products from €30 T-shirts to silk crepe gowns worth thousands of euro. Around 2 million customers, mainly affluent women, log on to Net-a-Porter every month to browse a range of pieces from 300 top global designers, such as Jimmy Choo, Alexander McQueen, Stella McCartney and Givenchy.[14] A decade ago women only bought clothes they had seen, touched and tried on. Now millions buy their designer labels online at Net-a-porter – a company which has been called the one-click wonder. Massenet, former fashion editor at Tatler, who created Net-a-Porter, is one of the leading success stories of the digital era. She launched the company from a minuscule artist's studio in Chelsea, London a decade ago. Since then the company has mushroomed, and it currently has an estimated turnover of around €120 million and 600 employees in London and New York. The website has won plaudits for revolutionising high-end shopping, allowing women, no matter where they live, to immediately and easily access this season's most cutting-edge design fashion trends. It now ships luxurious fashions to 170 countries around the world.

The Net-a-Porter website is well designed with good content, functionality and easy-to-use navigation.
Source: www.net-a-porter.com

Customer-managed brands

Marketers have to rethink how they view their brands and stop trying to control their brands, but rather should allow customers to engage with them in creative ways, letting the brands become customer managed brands. Companies such as BMW, Converse and Mars have embraced this idea and allow their brands to serve as blank canvases for personal expression. Consumers can designate the exact features, colours and designs of their Mini Cooper cars and Converse sneakers, and brides can serve monogrammed M&M'S at their weddings (See Audi on the next page). This collaborative revolution impacts on brands and brand management; it changes the way that companies do business. Don Tapscott and Anthony Williams write in the best-selling book *Wikinomics: How Mass Collaboration Changes Everything* that the traditional 'plan and push' mentality is being replaced by an 'engage and co-create' economy.[15] The marketing memo below discusses how to influence the brand experience in the digital environment.

This new world of mass collaboration is based on openness and global sharing. Companies such as P&G, Dell and Apple, which foster sharing and openness with customers, have found that this collaboration also drives innovation – an alignment of open innovation and social networking that can benefit both the customer and the company. **Open innovation** suggests that companies can and should use external ideas as well as internal ideas, and internal and external paths to market. The boundaries between a company and its environment have become more permeable; innovations can easily transfer inward and outward. The central idea behind open innovation is that, in a world of widely distributed knowledge, companies cannot afford to rely entirely on their own research and that often customers are great sources of information and research.[17]

Marketing memo

Understanding the digital experience

Brand-builders need to care about consumers' technological and online experiences because all of them – good, bad or indifferent – influence consumer perceptions of a company's brand. Technology-based initiatives can build on the following brand promises:[16]

- **The promise of convenience:** making a purchase experience more convenient than the real world. Tesco online shopping and home delivery offers convenience and support to many customers, some of whom cannot go to the shops, whether through illness or old age, and for others who just like the convenience of home shopping.

- **The promise of achievement:** to assist consumers in achieving their goals. Online booking and seat selection on airlines allows the brand to co-create experiences with the customer which align to their goal of less queuing and more comfort in travel.

- **The promise of fun and adventure:** creating a brand experience for the consumer that brings

excitement and fun. The LEGO site allows customers to design, create and build LEGO online and then order the bricks so that this can be recreated offline.

- **The promise of self-expression and recognition:** provided by personalisation services such as My Yahoo! where consumers can build their own website and express their own views through blogs. Nike's website encourages customers to design their own running shoes, which is fun, enjoyable and engages with the customer. On www.mygoogle.com, consumers can send their homepage to Google, and personalise it with websites of their own interest that provide the latest local news, weather, horoscopes or joke of the day.

- **The promise of belonging:** this is provided by online communities and explains why social networking sites such as Facebook and StudioZ are so popular. Brand communities online can be very powerful and are ignored at the company's peril.

Audi

Audi ran an absolutely phenomenal digital branding campaign which was creative and innovative and encouraged consumer engagement. Knowing that its audience loved to talk about cars, it posted images of its new model – called the A1 – across the web. Audi then collected people's responses from social networks and reposted them on an Audi site which also allowed users to customise their own Audi A1 – and then encouraged them to share that as well. Almost 40,000 people created customised versions of the new model. In total, 5.5 million people visited the site 119 million times, and the company reports that the campaign helped generate the largest number of car pre-orders in its history.[18] This branding campaign gave users a customised impression of the new brand (by letting them customise the car) and it was intelligently distributed through a huge number of social networking sites. This is a shift from the company giving information to the customer to the customer as the information giver and the designer of their own product.

Branding and social networking

Social networking technologies (see Chapter 4) have led to a revolution in user-generated content, global communities and the widespread publishing of consumer opinion. **Social networking** is 'the activities, practices, and behaviours among communities of people who gather online to share information, knowledge and opinions'.[19] The information within social networking is largely *user-generated content* where the customer develops and posts their own information on the web, which became possible through developments in web technology called Web 2.0. The advent of user-generated content marked a shift from companies and media organisations creating online content to customers creating their own content, publishing their own content easily and immediately, with customers trusting other customers and their peers more than company information. People post everything from Flickr photos and YouTube videos to blog comments, Twitter posts, and reviews on sites such as TripAdvisor or Amazon. User-generated content means that the company has little or no control of the content posted. Value creation practices in social networking take place under four categories, summarised in Table 13.1, which reinforce members escalating engagement with the brand community.

Some 25 per cent of search results for the world's 20 largest brands are linked to user-generated content. Brands are managed within these user-managed environments while staying focused on customer needs and their brand promise.[20] According to a recent Nielsen report, users now spend 22 per cent of their time online (or one in every four-and-a-half minutes) on social networking sites like Facebook, YouTube and Wikipedia. Nielsen also reports that 'for the first time ever, social network or blog sites are visited by three quarters of global consumers who go online. Users on Facebook spent an average of 6 hours on the site in the past year. This is far and away the longest amount of time that users spent with an online brand'.[21]

Social media provide rich customer insights faster than ever before. They provide marketers with powerful new ways to explore consumer lives; to study new product and service developments; to build brand awareness; and to trial and sell brands.[22] Using social media to support the brand is a challenge for marketers in knowing what to use and when to use it – particularly as they must be sensitive to this customer-controlled world. It is important to manage from a customer support perspective and to integrate with the brand promise – see the case of Virgin Airways on the next page.

Table 13.1 Value Creation Practices which reinforce members escalating engagement with the brand community

Social networking

Welcoming	Greeting new members, beckoning them into the fold, and assisting in their brand learning and community socialisation.
Empathising	Lending emotional and/or physical support to other members, including support for brand-related trials (e.g. product failure, customising) and/or for non-brand-related life issues (e.g. illness, death, job).
Governing	Articulating the behavioural expectations within the brand community.

Impression management

Evangelising	Sharing the brand 'good news' inspiring others to use, and may involve negative as well as positive comments.
Justifying	Deploying rationales generally for devoting time and effort to the brand and collectively to outsiders and marginal members in the boundary.

Community engagement

Staking	Recognising variance within the brand community membership and marking intragroup distinction and similarity.
Milestoning	Noting seminal events in brand ownership and consumption.
Badging	Translating milestones into symbols and artefacts.
Documenting	Detailing the brand relationship journey in a narrative way, often anchored by and peppered with milestones.

Brand use

Grooming	Cleaning, caring for and maintaining the brand or systematising optimal use patterns.
Customising	Modifying the brand to suit group-level or individual needs. This includes all efforts to change the factory specs of the product to enhance performance.
Commoditising	Distancing/approaching the marketplace in positive or negative ways. May be directed at other members (e.g. you should sell/should not sell that) or may be directed at the firm through explicit link or through presumed monitoring of the site (e.g. you should fix this/ do this/change this).

Source: Adapted from Hope J. Schau, Albert M. Muniz, and Eric J. Arnould, How brand community practices create value, *Journal of Marketing* 73 (September 2009), 30–51.

Virgin Airways

A recent study of Virgin Atlantic Airways showed how using social networking can influence purchasing habits and enhance the customer experience, once social networking has been embedded at key customer touchpoints.[23]

- **Virgin Airways offers and communicates a clear, relevant customer promise.** Customers expect that Virgin Atlantic Airways will provide an honest, caring, informal, fun and innovative service. The most read section of Virgin's Facebook page is the section with travel tips from crew members – communications which come across as honest and caring.
- **It builds trust by delivering on that promise.** For Virgin, trust relates to its service delivery and keeping the customer informed during the delivery process – particularly

when there are any issues. During the volcanic ash disruptions, Virgin used Twitter and Facebook to keep passengers up to date.

- **It drives the market by continually improving the promise.** Social media should supply insights which drive continual improvements. Virgin uses social media communication to improve passenger experience. When social networking discussion showed that customers did not like repeated security questioning during their loyalty scheme renewal process, it introduced a secure opt-in service to eliminate this step in the process. It also facilitated taxi sharing for customers from the same flight after it monitored a thread of discussion on a social networking site on this item.
- **It seeks further advantage by innovating beyond the familiar.** Virgin is known for being innovative and has launched many digital innovations including the first iPhone application and the Flying Club and Facebook Flight Status application – both of which have been successful. Virgin's launching of its iPhone app was accompanied by an innovative viral campaign called 'Love is in the air'.[24]

Linking social networking and the consumer decision journey

Social networking is and can be used throughout the stages of the consumer decision journey from the initial consideration to the postpurchase experience (see Figure 13.3).

- **Initial consideration.** Something has triggered a need for the customer to start thinking about making a purchase. The consumer considers an initial set of brands based on brand perceptions and exposure to recent touchpoints.

  How can social networking be used? According to McKinsey, people are three times more likely to purchase a brand that was in the initial stages of their purchasing

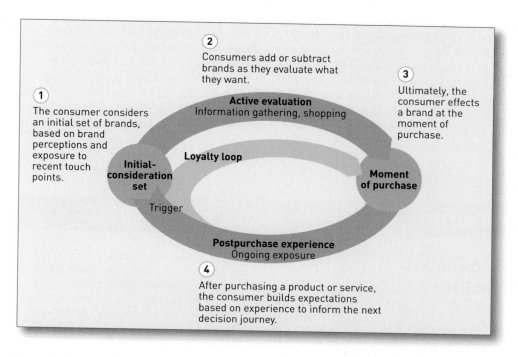

Figure 13.3 Aligning social networking and the consumer decision journey
Source: D. Court, D. Elzinga, S. Mulder and O. Jørgen Vetvik (2009) The consumer decision journey, *McKinsey Quarterly*, 3, 96–107.

journey in comparison with those that were added later. Social networking can play a part in this early stage by positioning a brand in the forefront of consumers' minds at all times. This might happen by stumbling across a brand on a Facebook page, reading a tweet about a good experience someone has had with a brand, or reading a blog post or forum thread online about a branded product or service. Not only does this help spread word-of-mouth, but the brand that a consumer is most likely to recall is one that has a constant place in their mind.

- **Active evaluation.** The consumer is actively seeking more information about the products or services they have in mind. Consumers add or subtract brands as they evaluate what they want and don't want.

  How can social networking be used? Two-thirds of the touchpoints during the active-evaluation phase involve consumer-driven marketing initiatives – something at which social media excels. Reviews and recommendations from 'people like me' play an integral part in the customer decision-making process. A good review by an influential blogger, or a comment by a social networking influencer, who appeals to the consumer audience, can be more valuable than thousands of euros' worth of advertising. By interacting and engaging with influencers, brands can build up their presence and appeal among their target audience.

- **Post-purchase experience.** After purchasing a product or service, the consumer builds expectations based on their previous experience, as well as hands-on experience of it themselves, to inform the rest of their journey.

  How can social networking be used? Post-purchase relations are very important. According to McKinsey, more than 60 per cent of consumers (of facial skin care products) go online to conduct further research after purchase. If a product is promoted effectively online, or has been reviewed or discussed in social media, its most useful functions and features can be discovered at this touchpoint.

- **Loyalty loop.** This is where a consumer moves from making a one-off purchase to developing loyalty with a brand.

  How can social media be used? Social media can be the glue that keeps customers loyal to a brand. A customer who has liked your Facebook page, follows you on Twitter and contributes to your company blog is half-way to becoming brand loyal. A careful balance of interaction with consumers through social media and a great product or service could be the extra step needed to maintain loyalty, turning impulse one-off purchasers into loyal customers. Happy customers can also turn into brand advocates, and focusing on retaining repeat consumers can help attract new or prospective customers.[25] Marketers can overemphasise the 'consider' and 'buy' stages when the 'evaluate' and 'advocate and bond' stages have now become so critical.

Marketing memo

Social networking goals, objectives and metrics

Building strong relationships is vital. As more and more customers trust other customers and/or their peers, there is a need to deepen relationships, learn from the community and drive purchase intention (see Table 13.2). Social networking has been called the 'Relationship Web'[26] where organisations use applications to attract, create, build and deepen relationships with people. In order to remain a strong competitor, a business needs to forge tighter links with their customers where they are – which is on social networking sites. The scale and speed of this social networking means that the business must learn to listen to its customers as falling short can be instantly painful for a company.[27]

> ▶ **Marketing memo** *(continued)*

Table 13.2 Social networking goals, objectives and metrics

Goals	Objectives	Metrics
Deepen relationship with customers	Achieve a critical mass of audience through social media	• No. of advocates (fans, followers, authors) • No. of comments posted
	Encourage ongoing interaction with the brand	• Comments/advocates • Advocate influence profile
Learn from the community	Uncover common themes among interactions	• Rank of topics discussed • Decipher positive versus negative sentiment
Drive purchase intent	Persuade engagement with website content and utility	• Leads to ecommerce partners • Retail locater results activity • Product brochure downloads

Source: C. Murdough (2009) Social media measurement: it's not impossible, *Journal of Interactive Advertising*, 10(1), 1–10.

Digital brand communities

A **brand community** is a group of people who share an interest in a specific brand and create a parallel social universe with its own values, rituals, vocabulary and hierarchy.[28] Ultimately, for a brand community to be successful, it should help build the brand. A **digital brand community**, also called an online or virtual community, is a social network of individuals who interact through specific technologies, potentially crossing geographical and political boundaries in order to pursue a mutual interest in a specific brand. It is a non-geographical, digitally supported community.

While brand communities are found both online and offline, only online/digital/virtual communities allow consumers to 'gather' independently of geographical location and time zones.[29] Nevertheless, brand communities may also meet outside the virtual world to enjoy their brands together in real life – be it cars, motorbikes, toys, books, games based on movies or even food products or cooking. Take the Mini Cooper club where mini enthusiasts meet to enjoy their cars together. Online communities can also meet offline: for example, in the gaming world large multiplayer activities are enjoyed in real life around the world at conferences and seminars. Last year's attendance at Gamescom topped 250,000 fans, exhibitors and journalists, making it the world's largest gaming event.

Three kinds of brand community can exist:

1 exclusively consumer driven with no accepted interference from companies (e.g. fan clubs such as Star Trek);
2 company driven with input from consumers or customers (e.g. Saatchi & Saatchi's lovemarks.com – a site attributed to brands that are high in customer respect and love);
3 customer–company 'joint ventures' (e.g. the LEGO community websites).[30]

Sustaining brand communities depends on people visiting the site, facilitating social interaction among community members and, most significantly, enhancing the loyalty of community members.[31] Studies of offline and online brand communities reveal that much of the value gained by community members stems not from the brand itself, but from the social links formed as a result of using the brand.[32]

Marketing professor Suzanne C. Beckmann from Copenhagen Business School, Denmark and Martin Gjerløff from DDB Needham Denmark suggest that companies seeking to communicate with brand communities may do so by following one or more of five approaches:

1   **Fight**. Many communities are positioning themselves as an opposition to another group: what would life be as a Real Madrid fan without Barcelona? The sense of 'us versus them' influences how community members think, feel and act. The internet music file-sharing service Napster, one of the first virtual brand communities, is an example of a fight strategy. Napster achieved its success by developing an ingenious anti-establishment attitude, not just by offering great technology. Napster later paved the way for decentralised peer-to-peer file-sharing programmes such as Kazaa, Limewire, iMesh, Morpheus and BearShare.[33]

2   **Role models**. The main function for role models is to be both a catalyst and a backbone for a community: somebody to identify with, to be inspired by, and to aspire to. Role models can therefore be used to create unified feelings among community members. A typical example is communities based on information exchange, brought together by a prominent person such as Jamie Oliver, who promoted the idea of healthy food in UK schools with the 'Feed Me Better' campaign.[34]

3   **Exchange**. Exchange ranges from gift giving and knowledge sharing to strategic networks and alliances. Exchange, as a central driver of brand communities, is found in both consumer- and company-driven communities, and quite often results in a 'joint venture' between the two parties. An example of a primarily exchange-based community is the International LEGO Users Group Network 'Lugnet' (www.lugnet.com), where the members support and help each other, have fun and provide advice.

4   **Manifestation**. Manifestation builds on the human need for the traditions, rituals, symbols and icons around which groups gather. From a company perspective, such human needs may be an attractive venue for relationship-marketing activities. A campaign dedicated to increasing consumption of milk provides an example of how manifestations may be used. Ads displayed people in daily situations, but only their head and feet were exposed in order to symbolise the impossibility of doing anything without a body. 'Don't take your body for granted. Drink milk'. The ads were used as a springboard for the young target group to start talking about milk in online forums such as snowboard competitions and music events.

5   **Progression**. Progression means looking forward, constantly striving for development and innovation. Consider the case of Adidas.

Adidas

Adidas Originals has created a unique application for providing first-of-its-kind access to the brand via the iPhone®. With the help of special 3D image recognition software, users get their recommendation for a new pair of sports shoes by taking a snapshot of a pair of shoes that they like. Then the application chooses the closest matching product that is available from the iconic sportswear label and sends it back to the customer. The snapshot is just the entry point into the mobile Adidas Originals world, where users can also check out the nearest Adidas shop, flip through the product catalogue, or become one of the 10.5 million fans on the Adidas Originals Facebook page.

Online brand communities member characteristics

Within online brand communities, members engage in a lot of work. They write new text, design and rework products and services, create original artwork and music, disseminate podcasts, upload video content, sell products and services, write reviews and rate products and services, program and debug software, offer advice, edit photographs and set up specialist blogs, to name but a few tasks.[35]

In general, the following features characterise an online brand community:[36]

- **Consciousness of kind.** A characteristic of a community is consciousness of kind, which refers to the feeling that binds every individual to the other community members and the community brand (e.g. admiration for Nelson Mandela, a passion for beer or red wine). For example, Citroën in Greece – www.citroen.gr – includes a list of venues and dates where Citroën fans can meet, and an online forum to discuss different Citroën models, features and repairs. Two factors determine consciousness of kind: legitimisation (distinguishing between true and false members) and opposition to other brands – BMW versus Mercedes; Apple versus Microsoft;

- **Rituals and traditions.** There is evidence of rituals and traditions that surround the brand. These characteristics reproduce and transmit the community meaning in and out of the community. Members relate to each other with the memory of major events in the history of the brand.

- **A sense of moral responsibility.** The members have an obligation to the brand community. There is a sense of obligation to the community and its members that is often, but not always, shared by members of the group (e.g. in regard to product repairs or personal services). PlayStation gamers may give online community tips about different games. Other communities may share bad experiences suffered by individuals who have chosen different brands.

Figure 13.4 describes a typology of the different ways in which consumers behave as participatory, creative collectives in online communities and provides examples of each.

- *Crowds* are large, organised groups that gather together for a specific competition or project.
- *Hives* refers to members of a specialised community who have expert knowledge on a certain product or service.
- *Mobs* are innovative and playful communities who have a specialist interest.
- Finally, *swarms* are when large groups of members individually contribute something small to the community.

Building a positive productive brand community requires careful thought and implementation. Branding experts Susan Fournier and Lara Lee have identified seven common myths about brand communities and suggest the reality in each case (see Table 13.3).

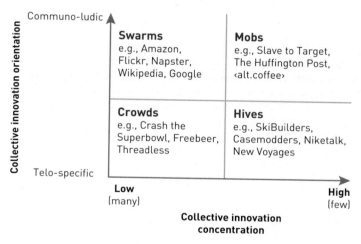

Figure 13.4 A typology of the different ways consumers behave as participatory, creative collectives in online communities

Source: R. V. Kozinets, A. Hemetsberger and H. J. Schau (2008) The wisdom of consumer crowds: collective innovation in the age of networked marketing, *Journal of Macromarketing*, 28(4). Copyright © 2008 Sage Publications, Inc. Reprinted with permission.

Table 13.3 The Myths and Realities of Brand Communities

Myth: Brand community is a marketing strategy.	**Reality:** Brand community is a business strategy. The entire business model must support the community brand.
Myth: Brand communities exist to serve the business.	**Reality:** Brand communities exist to serve the people who comprise them. Brand communities are a means to an end, not the ends themselves.
Myth: Build the brand, and the community will follow.	**Reality:** Cultivate the community and the brand will grow; engineer the community and the brand will be strong.
Myth: Brand communities should be love fests for faithful brand advocates.	**Reality:** Communities are inherently political and this reality must be confronted with honesty and authenticity head-on; smart companies embrace the conflicts that make communities thrive.
Myth: Focus on opinion leaders to build a strong community.	**Reality:** Strong communities take care of all of their members; everyone in the community plays an important role.
Myth: Online social networks are the best way to build community.	**Reality:** Social networks are one community tool, but the tool is not the strategy.
Myth: Successful brand communities are tightly managed and controlled.	**Reality:** Control is an illusion; brand community success requires opening up and letting go, of and by the people; communities defy managerial control.

Sources: Susan Fournier and Lara Lee (2008) *The Seven Deadly Sins of Brand Community*, Marketing Science Institute Special Report 08-208; Susan Fournier and Lara Lee (2009) Getting brand communities right, *Harvard Business Review*, April 105–11.

Digital branding, virtual worlds and gaming

The internet and the technology environment of computer games and interactive technologies provide global brands with an interactive medium through which they can deliver on their promises, quickly, reliably and rewardingly.[37] Interactive global game worlds are set to be the new way to reach future generations of consumers. Sony's online game EverQuest has millions of players, as does the game World of Warcraft with over 6 million paying subscribers. The most successful tabletop war game is Warhammer, a British brand that has reached global status.[38] Adidas, Evian, Corona, Diesel and Sony are all brands that have recognised branding opportunities in these distinctively themed online communities. Branding in this territory is in its early, experimental stage; global brands still have to learn more about this new brand playground.[39] Nike successfully incorporated its brand into the game *There*, selling its virtual sports shoes which allow avatars wearing them to outrun others.[40] Corona beer is now for sale at a Second Life bar – the bar also displays a neon Budweiser sign on the wall.[41] Brand placement within these virtual worlds must take care not to burst the 'fantasy' bubble that virtual games offer users. The avatar 'represents a distinctly different "shadow" consumer, one able to influence its creator's purchase of real-world products and services and conceivably make its own real-world purchases in the virtual world'. Furthermore, many users of virtual worlds import their own examples of real-world company logos as props or decorations. Coke machines are common in virtual worlds.

Red Bull, the Austrian energy drinks company, uses online gaming and virtual worlds that successfully gave its product virtual 'wings'. Since its launch it has kept its cool brand image by having a strong online presence and youth focus. This is a clever strategy, considering that it is an energy drink, and staying up for hours to play online requires that you stay awake. Red Bull teamed up with Sony PlayStation and the brand featured in its games, promoted as a way to 'rock out and relax' between the games' levels.[42] The virtual gaming world offers consumers and global brands opportunities to create new identities. For brands, computer games are a way to increase brand awareness on a global scale; for consumers, brands can enhance the realism of a game environment or their game character.[43] The subscribed players of virtual worlds such as Second Life, EverQuest, There and the Sims Online present marketers with highly invested, engaged, captive audiences for branded experiences.[44] Brands need to be well integrated into the game's landscape in order for it to be perceived as heightening the entertainment as opposed to being perceived as 'three-dimensional spam'.[45]

Managing global brands

More and more brands are now global, from fast food to cars, from fashion to music, from banking to biking. When a brand is marketed around the world, that fact alone can give it an aura of excellence. A **global brand** is one that is available in many nations and, though it may differ from country to country, the localised versions have a common goal and a similar identity[46]. Global brands are brands that customers can find – often under the same name – in multiple countries with generally similar and centrally coordinated marketing strategies.[47] The marketing mix elements may change but the substantial brand values are comparable across countries. Global brands may make slight alterations to their logo or image, depending on the market they are in, but ultimately the brand image and values are *consistent* in all markets.

For a brand to be judged as global it must achieve more than one-third of its sales from outside its home country and have a visible external marketing presence.[48] Alternatively, the brands must be available in all four of the main regions of the world: Europe/the Middle East and Africa (EMEA), North America, Latin America and Asia.

Certain consumer segments buy global brands as badges of membership to a 'global mall', and to reflect a cosmopolitan consumer culture.[49] Global branding is about ensuring that people from different cultures, speaking different languages, recognise and want to purchase the brand.[50] Global brands are a way for people from different countries to connect with each other; the global brand is a key symbol in this global community.[51] As Oxford Professor of Marketing Douglas Holt notes:

> **Many consumers are awed by the political power of companies that have sales greater than the GDP of small nations and that have a powerful impact on people's lives as well as the welfare of communities, nations and the planet itself.**

A **global community** is where people around the world view themselves as potential partners or even family members in a vast increasingly interconnected human family.[52] To build a global brand is to build a brand that has a 'voice'. Brands talk. Global brands talk a lot. They talk to millions of people and are talked about by millions of people.

Companies contemplating a global branding strategy need to be clear in their motives and ambitions. Any company wanting to develop international or global brands should have a clear idea of why and what it is trying to achieve. MasterCard – the global credit card company – has a vision 'to advance commerce globally'. Google's mission is 'to organise the world's information and make it universally accessible and useful'. Both of these companies have global visions.

Global branding is not new. Many companies have a deep-rooted history in global branding strategy. Many of Europe's top brands were developed over 100 years ago and still survive today. For example, Cadbury's was first introduced in 1905 and today sells over 250 million chocolate bars annually. BT is the world's oldest communications company, emanating from the Electric Telegraph Company that was established in 1846. Lyle's Golden Syrup, manufactured by British company Tate & Lyle, is in the *Guinness Book of Records* as the world's oldest brand – founded in 1885. The dairy brand Friesche Vlag is an established brand in the Netherlands, originating in 1913 and still popular today. Another example is the Swedish company H&M.

H&M

H&M is a fashion retailer that prides itself on delivering fashionable clothing at a low price. Originally founded in Sweden in 1947, H&M has almost 2,200 stores in 38 countries and as of 2011 it employed around 87,000 people. Beginning with its first location in Stockholm, H&M has never lost sight of its core brand values of combining affordability and fashion. While its headquarters are still located in Sweden, H&M operates a global organisation, though all fashion designs are made in-house in Stockholm. H&M has a global supply network with manufacturing facilities outsourced to lower-wage areas such as Bangladesh, China and Turkey, in order to reduce costs. H&M has been able to market its brand values successfully to many cultures through its ability to adapt to the differences in each new market.

When deciding to go global, culture becomes important. **Culture** can be defined as the set of basic values, perceptions, wants and behaviours in a society. Each country has its own *traditions, norms of behaviour and taboos.* For example, the Germans and the French eat more packaged, branded spaghetti than do Italians. Italian children like to eat chocolate bars between slices of bread as a snack – Nutella has a uniquely Italian website as Italians are huge fans of both chocolate and the brand. In Belgium, baby clothes for girls are trimmed with blue while baby clothes for boys are trimmed with pink. Marketers must understand how culture affects consumer reactions in each of the markets they enter for their brand to be successful in new markets. Building cultural empathy helps companies to avoid embarrassing mistakes and *optimise* their chances of being successful on a global scale. See the marketing insight box below.

Marketing insight

Global consumer segments and characteristics of global brands

Status and prestige are often associated with global brands, with research showing that global brands have more cachet.[53] Recent research found that global brands tend to have an 'esteem' dividend. This esteem is associated with familiarity that leads to comfort and feelings of prestige when buying or using the brand.[54]

In a European and Asian survey, consumers were grouped into four separate segments:

1 Global citizens: 55 per cent of respondents rely on the global brands' success as a signal of quality and innovation. They also have some concerns for corporate socially responsible behaviour by global companies.

2 Global dreamers: 23 per cent of respondents consisted of consumers who are less discerning and really embrace the global brand images as portrayed by the companies.

3 Anti-globals: 13 per cent of respondents are sceptical about claims of higher quality and dislike brands that preach more global or, in many cases, US values. They do not trust global brands and try to avoid purchasing them.

4 Global agnostics: 8 per cent of respondents evaluate the global product or service by the same criteria as the local brand.

► **Marketing insight** *(continued)*

Consumers worldwide are seen to associate global brands with three main characteristics which account for 64 per cent of global brand preference:

1 Quality signal (44 per cent). Most consumers equate global with quality and use the globalness of the brand rather than the country of origin as evidence of quality. For example, consumers will pay a higher premium for a Renault car or L'Oréal shampoo due to their global brand equity.

2 Global myths (12 per cent). Some consumers use global brands to create an imagined global identity that they share with like-minded people, reflecting an attitude that 'local brands show what we are; global brands show what we want to be'. For example, in Japan over 80 per cent of Japanese women between the ages of 18 and 24 own a piece of Louis Vuitton luggage.

3 Social responsibility (8 per cent). Only a small number of customers expect companies they buy from to address social problems. This group dislikes the low levels of corporate social responsibility. Many consumers still remember Nestlé's baby formula sales in Africa or Shell's use of resources in Nigeria.

Certain consumers use global brands to develop 'an imagined global identity that [is] shared with like-minded people'.[55] There is often conflict between supporting local brands and the desire for the global brand. Despite the advent of a global culture, there is often still a desire for local culture. Studies have shown that many consumers like to support local products and services. By adapting and using brands to appeal to local consumers' appetite for imported or western products or services, a multinational can distinguish its products or services and avoid competing directly with local groups that know the market better.

By aligning brand image to the cultural ideals of a market, companies can capture market share. For example, L'Oréal has developed a formula for global success by conveying its understanding of different cultures through product design, their communication strategy and their targeting. Whether L'Oréal advertisements are evoking French beauty, Italian style or oriental elegance, the brand *attracts* consumers across borders and cultures. More and more global brands try to have a 'think local, act local' strategy to make their brands more locally oriented in foreign markets. Most brands are adapted to some extent to reflect significant differences in consumer behaviour, brand development, competitive forces and the legal or political environment.[56] Even global brands undergo some changes in product features, service design, packaging, channels, pricing or communications in different global markets.[57] Barbie has a doll dressed in Muslim attire; Fanta offers country-specific flavours – Chinese consumers enjoy green apple Fanta, while customers in Portugal and Spain have watermelon Fanta, and Fanta Shokata – an elderflower cordial – is available in Romania.

Taking a brand global is a difficult step to reverse, and marketing or brand managers run the risk of damaging the brand's domestic image if they are unsuccessful in creating a global branding strategy. The risks of taking a brand into international markets are as follows:

- Foreign markets can have different operating *environments*.
- Foreign markets can have different cultural *histories and social institutions*.
- Brands designed for global markets are not very *customer oriented* and thus they may not outclass other products or services to the extent they did in the home market.[58]

Factors leading to increased global branding

Many factors have encouraged the phenomenal growth in global brands, including increased communication, travel, technology and marketing skill. Some more specific factors are as follows:

- In the last 15 years, economic, cultural and media globalisation has become widespread, meaning that consumers have started to become more mentally similar to one another. Meaningful segments are developing around the world with consumers with similar needs and tastes.

- For decades media communications circulated within national boundaries but now this has become global and increasingly expanding due to the internet and other media. Due to media consumption, a teenager in Paris may have more in common with a teenager in London or Sydney than with his own parents. The younger generation is more influenced by worldwide trends and broad cultural movements fuelled by exposure to social media, TV, movies and the internet.
- Similarly, though supply networks have been in operation for centuries, the speed and agility of supply means that the ability to move products and services all over the world at speed is now phenomenal.
- Many products and services face saturation in the markets in which they operate. With oversaturated markets in Europe, marketers need to look aboard for growth. It is for this reason that companies may embark on a global branding strategy in order to enhance their future prospects. Shareholder desire for growth can encourage a global marketing deployment.
- The fall of Communism meant that previously inaccessible markets in Russia, China and eastern Europe suddenly became much more available to marketers in the West. Often companies found consumers globally had been waiting for the chance to buy western products and services. Russia's appetite for western goods means that Moscow now offers most of the shopping facilities of a large, modern western city. There are supermarkets, department stores stocking imported goods and exclusive boutiques with French and Italian designer clothes and shoes for the middle classes and the new rich.
- India, China and growing consumer societies all over the world are hungry for western brands and have the disposable income to buy them. For example and despite the global recession, China's appetite for luxury goods fuelled a record year for sales and profits in 2011 with LVMH (Louis Vuitton) taking the top spot. The French luxury giant Hermès, for instance, recently opened a boutique in Shanghai for its new Chinese brand, Shang Xai. The Chinese already buy more cars and televisions than anyone else, and they are No. 2 when it comes to PC sales.
- There is a global dissemination of popular culture. The increasing popularity of western popular culture fuels demand for brands from the West.
- The competitive environment means that if *competitors* are global then a business may need to be global too.[59]
- The world's population has increased significantly in the last 50 years, mainly due to medical advances and substantial increases in agricultural productivity. The world population is estimated to have reached 7 billion, up from 1.5 billion in 1900.[60] Europe's 733 million people make up 11 per cent of the world's population.

Although the world has grown accustomed to the omnipresence of global brands such as the BBC, Volkswagen, Puma and Adidas, and service brands like banking, hotels and airlines, retailers, particularly those that cater to daily household needs, have been slow to reach out to consumers outside their own country. Exceptions are Tesco, Carrefour and Ahold.

Tesco, Carrefour and Ahold: global retailers

Tesco is a good example of a service company going global. Tesco, along with other European retailers, has decided to pursue a global strategy. Tesco now has 26 per cent of its floor space located outside its traditional UK market – UK 74 per cent, Europe 15 per cent and the rest of the world 11 per cent. Under the name Fresh & Easy, Tesco entered the United States market in 2007, opening a chain of grocery convenience stores on the West Coast (Arizona, California and Nevada). It currently has more than 163 shops there.

Many other big-name European retailers such as France's Carrefour SA and the Netherlands' Royal Ahold NV are also global service brands. Carrefour is one of the largest hypermarket chains in the world with over 1,400 hypermarkets, the second largest retail group in the world in terms of revenue and the third largest in profit after Wal-Mart and Tesco. Ahold, headquartered in Holland, has almost 3,000 shops and 213,000 employees. Albert Heijn, the grandson of the founder of the Dutch supermarket that bears his name, was the driving force behind the expansion of the Netherlands-based grocery chain operator Royal Ahold NV into international markets which include the USA, Sweden and Czech Republic. Albert Heijn, the flagship chain of Royal Ahold NV, was founded in 1887 and today is one of the leading food retailers and most recognised brands in the Netherlands, operating 800 stores with a market share of 33 per cent. These European retailers built their reputations and market share in home or domestic markets and then went global.

Managing iconic global brands

Many of the major global brands are also iconic brands. **Iconic brands** are those brands that customers 'regard with awe'. They are the brands that have conquered the world with ease and enthusiasm. Examples of European brand icons are Zara, Mercedes, Cartier, Rolex, Gucci and Hermès. The marketing managers of these companies understand and have a deep connection with the culture of the customer. The companies are totally focused on preserving and promoting their brands. When companies change these iconic brands, customers can be very upset. British Airways found this out to its cost when it removed the British flag from its planes in an attempt to both modernise the brand and move to a more ethnic image. Customers were very angry and confused, sales fell, and British Airways had to replace the flags on their planes.

Becoming a brand icon is not something a marketing manager can prescribe – it requires *outperforming* everyone else to have the best brand and marketing around. There are five aspects required for a brand to gain iconic status:[61]

1 Target national contradictions – iconic brands speak to mass society by *challenging* anxieties and desires in society. They tap into the sense of desire – like the L'Oréal slogan – 'Because you're worth it'.

2 Create *myths* that lead culture – icons lead popular culture; this sets them apart from conventional branders, who tend to mimic it. *The Simpsons* show is a particularly good example of this unconventional view, forcing audiences to think differently about existing cultural material.

3 Speak with a *rebel's voice*: iconic brands don't try to mimic their customers' tastes and feelings; instead they challenge them. The most successful icons rely on an intimate and credible relationship with a rebel world – such as Nike with the ghetto or Volkswagen with bohemian artists. The 'Wicked Vodka' campaign from Smirnoff also has this irreverent tone.

4 Draw on *political authority* to rebuild the myth: icons must be revitalised when ideology shatters; they can draw on the goodwill of the brand to rejuvenate ideas.

5 Draw on *cultural knowledge*, which is vital for building icons. Understanding what is happening in a culture and responding to that, learning to anticipate new contradictions and to select the one that best aligns with the brand's identity is a challenge. Bulmer's Cider placed an advertisement over the river Liffey in Dublin that read 'North Cider or South Cider?'[62] This slogan only has cultural significance in Dublin, where the city is divided into north and south both culturally and geographically by the river Liffey.

Some brands are seen as global icons as well as strong national brands, while others are strong locally but not globally. Take the Dutch drinks company Heineken. Heineken is both a strong local and a strong global brand. There are, however, other strong Dutch brands that do not have a strong global appeal – such as the Dutch iconic peanut butter brand Calve. Alternatively, Sony is seen as a global brand but is not an icon of Japanese culture.[63] To achieve iconic global status, brands must stay close to the customer but explore and understand culture now and into the future. With the global recession, brands repositioned into a need for austerity. An example is the Range Rover advertisement which suggested that 'The inherent value of a Range Rover Sport easily handles the ups and downs of sand, mud and the economy'; Ragu Spagetti uses the wording – 'The perfect meal when your family is growing and the economy is shrinking'. 'Consumer marketers are focusing their most recent ad campaigns not just on the bargains they're able to offer, but also on the economic value they can deliver at a time when the country is acutely aware of what it's spending and where,' writes Tessa Wegert on the ClickZ website for digital marketers. 'Ads that take a decidedly cash-conscious spin are cropping up on television, in print, and of course, online.' Hyundai, the Korean car manufacturer, is running an advertisement in which the voiceover intones: 'Buy any new Hyundai and if in the next year you lose your income, we'll let you return it.' Because, the ad continues, 'We're all in this together. And we'll all get through it together.'[64]

Operating a global brand strategy

Increasingly marketers must properly define and implement a global branding strategy. In designing and implementing a marketing programme to create a strong global brand, marketers want to realise the advantages of a global marketing programme while suffering as few of its disadvantages as possible.[65] The ten steps below are the guidelines that a company should follow when taking a brand global.

1 Understand the similarities and differences in the global branding landscape.
2 Don't take shortcuts in brand building.
3 Use all elements of the marketing mix.
4 Embrace integrated marketing communications.
5 Cultivate brand partnerships and establish interfaces.
6 Balance standardisation and customisation.
7 Balance global and local management control.
8 Establish operable guidelines.
9 Implement a global brand equity measurement system.
10 Leverage brand elements.

We will consider each of these in turn.

Understand the similarities and differences in the global branding landscape

The first – and most fundamental – guideline is to recognise that international markets can vary in terms of brand development, consumer behaviour, marketing infrastructure, competitive activity, legal restrictions and so on. Virtually every top global brand and company adjusts its marketing activities programme in some way across some markets, but holds the parameters fixed in other markets. Not understanding and reacting to the desires of the local market can have huge consequences. When Vodafone entered Japan with Vodafone Japan, it offered the same limited product range that worked in other countries. This failed to reflect the desire by the Japanese for many different models with fancy features, and Vodafone therefore failed to capture the expected market share in that market.

The best global brands often retain thematic consistency and alter specific elements of the marketing mix in accordance with consumer behaviour and the competitive situation in each country. Snuggle fabric softener changed its name to Cajoline in France, Coccolino in Italy and Miumosin in Spain – all names meaning softness in each language – to reflect the national language and to maintain the same brand positioning around the world.

Don't take shortcuts in brand buildings

One of the major pitfalls that global marketers can fall into is a mistaken belief that their strong position in a domestic market can easily – and even automatically – translate into a strong position in a foreign market, especially with respect to the brand associations held by consumers. Marketers must create brand awareness and a positive brand image in each country in which the brand is sold. The means may differ from country to country, or the actual sources of brand equity themselves may vary. Nevertheless it is critically important to have sufficient levels of brand awareness and strong, favourable and unique brand associations within each country. There is a danger that the company might take short-cuts and fail to build the brand sufficiently in each country. This often happens through inappropriately exporting marketing programmes from other countries. Building a brand in new markets must be done from the bottom up. Strategically, that means concentrating on building awareness first before the brand image. Tactically or operationally, it means determining how best to create sources of brand equity in different markets. The way a brand is built in one market with distribution, communications and pricing strategies may not be appropriate in another market, even if the same overall brand image is desired. Take the Vauxhall Nova car, which was marketed all across Europe. The term 'nova' means 'don't go' in Spanish.

Use all elements of the marketing mix

All aspects of marketing mix activities must align with the brand promise. Marketers must consider the full range of marketing mix variables to see where adaptations to the product, the services, the pricing, the promotion, the service process, and so on, may be needed. Any aspect of the mix activities could be crucial for the brand promise in different markets. McDonald's has adapted its global marketing and has beer in its product range in Germany, wine in France, mutton pies in Australia and McSpaghetti in the Philippines. Coca Cola had to promote their diet coke as light coke in Japan. They focused on weight maintenance because promoting it as a diet drink would not be popular in a region where the population is not overweight by European standards.

Embrace integrated marketing communications

Top global companies use an extensive integrated marketing communications programme. **Integrated marketing communications** (IMC) is the coordination and integration of all marketing communication tools, avenues, functions and sources within a company into a seamless programme that maximises the impact on consumers and other end users at a minimal cost. Each country has its own unique marketing communication challenges. In India only one-third of the population have television sets. In Europe, although television ownership is nearly universal, eBay shunned TV advertising for its launch into Europe and instead used the grassroots approach which cost less and also produced better customers. Germany is now the second largest eBay market after the USA, accounting for €1.14 billion, or 13 percent, of its total net revenue. So although the brand positioning may be the same in different countries, creative strategies in advertising may have to differ. Red Bull uses the same basic template for marketing in any country it sells in, to reinforce its positioning as an energy drink – using quirky, hand-drawn cartoon commercials extolling the fact that Red Bull 'gives you wiiiiiiiings'. Yet Red Bull adapts this template for local markets, translating the ad into local languages, and selecting local athletes and events to sponsor.

Different countries can be more or less receptive to different creative styles. For example, humour is more common in the UK than in Germany, while France and Italy are more tolerant of sex appeal and nudity in advertising. An ad for Camay – the soap product – which was shown in France and Italy, with the husband talking to the wife while she was in the bath, was considered in bad taste in the Japanese market.

Cultivate brand partnerships and establish interfaces

Most global brands have marketing partners of some form in their international markets, ranging from joint venture partners, licensees or franchisees and distributors to ad agencies and other marketing support personnel. One common reason for establishing brand partnerships is to gain access to distribution. For example, Guinness has used partnerships

	Criteria for evaluation		
Strategy	**Speed**	**Control**	**Investment**
Geographic extension	Slow	High	Medium
Brand acquisition	Fast	Medium	High
Brand alliance	Moderate	Low	Low

Figure 13.5 Trade-offs in market entry strategies
Source: Keller, Kevin, *Strategic Brand Management, 3rd*, © 2008. Printed and Electronically reproduced by permission of Pearson Education, Inc., Upper Saddle River, New Jersey.

very strategically to develop markets or provide the expertise it lacked. Joint venture partners such as Moet Hennessey have provided access to distribution abroad that otherwise would have been hard to achieve within the same time constraints. These partnerships have been crucial for Guinness as it expands operations into developing countries, from where almost half its profits are now derived.

A critical success factor for many global brands has been their manufacturing, distribution and logistical advantages. Often the appropriate marketing infrastructure must be developed from scratch, if necessary, as well as adapted to capitalise on the existing marketing infrastructure in other countries. Many companies have had to adapt operations, invest in foreign partners or both in order to succeed abroad. In many cases, production and distribution were the keys to success of a global marketing programme. Concerned about poor refrigeration in European stores, Häagen-Dasz ended up supplying thousands of free freezers to retailers across Europe. Sometimes companies mistakenly adapt strategies that were critical factors to success, only to discover that they eroded the brand's competitive advantage. Burberry changed its channels of distribution and lost control of production and distribution, resulting in its brand going down market and away from its luxury brand positioning.

There are three alternative ways to enter a new global market:

1 exporting existing brands into the new market (geographic extension);
2 acquiring existing brands already sold in the new market but not owned by the firm (brand acquisition); and
3 creating some form of brand alliance with another firm (joint venture, partnership or licensing agreement) (brand alliance).

Three key criteria – speed, control and investment – are aligned to these alternatives, to judge the different entry strategies – see Figure 13.5. This choice among these different entry strategies depends in part on how the resources and objectives of the firm match up with each strategy's cost and benefits.

Heineken

Heineken is a Dutch beer made by Heineken International since 1873. Heineken has a sequential entry strategy. The company first enters a new market by exporting to build brand awareness and image. If the market response is deemed satisfactory, the company will then license its brands to a local brewery in the hope of expanding volume. If that relationship is successful, Heineken may then take an equity stake or forge a joint venture. In doing so Heineken piggybacks sales of its high-priced Heineken brand with an established local brand. As a result, Heineken now sells in more that 170 countries with a product portfolio of over 80 brands. With more than 110 breweries in over 50 countries and export activities all over the world, Heineken is the most international brewery group in the world.

Balance standardisation and customisation

One implication of similarities and differences across international markets is that marketers need to blend local and global elements in the marketing progrmmes. The challenge, of course, is to get the right balance – to know which elements to customise or adapt and which to standardise. However, global marketers must address a number of issues in their marketing strategy to ensure their brand will be successful worldwide. Examples of these issues include differences in economic environments, political environments and cultures around the world. Global marketing strategies aim to maximise *standardisation, homogenisation* and *integration* of marketing activities across markets throughout the world.[66]

Standardisation means 'one size fits all' and helps keep the costs low by using the same activities and reaching out to as many people as possible with the same marketing. While the theory of standardisation of marketing activities can work on a strategic level, it is often not suitable for the richness of detail needed on operative and tactical levels. Most marketing activities will be more successful when *adapted* to local conditions and circumstances in the marketplace. In this way a pure global marketing strategy is not ideal as it does not take locally related issues into account. Marketers need to understand how their brand is meeting the needs of customers and how successful their marketing efforts are in individual countries.[67] The weakness of standardised global marketing is that it does not allow for differences in:

- consumer needs and wants;
- consumer values, attitudes and behaviour;
- economies, politics and cultures; and
- consumer responses to marketing mix elements.

A key issue to be considered when devising a global branding strategy is how the core values of the brand are to be represented in different markets.[68] Quite often what works in one country won't work in another. Many global brands need simultaneously to project a global image and create localised empathy in targeted consumer segments. Marketers are often required to harmonise centralised global branding strategies and local market conditions.[69] Take the example of the BBC.

The BBC

For decades BBC TV, Radio and, importantly, the BBC World Service have been broadcast around the globe, and the BBC is still a successful major global brand today. The BBC brand is the BBC service and the BBC strategy is the BBC brand. No matter where in the world, the BBC invokes a sense that is very British – or the positive stereotypes of what Britishness symbolises.[70] The brand's primary success lies in consistency. All markets experience Britishness but it has been adapted to their taste. In India the BBC has an Indian *Mastermind* presenter, rather than John Humphrys, and in Argentina the news is presented by a Latin American, in English.

There are aspects of the company and its culture that cannot be transferred from the home country to the new market. Examples of this include symbols, corporate culture, rituals, routines and control systems. Are there any aspects of the brand that would be offensive, not suitable or irrelevant to the target market's culture in the world market? Take Mukk yogurt from Italy and Zit lemonade from Germany. Another classic example is Gerber Baby Food – gerber means 'to throw up' in colloquial French. Nintendo's 'Wii' raised a few eyebrows in England and Ireland. There have been many classic global blunders in marketing – see Table 13.4.

Table 13.4 Classic blunders in global marketing

- Hallmark cards failed in France, where consumers dislike syrupy sentiment and prefer writing their own cards.
- Philips became profitable in Japan only after reducing the size of its coffeemakers to fit smaller kitchens and its shavers to fit smaller hands.
- Coca-Cola withdrew its big two-litre bottle in Spain after discovering that few Spaniards owned refrigerators that could accommodate it.
- General Foods' Tang initially failed in France when positioned as a substitute for orange juice at breakfast. The French drink little orange juice and almost never at breakfast.
- Kellogg's Pop-Tarts initially failed in Britain because fewer homes have toasters than in the United States, and the product was too sweet for British tastes.
- The US campaign for Procter & Gamble's Crest toothpaste initially failed in Mexico. Mexicans did not care as much about the decay-prevention benefit; nor did scientifically oriented advertising appeal.
- General Foods squandered millions trying to introduce packaged cake mixes to Japan, where only 3 per cent of homes at the time were equipped with ovens.
- S.C. Johnson's wax floor polish initially failed in Japan. It made floors too slippery for a culture where people do not wear shoes at home.

Brand managers need to decide whether the same kind of brand discrimination will be transferred from the home country to the new market or if a different approach should be taken. Brands often need to have some novelty feature to set them apart from other brands, particularly if consumers in the market demonstrate loyalty to local brands.

Balance global and local management control

Building brands in a global context must be a carefully designed and implemented process. A key decision in developing a global marketing programme is choosing the most appropriate organisation structure for managing the global brands. In general, there are three main approaches to organisation for a global marketing effort:

1 centralised at home office or headquarters;
2 decentralisation of decision making to local foreign markets; and
3 some combination of centralisation and decentralisation.

Firms tend to adopt a combination of centralisation and decentralisation to better balance local adaption and global standardisation.

A **glocal strategy** standardises certain core elements and localises other elements. It is a compromise between global and local (domestic) marketing strategies.[71] **Glocal marketing** reflects both the ideal of a pure global marketing strategy and the recognition that locally related issues need to be considered. In other words, this concept prescribes that in order to be successful globally, marketing managers must act locally in the different markets they choose to enter. In a glocal strategy, the corporate level gives strategic direction while local units focus on the local consumer differences. Glocal marketing allows for local and global marketing activities to be optimised simultaneously. Continuing the Tesco example from earlier in the chapter, this UK retailer goes global by adapting its product range to local food requirements.

Global companies understand that they often need to customise their products or services to a certain extent.

The advantages of glocal marketing are as follows:

- Consumers feel that the brand is relevant to them and is tailored to their needs and wants.

Tesco: European expansion

Tesco has expanded into central Europe and Asia, where it now has more than 139 stores. Tesco operates a glocal strategy. Shopping in the delicatessen aisle of Tesco's hypermarket in Warsaw is a strikingly Polish experience. Eight barrels of pickles stand at the end of one row, with all types of salami and sausages on display. It is not the sort of food you would find in any of the UK shops, where Tesco is seen as a quintessential British store. Tesco in Warsaw is catering to local tastes. 'Deli foods are very important to us,' says an elderly Polish shopper appreciatively.

Source: Tesco Stores Ltd

- There is harmony and balance between the different levels of marketing activity: strategic, tactical and operative.
- Brands gain greater market share.

Glocal marketing managers have the task of balancing demands from headquarters with those of local branches and taking full advantage of local expertise, knowledge and information.[72] There are four levels of adaptation:

1 The branding strategy can be tailored to suit a *region*. For example, in Asia, Nivea adapted its product to cater for the demand for pale skin.
2 The branding strategy can be tailored to suit a *country*. For example, in Russia, L'Oréal targets mothers and daughters with oil-based products focusing on red hair colouring – the most popular hair colour in Russia. Oil-based products would not be popular in other parts of Europe, where they would be considered greasy. Mr Clean, the household cleaner, becomes M. Propre in the French market.
3 The branding strategy can be tailored to suit a *city*.
4 The branding strategy can be tailored to suit a *retailer*. For example, the Stella McCartney fashion label adjusted her luxury fashion brand to suit the pockets of H&M's customers.

Establish operable guidelines

Brand definitions and guidelines must be established, communicated and properly enforced so that marketers in different regions have a good understanding of what they are and are not expected to do. The goal is for everyone within the organisation to understand the brand's meaning and be able to translate it to satisfy local consumer preferences. Brand definition and communication often revolve around two related issues. First, a document such as a **brand charter** should detail what the brand is and what it is not. Secondly, the product or service line should reflect only those products or services consistent with the brand definition. To assist in co-ordination, a sophisticated IT system is often put in place to support the brand. The goal of this integrated information system is to facilitate the local manager's ability to tap into what constitutes 'relevance' in any particular country and then communicate those ideals to headquarters. It also allows headquarters to control many aspects of the brand and to ensure that the brand image is consistent.

Implement a global brand equity measurement system

A **global brand equity measurement system** is a set of research procedures designed to provide timely, accurate and actionable information for marketers on brands, so that they can make the best possible tactical decisions in the short run and strategic decisions in the long run in all relevant markets. As part of this system, a global brand equity management system defines the brand equity charter in a global context, outlining how to interpret the brand positioning and resulting marketing programme in different markets. With the global brand strategy template in place, brand tracking can assess progress especially in terms of creating the desired positioning, eliciting the proper response and developing brand resonance.

Leverage brand elements

Proper design and implementation of brand elements (the brand name and all related trademarked brand identifiers) can often be critical to the successful building of global brand equity. In general, non-verbal brand elements such as logos, symbols and characters are more likely to directly transfer effectively – at least as long as the meaning is clear – than the verbal brand elements, which may need to be translated into another language. Germany's largest pharmaceutical manufacturer advertised a headache pill on billboards throughout the Middle East showing three photos: on the left, a picture of a grim-looking man with a bad headache; in the middle, a photo of the man taking a pill; on the right, a photo of the man smiling, looking relieved and happy. The campaign failed miserably because Arabic is read from right to left, not left to right. So the message was reversed. Feeling good? Take our pills and get a really bad headache.

If the meaning of a brand element is visually clear, it can be an invaluable source of brand equity worldwide. Take the MasterCard symbols or the M&M characters – they need no translation. The images can carry worldwide, like the Mercedes star which has connotations of status and prestige everywhere.

The Marketing memo lists these ten commandments of global branding to help guide effective global brand management.

Marketing memo

The ten commandments of global branding

A global branding programme can lower marketing costs, realise greater economies of scale in production and other variables, and provide a long-term source of growth. If not designed and implemented properly, however, it may ignore important differences in consumer behaviour and/or the competitive environment in individual countries. The following ten suggestions can help a company retain the advantages of global branding while minimising potential disadvantages:

1 Understand the similarities and differences in the global branding landscape. International

▶ Marketing memo *(continued)*

markets can vary in terms of brand development, consumer behaviour, consumer culture, competitive activity, legal restrictions and so on.

2 **Don't take shortcuts in brand building.** Build a brand in new markets from the 'bottom up', both strategically (building awareness before brand image) and tactically (creating sources of brand equity in new markets).

3 **Use all elements of the marketing mix.** Marketers must consider the full range of marketing mix variables to see where adaptations to the product, the services, the pricing, the promotion, the distribution, process, etc. may be needed.

4 **Embrace integrated marketing communications.** This means coordinating and integrating all marketing communication tools, avenues, functions and sources into a seamless programme that maximises the impact on consumers and other end users at a minimal cost.

5 **Cultivate brand partnerships and establish interfaces.** Most global brands have marketing partners in their international markets that help companies achieve advantages in distribution, profitability and added value.

6 **Balance standardisation and customisation.** Some elements of a marketing programme can be standardised (packaging, brand name); others typically require greater customisation (distribution channels). A company must often use many forms of communication in overseas markets, not just advertising.

7 **Balance global and local management control.** Companies must balance global and local control within the organisation and distribute decision making between global and local managers.

8 **Establish global brand operable guidelines.** Brand definition and guidelines must be established, communicated and properly enforced so everyone who is connected with the brand everywhere knows what they are expected to do and not to do. The goal is to set rules for how the brand should be positioned and marketed.

9 **Implement a global brand equity measurement system.** A global brand equity system is a set of research procedures designed to provide timely, accurate and actionable information for marketers so they can make the best possible short-run tactical decisions and long-run strategic decisions.

10 **Leverage brand elements.** Proper design and implementation of brand elements (brand name and trademarked brand identifiers) can be an invaluable source of brand equity worldwide.

Source: Adapted from K. Keller, (2008) *Strategic Brand Management*, New York: Pearson, K. L. Keller and S. Sood (2001) The ten commandments of global branding, *Asian Journal of Marketing*, 8(2), 97–108.

Branding in developing economies

As more and more European companies enter the markets of the developing world – lured by their large populations, growing economies and the possibility of high returns – managing brands effectively in these developing economies requires an understanding of consumer behaviour, marketing infrastructure and competitive frames of reference in often profoundly different environments. The developing world economies are becoming more and more important, most notably the so-called BRIC economies, the rapidly growing economies of Brazil, Russia, India and China.[73] These four countries, combined, currently account for more than a quarter of the world's land area and more than 40 per cent of the world's population. It has been suggested that by 2050 their combined economies could eclipse the combined economies of the current richest countries of the world.

Table 13.5 explores the major countries of China and India. The sheer size of these markets makes them hard to ignore from a marketing perspective.

Table 13.5 The markets of the future: China versus India 2030 – a global forecast

	China	India
Size of economy in global terms	2nd	4th
Global position in purchasing power parity	2nd	3rd
Global ranking among fastest-growing economies	20th	12th
Per capita income (US$)	10,700	8,900
World per capita income ranking	80th	88th
Number of workers (millions)	175	600
Population growth rate	0.82%	1.01%
Total population in global terms	19%	21.5%
Percentage of global trade	8%	5.5%
Global trade (US$bn, 2008)	9,824	4,500
Total rail track (km)	200,000	130,000
Total highway length (km in millions)	1.8	0.9
Total number of English speakers (millions)	10	250

Source: V. Dholakia (2011) India and China – comparison of two Asian giants, Trak.in, 6 April.

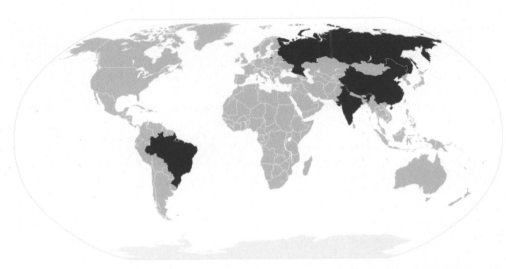

The term BRIC was first prominently used by Jim O'Neill, head of global economic research at Goldman Sachs in his 2003 thesis, Dreaming with BRICs.
Source: J. O'Neill (2003) Dreaming with BRICs: the path to 2050, Goldman Sachs Global Economics Paper No. 99, October (www2.goldmansachs.com/ideas/brics/book/99-dreaming.pdf).

Developing countries are a highly diverse group, often with very different views and concerns. About two-thirds of the World Trade Organization's 150 members are developing countries. A **developing country** is a country that has a relatively low standard of living, an undeveloped industrial base and a moderate to low Human Development Index (HDI) score and per capita income, but is in a phase of economic development. Another way of looking at developing countries is that 14 per cent of the world live in countries with per capita gross national product of more than €15,000, while 86 per cent of the world live in areas with less than that – the developing world.[74] According to a recent article, the 18 largest developing nations are home to some 680 million families earning €4,000 a year or less.[75]

Vital branding tools such as market research, technology links, supply networks and media development are still in their infancy in the developing world. Although the markets of developing countries have grown rapidly in recent years, companies still struggle to get reliable information about consumers, particularly about those consumers with low incomes. It can be difficult to find the deep databases on consumption patterns that allow the segmentation of consumers in more developed markets. Marketers also need to change their view of consumers based on disposable income and reinvent consumer value propositions when looking to the developing world.

- In Brazil, fast-moving consumer goods giant Unilever has developed Ala, a brand of detergent created specifically to meet the needs of low-income consumers who want an affordable yet effective product for laundry that is often washed by hand in river water.
- In India, Unilever successfully markets Sunsil and Lux shampoo sachets sold in units of 2–4 cents; Clinic All Clear anti-dandruff shampoo sachets at 2.5 rupees each; and 16-cent Rexona deodorant sticks. In Tanzania, Key soap (originally owned by Port Sunlight in the UK) is sold in small units for a few cents.
- Whirlpool has a line of inexpensive yet stylish washing machines in Brazil, India and China. In Brazil, customers want to see the machine operate, so Whirlpool made a transparent acrylic lid. In China, where washing machines are considered status symbols and are often placed in living rooms due to lack of space, extra attention was paid to sleek looks. In India the delicate wash cycle is called the 'sari' cycle.

The acceptance of local and global brands and the country of origin of a brand can be very important in developing countries. Brands coming from the West are generally held in high esteem, especially in developing countries where status is important culturally.[76] Research into brand preferences across the world found large differences (see Table 13.6).

As with the decision to enter any new market, marketing managers looking to enter developing economy markets have three strategy choices:[77]

1 Adapt the strategy. The company can adapt its business model to countries while keeping their core value propositions constant. They must start by identifying the value propositions that they will not modify whatever the context. If the company changes its brand too radically, it could lose its advantage of global scale and global branding.

2 Change the contexts. Some multinationals are powerful enough to change the context in which they operate.

3 Stay away. In some cases it is just impractical or uneconomical for a brand to enter the emerging market(s). Sometimes it is just that the time is not right.

Table 13.6 Brand perceptions by global region

- *Europe/USA*: markets are mature and have strong local and global brands. The profusion of brands clutters consumer choice.
- *Brazil*: consumers accept both local and global brands.
- *Russia*: consumers prefer global brands in cars and high tech. Local brands thrive in the food and beverage sectors.
- *India*: consumers buy both local and global brands.
- *China*: consumers prefer to buy products from US, European and Japanese companies.

Source: Reprinted by permission of *Harvard Business Review*. From Strategies that fit emerging markets by Khanna, T., Palepu, K. G. and Sinha, J., 83(6) 2005. Copyright © 2005 by the Harvard Business School Publishing Corporation; all rights reserved.

Take the case of Danone and the challenges it had entering a developing market.

Danone

China has a long history and a complex culture which is still unfamiliar to many in the West. Danone is a good example of a company that succeeded in entering the Chinese market after an initial failure. The Danone Group (DG) is a global French company founded in 1919. Danone is the brand name in most of Europe but it is called Doanonino in Latin America and Dannon and Danimals in the United States.[78] In 1987 when DG entered the Chinese market with its Yogurt brand, it applied a standardised global strategy of offering an almost identical product to the one in its home market. This caused problems as very few Chinese had a fridge and they eat using chop sticks (very difficult to eat yogurt that way!). Also, reflecting their non-dairy diet, they tend to be lactose intolerant. Having reviewed these issues, a new marketing programme was introduced. Danone began by creating multiple joint ventures with local firms, buying local dairy facilities and entering the market by paying attention to China's idiosyncratic distribution networks. It also offered free fridges, attached spoons to the yogurt pots and developed products with reduced lactose to suit the Chinese biological condition. Following these changes, which showed a better understanding of the consumer and the market, the Danone Group is now in second place in the Chinese dairy market.

Celebrity branding

Celebrities with worldwide popularity and recognition can help overcome cultural barriers in global marketing communications. The universal appeal of celebrities is key to their successful use as brand ambassadors. Manchester United – the UK premier league football club – has completed several pre-season tours to exploit the lucrative markets of the United States and the Far East. Through the marketing of its world-famous players, the Manchester United brand has become a hugely successful global brand. Many football players endorse other brands, from sunglasses to cars to hair gel.

The marketing insight box looks at how the popular English chef Jamie Oliver has become a brand in his own right.

Marketing insight

Brand cooking with Jamie Oliver

In 1997 Jamie Oliver got his start as a chef at London's River Café, when he was prominently featured in a TV documentary about the restaurant. His engaging personality led five different TV production companies to contact him the next day. His resulting television show on cooking, *The Naked Chef*, became a worldwide hit and a celebrity chef was born. Oliver has since leveraged his cooking fame and reputation to launch a number of successful new products and services:

- 7 books published internationally in 26 languages, with over 14 million sold worldwide;
- 11 different television series, with over 123 episodes shown in over 60 countries;

- 11 DVDs distributed in 25 countries;
- two UK-based newspaper columns syndicated in five countries;
- the Jamie Oliver Professional Series of pots and pans, bakeware and kitchen accessories, licensed by Tefal and sold in department stores in 15 countries;
- porcelain tableware and serveware licensed by Royal Worcester;
- new products such as the Flavour Shaker, traditional Italian pasta sauces, antipasti, olive oils and vinegars; and
- a website, www.jamieoliver.com, that logs 250,000 unique visitors per month.

> ▶ **Marketing insight** *(continued)*

Oliver also has a line of non-stick pans and cookware for Tefal and has appeared in Australian television commercials for Yalumba wines, using Del Boy's catchphrase of 'Lovely Jubbly'.

A celebrity endorser for UK supermarket giant Sainsbury's since 2000, Jamie Oliver is also credited with helping the chain's 'Recipe for Success' campaign deliver a staggering £1.12 billion of incremental revenue. The company says that the campaign has been 65 per cent more effective than any of its other campaigns.

Jamie's School Dinners was a four-part documentary series. Oliver took responsibility for running the kitchen meals in Kidbrooke School, Greenwich, England for a year. Disgusted by the unhealthy food being served to schoolchildren and the lack of healthy alternatives on offer, Oliver began a campaign to improve the standard of Britain's school meals. Public awareness was raised and subsequent to Oliver's efforts, the British government pledged to spend £280 million on school dinners (spread over three years).

Jamie Oliver clearly has a strong brand. Like any strong brand, his has a well-defined brand image and appealing brand promise.

Celebrity branding is not new.[79] What is new about celebrity branding is that it has become so commonplace in society. The popularity and voyeuristic nature of celebrity magazines means that images of celebrities are dissected to investigate which brands they wear and use, which can endow the brand with credibility and authenticity. This leads to a growing role for celebrities in global branding decisions. Nowadays, approximately 25 per cent of TV advertisements feature celebrities.[80] In a memorable incident during the World Cup, one commercial break featured top celebrity and soccer player David Beckham in four separate advertisements.[81] The *longevity* of celebrity endorsements is not surprising given that their correct use has many advantages for the brand.

How to use celebrities successfully

The celebrity should have high recognition. In other words, the endorser must have a *clear and popular image*.[82] The celebrity's perceived *credibility* must be high in consumers' minds. Consumers must trust a celebrity's motives for endorsing a product or service in order for the advertisement to be believed. The celebrity's image and that of the brand he or she endorses should be appropriate to each other: that is, *they must match up*.

The advantages of celebrity endorsements

Celebrity endorsements have several benefits:

- They enhance both the company image and brand attitudes.
- Celebrities help breathe new life into a company's advertising for a particular brand. Furthermore successful personalities add character to a brand. The British Post Office used boy band Westlife to position the Post Office as more appealing to a 'prime-time' audience. The point of using Westlife was to 'uncover the essence of the Post Office' and show that it is 'on the people's side'.
- Above all, celebrity endorsements can lead to increased profits and sales. Table 13.7 highlights the many successful celebrity-endorsed campaigns.
- Brands use celebrities to endorse their products by sending them gifts or loans of their products to wear to premieres, press interviews, television interviews or weddings, or just to use on a daily basis.
- They can make advertising campaigns stand out from the clutter and draw increased attention from the audience.[83]

Celebrity endorsement of products and services is a major branding development. European stars who have become global brands are Germany's Claudia Schiffer, Spain's Penelope Cruz and from Wales, Catherine Zeta-Jones.
Source: David Fisher/Rex Features (left); Most Wanted/Rex Features (centre); Carolyn Contino/BEV/Rex Features (right).

Table 13.7 Most successful celebrity campaigns in the United Kingdom

Celebrity	Company	ROI	Incremental value (£)
Prunella Scales and Jane Horrocks	Tesco	2.25:1	2.2 billion
Jamie Oliver	Sainsbury's	27:1	1.12 billion
Stephen Fry and Hugh Laurie	Alliance & Leicester	30:1	656 million
Bob Hoskins	BT	6:1	297 million
Vic Reeves and Bob Mortimer	FirstDirect	18:1	223 million
Ian Wright, Martin Luther King, Kate Moss, Elvis Presley, John McCarthy, Yuri Gagarin	One2One	5.4:1	199 million
Martin Clunes, Caroline Quentin, Jonah Lomu, Caprice, Jonathan Ross	Pizza Hut	3:1	55 million
Pauline Quirke and Linda Robson	Surf	2:1	42 million
George Best, Chris Eubank, Rolf Harris, Prince Naseem	The Dairy Council	2:5	21 million
The Simpsons	Domino's Pizza	5:3	13 million

Source: Institute of Practitioners in Advertising (IPA), IPA Effectiveness Awards databank (www.ipa.co.uk/databank). Reproduced with permission.

Multiple brand celebrity endorsers

Many celebrities are now shared by companies: that is, they are promoting more than one brand. Research shows that the endorsement of four or more products and services negatively influences the credibility of the celebrity endorser. This weakens the message of the advertisement and the projection of the brand's image to the consumer. Victoria's Secret model Gisele Bundchen is the highest-paid model in the world, with 20 fashion contracts including Ebel watches, Vogue Eyewear and Dolce & Gabbana.

Celebrity dangers

In a society becoming increasingly obsessed with celebrity culture, the lives of celebrities have been placed under a microscope. Europe has a profusion of magazines devoted to chronicling even the smallest activities of celebrities, from ¡Hola! in Spain to OK! and Heat in the United Kingdom. Under such constant examination it is easy for the image of the celebrity to be negatively portrayed or reported. If the celebrity's image is negatively portrayed then so is the brand associated with it. Brand managers must be reactive and wary of this. Most celebrity endorsement contracts now contain a 'morality clause' that allows the company to drop the celebrity if warranted by inappropriate behaviour. Supermodel Kate Moss's public dismissal from campaigns with H&M, Chanel and Burberry after being photographed allegedly using cocaine is a reflection of the risks of linking brands and celebrities. Reviled for having money but no taste, the wives and girlfriends (WAGs) of the England football team can kill a brand with a single approving nod. Being 'Wagged' can *damage* the brand's credibility. According to one source,[84] the images of Chloe and Jimmy Choo have been tarnished through the WAGs' public use of them.

Celebrities as brands

Many celebrities have completed the journey from featuring in advertising campaigns to being the 'face' of a brand to becoming brands themselves. In today's fame-obsessed culture, celebrities exist in the mind of the consumer in the same way packaged goods' brands do. Brand managers must be careful that they are not creating future competition for themselves through the immediate benefits of utilising celebrity endorsements. For example, in the perfume industry *celebrity scents* have increased by 2000 per cent. Perfumes have been launched by both of the Beckhams, Jude Law, Katie Price (Jordan) and many others. Over 40 per cent of the £638 million UK women's fragrance market is accounted for by celebrity fragrances[85] – 16 per cent of UK women, 11 per cent of German women and only 4 per cent of French women own a celebrity fragrance. Celebrity brands can become competition for established brands, or established brands can use a celebrity to front their brand – like Keira Knightly for Coco Mademoiselle from Chanel.

Perhaps the most famous celebrity brand is 'Brand Beckham', which is a joint branding effort between David and Victoria Beckham. At 17 years of age, Posh was asked what she would like to be when she grew up and she said, 'I would like to be more famous than Persil Automatic.'[86] This statement shows her desire to become a global brand.

Countries and places as brands

The idea of considering a *country* or *place* from a brand perspective only took hold in the last two decades.[87] There are now many *deliberately managed* country brands. This type of marketing is often called place, country or tourism marketing.

For effective country brand management, there must be agreement on what the country stands for, ensuring *consistency of communication* in delivering the brand message and planning for the long term. Country's branding is infinitely more complex than product or service branding. A country's image impacts on people's decisions in relation to purchasing products or services from that country, investing, living and visiting or tourism.[88] Take the unrest in the Middle East which affected tourist travel to that region, benefiting regions like Spain and Portugal.

The branding of countries is a contemporary branding challenge.
Source: Courtesy of the organisations shown.

The Olympics is not just a huge event but also offers revenue generation opportunities for businesses, particularly sport, leisure and tourism-related businesses. As the Department for Culture, Media and Sport (DCMS) puts it:

The London 2012 Olympic and Paralympic Games will be more than a major sporting occasion. They provide us with a unique opportunity to showcase all that Britain has to offer – both to visitors new to our country and to the large number of us who take at least some of our holidays at home. And it is a unique opportunity to ensure that our accommodation and tourist facilities match the best in the world.

Spain also benefited through winning the football World Cup in South Africa.

Many countries have strong associations, such as Scotland with Scotch Whisky, Germany with cars, Italy with fashion, France with cosmetics and perfumery, Switzerland with banking, the Czech Republic with beer, Germany with sausages, and Russia with vodka. Places too can have strong associations, such as Cambridge for its university, Waterford for crystal, Evian for water and Parma for ham. The entertainment industry and the media play an important role in shaping people's perceptions of places.[89]

Spain winning the world cup – country branding benefits greatly from sporting achievements.
Source: JAVIER SORIANO/AFP/Getty Images

An effective country brand management strategy requires the following:[90]

- carrying out an analysis to determine the country's chief strengths, weaknesses, opportunities and threats;
- selecting some industries, personalities, natural landmarks and historical events that could provide a basis for strong branding and storytelling;
- developing an umbrella concept of the country brand that covers, and is consistent with, all of its separate branding activities;
- allocation of sufficient national funds to carry out the branding strategy;
- through export controls, making sure that every exported product or service is reliable and delivers the promised level of performance.

The Anholt-GfK Roper Nation Brands Index measures the power and quality of each country's 'brand image' by combining the following six dimensions:

1 **Exports**. This determines the public's image of products and services from each country and the extent to which consumers proactively seek or avoid products from each country-of-origin.
2 **Governance**. This measures public opinion regarding the level of national government competency and fairness, and describes individuals' beliefs about each country's government, as well as its perceived commitment to global issues such as democracy, justice, poverty and the environment.
3 **Culture and heritage**. This reveals global perceptions of each nation's heritage and appreciation for its contemporary culture, including film, music, art, sport and literature.
4 **People**. This measures the population's reputation for competence, education, openness and friendliness and other qualities, as well as perceived levels of potential hostility and discrimination.
5 **Tourism**. This captures the level of interest in visiting a country and the interest in visiting its natural and man-made tourist attractions.
6 **Investment and immigration**. This determines the power to attract people to live, work or study in each country and reveals how people perceive a country's economic and social situation.

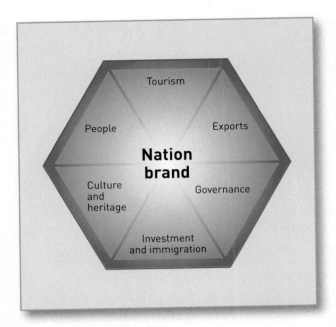

Figure 13.6 Nation Brand Hexagon
Source: The Nation Brand Hexagon, Simon Anholt 2000.

Figure 13.6 portrays the Nation Brand Hexagon, which provides a nation's brand scores at-a-glance. The Nation Brand Hexagon scores each country across the six dimensions and then provides a visual rendering of the total index score. The site provides a device to check perceptions, as shown below.

How highly do people in... United Kingdom
Rank the people in... France
Go

They rate them 21st out of 50.

How highly do people in... Sweden
Rank products from... Germany
Go

They rate them 4th out of 50.

How highly do people in... Germany
Rank a holiday in... Ireland
Go

They rate it 14th out of 50.

Source: Anholt-GFK Roper Nation Brands Index, http://www.simonanholt.com/Research/research-introduction.aspx

This easy-to-understand tool provides a consistent framework for country-to-country comparisons against the key factors impacting a nation's reputation, so you can see just where your nation's brand ranks and why. Together with the Index analysis, the Nation Brand Hexagon provides a thorough assessment of a country's standing, making it one of the most effective tools available for managing a country's brand.[91]

SUMMARY

1 Digital branding is the creation and management of brands through the use of all forms of digital technologies, many of which are controlled by the consumer.

2 The phenomenal reach speed and interactivity of digital technology mean that there are more touchpoints than ever from the internet – websites and social networking, mobile and self-service technologies. Close attention to the online (digital) and offline (human/physical) brand experience is essential, and marketing needs to understand, monitor and manage this 24/7.

3 A compelling digital experience requires that the brand and digital technology are integrated. Social networking puts the power into consumers' hands, where user-generated content – where the consumer develops and posts their own information on the web – is a shift to consumer-managed rather than company-managed brands.

4 Social networking, where the consumer uses technology to post, discuss, share and evaluate brands, must be managed and understood through each stage of the consumer decision journey from initial consideration to moment of purchase and beyond.

5 The consumer decision journey includes consider, evaluate and buy – but also a loyalty loop of bond, advocate and enjoy, changing how the brand needs to be managed.

6 A brand community refers to a group of people who share their interest in a specific brand and create a parallel social universe with its own values, rituals, hierarchy and vocabulary; it is non-geographical. Many of these are now digital brand communities, of three types: exclusively consumer driven, company driven or a mix of both.

7 A global brand is a brand that in most countries shares the same strategic principles, even though some of the marketing mix elements might change. There are ten global steps for marketing managers when taking a brand global.

8 Glocal strategies mean changing some aspects of the brand to reflect the market in which it is operating, with a 'think global but act local' orientation.

9 Many global brands are entering the developing world, which means managing brands through understanding very different consumer behaviours, marketing infrastructures and competitive environments, often in profoundly different geographical environments.

10 Global brands are often aligned with celebrities, as using the worldwide popularity and recognition of a celebrity can help to overcome cultural barriers.

11 Country branding means considering a country as a brand and deliberately managing it as a brand. A country's brand image is a combination of six dimensions – exports, governance, culture and heritage, people, tourism, and investment and immigration.

FURTHER READING

D. Edelman (2010) Branding in the digital era, *Harvard Business Review*, December, 62–9.

This is an excellent study of how consumers have changed fundamentally due to the internet and the digital age. It shows how consumers still want a clear brand promise and offerings that they value. What has changed is that they have so many touchpoints nowadays – many of them digital technologies – myriads of ways to interact with them and for them to engage with the brand. As a result of the internet, social networking, self-service technologies, mobile technology and so on, the traditional method of building brand awareness and waiting for the customers to purchase will not work. The consumer decision journey has changed. Nowadays before and after the buy stage customers consider, evaluate, bond, advocate and enjoy – with the getting and sharing of information online a core feature of the purchasing process. The article suggests how consumers act and how marketers should react and manage this experience, including having a customer experience plan – a deep investigation of the decision journey. The new roles for marketing includes:

- **Orchestrator:** managing all the touchpoints, whether owned by the company or customer-to-customer managed.

- **Publisher:** providing content in real time, which for one company was 160 pieces of content across 30 different touchpoints for one new product release.
- **Market intelligence leader:** managing the customer data and distributing and acting on customer insights throughout the organisation.

APPLICATIONS

Marketing debate

The digital era has changed the way marketers manage their brands. Debate the argument that: Online branding has made it easier to manage global brands *versus* Online branding has made it more challenging to manage global brands.

Marketing discussion

Explore the ten global branding strategies that must be followed to ensure success in global branding.

REFERENCES

[1]European Brand Institute (2010) Top 25 most valuable European single brands, www.rankingthebrands.com/The-Brand-Rankings.aspx?rankingID=22&year=221.

[2]L. Crombie and A. Simmons (2008) Beyond the buzz: designing an effective digital brand experience, www.landor.com/?do=thinking.article&storyid=571.

[3]Ibid.

[4]Ibid.

[5]http://en.wikipedia.org/wiki/The_Hire.

[6]Crombie and Simmons (2008) op. cit.

[7]Ibid.

[8]C. Stutzman, D. Cooperstein and C. Madigan (2011) Managing brand health in the digital age: how to diagnose and treat your brand's resilience and responsiveness, Forrester Research, www.forrester.com/rb/Research/managing_brand_health_in_digital_age/q/id/58691/t/2.

[9]Ibid.

[10]D. Edelman (2010) Branding in the digital era, *Harvard Business Review*, December, 62–9.

[11]Ibid.

[12]Ibid.

[13]Crombie and Simmons (2008) op. cit.

[14]I. Beuker (2009) How digital brands can succeed and thrive in the engaged era: an interview with Igor Beuker, founder of Grupo LaComunidad, *Journal of Digital Asset Management*, 5(6), 375–83.

[15]D. Tapscott and A. Williams (200) *Wikinomics: How Mass Collaboration Changes Everything*, New York: Portfolio.

[16]S. Dayal, H. Landesberg and M. Zeisser (2000) Building digital brands, *McKinsey Quarterly*, 2, 42–51.

[17]H. W. Chesbrough (2003) *Open Innovation: The New Imperative for Creating and Profiting from Technology*. Boston, MA: Harvard Business School Press.

[18]N. Elliott (2010) Winners of the 2010 Forrester Groundswell Awards (Consumer International) Forrester Blog, 19 November, http://blogs.forrester.com/nate_elliott/10-11-19-winners_of_the_2010_forrester_groundswell_awards_consumer_international.

[19]L. Safko and D. Brake (2009) *The Social Media Bible: Tactics, Tools, and Strategies for Business Success*, New York: Wiley.

[20]P. Barwise and S. Meehan (2010) The one thing you must get right when building a brand, *Harvard Business Review*, December, 80–4.

[21]Nielsen Blog (2010) Social networks/blogs now account for one in every four and a half minutes online, http://blog.nielsen.com/nielsenwire/global/social-media-accounts-for-22-percent-of-time-online/.

[22]Barwise and Meehan (2010) op. cit.

[23]www.freshnetworks.com/blog/2011/04/how-to-use-social-media-at-key-customer-touchpoints.

[24]Marketing Alchemist (2011) Virgin launches viral marketing campaign for-iphone app, www.marketingalchemist.co.uk/virgin-launches-viral-marketing-campaign-for-iphone-app/; Barwise and Meehan (2010) op. cit.

[25]www.freshnetworks.com/blog/2011/04/how-to-use-social-media-at-key-customer-touchpoints.

[26]R. Kozinets, S. Wilner, A. Wojnicki and K. de Valck (2010) Networks of narrativity: understanding word-of-mouth marketing in online communities, *Journal of Marketing*, 74(2), 71–89.

[27]Barwise and Meehan (2010) op. cit.

[28]A. Wipperfürth (2005) *Brand Hijack: Marketing Without Marketing*, London: Portfolio; A. Muniz and T. C. O'Guinn (2001) Brand community, *Journal of Consumer Research*, 27 (March), 412–32.

[29]S. C. Beckmann and M. Gjerløff (2007) A framework for communicating with brand communities, 3Rs – reputation, responsibility and relevance, ANZMAC Conference 2007, Dunedin, 1710–16.

[30]Beckmann and Gjerløff (2007) op. cit.

[31]H.-F. Lin (2007) The role of online and offline features in sustaining virtual communities: an empirical study, *Internet Research*, 17(2), 119–38.

[32]See J. Brown, A. J. Broderick and N. Lee (2007) Word of mouth communication within online communities: conceptualizing the online social network, *Journal of Interactive Marketing*, 21(3), 2–20.

[33]See http://en.wikipedia.org/wiki/Napster.

[34]http://community.channel4.com/eve/forums/a/ frm/f/4890059651.

[35]R. V. Kozinets, A. Hemetsberger and H. J. Schau (2008) The wisdom of consumer crowds: collective innovation in the age of networked marketing, *Journal of Macromarketing*, 28(4), 339–54.

[36]C. Flavián and M. Guinalíu (2005) The influence of virtual communities on distribution strategies in the internet, *International Journal of Retail and Distribution Management*, 33(6), 405–25; A. Muniz and T. C. O'Guinn (2001) Brand community, *Journal of Consumer Research*, 27 (March), 412–32.

[37]Ibid.

[38]B. Cova, S. Pace and D. J. Park (2007) Global brand communities across borders: the Warhammer case, *International Marketing Review*, 24(3), 313–29.

[39]P. Hemp (2006) Avatar-based marketing, *Harvard Business Review*, June, 48–57.

[40]Ibid.

[41]Ibid.

[42]M. Lindstrom (2010) *Buyology: Truth and Lies About Why We Buy*, New York: Crown Business; M. Lindstrom (2004) Branding is no longer child's play! *Journal of Consumer Marketing*, 21(3), 175–82; M. Lindstrom (2005) *BrandSense*, New York: Free Press.

[43]M. Nelson (2002) Recall of brand placements in computer/ video games, *Journal of Advertising Research*, 42(2), 80–92.

[44]Ibid.

[45]P. Hemp (2006) Avatar-based marketing, *Harvard Business Review*, June, 48–57.

[46]Interbrand (2006) Lessons learned from global brands, *Best Global Brands*, www.brandchannel.com/papers_review.asp?sp_id=1260.

[47]J. B. Steenkamp, R. Batra and D. Alden (2003) How perceived brand globalness creates brand value, *Journal of International Business Studies*, 34, 53–63.

[48]Ibid.

[49]N. Klein (2000) *No Logo*, London: Flamingo.

[50]M. Neumeier (2006) *The Brand Gap: How to Bridge the Distance Between Business Strategy and Design: A Whiteboard Overview*, Berkeley, CA: New Riders; London: Pearson Education.

[51]Holt, Quelch and Taylor (2004) op. cit.

[52]C. L. Borgman (2003) *From Gutenberg to the Global Information Infrastructure: Access to Information in the Networked World*, Boston, MA: MIT Press.

[53]J. Johansson and I. Ronkainen (2005) The esteem of global brands, *Journal of Brand Management*, 12(5), 339–54.

[54]Ibid.

[55]B. Cova, S. Pace and D. J. Park (2007) Global brand communities across borders: the Warhammer case, *International Marketing Review*, 24(3), 313–29.

[56]For some recent treatments of branding in Asia in particular, see M. Roll (2006) *Asian Brand Strategy: How Asia Builds Strong Brands*, New York: Palgrave Macmillan; P. Temporal (2001) *Branding in Asia: The Creation, Development and Management of Asian Brands for the Global Market*, Singapore: John Wiley & Sons; S. R. Kumar (2007) *Marketing and Branding: The Indian Scenario*, Delhi: Pearson Education.

[57]P. Ghemawat (2003) Globalization: the strategy of differences, Harvard Business School Working Knowledge, 10 November; P. Ghemawat (2003) The forgotten strategy, *Harvard Business Review*, 81 (November), 76–84.

[58]T. C. Melewar and C. Walker (2003) Global corporate brand building: guidelines and case studies, *Journal of Brand Management*, 11(2), 157–70.

[59]D. Holt, J. A. Quelch, and E. L. Taylor (2004) How global brands compete, *Harvard Business Review*, September, 69–75.

[60]http://en.wikipedia.org/wiki/World_population.

[61]Holt, Quelch and Taylor (2004) op. cit.

[62]J. Fanning (2006) *The Importance of Being Branded: An Irish Perspective*, Dublin: Liffey Press.

[63]Steenkamp, Batra and Alden (2003) op. cit.

[64]NPR (2009) Marc Fleishhacker of the ad firm Ogilvy & Mather talks with host Jacki Lyden, www.npr.org/templates/story/story.php?storyId=102211267

[65]K. Keller (2008) *Strategic Marketing Management*, International Edition, New York: Pearson.

[66]G. Svensson (2002) Beyond global marketing and the globalization of marketing activities, *Management Decision*, 40(5/6), 574–84.

[67]G. McGovern, D. Court, J. Quelch and B. Crawford (2004) Bringing customers into the boardroom, *Harvard Business Review*, November, 1–10.

[68]M. Desbordes (2006) *Marketing and Football: An International Perspective*, Boston, MA: Elsevier.

[69]J. Barron and J. Hollingshead (2004) Brand globally, market locally, *Journal of Business Strategy*, 25(1), 9–15.

[70]Melewar and Walker (2003) op. cit.

[71]Svensson (2002) op. cit.

[72]C. Macrae and M. D. Uncles (1997) Rethinking brand management: the role of brand chartering, *Journal of Product and Brand Management*, 6(1), 64–77.

[73]J. O'Neill (2003) Dreaming with BRICS: the path to 2050, Goldman Sachs Global Economics Paper No. 99, October (www2.goldmansachs.com/ideas/brics/book/99-dreaming.pdf).

[74]G. Wyner (2008) A changing climate, *Marketing Management*, January–February, 8–9.

[75]C. K. Prahalad and A. Hammond (2004) Selling to the poor, Foreign Policy, May–June (www.ckprahalad.com/2006/01/29/selling-to-the-poor-by-allen-l-hammond-ck-prahalad/).

[76]R. Batra, V. Ramaswamy, D. L. Alden, J.-Steenkamp and S. Ramachander (2000) Effects of brand local and nonlocal

origin on consumer attitudes in developing countries, *Journal of Consumer Psychology*, 9(2), 83–5.

[77]T. Khanna, K. G. Palepu and J. Sinha (2005) Strategies that fit emerging markets, *Harvard Business Review*, 83(6), 63–81.

[78]T. Melewar, E. Badal and J. Small (2006) Danone branding stategy in China, *Brand Management*, 13(6), 407–17.

[79]D. Cave (2005) How breweth Java with Jesus? *New York Times*, 23 October.

[80]T. Shimp (2000) *Advertising and Promotion: Supplemental Aspects of Integrated Marketing Communications*, Fort Worth, TX: Dryden Press.

[81]S. Moon (2006) Beckham the world brand, *This Is Money* (*Daily Mail*), 8 June (www.thisismoney.co.uk/news/special-report/article.html?in_article_id=409642&in_page_id=108).

[82]M. R. Solomon (1999) *Consumer Behavior*, 4th edn, Englewood Cliffs, NJ: Prentice Hall.

[83]Ibid.

[84]C. Coulson (2006) You've been WAGGED! *Telegraph*, 9 August, http://fashion.telegraph.co.uk/article/TMG3355473/you've-been-WAGGED.html.

[85]Celebrity-endorsed perfumes on the rise, *The Economic Times*, 24 October 2007 (http://economictimes.indiatimes.com/articleshow/2484543.cms).

[86]Extract from V. Beckham (2001) *Learning to Fly*, (www.wpp.com/wpp/marketing/branding/articles_poshspice.htm).

[87]P. Kotler and D. Gertner (2002) Country as brand, product, and beyond: a place marketing and brand management perspective, *Journal of Brand Management*, 9(4/5), 249–61.

[88]Ibid

[89]Ibid

[90]Ibid

[91]The Anholt-GfK Roper Nation Brands Index, www.gfkamerica.com/practice_areas/roper_pam/nbi_index/index.en.html.

Shaping the market offering

Video documentary for Part 5

Go to **www.pearsoned.co.uk/ marketingmanagementeurope** to watch the video documentary that relates to Part 5 and consider the issues raised below.

Essentially there are two key components in a product offer – a *package* which is offered for sale at a stated *price*.

Part 5: Shaping the market offering explores three important themes:

1 **managing products and services;**
2 **creating new products; and**
3 **developing pricing strategies.**

Pricing is a sensitive concern that in the customer's eyes reflects perceived value in the offering and that must deliver a long-term sustainable competitive advantage to the supplier. In highly competitive markets, customers exert considerable influence on the packages that companies bring to market. The modern concept of customer-perceived value dictates that customers expect their purchases to contain both product (tangible) and service (intangible) attributes and benefits. Well-perceived value packages result in pleasant buying experiences in both consumer and business markets.

Developing new products or customer-perceived value packages is an ongoing process in modern markets. When watching the video documentary that accompanies Part 5, consider how HSBC stresses its concern for customers' expectations and how they are of paramount importance. Each company acknowledges in its own way that due attention should be paid to current and anticipated changes in the market and the activities of the competition.

Hear a variety of top marketing executives from a wide range of organisations offer their own interesting and varied perspectives on the key themes of Part 5 including: Phil Popham, Global Managing Director, Land Rover (top); Neil Rami, Managing Director, Marketing Birmingham (centre); and Friday's Farms, a family business producing over 4 billion eggs a year (bottom).

Chapter 14

Designing, developing and managing market offerings

IN THIS CHAPTER, WE WILL ADDRESS THE FOLLOWING QUESTIONS:

1 What marketing strategies are appropriate at each stage of the product life cycle?

2 What are the implications of market evolution for marketing strategies?

3 What are the characteristics of market products and how do marketers classify products?

4 How can companies differentiate products and manage their product mix and product lines?

5 How can companies use packaging, labelling, warranties and guarantees as marketing tools?

High-performance equipment backed by superior sales and service functions is at the heart of Caterpillar's successful product strategy.

Source: Douglas C. Pizac/AP Wide World Photos.

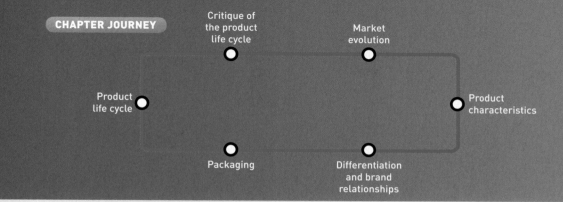

M arketing begins with formulating a customer-perceived value (CPV) offering to meet target customers' needs or wants. The offer will be judged in terms of the relative degree of customer satisfaction that the offering delivers. This chapter examines how successful companies design, develop and manage their CPV portfolio offerings.

Caterpillar has become a leading firm by maximising total customer-perceived value in the construction equipment industry, despite challenges from a number of able competitors such as John Deere, J. I. Case, Komatsu, Volvo and Hitachi. First, Caterpillar produces high-performance equipment known for its reliability and durability – key purchase considerations in the choice of heavy industrial equipment. The firm also makes it easy for customers to find the right product by providing a full line of construction equipment and offering a wide range of financial terms. Caterpillar maintains the largest number of independent construction equipment dealers in the industry. These dealers all carry a complete line of Caterpillar products and are typically better trained and perform more reliably than competitors' dealers. Caterpillar has also built an impressive worldwide parts and service system. As the company offers CPV packages, it is able to command a premium price in the marketplace.[1]

Markets are becoming increasingly dynamic. As a result product life cycles shorten dramatically.

Product life-cycle marketing strategies

The traditional term **product** can lead to confusion as buyers' market conditions normally require companies to offer a package of tangible (traditional product attributes and benefits) and supportive intangible (traditional service attributes and benefits) to meet customer-perceived value requirements and expectations (see Chapters 10 and 11). This is why the text frequently refers to the term **market offering**, which embodies the tangible and intangible components of this newly defined product. The terms 'product' and 'market offering' are interchangeable. A company's positioning and differentiation strategy must change as the product/market offering, market and competitors change over the *product life cycle* (PLC). To say that a product (market offering) has a life cycle is to assert four things:

1 Products (market offerings) have a limited life.
2 Sales pass through distinct stages, each posing different challenges, opportunities and problems to the seller.
3 Profits rise and fall at different stages of the product life cycle.
4 Products require different marketing, financial, manufacturing, purchasing and human resource strategies in each life cycle stage.

Product life cycles

Most product life cycle (PLC) curves are portrayed as bell-shaped (see Figure 14.1). This curve is typically divided into four stages: introduction, growth, maturity and decline.

1 **Introduction**: a period of slow sales growth as the product (market offering) is introduced into the market. Profits are non-existent because of the heavy expenses associated with market introduction.
2 **Growth**: a period of rapid market acceptance and substantial profit improvement.
3 **Maturity**: a slowdown in sales growth because the product (market offering) has achieved acceptance by most potential buyers. Profits stabilise or decline because of increased competition.
4 **Decline**: sales show a downward drift and profits decline.

The PLC concept can be applied to analyse a product category (alcohol), a product form (white alcohol), a product (vodka) or a brand (Smirnoff). Not all products exhibit a bell-shaped PLC. Three common alternative patterns are shown in Figure 14.2.

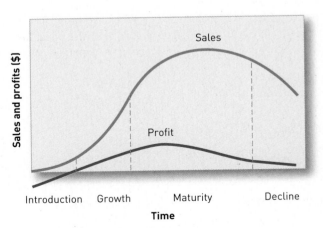

Figure 14.1 Long-range product market expansion strategy (P1 = product 1; M1 = market 1)

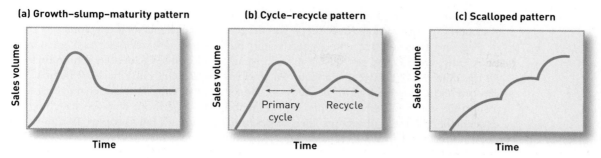

Figure 14.2 Common product life-cycle patterns

Figure 14.2(a) shows a *growth–slump–maturity pattern*, often characteristic of small kitchen appliances, such as handheld mixers and bread-makers. Sales grow rapidly when the item is first introduced and then fall to a residual level that is sustained by late adopters buying for the first time and early adopters replacing it.

The *cycle–recycle pattern* in Figure 14.2(b) often describes the sales of new drugs. The pharmaceutical company aggressively promotes its new drug, and this produces the first cycle. Later, sales start declining and the company responds by triggering another market-ing communication push, which produces a second cycle (usually of smaller magnitude and duration).

Another common pattern is the *scalloped PLC* in Figure 14.2(c). Here sales pass through a succession of life cycles based on the discovery of new product/market offering charac-teristics, uses or users. The sale of nylon, for example, shows a scalloped pattern because of the many new uses – parachutes, hosiery, shirts, carpeting, boat sails, car tyres – that continue to be discovered over time.

Style, fashion and fad life cycles

Three special categories of product life cycles – styles, fashions and fads – can be distin-guished (Figure 14.3). A *style* is a basic and distinctive mode of expression. Styles appear in homes (French, Italian, Scandinavian and Spanish); clothing (formal, casual); and art (realistic, surrealistic, abstract). A style can last for generations and go in and out of vogue. A *fashion* is a currently accepted or popular style in a given field. Fashions pass through four stages: distinctiveness, emulation, mass fashion and decline.[2]

The length of a fashion cycle is hard to predict. One point of view is that fashions end because they represent a purchase compromise, and consumers start looking for the missing attributes and benefits. For example, as cars become smaller, they become less comfortable, and then a growing number of buyers start wanting larger cars. Another explanation is that too many consumers adopt fashion clothes, as catwalk designs reach the fast fashion stores such as Zara causing others to seek the latest fashion releases. Still another is that the length of a particular fashion cycle depends on the extent to which

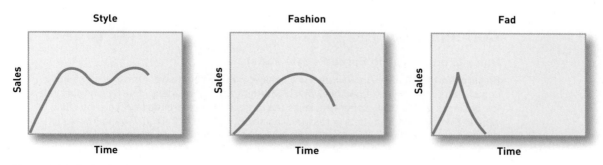

Figure 14.3 Style, fashion and fad life cycles

the fashion meets a genuine need, is consistent with other trends in the society, satisfies societal norms and values, and keeps within technological limits as it develops.

Fads are fashions that come quickly into public view, are adopted with great zeal, peak early, and decline very fast. Every Christmas in the United Kingdom certain toys are all the rage: Buzz Lightyear, Cabbage Patch dolls and Rubik's cube have all been at the top of children's wish lists in recent years. Generally speaking, fads are characterised by a short life cycle and tend to attract only a limited following, those who are searching for excitement or want to distinguish themselves from others. Fads fail to survive because they don't normally satisfy a strong need. The marketing winners are those who recognise fads early and leverage them into products (market offerings) with staying power: for example, successful rock bands such as Abba, the Beatles and the Rolling Stones.

Marketing strategies: the introduction stage and the pioneer advantage

Because it takes time to roll out a new product/market offering, work out the technical problems, fill dealer pipelines and gain consumer acceptance, sales growth tends to be slow in the introduction stage. Profits are negative or low, while promotional marketing communications expenditures are at their highest ratio to sales because of the need to: (1) inform potential consumers; (2) induce customers to trial the market offering; and (3) secure distribution in retail outlets.[3] Firms focus on those buyers who are the most ready to purchase. Prices tend to be high because costs are high.

Companies that plan to introduce a new market offering must decide when to enter the market. To be first can be rewarding, but risky and expensive. To come in later makes sense if the firm can bring superior technology, quality or brand strength. Speeding up innovation time is essential in an age of shortening product life cycles. Being early has been shown to pay. Nokia is a good illustration of a fast-track innovator. In many cases the market pioneer gains the greatest advantage. Companies such as Amazon, Nintendo, Sony and Swatch developed sustained market dominance.

What are the sources of the pioneer's advantage? Early users will recall the pioneer's brand name (as in the case of Hoover, whose brand name became the generic term for vacuum cleaners for several years in the United Kingdom) if the product satisfies them. The pioneer's brand also establishes the attributes the product class should possess. The pioneer's brand normally aims at the middle of the market and so captures more users. Customer inertia also plays a role; and there are producer advantages: economies of scale, technological leadership, patents, ownership of scarce assets, and other barriers to entry. Furthermore, pioneers can benefit from effective marketing communications and enjoy higher rates of consumer repeat purchases.

However, pioneer advantage is not inevitable. Look at the fate of Amstrad (low-cost personal computers), Apple's Newton (personal digital assistant) and Netscape (web browser), which were all market pioneers overtaken by later entrants. First movers also have to watch out for what some have called the 'second mover advantage'.

Coffeeheaven

Quick to plug a gap in Europe's café society

Richard Worthington was in Warsaw for a business deal when he went in search of a good cup of coffee. He could not find one, which gave him a great business idea. Seven years later the business he founded, Coffeeheaven, is the largest modern branded coffee shop chain in central Europe, with 59 outlets across the region, 39 of them in Poland. 'To me it was just a question of time before coffee bars appeared here. When we looked around central Europe, we saw fragmented markets, unfriendly staff, women-unfriendly restaurants and bad coffee. It was an enormous opportunity,' says the British entrepreneur.

For the moment, Coffeeheaven is more or less alone in a region with 140 million consumers. Older, more established coffee operations have skipped central Europe, jumping from Germany to oil-booming Moscow. Worthington's idea was not particularly ground breaking. Anyone walking down a North American or British street in the past decade would have noticed the trend to smart coffee bars that serve food, in a pleasant atmosphere that encourages lounging with a book or a laptop.

Central Europe is still fertile ground for adopting well-established western business models wholesale for increasingly wealthy customers, who are familiar with offerings in western Europe. The trick was to see that central Europe would rapidly become much more like western Europe in its tastes, in its expectations of service and quality, and eventually in its spending patterns.

The model Worthington chose was Britain's Café Nero, which stresses its food as well as its coffee. The first Coffeeheaven opened in 2000, followed in 2001 by an outlet in Galeria Mokotow, a new high-end shopping mall in southern Warsaw. That branch recouped its initial investment in 37 weeks. Since then the chain has grown by setting up in Warsaw's airport and main railway station as well as in cinemas. It is also looking at closer cooperation with Empik, a leading bookseller that is also a shareholder. In 2007, the chain reported sales of £6.4 million and a loss of about £700,000. It made its first profit in 2008, as it expanded in the Czech Republic, Slovakia, Bulgaria, Romania and Latvia. It is listed on the Alternative Investment Market (AIM) in London.

But Coffeeheaven's unchallenged expansion throughout the region is coming to an end. Costa Coffee, the coffee chain owned by Britain's Whitbread, announced in 2008 that it is to move into Romania, Bulgaria and Poland, with the aim of opening 200 shops in the first five years of its planned expansion programme. Other large coffee chains are also taking a second look at central Europe. However, late entrants will face several hurdles. The first is that Coffeeheaven already has choice locations in most of the region's new shopping malls. 'We have a first-mover advantage,' says Worthington. 'The action here is in the malls, and outsiders will have to buy someone out if they want to get in.'

Coffeeheaven has avoided the fate of many other pioneers entering new markets which take advantage of their status to make quick profits with an inferior offering. Even if the competition does make an appearance in a region where people drink only about half as much coffee as in western Europe, the company should be able to sustain fairly robust rivalry. There are also plans to expand into the Ukraine. In December 2009 Whitbread gave its network of Costa Coffee shops in central and eastern Europe a boost by acquiring Coffeeheaven for £36 million. John Derkach, the managing director of Costa, said: 'It is an important step forward in achieving Costa's strategic objectives and international growth ambitions. This transaction will give Costa a strong position in the important and rapidly growing central and eastern European market.' Founded in 2000, the AIM-listed Coffeeheaven has 62 shops in Poland, 14 in the Czech Republic and 14 across Bulgaria, Hungary and Latvia.

Source: J. Cienski (2006) Jan Cienski in Warsaw, *Financial Times,* 20 December; *Independent,* 16 December 2009.

Jaguar

Premium sports car

Jaguar was looking to replace the flagship of its range, the XK8/XKR high-performance sports car. It was imperative that the new model strongly communicated the core brand values of beauty, luxury and sportiness. The specialist agency Innovia was asked to create ideas for new features and attributes that would be worthy of the pedigree and would keep the trade press buzzing. Innovia explored the different associations of luxury and sportiness in the consumer's mind, and then created concepts that exploited the synergies and overcame the contradictions. It identified emerging technologies and created a range of features that could help the new model build a leading market position.

Jaguar's XK8/XKR high-performance sports car
Source: © Mark Scheuern/Alamy.

The new car was launched to widespread acclaim in March 2006 and won the UK's BBC *Top Gear*'s 'Car of the Year' Award in 2007. However, the company continued to lose money and in March 2008 Jaguar was acquired by the Indian conglomerate Tata.

Source: www.innoviatech.com/projects/articles/9/premium-sports-car.

If a company wants to win, it needs to be the first, surely? The first mover advantage theory states that the first company entering a certain market will gain massive market share due to the competitive advantages developed and will also be able to defend its leadership position from new entrants. The reasoning behind it is quite intuitive, it goes a long way with conventional wisdom and, if that was not enough, the principle has also been proposed by academics and managers around the world. Andrew Grove, Intel's ex-CEO, defended that 'the first mover and only the first mover, the company that acts while others dither, has a true opportunity to gain time over its competitors; and time advantage, in this business, is the surest way to gain market share'.[4]

There is a lot of theoretical evidence supporting the model, but does this evidence emerge empirically as well? Not quite. Consider the markets for safety razors, disposable nappies, photographic film, laser printers, games consoles, VCRs, energy drinks, personal computers, internet browsers, operating systems, search engines, online bookstores, online auctions, VoIP (a protocol optimised for the transmission of the voice through the internet) services – and the list goes on. In each and every one of these markets, the leader position is held by a company that was a late entrant to the market.

The question then becomes: why, despite the lack of empirical evidence, do people still embrace the idea that being the first to enter a market is extremely important? There are three main reasons: the industrial age environment, natural monopolies and the bias towards winners.

Industrial age environment

Until the 1980s, during the era of sellers' markets the pace of change in many industries was much slower. Being the first to enter a market characterised by stability and predictable incremental changes could actually yield significant advantages. In the information age, however, discontinuities and market innovations are becoming the norm. As a consequence, success often comes no longer from being the first to market but from rapidly evolving the product to become the dominant design. JVC's VHS recording technology came to the market almost two years after Sony's Betamax. Nonetheless by licensing out the technology to other producers, creating alliances with content creators and adapting the features to address the needs of customers and rental stores, JVC managed to establish the VHS as the standard for video recording, driving Betamax out of the market.

Natural monopolies

Some markets present predominant capital costs and infrastructure constraints, meaning that the first mover can actually build a strong competitive position by merely entering the market before other players. This is the case for oil and gas distribution, water services and electricity. Natural monopolies represent exceptions in most countries. In modern economies, being able to understand customers, manage innovation and adapt quickly to market discontinuities is much more important than being the first to enter a market. The most evident example is the internet. Google was not the first search engine. Amazon was not the first online bookstore. eBay was not the first online auction site. All these companies were focused on understanding their customers, innovating and adapting their strategies to reflect market changes, thus enabling them to build strong leadership positions.

Bias towards winners

Over the long term there is a natural tendency to forget failures and to over-celebrate successes. It is not surprising, therefore, that people wrongly associate long-term market leaders with the first to enter a certain segment. Consider the case of laser printers. In 1971 Xerox developed the first working model. IBM, on the other hand, was the first company to commercialise it in 1976. Hewlett-Packard entered the market almost ten years later, developed laser printers rapidly to suit mass market requirements and managed to become the clear winner. Hewlett-Packard has sold more than 100 million units – no wonder people think it was the first company to commercialise laser printers.

Entering a new market too early can prove to be disappointing. Many companies have found that it pays to learn from the experience of first movers and then enter the market before a dominant branded design emerges. Contrary to what most people think, King Gillette was not the first to market safety razors. They were invented in New York in 1880 by the Kampfe brothers, and a decade before King Gillette opened his company there were already commercial safety razors being sold. Gillette, however, evolved the product rapidly both by improving the design and by creating a business model where the profits would be made with the disposable blades. Neatly crafted business strategy, good understanding of customer needs and marketing enabled Gillette to dominate the safety razor market for a long period, after being a late market entrant.

Schnaars studied 28 industries where the imitators surpassed the innovators.[5] He found several weaknesses among the failing pioneers, including new products that were too crude, were improperly positioned or appeared before there was strong demand; product development costs that exhausted the innovator's resources; a lack of resources to compete against entering larger firms; and managerial incompetence or unhealthy complacency. Successful imitators thrived by offering lower prices, improving the product more continuously or using hard market power to overtake the pioneer. None of the companies that now dominate in the manufacture of personal computers – including Dell, Packard-Bell and Compaq – were first movers.[6]

Golder and Tellis raise further doubts about the pioneer advantage.[7] They distinguish between an *inventor*, first to develop patents in a new product category; a *product pioneer*, first to develop a working model; and a *market pioneer*, first to sell in the new product category. They also include non-surviving pioneers in their sample. They conclude that although pioneers may still have an advantage, a larger number of market pioneers fail than has been reported, and a larger number of early market leaders (though not pioneers) succeed. Examples of later entrants overtaking market pioneers are IBM over Sperry in mainframe computers and Matsushita over Sony in VCRs.

In a more recent study, Tellis and Golder identify the following five factors as underpinning long-term market leadership: vision of a mass market, persistence, relentless innovation, financial commitment and asset leverage.[8] Other research has highlighted the importance of the novelty of product innovation.[9] When a pioneer starts a market with a breakthrough, as was the case with the Dyson Cyclone vacuum cleaner, survival can be very challenging. In contrast, when the market is started by an incremental innovation, as was the case with MP3 players with video capabilities, pioneers' survival rates are much higher.

The pioneer should visualise the various product markets it could initially enter, knowing it cannot enter all of them at once. Suppose market-segmentation analysis reveals the product market segments shown in Figure 14.4. The pioneer should analyse the profit potential of each product market singly and in combination and decide on a market expansion path. Thus the pioneer in Figure 14.4 plans first to enter product market P_1M_1, then move the product into a second market (P_1M_2), then surprise the competition by developing a second product for the second market (P_2M_2), then take the second product back into the first market (P_2M_1), and then launch a third product for the first market (P_3M_1). If this game plan works, the pioneer firm will own a good part of the first two segments and serve them with two or three profitable product/service market offerings.

Marketing strategies: the growth stage

The growth stage is marked by a rapid climb in sales. Early adopters like the market offering, and new consumers start purchasing from the firm. New competitors enter, attracted by the opportunities. They introduce new product features (and market offering value attributes) and expand distribution.

Prices remain where they are or fall slightly, depending on how quickly demand increases. Companies maintain their promotional marketing communcation expenditures at the same or at a slightly increased level to meet competition and to continue to educate the market. Sales rise much faster than expenditures, causing a welcome decline in

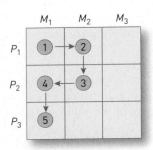

Figure 14.4 Long-range product market expansion strategy (p_i = product *i*; m_j = market *j*)

the promotion–sales ratio. Profits increase during this stage as marketing communications costs are spread over a larger volume and unit manufacturing costs fall faster than price declines, owing to the producer learning or experience curve effect. Firms have to watch for a change from an accelerating to a decelerating rate of growth in order to prepare new strategies. The European internet service provider market has grown rapidly since 2001 and by late 2007 moved into the mature stage.

ISP UK market

Consumers are highly fickle with their choice of internet provider, with nearly one in four people switching companies every year. People are far more likely to change their internet company than their power supplier, bank or mortgage provider, according to research from Group 1 Software, a division of the Pitney Bowes office technology group. Customer churn rates among internet service providers are about 24 per cent each year, far higher than a cross-industry average of about 19 per cent. Power utilities and mortgage lenders have a customer churn rate of less than 14 per cent, while banks see about 20 per cent of customers swap each year. The only sector with a higher churn rate is the mobile phone industry, where about one-third of customers change providers every year. Increasing customer disloyalty in the internet service market comes as competition, especially over price, intensifies. The Carphone Warehouse delivered the latest shakeup to the market when it announced an offer of 'free' high-speed internet access for customers who signed up to its landline telephone service.

Competition in the United Kingdom has increased, in particular after Ofcom, the communications regulator, ruled that the British Telecom Group should open its telecommunications exchanges to competitors, giving them control over the entire telephone line direct to the customer's home. This has made it easier for British Telecom's rivals to offer higher-speed internet connections at a lower cost. As a result the United Kingdom has become one of Europe's largest broadband markets, with more than 10 million connections, and about 70,000 new customers signing up every week. Brian Ahearne, of the Internet Service Providers' Association, said: 'We have a very competitive industry now with a wide variety of packages and contracts tailored to different needs. This is making people shop around.' Ofcom is also keeping a close watch to ensure that customers can easily change their ISP. More than 40 UK internet companies have signed up to a voluntary code that helps make customer migration easier, and Ofcom periodically investigates its effectiveness.

Though good for consumer choice, high churn rates are proving a headache for internet service companies, which have to spend increasing amounts of money to attract and retain customers. A number of them, such as Orange and O_2, have begun running loyalty reward schemes, where customers can win CDs, DVDs and gadgets if they stay with the same provider. Softpoint Multimedia, a firm that runs loyalty schemes for companies in a number of sectors, says internet service providers have become their single biggest client group, driving annual revenue growth of about 68 per cent.[10]

During the growth stage, the firm uses several strategies to sustain rapid market growth:

- It improves product quality and adds new product features and improved styling.
- It adds new models, accessory items and personalising options (i.e. market offerings of different sizes, flavours and so forth that protect the main product/service CPV offerings).
- It enters new market segments.
- It increases its distribution coverage and enters new distribution channels.
- It shifts from product-awareness advertising to product-preference advertising.
- It lowers prices to attract the next layer of price-sensitive buyers.

These market expansion strategies strengthen the firm's competitive position. Consider how Google has fuelled growth.

Google

Beginning in 1996, Stanford University graduate students Larry Page and Sergey Brin built a search engine called 'BackRub' that used links to determine the importance of individual web pages. By 1998 they had formalised their work, creating the company known today as Google.

Since then, Google has grown by leaps and bounds. From offering search in a single language, it now offers dozens of products and services – including various forms of advertising and web applications for all kinds of tasks – in scores of languages. Having rapidly become the market leader, Google has had to face stiff challenges from competitors such as Microsoft's Bing and is continually being accused of abusing its dominant search position.

A firm in the growth stage faces a trade-off between high market share and high current profit. By spending money on product improvement, a strong marketing communications programme and distribution, it can capture a dominant position. It forgoes maximum current profit in the hope of making even greater profits in the next stage.

Marketing strategies: the maturity stage

At some point the rate of sales growth will slow, and the product will enter a stage of relative maturity. This stage normally lasts longer than the previous stages and poses big challenges to marketing management. Most market offerings are in the maturity stage of the life cycle.

The maturity stage divides into three phases: growth, stable and decaying maturity. In the first phase, the sales growth rate starts to decline. There are no new distribution channels to fill. New competitive forces emerge (see the marketing insight box). In the second phase, sales flatten on a *per capita* basis because of market saturation. Most potential consumers have tried the product (market offering), and future sales are governed by population growth and replacement demand. In the third phase, decaying maturity, the absolute level of sales starts to decline, and customers begin switching to other market offerings.

Marketing insight

Competitive category dynamics

One of marketing's most astute observers, Professor David Aaker, notes that because new categories can represent strategically important threats or opportunities, marketers have to be very attentive to the forces that drive their emergence. He cites seven such dynamics that result in new categories:

1 A new product or service dimension expands the boundaries of an existing category. This is exemplified by the introduction of 'new' and claimed healthy yogurt derivatives such as Danone's Actimel yogurt drink.

2 A new product or set of products carves out a fresh niche in an existing category. Red Bull took the energy drinks market by storm and rapidly assumed market leadership in the United Kingdom.

3 A new competitor devises a way to bundle existing categories into a super category. In the late 1990s, Siebel created internet-based customer relationship management software by pulling together a host of applications, including customer loyalty programmes, customer acquisition, call centres, customer service, customer contact and sales force automation. In doing so, Siebel rendered irrelevant, for some customers, the more specialised application programmes of competitors.

4 A new competitor repositions existing products or services to create an original category. In the United Kingdom, Ford positioned its Galaxy minivan in relation to first-class air travel – comfortable enough to be suitable for busy executives. By highlighting attributes far different from those that would appeal to a buyer looking for a family vehicle, the car maker created a new minivan subcategory.

5 Customer needs propel a new product category or subcategory. Dual trends – wellness and the use of herbs and natural supplements – have supported a huge new beverage category, healthy refreshment drinks. It now contains a host of subcategories, including enhanced teas, fruit drinks, soya-based drinks and speciality waters.

> ▶ **Marketing insight** *(continued)*

6 A new technology leads the development of a product category or subcategory. The introduction of a low-cost, manual, battery-powered toothbrush by Oral-B Pulsar extended the product life cycle of the conventional manual toothbrush market. The new technology pulses the brush bristles to produce a deep-cleaning action that removes plaque and food particles from between teeth.

7 A company exploits changing technologies to invent a new category. Nintendo created a whole new market in portable entertainment with its DS Lite and Wii electronic gaming equipment.

Source: From D. A. Aaker (2004) The relevance of brand relevance, *Strategy Business*, 35, Summer, 1–10. Reproduced with permission. See also D. A. Aaker (2004) *Brand Portfolio Strategy: Creating Relevance, Differentiation, Energy, Leverage, Clarity*, New York: Free Press.

The third phase of maturity poses the most challenges. The sales slowdown creates overcapacity in the industry, which leads to intensified competition. Competitors scramble to find niches. They engage in frequent price reductions and sales promotions. They increase advertising and trade and consumer promotion. They increase R & D budgets to develop product (market offering) improvements and line extensions. They make deals to supply private brands and weaker competitors withdraw. The industry eventually consists of well-entrenched competitors whose basic drive is to gain or maintain market share to build a sustainable competitive advantage in the market.

Dominating the industry are a few giant firms – perhaps a quality leader, a service leader and a cost leader – that serve the whole market and make their profits mainly through high volume and lower costs. Surrounding these dominant firms is a multitude of market nichers, including market specialists, product specialists and customising firms. The issue facing a firm in a mature market is whether to struggle to become one of the 'big three' and achieve profits through high volume and low cost, or to pursue a niching strategy and achieve profits through low volume and a high margin. Sometimes, however, the market becomes polarised between low- and high-end segments and the firms in the middle see their market share steadily erode. Here is how Swedish appliance manufacturer, Electrolux, has coped with this situation.

Electrolux AB

In 2002 Electrolux began facing a rapidly polarising appliance market. At one end, low-cost Asian companies such as Haier, LG and Samsung were applying downward price pressure. At the other end, premium competitors such as Bosch, Sub-Zero and Viking were continuing to grow at the expense of the middle-of-the-road brands. Electrolux's new CEO Hans Stråberg, who took over the reins just as the middle was dropping out of the market, decided to escape the middle by rethinking Electrolux's customers' wants and needs. For instance, rather than accept the stratification between low and high, Stråberg segmented the market according to the lifestyle and purchasing patterns of about 20 different types of consumer – '20 product positions', as he calls them. Electrolux now successfully markets its steam ovens to health-oriented consumers, for example, and its compact dishwashers, originally developed for smaller kitchens, to a broader consumer segment interested in washing dishes more often. To companies finding themselves stuck in the middle of a mature market, Stråberg offers these words of advice:

> Start with consumers and understand what their latent needs are and what problems they experience . . . then put the puzzle together yourself to discover what people really want to have. Henry Ford is supposed to have said, 'If I had asked people what they really wanted, I would have made faster horses' or something like that. You have to figure out what people really want, although they can't express it.[11]

Table 14.1 Alternative ways to increase sales volume

Expand the number of brand users	Increase the usage rates among users
• *Convert non-users.* The key to the growth of air freight service is the constant search for new users to whom air carriers can demonstrate the benefits of using air freight rather than ground transportation.	• *Have consumers use the product on more occasions.* Serve yogurt for a snack.
• *Enter new market segments.* The major supermarket chains across Europe are increasingly placing more and higher value non-food lines on their shelves.	• *Have consumers use more of the product on each occasion.* Drink a larger glass of orange juice.
• *Attract competitors' customers.* Shops on garage forecourts generate profitable sales in food and non-food items as drivers pay for their petrol.	• *Have consumers use the product in new ways.* Use washing-up liquid to clean windows.

Some companies abandon weaker products to concentrate on more profitable and new products. Yet they may be ignoring the high potential many mature markets and old products still have. Industries widely thought to be mature – cars, motorcycles, televisions, watches, cameras – were proved otherwise by the Japanese, who found ways to offer new value to customers. The seemingly moribund brand Lucozade has achieved a sales revival by repositioning as an isotonic sports drink aimed at young people.

Three potentially useful ways to change the course for a brand are market, product and marketing programme modifications.

Market modification

A company might try to expand the market for its mature brand by working with the two factors that make up sales volume: volume = number of brand users × usage rate per user, as in Table 14.1.

Product modification

Managers also try to stimulate sales by modifying the market offering attributes and benefits through quality improvement feature improvement or style improvement.

Quality improvement aims at increasing functional performance. A manufacturer can often overtake its competition by launching a 'new and improved' CPV package. Grocery manufacturers call this a 'plus launch' and promote a new additive or advertise something as 'stronger', 'bigger' or 'better'. This strategy is effective to the extent that the quality is improved, buyers accept the claim, and a sufficient number will pay for it. In the case of the tinned coffee industry, manufacturers are using 'freshness' to better position their brands in the face of fierce competition from premium rivals, such as store brands that let customers grind their own beans in the store. Coffee brands are increasingly becoming available in 'seal-easy' packaging to keep the beans fresh.

Feature improvement aims at adding new features (attributes and benefits), such as size, weight, materials, additives and accessories that expand the product use performance, versatility, safety or convenience. This strategy has several advantages. New features build the company's image as an innovator and win the loyalty of market segments that value these features. They provide an opportunity for free publicity and they generate sales force and distributor enthusiasm. The chief disadvantage is that feature improvements are easily imitated; unless the marketer realises a permanent gain from being first, the feature improvement might not pay off in the long run.

Style improvement aims at increasing aesthetic appeal. The periodic introduction of new car models is largely about style competition, as is the introduction of new packaging for consumer goods. A style strategy might give the product (market offering) a unique market identity. Yet style competition has problems. First, it is difficult to predict whether people – and which people – will like a new style. Second, a style change usually requires discontinuing the old style, and the company risks losing customers.

Regardless of the type of improvement, marketers must beware of a possible backlash. Customers are not always willing to accept an 'improved' product, as the now-classic tale of New Coke illustrates.

Coca-Cola

Battered by competition from the sweeter Pepsi-Cola, Coca-Cola decided in 1985 to replace its old formula with a sweeter variation, dubbed New Coke. Coca-Cola spent US$4 million on market research. Blind taste tests showed that Coke drinkers preferred the new, sweeter formula, but the launch of New Coke provoked a national uproar. Market researchers had measured the taste but had failed to measure the emotional attachment consumers had to the original Coca-Cola. There were angry letters, formal protests and even lawsuit threats, to force the retention of 'The Real Thing'. Ten weeks later, the company withdrew New Coke and reintroduced its century-old formula as 'Classic Coke', giving the old formula even stronger status in the marketplace.

Marketing programme modification

Marketing managers might also try to stimulate sales by modifying other marketing programme elements. They should ask the following questions:

- **Prices.** Would a price cut attract new buyers? If so, should the list price be lowered, or should prices be lowered through price specials, volume or early purchase discounts, freight cost absorption or easier credit terms? Or would it be better to *raise* the price, to signal higher quality?
- **Distribution.** Can the company obtain more product support and display in existing outlets? Can it penetrate more outlets? Can the company introduce the product into new distribution channels?
- **Advertising.** Should advertising expenditure be increased? Should the message or advertising copy be improved? Or the media mix? Or the timing, frequency or size of advertisements?
- **Sales promotion.** Should the company step up sales promotion – trade deals, money-off coupons, rebates, warranties, gifts and contests?
- **Personal selling.** Should the number or quality of salespeople be increased? Should sales force duties be changed? Or sales territories and sales force incentives be revised? Can sales-call planning be improved?
- **Services.** Can the company speed up delivery? Can more technical assistance or better credit deals be given to customers?

Marketing strategies: the decline stage

Sales decline for a number of reasons, including technological advances, shifts in consumer tastes and increased domestic and foreign competition. All can lead to overcapacity, increased price cutting and profit erosion. The decline might be slow, as in the case of sewing machines; or rapid, as in the case of floppy disks. Sales may plunge to zero, or they may stagnate at a low level. As sales and profits decline, some firms withdraw from the market. Those remaining may reduce the number of items they offer. They may withdraw from smaller market segments and weaker trade channels, and they may cut their promotion budgets and reduce prices further. Unfortunately, most companies have not developed a policy for handling ageing products.

Unless strong reasons for retention exist, carrying a weak product is very costly to the firm – and not just by the amount of uncovered overhead and profit: there are many hidden costs. Weak products often consume a disproportionate amount of management's time; require frequent price and inventory adjustments; incur expensive set-up for short production runs; draw both advertising and sales force attention that might be better used to make healthy products more profitable; and cast a shadow on the company's image. The biggest cost might well lie in the future. Failing to eliminate weak market offerings delays the aggressive search for replacements.

In handling ageing product/service market offerings, a company faces a number of tasks and decisions. The first is to establish a system for identifying weak market offerings. Many companies appoint a review committee with representatives from marketing, R&D, manufacturing and finance who, based on all available information make a recommendation for each item in the firm's portfolio – leave it alone, modify its marketing strategy or drop it.[12]

Some firms abandon declining markets earlier than others. Much depends on the height and extent of exit barriers in the industry.[13] The lower the exit barriers, the easier it is for firms to leave the industry, and the more tempting it is for the remaining ones to stay and attract the withdrawing firms' customers. For example, Procter & Gamble stayed in the declining liquid soap business and improved its profits as others withdrew.

The appropriate strategy also depends on the industry's relative attractiveness and the company's competitive strength in that industry. A company that is in an unattractive industry but possesses competitive strength should consider shrinking selectively. A company that is in an attractive industry but has competitive strength should consider strengthening its investment. Companies that successfully reposition or rejuvenate a mature product often do so by adding value to the original offering.

If the company were choosing between harvesting and divesting, its strategies would be quite different. *Harvesting* calls for gradually reducing a product or business's costs while trying to maintain sales. The first step is to cut research and development costs and plant and equipment investment. The company might also reduce product quality, sales force size, marginal services and advertising expenditure. It would try to cut these costs without letting customers, competitors and employees know what is happening. Harvesting is difficult to execute. Yet many mature products warrant this strategy. It can substantially increase the company's current cash flow.[14]

When a company decides to drop a market offering, it faces further decisions. If it has strong distribution and residual goodwill, the company can probably sell it to another firm. In 2008 Ford sold on the famous UK car marques of Jaguar and Land Rover to Tata Steel of India. If the company cannot find any buyers, it must decide whether to liquidate the brand quickly or slowly. It must also decide on how much inventory and after-sales service support to maintain for past customers.

Evidence on the product life cycle concept

Based on the above discussion, Table 14.2 summarises the characteristics, marketing objectives and marketing strategies of the four stages of the PLC. The PLC concept helps marketers interpret product and market dynamics, conduct planning and control, and perform forecasting. One recent research study of 30 product categories unearthed a number of interesting findings concerning the PLC.[15]

- New consumer durables show a distinct take-off, after which sales increase by roughly 45 per cent a year, but also show a distinct slow-down, when sales decline by roughly 15 per cent a year.
- Slow-down occurs at 34 per cent penetration on average, well before the majority of households own a new product.

Table 14.2 Summary of product life cycle characteristics, objectives and strategies

	Introduction	Growth	Maturity	Decline
Characteristics				
Sales	Low sales	Rapidly rising sales	Peak sales	Declining sales
Costs	High cost per customer	Average cost per customer	Low cost per customer	Low cost per customer
Profits	Negative	Rising profits	High profits	Declining profits
Customers	Innovators	Early adopters	Middle majority	Laggards
Competitors	Few	Growing number	Stable number beginning to decline	Declining number
Marketing objectives				
	Create product awareness and trial	Maximise market share	Maximise profit while defending market share	Reduce expenditure and milk the brand
Strategies				
Product	Offer a basic product	Offer product extensions, service, warranty	Diversify brands and items models	Phase out weak products
Price	Charge cost-plus	Price to penetrate market	Price to match or best competitors'	Cut price
Distribution	Build selective distribution	Build intensive distribution	Build more intensive distribution	Go selective: phase out unprofitable outlets
Advertising	Build product awareness among early adopters and dealers	Build awareness and interest in the mass and dealers markets	Stress brand differences and benefits	Reduce to level needed to retain hard-core loyals
Sales promotion	Use heavy sales promotion to entice trial	Reduce to take advantage of heavy consumer demand	Increase to encourage brand switching	Reduce to minimal level

Sources: C. R. Wasson (1978) *Dynamic Competitive Strategy and Product Life Cycles*, Austin, TX: Austin Press; J. A. Weber (1976) Planning corporate growth with inverted product life cycles, *Long Range Planning*, October, 12–29; P. Doyle (1976) The realities of the product life cycle, *Quarterly Review of Marketing*, Summer.

- The growth stage lasts a little over eight years and does not seem to shorten over time.
- Informational cascades exist, meaning that people are more likely to adopt over time if others have bought, instead of by making careful product evaluations. One implication, however, is that product categories with large sales increases at take-off tend to have larger sales decline at slow-down.

Critique of the product life cycle concept

PLC theory has its share of critics. Crawford argued that what had traditionally been recognised as the PLC was actually a special case of the new, broader product evolutionary cycle.[16] The evolutionary concept borrowed from biology is useful in solving problems in the fixed cycle sequence: but still no simple solutions exist.[17]

The critics claim that life cycle patterns are too variable in shape and duration to be generalised, and that marketers can seldom tell what stage their product is in. A product may appear to be mature when actually it has reached a plateau prior to another upsurge. They also charge that, rather than an inevitable course that sales must follow, the PLC pattern is the self-fulfilling result of marketing strategies, and that skilful marketing can in fact lead to continued growth. The marketing memo provides ten rules for long-term marketing success.

Marketing memo

How to build a breakaway brand

Marketing experts Kelly and Silverstein define a *breakaway brand* as one that stands out, not just in its own product category, but from all other brands, and which achieves significant results in the marketplace. Here is a summary of their ten tips for building a breakaway brand:

1 **Make a commitment.** The entire organisation, from the top down, needs to make a commitment to build and support a breakaway brand and to develop new products that have breakaway attributes.

2 **Get a 'chief' behind it.** Few breakaway branding initiatives have a chance of success without the enthusiastic support of the company's CEO, chief operations officer (COO) or chief marketing officer (CMO). A senior executive must play the role of brand visionary, brand champion and brand architect.

3 **Find your brand truth.** Ultimately, the DNA of a breakaway brand is its brand truth. It is what defines and differentiates every breakaway brand. It is the single most important weapon a brand will ever have in the battle for increased awareness, profitability, market share and even share price.

4 **Target a winning mindset.** The winning mindset is the potent, aspirational, shared 'view of life' among all core audience segments. It should inspire all of the company's advertising and promotional activities.

5 **Create a category of one.** To be a breakaway brand, your brand needs not only to stand apart from others in its own category but also to transcend categories and open a defining gap between itself and its competitors. Then it becomes a category of one.

6 **Demand a great campaign.** Great campaigns are a team sport – they require a partnership between the company and its agencies to create a campaign that breaks away. Never compromise on a campaign, because without a great campaign, the potential breakaway brand is likely to fail to take off.

7 **Tirelessly integrate.** Integration is the name of the game. Depending on the audience a company is trying to reach, the campaign might feature an integrated marketing communication with both network and cable TV, print and online advertising, direct mail, email, radio and non-traditional media – from street marketing to publicity stunts to contests.

8 **Take risks.** Today, 80 per cent of brands are just about holding their own. Only 20 per cent are doing well.

9 **Accelerate new product development.** Nothing is more important than differentiating a product in the marketplace – but the only way to rise above me-too branding is to innovate and do something different and unique with the product. It may mean throwing away an old brand and reinventing it. Or it may mean introducing a new branded product.

10 **Invest as if the brand depends on it.** Building a breakaway brand is serious business, so it takes a serious business investment. Invest in the product, of course – but also in the packaging and a smart, integrated marketing campaign. Invest wisely . . . as the brand depends on it.

Source: Adapted from F. J. Kelly III and B. Silverstein (2005) *The Breakaway Brand*, New York: McGraw-Hill. Copyright © 2005 The McGraw-Hill Companies.

Market evolution

Because the PLC focuses on what is happening to a particular market offering or brand rather than on what is happening to the overall market, it yields a product-oriented picture rather than a market-oriented picture. Firms also need to visualise a *market's* evolutionary path as it is affected by new needs, competitors, technology, channels and other developments.[18] In the course of a market offering's or brand's existence, its positioning must change to keep pace with market developments. Markets evolve through four stages: emergence, growth, maturity and decline.

Emergence

Before a market materialises, it exists as a latent market. For example, for centuries people have wanted faster means of calculation. The market satisfied this need with abacuses, slide rules and large adding machines. Suppose an entrepreneur recognises this need and imagines a technological solution in the form of a small, handheld electronic calculator. He now has to determine the product attributes, including physical size and number of mathematical functions. Because he is market oriented, he interviews potential buyers and finds that target customers vary greatly in their preferences. Some want a four-function calculator (adding, subtracting, multiplying and dividing) and others want more functions (calculating percentages, square roots and logarithms). Some want a small handheld calculator and others want a large one. This type of market, in which buyer preferences scatter evenly, is called a *diffused-preference market*.

The entrepreneur's problem is to design an optimal package for this market. He or she has three options:

1 Design the new market offering to meet the preferences of one of the corners of the market – *a single-niche strategy.*
2 Launch two or more market offerings simultaneously to capture two or more parts of the market – *a multiple-niche strategy.*
3 Design the new market offering for the middle of the market – *a mass-market strategy.*

A small firm does not have the resources for capturing and holding the mass market, so a single-niche market strategy makes the most sense. A large firm might aim for the mass market by designing an item that is medium in size and number of functions. Assume a pioneer firm is large and designs for the mass market. Once it has launched the market offering, the *emergence* stage begins.

Growth

If the new offering sells well, new firms will enter the market, ushering in a *market-growth stage*. Where will a second firm enter the market, assuming the first firm established itself in the centre? If the second firm is small, it is likely to avoid head-on competition with the pioneer and to launch its brand in one of the market corners. If the second firm is large, it might launch its brand in the centre against the pioneer. The two firms can easily end up sharing the mass market. Or a large second firm can implement a multiple-niche strategy and surround and box in the pioneer.

Maturity

Eventually, the competitors cover and serve all the major segments and the market enters the *maturity stage*. In fact, the competitors go further and invade each other's segments, reducing everyone's profits in the process. As market growth slows down, the market splits into finer segments and high *market fragmentation* occurs. This situation is illustrated in Figure 14.5(a) where the letters represent different companies supplying various segments. Note that two segments are unserved because they are too small to yield a profit.

Market fragmentation is often followed by a *market consolidation*, caused by the emergence of a new customer-perceived value attribute that has strong appeal. This situation is illustrated in Figure 14.5(b) by the expansive size of the X territory.

However, even a consolidated market condition will not last. Other companies will copy a successful brand, and the market will eventually splinter again. Mature markets swing between fragmentation brought about by competition, and consolidation brought about by innovation. Consider the evolution of the paper towel market.

(a) Market fragmentation stage

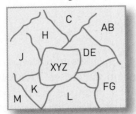

(b) Market consolidation stage

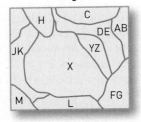

Figure 14.5 Market fragmentation and market consolidation strategies

Paper towels

Originally, homemakers used cotton and linen dishcloths and towels in their kitchens. A paper company, looking for new markets, developed paper towels. This development crystallised a latent market, and other manufacturers entered. The number of brands grew and created market fragmentation. Industry overcapacity led manufacturers to search for new features. One manufacturer, hearing consumers complain that paper towels were not absorbent, introduced 'absorbent' towels and increased its market share. This market consolidation did not last long because competitors came out with their own versions of absorbent paper towels. The market fragmented again. Then another manufacturer introduced a 'super strength' towel. It was soon copied. Another manufacturer introduced a 'lint-free' paper towel, which was subsequently copied. Thus paper towels evolved from a single product to one with various absorbencies, strengths and applications. Market evolution was driven by the forces of innovation and competition.

Decline

Eventually, demand for the current portfolio of offerings will begin to decrease, and the market will enter the *decline stage*. Either society's total need level declines, or a new technology replaces the old. For example, shifts in tradition and a trend towards cremation have caused coffin makers and funeral homes to reconsider how to conduct their business.[19]

Product characteristics and classifications

The traditional term **product** is a confusing one in today's highly competitive global markets. Many people think a product is a single, tangible offering – but it is more than that. Broadly, a product is anything that can be offered to a market to satisfy a want or need, and consists of a set of attributes, including physical goods, services, experiences,

Figure 14.6 Components of the market offering

events, persons, places, properties, organisations, information and ideas (see Figure 14.6) that can deliver the desired customer-perceived value. In current buyers' markets, where customers have a wide choice of suppliers, it is usually insufficient to provide tangible goods alone. As most markets are fiercely competitive, firms have to surround their core product with a set of carefully selected additional attributes and benefits, both tangible (e.g. attractive design, packaging) and intangible (e.g. prompt polite and efficient service). This mix of attributes and benefits makes up the desirable market offering.

Product levels: the customer-perceived value hierarchy

In planning its market offering, the marketer needs to address five CPV benefit levels (see Figure 14.7).[20] Each level adds more customer-perceived value.

1 The fundamental level is the **core benefit**: the benefit the customer is really buying. A hotel guest is buying 'rest and sleep'. The purchaser of a drill is buying 'holes'. Marketers must see themselves as benefit providers.

2 At the second level, the marketer must turn the core benefit into a **basic product**. Thus a hotel room includes a bed, bathroom, towels, desk and wardrobe.

3 At the third level, the marketer prepares an **expected product**, a set of attributes and conditions that buyers normally expect when they purchase this product. Hotel guests expect a clean bed, fresh towels, working lamps and a relative degree of quiet.

4 At the fourth level, the marketer prepares an **augmented product** that exceeds customer expectations. A hotel provides a Wi-fi connection and a flat-screen TV.

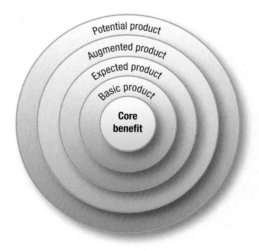

Figure 14.7 Five product levels

Marketing insight

Metamarkets and metamediaries

There are some products whose purchase necessitates other product purchases. The new car market is a good example of a 'metamarket'. The customer chooses a car but then also needs to buy insurance from an insurance company and often has to get a loan from a bank. A smart car company or dealer would make all three purchases easy for the buyer by partnering with an insurance company and a bank, thus acting as a 'metamediary'.

The wedding market is also a metamarket. The bride and groom need a bridal gown and suit respectively, a venue for the marriage and wedding reception, a caterer and possibly a wedding consultant. Here the wedding dress seller or the wedding consultant could well act as a wedding metamediary.

Metamarkets are the result of marketers observing the total consumption system and 'packaging' a collection of CPV offerings that simplifies the purchase process. A metamarket has been defined as 'a set of products and services that consumers need to perform a *cognitively related* set of activities'. Other metamarkets that are organised around major assets or major life events include:

- buying a home;
- giving birth to a child;
- getting a divorce;
- planning a holiday; and
- planning funeral arrangements.

Source: Adapted from M. Sawhney (1999) Rethinking marketing and mediation in the networked economy, Winning strategies for ecommerce lecture at the Kellogg School of Management, 7–10 April.

5 At the fifth level stands the **potential product**, which encompasses all the possible augmentations and transformations that the product or offering might undergo in the future. Here is where companies search for new ways to satisfy customers and distinguish their offering. The hotel staff provide a free fruit bowl and petit four tray every night.

Differentiation arises and competition increasingly occurs on the basis of the additional augmented and potential benefit attributes that comprise market offerings. This stimulates marketers to look at the user's total **consumption system**: the way the end customer obtains and uses such CPV offerings. Each augmentation and potential additional benefit attribute raises the supplier's cost. As customers strive to increase the perceived value for their money, augmented and potential benefits soon become expected necessary points-of-parity. Today's hotel guests expect cable or satellite television with a remote control and high-speed internet access or two phone lines. This means competitors must search continually for still other features and benefits in order to gain a market edge.

As some companies raise the price of their augmented and potential product market offerings, others offer a lower, less expensive, version. Thus, alongside the growth of five-star hotels there is a demand in many locations for modest hotels and motels such as Novatel.

Sultzer Pumps

The company is a subsidiary of the Swiss engineering group and is one of the world's leading pump manufacturers, recognised for excellent product quality, performance reliability and technical innovation. The company provides a full line of pumps, equipment and related technologies to the oil and gas, hydrocarbon processing, power generation and pulp and paper industries, individually designed to meet the needs of customers operating in adverse environments. 'We offer differentiation – highly engineered products. We focus on engineered solutions and on demonstrating that they will work in arduous conditions,' says the company's managing director.[21]

Product classifications

Marketers have traditionally classified products (market offerings) on the basis of durability, tangibility and use (consumer or industrial). Each type of offering has an appropriate marketing mix strategy.

Durability and tangibility

Marketers traditionally classify market offerings in three categories on the basis of durability and tangibility:

1 **Non-durable goods**: offerings, usually termed *fast-moving consumer goods* (fmcgs), which are normally consumed in one or a few uses. They include offerings such as beer and soap. Because these offerings are purchased frequently, the appropriate strategy is to make them available in many locations, charge only a small mark-up, and advertise heavily to induce trial and build preference.

2 **Durable goods**: market offerings that have a longer use lifetime, such as refrigerators, machine tools and clothing. These require more personal selling and service, command a higher margin, and require more provider guarantees.

3 **Services**: traditionally viewed as intangible, inseparable, variable and perishable offerings. Services normally require more quality control, supplier credibility and adaptability. Examples include haircuts, legal advice and appliance repairs. In reality, service offerings contain both tangible and intangible attributes and benefits, so are best considered as CPV packages.

Consumer goods classification

The array of market offerings that consumers buy can be classified on the basis of shopping habits.

Consumers usually purchase **convenience goods** frequently, immediately and with a minimum of effort. Examples include soft drinks, soaps and newspapers. Convenience goods can be further segmented. *Staples* are goods that consumers purchase on a regular basis. A buyer might routinely purchase bread, toothpaste and yogurt. *Impulse goods* are purchased without any planning or search effort. Confectionery and magazines can be impulse goods. *Emergency goods* are purchased when a need is urgent – umbrellas during a rainstorm, boots and shovels during the first winter snow. Manufacturers of impulse and emergency goods will place them in those outlets (e.g. petrol stations) where consumers are likely to make an impulse purchase.

Shopping goods are goods that customers characteristically evaluate on such criteria as suitability, quality, price and style. Examples include furniture, clothing, used cars and

Marketers rely on well-trained salespeople to help customers compare quality and features of shopping such as home appliances.
Source: © Jupiter Images/ Brand X/Alamy.

major appliances. *Homogeneous shopping goods* are similar in quality but different enough in price to justify shopping comparisons. *Heterogeneous shopping goods* differ by offering high customer-perceived value and a strong brand association: for example, offerings stocked by quality department stores. The seller of heterogeneous shopping goods carries a wide assortment to satisfy individual tastes and must have well-trained salespeople to inform and advise customers.

Speciality goods have unique characteristics or brand identification for which a sufficient number of buyers are willing to make a special purchasing effort. Examples include cars, stereo components, photographic equipment and men's suits. A Mercedes car and a Bang & Olufsen home cinema system are speciality products because interested buyers will travel far to buy one.

Unsought goods are those the customer does not know about or does not normally think of buying, such as smoke detectors. Classic examples of unsought products include life insurance, coffins and gravestones. Unsought goods require advertising and personal selling support.

Industrial goods classification

Industrial products can be classified in terms of their relative cost and how they enter the production process: materials and parts, capital items, and supplies and business services.

Materials and parts are goods that become part of a complete manufacturer's product/market offering. They fall into two classes: raw materials, and manufactured materials and parts. *Raw materials* fall into two major groups: *farm products* (wheat, cotton, livestock, fruit and vegetables) and *natural products* (fish, lumber, crude petroleum, iron ore). Farm products are supplied by many producers, which turn them over to marketing intermediaries, which provide assembly, grading, storage, transportation and selling services. Their perishable and seasonal nature gives rise to special marketing practices, whereas their commodity character results in relatively little advertising and promotional activity, with some exceptions. At times, commodity groups will launch campaigns to promote their product – potatoes, cheese and beef. Some producers such as Chiquita bananas and Jaffa oranges brand their products.

Natural products are limited in supply. They usually have great bulk and low unit value and must be moved from producer to user. Fewer and larger producers often market them directly to industrial users. Because users depend on these materials, long-term supply contracts are common. The homogeneity of natural materials makes it more difficult for suppliers to raise the value level of their products.

Manufactured materials and parts fall into two categories: component materials (iron, yarn, cement and wire) and component parts (small motors, tyres, castings). *Component materials* are usually fabricated further – pig iron is made into steel, and yarn is woven into cloth. The standardised nature of component materials usually means that price and supplier reliability are key purchase factors. *Component parts* enter the finished market offering with no further change in form, as when small motors are put into vacuum cleaners, and tyres are put on vehicles. Most manufactured materials and parts are sold directly to industrial users. Price and service are major marketing considerations, and branding and advertising tend to be less important.

Capital items are long-lasting goods that facilitate developing or managing the finished CPV offering. They include two groups: installations and equipment. *Installations* consist of buildings (factories, offices) and heavy equipment (generators, drill presses, mainframe computers, lifts). Installations are major purchases. They are usually bought directly from the producer, whose sales force includes technical personnel, and a long negotiation period precedes the typical sale. Producers must be willing to design to specification and to supply after-sales services. Personal selling is generally more important in these markets than advertising.

Equipment includes portable factory equipment and tools (hand tools, lift trucks) and office equipment (personal computers, desks). These do not become part of a finished product. They have a shorter life than installations but a longer life than operating supplies. Although some equipment manufacturers sell direct, more often they use intermediaries because the market is geographically dispersed, the buyers are numerous and the orders are small. Quality, price and service standards are usually major considerations. The sales force tends to be more important than advertising, although advertising can be used effectively.

Supplies and business services are short-term goods and services that facilitate developing or managing the finished product. Supplies are of two kinds: *maintenance and repair items* (paint, nails and brooms) and *operating supplies* (lubricants, coal, writing paper, pencils). Together, they go under the name of MRO goods. Supplies are the equivalent of convenience; goods that are usually purchased with minimum effort on a straight rebuy basis. They are normally marketed through intermediaries because of their low unit cost and the great number and geographic dispersion of customers. Price and service are important considerations because suppliers are standardised and brand preference is not high.

Business services include *maintenance and repair services* (window cleaning, copier repair) and *business advisory services* (legal, management consulting and advertising). Maintenance and repair services are usually supplied under contract by small producers or are available from the manufacturers of the original equipment. Business advisory services are usually purchased on the basis of the supplier's reputation and staff.

Differentiation

Branding enables market offerings to be positively differentiated. This is possible with every market offering that has a preferred CPV. The humble aspirin can be as positively branded by a generic firm as it can by a strongly branded firm such as Bayer. Firms often offer a portfolio of market offerings to cover many market segments. Procter & Gamble and Unilever offer a variety of detergents, each with a separate brand identity. Some products, such as cars, commercial buildings and furniture, are capable of high differentiation. This is achieved by the seller developing a rich mix of customer perceived benefit attributes. These can include such attributes and benefits as form, features, customisation, performance quality, conformance quality, durability, reliability, repairability and style. Over the last decade, design has become an increasingly important means of differentiation.

Product (market offering) differentiation

Form

Many market offerings can be differentiated in **form** – the size, shape or physical structure of an offering. Consider the many possible forms taken by items such as aspirin. Although aspirin is essentially a commodity, it can be differentiated by dosage size, shape, colour, coating or action time.

Features

Most market offerings can be marketed with varying **attributes** and **benefits** that supplement their basic function. A company can identify and select appropriate new attributes by surveying recent buyers and then assessing the package of *customer benefits* versus *company cost* for each potential featured value attribute. The company should also consider how many people want each attribute feature, how long it would take to introduce it, and whether competitors could easily copy it. To avoid 'feature fatigue' the company must also be careful to prioritise those attributes that are included and find unobtrusive ways to provide information about how consumers can use and benefit from them.[22] Companies must also think in terms of several product bundles or packages. Car manufacturers offer cars at several CPV 'trim levels'. Each company must decide in which market segment to compete and use market research techniques to discover the appropriate value-offering specifications.

Customisation

Marketers can differentiate products by customising. As companies have grown proficient at gathering information about individual customers and business partners (suppliers, distributors, retailers), and as their factories are being designed more flexibly, they have increased their ability to individualise products, messages and media. For example, publishers of academic texts customise books for selected college and university courses. **Mass customisation** is the ability of a company to meet each customer's requirements – to prepare on a mass basis individually designed products, services, programmes and communications.[23]

Although Levi's and Lands' End were among the first clothing manufacturers to introduce custom jeans; other players have introduced mass customisation into other markets. BMW customises over half the Minis it markets in Europe.[24] LEGO has customised its offering from the beginning.

LEGO

In a sense, LEGO of Billund, Denmark, has always been mass customised. Every child who has ever had a set of the most basic LEGO has built his or her own unique and amazing creations, brick by plastic brick. Many wrongly believe that the name LEGO stems from the Latin word for 'I put together'. In reality it comes from *leg godt*, Danish for 'play well'. However, in 2005, Lego set up The Lego Factory, which, as it says on the company website, 'lets you design, share, and build your very own custom LEGO products'. Using LEGO's freely downloadable Digital Designer Software, customers can create any structure. The creations can exist – and be shared with other enthusiasts – solely online or, if customers want to build them, the software tabulates the pieces required and sends an order to its nearest LEGO warehouse. The employees there put all the pieces into a box and send it back to the customer. LEGO Factory customers have the pride of building their own creations, but they can also earn royalties if LEGO decides the design is good enough to include in its own catalogue. In 2006, The LEGO Factory initiated a design competition in which eight contestants competed to be profiled on the LEGO Factory website along with their creations.[25]

Performance quality

Most market offerings are established at one of four performance levels: low, average, high or superior. **Performance value** is the level at which the market offering's primary characteristic attributes operate. Customer-perceived quality is becoming an increasingly important dimension for differentiation, as companies seek to meet and preferably exceed customers' expectations in the marketplace. Continuously improving the market offering can produce high returns and market share; failing to do so can have negative consequences.

Mercedes-Benz

From 2003 to 2006 Mercedes-Benz endured one of the most painful periods in its 127-year history, as its quality reputation took a beating in independent quality reviews. BMW surpassed it in global sales. As a consequence, DaimlerChrysler's chief executive Dieter Zetsche and his new management team initiated a major restructuring, organising the company around functional elements of the car – motors, chassis and electronic systems – instead of by model lines. To improve customer perceived quality, the company also made a number of changes in product development. Engineers begin testing electronic systems a year earlier than in the past. Laboratory workers put each new model's electronic system through a battery of 10,000 tests that ran 24 hours a day for three weeks. Trying to uncover even the most unlikely event, Mercedes found over 1,000 errors in the new S-Class. Mercedes now uses three times as many prototypes of new designs, allowing engineers to drive a new model 3 million miles before it goes into production. As a result of these and other changes, the number of flaws in the cars has dropped 72 per cent from its peak in 2002 and warranty costs have also decreased by 25 per cent.[26]

Performance quality is such a critical part of Mercedes-Benz's product strategy that the company undertook a series of sweeping changes in its quality control processes to reduce errors and flaws when its quality ratings slipped.
Source: Courtesy of Daimler AG.

Conformance quality

Buyers expect products to have a high **conformance quality**, which is the degree to which all market offerings meet the promised specifications. Suppose a Porsche 911 is designed to accelerate to 60 miles per hour within ten seconds. If every Porsche 911 coming off the assembly line does this, the model is said to have high conformance quality. If the model fails to perform as claimed, the low performance quality will disappoint some buyers.

Durability

Durability, a measure of the product's expected operating life under natural or stressful conditions, is usually a key value attribute/benefit. Customers will generally pay more for vehicles and kitchen appliances that have a reputation for being long lasting.

Reliability

Buyers will normally pay a premium for more reliable products. **Reliability** is a measure of the probability that a key benefit or valued attribute will not malfunction or will fail within a specified time period. Bosch, Liebherr and Miele, whose portfolios include major home appliances, have earnt an outstanding reputation for creating reliable appliances. The breakthrough marketing box describes how that company has excelled at making and selling high-quality, dependable motor vehicles.

Breakthrough marketing

Toyota

Toyota may have begun making cars by being a fast follower, but it is now a leading innovator. Toyota offers a full line of cars covering the market, from family cars to 4 × 4s to trucks and minivans. The company offers cars in the entry, middle and niche markets. Designing these different products (market offerings) entails listening to different customers, building the cars they want and then customising them to reinforce each model's image.

Toyota's marketing strategy for the Lexus line focuses on perfection. The tagline for the global strategy is 'Passionate pursuit of perfection'. Toyota markets Lexus globally and understands that each country defines perfection differently. In Europe, luxury means attention to detail and brand heritage. Therefore, although the core of Lexus marketing is similar (a consistent Lexus visual vocabulary, logo, font and overall communication), the advertising varies by country.

One big reason behind Toyota's success is its manufacturing. Toyota's combination of manufacturing speed and flexibility is world class. It is the master of lean manufacturing and continuous improvement. Its plants can make as many as eight different models at the same time, which brings Toyota huge increases in productivity and market responsiveness. It is also a continuous innovator. A typical Toyota assembly line makes thousands of operational changes in the course of a single year. Toyota employees see their purpose as threefold: making cars, making cars better, and teaching everyone how to make cars better. The company encourages creative problem solving, always looking to improve its thinking to enable it to improve its operational processes.

Toyota is integrating its assembly plants around the world into a single giant network. The plants will customise cars for local markets and be able to shift production quickly to satisfy any surges in demand from markets worldwide. With a manufacturing network, Toyota can build a wide variety of models much more inexpensively. That means Toyota will be able to fill market niches as they emerge without building whole new assembly operations. As buyers' markets are characterised by consumers who demand high levels of customer-perceived value in a car, Toyota's ability to meet individual country and customer requirements gives it a distinctly powerful competitive edge.

In the first quarter of 2007, Toyota edged past General Motors to become the world's largest car maker. In 2010 Toyota recalled several thousand cars as its quality reputation looked to be seriously undermined by a series of quality problems affecting carpets that were not clipped down and sticky pedals. On examination

these problems turned out to be largely emotional and had little to do with the actual facts, concluded Liker, who carried out a thorough review of the company's overall quality standards.

Toyota's product strategy is built on innovation and agility and has recently placed the firm into the number-one spot in the industry for the first time.
Source: John van Hasselt/Corbis.

Sources: M. Zimmerman (2007) Toyota's first quarter global sales beat GM's preliminary numbers, *Los Angeles Times*, 24 April; C. Fishman (2006) No satisfaction at Toyota, *Fast Company*, December–January, 82–90; S. F. Brown (2004) Toyota's global body shop, *Fortune*, 9 February, 120; J. B. Treece (2004) Ford down; Toyota aims for no. 1, *Automotive News*, 2 February, 1; B. Bemner and C. Dawson (2003) Can anything stop Toyota?, *BusinessWeek*, 17 November, 114–22; www.toyota.com; J. Liker (2010) Toyota's lost its quality edge? Not so fast, *BusinessWeek*, 28 January.

Repairability

Repairability is a measure of the ease of putting right a market offering when it malfunctions or fails. Ideal repairability would exist if users could fix the problem themselves with little cost in money or time. Some products include a diagnostic feature that allows service people to correct a problem over the telephone or advise the user how to correct it. Many computer hardware and software companies offer technical support over the phone, by fax or email, or by real-time 'chat' online.

Style

Style describes the market offering's look and feel to the buyer. Car buyers, for example, pay a premium for a Jaguar or a Lexus as they value their unique appeal. Aesthetics also play a key role in such brands as Absolut vodka, Apple computers, Montblanc pens, Lindt chocolate and Harley-Davidson motorcycles. Style has the advantage of creating distinctiveness that is difficult to copy. On the negative side, strong style does not always mean high-use performance. A car, such as a Lotus, may look sensational but spend a lot of time in a dealer's garage.

Design

As competition intensifies, design offers a potent way to differentiate and position a company's market offerings.[27] In increasingly fast-paced markets, design is the attribute that will often give a company its competitive edge. **Design** is the mix of features that affect how a market offering looks, feels and functions in terms of customer requirements.

Design is particularly important in making and marketing retail services, clothes and shoes, packaged goods and durable equipment. The designer decides how much to invest in attributes such as form, feature development, performance, conformance, durability, reliability, repairability and style. To the company, a well-designed market offering is one that is easy to manufacture and distribute. To the customer, a well-designed market offering is one that is pleasant to look at and easy to open, install, use, repair and dispose of. The designer must take all these customer-perceived benefit value attribute factors into account.

The arguments for good design are particularly compelling for smaller consumer companies and start-ups operating in consumer markets such as upmarket 'real-wood' furniture firms such as Ercol.

Certain countries and companies are design leaders: Italian design in clothing and furniture; Scandinavian design for functionality, aesthetics and environmental consciousness. Finland's Nokia was the first to introduce user-changeable covers for mobile phones, the first to have elliptical shaped, soft and friendly forms, and the first with big screens, all contributing to its remarkable market success. Braun, a German division of Gillette, has elevated design to a high art in its electric shavers, coffee makers, hair dryers and food processors. The company's design department enjoys equal status with engineering and manufacturing. The Danish firm Bang & Olufsen has received considerable recognition for the design of its stereos, TV equipment and telephones.

Firms should seek new designs to create differentiation and establish a more complete connection with consumers. Holistic marketers recognise the emotional power of design and the importance to consumers of how things look and feel. In an increasingly visually oriented culture, translating brand meaning and positioning through design is critical. A bad design can also ruin a product's prospects.

Service differentiation

When a market offering cannot easily be differentiated, the key to competitive success may lie in adding to the service attributes that comprise the customer-perceived value package. Rolls-Royce plc ensures that its aircraft engines are in high demand by continuously monitoring the health of its 3,000 engines for 45 airlines through live satellite feeds. Under its TotalCare programme, airlines pay a fee for every hour an engine is in flight, and the company assumes responsibility for downtime and repairs expenses.[28]

The main service benefit attribute differentiators are: ordering ease, delivery, installation, customer training, customer consulting, and maintenance and repair.

Ordering ease

Ordering ease refers to how easy it is for the customer to place an order with the company. Many financial service institutions offer secure online sites to help customers obtain information and complete transactions more efficiently.

Delivery

Delivery refers to how well the market offering is brought to the customer. It includes speed, accuracy and care throughout the process. Today's customers have grown to expect delivery speed: pizza delivered in half an hour, film developed in one hour, spectacles made in one hour, cars lubricated in 15 minutes. Levi Strauss and Benetton have adopted computerised *quick response systems* (QRS) that link the information systems of their suppliers, manufacturing plants, distribution centres and retailing outlets.

Installation

Installation refers to the service work done to make a product operational in its planned location. Buyers of heavy equipment expect good installation service. Differentiating at this point in the consumption chain is particularly important for companies with complex products. Ease of installation becomes a true selling point, especially when the target market contains many technological novices, as is frequently the case in the home PC market.

Customer training

Customer training refers to training the customer's employees to use the vendor's equipment properly and efficiently. One example is McDonald's, which requires its new European franchisees to attend its Hamburger University in the United States for a two-week franchise management training course.

Customer consulting

Customer consulting refers to data, information systems and advice services that sellers offer buyers.

Maintenance and repair

Maintenance and repair describes the service programme for helping customers keep purchases in good working order. Hewlett-Packard offers online technical support, or 'esupport', for its customers. In the event of a service problem, customers can use various online tools to find a solution. Those aware of the specific problem can search an online database for solutions; those unaware can use diagnostic software that finds the problem and searches the online database for an automatic repair. Customers can also seek online help from a technician.

Returns

Although returns are undoubtedly a nuisance to customers, manufacturers, retailers and distributors alike, they are also an unavoidable reality of doing business, especially with online purchases. Although the average return rate for online sales is relatively small – roughly 5 per cent – return and exchange policies are estimated to serve as a deterrent for one-third to one-half of online customers. The cost of processing a return can be two to three times that of an outbound shipment.

Returned items can be considered in two ways:[29]

- **Controllable returns**: result from problems, difficulties or errors of the seller or customer and can mostly be eliminated with proper strategies and programmes by the company or its value chain partners. Improved handling or storage, better packaging and improved transportation and forward logistics can eliminate problems before they happen.
- **Uncontrollable returns**: cannot be eliminated by the company in the short run through any of these means.

A basic returns strategy that companies can adopt is to attempt to eliminate the root causes of controllable returns, while at the same time developing processes for handling uncontrollable returns. The aim of a product return strategy is to have fewer items returned and a higher percentage of returns that can go back into the distribution pipeline to be sold again.

Product and brand relationships

Each market offering can be compared to competitive ones to ensure that a firm is performing effectively in the marketplace.

The product hierarchy

The hierarchy stretches from basic needs to particular value attributes and benefits that satisfy those needs. Six hierarchy levels can be identified, using life insurance as an example:

1 **Need family**: the core need that underlies the existence of a family policy. Example: security.
2 **Product family**: all the product classes that can satisfy a core need with reasonable effectiveness. Example: savings and income.
3 **Product class**: a group of products within the product family recognised as having a certain functional coherence; Also known as a product category. Example: financial instruments.
4 **Product line**: a group of products within a product class that are closely related because they perform a similar function, are sold to the same customer groups, are marketed through the same outlets or channels, or fall within given price ranges. A product line may consist of different brands, or a single family brand, or an individual brand that has been developed from a line extension. Example: house and property insurance.
5 **Product type**: a group of items within a product line that share one of several possible forms of the market offering. Example: life insurance.
6 **Item** (also called *stock keeping unit* or *product variant*): a distinct unit within a brand or product line distinguishable by size, price, appearance or some other attribute. Example: renewable life insurance.

Product systems and mixes

A **product system** is a group of diverse but related items that function in a compatible manner. For example, the PalmOne handheld and smartphones come with attachable items including headsets, cameras, keyboards, presentation projectors, ebooks, MP3 players

To read about French carmaker Renault and its strategy for pursuing international growth, visit **www.pearsoned. co.uk/marketingmanagementeurope**.

and voice recorders. A **product mix** (also called a **product assortment**) is the complete set of all products and items that a company brings to the marketplace.

A product mix consists of various product lines. Seagate now makes 29 kinds of drive that are essential to servers, PCs and consumer electronic products such as video games, digital video recorders and cameras. Michelin has three product lines: tyres, maps and restaurant-rating services. A company's product mix has a certain width, length, depth and consistency.

- The *width* of a market of a product mix refers to how many different product lines the company carries. Table 14.3 shows the four lines that make up Nivea's Sun Care range.
- The *length* of a product mix refers to the total number of items in the mix. Nivea has four items in its Children's Protection line.
- The *depth* of a product mix refers to how many variants there are in the market offering/product mix portfolio. Nivea has 15 in its Sun Care portfolio.
- The *consistency* of the product mix refers to how closely related the various lines are in end use, production requirements or distribution channels, or in some other way. Nivea's product lines are consistent so far as they are consumer goods that go through the same distribution channels.

The four product-mixed dimensions enable the company to expand its business in four ways. It can add new product lines, thus widening its product mix. It can lengthen each line. It can add more variants to each product and deepen its product mix. Finally, a company can pursue more product-line consistency. To make these product and brand decisions, it is useful to conduct product-line analysis.

Product-line analysis

When designing a product line, companies normally develop a basic platform and modules that can be added to meet different customer requirements. Car manufacturers build their cars around a basic platform. Homebuilders show a model home to which buyers can add additional features. This modular approach enables the company to position itself optimally by offering variety (to exhibit effectiveness in the marketplace) and to lower production costs (to become effective with its resources).

Table 14.3 Product-mix width and product line length for Nivea Sun Care

	Product-mix width			
	Protection	**Children's Protection**	**After Sun**	**'Sunntouch' Self-Tan**
PRODUCT LINE LENGTH	Light Feeling Sun Lotion	Baby Sun Lotion 501	Cooling After Sun Spray	Quick & Easy Tan Spray (Fair Skin)
	Firming Sun Lotion	Children's Lotion	Regenerating After Sun Balm	Self-Tan Spray
	Moisturising Sun Spray	Children's Sun Spray	Tan Prolonging After Sun Lotion	Self-Tan Lotion
	Oil Spray	Moisturising After Sun Lotion		Self-Tan Cream

Source: Beiersdorf GmbH.

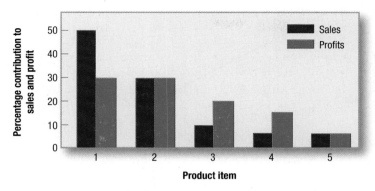

Figure 14.8 Product-item contributions to a product line's total sales and profits

Product-line managers need to know the sales and profits of each market offering in their line in order to determine which items to build, maintain, harvest or divest.[30] They also need to understand each product line's market profile.

Sales and profits

Figure 14.8 shows a sales and profit report for a five-item product line. The first item accounts for 50 per cent of total sales and 30 per cent of total profits. The first two items account for 80 per cent of total sales and 60 per cent of total profits. If these two items were suddenly attacked by a competitor, the line's sales and profitability could collapse. These items must be carefully monitored and protected. Finally, the last item delivers only 5 per cent of the line's sales and profits. The firm may consider dropping this item unless it has strong growth potential.

Every company's product portfolio contains offers with different margins. Supermarkets make almost no margin on bread and milk; reasonable margins on tinned and frozen foods; and better margins on flowers, ethnic food lines, freshly baked goods and dry goods. A telephone company makes different margins on its core telephone, call waiting, caller ID and voicemail services.

A company can classify its products into four types that yield different gross margins, depending on sales volume and promotion. To illustrate with laptop computers:

1 **Core product offerings**: basic laptop computers that produce high sales volume and are heavily promoted but with low margins because they are viewed as undifferentiated commodities.
2 **Staples**: items with lower sales volume and no promotion, such as faster central processing units (CPUs) or bigger memories. These yield a somewhat higher margin.
3 **Specialities**: items with lower sales volume but that might be highly promoted, such as digital film-making equipment; or which might generate income for services, such as personal delivery, installation or on-site training.
4 **Convenience items**: peripheral items that sell in high volume but receive less promotion, such as carrying cases and accessories, top-quality video or sound cards, and software. Consumers tend to buy them where they buy the original equipment because it is more convenient than making further shopping trips. These items can carry higher margins.

The main point is that companies should recognise that these items differ in their potential for justifying higher prices and increased advertising expenditure margins to increase sales and margins.[31]

Market profile

The product-line manager must review how the line is positioned against competitors' lines. Consider Paper Company X with a paperboard product line.[32] Two paperboard

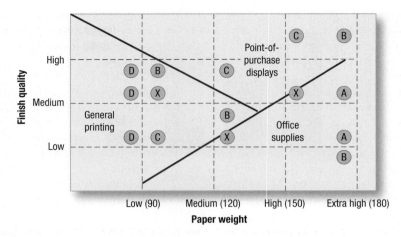

Figure 14.9 Product map for a paper-product line
Source: B. P. Shapiro (2003) Industrial product policy: managing the existing product line, Cambridge, MA: Marketing Science Institute (Report No. 77-110). Copyright © 2003.

attributes are weight and finish quality. Paper is usually offered at standard levels of 90, 120, 150 and 180 g/m² weight. Finish quality is offered at low, medium and high levels. Figure 14.9 shows the location of the various product-line items of company X and four competitors, A, B, C and D. Competitor A sells two product items in the extra-high weight class, ranging from medium to low finish quality. Competitor B sells four items that vary in weight and finish quality. Competitor C sells three items in which the greater the weight, the greater the finish quality. Competitor D sells three items, all lightweight but varying in finish quality. Company X offers three items that vary in weight and finish quality.

The **product map** shows which competitors' items are competing against company X's items. For example, company X's low-weight, medium-quality paper competes against competitor D's and B's papers, but its high-weight, medium-quality paper has no direct competitor. The map also reveals possible locations for new items. No manufacturer offers a high-weight, low-quality paper. If company X estimates a strong unmet demand and can produce and price this paper at low cost, it could consider adding this item to its line.

Another benefit of product mapping is that it identifies market segments. Figure 14.9 shows the types of paper, by weight and quality, preferred by the general printing industry, the point-of-purchase display industry and the office supply industry. The map shows that company X is well positioned to serve the needs of the general printing industry but is less effective in serving the other two industries.

Product-line analysis provides information for two key decision areas – product-line length and product-mix pricing.

Product-line length

Company objectives influence product-line length. One objective is to create a line to induce customers to trade up. Thus General Motors would like to move customers up from its entry market Chevrolet to an Opel or Vauxhall. A different objective is to create a line that facilitates cross-selling: Hewlett-Packard sells printers as well as computers. Still another objective is to create a product line that protects against economic cycles; Electrolux offers white goods such as refrigerators, dishwashers and vacuum cleaners under different brand names in the discount, middle-market and niche segments.[33] Companies seeking high market share and market growth will generally carry longer lines. Companies that emphasise high profitability will carry shorter lines consisting of carefully chosen items.

Product lines tend to lengthen over time. Excess manufacturing capacity puts pressure on firms to develop new items. The sales force and distributors also pressure the company for a more complete portfolio of market offerings to satisfy customers. However, as items are added, costs rise: design and engineering costs, inventory-carrying costs, manufacturing-changeover costs, order-processing costs, transportation costs and new item promotional costs. Eventually, someone calls a halt: top management may stop development because of insufficient funds or manufacturing capacity. The controller may call for a study of money-losing items. A pattern of market offering/product-line growth followed by massive pruning may repeat itself many times. Increasingly, consumers are growing weary of dense market offering/product lines, overextended brands and feature-laden market offerings (see the marketing insight box).

A company lengthens its product line in two ways: line stretching and line filling.

Line stretching

Every company's product line covers a certain part of the total possible range. For example, Mercedes and Porsche cars are located in the upper price niche segment of the car market. **Line stretching** occurs when a company lengthens its line beyond its current range. The company can stretch its line down market, up market, or both ways.

Marketing insight

When less is more

Although many customers find the notion of having more choices appealing, the reality is that customers can sometimes be overwhelmed by the choices involved. With thousands of new products introduced each year, customers find it harder and harder to navigate shop aisles successfully. Although customers with well-defined preferences may benefit from more differentiated offers with specific benefits to better suit their needs, too much choice may be a source of frustration, confusion and regret for other customers. Product proliferation has another disadvantage. Exposing the customer to constant offer changes and introductions may nudge them into reconsidering their choices, resulting in their switching to a competitor as a result.

Also, not all the new choices may be winners anyway, as Nestlé found out with its KitKat bars, among the best-selling confectionery bars in the United Kingdom since they were invented there in the 1930s. To increase sales in 2004, the company rolled out a vast array of new flavours. The summer saw the launch of strawberries and cream, passion fruit and mango, and red berry versions; with winter came Christmas pudding, tiramisu (with real wine and mascarpone), and low-carbohydrate versions. The new flavours were a disaster – the tastes were too sweet and unusual for many – and even worse,

some consumers could not find the classic KitKat bars among all the new varieties. An ill-timed switch from the classic slogan, 'Have a break, have a KitKat', didn't help, and sales dropped 18 per cent as a result. The new flavours were then discontinued.

Perceptive marketers are also realising that it is not just the lines that are confusing customers – many items are just too complicated for the average consumer. Royal Philips Electronics learned its lesson when the company asked 100 top managers to take various Philips electronic products home one weekend and see whether they could make them work. The number of executives who returned frustrated and angry spoke volumes about the challenges the ordinary consumer faced.

Sources: D. Ball (2006) Flavor experiment for KitKat leaves Nestlé with a bad taste, *Wall Street Journal*, 6 July; B. Schwartz (2004) *The Paradox of Choice: Why More Is Less*, New York: HarperCollins Ecco; F. Endt (2004) It is rocket science, *Newsweek*, 18 October, E8; A. Chernev (2003) When more is less and less is more: the role of ideal point availability and assortment in choice, *Journal of Consumer Research*, 30 September, 170–83; S. S. Iyengar and M. R. Lepper (2000) When choice is demotivating: can one desire too much of a good thing?, *Journal of Personality and Social Psychology*, 79(6), 995–1006; R. Dhar (1997) Consumer preference for a no-choice option, *Journal of Consumer Research*, 27 September, 233–48.

Down-market stretch A company positioned in the middle market may want to introduce a lower-priced line for any of three reasons:

1 The company may notice strong growth opportunities as mass retailers such as Carrefour, Tesco and others attract a growing number of shoppers who want lower-priced goods.
2 The company may wish to tie up lower-end competitors that might otherwise try to move up market. If the company has been attacked by a low-end competitor, it often decides to counterattack by entering the low end of the market.
3 The company may find that the middle market is stagnating or declining.

A company faces a number of naming choices in deciding to move a brand down market:

- Use the parent brand name on all its offerings. Sony has used its name on products in a variety of price tiers.
- Introduce lower-priced offerings using a sub-brand name, such as General Motors's Chevrolet models in Europe.
- Introduce the lower-priced offerings under a different name, as VW did with Seat and Skoda. This strategy is expensive to implement, and consumers may not accept a new brand that lacks the equity of the parent brand name.

Moving down market carries risks. Kodak introduced Kodak Funtime film to counter lower-priced brands, but it did not price it low enough to match the lower-priced film. It also found some of its regular customers buying Funtime, so it was cannibalising its core brand. Kodak withdrew the product and may also have lost some of its quality image in the process. On the other hand, Mercedes successfully introduced its C-class cars without injuring its ability to sell other top-priced Mercedes cars. In these cases, consumers may have been better able to compartmentalise the different brand offerings and understand and rationalise functional differences between offerings in higher and lower price tiers.

Up-market stretch Companies may wish to enter the high end of the market to achieve more growth, either to realise higher margins or simply to position themselves as full-line manufacturers. Many markets have spawned surprising upmarket segments: Starbucks in coffee, Mövenpick in ice cream, and Danone's Evian in bottled water. However, other companies have included their own name in moving up market, as is evidenced by super-market premium lines.

Two-way stretch Companies serving the middle market might decide to stretch their line in both directions. Pet food companies have stretched up and down to create a portfolio to offer varieties in the entry, middle and niche market segments.

Holiday Inn

Holiday Inn Worldwide has also performed a two-way stretch of its hotel product line. The hotel chain segmented its domestic hotels into five separate chains to tap into five different benefit segments – the upscale Crowne Plaza, the traditional Holiday Inn, the budget Holiday Inn Express, and the business-oriented Holiday Inn Select and Holiday Inn Suites & Rooms. Different branded chains received different marketing programmes and emphasis. Holiday Inn Express has been advertised with a humorous advertising campaign. By basing the development of these brands on distinct consumer targets with unique needs, Holiday Inn is able to insure against overlap between brands.

The relative position of a brand and its competitor context will also affect consumer acceptance. Research has shown that a high-end model of a low-end brand is favoured over a low-end model of a high-end brand, even when information about competing categories is made available.[34]

Line filling

A firm can also lengthen its product line by adding more items within the present range. There are several motives for *line filling*: reaching for incremental profits, trying to satisfy dealers who complain about lost sales because of missing items in the line, trying to utilise excess capacity, trying to be the leading full-line company, and trying to plug holes to keep out competitors.

Line filling is overdone if it results in self-cannibalisation and customer confusion. The company needs to differentiate each item in the consumer's mind with a *just-noticeable difference*. The company should also check that the proposed product meets a market need.

BMW AG

In four years BMW has evolved from a one-brand, five-model car maker into a three-brand, multi-model powerhouse. Not only has the car maker expanded its product range downwards with Mini Coopers and its compact 1-series models, but it has also built it upwards with Rolls-Royce and filled the gaps in between with its X3 and X5 sports activity vehicles, the Z3 and Z4 roadsters, and a 6-series coupé. The company has used line filling successfully to boost its appeal to the rich, the super-rich and the 'wannabe-rich', all without departing from its pure premium positioning.[35]

Line modernisation, featuring and pruning

Product lines need to be modernised. The issue is whether to overhaul the line piecemeal or all at once. A piecemeal approach allows the company to see how customers and dealers take to the new style. It is also less draining on the company's cash flow, but it allows competitors to see changes and to start redesigning their own lines.

In rapidly changing markets, modernisation is continuous. Companies plan improvements to encourage customer migration to higher-valued, higher-priced items. Microprocessor companies such as Intel and AMD, and software companies such as Microsoft and Sage, continually introduce more advanced versions of their products. A major issue is *timing* improvements so they do not appear too early (damaging sales of the current line) or too late (after the competition has established a strong reputation for more advanced equipment).

Firms must periodically review the line for products that are depressing profits.[36] The weak items can be identified through sales and cost analysis. One study found that for a big Dutch retailer, a major assortment reduction led to a short-term drop in category sales, caused mainly by fewer category purchases by former buyers, but it also attracted new category buyers at the same time. These new buyers partially offset the sales losses among former buyers of the delisted items.[37]

In 1999, Unilever announced its 'Path to Growth' programme designed to get the most value from its brand portfolio by eliminating three-quarters of its 1,600 distinct brands by 2003.[38] More than 90 per cent of its profits came from just 400 brands, prompting Unilever co-chairman Niall FitzGerald to liken the brand reduction to weeding a garden, so 'the light and air get into the blooms which are likely to grow the best'. The company retained global brands such as Lipton, as well as regional brands and 'local jewels' such as Persil, the leading detergent in the United Kingdom.

Multibrand companies all over the world are attempting to optimise their brand portfolios. In many cases, this has led to a greater focus on core brand growth and to concentrating energy and resources on the biggest and most established brands.

Pruning slow-selling brands from product lines often benefits the brands that are left, such as Unilever's global bestsellers including Lipton worldwide and Persil in the United Kingdom. Source: Martin Meissner/AP Wide World Photos.

VW

VW has four different brands to manage in its European portfolio. Initially, Audi and Seat had a sporty image and VW and Skoda had a family-car image. Audi and VW were in a higher price-quality tier than their respective counterparts. Skoda and Seat, with their basic spartan interiors and utilitarian engine performance, were clearly differentiated. With the goal of reducing costs, streamlining parts/systems designs and eliminating redundancies, Volkswagen upgraded the Seat and Skoda brands. Once viewed as below-par products by European consumers, Skoda and Seat have captured market share with attractive interiors, a full array of safety systems and reliable power-trains borrowed from Volkswagen. The danger, of course, is that by borrowing from its upper-echelon Audi and Volkswagen products, Volkswagen may have diluted their cachet. Frugal European car buyers may convince themselves that a Seat or Skoda is almost identical to a VW, but it is several thousand euro cheaper.[39]

Product-mix pricing

Chapter 16 discusses pricing concepts in detail, but a short summary of some basic market offering/product-mix pricing issues is given here. Marketers must modify their price-setting logic when the offering is part of a product mix. In product-mix pricing, the firm searches for a set of prices that maximises profits on the total mix. Pricing is difficult because the various products have demand and cost interrelationships and are subject to different degrees of competition. Six situations calling for product-mix pricing can be categorised: product-line pricing, optional-feature pricing, captive-product pricing, two-part pricing, by-product pricing and product-bundling pricing.

Product-line pricing

Companies normally develop product lines rather than single products, and introduce price steps. In many lines of trade, sellers use well-established price points for the products in their line. A men's clothing store might carry men's suits at three price levels: €200, €400 and €600. Customers will associate low-, average- and high-quality suits with the three price points. The marketer's task is to establish customer-perceived quality differences that justify the price differences.

Optional-feature pricing

Many companies offer optional products, features and services along with their main product. The car buyer can order power window controls, remote adjustable mirrors, a sunroof, an electronic parking aid and theft protection. Pricing is a serious problem because companies must decide which items to include in the standard price and which to offer as options.

Restaurants face a similar pricing problem. Many charge premium prices for their wine and alcoholic drinks. The food revenue covers costs, and the drinks produce the profit. This explains why waiters and waitresses often press hard to get customers to order drinks. Other restaurants offer low-price drinks and charge premium prices for their food.

Captive-product pricing

Some products require the use of ancillary products, or **captive products**. Manufacturers of razors, cameras and computer printers often price them low and set high mark-ups on razor blades, film and ink cartridges.

Hewlett-Packard

In 1996, Hewlett-Packard (HP) began drastically cutting prices on its printers, by as much as 60 per cent in some cases. HP could afford to make such dramatic cuts because customers typically spend twice as much on replacement ink cartridges, toner and speciality paper as on the actual printer over the life of the product. As the price of printers dropped, printer sales rose, as did the number of after-market sales. HP now owns about 40 per cent of the worldwide printer business. Its inkjet supplies command a 35 per cent profit margin and generated US $2.2 billion in operating profits in 2002 – over 70 per cent of the company's total.[40]

There is a danger in pricing the captive product too high in the after market, however. If parts and service are too expensive, counterfeiting and substitutions can erode sales. Consumers can now buy cartridge refills for their printers from discount suppliers and save 20–30 per cent of the price of the manufacturer's cartridges.

Two-part pricing

Firms in service sectors engage in **two-part pricing**, consisting of a fixed fee plus a variable usage fee. Mobile telephone users pay a monthly fee plus additional tariffs for different calls, and internet plans. Amusement parks charge an admission fee plus fees for rides over a certain minimum. The service firm faces a problem similar to captive-product pricing – namely, how much to charge for the basic service and how much for the variable usage. The fixed fee should be low enough to induce purchase of the service; the profit can then come from the usage fees.

By-product pricing

The production of certain goods – meats, petroleum products and other chemicals – often results in by-products. If the by-products have value to a customer group, they should be priced to reflect customer-perceived value. Any income earned on the by-products will make it easier for the company to charge a lower price on its main product if competition forces it to do so.

Product-bundling pricing

Sellers often bundle products and features. **Pure bundling** occurs when a firm offers its products only as a bundle. Many computer software companies do this with the twin aims of attracting additional custom through a sales promotion and running down excess stocks. In **mixed bundling**, the seller offers goods both individually and in bundles. When offering a mixed bundle, the seller normally charges less for the bundle than if the items were purchased separately. A car manufacturer might offer an option package at less than the cost of buying all the options separately. A magazine publisher will price an annual subscription at less than the cost of buying 12 issues.[41]

Some customers will want less than the whole bundle. Suppose a medical equipment supplier's offer includes free delivery and training. A particular customer might ask to forgo the free delivery and training in exchange for a lower price. The customer is asking the seller to 'unbundle' or 'rebundle' its offer. If a supplier saves €100 by not supplying delivery and reduces the customer's price by €80, the supplier has kept the customer happy while increasing its profit by €20.

Experience has shown that as promotional activity increases on individual items in the bundle, buyers perceive less saving and so are less likely to be attracted by the offer. This research suggests the following guidelines for correctly implementing a bundling strategy:[42]

- It is unwise to promote individual products in a package as frequently and cheaply as the bundle. The bundle price should be much lower than the sum of individual products or the consumer will not perceive its attractiveness.
- It is best to limit sales promotions to a single item in the mix if the company wants to promote individual products. Another option: alternate sales promotions, one after another, in order to avoid running conflicting promotions.
- If firms offer large rebates on individual products, it is best to do so with discretion and make them the sole exception. Otherwise, the consumer uses the price of individual products as an external reference for the bundle, which then loses value.

Co-branding and ingredient branding

Co-branding

Marketers often combine their products with products from other companies in various ways. In **co-branding** – also called dual branding or brand bundling – two or more well-known brands are combined into a joint market offering or marketed together in some fashion. One form of co-branding is *same-company co-branding*, as when the Danone Group advertises Activia Yogurt and Actimel. Still another form is *joint-venture co-branding*, such as British Gas energy and engineering and Bosch Worcester gas boilers in the United Kingdom. There is also *multiple-sponsor co-branding* that is evident when football clubs grant after-match interviews with the media in a room full of sponsors' displayed logos. Finally, there is *retail co-branding* where several retail establishments use the same location as a way to optimise both space and profits, as is the case in discount retail parks throughout Europe.

The main advantage of co-branding is that a market offering/product may be convincingly positioned by virtue of the multiple brands. Co-branding can generate greater sales from the existing target market as well as opening additional opportunities for new consumers and channels. It can also reduce the cost of introducing a new market offer, because it combines two well-known images and speeds adoption. And co-branding may be a valuable means to learn about consumers and how other companies approach them. Companies within the motor industry have reaped all these benefits of co-branding.

The potential disadvantages of co-branding are the risks and lack of control in becoming aligned with another brand in the minds of consumers. Consumer expectations about the level of involvement and commitment with co-brands are likely to be high, so unsatisfactory performance could have negative repercussions for both brands. If the other brand has entered into a number of co-branding arrangements, overexposure may dilute the transfer of any association. It may also result in a lack of focus on existing brands.

For co-branding to succeed, the two brands must separately have brand equity – adequate brand awareness and a sufficiently positive brand image. The most important requirement is a logical fit between the two brands, such that the combined brand or marketing activity maximises the advantages of each while minimising their disadvantages. Research studies show that consumers are more apt to perceive co-brands favourably if the two brands are complementary rather than similar.[43]

Besides remembering these strategic considerations, managers must enter into co-branding ventures carefully. There must be the right kind of fit in values, capabilities and goals, in addition to an appropriate balance of brand equity. There must be detailed plans to legalise contracts, make financial arrangements and coordinate marketing programmes. The financial arrangement between brands may vary, although one common approach is for the brand more deeply involved in the production process to pay a licensing fee and royalty.

Brand alliances require a number of decisions. What capabilities does a firm lack? What resource constraints is the firm facing (people, time, money, etc.)? What are the growth goals or revenue needs? In assessing a joint branding opportunity, a firm should satisfy itself that it is a profitable business venture. How might it help maintain or strengthen brand equity? Is there any risk of dilution of brand equity? Does the opportunity offer any extrinsic advantages such as learning opportunities?

Ingredient branding

Ingredient branding is a special case of co-branding. It creates brand equity for materials, components or parts that are necessarily contained within other branded products. Some successful ingredient brands include Dolby noise reduction, Gore-Tex water-resistant fibres,[44] Intel processors and Scotchgard fabrics. Ingredient branding is growing in an area known as 'nutraceuticals' – food products, such as Actimel, that claim they deliver health benefit properties.

An interesting variation on ingredient branding is 'self-branding', in which companies advertise and even trademark their own branded ingredients. For instance, stately homes all over Europe advertise crockery, foodstuffs and linen bearing their insignia in site-based shops and specialist magazines. If it can be done well, it makes much more sense to self-brand ingredients because you have more control and can develop the ingredient to suit your purposes.[45] Ingredient brands try to create enough awareness and preference for their market offerings so consumers will not buy a 'host' product that does not contain the brand badge.

Many manufacturers make components or materials that enter into final branded products but lose their individual identity. One of the few component branders that have succeeded in building a separate identity is Intel. Intel's consumer-directed brand

Marketing memo

Making ingredient branding work

What are the requirements for success in ingredient branding?

1 Customers must perceive that the ingredient matters to the performance and success of the end product. Ideally, this intrinsic value is easily seen or experienced.

2 Customers must be convinced that not all ingredient brands are the same and that the ingredient is superior.

3 A distinctive symbol or logo must clearly signal to customers that the host product contains the ingredient. Ideally, the symbol or logo would function like a 'seal', be simple and versatile, and credibly communicate quality and confidence.

4 A coordinated 'pull' and 'push' programme must help customers understand the importance and advantages of the branded ingredient. Channel members must offer full support. Often this will require consumer advertising and promotions and – sometimes in collaboration with manufacturers – retail merchandising and promotion programmes.

Sources: K. L. Keller (2008) *Strategic Brand Management*, 3rd edn, Upper Saddle River, NJ: Prentice Hall; P. Kotler and W. Pfoertsch (2006) *B2B Brand Management*, New York: Springer; P. F. Nunes, S. F. Dull and P. D. Lynch (2003) When two brands are better than one, *Outlook*, January, 14–23.

campaign convinced many personal computer buyers to buy only computer brands with 'Intel Inside'. As a result, major PC manufacturers – IBM, Dell, Compaq – purchase their chips from Intel at a premium price rather than buy equivalent chips from an unknown supplier. Most component manufacturers, however, would find it difficult to create a successful ingredient brand. The marketing memo outlines the characteristics of successful ingredient branding.

Packaging, labelling, warranties and guarantees

Most physical items must be packaged and labelled. Some packages – such as the Coke bottle and the L'eggs ladies' tights egg-shaped pack – are world famous. Many marketers have called packaging a fifth P, along with price, product, place and promotion. Most marketers, however, treat packaging and labelling as an important element of product strategy. It could also be seen as an important part of marketing communications and distribution. Cost is an important consideration too. So it is best to see packaging as part of the overall activity of companies that seeks to develop highly regarded customer-perceived value offerings which enable businesses to achieve a sustainable competitive advantage. Warranties and guarantees can also be an important part of the market offering, as they often appear on the packaging.

Packaging

Packaging is traditionally defined as all the activities of designing and producing the container for a product or market offering. Packages might include up to three levels of material – beer comes in a bottle or can (*primary package*) in a cardboard box (*secondary package*) and in a palette box (*shipping package*).

Well-designed packages can build brand equity and drive sales. The package is the customers' first encounter with the item and either impresses or disinterests them. Absolut vodka and Coca-Cola are world famous for their distinctive bottles. Toblerone confectionery is well known for its famous triangular shape and packaging. Expensive cereals feature see-through plastic windows in packaging to emphasise the quality of the contents. Packaging also affects consumers' later product experiences – good packaging, for example, protects the item after first opening and keeps it in good condition for subsequent use. Various factors have contributed to the growing use of packaging as a marketing tool:

- **Self-service.** An increasing number of product items are sold on a self-service basis. In an average supermarket, which stocks 15,000 items, the typical shopper passes by some 300 items per minute. Given that 50–70 per cent of all purchases are made in the shop, the effective package must perform many of the sales tasks: attract attention, describe the product's features, create consumer confidence and make a favourable overall impression.
- **Consumer affluence.** Rising consumer affluence means consumers are willing to pay a little more for the convenience, appearance, dependability and prestige of the better-packaged items.
- **Company and brand image.** Packages contribute to instant recognition of the company or brand. In a shop they can effectively advertise the item.
- **Innovation opportunity.** Innovative and unique packaging design can bring large benefits to consumers and profits to producers. Companies are incorporating materials and features such as tamper-proof packs.

From the perspective of both the firm and consumers, packaging must achieve six objectives:[46]

1 identify the brand in an attractive way;
2 convey descriptive and persuasive information;
3 provide protection to facilitate transportation;
4 assist at-home storage;
5 aid product consumption; and
6 be environmentally friendly on disposal.

To achieve the marketing objectives for the brand and satisfy the desires of consumers, marketers must choose the aesthetic and functional components of packaging correctly. Aesthetic considerations relate to a package's size and shape, material, colour, text and graphics. Blue is cool and serene, red is active and lively, yellow is medicinal and weak, pastel colours are feminine, dark colours are masculine. Functionally, structural design is crucial. For example, innovations with food products over the years have resulted in packages that are resealable, tamper-proof, and more convenient to use (easy to hold, easy to open, or squeezable). The packaging elements must harmonise with each other and with pricing, advertising and other parts of the marketing programme.

Packaging changes can have an immediate impact on sales. A good example is the book publishing industry, where customers often quite literally choose a book by its cover: Penguin Books has repackaged most of its titles and promoted them under the banner, 'Classic Books, Fresh Looks'.[47] Packaging changes can come in all forms. Kleenex tissues' seasonally themed oval-shaped boxes and Crest toothpaste's beauty-product-inspired Vivid White packaging all led to sales increases.[48]

After the company designs its packaging, it must test it. *Engineering tests* ensure that the package stands up under normal conditions; *visual tests*, that the script is legible and the colours harmonious; *dealer tests*, that dealers find the packages attractive and easy to handle; and *consumer tests*, that buyers will respond favourably. Eye tracking by hidden cameras can assess how much consumers notice and examine packages.[49]

Environmental costs of packaging
Source: Serif

Although developing effective packaging may be expensive and take several months to complete, companies must pay attention to growing environmental and safety concerns to reduce packaging. Increasingly, many companies are recognising the importance of going 'green' and are finding new ways to develop their packaging. Disposal of used packaging is rapidly becoming a major concern in many countries as landfill sites come under strain and as the EU fines for poor recycling practices begin to bite. In the United Kingdom many supermarkets either choose not to supply plastic carrier bags or sell temporary shopping bags at a slight penalty cost. Most, however, also promote the sales of environmentally friendly multiple-use bags, often sourced in underdeveloped economies.

Plastic packaging: an ecological disaster?

The overuse of plastic materials in packaging is stimulating passionate debate as they are not easily biodegraded. Many cardboard packs have plastic lids or spouts. Few drinks such as milk and fruit juice seem to be offered in glass bottles that are biodegradable. Most of the popular mineral waters such as Evian and Volvic are supplied in plastic polyethylene terephthalate (PET) bottles and even the niche brands such as San Pellegrino and Perrier seem to be abandoning their glass bottles. All is not doom and gloom, however, as some ecologically sensitive companies are starting to experiment with the use of reusable packaging. Danone, for example, is now supplying supermarkets in Belgium with yogurts in small brown earthenware pots that can be washed out and reused.[50]

In 2008 the UK produced around 2 million tonnes of plastic waste, twice as much as in the early 1990s. In 2008, total generation of post-consumer plastic waste in the EU-27, Norway and Switzerland was 24.9 Mt. Packaging is by far the largest contributor to plastic waste at 63 per cent. Average EU-27 per-capita generation of plastic packaging waste was 30.6 kg in 2007. Several end-of-life options exist to deal with plastic waste, including recycling, disposal and incineration with or without energy recovery. The plastics recycling rate was 21.3 per cent in 2008, helping to drive total recovery (energy recovery and recycling) to 51.3 per cent. The highest rate of recycling is seen in Germany at 34 per cent and the lowest in Greece at 8 per cent. The very qualities of plastic – its cheapness, its indestructible aura – make it hubristic, perhaps a reproachful symbol of an unsustainable way of life. However, plastics do have their plus points. There are more than 20 types of polymer to choose from and many can be blended to offer designers and manufacturers a limitless variety of options. There is the clarity of PET, used in most plastic bottles and trays; the strength of high-density polyethylene (HDPE), the cloudier polymer that is used in milk bottles; and easy-sealing polypropylene (PP), which is used to make bags and films.

Kimberly-Clark has dressed up its Kleenex products in any number of vivid new package designs including boxes with seasonal themes.
Source: Bill Aron/PhotoEdit Inc.

Plastics even have an important positive ecological advantage – a little of the material goes a long way. Furthermore, plastic materials are light and while they encase over 50 per cent of the items that are bought, they only account for 20 per cent by weight of the packaging that is consumed. Thus less energy is needed to transport plastic-packed goods. This is the main reason why it remains the packaging material of choice for many product offerings. It is actually good for the environment as it reduces the carbon footprint – a classic case of there being two sides to every story. Now the righteous indignation of the ecologists may begin to look irrational.

Might it be possible to gain the benefits of plastic packaging without its associated recycling problems? Curiously enough, the answer is yes. Cellulose, the most abundant organic compound on earth, is the main ingredient of cellophane, which was first used in Switzerland after its invention there in 1908. So why not consider abandoning oil-based plastics in favour of biodegradable ones? Research into environmentally renewable polymers has been gathering pace since the 1980s. Polyactic acid (PLA) and other starch-based polymers from sugar cane, potatoes, corn and wheat have emerged as the likeliest packaging materials. Worldwide polymer production increased from 20,000 tons a year in 1996 to over 400,000 tons in 2008 before falling back as a result of the financial crisis that followed the collapse and near collapse of many banks.[51]

However, there is a real problem with biodegradable plastic packaging – it looks the same as oil-based plastic packaging and so presents an insurmountable recycling problem. Perhaps this could be solved by households all over Europe being supplied with a separate recycling bin and by biodegradable plastic packaging carrying a distinctive image on the label.

Cordier Mestrezat breaks with tradition and packages Bordeaux in plastic cartons

Purists have been challenged by a French fine wine brand to sip their wine through a straw rather than pour it from a bottle into a wine glass. In June 2008 Cordier began supplying the new packs to supermarkets in a determined effort by the company to boost wine consumption among young urbanites. The new packs are biodegradable and come with a 'sensory straw' to send a spray of wine around the palate and to 'ensure that customers enjoy the same sensations as with a wine glass'. Wine experts have expressed their horror, as the wine's bouquet and colour will not be able to be appreciated in the conventional way. Cordier responded to the purists' protests by emphasising the serious state of the wine industry in France, where consumption is falling from 100 litres per person to 54 litres, and the need to move with the times.

Source: A. Sage (2008) Is Bordeaux in cartons the last straw for French wine?, *The Times*, 16 May.

Cardboard packaging is more ecologically friendly

The fast-food burger chain McDonald's has franchised many restaurants across Europe and this has generated a considerable amount of packaging. The company has gone to considerable trouble to see that its packaging is biodegradable and recycled.

McDonald's burger and fries cardboard packaging is environmentally friendly.
Source: © mediablitzimages (UK) Ltd/Alamy.

Packaging power

Special packs are often designed for low-risk trial. The UK Dulux paint company offers mini-pots to enable potential customers to see what the paint colours and textures will look like in the at-home situation. Multiple packs are increasingly found in supermarkets across Europe and seek to sell more and more alcoholic and non-alcoholic drinks. As a fully integrated marketing communications campaign is usually expensive (see Chapter 19), many companies pay particular attention to developing effective and efficient packaging. At certain times during the year, the pack assumes a great deal of importance. In the United Kingdom, chocolate Easter eggs are presented in elaborately designed packaging; and high-value items such as expensive jewellery and watches usually feature expensive packaging.

Distinctive packaging is usually protected in European countries by law to prevent pirating. In the United Kingdom packaging is covered by the 1994 Trade Marks Act. To convey value to the buyer, some companies place their offerings in over-size boxes, which is a practice that can be challenged in the EU.

Labelling

The label may be a simple tag attached to the item or an elaborately designed graphic that is part of the package. It might carry only the brand name, or a great deal of information. Even if the seller prefers a simple label, the legal regulations may require more.

Labels perform five functions:[52]

1 The label *identifies* the product or brand – for instance, the name Jaffa stamped on oranges. It also states the ingredients.
2 The label might also *grade* the item.
3 The label might *describe* the item: who made it, where it was made, when it was made, what it contains, how it is to be used, and how to use it safely. Cigarette packs in the United Kingdom warn buyers that smoking can damage their health.
4 The labels on food items increasingly *carry messages* about healthy eating.
5 The label might *promote* the product through attractive graphics. New technology allows for 360-degree shrink-wrapped labels to surround containers with bright graphics and accommodate more on-pack product information, replacing paper labels glued on to cans and bottles.

Quality labels usually indicate a quality market offering. Eventually they become outmoded and need freshening up. Companies with labels that have become icons need to tread very carefully when initiating a redesign.

The Campbell Soup Company

The Campbell Soup Company has estimated that the average shopper sees its familiar red-and-white can 76 times a year, creating the equivalent of millions of dollars' worth of advertising. Its label is such an icon that pop artist Andy Warhol immortalised it in one of his silk screens in the 1960s. The original Campbell's Soup label – with its scripted name and signature red and white – was designed in 1898, and the company did not redesign it until more than a century later, in 1999. With the goal of making the label more contemporary and making it easier for customers to find individual soups, Campbell made the famous script logo smaller and featured a photo of a steaming bowl of the soup flavour. In addition to the new graphic, the company put nutritional information on the packaging, with serving suggestions, quick dinner ideas and coloured bands that identify the six subgroups of condensed soup: that is, creams, broths and so on.[53]

The company's European business in greater Europe is headquartered in Puurs, Belgium, and includes businesses in Belgium, France, Germany, Russia and Scandinavia. Campbell's has production facilities in Puurs, Belgium; LePontet, France; Utrecht, Netherlands; and Lübeck, Germany.

While attractive and clear labelling reinforces a company's brand, it can also be used to mislead potential customers. Some firms claim that their wares are made in the home country, whereas they may be made elsewhere and merely packaged in the domestic market. Some food packs are deliberately scented in order to provide a pleasurable experience when the package is opened. Foods may carry evocative claims such as 'country fresh' or make questionable health claims. In the United Kingdom, the Food Standards Agency keeps a wary eye on labelling practice. Throughout Europe, national and EU laws protect consumers from the worst labelling practices.

Warranties and guarantees

Even the best businesses are sometimes faced with a customer who is not satisfied with the goods they have bought or who simply wants their money back. Alongside improved consumer protection legislation, awareness of consumer rights has increased dramatically over the last 30 years – and so have people's expectations of the sort of redress they can expect when the market offerings are not up to an acceptable standard. Anyone in business who provides market offerings should be aware of their obligations to customers.

All sellers are legally responsible for fulfilling a buyer's normal or reasonable expectations. **Warranties** are formal statements of expected product/market offering performance by the manufacturer. Products under warranty can be returned to the manufacturer or designated repair centre for repair, replacement or refund. Whether expressed or implied, warranties are legally enforceable. Wise companies will extend their warranties if there are good reasons to do so. In some cases they are obliged to do so to retain market credibility if they have been unfavourably exposed by a consumer body. Samsung decided to extend the warranty on its R21 refrigerator in the United Kingdom in May 2008 after a fault was exposed in the popular BBC TV consumer affairs programme *Watchdog*. Similarly, when several viewers complained of skin irritation (subsequently found to be caused by a fungicide sachet) after buying leather sofas manufactured by Linkwise, retailers Argos, Land of Leather and the high street chain Walmsley's eventually agreed to return customers' money and to stop trading with Linkwise.

Extended warranties – are they all they claim to be?

The UK government's Consumer Direct Unit urges people to think carefully about the value for money they are offered by an extended warranty because it is likely to be expensive compared with the amount customers could normally pay out in repair costs. Some people forget that the goods they buy new have a manufacturer's guarantee which usually lasts for one year, so there is no need to buy an extended warranty when they buy the goods.

If consumers decide that they would like a warranty, they do not have to buy one at the shop where they bought the goods. There are a number of firms – including insurance companies and the manufacturers themselves – that sell extended warranties on everyday household goods, from toasters to computers. In some cases they may be cheaper and more comprehensive than retailers' extended warranties. It is now also possible to buy warranties that cover a number of appliances, such as all the electrical equipment in the kitchen. So it is certainly a good idea to shop around for some quotes before signing up to a warranty.

The law also requires retailers to provide certain information on warranties they are selling, and consumers may get rights to cancel their extended warranty if they choose to do so. Consumer Direct offers advice on its website.

Source: Consumer Direct: www.consumerdirect.gov.uk/

Extended warranties can be extremely lucrative for manufacturers and retailers. Despite being regularly challenged as to their real worth in the United Kingdom, many retailers still attempt to market them robustly. Electrical appliance stores and home computer shops have become infamous for pushing (bullying) customers into purchasing additional 'peace of mind' cover. Many sellers offer either general guarantees or specific guarantees. A company such as Procter & Gamble promises general or complete satisfaction without being more specific – 'If you are not satisfied for any reason, return for replacement, exchange or refund.' Other companies offer specific and in some cases extraordinary guarantees:

- The John Lewis Partnership promises that it is 'never knowingly undersold' and if challenged on price will investigate. If the customer is right, it will immediately lower its price.
- Marks & Spencer will exchange clothing items that are found to be the wrong size provided the goods are returned in good condition with the appropriate invoice.
- British Gas guarantees its domestic central heating installations and promises prompt and efficient service if anything goes wrong.

Guarantees reduce the buyer's perceived risk. They suggest that the product is of high quality and that the company and its service performance are dependable. They can be especially helpful when the company or product (market offering) is not that well known or when the product's quality is superior to competitors.

SUMMARY

1 Because economic conditions change and competitive activity varies, companies normally find it necessary to reformulate their marketing strategy several times during a product's life cycle. Technologies, product forms and brands also exhibit life cycles with distinct stages. The general sequence of stages in any life cycle is introduction, growth, maturity and decline. The majority of products today are in the maturity stage.

2 Each stage of the product life cycle calls for different marketing strategies. The introduction stage is marked by slow growth and minimal profits. If successful, the product enters a growth stage marked by rapid sales growth and increasing profits. There follows a maturity stage in which sales growth slows and profits stabilise. Finally, the product enters a decline stage. The company's task is to identify the truly weak products, develop a strategy for each one, and phase out weak products in a way that minimises the hardship to company profits, employees and customers.

3 Like products, markets evolve through four stages: emergence, growth, maturity and decline. This necessitates coordinated decisions on product mixes, product lines, brands, and packaging and labelling.

4 In planning its market offering, the marketer needs to think through the five levels of the product: the core benefit, the basic product, the expected product, the augmented product and the potential product, which encompasses all the augmentations and transformations that the product might ultimately undergo.

5 Products can be classified in several ways. In terms of durability and reliability, products can be non-durable goods, durable goods or services. In the consumer goods category, products are convenience goods (staples, impulse goods and emergency goods), shopping goods (homogeneous and heterogeneous), speciality goods or unsought goods. In the industrial goods category, products fall into one of three categories: materials and parts (raw materials and manufactured materials and parts), capital items (installations and equipment), or supplies and business services (operating supplies, maintenance and repair items, maintenance and repair services, and business advisory services).

6 Brands can be differentiated on the basis of a number of different product or service dimensions: product form, features, performance, conformance, durability, reliability, repair ability, style and design, as well as such service dimensions as ordering ease, delivery, installation, customer training, customer consulting, and maintenance and repair.

7 Most companies sell more than one product. A product mix can be classified according to width, length, depth and consistency. These four dimensions are the tools for developing the company's marketing strategy and deciding which product lines to grow,

maintain, harvest and divest. To analyse a product line and decide how many resources should be invested in that line, product-line managers need to look at sales and profits and market profile.

8 A company can change the product component of its marketing mix by lengthening its product via line stretching (down market, up market, or both) or line filling, by modernising its products, by featuring certain products, and by pruning its products to eliminate the least profitable.

9 Brands are often sold or marketed jointly with other brands. Ingredient brands and co-brands can add value, assuming they have equity and are perceived as fitting appropriately.

10 Physical products must be packaged and labelled. Well-designed packages can create convenience value for customers and promotional value for producers. In effect, they can act as 'five-second commercials' for the product. Warranties and guarantees can offer further assurance to consumers.

APPLICATIONS

Marketing debate

With products, is it form or function? The 'form versus function' debate applies in many arenas, including marketing. Some marketers believe that product performance is the be all and end all. Other marketers maintain that the looks, feel and other design elements of products are what really make the difference.

Take a position: Product functionality is the key to brand success *versus* Product design is the key to brand success.

Marketing discussion

Can products be totally differentiated from services? Can products (i.e. tangible items) and services (intangible items) really be separated from customer-perceived value offerings in contemporary sellers' markets? (See argument in Chapters 3, 10 and 11.)

REFERENCES

[1]B. Upton (1999) Sharpening the claws, *Forbes*, 26 July, 102–5.

[2]R. Reed (1987) Fashion life-cycles and extension theory, *European Journal of Marketing*, 21(3), 52–62; T. Clark (2004) The fashion of management fashion: a surge too far? *Organization*, 11(2), 297–306.

[3]R. J. Chandy, G. J. Tellis, D. J. MacInnis and P. Thaivanich (2001) What to say when: advertising appeals in evolving markets, *Journal of Marketing Research*, November, 399–414; H-K. Wong and P. D. Ellis (2007) Is market orientation affected by the product life cycle? *Journal of World Business*, 42(2), 145–56.

[4]C. Nuttall (2005) Intel ventures beyond PCs, *Financial Times*, 12 November; C. Edwards (2006) Inside Intel, *BusinessWeek*, 9 January, 52–3; C. Edwards (2006) AMD: chipping away at Intels's lead, *BusinessWeek*, 12 June, 72–3.

[5]S. P. Schnaars (1994) *Managing Imitation Strategies*, New York: Free Press. See also J. K. Han, N. Kim and H. B. Kin (2001) Entry barriers: a dull-, one-, or two-edged sword for incumbents? Unravelling the paradox from a contingency perspective, *Journal of Marketing*, January, 1–14.

[6]V. Kegan (2002) Second sight: second movers take all, *Guardian*, 10 October; M. Kopel and C. Löffler (2008) Commitment, first-mover-, and second-mover advantage, *Journal of Economics*, 94(2), 143–66.

[7]P. N. Golder (2000) Historical method of marketing research with new evidence on long-term of marketing share stability, *Journal of Marketing Research*, 37 (May), 156–72.

[8]G. Tellis and P. Golder (2001) *Will and Vision: How Latecomers Can Grow to Dominate Markets*, New York: McGraw-Hill; P. N. Golder and G. J. Tellis (2004) Growing, growing, gone: cascades, diffusion, and turning points in the product life cycle, *Marketing Science*, 23(2), 207–18.

[9]S. Min, M. U. Kalwani and W. Robinson (2006) Market pioneer and early follower survival risks: a contingency analysis of really new versus incrementally new product-markets, *Journal of Marketing*, 70 (January), 15–35. See also R. Srinwasan, G. L. Lilien and A. Rangaswamy (2004) First in, first out? The effects of network externalities on pioneer survival, *Journal of Marketing*, 68 (January), 41–58; L. Löfqvist (2010) Product and process novelty in small companies' design processes, *Creativity and Innovation Management*, 19(4), 405–16.

[10]M. Palmer (2006) Internal provider loyalty hard to find, *Financial Times*, April.

[11]R. B. Trond (2006) Escaping the middle-market trap: an interview with the CEO of Electrolux, *McKinsey Quarterly*, 4, 72–9.

[12]P. Kotler (1965) Phasing out weak products, *Harvard Business Review*, March–April, 107–18; R. Varadarajan, M. P. DeFanti

and P. S. Busch (2006) Brand portfolio, corporate image, and reputation: managing brand deletions, *Journal of the Academy of Marketing Science*, 34 (Spring), 195–205; N. Kumar (2003) Kill a brand, keep a customer, *Harvard Business Review*, 81 (December), 86–95; H. Mao, X. Luo and S. P. Jain (2009) Consumer responses to brand elimination: an attributional perspective, *Journal of Consumer Psychology*, 19(3), 280–9; C. Homburg, A. Fürst and J-K. Prigge (2010) A customer perspective on product eliminations: how the removal of products affects customers and business relationships, *Journal of the Academy of Marketing Science*, 38(5), 531–49.

[13]K. R. Harrigan (1980) The effect of exit barriers upon strategic flexibility, *Strategic Management Journal*, 1, 165–76; R. Baptista and M. Karaöz (2011) Turbulence in growing and declining industries, *Small Business Economics*, 36(3), 249–70.

[14]P. Kotler (1978) Harvesting strategies for weak products, *Business Horizons*, August, 15–22; L. P. Feldman and A. L. Page (1985) Harvesting: the misunderstood market exit strategy, *Journal of Business Strategy*, Spring, 79–85.

[15]Golder and Tellis (2004) op. cit.

[16]C. Crawford (1992) Business took the wrong life cycle from biology, *Journal of Product and Brand Management*, 1, 51–7; L. M. Grantham (1997) The validity of the product life cycle in the high-tech industry, *Journal of Marketing Intelligence and Planning*, 15(1), 4–10.

[17]Y. Moon (2005) Break free from the product life cycle, *Harvard Business Review*, May, 87–94.

[18]R. D. Buzzell (1999) Market functions and market evolution, *Journal of Marketing*, 63 (Special Issue), 61–3; H. Gatignon and D. Soberman (2002) Competitive response and market evolution, in B. A. Weitz and R. Wensley (eds), *Handbook of Marketing*, London: Sage, 126–47; F. Wang and X-P. Zhang (2008) Reasons for market evolution and budgeting implications, *Journal of Marketing*, 72(5), 15–30; I. Abel (2008) From technology imitation to market dominance: the case of iPod, *Competitiveness Review*, 18(3), 257–74.

[19]D. Fisher (2003) Six feet under, *Forbes*, 7 July; see also for strategic moves in mature and declining markets, www.scribd.com/doc/39546372/Mature-and-Declining-Markets, 66–8.

[20]This discussion is adapted from T. Levitt (1980) Marketing success through differentiation: of anything, *Harvard Business Review*, January–February, 83–91. The first level, core benefit, has been added to Levitt's discussion.

[21]J. Willman and W. MacNamara (2007) An uplifting experience, *Financial Times*, 6 September; see also www.sulzerpumps.com/desktopdefault.aspx.

[22]P. Kedrosky (2005) Feature fatigue: when product capabilities become too much of a good thing, *Journal of Marketing Research*, 42 (November), 431–42.

[23]J. H. Gilmore and B. J. Pine (2000) *Markets of One: Creating Customer-Unique Value through Mass Customization*, Boston, MA: Harvard Business School Press; R. I. McIntosh, J. Matthews, G. Mullineux and A. J. Medland (2010) Late customisation: issues of mass customisation in the food industry, *International Journal of Production Research*, 48(6), 1557–74.

[24]S. Elliott (2006) Letting consumers control marketing: priceless, *New York Times*, 9 October.

[25]P. Grimaldi (2006) Consumers design products their way, *Knight Rider Tribune Business News*, 25 November; M. A. Prospero (2005) *Fast Company*, September, 35.

[26]G. Edmundson (2006) Mercedes gets back up to speed, *BusinessWeek*, 12 November, 46–7.

[27]B. Nussbaum (2004) The power of design, *BusinessWeek*, 17 May, 88–94. See also P. Kotler (1984) Design: a powerful but neglected strategic tool, *Journal of Business Strategy*, Fall, 16–21; G. Gabrielsen, T. Kristensen and J. L. Zaichkowsky (2010) Whose design is it anyway?, *International Journal of Market Research*, 52(1), 89–110.

[28]S. Reed (2005) Rolls-Royce at your service, *BusinessWeek*, 15 November, 92–3.

[29]This section is based on a comprehensive treatment of product returns: J. Stock and T. Speh (2006) Managing product returns for competitive advantage, *MIT Sloan Management Review*, Fall, 57–62; J. D. Shulman, A. T. Coughlan and R. C. Savaskan (2010) Optimal reverse channel structure for consumer product returns, *Marketing Science*, 29(6), 1071–85; R. Ramanathan (2011) An empirical analysis on the influence of risk on relationships between handling of product returns and customer loyalty in E-commerce, *International Journal of Production Economics*, 130(2), 255–61.

[30]R. Bordley (2003) Determining the appropriate depth and breadth of a firm's product portfolio, *Journal of Marketing Research*, 40 (February), 39–53; P. Boatwright and J. C. Nunes (2001) Reducing assortment: an attitude-based approach, *Journal of Marketing*, 65 (July), 50–63.

[31]Adapted from a Hamilton Consultants White Paper, 1 December 2000.

[32]This illustration is found in B. P. Shapiro (1977) *Industrial Product Policy: Managing the Existing Product Line*, Cambridge, MA: Marketing Science Institute, 3–5, 98–101.

[33]Brand challenge (2002) *The Economist*, 6 April, 68.

[34]F. Leclerc, C. K. Hsee and J. C. Nunes (2005) Narrow focusing: why the relative position of a good in its category matters more than it should, *Marketing Science*, 24 (Spring), 194–205.

[35]N. E. Boudette (2005) BMW's push to broaden line hits some bumps in the road, *Wall Street Journal*, 25 January; A. Taylor III (2004) The ultimate fairly inexpensive driving machine, *Fortune*, 1 November, 130–40.

[36]N. Kumar (2003) Kill a brand, keep a customer, *Harvard Business Review*, December, 86–95; B. Stone (2003) Back to basics, *Newsweek*, 4 August, 42–4; C. Eckel and J. P. Neary (2010) Multiproduct firms and flexible manufacturing in the global economy, *Review of Economic Studies*, 77(1), 188–217.

[37]L. M. Sloot, D. Fok and P. Verhoef (2006) The short- and long-term impact of an assortment reduction on category sales, *Journal of Marketing Research*, 43 (November), 536–48.

[38]P. O'Connell (2001) A chat with Unilever's Niall Fitzgerald, *BusinessWeek* Online, 2 August; J. Willman (2000) Leaner, cleaner and healthier is the stated aim, *Financial Times*, 23 February; Unilever's goal: power brands, *Advertising Age*, 3 January 2000; see also Unilever investor seminar (2007).

[39]G. Radler, J. Kubes and B. Wojnar (2006) Skoda auto: from 'no-class' to world-class in a decade, *Critical EYE*, 15 July.

[40]B. Elgin (2003) Can HP's printer biz keep printing money?, *BusinessWeek*, 14 July, 68–70.

[41]D. Soman and J. T. Gourville (2001) Transaction decoupling: how price bundling affects the decision to consume, *Journal of Marketing Research*, 38 (February), 30–44; J. Kim, D. C. Bojanic and R. B. Warnick (2009) Price bundling and travel product pricing practices used by online channels of distribution, *Journal of Travel Research*, 47(4), 403–12; R. Arora (2011) Bundling or unbundling frequently purchased products: a mixed method approach, *Journal of Consumer Marketing*, 28(1), 67–75.

[42]Adapted from G. Wuebeker (2002) Bundles effectiveness often undermined, *Marketing News*, 18 March, 9–12; S. Stremersch and G. J. Trellis (2002) Strategic bundling of products and prices, *Journal of Marketing*, 66 (January), 55–72.

[43]L. Leuthesser, C. Kohli and R. Suri (2003) 2 + 2 = 5? A framework for using co-branding to leverage a brand, *Journal of Brand Management*, 2(1), 35–47; A. Besharat (2010) How co-branding versus brand extensions drive consumers' evaluations of new products: a brand equity approach, *Industrial Marketing Management*, 39(8), 1240–9 ; P. C. M. Cornelis (2010) Effects of co-branding in the theme park industry: a preliminary study, *International Journal of Contemporary Hospitality Management*, 22(6), 775–96; A. Stokes and T. D. Jensen (2011) Co-branding: the effects of e-tailer and delivery carrier familiarity on price and e-tailer perceptions, *Journal of Marketing Theory and Practice*, 19(1), 97–100.

[44]WL Gore and Associates: GoreTex manufacturer (2007) *The Sunday Times*, 11 March; S. Erevelles, Sunil, T. H. Stevenson, S. Shuba and N. Fukawa (2008) An analysis of B2B ingredient co-branding relationships, *Industrial Marketing Management*, 37(8), 940–52.

[45]K. K. Desai and K. L. Keller (2002) The effects of brand expansions and ingredient branding strategies on host brand extendibility, *Journal of Marketing*, 66 (January), 73–93.

[46]P. Gander (2008) Waste not, want not, *Design Week*, 6 December Supplement, 9–11; for objectives of packaging and labelling, see also www.newworldencyclopedia.org/entry/Packaging_and_labeling

[47]K. Springen (2004) Nancy's still nice, *Newsweek*, 16 February; J. Rosen (2003) Classics' strategies: classics' sales, *Publishers Weekly*, 6 October, 16–18; O. Ampuero and N. Vila (2006) Consumer perceptions of product packaging, *Journal of Consumer Marketing*, 23(2), 100–12.

[48]S. Hamner (2006) Packaging that pays, *Business 2.0*, July, 68–9.

[49]M. Frazier (2006) How can your package stand out? Eye tracking looks hard for answers, *Advertising Age*, 16 October, 14; J. Park (2008) September Research form puts shoppers' gaze in focus, *Packaging News*, 28.

[50]N. Tait (2008) I gave up plastic for Lent, *Financial Times*, 26 April.

[51]S. Knight (2008) Plastic: the elephant in the room, *Financial Times Arts and Weekend Magazine*, 25 April.

[52]S. Hartlieb and B. Jones (2009) Humanising business through ethical labelling: progress and paradoxes in the UK, *Journal of Business Ethics*, 88(3), 583–600; S. Katz (2010) When function trumps form, *Beauty Packaging*, 15(8), 16–24.

[53]K. Novack (2004) Tomato soup with a side of pop art, *Time*, 10 May; Campbell Soup Co. changes the look of its famous cans (1999) *Wall Street Journal*, 26 August.

Chapter 15

Introducing new market offerings

IN THIS CHAPTER, WE WILL ADDRESS THE FOLLOWING QUESTIONS:

1 What challenges does a company face in developing new customer-perceived value (CPV) offerings (products and services)?

2 What organisational structures and processes do managers use to develop new market offerings?

3 What are the main stages in developing new market offerings?

4 What is the best way to manage the process of developing new market offerings?

5 What factors affect the rate of diffusion and consumer adoption of newly launched market offerings?

Dyson knows the value of innovation and new-product development. The company's engineers are continuously seeking to innovate and see the establishment of the new design and engineering school in 2010 as a major part of the Dyson mission.

Source: Rex Features.

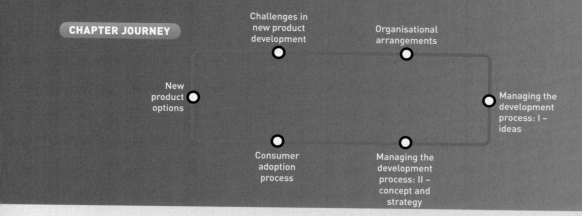

CHAPTER JOURNEY

Challenges in new product development

Organisational arrangements

New product options

Managing the development process: I – ideas

Consumer adoption process

Managing the development process: II – concept and strategy

Firms all over the world are challenged by the need in highly competitive buyers' markets to innovate new products. The term 'product' in this chapter, following the argument in Chapter 14, refers to a market offering that is a package of tangible (product) and intangible (service) attributes and benefits. Marketers play a key role in the development of new market offerings by identifying and evaluating new ideas and working with R & D personnel and other functional areas in every stage of development. Companies need to grow their revenue over time by developing new market offerings (products) and by expanding into new markets. New product development shapes the company's future. Improved or replacement products can maintain or build sales; new-to-the-world products can transform industries and companies and change lives. However, the low success rate of new products and services points to the many challenges involved. More and more companies are doing more than just talking about innovation. They are fundamentally changing the way they develop their new CPV market offerings.

Look how Sir James Dyson has and is approaching this all-important task.

To encourage and to improve the speed of development of new product innovations Sir James Dyson, who invented the 'bagless' vacuum cleaner, remains keen to encourage design and engineering education and training, despite having his plans for a school turned down when the UK government rejected his funding bid in 2008. The main Dyson website carries an invitation for young would-be engineers to spend some time with the company and learn what they do.

The dual cyclone 'bagless' cleaner took five years to develop and it was a further two years before Sir James managed to obtain financial backing in Japan. Using income from the Japanese licence, he began to manufacture a new model under his own name in the United Kingdom in 1993. The new concept and colourful design of his cleaners resulted in much popular acclaim and his 'bagless' vacuum cleaners now have 46 per cent of the UK market. In addition to the cleaners, Sir James has a number of other inventions carrying his name, including the Sea Truck, the award-winning Ballbarrow, as well as the Trolleyball, a trolley that makes it easier to launch boats, and the less successful Wheelboat, which can travel at speeds of up to 64 km/h on both land and water. To revive falling sales in the vacuum cleaner business in 2005, Sir James incorporated his Dyson Ball™ technology into a new version of the Dyson vacuum cleaner principle to create the more manoeuvrable

DC25 model. This offers the tried and trusted benefits from Root Cyclone™ technology and is easy to operate as it has no wheels and can pivot easily round awkward corners as it cleans.

However, Dyson has suffered several setbacks on its way to becoming an iconic company. Sir James advises companies to 'Enjoy failure and learn from it. You can never learn from success.' The most notable was the early failure of the company's venture into the washing machine market. After making heavy losses, the company pulled out of the market but it has recently announced a determination to re-enter it. Sir James hopes that his enthusiastic support of the need to train new designers and engineers will do much to reclaim some of the lost appeal following the company's decision for economic reasons to move its manufacturing base from the United Kingdom to Malaysia.[1]

New market offering options

The following sections review several ways in which companies innovate as they strive to achieve an evolving portfolio of new market offerings. Is there one best way to manage this process that involves specific managers and executives? Or perhaps the creation of new products is really about a coordinated effort involving everyone within the company as well as key organisations in the company's value chain.

The celebrated guru Peter Drucker believed that a continual determination to develop new products was a crucial matter for all organisations.

> **If the prime purpose is to create a customer, the business has two – and only two – functions: marketing and innovation. Marketing and innovation produce results. Everything else is a cost.**[2]

Make or buy?

A company can add new products through acquisition or by innovative development. The acquisition route can take three forms. The company can buy other companies, it can acquire patents from other companies, or it can buy a licence or franchise from another company.

However, firms can make only so many acqusitions successfully. At some point, there becomes a pressing need for *organic growth* – the development of new products from within the company. New products can evolve in its own organisation or it can contract with independent researchers or specialist agencies to develop specific new products or provide new technology. Many firms have engaged consultants to provide fresh insights and different points of view.[3]

Types of new product

New products range from completely new items that create an entirely new market at one end, to minor improvements or revisions of existing products at the other. Most new product development activity is devoted to the improvement of existing products. At Sony, over 80 per cent of such activity is modifying and improving existing products. Some of the most successful new consumer products in recent years have been brand extensions.

In many categories, it is becoming increasingly difficult to identify high-potential products that will transform a market. However, continuous innovation to improve customer satisfaction can force competitors to retaliate.[4] Continually launching new products as brand extensions into related offering categories can also broaden the brand meaning. Nike started as a running-shoe manufacturer but now competes in the sports market with all types of athletic shoes, clothing and equipment. Armstrong World Industries moved from selling floor coverings to selling finishes for ceilings and to total interior surface decoration. Product innovation and effective marketing programmes have allowed these firms to expand their 'market footprint'. (See also Chapters 12 and 13.)

Comparatively few new products are truly innovative and so really new. These incur the greatest cost and risk because they are new to both the company and the market-place.[5] Radical innovations can strain the company's profit performance in the short term, but their successful addition to a company's portfolio of products can create a greater sustainable competitive advantage than existing conventional products. Companies typically must create a strong R & D and marketing partnership to achieve radical innovations.[6] Few reliable techniques exist for estimating demand for these innovations. Focus groups will provide some perspectives on customer interest and need, but marketers may need to use a 'probe and learn' approach based on observation and feedback of early users' experiences and other suitable means.[7]

Many high-tech firms strive for radical innovation.[8] High-tech covers a wide range of industries – telecommunications, computers, consumer electronics, biotech and software. High-tech marketers face a number of challenges in launching their products: high technological uncertainty; high market uncertainty; high competitive volatility; high investment costs; short product life cycles; and difficulty in finding funding sources for risky projects.[9]

Challenges in new product development

New product introductions have accelerated in recent years. In many industries, such as retailing, consumer goods, electronics and cars, among others, the time it takes to introduce new products has been halved.[10] Luxury leather-goods maker Louis Vuitton implemented a new factory format dubbed Pégase so that it could ship fresh collections to its boutiques every six weeks – more than twice as frequently as in the past – offering customers a choice of more new 'looks'.[11]

The innovation imperative

In strong buyers' markets many products fall into decline – as a result of technological developments, severe competition, changing market and societal factors, and customer purchase experiences – making innovation a necessity. Highly innovative firms are able to identify and quickly seize new market opportunities. In a Special Report published by *BusinessWeek*, featuring the top 50 most innovative companies in the world, just four (Nokia at 9; Volkswagen at 18; BMW at 20 and Vodafone at 25) were based in Europe[12] (see Table 15.1). Innovative firms, such as Vodafone, which has a special business unit solely devoted to increasing innovation, creates a positive attitude towards innovation and risk taking, streamlines the innovation process, practises teamwork and allows its people to experiment and even fail. Overall 14 out of the top 50 innovative companies were based in Europe.

Table 15.1 The world's top 50 most innovative companies

2009 rank	2008 rank	Company	HQ country	HQ continent	Stock returns 2005–8 *(in %)	Revenue growth 2005–8 **(%)	Margin growth 2005–8 ***(in %)	Known for its most innovative (%)
1	1	Apple	USA	North America	5.9	30.4	15.8	Product (47%)
2	2	Google	USA	North America	−9.5	52.6	−8.2	Customer experience (26%)
3	3	Toyota Motor	Japan	Asia	−20.7	4.2	−35.9	Process (35%)
4	5	Microsoft	USA	North America	−8	13.5	−1.3	Process (26%)
5	7	Nintendo	Japan	Asia	36.7	61.1	20.6	Product (48%)
6	12	IBM	USA	North America	2.3	4.4	14.3	Process (31%)
7	15	Hewlett-Packard	USA	North America	9.1	10.9	31.6	Process (39%)
8	13	Research In Motion	Canada	North America	24.6	74.1	11.2	Product (53%)
9	10	Nokia	Finland	Europe	−8.3	14	−10.3	Product (38%)
10	23	Wal-Mart Stores	USA	North America	8	9.1	−2.1	Process (49%)
11	11	Amazon.com	USA	North America	2.8	31.2	−4.8	Customer experience (41%)
12	8	Procter & Gamble	USA	North America	4.5	11.7	2.4	Process (27%)
13	6	Tata Group	India	Asia	Private	Private	Private	Product (44%)
14	9	Sony	Japan	Asia	−25.8	3.1	−41.1	Product (40%)
15	19	Reliance Industries	India	Asia	22.6	28.5	11.9	Business model (35%)
16	26	Samsung Electronics	South Korea	Asia	−10.8	10.5	−1.5	Product (41%)
17	4	General Electric	USA	North America	−19.7	10.1	−12.2	Process (36%)
18	NR	Volkswagen	Germany	Europe	−14.4	7.1	33.6	Customer experience (38%)
19	30	McDonald's	USA	North America	25.8	7.2	9.5	Customer experience (55%)
20	14	BMW	Germany	Europe	−14.8	6.9	−14.6	Customer experience (37%)
21	17	Walt Disney	USA	North America	−0.2	6.4	17.2	Customer experience (68%)
22	16	Honda Motor	Japan	Asia	−15.4	4.8	−14.6	Product (47%)
23	27	AT&T	USA	North America	9.9	41.5	9.7	Product (33%)
24	NR	Coca-Cola	USA	North America	6.8	11.4	0.1	Customer experience (38%)
25	47	Vodafone	Britain	Europe	8.6	10.2	NA	Product (25%)
26	NR	Infosys	India	Asia	−8.1	32.4	2	Process (40%)
27	NR	LG Electronics	South Korea	Asia	−5	9.6	17	Product (46%)
28	NR	Telefónica	Spain	Europe	12.2	17	−2	Business model (40%)
29	31	Daimler	Germany	Europe	−11.9	1.5	39	Product (40%)
30	34	Verizon Communications	USA	North America	10.4	11.9	−1	Customer experience (38%)
31	NR	Ford Motor	USA	North America	−32.6	−3.3	NA	Product (36%)
32	35	Cisco Systems	USA	North America	−1.6	14.3	−8	Process (27%)
33	48	Intel	USA	North America	−14.3	−1.1	−8	Process (35%)
34	28	Virgin Group	Britain	Europe	Private	Private	Private	Customer experience (45%)
35	NR	ArcelorMittal	Luxembourg	Europe	−6.7	64.4	−18	Business model (63%)

Table 15.1 (*Continued*)

2009 rank	2008 rank	Company	HQ country	HQ continent	Stock returns 2005–8 *(in %)	Revenue growth 2005–8 **(%)	Margin growth 2005–8 ***(in %)	Known for its most innovative (%)
36	40	HSBC Holdings	Britain	Europe	−6.1	20.3	−18	Process (32%)
37	42	ExxonMobil	USA	North America	14.5	8.8	2	Process (47%)
38	NR	Nestlé	Switzerland	Europe	4.3	6.5	−14	Product (47%)
39	NR	Iberdrola	Spain	Europe	7.5	54	−14	Customer experience (40%)
40	25	Facebook	USA	North America	Private	Private	Private	Customer experience (51%)
41	22	3M	USA	North America	−7.2	6.1	−3	Product (44%)
42	NR	Banco Santander	Spain	Europe	−9.3	11.8	2	Business model (37%)
43	45	Nike	USA	North America	7.1	11.5	−4	Customer experience and Product (36% each)
44	NR	Johnson & Johnson	USA	North America	2.4	8.1	1	Customer experience (42%)
45	49	Southwest Airlines	USA	North America	−19.2	13.3	−25	Customer experience (45%)
46	NR	Lenovo	China	Asia	−14.2	6.6	4	Business model (35%)
47	NR	JPMorgan Chase	USA	North America	−4.4	−2.6	NA	Process (62%)
48	NR	Fiat	Italy	Europe	−13.5	8.5	2	Product (30%)
49	24	Target	USA	North America	−13.5	8.1	2	Customer experience (60%)
50	NR	Royal Dutch Shell	Netherlands	Europe	4.7	14.3	−8	Process (45%)

Notes: Analysis and data provided in collaboration with the innovation practice of the Boston Consulting Group and BCG-ValueScience. Reuters and Compustat were used for financial and industry data and Bloomberg for total shareholder returns. *Stock returns are annualised, 31 Dec. 2005 to 31 Dec. 2008, and account for price appreciation and dividends. **Revenue and operating margin growth are annualised based on 2005–8 fiscal years. Margin growth is earnings before interest and taxes as a percentage of revenues reported in most recent statements or filings. Where possible, quarterly and semiannual data were used to bring performance for pre-June year-ends closer to December 2008. Financial figures were calculated in local currency. ***Calculating three-year compound annual growth rate for operating margins was not possible when either figure was negative. NR: Not Rated.

Source: The World's Fifty Most Innovative Companies (2009), Special Report, BusinessWeek, 9 May. Used with permission of Bloomberg L.P. Copyright © 2012. All rights reserved.

W. L. Gore

W. L. Gore, best known for its durable Gore-Tex outdoor fabric, has innovated breakthrough new products in a number of diverse areas – guitar strings, dental floss, medical devices and fuel cells. It has adopted several principles to guide its new product development. First, it works with potential customers. Its thoracic graft, designed to combat heart disease, was developed in close collaboration with physicians. Second, it lets employees choose projects and appoints few of its actual product leaders and teams. Gore likes to nurture 'passionate champions' who convince others a project is worth their time and commitment. The development of the fuel cell rallied over 100 of the company's 6,000 research associates. Third, Gore gives employees 'dabble' time. All research associates spend 10 per cent of their work hours developing their own ideas. Promising ideas are pushed forward and judged according to a 'Real, Win, Worth' exercise: Is the opportunity real? Can we win? Can we make money? Fourth, it knows when to let go. Sometimes dead ends in one area can spark an innovation in another. Elixir acoustic guitar strings were a result of a failed venture into bike cables. Even successful ventures may need to move on. Glide shred-resistant dental floss was sold to Procter & Gamble because Gore-Tex knew that retailers would want to deal with a company selling a whole family of health care products.[13]

Table 15.2 Kodak CEO Antonio Perez's seven notions of innovation

1   See the future through the eyes of your customer.
2   Intellectual property and brand power are key assets.
3   Use digital technology to create tools for customers.
4   Build a championship team, not a group of champions.
5   Innovation is a state of mind.
6   Speed is critical, so push your organisation.
7   Partner up if you're not the best in something.

Source: Based on S. Hamm and W. C. Symonds (2006) Mistakes made on the road to innovation, *BusinessWeek IN Inside Innovation*, November, 27–31.

Companies that fail to develop new products put themselves at risk. Their existing products are vulnerable to changing customer needs and tastes, new technologies, shortened product life cycles and increased domestic and foreign competition. New technologies are especially threatening. Kodak has worked hard to develop a new business model and product-development processes that work well in a digital photography world. Its new goal is to do for photos what Apple does for music by helping people to organise and manage their personal libraries of images. Table 15.2 displays the company's philosophy of innovation and transformation.

New product success

Most established companies focus on *incremental innovation*. Incremental innovation can allow companies to enter new markets by adapting existing market offerings for new customers, use variations on a core product to stay one step ahead of the market, and create interim solutions for industry-wide problems.[14]

Newer companies create *disruptive technologies* that are cheaper and more likely to challenge the competitive space. Established companies can be slow to react or to invest in these disruptive technologies because they threaten their existing business. As a result they may find themselves facing formidable new competitors, and many fail.[15] To avoid this trap, firms must carefully monitor the preferences of both customers and potential customers to discover new viable market opportunities.[16]

What else can a company do to develop successful new products? In a study of US industrial products, the new products specialist agency Cooper & Kleinschmidt found that the main success factor was a unique, superior product. Another key factor is a well-defined product concept. The company carefully defines and assesses the target market, product requirements and benefits before proceeding. Other success factors are technological and marketing synergy, quality of execution in all stages, and market attractiveness.

The study also found that products designed solely for the domestic market tend to show a high failure rate, low market share and low growth. On the other hand, products designed for foreign markets achieved significantly better profits. Yet few of the new products in their study were designed specifically for export markets. A study of small and medium-sized firms in Finland, Germany, Japan, South Korea and South Africa found that committed management leadership resulted in significant success in foreign markets. The implication is that companies should adopt an international focus in designing and developing new products.[17]

New product failure

New product development can be risky. New products continue to fail at a disturbing rate. Recent studies put the rate as high as 50 per cent and potentially as high as 95 per cent in

Table 15.3 Causes of new product failure

1 Market/marketing failure
 • Small size of the potential market
 • No clear product differentiation
 • Poor positioning
 • Misunderstanding of customer needs
2 Financial failure
 • Low return on investment
3 Timing failure
 • Late in the market
 • 'Too early' – market not yet developed
4 Technical failure
 • Product did not work
 • Bad design
5 Organisational failure
 • Poor fit with the organisation's culture
 • Lack of organisational support
6 Environmental failure
 • Government regulations
 • Macroeconomic factors

Source: D. Jain (2001) Managing new-product development for strategic competitive advantage, in D. Iacobucci (ed.), *Kellogg on Marketing*, New York: Wiley, Table 6.1, p. 131. Reproduced with permission.

the United States and 90 per cent in Europe.[18] Failure can result for many reasons: ignored or misinterpreted market research; overestimates of market size; high development costs; poor design; incorrect positioning, ineffective advertising or wrong pricing; insufficient distribution support; and competitors that retaliate fiercely. Some additional factors hindering new product development are:

• **Shortage of important ideas in certain areas.** There may be few ways left to improve some basic market (such as steel or detergents).

• **Fragmented markets.** Companies must aim their new products at smaller market segments, and this can mean lower sales and profits for each product.

• **Social and governmental constraints.** New products must satisfy consumer safety and environmental concerns.

• **Cost of development.** A company must typically generate many ideas to find just one worthy of development and often faces high R & D, manufacturing and marketing costs.

• **Capital shortages.** Some companies with good ideas cannot raise the funds needed to research and launch them.

• **Shorter required development time.** Companies must learn how to compress development time by using new techniques, strategic partners, early concept tests and advanced marketing planning.

• **Shorter product life cycles.** When a new product is successful, rivals are quick to copy it. Sony used to enjoy a three-year lead on its new products. Now Matsushita will copy the product within six months, barely leaving time for Sony to recoup its investment.

• **Hostile reception by the media.** Coca-Cola successfully launched a new brand of mineral water in the United States called Dasani but failed to gain any success in the United Kingdom and was forced to withdraw the product from all distribution outlets. The media criticised Dasani as being 'rebottled tap water' following the broadcast of an episode of the UK TV hit comedy programme *Only Fools and Horses*, which featured the lead character filling bottles from tap water and branding the product as 'Peckham Springs'.

Failure comes with the task, and truly innovative firms accept it as part of what is required to be successful (see the chapter-opening vignette). Many web companies are the result of failed business ventures and experience numerous failed initiatives as they evolve their products and services.

Initial failure is not always the end of the road for an idea. Recognising that 90 per cent of experimental drugs fail, ethical pharmaceutical companies have established a corporate culture that looks at failure as an inevitable part of discovery, and its scientists are encouraged to look for new uses for compounds that fail at any stage in a human clinical trial.[19]

Organisational arrangements

(See also Chapters 3 and 21.)
Many companies use *customer-driven engineering* to design new market offerings. This strategy attaches high importance to incorporating customer value preferences in the final design.

Xerox

Xerox traditionally developed new products as many firms did in the past: come up with an idea, develop a prototype, and get some consumer feedback. When Xerox researchers first came up with the idea for a dual-engine commercial printer, it decided to first go straight to the consumer to collect feedback before even developing any prototypes. Lucky it did. Although the Xerox team thought customers would want a second engine for special purposes, the fact that the second engine would be a back-up if the main engine failed turned out to be the biggest draw. In introducing the dual-engine Nuvera 288 Digital Perfecting System in April 2007, 'customer-led innovation' was cited as a critical driver. Xerox now believes in **brainstorming**, or 'dreaming with the customer', by combining company experts who know technology with customers who know the problem areas and what the most valuable product features can be. In addition, scientists and engineers are encouraged to meet face to face with customers, in some cases working on-site for a few weeks to see how customers interact with products.[20]

Xerox's popular new dual-engine printer was a response to customers' feedback on the value of a commercial printer with a back-up engine.
Source: Courtesy of the Xerox Corporation.

Unilever

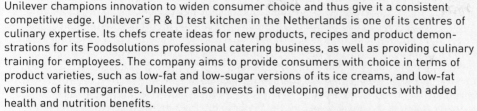

Unilever champions innovation to widen consumer choice and thus give it a consistent competitive edge. Unilever's R & D test kitchen in the Netherlands is one of its centres of culinary expertise. Its chefs create ideas for new products, recipes and product demonstrations for its Foodsolutions professional catering business, as well as providing culinary training for employees. The company aims to provide consumers with choice in terms of product varieties, such as low-fat and low-sugar versions of its ice creams, and low-fat versions of its margarines. Unilever also invests in developing new products with added health and nutrition benefits.

The work is led by the Unilever Food and Health Research Institute, which employs around 450 scientific staff and collaborates with external experts on product innovation and enhancement. The Institute is part of the company's wider commitment to research and development across both its Foods and Home and Personal Care categories. Around 6,000 Unilever scientists and product developers work on the discovery and development of new ingredients and processes for products that provide proven benefits in nutrition, hygiene and personal care for consumers while minimising environmental impacts. In 2007, Unilever invested €868 million in R & D, equivalent to 2.2 per cent of sales.

Here are some examples of recent innovations.

Knorr Vie – increasing fruit and vegetable intake

People the world over do not eat enough fruit and vegetables. The World Health Organization and the UN Food and Agriculture Organization recommend a minimum intake of 400 g/day, but the average is only 100 g/day in developing countries and around 300 g/day in the western world. In 2005 Unilever launched Knorr Vie in Europe, a smoothie-style shot made from concentrated vegetable and fruit juices without any additives. In a 100 ml bottle, it provides half the recommended daily intake of fruit and vegetables. Sales of Knorr Vie fruit and vegetable shots continue to grow, increasing by 67 per cent with around 162 million bottles sold in Europe in 2007.

Ice cream – a choice

Unilever invests around €50 million in ice cream R & D each year, and 40 per cent of this is now devoted to opportunities in the fast-growing health and wellness sector. Ice cream is primarily about pleasure and indulgence, but eaten sensibly it can form part of a nutritionally balanced diet. The company provides a broad range of options, with light, low-fat and no-sugar-added versions. Many brands, such as Cornetto and Magnum, are available in snack size, too, to help with calorie control. Moo is a range of children's ice creams based on the goodness of milk, with each ice cream containing as much calcium as in 100 ml of milk. Since 2006, most of Unilever's ice creams have been labelled with the values for eight nutrients, including energy, protein, fat and sugars.

After successful test marketing in Belgium and Ireland in 2006, Frusì, Unilever's frozen yogurt brand, has been rolled out in France, Italy, the United Kingdom and the Netherlands. Frusì contains 110 calories or less per 100 ml pot and just 2.4 g of fat. Each pot also provides 50 per cent of the recommended daily allowance of vitamin C. The Solero range of products is made with fruit juice and fruit pieces and has a maximum of 99 kilo calories per product.

The company has also developed non-dairy alternatives for ice cream, such as Carte d'Or, Soy and Ades ice creams.

Source: Paul Aresu/PunchStock.

Becel/Flora pro-activ – improving heart health

According to the World Health Organization, heart disease is the principal cause of premature death worldwide. Reducing cholesterol is key to minimising the risks of heart disease. Since 2003 the company has worked in partnership with the World Heart Federation and national groups to promote heart health. Becel/Flora's Love your Heart campaign focuses on raising awareness and has distributed 4.5 million heart health leaflets to consumers and health professionals. It also offers free cholesterol testing, for example in Greece, where 25,000 people have been tested. Becel/Flora pro-activ was originally launched as a spread to help people reduce cholesterol levels – it is proven to lower blood cholesterol levels by 10–15 per cent. The healthy heart foods market is growing fast and the pro-activ range has been extended to include milk drinks and yogurt products. Between 2003 and 2005 sales of pro-activ grew by 40 per cent and it now reaches over 13 million households.

Source: Adapted from Unilever website: www.unilever.com/ourvalues/environment-society/ sustainabledevelopment-report/nutrition-hygiene-wellbeing/nutrition/innovation.asp?print=true. Reproduced with kind permission of Unilever PLC and group companies.

New product development requires senior management to define business domains, product categories and specific criteria for success. Most importantly, they need to be willing to devote significant financial and management support over the medium to long term. For example, Siemens VAI, one of the largest metallurgical firms in the world, took 12 years to develop COREX, a direct reduction technology for iron production that cuts costs and improves the production environment.

Budgeting for new product development

Senior management also need to decide how much to budget for new product development. R & D outcomes are so uncertain that it is difficult to use normal investment criteria. Some companies solve this problem by financing as many projects as possible, hoping to achieve a few winners. Other companies apply a conventional percentage-of-sales figure or spend what the competition spends. Still other companies decide how many successful new products they need and work backwards to estimate the required investment. In either case, new product development is an expensive activity as several ideas need to be generated and screened for their potential in order to identify one strong runner.

Success rates vary. Inventor Sir James Dyson claims he made 5,127 prototypes of his bagless, transparent vacuum cleaner before finally achieving success. However, he does not regret his failures: 'If you want to discover something that other people haven't, you need to do things the wrong way . . . watching why that fails can take you on a completely different path.' Toshiba had great expectations of leading the way when it launched its cutting-edge, high-definition TV in 2007 but by early 2008 that had been comprehensively outsold by the Sony-developed Blu-ray system.[21]

Organising new product development

Companies handle the organisational aspect of new product development in several ways. Many assign responsibility for new ideas to *product managers*. However, product managers are often so busy managing existing lines that they give little thought to new projects other than line extensions.[22] They also lack the specific skills and knowledge needed to develop and critique potential new products. Some companies have a *high-level management committee* charged with reviewing and approving proposals. Large companies often establish a new product development department headed by an executive who has direct access to top management. The department's major responsibilities include generating and screening new ideas, working with the R & D department, and carrying out field testing and final marketing.

Adobe Systems, Inc.

A developer of software solutions for graphic designers and publishers, Adobe established a task force in 2004 to identify all the obstacles that company innovators faced in trying to develop new products. The team found that the corporate hierarchy resisted ideas needing a new sales channel, new business model or even new packaging, and the company had grown so large that ideas originating in branch offices were not getting a fair hearing. The company then established a New Business Initiatives Group that holds quarterly Adobe Idea Champion Showcases. About 20 product managers and other employees (except top executives, who are barred from the proceedings) watch as potential employee-entrepreneurs give brief presentations and Q & A sessions. The ideas are vetted by Adobe entrepreneurs-in-residence, but even one who is turned down can still get a hearing on the company's brainstorming site. Since the new initiative was formed, the event has become extremely popular within Adobe.[23]

Some companies assign new product development work to **venture teams**, cross-functional groups charged with developing a specific product or business. These 'intrapreneurs' are relieved of their other duties and given a budget, time frame and 'skunkworks' setting. (*Skunkworks* are informal workplaces, sometimes garages, where intrapreneurial teams attempt to develop new products.)

Cross-functional teams can collaborate and use concurrent new offering development to push new offerings to market.[24] Concurrent product development resembles a football match, with team members passing the new market offering back and forth as they head towards the goal.

Many top companies use the *stage-gate system* to manage the innovation process.[25] The system enables companies to strike a considered balance between entrepreneurial creativity and business acumen. They divide the process into stages, at the end of each being a gate or checkpoint. The project leader, working with a cross-functional team, must bring a set of known deliverables to each gate before the project can pass to the next stage. To move from the business plan stage into offering development requires a convincing market research study of consumer needs and interests, a competitive analysis and a technical appraisal. Senior managers review the criteria at each gate to make one of four decisions: *go, kill, hold* or *recycle*. Stage-gate systems make the innovation process visible to all involved and clarify the project leader's and team's responsibilities at each stage.[26]

The stages in the new product development process are shown in Figure 15.1. Many firms have parallel sets of projects working through the process, each at a different stage. Think of the process as a *funnel*: a large number of initial new product ideas and concepts are winnowed down to a few high-potential products that are ultimately launched. However, the process is not always linear. Many firms use a *spiral development process* that recognises the value of returning to an earlier stage to make improvements before moving forward.[27]

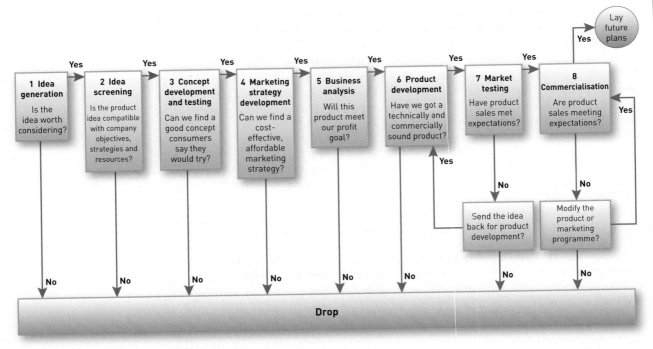

Figure 15.1 The new product development decision process

Managing the development process I: ideas

Process stages

Introducing a new product to the marketplace requires a firm to manage three process activities:

![icon]
To learn more about the extension of Richard's Branson's Virgin umbrella brand into Virgin Media, set up as rival to Rupert Murdoch's BSkyB, visit www.pearsoned.co.uk/marketingmanagementeurope.

1 managing idea generation and screening;
2 managing activities as selected ideas develop from concepts to strategy, paying particular attention to concept development and timing, marketing strategy development and business analysis;
3 managing the introduction of the new product to the marketplace with particular reference to product development, market testing and commercialisation.

Idea generation

The new product development process starts with the search for ideas. Some marketing experts believe the greatest opportunities and best advantages with new products are found by uncovering the best possible set of unmet customer needs or technological innovations.[28]

Inventions and innovations

The term 'invention' traditionally refers to turning money into ideas; innovation is turning ideas into money. There is a fine line between these two essential new product activities. Patent offices provide a testimony to the creative activity of individuals. Some are just interesting ideas that inventors have patented. Inventions that are taken up by businesses and developed from ideas to products that are capable of being marketed have to meet real customer needs if they are to become innovations. Innovation is the first practical application of a new mode of thought that can generate a better solution to an existing need (for example, the invention and subsequent commercialisation of electric washing machines revolutionised domestic clothes washing) or completely transform traditional practices (in the way mobile phones have done).

In many ways the days of the mad inventor have given way to the age of innovation, and existing ideas are being improved and applied more efficiently to meet known and perceived customer needs. New presentations of existing technology through clever design are increasingly capturing customers' attention and becoming 'must-have' items. The technology behind the Apple iPod is not that new. What makes it a successful new product is how the technology is packaged – in other words, the design and the marketing skills.

Ideas can come from interacting with various groups and using creativity-generating techniques (see the marketing memo).

Interacting with others

Encouraged by the *open innovation* movement, many firms are increasingly going outside the company to gather sources of new ideas,[29] including customers, employees, scientists, engineers, channel members, marketing agencies, top management and even competitors.

A true innovation is a product which brings a new solution to consumers' problems by offering more customer-perceived value than the usual solution or by offering a totally different conceptual solution. A better conventional vacuum cleaner or the Dyson DC25 roller ball model? The Dyson engineers are seeking to make the company's vacuum machines smaller and easier to handle while keeping and if possible improving on their performance. The Gallup Organisation has produced a series of audits or Innobarometers to assist the EU civil service and politicians to audit the degree of innovation evident within the EU member states. The Innobarometer 2009 researched 'the experience of European managers in innovative activities'. It sought to discover the degree of 'innovative readiness in Europe'.

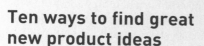

Marketing memo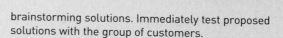

Ten ways to find great new product ideas

1 Run informal sessions where groups of customers meet with company engineers and designers to discuss problems and needs and brainstorm potential solutions.

2 Allow time off – scouting time – for technical people to discuss their own pet projects.

3 Make a customer brainstorming session a standard feature of plant tours.

4 Survey your customers: find out what they like and dislike in your and your competitors' products.

5 Encourage spontaneous ideas and hold idea-generating away-day meetings with key customers.

6 Use iterative rounds: a group of customers in one room, focusing on identifying problems; and a group of technical people in the next room, listening and brainstorming solutions. Immediately test proposed solutions with the group of customers.

7 Set up a keyword search that routinely scans trade publications in multiple countries for new offering announcements.

8 Treat trade shows as intelligence missions, where you view all that is new in your industry under one roof.

9 Have your technical and marketing people visit your suppliers' labs and spend time with their technical people – find out what's new.

10 Set up an ideas workshop, and make it open and easily accessed. Allow employees to review the ideas and add constructively to them.

Source: Adapted from R. Cooper (1998) *Product Leadership: Creating and Launching Superior New Products*, New York: Basic Books. Copyright © 1998 Robert G. Cooper. Reprinted by permission of Basic Books, a member of the Perseus Books Group.

The research showed that only 10 per cent of the EU-15 companies surveyed were deemed to be 'highly innovative' with over half of their turnover being generated by new products and services. Twice this percentage were found to be 'non-innovator' companies. A country-by-country comparison reveals Portugal, the United Kingdom and Spain as having the highest proportion of innovative companies, while Belgium, Greece and France have the most non-innovator companies.

The latest 2009 Innobarometer survey focused on innovation spending. Table 15.4 presents some summary data showing how some of the long-standing members of the EU have altered their expenditure on innovation as a result of the economic downturn. Based on the Summary Innovation Index, the EU member states fall into the following four groupings:

- **Group 1**: Denmark, Finland, Germany and Sweden all show a performance above that of the EU-27. These countries are the *innovation leaders*.
- **Group 2**: Austria, Belgium, Cyprus, Estonia, France, Ireland, Luxembourg, Netherlands, Slovenia and the UK all show a performance close to that of the EU-27. These countries are *innovation followers*.
- **Group 3**: The performance of the Czech Republic, Greece, Hungary, Italy, Malta, Poland, Slovakia and Spain is below that of the EU-27. These countries are *moderate innovators*.
- **Group 4**: The performance of Bulgaria, Latvia, Lithuania and Romania is well below that of the EU-27. These countries are classified as *catching-up countries*.

Customer needs and wants are the logical place to start the search for new ideas. One-to-one interviews and focus group discussions can explore needs and reactions. Griffin and Hauser suggest that conducting 10–20 in-depth experiential interviews per market segment often uncovers the vast majority of customer needs.[30] But many additional approaches can be profitable (see the marketing memo on p. 624).

The traditional company-centric approach to innovation is giving way to a world in which companies co-create products with customers.[31] Companies are increasingly turning to 'crowd sourcing' to generate new ideas and to create consumer-generated marketing campaigns. Crowd sourcing means inviting the internet community to help create content or software, often with prize money or a celebratory moment involved. This strategy has helped create new offerings and companies such as Wikipedia and Google's popular video website YouTube.

Regular users of a product can be a good source of input when they innovate without the consent or even the knowledge of the companies that produce them. Mountain bikes developed as a result of young people taking their bicycles up to the top of a mountain and riding down. When the bicycles broke, the young riders began building more durable machines and adding such things as motorcycle brakes, improved suspension and accessories. The young cyclists, not the companies, developed these innovations. Some companies, particularly those that want to appeal to young consumers, bring the lead users into their product design process.[32]

Technical companies can learn a great deal by studying customers who make the most advanced use of the company's products and who recognise the need for improvements before other customers do. Employees throughout the company can be a source of ideas for improving production, and development of new products and services. Toyota claims its employees submit 2 million ideas annually (about 35 suggestions per employee), over 85 per cent of which are implemented. Many firms, such as Kodak and Oticon, the Danish hearing aid company, give monetary, holiday or other recognition awards to employees who submit the best ideas. Nokia inducts engineers with at least ten patents into its 'Club 10', recognising them each year in a formal awards ceremony hosted by the company's CEO.[33]

A company can motivate its employees to submit new ideas to an *idea manager* whose name and phone number are widely circulated or by means of the traditional *suggestion box*. Internal brainstorming sessions also can be quite effective – if they are conducted correctly. The marketing memo on p. 625 provides some brainstorming guidelines.

Marketing insight

Reckitt Benckiser's connect-and-develop approach to innovation

Since its creation in 1999 through the merger of the UK's Reckitt & Colman and Benckiser of Germany, although listed on the Netherlands' stock exchange, profits almost doubled by 2004 and the share price has more than doubled since the start of the millennium. In 2006 revenues of €6.5 billion were achieved together with profits of €910 million. The company has achieved this by fostering an innovative approach which has developed several new products that customers never knew they needed. So where do these ideas come from? According to the company's chief executive during this period, Bart Becht:

> Consumers will generally not come up with the next innovation. So we try to have ideas that

target consumers in specific areas. Then we screen them. We go through literally thousands of ideas every quarter. Then we ask consumers about the ideas.

This relentless quest to find and exploit new market offering/product ideas generated over 35 per cent of the company's sales between 2004 and 2007. To ensure that consumers know about these ideas Reckitt Benckiser spends over 12 per cent of its entire revenue on media and significantly more when other aspects of marketing are included such as education programmes, marketing to professionals and PR. The company aims to double its sales by 2012 and double its profit margins to more than 30 per cent.

The key word, never omitted from any Reckitt Benckiser presentation, is 'powerbrands'. In February 2008 there were 18 such brands – the best known in Britain being Veet hair remover, Dettol, Nurofen, Strepsils, Calgon, Vanish, Woolite, Cillit Bang, Harpic, Finish, AirWick, Lemsip and Gaviscon.

An important contributor to the company's success has been its development of a strong innovative culture across all of its branded offerings. The company seeks to generate 40 per cent of its revenues from market offerings/products launched in the previous three years. Its culture values swift decision making, innovation and a focus on financial results. Managers' pay is closely linked to individual performance and – to foster teamwork – to that of their colleagues.

Cillit Bang is a good example of well-known technology that has been given a new set of clothes and a clever slogan which most people remember.

Two of Reckitt Benckiser brands that are markedly imaginative: Cillit Bang ' . . . and the dirt is gone!' and 'Dettol kills all known germs stone dead!'
Source: Courtesy of Reckitt Benckiser Group plc.

Sources: M. Urry (2008) Reckitt's strongly flavoured essence, *Financial Times*, 21 January; Cleaning up, *The Economist*, 14 February 2008; B. Laurence (2008) Reckitt Benckiser cleans up with research to boost global sales, *Sunday Times*, 17 February.

Table 15.4 Innovation in Europe: expenditure on innovation, 2006–8

Country	% decreased	% increased	No change
Belgium	9.3	40.2	50.5
Denmark	10.4	35.3	54.4
Germany	5.3	43.1	51.6
Greece	15.0	45.7	39.2
Spain	11.1	28.8	60.0
France	7.0	35.3	57.7
Ireland	14.9	30.8	54.3
Italy	13.4	35.8	50.8
Luxembourg	6.6	31.6	61.8
Netherlands	8.7	35.5	55.7
Austria	5.8	40.8	53.4
Portugal	14.0	37.2	48.8
Finland	6.4	42.7	50.9
Sweden	5.8	54.2	40.0
United Kingdom	9.6	32.9	57.5
EU-15	9.6	38.0	52.4

Source: Adapted from Flash EB No. 267 – 2009 Innobarometer.

Companies can find good ideas by researching the market offerings of competitors and other companies. They can find out what customers like and dislike about competitors' products. They can buy their competitors' products, take them apart, and build better ones. Company sales representatives and intermediaries are a particularly good source of ideas. These groups have first-hand exposure to customers and are often the first to learn about competitive developments.

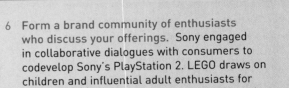

Marketing memo

Seven ways to draw new ideas from your customers

1 Observe how your customers are using your products.

2 Ask your customers about their problems with your products.

3 Ask your customers about their dream goods. Ask your customers what they want your product to do, even if the ideal sounds impossible.

4 Use a customer advisory board to comment on your company's ideas.

5 Use websites for new ideas. Companies can use specialised search engines to find blogs and postings relevant to their businesses.

6 Form a brand community of enthusiasts who discuss your offerings. Sony engaged in collaborative dialogues with consumers to codevelop Sony's PlayStation 2. LEGO draws on children and influential adult enthusiasts for feedback on new product concepts in the early stages of development.

7 Encourage or challenge your customers to change or improve your products. BMW posted a toolkit on its website to let customers develop ideas using telematics and in-car online services.

Source: From an unpublished paper, P. Kotler (2007) Drawing new ideas from your customers.

Marketing memo

How to run a successful creative problem-solving session

Group creative problem-solving (CPS) sessions have much to recommend them, but also some drawbacks. If carried out incorrectly, they can frustrate and antagonise participants; if carried out correctly, however, they can create insights, ideas and solutions that would have been impossible without everyone's participation. To ensure success, experts recommend the following guidelines:

1 There should be a trained facilitator to guide the session.

2 Participants must feel that they can express themselves freely.

3 Participants must see themselves as collaborators working towards a common goal.

4 Rules need to be set up and followed, so conversations do not stray.

5 Participants must be given proper background preparation and materials so that they can get into the task quickly.

6 Individual sessions before and after the CPS workshop can be useful to think and learn about the topic ahead of time as well as to reflect afterwards on what happened.

7 CPS sessions must lead to a clear plan of action and implementation, so the ideas that materialise can provide tangible value.

8 CPS sessions can do more than just generate ideas – they can help build teams and leave participants better informed and energised.

Source: Based on L. Tischler (2007) Be creative: you have 30 seconds, *Fast Company*, May, 47–50.

Top management can be another major source of ideas. Some company leaders, such as the former CEO of Intel, take personal responsibility for technological innovation in their companies. Ideas can come from inventors, patent lawyers, university and commercial laboratories, industrial consultants, advertising agencies, marketing research firms and industrial publications. However, although ideas can flow from many sources, their chances of receiving serious attention often depend on whether the company has a formal screening system and new offering responsibility.

Table 15.5 summarises data from the 2009 Innovator report on actions taken by companies to integrate activities in support of innovation by the EU-15 countries.

Creativity techniques

The following list presents a sample of techniques for stimulating creativity in individuals and groups.[34]

- **Attribute listing.** List the attributes of an object, such as a screwdriver. Then modify each attribute, such as replacing the wooden handle with plastic, providing torque power, adding different screw heads, and so on.

- **Forced relationships.** List several ideas and consider each in relation to each other one. In designing new office furniture, for example, consider a desk, bookcase and filing cabinet as separate ideas. Then imagine a desk with a built-in bookcase or a desk with built-in files or a bookcase with built-in files.

- **Morphological analysis.** Start with a problem, such as 'getting something from one place to another via a powered vehicle'. Now think of dimensions, such as the type of platform (cart, chair, sling, bed), the medium (air, water, oil, rails), and the power source (compressed air, electric motor, magnetic fields). By listing every possible combination, many new solutions can be generated.

- **Reverse assumption analysis.** List all the normal assumptions about an entity and then reverse them. Instead of assuming that a restaurant has menus, charges for and serves food, reverse each assumption. The new restaurant may decide to serve only what the chef bought that morning and cooked; it may provide some food and charge only for how long the person sits at the table; or it may design an exotic atmosphere and rent out the space to people who bring their own food and beverages.

Table 15.5 Integration activities in support of innovation in the EU-15

Country	Knowledge management systems	Internal mechanisms for employees to submit innovative ideas	Staff rotations or secondments between different functions	Creation of cross-functional or cross-departmental teams on innovation projects
Belgium	34.9	45.6	40.2	35.2
Denmark	34.7	43.9	51.1	45.1
Germany	24.7	52.3	28.7	44.8
Greece	48.4	42.8	38.0	28.4
Spain	47.1	53.6	51.5	45.0
France	37.8	49.1	39.6	22.8
Ireland	41.3	45.7	45.5	51.9
Italy	24.0	38.2	48.4	26.8
Luxembourg	44.8	55.9	52.2	33.6
Netherlands	32.8	39.3	29.6	33.8
Austria	31.5	53.7	42.7	45.8
Portugal	48.5	43.6	51.6	36.2
Finland	55.4	40.7	53.4	45.6
Sweden	30.9	50.5	47.0	29.3
United Kingdom	40.2	35.2	34.2	37.9

Source: Adapted from Flash EB No. 267 – 2009 Innobarometer.

'I've got a great idea!'

'It won't work here.'

'We've tried it before.'

'This isn't the right time.'

'It can't be done.'

'It's not the way we do things.'

'We've done all right without it.'

'It will cost too much.'

'Let's discuss it at our next meeting.'

Figure 15.2 Forces fighting new ideas

Source: Jerold Panas, Young & Partners. Reproduced with permission.

A cyber café: cafeteria + internet
Source: image 100/Corbis.

- **New contexts**. Take familiar processes, such as people-helping services, and put them into a new context. Imagine helping dogs and cats instead of people with day-care service, stress reduction, psychotherapy, animal funerals, and so on. As another example, instead of sending hotel guests to the front desk to check in, greet them at kerb side and use a wireless device to register them.
- **Mind mapping**. Start with a thought, such as a car, write it on a piece of paper, then think of the next thought that comes up (say Mercedes); link it to car, then think of the next association (Germany); and do this with all associations that come up with each new word. Perhaps a whole new idea will materialise.

Increasingly, offering ideas arise from *lateral marketing* that combines two value concepts or ideas to create a new offering. Here are some successful examples:

- petrol station shops = petrol stations + food
- cyber cafés = cafeteria + internet
- cereal bars = cereal + snacking
- Kinder Surprise = confectionery + toy
- Sony Walkman = audio + portable.

Idea screening

In screening ideas the company must avoid two types of error. A *DROP-error* occurs when the company dismisses a good idea. It is extremely easy to find fault with other people's ideas (see Figure 15.2). Some companies shudder when they look back at ideas they dismissed or breathe sighs of relief when they realise how close they came to dropping what eventually became a huge success. This was the case with the hit television show *Friends*.

Friends

An idea that did not get off the storyboard was the pilot for *Friends*, one of the longest-running hit comedies on television. Dismissing an idea that later proves successful is a marketer's nightmare and is called a DROP error.
Source: Warner Brothers TV/ Bright/Crane Pro/The Kobal Collection/Chris Haston.

The US NBC situation comedy *Friends* enjoyed a ten-year run from 1994 to 2004 as a perennial ratings powerhouse. But the show almost did not see the light of day. According to an internal NBC research report, the pilot episode was described as 'not very entertaining, clever or original' and was given a failing grade, scoring 41 out of 100. Ironically, the pilot for an earlier hit sit-com, *Seinfeld,* was also rated 'weak', although the pilot for the medical drama *ER* scored a healthy 91. Courtney Cox's Monica was the *Friends* character who scored best with test audiences, but characters portrayed by Lisa Kudrow and Matthew Perry were deemed to have marginal appeal, and the Rachel, Ross and Joey characters scored even lower. Adults 35 and over in the sample found the characters as a whole 'smug, superficial and self-absorbed'.[35]

Friends was a substantial success in the United Kingdom but another US comedy import, *Pushing Daisies*, while a success in the United States, obtained poor viewing figures elsewhere.

A *GO-error* occurs when the company permits a poor idea to move into development and commercialisation. An *absolute product failure* loses money; its sales do not cover variable costs. A *partial product failure* loses money, but its sales cover all its variable costs and some of its fixed costs. A *relative product failure* yields a profit lower than the company's target rate of return.

The purpose of screening is to drop poor ideas as early as possible. The rationale is that development costs rise substantially with each successive development stage. Most companies require ideas to be described on a standard form for a review. The description states the idea, the target market and the competition, and roughly estimates market size, product price, development time and costs, manufacturing costs and rate of return.

The executive committee then reviews each idea against a set of criteria. Does the product meet a need? Would it offer superior in-use value? Can it be distinctively advertised? Does the company have the necessary know-how and capital? Will the new product deliver the expected sales volume, sales growth and profit? Consumer input may be necessary to tap into marketplace realities.[36]

Management can rate the surviving ideas using a weighted-index method such as that in Table 15.6. The first column lists factors required for successful product launches, and the second column assigns importance weights. The third column scores the product idea on a scale from 0 to 1.0, with 1.0 the highest score. The final step multiplies each factor's importance by the product score to obtain an overall rating. In this example, the product idea scores 0.69, which places it in the 'good idea' level. The purpose of this basic rating device is to promote systematic evaluation and discussion. It is not supposed to make the decision for management.

Table 15.6 Product–idea rating device

Product success requirements	Relative weight (a)	Product score (b)	Product rating (c) = (a) × (b)
Unique or superior product	0.40	0.8	0.32
High performance-to-cost ratio	0.30	0.6	0.18
High marketing euro support	0.20	0.7	0.14
Lack of strong competition	0.10	0.5	0.05
Total	1.00		0.69[a]

[a]Rating scale: .00–.30 poor; .31–.60 fair; .61–.80 good. Minimum acceptance rate: .61

As the idea moves through development, the company will constantly need to revise its estimate of the product's overall probability of success, using the following formula:

$$\begin{array}{c}\text{Overall}\\\text{probability of}\\\text{success}\end{array} = \begin{array}{c}\text{Probability}\\\text{of technical}\\\text{completion}\end{array} \times \begin{array}{c}\text{Probability of}\\\text{commercialisation}\\\text{given technical}\\\text{completion}\end{array} \times \begin{array}{c}\text{Probability of}\\\text{economic}\\\text{success given}\\\text{commercialisation}\end{array}$$

For example, if the three probabilities are estimated as 0.50, 0.65 and 0.74, respectively, the overall probability of success is 0.24. The company must then judge whether this probability is high enough to warrant continued development.

Managing the development process II: concept to strategy

Attractive ideas must be refined into testable product concepts. An *idea* is a possible product that the company might introduce to the market. A *product concept* is a statement of the idea expressed in customer-perceived value terms.

Concept development and testing

Concept development

This can be illustrated by considering concept development as follows: a large food-processing company has the idea of producing a powder to add to milk to increase its nutritional value and taste. This is a product *idea*, but customers do not buy such ideas; they buy product *concepts*.

A product idea can be turned into several concepts. The first question is: who will use this product? The powder can be targeted at infants, children, teenagers, young or middle-aged adults or older adults. Second, what primary benefit should this product provide? Taste, nutrition, refreshment, energy? Third, when will people consume this drink? Breakfast, mid-morning, lunch, mid-afternoon, dinner, late evening? By answering these questions, a company can form several concepts:

- **Concept 1**: an instant breakfast drink for adults who want a quick, nutritious breakfast without preparation.
- **Concept 2**: a tasty snack for children to drink as a midday refreshment.
- **Concept 3**: a health supplement for older adults to drink in the late evening before they go to bed.

Each concept represents a *category concept* that defines the product's competition. An instant breakfast drink would compete against bacon and eggs, breakfast cereals, coffee and pastry, and other breakfast alternatives. A tasty snack drink would compete against soft drinks, fruit juices, sports drinks and other thirst quenchers.

Suppose the instant-breakfast-drink concept looks best. The next task is to show where this powdered product would stand in relationship to other breakfast products. *Perceptual maps* are a visual way to display consumer perceptions and preferences (see Chapter 10). They provide quantitative portrayals of market situations and how consumers see different market products, services and brands. By overlaying consumer preferences with brand perceptions, marketers can reveal 'holes' or 'openings' that suggest unmet customer needs.

Figure 15.3(a) uses the two dimensions of cost and preparation time to create a *product-positioning map* for the breakfast drink. An instant breakfast drink offers low cost and

(a) Product-positioning map (breakfast market)

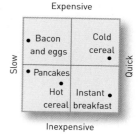

(b) Brand-positioning map (instant breakfast market)

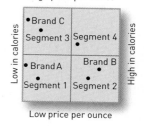

Figure 15.3 Product and brand positioning

quick preparation. Its nearest competitor is cold cereal or breakfast bars; its most distant competitor is bacon and eggs. These contrasts can help communicate and promote the concept to the market.

Next, the product concept becomes a *brand concept* (see Chapters 12 and 13). Figure 15.3(b) is a *brand-positioning map*, a perceptual map showing the current positions of three existing brands of instant breakfast drinks (A–C), as seen by consumers. It can also be useful to overlay consumer preferences on to the map in terms of their current or desired preferences. Figure 15.3(b) also shows that there are four segments of consumers (1–4) whose preferences are clustered around the points displayed on the map.

The brand-positioning map helps the company to decide how much to charge and how calorific to make its drink. Three segments (1–3) are well served by existing brands (A–C). The company would not want to position itself next to one of those existing brands, unless that brand is weak or inferior or market demand was high enough to be shared. As it turns out, the new brand would be distinctive in the medium-price, medium-calorie market or in the high-price, high-calorie market. There is also a segment of consumers (4) clustered fairly near the medium-price, medium-calorie market, suggesting that it may offer the greatest opportunity.

Concept testing

Concept testing involves presenting the product idea concept, symbolically or physically, to target consumers and getting their reactions. The more the tested concepts resemble the final market offering or experience, the more dependable concept testing is. Concept testing of prototypes can help avoid costly mistakes and can be especially challenging with radically different, innovative products.[37] In the past, creating physical prototypes was costly and time consuming, but today firms can use *rapid prototyping* to design products on a computer, and then produce outline models to show potential customers for their reactions. Companies are also using *virtual reality* to test product concepts. Virtual reality programmes use computers and sensory devices (such as gloves or goggles) to simulate real-time experiences.

Concept testing presents customers with a version of the product concept that they can experience. In the case of Concept 1 in the milk example, the expanded concept might look like this:

> **The market product idea is a powdered mixture added to milk to make an instant breakfast that gives the person all the day's needed nutrition along with good taste and high convenience. The product comes in three flavours (chocolate, vanilla and strawberry) and individual packets, six to a box, at €5 a box.**

After receiving this information, researchers measure the new product dimensions by asking customers to respond to the following types of question:

1 **Communicability and believability.** Are the CPV benefits clear and believable? If the scores are low, the concept must be refined or revised.
2 **Need level.** Does the proposed product solve a problem or fill a need? The stronger the need, the higher the expected customer and consumer interest.
3 **Gap level.** Do any other products currently meet this need and are they satisfactory? The greater the gap, the higher the expected customer interest. Marketers can multiply the need level by the gap level to produce a *need-gap score*. A high score means the customer sees the proposed product as filling a strong need not satisfied by available alternatives.
4 **Customer-perceived value.** Is the potential benefit of the proposed product (using the term product to mean a market offering that is a mix of tangible and intangible benefits) acceptable? The higher the value, the higher is the expected customer and consumer interest.

5 Purchase intention. Would the respondents (definitely, probably, probably not, definitely not) buy the product? Customers who answered the first three questions positively should answer 'Definitely' here.

6 User targets, purchase occasions, purchasing frequency. Who would use this product, when and how often?

Respondents' answers indicate whether the concept has a strong customer and consumer appeal, what rival market products it competes against, and which customers are the best targets. The need-gap levels and purchase-intention levels can be checked against norms for the market category to see whether the concept appears to be a winner, a long shot or a loser.

Conjoint analysis

This is a scaling technique method for deriving the use benefit values that consumers attach to varying levels of a product's CPV value attributes. It is also called trade-off analysis as it models the relative customer-perceived value of competing products and throws light on how customers decide what CPV value attributes (quality or transaction) can be offset. The technique has become one of the most popular concept development and testing tools. With conjoint analysis, respondents see and rank different hypothetical products formed by combining varying combinations of CPV attributes. Management can then identify the most appealing product's CPV attributes and its estimated market share and profit.

Suppose the new product marketer is considering five CPV attribute benefit design elements:

1 three package designs (A, B, C – see Figure 15.4);
2 three brands (Euro 1, Euro 2 and Euro 3);
3 three retail prices (€1.20, €1.40 and €1.60);
4 a possible seal of approval such as *Good Housekeeping* magazine in the United Kingdom (yes, no); and
5 a possible money-back guarantee (yes, no).

Although the researcher can form 108 possible product concepts ($3 \times 3 \times 3 \times 2 \times 2$), it would be too much to ask customers to rank 108 concepts. A sample of, say, 18 contracting product concepts is feasible, and customers would rank them from the most to the least preferred.

The marketer can then use a statistical software program to discover the customer's preferred utility functions for each of the five attributes (see Figure 15.5). Utility ranges between 0 and 1; the higher the utility, the stronger the consumer's preference for that level of the attribute. Looking at packaging, it is clear that package B is the most favoured, followed by C and then A, which has hardly any perceived utility. The preferred brands are Bissell, K2R and Glory, in that order. The consumer's utility varies inversely with price. A *Good Housekeeping* seal is preferred, but it does not add that much utility and may not be worth the effort to obtain it. A money-back guarantee is strongly preferred.

The consumer's most desired market offering is package design B, brand name Bissell, priced at €1, with a *Good Housekeeping* seal and a money-back guarantee. It is also possible to determine the relative importance of each attribute to this consumer – the difference between the highest and lowest utility level for that attribute. The greater the difference, the more important the attribute. Clearly this consumer sees price and package design as the most important attributes, followed by money-back guarantee, brand name and a *Good Housekeeping* seal.

CPV preference data from a sufficient sample of target consumers help the company to estimate the market share any specific offer is likely to achieve, given any assumptions about competitive responses. Still, the organisation may not launch the market offering

Figure 15.4 Vacuum cleaner samples for conjoint analysis

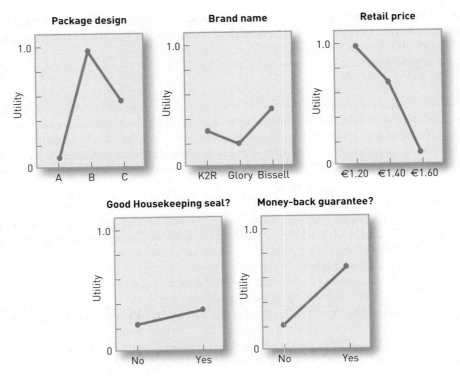

Figure 15.5 Utility functions based on conjoint analysis

that promises to gain the greatest market share, because of cost considerations. The most customer-appealing product (in CPV terms) is not always the most profitable one to bring to market.

Under some conditions, researchers will collect the data without a full-profile description of each product, by presenting two factors at a time. For example, respondents may see a table with three price levels and three package types and indicate which of the nine combinations they would like most, second best and so on. A further table consists of trade-offs between two other variables. The trade-off approach may be easier to use when there are many variables and possible offers. However, it is less realistic in that respondents are focusing on only two variables at a time. Adaptive conjoint analysis (ACA) is a 'hybrid' data collection technique that combines self-explicated importance ratings with pair-wise trade-off tasks.[38]

Marketing strategy development

Following a successful concept test, the firm will develop a preliminary three-part strategy plan for introducing the new product offering to the market. The first part describes the target market's size, structure and behaviour; the planned positioning; and the sales, market share and profit goals sought in the first few years:

> The target market for the instant breakfast drink is families with children who are receptive to a new, convenient, nutritious and inexpensive form of breakfast. The company's brand will be positioned at the higher-price, higher-quality end of the instant breakfast drink category. The company will initially aim to sell 500,000 cases or 10 per cent of the market, with a loss in the first year not exceeding €1.5 million. The second year will aim for 700,000 cases or 14 per cent of the market, with a planned profit of €2.2 million.

The second part outlines the planned price, distribution strategy and marketing budget for the first year:

> The product will be offered in chocolate, vanilla and strawberry in individual packets of six to a box, at a retail price of €2.49 a box. There will be 48 boxes per case, and the case price to distributors will be €24. For the first two months, dealers will be offered one case free for every four cases bought, plus cooperative advertising allowances. Free samples will be distributed door to door. Money-off coupons will appear in newspapers. The total sales promotional budget will be €2.9 million. An advertising budget of €6 million will be split 50:50 between national and local. Two-thirds will go into television and one-third into newspapers. Advertising copy will emphasise the benefit concepts of nutrition and convenience. The advertising execution concept will revolve around a small boy who drinks instant breakfast and grows strong. During the first year, €100,000 will be spent on marketing research to buy store audits and consumer-panel information to monitor market reaction and buying rates.

The third part of the marketing strategy plan describes the long-run sales and profit goals and marketing mix strategy over time:

> The company intends to win a 25 per cent market share and realise an after-tax return on investment of 12 per cent. To achieve this return, product quality will start high and be improved over time through technical research. Price will initially be set at a high level and lowered gradually to expand the market and meet competition. The total promotion budget will be boosted each year by about 20 per cent, with the initial advertising–sales promotion split of 65:35 evolving eventually to 50:50. Marketing research will be reduced to €60,000 per year after the first year.

Business analysis

After management develops the product concept and marketing strategy, it can evaluate the business attractiveness of the proposal. Management needs to prepare sales, cost and profit projections to determine whether they satisfy company objectives. If they do, the concept can move to the development stage. As new information comes in, the business analysis will undergo revision and expansion.

Estimating total sales

Total estimated sales are the sum of estimated first-time sales, replacement sales and repeat sales. Sales estimation methods depend on whether the product is purchased once (such as an engagement ring or retirement home), infrequently or often. For one-time products, sales rise at the beginning, peak, and approach zero as the number of potential buyers is exhausted (see Figure 15.6(a)). If new buyers keep entering the market, the curve will not go down to zero.

Infrequently purchased products – such as cars, toasters and industrial equipment – exhibit replacement cycles dictated by physical wear or obsolescence associated with changing styles, features and performance. Sales forecasting for this category calls for estimating first-time sales and replacement sales separately (see Figure 15.6(b)).

Frequently purchased products, such as consumer and industrial non-durables, have product life cycle sales resembling Figure 15.6(c). The number of first-time buyers initially increases and then decreases as fewer buyers are left (assuming a fixed population). Repeat purchases occur soon, providing the product satisfies some buyers. The sales curve eventually falls to a plateau representing a level of steady repeat-purchase volume; by this time, the product market offering is no longer a new product.

In estimating sales, the manager's first task is to estimate first-time purchases of the new product in each period. To estimate replacement sales, management researches the

(a) One-time purchased product

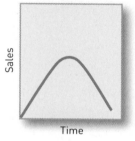

(b) Infrequently purchased product

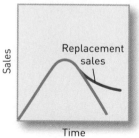

(c) Frequently purchased product

Figure 15.6 Product life cycle sales for three types of product

products' *survival-age distribution* – that is, the number of units that fail in year 1, 2, 3, and so on. The low end of the distribution indicates when the first replacement sales will take place. Replacement sales can be difficult to estimate before the product is in use; some manufacturers therefore base the decision to launch a new offering solely on the estimate of first-time sales.

For a frequently purchased new product, the seller estimates repeat sales as well as first-time sales. A high rate of repeat purchasing means customers are satisfied; sales are likely to stay high even after all first-time purchases take place. The seller should note the percentage of repeat purchases in each repeat-purchase class: those who rebuy once, twice, three times and so on. Some products and brands are bought a few times and then dropped.[39]

Estimating costs and profits

Costs are estimated by the R & D, manufacturing, marketing and finance departments. Table 15.7 illustrates a five-year projection of sales, costs and profits for a company marketing an instant breakfast drink.

Row 1 shows projected sales revenue over the five-year period. The company expects to sell €11,889,000 (approximately 500,000 cases at €24 per case) in the first year. Behind this projection is a set of assumptions about the rate of market growth, the company's market share and the ex-factory price. *Row 2* shows the cost of goods sold, which hovers around 33 per cent of sales revenue. This cost is calculated by estimating the average cost of labour, ingredients and packaging per case. *Row 3* shows the expected gross margin, the difference between sales revenue and cost of goods sold.

Row 4 shows anticipated development costs of €3.5 million, including product development costs, marketing research costs and manufacturing development costs. *Row 5* shows the estimated marketing costs over the five-year period to cover advertising, sales promotion and marketing research, and an amount allocated for sales force coverage and marketing administration. *Row 6* shows the allocated overhead to this new product to cover its share of the cost of executive salaries, heat, light and so on.

Row 7, the gross contribution, is gross margin minus the preceding three costs. *Row 8*, supplementary contribution, lists any change in income from other company products caused by the new product introduction. *Dragalong income* is additional income to them, and *cannibalised income* is reduced income. Table 15.7 assumes no

Table 15.7 Projected five-year cash-flow statement (in €000)

	Year 0	Year 1	Year 2	Year 3	Year 4	Year 5
1 Sales revenue	0	11,889	15,381	19,654	28,253	32,491
2 Cost of goods sold	0	3,981	5,150	6,581	9,461	10,880
3 Gross margin	0	7,908	10,231	13,073	18,792	21,611
4 Development costs	−3,500	0	0	0	0	0
5 Marketing costs	0	8,000	6,460	8,255	11,866	13,646
6 Allocated overhead	0	1,189	1,538	1,965	2,825	3,249
7 Gross contribution	−3,500	−1,281	2,233	2,853	4,101	4,716
8 Supplementary contribution	0	0	0	0	0	0
9 Net contribution	−3,500	−1,281	2,233	2,853	4,101	4,716
10 Discounted contribution (15%)	−3,500	−1,113	1,691	1,877	2,343	2,346
11 Cumulative discounted cash flow	−3,500	−4,613	−2,922	−1,045	1,298	3,644

supplementary contributions. *Row 9* shows net contribution, which in this case is the same as gross contribution. *Row 10* shows discounted contribution – that is, the present value of each future contribution discounted at 15 per cent per annum. For example, the company will not receive €4,716,000 until the fifth year. This amount is worth only €2,345,000 today if the company can earn 15 per cent on its money through other investments.[40]

Finally, *row 11* shows the cumulative discounted cash flow, the accumulation of the annual contributions in row 10. Two things are of central interest. The first is the maximum investment exposure, the highest loss the project can create. The company will be in a maximum loss position of €4,613,000 in year 1. The second is the payback period, the time when the company recovers all its investment, including the built-in return of 15 per cent. The payback period here is about three and a half years. Management must decide whether to risk a maximum investment loss of €4.6 million and a possible payback period of three and a half years.

Companies use other financial measures to evaluate the merit of a new product proposal. The simplest is **breakeven analysis**, which estimates how many units the company must sell (or how many years it will take) to break even with the given price and cost structure. If management believes sales could easily reach the break-even number, it is likely to develop the new offering.

A more complex method of estimating profit is **risk analysis**. Here three estimates are obtained (optimistic, pessimistic and most likely) for each uncertain variable affecting profitability, under an assumed marketing environment and marketing strategy for the planning period. The computer simulates possible outcomes and computes a distribution showing the range of possible rates of return and their probabilities.

Managing the development process III: development to commercialisation

Up to now, the new market offering has existed only as a description of an idea, a drawing or a prototype. The next step represents a jump in investment that dwarfs the costs incurred so far. The company will determine whether the new idea can translate into a technically and commercially feasible CPV market offering. If not, the accumulated project cost will be lost, except for any useful information gained in the process.

Product and market development

The job of translating target customer requirements into a working prototype is helped by a set of methods known as *quality function deployment* (QFD). The methodology takes the list of desired *customer attributes* (CAs) generated by market research and turns them into a list of *engineering attributes* (EEs) that engineers can use. For example, customers of a proposed truck may want a certain acceleration rate (CA). Engineers can turn this into the required horsepower and other engineering equivalents (EEs). The methodology measures the trade-offs and costs of meeting customer requirements. A major contribution of QFD is improved communication between marketers, engineers and manufacturing people.[41]

Physical prototypes

The R & D department will develop one or more versions of the core offer product concept. Its goal is to develop a prototype that embodies the key customer-perceived (CPV) attributes and benefits described in the product concept statement. The prototype must perform safely under normal use and conditions and be produced within budgeted manufacturing costs. In the past, developing and manufacturing a successful prototype could take days, weeks, months or even years. The web now permits more rapid prototyping and more flexible development processes.[42] Sophisticated virtual-reality technology is also speeding up the process. By designing and testing product designs through simulation, for example, companies can achieve the flexibility to respond to new information and resolve uncertainties by exploring alternatives.

Boeing

Boeing designed its 777 aircraft on a totally digital basis. Engineers, designers and more than 500 suppliers designed the aircraft on a special computer network without ever making a blueprint on paper. Project partners were connected by an extranet enabling them to communicate, share ideas and work on the design at a distance. A computer-generated 'human' could climb inside the three-dimensional design on-screen to show how difficult maintenance access would be for a live mechanic. Such computer modelling allowed engineers to spot design errors that otherwise would have remained undiscovered until a person began to work on a physical prototype. Avoiding the time and cost of building physical prototypes reduced development time, wastage and rework by 60–90 per cent.[43]

Scientists must not only design the new product's functional characteristics, but also communicate its psychological aspects and brand image through physical cues. How will consumers react to different colours, sizes and weights? Marketers need to supply design and development staff with information about what CPV attributes consumers seek and how consumers judge whether these attributes are present.

Customer tests

When the prototypes are ready, they must be put through rigorous functional tests and customer tests before they enter the marketplace. *Alpha testing* is testing the proposed new product within the firm to see how it performs in different applications. After refining the prototype, the company moves to *beta testing* with customers.[44] Consumer testing can take several forms, from bringing potential customers into a laboratory to giving them samples to use in their homes. Procter & Gamble has on-site labs such as a nappy-testing centre where dozens of mothers bring their babies to be studied. In-home placement tests are common for products ranging from ice cream flavours to new appliances.

How are customer preferences measured? The *rank-order* method asks the consumer to rank the options. The *paired-comparison* method presents pairs of options and asks the consumer which one is preferred in each pair. The *monadic-rating* method asks the consumer to rate each product on a scale so marketers can derive the individual's preference order and levels.

Market testing

After management is satisfied with functional and psychological performance, the new product is ready to be branded, packaged and market tested. In an authentic setting, marketers can learn how large the market is and see how consumers and dealers react to handling, using and repurchasing the new product.

Not all companies undertake market testing but many believe it can yield valuable information about buyers, dealers, marketing programme effectiveness and market potential. The main issues are: how much market testing should be done, and what kind(s)?

The amount of market testing is influenced by the investment cost and risk on the one hand, and the time pressure and research cost on the other. High-investment–high-risk new products, where the chance of failure is high, must be market tested; the cost of the market tests will be an insignificant percentage of total project cost. High-risk products – those that create really new product categories (first instant breakfast drink) or have novel features (first gum-strengthening toothpaste) – warrant more market testing than modified new products (another toothpaste brand).

The amount of market testing may be severely reduced if the company is under great time pressure because the season is just starting, or because competitors are about to launch their brands. The company may prefer the risk of a new product failure to the risk of losing distribution or market penetration on a highly successful product.

Consumer goods market testing

Consumer new product tests seek to estimate four variables: *trial, first repeat, adoption* and *purchase frequency*. The company hopes to find all these variables at high levels. Many consumers may try the new product but few rebuy it; or it might achieve high permanent adoption but low purchase frequency (e.g. gourmet frozen foods).

Here are four major methods of consumer goods market testing, from least to most costly.

Sales-wave research In sales-wave research, consumers who initially try the new product at no cost are reoffered it, or a competitor's product, at slightly reduced prices. The offer may be made as many as five times (sales waves), while the company notes how many customers selected that product again and their reported level of satisfaction. Sales-wave research can also expose consumers to one or more advertising concepts to measure the impact of that advertising on repeat purchase.

Sales-wave research can be implemented quickly and conducted with a fair amount of security. It can be carried out without final packaging and advertising. However, it does not indicate trial rates that the new product would achieve with different sales promotion incentives, as the consumers are pre-selected to try the product. Nor does it indicate the brand's power to gain distribution and a favourable shelf position.

Simulated test marketing Simulated test marketing calls for finding 30–40 qualified shoppers and questioning them about brand familiarity and preferences in a specific product category. These consumers attend a brief screening of both well-known and new TV commercials or print advertisements. One advertisement promotes the new product but is not singled out for attention. Consumers receive a small amount of money and are invited into a store where they may buy any items. The company notes how many consumers buy the new product brand and competing brands. This provides a measure of the advertisement's relative effectiveness against competing advertisements in stimulating customer trials. Consumers are asked the reasons for their purchases or non-purchases. Those who did not buy the new product are given a free sample. Some weeks later, they are interviewed by phone to determine product attitudes, usage, satisfaction and repurchase intention, and are offered an opportunity to repurchase the new product.

This method gives fairly accurate results on advertising effectiveness and trial rates (and repeat rates if extended) in a much shorter time and at a fraction of the cost of using real test markets. The results are incorporated into new product forecasting models to project ultimate sales levels. Marketing research firms have reported surprisingly accurate predictions of sales levels of new market offerings/products that are subsequently launched in the market.[45] In a world where media and channels have become highly fragmented, however, it will become increasingly hard for simulated test marketing to truly simulate market conditions with only traditional approaches.

Controlled test marketing In controlled test marketing, a research firm manages a panel of stores that will carry new products for a fee. The company with the new product specifies the number of stores and geographic locations it wants to test. The research firm delivers the new product to the participating stores and controls shelf position; number of facings, displays and point-of-purchase promotions; and pricing. Electronic scanners measure sales at checkout. The company can also evaluate the impact of local advertising and promotions.

Controlled test marketing allows the company to test the impact of in-store factors and limited advertising on buying behaviour. A sample of consumers can be interviewed later to give their impressions of the new product. The company does not have to use its own sales force, give trade allowances or 'buy' distribution. However, controlled test marketing provides no information on how to persuade the trade to carry the new product. This technique also exposes the product and its features to competitors' scrutiny.

Test markets The ultimate way to test a new consumer product is to put it into full-scale test markets. The company chooses a few representative cities, and the sales force tries to persuade the trade to carry the new product and give it good shelf exposure. The company puts on a full advertising and promotion campaign similar to the one it would use in national marketing. Test marketing also measures the impact of alternative marketing plans by varying the marketing programme in different cities and or/regions: a full-scale test can cost over €1 million, depending on the number of test areas, the test duration, and the amount of data the company wants to collect.

Management faces several decisions:

- **How many test sites?** Most tests use two to six sites. The greater the possible loss, the greater the number of contending marketing strategies, the greater the regional differences and the greater the chance of test-market interference by competitors, the more sites management should test.
- **Which sites?** Each company must develop selection criteria such as having good media coverage, cooperative chain stores and average competitive activity. How representative the site is of other markets must also be considered.
- **Length of test?** Market tests last anywhere from a few months to a year. The longer the average repurchase period, the longer the test period.
- **What information to collect?** Warehouse shipment data will show gross stock buying but will not indicate weekly sales at the retail level. Store audits will show retail sales and competitors' market shares but will not reveal buyer characteristics. Consumer panels will indicate which people are buying which brands and their loyalty and switching rates. Buyer surveys will yield in-depth information about consumer attitudes, usage and satisfaction.
- **What action to take?** If the test markets show high trial and repurchase rates, the marketer should launch the new product nationally; if a high trial rate and low repurchase rate, redesign or drop the new product; if a low trial rate and high repurchase rate, develop marketing communications to convince more people to try it. If trial and repurchase rates are both low, abandon the new product. Many managers find it difficult to kill a project that created much effort and attention even if they should, resulting in an unfortunate (and typically unsuccessful and expensive) escalation of commitment.[46]

In spite of its benefits, many companies today do not do any test marketing and rely on faster and more economical testing methods. Absolut vodka and Colgate-Palmolive often launch a new product in a set of small 'lead countries' and keep rolling it out if it proves successful.

Business-product market testing

New business products (market offerings) can also benefit from market testing. Expensive industrial new products and new technologies will normally undergo alpha testing (within the company) and beta testing (with outside customers). During beta testing, the company's technical people observe how test customers use the new product, a practice that often exposes unanticipated problems of safety and servicing, and alerts the company to customer training and service support requirements. The company can also observe how much CPV the equipment adds to the customer's operation as a clue to subsequent pricing.

The company will ask test customers to express their purchase intention and other reactions after the test. Companies must interpret beta test results carefully because only a small number of test customers are used, they are not randomly drawn, and tests are somewhat customised to each site. Another risk is that test customers who are unimpressed with the new product may leak unfavourable reports about it.

A second common test method for business new products is to introduce them at trade shows. The company can observe how much interest buyers show in the new product, how they react to various CPV attributes and benefits, and how many express purchase intentions or place orders.

New industrial products can be tested in distributor and dealer display rooms, where they may stand next to the manufacturer's other products and possibly competitors' products. This method yields preference and pricing information in the product's normal selling atmosphere. The disadvantages are that customers might want to place early orders that cannot be fulfilled, and those customers who come in might not represent the target market.

Industrial manufacturers come close to using full test marketing when they give a limited supply of the new product to the sales force to sell in a limited number of areas that receive sales promotion support and printed catalogue sheets.

Commercialisation and new product launch

If the company goes ahead with commercialisation, it will face its largest costs to date.[47] It will need to contract for manufacture or build or rent a full-scale manufacturing facility. Another major cost is marketing. To introduce a major new consumer packaged product into the national market can cost from €25 million to as much as €100 million in advertising, promotion and other marketing communications in the first year. In the introduction of new food products, marketing expenditures typically represent 57 per cent of sales during the first year. Most new product campaigns rely on a sequenced mix of marketing communication tools.

When (timing)

In commercialising a new product, market-entry timing is critical. Suppose a company has almost completed the development work on its new product and learns that a competitor is nearing the end of *its* development work. The company faces three choices:

1 **First entry**. The first firm entering a market usually enjoys the 'first mover advantages' of locking up key distributors and customers and gaining leadership. But if the new product is rushed to market before it is ready, the first entry can backfire.
2 **Parallel entry**. The firm might time its entry to coincide with the competitor's entry. The market may pay more attention when two companies are advertising the new products.[48]
3 **Late entry**. The firm might delay its launch until after the competitor has entered. The competitor will have borne the cost of educating the market, and its new product may reveal faults the late entrant can avoid. The late entrant can also learn the size of the market.

The timing decision requires additional considerations.[49] If a new product replaces an older product, the company might delay the introduction until the old product's stock is drawn down. If the product is seasonal, it might be delayed until the right season arrives; often a new product waits for a 'killer application' to occur. Complicating new product launches, many companies are encountering competitive 'design-arounds' – rivals are imitating inventions but making their own versions just different enough to avoid patent infringement and the need to pay royalties.

Where (geographic strategy)

The company must decide whether to launch the new product in a single locality, a region, several regions, the national market or the international market. Most will develop a planned market roll-out over time. Company size is an important factor here. Small companies will select an attractive site area and put on a blitz campaign, entering other sites one at a time. Large companies will introduce their new product into a whole region and then move to the next region or country. Companies with national distribution networks, such as car companies, will launch their new models in the national market.

Most companies design new products to sell primarily in the domestic market. If the product does well, the company considers exporting to neighbouring countries or the world market, redesigning if necessary. In choosing roll-out markets, the major criteria are: market potential; the company's local reputation; the cost of setting up the supply channels; the cost of communication media; the influence of the area on other areas; and the strength of competition.

With the web connecting near and distant parts of the globe, competition is more likely to cross national borders. Companies are increasingly rolling out new products simultaneously across the globe, rather than nationally or even regionally. However, masterminding a global launch poses challenges, and a sequential roll-out across countries may still be the best option.[50]

To whom (target-market prospects)

Within the roll-out markets, the company must adopt a customer relationship approach and target its initial distribution and marketing communications to appeal to the best prospect groups. The company will have profiled these, and ideally they should be early adopters, heavy users and opinion leaders who can be reached at low cost.[51] Few groups have all these characteristics. The company should rate the various prospect groups on these characteristics and target the best group. The aim is to generate strong sales as soon as possible to attract further prospects.

How (introductory market strategy)

The company must develop an action plan for introducing the new product. Because new product launches often take longer and cost more money than expected, many potentially successful offerings suffer from underfunding. It is important to allocate sufficient time and resource as the new product gains a foothold in the marketplace.[52]

A master of new product introductions, Apple Computers staged a massive marketing blitz in 1998 to launch the iMac, its re-entry into the computer PC business after a hiatus of 14 years. Five years later, Apple struck gold again with the launch of the iPod. The company continues to set a fast pace and in the spring of 2010 launched its iPad which is a design leader as well as a technological first that can provide entertainment and business-related features.

To coordinate the many activities involved in launching a new product, management can use network-planning techniques such as **critical path scheduling**. This calls for developing a master chart showing the simultaneous and sequential activities that must take place to launch the product. By estimating how much time each activity takes, the planners estimate completion time for the entire project. Any delay in any activity on the critical path – the shortest route to completion – will cause the project to become overdue.[53]

Breakthrough marketing

Apple iPad

Hundreds of people gathered on 1 March 2011 at Apple's flagship store in London to be among the first to buy the company's latest new offering – the iPad – following a delayed launch caused by unexpected high demand in the USA.

Financial Times technology reporter Jonathan Fildes, who went along to the Apple store, said it was besieged with hundreds of people, the police were on hand to keep people in order, and every time a new owner of an iPad emerged they won a cheer from the crowd. He said there was a 'carnival' atmosphere outside the store aided by the appearance of the world's tallest married couple, Wilco van-Kleef and Keisha Bolton, who turned up to promote the Guinness World Records iPad app. Long-standing Apple fan Stephen Fry also turned up to buy a 3G version of the iPad.

Despite the success of the iPad's launch in the USA, some have criticised it for being a closed system that limited what people could do with the books, magazines, music and video they enjoy. The BBC's technology correspondent Rory Cellan-Jones commented that 'magazine editors were enthusing about the possibility of glossy interactive editions which will convince premium advertisers to keep spending'. The tablet-device is also starting to see competition from other devices such as the Dell Streak and the established Archos media tablets. Similar devices that run Google's Android operating system were launched in the final three months of 2010. Two versions of the iPad are available and prices start at £429 including VAT. One model only uses wi-fi to connect to the net and the other can use both wi-fi and 3G mobile technology. The iPad went on sale in continental Europe on 28 May. In the UK mobile phone providers Vodafone, Orange, O2 and 3 revealed details of the price plans for the 3G version which requires a separate micro-Sim card in order to connect to the internet. The 3G version requires owners to buy airtime to use the gadget while out and about.

The iPad is essentially an emotional luxury product – a purchase that is not really needed, as many of the things the iPad offers can be done on other gadgets such as phones and laptops. Most of the people in the world do not interact with content, they just consume it, and the iPad is a great device for consuming content but not great for creating it. In an attempt to retain its lead in the market with the iPad in the face of emerging competition, Apple launched its iPad 2 in March 2011. The new device features front- and back-facing cameras and a gyroscope, and is dramatically faster with a A5 dual-core processor. It is 33 per cent thinner at 8.8 mm – slimmer than the iPhone 4. It also fell in weight from 1.5 pounds to 1.3 pounds.

Source: BBC, 28 February 2010; *Financial Times*, 2 March 2011 (Tim Bradshaw, Chris Nuttall and Shannon Bond).

The campaign for the Apple iPad was a masterful new product introduction that helped it quickly achieve a dominant market share.
Source: Chris Batson/Alamy.

The consumer adoption process

Adoption is an individual's decision to become a regular user of a product. The *consumer adoption process* is followed by the *consumer loyalty process*, which is the concern of the established producer. Years ago, new product marketers used a *mass market approach* to launch products, which had two main drawbacks: it called for heavy marketing expenditures, and it wasted many exposures. These drawbacks led to a second approach, *heavy-user target marketing*. This approach makes sense, provided that heavy users are identifiable and are early adopters. However, even within the heavy-user group, many heavy users are loyal to existing brands. New product marketers now aim at early adopters and use the theory of innovation diffusion and customer adoption to identify them. Mozilla launched its new Firefox 3 Web browser in the United Kingdom in the summer of 2008 and hopes to build on its encouraging market share in Europe with its new software that is claimed to be more user friendly and adaptable than Microsoft's Internet Explorer's web browser.

Stages in the adoption process

An **innovation** is any good, service or idea that someone *perceives* as new, no matter how long its history. Innovations take time to spread. Rogers defines the **innovation diffusion process** as 'the spread of a new idea from its source of invention or creation to its ultimate users or adopters'.[54] The consumer adoption process tracks the steps an individual takes from first hearing about an innovation to its final adoption.[55]

Adopters of new products move through five stages:

1 **Awareness**. The consumer becomes aware of the innovation but lacks information about it.
2 **Interest**. The consumer is stimulated to seek information about the innovation.
3 **Evaluation**. The consumer considers whether to try the innovation.
4 **Trial**. The consumer tries the innovation to improve his or her estimate of its value.
5 **Adoption**. The consumer decides to make full and regular use of the innovation.

The new product marketer should facilitate movement through these stages. A portable electric dishwasher manufacturer might discover that many customers are stuck in the interest stage; they do not buy because of their uncertainty and the large investment cost.[56] But these same customers would be willing to use an electric dishwasher on a trial basis for a small monthly fee. The manufacturer should consider offering a trial-use plan with an option to buy.

Factors influencing the adoption process

Marketers recognise the following characteristics of the adoption process: differences in individual readiness to try new products; the effect of personal influence; differing rates of adoption; and differences in organisations' readiness to try new products. Some researchers are focusing on use-diffusion processes as a complement to adoption process models, to see how consumers actually use new products.[57]

Readiness to try new products and personal influence

Rogers[58] defines a person's level of innovativeness as 'the degree to which an individual is relatively earlier in adopting new ideas than the other members of his social system'. In each product area, there are pioneers and early adopters. Some people are the first to adopt new clothing fashions or new appliances; some doctors are the first to prescribe new medicines; some farmers are the first to adopt new farming methods.[59] People fall

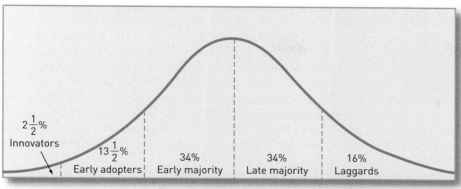

Time of adoption of innovations

Figure 15.7 Adopter categorisation on the basis of relative time of adoption of innovations

into the adopter categories shown in Figure 15.7. After a slow start, an increasing number of people adopt the innovation, the number reaches a peak, and then it diminishes as fewer non-adopters remain. The five adopter groups differ in their value orientations and their motives for adopting or resisting the new product.[60]

- **Innovators**: technology enthusiasts; they are venturesome and enjoy tinkering with new products and mastering their intricacies. In return for low prices, they are happy to conduct alpha and beta testing and report on early weaknesses.
- **Early adopters**: opinion leaders who carefully search for new technologies that might give them a dramatic competitive advantage. They are less price sensitive and willing to adopt the product if given personalised solutions and good service support.
- **Early majority**: deliberate pragmatists who adopt the new technology when its benefits are proven and a lot of adoption has already taken place. They make up the mainstream market.
- **Late majority**: sceptical conservatives who are risk averse, technology shy and price sensitive.
- **Laggards**: tradition bound and resist the innovation until they find that the status quo is no longer defensible.

Each group must be approached with a different type of marketing if the firm wants to move its innovation through the stages of the full product life cycle.[61]

Personal influence is the effect one person has on another's attitude or purchase probability. Its significance is greater in some situations and for some individuals than others, and it is more important in the evaluation stage than the other stages. It has more influence on late adopters than early adopters and is more important in risky situations.

Companies often target innovators and early adopters with product introductions. For Vespa scooters, the Italian company Piaggio has hired models to go around cafés and clubs to publicise the new scooters.[62]

Characteristics of the innovation

Some products are an instant success (rollerblades), whereas others take a long time to gain acceptance (diesel engine cars).[63] Five characteristics influence the rate of adoption of an innovation. These are considered in relation to personal video recorders (PVRs) for home use.

The first characteristic is *relative advantage* – the degree to which the innovation appears superior to existing products. The greater the perceived relative advantage of using a PVR, say for easily recording favourite shows, pausing live TV or skipping commercials, the more quickly it will be adopted. The second is *compatibility* – the degree to which the innovation matches the values and experiences of the individuals. PVRs, for example, are highly compatible with the preferences of avid television watchers. Third is *complexity* – the degree to which the innovation is difficult to understand or use. PVRs are somewhat complex and will therefore take a slightly longer time to penetrate into home use. Fourth is *divisibility* – the degree to which the innovation can be tried on a limited basis. This provides a sizeable challenge for PVRs – sampling can only occur in a retail store or perhaps a friend's house. Fifth is *communicability* – the degree to which the benefits of use are observable or describable to others. The fact that PVRs have some clear advantages can help create interest and curiosity.

Other characteristics that influence the rate of adoption include cost, risk and uncertainty; scientific credibility and social approval. The new product marketer must research all these factors and give the key ones maximum attention in designing the new product and marketing programme.

Organisations' readiness to adopt innovations

The creator of a new teaching method would want to identify innovative schools. The producer of a new piece of medical equipment would want to identify innovative hospitals. Adoption is associated with variables in the organisation's environment (community progressiveness, community income), the organisation itself (size, profits, pressure to change) and the administrators (education level, age, sophistication). Other forces come into play in trying to get a product adopted into organisations that receive the bulk of their funding from the government, such as state schools and hospitals in the United Kingdom. A controversial or innovative new product offering can be seriously damaged by negative public opinion.

SUMMARY

1 Once a company has segmented the market, chosen its target customer groups and identified their needs, and determined its desired market positioning, it is ready to develop and launch appropriate new market offerings. Marketing should participate with other departments in every stage of the development of new value offerings.

2 Successful new product/market offering development requires the company to establish an effective organisation for managing the process. Traditionally, companies have chosen to use product managers, new product managers, new product committees, new product departments or new product venture teams. Increasingly, companies are adopting cross-functional teams, connecting to individuals and organisations outside the company, and developing multiple market offerings as they accept that the right CPV requires the coordinated effort of all internal and external parties.

3 Eight stages take place in the new product/ market offering development process: idea generation, screening, concept development and testing, marketing strategy development, business analysis, product/offer development, market testing and commercialisation. At each stage, the company must determine whether the idea should be dropped or moved to the next stage.

4 The consumer adoption process is the process by which customers learn about new market offerings, try them, and adopt or reject them. Today many marketers are targeting heavy users and early adopters of new products, because both groups can be reached by specific media and tend to be opinion leaders. The consumer adoption process is influenced by many factors beyond the marketer's control, including consumers' and organisations' willingness to try new market offerings.

APPLICATIONS

Marketing debate

Whom should you target with new products? Some new product experts maintain that getting close to customers through intensive research is the only way to develop successful new products. Other experts disagree and maintain that customers cannot possibly provide useful feedback on what they don't know and cannot provide insights that will lead to breakthrough products.

Take a position: Consumer research is critical to new product development *versus* Consumer research may not be all that helpful in new product development.

Marketing discussion

Think about the last new product you bought. How do you think its success will be affected by the five characteristics of an innovation: relative advantage, compatibility, complexity, divisibility and communicability?

REFERENCES

[1]James Dyson (2002) Business whirlwind, *BBC Business News*, 5 February; P. Marsh (2006) Dyson keeps its wash day hopes alive, *Financial Times*, 27 June; Sir James Dyson and family (2008) *Sunday Times* online, 27 April.

[2]For some scholarly reviews, see P. Drucker (2001) *The Essential Drucker*, Oxford: Butterworth-Heinemann; E. Dahan and J. R. Hauser (2002) Product development: managing a dispersed process, in B. Weitz and R. Wensley (eds), *Handbook of Marketing*, London: Sage, 179–222.

[3]P. Cameron (2007) Innovation and new product development: Sky1 – a mini case study, *Marketing Review*, 7(4), 313–23; S. J. Carson (2007) When to give up control of outsourced new product development, *Journal of Marketing*, January, 71(1), 49–66.

[4]Don't laugh at gilded butterflies, *The Economist*, 24 April 2004, 71. For some academic discussion of the effects of new product introduction on markets, see H. J. Van Heerde, C. F. Mela and P. Manchanda (2004) The dynamic effect of innovation on market structure, *Journal of Marketing Research*, 41 (May), 166–83.

[5]S. Min, M. U. Kalwani and W. T. Robinson (2006) Market pioneer and early follower survival risks: a contingency of new versus incrementally new-product markets, *Journal of Marketing*, 70 (January), 15–33; C. P. Moreau, A. B. Markman and D. R. Lehmann (2001) What is it? Category flexibility and consumers' response to really new products, *Journal of Consumer Research*, 27 (March), 489–98; M. Zhao, S. Hoeffler and D. W. Dahl (2009) The role of imagination-focused visualization on new product evaluation, *Journal of Marketing Research (JMR)*, 46(I) 1, 46–55.

[6]S. Wuyts, S. Dutta and S. Stremersch (2004) Portfolios of interfirm agreements in technology-intensive markets: consequences for innovation and profitability, *Journal of Marketing*, 68 (April), 88–100; H. Perks, K. Kahn and C. Zhang (2009) An empirical evaluation of R & D–marketing NPD integration in Chinese firms: the Guanxi effect, *Journal of Product Innovation Management*, 26(6), 640–51.

[7]C. Hui-Chun (2010) Linkage community based innovation and speed to market: the mediating role of new product development

process, *International Journal of Organizational Innovation*, 2(4), 49–60.

[8]A. Sood and G. J. Tellis (2005) Technological evolution and radical innovation, *Journal of Marketing*, 69 (July), 152–68; P. N. Golder, R. Shacham and D. Mitra (2009) Innovations' origins: when, by whom, and how are radical innovations developed?, *Marketing Science*, 28(1), 166–79; V. Story, S. Hart and L. O'Malley (2009) Relational resources and competences for radical product innovation, *Journal of Marketing Management*, 25(6), 461–81.

[9]See S. E. Reid and U. de Brentani (2010) Market vision and market visioning competence: impact on early performance for radically new, high-tech products, *Journal of Product Innovation Management*, 27(4), 500–18.

[10]M. R. Murray and D. Wilemon (2010) The impact of changing markets and competition on the NPD speed/market success relationship, *International Journal of Innovation Management*, 14(5), 841–70; M. R. Millson and D. Wilemon (2010) The impact of changing markets and competition on the NPD speed/market success relationship, *International Journal of Innovation Management*, 14(5), 841–70.

[11]C. Passariello (2006) Brand new bag: Louis Vuitton tries modern methods on factory lines, *Wall Street Journal*, 9 October.

[12]The world's fifty most innovative companies (2007) Special Report, *BusinessWeek*, 9 May.

[13]B. Weiners (2004) Gore-Tex tackles the great indoors, *Business 2.0*, April, 32; A. Harrington (2003) Who's afraid of a new product?, *Fortune*, 10 November, 189–92; W. L. Gore & Associates, *The Times* online, 11 March.

[14]D. G. McKendrick and J. B. Wade (2010) Frequent incremental change, organizational size, and mortality in high-technology competition, *Industrial & Corporate Change*, 19(3), 613–39.

[15]D. Lange, S. Boivie and A. D. Henderson (2009) The parenting paradox: how multibusiness diversifiers endorse disruptive technologies while their corporate children struggle. *Academy of Management Journal*, 52(1), 179–98.

[16]T.-J. Chang, W. C. Chen, L. Wen-Chiang, L. Z. Lin and J. S.-K. Chiu (2010) The impact of market orientation on customer knowledge development and NPD success, *International Journal of Innovation and Technology Management*, 7(4), 303–27.

[17]S. Salomo, E. J. Keinschmidt, J. Elko and U. de Brentani (2010) Managing new product development teams in a globally dispersed NPD program, *Journal of Product Innovation Management*, 27(7), 955–71; U. de Brentani, E. J. Kleinschmidt and S. Salomo (2010) Success in global new product development: impact of strategy and the behavioral environment of the firm, *Journal of Product Innovation Management*, 27(2), 143–60.

[18]S. Ogama and F. T. Pillar (2006) Reducing the risks of new-product development, *MIT Sloan Management Review*, Winter, 65–71; J. Hlavacek, C. Maxwell and J. Williams, Jr (2009) Learn from new product failures, *Research Technology Management*, 52(4), 31–9.

[19]T. N. Burton (2004) By learning from failures Lilly keeps drug pipelines full, *Wall Street Journal*, 21 April.

[20]N. Byrnes (2007) Xerox's new design team customers, *BusinessWeek*, 7 May, 71.

[21]D. Sabbagh (2008) Blu-ray delivers fatal sting to rival in battle of high definition DVD, *The Times*, 19 February.

[22]B. S. Blichfeldt (2005) On the development of brand and line extensions, *Journal of Brand Management*, 12(3), 177–90; A.E. Akgün, H. Keskin and J. C. Byrne (2010) Procedural justice climate in new product development teams: antecedents and consequences, *Journal of Product Innovation Management*, 27(7), 1096–111.

[23]D. Sacks, C. Salter, A. Deutschmann and S. Kirsner (2007) Innovation scouts, *Fast Company*, May, 90.

[24]H. Ernst, W. D. and C. Rübsaamen (2010) Sales, marketing, and research-and-development cooperation across new product development stages: implications for success, *Journal of Marketing*, 74(5), 80–92; R. Bunduchi (2009) Implementing best practices to support creativity in NPD cross-functional teams, *International Journal of Innovation Management*, 13(4), 537–54; C. Nakata and S. Im (2010) Spurring cross-functional integration for higher new product performance: a group effectiveness perspective, *Journal of Product Innovation Management*, 27(4), 554–71; G. Gemser and M. A. A. M. Leenders, Managing cross-functional cooperation for new product development success, *Long Range Planning*, 44(1), 26–41.

[25]J. Grönlund, D. Sjödin and F. J. Rönnberg (2010) Open innovation and the stage-gate process: a revised model for new product development, *California Management Review*, 52(3), 106–31.

[26]K. van Oorschot, K. Sengupta, H. Akkermans and L. van Wassenhove (2010) Get fat fast: surviving stage-gate® in NPD, *Journal of Product Innovation Management*, 27(6), 828–39.

[27]An alternative approach to the funnel process advocates 'rocketing'. See D. Nichols, *Return on Ideas*, Chichester: John Wiley & Sons.

[28]J. Hauser, G. J. Tellis and A. Griffin (2006) Research on innovation: a review and agenda for Marketing Science, *Marketing Science*, 25 (November–December), 687–717.

[29]H. Chesbrough (2006) *Open Business Models: How to Thrive in the New Innovation Landscape*, Boston, MA: Harvard University Press; E. Von Hipple (2005) *Democratizing Innovation*, Cambridge, MA: MIT Press; B. Helm (2005) Inside a white-hot idea factory, *BusinessWeek*, 15 January, 72–1; C. K. Prahalad and V. Ramaswamy (2004) *The Future of Competition: Co-creating Unique Value with Customers*, Boston, MA: Harvard University Press.

[30]A. J. Griffin and J. Hauser (1993) The voice of the customer, *Marketing Science*, Winter, 1–27.

[31]P. C. Hoenbein and R. F. Cammarano (2006) Customers at work, *Marketing Management*, January–February, 26–31.

[32]P. Seybold (2007) Customer-controlled innovation: collaboration with customers is transforming product-development strategies and unlocking new ways for companies to innovate, *Optimize*, 6(2), 26.

[33]*BusinessWeek* (2007) op. cit.

[34]D. W. Dahl and P. Moreau (2002) The influence and value of analogical thinking during new-product ideation, *Journal of Marketing Research*, 39 (February), 47–60; M. Goodman (1995) *Creative Management*, Hemel Hempstead: Prentice Hall International.

[35]See www.smokinggun.com.

[36]O. Toubia and L. Flores (2007) Adaptive idea screening using consumers, *Marketing Science*, 26 (May–June), 342–60.

[37]Hoeffler (2003) op. cit.; Dahl and Moreau (2002) op. cit.; J. Sharan, J. Kamel and M. Jamil (2007) A multibrand concept-testing methodology for new product strategy, *Journal of Product Management*, 24(1), 34–51.

[38]For additional information see D. Bakken and C. L. Frazier (2006) Conjoint analysis: understanding consumer decision making, in R. Grover and M. Vriens (eds), *The Handbook of Marketing Research*, Thousand Oaks, CA: Sage; V. T. Rao and J. R. Hauser (2004) Conjoint analysis, related modeling and application, in Y. Wind and P. E. Green (eds), *Market Research and Modeling: Progress and Prospects – A Tribute to Paul Green*, New York: Springer, 141–68.

[39]P. N. Golder and G. J. Tellis (1997) Will it ever fly? Modeling the takeoff of really new durables, *Marketing Science*, 16(3), 256–70.

[40]The present value (V) of a future sum (I) to be received t years from today and discounted at the interest rate (r) is given by $V = I_t/(1 + r)^t$. Thus €4,716,000/$(1.15)^5$ = €2,345,000.

[41]See L. R. Guinta and N. C. Praizler (1993) *The QFD Book: The Team Approach to Solving Problems and Satisfying Customers through Quality Function Deployment*, New York: AMACOM.

[42]Peters (1997) *The Circle of Innovation*, New York: Alfred A. Knopf; K. Zheng Zhou, Y. Chi Kin and D. K. Tse (2005) The effects of strategic orientations on technology and market-based breakthrough innovations, *Journal of Marketing*, 2, 42–60.

[43]M. Iansiti and A. MacCormack (1997) Developing products on internet time, *Harvard Business Review*, September–October, 108–17.

[44]Peters (1997) op. cit., 96.

[45]K. J. Clancy, P. C. Krieg and M. M. Wolf (2005) *Marketing New Products Successfully: Using Simulated Test Marketing Methodology*, New York: Lexington Books.

[46]E. Biyalogorski, W. Boulding and R. Staelin (2006) Stuck in the past: why managers persist with new-product failures, *Journal of Marketing*, 70 (April), 108–21.

[47]R. Chandy, B. Hopstaken, O. Narasimhan and J. Prabhu (2006) From invention to innovation: conversion in product development, *Journal of Marketing Research*, 43 (August), 404–508.

[48]R. Prins and P. C. Verhoef (2007) Marketing communication drivers of adoption timing of a new e-service among existing customers, *Journal of Marketing*, 71 (April), 169–83.

[49]For further discussion, see Y. Wu, S. Balasubramanian and V. Mahajan (2004) When is a pre-announced new product likely to be

delayed?, *Journal of Marketing*, 68 (April), 104–13; R. Srinivasan, G. L. Lilien and A. Rangaswamy (2004) First in first out? The effects of network externalities on pioneer survival, *Journal of Marketing*, 68 (January), 41–58; B. L. Bayus, S. Jain and A. Rao (2001) Consequences: an analysis of truth or vaporware and new-product announcements, *Journal of Marketing Research*, February, 3–13.

[50]K. Gielens and J.-B. E. M. Steenkamp (2007) Drivers of consumer acceptance of new packaged goods: an investigation across products and countries, *International Journal of Research in Marketing*, 97–111.

[51]P. Kotler and G. Zaltman (1976) Targeting prospects for a new product, *Journal of Advertising Research*, February, 7–20; E. Gummesson (1998) Implementation requires a relationship marketing paradigm, *Journal of the Academy of Marketing Science*, 26(3), 242–9.

[52]M. Leslie and C. A. Holloway (2006) The sales learning curve, *Harvard Business Review*, July–August, 114–23.

[53]For details, see K. G. Lockyer (1984) *Critical Path Analysis and Other Project Network Techniques*, London: Pitman. Also see A. Rangasway and G. L. Lilien (1997) Software tools for new-product development, *Journal of Marketing Research*, February, 177–84.

[54]The following discussion is based on E. M. Rogers (1962) *Diffusion of Innovations*, New York: Free Press. Also see the 3rd edn published in 1973.

[55]C. P. Moreau, D. R. Lehmann and A. B. Markman (2001) Entrenched knowledge structures and consumer response to new products, *Journal of Marketing Research*, 38 (February), 14–29.

[56]J. T. Gourville (2006) Eager sellers and stony buyers, *Harvard Business Review*, June, 99–106.

[57]C.-F. Shih and A. Ventkatesh (2004) Beyond adoption: development and application of a use-diffusion model, *Journal of Marketing*, 68 (January), 59–72.

[58]E. M. Rogers (1962) *Diffusion of Innovations*, New York: Free Press, 1962; see also his 3rd edn published in 1983.

[59]M. Hertzenstein, S. S. Posavac and J. J. Brakuz (2007) Adoption of new and really new products: the effects of self regulation systems and risk salience, *Journal of Marketing Research*, 44 (May), 251–60; C. Van den Bulte and Y. V. Joshi (2007) New-product diffusion with influentials and imitators, *Marketing Science*, 26 (May–June), 400–21; Hoeffler (2003) op. cit.

[60]Rogers (1962) op. cit. 192; G. A. Moore (1999) *Crossing the Chasm: Marketing and Selling High-Tech Products to Mainstream Customers*, New York: HarperBusiness.

[61]A. Parasuraman and C. L. Colby (2001) *Techno-ready Marketing*, New York: Free Press; Mohr (2001) op. cit.

[62]M. M. Hall, Selling by stealth, *Business Life*, November, 51–55.

[63]B. Kamrad, S. S. Lele, A. Siddique and R. J. Thomas (2005) Innovation diffusion uncertainty, advertising and pricing policies, *European Journal of Operational Research*, 164(3), 829–50; G. B. Voss, M. Montoya-Weiss and Z. G. Voss (2006) Aligning innovation with market characteristics in the non-profit professional theatre industry, *Journal of Marketing Research*, 43(2), 296–302; M. J. Brand and E. K. R. E. Hurzingh (2008) Into the drivers of innovation adoption: what is the impact of the current level of adoption?, *European Journal of Innovation Management*, 11(1), 5–21; A. Murray and D. Demick (2006) Wine retailing in Ireland: the diffusion of innovation, *International Journal of Wine Marketing*, 18(3); G. Yaleinkaya (2008) A culture-based approach to understanding the adoption and diffusion of new products across countries, *International Marketing Review*, 25(2), 202–14.

Chapter 16

Developing and managing pricing strategies

IN THIS CHAPTER, WE WILL ADDRESS THE FOLLOWING QUESTIONS:

1 How do consumers process and evaluate prices?

2 How should a company initially set prices for products or services?

3 How should a company adapt prices to meet varying circumstances and opportunities?

4 When should a company initiate a price change?

5 How should a company respond to a competitor's price change?

Even though it cannot access the internet or take pictures, the top luxury edition of the 'Æ+Y' mobile phone costs no less than €42,000.

Source: Æ+Y phone by Æsir.

CHAPTER JOURNEY

Understanding
pricing

Setting
the price

Adapting
the price

Initiating and
responding to
price changes

P rice is the one element of the marketing mix that produces revenue; the other elements produce costs. Prices are perhaps the easiest element of the marketing programme to adjust; product features, channels and even promotion take more time. Price also communicates to the market the company's intended value positioning of its product or brand.

Consider the Æ+Y mobile phone.

Even though it cannot go on the internet or take pictures, the top luxury edition of the 'Æ+Y' mobile phone developed by the Danish company Æsir costs no less than €42,000. 'Our mobile phone is an alternative for those who want a phone in an exciting and timeless design. Unlike the mass-produced phones we have made a telephone that favors design more than technology,' says Thomas Møller Jensen, founder of Æsir.The Æ+Y phone is available in either 18 carat gold and ceramic (€42,000) or stainless steel (€7,250). While other mobile phone companies, such as Nokia, also offer luxury editions of some of their mobile phones Æ+Y is among the first mobile phones to emphasise quality, craftsmanship and design more than technological functionalities. 'Our aim is not to compete with iPhones and other smartphones. Instead, we seek to attract people who value beauty and design and who can afford to pay accordingly,' Thomas Møller Jensen says. Despite the high prices, people who are interested in purchasing an Æ+Y phone could end up using their time in vain as the phone will be produced only in a few thousand units.[1]

Pricing decisions are clearly complex and difficult, and many marketers neglect their pricing strategies[2] and the effect they might have on the market and on the public. Holistic marketers must take into account many factors in making pricing decisions – the company, the customers, the competition and the marketing environment. Pricing decisions must be consistent with the firm's marketing strategy and its target markets and brand positionings.

In this chapter, we provide concepts and tools to facilitate the setting of initial prices and adjusting prices over time and markets.

Understanding pricing

Price is not just a number on a tag. Price comes in many forms and performs many functions. Rent, tuition, fares, fees, rates, tolls, wages and commissions may all in some way be the price you pay for some good or service. Price is also made up of many components. If you buy a new car, the sticker price may be adjusted by rebates and dealer incentives. Some firms allow for payment through multiple forms, such as €120 plus 25,000 frequent flier miles from an airline loyalty programme.[3]

Throughout most of history, prices were set by negotiation between buyers and sellers. Bargaining is still a sport in some areas and countries, and takes place in both consumer and business markets. Companies may proactively seek to increase their bargaining power. For instance, the introduction of private labels may enhance a retailer's bargaining power with respect to manufacturers.[4] Setting one price for all buyers is a relatively modern idea that arose with the development of large-scale retailing in the second half of the nineteenth century. European department stores such as Le Bon Marché (France), Delaney's New Mart (Ireland), Whiteleys (England) and others introduced fixed-price policies (accompanied by guarantees allowing exchanges and refunds), because they carried so many items and supervised so many employees.

Traditionally, price has operated as one of the major determinants of buyer choice. Consumers and purchasing agents have more access to price information and price discounters. Consumers and competition put pressure on retailers to lower their prices. Retailers put pressure on manufacturers to lower their prices. The result is a marketplace characterised by heavy discounting and sales promotion.

A changing pricing environment

Pricing practices have changed significantly. At the turn of the 21st century, consumers had easy access to credit, so by combining unique product formulations with enticing marketing campaigns, many firms successfully traded consumers up to more expensive products and services. However, the onset of the recent recession – a recession more severe than previous recessions, and which resulted in many jobs lost and many businesses and consumers unable to receive loans due to their poorly leveraged situations – changed things.

A combination of environmentalism, renewed frugality and concern about jobs and home values forced many European consumers to rethink how they spent their money. They replaced luxury purchases with basics. They bought fewer accessories like jewellery, watches and bags. They ate at home more often and purchased espresso machines to make lattes in their kitchens instead of buying them at expensive cafés. If they bought a new car at all, they downsized to smaller, more fuel-efficient models. They even cut back spending on hobbies and sports activities.

Downward price pressure from a changing economic environment coincided with some longer-term trends in the technological environment. For some years now, the internet has been changing how buyers and sellers interact. Here is a short list of how the internet allows sellers to discriminate between buyers, and buyers to discriminate between sellers.[5]

Buyers can:

- **Get instant price comparisons from thousands of vendors.** Customers can compare the prices offered by over two dozen online bookstores just by clicking mySimon. com. PriceScan.com lures thousands of visitors a day, most of them corporate buyers. Intelligent shopping agents ('bots') take price comparison a step further and seek out products, prices and reviews from hundreds if not thousands of merchants.

Among the marketers attempting to swim against the trend towards low prices is Clinomyn toothpaste for smokers.
Source: CCS Healthcare AB, Sweden.

- **Name their price and have it met.** On Priceline.com, the customer states the price he or she wants to pay for an airline ticket, hotel or rental car, and Priceline checks whether any seller is willing to meet that price. Volume-aggregating sites combine the orders of many customers and press the supplier for a deeper discount.
- **Get products free.** Open Source, the free software movement that started with Linux, will erode margins for just about any company creating software. The biggest challenge confronting Microsoft, Oracle, IBM and virtually every other major software producer is: how do you compete with programs that can be had for free? The marketing insight box on p. 652 describes how different firms have been successful with essentially free offerings.

Sellers can:

- **Monitor customer behaviour and tailor offers to individuals.** The JSTOR (Journal Storage) project, a non-profit venture that makes available electronic versions of archived issues of scholarly journals, monitors usage data to determine prices to individual customers. More than 2,000 international educational institutions, including those from most European countries, have become participants in the project.[6] Educational institutions are charged prices based on the value to the school, not the number of copies sold. So, a large institution where users view articles many times pays more.
- **Give certain customers access to special prices.** CD WOW!, an online vendor of music albums, emails certain buyers a special website address with lower prices. Ruelala is a members-only website that sells upscale women's fashion, accessories and footwear through limited-time sales, usually two-day events. Business marketers are already using extranets to get a precise handle on inventory, costs and demand at any given moment in order to adjust prices instantly.
- **Let customers decide the price.** British rock band Radiohead distributed its album, *In Rainbows*, on the band's website, applying an 'honesty box' principle. Consumers were given the choice of how much they wanted to pay for Radiohead's new album – anything between nothing at all and £100 (€130).[7] An internet survey of 3,000 people who downloaded the album found that most paid an average of £4 (€5), although there was a hardcore of 67 fans who thought that the record was worth more than £10 (€13) and a further 12 who claimed to have paid more than £40 (€50).[8]

Both buyers and sellers can:

- **Negotiate prices in online auctions and exchanges.** Want to sell hundreds of excess and slightly worn widgets? Post a sale on eBay. Want to purchase vintage baseball cards at a bargain price? Go to www.baseballplanet.com.

How companies price

Companies do their pricing in a variety of ways. In small companies, prices are often set by the boss. In large companies, pricing is handled by division and product line managers. Even here, top management sets general pricing objectives and policies, and often approves the prices proposed by lower levels of management. In industries where pricing is a key factor (aerospace, railways, oil companies), companies will often establish a pricing department to set or assist others in determining appropriate prices. This department reports to the marketing department, finance department or top management. Others who exert an influence on pricing include sales managers, production managers, finance managers and accountants.

Executives complain that pricing is a big headache – and one that is getting worse by the day. Many companies do not handle pricing well and throw up their hands with 'strategies' such as this: 'We determine our costs and take our industry's traditional margins.' Other common mistakes are: not revising price often enough to capitalise on market changes; setting price independently of the rest of the marketing mix rather than as an intrinsic element of market-positioning strategy; and not varying price enough for different product items, market segments, distribution channels and purchase occasions. Setting the price 'correctly' will not only bring satisfactory returns but will also help strengthen sales and accurately reflect the value provided to customers. Not surprisingly, that ideal price cannot be identified only by focusing on the cost of doing business or on competitors' pricing decisions. Rather, developing a pricing strategy should begin with determining the true value of a company's offerings to its customers. There is often a gap between what customers will pay and what a business charges.

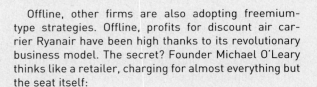

Marketing insight

Giving it all away

Giving away products for free via sampling has been a successful marketing tactic for years. Estée Lauder gave free samples of cosmetics to celebrities, and organisers at awards shows to this day like to lavish winners with extensive free items or gifts known as 'swag'. Other manufacturers, such as Gillette and HP, have built their business model around selling the host product essentially at cost and making money on the sale of necessary supplies, such as razor blades and printer ink.

With the advent of the internet, software companies began to adopt similar practices. Adobe gave away PDF Reader for free in 1994, as did Macromedia with its Shockwave player in 1995. More recently, internet start-ups such as the Blogger Weblog publishing tool, MySpace online community and Skype internet phone calls have all achieved some success with a 'freemium' strategy – free online services with a premium component. Venture capitalists and entrepreneurs believe that successful online freemium strategies of this kind depend on a number of factors (see Figure 16.1).

Offline, other firms are also adopting freemium-type strategies. Offline, profits for discount air carrier Ryanair have been high thanks to its revolutionary business model. The secret? Founder Michael O'Leary thinks like a retailer, charging for almost everything but the seat itself:

1 A quarter of Ryanair's seats are free. O'Leary wants to double that within five years, with the ultimate goal of all seats for free. Passengers pay only taxes and fees of about €7–18, with an average one-way fare of roughly €35.

2 Passengers pay extra for basically everything else on the flight: checked luggage (€6 per bag); snacks (€4 for a hot dog, €3 for chicken soup and €2.50 for water); and bus or train transportation into town from the far-flung airports that Ryanair uses.

3 Flight attendants sell a variety of merchandise, including digital cameras (€100) and iPocket MP3 players (€120). On-board gambling and a mobile phone service are projected new revenue sources.

▶ Marketing insight *(continued)*

1. **Mix free and paid elements.** The essence of a freemium strategy is one that mixes free and paid elements (premiums) of some kind. The paid elements could include another form of exchange such as users' personal data or their time but might also be in the form of a fee paid by users.
2. **Product differentiation.** It is important that your product stands out from the crowd. It should be superior to other market offerings. Remember that a freemium model is quite mainstream these days.
3. **Low costs.** For both free and paid elements the costs of producing and supporting the service should be kept to a minimum.
4. **Bottom up.** Services in a freemium package must be designed from the bottom up so that the free and paid elements are balanced and complementary. Basically, freemium refers to a marketing strategy that allows consumers to use a basic version of a product or service for nothing, in the hope that they will go on to pay a premium for the whole thing.
5. **Easy access.** Make sure that your product can be easily accessed by customers. For instance, if it is time-consuming to download registration forms online customers may get bored or frustrated and abort.
6. **Understand the customer.** Remember that the key freemium driver is the basic fact that customers like and are attracted to things that are free.
7. **Timing is everything.** The revenue from your freemium strategy should soon cover the costs of your free service. If not, cut your losses and move further to the next start-up.
8. **Focus on your main goal.** Remember that your main goal is to pull people into the funnel in hopes of turning a fraction of them into paying customers. 'If we can focus on getting people to listen to more music than they were before and they're building more playlists, they eventually will convert' says Spotify CEO, Daniel Ek

Figure 16.1 Guidelines for a successful freemium strategy
Source: E. Zoller (2011) Winning with 'freemium' content, *Forum*, April, p. 30; Word worth freemium (2001), *Management Today*, May, p. 13; K. Heires (2006) Why it pays to give away the store, Business 2.0, October, 36-7; G. Peoples (2011) A New Kind of Free, *Billboard*, 123(46), p. 30.

Other strategies cut costs or generate outside revenue:

4 Seats don't recline, window shades and seat-back pockets have been removed, and there is no entertainment. Seat-back trays now carry advertisements, and the exteriors of the planes are giant billboards for Vodafone Group, Jaguar, Hertz and others.

5 More than 99 per cent of tickets are sold online. Ryanair's website also offers travel insurance, hotels, ski packages and car rentals.

6 Only Boeing 737–800 jets are flown to reduce maintenance, and flight crews buy their own uniforms.

The formula works for Ryanair's customers, and the airline flies 58 million passengers to over 150 airports each year. All the extras add up to 20 per cent of revenue. Ryanair enjoys net margins of 25 per cent, which are high in the competitive airline business. Some industry pundits even refer to Ryanair as 'Wal-Mart with Wings'. European discount carrier easyJet has adopted many of the same practices. Other European – as well as US – airlines have now taken notice. Fellow discount carrier Spirit Airlines has begun to charge for checking bags and all drinks; and even non-discount carriers such as SAS, Cimber-Sterling Airways and Air France have begun to charge extra for headsets and snacks.

Sources: C. Anderson, *Free: The Future of a Radical Price* (New York: Hyperion, 2009); P. J. Howe (2007) The next pinch: fees to check bags, *Boston Globe*, 8 March; K. Heires (2006) Why it pays to give away the store, *Business 2.0*, October, 36–7; K. Capel (2006) Wal-Mart with wings, *BusinessWeek*, 27 November, 44–5; M. Maier (2006) A radical fix for airlines: make flying free, *Business 2.0*, April, 32–4; G. Stoller (1996) Would you like some golf balls with that ticket?, *USA Today*, 30 October.

There are many ways to find out how much customers value a company's offerings:

- One tactic is to employ researchers to perform so-called discrete choice analysis. In this scenario, customers view different products with different features and are asked to judge the varying prices researchers attach to them. Those findings help a company settle on an attractive mix of features and price them accordingly.
- A simpler, less expensive way to get good pricing information is to ask customers directly. Through qualitative measures, a company can ask customers what they would substitute for a specific product if it did not exist. This will show if customers have alternative options and how good those options are, which reveals the true value of a product or service.
- Another important source of information is company employees. A company's sales force knows a lot about what customers want, need and value in a product, but often they don't have an avenue to share these insights.[9]

Changing a company's pricing strategy often demands a shift in organisational culture. One key to drive such a change in culture is to convince the sales team that low prices or discounts are not always the answer to closing sales, and to ensure that any employee who works directly with customers must be able to explain the value of the product. Ideally, reconsidering pricing will force a company to focus more on its customers' needs and wants.

For any organisation, effectively designing and implementing pricing strategies requires a thorough understanding of consumer pricing psychology and a systematic approach to setting, adapting and changing prices.

Consumer psychology and pricing

Many economists assume that consumers are 'price takers' and accept prices at 'face value' or as given. Marketers recognise that consumers often actively process price information, interpreting prices in terms of their knowledge from prior purchasing experience, formal communications (advertising, sales calls and brochures), informal communications (friends, colleagues or family members), point-of-purchase or online resources, or other factors.[10]

Purchase decisions are based on how consumers perceive prices and what they consider the current actual price to be – *not* the marketer's stated price. Customers may have a lower price threshold below which prices signal inferior or unacceptable quality, as well as an upper price threshold above which prices are prohibitive and seen as not worth the money. The following example helps illustrate the large part consumer psychology plays in determining three different prices for essentially the same item: a black T-shirt.

Armani, Gap, H&M

The black Armani T-shirt for women looks pretty ordinary. In fact, it is not that different from the black T-shirt sold by Gap and by Swedish discount clothing chain H&M. Yet the black Armani T-shirt costs €210.00 whereas the Gap item costs €11.25 and the H&M one €6.00. Customers who purchase the Armani T-shirt are paying for a T-shirt made of 70 per cent nylon, 25 per cent polyester and 5 per cent Elastane, whereas the Gap and H&M shirts are made mainly of cotton. True, the Armani T is a bit more stylishly cut than the other two and sports a 'Made in Italy' label, but how does it command a €210 price tag? A luxury brand, Armani is primarily known for its suits, handbags and evening gowns that it sells for thousands of euro. In that context, it can hardly sell its T-shirts for €10 or even €70. And because there are not many takers for €210 T-shirts, Armani does not make many, thus further enhancing the appeal for status seekers who like the idea of having a 'limited edition' T-shirt. 'Value is not only quality, function, utility, channel of distribution,' says Arnold Aronson, managing director of retail strategies for Kurt Salmon Associates and former CEO of Saks Fifth Avenue, 'it's also a customer's perception of a brand's luxury connotations.'[11]

Consumer attitudes about pricing took a dramatic shift in the recent economic down-turn as many found themselves unable to sustain their lifestyles.[12] Consumers began to buy more for need than desire and to trade down more frequently in price. They shunned conspicious consumption, and sales of luxury goods suffered. Even purchases that had never been challenged before were scrutinised. Even in a recession, however, some companies can command a price premium if their offerings are unique and relevant enough to a large enough market segment. Understanding how consumers arrive at their perceptions of prices is an important marketing priority. Here we consider three key topics – reference prices, price–quality inferences and price endings.

Reference prices

Research has shown that although consumers may have fairly good knowledge of the range of prices involved, surprisingly few can accurately recall specific prices of products.[13] When examining products, however, consumers often employ **reference prices**, comparing an observed price to an internal reference price they remember or to an external frame of reference such as a posted 'regular retail price'.[14]

All types of reference prices are possible (see Table 16.1), and sellers often attempt to manipulate them. For example, a seller can situate its product among expensive competitors to imply that it belongs in the same class. Department stores will display women's apparel in separate departments differentiated by price; dresses found in the more expensive department are assumed to be of better quality. Marketers also encourage reference-price thinking by stating a high manufacturer's suggested price, or by indicating that the product was priced much higher originally, or by pointing to a competitor's high price. When consumers evoke one or more of these frames of reference, their perceived price can vary from the stated price. Research on reference prices has found that 'unpleasant surprises' – when perceived price is lower than the stated price – can have a greater impact on purchase likelihood than pleasant surprises.[15] Consumer expectations can also play a key role in price response. In the case of internet auction sites such as eBay, when consumers know similar goods will be available in future auctions, they will bid less in the current auction.[16]

Clever marketers try to frame the price to signal the best value possible: for example, a relatively more expensive item can look less expensive if the price is broken down into smaller units. A €350 annual membership may look more expensive than 'under €30 a month' even if the totals are the same.[17]

Price–quality inferences

Many consumers use price as an indicator of quality. Image pricing is especially effective with ego-sensitive products such as perfumes, expensive cars and Armani T-shirts. A €100

Table 16.1 Possible consumer reference prices

- fair price (what the product should cost)

- typical price

- last price paid

- upper-bound price (reservation price or what most consumers would pay)

- lower-bound price (lower threshold price or the least consumers would pay)

- competitor prices

- expected future price

- usual discounted price

Source: Adapted from R. S. Winer (1988) Behavioral perspectives on pricing: buyers' subjective perceptions of price revisited, in T. Devinney (ed.), *Issues in Pricing: Theory and Research*, Lexington, MA: Lexington Books, 35–57. Copyright © 1988 Lexington Books. Reproduced with permission.

bottle of perfume might contain €10 worth of scent, but gift givers pay €100 to communicate their high regard for the receiver. The price of a product serves therefore at least two consumer functions: (1) a higher price may signal higher quality (the 'positive' function of price), (2) the price denotes the monetary sacrifice the consumer must make to obtain the product (the 'negative' function of price).

Price and quality perceptions of cars interact.[18] Higher-priced cars are perceived to possess high quality. Higher-quality cars are likewise perceived to be higher priced than they actually are; as illustrated by this note from a dedicated supporter of the luxury car brand Rolls-Royce: 'If you think *I would love to buy a Rolls-Royce to fullfill my dream, but I cannot afford it!* then think again.'[19] When information about true quality is available, price becomes a less significant indicator of quality and merely functions as a cost component. When this information is not available, price also acts as a signal of quality. Some brands adopt exclusivity and scarcity as a means to signify uniqueness and justify premium pricing. Luxury-goods makers of watches, jewellery, perfume and other products often emphasise exclusivity in their communication messages and channel strategies. For luxury-goods customers who desire uniqueness, demand may actually increase with higher prices, as they may believe that fewer other customers will be able to afford to purchase the product.[20]

Tiffany

For its entire century-and-a-half history, Tiffany's name has connoted diamonds and luxury. As a cultural icon – its Tiffany Blue colour is even trademarked – Tiffany has survived the economy's numerous ups and downs through the years. With the emergence in the late 1990s of the notion of 'affordable luxuries', Tiffany seized the moment by creating a line of cheaper silver jewellery. Its 'Return to Tiffany' silver bracelet became a must-have item for teens of a certain set. Earnings skyrocketed for the next five years, but the affordable jewellery brought both an image and a pricing crisis for the company: what if all those teens who bought Tiffany charm bracelets grew up to think of Tiffany only as a place where they got the jewellery of their girlhood? Starting in 2002, the company began hiking prices again. At the same time, it launched higher-end collections, renovated stores to feature expensive items appealing to mature buyers, and expanded agressively into new cities and shopping malls. When the recession began in 2008, the firm knew it had to be careful not to dilute its high-end appeal. Tiffany offset softer sales largely with cost-cutting and inventory management, and – very quietly – it lowered prices on its best-selling engagement rings only, by roughly 10 per cent.[21]

Price endings

Many sellers believe prices should end in an odd number. Customers see an item priced at €299 in the €200 rather than the €300 range; they tend to process prices in a 'left-to-right' manner rather than by rounding.[22] Price encoding in this fashion is important if there is a mental price break at the higher, rounded price.

Another explanation for the popularity of '9' endings is that they convey the notion of a discount or bargain, suggesting that if a company wants a high-price image, it should avoid the odd-ending tactic.[23] One study even showed that demand was actually increased one-third when the price of a dress *rose* from €34 to €39 but was unchanged when the price increased from €34 to €44.[24] Findings from another study indicate that changes between just-below (e.g. €29.99 and €39.99) and round (e.g., €30 and €40) pricing affect choice, with just-below pricing shifting share towards lower-priced alternatives.[25]

Prices that end with 0 and 5 are also common in the marketplace; they are thought to be easier for consumers to process and retrieve from memory.[26] 'Sale' signs next to prices have been shown to spur demand, but only if not overused. Total category sales are

Prices that end with '9' convey the notion of a discount or bargain
Source: Michele Constantini Photo Alto Agency RF collections/Getty Images

highest when some, but not all, items in a category have sale signs; past a certain point, sale signs may cause total category sales to fall.[27]

Pricing cues such as sale signs and prices that end in 9 become less effective the more they are employed. They are more influential when consumers' price knowledge is poor, when they purchase the item infrequently or are new to the category, and when product designs vary over time, prices vary seasonally or quality or sizes vary across stores.[28] Limited availability (for example, 'three days only') can also spur sales among consumers actively shopping for a product.[29]

Setting the price

A firm must set a price for the first time when it develops a new product, when it introduces its regular product into a new distribution channel or geographical area, and when it enters bids on new contract work. The firm must decide where to position its product on quality and price.

Most markets have three to five price points or tiers. Operating in nearly 100 countries, French Accor Hotels is a European leader. Accor Hotels is good at developing different brands for different price points: Sofitel luxury hotels (highest price), Pullman Hotels and Resorts (high price), Novotel (high–medium price), Mercure (medium–high price), Suitehotel (medium price), Ibis (medium–low price), and Etap and Formule 1 (low price). Consumers often rank brands according to these price tiers in a category.[30]

A firm must consider many factors in setting its pricing policy.[31] Let's look in some detail at a six-step procedure: (1) selecting the pricing objective; (2) determining demand; (3) estimating costs; (4) analysing competitors' costs, prices and offers; (5) selecting a pricing method; and (6) selecting the final price.

Step 1: selecting the pricing objective

The company first decides where it wants to position its market offering. The clearer a firm's objectives, the easier it is to set a price. Five major objectives are: survival, maximum current profit, maximum market share, maximum market skimming, and product-quality leadership.

Survival

Companies pursue survival as their major objective if they are plagued with overcapacity, intense competition or changing consumer wants. As long as prices cover variable costs and some fixed costs, the company stays in business. Survival is a short-run objective; in the long run, the firm must learn how to add value or face extinction.

Maximum current profit

Many companies try to set a price that will maximise current profits. They estimate the demand and costs associated with alternative prices and choose the price that produces maximum current profit, cash flow or rate of return on investment. This strategy assumes that the firm has knowledge of its demand and cost functions; in reality, these are difficult to estimate. In emphasising current performance, the company may sacrifice long-run performance by ignoring the effects of other marketing-mix variables, competitors' reactions and legal restraints on price.

Maximum market share

Some companies want to maximise their market share. They believe that a higher sales volume will lead to lower unit costs and higher long-run profit. They set the lowest price, assuming the market is price sensitive. Texas Instruments practised this **market-penetration pricing** for years. TI would build a large plant, set its price as low as possible, win a large market share, experience falling costs, and cut its price further as costs fell. The following conditions favour adopting a market-penetration pricing strategy: (1) the market is highly price sensitive and a low price stimulates market growth; (2) production and distribution costs fall with accumulated production experience; and (3) a low price discourages actual and potential competition.

Maximum market skimming

Companies unveiling a new technology favour setting high prices to *maximise market skimming*. Sony is a frequent practitioner of **market-skimming pricing**, in which prices start high and slowly drop over time. When Sony introduced the world's first high-definition television (HDTV) to the Japanese market in 1990, it had a price corresponding to €29,000. So that Sony could 'skim' the maximum amount of revenue from the various segments of the market, the price dropped steadily over the years – a 28-inch Sony HDTV cost just over €4,000 in 1993, but a 40-inch Sony HDTV costs just about €500 in 2011. In 2015, experts expect that the price of an iPad or a Galaxy Tab will be only half the level of today's price.[32]

This strategy can be fatal, however, if a worthy competitor decides to price low. When Philips, the Dutch electronics manufacturer, priced its videodisc players to make a profit on each player, Japanese competitors priced low and succeeded in building their market share rapidly, which in turn pushed down their costs substantially.

Market skimming makes sense under the following conditions: (1) a sufficient number of buyers have a high current demand; (2) the unit costs of producing a small volume are not so high that they cancel the advantage of charging what the traffic will bear; (3) the high initial price does not attract more competitors to the market; (4) the high price communicates the image of a superior product.

Product-quality leadership

A company might aim to be the *product-quality leader* in the market. Many brands strive to be 'affordable luxuries' – products or services characterised by high levels of perceived quality, taste and status with a price just high enough not to be out of consumers' reach. Brands such as Starbucks coffee, Aveda shampoo, Victoria's Secret lingerie, BMW cars and Viking ranges have been able to position themselves as quality leaders in their categories, combining quality, luxury and premium prices with an intensely loyal customer base.

Other objectives

Non-profit and public organisations may have other pricing objectives. A university aims for *partial cost recovery*, knowing that it must rely on private gifts and public grants to cover its remaining costs. A non-profit hospital may aim for full cost recovery in its pricing. A non-profit theatre company may price its productions to fill the maximum number of theatre seats. A social service agency may set a service price geared to client income.

Whatever the specific objective, businesses that use price as a strategic tool will profit more than those which simply let costs or the market determine their pricing. For art museums, which earn only an average of 5 per cent of their revenues from admission charges, pricing can send a message that affects their public image and the number of donations and sponsorships they receive.

Museums for free?

Should art museums be free? This question arose when it was found that two-thirds of all visitors to French national museums such as the Louvre and the Musée d'Orsay are foreign tourists, and that three-quarters of visitors are between the ages of 18 and 25. With a view to persuading more French people to visit their museums, the French government is considering following the British and Danish examples of allowing free access to the permanent collections of major museums. Attendance at British museums has doubled since free admission was introduced in 2001. And the diversity of visitors has increased, with the number of young people and people of ethnic minorities on the rise. Temporary shows, for which ticket prices can exceed €15, have also benefited from the free access given to permanent collections.

Still, a number of French museum experts are sceptical that free admission will in fact attract people who never set foot in museums in the first place. France's minister of culture, Christine Albanel, says: 'The question has been asked for 30 years. Is free access the best solution? Or is it to have more free visiting hours or more attractive prices for different age groups?' Currently, museums are not for free in France – but other initiatives have been taken, including the Paris Museum Pass (two consecutive days cost €50). With this pass there is no entrance fee at 60 museums and historic places in and around Paris. The Paris Museum Pass comes with priority admission, so pass holders will not waste time waiting in line at The Louvre, Notre Dame, Musée d'Orsay, Château de Versailles, Musée National Picasso, Centre Pompidou, Musée Rodin, Château de Rambouillet and other must-sees.[33]

Should access to museums be free to the public?
Source: A&L Sinibaldi/Stone/Getty Images

Figure 16.2 Inelastic and elastic demand

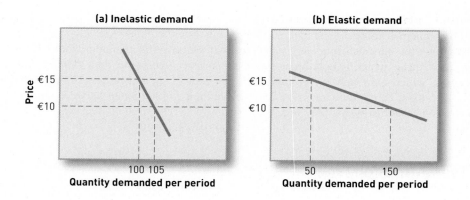

Step 2: determining demand

Each price will lead to a different level of demand and will therefore have a different impact on a company's marketing objectives. The relationship between price and demand is captured in a demand curve (see Figure 16.2). In the normal case, the two are inversely related: the higher the price, the lower the demand. In the case of prestige goods, the demand curve sometimes slopes upwards. One perfume company raised its price and sold more perfume rather than less! Some consumers take the higher price to signify a better product. However, if the price is too high, the level of demand may fall.

Price sensitivity

The demand curve shows the market's probable purchase quantity at alternative prices. It sums the reactions of many individuals who have different price sensitivities. The first step in estimating demand is to understand what affects price sensitivity. Generally speaking, customers are less price sensitive to low-cost items or items they buy infrequently. They are also less price sensitive when: (1) there are few or no substitutes or competitors; (2) they do not readily notice the higher price; (3) they are slow to change their buying habits; (4) they think the higher prices are justified; and (5) price is only a small part of the total cost of obtaining, operating and servicing the product over its lifetime.

A seller can charge a higher price than competitors and still get the business if it can convince the customer that it offers the lowest *total cost of ownership* (TCO). Marketers often do not realise the value they actually provide but think only in terms of product features. They treat the service elements in a product offering as sales incentives rather than as value-enhancing augmentations for which they can charge. In fact, pricing expert Tom Nagle believes the most common mistake manufacturers have made in recent years has been to offer all sorts of services to differentiate their products without charging for them in any way.[34]

Of course, companies prefer customers who are less price sensitive. Table 16.2 lists some characteristics associated with decreased price sensitivity. On the other hand, the internet has the potential to *increase* price sensitivity. In some established, fairly big-ticket categories such as car retailing and term insurance, consumers pay lower prices as a result of the internet. Car buyers use the internet to gather information and to use the negotiating clout of an online buying service.[35] But customers must visit multiple sites to realise these savings, and they don't always do so. Targeting only price-sensitive consumers may in fact be 'leaving money on the table'.

Estimating demand curves

Most companies make some attempt to measure their demand curves, using several different methods:

- **Surveys** can explore how many units consumers would buy at different proposed prices, although there is always the chance they might understate their purchase intentions at higher prices to discourage the company from setting higher prices.

Table 16.2 Factors leading to less price sensitivity

- The product is more distinctive.
- Buyers are less aware of substitutes.
- Buyers cannot easily compare the quality of substitutes.
- The expenditure is a smaller part of the buyer's total income.
- The expenditure is small compared to the total cost of the end product.
- Part of the cost is borne by another party.
- The product is used in conjunction with assets bought previously.
- The product is assumed to have more quality, prestige or exclusiveness.
- Buyers cannot store the product.

Source: Adapted from T. T. Nagle and R. K. Holden (2001) *The Strategy and Tactics of Pricing*, 3rd edn, Chapter 4. Copyright © 2001. Reprinted by permission of Pearson Education, Inc., Upper Saddle River, NJ.

- **Price experiments** can vary the prices of different products in a shop or charge different prices for the same product in similar territories to see how the change affects sales. Another approach is to use the internet. An ebusiness could test the impact of a 5 per cent price increase by quoting a higher price to every 40th visitor to compare the purchase response. However, it must do this carefully and not alienate customers.
- **Statistical analysis** of past prices, quantities sold and other factors can reveal their relationships. The data can be longitudinal (over time) or cross-sectional (from different locations at the same time). Building the appropriate model and fitting the data with the proper statistical techniques calls for considerable skill.

Advances in database management have improved marketers' abilities to optimise pricing. A large retail chain uncovered a new strategy by analysing its data. It sold three similar power drills: one for about £45 (€57), a purportedly better one at £60 (€76) and a top-tier one at £65 (€82). The higher the price, the more the store profited. But while drill know-it-alls flocked to the £65 model and price fretters grabbed its £45 cousin, shoppers often ignored the middle one. After analysing an array of variables, including sales history and competitors' prices, the retailer cut the middle drill to £55 (€70). Drill aficionados still chose the £65 option and sales of that drill did not change. However, now that the £45 version seemed less of a bargain, the store sold 4 per cent fewer low-end drills – and 11 per cent more of the mid-range model. As a result, profits rose.[36]

In measuring the price–demand relationship, the market researcher must control for various factors that will influence demand.[37] The competitor's response will make a difference. Also, if the company changes other marketing-mix factors besides price, the effect of the price change itself will be hard to isolate.

Price elasticity of demand

Marketers need to know how responsive, or elastic, demand would be to a change in price. Consider the two demand curves in Figure 16.2. In demand curve (a), a price increase from €10 to €15 leads to a relatively small decline in demand from 105 to 100. In demand curve (b), the same price increase leads to a substantial drop in demand from 150 to 50. If demand hardly changes with a small change in price, we say the demand is *inelastic*. If demand changes considerably, demand is *elastic*.

The higher the elasticity, the greater the volume growth resulting from a 1 per cent price reduction. If demand is elastic, sellers will consider lowering the price. A lower price will produce more total revenue. This makes sense as long as the costs of producing and selling more units do not increase disproportionately.

Price elasticity depends on the magnitude and direction of the contemplated price change. It may be negligible with a small price change and substantial with a large price change. It may differ for a price cut versus a price increase, and there may be a *price indifference band* within which price changes have little or no effect.

Finally, long-run price elasticity may differ from short-run elasticity. Buyers may continue to buy from a current supplier after a price increase, but they may eventually switch suppliers. Here demand is more elastic in the long run than in the short run, or the reverse may happen: buyers may drop a supplier after being notified of a price increase but return later. The distinction between short-run and long-run elasticity means that sellers will not know the total effect of a price change until time passes.

One comprehensive study reviewing a 40-year period of academic research projects that investigated price elasticity yielded a number of interesting findings:[38]

- The average price elasticity across all products, markets and time periods studied was 22.62.
- Price elasticity magnitudes were higher for durable goods than for other goods, and higher for products in the introduction/growth stages of the product life cycle than in the mature/decline stages.
- Inflation led to substantially higher price elasticities, especially in the short run.
- Promotional price elasticities were higher than actual price elasticities in the short run (although the reverse was true in the long run).
- Price elasticities were higher at the individual item or Stock Keeping Unit (SKU) level than at the overall brand level.

Step 3: estimating costs

Demand sets a ceiling on the price the company can charge for its product. Costs set the floor. The company wants to charge a price that covers its cost of producing, distributing and selling the product, including a fair return for its effort and risk. Yet, when companies price products to cover their full costs, profitability is not always the net result.

Types of costs and levels of production

A company's costs take two forms: fixed and variable. **Fixed** (also known as **overhead**) **costs** are costs that do not vary with production level or sales revenue. A company must pay bills each month for rent, heat, interest, salaries and so on, regardless of output.

Variable costs vary directly with the level of production. For example, each handheld calculator produced by Texas Instruments incurs the cost of plastic, microprocessor chips and packaging. These costs tend to be constant per unit produced, but they are called *variable* because their total varies with the number of units produced.

Total costs consist of the sum of the fixed and variable costs for any given level of production. **Average cost** is the cost per unit at that level of production; it equals total costs divided by production. Management wants to charge a price that will at least cover the total production costs at a given level of production.

To price intelligently, management needs to know how its costs vary with different levels of production. Take the case in which a company such as TI has built a fixed-size plant to produce 1,000 handheld calculators a day. The cost per unit is high if few units are produced per day. As production approaches 1,000 units per day, the average cost falls because the fixed costs are spread over more units. Short-run average cost (*SRAC*) *increases* after 1,000 units, however, because the plant becomes inefficient: workers must line up for machines, getting in each other's way, and machines break down more often (see Figure 16.3(a)).

If TI believes it can sell 2,000 units per day, it should consider building a larger plant. The plant will use more efficient machinery and work arrangements, and the unit cost of producing 2,000 units per day will be lower than the unit cost of producing 1,000 units per day. This is shown in the long-run average cost (*LRAC*) curve in Figure 16.3(b). In fact, a 3,000-capacity plant would be even more efficient according to Figure 16.3(b), but a 4,000-daily production plant would be less so because of increasing diseconomies

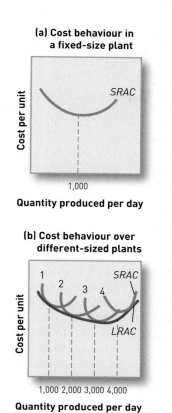

(a) Cost behaviour in a fixed-size plant

(b) Cost behaviour over different-sized plants

Figure 16.3 Cost per unit at different levels of production per period

of scale: there are too many workers to manage and paperwork slows things down. Figure 16.3(b) indicates that a 3,000-daily production plant is the optimal size if demand is strong enough to support this level of production.

There are more costs than those associated with manufacturing. To estimate the real profitability of selling to different types of retailer or customer, the manufacturer needs to use **activity-based cost (ABC) accounting** instead of standard cost accounting. ABC accounting tries to identify the real costs associated with serving each customer. It allocates indirect costs, such as clerical costs, office expenses, supplies and so on, to the activities that use them, rather than in some proportion to direct costs. Both variable and overhead costs are tagged back to each customer.

Companies that fail to measure their costs correctly are also not measuring their profit correctly and are likely to misallocate their marketing effort. The key to employing ABC effectively is to define and judge 'activities' properly. One proposed time-based solution calculates the cost of one minute of overhead and then decides how much of this cost each activity uses.[39]

Accumulated production

Suppose TI runs a plant that produces 3,000 handheld calculators per day. As TI gains experience in producing handheld calculators, its methods improve. Workers learn shortcuts, materials flow more smoothly and procurement costs fall. The result, as Figure 16.4 shows, is that average cost falls with accumulated production experience. Thus the average cost of producing the first 100,000 handheld calculators is €10 per calculator. When the company has produced the first 200,000 calculators, the average cost falls to €9. After its accumulated production experience doubles again to 400,000, the average cost is €8. This decline in the average cost with accumulated production experience is called the **experience curve** or **learning curve**.

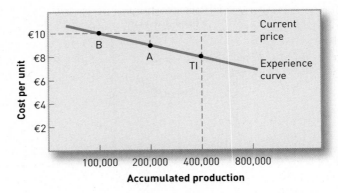

Figure 16.4 Cost per unit as a function of accumulated production: the experience curve

Now suppose three firms compete in this industry, TI, A and B. TI is the lowest-cost producer at €8, having produced 400,000 units in the past. If all three firms sell the calculator for €10, TI makes €2 profit per unit, A makes €1 per unit, and B breaks even. The smart move for TI would be to lower its price to €9. This will drive B out of the market, and even A may consider leaving. TI will pick up the business that would have gone to B (and possibly A). Furthermore, price-sensitive customers will enter the market at the lower price. As production increases beyond 400,000 units, TI's costs will drop still further and faster and will more than restore its profits, even at a price of €9. TI has used this aggressive pricing strategy repeatedly to gain market share and drive others out of the industry.

Experience-curve pricing nevertheless carries major risks. Aggressive pricing might give the product a cheap image. The strategy also assumes that competitors are weak followers. It leads the company into building more plants to meet demand, but a competitor may choose to innovate with a lower-cost technology. The market leader is now stuck with the old technology.

Most experience-curve pricing has focused on manufacturing costs, but all costs can be improved on, including marketing costs. If three firms are each investing a large sum of money in marketing, the firm that has used it the longest might achieve the lowest costs. This firm can charge a little less for its product and still earn the same return, all other costs being equal.[40]

Target costing

Costs change with production scale and experience. They can also change as a result of a concentrated effort by designers, engineers and purchasing agents to reduce them through **target costing**.[41] Market research establishes a new product's desired functions and the price at which the product will sell, given its appeal and competitors' prices. Deducting the desired profit margin from this price leaves the target cost the marketer must achieve.

The firm must examine each cost element – design, engineering, manufacturing, sales – and consider different ways to bring down costs so the final cost projections are in the target

Aldi

Germany's Aldi follows a simple formula globally. It stocks only about 1,000 of the most popular everyday grocery and household items, compared with more than 20,000 at a traditional grocer such as Royal Ahold's Albert Heijn. Almost all the products carry Aldi's own exclusive label. Because it sells so few items, Aldi can exert strong control over quality and price and simplify shipping and handling, leading to high margins. With more than 8,200 stores worldwide currently, Aldi brings in almost €50 billion in annual sales.[42]

cost range. If this is not possible, it may be necessary to stop developing the product because it cannot sell for the target price and make the target profit. To hit price and margin targets, marketers of the 9Lives® brand of cat food employed target costing to bring their price down to 'four cans for a euro' through a reshaped package and redesigned manufacturing processes. Even with lower prices, profits for the brand doubled. Other companies such as Aldi take advantage of global scope.

Step 4: analysing competitors' costs, prices and offers

Within the range of possible prices determined by market demand and company costs, the firm must take competitors' costs, prices and possible price reactions into account. The firm should first consider the nearest competitor's price. If the firm's offer contains features not offered by the nearest competitor, it should evaluate their worth to the customer and add that value to the competitor's price. If the competitor's offer contains some features not offered by the firm, the firm should subtract their value from its own price. Now the firm can decide whether it can charge more than, the same as, or less than the competitor.

The introduction of any price or the change of any existing price can provoke a response from customers, competitors, distributors, suppliers and even government. Competitors are most likely to react when the number of firms are few, the product is homogeneous (i.e. when no important differences between the product and competing products are perceived by buyers), and buyers are highly informed. Competitor reactions can be a special problem when these firms have a strong value proposition. Sony's Blu-ray format was able to exclude market pioneer Toshiba (backed by Microsoft) with its HD DVD format from the market and command a price premium in the process. This was due to the success of the Blu-ray team with winning the backing of the major film studios – after all, consumers will buy the technology only if they believe most of the films they want will be available.[43]

How can a firm anticipate a competitor's reactions? One way is to assume the competitor reacts in the standard way to a price being set or changed. Another is to assume the competitor treats each price difference or change as a fresh challenge and reacts according to self-interest at the time. Now the company will need to research the competitor's current financial situation, recent sales, customer loyalty and corporate objectives. If the competitor has a market share objective, it is likely to match price differences or changes.[44] If it has a profit-maximisation objective, it may react by increasing the advertising budget or improving product quality.

The problem is complicated because the competitor can put different interpretations on lowered prices or a price cut: that the company is trying to steal the market, that the company is doing poorly and trying to boost its sales, or that the company wants the whole industry to reduce prices to stimulate total demand.

Step 5: selecting a pricing method

Given the customers' demand schedule, the cost function, and competitors' prices, the company is now ready to select a price. Figure 16.5 summarises the three major considerations in price setting: costs set a floor to the price. Competitors' prices and the price of substitutes provide an orienting point. Customers' assessment of unique features establishes the price ceiling.

Companies select a pricing method that includes one or more of these three considerations. We will examine six price-setting methods: mark-up pricing, target-return pricing, perceived-value pricing, value pricing, going-rate pricing and auction-type pricing.

Mark-up pricing

The most elementary pricing method is to add a standard **mark-up** to the product's cost. Construction companies submit job bids by estimating the total project cost and adding a standard mark-up for profit. Lawyers and accountants typically price by adding a standard mark-up on their time and costs.

Figure 16.5 The three Cs model for price setting

Suppose a toaster manufacturer has the following costs and sales expectations:

Variable cost per unit	€10
Fixed costs	€300,000
Expected unit sales	50,000

The manufacturer's unit cost is given by:

$$\text{Unit cost} = \text{variable cost} + \frac{\text{fixed cost}}{\text{unit sales}} = €10 + \frac{€300,000}{50,000} = €16$$

Now assume the manufacturer wants to earn a 20 per cent mark-up on sales. The manufacturer's mark-up price is given by:

$$\text{Markup price} = \frac{\text{unit cost}}{(1 - \text{desired return on sales})} = \frac{€16}{1 - 0.2} = €20$$

The manufacturer would charge dealers €20 per toaster and make a profit of €4 per unit. The dealers in turn will mark up the toaster. If dealers want to earn 60 per cent on their selling price, they will mark up the toaster 100 per cent to €40. Mark-ups are generally higher on seasonal items (to cover the risk of not selling), speciality items, slower-moving items, items with high storage and handling costs, and demand-inelastic items, such as prescription drugs.

Does the use of standard mark-ups make logical sense? Generally, no. Any pricing method that ignores current demand, perceived value and competition is not likely to lead to the optimal price. Mark-up pricing works only if the marked-up price actually brings in the expected level of sales. Still, mark-up pricing remains popular. First, sellers can determine costs much more easily than they can estimate demand. By tying the price to cost, sellers simplify the pricing task. Second, where all firms in the industry use this pricing method, prices tend to be similar and price competition is minimised.[45] Third, many people feel that cost-plus pricing is fairer to both buyers and sellers. Sellers do not take advantage of buyers when the latter's demand becomes acute, and sellers earn a fair return on investment.

Target-return pricing

In **target-return pricing**, the firm determines the price that would yield its target rate of return on investment. General Motors has priced its automobiles to achieve a 15–20 per cent ROI. Public utilities, which need to make a fair return on investment, can also use this method (see Chapter 22 for more on ROI).

Suppose the toaster manufacturer has invested €1 million in the business and wants to set a price to earn a 20 per cent ROI, specifically €200,000. The target-return price is given by the following formula:

$$\text{Target-return price} = \text{unit cost} + \frac{\text{desired return} \times \text{invested capital}}{\text{unit sales}}$$

$$= €16 + \frac{0.20 \times €1,000,000}{50,000} = €20$$

The manufacturer will realise this 20 per cent ROI provided its costs and estimated sales turn out to be accurate. But what if sales don't reach 50,000 units? The manufacturer can prepare a break-even chart to learn what would happen at other sales levels (see Figure 16.6). Fixed costs are €300,000 regardless of sales volume. Variable costs, not shown in the figure, rise with volume. Total costs equal the sum of fixed costs and variable costs. The total revenue curve starts at zero and rises with each unit sold.

The total revenue and total cost curves cross at 30,000 units. This is the break-even volume. We can verify it by the following formula:

$$\text{Break-even volume} = \frac{\text{fixed cost}}{(\text{price} - \text{varible cost})} = \frac{€300,000}{€20 - €10} = 30,000$$

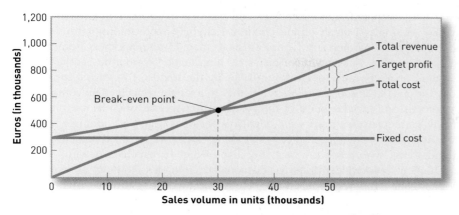

Figure 16.6 Break-even chart for determining target-return price and break-even volume

The manufacturer, of course, is hoping the market will buy 50,000 units at €20, in which case it earns €200,000 on its €1 million investment, but much depends on price elasticity and competitors' prices. Unfortunately, target-return pricing tends to ignore these considerations. The manufacturer needs to consider different prices and estimate their probable impacts on sales volume and profits. The manufacturer should also search for ways to lower its fixed or variable costs, because lower costs will decrease its required break-even volume. Acer has been gaining share in the netbook market through rock-bottom prices made possible because of its bare-bones cost strategy. Acer sells only via retailers and other outlets and outsources all manufacturing and assembly, reducing its overhead to 8 per cent of sales vs. 14 per cent at Dell and 15 per cent at HP.[46]

Perceived-value pricing

An increasing number of companies now base their price on the customer's **perceived value**. Perceived value is made up of several elements, such as the buyer's image of the product performance, the ability to deliver on time, the warranty quality, customer support and softer attributes such as the supplier's reputation, trustworthiness and esteem. Companies must deliver the value promised by their value proposition, and the customer must perceive this value. Firms use the other marketing-mix elements, such as advertising and sales force, to communicate and enhance perceived value in buyers' minds.[47]

Caterpillar uses perceived value to set prices on its construction equipment. It might price its tractor at €100,000, although a similar competitor's tractor might be priced at €90,000. When a prospective customer asks a Caterpillar dealer why he should pay €10,000 more for the Caterpillar tractor, the dealer answers:

€ 90,000 is the tractor's price if it is only equivalent to the competitor's tractor

€   7,000 Is the price premium for Caterpillar's superior durability

€   6,000 is the price premium for Caterpillar's superior reliability

€   5,000 is the price premium for Caterpillar's superior service

€   2,000 is the price premium for Caterpillar's longer warranty on parts

€110,000 is the normal price to cover Caterpillar's superior value

€ 10,000 is the discount

€100,000 is the final price.

The Caterpillar dealer is able to indicate why Caterpillar's tractor delivers more value than the competitor's. Although the customer is asked to pay a €10,000 premium, he is actually getting €20,000 extra value. He chooses the Caterpillar tractor because he is convinced that its lifetime operating costs will be lower.

Ensuring that customers appreciate the total value of a product or service offering is crucial. For example, Danish online children's clothing store 'mormor.nu' (*mormor. nu* is Danish for grandmother now) employs more than 75 grandmothers from all parts of Denmark who create handmade children's clothing items. Mormor.nu is able to command premium prices because of its skill in bringing the trends of nostalgia, storytelling, authenticity, design, style and uniqueness together in a single concept. The company has a relentless focus on crucial aspects of the customer experience, such as creating handmade quality garments from pure wool, alpaca wool or cotton, and adding a sense of uniqueness and authenticity – each piece of clothing comes with a small name-tag signed by the grandmother who made the item. Because of higher perceived quality – making the products meet modern demands for fashionable children's clothing, as well as for old-fashioned quality and honest materials – the higher prices (e.g. €16 for a pair of baby socks or €160 for a baby shawl) come to match the product offer in the mind of the consumer. Mormor.nu even bucks the commoditisation trend by custom-designing clothing items to individual specifications.[48]

Mormor.nu creates handmade children's clothing items
Source: Monika Elena Photo

Yet even when a company claims that its offering delivers more total value, not all customers will respond positively. There is always a segment of buyers who care only about the price. Other buyers suspect the company is exaggerating its product quality and services. One company installed its software system in one or two plants operated by a customer. The substantial and well-documented cost savings convinced the customer to buy the software for its other plants.

The key to perceived-value pricing is to deliver more value than the competitor and to demonstrate this to prospective buyers. Basically, a company needs to understand the customer's decision-making process. The company can try to determine the value of its offering in several ways: managerial judgements within the company, consumer ratings data, value of similar products, focus groups, surveys, experimentation, analysis of historical data and conjoint analysis.[49] Table 16.3 contains six key considerations in developing value-based pricing.

Value pricing

In recent years, several companies have adopted **value pricing**. They win loyal customers by charging a fairly low price for a high-quality offering. Value pricing is thus not a matter of simply setting lower prices; it is a matter of re-engineering the company's operations to become a low-cost producer without sacrificing quality, to attract a large number of

Table 16.3 A framework of questions for practising value-based pricing

1   What is the market strategy for the segment? (What does the supplier want to accomplish? What would the supplier like to have happen?)

2   What is the differential value that is *transparent* to target customers? ('Transparent' means that target customers easily understand how the supplier calculates the differential value between its offering and the next best alternative, and that the differential value can be verified with the customer's own data.)

3   What is the price of the next best alternative offering?

4   What is the cost of the supplier's marketing offering?

5   What pricing tactics will be used initially or eventually? ('Pricing tactics' are changes from a price that a supplier has set for its marketing offering – such as discounts – that motivate customers to take actions that benefit the supplier.)

6   What is the customer's expectation of a 'fair' price?

Source: J. C. Anderson, M. Wouters and W. Van Rossum (2010) Why the highest price isn't the best price, *MIT Sloan Management Review*, Winter 69–76. © 2010 from MIT Sloan Management Review/Massachusetts Institute of Technology. All rights reserved. Distributed by Tribune Media Services.

value-conscious customers. Among the best practitioners of value pricing are IKEA, airlines such as easyJet and Ryanair, and supermarket chains Tesco and ASDA.

Value pricing can change the manner by which a company sets prices too. One company that sold and maintained switch boxes in a variety of sizes for telephone lines found that the probability of failure – and thus maintenance costs – was proportional to the number of switches customers had in their boxes rather than to the dollar value of the installed boxes. The number of switches could vary in a box, though. Therefore, rather than charging customers based on the total spent on their installation, the company began charging based on the total number of switches needing servicing.[50]

An important type of value pricing is **everyday low pricing** (EDLP), which takes place at the retail level. A retailer that holds to an EDLP pricing policy charges a constant low price with little or no price promotions and special sales. These constant prices eliminate week-to-week price uncertainty and the 'high–low' pricing of promotion-oriented competitors. In **high–low pricing**, the retailer charges higher prices on an everyday basis but then runs frequent promotions in which prices are temporarily lowered below the EDLP level.[51] The two different pricing strategies have been shown to affect consumer price judgements – deep discounts (EDLP) can lead customers to perceive lower prices over time than can frequent, shallow discounts (high–low), even if the actual averages are the same.[52]

Greggs

Greggs plc is a UK-based retail bakery food service operator with its core Greggs retail fascia complemented by its eat-in Baker's Oven brand. It has grown in the space of eight decades from a one shop outfit into a chain of more than 1,200 stores (under the Greggs fascia) covering most of Great Britain, with the exception of Northern Ireland and south-west England, which offer it scope for further growth. It suffered volatile trading conditions in the first decade of the 21st century, but while rivals are struggling, Greggs is now growing sales due to its everyday low pricing and greater variety in its menus, both of which are finding favour with UK consumers.[53]

In recent years, high–low pricing has given way to EDLP at widely different venues, including hardware stores such as Bauhaus (an international chain with more than 220 outlets across Europe and with a head office in Zug, Switzerland) and kitchen companies such as Kvik (part of the Swedish group Ballingslöv); but in European grocery retailing, so-called 'hard discounters' such as Aldi, Lidl and Netto have been committed to a long-term strategy of offering everyday low prices on major brands since the beginning of the 1990s. Having enjoyed annual growth of around 7 per cent since 1991, these discounters have come to comprise a major force in European retailing, and now command high market shares in, for example, Germany, Belgium and Austria.[54]

Some retailers have even based their entire marketing strategy around what could be called *extreme* everyday low pricing. Partly fuelled by an economic downturn, and partly by changes in consumer habits (where shoppers reject price premiums yet are willing to pay more where they perceive value), once-unfashionable 'dollar stores' are gaining popularity.

Tiger shops

In recent years, 'Tiger' shops have been breaking the boundaries for what is possible to buy for 10, 20, 50 or 100 Danish kroner (DKK). €1 equals approximately DKK8. The word 'tiger' sounds like 'ti'er', which is short for DKK10. This ultra-discount chain does not consist of DKK10 stores in the strict sense of the word – Tiger shops sell many items over DKK10, although the highest price is DKK100. The Tiger chain has developed a successful formula for drawing in customers: build small, easy-to-navigate stores; keep overheads low by maintaining only a limited inventory; spend sparingly on store decor and get a lot of free word-of-mouth publicity. Sales have grown tremendously since Tiger started to send out a monthly catalogue to more than 1 million households. This has made customers aware that Tiger stocks kitchenware, office ware, beauty aids, make-up, toys, games, films, socks, underwear, reading glasses, spices, candles and many other products. Among these, some are surplus stock of well-known brands, but most of the products are bought directly from the factory to keep costs down. A majority of Tiger shoppers are women, who shop in Tiger for small presents for Christmas stockings, for children's birthday parties, or on impulse. But there are also customers who shop for low-priced everyday necessities – particularly in the provinces. The Tiger chain now has over 90 Tiger shops in ten countries: Denmark, England, Germany, Greece, Iceland, Latvia, Lithuania, Netherlands, Spain and Sweden.[55]

The most important reason why retailers adopt EDLP is that constant sales and promotions are costly and have eroded consumer confidence in the credibility of everyday shelf prices. Consumers also have less time and patience for such time-honoured traditions as watching for supermarket specials and clipping coupons. Yet there is no denying that promotions create excitement and draw shoppers. For this reason, EDLP is not a guarantee of success. As supermarkets face heightened competition from their counterparts and from alternative channels, many find that the key to drawing shoppers is using a combination of high-low and everyday low pricing strategies, with increased advertising and promotions.

Going-rate pricing

In **going-rate pricing**, the firm bases its price largely on competitors' prices, charging the same as, more than or less than major competitor(s). In oligopolistic industries (i.e. industries dominated by a small number of sellers) that sell a commodity such as steel, paper or fertiliser, all firms normally charge the same price. The smaller firms 'follow the leader', changing their prices when the market leader's prices change rather than when their own demand or costs change. Some firms may charge a slight premium or slight discount, but they preserve the amount of difference. Thus minor petrol stations usually charge a few pence less per gallon than the major oil companies, without letting the difference increase or decrease.

Going-rate pricing is quite popular. Where costs are difficult to measure or competitive response is uncertain, firms feel the going price is a good solution because it is thought to reflect the industry's collective wisdom.

Auction-type pricing

Auction-type pricing is growing more popular, especially with the growth of the internet. There are over 2,000 electronic marketplaces selling everything from pigs to used vehicles and cargo to chemicals. One major purpose of auctions is to dispose of excess inventories

Breakthrough marketing

Private labels

Consumers are frequently faced with judging the quality of various products when determining what to buy, in what amount. It may, however, be difficult for consumers to assess the importance of various quality-aspects in relation to each other and in relation to requirements rooted in the intended use of the products. Therefore, consumers are often faced with uncertainty when making judgements of the quality of products. In that respect, consumers have for years used product brands to infer the quality of many products, and supermarkets wishing to market their own brands (private labels) have faced difficult times. However, it seems that the days of branded FMCG goods overshadowing the cheap private labels are numbered. Based on a large survey comprising 27,000 consumers in 51 countries, a recent AC Nielsen report finds that 60 per cent of all Europeans have increased their purchase of private label products. And, even more important, 90 per cent say that they will continue purchasing the same amount of private labels even when the economy has fully recovered. These findings are consistent with results from Lightspeed Research revealing that nearly every other UK consumer buys more private label products.

Clearly, an advantage of private labels today is that supermarkets have managed simultaneously to close the quality gap and hold the price gap between branded FMCG manufacturers and private labels. In addition, increasing globalisation, the emergence of the internet (making information and price comparisons readily available), and the consequent increasing market shares of private labels have contributed to their increased popularity.

While consumers seem to be impressed by the quality of supermarkets' premium brand names, they are less confident about the products' prestige. Most consumers find that supermarket brands are less suitable than named brands when purchasing gifts. A similar picture is found when consumers are asked to buy food for others. In such situations, only 21 per cent would buy a premium supermarket product, while 69 per cent would buy a named brand. And only 9 per cent would buy something from a regular supermarket range.

Own-label brands still lack 'the cool factor or the posh factor' of other brands, says Ralph Risk, marketing director for EMEA at Lightspeed. 'Supermarkets have to be very careful not to degrade the image of premium own-label goods and their brand values by giving it too much discount, or making the cost too cheap. I think it is a balancing act to encourage people to purchase them without actually damaging the brand by making it look like it is a cheaper brand.'

To compete with private labels, manufacturers of branded FMCG goods may wish to launch value versions of branded goods or to open their own stores. Alternatively, branded goods manufacturers may cooperate with retailers to create a lower-priced branded option – in fact, many large manufacturers have developed products as private labels, suggesting that the relationship between branded goods manufacturers and private labels should not be understood as competitive, or they may seek to innovate and improve their products at a rate that prevents labels from keeping up and copying the design.

Sainsbury's has developed a powerful private label programme
Source: Sainsbury's Supermarket Limited

▶ **Breakthrough marketing** *(continued)*

Questions

1. Elaborate on the introduction of private labels. Why is it working so well for supermarkets nowadays?

2. Private labels do very well when the economy turns sour. What competitive actions can be taken by FMCG managers when the economy is on the rise? Explain.

Sources: M. Barnett (2010) Premium lines offer quality at a lower price, *Marketing Week*, 16 December; J. K. Jørgensen (2011) Supermarkeder storsælger egne mærker, *EPN*, 3 March; M. Hubert (2009) Quo vadis manufacturers? Private label strategy: how to meet the store brand challenge, *International Journal of Retail and Distribution Management*, 37(11), 1008.

or used goods. Companies need to be aware of the three major types of auction and their separate pricing procedures.

- **English auctions (ascending bids)**: one seller and many buyers. On sites such as Yahoo! and eBay, the seller puts up an item and bidders raise the offer price until the top price is reached. The highest bidder gets the item. English auctions (the term commonly used for these kinds of auction – but known also as 'ascending-price' auctions) are used today for selling antiques, cattle, property, and used equipment and vehicles. After seeing eBay and other ticket brokers, scalpers and middlemen reap millions by charging what the market would bear, Ticketmaster Corp. has overhauled the way it sells tickets, including running auctions for 30 per cent of major music tours by popular artists such as Barbra Streisand and Madonna, and allowing some customers to resell their seats at its website.[56]

- **Dutch auctions (descending bids)**: one seller and many buyers, or one buyer and many sellers. In the first kind, an auctioneer announces a high price for a product and then slowly decreases the price until a bidder accepts the price. In the other, the buyer announces something he or she wants to buy, and potential sellers compete to get the sale by offering the lowest price. Each seller sees what the last bid is and decides whether to go lower. FreeMarkets.com – later acquired by Ariba – helped Royal Mail Group plc, the United Kingdom's public postal service company, save approximately £2.5 million, in part via an auction where 25 airlines bid for its international freight business.[57]

- **Sealed-bid auctions**: would-be suppliers can submit only one bid and cannot know the other bids. Governments often use this method to procure supplies (see Chapter 8). A supplier will not bid below its cost but cannot bid too high for fear of losing the job. The net effect of these two pulls can be described in terms of the bid's expected profit. Using expected profit for setting price makes sense for the seller that makes many bids. The seller who bids only occasionally or who needs a particular contract badly will not find it advantageous to use expected profit. This criterion does not distinguish between a €1,000 profit with a 0.10 probability and a €125 profit with a 0.80 probability. Yet the firm that wants to keep production going would prefer the second contract to the first.

As more and more firms use online auctions for industrial buying, they need to recognise the possible effects they can have on their suppliers. If the increased savings a firm obtains in an online auction translate into decreased margins for an incumbent supplier, the supplier may feel the firm is opportunistically squeezing out price concessions.[58] Online auctions with a large number of bidders, greater economic stakes and less visibility in pricing have been shown to result in greater overall satisfaction, more positive future expectations and fewer perceptions of opportunism.

Step 6: selecting the final price

Pricing methods narrow the range from which the company must select its final price. In selecting that price, the company must consider additional factors, including the impact of other marketing activities, company pricing policies, gain-and-risk-sharing pricing and the impact of price on other parties.

Impact of other marketing activities

The final price must take into account the brand's quality and advertising relative to the competition. In a classic study, Farris and Reibstein examined the relationships among relative price, relative quality and relative advertising for 227 consumer businesses and found the following:

- Brands with average relative quality but high relative advertising budgets were able to charge premium prices. Consumers were willing to pay higher prices for known products than for unknown products.
- Brands with high relative quality and high relative advertising obtained the highest prices. Conversely, brands with low quality and low advertising charged the lowest prices.
- The positive relationship between high prices and high advertising held most strongly in the later stages of the product life cycle for market leaders.[59]

Company pricing policies

The price must be consistent with company pricing policies. At the same time, companies are not averse to establishing pricing penalties under certain circumstances.[60]

Banks charge fees for too many withdrawals in a month or for early withdrawal of a certificate of deposit. Dentists, hotels, car rental companies and other service providers charge penalties for no-shows who miss appointments or reservations. Although these policies are often justifiable, marketers must use them judiciously so as not to alienate customers unnecessarily (see the marketing insight box).

Marketing insight

Stealth price increases

With consumers stubbornly resisting higher prices, companies are trying to figure out how to increase revenue without really raising prices. Increasingly, the solution has been through the addition of fees for what had once been free features. Although some consumers abhor 'nickel-and-dime' pricing strategies, small additional charges can add up to a substantial source of revenue. The telecommunications industry in general has been aggressive at adding fees for set-up, change-of-service, service termination, directory assistance, regulatory assessment, number portability, and cable hook-up and equipment, costing consumers billions of euro.

This usage of fees has a number of implications. Given that list prices stay fixed, they may understate inflation. They also make it harder for consumers to compare competitive offerings. Although various citizens' groups have been formed to pressure companies to roll back some of these fees, they don't always get a sympathetic ear from national and local governments, which have been guilty of using their own array of fees, fines and penalties to raise necessary revenue.

Companies justify the extra fees as the only fair and viable way to cover expenses without losing customers. Many argue that it makes sense to charge a premium for added services that cost more to provide, rather than charging all customers the same amount whether or not they use the extra service. Breaking out charges and fees according to the related services is a way to keep basic costs low. Companies also use fees as a means to weed out unprofitable customers or get them to change their behaviour.

Ultimately, the viability of extra fees will be decided in the marketplace, and by the willingness of consumers to vote with their wallets and pay the fees, or vote with their feet and move on.

Sources: A. Leondis and J. Plungis, The latest credit card tricks, *Bloomberg BusinessWeek*, 28 December 2009 and 4 January 2010, 95; The price is wrong, *The Economist*, 25 May 2002, 59–60; Once more unto the branch, *The Economist*, 2 August 2007; British banks come under fire over fees, *International Herald Tribune*, 6 April 2006; H. Spongenberg (2007) EU clinches deal on roaming prices, *BusinessWeek*, 17 May; EU close to mobile roaming fee cut deal, *BusinessWeek*, 16 March 2007; C. Barker (2006) EU to slash mobile roaming rates, *BusinessWeek*, 29 March; www.euobserver.com.

Many companies set up a pricing department to develop policies and establish or approve decisions. The aim is to ensure that salespeople quote prices that are reasonable to customers and profitable to the company.

Gain-and-risk-sharing pricing

Buyers may resist accepting a seller's proposal because of a high perceived level of risk. The seller has the option of offering to absorb part or all the risk if it does not deliver the full promised value. Aircraft manufacturer Bombardier Aerospace was able to secure a contract for the delivery of 27 regional and turboprop planes to Scandinavian Airlines (SAS), by giving SAS more than €106.4 million in cash and credit compensation for future aircraft orders. The compensation was due to the fact that the year before SAS had to ground the airline's entire fleet of 27 Bombardier Dash 8 Q400 aircraft after suffering three landing accidents.[61]

Impact of price on other parties

Management must also consider the reactions of other parties to the contemplated price.[62] How will distributors and dealers feel about it? If they don't make enough profit, they may not choose to bring the product to market. Will the sales force be willing to sell at that price? How will competitors react? Will suppliers raise their prices when they see the company's price? Will the government intervene and prevent this price from being charged?

Marketers need to know the laws regulating pricing. EU competition law states that sellers must set prices without talking to competitors: price fixing is illegal to protect consumers against deceptive pricing practices. Also, it is illegal to exploit a dominant market position in order to directly or indirectly impose unfair purchase or selling prices or other unfair trading conditions.

Very often companies must take into account the many variations in their surroundings when setting price(s). This is considered in the next section.

Adapting the price

Companies usually do not set a single price, but rather develop a pricing structure that reflects variations in geographical demand and costs, market-segment requirements, purchase timing, order levels, delivery frequency, guarantees, service contracts and other factors. As a result of discounts, allowances and promotional support, a company rarely realises the same profit from each unit of a product that it sells. Here we will examine several price-adaptation strategies: geographical pricing, price discounts and allowances, promotional pricing and differentiated pricing.

Geographical pricing (cash, countertrade, barter)

In geographical pricing, the company decides how to price its products to different customers in different locations and countries. Should the company charge higher prices to distant customers to cover the higher shipping costs, or a lower price to win additional business? How should it account for exchange rates and the strength of different currencies?

Another question is how to get paid. This issue is critical when buyers lack sufficient hard currency to pay for their purchases. Many buyers want to offer other items in payment, a practice known as **countertrade**. Countertrade may account for 15–25 per cent of world trade and takes several forms:[63]

- **Barter.** The buyer and seller directly exchange goods, with no money and no third party involved.
- **Compensation deal.** The seller receives some percentage of the payment in cash and the rest in products. A British aircraft manufacturer sold planes to Brazil for 70 per cent cash and the rest in coffee.

- **Buyback arrangement**. The seller sells plant, equipment or technology to another country and agrees to accept as partial payment products manufactured with the supplied equipment. For example, a chemical company builds a plant for an Indian company and accepts partial payment in cash and the remainder in chemicals manufactured at the plant.
- **Offset**. The seller receives full payment in cash but agrees to spend a substantial amount of the money in that country within a stated time period. For example, PepsiCo sells its cola syrup to Russia for rubles and agrees to buy Russian vodka at a certain rate for sale in the United States.

Price discounts and allowances

Most companies will adjust their list price and give discounts and allowances for early payment, volume purchases and off-season buying (see Table 16.4).[64] Companies must do this carefully or they will find their profits much lower than planned.[65]

Discount pricing has become the modus operandi of a surprising number of companies offering both products and services. Some product categories tend to self-destruct by always being on sale. Salespeople, in particular, are quick to give discounts in order to close a sale. But word can get around fast that the company's list price is 'soft', and discounting becomes the norm. The discounts undermine the value perceptions of the offerings. Some product categories self-destruct by always being on sale.

Some companies with overcapacity are tempted to give discounts or even begin to supply a retailer with a store-brand version of their product at a deep discount. Because the store brand is priced lower, however, it may start making inroads on the manufacturer's brand. Manufacturers should stop to consider the implications of supplying products to retailers at a discount, because they may end up losing long-run profits in an effort to meet short-run volume goals.

At the same time, discounting can be a useful tool if a company can gain concessions in return, such as when the customer agrees to sign a longer contract, is willing to order electronically, thus saving the company money, or agrees to buy in truckload quantities.

Table 16.4 Price discounts and allowances

Cash discount	A price reduction to buyers who pay bills promptly. A typical example is '2/10, net 30', which means that payment is due within 30 days and that the buyer can deduct 2 per cent by paying the bill within 10 days.
Quantity discount	A price reduction to those who buy large volumes. A typical example is '€10 per unit for fewer than 100 units; €9 per unit for 100 or more units'. Quantity discounts must be offered equally to all customers and must not exceed the cost savings to the seller. They can be offered on each order placed or on the number of units ordered over a given period.
Functional discount	Discount (also called *trade discount*) offered by a manufacturer to trade-channel members if they will perform certain functions, such as selling, storing and record keeping. Manufacturers must offer the same functional discounts within each channel.
Seasonal discount	A price reduction to those who buy merchandise or services out of season. Hotels, motels and airlines offer seasonal discounts in slow selling periods.
Allowance	An extra payment designed to gain reseller participation in special programmes. *Trade-in allowances* are granted for turning in an old item when buying a new one. *Promotional allowances* reward dealers for participating in advertising and sales support programmes.

Sales management needs to monitor the proportion of customers who are receiving discounts, the average discount and the particular salespeople who are overrelying on discounting. Higher levels of management should conduct a **net price analysis** to arrive at the 'real price' of the offering. The real price is affected not only by discounts but also by many other expenses that reduce the realised price (see promotional pricing section). Suppose the company's list price is €3,000. The average discount is €300. The company's promotional spending averages €450 (15 per cent of the list price). Co-op advertising money of €150 is given to retailers to back the product. The company's net price is €2,100, not €3,000.

Promotional pricing

Companies can use several pricing techniques to stimulate early purchase:

- **Loss-leader pricing.** Supermarkets and department stores often drop the price on well-known brands to stimulate additional store traffic. This pays if the revenue on the additional sales compensates for the lower margins on the loss-leader items. Manufacturers of loss-leader brands typically object because this practice can dilute the brand image and bring complaints from retailers who charge the list price. Manufacturers have tried to restrain intermediaries from loss-leader pricing through lobbying for retail price maintenance laws, but these laws have been revoked.
- **Special-event pricing.** Sellers will establish special prices in certain seasons to draw in more customers. Every August, there are back-to-school sales.
- **Cash rebates.** Car companies and other consumer goods companies offer cash rebates to encourage purchase of the manufacturers' products within a specified time period. Rebates can help clear inventories without cutting the stated list price.
- **Low-interest financing.** Instead of cutting its price, the company can offer customers low-interest financing. Bang & Olufsen used no-interest financing in trying to attract more customers (see Chapter 9).
- **Longer payment terms.** Sellers, especially mortgage lenders and car manufacturers/dealers, stretch loans over longer periods and thus lower the monthly payments. Consumers often worry less about the cost (the interest rate) of a loan and more about whether they can afford the monthly payment.
- **Warranties and service contracts.** Companies can promote sales by adding a free or low-cost warranty or service contract.
- **Psychological discounting.** This strategy sets an artificially high price and then offers the product at substantial savings: for example, 'Was €359, now €299'. Most governments fight such misleading discount tactics. Discounts from normal prices are a legitimate form of promotional pricing.

Promotional-pricing strategies are often a zero-sum game. If they work, competitors copy them and they lose their effectiveness. If they don't work, they waste money that could have been put into other marketing tools, such as building up product quality and service or strengthening product image through advertising.

Differentiated pricing

Companies often adjust their basic price to accommodate differences in target consumers, products, locations and so on. Designer Donna Karan creates women's clothes in different price classes. The Donna Karan main line is expensive, but also the ultimate in relaxed chic, whereas the lower-priced line, DKNY, is more affordable. A woman's black dress from the DKNY line may cost €215, while a black dress from the Donna Karan Collection may cost as much as €2700.[66]

Price discrimination occurs when a company sells a product or service at two or more prices that do not reflect a proportional difference in costs. In first-degree price discrimination, the seller charges a separate price to each customer depending on the intensity of his or her demand. In second-degree price discrimination, the seller charges less to buyers who buy a larger volume. In third-degree price discrimination, the seller charges different amounts to different classes of buyers, as in the following cases:

- **Customer-segment pricing.** Different customer groups pay different prices for the same product or service. For example, museums often charge a lower admission fee to students and senior citizens.
- **Product-form pricing.** Different versions of the product are priced differently, but not proportionately to their costs. Evian prices a 48-ounce bottle of its mineral water at €1.50. It takes the same water and packages 1.7 ounces in a moisturiser spray for €4.00. Through product-form pricing, Evian manages to charge €2.50 an ounce in one form and about €0.03 an ounce in another.
- **Image pricing.** Some companies price the same product at two different levels based on image differences. A perfume manufacturer can put the perfume in one bottle, give it a name and image, and price it at €10. It can put the same perfume in another bottle with a different name and image and price it at €30.
- **Channel pricing.** Coca-Cola carries a different price depending on whether the consumer purchases it in a fine restaurant, a fast-food restaurant or a vending machine.
- **Location pricing.** The same product is priced differently at different locations even though the cost of offering it at each location is the same. A theatre varies its seat prices according to audience preferences for different locations.
- **Time pricing.** Prices are varied by season, day or hour. Public utilities vary energy rates to commercial users by time of day and weekend versus weekday. Restaurants charge less to 'early bird' customers, and some hotels charge less on weekends.

The airline and hospitality industries use yield management systems and **yield pricing**, by which they offer discounted but limited early purchases, higher-priced late purchases, and the lowest rates on unsold inventory just before it expires. Airlines charge different fares to passengers on the same flight, depending on the seating class; the time of day (morning or night flight); the day of the week (workday or weekend); the season; the person's employer, past business or status (youth, military, senior citizen); and so on.

That is why on a flight from Oslo to Rome you might have paid €93 and be sitting across from someone who has paid €526. At any given moment the global airline market has more than 7 million prices. And in a system that tracks the difference in prices and the price of competitors' offerings, airlines collectively change 75,000 different prices a day. It is a system designed to punish procrastinators by charging them the highest possible prices.

The phenomenon of offering different pricing schedules to different consumers and dynamically adjusting prices is exploding.[67] Many companies are using software packages that provide real-time controlled tests of actual consumer response to different pricing schedules. Constant price variation, however, can be tricky where consumer relationships are concerned. Research shows it tends to work best in situations where there is no bond between the buyer and the seller. One way to make it work is to offer customers a unique bundle of products and services to meet their needs precisely, making it harder for them to make price comparisons.

The tactic most companies favour, however, is to use variable prices as a reward for good behaviour rather than as a penalty. Customers are also getting more savvy about how to avoid buyer's remorse from overpaying. They are changing their buying behaviour to accommodate the new realities of dynamic pricing – where prices vary frequently by channels, products, customers and time.

Some forms of price discrimination (in which sellers offer different price terms to different people within the same trade group) are illegal. However, price discrimination is legal if the seller can prove that its costs are different when selling different volumes or different qualities of the same product to different retailers. Predatory pricing – selling below cost with the intention of destroying competition – is unlawful.[68] Even if legal, some differentiated pricing may meet with a hostile reaction. Coca-Cola considered using wireless technology to raise its vending machine drinks prices on hot days and lower them on cold days. Customers so disliked the idea that Coke abandoned it.

For price discrimination to work, certain conditions must exist. First, the market must be segmentable and the segments must show different intensities of demand. Second, members in the lower-price segment must not be able to resell the product to the higher-price segment. Third, competitors must not be able to undersell the firm in the higher-price segment. Fourth, the cost of segmenting and policing the market must not exceed the extra revenue derived from price discrimination. Fifth, the practice must not breed customer resentment and ill will. Sixth, of course, the particular form of price discrimination must not be illegal.[69]

While this section has examined several price-adaptation strategies, the next section reviews circumstances where companies may initiate and respond to price changes.

Initiating and responding to price changes

Initiating price cuts

Several circumstances might lead a firm to cut prices. One is *excess plant capacity*: the firm needs additional business and cannot generate it through increased sales effort, product improvement or other measures. Companies sometimes initiate price cuts in a *drive to dominate the market through lower costs*. Either the company starts with lower costs than its competitors, or it initiates price cuts in the hope of gaining market share and lower costs.

Cutting prices to keep customers or beat competitors often encourages customers to demand price concessions, however, and trains salespeople to offer them.[70] A price-cutting strategy can lead to other possible traps:

- **Low-quality trap**. Consumers assume quality is low.
- **Fragile market-share trap**. A low price buys market share but not market loyalty. The same customers will shift to any lower-priced firm that comes along.
- **Shallow-pockets trap**. Higher-priced competitors match the lower prices but have longer staying power because of deeper cash reserves.
- **Price-war trap**. Competitors respond by lowering their prices even more, triggering a price war.

Customers often question the motivation behind price changes.[71] They may assume the item is about to be replaced by a new model; the item is faulty and not selling well; the firm is in financial trouble; the price will come down even further; or the quality has been reduced. The firm must monitor these attributions carefully.

Initiating price increases

A successful price increase can raise profits considerably. For example, if the company's profit margin is 3 per cent of sales, a 1 per cent price increase will increase profits by 33 per cent if sales volume is unaffected. This situation is illustrated in Table 16.5. The assumption is that a company charged €10 and sold 100 units and had costs of €970, leaving a profit of €30, or 3 per cent on sales. By raising its price by 10 cents (a 1 per cent price increase), it boosted its profits by 33 per cent, assuming the same sales volume.

A major circumstance provoking price increases is *cost inflation*. Rising costs unmatched by productivity gains squeeze profit margins and

European low-cost airlines such as Sterling and SAS have different views on their respective future pricing strategies. To learn more, visit www.pearsoned. co.uk/marketingmanagementeurope.

Table 16.5 Profits before and after a price increase

	Before	**After**
Price	€10	€10.10 (a 1% price increase)
Units sold	100	100
Revenue	€1,000	€1,010
Costs	−€970	−€970
Profit	€30	€40 (a $33\frac{1}{3}$% profit increase)

lead companies to regular rounds of price increases. Companies often raise their prices by more than the cost increase, in anticipation of further inflation or government price controls, in a practice called *anticipatory pricing*.

Another factor leading to price increases is *overdemand*. When a company cannot supply all its customers, it can raise its prices, ration supplies to customers, or both. The price can be increased in the following ways, each of which has a different impact on buyers.

- **Delayed quotation pricing.** The company does not set a final price until the product is finished or delivered. This pricing is prevalent in industries with long production lead times, such as industrial construction and heavy equipment.
- **Escalator clauses.** The company requires the customer to pay today's price and all or part of any inflation increase that takes place before delivery. An escalator clause bases price increases on some specified price index. Escalator clauses are found in contracts for major industrial projects, such as aircraft construction and bridge building.
- **Unbundling.** The company maintains its price but removes or prices separately one or more elements that were part of the former offer, such as free delivery or installation. Car companies sometimes add antilock brakes and passenger-side airbags as supplementary extras to their vehicles.
- **Reduction of discounts.** The company instructs its sales force not to offer its normal cash and quantity discounts.

Although there is always a chance that a price increase can carry some positive meanings to customers – for example, that the item is 'hot' and represents unusually good value – consumers generally dislike higher prices. In passing price increases on to customers, the company must avoid looking like a price 'gouger'.[72] Consumer concern and dissatisfaction with high petrol, food and prescription drug prices, and Amazon.com's dynamic pricing experiment whereby prices varied by purchase occasion have become front-page news. The more similar the products or offerings from a company, the more likely consumers are to interpret any pricing differences as unfair. Product customisation and differentiation and communications that clarify differences are thus critical.[73]

Generally, consumers prefer small price increases on a regular basis to sudden, sharp increases. Their memories are long, and they can turn against companies they perceive as price gougers. Price hikes without corresponding investments in the value of the brand increase vulnerability to lower-priced competition. Consumers may be willing to 'trade down' because they can no longer justify to themselves that the higher-priced brand is worth it.

Several techniques help consumers avoid sticker shock and a hostile reaction when prices rise: one is that a sense of fairness must surround any price increase, and customers must be given advance notice so they can do forward buying or shop around. Sharp price increases need to be explained in understandable terms. Making low-visibility price moves first is also a good technique: eliminating discounts, increasing minimum order sizes and curtailing production of low-margin products are some examples; and contracts or bids for long-term projects should contain escalator clauses based on such factors as increases in recognised national price indexes.[74]

Given strong consumer resistance to price hikes, marketers go to great lengths to find alternative approaches that will allow them to avoid increasing prices when they would otherwise have done so. Here are a few popular ones.

- **Shrinking the amount of product instead of raising the price.** Hershey Foods maintained its chocolate bar price but trimmed its size. Nestlé maintained its size but raised the price.
- **Substituting less expensive materials or ingredients.** Many confectionery companies substituted synthetic chocolate for real chocolate to fight price increases in cocoa.
- **Reducing or removing product features.** Full-service air carriers such as British Airways have changed their services by simplifying fare structures and introducing ticketless travel.[75]
- **Removing or reducing product services.** These services might include installation or free delivery.
- **Using less expensive packaging material or larger package sizes.**
- **Reducing the number of sizes and models offered.**
- **Creating new economy brands.** Jewel food stores introduced 170 generic items selling at 10–30 per cent less than national brands.

When setting the price it is important that the company pays attention to competitors' price changes and responds to these when appropriate. How a firm should respond to a price cut initiated by a competitor is considered in the next section.

Responding to competitors' price changes

In general, the best response to competitors' price changes varies with the situation. The company must consider the product's stage in the life cycle, its importance in the company's portfolio, the competitor's intentions and resources, the market's price and quality sensitivity, the behaviour of costs with volume, and the company's alternative opportunities.

In markets characterised by high product homogeneity, the firm can search for ways to enhance its augmented product. If it cannot find any, it may need to meet the price reduction. If the competitor raises its price in a homogeneous product market, other firms might not match it if the increase will not benefit the industry as a whole. Then the leader will need to roll back the increase. In non-homogeneous product markets, a firm has more latitude. It needs to consider the following issues: (1) Why did the competitor change the price? To steal the market, to utilise excess capacity, to meet changing cost conditions, or to lead an industry-wide price change? (2) Does the competitor plan to make the price change temporary or permanent? (3) What will happen to the company's market share and profits if it does not respond? Are other companies going to respond? (4) What are the competitors' and other firms' responses likely to be to each possible reaction?

Market leaders often face aggressive price cutting by smaller firms trying to build market share. Using price, Fuji has attacked Kodak, Schick has attacked Gillette, and AMD has attacked Intel. Brand leaders also face competition from lower-priced, private-label store brands. The brand leader can respond in several ways. The marketing memo highlights some possible responses.

An extended analysis of alternatives may not always be feasible when the attack occurs. The company may have to react decisively within hours or days, especially in those industries where price changes occur with some frequency and where it is important to react quickly, such as the meatpacking, lumber or oil industries. It would make better sense to anticipate possible competitors' price changes and prepare contingent responses.

Marketing memo

How to fight low-cost rivals

London Business School's Nirmalya Kumar spent five years studying 50 incumbents and 25 low-cost businesses to better understand the threats posed by disruptive, low-cost competitors. He notes that successful price warriors, such as Germany's Aldi supermarkets, India's Aravind Eye Hospitals and Israel's Teva Pharmaceuticals, are changing the nature of competition all over the world by employing several key tactics, such as focusing on just one or a few consumer segments, delivering the basic product or providing one benefit better than rivals do, and backing low prices with super-efficient operations.

Kumar believes ignoring low-cost rivals is a mistake because they eventually force companies to vacate entire market segments. He does not see price wars as the answer either: slashing prices usually lowers profits for incumbents without driving the low-cost entrants out of business. In the race to the bottom, he says, the challengers always come out ahead of the incumbents. Instead, he offers three possible responses that will vary in their success depending on different factors, as outlined in Figure 16.7.

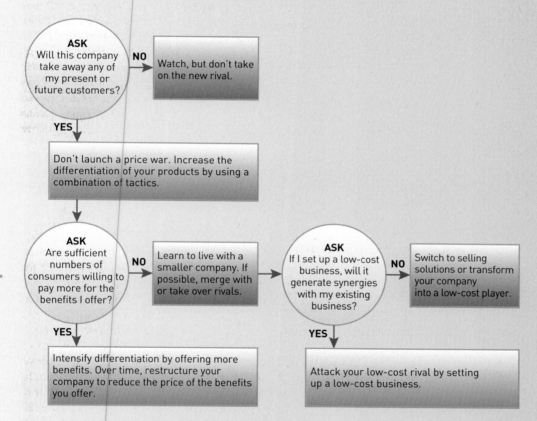

Figure 16.7 A framework for responding to low-cost rivals

Source: Reprinted by permission of *Harvard Business Review*. From Strategies to fight low-cost rivals by Kumar, N., December 2006. Copyright © by the Harvard Business School Publishing Corporation; all rights reserved.

The first approach to competing against cut-price players is to differentiate the product or service through various means:

- design 'cool' products (Apple; Bang & Olufsen);
- continually innovate (Gillette; 3M);
- offer unique product mix (Sharper Image; Whole Foods);

- brand a community (Harley-Davidson; Red Bull);
- sell experiences (Four Seasons; Starbucks).

Kumar cautions that three conditions will determine the success of a differentiation response:

1 **Companies must not use differentiation tactics in isolation.** Bang & Olufsen has competed effectively against low-cost electronics manufacturers in part because of its strong design capabilities, but also because the company continually introduces new products, cultivates an upscale brand image, and supports modern-looking retail outlets.
2 **Companies must be able to persuade consumers to pay for added benefits.** Charging a small premium for greater services or benefits can be a powerful defence.
3 **Companies must first bring costs and benefits in line.** HP's resurgence in the PC industry can be attributed in part to its success in cutting Dell's cost advantage from 20 per cent to 10 per cent.

Kumar cautions that unless sizeable numbers of consumers demand additional benefits, companies may need to yield some markets to price warriors. For example, British Airways has relinquished some short-haul routes to low-cost rivals easyJet and Ryanair. Kumar also believes strategies that help an incumbent firm coexist with low-cost rivals can work initially, but over the long haul consumers migrate to low-cost options as they become more familiar with them.

Another approach that many companies have tried in responding to low-cost competitors is to introduce a low-cost venture themselves. Citing the failure of no-frills second carriers such as Continental Lite, Delta's Song, KLM's Buzz, SAS's Snowflake, US Airways' MetroJet, and United's Shuttle, however, Kumar asserts that companies should set up low-cost operations only if: (1) the traditional operation will become more competitive as a result; and (2) the new business will derive some advantages that it would not have gained as an independent entity.

A dual strategy succeeds only if companies can generate synergies between the existing businesses and the new ventures, as financial service providers HSBC and ING did. The low-cost venture probably includes a unique brand name or identity, adequate resources and a willingness to endure some cannibalisation between the two businesses.

If there are no synergies between traditional and low-cost businesses, companies should consider two other options. They can switch from selling products to selling solutions, or even convert themselves into low-cost players. In the former approach, Kumar believes that by offering products and services as an integrated package, companies can expand the segment of the market that is willing to pay more for additional benefits. Selling solutions requires managing customers' processes and increasing their revenues or lowering their costs and risks.

And if all else fails, the best solution may be reinvention as a low-cost player. After all, as noted above, Ryanair was an unprofitable, high-cost traditional airline before it completely – and quite successfully – transformed itself into a low-cost carrier.

SUMMARY

1 Despite the increased role of non-price factors in modern marketing, price remains a critical element of the marketing mix. Price is the only element that produces revenue; the others produce costs.

2 Consumer attitudes about pricing took a dramatic shift in the recent economic downturn as many found themselves unable to sustain their lifestyles. Consumers began to buy more for need than desire and to trade down more frequently in price. They shunned conspicious consumption, and sales of luxury goods suffered. Even purchases that had never been challenged before were scrutinised.

3 In setting pricing policy, a company follows a six-step procedure. It selects its pricing objective. It estimates the demand curve – the probable quantities it will sell at each possible price. It estimates how its costs vary at different levels of output, at different levels of accumulated production experience and for differentiated marketing offers. It examines competitors' costs, prices and offers. It selects a pricing method. It selects the final price.

4 Companies do not usually set a single price, but rather a pricing structure that reflects variations in geographical demand and costs, market-segment requirements, purchase timing, order levels and other

factors. Several price-adaptation strategies are available: (1) geographical pricing; (2) price discounts and allowances; (3) promotional pricing; and (4) discriminatory pricing.

5 After developing pricing strategies, firms often face situations in which they need to change prices. A price decrease might be brought about by excess plant capacity, declining market share, a desire to dominate the market through lower costs, or economic recession. A price increase might be brought about by cost inflation or overdemand. Companies must carefully manage customer perceptions in raising prices.

6 Companies must anticipate competitor price changes and prepare contingent responses. A number of responses are possible in terms of maintaining or changing price or quality.

7 The firm facing a competitor's price change must try to understand the competitor's intent and the likely duration of the change. Strategy often depends on whether a firm is producing homogeneous or non-homogeneous products. A market leader attacked by lower-priced competitors can seek to better differentiate itself, introduce its own low-cost competitor, or transform itself more completely.

APPLICATIONS

Marketing debate

Is the right price a fair price? Prices are often set to satisfy demand or to reflect the premium that consumers are willing to pay for a product or service. Some critics shudder, however, at the thought of €1.50 bottles of water, €150 running shoes and €400 concert tickets.
Take a position: Prices should reflect the value that consumers are willing to pay *versus* Prices should primarily just reflect the cost involved in making a product or service.

Marketing discussion

Think of the various pricing methods described in this chapter – mark-up pricing, target-return pricing, perceived-value pricing, value pricing, going-rate pricing and auction-type pricing. As a consumer, which method do you personally prefer to deal with? Why? If the average price were to stay the same, which would you prefer: (1) for firms to set one price and not deviate; or (2) for firms to employ slightly higher prices most of the year, but slightly lower discounted prices or specials for certain occasions?

REFERENCES

[1] T. Y. Mørch (2011) Design, *Berlingske Tidende*, 3 April, 9–10.

[2] The price is wrong (2002) *The Economist*, 25 May, 59–60.

[3] X. Dreze and J. C. Nunes (2004) Using combined-currency prices to lower consumers' perceived cost, *Journal of Marketing Research*, 41 (February), 59–72.

[4] F. Bergés-Sennou (2006) Store loyalty, bargaining power and the private label production issue, *European Review of Agricultural Economics*, 33(3), 315–35.

[5] J. B. Kim, P. Albuquerque and B. Bronnenberg (2010) Online demand under limited consumer search, *Marketing Science*,

29(6), 1001–23; W. K. Darley, C. Blankson and D. J. Luethge (2010) Toward an integrated framework for online consumer behavior and decision making process: a review, *Psychology and Marketing*, 27(2), 94–116; P. Markillie (2004) A perfect market: a survey of e-commerce, *The Economist*, 15 May, 3–20; D. Kirpatrick (2004) How the open-source world plans to smack down Microsoft, and Oracle, and. . ., *Fortune*, 23 February, 92–100; F. Keenan (2003) The price is really right, *BusinessWeek*, 31 March, 61–7; M. Menduno (2001) Priced to perfection, *Business 2.0*, 6 March, 40–2; A. E. Cortese (1998) Good-bye to fixed pricing?, *BusinessWeek*, 4 May, 71–84. For a discussion of some of the academic issues involved, see F. Zettelmeyer (2000) Expanding to the internet: pricing and communication strategies when firms compete on multiple channels, *Journal of Marketing Research*, 37 (August), 292–308; J. G. Lynch, Jr and D. Ariely (2000) Wine online: search costs affect competition on price, quality, and distribution, *Marketing Science*, 19(1), 83–103; R. Lal and M. Sarvary (1999) When and how is the internet likely to decrease price competition?, *Marketing Science*, 18(4), 485–503.

6See www.jstor.org.

7J. Brown (2007) Radiohead album goes live on the internet, *Independent*, Music, 11 October, www.independent.co.uk/arts-entertainment/music/news/radiohead-album-goes-live-on-the-internet-396544.html.

8A. Sherwin (2007) How much is Radiohead's online album worth?, *The Times*, 11 October, 10–13.

9Based or pricing: the magic number (2006) *BusinessWeek*, Winter, www.businessweek.com/magazine/content/06_52/b4015452.htm?chan=search.

10For a thorough, up-to-date review of pricing research, see H. Yuan and S. Han (2010) The effects of consumers' price expectations on sellers' dynamic pricing strategies, *Journal of Marketing Research*, 48(1), 48–61; C. Ofir and R. S. Winer (2002) Pricing: economic and behavioral models, in B. Weitz and R. Wensley (eds), *Handbook of Marketing*, London: Sage.

11P. Sarkar (2007) Which shirt costs $275? Brand loyalty, bargain hunting, and unbridled luxury all play a part in the price you'll pay for a T-shirt, *Final Edition*, 15 March, C1. Reprinted by permission.

12J. Fernandez (2010) Consumers still focusing on frugality and value despite economic recovery, *Marketing Week*, 22 April; B. Horovitz (2010) Sale, sale, sale: today everyone wants a deal, *USA TODAY*, 21 April, 1A, 2A.

13P. R. Dickson and A. G. Sawyer (1990) The price knowledge and search of supermarket shoppers, *Journal of Marketing*, July, 42–53. For a methodological qualification, however, see H. Estalami, A. Holden and D. R. Lehmann (2001) Macro-economic determinants of consumer price knowledge: a meta-analysis of four decades of research, *International Journal of Research in Marketing*, 18 (December), 341–55.

14For a comprehensive review, see B. Lowe and F. Alpert (2010) Pricing strategy and the formation and evolution of reference price perceptions in new product categories, *Psychology and Marketing*, 27(9), 846–73; T. Mazumdar, S. P. Raj and I. Sinha (2005) Reference price research: review and propositions, *Journal of Marketing*, 69 (October), 84–102. For a different point of view, see C. Janiszewski and D. R. Lichtenstein (1999) A range theory account of price perception, *Journal of Consumer Research*, March, 353–68.

15G. E. Mayhew and R. S. Winer (1992) An empirical analysis of internal and external reference-price effects using scanner data, *Journal of Consumer Research*, June, 62–70.

16R. Ziethammer (2006) Forward-looking buying in online auctions, *Journal of Marketing Research*, 43 (August), 462–76.

17J. T. Gourville (1998) Pennies-a-day: the effect of temporal reframing on transaction evaluation, *Journal of Consumer Research*, March, 395–408.

18E. C. Jackson and R. Narasimhan (2010) A dynamic pricing game investigating the interaction of price and quality on sales response, *Journal of Business and Economics Research*, 8(9), 37–52; G. M. Erickson and J. K. Johansson (1985) The role of price in multi-attribute product-evaluations, *Journal of Consumer Research*, September, 195–9.

19www.rolls-royce.150m.com/maintenance_cost/indexen.html.

20W. Amaldoss and S. Jain (2005) Pricing of conspicuous goods: a competitive analysis of social effects, *Journal of Marketing Research*, 42 (February), 30–42. A. Chao and J. B. Schor (1998) Empirical tests of status consumption: evidence from women's cosmetics, *Journal of Economic Psychology*, 19(4), 107–31.

21B. Burnsed (2009) Where discounting can be dangerous, *BusinessWeek*, 3 August, 49; Tiffany's profit tops expectations, *Associated Press*, 26 November 2009; C. Wilson (2009) If bling had a hall of fame, *New York Times*, 30 July; E. Byron (2007). Fashion victim: to refurbish its image, Tiffany risks profits, *Wall Street Journal*, 10 January A1.

22M. Stiving and R. S. Winer (1997) An empirical analysis of price endings with scanner data, *Journal of Consumer Research*, June, 57–68.

23E. T. Anderson and D. Simester (2003) Effects of $19 price endings on retail sales: evidence from field experiments, *Quantitative Marketing and Economics*, 1(1), 93–110.

24E. Anderson and D. Simester (2003) Mind your pricing cues, *Harvard Business Review*, September, 96–103.

25K. C. Manning and D. E. Sprott (2009) Price endings, left-digit effects, and choice, *Journal of Consumer Research*, 36, 328–35.

26R. M. Schindler and P. N. Kirby (1997) Patterns of rightmost digits used in advertised prices: implications for nine-ending effects, *Journal of Consumer Research*, September, 192–201.

27Anderson and Simester (2003) op. cit.

28Ibid.

29D. J. Howard and R. A. Kerin (2006) Broadening the scope of reference-price advertising research: a field study of consumer shopping involvement, *Journal of Marketing*, 70 (October), 185–204.

30W. W. Moe and P. S. Fader (2009) The role of price tiers in advance purchasing of event tickets, *Journal of Service Research*, 12(1), 73–86; R. C. Blattberg and K. Wisniewski (1989) Price-induced patterns of competition, *Marketing Science*, 8 (Fall), 291–309.

31S. Dutta, M. J. Zbaracki and M. Bergen (2003) Pricing process as a capability: a resource-based perspective, *Strategic Management Journal*, 24(7), 615–30.

32T. Breinstrup (2011) Prisen på iPad og konkurrenterne rasler ned, *Business.dk*, 4 April.

33www.raileurope.com/activities/paris-museum-pass/index.html.

34T. Aeppel (2007) Seeking perfect prices, CEO tears up the rules, *Wall Street Journal*, 27 March.

35F. Zettelmeyer, F. S. Morton and J. Silva-Risso (2006) How the internet lowers prices: evidence from matched survey and automobile transaction data, *Journal of Marketing Research*, 43(May), 168–81; J. R. Brown and A. Goolsbee (2002) Does the internet make markets more competitive? Evidence from the life insurance industry, *Journal of Political Economy*, 110(5), 481–507.

[36]B. Bergstein (2007) Pricing software could reshape retail, *Forbes*, 27 April.

[37]T. T. Nagle and R. K. Holden (2002) *The Strategy and Tactics of Pricing*, 3rd edn, Upper Saddle River, NJ: Prentice Hall.

[38]T. H. A. Bijmolt, H. J. Van Heerde and R. G. M. Pieters (2005) New empirical generalizations on the determinants of price elasticity, *Journal of Marketing Research*, 42 (May), 141–56. Easier Than ABC (2003) *The Economist*, 25 October, 56.

[39]Easier than ABC (2003) *The Economist*, 25 October, 56.

[40]W. W. Alberts (1989) The experience curve doctrine reconsidered, *Journal of Marketing*, July, 36–49.

[41]M. Sivy (1991) Japan's smart secret weapon, *Fortune*, 12 August, 75.

[42]J. Ewing (2004) The next Wal-Mart?, *BusinessWeek*, 26 April, 60–2; German discounter Aldi aims to profit from belt-tightening in US, *DW World.de.*, www.dw-world.de, 15 January 2009; www.aldi.com.

[43]R. Grover and C. Edwards (2007) Next-gen DVDs: advantage, Sony, *BusinessWeek*, 6 December; adapted from R. J. Dolan and H. Simon (1997) Power pricers, *Across the Board*, May, 18–19.

[44]K. L. Ailawadi, D. R. Lehmann and S. A. Neslin (2001) Market response to a major policy change in the marketing mix: learning from Procter & Gamble's value pricing strategy, *Journal of Marketing*, 65(January), 44–61.

[45]M. Copaciu, F. Neagu and H. Braun-Erdei (2010) Survey evidence on price-setting patterns of Romanian firms, *Managerial and Decision Economics*, 31(2/3), 235–47.

[46]B. Einhorn (2009) Acer's game-changing PC offensive, *BusinessWeek*, 20 April, 65; B. Einhorn and T. Culpan (2010) With Dell in the dust, Acer chases HP, *Bloomberg BusinessWeek*, 8 March, 58–9.

[47]H. He and Y. Li (2011) Key service drivers for high-tech service brand equity: the mediating role of overall service quality and perceived value, *Journal of Marketing Management*, 27(1/2), 77–99; Tung-Zong Chang and A. R. Wildt (1994) Price, product information, and purchase intention: an empirical study, *Journal of the Academy of Marketing Science*, Winter, 16–27. See also G. D. Kortge and P. A. Okonkwo (1993) Perceived value approach to pricing, *Industrial Marketing Management*, May, 133–40.

[48]H. J. Larsen (2006) Mormor, www.springwise.com, 6 February; www.mormor.nu.

[49]L. Xinxin and L. M. Hitt (2010) Price effects in online product reviews: an analytical model and empirical results, *MIS Quarterly*, 34(4), 809–A5; J. C. Anderson, D. C. Jain and P. K. Chintagunta (1993) Customer value assessment in business markets: a state-of-practice study, *Journal of Business-to-Business Marketing*, 1(1), 3–29.

[50]E. Sullivan (2008) Value pricing, *Marketing News*, 15 January, 08.

[51]S. J. Hoch, X. Dreze and M. J. Purk (1994) EDLP, Hi-Lo, and margin arithmetic, *Journal of Marketing*, October, 16–27; R. Lal and R. Rao (1997) Supermarket competition: the case of everyday low pricing, *Marketing Science*, 16(1), 60–80.

[52]J. W. Alba, C. F. Mela, T. A. Shimp and J. E. Urbany (1999) The effect of discount frequency and depth on consumer price judgments, *Journal of Consumer Research*, September, 99–114.

[53]Adapted from Greggs case study (2009), Datamonitor Case Studies, March.

[54]M. Duff (2005) European retailers reckon with hard discounters' formidable potential, *DSN Retailing Today*, 10 January.

[55]J. E. Rasmussen (2006) Succes ved en tilfældighed, *Erhverv og Økonomi*, 6 March; www.tiger.dk/butikker.html.

[56]E. Smith and S. Silver (2006) To protect its box-office turf, Ticketmaster plays rivals' tune, *Wall Street Journal*, 12 September.

[57]Royal Mail drives major cost savings through free markets (2003) Free Markets press release, 15 December.

[58]S. D. Jap (2007) The impact of online reverse auction design on buyer–supplier relationships, *Journal of Marketing*, 71 (January), 146–59; S. D. Jap (2003) An exploratory study of the introduction of online reverse auctions, *Journal of Marketing*, 67 (July), 96–107.

[59]P. W. Farris and D. J. Reibstein (1879) How prices, expenditures, and profits are linked, *Harvard Business Review*, November–December, 173–84. See also M. Abe (1995) Price and advertising strategy of a national brand against its private-label clone: a signaling game approach, *Journal of Business Research*, July, 241–50.

[60]Y. Xu, J. C. S. Lui and D-M. Chiu (2010) On oligopoly spectrum allocation in cognitive ration networks with capacity constraints, *Computer Networks*, 54(6), 925–43; E. H. Fram and M. S. McCarthy (1999) The true price of penalties, *Marketing Management*, October, 49–56.

[61]Airline SAS gets 1 billion kronor in compensation from Bombardier, Associated Press, 10 March.

[62]J. E. Urbany (2001) Justifying profitable pricing, *Journal of Product and Brand Management*, 10(3), 141–57; C. Fishman (2003) The Wal-Mart you don't know, *Fast Company*, December, 68–80.

[63]P. N. Agarwala (1991) *Countertrade: A Global Perspective*, New Delhi: Vikas; M. Rowe (1989) *Countertrade*, London: Euromoney Books; C. M. Korth (ed.) (1987) *International Countertrade*, New York: Quorum Books.

[64]For an interesting discussion of a quantity surcharge, see D. E. Sprott, K. C. Manning and A. Miyazaki (2003) Grocery price settings and quantity surcharges, *Journal of Marketing*, 67 (July), 34–46.

[65]M. V. Marn and R. L. Rosiello (1992) Managing price, gaining profit, *Harvard Business Review*, September–October, 84–94. See also K. L. Ailawadi, S. A. Neslin and K. Gedenk (2001) Pursuing the value-conscious consumer: store brands versus national-brand promotions, *Journal of Marketing*, 65 (January), 71–89; G. J. Tellis (1995) Tackling the retailer decision maze: which brands to discount, how much, when, and why?, *Marketing Science*, 14(3), 271–99.

[66]www.donnakaran.com; www.dkny.com; L. Smilth (1990) Donna Karan's fashions hit London, *The Times*, 20 February.

[67]C. Yongmin and J. Pearcy (2010) Dynamic pricing: when to entice brand switching and when to reward consumer loyalty, *RAND Journal of Economics*, 41(4), 674–85; C. Fishman (2003) Which price is right?, *Fast Company*, March, 92–102; B. Tedeschi (2002) E-commerce report, *New York Times*, 2 September; F. Keenan (2003) The price is really right, *BusinessWeek*, 31 March, 62–7; P. Coy (2000) The power of smart pricing, *BusinessWeek*, 10 April, 160–4. For a review of recent and seminal work linking pricing decisions with operational insights, see M. Fleischmann, J. M. Hall and D. F. Pyke (2004) Research brief: smart pricing, *MIT Sloan Management Review*, Winter, 9–13.

[68]Article 82 (formerly Article 86) of the EC Treaty prohibits predatory pricing. See also M. France (1998) Does predatory pricing make Microsoft a predator?, *BusinessWeek*, 23 November, 130–2. Also see J. P. Guiltinan and G. T. Gundlack (1996) Aggressive and predatory pricing: a framework for analysis, *Journal of Advertising*, July, 87–102.

[69]For more information on specific types of price discrimination that are illegal, see H. Cheesman (2007) *Business Law*, 6th edn, Upper Saddle River, NJ: Prentice Hall.

[70]B. Donath (2003) Dispel major myths about pricing, *Marketing News*, 3 February, 10.

[71]For a classic review, see K. B. Monroe (1973) Buyers' subjective perceptions of price, *Journal of Marketing Research*, February, 70–80. See also Z. J. Zhang, F. Feinberg and A. Krishna (2002) Do we care what others get? A behaviorist approach to targeted promotions, *Journal of Marketing Research*, 39 (August), 277–91.

[72]M. C. Campbell (1999) Perceptions of pricing unfairness: antecedents and consequences, *Journal of Marketing Research*, 36 (May), 187–99.

[73]Lan Xia, K. B. Monroe and J. L. Cox (2004) The price is unfair! A conceptual framework of price fairness perceptions, *Journal of Marketing*, 68 (October), 1–15.

[74]E. Mitchell (1990) How not to raise prices, *Small Business Reports*, November, 64–7.

[75]R. Collis (2002) The frequent traveler: getting frills for the cost of a no-frills ticket, *International Herald Tribune*, 5 July.

Delivering value

Video documentary for Part 6

Go to **www.pearsoned.co.uk/ marketingmanagementeurope** to watch the video documentary that relates to Part 6 and consider the issues raised below.

Once a company has researched and then developed an attractive value package, it is important to ensure that it reaches customers in the marketplace quickly and efficiently.

Part 6: Delivering value explores three important themes:

1   selecting and managing channels;
2   analysing channel members; and
3   charting the rise of new channels.

Different national markets and different target markets require many companies to design, develop and operate multichannel distribution networks. This provides a real challenge to marketing management of maintaining their corporate brand values.

The rapid growth in digital marketing techniques has helped to speed up order placement, processing, and online and physical delivery logistics as well as opening up new markets and new intermediaries.

When watching the video documentary that accompanies Part 6, consider how the companies being interviewed either seek to do as much as possible 'in-house', or take care to build loyal value chains before moving finished value packages as efficiently as possible to their customers. As distribution channel members are in direct contact with trading customers (their intermediaries) or the final customer, they are in an ideal position to gather and communicate important customer information that has a bearing on the perceived value of the branded offering. Attention to the constant improvement of the customer interface with the supply and delivery network is a vital management concern in competitive market places.

Hear a variety of top marketing executives from a range of organisations offer their own interesting and varied perspectives on the key themes of Part 6 including: Josephine Rydberg-Dumont, President, IKEA Sweden (top); Mats Ronne, European Media Director, Electrolux (centre); and Royal Enfield, the Indian-based manufacturer of motorcycles (bottom).

Chapter 17

Designing and managing integrated marketing channels and global value networks

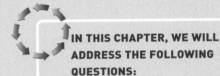

IN THIS CHAPTER, WE WILL ADDRESS THE FOLLOWING QUESTIONS:

1 What is a marketing channel system and value network?
2 What work do marketing channels perform?
3 How should channels be designed?
4 What decisions do marketers face in managing their channels?
5 How should marketers integrate channels and manage channel conflict?
6 What are the key issues with digital technologies, online channels and m-commerce?

The Smartville network of companies are all linked together to manufacture the Smart car
Source: Courtesy of Daimler AG.

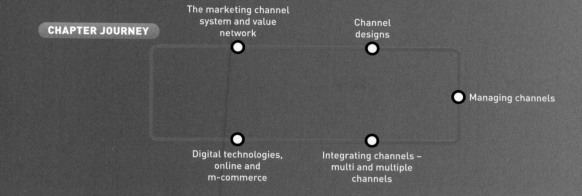

The marketing channel
system and value
network

Channel
designs

Managing channels

Digital technologies,
online and
m-commerce

Integrating channels –
multi and multiple
channels

Successful value creation needs successful value delivery. Holistic marketers are increasingly taking a value network view of their businesses. Instead of limiting their focus to their immediate suppliers, distributors and customers, they are examining the whole supply network that links raw materials, components and manufactured products and services, and exploring how they move towards the final consumers. Companies are looking at their suppliers' suppliers upstream and at their distributors' customers downstream. They are looking at customer segments and considering a wide range of new and different means to sell, distribute and manage their offerings.

Take the Smart car.

The Smart car, named after Swatch, Mercedes and Art, was the brainchild of Nicolas Hayek, perhaps better known as CEO of Swatch, the watch company. Hayek's dream was the Swatchmobile, which would do for the small car what he had done for the watch: a car that would be fun, cheap and simple, yet environmentally sound, running on hybrid power. For young elites the Smart car is a mix of German engineering and technology which is also energy-efficient. It is a small luxury car with sophisticated style and flexibility around town – innovative, functional and geared to the joy of driving. The Smart car, which is now owned by DaimlerChrysler, the parent company of Mercedes-Benz, is a two-seat, 2.5 m long by 1.5 m wide car – small enough that two or even three Smart cars can squeeze into a standard parking space. The Smart car is managed as part of a unique value network with all the suppliers and channels of distribution or marketing channels tightly linked together. The Smart car is built at one of the most modern car manufacturing network complexes in the world – called Smartville, located at Hambach in Lorraine, France. The cross-shaped assembly building is surrounded by individual companies who are the main suppliers of the parts to build the car – see image on previous page. There are over 1,900 people in 11 independent companies who work together in this network to build the Smart car.[1] The companies include: Magna (space frame), Magna Uniport (Ymos) (doors), Surtema Eisenmann (paintshop); Bosch (front powertrain, breaks, lights), Mannesmann VDO (cockpit), Dynamit Nobel (plastic body panels) and Krupp Automotive Systems (rear powertrain). In addition, there are three on-site logistics partners: TNT Logistics (spare part facility), Rhenus (storage for small parts) and MTL (moves finished cars to dealers).

The channels of distribution used for the Smart car are innovative, featuring round, transparent towers with Smart cars inside them. Smart was also the first manufacturer to sell cars over the internet. The Smart small car is very popular in major European cities, although distributor challenges have prevailed in the USA, showcasing many of the channel management issues. Even a Smart House in Los Angeles to showcase the car has not impacted on sales in the USA.[2]

Companies today must build and manage a continuously evolving and increasingly complex channel system and value network. In this chapter, we consider strategic and tactical issues in integrating marketing channels and developing value networks.

Marketing channels and value networks

Most producers do not sell their products or services directly to the final users; between them stands a set of intermediaries performing a variety of functions. These intermediaries constitute a marketing channel (also called a trade channel or distribution channel). Formally, **marketing channels** are sets of interdependent organisations participating in the process of making a product or service available for use or consumption. They are the set of pathways a product or service follows after production, culminating in purchase and consumption by the final end user.[3]

Some intermediaries – such as wholesalers and retailers – buy, take title to, and resell the merchandise; they are called *merchants*. Others – brokers, manufacturers' representatives, sales agents – search for customers and may negotiate on the producer's behalf but do not take title to the goods; they are called *agents*. Still others – transportation companies, independent warehouses, banks, advertising agencies – assist in the distribution process but neither take title to goods nor negotiate purchases or sales; they are called *facilitators*.

Channels of all types play an important role in the success of a company and affect all other marketing decisions. Marketers should judge them in the context of the entire process by which their products and services are made, distributed, sold and serviced. We consider all these issues in the following sections.

The importance of channels

A **marketing channel system** is the particular set of marketing channels a firm employs, and decisions about it are among the most critical ones management faces. Channel members collectively have earned margins that account for 30 to 50 per cent of the ultimate selling price. In contrast, advertising typically has accounted for less than 5 to 7 per cent of the final price.[4] Marketing channels also represent a substantial opportunity cost. One of their chief roles is to convert potential buyers into profitable customers. Marketing channels must not just *serve* markets; they must also *make* markets.[5]

The channels chosen affect all other marketing decisions. The company's pricing depends on whether it uses online discounters or high-quality boutiques. Its sales force and advertising decisions depend on how much training and motivation dealers need. In addition, channel decisions include relatively long-term commitments with other firms as well as a set of policies and procedures. When a car company signs up independent dealers to sell its car, it cannot buy them out the next day and replace them with company-owned outlets. At the same time, channel choices themselves depend on the company's marketing strategy with respect to segmentation, targeting and positioning. Holistic marketers ensure that marketing decisions in all these different areas are made to collectively maximise value.

In managing its intermediaries, the firm must decide how much effort to devote to push versus pull marketing. A **push strategy** uses the manufacturer's sales force, trade promotion money or other means to induce intermediaries to carry, promote and sell the product or service to end users. A push strategy is particularly appropriate when there is low brand loyalty in a category, brand choice is made in the shop, the product is an impulse item, and product benefits are well understood. In a **pull strategy** the manufacturer uses advertising, promotion and other forms of communication to persuade consumers to demand the product from intermediaries, thus inducing the intermediaries to order it. A pull strategy is particularly appropriate when there is high brand loyalty and high involvement in the category, when consumers are able to perceive differences between brands, and when they choose the brand before they go to the shop.

Top marketing companies such as Red Bull, Samsung and Gucci skilfully employ both push and pull strategies. A push strategy is more effective when accompanied by a well-designed and well-executed pull strategy that activates consumer demand. On the other hand, without at least some consumer interest, it can be very difficult to gain much channel acceptance and support, and vice versa for that matter.

Multichannel distribution systems

Today's successful companies typically employ hybrid channels and multichannel marketing, multiplying the number of 'go-to-market' channels in any one market area. Hybrid channels or **multichannel distribution systems** occur when a single firm uses two or more marketing channels to reach customer segments. HP uses its sales force to sell to large accounts, outbound telemarketing to sell to medium-sized accounts, direct mail with an inbound number to sell to small accounts, retailers to sell to still smaller accounts, and the internet to sell specialty items. Philips also is a multichannel marketer.

PHILIPS

Royal Philips Electronics of the Netherlands is one of the world's biggest electronics companies and Europe's largest, with sales of over €25 billion in 2010. The company employs 119,000 people in more than 60 countries. Established in 1891, it now has over 100 different businesses and over 200 production sites, and carries out research and development in more than 40 countries. Its sales and service outlets cover 150 countries, and it has a total workforce upwards of 230,000 employees. It has a strong technology base, spending over 5 per cent of sales on research and development, and owning some 10,000 patents. Philips' electronics products are channelled towards the consumer primarily through local and international retailers. The company offers a broad range of products from high to low price/value quartiles, relying on a diverse distribution model that includes mass merchants, retail chains, independents and small specialty shops. To work most effectively with these retail channels, Philips has created an organisation designed around its retail customers, with dedicated global key account managers serving leading retailers such as Carrefour, Dixons and Tesco. Like many modern firms, Philips also sells via the web through its own online store as well as through a number of other online retailers.[6]

In multichannel marketing, each channel targets a different segment of buyers, or different need states for one buyer, and delivers the right products in the right places in the right way at the least cost. When this does not happen, there can be channel conflict, excessive cost or insufficient supply.

Companies that manage hybrid channels clearly must make sure their channels work well together and match each target customer's preferred ways of doing business. Customers expect *channel integration*, which allows them to:

* order a product online and pick it up at a convenient retail location;
* return an online-ordered product to a nearby shop of the retailer;
* receive discounts and promotional offers based on total online and off-line purchases.

Fnac is a company that has carefully managed its multiple channels.

Fnac

Fnac, the leading French bookshop, has been lauded by industry analysts for its seamless integration of a range of channels including its retail shops, website, internet kiosks, mail-order catalogues, self-service technology use and call centres. Fnac ventured rather hesitantly into e-commerce or internet sales for fear of cannibalising its traditional brick-and-mortar stores. But ever since its inception, Fnac Direct, the retailer's e-business venture, had posted stellar growth. If an item is out of stock in the shop, all customers need do is tap into the shop's internet kiosk to order it from Fnac's website. Less internet-savvy customers can get staff to place the order for them at the checkout counters. Fnac not only generates store-to-internet traffic; it also sends internet shoppers into its stores. If a customer browses Fnac's site and reads a Fnac review, the site will highlight an in-store promotion which the customer can redeem in the shop – linking all the channels together.

Technology plays a dominant role in Fnac's channel strategy. As the number one distributor of entertainment tickets in France, it manages more than 6,000 cultural events and a total of almost 50,000 individual performances a year. The Billetel software solution used by Fnac is installed in all 350 Fnac ticket offices in France, Belgium and Switzerland, and also controls the company's direct sales via the web and by telephone – providing an integrated technological solution.

Like many retailers, Fnac has found that dual-channel shoppers spend significantly more than single-channel shoppers, and multi-channel shoppers spend even more.[7]

Fnac manages a multiple channel strategy, utilising retail shops, websites, internet kiosks and self-service technologies, and linking all these channels together

Source: © Ian Canham/Alamy.

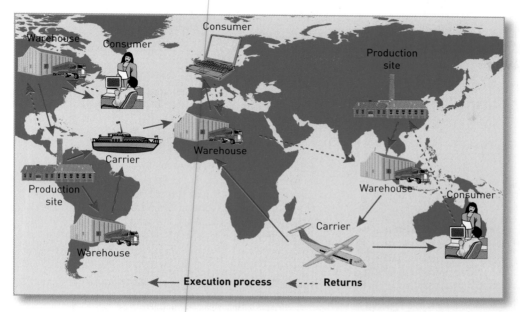

Figure 17.1 Global supply networks: coordinating road, rail, shipping, airlines and the internet

Value networks

A **supply chain** view of a firm sees markets as destination points and amounts to a linear view of the flow of ingredients and components through the production process to their ultimate sale to customers. The company should first think of the target market, however, and then design the supply chain backwards from that point. This strategy has been called **demand chain planning**.[8]

A broader view sees a company at the centre of a **value network** – a system of partnerships and alliances that a firm creates to source, augment and deliver its offerings. A **value network** includes a firm's suppliers and its suppliers' suppliers, its distributors and ultimately their end customers, who 'partner' each other to improve the performance of the entire network in delivering customer value. Figure 17.2 shows the value network for a hotel group.

The value network includes valued relationships with a range of suppliers, distributors and retailers – see the marketing insight box.

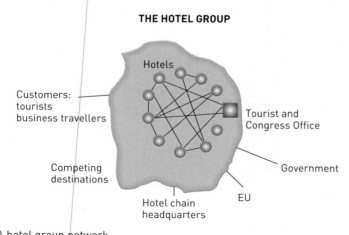

Figure 17.2 A hotel group network

Source: Y. von Friedrichs Grängsjö and E. Gummesson (2008) Hotel networks and social capital in destination marketing, *International Journal of Service Industry Management*, 17(1), 58–75.

Marketing insight

Cadbury's global supply network of channel members

Cadbury's has an extensive global supply network designed to create delicious chocolate.
Source: Courtesy of Cadbury plc.

The global supply network involved in making a Cadbury's Dairy Milk Fruit & Nut bar, at Bournville in the United Kingdom, gives a good illustration of how supply networks, and relationships within them, can differ.

- **Milk – two steps away.** The milk that goes into the chocolate bar comes from the United Kingdom. Cadbury's buys it from farmer-run co-operatives and has direct dealings with the co-operatives but not with the individual farmers, which means the farmers who produce the milk are two steps away from the company.

- **Raisins – two steps away.** The raisins come from Turkey. Cadbury's buys the raisins from a family-owned Turkish processing plant near Izmir, which buys its raisins from around 1,000 small farmers. The raisins are traceable back to the original farms. The processing plant maintains close relations with the farmers to ensure quality. The company is two steps away from these small farmers.

- **Almonds – two steps away.** The almonds come from California. Cadbury's buys the almonds from a processor, who in turn buys them from the farmer. Here the company is two steps away from the original producers, the Californian almond growers.

- **Sugar – two steps away.** The sugar comes from the United Kingdom and mainland Europe. The company buys it from sugar processors, who buy sugar beet direct from the farmer. The farmers who grow the sugar beet are therefore two steps away from the company.

- **Cocoa – three or more steps away.** Cocoa is sourced from Ghana. Cadbury's buys cocoa from the Ghanaian Government Cocoa Board (COCOBOD), which controls the cocoa trade in Ghana. Between COCOBOD and the farmer there are licensed buying companies. They buy cocoa from the farmer and transport it to the seaport. Here Cadbury's is three steps or more away from more than half a million farmers.

- **Distribution.** Cadbury's uses distributors and also vending machines at train stations and airports focusing on extensive distribution.

- **Wholesalers.** Cadbury's uses wholesalers to distribute its products to the retailers.

- **Retailers.** The wholesalers deliver to retailers all over Europe, including Carrefour in France, Tesco and Spar. Retailers make the product available to consumers by stacking them on shelves.

The amount of influence Cadbury's can exert on particular supply network members varies. As a major buyer of a product, or where it buys directly from the producer, the company's influence can be great. When it is not a major buyer, or where it is several steps away from the producer, its influence tends to be more limited. Nevertheless it must still recognise its responsibilities for each link in the supply network which it manages as a value network, ensuring benefits for all throughout the network. Since its network is so extensive and wide ranging, the number of groups with which Cadbury's can engage, and the degree of engagement, varies according to circumstances. It is also greater where the company believes it can have most effect, for suppliers whose products and services are more central to Cadbury's brands, and for those operating in countries or sectors typically known to face the most significant human and labour rights issues. Distribution channels and supply networks in the developing regions tend to be rather multi-tiered and complex.[9]

To help manage its value network, Cadbury's categorises and prioritises its suppliers into three tiers, according to risk as well as the importance of the product or service to the company and its brands.[10]

A **network** *consists of relationships within which interaction takes place. It can accommodate movement in any direction; it can change into any number of shapes; it is scale-free, it defines structure but also process and change. Its nodes include people, organisations, machines, events or activities. We can choose to focus on any of its parts without losing*

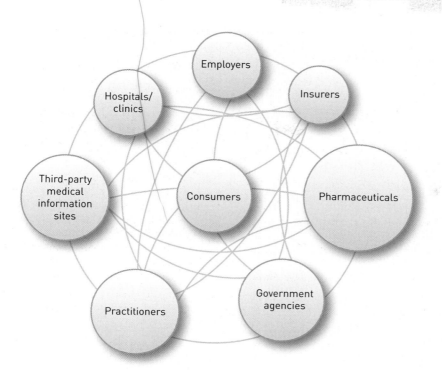

Figure 17.3 The health-care network
Source: H. J. Schau, M. F. Smith and P. I. Schau (2005) The healthcare network economy: the role of internet information transfer and implications for pricing, *Industrial Marketing Management*, 34, 147–56. Reproduced with permission.

sight of the systemic context. A network can support a strict mode of operation which is cost-effective in mass production, but it can equally well be flexible to a customer's individual value creation.[11] Figure 17.3 shows a supply network for the health care sector.[12]

As you can see from Figure 17.3, all the members in the network interlink and each member has to reflect or be aware of other members and their needs. Nokia, the Swedish mobile phone company, was ranked number one in the top 25 supply networks. Nokia excels at supplier collaboration while still pursuing technology and design innovations. Nokia manufactures and delivers mobile phones to almost 1 billion customers worldwide due to its ability to manage complexity, understand consumer needs and relate to the needs of its market and its network of suppliers and distributors. Nokia insists that:

close cooperation with customers and suppliers is one of our core development principles. It encourages end-to-end efficiency and speed – key success factors for the entire supply chain [network]. Openness and trust are important aspects when working together with suppliers and driving compliance.[13]

Leading companies are jumping ahead of their slower rivals and are establishing positions of dominance, based in large part on their ability to work collaboratively with carefully selected trading partners, but also on their greater understanding of customer needs and wants, and delivering to them when they want and need. Companies such as Zara, Nokia, Heineken and Unilever are examples of firms that focus on their customers and then their supply network. In contrast, some companies still focus their supply network efforts entirely inwardly. They rely on internally generated process improvements aimed at reducing costs in specific functional areas rather than having an external focus on what the market needs and wants. Many marketers are still struggling to reach the more advanced stage of supply network management, in which collaboration and the use of technology link all members.[14] A company needs to orchestrate these parties in order to deliver superior value to the target market.

Customers can play a more integrated or co-creation role in networks where customers can be seen as co-developers. Oracle relies on 5.2 million developers and 400,000

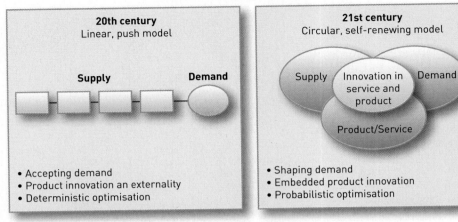

Figure 17.4 Demand-driven supply networks

discussion forum threads to advance its products.[15] Apple's Developer Connection – where customers who are technology enthusiasts create iPhone Apps and the like – has 50,000 members at different levels of membership.[16] Developers keep 70 per cent of any revenue that their products generate and Apple gets 30 per cent.

Demand-driven supply networks (DDSN) move away from the linear model of supply chains to a network focus – see Figure 17.4.

These demand-driven supply networks yield several insights.[17] First, the company can estimate whether more money is made upstream or downstream, and decide whether to integrate backwards or forwards. Second, the company is more aware of disturbances anywhere in the supply chain that might change costs, prices or supplies. Third, companies can use technology and go online with their business partners to speed communications, transactions and payments, reduce costs and increase accuracy. Ford not only manages numerous supply networks but also sponsors or operates on many B2B websites and exchanges.

Managing a value network means making increasing investments in information technology (IT) and software. Firms have introduced supply chain management (SCM) software and invited such software firms as SAP and Oracle to design comprehensive *enterprise resource planning* (ERP) systems to manage cash flow, manufacturing, human resources, purchasing and other major functions within a unified framework. They hope to break up departmental silos – where each department only acts in its own self-interest – and carry out core business processes more seamlessly. Most, however, are still a long way from truly comprehensive ERP systems. Companies now operate technological networks, managing all their operations. The marketing memo showcases an intranet-based network for the Finnish steel manufacturing industry.

Technology can increase efficiency particularly in operations or logistics, but it can also create barriers to relationships and change the power of relationships within the network. There are also emerging technologies, such as RFID (radio frequency identification devices), that can provide real-time and context-specific information continuously flowing from the product or service tagged to the company – see the marketing insight box.

Marketers, for their part, have traditionally focused on the side of the value network that looks towards the customer, adopting customer relationship management (CRM) software and practices. In the future, they will increasingly participate in and influence their companies' upstream activities and become network managers, not just product and customer managers.

Marketing memo

A network of technology-based communications

The Finnish steel manufacturing industry provides an example on how internet-based computing and communications may assist company partners in dealing with complex issues. A group of small and medium-sized companies, all located in northern Finland, operate in cooperation with a large steel producer with a turnover of €2,900 million. Before going into the internet-based communications project, information exchange between companies was limited to mail, email, phone calls and company visits. The market demand for steel plate components is expected to increase rapidly – led by buoyant activity in Asian markets[18] – and this volume increase required efficiency improvements (e.g. reducing delivery lead time, reducing production and logistics costs) in the whole network. To facilitate this aim, a new digital business design – the SteelNet system – was created (see Figure 17.5).[19]

The SteelNet system can easily communicate with the partners' own planning systems. The SteelNet system can transmit mutually agreed information and can be used via a web browser. Each of the participating companies has equal rights and responsibilities in the system. Moreover, company representatives from a broad range of company functionalities (e.g. manufacturing, management and transportation) can communicate and collaborate within the system and with representatives from other companies through the internet, and relevant information is timely and accurately available to all SteelNet members. Metcalfe's Law[20] states that, 'the value of any communication technology is proportional to the square of the number of users of the system'. Thus, creating the SteelNet enhances the possibility of reaping the full benefits of ebusiness.

Source: Based on P. Iskanius and H. Kilpala (2006) One step closer towards e-business: the implementation of a supporting ICT system, *International Journal of Logistics: Research and Applications*, 9(3), 289; J. Hendler and J. Golbeck, Metcalfe's Law, Web 2.0, and the semantic Web, available at www.cs.umd.edu/~golbeck/downloads/Web20-SW-JWS-webVersion.pdf, accessed March 2008. M. R. Fellenz, C. Augustenborg, M. Brady and J. Greene (2009) Requirements for an evolving model of supply chain finance: a technology and service providers perspective, *Communications of the IBIMA*, 10, 227, 235.

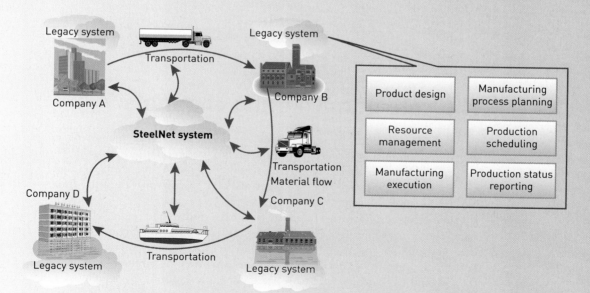

Figure 17.5 The SteelNet system
Source: Adapted from P. Iskanius and H. Kilpala (2006) One step closer towards e-business: the implementation of a supporting ICT system, *International Journal of Logistics: Research and Applications*, 9(3), 289. Reproduced with permission.

Marketing insight

Using RFID for real-time information along value networks

Radio frequency identification devices (RFID) systems are made up of 'smart' tags – which have microchips attached to tiny radio antennas – and electronic readers. Chips are about the size of a dot. The tags allow companies to read out of line of sight and to gather a range of information including temperature, position and surroundings. The smart tags can be embedded in products, services or people (normally stuck on labels or worn by a person). Legoland in Denmark has RFID armbands for all children similar to those used by Disney. Alton Towers in England uses RFID to track visitors through the park in order to be able to make DVDs of their visit should they wish to have them. Many toll roads use RFID on their easy pass systems to allow cars to drive through at speed and download payment automatically from the internet.

When the RFID tag is near a reader, the tag transmits a unique identifying number to its computer database.[21] Radio-tagging products allow retailers to alert manufacturers before shelves go bare, and consumer goods manufacturers can further perfect their supply networks so they don't produce or distribute too few or too many goods.

The ability to link product IDs with databases containing the life histories and whereabouts of products, equipment or even people makes RFID useful for all sorts of marketing along with preventing counterfeiting and ensuring food and drug safety. Although a potential boon to marketers, smart tags raise issues of consumer privacy. Take tagged medications. Electronic readers in office buildings might detect the type of medication carried by employees – an invasion of privacy. Or what about RFID-enabled customer loyalty cards that encode all sorts of personal and financial data? Already a group of more than 40 public interest groups has called for strict public notification rules, the right to demand deactivation of the tag when people leave shops, and overall limits on the technology's use until privacy concerns have been better addressed.[22]

Radio frequency identification devices could offer many benefits along value networks, tracking products and services throughout the journey. Gillette uses smart tags to improve logistics and shipping from factories. RFID technology enabled Gillette to get the new Fusion razor on store shelves 11 days faster than its normal turnaround time. Gillette forecasts a 25 per cent return on its RFID investment over the next ten years, through increased sales and productivity savings.[23]

The role of marketing channels

Why would a producer or service provider delegate some of the selling job to intermediaries, relinquishing control over how and to whom offerings are sold? Through their contacts, experience, specialisation and scale of operation, intermediaries make offerings widely available and accessible to target markets, usually providing the firm with more effectiveness and efficiency than it can achieve on its own.[24]

Many producers lack the financial resources and expertise to sell directly on their own. The manufacturers of Red Bull would not find it practical to establish small retail Red Bull shops throughout Europe to sell their energy drink. It is easier to work through the extensive network of privately owned distribution organisations. Even BMW would be hard-pressed to replace all the tasks done by its almost 1,000 dealer outlets worldwide.

Channel functions and flows

A marketing channel performs the work of moving products and services from producers to consumers. It overcomes the time, place and possession gaps that separate goods and services from those who need or want them. Members of the marketing channel perform a number of key functions (see Table 17.1).

Table 17.1 Channel member functions

- Gather information about potential and current customers, competitors, and other actors and forces in the marketing environment.
- Develop and disseminate persuasive communications to stimulate purchasing.
- Negotiate and reach agreements on price and other terms so that transfer of ownership or possession can be affected.
- Place orders with manufacturers or service providers.
- Acquire the funds to finance inventories at different levels in the marketing channel.
- Assume risks connected with carrying out channel work.
- Provide for the successive storage and movement of physical products or services.
- Provide for buyers' payment of their bills through banks and other financial institutions.
- Oversee actual transfer of ownership from one organisation or person to another.

Some of these functions (storage and movement, title and communications) constitute a *forward flow* of activity from the company to the customer; other functions (ordering and payment) constitute a *backward flow* from customers to the company. Still others (information, negotiation, finance and risk taking) occur in both directions. Five flows are illustrated in Figure 17.6 for the marketing of forklift trucks. If these flows were superimposed in one diagram, we would see the tremendous complexity of even simple marketing channels.

A manufacturer selling a physical product and services might require three channels: a *sales channel,* a *delivery channel* and a *service channel.* To sell its Nokia mobile phone Nokia has historically emphasised retail purchases via television infomercials and ads, inbound/outbound call centres, response mailings and the internet as sales channels; UPS ground service as the delivery channel; and local repair people as the service channel. Reflecting shifting consumer buying habits, Nokia now sells through commercial, retail and specialty retail channels.

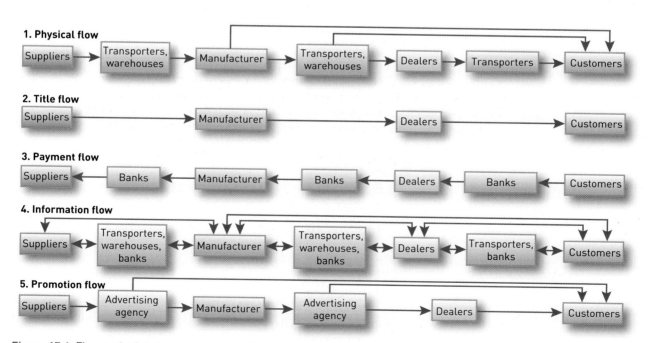

Figure 17.6 Five marketing flows in the marketing channel for forklift trucks

The question for marketers is not *whether* various channel functions need to be performed – they must be – but rather, *who* is to perform them. All channel functions have three things in common: they use up scarce resources; they can often be performed better through specialisation; and they can be shifted among channel members. Shifting some functions to intermediaries lowers the producer's costs and prices, but the intermediary must add a charge to cover its work. If the intermediaries are more efficient than the manufacturer, prices to consumers should be lower. If consumers perform some functions themselves, they should enjoy even lower prices. Changes in channel institutions thus largely reflect the discovery of more efficient ways to combine or separate the economic functions that provide assortments of goods to target customers.

Channel levels

The producer and the final customer are part of every channel. We will use the number of intermediary levels to designate the length of a channel. Figure 17.7(a) illustrates several consumer-goods marketing channels of different lengths.

A **zero-level channel** consists of a manufacturer selling directly to the final customer. The major examples are internet, manufactured owned shops, home parties, mail order, tele-marketing, TV selling and door-to-door sales. The *Encyclopedia Britannica* was traditionally sold door to door and is now sold over the internet, though with major competition from Wikipedia – the free encyclopedia – and Google or Firefox search engines as sources of information.

Some examples of zero-level channels are:

- the growth of food markets in Europe;
- the Yellow (Golden) Pages, which uses the telephone to prospect for new customers or to sell advertising to existing customers;
- Time-Life, which sells music and video collections through TV commercials or longer 'infomercials';
- Franc and Ticket Master, which sell tickets online;
- Apple, which sells computers, iPods and iPads and other consumer electronics through its own retail outlets.

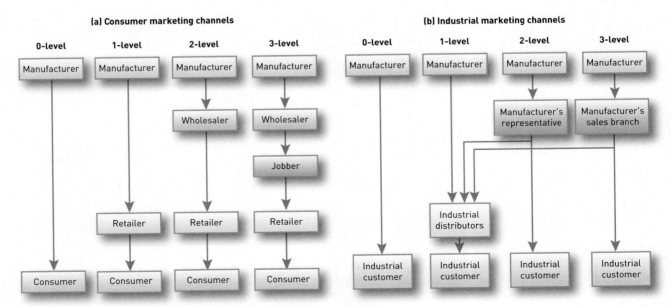

Figure 17.7 Consumer and industrial marketing channels

Many firms now sell directly to customers in more ways than one, via online, telephone or direct mail, etc.

A *one-level channel* contains one selling intermediary, such as a retailer. A *two-level channel* contains two intermediaries. In consumer markets, these are typically a wholesaler and a retailer. A *three-level channel* contains three intermediaries. In the meatpacking industry, wholesalers sell to *jobbers*, essentially small-scale wholesalers, which sell to small retailers. In Japan, food distribution may include as many as six levels. Obtaining information about end users and exercising control becomes more difficult for the producer as the number of channel levels increases.

Figure 17.7(b) shows channels commonly used in B2B marketing. An industrial-goods manufacturer can use its sales force to sell directly to industrial customers; or it can sell to industrial distributors which sell to industrial customers; or it can sell through manufacturer's representatives or its own sales branches directly to industrial customers, or indirectly to industrial customers through industrial distributors. Zero-, one-, and two-level marketing channels are quite common.

Channels normally describe a forward movement of products from source to user, but *reverse-flow channels* are also important: (1) to reuse products or containers (such as refillable chemical-carrying drums); (2) to refurbish products for resale (such as circuit boards or computers); (3) to recycle products (such as paper); and (4) to dispose of products and packaging. Reverse-flow intermediaries include manufacturers' redemption centres, community groups, rubbish or waste-collection specialists, recycling centres, rubbish-recycling brokers and central processing warehousing.[25]

Recycling Ireland

Six years ago Irish people discarded fridges, cookers, TV sets, deep fat fryers and other electrical goods to the dump, where they were thrown into a deep hole along with other waste and eventually covered over. Now, however, the whole idea is to divert such goods away from dumps (landfills). The main method is to give them to a retailer when purchasing the replacement. Indeed, the Irish are among the best in Europe at doing this and are recycling almost twice as many electrical items as Britain. In just five years, the Irish have brought the average electric recyclables to 9.5 kg per person compared to the EU average of 5 kg. Elizabeth O'Reilly, compliance manager with WEEE Ireland (Waste Electrical and Electronic Equipment), says one of the main reasons for the success is that it has been made as easy as possible for people to recycle. Firstly, people can bring back old goods to retailers when they are purchasing something new; secondly, they can bring used goods to regular recycling centres; and thirdly, collection days are arranged in areas around the country where recycling facilities are not readily available.[26]

Service sector channels

Traditionally, supply chains have been product focused, assuming a tangible product with a customer at the end of the process. Producers of services and ideas also face the problem of making their output available and accessible to target populations. More and more, supply networks are based on services. For hospitals we have 'health-delivery systems: that is, moving from the patient going to the hospital to remote diagnostics and care in the community as different channels.

Figure 17.8 shows how the consumer often plays a central role in services and the shaded area of the diagram shows how the consumer is often part of the supply network as a **co-creator** or **prosumer**. A **prosumer** is a composite of production and consumer – to denote the concept that the consumer could be both the producer and the consumer.[27]

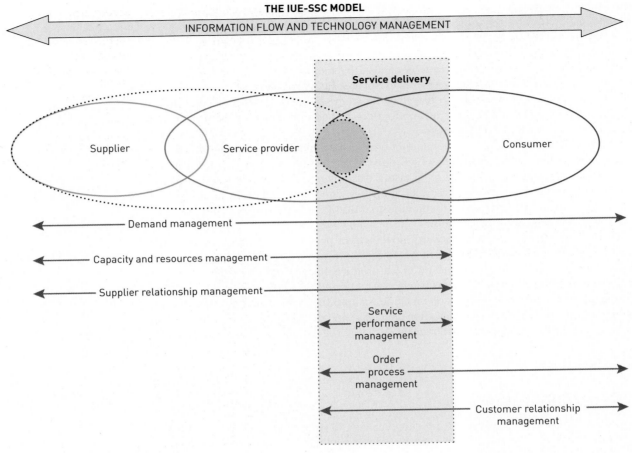

Figure 17.8 The service supply chain
Source: T. Baltacioglu, E. Ada, M. Kaplan, O. Yurt and Y. Kaplan (2007) A new framework for service supply chains, *Service Industries Journal*, 27(2), 105–24. Reproduced with permission.

The dividing line between the supplier and the customer has become blurred or partly erased. The customer is part of the supply chain and not simply a wallet at the end of it. Therefore, as we assemble our IKEA furniture we are part of the process and co-create the value of the product for ourselves. Self-service restaurants and self-care in the medical area where customers act as both nurse and patient – self-managing through home help and sensor supports – are other examples.

As internet and other technologies advance, service industries such as banking, insurance, travel and stock buying and selling are operating through new channels. Kodak offers its customers four ways to print their digital photos – minilabs in retail outlets, home printers, online services at its Ofoto website, and self-service kiosks. Kodak in-store kiosks also allow photo printing directly from Picasa. The world leader with 80,000 kiosks, Kodak makes money both by selling the units and by supplying the chemical and paper they use to make the prints.[28]

The increased use of technology has changed the entertainment industry. Besides live and programmed entertainment, entertainers, musicians and other artists can reach prospective and existing fans online in many ways – through their own websites, social networking sites such as Facebook and Twitter, and third-party websites. Politicians also must choose a mix of channels – mass media, rallies, coffee hours, TV ads, direct mail, billboards, faxes, email, blogs, podcasts, websites and social networking sites – for delivering

Service innovation in distribution: coproduction with the customer across many channels, including a photoframe which plays digital photos
Source: Reproduced by kind permission of Eastman kodak Company, trademark and copyright owner.

their messages to voters. The Obama campaign for president of the USA produced 2,000 official videos, which were viewed 80 million times on YouTube, and generated 244,000 unofficial video responses. It integrated communications by email (13 million registrations), mobile (3 million subscribers) and social networking (5 million 'friends').

Non-profit service organisations such as schools develop 'educational-dissemination systems' and hospitals develop 'health-delivery systems'.

Channel-design decisions

In designing a marketing channel system, marketers analyse customer needs and wants, establish channel objectives and constraints, and identify and evaluate major channel alternatives.

Analysing customer needs and wants

Consumers may choose the channels they prefer based on price, product assortment and convenience, as well as their own shopping goals (economic, social or experiential).[29] Segmentations exists, and marketers must be aware that different consumers have different needs during the purchase process.

One study of 40 grocery and clothing retailers in France, Germany and the United Kingdom found that they served three types of shopper: (1) *service/quality customers* who cared most about the variety and performance of products and service; (2) *price/value customers* who were most concerned about spending wisely; and (3) *affinity customers* who primarily sought shops that suited people like themselves or groups they aspired to join. As Figure 17.9 shows, customer profiles differed across the three markets: in France, shoppers stressed service and quality, in the United Kingdom, affinity, and in Germany, price and value.[30]

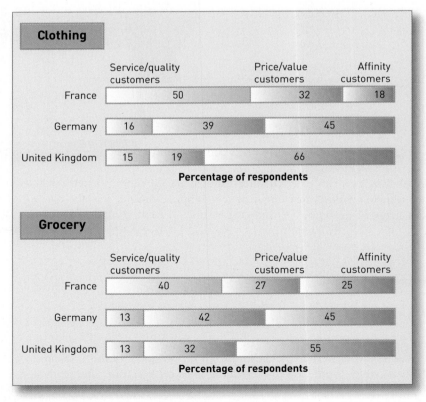

Figure 17.9 What do European consumers value?
Source: Peter N. Child, Suzanne Heywood and Michael Kliger (2002) Do retail brands travel?, *The McKinsey Quarterly*, 1, 11–13. All rights reserved.

Even the same consumer, though, may choose different channels for different functions in a purchase, browsing a catalogue before visiting a shop or test driving a car at a dealer before ordering online. Some consumers are willing to 'trade up' to retailers offering higher-end goods such as TAG Heuer watches or Callaway golf clubs and 'trade down' to discount retailers for private-label paper towels, detergent or vitamins, and this was particularly noticeable during the recent recession.[31]

Channels produce five service outputs:

1 **Lot size**: the number of units the channel permits a typical customer to purchase on one occasion. In buying cars for its fleet, Hertz prefers a channel from which it can buy a large lot size; a household wants a channel that permits a lot size of 1.

2 **Waiting and delivery time**: the average time customers wait for receipt of goods. Customers increasingly prefer faster delivery channels.

3 **Spatial convenience**: the degree to which the marketing channel makes it easy for customers to purchase the product. Toyota offers greater spatial convenience than Lexus because there are more Toyota dealers, helping customers save on transportation and search costs in buying and repairing an automobile. The Lexus, as the more upmarket brand, is only available through a limited number of dealers in well-targeted areas.

4 **Product variety**: the assortment provided by the marketing channel. Normally, customers prefer a greater assortment because more choices increase the chance of finding what they need, although too many choices can sometimes create a negative effect.[32]

5 **Service backup**: add-on services (credit, delivery, installation, repairs) provided by the channel. The greater the service backup, the greater the work provided by the channel.[33]

Providing greater service outputs also means increasing channel costs and raising prices. The success of discount stores such as Aldi and Lidl indicates that many consumers are willing to accept smaller service outputs if they can save money.

Establishing objectives and constraints

Marketers should state their channel objectives in terms of service output levels and associated cost and support levels. Under competitive conditions, channel members should arrange their functional tasks to minimise costs and still provide desired levels of service.[34] Usually, planners can identify several market segments based on desired service and choose the best channels for each.

Channel objectives vary with product characteristics. Bulky products, such as building materials, require channels that minimise the shipping distance and the amount of handling. Non-standard products such as custom-built machinery are sold directly by sales representatives. Products requiring installation or maintenance services, such as heating and cooling systems, are usually sold and maintained by the company or by franchised dealers. High-unit-value products such as generators and turbines are often sold through a company's sales force rather than intermediaries.

Marketers must adapt their channel objectives to the larger environment. When economic conditions are depressed, producers want to move goods to market using shorter channels and without services that add to the final price. Legal regulations and restrictions also affect channel design. European law looks unfavourably on channel arrangements that substantially lessen competition or create a monopoly.

In entering new markets, firms often closely observe what other firms are doing. France's Auchan considered the presence of its French rivals Leclerc and Casino in Poland as key to its decision to also enter that market.[35] Apple's channel objective of creating a dynamic retail experience for consumers was not being met by existing channels, so it chose to open its own stores.[36]

Apple shops

Within the European market, Apple opened its first retail shop in London in November 2004 and its largest shop inside the FNAC Digital store on the chic Boulevard Saint Germain in central Paris in 2007, with Apple shops opened in Barcelona, Strasbourg and Florence in 2011. When Apple stores were launched, many questioned their prospects and *BusinessWeek* published an article titled, 'Sorry Steve, here's why Apple Stores won't work'. The typical Apple retail location sells about 21 Mac computers every day versus less then two a day for many less specialised electronics shops. This amounts to about 8,000 Macs per shop per year, and played a crucial role in expanding the Mac's appeal. It is estimated that about two-thirds of shop revenues came from the computers and earned Apple the lion's share of its converts. Bernstein Research senior analyst Sacconaghi says that 'We estimate that the shops, which collectively represent just 2.5 per cent of the Mac's global distribution points, drove more than one-third of its market share gain during the year'[37]. With almost 300 locations by 2011, net revenue from stores totalled €4.5 billion and represented roughly 20 per cent of total corporate revenue. Anyway you look at it, Apple shops have been an unqualified success. Designed to fuel excitement for the brand, they let people see and touch Apple products – and experience what Apple can do for them – making it more likely that they will become Apple customers. They target tech-savvy customers with in-store product presentations and workshops; a full line of Apple products, software, and accessories; and a 'Genius Bar' staffed by Apple specialists who provide technical support, often free of charge. Although the shops – as a new marketing channel – upset existing retailers, Apple has worked hard to smooth relationships, in part justifying the decision as a natural evolution of its existing online sales channel.

Identifying major channel alternatives

Each channel, from sales forces to agents, distributors, dealers, direct mail, telemarketing and the internet, has unique strengths and weaknesses. Sales forces can handle complex products and transactions, but they are expensive. The internet is inexpensive but may not be as effective with complex products and services. Distributors can create sales, but the company loses direct contact with customers. Several clients can share the cost of manufacturers' reps, but the selling effort is less intense than company reps provide.

Channel alternatives differ in three ways: types of intermediary, the number needed and the terms and responsibilities of each. Let's look at these factors.

Types of intermediary

Consider the channel alternatives identified by a consumer electronics company that produces satellite radios. It could sell its players directly to car manufacturers to be installed as original equipment, or to car dealers, rental car companies, or satellite radio specialist dealers through a direct sales force or through distributors. It could also sell its players through company stores, online retailers, mail-order catalogues or mass merchandisers such as Dixon.

Companies should search for innovative marketing channels. CDNow has successfully sold CDs through the mail and internet. Companies like www.Direct2Florists.co.uk have creatively sold flowers through direct delivery, and DHL has been innovative in parcel management and monitoring.

Sometimes a company chooses a new or unconventional channel because of the difficulty, cost or ineffectiveness of working with the dominant channel. One advantage is often reduced competition, at least at first. Austrian energy drink Red Bull built its market share by unconventional channels, including a network of student sales representatives who managed all the distribution and visited the hot spots and discos to increase sales, before then moving slowly into the mainstream of traditional convenience stores and supermarkets. It now distributes over 4 billion cans of Red Bull annually in over 130 countries.

Number of intermediaries

Three strategies based on the number of intermediaries are exclusive distribution, selective distribution and intensive distribution.

Exclusive distribution means severely limiting the number of intermediaries. It is appropriate when the producer wants to maintain control over the service level and outputs offered by the resellers, and it often includes *exclusive dealing* arrangements. By granting exclusive distribution, the producer hopes to obtain more dedicated and knowledgeable selling. It requires a closer partnership between seller and reseller and is used in the distribution of new cars, some major appliances and some women's fashion brands. Rolex watches are only available through its exclusive distribution arrangements at shops such as Harrods of London and Les Galleries Lafayette in Paris.

Exclusive deals are becoming a mainstay for specialists looking for an edge in markets increasingly driven by price.[38] When the legendary Italian designer label Gucci found its image severely tarnished by overexposure from licensing and discount stores, it decided to end contracts with third-party suppliers, control its distribution and open its own shops to bring back some of the lustre.[39]

Selective distribution relies on only some of the intermediaries being willing to carry a particular product. Whether established or new, the company does not need to worry about having too many outlets; it can gain adequate market coverage with more control and less cost than intensive distribution. Stihl is a good example of selective distribution.

STIHL

The STIHL Group, the Stuttgart-based manufacturer of handheld outdoor power equipment, manufactures under two brand names: STIHL and VIKING. STIHL does not make private-label products for other companies. The company produces the world's best-selling brand of chain saws and is the only chain saw manufacturer to make its own saw chains and guide bars. Though best known for chain saws, it has expanded into string trimmers, blowers, hedge trimmers and cut-off machines. VIKING is a wholly-owned member of the STIHL Group and produces garden power tools (lawn mowers, shredders, tillers) from its base in Kufstein, Austria. VIKING products are sold through the STIHL Approved Dealer network.

The STIHL Group distributes its products through a global network of 38,000 Approved Dealers in over 160 countries. It has 32 sales and marketing subsidiaries of its own as well as more than 120 importers. STIHL is one of the few outdoor-power-equipment companies that do not sell through mass merchants, catalogues or the internet.[40]

Source: Courtesy of Stihl GB.

Intensive distribution places the goods or services in as many outlets as possible. This strategy serves well for snack foods, soft drinks, newspapers and sweets – products that consumers buy frequently or in a variety of locations. Convenience stores such as Spar, Wizzl (Netherlands) Deli de Luca (Norway) have survived by selling items that provide just that – location and time convenience.

Manufacturers are constantly tempted to move from exclusive or selective distribution to more intensive distribution to increase coverage and sales. This strategy may help in the short term, but if not done properly, it can hurt long-term performance by encouraging retailers to compete aggressively. Price wars can then erode profitability, dampening retailer interest and harming brand equity. Some firms do not want to be sold everywhere.

Terms and responsibilities of channel members

Each channel member must be treated respectfully and given the opportunity to be profitable. The main elements in the 'trade-relations mix' are price policies, conditions of sale, territorial rights and specific services to be performed by each party.

- **Price policy**: calls for the producer to establish a price list and schedule of discounts and allowances that intermediaries see as equitable and sufficient.
- **Conditions of sale**: refers to payment terms and producer guarantees. Most producers grant cash discounts to distributors for early payment. They might also offer a guarantee against defective merchandise or price declines, creating an incentive to buy larger quantities.
- **Distributors' territorial rights**: define the distributors' territories and the terms under which the producer will enfranchise other distributors. Distributors normally expect to receive full credit for all sales in their territory, whether or not they did the selling.
- **Mutual services and responsibilities**: must be carefully spelled out, especially in franchised and exclusive-agency channels. Eurocar, the car hire company, provides franchisees with a building, promotional support, a record-keeping system, training, and general administrative and technical assistance. In turn, franchisees are expected to satisfy company standards for the physical facilities, cooperate with new promotional programmes, furnish requested information, and buy supplies from specified vendors.

Evaluating major channel alternatives

Each channel alternative needs to be evaluated against economic, control and adaptive criteria.

Economic Criteria

Each channel alternative will produce a different level of sales and costs. Figure 17.10 shows how six different sales channels stack up in terms of the value added per sale and the cost per transaction. For example, in the sale of industrial products costing between €2,000 and €5,000, the cost per transaction has been estimated at €500 (field sales), €200 (distributors), €50 (telesales) and €10 (internet). In retail banking services, a Booz, Allen, Hamilton worldwide study shows the average transaction of a full-service branch: it costs €0.69 to handle a transaction in a bank branch, about €0.35 on the phone, €0.16 through an ATM, and just €0.1 on the internet.[41]

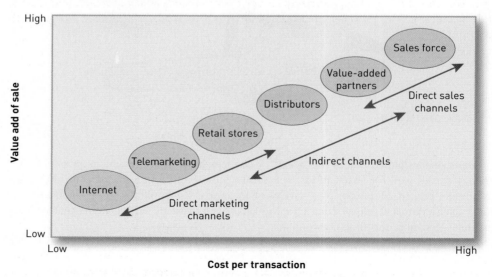

Figure 17.10 The value adds versus the costs of different channels

Firms will try to align customers and channels to maximise demand at the lowest overall cost. Clearly, sellers try to replace high-cost channels with low-cost channels as long as the value added per sale is sufficient. Consider the following situation:

A German furniture manufacturer wants to sell its furniture to retailers in France. One alternative is to hire ten new sales representatives to operate out of a sales office in France and receive a base salary plus commissions. The other alternative is to use a French-based manufacturers' sales agency that has extensive contacts with retailers. The sales agency has 30 sales representatives who receive a commission based on their sales.

The first step is to estimate how many sales each alternative is likely to generate. A company sales force will concentrate on the company's products; be better trained to sell them; be more aggressive because each rep's future depends on the company's success; and be more successful because many customers prefer to deal directly with the company. The sales agency, however, has 30 representatives, not just 10; it may be just as aggressive, depending on the commission level; customers may appreciate its independence; and it may have extensive contacts and market knowledge. The marketer needs to evaluate all these factors in formulating a demand function for the two different channels.

The next step is to estimate the costs of selling different volumes through each channel. The cost schedules are shown in Figure 17.11. Engaging a sales agency is less expensive than establishing a new company sales office, but costs rise faster through an agency because sales agents get larger commissions.

The final step is comparing sales and costs. As Figure 17.12 shows, there is one sales level (S_B) at which selling costs are the same for the two channels. The sales agency is thus the better channel for any sales volume below S_B, and the company sales branch is better at any volume above S_B. Given this information, it is not surprising that sales agents tend to be used by smaller firms, or by large firms in smaller territories where the volume is low.

Control and adaptive criteria

Using a sales agency can pose a control problem. Agents may concentrate on the customers who buy the most, not necessarily those who buy the manufacturer's goods. They might not master the technical details of the company's product or handle its promotion materials effectively.

To develop a channel, members must commit to each other for a specified period of time. Yet these commitments invariably reduce the producer's ability to respond to change and uncertainty. The producer needs channel structures and policies that provide high adaptability.

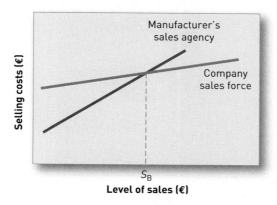

Figure 17.11 Break-even cost chart for the choice between a company sales force and a manufacturer's sales agency

Channel-management decisions

After a company has chosen a channel system, it must select, train, motivate and evaluate individual intermediaries for each channel. It must also modify channel design and arrangements over time. As the company grows, it can also consider channel expansion into international markets.

Selecting channel members

To customers, the channels are the company. Consider the negative impression customers would get if a Volvo dealer appeared dirty, inefficient or unpleasant.

To facilitate channel member selection, producers should determine what characteristics distinguish the better intermediaries – number of years in business, other lines carried, growth and profit record, financial strength, cooperativeness and service reputation. If the intermediaries are sales agents, producers should evaluate the number and character of other lines carried and the size and quality of the sales force. If the intermediaries are department stores that want exclusive distribution, their locations, future growth potential and type of clientele will matter.

Training and motivating channel members

A company needs to view its intermediaries in the same way that it views its end users. It should determine their needs and wants and tailor its channel offering to provide them with superior value.

Carefully implemented training, market research and other capability-building programmes can motivate and improve intermediaries' performance. The company must constantly communicate that intermediaries are crucial partners in a joint effort to satisfy end users of the product. Microsoft requires its third-party service engineers to complete

The strength of the Volvo dealer network is built around supporting the customer not just at the time of purchase, but throughout the life of their Volvo purchase.

Source: Courtesy of Volvo Car Corporation

a set of courses and take certification exams. Those who pass are formally recognised as Microsoft Certified Professionals and can use this designation to promote their own business. Other firms use customer surveys rather than exams.

Channel power

Producers vary greatly in their skill in managing distributors. **Channel power** is the ability to alter channel members' behaviour so that they take actions they would not have taken otherwise.[42] Manufacturers can draw on the following types of power to elicit cooperation:

- **Coercive power.** A manufacturer threatens to withdraw a resource or terminate a relationship if intermediaries fail to cooperate. This power can be effective, but its exercise produces resentment and can lead the intermediaries to organise countervailing power.
- **Reward power.** The manufacturer offers intermediaries an extra benefit for performing specific acts or functions. Reward power typically produces better results than coercive power, but intermediaries may come to expect a reward every time the manufacturer wants a certain behaviour to occur.
- **Legitimate power.** The manufacturer requests a behaviour that is warranted under the contract. As long as the intermediaries view the manufacturer as a legitimate leader, legitimate power works.
- **Expert power.** The manufacturer has special knowledge that the intermediaries value. Once the intermediaries acquire this expertise, however, expert power weakens. The manufacturer must continue to develop new expertise so that intermediaries will want to continue cooperating.
- **Referent power.** The manufacturer is so highly respected that intermediaries are proud to be associated with it. Companies such as Airbus, Sap and Caterpillar have high referent power.[43]

Coercive and reward power are objectively observable; legitimate, expert and referent power are more subjective and depend on the ability and willingness of parties to recognise them.

Most producers see gaining intermediaries' cooperation as a huge challenge. They often use positive motivators, such as higher margins, special deals, premiums, cooperative advertising allowances, display allowances and sales contests. At times they will apply negative sanctions, such as threatening to reduce margins, slow down delivery or terminate the relationship. The weakness of this approach is that the producer is using crude, stimulus–response thinking.

In many cases, retailers hold the power. Manufacturers offer the nation's supermarkets between 150 and 250 new items each week, of which store buyers reject over 70 per cent. Manufacturers need to know the acceptance criteria that buyers, buying committees and store managers use. ACNielsen interviews found that store managers were most influenced by (in order of importance): strong evidence of consumer acceptance, a well-designed advertising and sales promotion plan, and generous financial incentives.

Channel partnerships

More sophisticated companies try to forge a long-term partnership with distributors.[44] The manufacturer clearly communicates what it wants from its distributors in the way of market coverage, inventory levels, marketing development, account solicitation, technical advice and services, and marketing information, and may introduce a compensation plan for adhering to the policies.

To streamline the supply chain and cut costs, many manufacturers and retailers have adopted *efficient consumer response (ECR) practices* to organise their relationships in three areas: (1) *demand-side management* or collaborative practices to stimulate consumer demand by promoting joint marketing and sales activities; (2) *supply-side management* or collaborative practices to optimise supply (with a focus on joint logistics and supply chain activities); and (3) *enablers and integrators*, or collaborative information technology and process improvement tools to support joint activities that reduce operational problems, allow greater standardisation and so on.

Research has shown that although ECR has a positive impact on manufacturers' economic performance and capability development, manufacturers may also feel they are inequitably sharing the burdens of adopting it and not getting as much as they deserve from retailers.[45]

Evaluating channel members

Producers must periodically evaluate intermediaries' performance against such standards as sales-quota attainment, average inventory levels, customer delivery time, treatment of damaged and lost goods, and cooperation in promotional and training programmes. A producer will occasionally discover it is overpaying particular intermediaries for what they are actually doing. One manufacturer compensating a distributor for holding inventories found that the inventories were actually held in a public warehouse at its own expense. Producers should set up functional discounts in which they pay specified amounts for the trade channel's performance of each agreed service. Underperformers need to be counselled, retrained, motivated or terminated. Consider the case of Mercedes-Benz and the Smart car below.

Modifying channel design and arrangements

No channel strategy remains effective over the whole product life cycle. In competitive markets with low entry barriers, the optimal channel structure will inevitably change over time. The change could mean adding or dropping individual market channels or channel members, or developing a totally new way to distribute.

Channel evolution

A new firm typically starts as a local operation selling in a fairly circumscribed market, using a few existing intermediaries. Identifying the best channels might not be a problem; the problem is often to convince the available intermediaries to handle the firm's line.

If the firm is successful, it might branch into new markets with different channels. In smaller markets, the firm might sell directly to retailers; in larger markets, through distributors. In rural areas, it might work with general-goods merchants; in urban areas, with limited-line merchants. It might grant exclusive franchises or sell through all willing

Smart Car Distribution Challenges

Managing distributors across geographical markets can be a challenge. Take the Smart car, owned by Daimler, which has enjoyed phenomenal success in many European markets but encountered distribution challenges when they entered the North American market. Their choice here was to hire a distributor and therefore in 2008 they chose a dealer to manage the brand and the distribution. It was always going to be challenging to market a small car to the nation who love their large cars and where bigger is often considered better but that was the task. Sales started well, helped by high petrol prices but then declined. Sales of the car peaked at 24,622 in 2008 but then fell almost 60 per cent to just below 6,000 in 2010. The company decided to act and in 2011 they moved distribution in-house to the Mercedes-Benz division of Daimler and cancelled the dealer contract. Both the dealer and the company say that poor sales were not the reason for the cancelled contract.[46]

After originally trying a distributor, Mercedes-Benz are now managing their own distribution of the Smart car in the US Market

Source: Daimler AG

outlets. In one country, it might use international sales agents; in another, it might partner a local firm.

Early buyers might be willing to pay for high-value-added channels, but later buyers will switch to lower-cost channels. Small office copiers were first sold by manufacturers' direct sales forces, later through office equipment dealers, still later through mass merchandisers, and now by mail-order firms and internet marketers.

In short, the channel system evolves as a function of local opportunities and conditions, emerging threats and opportunities, company resources and capabilities, and other factors. Consider some of the changes that Kurt Geiger has faced in growing its business.

Kurt Geiger

High demand for fashion-forward shoes helped Kurt Geiger, the British footwear retailer, increase operating profits by selling more than 2 million shoes annually – divided between sales of its own brands and distribution for many top brands. The strong results were boosted by the opening of 12 new stand-alone Kurt Geiger stores during the past financial year, bringing the total up to 63 worldwide. Kurt Geiger sells own-brand and third-party women's and men's shoes internationally through a number of distribution channels. As well as the main Kurt Geiger brand, it owns KG by Kurt Geiger and Carvela.

It operates shops under the Kurt Geiger brand, runs concessions in a number of department store chains, and has wholesale agreements with other footwear companies including high-end designers such as Gucci, Prada and Jimmy Choo. Last year, it signed a long-term wholesale distribution agreement with Nine West.[47]

Channel modification decisions

A producer must periodically review and modify its channel design and arrangements.[48] The distribution channel may not work as planned, consumer buying patterns change, the market expands, new competition arises, innovative distribution channels emerge, and the product moves into later stages in the product life cycle.[49]

Adding or dropping individual channel members requires an incremental analysis. Increasingly, technology including detailed customer databases and sophisticated analysis tools can provide guidance into those decisions.[50] A basic question is: what would the firm's sales and profits look like with and without this intermediary?

Perhaps the most difficult decision is whether to revise the overall channel strategy.[51] Avon, the pioneer in door-to-door selling of cosmetics, was modified as more women entered the workforce and it now includes house parties and online marketing. Despite the convenience of automated teller machines, online banking and telephone call centres, many bank customers still want 'high touch' over 'high tech', or at least they want the choice.

Global channel considerations

International markets pose distinct challenges, including variations in customers' shopping habits, but opportunities at the same time.[52] In India, sales from 'organised retail' – hypermarkets, supermarkets and department stores – make up only 4 per cent of the €223 billion market. Most shopping still takes place in millions of independent grocery shops or *kirana* shops, run by an owner and one or perhaps two other people.[53] Many top global retailers such as Germany's Aldi, the United Kingdom's Tesco and Spain's Zara have tailored their image to local needs and wants when entering a new market. Tesco entered the US market with the name Fresh & Easy shops but unfortunately has struggled to gain a foothold in the market and has made some fundamental errors, such as opening shops on the wrong side of the road, eliminating discount coupons, and decorating in a spare style more suited to a hospital than a food retailer.[54]

Franchised companies such as Curves women's fitness centres and Subway sandwich makers have experienced double-digit growth in international markets, especially in developing markets such as Brazil and central and eastern Europe. In some cases, *master franchisees* pay a significant fee to acquire a territory or country where they operate as a 'mini-franchiser'

Carrefour, the world's second largest retailer, has encountered stiff competition in its home market and has expanded internationally

Source: OMAR TORRES/ AFP/Getty Images

in their own right. More knowledgeable about local laws, customs and consumer needs than foreign companies, they sell and oversee franchises and collect royalties.[55]

But many pitfalls exist in global expansion, and retailers must also be able to defend their home turf from the entry of foreign retailers. Selling everything from food to televisions, France's Carrefour, the world's second-biggest retailer, has encountered stiff competition in its home markets from smaller supermarkets for groceries and from specialist retailers such as IKEA and FNAC for other goods. Although strong in parts of Europe, Asia and Latin America, Carrefour (which means 'crossroads' in French) has been forced to cease operations in a number of countries, such as Japan, South Korea, Mexico, the Czech Republic, Slovakia, Russia, Switzerland and Portugal. Another of France's mega-retailers, Auchan, has been quite successful in entering emerging markets like China while unable to crack markets in the United States and Britain.[56]

The first step in global channel planning, as is often the case in marketing, is to get close to customers. To adapt its clothing lines to better suit European tastes, Philadelphia-based Urban Outfitter set up a separate design and merchandising unit in London before it opened its first store in Europe. Although this increased costs, the blended American and European looks helped the retailer stand out.[57] A good retail strategy that offers customers a positive shopping experience and unique value, if properly adapted, is likely to find success in more than one market. Take Topshop, for instance.

Topshop

Founded by Sir Richard Green in the UK in 1994, clothing retailer Topshop is a chain of 310 UK stores and 116 international franchisees that commands intense loyalty from its trendy, style-obsessed customer base. Selling primarily party clothes, accessories and daywear to women, Topshop blends English street fashion, reasonable prices and fun services. A higher-end, quirkier version of fast-fashion chains H&M and Zara, Topshop allows middle-market consumers to dress upscale affordably, partnering with style icons Kate Moss, Stella Vine and Celia Birtwell to create the latest designs. Topshop offers style advisers, Topshop-to-Go (a Tupperware-type party that brings a style adviser to a customer's home with outfits for up to ten people), and Topshop Express (an express delivery service via Vespa scooters for fashion 'emergencies').[58]

Channel integration and systems

Distribution channels don't stand still. Here we will look at the recent growth of vertical, horizontal and multichannel marketing systems.

Vertical marketing systems

A **conventional marketing channel** consists of an independent producer, wholesaler(s) and retailer(s). Each is a separate business seeking to maximise its own profits, even if this goal reduces profit for the system as a whole. No channel member has complete or substantial control over other members.

A **vertical marketing system (VMS)**, by contrast, includes the producer, wholesaler(s) and retailer(s) acting as a unified system. One channel member, the *channel captain*, owns or franchises the others, or has so much power that they all cooperate. The marketing insight box provides some perspective on how a channel caption, or *channel stewards*, a closely related concept, can work.

Marketing insight

Channel stewards take charge

Harvard University's V. Kasturi Rangan suggests that companies should adopt a new approach to going to market – channel stewardship. Rangan defines **channel stewardship** as the ability of a given participant in a distribution channel – a steward – to create a go-to-market strategy that simultaneously addresses customers' best interests and drives profits for all channel partners. The channel steward accomplishes channel coordination without issuing commands or directives, by persuading channel partners to act in the best interest of all.

A channel steward might be the maker of the product or service (Unilever or Luftansa Airlines); the maker of a key component (microchip maker Intel); the supplier or assembler (Dell or Arrow Electronics EMEA); or the distributor (Wick Hill) or retailer (Dixon). Within a company, stewardship might rest with the CEO, a top manager or a team of senior managers.

Channel stewardship should appeal to any organisation that wants to bring a disciplined approach to channel strategy. With the customer's point of view in mind, the steward advocates for change among all participants, transforming them into partners with a common purpose.

Channel stewardship has two important outcomes. First, it expands value for the steward's customers, enlarging the market or existing customers' purchases through the channel. A second outcome is to create a more tightly woven and yet adaptable channel, in which valuable members are rewarded and the less valuable members are weeded out.

Rangan outlines three key disciplines of channel management:

1 *Mapping* at the industry level provides a comprehensive view of the key determinants of channel strategy and how they are evolving. It identifies current best practices and gaps, and it projects future requirements.

2 *Building and editing* assesses the producer's own channels to identify any deficits in meeting customers' needs and/or competitive best practices to put together a new and improved overall system.

3 *Aligning and influencing* closes the gaps and works out a compensation package in tune with effort and performance for channel members that add or could add value.

Channel stewardship works at the customer level, not at the level of channel institutions. Thus, channel managers can adapt their fulfilment of customer needs without having to change channel structure all at once. An evolutionary approach to channel change, stewardship requires constant monitoring, learning and adaptation, but all in the best interests of customers, channel partners and the channel steward. A channel steward need not be a huge company or market leader; it can also be a smaller player, such as Haworth the office furniture provider as well as distributors and retailers such as Tesco, Dixon and Carrefour.

Source: V. Kasturi Rangan (2006) *Transforming Your Go-to-Market Strategy: The Three Disciplines of Channel Management,* Boston, MA: Harvard Business School Press; K. Rangan, Channel stewardship: an introductory guide, www.channelstewardship. com; P. Rose and R. Dey, (2007) Channel stewardship: driving profitable revenue growth in high-tech with multi-channel management, *Infosys ViewPoint*, August.

Vertical marketing systems (VMSs) arose from strong channel members' attempts to control channel behaviour and eliminate conflict over independent members pursuing their own objectives. VMSs achieve economies through size, bargaining power and elimination of duplicated services. Business buyers of complex products and systems value the extensive exchange of information they can obtain from a VMS,[59] and VMSs have become the dominant mode of distribution in the European consumer marketplace, serving 70 to 80 per cent of the market. There are three types: corporate, administered and contractual.

Corporate VMS

A *corporate VMS* combines successive stages of production and distribution under single ownership. In grocery shops in Europe, own-label brands account for as much as 40 per cent of the items sold. In Britain, the largest food chains, Sainsbury's and Tesco, obtain over half the goods they sell from companies they partly or wholly own – roughly half of the products on their shelves are own-label goods.

Administered VMS

An *administered VMS* coordinates successive stages of production and distribution through the size and power of one of the members. Manufacturers of dominant brands can secure strong trade cooperation and support from resellers. Germany's Dr Oetker, manufacturer of pizza, yogurt and frozen meals, is able to command high levels of cooperation from its resellers in connection with displays, shelf space, promotions and price policies. Similarly, Hellmann's Mayonnaise, Magnum and Dove – Unilever products – command high levels of cooperation from their resellers in connection with displays, shelf space, promotions and price policies. The most advanced supply–distributor arrangement for administered VMSs relies on **distribution programming**, which builds a planned, professionally managed, vertical marketing system that meets the needs of both manufacturer and distributors.

Contractual VMS

A *contractual VMS* consists of independent firms at different levels of production and distribution, integrating their programme on a contractual basis to obtain more economies or sales impact than they could achieve alone.[60] Sometimes thought of as 'value-adding partnerships' (VAPs), contractual VMSs come in three types:

1 **Wholesaler-sponsored voluntary chains**. Wholesalers organise voluntary chains of independent retailers to help standardise their selling practices and achieve buying economies in competing with large chain organisations.
2 **Retailer cooperatives**. Retailers take the initiative and organise a new business entity to carry on wholesaling and possibly some production. Members concentrate their purchases through the retailer co-op and plan their advertising jointly. Profits pass back to members in proportion to their purchases. Non-member retailers can also buy through the co-op but do not share in the profits.
3 **Franchise organisations**. A channel member called a *franchisor* might link several successive stages in the production–distribution process. Franchising has been the fastest-growing retailing development in recent years.

Although the basic idea is an old one, some forms of franchising are quite new. The traditional system is the *manufacturer-sponsored retailer franchise*. BMW licenses independent businesspeople, who agree to meet specified conditions of sales and services, to sell its cars. Another system is the *manufacturer-sponsored wholesaler franchise*. Coca-Cola licenses bottlers (wholesalers) in various markets that buy its syrup concentrate and then carbonate, bottle and sell it to retailers in local markets. A newer system is the *service-firm-sponsored retailer franchise*, organised by a service firm to bring its service efficiently to consumers. We find examples in car hire (Avis and Europcar), clothing (Benetton and Mango), food (Euromarche, Champion and Leonidas). In a dual distribution system, firms use both vertical integration (the franchisor actually owns and runs the units) and market governance (the franchisor licenses the units to other franchisees).[61]

The new competition in retailing

Many independent retailers that have not joined VMSs have developed speciality stores serving special market segments. The result is a polarisation in retailing between large vertical marketing organisations and independent speciality stores, which creates a problem for manufacturers. They are strongly tied to independent intermediaries but must eventually realign themselves with the high-growth vertical marketing systems on less attractive terms. Furthermore, vertical marketing systems constantly threaten to bypass large manufacturers and set up their own manufacturing. The new competition in retailing is no longer between independent business units but between whole systems of centrally programmed networks (corporate, administered and contractual), competing against one another to achieve the best cost economies and customer response.

Horizontal marketing systems

Another channel development is the **horizontal marketing system**, in which two or more unrelated companies put together resources or programmes to exploit an emerging marketing opportunity. Each company lacks the capital, know-how, production or marketing resources to venture alone, or is afraid of the risk. The companies might work together on a temporary or permanent basis, or create a joint venture company.

For example, many supermarket chains have arrangements with local banks to offer in-shop banking. The Royal Bank of Scotland has teamed up with Tesco to offer banking facilities in over 600 Tesco shops across the UK.

Integrating multichannel marketing systems

Most companies today have adopted multichannel marketing.[62]

An **integrated marketing channel system** is one in which the strategies and tactics of selling through one channel reflect the strategies and tactics of selling through one or more other channels. Adding more channels gives companies three important benefits. The first is increased market coverage. Not only are more customers able to shop for the company's products in more places, but those who buy in more than one channel are often more profitable than single-channel customers.[63] The second benefit is lower channel cost – selling by phone is cheaper than personal selling to small customers. The third is more customised selling – such as by adding a technical sales force to sell complex equipment.

There is a trade-off, however. New channels typically introduce conflict and problems with control and cooperation. Two or more may end up competing for the same customers.

Clearly, companies need to think through their channel architecture and determine which channels should perform which functions. Figure 17.12 shows a simple grid to help make channel architecture decisions. The grid consists of major marketing channels (as rows) and the major channel tasks to be completed (as columns).[64]

The grid illustrates why using only one channel is not efficient. Consider a direct sales force. A salesperson would have to find leads, qualify them, presell, close the sale, provide service, and manage account growth. The company's marketing department could run a preselling campaign informing prospects about the company's products through advertising, direct mail and telemarketing; generate leads through telemarketing, direct mail, advertising and trade shows; and qualify leads into hot, warm and cool. The salesperson enters when the prospect is ready to talk business and invests his or her costly time primarily in closing the sale. This multichannel architecture optimises coverage, customisation and control while minimising cost and conflict.

Companies should use different sales channels for different-sized business customers – a direct sales force for large customers, telemarketing for midsize customers, and distributors for small customers – but be alert for conflict over account ownership. For example,

Demand-generation tasks

		Gather relevant information	Develop & disseminate communications	Reach price agreements	Place orders	Acquire funds for inventories	Assume risks	Facilitate product storage & movement	Facilitate payment	Oversee ownership transfer	
	Internet										
	National account management										
	Direct sales										
VENDOR	Telemarketing										**CUSTOMER**
	Direct mail										
	Retail stores										
	Distributors										
	Dealers and value-added resellers										

Marketing channels and methods

Figure 17.12 The hybrid grid

territory-based sales representatives may want credit for all sales in their territories, regardless of the marketing channel used.

Multichannel marketers also need to decide how much of their product to offer in each of the channels. Many outdoor clothing specialists use the web as the ideal channel for showing off their entire line of goods, given that their shops are limited by space to offering a selection only, and even catalogues cannot always promote all of the merchandise.[65] Other marketers prefer to limit their online offerings, theorising that customers look to websites and catalogues for a 'best of' array of merchandise and don't want to have to click through dozens of pages.

Multichannel and channel multiplicity

Multichannel marketing occurs when a company uses two or more distribution channels to reach one or more customer segments. A **multi marketing channel strategy** is one in which the strategies and tactics of distribution and sales through one channel reflect the strategies and tactics of distribution and sales through other channels. There is a real choice between multiple channels and a multichannel strategy. A **multiple channels strategy** simply provides multiple channels for the consumer, while a **multichannel strategy** has cross-channel benefits based on the management of the multiple channels. A McKinsey report showed that customers who use multiple channels for purchasing spend two to four times more than the spend of those using one channel. Similarly, in banking multichannel customers are 25–50 per cent more profitable than single-channel users.[66]

Customers want to get products and services when they need them and have these delivered in the many different ways that suit them. To respond to this diversity of needs and situations, marketers need to create multiple points of presence, fully integrated to deliver a seamless customer experience. They need to treat every customer as a unique individual instead of treating all customers alike and discriminating among customers based on the channel they use. At times, it seems, marketers are beholden to their channels but agnostic when it comes to their customers. Remember, a channel is merely a means to an end. What matters is not only the channel through which the customer purchases but

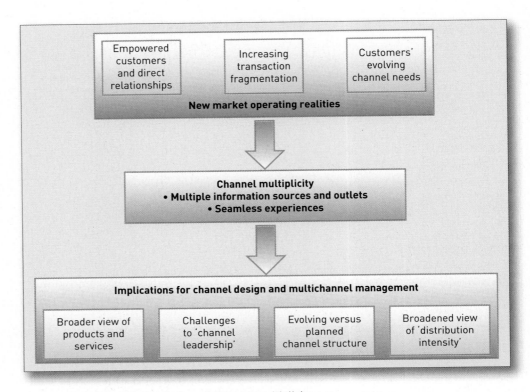

Figure 17.13 Conceptual overview of channel multiplicity
Source: G. H. Van Bruggen, K. D. Antia, S. D. Jap, W. J. Reinartz and F. Pallas (2010) Managing marketing channel multiplicity, *Journal of Service Research*, 13(3), 331–40.

rather, it is the ability to capture, store and track all interactions and transactions with that customer across all touchpoints to create a seamless, context-rich conversation. Companies need to be everywhere that customers want them to be. They need to market in all the ways that customers want to be reached, in all the ways that customers want to buy, and provide support in all the ways that customers want to be supported. Take the customer who reviews a hotel through Travel Advisor online, checks with their friends offline, phones the hotels for rates and then finally books the hotel through a booking site. Many of these channels are not even managed by the company. This is called the multiplicity of channels. The **multiplicity of channels** is the emerging phenomenon of customers seeking information and demanding products and services from an ever-increasing range of sources.[67] One of the many consequences of channel multiplicity is the need for a sound multichannel management strategy. The former reflects the behaviour of the customer and the latter reflects the company's response to that behaviour.[68]

The immediate result of channel multiplicity is a change not only in the way firms must design and manage their marketing channels and coordinate and create incentives for the channel partners, but also in how they view products, services and channels. Add to this the ever-increasing level of digital technology and the corresponding growth in information-based offerings and the result can be uncontrolled chaos or unbridled opportunity.[69] Much of channel multiplicity is externally controlled rather than internally controlled by the company itself.[70]

Customers should not be forced to stay with the channel with which they originated, as if they were driving along a motorway where cars are prohibited from changing lanes. Marketers know that they need to break down the channel walls and allow data that were captured through one channel or customer touchpoint to migrate instantly to all other channels and touchpoints. Sometimes customers want to talk to a support rep; at

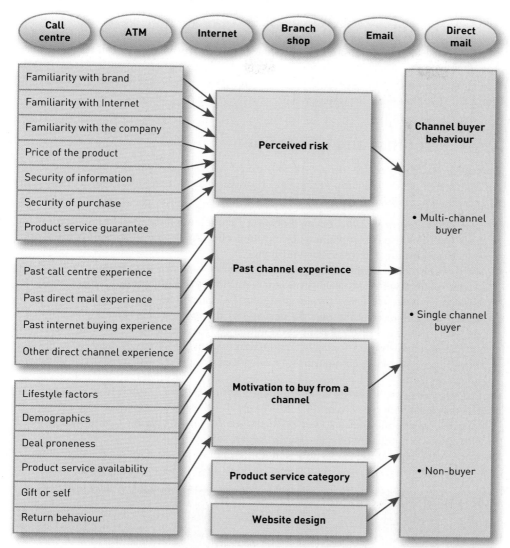

Figure 17.14 Multi-channel shopping behaviour
Source: Adapted from D. Schoenbachler and G. Gordon (2002) Multi-channel shopping: understanding what drives channel choice, *Journal of Consumer Marketing*, 19(1), 42–53. Reproduced with permission.

other times they want self-service. Sometimes they want to buy online; at other times, in a shop. Sometimes they want to return products through the post; at other times, to a shop. Figure 17.14 shows the range of channels available and the decision making that customers go through when deciding to be a multi- or single-channel buyer.

Conflict, cooperation and competition

No matter how well channels are designed and managed, there will be some conflict, if only because the interests of independent business entities do not always coincide. **Channel conflict** is generated when one channel member's actions prevent another channel from achieving its goal. Software giant Oracle Corp., plagued by channel conflict between its sales force and its vendor partners, decided to roll out new 'All Partner Territories' where all deals except for specific strategic accounts would go through select Oracle partners.[71]

Channel coordination occurs when channel members are brought together to advance the goals of the channel, as opposed to their own potentially incompatible goals.[72] Here we examine three questions: What types of conflict arise in channels? What causes conflict? What can marketers do to resolve it?

Types of conflict and competition

Suppose a manufacturer sets up a vertical channel consisting of wholesalers and retailers, hoping for channel cooperation and greater profits for each member. Yet horizontal, vertical and multichannel conflict can occur.

- *Horizontal channel conflict* occurs between channel members at the same level. Some Pizza Inn franchisees complained about others cheating on ingredients, providing poor service and hurting the overall brand image.
- *Vertical channel conflict* occurs between different levels of the channel. When Estée Lauder set up a website to sell its Clinique and Bobbi Brown brands, department stores reduced its space for Estée Lauder products.[73] Greater retailer consolidation – the ten largest retailers account for over 80 per cent of the average manufacturer's business – has led to increased price pressure and influence from retailers.[74] Carrefour and Tesco are the principal buyers for many manufacturers, including Green Isle and Campbell Soups, and are able to command reduced prices or quantity discounts from these and other suppliers.[75]
- *Multichannel conflict* exists when the manufacturer has established two or more channels that sell to the same market.[76] It is likely to be especially intense when the members of one channel get a lower price (based on larger-volume purchases) or work with a lower margin. When Goodyear began selling its popular tyre brands through major retailers, it angered its independent dealers and eventually placated them by offering exclusive tyre models not sold in other retail outlets.

When Goodyear sold their tyres through major retailers this was in direct conflict with independent tyre companies
Source: Todd Warshaw/Getty Images

Causes of channel conflict

Some causes of channel conflict are easy to resolve, others are not. Conflict may arise from:

- **Goal incompatibility.** The manufacturer may want to achieve rapid market penetration through a low-price policy. Dealers, in contrast, may prefer to work with high margins and pursue short-run profitability.
- **Unclear roles and rights.** HP may sell personal computers to large accounts through its own sales force, but its licensed dealers may also be trying to sell to large accounts. Territory boundaries and credit for sales often produce conflict.
- **Differences in perception.** The manufacturer may be optimistic about the short-term economic outlook and want dealers to carry higher inventory. Dealers may be pessimistic. In the beverage category, it is not uncommon for disputes to arise between manufacturers and their distributors about the optimal advertising strategy.
- **Intermediaries' dependence on the manufacturer.** The fortunes of exclusive dealers, such as car dealers, are profoundly affected by the manufacturer's product and pricing decisions. This situation creates a high potential for conflict.

Managing channel conflict

Some channel conflict can be constructive and lead to better adaptation to a changing environment, but too much is dysfunctional.[77] The challenge is not to eliminate all conflict, which is impossible, but to manage it better. There are a number of mechanisms for effective conflict management (see Table 17.2).[78]

- **Strategic justification.** In some cases, a convincing strategic justification that they serve distinctive segments can reduce potential for conflict among channel members. Developing special versions of products for different channel members is a clear way to demonstrate that distinctiveness.
- **Dual compensation.** Dual compensation pays existing channels for sales made through new channels. When insurance companies started selling insurance online, they agreed to pay agents a 2 per cent commission for face-to-face service to customers who got their quotes on the web. Although lower than the agents' typical 10 per cent commission for offline transactions, it did reduce tensions.[79]
- **Superordinate goals.** Channel members can come to an agreement on the fundamental or superordinate goal they are jointly seeking, whether it is survival, market share, high quality or customer satisfaction. They usually do this when the channel faces an outside threat, such as a more efficient competing channel, an adverse piece of legislation or a shift in consumer desires.
- **Employee exchange.** A useful step is to exchange persons between two or more channel levels. BMW executives might agree to work for a short time in some dealerships, and some dealership owners might work in BMW's dealer policy department. Thus participants can grow to appreciate each other's point of view.

Table 17.2 Strategies to manage channel conflict

- Strategic justification
- Dual compensation
- Superordinate goals
- Employee exchange
- Joint memberships
- Co-optation
- Diplomacy, mediation or arbitration
- Legal recourse

- **Joint memberships.** Similarly, marketers can encourage joint memberships in trade associations. Good cooperation between the Food Associations – both retailing and manufacturing across Europe – which represents most of the food chains, could highlight issues between food manufacturers and retailers and resolve them in an orderly way.
- **Co-optation.** *Co-optation* is an effort by one organisation to win the support of the leaders of another by including them in advisory councils, boards of directors and the like. If the organisation treats invited leaders seriously and listens to their opinions, co-optation can reduce conflict, but the initiator may need to compromise its policies and plans to win outsiders' support.
- **Diplomacy, mediation and arbitration.** When conflict is chronic or acute, the parties may need to resort to stronger means. *Diplomacy* takes place when each side sends a person or group to meet with its counterpart to resolve the conflict. *Mediation* relies on a neutral third party skilled in conciliating the two parties' interests. In *arbitration* two parties agree to present their arguments to one or more arbitrators and accept their decision.
- **Legal recourse.** If nothing else proves effective, a channel partner may choose to file a lawsuit.

Dilution and cannibalisation

Marketers must be careful not to dilute their brands through inappropriate channels, particularly luxury brands whose images often rest on exclusivity and personalised service. Burberry, Calvin Klein and Tommy Hilfiger took a hit when they sold too many of their products in discount channels.

To reach affluent shoppers who have little time to shop, high-end fashion brands such as Dior, Louis Vuitton and Fendi use e-commerce sites as a way for customers to research items before going to a shop, and a means to help combat fakes sold on the internet. Given the lengths to which these brands go to pamper customers in their shops – doormen, glasses of champagne, extravagant surroundings – they have had to work hard to provide a high-quality experience online.[80]

Legal and ethical issues in channel relations

Companies are generally free to develop whatever channel arrangements suit them. In fact, the law seeks to prevent them from using exclusionary tactics that might keep competitors from using a channel. Here we briefly consider the legality of certain practices, including exclusive dealing, exclusive territories, tying agreements and dealers' rights.

With *exclusive distribution*, only certain outlets are allowed to carry a seller's products. Requiring that these dealers do not handle competitors' products is called *exclusive dealing*. Both parties benefit from exclusive arrangements: the seller obtains more loyal and dependable outlets, and the dealers obtain a steady supply of special products and stronger seller support. Exclusive arrangements are legal as long as they do not substantially lessen competition or tend to create a monopoly, and as long as both parties enter into them voluntarily.

Exclusive dealing often includes exclusive territorial agreements. The producer may agree not to sell to other dealers in a given area, or the buyer may agree to sell only in its own territory. The first practice increases dealer enthusiasm and commitment. It is also perfectly legal – a seller has no legal obligation to sell through more outlets than it wishes. The second practice, whereby the producer tries to keep a dealer from selling outside its territory, has become a major legal issue. European car dealers have lobbied to control sales within territories.

European car dealers

Car dealers use multiple channels to market: customers can use car dealers, agent web-sites, the telephone, the companies' or dealers own internet sites. The internet gives car dealers and customers new opportunities to take advantage of differential pricing across Europe, but this can also damage business within countries. For example, there has been an increasing trend of car exports from Germany and the Netherlands into the UK. Manu-facturers felt that they had to alter their policies to try and block this, and to protect prices in the UK. The following changes were made:

- Factory manufacturing times for cars, ordered by continental dealers, were increased from 4 to 6 weeks for popular models and to 26 weeks or more for all UK left-hand drive models.
- One European car company requires a specific UK code that automatically increases prices to UK levels for UK cars.
- Car manufacturers' websites have been altered to provide less information to UK cus-tomers wishing to make price comparisons.[81]

Producers of a strong brand sometimes sell it to dealers only if they will take some or all of the rest of the line. This practice is called *full-line forcing*. Such **tying agreements** are not necessarily illegal, but they do violate European law if they tend to lessen competition substantially.

Producers are free to select their dealers, but their right to terminate dealers is some-what restricted. In general, sellers can drop dealers 'for cause', but they cannot drop dealers if, for example, they refuse to cooperate in a doubtful legal arrangement, such as exclusive dealing or tying agreements.

Online channel marketing practices

Online marketing uses a website to transact or facilitate the sale of products and services online. Online retail sales or e-commerce have exploded in recent years, and it is easy to see why. Online retailers can predictably provide convenient, informative and personal-ised experiences for vastly different types of consumers and businesses. By saving the cost of retail floor space, staff and inventory, online retailers can profitably sell low-volume products to niche markets. Online retailers compete in three key aspects of a transaction: (1) customer interaction with the website; (2) delivery; and (3) ability to address problems when they occur.[82]

We can distinguish between **pure-click** companies, those that have launched a website without any previous existence as a firm, and **brick-and-click** companies, existing com-panies that have added an online site for information or e-commerce.

Pure-click companies

There are several kinds of pure-click companies: search engines sites like Google, internet service providers (ISPs), commerce sites, transaction sites, content sites and enabler sites. Commerce sites sell all types of products and services, notably books, music, toys, insur-ance, stocks, clothes, financial services and so on. They use various strategies to compete: AutoTrader is a leading metamediary of car-buying and related services; Bookings.com is the information leader in hotel reservations; French price comparison site Touslesprix.com leads on price; and UK site lastminute.com is great for last-minute offers, while mumsnet. co.uk is a single-category specialist site focusing on mums.

Online success factors

Companies must set up and operate their websites carefully. Customer service is critical. Online shoppers may select an item for purchase but fail to complete the transaction – one estimate of the conversion rate of internet shoppers is that only 35 per cent convert. Worse, only 2–3 per cent of visits to online retailers lead to sales, compared with 5 per cent of visits to department stores.[83] To improve conversion rates, firms should make the website fast, simple and easy to use. Something as simple as enlarging product images onscreen can increase perusal time and the amount customers buy.[84]

Consumer surveys suggest that the most significant inhibitors of online shopping are the absence of pleasurable experiences, social interaction, and personal consultation with a company representative.[85] Firms are responding. Many now offer live online chat to give potential customers immediate advice about products and suggest purchasing additional items. When a representative is active in the sale, the average amount per order is typically higher. B2B marketers also need to put a human face on their e-commerce presence, and some are taking advantage of Web 2.0 technologies such as virtual environments, blogs, online videos and click-to-chat.

To increase customer satisfaction and the entertainment and information value of web-based shopping experiences, some firms are employing **avatars**, graphical representations of virtual, animated characters that act as company representatives, personal shopping assistants, website guides or conversation partners. Avatars can enhance the effectiveness of a web-based sales channel, especially if they are seen as expert or attractive.[86]

Ensuring security and privacy online remains important. Customers must find the website trustworthy, even if it represents an already highly credible offline firm. Investments in website design and processes can help reassure customers sensitive to online risk.[87] Online retailers are also trying new technologies such as blogs, social networks and mobile marketing to attract new shoppers.

B2B online

Although business-to-consumer (B2C) websites have attracted much attention in the media, even more activity is being conducted on business-to-business (B2B) sites, which are changing the supplier–customer relationship in profound ways.

In the past, buyers exerted a lot of effort to gather information about worldwide suppliers. B2B sites make markets more efficient, giving buyers easy access to a great deal of information from: (1) supplier websites; (2) *infomediaries*, third parties that add value by aggregating information about alternatives; (3) *market makers*, third parties that link buyers and sellers; and (4) *customer communities*, where buyers can swap stories about suppliers' products and services.[88] Firms are using B2B auction sites, spot exchanges, online product catalogues, barter sites and other online resources to obtain better prices. Ironically, the largest of the B2B market makers is Alibaba, homegrown in China where businesses have faced decades of Communist antipathy to private enterprise.

Alibaba

The brainchild of Jack Ma, Alibaba began in 1999 and grew over the next decade to become the world's largest online B2B marketplace and Asia's most popular online auction site. Its numbers are staggering. The €6 billion company has 60 million registered users (45 million in China and 15 million internationally), and hosts more than 5.5 million shopfronts online. At any moment, more than 4 million businesses are trading. At Alibaba's heart are two B2B websites: www.alibaba.com, a marketplace for companies around the globe to buy and sell in English, and www.china.alibaba.com, a domestic Chinese marketplace. The Chinese powerhouse has a nationalist agenda: to build markets for China's vast number of small and medium-sized businesses. Alibaba enables these businesses to trade with each other and link to global supply networks. To establish customer trust, the company set up Trust-Pass, in which users pay Alibaba a fee to hire a third party that verifies them. Users must have five people vouch for them and provide a list of all their certificates/business licences. Anyone on Alibaba who has done business with a user is encouraged to comment on the firm, in the same way buyers comment on sellers on eBay's marketplace. Businesses are even starting to print 'TrustPass' on their business cards, a true sign of Alibaba's B2B credibility. Global growth has become a priority. Home pages in Spanish, German, Italian, French, Portuguese and Russian were launched in 2008 to complement Chinese and US options. After its IPO of €1.1 billion (second only to Google's among internet firms), Alibaba, says Jack Ma, will 'create the e-commerce platform for 10 million small enterprises creating 100 million jobs around the world and providing an online retail platform to supply the everyday needs of 1 billion people'[89].

The effect of these sites is to make prices more transparent.[90] For undifferentiated products, price pressure will increase. For highly differentiated products, buyers will gain a better picture of the items' true value. Suppliers of superior products will be able to offset price transparency with value transparency; suppliers of undifferentiated products will need to drive down their costs in order to compete.

Brick-and-click companies

Although many bricks-and-mortar companies may have initially debated whether to add an online channel for fear of channel conflict with their offline retailers, agents or their own shop, most have now added the internet as a distribution channel after seeing how much business was generated online.[91] Estée Lauder sells online in 11 European countries, including its newest market, Russia, along with the traditional physical channels of distribution.[92] Managing the online and offline channels has thus become a priority for many firms[93].

Adding an e-commerce channel does create the possibility of a backlash from retailers, brokers, agents and other intermediaries. The question is how to sell both through intermediaries and online. There are at least three strategies for trying to gain acceptance from intermediaries: first, offer different brands or products on the internet; secondly, offer offline partners higher commissions to cushion the negative impact on sales; thirdly, take orders on the website but have retailers deliver and collect payment. Harley-Davidson trod carefully before going online.

Harley-Davidson

Given that Harley sells more than €600 million worth of parts and accessories to its loyal followers, an online venture was an obvious next step to generate even more revenue. Harley needed to be careful, however, to avoid the wrath of 850 dealers who benefited from the high margins on those sales. Its solution was to send customers seeking to buy accessories online to the company's website. Before they can buy anything, they are prompted to select a participating Harley-Davidson dealer. When the customer places the order, it is transmitted to the selected dealer for fulfilment, ensuring that the dealer still remains the focal point of the customer experience. Dealers, in turn, agreed to a number of standards, such as checking for orders twice a day and shipping promptly. The website now gets more than one million visitors a month and includes a virtual tour of the restaurant.[94]

Many brick-and-click retailers are trying to give their customers more control over their shopping experiences by bringing web technologies into the store. The Metro store in Germany has experimented with personal scanners so that customers can keep track of their supermarket purchases. The IKEA store in the UK, part of the worldwide home furnishing group, has decided to enhance the customer experience by displaying IKEA UK's retail website on in-store kiosks. The kiosks also feature an Interactive Customer Service assistant called 'Anna' in an adjacent frame, allowing customers to ask questions and receive immediate replies without the need for human presence. Anna always remains helpful and IKEA focused.[95]

M-commerce marketing practices

M-commerce – driven by the widespread penetration of mobile phones and smartphones – there are currently more mobile phones than personal computers in the world – allows people to connect to the internet and place online orders on the move, through their mobile phones. Many see a big future in **m-commerce** (*m* for mobile).[96] The existence of mobile channels and media can keep consumers connected and interacting with a brand throughout their day-to-day lives. GPS-type features can help identify shopping or purchase opportunities for consumers for their favourite brands.

Smartphone adoption (including Blackberry and iPhone) in the EU (UK, France, Germany, Spain, Italy) has grown by 32 per cent to reach 51.6 million subscribers in 2010. The UK market strongly leads in growth of smartphone adoption over the past year, growing 70 per cent to more than 11 million subscribers. France ranks second in growth with the number of smartphone subscribers up 48 per cent to 7 million. Meanwhile, Italy boasts the largest number of smartphone subscribers overall (15 million).[97] Sales of smartphones are forecast to exceed those of regular phones soon. As their penetration and adoption of 3G increases, and as easy payment options and various apps for mobile phones are developed, m-commerce will take off. By 2015, more people are expected to access the internet with mobile phones than with PCs.[98]

In some countries, m-commerce already has a strong foothold. Millions of Japanese teenagers carry DoCoMo phones available from NTT (Nippon Telephone and Telegraph). They can also use their phones to order products and services. Each month, the subscriber receives a bill from NTT listing the monthly subscriber fee, the usage fee and the cost of all the transactions. Bills can be paid at the nearest 7-11 store.

Purchasing through the mobile phone in Europe remains low, with a mere 2 per cent of adults across the continent reporting purchasing products from their mobiles and only 5 per cent interested in doing so, according to research from Forrester Research based on a survey of more than 14,000 European online adults. Italian and Swedish online buyers have warmed up the most to mobile commerce, followed by the UK. Those in France and Germany show the least interest – as backed up by eBay's findings that UK consumers buy four times as much online as the French. Some European retailers — like Tesco, Zara and Albert Heijn — provide fully established mobile website options. Other European retailers — like La Redoute, FNAC and Ocado — have mobile applications aimed at capturing orders via a mobile phone. UK grocer Marks & Spencer recently launched a version of its website designed specifically for mobile devices, where mobile users can access the website through the original Marks & Spencer address (www.marksandspencer.com) without having to download any software or applications. Carrefour also launched m.carrefour.fr where users can see 360-degree product views, find in-store promotions, check inventory and order products. Fashion retailers Oasis and Net-A-Porter have launched iPhone applications that enable customers to shop and complete transactions via their mobile devices.[99]

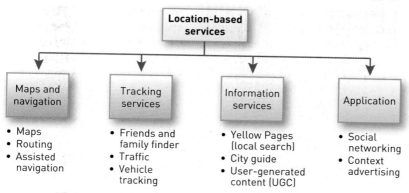

Figure 17.15 Location-based services

Source: M. Agrawal (2009) Introduction to location based services (LBS), www.telecomcircle.com/2009/06/introduction-to-lbs.

Mobile marketing can have influence inside the store too. Consumers are increasingly using a mobile phone to text a friend or relative about a product while shopping.

Here is how Intercontinental Hotel Group developed an m-commerce strategy to complement its broader marketing efforts.

The Intercontinental Group

For InterContinental Hotels Group (IHG), a mobile website is a must, according to Interactive Marketing Manager Marco De Rosa. Why? In a case study published by Google about IHG's European mobile programme, De Rosa points out that websites are more flexible across different platforms. Of course, apps have their place, and IHG launched one – called the Priority Club Reward app – which lets customers book hotel rooms, check their points balance and view reservations. IHG got the word out about its expanded mobile offerings via old school media, including print and on-premise signage. The result from the mobile focus was a 91 per cent year-over-year increase in mobile search revenues, and traffic to the company's mobile site jumps about 20 per cent every month.

GPS (global positioning system) technology enables customers to find companies and companies to target customers who are near their location. This is one of the most powerful uses of mobile phones and is called *location-based services* (LBS). The term denotes applications integrating geographic location (i.e. spatial coordinates) with the general notion of services (Chapter 18). LBS delivers multimedia and other content directly to the user of a mobile device dependent upon their location.

Examples of such applications include emergency services, car navigation systems, and tourist tour planning. It is a new form of service that delivers location-dependent (it depends where you are) and context-sensitive (what your particular needs are) information to mobile users. For example, a mobile phone can be used to search for a nearby restaurant that meets the criteria you entered. Foursquare is a company capitalising on this technology.

Foursquare

Foursquare is a location-based social networking website based on software for mobile devices. Four Square CEO Denis Crowley says that the company is designed to make cities easier to use and for people to have more fun in the cities. With nearly 9 million active users, Foursquare is one of the largest location-based social media platforms. Millions of people use Foursquare every day to find friends and explore new places through a process called 'checking in'. Whether users visit a new restaurant or clothing boutique, they share what they are doing and where they are with their social network. When users check in at a business, they can get rewards like 'badges' and points redeemable through Foursquare, and they can become 'mayors'.

A restaurant may offer 20 per cent off a meal or a free dessert to customers who check in at the restaurant. Through a dashboard, the number of check-ins can be counted and tracking statistics accessed that will help to gauge whether Foursquare is working for the customer. 'We now have over 250,000 businesses using our merchant platform,' Gleason said. 'As awareness about location-based social media as a marketing tool for business increases, we expect to see more and more businesses using the merchant platform to reach out to their customers.'[100]

Foursquare is a location-based social networking site where members note their locations with a mobile phone and can find out where friends are. Companies can also target them with location-specific information

Source: © NetPhotos /Alamy

SUMMARY

1 Most producers do not sell their goods directly to final users. Between producers and final users stands one or more marketing channels, a host of marketing intermediaries performing a variety of functions.

2 Marketing channel decisions are among the most critical decisions facing management. The company's

chosen channel(s) profoundly affect all other marketing decisions.

3 Companies use intermediaries when they lack the financial resources to carry out the tasks themselves, and when they can earn more by doing so. The most important functions performed

by intermediaries are information, promotion, negotiation, ordering, financing, risk taking, physical possession, payment and title.

4 Manufacturers have many alternatives for reaching a market. They can sell direct or use one-, two-, or three-level channels. Deciding which type(s) of channel to use calls for analysing customer needs, establishing channel objectives, and identifying and evaluating the major alternatives, including the types and numbers of intermediaries involved in the channel.

5 Effective channel management calls for selecting intermediaries, and training and motivating them. The goal is to build a long-term partnership that will be profitable for all channel members.

6 Marketing channels are characterised by continuous and sometimes dramatic change. Three of the most important trends are the growth of vertical marketing systems, horizontal marketing systems and multichannel marketing systems.

7 All marketing channels have the potential for conflict and competition resulting from such sources as goal incompatibility, poorly defined roles and rights, perceptual differences and interdependent relationships. There are a number of different approaches that companies can take to try to manage conflict.

8 Channel arrangements are up to the company, but there are certain legal and ethical issues to be considered with regard to practices such as exclusive dealing or territories, tying agreements and dealers' rights.

9 Online marketing has grown in importance as companies have adopted 'brick-and-click' channel systems. Channel integration must recognise the distinctive strengths of online and offline selling and maximise their joint contributions.

10 An area of increasing importance is m-commerce and marketing through mobile phones, and an increased use of location-based services targeting customers dependent on their location.

FURTHER READING

Gerrit H. Van Bruggen, Kersi D. Antia, Sandy D. Jap, Werner J. Reinartz and Florian Pallas (2010) Managing marketing channel multiplicity, *Journal of Service Research*, 13(3), 331–40.

This article discusses the concept of channel multiplicity as distinct from multichannel management. Channel multiplicity is the emerging phenomenon of customers seeking information and looking for products and services from an ever-increasing range of channels. Channel multiplicity is customer behaviour and multichannel behaviour is the firm's response to that behaviour.

APPLICATIONS

Marketing debate

Does it matter where you sell? Some marketers feel that the image of the particular channel in which they sell their products does not matter – all that matters is that the right customers shop there and the product is displayed in the right way. Others maintain that channel images, such as a dealer network or the retail shop, can be critical and must be consistent with the image of the product.

Take a position: Channel images do not really affect the brand images of the products they sell that much *versus* Channel images must be consistent with the brand image.

Marketing discussion

Think of your favourite retailers. How have they integrated their channel system? How would you like their channels to be integrated? Do you use multiple channels from them? Why?

REFERENCES

[1] www.5min.com/Video/The-History-of-the-Smart-Car-114252602; P. Kuhn (2002) The world according to Smart: a presentation by Paul Kuhn of DaimlerChrysler at Les Amis L'Ecole d'Paris (www.ecole.org).

[2] MLive. Com (2011) Penske hands off Smart car distribution to Mercedes as sales continue to nosedive, www.mlive.com/auto/index.ssf/2011/02/penske_hands_off_smart_car_dis.html.

[3] A. T. Coughlan, E. Anderson, L. W. Stern and A. I. El-Ansary (2007) *Marketing Channels,* 7th edn, upper Saddle River, NJ: Prentice Hall.

[4] L. W. Stern and B. A. Weitz, The revolution in distribution: challenges and opportunities, *Long Range Planning,* 30(6), 823–9.

[5] For an insightful summary of academic research, see E. Anderson and A. T. Coughlan (2002) Channel management: structure, governance, and relationship management, in B. Weitz and R. Wensley (eds), *Handbook of Marketing,* London: Sage, 223–47. See also G. L. Frazier, (1999) Organizing and managing channels of distribution, *Journal of the Academy of Marketing Sciences,* 27(2), 226–40.

[6] Philips - strengthening a global brand, www.brandingasia.com/cases/philips.htm; K. Capell (2006) Thinking simple at Philips, *BusinessWeek,* 11 December, 50; Royal Philips Electronics Annual Report, 2010; Simply making a difference, *brandchannel.com* (20 June 2005); J. L. Schenker (2002) Fine-tuning a fuzzy image, *TIMEeurope.com* (2002) (Spring).

[7] M. Wildberger (2002) Multichannel business basics for successful e-commerce, *Electronic Commerce News,* 16 September, 1; M. Haeberle (2003), REI overhauls its e-commerce, *Chain Store Age,* January, 64.

[8] C. S. Dev and D. E. Schultz (2005) In the mix: a customer-focused approach can bring the current marketing mix into the 21st century, *Marketing Management,* 14 (January–February).

[9] B. Ferrari (2010) Kraft foods facing considerable global supply chain challenges, www.theferrarigroup.com/supply-chain-matters/2010/02/18/kraft-foods-facing-considerable-global-supply-chain-challenges-part-two/; see http://csr2006.cadburyschweppes.com/ethical/supplychain.html.

[10] ibid.

[11] E. Gummesson (2007) Case study research and network theory: birds of a feather, *Qualitative Research in Organizations and Management,* 2(3), 226–48.

[12] H. J. Schau, M. F. Smith and P. I. Schau (2005) The healthcare network economy: the role of internet information transfer and implications for pricing, *Industrial Marketing Management,* 34, 147–56.

[13] See www.nokia.com/A4252213.

[14] M. R. Fellenz and M. Brady (2008) Managing the innovative deployment of information and communication technology (ICT) for global service organisations, *International Journal of Technology Marketing,* 3(1), 39–55. C. C. Poirier and F. J. Quinn (2003) A survey of supply chain progress, *Supply Chain Management Review,* 7(5), 40–9.

[15] www.oracle.com.

[16] www.apple.com.

[17] R. Shaw and P. Kotler (2009) Rethinking the chain, *Marketing Management,* July/August, 18–23.

[18] See www.oecd.org/document/10/0,3343,de_2649_201185_39732042_1_1_1_1,00.html.

[19] Adapted from P. Iskanius and H. Kilpala (2006) One step closer towards e-business – the implementation of a supporting ICT system, *International Journal of Logistics: Research and Applications,* 9(3), 282–92, diagram 289.

[20] See J. Hendler and J. Golbeck (in press) Metcalfe's law, Web 2.0, and the semantic web, available at www.cs.umd.edu/~golbeck/downloads/Web20-SW-JWS-webVersion.pdf.

[21] IDTechEx RFID market projections 2008 to 2018, IDTechEx, 4 February 2008 (www.idtechex.com/research/articles/idtechex_rfid_market_projections_2008_to_2018_00000813.asp).

[22] D. Anderson (2006) RFID technology getting static in New Hampshire, *Brandweek,* 23 January, 13.

[23] www.rfidjournal.com.

[24] Coughlan, Anderson, Stern and El-Ansary (2007) op.cit.

[25] For additional information on backward channels, see M. Jahre (1995) Household waste collection as a reverse channel: a theoretical perspective, *International Journal of Physical Distribution and Logistics,* 25(2), 39–55; T. L. Pohlen and M. T. Farris II (1992) Reverse logistics in plastics recycling, *International Journal of Physical Distribution and Logistics,* 22(7), 35–7.

[26] Read more: www.examiner.ie/opinion/columnists/donal-hickey/plugging-into-recycling-success-128551.html#ixzz1LxqLt692.

[27] A. Toffler (1980) *The Third Wave,* New York: Bantam Books.

[28] R. King (2011) Kodak in-store kiosks allow photo printing directly from Facebook, Picasa, www.zdnet.com/blog/digitalcameras/kodak-in-store-kiosks-allow-photo-printing-directly-from-facebook-picasa/3195; W. M. Bulkeley (2006) Kodak revamps Wal-Mart kiosks, *Wall Street Journal,* 6 September, B2; F. Keenan (2003) Big Yellow's digital dilemma, *BusinessWeek,* 24 March, 80–1.

[29] A. Ansari, C. F. Mela and S. A. Neslin (2008) Customer channel migration, *Journal of Marketing Research,* 45 (February), 60–76; J. S. Thomas and U. Y. Sullivan (2005) Managing marketing communications, *Journal of Marketing,* 69 (October), 239–51; S. Balasubramanian, R. Raghunathan and V. Mahajan (2005) Consumers in a multichannel environment: product utility, process utility, and channel choice, *Journal of Interactive Marketing,* 19(2), 12–30; E. J. Fox, A. L. Montgomery and L. M. Lodish (2004) Consumer shopping and spending across retail formats, *Journal of Business,* 77(2), S25–S60.

[30] P. Child, S. Heywood and M. Kilger (2002) Do retail brands travel? *McKinsey Quarterly,* January, 11–13. For another taxonomy of shoppers, see also P. F. Nunes and F. V. Cespedes (2003) The customer has escaped, *Harvard Business Review,* November, 96–105.

[31] J. Kollewe (2011) Discounters take over UK malls, *Guardian* online, 18 April; J. Helyar (2003), The only company Wal-Mart fears, *Fortune,* 24 November, 158–66. See also M. Silverstein and N. Fiske (2003) *Trading Up: The New American Luxury,* New York: Portfolio.

[32] S. Broniarczyk (2008) Product assortment, in C. Haugtvedt, P. Herr and F. Kardes (eds.), *Handbook of Consumer Psychology,* New York: Lawrence Erlbaum Associates, 755–79; A. Chernev and R. Hamilton (2009) Assortment size and option

attractiveness in consumer choice among retailers, *Journal of Marketing Research*, 46 (June), 410–20; R. A. Briesch, P. K. Chintagunta and E. J. Fox (2009) How does assortment affect grocery store choice?, *Journal of Marketing Research*, 46 (April), 176–89.

[33]Coughlan, Anderson, Stern and El-Ansary (2007) op. cit.

[34]L. P. Bucklin (1966) *A Theory of Distribution Channel Structure*, Berkeley: Institute of Business and Economic Research, University of California.

[35]K. Gielens and M. G. Dekimpe (2007) The entry strategy of retail firms into transition economies, *Journal of Marketing*, 71 (April), 196–212.

[36]A. Frankel (2007) Magic shop, *Fast Company*, November, 45–9; Apple reports fourth quarter results, www.apple.com, 19 October, 2009; J. Useem (2007) Simply irresistible, *Fortune*, 19 March, 107–12; N. Wingfield, (2006) How Apple's store strategy beat the odds, *Wall Street Journal*, 17 May; A. Z. Cuneo (2003), Apple transcends as lifestyle brand, *Advertising Age*, 15 June, S2, S6; T. Elkin (2001), Apple gambles with retail plan, *Advertising Age*, 24 June.

[37]See www.appleinsider.com/articles/08/01/07/report_apple_stores_mac_sales_beat_pc_stores_by_10_to_1.html.

[38]Exclusives becoming a common practice, *DSN Retailing Today*, 9 February 2004, 38, 44.

[39]Trouser suit, *Economist*, 24 November 2001, 56.

[40]www.stihlusa.com/corporate/corporate_facts.html.

[41]R. K. Heady (2004) Online bank offers best rates, *South Florida Sun-Sentinel*, 22 November.

[42]Anderson and Coughlan (2002) op. cit. M. Draganska, D. Klapper and S. B. Villa-Boas (2010) A larger slice or a larger pie? An empirical investigation of bargaining power in the distribution channel, *Marketing Science*, 29 (January–February), 57–74.

[43]These bases of power were identified in J. R. P. French and B. Raven (1959), The bases of social power, in D. Cartwright (ed), *Studies in Social Power*, Ann Arbor: University of Michigan Press, 1959, 150–67.

[44]J. Srivastava and D. Chakravarti (2009) Channel negotiations with information asymmetries: contingent influences of communication and trustworthiness reputations, *Journal of Marketing Research*, 46 (August), 557–72.

[45]D. Corsten and N. Kumar (2005) Do suppliers benefit from collaborative relationships with large retailers? An empirical investigation of efficient consumer response adoption, *Journal of Marketing*, 69 (July), 80–94; for some related research, see A. W. Joshi (2009), Continuous supplier performance improvement: effects of collaborative communication and control, *Journal of Marketing*, 73 (January), 133–50.

[46]Alt Energy Autos (2011) Mercedes-Benz To Control Smart Car Distribution in the US - Penske Relieved of Duties, http://altenergyautos.blogspot.com/2011/02/mercedes-benz-to-control-smart-car.html (accessed August, 2011); Levin, D., (2011) U.S. sales of Smart cars hit a wall, http://money.cnn.com/2011/02/18/autos/smart-car-penske-mercedes.fortune/index.htm.

[47]M. Serdarevic (2010) Fashion-forward shoes boost Kurt Geiger, *Financial Times*, 11 October.

[48]For a detailed case study example, see J. Shang, T. Pinar Yildrim, P. Tadikamalla, V. Mittal and L. Brown (2009) Distribution network redesign for marketing competitiveness, *Journal of Marketing* 73 (March), 146–63.

[49]X. Chen, G. John and O. Narasimhan (2008) Assessing the consequences of a channel switch, *Marketing Science*, 27 (May–June), 398–416.

[50]T. H. Davenport and J. G. Harris (2007) *Competing on Analytics: The New Science of Winning*, Boston, MA: Harvard Business School Press.

[51]J. Chu, P. K. Chintagunta and N. J. Vilcassim (2007) Assessing the economic value of distribution channels: an application to the personal computer industry, *Journal of Marketing Research* 44 (February), 29–41.

[52]B. Einhorn (2010) China: where retail dinosaurs are thriving, *Bloomberg BusinessWeek*, 1 and 8 February, 64.

[53]Unshackling the chain stores, *The Economist*, 31 May 2008, 69–70.

[54]J. A. Quelch (2010) Tesco plc: Fresh & Easy in the United States, *Harvard Business School Teaching Note 511–054*; M. Boyle and M. V. Copeland (2007) Tesco reinvents the 7-Eleven," *Fortune*, 26 November, 34.

[55]R. Gibson (2009) US franchises find opportunities to grow abroad, *Wall Street Journal*, 11 August, B5.

[56]Crossroads, *The Economist*, 17 March, 2007, 71–2; Shopped around, *The Economist*, 18 October 2008, 74; C. Matlack (2009) A French Wal-Mart's global blitz, *BusinessWeek*, 21 December 64–5.

[57]M. Arndt (2010) Urban outfitters grow-slow strategy, *Bloomberg BusinessWeek*, 1 March, 56; M. Arndt (2010) How to play it: apparel makers, *Bloomberg BusinessWeek*, 1 March, 61.

[58]J. Reingold (2008) The British (retail) invasion, *Fortune*, 7 July, 132–8; R. La Ferla (2006) But will it play in Manhattan?, *New York Times*, 21 June; D. Reece (2009) Topshop's injection of True Brit stirs up the Big Apple, *Daily Telegraph*, 2 April.

[59]S. Wuyts, S. Stremersch, C. Van Den Bulte and P. Hans Franses (2009) Vertical marketing systems for complex products: a triadic perspective, *Journal of Marketing Research*, 41 (November (1988), 479–87.

[60]R. Johnston and P. R. Lawrence (1988) Beyond vertical integration: the rise of the value-adding partnership, *Harvard Business Review* (July–August), 94–101. See also A. Bovik and G. John (2000) When does vertical coordination improve industrial purchasing relationships?, *Journal of Marketing* 64 (October), 52–64; J. A. Siguaw, P. M. Simpson and T. L. Baker (1998) Effects of supplier market orientation on distributor Market orientation and the channel relationship: the distribution perspective, *Journal of Marketing* July 99–111; N. Narayandas and M. U. Kalwani (1995) Long-term manufacturer–supplier relationships: do they pay off for supplier firms?, *Journal of Marketing*, January 1–16.

[61]R. Srinivasan (2006) Dual distribution and intangible firm value: franchising in restaurant chains, *Journal of Marketing* 70 (July), 120–35.

[62]www.disney.com; J. Cooney (2006) Mooney's kingdom, *License*, 1 October.

[63]R. Venkatesan, V. Kumar and N. Ravishanker (2007) Multichannel shopping: causes and consequences, *Journal of Marketing* 71 (April), 114–32.

[64]Based on R. T. Moriarty and U. Moran (1990) Marketing hybrid marketing systems, *Harvard Business Review*, November–December), 146–55.

[65]S. Casey (2007) Eminence green, *Fortune*, 2 April, 64–70.

[66]C. Yulinsky (2000) Multi-channel marketing, making 'bricks and clicks' stick, McKinsey Marketing Practice Series.

[67]G. H. Van Bruggen, K. D. Antia, S. D. Jap, W. J. Reinartz and F. Pallas (2010) Managing marketing channel multiplicity, *Journal of Service Research*, 13(3), 331–40.

[68]Ibid.

[69]Ibid.

[70]Ibid.

[71]B. Darow (2006) Oracle's new partner path, *CRN*, 21 August, 4.

[72]A. Coughlan and L. Stern (2001) Marketing channel design and management, in D. Lacobucci (ed.), *Kellogg on Marketing*, New York: John Wiley & Sons, 247–69.

[73]N. Kumar (2005) Some tips on channel management, rediff. com, 1 July.

[74]M. Boyle (2003) Brand killers, *Fortune*, 11 August, 51–6; for an opposing view, see A. J. Dukes, E. Gal-Or and K. Srinivasan (2006) Channel bargaining with retailer asymmetry, *Journal of Marketing Research* 43 (February), 84–97.

[75]J. Useem, J. Schlosser and H. Kim (2003) One nation under Wal-Mart, *Fortune* (Europe), 3 March.

[76]S. R. Bhaskaran and S. M. Gilbert (2009) Implications of channel structure for leasing or selling durable goods, *Marketing Science*, 28 (September–October), 918–34.

[77]For an example of when conflict can be viewed as helpful, see A. Arya and B. Mittendorf (2006) Benefits of channel discord in the sale of durable goods, *Marketing Science*, 25 (January–February), 91–6; and N. Kumar (2004) Living with channel conflict, *CMO Magazine*, October.

[78]This section draws on Coughlan, Anderson, Stern and El-Ansary (2007), op. cit., chapter 9. See also J. D. Hibbard, N. Kumar and L. W. Stern (2001) Examining the impact of destructive acts in marketing channel relationships, *Journal of Marketing Research*, 38 (February), 45–61; K. D. Antia and G. L. Frazier (2001) The severity of contract enforcement in interfirm channel relationships, *Journal of Marketing*, 65 (October), 67–81; J. R. Brown, C. S. Dev and Dong-Jin Lee (2001) Managing marketing channel opportunism: the efficiency of alternative governance mechanisms, *Journal of Marketing*, 64 (April), 51–65; A. Sa Vinhas and E. Anderson (2005) How potential conflict drives channel structure: concurrent (direct and indirect) Channels, *Journal of Marketing Research*, 42 (November), 507–15.

[79]N. Kumar (2004) op. cit.

[80]C. Passriello (2006) Fashionably late? Designer brands are starting to embrace e-commerce, *Wall Street Journal*, 19 May.

[81]G. Wootten (2003) Channel conflict and high involvement internet purchases – a qualitative cross cultural perspective of policing parallel importing, *Qualitative Market Research: An International Journal*, 6(1), 38–47.

[82]J. C. Collier and C. C. Bienstock (2006) How do customers judge quality in an e-tailer, *MIT Sloan Management Review*, Fall, 35–40.

[83]*Coremetrics Benchmark December US Retail* www.coremetrics.com/downloads/coremetrics-benchmark-industry-report-2008-12-us.pdf.

[84]J. Borden (2008) The right tools, *Marketing News*, 15 April, 19–21.

[85]A. K. J. Barlow, N. Q. Siddiqui and M. Mannion (2004) Development in information and communication technologies for retail marketing channels, *International Journal of Retail and Distribution Management*, 32 (March), 157–63; G&J Electronic Media Services (2001) *7th Wave of the GfK-Online-Monitor*, Hamburg: GfK Press.

[86]M. Holzwarth, C. Janiszewski and M. M. Newmann (2006) The influence of avatars on online consumer shopping behavior, *Journal of Marketing*,70 (October), 19–36.

[87]A. E. Schlosser, T. Barnett White and S. M. Lloyd (2006) Converting web site visitors into buyers: how web site investment increases consumer trusting beliefs and online purchase intentions, *Journal of Marketing* 70 (April), 133–48.

[88]R. Abler, J. S. Adams and P. Gould (1971) *Spatial Organizations: The Geographer's View of the World*, Upper Saddle River, NJ: Prentice Hall, 531–32.

[89]China's Pied Piper, *The Economist*, 23 September 2006, 80; www.alibaba.com; G. Barker, (2009) The treasure keeps coming for Alibaba, *The Age*, 27 October; 27, J. E. Vascellaro (2009) Alibaba.com plans US push, *Wall Street Journal*, 7 August; B. Einhorn (2009) At Alibaba, investors come last, *BusinessWeek*, 17 August, 50.

[90]For an in-depth academic examination, see J. G. Lynch, Jr and D. Ariely (2000) Wine online: search costs and competition on price, quality, and distribution, *Marketing Science*, 19 (Winter), 83–103.

[91]A. Chang (2010) Retailers fuse stores with e-commerce, *Los Angeles Times*, 27 June.

[92]M. Bohan (2011) Estee Lauder builds its European e-commerce house a brick at a time, *Internet Retailer*, 18 April, www.internetretailer.com.

[93]X. Zhang (2009) Retailer's multichannel and price advertising strategies, *Marketing Science*, 28 (November–December), 1080–94.

[94]www.harley-davidsoncafe.com; S. Fournier and L. Lee (2009) Getting brand communities right, *Harvard Business Review*, April 105–11; New Harley Davidson accessory and clothing store, PRLog, 21 July 2009; B. Tedeshi, How Harley revved online sales, *Business 2.0*, December 2002–January 2003, 44; J. W. Schouten and J. H. McAlexander (1993) Market impact of a consumption subculture: the Harley-Davidson mystique, in G. J. Bamossy and W. Fred van Raaij (eds), *European Advances in Consumer Research*, Provo, UT: Association for Consumer Research, 389–93.

[95]Tech Talk (2011) Anna, IKEA's Chatbot, graciously answers Proust questionnaire, curbed.com/archives/2010/09/23/anna-ikeas-chatbot-graciously-answers-proust-questionnaire.php; Kiosks Europe (2006) IKEA's instore kiosk assistant, *Kiosks Europe*, April, www.kioskeurope.com/content/ikeas-anna-has-answer.

[96]D. Lamont (2001) *Conquering the Wireless World: The Age of M-Commerce*, New York: Wiley; H. Nysveen, P. E. Pedersen, H. Thorbjørnsen and P. Berthon (2005) Mobilizing the Brand: the effects of mobile services on brand relationships and main channel use, *Journal of Service Research*, 7(3), 257–76; V. Shankar and S. Balasubramanian (2009) Mobile marketing: a synthesis and prognosis, *Journal of Interactive Marketing*, 23(2), 118–29; V. Shankar, A. Venkatesh, C. Hofacker and P. Naik, Mobile marketing in the retailing environment: current insights and future research avenues, special issue, *Journal of Interactive Marketing*, co-editors Venkatesh Shankar and Manjit Yadav, forthcoming.

[97]ComScore (2010) UK leads European countries in smartphone adoption with 70% growth in past 12 months, www.comscore.com/Press_Events/Press_Releases/2010/3/UK_Leads_European_Countries_in_Smartphone_Adoption_with_70_Growth_in_Past_12_Month.

[98]The Mobile Internet Report, www.morganstanley.com, accessed May 2010.

[99]P. Skeldon (2010) Adoption of m-commerce across Europe is as low as 2%, but growth will come, study shows, *Internet Retailing*, 26 July, 6–12.

[100]Technology Live (2011) Foursquare CEO on the future of mobile, 22 March, http://content.usatoday.com/communities/ technologylive/post/2011/03/video-foursquare-ceo-on-the-future-of-mobile/1; Miami Herald (2011) Find your path to success on foursquare, February, www.miamiherald. com/2011/05/02/2194438/find-your-path-to-success-on-foursquare.html#ixzz1LBeyiN00.

Chapter 18

Managing process, people and physical evidence at the consumer interface

IN THIS CHAPTER, WE WILL ADDRESS THE FOLLOWING QUESTIONS:

1 How is service process designed and managed?

2 What are the people management issues (both staff and consumers) at the customer interface?

3 How is the physical evidence and the experience environment managed?

4 What are the challenges for managing digital technologies at the customer interface?

Swiss International Air Lines named 'Best Airline for Europe'

Source: Copyright © Swiss International Air Lines.

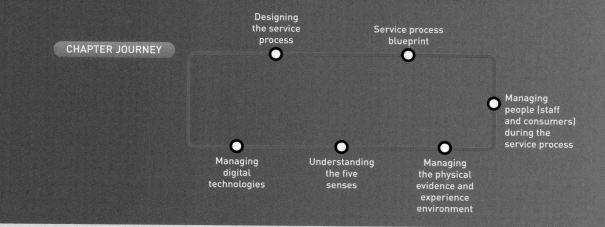

Designing the service process

Service process blueprint

Managing people (staff and consumers) during the service process

Managing digital technologies

Understanding the five senses

Managing the physical evidence and experience environment

C ustomers today are more involved, more educated and more demanding, have more choice and are less tolerant of poor performance. The customer experience is created by the process the customer goes through, the people they encounter and the physical environment that supports their value creation. Swiss International Air Lines exemplifies the importance of managing these aspects of the offering.

Swiss International Air Lines manages its service process, people and physical environment for a meaningful and memorable customer experience. Named 2010 Airline of the Year in the short-haul category, by Switzerland's *ReiseBlick* travel magazine, the airline prevailed over 51 competitors to earn the prestigious distinction.[1] 'We are particularly delighted to win this award because it has been bestowed directly by our customers,' said Swiss Chief Commercial Officer Holger Hätty. The head of marketing Europe, Alexander Arafa, observed that

> Our top placing confirms to us that we are delivering on our promise of making our customers feel at home whenever they're aboard. Personal care, quality in every detail and typical Swiss hospitality: these are the values that our staff embody and convey day in, day out. And it's to their tremendous work and commitment that we owe our success.[2]

For Swiss everything counts. The booking, checking-in and boarding processes, the colour and the texture of the seats, the style of the staff uniform, the music and the greeting are all designed to make the customer feel welcome and safe with Swiss International Air Lines. If the pilot was wearing jeans and a T-shirt or the music was loud rap, a different impression and experience for the customer would be created.

Process design and management

In a recent Bain & Co. survey, only 8 per cent of customers described their experience with companies as 'superior', while 80 per cent of the companies believed that the service they were supplying was superior.[3] There can be a large disparity between what the customer wants as service and what companies provide. Many companies find that what should be transparent, customer-centric strategies for delivering value to their customers have become company centric, unhelpful and damaging strategies for extracting value from customers.[4] The goal for marketing is to engage the company with the customers' processes to support value creation in those processes, in a mutually beneficial way.[5] Shops such as Spain's Zara, Sweden's H&M, Spain's Mango and Britain's Topshop have thrived in recent years, as they understand the role of the service process, the shopping environment and the staff in creating an enjoyable shopping experience. Zara, in particular, uses its store front and process as core marketing strategies.

Service process design describes and prescribes the procedures to be followed in service delivery – the way in which the service system operates. This includes how the service will be performed by both the customer and staff, and how they use or interact with other resources such as technology and equipment.[6] The interrelated chain of processes needs to be carefully designed, managed and controlled to deliver value to customers and the organisation. How customers board an aircraft, how they queue in a bank, how they get food in a restaurant, are examples of processes.[7] They must be designed so that it works for the customer, whose demand and needs are met, without squandering the company's or the customer's time, effort and resources.[8] Consider Virgin Mobile.

Virgin Mobile

Virgin Mobile, the UK-based mobile phone provider, was able to break into the US market by making its processes simpler and more transparent than its competitors, which was valued by the customer. It introduced a simple 'pay as you go' mobile phone service, with no hidden fees, no time or day restrictions and no contract. This was straightforward and the service that the customer wanted. So in a market where there were already major players and growth was slowing, Virgin Mobile was able to enter the market and capture 5 million customers in one year. Virgin's customer satisfaction rating has been above the 90th percentile since the service launched and many customers act as goodwill ambassadors for the brand. More than two-thirds of customers have recommended it to a friend. Virgin Mobile did all this with low brand recognition and an advertising budget of €50 million, which was less than one-tenth of the major players in the market.[9] It focused on the process – making it easy to understand and making it easy to leave the service – with the added advantage of no cancellation fee. Many small process improvements make the process easy and fun for the customer, resulting in big profits for the company.

Properly designed service systems allow relatively inexperienced people to perform very sophisticated tasks quickly – vaulting them over normal learning curve delays. Ideally, empowerment of both service providers and customers (often via self-service) results from a well-designed service process. Constructing a service process necessitates a number of decisions to be made within three key areas, as highlighted in Figure 18.1.[10]

1 **Service process design**: the way in which the service operates and is designed to fulfil customer needs and the objectives of the company.
2 **Service process delivery**: how and to whom the service is to be delivered. Not just customer service representatives, but all employees of a company are responsible

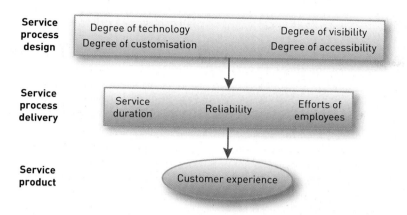

Figure 18.1 Three decision-making areas: design, delivery and customer experience
Source: H. Kasper, P. van Helsdingen and M. Gabbott (2006) *Services Marketing Management: A Strategic Perspective*, 2nd edn. Copyright © 2006 John Wiley & Sons Ltd. Reproduced with permission of John Wiley & Sons Ltd.

for delivering good customer service. Delivery means having dedicated, empowered, linked, informed, valued and experienced representatives who accept responsibility.

3 **Service product**: performance of the service aligns to the outcome or the customer's experience of the service – their level of satisfaction and their loyalty to the company.

Within service process design there are four issues:

1 **The degree of technology utilised.** How much human and how much technological interaction is there?

2 **The degree of visibility.** How much of the service is front office (what the customer can see) and how much is operations or back office (hidden from the customer)? Figure 18.2 shows how marketing can move the front and back office activities around. Technology can play a major role in this area. Take booking a airline ticket – this was traditionally a back office process performed by airline staff, but has now moved to a front office process performed by the customer through the internet.[11]

3 **The degree of customisation. Customisation** is making or providing an offering according to a customer's individual requirements. In a restaurant, a steak can be cooked to the customer's taste preference. **Mass customisation** (MC) represents a manufacturing paradigm which aims to provide a variety of customised products with cost, quality and delivery performance comparable to that achieved by mass production.[12] The outcome is mass customisation of products and services for individual customers at a mass production price, often led by technological advances. For example, cars, clothing and laptops are all now mass customised with self-choice for Apple covers and car design, with colour and features selection in the customer remit. This is dependent on the degree of complexity for the customer (the number of steps involved in the process) and the degree of process divergence (the amount of variety in the process).[13] Sometimes it is possible to allow customisation of some or all of the service: for example, most airlines allow passengers to choose their own seat. For other services or parts of services, this level of customisation would be impossible. For example, it would not be possible to allow passengers to decide what time the aeroplane departed.

4 **The degree of accessibility. Accessibility** is the degree of ease with which the customer can get to or avail themselves of a service. Once the customer is present, accessibility refers to how the service is laid out, where the queues are and how the service environment is designed.

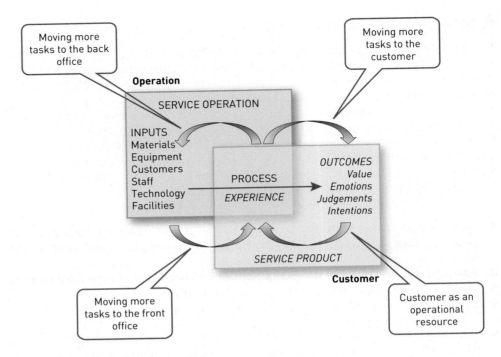

Figure 18.2 Managing the service process: from operation to customers
Source: R. Johnston and C. Graham (2005) *Service Operations Management: Improving Service Delivery*, 2nd edn, Harlow, England: Prentice Hall. Copyright © 2005 Pearson Education Ltd. Reproduced with permission.

Within service process delivery there are three issues:

1   **Duration**. This relates to the time it takes to provide the service and is a function of:
    - task time;
    - total process time;
    - customer contact time;
    - throughput time; and
    - waiting time.

    Time is usually connected to queues, both the physical, as in queuing, and the technological, as in online connection times or call waiting. Managing waiting can be a core element of service design. Customers can be scheduled to try and control this or the system can be operated on a first-come first-served basis. In general, the more waiting there is, the lower customers rate the service experience.

    A 'pace-of-life' study of time using three measures – walking speed on pavements, speed of response from a post office worker to a request for a stamp, and the accuracy of public clocks – showed that the five fastest-paced countries are Switzerland, Ireland, Germany, Japan and Italy. Because queuing, waiting, delivery and duration are intrinsically important, marketers need to be especially aware of consumers' attitudes to time in designing a process.[14]

2   **Efforts of employees**. The service personnel's ability to interact well with the customer is very important. Whether they smile and how pleasant they are correlate highly with how customers perceive service, whether face to face or over the phone.

3   **Reliability**. Customers like to receive expected outcomes. Reliability links to the consistency, integrity and dependability of the process. Does the customer receive the service promised? If a restaurant says there will be a table in ten minutes, is there a table within or before that time? Sometimes it is better to underpromise and overdeliver than overpromise and underdeliver.

A service process blueprint

To understand and design the process, a service blueprint is used. A **service blueprint** is a pictorial map of the essential components of the service performance. It identifies the customers, the service personnel (both front and back office), the points of interaction between the customer and the company, and any other evidence, processes or activities. Most importantly, the blueprint shows how these combine to create the service performance. Figure 18.3 shows a service process blueprint for a visit to a bar.[15] The service blueprint is designed as a flow chart and includes the line of visibility between customers and service provider. In service blueprinting, the line of visibility separates activities of the front office, where customers obtain tangible evidence of the service, from those of the back office, which is out of the customers' view.

The seven key steps in preparing a service blueprint are as follows:

1 **Identifying processes**: studying the service processes and presenting them in a diagrammatic form. The level of detail will depend on the complexity and nature of the service.
2 **Sequencing**: deciding on the number of steps or the complexity of the service process.
3 **Visibility**: deciding how much of the process is revealed to the customer.
4 **Timing**: setting standards against which the performance of the various steps might be measured – many blueprints include timings for each stage of the process.
5 **Tolerance**: the best-case scenario, when everything works well, but also the process for what happens when something goes wrong. These are the tolerance levels for how long the customer is prepared to wait.

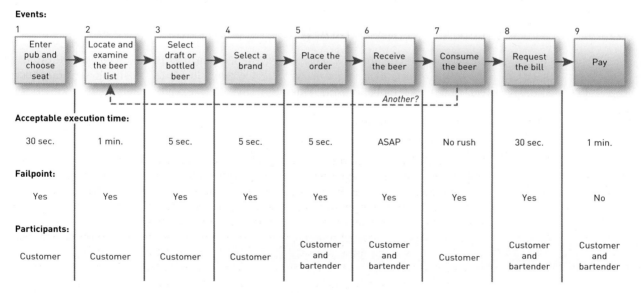

Events:								
1	2	3	4	5	6	7	8	9
Enter pub and choose seat	Locate and examine the beer list	Select draft or bottled beer	Select a brand	Place the order	Receive the beer	Consume the beer	Request the bill	Pay

Another?

Acceptable execution time:								
30 sec.	1 min.	5 sec.	5 sec.	5 sec.	ASAP	No rush	30 sec.	1 min.

Failpoint:								
Yes	Yes	Yes	Yes	Yes	Yes	Yes	Yes	No

Participants:								
Customer	Customer	Customer	Customer	Customer and bartender	Customer and bartender	Customer	Customer and bartender	Customer and bartender

Physical evidence: Tables, chairs, glassware, menus, wall decorations, etc.

Line of visibility to customers: FRONTSTAGE

BACKSTAGE

Physical evidence: Storage areas, refrigerators, kegs, kitchen equipment.

Key activities: Selecting, stocking and repurchasing materials; scheduling employees, etc.

Figure 18.3 A service process blueprint for a visit to a bar
Source: From Fisk. *Interactive Services Marketing*, 2E. © 2004 South-Western, a part of Cengage Learning, Inc. Reproduced by permission www.cengage.com/permissions.

6 **Fail point identification**: stages where things might go wrong. The actions necessary to correct these must be determined, and systems and procedures developed to reduce the likelihood of them occurring in the first instance or, importantly, occurring again.

7 **Profitability**: analysing the profitability of the service delivered, in terms of the number of customers served during a period of time.

The benefits of a service process blueprint

There are many benefits to providing a service process blueprint. The visual representation makes it easier to determine which activities are truly necessary, which can be deleted and which can be modified. Customer contact points are clearly identified. This helps to highlight activities that can be performed separately and identify where opportunities for co-creation of activities exist.

Marketers need to know where failures might occur and potential service failure points can be identified with a blueprint. This is helpful in developing plans to minimise the chance of a failure and in identifying possible corrective actions, if failure does occur.

A blueprint can be used to support staff and helps in training and motivation. Service personnel can see what activities must be performed and how, where failures are most likely to occur, and how to prevent and correct them. This links to the resources and technology that will be needed, which can be identified along with how best to manage the resources to facilitate services.

Service process blueprints are not static and can and should be updated regularly using feedback from customers and staff. They should also be used to evaluate and improve the service system over time, especially as new technologies become available and the services provided change or expand, or customer needs change.[16]

Creating an atmosphere

Atmosphere is the creation of a sense or experience. Businesses want to create the atmosphere which reflects their target market. Service operations such as shops, supermarkets, hotels, restaurants, clubs, doctors' waiting rooms and hospitals create an atmosphere for the customer which matches the service provision and manage their atmosphere through the 'look' or design of their premises. Take the Apple Stores. Apple introduced a new store layout and design with surgical-grade stainless steel walls and backlit signage. The new store design replaced the dedicated point-of-sale station with a handheld EasyPay system. Apple plans to trademark, patent and legally protect the 'distinctive design and layout' of Apple retail stores.[17]

The physical layout can make it hard or easy to move around (see the marketing memo).

Marketing memo

Helping shops design good processes

In pursuit of higher sales volume, retailers are studying their shop environments for ways to improve the shopper experience. Paco Underhill is managing director of the retail consultant Envirosell Inc., whose clients include McDonald's, Starbucks, Estée Lauder, Block-

buster, Citibank, The Gap and Burger King. Using a combination of in-shop video recording and observation, Underhill and his colleagues study 50,000 people each year as they shop. He offers the following advice for fine-tuning retail space:

• **Attract shoppers and keep them in the shop.** The amount of time shoppers spend in a shop is perhaps the single most important factor in determining

> ▶ **Marketing memo** *(continued)*

how much they buy. To increase shopping time, give shoppers a sense of community; recognise them in some way; give them ways to deal with their accessories, such as chairs in convenient locations for boyfriends, husbands, children or bags; and make the environment both familiar and fresh each time they come in.

- **Honour the 'transition zone'.** On entering a shop, people need to slow down and sort out the stimuli, and so they will probably be moving too fast to respond positively to signs, merchandise or sales clerks in the zone they cross before making that transition. Make sure there are clear sight lines. Create a focal point for information within the shop. Most right-handed people turn right upon entering a shop.

- **Avoid overdesign.** Shop fixtures, point-of-sales information, packaging, signage and flat-screen televisions can combine to create a visual cacophony. Use crisp and clear signage – 'Our best seller' or 'Our best student computer' – where people feel comfortable stopping and facing the right way. Window signs, displays and mannequins communicate best when angled 10–15 degrees to face the direction in which people are moving.

- **Don't make them hunt.** Put the most popular products up front to reward busy shoppers and encourage leisurely shoppers to look more. At Staples, ink cartridges are one of the first products that shoppers encounter after entering.

- **Make merchandise available to reach and touch.** It is hard to overemphasise the importance of customers' hands. If the shopper cannot reach or pick products up, much of their appeal can be lost.

- **Make children welcome.** If children feel welcome, parents will follow. Take a three-year-old's perspective and make sure there are engaging sights at eye level. A virtual hopscotch pattern or dinosaur on the floor can turn a boring shopping trip for a child into a friendly experience.

- **Note that men don't ask questions.** Men always move faster than women do through a shop's aisles. In many settings, it is hard to get them to look at anything they had not intended to buy. Men also do not like asking where things are. If a man cannot find the section he is looking for, he will wheel about once or twice, then leave the shop without ever asking for help.

- **Remember, women need space.** A shopper, especially a woman, is far less likely to buy an item if her derriere is brushed, even lightly, by another customer when she is looking at a display. Keeping aisles wide and clear is crucial.

- **Make checkout easy.** Be sure to have the right high-margin goods near cash registers to satisfy impulse shoppers. People love to buy sweets when they check out – so satisfy their sweet tooth. Alternatively, shops can opt for sweet-free aisles – ASDA, the UK supermarket chain, has sweet-free checkouts for parents who are seeking refuge from the pestering of their children while grocery shopping.

Some of Paco Underhill's additional words of wisdom for retailers include: (1) develop expertise in the mature market; (2) sell both to and through your customer; (3) localise your presence; (4) extend your brand – use your history better; (5) build on the internet-to-phone-to-shop connection; (6) find your customers where they are; (7) refine the details of each point of sale; and (8) go undercover as your reality check.

Sources: P. Underhill (2008) *Why We Buy: The Science of Shopping – Updated and Revised for the Internet, the Global Consumer, and Beyond*, New York: Simon & Schuster; B. Parks (2006) 5 rules of great design, *Business 2.0*, March, 47–9; Monday keynote: why they buy, *Loupe* online, 15 (Fall), envirosell.com; P. Underhill (2004) *Call of the Mall: The Geography of Shopping*, New York: Simon & Schuster; H. McGavin (2003) Parents pressure supermarket chain to try 'sweet-free checkouts' for children, *Independent*, 5 December.

Many department stores use a floor plan modelled along the lines of a racetrack. Designed to convey customers smoothly past all the products in the shop, an 8-foot-wide main aisle moves customers in a circle around the shop. The design also includes a middle aisle that hurried shoppers can use as a shortcut. The racetrack loop yields higher spending levels than many other layouts.[18] The image in the box about IKEA on the next page shows the maze design of an IKEA shop.

IKEA

Ikea's distinctive labyrinth-style floor plan where customers must follow a predesigned pathway has worked very well, encouraging purchasing and particularly impulse purchasing on each visit. The concept is based on the idea of keeping the customer in the shop for as long as possible. This gives the customer an opportunity to browse and for the company to highlight their full range of products in ideal settings. This gives customers design ideas and also encourages purchasing for each room of the house. The yellow paths indicate the direction that customer should take and the reality is that customers normally all walk in the same direction around the store even visiting areas that they have no interest in. According to Professor Alan Penn, Director of the Virtual Reality Centre for the Built Environment at University College London: 'In Ikea's case, you have to follow a set path past what is effectively their catalogue in physical form, with furniture placed in different settings which is meant to show you how adaptable it is'. The marketplace – a large shopping area near the end of the pathway – is packed full of low-cost items like glasses and flower pots, many of which are impulse purchases. It is suggested that as much as 60 per cent of Ikea purchases are for impulse items encouraged by the floor plan, low cost and design ideas.[19]

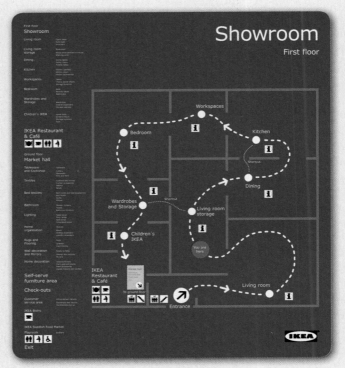

IKEA's shop design is focused on keeping the customer in the shop

Source: © Inter IKEA Systems B.V.

Managing flexibility within the service design

Some services are *extremely flexible* and allow the customer to choose how and when they avail themselves of the service. Net-A-Porter, the online high-fashion company, provides customers with the shopping experience from their own homes and when it suits them. Other service processes are much more *rigid and closely defined* in order to achieve benefits of consistency and efficiency. In call centre the process is formalised – the caller is welcomed by a standard greeting and much of what operators say is standardised to manage the call. Other service processes *depend a lot on the skills, knowledge and expertise* of the service provider, such as medical doctors or ski instructors. These options make greater or lesser use of technology and customer roles.

Managing variability

Since the specific usage of the process and the usage conditions can vary, the resultant variations in service performance can impact consumer preferences for and satisfaction with the service process. In manufacturing the focus is on eliminating variability but in services the customer often judges the service on the amount of variability that is allowed. So while some variability has a negative impact on customers, other kinds of variation may be preferred by customers.[20]

Coping with variability and the various requests and needs of customers in the service process is challenging. Unlike in manufacturing there is no single solution, but there are multiple ways to combat the effects of variability. What is needed is a systematic approach to diagnose problems and design and fine tune interventions to ensure effectiveness of the service. There are five forms of variability:[21]

1 **Arrival variability.** Customers like to arrive at different times, and the classic way to control this is to insist on reservations. There are some services that cannot be foreseen or pre-booked, such as car breakdowns or hospital accidents and emergencies. When times *can* be controlled, waiting time analysis and waiting time standards can be used by marketers. Domino's Pizza states that if you wait for longer than 30 minutes for delivery, you get a free pizza. There is also a tracking feature on the company's website that allows customers to track their pizza. Many call centres tell customers how long they will be waiting or where they are in the phone queue and also use the call-back facility. Airlines are particularly focused on 'on-time' arrival and many pride themselves on this feature.

2 **Request variability.** The fact that customers' desires are different can pose problems for services. Take Café Java – there are now up to 6,000 permutations of the type of coffee or tea that customers can order. Menus are one technique to avoid requests. Not agreeing to special orders reduces the complexity of the service, but agreeing to them can increase the service experience.

3 **Capability variability.** Customers themselves have different levels of ability within the process. Some customers perform tasks easily and others need to be managed through the process. Consider a visit to the doctor. How well a patient is able to describe their illness or how efficient they are at filling in medical forms can both affect service levels.

4 **Effort variability.** Customers will decide how much effort they are prepared to make. In gyms, many customers return the weights while others expect the gym staff or other customers to do that. To manage this, many marketers offer incentives. Customers who return a trolley at an airport get their money back as a means of thanking them for putting in the effort to return the trolley.

5 **Subjective preference variability.** Personal preferences of the customer are important. This means that different customers will experience the same service differently. In a bank, one customer may like being called by their first name while another may think that it is intrusive.

The less variability there is, the easier it is to manage. Marketers use either accommodation or reduction strategies to manage variability.

• **Accommodation:** allow variability in customer requests and set up methods to accommodate those requests. Employees often judge the level of service required and provide it. Certain customers get treated differently and the company bears the cost of the variability strategy. Airlines have the gold circle and divide the plane into different service levels – first class, business and economy. In first-class travel the customer can decide when their meal is served and when they would like to watch TV.

- **Reduction.** reduce variability and focus on the operations and getting the customer to accept the lack of variability and to conform to the operation rules. This can often be equated with price consciousness. Low-cost airlines are priced for less service, so all customers eat at the same time and watch TV together.

Ryanair

Ryanair – the low-cost airline – provides a reduced service level and charges less, and customers accept this trade-off. Problems arise when the service level desired and the service level paid for do not equate in the customer's mind. Michael O'Leary, the chief executive of Ryanair, states: 'They get the service they paid for.' A €1 flight does not give business-class service. Ryanair has in many ways trained customers to accept and expect less variability in service. Customers now know to arrive on time for flights, to pack within the kilo limits and not to expect anything free on the flight. These are all reduction techniques used by the airline to keep costs low.

Evert Gummesson, Professor of Marketing at Stockholm University, said: 'Customers co-create the value of the service to the benefit of themselves and the service provider. Unfortunately the providers may not see the contribution of this involvement and fail to support it.'[22] How would a manufacturing company operate if customers were walking around the factory all the time and changing things? Customers often want to do it their way, not necessarily the way the company wants it done. As customers provide varied inputs to the service process, service personnel cannot necessarily rely on past procedures and ways of doing things. They must be able to generate novel and appropriate solutions to customer requests. Watch customers queuing – some jump the queue; some jump from queue to queue, while others just wait their turn.

There are four techniques for managing customer-introduced variability: classic accommodation, low-cost accommodation, classic reduction and uncompromised reduction. Examples of each appear in Table 18.1. The desired outcome is that the situation will be managed without damaging the expected service experience.

The service process and customer satisfaction

A satisfactory outcome occurs when the customer is satisfied with their service and their interactions with a company: in other words, the process worked and the customer received the quality of service they expected. There are five stages to be aware of:

1 Avoid dissatisfaction.
2 Try to create satisfaction.
3 Monitor how satisfaction and dissatisfaction are linked: for example, making one customer satisfied but by doing so leaving another customer dissatisfied.
4 Try to involve the customer.
5 Try to create a feeling of achievement on the part of the customer.[23]

Satisfied customers will not only visit the service again but also act as service ambassadors, encouraging other customers to use the service.

Measuring how well a process is performed and how it relates to customer satisfaction is a balancing act which is difficult to achieve, especially during a downturn. Many companies respond to straitened economic circumstances by cutting costs, often in customer service, and sacrificing service quality in a quest to reach short-term financial targets. When the economy starts recovering, they invest again in customer service to try and win back customers. But often it is too late.[24] Nokia is a company that has invested in its customer experience during the recession and hopes to reap the benefits.

Table 18.1 Strategies for managing customer-introduced variability

Once a company has determined which type of customer-introduced variability is creating operational difficulties, it must choose which of four basic strategies to pursue. The chart outlines tactics that have proven to be effective in each category.

	Classic accommodation	Low-cost accommodation	Classic reduction	Uncompromised reduction
Arrival	• Make sure plenty of employees are on hand	• Hire lower-cost labour • Automate tasks • Outsource customer contact • Create self-service options	• Require reservations • Provide off-peak pricing • Limit service availability	• Create complementary demand to smooth arrivals without requiring customers to change their behaviour
Request	• Make sure many employees with specialised skills are on hand • Train employees to handle many kinds of requests	• Hire lower-cost specialised labour • Automate tasks • Create self-service options	• Require customers to make reservations for specific types of service • Persuade customers to compromise their requests • Limit service breadth	• Limit service breadth • Target customers on the basis of their requests
Capability	• Make sure employees are on hand who can adapt to customers' varied skill levels • Do work for customers	• Hire lower-cost labour • Create self-service options that require no special skills	• Require customers to increase their level of capability before they use the service	• Target customers on the basis of their capability
Effort	• Make sure employees are on hand who can compensate for customers' lack of effort • Do work for customers	• Hire lower-cost labour • Create self-service options with extensive automation	• Use rewards and penalties to get customers to increase their effort	• Target customers on the basis of motivation • Use a normative approach to get customers to increase their effort
Subjective preference	• Make sure employees are on hand who can diagnose differences in expectations and adapt accordingly	• Create self-service options that permit customisation	• Persuade customers to adjust their expectations to match the value proposition	• Target customers on the basis of their subjective preferences

Nokia

Nokia's retail experience and marketplace strategy includes more than 1,000 Nokia branded retail shops and more than 650,000 retail outlets globally. Today consumers expect more from their shopping experience. Not only do they want to spend money; they want to be informed, engaged and entertained. Nokia wanted to engage with customers by creating an immersive, interactive high-tech shop environment, which would both inform and entertain their customers at point of sale.[25] It created an interactive, multi-screen system to surround the customer in a total Nokia brand experience. By using moving imagery on screens throughout the Nokia shops and synchronising this with sound and lighting panels, it is able to create a visual, dynamic and exciting retail experience. Shoppers can interact with the system through texting and live phone displays. All content and ambient lighting changes are updated through the website – though shop managers have their own dedicated areas which allow them to manage their shop experience. Simple online tools allow each shop to tailor its own schedule and environment, while data-capture tools track customer interaction, helping the Nokia team to shape and inform these decisions and ensure optimum consumer engagement. Nokia has multiple sites around the globe, from tower screens at Heathrow's Terminal 5 to the LA Live Theatre, as well as rolling out smaller 'shop in shop' versions of the system in Nokia's key growth markets, including Brazil, India and Russia. Nokia is committed to delivering a 'best in class' customer experience.[26]

Managing efficiency within the service process

In manufacturing, measuring efficiency is quite easy – counting how many products were manufactured in a given period of time. The inputs are the raw material and the output is a product. Measuring efficiency is more difficult for service. How many customers were served? Customers have very different service skills, motivation, knowledge and expectations, and can be very different personally.[27] Therefore the service delivery system has to be flexible enough to cope with variability in (customer) inputs and also to understand that customers often want different outputs. Two customers can have very different experiences of the service process and both be content. Consider two dining experiences in the same restaurant – one group arrives with three children for a quick meal; the other is a romantic couple hoping for a three-hour meal. Both parties might be satisfied with the output, even if the objective time measurement is quite different.[28]

Trying to use objective manufacturing measures for efficiency in services can cause pitfalls. Trying to automate the service provision in a similar way to the manufacturing process has been successful for some companies – Waitrose uses a semi-manufacturing process within its restaurants – but unsuccessful for others. Take a call centre – measuring average call times would probably not be a measure of satisfied customers. Shorter calls may just be a reflection of staff who hurried the customer off the line, whereas measuring problems solved in a call (no callers returning with the same problem) might be a better measure, even if calls take longer. Consider Fujitsu and British Midlands.

Fujitsu and British Midlands

Fujitsu Limited is one of the largest providers of IT services in Europe, the Middle East and Africa, with 15,400 employees in 30 countries and revenues of €25.8 billion. It handles all calls to the BMI (British Midland International) call centre. Normal practice would be that the more calls that were answered, the more money the company would be paid. Fujitsu views its call centre operation very differently, and rather than answer as many complaint calls as possible it tries to reduce the number of such calls. Fujitsu, instead of being paid for each call handled, is paid a set fee on the *potential* number of calls. It focuses on the content of *all* calls and tries to find the root causes of the problems.

For example, one of the main problems (26 per cent of total calls) was the malfunction of printers when check-in staff issued boarding cards. Fujitsu convinced BMI senior managers to invest in new printers, and calls in relation to malfunctioning printers were cut by 80 per cent in 18 months. Answering complaint calls does not improve the service process. Understanding what the real problem is, and sorting out that problem – that is providing real service for customers and employees. 'Fujitsu has a very similar business culture to British Midland,' says Richard Dawson, IT Director, British Midland International. 'Both companies want to innovate and grow, and both see IT as critical to business success.'[29]

It is often very hard for customers to judge how well a service worked. Customer assessment of service process effectiveness and efficiency often relies on their perceived or subjective assessment – how a customer felt about the service – rather than on the actual experience or objective assessment, which is an exact measure of what occurred.[30] Hospitals may have delays in accident and emergency, but if they ultimately cure the pain, customers may feel that the service was excellent even if they waited for hours.[31] See zones of tolerance in the marketing memo below.

How customers evaluate service quality relates to the five issues below:

1 **Reliability**: the ability to perform the service dependably, accurately and consistently. Reliability is performing the service right the first time. This component has been found to be the most important to consumers.

2 **Responsiveness**: the ability to provide prompt service. Examples of responsiveness include calling the customer back quickly, serving lunch urgently to someone who is in a hurry, or emailing an order confirmation immediately.

3 **Assurance**: the knowledge and courtesy of employees and their ability to convey trust. Skilled employees who treat customers with respect and make customers feel that they can trust the company exemplify assurance.

4 **Empathy**: caring, individualised attention to customers. Firms whose employees recognise customers, smile at them, and learn their customers' specific requirements are providing empathy.

5 **Tangibles**: many services are intangible by nature – you cannot drop them on your foot – but the physical evidence of the service can be used to judge its quality. The tangible parts of a service and the physical aspects of the experience environment include design and furniture – the seating, the carpet and wallpaper.

Marketing memo

Customer service process expectation zones

Customers have expectations of levels of service.[32] At the top is what they desire and believe the company can and will deliver. At the bottom is the minimum they are willing to accept.[33] This is the **zone of tolerance**, defined as the range of customer perceptions of a service between desired and minimum acceptable standards. In essence, it is the range of service performance that a customer considers satisfactory. Performance below the zone is seen as dissatisfying and performance above the zone is seen as delighting. The importance of this zone of tolerance is that customers may accept variation within a range of performance, and any increase or decrease in performance within this area will have only a marginal effect on perceptions. Only when performance moves outside this range will it have any real effect on perceived service quality. If the service has better than desired levels, the customer will see it as very good and be delighted. If the service falls below the zone

of tolerance, the customer will be unhappy and may look elsewhere.

Zones of tolerance can vary across customers, reflecting different priorities in their service expectations, and also across occasions or contexts, reflecting different potential drivers of expectations. Customers' service expectations can be greatly influenced by what is promised, both explicitly and implicitly. There can be explicit promises in, for example, **service level agreements** – formal service contracts between companies. There can also be no formal agreement but implicit or vague service promises which are more difficult to address. In addition, customers' personal needs could affect their service expectations. Word-of-mouth communications and recommendations are also powerful determinants of service expectations. The perception of the alternative services that are available to customers will also affect their view of the services offered. Sometimes service levels can be affected by *situational factors*, which are factors beyond the service provider's control (e.g. a power failure). When service customers are made aware of such situational factors, they are often willing to be more understanding and to widen their zones of tolerance.

Service recovery

Service recovery can be defined as the way an organisation responds to what is perceived as a service failure. It focuses on the actions taken by the organisation to avoid or rectify the deviation, to prevent breaches in customer confidence and loyalty, and to return the customer to a state of satisfaction.[34]

There are two strategies: (1) a prevention, variation reduction approach, based on the idea of 'zero defect' environments, which is highly influenced by manufacturing processes; and (2) a service encounter approach, based on the human interaction that occurs when services fail, which is often inherent in something that is created and consumed simultaneously, through human interaction.[35]

Customer experience

The **customer experience** is all the experiences a customer has with a product or service, over the duration of their relationship with that company – from awareness, discovery, attraction, interaction and purchase, to use, cultivation and advocacy. It can also be used to mean an individual experience over one transaction; the distinction is usually clear in context. Studying the service process ensures that the service solutions are put in place to benefit the customer.[36]

Figure 18.4 shows the customer feelings from arrival at the airport to arrival at their destination and the service solutions that make up the customer experience. LEGO's WOW map for an executive's experience visiting LEGO is a tool called a 'customer experience wheel'.[37] 'we understand what is and what is not important to the customer in that experience and then we design a "wow" experience to improve it.'

The focus of customer experience should be on understanding, researching and improving the design and layout to provide the customer with an experience that they value. The case of Pizza Express is instructive.

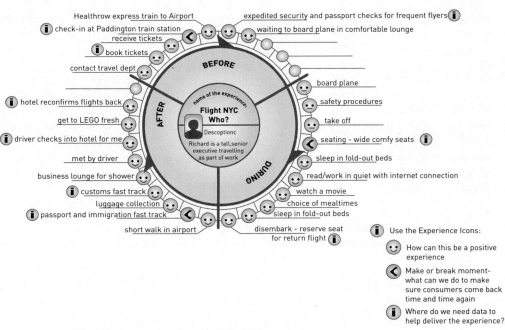

Figure 18.4 The customer experience wheel and how to improve it
Source: B. Temkin (2009) LEGO's building block for good experiences, http://experiencematters.wordpress.com/2009/03/03/legos-building-block-for-good-experiences/

Pizza Express

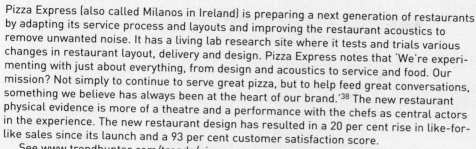

Pizza Express (also called Milanos in Ireland) is preparing a next generation of restaurants by adapting its service process and layouts and improving the restaurant acoustics to remove unwanted noise. It has a living lab research site where it tests and trials various changes in restaurant layout, delivery and design. Pizza Express notes that 'We're experimenting with just about everything, from design and acoustics to service and food. Our mission? Not simply to continue to serve great pizza, but to help feed great conversations, something we believe has always been at the heart of our brand.'[38] The new restaurant physical evidence is more of a theatre and a performance with the chefs as central actors in the experience. The new restaurant design has resulted in a 20 per cent rise in like-for-like sales since its launch and a 93 per cent customer satisfaction score.

See www.trendhunter.com/trends/pizza-express-concept-restaurant.

Managing people at the customer interface

The customer experience is more than an analysis of hard metrics about speed, availability and information, but also concerns the experience with the service personnel. Real progress in shaping the customer experience comes from addressing the emotional aspects of their interactions. People or service personnel are particularly important in services where, in the absence of clues from tangible products, the customer will form an impression of the company and service through the behaviour and attitude of its staff. **Service personnel** are any staff members whom customers see or encounter, and are often called front-line staff.

The key to success is fully to understand customers' needs and expectations. By doing so, companies can identify the most important interactions – what are called the 'moments of truth' – and prioritise delivery on these interactions.[39]

Consumer loyalty is often gained or lost in instances of customer service. Positive experiences can help increase customer confidence, and negative experiences result in consumers reducing their commitment to a brand. Companies need emotionally intelligent front-line workers who perform exceptional customer service and perform well in moments of truth.[40] **Moments of truth** are those few interactions (for instance, a lost credit card, a cancelled flight, a damaged piece of clothing, or investment advice) when customers invest a high amount of emotional energy in the outcome. Superb handling of these moments requires an instinctive front-line response that puts the customer's emotional needs ahead of the company's and the service personnel's agendas. The requirements are for service personnel to have:

- a strong sense of self-empowerment and self-regulation, which together help employees to make decisions on the spot if that should be necessary;
- a positive outlook, promoting constructive responses to the challenges of delivering the service;
- an awareness of their own and other people's feelings, creating empathy and facilitating better conversations with customers;
- a mastery of fear and anxiety, and the ability to tap into selfless motives, which make it possible for employees to express feelings of empathy and caring.

To no small degree, these are intrinsic features of a human being's personality. Even so, companies – particularly those with far-flung networks of thousands or even tens of thousands of employees – can take practical steps to encourage and enhance them.[41] The necessary steps include working to give front-line jobs real meaning, aligning structures and processes, focusing on learning by experience, developing front-line leaders and using them to serve as role models.[42]

Training service personnel

Service personnel have to have **task competency**. They have to be competent in the task they have to perform. They also have to provide guidance and help throughout the process and act as advisers: for example, when a waiter is asked to recommend a dish. Being able to do the job is not enough. They must also have **behaviour skills**, or the ability to interact well with customers. This has been called emotional intelligence. **Emotional intelligence** (EI) is an ability, skill or self-perceived ability to identify, assess and control the emotions of oneself, of others, and of groups.

Employee selection needs to focus on both the behaviour skills (emotional intelligence) and the task skills. Staff can be hired for service ability and trained for task competency. Training in task only or in behaviour only will not result in good service. If the service personnel are really nice, but completely ineffectual at their task, the service encounter (though pleasant) is not effective. Both are needed.

Service personnel need to display initiative, cope with stress (and other emotions), be interpersonally flexible and sensitive, and be more cooperative than manufacturing staff. Correct expressions and body language have an effect on the customer experience. This can be draining and stressful on the service personnel and has to be managed.[43] There need to be norms, values and a culture that focuses on the desired behaviour of the service personnel, so that they behave every time in ways that reflect the brand image of the service provider.[44] Porters in hotels are trained to be friendly, doctors are trained to listen and waitresses are trained to be polite. Human beings by nature are ever changing and have moods and humours that ebb and flow throughout the day. This can impact on the service provision that the customer will receive. Consider the example of Disneyland Paris.

Front-line employees need to monitor their behaviour constantly. The breakthrough marketing box explores six areas where service personnel can research their attitude and rank themselves: including customer orientation – enjoyment and needs; competence – task and social; surface and deep acting.

Disneyland Paris

Disneyland Paris is a holiday and recreation resort in Marne-la-Vallée, located 32 kilometres from the centre of Paris. It comprises two theme parks, a retail, dining and entertainment district, and seven Disney-owned hotels. With over 15 million visitors, it is France's and Europe's most visited tourist site. Euro Disney hires and trains close to 15,000 employees, with what are called casting centres set up in Paris, London and Amsterdam. Its employees represent nearly 100 different nationalities and more than 500 different trades, making the company one of the most dynamic recruiters in Europe. Disneyland Paris staff are asked to monitor their humour, when they start work and throughout the day, to ensure that the customer always gets a smile and a happy greeting. Disneyland Paris is very clear that customers enter another world when they come to this attraction – from the fairy castles to the Mickey Mouse staff, all are designed to create the experience of a lifetime.

Disneyland Paris understands that it is the staff who help to create the experience with the customers.

Source: Pascal Della Zuana/Corbis

Breakthrough marketing

A questionnaire for front-line staff

The suitability of people for service roles is commonly gauged by assessing particular skills, behaviours or personality traits to see if people understand what the customer and the firm want from the encounter. The questions below could guide service personnel in an understanding of their role and contribution to the customer experience.

Customer orientation

Likert scale: 'strongly disagree/strongly agree'

1 *Enjoyment dimension*
   I find it easy to smile at each of my customers.
   I enjoy remembering my customers' names.
   It comes naturally to have empathy for my customers.
   I enjoy responding quickly to my customers' requests.
   I get satisfaction from making my customers happy.
   I really enjoy serving my customers.

2 *Needs dimension*
   I try to help customers achieve their goals.
   I achieve my own goals by satisfying customers.
   I get customers to talk about their service needs with me.
   I take a problem-solving approach with my customers.
   I keep the best interests of the customer in mind.
   I am able to answer a customer's questions correctly.

▶ Breakthrough marketing *(continued)*

Competence
Likert scale: 'strongly disagree/strongly agree'

1 *Task competence*
I was capable.
I was efficient.
I was organised.
I was thorough.
I met the customer's needs.
I performed as I expected.

2 *Social competence*
I connected to the customer's life/experiences.
I revealed personal information.
I invited the customer to reveal personal information.
I paid special attention to the customer.
I went out of my way.
I was my own person.
I was genuine.

Surface acting
Likert scale: 'never/always'

1 On an average day at work, how frequently do you . . .
Resist expressing my true feelings?
Pretend to have emotions that I don't really have?
Hide my true feelings about a situation?

Deep acting
Likert scale: 'never/always'

1 On an average day at work, how frequently do you . . .
Make an effort to actually feel the emotions that I need to display to others?
Try to actually experience the emotions that I must show?
Really try to feel the emotions I have to show as part of my job?

Source: R. Mascio (2010) The service models of frontline employees, *Journal of Marketing*, 74(4), 63–80.

Hiring service personnel

Hiring of service personnel is usually the domain of the human resources department but marketing needs to be part of the process to ensure that the staff hired match the values of the brand and the service level. Marketing needs to ensure explicitly and systematically that people are hired who genuinely embrace the brand's values.

What you have to do is create an employment offering that attracts the right people – what is referred to as talent management. **Talent management** comprises the skills of attracting highly skilled staff, integrating new staff, and developing and retaining current staff to meet current and future business objectives. To attract and maintain the best staff, a company needs to be 'a place where people not only get paid "their due" but also get to initiate and execute great things'.[45] If companies want to hire young, cheerful and happy staff, they need to create an environment where they would like to work.

Google

Google, which ranks in the top ten best employers, focuses on recruiting and keeping the best staff. Google's new European engineering headquarters in Zurich is an exercise in lateral-thinking, creativity-run-wild interior design. Google's offices have a slide, a games room, a library in the style of an English country house, and a 'chill-out' aquarium where overworked Googlers can lie in a bath of red foam and stare at fish. It also provides free food, meeting 'pods' in the style of Swiss chalets and igloos, and firefighter poles – all part of the design to attract and maintain the best staff. The building was designed for – and partly by – the 300 engineers who work there.

Google says 'From our flexible, project-based approach to corporate structure to our innovative perks and benefits, we do everything we can to make sure our employees not only have great jobs, but great lives.'[46]

Service personnel failure and recovery

Due to the inseparability of the company and the customer, where service failures occur they often occur in real time while the customer is present and involved in the interaction. Failure means that the service did not meet the customer's expectation.[47] Often it is the customer service personnel who have both to notice the service failure and the unsatisfied customer (if possible) and to repair the failure – immediately (if possible). The picture gets complicated for management for several reasons:

- Customers may blame themselves for the failure (not wanting to complain).
- The cause for the failure may be the contact people charged with noticing and repairing the failure (causing potential role conflicts).
- Fixing a service is also different, due to intangibility and perishability. A broken TV can be repaired, but how can you give back time lost waiting?
- Compensations that customers are willing to accept and perceive as fair will vary.[48]

Several companies pre-authorise front-line employees to spend a capped amount to fix customer problems. Swisscom has a system in place where each employee is pre-authorised to spend up to €1,000 to solve a customer's problem, and employees at the Ritz-Carlton Hotel may spend up to €2,000 per incident. The principle behind this is that customers are more satisfied with their encounter if the first person they contact about a problem takes the initiative to fix things without having to send the request up the chain to their manager. It lets employees focus on solving problems.[49]

Customer participation

Customer participation must be accommodated, planned and designed into the service process.[50] The distinct roles of the customer and the company have evolved and they are more entwined than ever.[51] Customers are often very involved in the service process. Take a supermarket trip to Carrefour (France), an Albert Hein (Netherlands) or a Spar (United Kingdom). The customer does a lot of work – parking the car, finding a trolley, browsing the aisles and selecting products, loading them into the trolley, then loading products on to the conveyor belt and then, when the cashier has scanned them, putting them all back into the trolley. There are now self-service options available to perform self-scanning and payment.

Co-creation of value

Co-creation of value emphasises the generation and ongoing realisation of mutual firm–customer value. It views markets as forums for firms and active customers to share, combine and renew each other's resources and capabilities to create value through new forms of interaction, service and learning mechanisms. It is very evident in social networking, gaming and the virtual world. Wikipedia, for example, is co-created with customers who manage the content by updating, adding and amending entries. Social networking sites only work if people post, design and comment. From eBay to YouTube there is a battle of content between professional companies posting information to the internet and user-generated content from what could be called amateurs. Prahalad and Ramaswamy, leading authors in this area, suggest that 'high-quality interactions that enable an individual customer to co-create unique experiences with the company are the key to unlocking new sources of competitive advantage'.[52] Customers co-create value when they log on to the EuroDisney site and design their agenda for their trip. In many cases the customer (either by accident or by design) performs much of the service themselves. We can return again to the example of IKEA.

IKEA

IKEA, the Swedish furniture retailer, sees the customer as an integral part of the service process. Customers self-assemble the furniture in their own homes. This is an extreme version of the traditional DIY concept. Interestingly, the IKEA concept of self-service and build-your-own-furniture is partly coincidental. Back in the early days, insurance companies were complaining that too many of the IKEA furniture deliveries were damaged when they reached their final destination (IKEA customers). So IKEA designed self-assembly furniture, which was stronger and could not be damaged in transport. In relation to self-service, when IKEA opened its first showroom (IKEA was originally a mail order firm) an overwhelming number of customers showed up. There were too many for store personnel to handle and therefore customers were allowed to go to the storeroom and find the furniture themselves. And so these two winning service process strategies were born. IKEA has managed both of these very well and has created an award winning co-creation process out of necessity.

Level of engagement

The dividing line between the company and customer can also blur in relation to level of engagement – eBay, iTunes and YouTube customers expect to perform a lot of the service themselves. Other customers are used to companies providing the service and have to be persuaded to change. Think of petrol stations, which now have self-service for petrol and payment at the pump, rather than a petrol station attendant.

Successful service provision relates to the completion of the core service but also the personal aspects of the service. The service process can move through professional, casual and personal to friendship. The domain of the service can influence this. For example, financial and health care services are viewed as professional, while hairdressers are often viewed as friends rather than professional.[53] In many cases the service personnel and the customer can form an emotional attachment, seeking personal advice and socialising.[54]

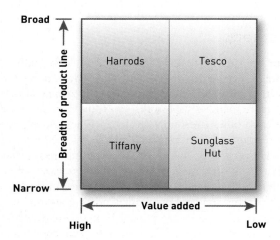

Figure 18.5 Retail positioning map
Source: Adapted from W. T. Gregor and E. M. Friars (1982) *Money Merchandising: Retail Revolution in Consumer Financial Service*, Cambridge, MA: The MAC Group.

Take celebrities who form friendships with their hairdressers. Victoria Beckham, David Beckham's wife and ex-Spice Girl band member, said that 'her two closest friends are her hairdresser and make-up artist'[55] – both service providers.

Within the retail environment, different levels of service are required. Retailers position themselves as offering one of four levels:

1 **Self-service.** Self-service is the cornerstone of most retail operations. Many customers are willing to carry out their own locate–compare–select process to save money.
2 **Self-selection.** Customers find their own products, although they can ask for assistance.
3 **Limited service.** These retailers carry more shopping products, and provide services such as credit and product-return privileges. Customers need more information and assistance.
4 **Full service.** Salespeople are ready to assist in every phase of the locate–compare–select process. Customers who like to be waited on prefer this type of shop. The high staffing costs, along with the higher proportion of speciality products and services, result in high-cost retailing.

By combining these different service levels with different assortment breadths, we can distinguish the four broad positioning strategies available to retailers, as shown in Figure 18.5.

1 **Harrods.** Shops that feature a broad product range and high value added pay close attention to shop design, product quality, service and image. Their profit margin is high, and if they have high enough volume they will be very profitable.
2 **Cartier.** Shops that feature a narrow product assortment and high value added cultivate an exclusive image and operate on high margin and low volume.
3 **Sunglass Hut.** Shops that feature a narrow line and low value added keep costs and prices low by centralising buying, merchandising, advertising and distribution.
4 **Tesco.** Shops that feature a broad line and low value added focus on keeping prices low and have the image of a place for good buys. High volume makes up for low margin.

Carrefour, the world's second-largest retailer and the largest in Europe, with over 12,500 shops and over 500,000 employees, operates four main grocery shop formats: hypermarkets, supermarkets, discount and convenience shops – all with different service levels.

Training customers

Many techniques can be used to manage the customer. This implies that customers can be trained. This training can be as simple as giving physical cues such as direction or operational signs: for example, 'Please wait to be seated' signs in a restaurant, 'Please queue to the right', or 'Please take one'. All these indications inform and guide the customer.

The two main customer management techniques are normative and instrumental behavioural control.[56]

Normative behaviour control focuses on the emotional rather than the rational and involves shame, blame or pride. It uses peer pressure, norms of behaviour and other social influences to shape behaviour in the service environment. eBay is a customer-to-customer domain where the customers are both the 'sellers' and the 'buyers' of online auction goods. Customer perception of the service level provided by other customers is a matter of public record. There is a rating scale for eBay customers and this influences behaviour. Both buyers and sellers found that there were consequences to their actions. For eBay this is a very low-cost policing method. Online communities often have their own norms of behaviour in relation to what is acceptable. Normative behaviour is best when a foundation of trust exists between the firm and the customer; when customer interdependence makes customer community a viable option; and when customers understand that their actions matter.

Directional signs are used to show customers how to process through the service encounter.
Source: © Mike Baldwin/Cornered www.CartoonStock.com

Instrumental controls are specific tangible costs and rewards designed to induce desired behaviour. Behavioural theory has long acknowledged two basic tools for influencing human behaviour – reward and punishment. Therefore banks asks customers to keep a certain balance in their account and if customers don't the banks punish them by charging interest for being overdrawn. There is an argument that banks should not let the person overdraw, but this is where the banks make their money.

Charging more or less money to promote behaviour that serves the company's interests is very common. This discourages behaviour that unintentionally increases the cost or decreases the quality of a service. Supermarkets have long had the policy of rewarding customers with money back for replacing the trolley in the trolley bay. This shows a lack of trust in relation to expected behaviour. Actually a payment for undesired behaviour does not always work. When a crèche introduced a fee for parents who were late collecting their children, parents were happier and happy to pay. They felt that their guilt was allayed – they could be late and just pay extra.

Sometimes both normative and instrumental techniques can be used. Take the use or non-use of yellow box junctions while driving. This can be influenced by normative behaviour – pressure from other drivers – but there can also be instrumental control with a fine from the police.

Managing customer-to-customer interactions

Customer-to-customer interactions during the process and while other customers are availing of the service are often crucial to the creation of the service and the levels of satisfaction with it. Take a music festival experience.

Sziget music festival in Hungary

Music festivals are a core part of the culture of young people all over Europe: for example, the Sziget music festival in Hungary attracts over 50,000 visitors. This festival takes place in a tented city on the Danube in Budapest. It is a huge service process, with innumerable stages featuring mainstream and other bands. The Sziget festival kicks off with one concert on 'Zero Day', followed by five days of bands such as Pulp, Dizzee Rascal, Rise Against, Smash Mouth, Flogging Molly, Interpol, The National, Gogol Bordello, the Chemical Brothers and Skunk Anansie. The success of these and other festival extravaganzas of camping, food and fun with thousands of other festival goers is very dependent on the festival goers (customers) themselves. How much fun is had relates to the other customers at the concert as much as the bands or the venue. At a music concert, everyone helps to create the atmosphere and also the enjoyment.

Many positive and negative outcomes can arise from **customer-to-customer encounters**. A UK case study by Harris and Baron found that conversations between train passengers really helped their mood, particularly when there were delays.[57] The study also found that in the absence of service personnel the passengers themselves often gave each other information in relation to timetables and platforms. Customers could be viewed as unsalaried part-time employees.

Managing the physical evidence and experience environment

The **physical evidence** – also called the servicescape or experience environment – is the surroundings where the service takes place. Buildings, furnishing, layout, colour, packaging, signs, uniforms and products associated with the service such as carrier bags, tickets, brochures, labels – all combine to create the brand image desired. The physical evidence includes the surroundings and any tangible item received during the process which will impact on both the customer's and the service provider's behaviour and experience of the service.[58] Both respond emotionally and physiologically to the perceived environment, and these responses ultimately impact upon behaviour. Some service environments can work for the customer and not for the employee and vice versa. For instance, queues help the service personnel but many customers do not like them. Many of the physical elements have a rational function – they are there for a reason (e.g. directional signs); while others have a more symbolic mission – they help define the role (e.g. wigs on judges or gowns on lecturers).

Two main emotional impacts of the physical environment are: pleasure–displeasure and degree of arousal. Pleasant environments are likely to be ones that people want to spend longer in and to return to. Conversely, unpleasant ones are avoided. Similarly, arousing environments (a lot of stimulation) are viewed positively and customers like to be there, unless of course arousal is accompanied by unpleasantness.[59]

The physical environment may assume a variety of strategic roles in services:

- The physical environment provides a visual metaphor for an organisation's total offering.
- The physical environment can assume a facilitator role by either helping or hindering the ability of customers and employees to carry out their respective activities.
- The physical environment can serve as a differentiator in signalling the intended market segment, positioning the organisation, and conveying distinctiveness from competitors.

To secure strategy advantages from physical environment, the needs of customers and the requirements of various company departments must be incorporated into environmental design decisions. Figure 18.6 shows the areas of influence of the experience space, which include the event, the context of the event, the involvement with the event and personal meaning.[60]

Physical evidence for a sporting event includes tickets with the team's logo; players wearing team colours; the stadium itself, which can be impressive and have an electrifying atmosphere; the colour of the seats; the food and drink. How parking is arranged, whether the seating is comfortable and the standard of the toilets and the refreshments all contribute to the experience the customer has of the environment. This relates to what are called hygiene or motivator factors.[61] Herzberg's motivation–hygiene theory states that there are certain factors in the workplace that cause job satisfaction, while a separate set of factors cause dissatisfaction. It was developed by Frederick Herzberg, a psychologist, who theorised that job satisfaction and job dissatisfaction act independently of each other. It can be used for customer enjoyment too.

- **Motivator factors** provide satisfaction and derive from the actual service or experience (e.g. entertainment from watching an event at a sports stadium). These factors are concerned with what customers actually get.

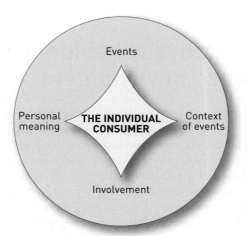

Figure 18.6 The experience space
Source: C. K. Prahalad and V. Ramaswamy (2003) The new frontier of experience innovation, *MIT Sloan Management Review*, 44(4), 12–18. © 2003 from MIT Sloan Management Review/Massachusetts Institute of Technology. All rights reserved. Distributed by Tribune Media Services.

- **Hygiene factors** can cause dissatisfaction if missing but do not necessarily satisfy if increased. For a sports stadium, the quality of the seating, the toilets and the car park could be hygiene factors. Customers expect the toilets to be clean and will notice if they are not. Research showed that visitors to a zoo in Denmark rated the hygiene factors, such as toilets and car parking, as more important than the motivators (the actual visit to the zoo) leading to dissatisfaction with the service when they were not provided to the expected levels.[62]

The retail environment is adopting practices as simple as calling each shopper a 'guest' and as grandiose as building an indoor amusement park. The Mall of the Emirates in Dubai has a ski slope in the desert shopping centre – an interesting attraction for shoppers used to 50-degree heat. The shop atmosphere should match the basic motivations of the shopper – if target consumers are more likely to be in a task-oriented and functional mindset, then a simpler, more restrained in-store environment may be better.[63] Consistent with this reasoning, some retailers of experiential products are creating in-store entertainment to attract customers who want fun and excitement. Other companies, like Virgin Airlines, concentrate on comfort, service and luxury for certain customer target markets, and fun and enjoyment for others.

Virgin Atlantic

Virgin Atlantic created a flagship £11 million Heathrow Clubhouse lounge. This lounge is more than double the size of the previous one and sets a whole new standard for business-class travellers. It includes a myriad of features ranging from a long bar, a deli, a brasserie, a poolside lounge, a library and a rooftop garden through to a spa that houses four massage bays, a sauna, six steam-shower rooms, suntan booths and, for those fancying a quick dip before flying, a hydro-pool. On board there are a selection of service levels and entertainment:

- *Flying in economy* is all about fun and value, from the free amenity kit to the seat-back TVs.
- *Premium economy* seats are bigger and wider and there is a separate cabin dedicated to Premium Economy passengers.
- The *Upper Class Suite* has beds, tables and plenty of leg room. It is perfect for stretching out or curling up to sleep. The Upper Class Suite has one of the longest fully flat beds when compared with other airlines' business class.

Senses management

The best marketers understand that customers use all five sensual dimensions – sight, sound, touch, taste and smell – to purchase, stay loyal and have an emotional connection with the service experience. 'We are not buying products and services but experiences and dreams.'[64] A study by Millward Brown revealed that 83 per cent of all brand communication is focused on two senses: what we hear and what we see. All brands must try to build two or more senses into the brand appeal. Martin Lindstrom, a Dutch branding expert, noted that only 10 per cent of the world's top 200 brands use all five senses. He noted that businesses often overlook the fact that 75 per cent of day-to-day emotions are influenced by smell, and there can be a 65 per cent chance of a mood change when exposed to a positive sound.[65] Managing the sensory experience makes good sense relating to services, products and brand image creation and management. For example, blindfolded customers can recognise a Coke bottle or a Barbie doll just from touch.[66]

Supermarkets have found that varying the tempo of music affects the average time spent in the shop and average expenditure. Retailers are adding fragrances to stimulate certain moods. SonyStyle shops have a specially designed subtle vanilla and mandarin orange fragrance. Every surface in a SonyStyle shop is also designed to be touchable, from etched glass with bevelled edges on countertops to silk paper and maple panelling. Bloomingdales uses essences in different departments: baby powder in the baby department and suntan lotion in the swimwear department.[67]

Managing sight

Sight or vision is our primary sense and is aligned to colour and aesthetics: 85 per cent of all communications from companies is linked to sight only. This is connected to how customers see service, the product, the environment and particularly the interior design of the company when they visit it. For business-class passengers, Air France-KLM has leather seats and plush carpets, leading to an impression of luxury and comfort, while Ryanair – the low-cost airline – has plastic seats with blue and yellow as the dominant colours, reinforcing the cheap, low-cost, no-frills positioning.

The setting where the service is simultaneously produced and consumed has a significant effect on the customer's service experience. Compare the experience of a meal at the best restaurant in Europe, elBulli, a three Michelin-starred restaurant on the Costa Brava in, Spain. The small restaurant overlooks the Cala Monjoi bay, and the head chef has been described as 'the most imaginative generator of haute cuisine on the planet'. ElBulli has subdued lighting and expensive art deco, in contrast to the fast-food sector that uses bright colours and bright lights to discourage customers from sitting around and occupying seating needed by the next customers. Customers will not linger on chairs that are brightly coloured but are more inclined to stay on neutral-coloured chairs. Take Safeway, which redesigned its shops to increase profits by thoroughly reinventing the look of its stores:[68]

- **Walls**: replaced plain old white walls with earthy tones to convey freshness and wholesomeness.
- **Lighting**: replaced bright glaring lights with warm accent lights that direct attention to products and departments.
- **Signage**: added big pictures of healthy food, as well as display stations throughout the store to suggest meal ideas for time-starved shoppers.
- **Produce department**: enlarged the organic section, moving it from against the wall to wooden crates at the centre of the floor space, suggesting a farmer's market.
- **Floors**: installed hardwood floors in perishables department to provide a natural feel.
- **Bakery**: knocked down walls to show off bread baking in wood-fired oven, and added an island in the centre of the department that offers custom bread slicing.

For many service encounters, staff wear uniforms which suggest their role and how the interaction should occur. We immediately react to police officers, fire personnel and many others because the uniform is reflective of their position and authority. Doctors wear white coats and a stethoscope around their neck, which provides an air of professionalism and authority. Sometimes a lot of thought goes into designing these uniforms. For example, Air Italia uniforms are designed by Giorgio Armani, while Air France and British Airways use Christian Lacroix and Julian McDonald respectively – all helping to create the impression of luxury for these brands. In Asian and Islamic countries the airline uniforms are a mix of fashion and modesty to reflect the culture of those countries.

Managing sound

Customers are familiar with piped music in shops and also music in aircraft to calm passengers before the flight. In a recent study the effect of music (tempo and type) on customer perceptions and behavioural outcomes in women's fashion retailing was tested.[69] The results revealed that customers who liked the music being played were more likely to feel happy and to rate highly the quality of service and products on offer. On music *type*, when classical music or slow songs from the Top 40 were played, shoppers had a higher perception of service quality and pleasure than when the music was fast. Music tempo can suggest the type of business – classical music for an older target market and boy bands for the teenage market.

Companies can patent sounds that are core to their product or service. Kellogg's has patented the crackle sounds when you open a bag of cornflakes and Mercedes-Benz the sound of the car door as it closes. That 'cluck' sound has been shown to be an effective criterion that customers use to judge the quality of a car.[70] Intel has spent millions promoting the Intel Inside sound to link to the customers' senses when they hear that sound and make them think Intel.

Managing smells

The sense of smell is the strongest sense and one that can trigger dormant memories and associations. Around 75 per cent of our emotions are generated by smell.[71] A smell can have long-lasting associations that are cognitive (mental processes), behavioural and also emotional. The poet Diane Ackerman noted that 'hit a tripwire of smell and memories explode at once'.[72] Customers often equate the newness of a car with its smell, which by the way is a manufactured smell and does not exist. Rolls-Royce found that the sales of its new car increased after it created and sprayed the same distinctive fragrance that it used for the 1965 Silver Cloud.[73]

Customers expect what is called the **ambient smell**, which is the smell that creates an ambience – like the smell of coffee beans in a coffee shop. Many supermarkets smell of freshly baked bread. It is not that they are baking all day, but the smell is piped into the shop as the smell of fresh bread has positive connotations and also promotes hunger, which can encourage people to buy more. Other examples:

- Some Barclays Bank branches in the United Kingdom offer freshly brewed coffee so that the customer has the sense that they are at home in the bank.
- Thomas Pink, which has branches in the United Kingdom, Ireland, France and Turkey, sprays the smell of fresh laundry and cotton in its shops to create that 'fresh' ambience.
- Singapore Airlines has developed a signature scent called Stefan Floridian Waters, which is sprayed in all its aeroplanes, worn by its staff and also sprayed on the hot towels handed out to passengers during flights.

A pleasant or unpleasant smell will reflect either positively or negatively on the service. A German study for Nike trainers found that 85 per cent of respondents preferred trainers displayed in a room with a light smell over the exact same shoe displayed in a room with no smell – and also were prepared to spend more to buy them.[74] Casinos have also noted an increase in gambling if there is a citrus smell.[75] In a recent study the diffusion of scents was studied to see if there was a positive change to the evaluations of a service experience and perceptions of personal wellness in a health service environment. Three situations in a children's hospital were examined: no scent situation, relaxing scent situation and stimulating scent situation. The study revealed that both a relaxing and a stimulating odour improved the evaluation of the service experience in the paediatric service. It showed that the use of scent is helpful in creating an experiential context, allowing the children to be more positive about their hospital stay.[76]

Managing touch

Customers like to touch, to feel, to experience for themselves. In a recent survey of mobile phone purchasers, 35 per cent of consumers stated that the feel of the phone was more important than the look. In a similar study, 46 per cent of consumers said that the weight of the phone was more important than the look.[77] When customers touch fabrics or furniture they create images in their minds. The touch or texture can trigger connections to quality, as in the fine cotton dining cloth in a restaurant, or the opposite – a fast-food outlet with a plastic table top. Nokia also values touch and sound in its product design.

Managing taste

Taste is the weakest of the five senses and relates to flavour. The roof of the mouth and the tongue are covered with thousands of tiny taste buds. There are four basic tastes:

sweet, salty, sour and bitter. Customers experience thousands of tastes and they play an important part in helping customers enjoy the many products that they eat. There are many reasons why we consume food, the obvious and most important one being to obtain nutrition for a healthy and happy body. However, in a society where food supply, safety and nutrition are more than adequately provided for, other issues relating to consumers' food choice have grown in importance.[78] Many tastes are designed to make food so tasty and addictive that customers want to eat more and more almost addictively. Products such as coffee, chocolate, ice cream and, of course, alcohol are often consumed to change the state of mind rather than for hunger or nutrition.

Marketing managers need to manage all the senses to create the total environment for the service experience, as the case of Ritz Carlton illustrates.

Ritz Carlton

Take the Ritz Hotel, where the sound is kept subdued and quiet. Noise from other hotel guests can really impact on guests' enjoyment. The texture of the bedclothes and the towels are all of the highest quality to reflect the brand image of luxury. All the decor and imagery in the hotel is designed for the refined taste of the clientele. All the food is fine dining with a focus on exquisite tastes. The smell within the hotel is complemented by fresh flowers on all floors. All the senses are managed well to create the image of luxury.

Marketing insight

Martin Lindstrom, *Brand Sense*

Dutchman Martin Lindstrom is one of the world's leading experts on branding and the senses. He is the author of three influential books: *Brand Sense: Sensory Secrets Behind the Stuff We Buy*; *Buyology: Truth and Lies About Why We Buy*; and *Brand Sense: How to Build Powerful Brands through Touch, Taste, Smell, Sight, and Sound*. He has always been a free thinker and entrepreneurial. As a child he developed a LEGO house which attracted hundreds of visitors and also the attention of LEGO, which hired him. At 12 years of age he founded his first advertising agency and started to explore the lack of use of senses in branding and marketing. He suggests a six-step approach to crafting a sensory brand across all touchpoints:

1 synergy across sensory touchpoints;

2 innovative sensory thinking ahead of competitors;

3 sensory consistency;

4 sensory authenticity;

5 positive sensory ownership; and

6 constant progress across sensory touchpoints.

Abercrombie and Fitch use their own scent – spraying it outside their shops, on their clothes and in their shop all day. They also have loud music and the sense of a dark cave or disco to entice their target market to stay and shop. To understand how to use senses to enhance the brand and the customer experience, why not listen to Martin Lindstrom talk about how our senses interact when shopping, playing and on the go – log onto www.brandsense.com.

Managing digital technology at the customer interface

Service processes, people and physical evidence of the service environment have all been impacted by digital technology. Technology allows service to be delivered at a geographical or physical distance from the company. Self-check-out at retail stores and supermarkets,

Marketing insight

Air transport self service technologies

In a 2011 Passenger Self-Service Survey of passengers' use of air transport self-service technology, it was revealed that self-service options are gaining ground throughout the passenger journey – from online booking and check-in to baggage processing and security. While some of these steps still need to be fully addressed, passengers are showing an encouraging interest. The survey found popular demand for non-traditional areas of self-service as passengers are increasingly comfortable with online, kiosk and mobile phone channels. While online booking and check-in are nearing their full potential, there is now a clear demand for self-service during other steps of the passenger journey or service process design. These include automated security checks and automatic boarding gates. The survey found that:

- 71% of respondents have used *kiosk check-in*;
- 70% of respondents said *automated security checks* are acceptable – up from 58% in the previous year's survey;
- 70% of respondents prefer *automatic boarding gates* – up from 57% in the previous year;
- 66% of respondents would use *kiosks for booking/ changing a flight,* purchasing additional services, printing bag tags, self-transfer and claiming delayed baggage;
- 61% of respondents have used *online check-in*;
- 38% of respondents have used airline websites to book hotels – up from 21% for the previous year; and
- 35% of respondents have used airline websites to book car rental – up from 19% in the previous year.

Source : Passenger Self-Service Survey (2010) www.sita.aero/content/passenger-self-service-survey-2010.

pay-at-the-pump petrol stations, self-check-ins at airports and hotels, online banking and stock trading, self-order entry at restaurants, and an array of dedicated devices (photo kiosks, DVD rentals, ticket machines, etc.) are commonplace across Europe.[79] Self-service technologies are replacing many face-to-face service interactions with the intention to make service transactions more accurate, more convenient and faster. **Self-service technologies**, which automate routine interactions between companies and customers, should be a source of convenience and efficiency to both parties. The marketing insight box discusses the adoption of self-service technologies in the European airline industry.

Self-service technologies offer many benefits but also have associated problems. Questions need to be asked. Take the situation of grocery shopping online:

- How does this affect the overall operation?
- What are the costs connected with it?
- Does it stop impulse purchases, which are a core part of any supermarket's revenues?

The substitution of self-service technology for staff labour is often used to reduce costs but should be designed for increased service provision and benefits for the consumer as well as cost savings. For example, self-service check-in at airports around the world saves the industry as much as €2.50 per check-in, while also improving customer service.[80] Many consumers appreciate the control they have over the self-service process.

Managing the internet at the customer interface

Service encounters increasingly take place on the internet or in the digital or cyberspace arena, as opposed to the physical marketspace.[81] Designing and planning the virtual environment so as to 'control', show empathy and create optimal experiences for browsers is therefore as important in cyberspace or digital space as in real space. First, there is a need to focus and target site content at particular customers. Designers and publishers cannot expect to satisfy a wide and diverse audience with single sites. Secondly, there is

Marketing insight

Avatars

Online virtual worlds offer untapped marketing potential for real-world products and services, particularly because of their ability to generate sustained consumer engagement with a brand. This occurs through interactions with 'avatars', the beings that users create as representations of themselves and through which they live and relate to others in these worlds.

The stage for real-world marketing has been set in virtual worlds like Second Life. There, residents run businesses that sell virtual products and services priced in Second Life's Linden dollars, which are convertible into real-world currency on various internet exchanges.

Coke Studios is a teen-oriented virtual world run by Coca-Cola. In this world, users' avatars interact – through conversation in text boxes – and accumulate points through primarily music-related activities. For example, you get five decibels for each thumbs-up from a fellow avatar for your selection of dance music in your role as virtual DJ in one of the public studios. You can use these points to buy furniture and accessories for your online home.

Virtual worlds also allow companies to tap the innovative potential of consumers and consumer communities to design or suggest innovation. For example, Osram, a light manufacturer, started an idea contest and invited Second Life residents to contribute ideas on the topic of lighting. Toyota Scion launched a virtual car model and encouraged participants to modify and customise their cars. Aloft, a new hotel concept from Starwood Hotels, provides a virtual mock-up of a new hotel which was discussed, evaluated, modified and developed further in Second Life. Based on the feedback, several changes to the overall design of Aloft hotels occurred.

Sources: T. Kohler, J. Fueller, D. Stieger and K. Matzler (2011) Avatar-based innovation: consequences of the virtual co-creation experience, *Computers in Human Behavior*, 27, 160–8; P. Hemp (2006) Avatar-based marketing, *Harvard Review*, June, 407–58; T. Kohler, K. Matzler and J. Füller (2009) Avatar-based innovation: using virtual worlds for real-world innovation, *Technovation*, 29(6–7), 395–400.

---

a need to offer vividness, providing most notably a depth of sensory information. This provides 'presence', a factor also enhanced by interactivity. Interactivity should allow the browser a sense of control. This may come from allowing the browser to match skills with challenges and also to structure the flow of information. There is a need to understand the customer expectation so as to avoid negative disconfirmation and frustration.[82]

To increase the entertainment and information value and customer satisfaction from web-based shopping experiences, some firms are employing *avatars*, graphical representations of animated characters that can act as company representatives. Avatars can provide a more interpersonal shopping experience by serving as identification figures, personal shopping assistants, website guides or conversation partners. Research has shown that avatars can enhance the effectiveness of a web channel, especially if they are seen as expert or attractive.[83] See the marketing insight box.

Managing vending machines

The first known use of vending machines was probably about 200 BC when Hero of Alexandria used a coin-operated device which provided holy water at an Egyptian temple. Automatic vending offers a variety of products and services, including impulse items such as call credit, stamps, soft drinks, coffee, sweets, newspapers, magazines, cosmetics, hot food and paperbacks. The expectation is that vending machines expenditure will continue to grow as shown in Figure 18.7.

Besides airline check-in, consumers would like to see automated multipurpose kiosks that let them renew drivers' licences or vehicle registration, checking the status of items ordered online, purchasing airline tickets, making photocopies and ordering flowers, books and other items.[84] Many services normally involve person-to-person contact at some level, such as hairdresser, doctor and pizza delivery. All now have vending machine versions that change the service process.

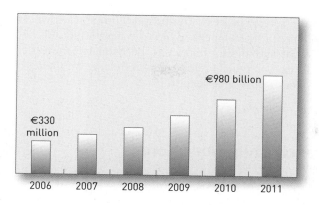

Figure 18.7 Projected spending on self-service kiosks
Source: Adapted from L. Holman and G. Buzek (2008) *North American Self-Service Kiosks Market Study*, Franklin, TN: IHL Consulting Group. Reproduced with permission.

- For hairdressing, customers can use the GHD (good hair day) machine in cloakrooms to perfect their hair in minutes.
- Want to check on your health? Kiosks are available to do that just by reading a pulse, a retina and a finger, and making a heart rate analysis.
- There are even pizza vending machines, as shown in the picture below.

Traditional services are now moving to self-service – even pizzas in Italy.
Source: Phil Yeomans/ Rex Features.

RFID at the customer interface

Radio frequency identification device (RFID) systems are 'smart' tags that can be read in real time and at a distance. Though normally focused on products, these smart tags can be embedded within the service process. Throughout Europe, car owners can purchase toll cards with RFID chips for windscreens, which are read at the toll booths automatically, allowing them fast passage and the money to be deducted from their online accounts. The same system is used on trams in Portugal and Ireland. An interesting example of this technology comes from its use in a Spanish disco.

The Baja Beach Club, Barcelona

VIP customers of this nightclub have RFID microchips implanted in their bodies to avoid queues and to make paying easier.[85] On entrance to the club, and each time they order drinks from the bar, customers simply wave their arm over a microchip scanner. This automatically deducts the amount from their bank account. Customers pay €125 to have the chips implanted. They are programmed with a ten-digit number that can be linked to the customer's bank account. Clearly these consumers are not worried about the lack of privacy entailed in this practice. Whatever they buy can be traced, and of course their presence in the club is recorded. The service provision and the customer are tightly intertwined.[86]

The radio tagging of products allows retailers to improve their service process by alerting manufacturers or their warehouses before shelves go bare. Coca-Cola is embedding RFID readers in 200,000 of its 1 million vending machines in Japan to allow consumers to buy a Coke using wallet phones with RFID chips. Dutch bookseller Selexyz inserted RFID tags into every book after a study showed a 25 per cent increase in sales and also easier inventory control, consumer search and checkout at the register.

We are nearing the day when a customer will be able to shop and walk out of a shop, as a scanner will read all the RFID chips on the groceries and then take payment straight out of the customer's bank account through the mobile phone chip. No stopping, or really shopping, at all. If RFID chips were in fridges, they could report their contents to the supermarket for reordering, and interactive televisions with RFID could select advertisements based on the contents of a person's fridge.

The Metro Store – Germany's largest retailer and the fifth largest retailer in the world – has opened a Future Store in Rheninberg in Germany that reflects future technology and also some of the challenges which marketing will face.

Metro

Metro has opened a Future Store that is a high-tech heaven and provides a unique service experience. It provides personal shopping assistants (PSAs), which are small Wincor Nixdorf table computers, clipped to the shopping trolley and activated with a loyalty card. Type 'ice cream' on the touch screen and you are directed to the correct aisle – floor plan included. Regular purchases show up on a favourites list with price and location. Special offers are flagged as you move from section to section. If you write a shopping list online, you can automatically download it to the PSA. The customer trolley has an intelligent Scale, which can identify and scan items by sight. In key sections such as baby care, hair colour, wine and meats, touch screen terminals provide in-depth information on the product or suggestions for other uses. The integrated scanner gives you a running total of your shopping and fast-track treatment at the checkout. The shop's shelves sport 30,000 wireless electronic price labels that can be changed at the push of a button.

With its network of technology and RFID systems, Metro, the German retail shop, is a leading innovator in this area.

Source: Ulrich Baumgarten/vario images GmbH & Co. KG/Alamy.

SUMMARY

1 Identifying and managing the service process, design and delivery to create value for the company and the customer is a core marketing requirement. Service process design uses a blueprint of the service process.

2 A service process design describes the procedures to be followed in service delivery and links to the degree of technology, visibility customisation and accessibility.

3 A service blueprint is a pictorial map of the essential components of the service performance, including the front office and back office elements.

4 Strategies for managing customer-introduced variability centre on accommodation or reduction.

5 Managing and training service personnel and customers to create the expected service provision demands skill

and empowerment, self-regulation and management support.

6 Co-creation of value is the generation and ongoing realisation of mutual firm–customer value.

7 Creating and managing the physical evidence or service environment relies on understanding how customers use their five senses to experience the service environment, and how each element of the physical evidence can help to form the brand image of the company.

8 Understanding the role of technology, particularly the growing self-service technology, the internet and more innovations in vending and RFID, is core as customer experiences move into the digital world.

FURTHER READING

R. Di Mascio (2010) The service models of frontline employees, *Journal of Marketing*, 74 (4), 63–80.

This paper studies the suitability of people for service roles aligned to their particular skills, behaviours or personality traits. These methods implicitly assume that job candidates have a common interpretation of what customer service is. This study suggests that assessment of job candidates' service models can complement these other methods. Thus, if a firm aims to develop collaborative, problem-solving relationships with customers to deliver customised offerings, job candidates subscribing to a win–win service model would be most suitable. The service models of job candidates can be discerned by probing how they view themselves and customers, their objective during a service encounter, and how they judge their service quality.

Another implication is related to customer service training. Consider the value of training that encourages front line employees (FLEs) to think of their jobs as acting or that measures how often they exhibit certain behaviours, such as saying customer names. This study shows that staff who liken service to acting are less competent than those who do not, and it is easy to imagine efficiency-oriented FLEs happily following instructions to say customers' names but not necessarily establishing the 'relationship side' of customer service.

APPLICATIONS

Marketing debate

Marketers should use all the senses to target customers *versus* Marketers should concentrate on the product or service only.

Marketing discussion

Design a service blueprint for a service you are familiar with. Explore the level of variability and accommodation you will allow within the service process design.

REFERENCES

[1] SwissAir (2011) SWISS named Best Airline for Europe and to North and South America in the latest Business Traveller Award, www.swiss.com/web/EN/about_swiss/media/press_releases/Pages/pr_20110114.aspx.

[2] Swiss named 'Best Airline for Europe', *eTurboNews*, 21 January 2008 (www.eturbonews.com/946/swiss-named-%E2%80%9Cbest-airline-europe%E2%80%9D).

[3] C. Meyer and A. Schwager (2007) Understanding customer experience, *Harvard Business Review*, 85(2), 116–26.

[4] M. Brady, M. R. Fellenz and M. Cholakova (2007) Towards an IT enabled customer centric service supply chain, Academy of Marketing Conference (UK) Kingston University, July; G. McGovern and Y. Moon (2007) Companies and the customers who hate them, *Harvard Business Review*, June, 2–7.

[5] C. Gronroos and P. Helle (2010) Adopting a service logic in manufacturing. Conceptual foundation and metrics for mutual value creation, *Journal of Service Management*, 21(5), 564–90. C. Gronroos (2008) Service logic revisited: who creates value? And who co-creates? *European Business Review*, (20)4, 298–314.

[6] R. Johnson (2008) Internal service: barriers, flows and assessment, *International Journal of Service Industry Management*, 19(2), 210–31; R. Johnston and G. Clark (2005) *Service Operations Management: Improving Service Delivery*, 2nd edn, Harlow: Prentice Hall.

[7] C. Gronroos (2000) Creating a relationship dialogue, *Marketing Review*, 1(1), 5–14.

[8] J. Womack and D. Jones (2005) Lean consumption, *Harvard Business Review*, March, 2–13.

[9] McGovern and Moon (2007) op. cit.

[10] H. Kasper, P. van Helsdingen and M. Gabbott (2006) *Services Marketing Management: A Strategic Perspective*, 2nd edn, Chichester: John Wiley & Sons.

[11] Johnston and Clark (2005) op. cit.

[12] M. Murat Kristal, X. Huang and R. G. Schroeder (2010) The effect of quality management on mass customization capability, *International Journal of Operations and Production Management*, 30(9), 900–22.

[13] G. L. Shostack (1987) Service positioning through structural change, *Journal of Marketing*, 54(1), 34–44.

[14] C. Ezzell (2002) Clocking cultures, *Scientific American* (special edition), 287(3), 56–8; R. Wiseman, Pace of Life Study www.richardwiseman.com/quirkology/pace_home.htm.

[15] R. Fisk, S. J. Grove and J. John (2008) *Interactive Services Marketing*, 3rd edn, Boston MA: Houghton-Mifflin.

[16] A. Shahin (2010) Service blueprinting: an effective approach for targeting critical service processes – with a case study in a four-star international hotel, *Journal of Management Research*, 2(2), 1–16

[17] C. Davis (2010) Apple attempt to trademark 'distinctive' Apple Store design, 18 May, www.slashgear.com/apple-attempt-to-trademark-distinctive-apple-store-design-1885991/.

[18]J. Tozer (2011) Why shoppers find it so hard to escape from Ikea: Flatpack furniture stores are designed just like a maze, *Daily Mail* online, 24 January; C. Coleman (2000) Kohl's retail racetrack, *Wall Street Journal*, 1 March.

[19]J. Tozer (2011) Why shoppers find it so hard to escape from Ikea: Flatpack furniture stores are designed just like a maze; *Daily Mail* Online, 24th January http://www.dailymail.co.uk/femail/article-1349831/Ikea-design-stores-mazes-stop-shoppers-leaving-end-buying-more.html#ixzz1VqPnP4BN (accessed August 2011); C. Coleman (2000) Kohl's retail racetrack, *Wall Street Journal*, 1 March; http://www.90percentofeverything.com/2011/04/10/alan-penn-on-shop-floor-plan-design-ikea-and-dark-patterns/ (Accessed march, 2012).

[20]P. K. Kannan and J. F. Proença (2010) Design of service systems under variability: research, *Information Systems E-Business Management*, 8, 1–11.

[21]F. Frei (2006) Breaking the trade off between efficiency and service, *Harvard Business Review*, 84(11), 93–101.

[22]E. Gummesson and C. Mele (2010) Marketing as value co-creation through network interaction and resource integration, *Journal of Business Market Management*, 4(4), 181–98; E. Gummesson (2007) Case study research and network theory: birds of a feather, *Qualitative Research in Organizations and Management*, 2(3), 226–48.

[23]B. D. Gelb (1987) How marketers of intangibles can raise the odds for consumer, *Journal of Services Marketing*, 1(1), 11–18.

[24]M. Kovac, J. Chernoff, J. Denneen and P. Rratap (2009) Strike the right balance between service efficiency and customer satisfaction, *Network Journal*, 2 February, www.tnj.com/node/1483.

[25]Nokia Retail Content System, http://ny.beam.tv/case-studies/nokia-retail-content-system.

[26]S. Bicheno (2009) Nokia focuses its retail strategy to boost the consumer experience, http://channel.hexus.net/content/item.php?item=21577.

[27]J. Bowen and R. C. Ford (2002) Managing service organizations: does having a 'thing' make a difference?, *Journal of Management*, 28(3), 447–69.

[28]Ibid.

[29]www.fujitsu.com/downloads/WWW2/BMI.pdf.

[30]Bowen and Ford (2002) op. cit.

[31]Ibid.

[32]V. A. Zeithaml, L. L. Berry and A. Parasuraman (1996) The behavioral consequences of service quality, *Journal of Marketing*, 60, 31–46.

[33]Ibid.

[34]Sparks and McColl-Kennedy (2001) op. cit.

[35]M. Pina e Cunha, A. Rego and K. Kamoche (2009) Improvisation in service recovery, *Managing Service Quality*, 19(6), 657–69.

[36]D. McGinn (2011) Welcome to creating a customer-centered organization, 18 April, *Harvard Business Review*, http://blogs.hbr.org/cs/2011/04/welcome_to_creating_a_customer.html.

[37]B. Temkin (2009) LEGO's building block for good experiences, http://experiencematters.wordpress.com/2009/03/03/legos-building-block-for-good-experiences.

[38]Marketing Week (2011) 24 February, www.marketingweek.co.uk.

[39]R. Heffernan and S. LaValle (2007) Emotional interactions: the frontier of the customer-focused enterprise, *Strategy and Leadership*, 35(3), 3–5.

[40]M. Beaujean, J. Davidson and S. Madge (2006) The 'moment of truth' in customer service, *McKinsey Quarterly*, 1, 62–73.

[41]Ibid.

[42]Ibid.

[43]Bowen and Ford (2002) op. cit.

[44]Ibid.

[45]T. Peters (2006) *Reimagine! Business Excellence in a Disruptive Age*, London: DK Adult.

[46]See www.google.ch/intl/en/jobs/index.html.

[47]Bowen and Ford (2002) op. cit.

[48]Ibid.

[49]F. Segelström and J. Howar (2010) Understanding service recovery, *designforservice*, www.wordpress.com/understanding-service-recovery; F. Segelstrom (2010) Service management as seen from a service design perspective, www.ida.liu.se/~fabse/papers/termpaper-service_management.pdf.

[50]J. A. Fitzsimmons and M. J. Fitzsimmons (2001) *Service Management: Operations, Strategy and Information Technology*, New York: McGraw-Hill.

[51]C. Robin and M. Ligas (2004) A typology of customer-service provider relationships: the role of relational factors in customers, *Journal of Services Marketing*, 18(6), 482–93.

[52]Prahalad and Ramaswamy (2003) op. cit.

[53]Robin and Ligas (2004) op. cit.

[54]Ibid.

[55]Victoria comes to America . . . Zara Rabinowicz on www.startrip.tv/2007/07/victoria-comes-.html, 18 July 2007.

[56]Frei (2006) op. cit.

[57]K. Harris and S. Baron (2004) Consumer-to-consumer conversations in service settings, *Journal of Service Research*, 6(3), 287–303.

[58]B. Booms and M. Bitner (1982) Marketing services by managing the environment, *Cornell Hotel and Restaurant Administration Quarterly*, 23(1), 35–40.

[59]M. J. Bitner, B. Booms and M. Tetrault (1990) The service encounter: diagnosing favorable and unfavorable incidents, *Journal of Marketing*, 54(1), 71–84.

[60]M. J. Bitner (1992) Servicescape: the impact of physical surrounding on customers and employees, *Journal of Marketing*, 56, 57–71.

[61]J. Møller Jensen (2007) The relationships between hygiene factors, motivators, satisfaction and response among visitors to zoos and aquaria, *Tourism Review International*, special issue on zoos, aquaria and other captive wildlife attractions, 11(3), 307–16.

[62]Ibid.

[63]V. D. Kaltcheva and B. Weitz (2006) When should a retailer create an exciting store environment?, *Journal of Marketing*, 70 (January), 107–18.

[64]Gummesson (2010) op. cit.

[65]M. Lindstrom (2010) *Brand Sense: Sensory Secrets Behind the Stuff We Buy*, New York: Free Press; M. Lindstrom (2008) *Buyology: Truth and Lies About Why We Buy*, New York: Crown Business; M. Lindstrom (2005) *Brand Sense: Build Powerful Brands through Touch, Taste, Smell, Sight, and Sound*, New York: Free Press.

66Ibid.

67M. Fetterman and J. O'Donnell (2006) Just browsing at the mall? That's what you think, *USA Today*, 1 September, 1B, 2B.

68J. Hibbard (2006) Put your money where your mouth is, *BusinessWeek*,18 September, 61–3.

69J. C. Sweeney and F. Wyber (2002) The role of cognition and emotions in the music-approach–avoidance behaviour relationship, *Journal of Services Marketing*, 16(1), 51–69.

70Lindstrom (2010) op. cit.

71See www.ameinfo.com/82230.html.

72L. Goldkuhl and M. Styven (2007) Sensing the scent of service success, *European Journal of Marketing*, 41(11/12), 1297–1305.

73Lindstrom (2010) op. cit.

74Goldkuhl and Styven (2007) op. cit.

75Lindstrom (2010) and (2005) op. cit.

76J. Bree, M. Naja and J. Zaïchkowski (2011) The use of ambient scent to improve children's hospital experience, 10th International Congress on Marketing Trends.

77Lindstrom (2010) op. cit.

78J. Clarke (1998) Taste and flavour: their importance in food choice and acceptance, Nutrition Society, www.fantastic-flavour.com/files-downloads/Taste_and_flavour_food_choice_acceptance.pdf.

79V. Zeithaml, M. J. Bitner and D. D. Gremler *Services Marketing*, 5th edn, New York: McGraw-Hill.

80Adapting to survive: an industry overview, airport-technology.com, 1 March 2006 (www.airport-technology.com/features/feature565/).

81R. Williams and M. Dargel (2004) From servicescape to 'cyberscape', *Marketing Intelligence and Planning*, 22(2/3), 310–20.

82Ibid.

83M. Holzwarth, C. Janiszewski and M. M. Newmann (2006) The influence of avatars on online consumer shopping behavior, *Journal of Marketing*, 70 (October), 19–36.

84E. Morphy (2008) Self-service kiosks: bane or boon?, *CRM Buyer*, 28 July (www.crmbuyer.com/story/63949.html).

85G. Keeley (2006) Now we can start paying by chip in skin, *London Evening Standard*, 11 October, p. 22.

86Ibid.

Communicating value

Video documentary for Part 7

Go to **www.pearsoned.co.uk/ marketingmanagementeurope** to watch the video documentary that relates to Part 7 and consider the issues raised below.

Value packages need to be effectively and efficiently communicated to targeted audiences and this is achieved by a mix of tools that are usually termed the marketing communications mix.

Part 7: Communicating value explores four important themes:

1 managing advertising;
2 managing direct marketing;
3 managing sponsorship; and
4 exploring the potential of word of mouth.

Marketing communications are tailored to resonate with national cultures and value sets. When watching the video documentary for Part 7, consider how Royal Enfield's tag line 'Everyone makes way for the bullet' is appropriate for the Indian market but inappropriate for other markets where emphasis on heritage and the low cost of ownership carry more meaning. Advertising seeks to achieve 'top of the mind awareness' according to IKEA and can feature a variety of media (press, the internet, posters, TV and radio). The rise of web-based advertising has caused a significant shift from traditional 'pull strategies' to modern 'push strategies', as web-based activities facilitate a customer 'call to action'.

An important tool in a modern marketing communications mix is sponsorship activity, as this brings a company's value offerings directly into the real theatres of targeted customer's lives.

However, many would agree that the best form of advertising is word of mouth with its implied third-party recommendation.

Hear a variety of top marketing executives from a wide range of organisations offer their own interesting and varied perspectives on the key themes of Part 7 including: Vicky Starnes, Head of Marketing, VSO (top); Acme Whistles, an SME facing fierce global competition (centre); and Marketing Birmingham manage a brand that is constantly changing (bottom).

Chapter 19

Designing and managing marketing communications

IN THIS CHAPTER, WE WILL ADDRESS THE FOLLOWING QUESTIONS:

1 What is the role of marketing communications?

2 How do marketing communications work?

3 What are the major steps in developing effective marketing communications?

4 What is the marketing communications mix and how should it be set?

5 What is an integrated marketing communications programme?

The 'Evolution' advertising video, transforming an ordinary-looking woman's face into the image of a supermodel, was just one of the creative marketing communications that sparked Dove's recent shift in marketing strategy.

Source: Reproduced with kind permission of Unilever PLC and Group Companies.

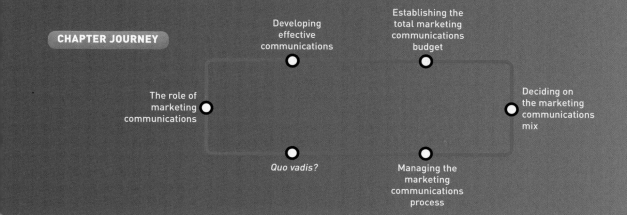

Developing
effective
communications

Establishing the
total marketing
communications
budget

The role of
marketing
communications

Deciding on
the marketing
communications
mix

Quo vadis?

Managing the
marketing
communications
process

Modern marketing calls for more than developing a good market offering, pricing it attractively and making it accessible. Companies must also communicate with present and potential customers, stakeholders and the general public. For most, therefore, the question is not whether to communicate but rather what to say, how and when to say it, to whom and how often. However, communication becomes progressively more difficult as more companies clamour to attract an increasingly empowered consumer's divided attention. Consumers are taking a more active role in the communication process. They are deciding what communications they want to receive and how they want to communicate to others about the market offerings they choose to purchase and use. To reach and influence target markets effectively, holistic marketers are creatively employing multiple forms of communications.

Dove has been a Unilever stalwart for decades, backed by traditional advertising emphasising the brand's benefit of one-quarter moisturising cream and exhorting women to take the seven-day Dove test to discover its effects. A significant shift in strategy occurred for Dove in 2003 with the launch of the Real Beauty campaign, which celebrated 'real women' of all shapes, sizes, ages and colours. The campaign arose from research revealing that only 2 per cent of women *worldwide* considered themselves beautiful. It featured candid and confident images of curvy, full-bodied women – not traditional models. The advertisements promoted Dove skin products such as Intensive Firming Cream, Lotion, and Body Wash. The multimedia campaign was thoroughly integrated. Traditional TV and print advertisements were combined with all forms of new media, such as real-time voting for models on mobile phones and tabulated displays of results on giant billboards. PR was scaled up; paid media were scaled down. The internet was crucial for creating a dialogue with women. A website was launched and supplemented with advertising videos. The Dove 'Evolution' video showed a rapid-motion view of an ordinary-looking woman transformed by make-up artists, hairdressers, lighting and digital retouching to look like a model. When it was uploaded to YouTube by Dove's advertising agency Ogilvy & Mather, it was an instant hit, drawing 2.5 million views. A subsequent advertisement, 'No Age Limit', featuring older, naked women, also aimed for a primarily online audience. Although the campaign sparked much debate, it was credited with boosting Dove sales and share in every country in which it was launched.[1]

Conducted correctly, marketing communications are hugely valuable. This chapter describes how they work, discusses the importance of word-of-mouth marketing and demonstrates what marketing communications can achieve for a company.

It also addresses how holistic marketers combine and integrate marketing communication (IMC). Chapter 20 examines the different forms of mass (non-personal) marketing communications (advertising, sales promotion, events and experiences, and public relations and publicity) and the different forms of personal marketing communications (direct and interactive marketing and personal selling).

The role of marketing communications

Marketing communications are the means by which firms attempt to inform, persuade and remind customers – directly or indirectly – about the brands they market. In a sense, marketing communications represent the 'voice' of the company and its brands, and are the ways in which it can establish a dialogue and build relationships with customers.

Marketing communications also perform many functions for customers. They can inform or show customers how and why a market offering is used, by what kind of person, and where and when. Customers can discover who develops and supplies the market offering and judge the reputation of the company's brand. There could also be an incentive or reward for trial or usage. Marketing communications allow companies to link their brands to other people, places, events, brands, experiences, feelings and things. They can contribute to brand equity – by establishing the brand in long-term memory and creating a brand image – as well as drive sales and affect shareholder value.[2]

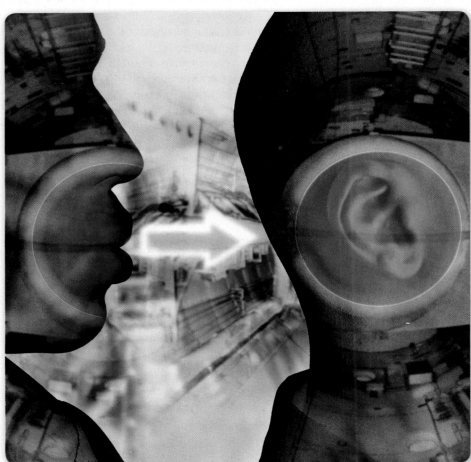

Go forth and tell: the importance of effective communication
Source: Serif.

The changing marketing communication environment

Although marketing communications can play a number of crucial roles, they must do so in an increasingly difficult environment. Technology and other factors have profoundly changed the way customers process information and whether they choose to process it at all. The rapid diffusion of powerful broadband internet connections, advertising-skipping digital video recorders, multipurpose mobile phones, and portable music and video players have forced marketers to rethink a number of their traditional practices.[3] These dramatic changes have eroded the effectiveness in terms of impact and use of the traditional marketing communication tools.

Two forces have caused the demise of TV advertising, which used to be the most powerful means of communicating effectively with customers. One is the fragmentation of target audiences and the other is the advent of digital technology and the internet. As a result, prime-time TV advertisement ratings and press advertisement circulations have shown a downward trend since the 1970s.

What *is* new is the proliferation of media and entertainment options – from hundreds of cable and satellite TV and radio stations and thousands of magazines and webzines to numerous websites, blogs, video games and mobile phone screens. Marketers have a wide selection of media to use and consumers have a choice about whether and how they want to receive commercial content. Additionally, digital or personal video recorders (DVR/PVRs), which allow consumers to eliminate commercials with the push of a fast-forward button, are part of the second force that is lessening the effectiveness of the 30-second TV advertising spot.

However, as some marketers flee the traditional media options, they still encounter challenges. Commercial *clutter* (i.e. confusion or *noise* caused by multiple messages in multiple media) is rampant. As consumers become increasingly selective both in their choice of media and in the messages that appeal, marketers are continually being challenged in their attempts to gain their attention. The average city dweller is now exposed to between 3,000 and 5,000 advertising messages a day. Advertisements are on the back of bus tickets, parking vouchers and plastic carrier bags. Brand logos are designed to be worn on the outside of clothing or shoes (e.g. the Timberland logo and Nike's swoosh). Advertisements in almost every medium and form have been on the ascendancy and some consumers feel they are becoming increasingly invasive.[4]

Marketing communications, brand equity and sales

In this new communications environment, although advertising is often a central element of a marketing communications programme, it is usually not the only one – or even the most important one – in terms of building brand equity and boosting sales.

Marketing communications mix

The **marketing communications mix** consists of eight major modes of communication:[5]

1 **Advertising**: any paid form of non-personal presentation of ideas, goods or services by an identified sponsor.
2 **Sales promotion**: a variety of short-term incentives to encourage trial or purchase of a product/service (market offering).
3 **Events and experiences**: company-sponsored activities and programmes designed to create daily or special brand-related interactions.
4 **Public relations and publicity**: a variety of programmes designed to present or protect a company's image or its individual market offerings.
5 **Direct marketing**: use of mail, telephone, fax, email or the internet to communicate directly with or solicit response or dialogue from specific customers and prospects.
6 **Interactive marketing**: online activities and programmes designed to engage customers or prospects and directly or indirectly raise awareness, improve image or elicit sales of market offerings (value packages, i.e. combinations of products and service attributes).

Table 19.1 Common communication platforms

Advertising	Sales promotion	Events and experiences	Public relations and publicity	Direct and interactive marketing	Word-of-mouth marketing	Personal selling
Print and broadcast advertisements	Contests, games, sweepstakes, lotteries	Sports	Press kits	Catalogues	Person to person	Sales presentations
Packaging – outer	Premiums and gifts	Entertainment	Speeches	Mailings	Chatrooms	Sales meetings
Packaging inserts	Sampling	Festivals	Seminars	Telemarketing	Blogs	Incentive programmes
Motion pictures	Fairs and trade shows	Arts	Annual reports	Electronic shopping		Samples
Brochures and booklets	Exhibits	Causes	Charitable donations	TV shopping		Fairs and trade shows
Posters and leaflets	Demonstrations	Factory tours	Publications	Fax		
Directories	Coupons	Company museums	Community relations	Email		
Reprints of advertisements	Rebates	Street activities	Lobbying	Voicemail		
Billboards	Low-interest financing		Identity media	Blogs		
Display signs	Entertainment		Company magazine	Websites		
Point-of-purchase displays	Trade-in allowances					
Audiovisual material	Continuity programmes					
Symbols and logos	Tie-ins					
Videotapes						

7 Word-of-mouth marketing: people-to-people oral, written or electronic communications that relate to the merits or experiences of purchasing and consuming market offerings.

8 Personal selling: face-to-face interaction with one or more prospective purchasers for the purpose of making presentations, answering questions and procuring orders.

Table 19.1 lists several communication platforms. Company communication goes beyond those specific platforms. The market offering's styling and price, the shape and colour of the package, the salesperson's manner and dress, the store decor, the company's stationery – all communicate value that can be perceived by buyers. Every brand contact delivers an impression that can strengthen or weaken a customer's view of the company.[6] So wise firms carefully develop their brands to reflect these customer-perceived values (see Chapter 11).

As Figure 19.1 shows, marketing communications activities contribute to brand equity and drive sales in many ways: by creating awareness of the brand; linking the right associations to the brand image in consumers' long-term memory; eliciting positive brand judgements or feelings; and/or facilitating a stronger consumer–brand connection.

Marketing communication effects

The manner in which brand associations are formed is unimportant. For example, some consumers may have a strong, favourable and unique brand association of Land Rover and identify the vehicle with characteristic concepts of environmental pursuits such as 'outdoors', 'active' and 'rugged' because of exposure to TV advertisements that show the

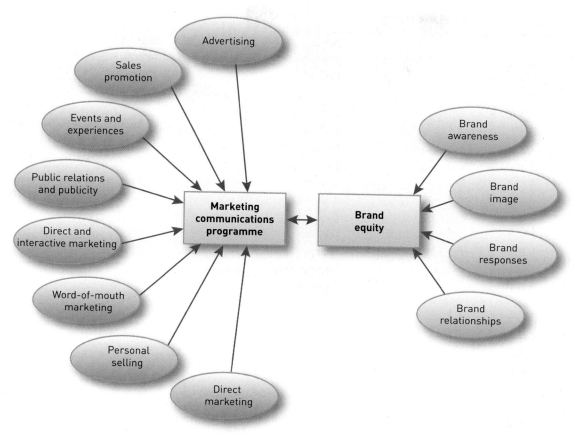

Figure 19.1 Integrating marketing communications to build brand equity

vehicle driving over rugged terrain at different times of the year. Others may prefer a Land Rover because they seek a comfortable vehicle for country roads.

These marketing communications activities must be integrated to deliver a consistent message to achieve the appropriate strategic positioning (see Chapter 10). The starting point in planning marketing communications is an audit of all the potential interactions that customers in the target market may have with the company and all its market offerings. For example, someone interested in purchasing a new laptop computer might talk to others, see television advertisements, read articles, look for information on the internet and look at laptops in a local computer dealership.

Marketers need to assess which experiences and impressions will have the most influence at each stage of the buying process. This understanding will help them allocate the budget for marketing communications more efficiently and to design and implement the right communications programmes. Armed with these insights, marketers can judge marketing communications according to their ability to affect experiences and impressions, build brand equity and drive brand sales. For example, how well does a proposed advertising campaign contribute to awareness or to creating, maintaining or strengthening brand associations? Does sponsorship cause customers to have more favourable brand judgements and feelings? To what extent does a sales promotion encourage consumers to buy more of a market offering?

From the perspective of building brand equity, marketers should be 'media neutral' and evaluate *all* the different possible communication options according to *effectiveness* criteria (how well does it work?) as well as *efficiency* considerations (how much does it cost?). This broad view of brand-building activities is especially relevant when marketers are considering strategies to improve brand awareness.

Anything that causes the consumer to notice and pay attention to a brand – such as sponsorship and advertising – can increase **brand awareness**, at least in terms of brand

Driving on the edge!
Source: Courtesy of Land
Rover.

recognition. To enhance *brand recall*, however, more intense and elaborate processing may be necessary, so that stronger brand links to the market offering, category or customer needs are established to improve memory performance.

The communications process models

Marketers should understand the fundamental elements of effective communications. Two models are useful: a macro- and a micromodel.

Macromodel of the communications process

Figure 19.2 shows a communications macromodel with nine elements. Two represent the major parties in a communication – *sender* and *receiver*. Two represent the major communication tools – *message* and *media*. Four represent major communication functions – *encoding, decoding, response* and *feedback*. The last element in the system is *noise* (random and competing messages that may interfere with the intended communication).

The model emphasises the key factors in effective communication. Senders must know what audiences they want to reach and what responses they want to achieve. They must encode their messages so the target audience can decode them; then transmit the message through media that reach the target audience and develop feedback channels to monitor the responses. The more the sender's field of experience overlaps that of the receiver, the more *effective* the message is likely to be. Note that selective attention, distortion and retention processes – concepts first introduced in Chapter 7 – may be operating during communication.

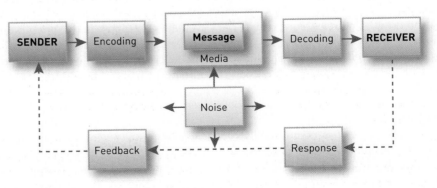

Figure 19.2 Elements in the communication process

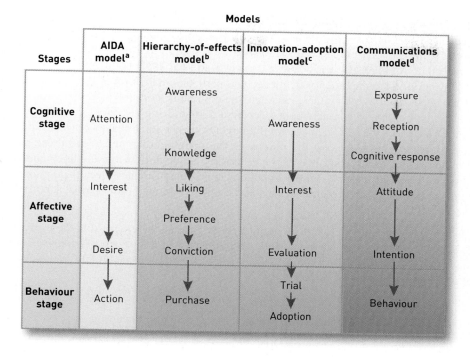

Figure 19.3 Response hierarchy models
Sources: [a]E. K. Strong (1925) *The Psychology of Selling*, New York: McGraw-Hill, 9; [b]R. J. Lavidge and G. A. Steiner (1961) A model for predictive measurements of advertising effectiveness, *Journal of Marketing*, October, 61; [c]E. M. Rogers (1962) *Diffusion of Innovation*, New York: Free Press, 79–86; [d]various sources.

Micromodel of consumer responses

Micromodels of marketing communications concentrate on customers' specific responses to communications. Figure 19.3 summarises four classic *response hierarchy models*.

All these models assume that the buyer passes through a cognitive, affective and behavioural stage, in that order. This 'learn–feel–do' sequence is appropriate when the audience has high involvement with a product (market offering) category perceived to have high differentiation, such as a car or house. An alternative sequence, 'do–feel–learn', is relevant when the audience has high involvement but perceives little or no differentiation within the product category, such as an airline ticket or personal computer. A third sequence, 'learn–do–feel', is relevant when the audience has low involvement and perceives little differentiation within the market offering category, as with salt or batteries. By choosing the right sequence the marketer can fine tune marketing communications.[7]

Assuming that the buyer has high involvement with the market offering category and perceives a high differentiation within it, the *hierarchy-of-effects model* (in the second column of Figure 19.3) sheds valuable light on the development of a marketing communications campaign for a small university named Logos.

- **Awareness.** If most of the target audience is unaware of the object, the communicator's task is to build awareness. Suppose Logos seeks applicants from Europe but has no name recognition there. There are many thousand potential students in Europe who may be interested in studying at Logos. The university might set the objective of making 70 per cent of these students aware of its name within one year by an e-marketing campaign.

- **Knowledge.** The target audience might have brand awareness but not know much more. Logos may want its target audience to know that it is a prestigious institution with excellent programmes in several languages and history. It needs to learn how many people in the target audience have little, some or much knowledge about the university. If knowledge is weak, Logos may decide to select brand knowledge as its main communications objective.

- **Liking.** If target members know the brand, how do they feel about it? If the target audience looks unfavourably on Logos, the communicator needs to find out why. If the unfavourable view is based on real problems, the university will need to attend to these and then communicate anew. Good public relations call for 'good deeds followed by good words'.

- **Preference**. The target audience might quite like Logos but not prefer it to other universities. In this case, the communicator must try to build consumer preference by comparing customer-perceived value (see CPV section in Chapter 11), performance and other attribute features where it can claim to beat likely competitors.
- **Conviction**. A target audience might prefer a particular market offering but not develop a conviction about buying it. In this case the communicator's job is to build conviction and purchase intent among students interested in studying at Logos.
- **Purchase**. Finally, some members of the target audience might have conviction but not quite get around to making the purchase. The communicator must lead these potential customers to take the final step, perhaps by employing 'below-the-line' marketing activity such as press and public relations. Logos might invite selected potential students to visit the campus and attend some classes, or it might offer partial scholarships to deserving students.

To show how fragile the whole communications process is, assume that the probability of *each* of the six steps being successfully accomplished is 50 per cent. The laws of probability suggest that the probability of *all* six steps occurring successfully (assuming they are independent events) is

$$0.5 \times 0.5 \times 0.5 \times 0.5 \times 0.5 \times 0.5$$

which equals 1.5625 per cent. If the probability of each step occurring was, on average, a more moderate 10 per cent, then the joint probability of all six events occurring would be 0.0001 per cent – in other words, only 1 in 1,000,000!

To increase the odds for a successful marketing communications campaign, marketers must attempt to increase the likelihood that *each* step occurs. For example, from an advertising standpoint, the ideal advertising campaign would ensure that:

- The right customer is exposed to the right message at the right place and at the right time.
- The advertisement causes the customer to pay attention to it but does not distract from the intended message.
- The advertisement properly reflects the customer's level of understanding and appreciation of the customer-perceived value of the branded market offering.
- The advertisement correctly positions the brand in terms of desirable and deliverable points-of-difference and points-of-parity.
- The advertisement motivates consumers to consider purchase of the market offering.
- The advertisement creates strong brand associations with all these stored communications effects so that they can have an impact when consumers are considering making a purchase.

Developing effective communications

Effective communications should accomplish four things: establish a *connection*, promise a *reward*, inspire *action* and stick in the *memory*. The Cillit Bang campaign (see Chapter 15) provides a good example of effective communication. Figure 19.4 shows the eight key steps in developing effective communications: identifying the target audience; determining the objectives; designing the communications; selecting the channels; establishing the budget; deciding on the media mix; measuring results; and managing integrated marketing communications.

Identify the target audience

The process must start with a clear target audience in mind: potential buyers of the company's market offerings, current users, deciders or influencers; individuals, groups, particular publics or the general public. The target audience is a critical influence on the communicator's decisions about what to say, how, when, where and to whom.

It is often useful to identify the target audience in terms of any of the market segments identified in Chapter 10 as regards usage and loyalty. Is the target new to the category

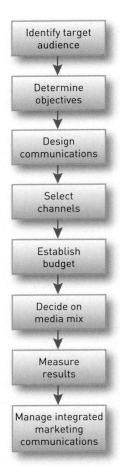

Figure 19.4 Steps in developing effective communications

or a current user? Is the target loyal to the brand, loyal to a competitor, or someone who switches between brands? If a brand user, is he or she a heavy or light user? Communication strategy will differ depending on the answers. An *image analysis* can provide further insight, by profiling the target audience in terms of brand knowledge.

Determine the communications objectives

Marketers can set marketing communications objectives at any level of the hierarchy-of-effects model. Rossiter and Percy identify four possible objectives, as follows:[8]

1 **Category need**: establishing a product/service (market offering) category as necessary to remove or satisfy a perceived discrepancy between a current motivational state and a desired emotional state. A new-to-the-world item, such as electric cars, would always begin with a communications objective of establishing a category need.

2 **Brand awareness**: developing the ability to identify (recognise or recall) the brand within the category in sufficient detail to make a purchase. Recognition is easier to achieve than recall. Brand recall is important outside the store; brand recognition is important inside the store. Brand awareness provides a foundation for brand equity.

3 **Brand attitude**: evaluating the brand with respect to its perceived ability to meet a current relevant need. Relevant brand needs may be negatively oriented (problem removal, problem avoidance, incomplete satisfaction normal depletion) or positively oriented (sensory gratification, intellectual stimulation, social approval). Household cleaning products (market offerings) often use problem solution; food products, on the other hand, often use sensory-oriented advertisements emphasising appetite appeal.

4 **Brand purchase intention**: self-instructions to purchase the brand or to take purchase-related action. Promotional offers in the form of coupons or two-for-one deals encourage consumers to make a mental commitment to buy a product. However, many consumers do not have an expressed category need and may not be in the market when exposed to an advertisement, so they are unlikely to form purchase intentions. For example, in any given week, only about 20 per cent of adults may be planning to buy detergent; only 2 per cent may be planning to buy a carpet cleaner; and only 0.25 per cent may be planning to buy a car.

In most cases, companies are intent on achieving multiple communications objectives.

Design the communications

Formulating the communications to achieve the desired response will require solving three problems: what to say (message strategy), how to say it (creative strategy), and who should say it (message source).

Message strategy

In determining message strategy, management searches for appeals, themes or ideas that will connect with the brand positioning and help to establish points-of-parity or points-of-difference. Some of these may be related directly to purchase and use experience (the quality, economy or value of the brand), whereas others may relate to more extrinsic considerations (the brand as being contemporary, popular or traditional).

Buyers expect one of four types of reward from a market offering: rational, sensory, social or ego satisfaction.[9] Buyers might visualise these rewards from results-of-use experience, product-in-use experience or incidental-to-use experience. Analysing the four types of reward with the three types of experience generates 12 types of message. For example, the appeal 'gets clothes cleaner' is a rational-reward promise following results-of-use experience. The phrase 'real beer taste in a great light beer' is a sensory-reward promise connected with product-in-use experience.

Creative strategy

Communications effectiveness depends on how a message is being expressed, as well as on the content of the message itself. If a communication is ineffective, it may mean the wrong message was used, or the right one was just poorly expressed. *Creative strategies* are the way marketers translate their messages into a specific communication. They can be broadly classified as either *informational* or *transformational appeals*. These two general categories each cover several different specific creative approaches.

Informational appeals An informational appeal elaborates on market offering quality and payment attributes or benefits. Examples in advertising are advertisements that provide a solution (Nurofen stops the toughest headache pain), demonstrate a clear benefit (use Cillit Bang 'and the dirt is gone'), offer product comparison (Sky TV offers the best satellite programmes), and testimonials from unknown or celebrity endorsers, such as famous film stars or sports personalities (Jane Fonda recommending the use of L'Oréal's anti-ageing creams – see Chapter 11). Informational appeals assume very rational processing of the communication on the part of the consumer. Logic and reason rule.

Hovland's research has shed light on informational appeals and their relationship to such issues as conclusion drawing, one-sided versus two-sided arguments and order of argument presentation. Some early experiments supported stating conclusions for the audience. Subsequent research, however, indicates that the best advertisements ask questions and allow readers and viewers to form their own conclusions.[10] Some stimulus ambiguity can lead to a broader market definition and more spontaneous purchases.

It would be logical to assume that presentations which praise a market offering would be more effective than two-sided arguments that also mention shortcomings. Yet two-sided messages may be more appropriate, especially when negative associations must be overcome. Listerine (mouthwash) said 'Listerine tastes bad twice a day.' Two-sided messages are more effective with more educated audiences and those who are initially opposed.[11]

Finally, the order in which arguments are presented is important.[12] In a one-sided message, presenting the strongest argument first has the advantage of arousing attention and interest. This is important in media where the audience often does not attend to the whole message. With a captive audience, a climactic presentation might be more effective. In the case of a two-sided message, if the audience is initially opposed, the communicator might start with the other side's argument and conclude with his or her strongest argument.

Transformational appeals A transformational appeal elaborates on a non-market offering-related benefit or image. It might depict what kind of person uses a brand. Renault presents the Clio model as being attractive to female drivers and the Megane model (with its celebrated derrière) to male drivers. Transformational appeals often attempt to stir up emotions that will motivate purchase.

Communicators use negative appeals such as fear, guilt and shame to get people to do things (brush their teeth, have an annual health check-up) or stop doing things (smoking, alcohol abuse, overeating). Fear appeals work best when they are not too strong, when source credibility is high, and when the communication promises to relieve, in a believable and efficient way, the fear it arouses. Messages are most persuasive when they are moderately discrepant with what the audience believes. Stating only what the audience already believes at best only reinforces beliefs, and if the messages are too discrepant, audiences will counter-argue and disbelieve them.[13]

Communicators also use positive emotional appeals such as humour, love, pride and joy. Motivational or 'borrowed interest' devices – such as the presence of cute babies, attractive puppies (such as in the Andrex advertisements – see Chapter 20), popular music or provocative sex appeals – are often employed to attract consumer attention and raise their involvement with an advertisement. Borrowed-interest techniques are thought to be necessary in the tough new media environment characterised by low-involvement consumer processing and much competing advertisement and programming clutter.

Michelin's use of the Michelin Man brand character in its advertising helps to break through the clutter and reinforce the brand's key safety and trust messages.
Source: Michelin, North America, Inc.

Although these borrowed-interest approaches can attract attention and create more liking and belief in the sponsor, they may also detract from comprehension, wear out their welcome fast and overshadow the product.[14] Benetton, a retailer of colourful and fashionable clothes, attracted considerable attention (but much of it negative) when it posted a series of shocking images featuring graphic scenes of new-born babies, oil-infested seabirds, a man dying of Aids and copulating horses. Attention-getting tactics are often *too* effective and distract from brand claims. The advertisements were considered to be notoriously insensitive and damaged the company's brand image. A real challenge in arriving at the best creative strategy is working out how to 'break through the clutter' or 'noise' in the marketplace to attract the attention of customers – and still deliver the intended message effectively.

The magic of advertising is to bring concepts on a piece of paper to life in the minds of the target customer. In a print advertisement, the communicator must decide on headline, copy, illustration and colour.[15] For a radio message, the communicator must choose words, voice qualities and vocalisations. If the message is to be carried on television or in person, all these elements plus body language (non-verbal clues) must be planned. Presenters need to pay attention to facial expressions, gestures, dress, posture and hairstyle. If the message is carried by the market offering or its packaging, the communicator must pay attention to colour, texture, scent, size and shape.

Message source

Many communications do not use a source beyond the company itself. Others use known or unknown people. Messages delivered by attractive or popular sources can achieve higher attention and recall, which is why advertisers often use celebrities as spokes-people. Celebrities are likely to be effective when they are credible or personify a key market offering attribute. The retired England international footballer and current BBC TV presenter, Gary Lineker, has for years successfully advertised Walkers Crisps. The actress Annette Crosbie is currently advertising Vodafone in the United Kingdom. Tesco, on the other hand, is running TV advertisements that feature a variety of well-known names and voices to boost its image.

Gary Lineker and Jamie Oliver present for Walkers and Sainsbury's

Gary Lineker is regarded by many as being a typical Mr Nice Guy. He has successfully promoted Walkers Crisps for over a decade. For a time the company used his name to promote a sub-brand – Walkers Salt & Lineker (salt and vinegar flavoured crisps). His endorsement greatly helped the company to sell an additional 1.4 billion bags of crisps in seven years.

The celebrity chef Jamie Oliver has promoted Sainsbury's supermarkets in the United Kingdom since 2000. The association increased sales by £1 billion in the first two years and increased Sainsbury's gross profits by £200 million. Jamie has also successfully campaigned in a TV series to persuade the UK government to improve the quality of school meals.[16]

What *is* important is the spokesperson's credibility. What factors underlie source credibility? The three most often identified are expertise, trustworthiness and likeability.[17] *Expertise* is the specialised knowledge that the communicator possesses to back the claim. *Trustworthiness* is related to how objective and honest the source is perceived to be. Friends are trusted more than strangers or salespeople, and those who are not paid to endorse a market offering are viewed as more trustworthy than those who are.[18] *Likeability* describes the source's attractiveness. Qualities such as candour, humour and naturalness make a source more likeable.

Accenture

What better symbol for high performance than Tiger Woods, the world's number-one golfer? That's why business consulting firm, Accenture, was persistent in seeking to use the golfer as the main focus for its rebranding campaign. Enter Tiger Woods and the new tagline 'High performance delivered'. Accenture's message is that it can help client companies become 'high-performing business leaders', like the ones featured on its website. The Woods endorsement drives home the importance of high performance, just as Woods drives home in yet another tournament. The campaign includes advertisements in 27 countries, capitalising on Tiger Woods' international appeal; events and sponsorships that are aligned with the idea of high performance, such as the World Golf Championships; and an interactive website that users can personalise to get information and regular updates relevant to their industry. Accenture has also teamed up with the *Wall Street Journal* to produce a series of articles that explore different facets of high-performance business, written by seasoned journalists and featuring Accenture client companies.[19]

The most highly credible source would score high on all three dimensions – candour, humour and naturalness. Pharmaceutical companies want doctors to testify about product benefits because doctors have high credibility. The boxer George Foreman achieved fame in his recommendation of healthy grills. The marketing insight box on p. 788 focuses on the use of testimonials.

Salton and George Foreman

Salton was a little-known manufacturer of oddball appliances that gained temporary fame in the 1950s with its Salton Hot Tray, an essential item for every wedding list at the time. In the early 1990s, the company introduced an indoor grill that seemed destined for obscurity until two-time heavyweight boxing champion George Foreman chose not only to endorse it, but to join up with the company to sell it. Foreman and his Lean, Mean, Fat-Reducing Grilling Machine were a great success.[20] Since the launch, over 100 million grills have been sold.

George Foreman recommends fat-free grilled food.
Source: Spectrum Brands (UK) Ltd.

If a person has a positive attitude towards a source and a message, or a negative attitude towards both, a state of *congruity* is said to exist. What happens if the person holds one attitude towards the source and the opposite one towards the message? Suppose a customer hears a likeable celebrity praise a brand she dislikes. Osgood and Tannenbaum argue that *attitude change will take place in the direction of increasing the amount of congruity between the two evaluations*.[21] The consumer will end up respecting the celebrity somewhat less or respecting the brand somewhat more. If a person encounters the same celebrity praising other disliked brands, he or she will eventually develop a negative view of the celebrity and maintain negative attitudes towards the brands. The **principle of congruity** implies that communicators can use their good image to reduce some negative feelings towards a brand but in the process might lose some esteem with the audience.

Research at the University of Bath in the United Kingdom suggests that celebrity endorsements are becoming less effective for many market offerings.[22] Another study has shown that both endorser image and brand image serve as mediators in the equity and creation process of celebrity market offering endorsement.[23] UK supermarkets are shifting their advertising strategies away from campaigns featuring celebrities in favour of price promotions. ASDA has frozen its spend at £51 million, and will not commission any more celebrity advertisements that feature the actresses Victoria Wood and Julie Walters and the ex-Arsenal football pundit Ian Wright after 2008. Tesco also seems to be cooling its interest.

Marketing insight

Celebrity endorsements as a strategy

To reinforce its prestigious image, Chanel signed up Nicole Kidman to add a quality mystique to its famous No. 5 perfume.

The choice of the celebrity is critical. The celebrity should have high recognition, high positive affect and high appropriateness to the product. Paris Hilton, Kate Moss and Britney Spears have high recognition but negative affect among many groups. Robbie Williams has high recognition and high positive affect but might not be appropriate for advertising a World Peace Conference. The TV actor Hugh Laurie (of the US soap *House*) and model Claudia Schiffer could successfully advertise a large number of products because they have extremely high ratings for familiarity and likeability (known as the Q factor in the entertainment industry). Hugh Grant is currently promoting the Marie Curie Cancer Care Great Daffodil Appeal to show his gratitude for the care they gave to his late mother.[24]

Celebrities show up everywhere in the advertising of market offerings to children. Familiar cartoon characters are widely used on cereal packets and children's soft drinks. This lasting attraction can be given a boost by the inclusion of celebrity endorsements, even though the young audience does not always know who the celebrity is.[25]

Athletes commonly endorse athletic products, beverages and clothing. One of the premier athletic endorsers has been the US cyclist Lance Armstrong, who battled and beat testicular cancer on his way to winning six consecutive Tour de France championships. He has endorsed a number of bicycle and sports products and companies, including Trek, PowerBar and Nike. Armstrong's improbable 'against all odds' success story also enabled him to win multimillion-dollar endorsement contracts from companies not affiliated with sports, such as Bristol-Myers Squibb pharmaceuticals, Coca-Cola, Subaru and 24 Hour Fitness.

Celebrities can play a more strategic role for their brands, not only endorsing a product but also helping design, position and sell merchandise and services. Since signing Tiger Woods in 1996, Nike has seen its share of the golf ball market grow steadily. Woods has played a key role in developing a series of golf products and apparel that Nike has periodically altered to reflect his changing personality and design tastes.

Using celebrities poses certain risks. The celebrity might demand a larger fee at contract renewal time or withdraw. In common with some films and CDs, celebrity campaigns can sometimes be expensive failures. T-Mobile axed the film actress Catherine Zeta-Jones, citing celebrity fatigue due to her overexposure in the United States. The celebrity might lose popularity or, even worse, get caught in a scandal or embarrassing situation, as did the English film star Hugh Grant and more recently the late pop star Amy Winehouse.

Global adaptations

Multinational companies wrestle with a number of challenges in developing global marketing communications programmes. They must decide whether the market offering is appropriate for a country. They must make sure the market segment they address is both legal and customary. They must decide whether the style of the advertisement is acceptable, and whether advertisements should be created at headquarters or be locally specific.[26]

- **Product (market offering package).** Many items are restricted or forbidden in certain parts of the world. Beer, wine and spirits cannot be advertised or sold in many Muslim countries. Tobacco products are subject to strict regulation in many countries.
- **Market segment.** In Norway and Sweden, for example, TV advertisements may not be directed at children under 12. Sweden lobbied hard to extend that ban to all EU member countries in 2001 but failed. To play it safe, McDonald's advertises itself as a family restaurant in Sweden.
- **Style.** Comparative advertisements, acceptable and even common in the United States and Canada, are less commonly used in the United Kingdom, unacceptable in Japan, and illegal in India and Brazil. The EU seems to have a very low tolerance for comparative advertising, with a Comparative Advertising Directive that prohibits criticising rivals in advertisements.
- **Local or global.** Today, more and more multinational companies are attempting to build a global brand image by using the same advertising in all markets.

Companies that market their products to different cultures or in different countries must be prepared to vary their messages. In advertising its hair care products in different countries, Helene Curtis adjusts its messages. Middle-class British women wash their hair frequently, whereas the opposite is true among Spanish women. Japanese women avoid washing their hair too often for fear of removing protective oils. Car advertisements screened on UK TV often feature cars that are left-hand drive and so risk reducing the impact and positive recall.

Select the communications channels

Selecting efficient means to carry the message becomes more difficult as channels of communication become more fragmented and cluttered. Think of the challenges in the pharmaceutical industry. The industry has had to expand its range of communications channels to include advertisements in medical journals, direct mail (including audio and videotapes), free samples and even telemarketing. Pharmaceutical companies sponsor clinical conferences in which physicians are paid to spend a weekend listening to leading colleagues extol the virtues of their drug portfolios. Pharmaceuticals use all these channels in the hope of building physician preference for their branded therapeutic agent. They are also using new technologies to reach doctors through handheld devices, online services and videoconferencing equipment.[27]

Communications channels may be personal and non-personal and in each category there are many sub-channels. The best advice is to focus on connecting the company's cause to its targeted audience's values rather than telling people to value the company's cause – and reach people when they are in the best place, time and state of mind to get the best impact for the marketing communications budget. Put another way, a successful mantra is *concentrate and inundate* rather than *spray and pray*.

Personal communications channels

Personal communications channels let two or more persons communicate face-to-face, person-to-audience, over the telephone or through email. Instant messaging and independent sites to collect consumer reviews are another channel and one of growing importance in recent years. Personal communication channels derive their effectiveness through individualised presentation and feedback.

A further distinction can be made between advocate, expert and social communications channels. *Advocate channels* consist of company salespeople contacting buyers in the target market. *Expert channels* consist of independent experts making statements to target buyers. *Social channels* consist of neighbours, friends, family members and associates talking to target buyers. In a study of 7,000 consumers in seven European countries, 60 per cent said they were influenced to use a new brand by family and friends.[28]

Marketers have discovered that one influential person's word of mouth tends to affect the buying attitudes of two other people, on average. That circle of influence, however, jumps to eight online. Considerable consumer-to-consumer communication takes place on the web on a wide range of subjects. Online visitors also increasingly create product information, not just consume it. They join internet interest groups to share information, so that 'word of Web' is joining 'word of mouth' as an important buying influence. Word about good companies travels fast; word about bad companies travels even faster. As one marketer noted, 'You don't need to reach 2 million people to let them know about a new product – you just need to reach the right 2,000 people in the right way and they will help you reach 2 million.'[29]

Personal influence carries an especially great weight in two situations. One occurs when items are expensive, risky or purchased infrequently. The other arises when purchases may suggest something about the user's status or taste. People often ask others for a recommendation for a doctor, plumber, hotel, lawyer, accountant, architect, insurance agent, interior decorator or financial consultant. If they have confidence in the recommendation, they normally act on the referral. In such cases, the recommender has potentially benefited the provider as well as the customer. Service providers clearly have a strong interest in building referral sources that are prepared to recommend their high levels of customer-perceived satisfaction. Research indicates that 30–50 per cent of all brand switching occurs as a result of personal recommendation, as against 20 per cent for advertising, promotions and personal search.[30]

Word of mouth

Word of mouth (WOM) has been defined as an interpersonal communication of products/services (market offerings) where the receiver regards the communicator as impartial. Both positive and negative word of mouth has been shown by research to have a substantial impact on firms' fortunes and should be regularly monitored.[31] Markets can be regarded as conversations. The London School of Economics and Political Science and the Listening Company Agency found in a 2005 survey of a random sample of 1,256 adult consumers in the United Kingdom that WOM advocacy was a significant predictor of annual sales growth. Companies earning higher levels of WOM advocacy, such as HSBC, Asda, O2 and Honda, returned higher growth in the research period than their less fortunate competitors. Companies returning poor WOM scores at the time included Lloyds-TSB, Fiat and T-Mobile.[32]

Social networks, such as Facebook and Twitter, have become an important force in both business-to-consumer and business-to-business marketing. A key aspect of social networks is word of mouth and the number and nature of conversations and communications between different parties. Although many are media and entertainment items such as films, TV shows, publications, food items, travel offers and retail stores, many others are often mentioned. Although mega-networks such as Facebook and Twitter can provide the most exposure, niche social networks have the potential to spread the message more effectively to a targeted market segment.

Companies are becoming increasingly aware of the potential of word of mouth. Brands such as Hush Puppy shoes, Pret A Manger and the feature film *The Passion of Christ* benefited considerably through strong WOM, as have the reputations of Amazon, The Body Shop and Red Bull. In some cases word of mouth happens naturally with little support advertising, but in many cases it is managed and facilitated. It is particularly effective for smaller businesses with which customers may develop a more personal relationship. To facilitate goodwill many companies are seeking to form online virtual communities to forge and strengthen customer relationships.

Buzz and viral marketing

Some marketers highlight two particular forms of word of mouth – **buzz** and **viral marketing**. (See also Chapter 4.)

Buzz marketing generates excitement, creates publicity and conveys new relevant brand-related information through unexpected or even outrageous means. The advertiser reveals information about the market offering (product or service package) to only a few 'knowing' people in the target audience. By purposely seeking out one-to-one conversations with those who heavily influence their peers, buzz marketers create a sophisticated word-of-mouth campaign where consumers are flattered to be included in the elite group of those 'in the know' and willingly spread the word to their friends and colleagues.

Viral marketing is another form of word of mouth that encourages consumers to pass on company-developed impressions of company offers to others online.[33] By exploiting the power of peer-to-peer advertising, brands are able to raise their awareness and achieve valuable dwell time through attracting the full attention of their audience for minutes rather than seconds. This is undoubtedly a major strength of advertising online, when compared with most other traditional media.

The success of viral marketing is often based on the concept of 'cool' – if a recipient enjoys the content of an email, they will pass it on to their friends or colleagues.

Furthermore, if something is seen as particularly informative or useful, the same rule applies. A *buzz* can be created around a new product or service at a relatively low cost, by distributing a cleverly constructed campaign to a specific and targeted database of internet users. These can include funny videos, entertaining microsites, games, special offers, interesting stories or images that are passed around the online community.

If a viral campaign is based on offensive or controversial content, advertisers must be aware that this can damage brands. Essentially, what makes a successful viral campaign is intelligently created and delivered content in keeping with the values and tone of a brand's communications strategy. The classic example of successful viral marketing is MSN's Hotmail free email service. The company gave away free email addresses. At the end of every message it added the tag 'Get your private, free email at http://www.hotmail.com/'.

Opinion leaders

Communication researchers propose a social structure view of interpersonal communication. They see society as consisting of *cliques*, small groups whose members interact frequently. Clique members are similar and their closeness facilitates effective communication but also insulates the clique from new ideas. The challenge is to create more openness so that cliques exchange information with others in society. This can be helped by people who function as *liaisons* and connect two or more cliques without belonging to either, and *bridges*, people who belong to one clique and are linked to another. Companies can take several steps to stimulate personal influence channels to work on their behalf. The marketing memo describes some techniques.

Blogs

Regularly updated online journals or diaries have become an important outlet for word of mouth. They vary widely – some are personal for close friends and families, others are designed to appeal to and reach a large audience. Internet users are increasingly reading blogs, but many still regard market offer information from corporate websites as being more trustworthy. Procter & Gamble is a noteworthy user of this digital channel, encouraging users to participate in the development of its portfolio of brands.[34] (See also Chapter 4.)

Marketing memo

How to start a buzz fire

Marketers can take a number of positive steps to increase the likelihood of securing positive word-of-mouth advantages.

- **Identify influential individuals and companies and devote extra effort towards them.** Purchase influencers such as checkout counter staff and user focus groups can be contacted. In business-to-business markets, large corporate customers, industry analysts and journalists can be encouraged to spread the word.

- **Supply key 'influencers' with samples.**

- **Work with local influencers such as radio presenters and TV journalists.**

- **Develop word-of-mouth referral channels to build business.** Businesses can encourage customers to recommend them to others by offering incentives such as a saving on their next purchase.

- **Provide compelling information that customers want to tell friends and professional communities.**

Source: S. Moldavan, J. Goldenberg and A. Chattopadhyay (2006) What drives word of mouth? The roles of product quality and usefulness, MSI Report No. 06-111, Cambridge, MA: Marketing Science Institute. Also consider M. Hughes (2005) *Buzzmarketing: Get Your People to Talk About Your Stuff*, Harmondsworth: Penguin/Portfolio.

Non-personal communications channels

Non-personal channels are communications directed to more than one person and include media, sales promotions, events and experiences, and public relations.

- **Media**: consist of print media (newspapers and magazines); broadcast media (radio and television); network media (telephone, cable, satellite, wireless); electronic media (audiotape, videotape, videodisk, CD-ROM, web page); and display media (billboards, signs, posters). Most non-personal messages come through paid media.
- **Sales promotions**: consist of consumer promotions (such as samples, coupons and premiums); trade promotions (such as advertising and display allowances); and business and sales force promotions (contests for sales representatives).
- **Events and experiences**: include sports, arts, entertainment and 'good cause' events as well as less formal activities that create novel brand interactions with consumers.
- **Public relations**: include communications directed internally to employees of the company or externally to consumers, other firms, the government and media.

Much of the recent growth of non-personal channels has taken place through *events and experiences*. A company can build its brand image by creating or sponsoring events. Events marketers who once heavily favoured sports events are now using other venues such as art museums, zoos or ice shows to entertain clients and employees. HSBC and IBM sponsor symphony performances and art exhibits; and Harley-Davidson sponsors annual motorcycle rallies. Many famous consumer brands, e.g. Coca-Cola, Visa, Lloyds TSB, McDonald's, signed up to sponsor the 2012 Olympic Games in London.

Companies continually seek better ways to quantify the benefits of sponsorship and demand greater accountability from event owners and organisers. They are also creating events designed to surprise the public and create a buzz. Many amount to guerrilla marketing tactics. But if not done properly, they can backfire and have unintended consequences.

The increased use of attention-getting events is a response to the fragmentation of the media: people can turn to hundreds of cable channels, thousands of magazine titles and

Billboards can capture the attention of large audiences.
Source: Chris P. Batson/Alamy.

Guerrilla marketing – getting noticed

Guerrilla marketing is an unconventional approach originally intended to assist small businesses to get them noticed in markets where the conventional media are cluttered. It is now increasingly being used by large businesses to achieve an instant impact. People in Parliament Square in London were either amused or shocked one night in 1999 when they saw that a 60-foot high image of the actress Gail Porter's bare backside had been projected on to the Houses of Parliament. The deed was perpetrated by the magazine *FHM* to promote its poll to find the sexiest women in town. Although of short duration the stunt was successful, leading to increased sales of the magazine and boosting advertising revenue. Less outrageous have been the attention-seeking activities of firms such as First Group, National Van Rental and Thameslink.

Whilst the *FHM* magazine stunt amused many, Unilever suffered some bad WOM as a result of an internet guerrilla attack. Raunchy images from a commercial for its Lynx body spray were sliced into a Dove video urging parents to protect girls from negative images of women.[35]

millions of internet pages. Events can create attention, although whether they have a lasting effect on brand awareness, knowledge or preference will vary considerably, depending on the quality of sponsored products, the event itself, and its execution.

Integration of communications channels

Although one-to-one communication is often more effective than mass communication, mass media are the major means of communicating to large target audiences. Mass communications affect personal attitudes and behaviour through a two-step process. Ideas often flow from radio, television and print to opinion leaders, and from these to the less media-involved population groups. This two-step flow has several implications. First, the influence of mass media on public opinion is not as direct, powerful and automatic as marketers have supposed. It is mediated by opinion leaders, people whose opinions others seek, or who carry their opinions to others. Secondly, the two-step flow challenges the notion that consumption styles are primarily influenced by a 'trickle-down' or 'trickle-up' effect from mass media. People interact primarily within their own social groups and acquire ideas from opinion leaders in their groups. Thirdly, two-step communication suggests that mass communicators should direct messages specifically to opinion leaders and let them carry the message to others.

Establishing the total marketing communications budget

One of the most difficult marketing decisions is determining how much to spend on marketing communication. Expenditure might be 40–45 per cent of sales in the cosmetics industry and 5–10 per cent in the industrial equipment industry. Within a given industry, there are low- and high-spending companies. How do companies decide their budget? The most common methods are briefly described below.

Affordable method

Many companies set the budget at what they think the company can afford. The affordable method completely ignores the role of marketing communication as an investment and its potential impact on sales volume. It leads to an uncertain annual budget, which makes long-range planning difficult.

Percentage-of-sales method

Many companies set their budget at a specified percentage of sales (either current or anticipated) or of the sales price. Car manufacturers typically budget a fixed percentage for marketing communication based on the planned car price. Oil companies set the appropriation at a small fraction of a euro for each litre of petrol sold under their own label.

Supporters of the percentage-of-sales method see a number of advantages. First, expenditure will vary with what the company can afford. This satisfies financial managers, who believe expenses should be closely related to the movement of corporate sales over the business cycle. Secondly, it encourages management to think of the relationship between the cost of marketing communications, selling price and profit per unit. Thirdly, it encourages stability when competing firms spend approximately the same percentage of their sales on marketing communication.

In spite of these advantages, the percentage-of-sales method has little to justify it. It views sales as the determinant of marketing communication rather than as the result. It leads to a budget set by the availability of funds rather than by market opportunities. It discourages experimentation with countercyclical campaigns or aggressive spending. Dependence on year-to-year sales fluctuations interferes with long-range planning. There is no logical basis for choosing the specific percentage, except what has been done in the past or what competitors are doing. Finally, it does not encourage building the marketing communications budget by determining what each product (market offering) and territory deserves.

Competitive parity method

Some companies set their budgets to achieve share-of-voice parity with competitors. There are two supporting arguments. One is that competitors' expenditures represent the collective wisdom of the industry. The other is that maintaining competitive parity prevents *promotion* marketing communication wars. Neither argument is valid. There are no grounds for believing that competitors know better. Company reputations, resources, opportunities and objectives differ so much that budgets are hardly a guide. Furthermore, there is no evidence that budgets based on competitive parity discourage marketing communication wars.

Objective-and-task method

The objective-and-task method calls upon marketers to develop budgets by defining specific objectives, determining the tasks that must be performed to achieve these objectives, and estimating the costs of performing these tasks. The sum of these costs is the proposed budget.

For example, if a company wants to introduce a new market offering, it needs to:[36]

1 Establish the market share goal.
2 Determine the percentage of the market that should be reached.
3 Determine the percentage of aware prospects that should be persuaded to try the brand.
4 Determine the number of advertising impressions per 1 per cent trial rate.
5 Determine the number of gross rating points that would have to be purchased.
6 Determine the necessary marketing communications budget on the basis of the average cost of buying a gross rating point.

The objective-and-task method has the advantage of requiring management to declare its assumptions about the relationship between the amount spent, exposure levels, trial rates and regular usage.

A major question is how much weight marketing communications should receive in relation to alternatives such as market offering (product/service) improvement, lower prices or better service. The answer depends on where the company's market offerings/products are in their life cycles (see Chapter 11), whether they are commodities or highly differentiable products, whether they are routinely needed or must be 'sold', and other considerations. Marketing communications budgets tend to be higher when there is low channel support, considerable change in the marketing programme over time, many hard-to-reach customers, more complex customer decision making, differentiated products/

services and non-homogeneous customer needs, and frequent product purchases in small quantities.[37]

Other methods focus on financial considerations.

Modelling

This uses a variety of econometric and simulation techniques to model how various spend levels will affect performance in terms of awareness rating, revenue flow and profitability. An example is Unilever's AMTES market-testing model.

Payback period

This calculates the amount of exposure time needed to redeem the budgeted cost of the marketing communications.

Profit optimisation

This seeks to track the point at which the marginal revenue from the spend exceeds the marginal costs. While fine in theory, this approach is very difficult to implement in highly competitive markets, although hindsight can provide important lessons.

Ideally and in theory, marketing managers should establish the total marketing communications budget so that the marginal profit from the last communication euro just equals the marginal profit from the last euro in the best communication cases. Implementing this principle, however, is virtually impossible as customers' responses are influenced by a host of dynamic variables, many of which are beyond the control of marketing management.

Deciding on the marketing communications mix

Companies must allocate the marketing communications budget over the eight major modes of communication – advertising, sales promotion, public relations and publicity, events and experiences, direct marketing, interactive marketing, word-of-mouth marketing, and the sales force. Within the same industry, companies can differ considerably in their media and channel choices. The Avon cosmetics company concentrates its budget on personal selling, whereas Revlon spends heavily on advertising. Electrolux spent heavily on a door-to-door sales force for years, whereas Hoover has relied more on advertising. The Breakthrough marketing box shows how Ocean Spray has used a variety of marketing communication vehicles to turn its sales fortunes around.

Companies are always searching for ways to gain efficiency by replacing one marketing communication tool with others. Many companies are replacing some field sales activity with advertisements, direct mail and telemarketing.

Characteristics of the marketing communications mix

Each marketing communication tool has its own unique characteristics and costs. These are briefly reviewed here and discussed in more detail in Chapter 20.

Advertising

Advertising reaches geographically dispersed buyers. It can build up a long-term image for a product (for example, Cadbury's Dairy Milk advertisements) or trigger quick sales (the DFS furniture upholstery advertisements in the United Kingdom). Certain forms of advertising such as TV can require a large budget, whereas other forms such as newspapers do not. Just the presence of advertising might have an effect on sales: consumers might believe that a heavily advertised brand must offer 'good value'.[38] Because of the many

Breakthrough marketing

Ocean Spray

Ocean Spray faced a tough situation in 2004. Domestic sales had been flat for five years and sales in the juice category as a whole suffered from concerns over sugar, increased competition from other types of beverage that were adding juice, and growing consumer interest in consumption of other beverage such as water and sports drinks. Cranberry juice was known among women as an effective way to keep the urinary tract healthy – not necessarily a product benefit with broad appeal.

Ocean Spray, an agricultural cooperative of growers of cranberries in the United States, decided to make use of expert marketing consultancy to arrest the decline in sales. The cranberry was repositioned as a 'surprisingly versatile little fruit that supplies modern-day benefits', through a true '360-degree' campaign that used all facets of marketing communications to reach consumers in a variety of settings. The intent was to support the full range of market offerings – cranberry sauce, fruit juices, and dried cranberries in different forms.

The advertising strategy promoted the unique DNA of the Ocean Spray Cooperative and the realisation that the heart of the brand was born in the cranberry bogs and remained there still. The agency decided to focus on the bog to tell an authentic, honest and perhaps surprising story dubbed 'Straight from the bog'. The campaign was designed also to reinforce two key brand benefits – that Ocean Spray products tasted good and were good for you.

PR played a crucial role. Miniature bogs were brought to New York and were featured on a local TV show (*NBC Today*) morning segment. The event reached over 23 million people through related media pick-up. A 'Bogs across America Tour' brought the experience to Los Angeles, Chicago and even London. Television and print advertising featured two natural-looking and natural-sounding growers (depicted by actors) standing waist deep in a bog talking, often humorously, about what they did. The advertisements were the highest rated ever for Ocean Spray and improved both awareness and persuasion for the two key benefits.

Despite a decline in sales of the entire fruit juice category, Ocean Spray's inventive campaign grew sales of all its cranberry products by a remarkable 10 per cent.

Source: Photographer William Huber. Used by permission of Ocean Spray Cranberries, Inc.

The campaign also included a website, in-store displays and external events for consumers as well as internal ones for members of the growers' cooperative itself. The campaign hit the mark, lifting sales by 10 per cent despite continued decline in the fruit juice category.

Sources: L. Peterson (2006) Breakaway brands: Ocean Spray tells it straight from the bog, *MediaPost*, 9 October; F. J. Kelly III and B. Silverstein (2005) *The Breakaway Brand*, New York: McGraw-Hill.

forms and uses of advertising, it is difficult to make generalisations about it.[39] Yet a few observations are worthwhile:

- **Pervasiveness**. Advertising permits the seller to repeat a message many times. It also allows the buyer to receive and compare the messages of various competitors. Large-scale advertising says something positive about the seller's size, power and success.
- **Amplified expressiveness**. Advertising provides opportunities for dramatising the company and its products/service offerings through the artful use of print, sound and colour.
- **Impersonality**. The audience does not feel obligated to pay attention or respond to advertising. Advertising is a monologue in front of, not a dialogue with, the audience.

Sales promotion

Companies use sales promotion tools – coupons, contests, premiums, and so on – to draw a stronger and quicker buyer response, including short-run effects such as highlighting product offers and boosting sagging sales. Sales promotion tools offer three distinctive benefits:

1 **Communication.** They gain attention and may lead the consumer to the product.
2 **Incentive.** They incorporate some concession, inducement or contribution that gives value to the consumer.
3 **Invitation.** They include a distinct invitation to engage in the transaction now.

Public relations and publicity

Marketers tend to underuse public relations, yet a well-thought-out programme coordinated with the other marketing communications mix elements can be extremely effective, especially if a company needs to challenge consumers' misconceptions.

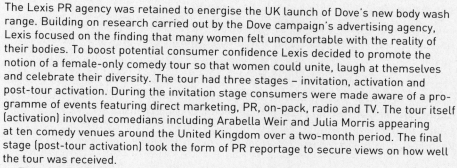

Dove: comedy tour

The Lexis PR agency was retained to energise the UK launch of Dove's new body wash range. Building on research carried out by the Dove campaign's advertising agency, Lexis focused on the finding that many women felt uncomfortable with the reality of their bodies. To boost potential consumer confidence Lexis decided to promote the notion of a female-only comedy tour so that women could unite, laugh at themselves and celebrate their diversity. The tour had three stages – invitation, activation and post-tour activation. During the invitation stage consumers were made aware of a programme of events featuring direct marketing, PR, on-pack, radio and TV. The tour itself (activation) involved comedians including Arabella Weir and Julia Morris appearing at ten comedy venues around the United Kingdom over a two-month period. The final stage (post-tour activation) took the form of PR reportage to secure views on how well the tour was received.

The tour was a great success with both the media and consumers. The PR platform generated PR coverage from 13 national sources, 57 regional sources, 6 women's consumer titles, 5 **advertorials**, 18 competitions, 59 pieces of broadcast coverage and 25 pieces of online coverage. Consumers who attended the events were given samples (2,500). The news value of the campaign created further post-tour 'talkability' in the media.[40]

The appeal of public relations and publicity is based on three distinctive qualities:

1 **High credibility.** News stories and features are more authentic and credible to readers than advertisements.
2 **Ability to catch buyers off guard.** Public relations can reach prospects who prefer to avoid salespeople and advertisements.
3 **Dramatisation.** Public relations has the potential for dramatising a company's market communication activities.

Events and experiences

There are many advantages to events and experiences, among which are:

1 **Relevance.** A well-chosen event or experience can be seen as highly relevant because the consumer gets personally involved.
2 **Involvement.** Their live, real-time quality means that, events and experiences are more actively engaging for consumers.
3 **Implicitness.** Events are an indirect 'soft sell'.

Direct and interactive marketing

Direct and interactive marketing takes many forms – over the phone, online or in person. They share three distinctive characteristics. Direct and interactive marketing messages are:

1 **Customised.** The message can be prepared to appeal to the addressed individual.
2 **Up to date.** A message can be prepared very quickly.
3 **Interactive.** The message can be changed depending on the person's response.

Word-of-mouth marketing

Word of mouth also takes many forms online or offline. Three noteworthy characteristics are that it is:

1 **Credible.** Because people trust others they know and respect, word of mouth can be highly influential.
2 **Personal.** Word of mouth can be a very intimate dialogue that reflects personal facts, opinions and experiences.
3 **Timely.** It occurs when people want it to and when they are most interested, and it often follows noteworthy or meaningful events or experiences.

Personal selling

Personal selling is the most effective tool in later stages of the buying process, particularly in building up buyer preference, conviction and action. Personal selling has three distinctive qualities:

1 **Personal interaction.** Personal selling creates an immediate and interactive episode between two or more persons. Each party is able to observe the other's reactions.
2 **Cultivation.** Personal selling also permits all kinds of relationships to spring up, ranging from a matter-of-fact selling relationship to a deep personal friendship.
3 **Response.** The buyer feels under some obligation following the sales talk.

Factors in setting the marketing communications mix

Companies must consider several factors in developing their communications mix: type of market offering, consumer readiness to make a purchase, and stage in the traditional product life cycle. Also important is the company's market ranking.

Type of market

Communications mix allocations vary between consumer and business markets. Consumer marketers tend to spend comparatively more on sales promotion and advertising; business marketers tend to spend comparatively more on personal selling. In general, personal selling is used more with complex, expensive and risky purchases and in markets with fewer and larger sellers (hence, business markets).

Although marketers use advertising less than sales calls in business-to-business markets, advertising still plays a significant role:

• Advertising can provide an introduction to the company and its product portfolio.
• If the product/service offering has new features, advertising can explain them.
• Reminder advertising is more economical than sales calls.
• Advertisements offering brochures and carrying the company's phone number are an effective way to generate leads for sales representatives.
• Sales representatives can use copies of the company's advertisements to legitimise their company and its product/service offerings.
• Advertising can remind customers how to use and benefit from product/service offerings and reassure them about their purchase.

A number of studies have underscored advertising's role in business-to-business markets. Corporate advertising can improve a company's reputation and improve the sales force's chances of obtaining a favourable first hearing and early adoption of the product.[41] It can also help to position or reposition a business-to-business market offering.

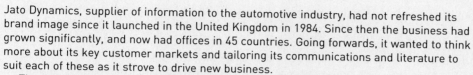

Jato Dynamics

Jato Dynamics, supplier of information to the automotive industry, had not refreshed its brand image since it launched in the United Kingdom in 1984. Since then the business had grown significantly, and now had offices in 45 countries. Going forwards, it wanted to think more about its key customer markets and tailoring its communications and literature to suit each of these as it strove to drive new business.

There is a general perception that if there's a choice of 'evolution' or 'revolution' then branding companies will go for the less risky visual 'revolution'. Classic examples of the suitability of both are the visual histories of BP and Shell. BP's one big change triggered by merger and repositioning, and Shell's nine visual updates since 1990 (an average of one every two years) symbolise a reaction to change. Both could argue that they are right.[42]

Personal selling can also make a strong contribution in consumer goods marketing. Some consumer marketers use the sales force mainly to collect weekly orders from dealers and to see that sufficient stock is on the shelf. Yet an effectively trained company sales force can make four important contributions:

1 **Increased stock position.** Sales representatives can persuade dealers to take more stock and devote more shelf space to the company's brand.
2 **Enthusiasm building.** Sales representatives can build dealer enthusiasm by dramatising planned advertising and sales promotion back-up.
3 **Missionary selling.** Sales representatives can sign up more dealers.
4 **Key account management.** Sales representatives can take responsibility for growing business with the most important accounts.

Buyer readiness stage

Marketing communication tools vary in cost effectiveness at different stages of buyer readiness. Figure 19.5 shows the relative cost effectiveness of three marketing communication tools. Advertising and publicity play the most important roles in the awareness-building stage. Customer comprehension is primarily affected by advertising and

Figure 19.5 Cost effectiveness of three different communication tools at different buyer readiness stages

personal selling. Customer conviction is influenced mostly by personal selling. Closing the sale is influenced mostly by personal selling and sales promotion. Reordering is also affected mostly by personal selling and sales promotion, and somewhat by reminder advertising.

Product life cycle stage

Communication tools also vary in cost effectiveness at different stages of the product life cycle (see Chapter 14). In the introduction stage, advertising, events and experiences, and publicity have the highest cost effectiveness, followed by personal selling to gain distribution coverage, and sales promotion and direct marketing to induce trial. In the growth stage, demand has its own momentum through word of mouth. In the maturity stage, advertising, events and experiences, and personal selling all become more important. In the decline stage, sales promotion continues to be strong, other marketing communication tools are reduced, and salespeople give the product only minimal attention.

Measuring marketing communication results

Senior managers want to know the *outcomes* and *revenues* resulting from their marketing communications investments. Too often, however, their marketing communications specialists supply only *outputs* and *expenses*: press clipping counts, numbers of advertisements placed and media costs. In fairness, the specialists try to report progress in terms such as reach and frequency, recall and recognition scores, persuasion changes and cost-per-thousand calculations. Ultimately, however, behaviour change measures capture the reward from effective marketing communications activity.

After implementing the marketing communications plan, specialists must measure its impact on the target audience. Members of the target audience are asked whether they recognise or recall the message, how many times they saw it, what points they recall, how they felt about the message, and their previous and current attitudes towards the product and the company. The specialist should also collect behavioural measures of audience response, such as how many people bought the product/service offer, liked it and talked to others about it.

Figure 19.6 provides an example of good feedback measurement. In this case 80 per cent of customers in the total market are aware of brand A, 60 per cent have tried it, and only 20 per cent who have tried it are satisfied. This indicates that the marketing communications programme is effective in creating awareness, but the market offering fails to meet consumer expectations. In contrast, 40 per cent of the consumers in the total market are aware of brand B, and only 30 per cent have tried it, but 80 per cent of those who have tried it are satisfied. In this case, the marketing communications programme needs to be strengthened to take advantage of the brand's power.

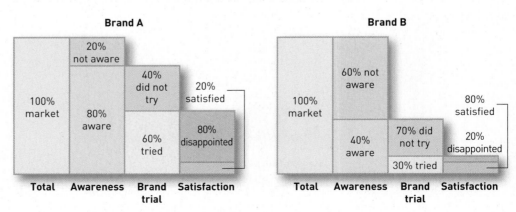

Figure 19.6 Current consumer states for two brands

Managing the integrated marketing communications process

As defined by the American Association of Advertising Agencies, **integrated marketing communications** (IMC) is a concept of marketing communications planning that recognises the added value of a comprehensive plan. Such a plan evaluates the strategic roles of a variety of marketing communications disciplines – for example, general advertising, direct response, sales promotion and public relations – and combines these disciplines to provide clarity, consistency and maximum impact through the seamless integration of messages. Nike has adopted the IMC concept and its vice-president for global and category management has gone on record saying that 'We create demand for our brand by being flexible about how we tell the story. We do not rigidly stay with one approach . . . We have an integrated marketing model that involves all elements of the marketing mix'.[43]

Unfortunately, many companies still rely on one or two marketing communication tools. This practice persists in spite of the fragmenting of mass markets into a multitude of minimarkets, each requiring its own approach; the proliferation of new types of media; and the growing sophistication of customers. The wide range of marketing communication tools, messages and audiences makes it imperative that companies move towards integrated IMC practice. However, despite its potential many firms seem to be slow to accept it seriously.[44] Companies must adopt a '360-degree view' of themselves and consumers to understand fully all the different ways that marketing communications can affect consumer behaviour and so benefit their businesses.

Media companies and advertising agencies are expanding their capabilities to offer multi-platform deals for marketers. For example, newspapers and magazines have been formulating digital strategies, such as adding videos to their homepages, to increase advertising revenue. In the United Kingdom, the *Daily Telegraph* and *Financial Times*, for instance, offer online video segments on their websites carrying topic, news and advertising material. These expanded capabilities make it easier for marketers to assemble various media properties in an IMC programme.

Coordinating media

Media coordination can occur across and within media types, but marketers should combine personal and non-personal marketing communications channels to achieve maximum impact. Imagine a marketer using a single tool in a 'one-shot' effort to reach and sell to a prospect. An example of a *single-vehicle, single-stage campaign* is a one-time mailing offering a cookware item. A *single-vehicle, multiple-stage campaign* would rely on successive mailings to the same prospect. Magazine publishers, for example, send about four renewal notices to a household before giving up. A more powerful approach is the *multiple-vehicle, multiple-stage campaign*. Consider the sequence in Figure 19.7.

Multiple media deployed within a tightly defined time frame can increase message reach and impact. This strategy is commonly seen in the marketing of financial services. Research has also shown that sales promotions can be more effective when combined with advertising.[45] The awareness and attitudes created by advertising campaigns can improve the success of more direct sales pitches. Many companies are coordinating their

Figure 19.7 Example of a multiple-vehicle, multiple-stage communication campaign

online and offline marketing communications activities. Listing web addresses in advertisements (especially print ones) and on packages allows people to explore a company's wares more fully, find store locations and get market offering information. For example, Danone makes it a priority to drive traffic to its Danone Yogurt homepage, so the company can benefit from the twin paybacks of (1) forging direct relationships with customers; and (2) building a database of its best customers, whose loyalty can be strengthened with more targeted coupon and direct mail promotional efforts.[46] When Dutch financial services firm ING Group launched its brand into other European countries, it paired TV and print advertisements with online advertisements.

Implementing IMC

IMC has been slow to take hold for several reasons. Large companies often employ several different communications specialists who may know comparatively little about the other marketing communication tools.[47] A Further complicating matter is that many global companies use a large number of advertising agencies located in different countries and serving different divisions, resulting in uncoordinated marketing communications and image diffusion. One company that has managed to coordinate the integrated marketing effort of a number of agencies and internal departments is British Gas.

British Gas

British Gas holds twice-monthly planning meetings with all the agencies working on various aspects of an integrated marketing campaign – from the advertising agency to the PR agency to the company's own internal communications department. These different factions are 'integrated' because British Gas retains them on a project basis and assigns a budget to a specific business initiative rather than to a media channel. Bringing planners from various disciplines together in an open forum to discuss their views shatters their preconceptions. In a recent British Gas campaign around energy efficiency, the company used this collaborative approach and logged 1 million responses from people who wanted to learn more about the issue. A spokesperson commented, 'We all got behind the single objective and message, starting with advertising, and followed by direct and online marketing. But integration is not just about marketing communications. It is about everything from PR to the service experience to internal communications.'[48]

Today, however, a few large agencies have substantially improved their integrated marketing communications provision. To facilitate one-stop shopping, major advertising agencies have acquired sales promotion agencies, public relations firms, package-design consultancies, website developers and direct mail houses. These agencies are redefining themselves as *marketing communications companies* that assist clients to improve their overall marketing communications effectiveness by offering strategic and practical advice on many forms of IMC. Many international clients have opted to put a substantial portion of their IMC work through one full-service agency. An example is IBM turning all its advertising over to Ogilvy to attain uniform branding. The result is integrated and more effective marketing communications at a much lower total communications cost.

IMC can produce stronger message consistency and help to build brand equity and create greater sales impact.[49] It forces management to think about every way the customer comes into contact with the company, how the company communicates its positioning, the relative importance of each vehicle, and timing issues. It gives someone the responsibility – where none existed before – to unify the company's brand images and messages as they progress through a host of company activities. IMC should improve the company's ability to reach the right customers with the right messages at the right time and in the right place.[50]

Quo vadis?

In today's buyers' markets, consumers expect quality and price attributes offered by companies to meet and – preferably – exceed their CPV requirements (see Chapter 11). They expect firms to deliver a desirable customer experience by integrating information technology, branding, communications and entertainment. The progression from the traditional FMCG marketing and branding approach towards *experiential marketing* is a key theme that is discussed in Chapter 21.

The marketing memo provides some guidelines.

Marketing memo

How integrated is your IMC programme?

In assessing the collective impact of an IMC programme, the marketer's overriding goal is to create the most effective and efficient marketing communications programme possible. The following six criteria can help determine whether marketing communications are truly integrated:

1 **Coverage.** Coverage is the proportion of the audience reached by each communication option employed, as well as how much overlap exists among communication options. In other words, to what extent do different communication options reach the designated target market and the same or different consumers making up that market?

2 **Contribution.** Contribution is the inherent ability of a marketing communication to create the desired response and communication effects from consumers in the absence of exposure to any other marketing communication option. How much does marketing communication affect consumer processing and build awareness, enhance image, elicit responses and induce sales?

3 **Commonality.** Commonality is the extent to which *common* associations are reinforced across communication options: that is, the extent to which information conveyed by different marketing communication options shares meaning. The consistency and cohesiveness of the brand image is important because it determines how easily existing associations and responses can be recalled and

how easily additional associations and responses can become linked to the brand in memory.

4 **Complementarity.** Marketing communication options are often more effective when used in tandem. Complementarity relates to the extent to which *different* associations and linkages are emphasised across marketing communication options. Different brand associations may be most effectively established by capitalising on those marketing communication options best suited to eliciting a particular consumer response or establishing a particular type of brand association.[51]

5 **Versatility.** In any integrated marketing communication programme, when consumers are exposed to a particular marketing communication, some will already have been exposed to other marketing communications for the brand, and some will not have had any prior exposure. Versatility refers to the extent to which a marketing communication option is robust and 'works' for different groups of consumers. The ability of a marketing communication to work at two levels – effectively communicating to consumers who have or have *not* seen other communications – is critically important.

6 **Cost.** Marketers must weigh evaluations of marketing communications on all these criteria against their cost to arrive at the most effective *and* efficient communications programme.

Source: Keller, Kevin, *Strategic Brand Management*, 3rd edn, © 2008 Printed and electronically reproduced by permission of Pearson Education, Inc., Upper Saddle River, NJ.

SUMMARY

1 Modern marketing calls for more than developing a good product, pricing it attractively and making it accessible to target customers. Companies must also communicate with present and potential stakeholders and with the general public.

2 The marketing communications mix consists of eight major modes of communication: advertising, sales promotion, public relations and publicity, events and experiences, direct marketing, interactive marketing, word-of-mouth marketing and personal selling.

3 The communications process consists of nine elements: sender, receiver, message, media, encoding, decoding, response, feedback and noise. To get their messages through, marketers must encode their messages in a way that takes into account how the target audience usually decodes messages. They must also transmit the message through efficient media that reach the target audience and develop feedback channels to monitor response to the message.

4 Developing effective communications involves eight steps: (1) identify the target audience; (2) determine the communications objectives; (3) design the communications; (4) select the communications channels; (5) establish the total communications budget; (6) decide on the communications mix; (7) measure the communications results; and (8) manage the integrated marketing communications process.

5 In identifying the target audience, the marketer needs to close any gap that exists between current public perception and the image sought. Communications objectives may involve category need, brand awareness, brand attitude or brand purchase intention.

Formulating the communication requires solving three problems: what to say (message strategy), how to say it (creative strategy), and who should say it (message source). Communications channels may be personal (advocate, expert and social channels) or non-personal (media, atmospheres and events). The objective-and-task method of setting the promotion budget, which calls upon marketers to develop their budgets by defining specific objectives, is the most desirable.

6 In deciding on the marketing communications mix, marketers must examine the distinct advantages and costs of each communication tool and the company's market rank. They must also consider the type of product market in which they are selling, how ready consumers are to make a purchase, and the product's stage in the product life cycle. Measuring the effectiveness of the marketing communications mix involves asking members of the target audience whether they recognise or recall the communication, how many times they saw it, what points they recall, how they felt about the communication, and their previous and current attitudes towards the product and the company.

7 Managing and coordinating the entire communications process calls for integrated marketing communications: marketing communications planning that recognises the added value of a comprehensive plan which evaluates the strategic roles of a variety of communications disciplines and combines these disciplines to provide clarity, consistency and maximum impact through the seamless integration of discrete messages.

APPLICATIONS

Marketing debate

Has TV advertising lost power? Long deemed the most successful medium, television advertising has received increased criticism for being too expensive and, even worse, no longer as effective as it used to be. Critics maintain that consumers tune out too many advertisements and that it is difficult to make a strong impression. The future, claim some, is with online advertising. Supporters of TV advertising disagree, contending that the multisensory impact of TV is unsurpassed and that no other media option offers the same potential impact.

Take a position: TV advertising has faded in importance *versus* TV advertising is still the most powerful advertising medium.

Marketing discussion

Pick a brand and go to its website. Locate as many forms of communication as you can find. Conduct an informal communications audit. What do you notice? How consistent are the different communications?

REFERENCES

[1]R. Rothenberg (2007) Dove effort gives packaged-goods marketers lessons for the future, *Advertising Age*, 5 March; T. Howard (2005) Ad campaign tells women to celebrate who they are, *USA Today*, 8 July; J. Neff (2004) In Dove ads, normal is the new beautiful, *Advertising Age*, 27 September; www.campaignforrealbeauty.com.

[2]X. Luo and N. Donthu (2006) Marketing's credibility: a longitudinal investigation of marketing communication productivity and shareholder value, *Journal of Marketing*, 70 (October), 70–91; P. C. Patel (2010) Measurement of brand equity of brand India, *Journal of Marketing and Communication*, 5(3), 12–15.

[3]D. Kiley (2005) Hey advertisers, TiVo is your friend, *BusinessWeek*, 17 October, 97–8; K. L. Keller (2009) Building strong brands in a modern marketing communications environment. *Journal of Marketing Communications*, 15 (2/3), 139–155; G. Simmons, B. Thomas and Y. Truong (2010) Managing i-branding to create brand equity, *European Journal of Marketing*, 44(9/10), 1260–85.

[4]L. Story (2007) Anywhere the eye can see, it's likely to see an ad, *New York Times*, 15 January; L. Petrecca (2006) Product placement: you can't escape it, *USA Today*, 11 October; Y. Yi-Hsin and Z. Jie (2010) The third-person perception and privacy-invasive advertising messages on social networking sites, *American Academy of Advertising Conference Proceedings*, 118.

[5]Some of these definitions are adapted from P. D. Bennett (ed.) (1995) *Dictionary of Marketing Terms*, Chicago: American Marketing Association.

[6]T. Duncan and S. Moriarty (2006) How integrated marketing communications 'touch points' can operationalize the service-dominant logic, in R. F. Lusch and S. L. Vargo (eds), *The Service-Dominant Logic of Marketing: Dialog, Debate, and Directions*, Armonk, NY: M. E. Sharpe; T. Duncan (2005) *Principles of Advertising and IMC*, 2nd edn, New York: McGraw-Hill/Irwin; F. Harrison (2009) Unravelling the Gordian knot of brand contact, *Market Leader*, (Fall) 46, 38–41.

[7]D. Vakratsas and T. Ambler (1999) How advertising works: what do we really know? *Journal of Marketing*, 63(1), 26–43.

[8]This section is based on J. R. Rossiter and L. Percy (1997) *Advertising and Promotion Management*, 2nd edn, New York: McGraw-Hill.

[9]J. F. Engel, R. D. Blackwell and P. W Minard (2001) *Consumer Behavior*, 9th edn, Fort Worth, TX: Dryden.

[10]C. I. Hovland, A. A. Lumsdaine and F. D. Sheffield (1948) *Experiments on Mass Communication*, Princeton, NJ: Princeton University Press, Volume 3, Chapter 8.

[11]H. E. Crowley and W. D. Hoyer (1994) An integrative framework for understanding two-sided persuasion, *Journal of Consumer Research*, March, 561–74; M. Eisend (2010) Explaining the joint effect of source credibility and negativity of information in two-sided messages, *Psychology and Marketing*, 27(11), 1032–49. For an alternative viewpoint see G. E. Belch (1983) The effects of message modality on one and two-sided advertising messages, in R. P. Bagozzi and A. M. Tybout (eds), *Advances in Consumer Research*, Ann Arbor, MI: Association for Consumer Research, 21–6.

[12]C. P. Haugtvedt and D. T. Wegener (1994) Message order effects in persuasion: an attitude strength perspective, *Journal of Consumer Research*, June, 205–18: H. R. Unnava, R. E. Burnkrant and S. Erevelles (1994) Effects of presentation order and communication modality on recall and attitude, *Journal of Consumer Research*, December, 48–90; S. Lijiang (2010) Mitigating psychological reactance: the role of message-induced empathy in persuasion,. *Human Communication Research*, 36(3), 397–42; C-T. Chang and Y-K. Lee (2010) Effects of message framing, vividness congruency and statistical framing on responses to charity advertising, *International Journal of Advertising*, 29(2), 195–220.

[13]M. R. Solomon, *Consumer Behavior*, 7th edn, Upper Saddle River, NJ: Prentice Hall.

[14]Some recent research on humour in advertising, for example, includes H. Shabbir and D. Thwaites (2007) The use of humor to mask deceptive advertising: it's no laughing matter, *Journal of Advertising*, 36 (Summer), 75–85; T. W. Cline and J. J. Kellaris (2007) The influence of humor strength and humor message relatedness on ad memorability: a dual process model, *Journal of Advertising*, 36 (Spring), 55–67; H. Shanker Krishnan and D. Chakravarti (2003) A process analysis of the effects of humorous advertising executions on brand claims memory, *Journal of Consumer Psychology*, 13(3), 230–45.

[15]R. Pieters and M. Wedel (2004) Attention capture and transfer in advertising: brand, pictorial, and text-size effects, *Journal of Marketing*, 68 (April), 36–50; L. M. Wakolbinger, M. Denk and K. Oberecker (2009) The effectiveness of combining online and print advertisements, *Journal of Advertising Research*, 49(3), 360–72; E. Plakoyiannaki and Y. Zotos (2009) Female role stereotypes in print advertising, *European Journal of Marketing*, 43(11/12), 1411–34; B. Kyunghee, K. Donghoon Kim and L. Seung-yon (2009) Determinants of visual forms used in advertising, *International Journal of Advertising*, 28(1), 13–47; J. E. Fisher, B. D. Till and S. M. Stanley (2010) Signaling trust in print advertisements: an empirical investigation, *Journal of Marketing Communications*, 16(3), 133–147.

[16]www.celebrityendorsements.co.uk; A. Byrne, M. Whitehead and S. Breen (2003) The naked truth of celebrity endorsement, *British Food Journal*, 105(4/5), 288–96; R. Adams and J. Finch (2003) Take one celebrity chef, *Guardian*, 1 January.

[17]H. C. Kelman and C. I. Hovland (1953) Reinstatement of the communication in delayed measurement of opinion change, *Journal of Abnormal and Social Psychology*, 48 (July), 327–35. See also K. O'Quinn (2009) The elements of persuasion: three principles that will strengthen any appeal, *Public Relations Tactics*, 16(2), 20.

[18]D. J. Moore, J. C. Mowen and R. Reardon (1994) Multiple sources in advertising appeals: when product endorsers are paid by the advertising sponsor, *Journal of the Academy of Marketing Science*, Summer, 234–43; A. B. Bower and S. L. Grau (2009) Explicit donations and inferred endorsements, *Journal of Advertising*, 38(3), 113–26.

[19]www.accenture.com; M. E. Podmolik (2004) Accenture turns to Tiger for global marketing effort, *BtoB*, 89(12), 25 October; S. Callahan (2003) Tiger tees off in new Accenture campaign, *BtoB*, 88(11), 13 October.

[20]J. Sloane (2003) Gorgeous George, *Fortune Small Business*, June, 36.

[21]C. E. Osgood and P. H. Tannenbaum (1995) The principles of congruity in the prediction of attitude change, *Psychological Review*, 62 (January), 42–55.

[22]Celebrity endorsements less effective for many products, says research, Press Release, 27 February 2007, Bath, England: University of Bath (www.bath.ac.uk/news/2007/2/27/celebrity-ads.html).

[23]M. Callow and L. Schiffman (2002) Implicit meaning in visual print advertisements: a cross-cultural examination of the contextual communication effect, *International Journal of Advertising*, 21(2), 259–77; D. Seno and B. A. Lukas (2007) The equity effect of product endorsement by celebrities: a conceptual framework, from a co-branding perspective, *European Journal of Marketing*, 41(1/2), 121–34.

[24]L. Carter (2008) Hugh Grant backs Marie Curie cancer case appeal in his mother's memory, *Daily Telegraph*, 25 February.

[25]A. Sherwin (2004) It's crunch time for cartoon adverts, *The Times*, 23 July.

[26] R. Snoddy (2004) WPP brings local touch to global operations, *The Times*, 12 January; L. Eagle, P. J. Kitche and S. Bulmer (2007) Insights into interpreting integrated marketing communications: a two-nation qualitative comparison, *European Journal of Marketing*, 41(7/8), 956–70; C. Dianoux and Z. Linhart (2010) The effectiveness of female nudity in advertising in three European countries, *International Marketing Review*, 27(5), 562–78.

[27]Rebirth of a salesman, *The Economist*, 14 April 2001.

[28]M. Kiely (1993) Word-of-mouth marketing, *Marketing*, September, 6. See also E. M. Rodger (2003) *Diffusion of Innovation*, 5th edn, New York: Free Press; A. Rindfleisch and C. Moorman (2001) The acquisition and utilization of information in new product alliances: a strength-of-ties perspective, *Journal of Marketing*, April, 1–18; R. East, K. Hammond, W. Lomax and H. Robinson (2005) What is the effect of a recommendation?, *Marketing Review*, 5(2), 145–57.

[29]I. Mount (2001) Marketing, *Business 2.0*, August–September, 84.

[30]P. R. Smith and J. Taylor (2004) *Marketing Communications: An Integrated Approach*, 4th edn, London: Kogan Page, 590; K. Nagar (2009) Evaluating the effect of consumer sales promotions on brand loyal and brand switching segments. *Vision (09722629)*, 13(4), 35–48; S. K. Lam, M. Ahearne, Y. Hu and N. Schillewaert (2010) Resistance to brand switching when a radically new brand is introduced: a social identity theory perspective, *Journal of Marketing*, 74 (6), 128–46.

[31]D. Stokes and W. Lomax (2002) Taking control of word of mouth marketing: the case of an entrepreneurial hotelier, *Journal of Small Business and Enterprise Development*, 9(4), 349–57; F. F. Reichheld (2003) The one number you need to grow, *Harvard Business Review* (December), 47–54; S. Y. Hong and S-U Yang (2009) Effects of reputation, relational satisfaction, and customer-company identification on positive word-of-mouth intentions, *Journal of Public Relations Research*, 21(4), 381–403; R. Lee and J. Romaniuk (2009) Relating switching costs to positive and negative word of mouth, *Journal of Consumer Satisfaction, Dissatisfaction and Complaining Behavior*, 22, 54–67; J. Berger, A. T. Sorensen and S. J. Rasmussen (2010) Positive effects of negative publicity: when negative reviews increase sales, *Marketing Science*, 29(5), 815–27; S. Bambauer-Sachse and S. Mangold (2011) Brand equity dilution through negative online word-of-mouth communication, *Journal of Retailing and Consumer Services*, 18(1), 38-45.

[32]J. Kirby and P. Marsden (2005) *Connected Marketing: The Viral Buzz and Word of Mouth Revolution*, London: Butterworth-Heinemann; J. Bughin, J. Doogan and O. J. Vetvik (2010) A new way to measure word of mouth marketing, *McKinsey Quarterly*, no. 2, 113–16.

[33]A good working definition of viral marketing can be found in A. Vilpponen, S. Winter and S. Sundqvist (2006) Electronic word-of-mouth in online environments: exploring referral network structure and adoption behaviour, *Journal of Interactive Advertising*, 6(2), 71–86 ; O. Toubia, A. T. Stephen and A. Freud (2009) Viral marketing: a large-scale field experiment, *INSEAD Working Papers Collection*, 48, 1–39; E. M. Notarantomo (2009) The effectiveness of a buzz marketing approach compared to traditional advertising: an explanation, *Journal of Promotion Management*, 15(4), 455–64.

[34]G. Silverman (2006) How can I help you?, *Financial Times*, 4 February, 16–21.

[35]C. Mortished (2007) Internet guerrilla attack exposes Unilever's 'hypocrisy' of Dove girls and dirty dancers, *The Times*, 3 December; M. Dahlén (2009) The consumer-perceived value of non-traditional media: effects of brand reputation, appropriateness and expense, 26 (3), 155–63; A. Roy and S. P. Chattopadhyay (2010) Stealth marketing as a strategy, *Business Horizons*, 53(1), 69–79.

[36]Adapted from G. Maxwell Ule (1957) A media plan for 'sputnik' cigarettes, *How to Plan Media Strategy*, American Association of Advertising Agencies, Regional Convention, 41–52; D. West and G. P. Prendergast (2009) Advertising and promotions budgeting and the role of risk, *European Journal of Marketing*, 43(11/12), 1457–76.

[37]T. C. Kinnear, K. L. Bernhardt and K. A. Krentler (1995) *Principles of Marketing*, 6th edn, New York: HarperCollins.

[38]K. Sridhar Moorthy and S. A. Hawkins (2005) Advertising repetition and quality perceptions, *Journal of Business Research*, 58 (March), 354–60; A. Kirmani and A. R. Rao (2000) No pain, no gain: a critical review of the literature on signaling unobservable product quality, *Journal of Marketing*, 64 (April), 66–79; L. Binet and P. Field (2009) Empirical generalizations about advertising campaign success,. *Journal of Advertising Research*, 49(2), 130–3.

[39]D. Vakratsas and T. Ambler (1999) How advertising works: what do we really know?, *Journal of Marketing*, 63(1), 26–43; L. Wood (2009) Short-term effects of advertising: some well-established empirical law-like patterns, *Journal of Advertising Research*, 49(2), 186–192; G. J. Tellis (2009) Generalizations about advertising effectiveness in markets, *Journal of Advertising Research*, 49(2), 240–5; R. Pieters, M. Wedel and R. Batra, (2010) The stopping power of advertising: measures and effects of visual complexity, *Journal of Marketing*, 74(5), 48–60.

[40]www.lexispr.com/case/show/52

[41]J. M. T. Balmer and S. A. Greyser (2006) Corporate marketing: integrating corporate identity, corporate branding, corporate communications, corporate image and corporate reputation, *European Journal of Marketing*, 40(7/8), 730–41; G. O'Malley (2006) Who's leading the way in web marketing? It's Nike, of course, *Advertising Age*, October, D3; M. Banham (2010) Reckitt Benckiser adspend aids profits,. *Marketing (00253650)*, 28 July, 3; R. Peterson and J. Jeong (2010) Exploring the impact of advertising and R&D expenditures on corporate brand value and firm-level financial performance, *Journal of the Academy of Marketing Science*, 38(6), 677–90.

[42]C. Weekes (2007) Jato Dynamics needed to rev up its image and show its motor industry customers that it was moving with the times, *B2B Marketing* online, 14 May.

[43]D. E. Schultz and H. E.Shultz (2003) *IMC the next generation*, New York: McGraw-Hill. Strategic Direction (2006) The importance of marketing strategy: gaining the competitive edge with integrated marketing communications, General Review, *Strategic Direction*, 22(8), 23–5.

[44]P. A. Naik, K. Raman and R. S. Winer (2005) Planning marketing-mix strategies in the presence of interaction effects, *Marketing Science*, 24 (January), 25–34; G. Hughes and C. Fill (2007) Redefining the nature and format of the marketing communications mix, *Marketing Review*, 7(1), 45–57; E. Luck and J. Moffatt (2009) IMC: has anything really changed? A new perspective on an old definition, *Journal of Marketing Communications*, 15(5), 311–25.

[45]E. Schultz and C. H. Patti (2009) The evolution of IMC: IMC in a customer-driven marketplace,. *Journal of Marketing Communications*, 15(2/3), 75–84.

[46]G. Khermouch (2003) The top 5 rules of the ad game, *Business-Week*, 20 January, 72–3.

[47]T. Duncan and F. Mulhern (eds) (2004) *A White Paper on the Status, Scope, and Future of IMC*, New York: McGraw-Hill; O. Holm (2006) Integrated marketing communication: from tactics to strategy, *Corporate Communications: An International Journal*, 11(1), 23–33; P. J. Kitchen (2005) New paradigm: IMC under fire, *Competitiveness Review: An International Journal of Global Competitiveness*, 15(1), 72–80; L. T. Christenson, S. Torp and A. F. Fuat (2005) Integrated marketing communication and postmodernity: an odd couple, *Corporate Communications: An International Journal*, 10(2), 156–67.

[48] S. Bashford (2006) Collaboration is imperative, *Marketing*, 13 December, 4.

[49]S. Madhavaram, V. Badrinarayanan and R. E. McDonald (2005) Integrated marketing communication (IMC) and brand identity as critical components of brand equity strategy, *Journal of Advertising*, 34 (Winter), 69–80; M. Reid, S. Luxton and F. Mavondo (2005) The relationship between integrated marketing communication, market orientation, and brand orientation, *Journal of Advertising*, 34 (Winter), 11–2; S. Mishra and S. Muralie (2010) Managing dynamism of IMC – anarchy to order, *Journal of Marketing and Communication*, 6(2), 29–37.

[50]D. E. Schultz and H. Schultz (2003) *IMC, The Next Generation: Five Steps for Delivering Value and Measuring Financial Returns*, New York: McGraw-Hill; A. Finne and C. Grönroos (2009) Rethinking marketing communication: from integrated marketing communication to relationship communication, *Journal of Marketing Communications*, 15(2/3), 179–95.

[51]K. L. Keller (2009) Building strong brands in a modern marketing communications environment, *Journal of Marketing Communications*, 15(2/3), 139–55; C. R. Taylor (2010) Integrated marketing communications in 2010 and beyond, *International Journal of Advertising*, 29(2), 161–4.

Chapter 20

Managing mass and personal communications

IN THIS CHAPTER, WE WILL ADDRESS THE FOLLOWING QUESTIONS:

1 What steps are required in developing an advertising programme?

2 How should sales promotion decisions be made?

3 What are the guidelines for effective brand-building events and experiences?

4 How can companies exploit the potential of public relations and publicity?

5 How can companies integrate direct marketing for competitive advantage?

6 How can companies practise effective interactive marketing?

7 What decisions do companies face in designing and managing a sales force?

8 How can salespeople improve their selling, negotiating and relationship marketing skills?

The iconic Andrex Labrador Retriever puppy has been the focus of the Andrex brand's mass and personal communications since 1972, designed to emphasise the attractiveness of Andrex's super-soft luxury toilet tissue.
Source: © Justin Kase z12z/Alamy.

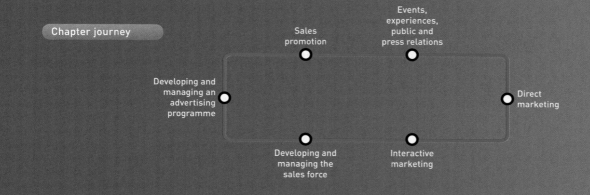

Sales promotion

Events, experiences, public and press relations

Developing and managing an advertising programme

Direct marketing

Developing and managing the sales force

Interactive marketing

Although there has been an increase in the use of personal communications by marketers in recent years (due to the rapid penetration of the internet and other factors), mass media, if used correctly, can still dramatically improve the fortunes of a brand or company.[1] Today, marketing communications increasingly occur as a kind of personal dialogue between the company and its customers. Companies must ask not only 'How should we reach our customers?' but also 'How should our customers reach us?' and even 'How can our customers reach each other?' Technological advances allow people and companies to communicate with each other through the internet, fax machines, mobile phones, pagers and wireless appliances. By increasing communication effectiveness and efficiency, new technologies have encouraged companies to move from mass communication to more targeted, two-way communications. Consumers now play a much more participatory role in the marketing process.

Kimberly-Clark, the owner of the leading Andrex brand, is the world's largest toilet tissue manufacturer. Since 1972 Andrex has featured an iconic Labrador Retriever puppy in its mass and personal marketing communications strategy. The memorable image of the puppy has been used to convey key value attributes. The luxury two-ply tissue is soft, strong and very long. In addition, it is family friendly. According to a poll published in September 2007, the Andrex puppy has become the UK's favourite TV advertising animal. The appeal of the bouncy, friendly puppy has enabled Kimberly-Clark over the years to develop a powerful sales promotion programme. The puppy has its own website, which offers a collection of items including fridge magnets, shoulder bags, toys, a calendar, mouse mat, screen saver, and competitions and interactive games. Over one and a half a million rolls of Andrex are used every day in the United Kingdom. Kimberly-Clark invested £2.5 million in 2007 on the launch of an even longer toilet tissue. The new longer-lasting toilet tissue branded Andrex Quilts is the only quilted roll on the market and features three plush white layers made into a light and airy quilt that combines the quality attributes of the regular Andrex toilet tissue with 50 per cent more sheets. Such is the popularity of the Andrex puppy that in September 2007 it was inducted into the famous London Wax Museum of Madame Tussauds.[2]

Some firms have had great success with advertising, but other marketers are trying to master how best to use mass media in the new communication environment.[3] This chapter examines the nature and use of four mass communication tools – advertising, sales promotion, events and experiences, and public relations and publicity – and how companies personalise their marketing communications. Personalising communications and creating dialogues by saying and doing the right thing to the right person at the right time is critical for marketing. The main elements of the personal communications mix are direct and interactive marketing, personal selling and the sales force.

Developing and managing an advertising programme

Advertising is any paid form of non-personal presentation and communication of market offerings (i.e. customer perceived value product/service packages) by an identified sponsor. Its realistic task is not to change what people think about your brand, which is always hard to achieve, but to have them think *about* your brand. As Dr Johnson said almost 300 years ago, 'Men more frequently require to be reminded than informed.' Advertisements are a cost-effective way to communicate messages. Even in today's challenging media environment, good advertisements can generate sales. Advertisements for Olay Definity anti-ageing products and Head & Shoulders Intensive Treatment shampoo helped both brands enjoy double-digit sales gains in recent years.

In developing an advertising programme, marketing managers must always start by identifying the target market and buyers' motives. Then they can make the five major decisions, known as 'the five Ms': *Mission*: What are our advertising objectives? *Money*: How much can we spend? *Message*: What message should we send? *Media*: What media should we use? *Measurement*: How should we evaluate the results? These decisions are summarised in Figure 20.1 and described in the following sections.

Setting objectives

The advertising objectives must flow from prior decisions on target markets (see Chapter 10) and brand positioning (see Chapter 11).

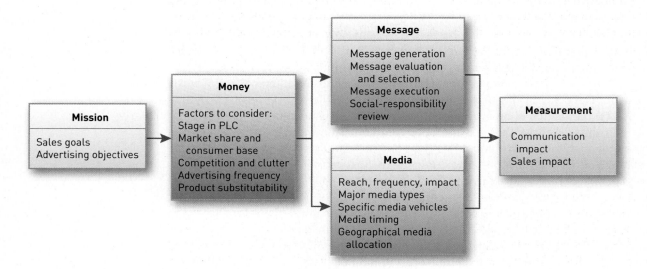

Figure 20.1 The five Ms of advertising

An **advertising goal** (or objective) is a communication targeted at a preselected audience at a specific time to stimulate increased sales. Advertising objectives can be classified according to whether their aim is to inform, persuade, remind or reinforce. These goals correspond to different stages in the *hierarchy-of-effects* model discussed in Chapter 19.

- **Informative advertising**: aims to create brand awareness and knowledge of new products/market offerings or upgraded existing product/market offerings.
- **Persuasive advertising**: aims to create liking, preference, conviction and purchase of a market offering. Some persuasive advertising uses comparative advertising, which makes an explicit comparison of the attributes of two or more brands. The UK supermarket ASDA ran a TV advertisement in which it claimed to offer more and better price reductions than a rival supermarket (Morrisons). However, comparative advertising is not favoured by the EU authorities.
- **Reminder advertising**: aims to stimulate repeat purchase of market offerings. Expensive, four-colour cosmetic advertisements in magazines such as the UK's *Radio Times* and the Sunday newspaper supplements are intended to remind people to purchase such items as skin creams and to invite them to 'love the skin you are in' (Olay).
- **Reinforcement advertising**: aims to convince current purchasers that they made the right choice. Advertisements for cars often depict satisfied customers enjoying special quality and cost attributes of their new car.

The advertising objective should emerge from studying the current marketing situation. If the market offering/product class is mature, the company is the market leader, and brand usage is low, the objective is to stimulate more usage. If the market offering/product class is new, the company is not the market leader, but the brand is superior to the leader, then the objective is to convince the market of the brand's superiority.

Deciding on the advertising budget and developing the advertising campaign

John Wanamaker, a celebrated nineteenth-century department store magnate, once quipped 'Half my advertising is wasted. I just don't know which half.'[4] How does a company know it is spending the right amount? Large consumer-packaged-goods firms tend to overspend on advertising as a form of insurance against not spending enough. On the other hand, business-to-business companies tend to underspend as they underrate the power of advertising as a means to boost their images.

Although advertising is often treated as a current expense, it is really an investment in building brand equity and customer loyalty. When a company spends €5 million on capital equipment, it may treat the equipment as a five-year depreciable asset and write off only one-fifth of the cost in the first year. When it spends €5 million on advertising to launch a new market offering, it is common for management to want to write off the entire cost in the first year.

Factors affecting budget decisions

Here are five specific factors to consider when *setting* the advertising budget.

1 **Stage in the product life cycle.** New market offerings typically merit large advertising budgets to build awareness and to gain consumer trial. Established brands are usually supported with lower advertising budgets, measured as a ratio to sales.
2 **Market share and consumer base.** High-market-share brands usually require less advertising expenditure as a percentage of sales to maintain share. To build share by increasing market size requires larger expenditures.
3 **Competition and clutter.** In a market with a large number of competitors and high advertising spending, a brand must advertise more heavily to be noticed. Even simple distractions ('noise') from advertisements not directly competitive to the brand creates a need for heavier advertising.

4 Advertising frequency. The number of repetitions needed to convey the brand's message to consumers has an obvious impact on the advertising budget.

5 Product substitutability. Brands in less-well-differentiated or commodity-like classes such as beer, soft drinks, banks and airlines require heavy advertising to establish a differential image.

In one study of budget allocation, Low and Mohr found that managers allocated less to advertising as brands moved to the more mature phase of the product life cycle; when a brand was well differentiated from the competition; when managers were rewarded on short-term results; as retailers gained more power; and when managers had less experience with the company.[5]

Advertising elasticity

The predominant response function for advertising is often concave but can be S-shaped. When consumer response is S-shaped, some positive amount of advertising is necessary to generate any sales impact, but sales increases eventually flatten out.[6]

One classic study found that increasing TV advertising budgets had a measurable effect on sales only half the time. The success rate was higher on new market offerings or line extensions than on established brands, and when there were changes in copy or in media strategy (such as an expanded target market). When advertising was successful in increasing sales, its impact lasted up to two years after peak spending. Moreover, the long-term incremental sales generated were approximately double the incremental sales observed in the first year of an advertising spending increase.[7]

Other studies reinforce these conclusions. In a 2004 Information Resource Incorporated (IRI) study of 23 brands, advertising often did not increase sales for mature brands or categories in decline. A review of academic research found that advertising elasticities were estimated to be higher for new (0.3) than for established products (0.1).[8]

In designing and evaluating a campaign, marketers need to combine both art and science creatively to develop the *message strategy* or positioning of an advertisement: *what message* it conveys about the brand, its *creative strategy* and *how* the brand claims are expressed in it. Advertisers typically take three steps: message generation and evaluation; creative development and execution; and social-responsibility review.

Message generation and evaluation

Many advertisements for cars today have a sameness about them – a car drives at high speed on a curved mountain road or across a desert. The result is that only a weak link forms between the brand and the message. Advertisers are always seeking 'the big idea' that connects with consumers rationally and emotionally, sharply distinguishes the brand from competitors, and is broad and flexible enough to translate to different media, markets and time periods. Fresh insights are important for avoiding using the same appeals and positioning as competitors.

A good advertisement normally focuses on one or two core selling propositions. As part of refining the brand positioning, the advertiser should conduct market research to determine which appeal works best with its target audience and then prepare a *creative brief*. This is a development of the *positioning statement* (see Chapter 10) and includes: the key message, target audience, communications objectives (to do, to know, to believe), key brand benefits, supports for the brand promise, and media.

How many alternative themes should the advertiser create before making a choice? The more themes explored, the higher the probability of finding a highly successful one. The use of computers has substantially reduced the costs of advertisement development. Many alternative approaches can be created in a short time by drawing still and video images from computer files. Marketers can also cut costs dramatically by using consumers

Chanel No. 5 can make you look and feel like Nicole Kidman.

Source: Image courtesy of The Advertising Archives.

as their creative team, a strategy sometimes called 'open-source' or 'crowd-sourcing'. However, this technique can be either pure genius or a regrettable failure. Other marketers caution that the open-source model does not work for every company or every market offering. Chanel spent nearly £18 million on a three-minute prestigious TV commercial for its Chanel No. 5 brand, featuring Nicole Kidman, which was screened in the United Kingdom in late 2007.

Creative development and execution

According to Leo Burnett, founder of the famous Chicago-based advertising agency, 'The secret of all effective originality in advertising, is not the creation of new and tricky words and pictures but one of putting familiar words and pictures into new relationships' (www.leoburnett.com). Visual images, sound and motion can be combined to affect viewers' emotions and senses. The advertisement's *impact* depends not only on what it says, but particularly on *how* it says it. Execution can be decisive. Every advertising medium has advantages.

Television advertisements TV is generally acknowledged as the most powerful advertising medium and reaches a broad spectrum of consumers. The wide *reach* translates to low cost per exposure. TV advertising has two particularly important strengths. First, it can be an effective means of vividly demonstrating market offering attributes and persuasively explaining their corresponding consumer benefits. Secondly, it can dramatically portray user and usage imagery, brand personality and other intangibles.

Because of its fleeting nature, however, and the distracting creative elements often found in advertisements, it can sometimes fail to impact effectively. Moreover, the high volume of advertising and non-programming material on TV creates *clutter* ('noise') and advertisements can easily be forgotten or ignored. Despite high production and placement costs, research has shown that the number of viewers who said they paid attention to TV advertisements has dropped significantly in the past decade. Nevertheless, properly designed and executed TV advertisements can improve brand equity and affect sales and profits. A highly inspirational and professional TV commercial is still a powerful marketing tool.

Print advertisements Print media offer a stark contrast to broadcast advertisements. Magazines and newspapers can provide detailed market offering/product information and effectively communicate user and usage imagery. However, the static nature of the visual images in print media makes dynamic presentations or demonstrations difficult. The two main print media – magazines and newspapers – share many advantages and disadvantages. Although newspapers are timely and pervasive, magazines are typically more effective at building user and usage imagery. Although advertisers have some flexibility in designing and placing newspaper advertisements, poor reproduction quality and short shelf-life can diminish their impact.

Format elements, such as size, colour and illustration, also affect a print advertisement's impact. Larger ones gain more attention, though not necessarily by as much as their difference in cost. Four-colour illustrations increase both effectiveness and cost. New electronic eye-movement studies show that consumers can be led through an advertisement by the strategic placement of dominant elements. These are devices to focus the eye on the core values of the offering, such as the softness and length of the Andrex toilet tissue featured in the opening vignette.

Researchers studying print advertisements report that the *picture*, *headline* and *copy* matter in that order. The picture must be interesting enough to draw attention. The headline must reinforce the picture and lead the person to read the copy. The copy must be engaging and the brand's name sufficiently prominent. Even then, less than 50 per cent of the exposed audience will notice even a really outstanding advertisement. About 30 per cent might recall the headline's main point; about 25 per cent will remember the advertiser's name; and fewer than 10 per cent will read most of the body copy. Many advertisements fail to achieve even these results.

Nissan doodles all over London's entertainment pages

Nissan introduced the Qashqai as a competitor to the traditional hatchback with the 'personality of a 4 × 4' to engage a young, urban target audience. The agency art director created the freehand drawings, which embellished images of the Nissan

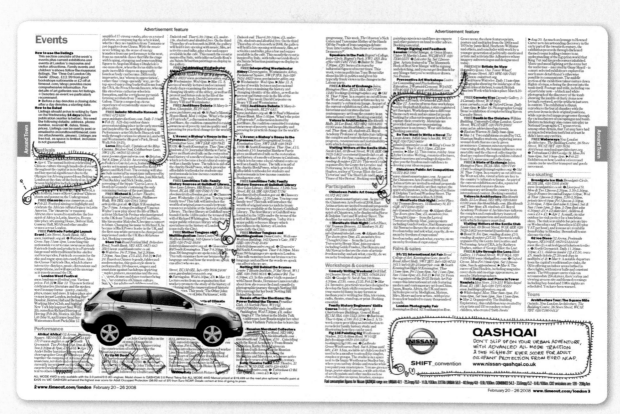

Getting audience attention before a print advertising campaign
Source: Nissan/Agency: TBWA London.

Qashqai with doodles to emphasise individual features. The 2007 campaign was part of an innovative approach to press advertisements for cars that usually featured big glossy advertisements with standard information about the vehicle and its specification. Each of the four double-page advertisements told a different story about the vehicle's design, handling or technology. The pen illustrations were focused on a shot of the car embedded in the editorial, while the main body copy of the advertisement was in the right-hand corner of the page and handwritten to draw attention to the doodle. The advertisements appeared on London Underground hoardings and *Time Out* magazine before the main press campaign was rolled out across the United Kingdom.[9]

Some clear implications emerge for marketers on how consumers process print advertisements, and these are summarised in the Marketing memo.

Radio advertising Radio is a pervasive medium. Perhaps its main advantage is flexibility – stations are highly targeted in terms of demographic, psychographic and geographic segmentation – and advertisements are relatively inexpensive to produce. Radio is a particularly effective medium at morning and evening commuting times. It can be especially useful for small local businesses and can assist larger national and international firms to achieve a balance between broad and localised market coverage.[10]

The obvious disadvantages of radio are the lack of visual images and the relatively passive nature of the consumer processing that results.[11] Nevertheless, radio advertisements can be extremely creative. Some see the lack of visual images as a plus because

Marketing memo

Print advertisement evaluation criteria

In judging the effectiveness of a print advertisement, in addition to considering the communication strategy (target market, communications objectives, message and creative strategy), marketers should be able to answer 'yes' to the following questions about the practical elements:

1 Is the message clear at a glance? Can you quickly tell what the advertisement is all about?

2 Is the benefit in the headline?

3 Does the illustration support the headline?

4 Does the first line of the copy support or explain the headline and illustration?

5 Is the advertisement easy to read and follow?

6 Is the market offering easily identified?

7 Is the brand or sponsor clearly identified?

Source: Based on P. W. Burton and S. C. Purvis (2002) *Which Ad Pulled Best*, 9th edn, Lincolnwood, IL: NTC Business Books.

---

they feel that the clever use of music, sound and other creative devices can tap into the listeners' imagination to create powerfully relevant, well-liked and consequently easily recalled images.

Legal and social issues

Advertisers and their agencies must be sure that advertising does not infringe social and legal norms. Public policy makers have developed a substantial body of laws and regulations to govern advertising. The problem is how to tell the difference between deception and exaggerations, which are not meant to be believed and are permitted by law.

To be socially responsible, advertisers must be careful not to offend the general public as well as any ethnic groups, racial minorities or special interest groups.[12] After choosing the message, the advertiser's next task is to choose media to carry it. The key steps are deciding on desired reach, frequency and impact; choosing among major media types; selecting specific media vehicles; deciding on media timing; and deciding on geographical media allocation. Then the marketer evaluates the results of these decisions.

Managing media matters

Media selection is finding the most cost-effective media to deliver the desired number and type of exposures to the target audience. The advertiser seeks a specified advertising objective and response from the target audience – for example, a target level of customer trial. This level depends on, among other things, level of brand awareness. Suppose the rate of customer trial increases at a diminishing rate with the level of audience awareness, as shown in Figure 20.2(a). If the advertiser seeks a product trial rate of T^*, it will be necessary to achieve a brand awareness level of A^*.

The next task is to find out how many exposures, E^*, will produce a level of audience awareness of A^*. The effect of exposures on audience awareness depends on the exposures' reach, frequency and impact:

- **Reach (R)**: the number of different persons or households exposed to a particular media schedule at least once during a specified time period.
- **Frequency (F)**: the number of times within the specified time period that an average person or household is exposed to the message.

(a) Relationship between product trial rate and audience awareness level

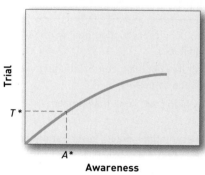

(b) Relationship between audience awareness level and exposure reach and frequency

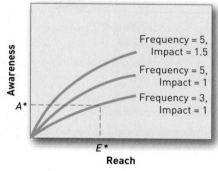

Figure 20.2 Relationship among trial, awareness and the exposure function

- **Impact (I)**: the qualitative value of an exposure through a given medium (thus a food advertisement in the UK's *Good Housekeeping* magazine would have a higher impact than in the UK's *Radio Times* magazine).

Figure 20.2(b) shows the relationship between audience awareness and reach. Audience awareness will be greater, the higher the exposures' reach, frequency and impact. The relationship between reach, frequency and impact is captured in the following concepts:

- **Total number of exposures (E)**. This is the reach times the average frequency: that is, $E = R \times F$, also called the gross rating points (GRP). If a given media schedule reaches 80 per cent of homes with an average exposure frequency of 3, the media schedule has a GRP of 240 (80 × 3). If another media schedule has a GRP of 300, it has more weight, but it is not possible to tell how this weight breaks down into reach and frequency.
- **Weighted number of exposures (WE)**. This is the reach times average frequency times average impact: that is, $WE = R \times F \times I$.

Reach is most important when launching new market offerings, or extensions of well-known brands or infrequently purchased brands, or prospecting an undefined target market. Frequency is most important where there are strong competitors, a complex story to tell, high consumer resistance or a frequent-purchase cycle. Many advertisers believe that a target audience needs a large number of exposures. Others believe that after people see the same advertisement a few times they act on it, get irritated by it or stop noticing it. Think of an advertisement that has recently irritated you. Was the advertisement effective? How would you change it if you had the opportunity to advise the client company? Another reason for repetition is forgetting. The higher the forgetting rate associated with a brand market offering message, the higher the warranted level of repetition. However, advertisers should not rest on a tired advertisement but insist on fresh effort from their advertising agency.[13]

The media planner must also know the capacity of the major advertising media types to deliver reach, frequency and impact. The major advertising media along with their costs, advantages and limitations are profiled in Table 20.1.

Media planners make their choices by considering the following variables:

- **Target audience media habits.** Radio and television are the most effective media for reaching teenagers.
- **Product characteristics.** Media types have different potential for demonstration, visualisation, explanation, believability and colour. Women's dresses are best shown in colour

Table 20.1 Profiles of major media types

Medium	Advantages	Limitations
Newspapers	Flexibility; timeliness; good local market coverage; broad acceptance; high believability	Short life; poor reproduction quality; small 'pass-along' audience
Television	Combines sight, sound and motion; appealing to the senses; high attention; high reach	High absolute cost; high clutter; fleeting exposure; less audience selectivity
Direct mail	Audience selectivity; flexibility; no ad competition within the same medium; personalisation	Relatively high cost; 'junk mail' image
Radio	Mass use; high geographic and demographic selectivity; low cost	Audio presentation only; lower attention than television; non-standardised rate structures; fleeting exposure
Magazines	High geographic and demographic selectivity; credibility and prestige; high-quality reproduction; long life; good pass-along readership	Long advert purchase lead time; some waste circulation; no guarantee of position
Outdoor	Flexibility; high repeat exposure; low cost; low competition	Limited audience selectivity; creative limitations
Yellow Pages	Excellent local coverage; high believability; wide reach; low cost	High competition; long advert purchase lead time; creative limitations
Newsletters	Very high selectivity; full control; interactive opportunities; relative low costs	Costs could run away
Brochures	Flexibility; full control; can dramatise messages	Overproduction could lead to runaway costs
Telephone	Many users; opportunity to give a personal touch	Relative high cost unless volunteers are used
Internet	High selectivity; interactive possibilities; relatively low cost	Relatively new media with a low number of users in some countries

magazines, but high-tech products requiring dynamic presentation, such as digital cameras, printers or mobile phones, are best demonstrated on television.

- **Message characteristics.** Timeliness and information content will influence media choice. A message announcing a major sale tomorrow will require radio, TV or newspaper advertising. A message containing a great deal of technical data might require specialised magazines or mailings.
- **Cost.** Television is very expensive, whereas newspaper advertising is relatively inexpensive. What counts is the cost per thousand exposures.

Given the abundance of media, the planner must first decide how to allocate the budget to the major media types. Customers are increasingly time starved. Attention is a scarce currency, and advertisers need strong devices to capture it.[14] In recent years, researchers have noticed a reduced effectiveness for television due to increased commercial clutter, increased 'zipping and zapping' of commercials, aided by the arrival of PVRs such as TiVo, and lower viewing owing to the growth in cable and satellite TV and DVDs/VCRs.

Place advertising

Place advertising, or **out-of-home advertising**, is a broad category including many creative and unexpected methods to capture consumers' attention. The rationale is that it is more effective to reach people where they work, play and, of course, shop. The main options include ambient advertising, billboards, public spaces, point of purchase and transport advertising.

A billboard advertisement with a difference!
Source: Patrick Stollarz/
AFP/Getty Images.

Billboards Billboards have been transformed and now use colourful, digitally produced graphics, backlighting, sounds, movement, and unusual – even three-dimensional – images. In Belgium, eBay posted 'Moved to eBay' stickers on empty storefronts; and in Germany, imaginary workers toiling inside vending machines, ATMs and photo booths were justification for a German job-hunting website to proclaim, 'Life is too short for the wrong job'.

BBC World

The Best Show winner at the OBIE awards sponsored by the Outdoor Advertising Association of America was the BBC World television channel and its advertising agency BBDO. The BBC World Voting Campaign featured interactive digital billboards designed to introduce BBC World to the US market. The interactive units showed images and headlines that reflected current events. Members of the public were then asked to use Bluetooth technology to select one of two available opinions, and a running tally was displayed.[15]

Public spaces or ambient advertising Advertisers are placing advertisements in unconventional places such as cinemas, airlines and lounges, as well as sports arenas, office and hotel lifts, and other public places. Billboard-type poster advertisements are appearing everywhere. Advertisements on buses, subways and metro and commuter trains have become valuable ways to reach consumers. 'Street furniture' – bus shelters, kiosks and public areas – is another fast-growing option.

Advertisers can buy space in stadia, arenas and on rubbish bins, bicycle racks, parking meters, airline snack packages, airport luggage carousels, lifts and petrol pumps. Volkswagen has used fuel pump nozzles to communicate the fuel efficiency of its Golf TDI model.

British Airports Authority

Advertising agency JCDecaux has worked alongside the British Airports Authority (BAA) and architects to build advertising into the very foundation of London Heathrow's new Terminal 5. Rather than advertising clutter to besiege the weary traveller, only a small number of advertising sites carry messages, but they will be massive, including light boxes larger than four double-decker buses. Over 300 digital advertising sites were installed in the terminal, taking up 50 per cent of the airport's advertising 'real estate', and departing from the usual B2B or corporate branding campaigns to introduce a whole range of consumer goods – from chocolates and clothing to perfumes and cosmetics. The intensive use of digital images also means that messages can be targeted to different audiences in different locations at different times of day. Advertisements can even appear in different languages to greet arriving and departing flights. BAA director of media, Duncan Tolson, says Terminal 5 is just the beginning: 'Terminal 5 will mark the start of a new generation of airport advertising. It will act as a blueprint for the future, and we are looking forward to rolling it out across all BAA airports.'[16]

Product placement

Product placement has been threatening to expand from films to all types of TV show. From 2011 product placement has been approved on UK TV. Marketers pay high fees so that their goods will make cameo appearances in films and on television. Sometimes placements are the result of a larger network advertising deal, but at other times they are the work of small product-placement shops that maintain ties with prop masters, set designers and production executives. 7-UP, Aston Martin, Finlandia, Visa and Omega all initiated major promotional campaigns based on product-placement tie-ins with the James Bond film *Die Another Day*. With over US$100 million paid for product-placement rights, some critics called the film 'Buy Another Day'. Product placements also featured strongly in *Sex in the City*, released in May 2008.

Some firms (such as Chanel and Louis Vuitton) get product placement at no cost by supplying their products to the film company. Nike, too, often supplies shoes, jackets, bags, etc.[17]

Marketers are finding inventive ways to advertise during real-time television broadcasts. Sports fans are familiar with virtual logos added digitally to the playing field. Invisible to spectators at the event, these advertisements look just like painted-on logos to viewers at home. **Advertorials** are print advertisements that offer editorial content reflecting favourably on the brand and are difficult to distinguish from newspaper or magazine content.[18] Many companies include advertising inserts in monthly bills. Some companies send CDs or DVDs to prospects.

Point of purchase

There are many ways to communicate with consumers at the **point of purchase** (POP). In-store advertising includes advertisements on shopping trolleys, aisles and shelves, as well as promotion options such as in-store demonstrations and live sampling. P-O-P radio provides FM-style programming and commercial messages to many stores and shops. Programming includes a store-selected music format, consumer tips and commercials. The appeal of point-of-purchase advertising lies in the fact that in many product categories consumers make the bulk of their final brand decisions in the store.

Evaluating alternative media

Advertisements now appear virtually anywhere. The main advantage of non-traditional media is that they can often reach a very precise and captive audience in a cost-effective manner. The message must be simple and direct. In fact, outdoor advertising is often called the '15-second sell'. It is more effective at enhancing brand awareness or brand image than creating new brand associations.

The challenge with non-traditional media is demonstrating their reach and effectiveness through credible, independent research. Unique advertising placements designed to break through clutter may also be perceived as invasive and obtrusive. Consumer backlash often results when people see advertisements in traditionally advertisement-free spaces, such as in dentists' and doctors' waiting rooms.

Not everyone is turned off by the proliferation of advertising. Branded merchandise is so much a part of teenagers' lives that they don't think twice about it. Perhaps because of its sheer pervasiveness, some consumers seem to be less bothered by non-traditional media now than in the past.

However, consumers must be favourably affected in some way to justify the marketing expenditures for non-traditional media. There will always be room for creative means of placing the brand before consumers. The possibilities are endless: The marketing insight box describes the emergence of yet another new media trend.

The media planner must search for the most cost-effective vehicles within each chosen media type. These choices are critical, as it can cost as much to run an advertisement once on network TV as to make it. In making choices, the planner must rely on measurement services that provide estimates of audience size, composition and media cost. Audience size has several possible measures:

- **Circulation**: the number of physical units carrying the advertising.
- **Audience**: the number of people exposed to the vehicle. (If the vehicle has pass-on readership, then the audience is larger than the circulation.)
- **Effective audience**: the number of people with target audience characteristics exposed to the vehicle.
- **Effective advertising-exposed audience**: the number of people with target audience characteristics who actually saw the advertisement.[19]

Media planners calculate the cost per thousand persons reached by a vehicle. The media planner ranks each magazine by cost per thousand and favours magazines with the lowest cost per thousand for reaching target consumers. The magazines themselves often put together a 'reader profile' for their advertisers, summarising the characteristics of the magazine's readers with respect to age, income, residence, marital status and leisure activities.

Marketing insight

Playing games with brands

Advergaming, the practice of incorporating an advertising message into an online game, is becoming an effective way to reach target audiences.

The central concept of advergaming is that if the game is fun, consumers are more likely not only to remember the brand or product itself, but to associate specific brand attributes with it. If the game is popular, players will challenge friends to try it or simply add it to their blogs.

Studies suggest that 50 per cent of recipients play the advergame for an average of 25 minutes and 90 per cent of players who receive a challenge from a friend to play the game respond back with their score or statistics.

At Web 2.0 websites like Multigames.com, users upload their own free flash games to the site, as users do with videos to sites such as YouTube. Once uploaded, the games are provided with embed codes, which can also accommodate Facebook features and other social bookmarking tools that encourage viral spread of the game.

'One of our most popular games is actually an advergame for Guitar Hero 2 by Red Octane', explains Multigames CEO Christian Lovstedt. 'It's a simplified version of the real Guitar Hero game that you play with your computer keyboards. This advergame is also the game that is being embedded the most so it's a very effective word of mouth communicator for Guitar Hero 2.'

'I am not sure if marketing departments are using the full potential of viral spread of advergames yet. The common set up is that a promotion site is launched with an advergame and the advertising company will spend time trying to drive traffic to that specific site. But you can attract a lot of attention to your product by letting the game "transport itself" virally over the internet. We hope to see more of Advergames on our site in the future', says Lovstedt.

The advergame industry is expected to generate US$312.2 million by 2009, up from US$83.6 million in 2004, according to Boston research firm Yankee Group.

Source: C. Lovstedt, Multigames Sweden AB (www.multigames.com).

Marketers need to apply several adjustments to the cost per thousand measure. First, they should adjust the measure for *audience quality*. For a baby lotion advertisement, a magazine read by 1 million young mothers has an exposure value of 1 million; if read by 1 million teenagers, it would have an exposure value of almost zero. Second, adjust the exposure value for the *audience-attention probability*. Readers of *Vogue* may pay more attention to advertisements than do readers of *The Economist*. Third, adjust for the magazine's *editorial quality* (prestige and trustworthiness). People are more likely to believe a TV or radio advertisement and to become more positively disposed towards the brand when the advertisement is placed within a programme they like. Fourth, adjust for the magazine's *advertising placement policies and extra services* (such as regional or occupational editions and lead-time requirements).

Media planners are increasingly using more sophisticated measures of effectiveness and employing them in mathematical models to arrive at the best media mix. Many advertising agencies use a computer program to select the initial media and then make further improvements based on subjective factors.

In choosing media, the advertiser faces both a macro-scheduling and a micro-scheduling problem. The *macro-scheduling problem* involves scheduling the advertising in relationship to seasons and the business cycle. Suppose 70 per cent of a product's sales occur between June and September. The firm can vary its advertising expenditures to follow the seasonal pattern, to oppose the seasonal pattern, or to be constant throughout the year.

The *micro-scheduling problem* calls for allocating advertising expenditures within a short period to obtain maximum impact. Suppose the firm decides to buy 30 radio spots in the month of September. Figure 20.3 shows several possible patterns. The left side shows that advertising messages for the month can be concentrated ('burst' advertising), dispersed continuously throughout the month, or dispersed intermittently. The top side shows that the advertising messages can be beamed with a level, rising, falling or alternating frequency.

The most effective pattern depends on the communications objectives in relationship to the nature of the market offering, target customers, distribution channels and other marketing factors. The timing pattern should consider three factors. *Buyer turnover*

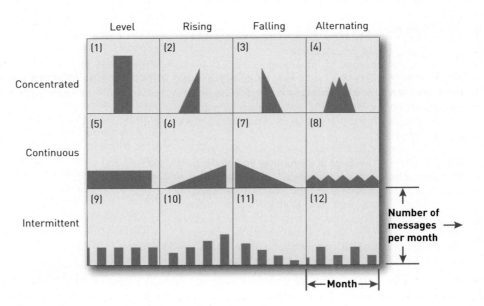

Figure 20.3 Classifications of marketing timing patterns

expresses the rate at which new buyers enter the market; the higher this rate, the more continuous the advertising should be. *Purchase frequency* is the number of times during the period that the average buyer buys the product; the higher the purchase frequency, the more continuous the advertising should be. The *forgetting rate* is the rate at which the buyer forgets the brand; the higher the forgetting rate, the more continuous the advertising should be.

In launching a new market offering, the advertiser must choose among continuity, concentration, flighting and pulsing.

- **Continuity**: exposures appear evenly throughout a given period. Generally, advertisers use continuous advertising in expanding market situations, with frequently purchased items, and in tightly defined buyer categories.
- **Concentration**: making the advertising spend in a single period. This makes sense for seasonal purchases such as fruit, vegetables, holidays and Christmas presents.
- **Flighting**: advertising for a period, followed by a period with no advertising, followed by a second period of advertising activity. It is useful when funding is limited, the purchase cycle is relatively infrequent, or items are seasonal.
- **Pulsing**: continuous advertising at low-weight levels reinforced periodically by waves of heavier activity. It draws on the strength of continuous advertising and flights to create a compromise scheduling strategy. Those who favour pulsing believe the audience will learn the message more thoroughly, and at a lower cost to the firm.

A company must decide how to allocate its advertising budget over space as well as over time. The company makes 'national buys' when it places advertisements on national TV networks or in nationally circulated magazines. It makes 'spot buys' when it buys TV time in just a few markets or in regional editions of magazines. These markets are called *areas of dominant influence* (ADIs) or *designated marketing areas* (DMAs). Advertisements reach a market 60–100 kilometres from a city centre. The company makes 'local buys' when it advertises in local newspapers, on radio or at outdoor sites.

Evaluating advertising effectiveness

Most advertisers try to measure the communication effect of an advertisement – that is, its potential effect on awareness, knowledge or preference. They would also like to measure the advertisement's sales effect.

Communication-effect research

Communication-effect research, called *copy testing*, seeks to determine whether an advertisement is communicating effectively. Marketers should perform this test both before an advertisement is put into media and after it is printed or broadcast.

There are three major methods of pre-testing. The *consumer feedback method* asks consumers questions such as these:

1 What is the main message you get from this advertisement?
2 What do you think they want you to know, believe or do?
3 How likely is it that this advertisement will influence you to undertake the action?
4 What works well in the advertisement and what works poorly?
5 How does the advertisement make you feel?
6 Where is the best place to reach you with this message?

Portfolio tests ask consumers to view or listen to a portfolio of advertisements. Consumers are then asked to recall all the advertisements and their content, aided or unaided by the interviewer. Recall level indicates an advertisement's ability to stand out and to have its message understood and remembered.

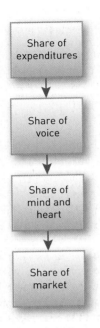

Figure 20.4 Formula for measuring sales impact of advertising

Laboratory tests use equipment to measure physiological reactions to an advertisement; or consumers may be asked to turn a knob to indicate their moment-to-moment liking or interest while viewing sequenced material.[20] These tests measure attention-getting power but reveal nothing about impact on beliefs, attitudes or intentions.[21]

Pre-test critics maintain that agencies can design advertisements which test well but may not necessarily perform well in the marketplace. Proponents of pre-testing maintain that useful diagnostic information can emerge and that pre-tests should not be used as the sole decision criterion. Widely acknowledged as being one of the most successful advertisers, Nike is notorious for doing very little advertising pre-testing.

Many advertisers use post-tests to assess the overall impact of a completed campaign. If a company hoped to increase brand awareness from 20 per cent to 50 per cent and succeeded in increasing it to only 30 per cent, then the company is not spending enough, its advertisements are poor, or it has overlooked some other factor.

Sales-effect research

What sales are generated by an advertisement that increases brand awareness by 20 per cent and brand preference by 10 per cent? The fewer or more controllable additional factors such as features and price are, the easier it is to measure advertising's effect on sales. The sales impact is easiest to measure in direct marketing situations and hardest in brand or corporate image-building advertising.

Companies are generally interested in finding out whether they are overspending or underspending on advertising. A company's *share of advertising expenditures* produces a *share of voice* (proportion of company advertising of that product to all advertising of that product) that earns a *share of consumers' minds and hearts* and, ultimately, a *share of market*.

Researchers try to measure the sales impact through analysing historical or experimental data. The *historical approach* involves correlating past sales to past advertising expenditures using advanced statistical techniques. Other researchers use an *experimental design* to measure advertising's sales impact.

Information Resources, Inc.

A growing number of researchers are striving to measure the sales effect of advertising expenditures instead of settling for communication-effect measures.[22] Millward Brown International has conducted tracking studies for years to help advertisers decide whether their advertising is benefiting their brand.[23] Another research pioneer, Nielsen, has begun tracking commercials electronically.[24]

Sales promotion

Sales promotion is a key ingredient in the marketing communications mix. Strictly speaking, it should be termed *sales promotion* and not *promotion* as the latter is a collective term for the complete marketing communications mix. It consists of a collection of incentive tools, mostly short term, designed to stimulate quicker or greater purchase of particular market offerings by consumers or the trade.[25]

Whereas advertising offers a *reason* to buy, sales promotion offers an *incentive* to buy. Sales promotion includes tools for *consumer promotion* (samples, coupons, cash refund offers, money off, premiums, prizes, patronage rewards, free trials, warranties, tie-in promotions, cross-promotions, point-of-purchase displays and demonstrations); *trade promotion* (money off, advertising and display allowances, and free goods); and *business* and *sales force promotion* (trade shows and conventions, sales force contests and speciality advertising).

Setting objectives

Sales promotion tools vary in their specific objectives. A free sample stimulates consumer trial, whereas a free management advisory service aims at cementing a long-term relationship with a retailer. Sellers use incentive-type promotions to attract new users, to reward loyal customers and to increase the repurchase rates of occasional users. Sales promotions often attract brand switchers, who are primarily looking for low price, good perceived value or premiums. If some of them would not otherwise have tried the brand, sales promotion can yield long-term increases in market share.[26]

Sales promotions in markets of high brand similarity can produce a high sales response in the short run but little permanent gain in brand preference over the longer term. In markets of high brand dissimilarity, they may be able to alter market shares permanently. In addition to brand switching, consumers may engage in stockpiling – purchasing earlier than usual (purchase acceleration) or purchasing extra quantities.[27] However, sales may then hit a post-sales-promotion dip.[28]

A number of sales promotion benefits flow to manufacturers and consumers. Manufacturers can adjust to short-term variations in supply and demand and test how high a list price they can charge, because they can always discount it. Promotions induce consumers to try new products and lead to more varied retail formats, such as everyday low pricing and promotional pricing. For retailers, promotions may increase sales of complementary categories (cake mix promotions may drive cake decoration sales) as well as induce store switching. They promote greater consumer awareness of prices. They help manufacturers and service providers (i.e. all market offering providers) sell more than normal at the list price and adapt programmes to different consumer segments.

Advertising versus sales promotion

A decade ago, the advertising-to-sales-promotion ratio was about 60:40. Today, in many consumer-packaged-goods companies, sales promotion accounts for 75 per cent of the combined budget (roughly 50 per cent is trade promotion and 25 per cent is consumer promotion). Sales promotion expenditure increased as a percentage of budget expenditure annually for almost two decades, although its growth has slowed down in recent years.

Several factors contributed to this rapid growth, particularly in consumer markets. Promotion became more accepted by top management as an effective sales tool; the number of brands increased; competitors used promotions frequently; many brands were seen as similar; consumers became more price value oriented; the trade demanded more deals from manufacturers; and advertising efficiency declined.

However, the rapid growth of sales promotion created clutter. Incessant price reductions, coupons, deals and premiums may devalue the product in buyers' minds. It is risky to overuse sales promotion for a well-known brand on promotion over 30 per cent of the time.[29] Dominant brands offer deals less frequently because most deals subsidise only current users.

Loyal brand buyers tend not to change their buying patterns as a result of competitive promotions. Advertising appears to be more effective at deepening brand loyalty, although added-value promotions can be distinguished from price promotions. Certain types of sales promotion may actually be able to enhance brand image.

Harveys Furniture Store

Harveys the UK furniture group, now part of the German Steinhoff Group, which sponsors the long-running UK TV soap *Coronation Street*, is offering discount vouchers to viewers visiting its dedicated area of the soap opera's interactive TV service. The sales promotion, created by the Eagle Eye Solutions agency, will encourage viewers to text in to receive an eight-digit short code to their mobile phone, which can be redeemed against discounts in selected Harveys stores. [30]

Harveys is the proud sponsor of the long-running UK TV soap *Coronation Street*.
Source: Harveys Darlington.

Ford Motor Company

As well as the time-honoured devices of price promotions and two for the price of one offers (BOGOFs), Ford of Britain conducted an unbranded survey of about 150,000 sporty male prospects in 2006 whom it had identified as a prospective target audience for the launch of its new S-MAX MPV across Europe. Recipients were incentivised with vouchers that appealed to their lifestyle, such as those for the outdoor retailer Snow+Rock. The response rate of 25,000 was greatly in excess of company expectations and 16,000 turned out to be 'hot' prospects for the new vehicle launch.[31]

Price promotions may not build permanent total category volume. One study of more than 1,000 promotions concluded that only 16 per cent were successful.[32] Small market share competitors find it advantageous to use sales promotion because they cannot afford to match the market leaders' large advertising budgets. Neither can they obtain shelf-space without offering trade allowances or stimulate consumer trial without offering incentives. The result is that many consumer-packaged-goods companies feel they are forced to use more sales promotion than they wish. They blame the heavy use of sales promotion for decreasing brand loyalty, increasing consumer price sensitivity, brand-quality-image dilution, and a focus on short-run marketing planning.

Major decisions

In using sales promotion a company must establish its objectives; select the tools; develop the programme; pre-test, implement and control it; and evaluate the results.

Establishing objectives

Sales promotion objectives derive from broader promotion objectives, which draw from more basic marketing objectives for the product/market offering. For consumers, objectives include encouraging purchase of larger-sized units, building trial among non-users and attracting switchers away from competitors' brands. Ideally, promotions with consumers would have short-run sales impact as well as long-run brand equity effects. For retailers, objectives include persuading retailers to carry new items and higher levels of inventory, encouraging off-season buying, encouraging stocking of related items, offsetting competitive promotions, building brand loyalty and gaining entry into new retail outlets. For the sales force, objectives include encouraging support of a new market offering or model, encouraging more prospecting and stimulating off-season sales.[33]

Selecting consumer promotion tools

The promotion planner should take into account the type of market, sales promotion objectives, competitive conditions, and each tool's cost effectiveness. The main consumer promotion tools are summarised in Table 20.2. *Manufacturer promotions* are, for instance in the motor industry, rebates, gifts to motivate test drives and purchases, and high-value trade-in credit. *Retailer promotions* include price cuts, feature advertising, retailer coupons and retailer contests or premiums.[34]

A distinction can also be made between sales promotion tools that are *consumer franchise building* and those that are not. The former impart a selling message along with the offer, such as free samples, frequency awards, coupons when they include a selling message, and premiums when they are related to the market offering/product. Sales promotion tools that typically are *not* brand building include 'money-off' packs, consumer premiums not related to a product, contests and sweepstakes, consumer refund offers, and trade allowances. Consumer franchise-building promotions offer the best of both worlds – they build brand equity and generate sales.

Selecting trade promotion tools Manufacturers use a number of trade promotion tools. Manufacturers award money to the trade: (1) to persuade the retailer or wholesaler to carry the brand; (2) to persuade the retailer or wholesaler to carry more units than the normal amount; (3) to induce retailers to promote the brand by featuring display and price reductions; and (4) to stimulate retailers to push the product.

The growing power of large retailers has increased their ability to demand trade promotion at the expense of consumer promotion and advertising.[35] The company's sales force and its brand managers are often at odds over trade promotion. The sales force says local retailers will not keep the company's products on the shelf unless they receive more trade promotion money, whereas brand managers want to spend the limited funds on consumer promotion and advertising.

Table 20.2 Major consumer promotion tools

Samples: offer of a free amount of a product or service delivered door to door, sent in the mail, picked up in a store, attached to another product or featured in an advertising offer.

Coupons: certificates entitling the bearer to a stated saving on the purchase of a specific product: mailed, enclosed in other products or attached to them, or inserted in magazine and newspaper ads.

Cash refund offers (rebates): provide a price reduction after purchase rather than at the retail shop. The consumer sends a specified 'proof of purchase' to the manufacturer, which 'refunds' part of the purchase price by mail.

Price packs (money-off deals): offers to consumers of savings off the regular price of a product, flagged on the label or package. A *reduced-price pack* is a single package sold at a reduced price (such as two for the price of one). A *banded pack* is two related products banded together (such as a toothbrush and toothpaste).

Premiums (gifts): merchandise offered at a relatively low cost or free as an incentive to purchase a particular product. A *with-pack premium* accompanies the product inside or on the package. A *free in-the-mail premium* is mailed to consumers, who send in a proof of purchase, such as a box top or bar code. A *self-liquidating premium* is sold below its normal retail price to consumers who request it.

Frequency programme: a programme providing rewards related to the consumer's frequency and intensity in purchasing the company's products or services.

Prizes (contests, sweepstakes, games): offers of the chance to win cash, trips or merchandise as a result of purchasing something. A *contest* calls for consumers to submit an entry to be examined by a panel of judges who will select the best entries. A *sweepstake* asks consumers to submit their names to a draw. A *game* presents consumers with something every time they buy – bingo numbers, missing letters – that might help them win a prize.

Patronage awards: values in cash or in other forms that are proportional to patronage of a certain vendor or group of vendors.

Free trials: inviting prospective purchasers to try the product without cost in the hope that they will buy.

Product warranties: explicit or implicit promises by sellers that the product will perform as specified or that the seller will fix it or refund the customer's money during a specified period.

Tie-in promotions: two or more brands or companies team up on coupons, refunds and contests to increase pulling power.

Cross-promotions: using one brand to advertise another, non-competing brand.

Point-of-purchase (P-O-P) displays and demonstrations: P-O-P displays and demonstrations take place at the point of purchase or sale.

Manufacturers face several challenges in managing trade promotions. First, they often find it difficult to persuade retailers to do what they agreed. Manufacturers are increasingly insisting on proof of performance before paying any allowances. Second, some retailers are *forward buying* – that is, buying a greater quantity during the deal period than they can immediately sell. In the light of these problems, many manufacturers feel that trade promotions have become a nightmare. They contain several offers, are complex to administer, and often lead to lost revenues.

Selecting business and sales force promotion tools Companies are increasingly spending on business and sales force promotion tools such as sales contests and speciality advertising to gather business leads, impress and reward customers, and motivate the sales force to greater effort. Typically they develop budgets for tools that remain fairly constant from year to year. For many new businesses that want to attract a targeted audience, especially in B2B markets, trade shows are an important tool, but the cost per contact is the highest of all communication options.

Developing the programme

In planning sales promotion programmes, marketers are increasingly blending several media into an integrated marketing communications campaign concept.

In deciding to use a particular incentive, marketers must first determine the *size* of the incentive. A certain minimum is necessary if the promotion is to succeed. Second, the marketing manager must establish *conditions* for participation. Incentives might be offered to everyone or to select groups. Third, the marketer must decide on the *duration* of the promotion. Fourth, the marketer must choose a *distribution vehicle*. A money-off coupon can be distributed in the package, in stores, by mail or in advertising. Fifth, the marketing manager must establish the *timing* of promotion. Finally, the marketer must determine the *total sales promotion budget*.

Pre-testing, implementing, controlling and evaluating the programme

Although most sales promotion programmes are designed on the basis of experience, pre-tests can determine whether the tools are appropriate, the incentive size optimal, and the presentation method efficient. Consumers can be asked to rate or rank different possible deals, or trial tests can be run in limited geographic areas.

Marketing managers must prepare implementation and control plans that cover lead time and sell-in time for each individual promotion. *Lead time* is the time necessary to prepare the programme prior to launching it. *Sell-in time* begins with the promotional launch and ends when approximately 95 per cent of the deal merchandise is in the hands of consumers.

Manufacturers can evaluate the programme using sales data, consumer surveys and experiments. Sales (scanner) data help analyse the types of people who took advantage of the promotion, what they bought before the promotion, and how they behaved later towards the brand and other brands. Sales promotions work best when they attract competitors' customers, who then switch. *Consumer surveys* can uncover how many recall the promotion, what they thought of it, how many took advantage of it, and how the promotion affected subsequent brand choice behaviour. *Experiments* vary such attributes as incentive value, duration and distribution media: for example, coupons can be sent to half the households in a consumer panel. Scanner data can track whether the coupons led more people to buy the product and when.

Additional costs beyond the cost of specific promotions include the risk that promotions might decrease long-run brand loyalty. Second, promotions can be more expensive than they appear. Some are inevitably distributed to the wrong consumers. Third are the costs of special production runs, extra sales force effort, and handling requirements. Finally, certain promotions irritate retailers, who may demand extra trade allowances or refuse to cooperate.

Events, experiences, public and press relations

Setting objectives

Sponsorship of sporting events, arts festivals, fairs, and annual and charity events involves becoming part of a personally relevant moment in consumers' lives that can broaden and deepen a company's relationship with the target market.

British Telecom sponsors the Isle of Wight Festival

British Telecom (BT) marked a strategic change in its sponsorship activity when it signed up to support the popular 'globally recognised' Isle of Wight Festival in June 2008. The event organiser agreed to BT advertising its association with the festival via its voice, broadband and Vision products and to display its branding across the 250-acre site. BT also issued tickets to the sold-out event, which featured big acts including NERD, Kaiser Chiefs and The Police.[36]

Red Bull

Red Bull is an energy drink that was launched in the United Kingdom in 1995. It is targeted at the young, such as sportspeople, students and clubbers, and has achieved a dominant market share by developing an effective integrated marketing communication programme. The opening TV advertising featured whimsical cartoons and ended with the tag line 'Red Bull gives *you* wings'. The IMC promotes an adventure/fun brand mystique message. The IMC mix includes whacky TV advertising, sponsorship of a number of high-profile events, such as UK athletics, and the £60 million (€84 million) purchase of the Formula One Jaguar racing team. Red Bull also runs a variety of fun events such as the *Flugtag* (where amateur 'pilots' attempt to launch home-made flying machines); and the Art of Can, featuring sculptures using Red Bull's distinctive blue and silver cans. It is identified by its target market as a 'cool drink' but has also attracted some adverse publicity when the ethics of its mystique have been challenged. However, it has successfully managed to generate and sustain high levels of added value, thus enabling it to be positively differentiated from rivals' products – a strategic focus in itself.[37]

Red Bull ... drink, wink and think excitement
Source: Red Bull Content Pool/Kevin Yang

Daily encounters with brands may also affect consumers' brand attitudes and beliefs. *Atmospheres* are 'packaged environments' that create or reinforce leanings towards market offering purchase. Law offices decorated with Oriental rugs and oak furniture communicate 'stability' and 'success'.[38] A five-star hotel will feature elegant chandeliers, marble columns and other tangible signs of luxury. Small brands, of necessity, are more likely to take less obvious and less expensive paths in sponsorship and communications.

Marketers report a number of reasons to sponsor events:

- **To identify with a particular target market or lifestyle.** Customers can be targeted geographically, demographically, psychographically or behaviourally according to events (see Chapters 10 and 11).
- **To increase awareness of company or product name.** Sponsorship often offers sustained exposure to a brand, a necessary condition to build brand recognition and enhance brand recall.
- **To create or reinforce perceptions of key brand image associations.** Events themselves have associations that help to create or reinforce brand associations.[39]
- **To enhance corporate image.** Sponsorship can improve perceptions that the company is likeable and prestigious.
- **To create experiences and evoke feelings.** The feelings engendered by an exciting or rewarding event may indirectly link to the brand.
- **To express commitment to the community, green or social issues.** Cause-related marketing sponsors non-profit organisations and charities. Ben & Jerry's (ice cream, now owned by Unilever) has been a consistent champion of green and social issues.

- **To entertain key clients or reward key employees.** Many events include lavish hospitality tents and other special services or activities for sponsors and their guests only. These engender goodwill and establish valuable business contacts. From an employee perspective, events can also build participation and morale or be used as an incentive.
- **To permit merchandising or promotional opportunities.** Many marketers include contests or sweepstakes, in-store merchandising, direct response or other marketing activities in an event.

Despite these potential advantages, the success of an event can still be unpredictable and beyond the control of the sponsor. Although many consumers will credit sponsors for providing the financial assistance to make an event possible, some may resent the commercialisation of events.

Major sponsorship experiences

Successful sponsorships require choosing the appropriate events, designing the optimal sponsorship programme and measuring the effects of sponsorship. Professional advice on sponsorship is available in most European countries.

Choosing events

Because of the number of opportunities and their huge cost, many marketers are becoming more selective about choosing sponsorship events.

The event must meet the marketing objectives and communication strategy defined for the brand. The audience must match the target market. The event must have sufficient awareness, possess the desired image and be capable of creating the desired effects. Consumers must see favourable attributions for the sponsor's engagement. An ideal event is unique, lends itself to ancillary marketing activities and reflects or enhances the sponsor's brand or corporate image. As marketing managers are keen to be identified with excellent, prestigious and global activities, many are attracted by events such as the Olympics and World Cup competitions. The Octagon agency specialises in marketing the Olympics, and over 20 years and nine Olympic Games across five continents, it has gained a depth of Olympic marketing expertise. Over the years many leaders – brands, athletes and governing bodies – have valued its skills, insight and creativity.

More firms are also using their names to sponsor the arenas, stadiums and other venues that hold the events. In the United Kingdom the Premier League football club Arsenal plays at the Emirates stadium in London, and Bolton football club plays at the Reebok stadium in Bolton.

Designing sponsorship programmes

Many marketers believe it is the marketing programme accompanying an event sponsorship that ultimately determines its success. At least two to three times the amount of the sponsorship expenditure should be spent on related marketing activities.

Event creation is a particularly important skill in publicising fund-raising drives for non-profit organisations. Fund-raisers have developed a large repertoire of special events, including anniversary celebrations, art exhibitions, auctions, benefit evenings, bingo games, book and cake sales, contests, dances, dinners, fairs, fashion shows, parties in unusual places, 'phonathons', jumble sales, tours and 'walkathons'. No sooner is one type of event created, such as a 'walkathon', than competitors spawn new versions, such as 'readathons', 'bikeathons' and 'jogathons'.

Measuring sponsorship activities

As with public relations, measurement of events is difficult. The *supply-side* measurement method focuses on potential exposure to the brand by assessing the extent of media coverage, while the *demand-side* method focuses on reported exposure from consumers.

Supply-side methods approximate the amount of time or space devoted to media coverage of an event: for example, the number of seconds the brand is clearly visible on a television screen, or column inches of press clippings covering an event that mention the brand. These potential 'impressions' translate into an equivalent value in advertising expenditure according to the fees associated in actually advertising in the particular media vehicle. Some industry consultants have estimated that 30 seconds of TV logo exposure during a televised event can be worth 6 per cent, 10 per cent or as much as 25 per cent of a 30-second TV advertisement.

Although supply-side exposure methods provide quantifiable measures, equating media coverage with advertising exposure ignores the content of the respective communications. The advertiser uses media space and time to communicate a strategically designed message. Media coverage and telecasts only expose the brand and don't necessarily embellish its meaning in any direct way. Although some public relations professionals maintain that positive editorial coverage can be worth 5–10 times the equivalent advertising value, sponsorship rarely provides such favourable treatment.

The demand-side method identifies the effect sponsorship has on consumers' brand knowledge. Marketers can survey event spectators to measure sponsor recall of the event as well as resulting attitudes and intentions towards the sponsor:

- **direct tracking of sponsorship-related promotions**: web data, call centre data, online event statistics, other consumer engagements etc.;
- **qualitative research**: on-site/in-market, pre/post and participant/non-participant, using a proprietary model for brand equity transfer and subsequent impact on purchase intent and;
- **quantitative analysis**: analysis to link sponsorship to brand awareness, sales and retention and to optimise tactics in sponsorship activation that maximise ROI.

Creating experiences

A large part of local marketing is experiential marketing, which not only communicates features and benefits but also connects a market offering with unique and interesting experiences. 'The idea is not to sell something, but to demonstrate how a brand can enrich a customer's life.'[40] The marketing insight box describes the concept of customer experience management.

Marketing insight

Experiential marketing

Bernd Schmitt has developed the concept of *customer experience management* (CEM) – the process of strategically managing a customer's entire experience with a market offering or company.[41] According to Schmitt, brands can help to create five different types of experience: sense, feel, think, act and relate. In each case, Schmitt distinguishes between hard-wired and acquired experiential response levels. He maintains that marketers can provide experiences for customers through a set of experience providers:

- **communications**: advertising, public relations, annual reports, brochures, newsletters and magalogues (a combination of a magazine and a catalogue);
- **visual/verbal identity**: names, logos, signage and transportation vehicles;
- **product presence**: product design, packaging and point-of-sale displays;
- **co-branding**: event marketing and sponsorships, alliances and partnerships, licensing, and product placement in films or on TV;
- **environments**: retail and public spaces, trade booths, corporate buildings, office interiors and factories;

▶ Marketing insight *(continued)*

- websites and electronic media: corporate sites, product or service sites, CD-ROMs, automated emails, online advertising and intranets;
- people: salespeople, customer service representatives, technical support or repair providers, company spokespersons, and CEOs and other executives.

The CEM framework is made up of five basic steps:

1 Analysing the experiential world of the customer: gaining insights into the sociocultural context of consumers or the business context of business customers.

2 Building the experiential platform: developing a strategy that includes the positioning for the kind of experience the brand stands for ('what'), the value proposition of what relevant experience to deliver ('why') and the overall implementation theme that will be communicated ('how').

3 Designing the brand experience: implementing the experiential platform in the look and feel of logos and signage, packaging, retail spaces, advertising, collaterals and online.

4 Structuring the customer interface: implementing the experiential platform in the dynamic and interactive interfaces, including face to face, in stores, during sales visits, at the check-in desk of a hotel, or in the e-commerce engine of a website.

5 Engaging in continuous innovation: implementing the experiential platform in new product development, creative marketing events for customers and fine tuning the experience at every point of contact.

Schmitt cites Pret A Manger, the UK-based sandwich company, as an example of an attractive brand experience, customer interface and ongoing innovation:

The Pret A Manger brand is about great tasting, handmade, natural products served by amazing people who are passionate about their work. The sandwiches and stores look appealing and attractive. The company hires only 5 per cent of those who apply and only after they have worked for a day in the shop. This process ensures good fit and good teamwork.

He also offers Singapore Airlines, Starbucks and Amazon.com as outstanding providers of customer experiences.

Sources: www.exgroup.com; B. Schmitt (2003) *Customer Experience Management: A Revolutionary Approach to Connecting with Your Customers*, New York: John Wiley and Sons; B. Schmitt, D. L. Rogers and K. Vrotsos (2003) *There's No Business That's Not Show Business: Marketing in an Experience Culture*, Upper Saddle River, NJ: Prentice Hall; B. Schmitt (1999) *Experiential Marketing: How to Get Companies to Sense, Feel, Think, Act, and Relate to Your Company and Brands*, New York: Free Press; B. Schmitt and A. Simonson (1997) *Marketing Aesthetics: The Strategic Management of Brands, Identity, and Image*, New York: Free Press.

Pine and Gilmore argue that marketers are on the threshold of the 'experience economy' (see also Chapter 22), a new economic era in which all businesses must orchestrate memorable events for their customers.[42] They assert:

- If you charge for stuff, then you are in the *commodity business.*
- If you charge for tangible things, then you are in the *goods business.*
- If you charge for the activities you perform, then you are in the *service business.*
- If you charge for the time customers spend with you, then and only then are you in the *experience* business.

Citing a range of companies from Disney to AOL, Pine and Gilmore maintain that saleable experiences come in four varieties: entertainment, education, aesthetic and escapist.

One survey showed that 80 per cent of respondents found participating in a live event more engaging than all other forms of communication. The vast majority also felt that experiential marketing gave them more information than other forms of communication and would make them more likely to tell others about participating in the event and to be receptive to other marketing for the brand.[43]

Companies can even create a strong image by inviting prospects and customers to visit their headquarters and factories. Cadbury's, Denby and Nissan all sponsor excellent company tours that draw many visitors a year. Companies such as the Dundee Sweet factory, Lakeland Pencils, Poole Pottery and Walkers Crisps have all built corporate museums at their headquarters that display their history and the drama of producing and marketing their products.

Major decisions in marketing and public relations

Not only must the company relate constructively to customers, suppliers and dealers; it must also relate to a large number of interested publics. A **public** is any group that has an actual or potential interest in or impact on a company's ability to achieve its objectives. **Public relations** (PR) includes a variety of programmes to promote or protect a company's image or individual products.

The wise company takes concrete steps to manage successful relationships with its key publics. Most companies have a public relations department that monitors the attitudes of the organisation's publics and distributes information and communications to build goodwill. The best PR departments counsel top management to adopt positive programmes and eliminate questionable practices so that negative publicity does not arise in the first place. They perform the following five functions:

To learn how an American Burger King franchise was started in Western Australia by a Canadian and grew to 210 outlets by 2003 before being consolidated under 'Happy Jacks', visit www.pearsoned.com.au/marketingmanagementaustralia.

1 **Press relations**: presenting news and information about the organisation in the most positive light.
2 **Goods/market offering publicity**: sponsoring efforts to publicise specific marketing offerings.
3 **Corporate communications**: promoting understanding of the organisation through internal and external communications.
4 **Lobbying**: dealing with legislators and government officials to promote or defeat legislation and regulation.
5 **Counselling**: advising management about public issues and company positions and image during good times and bad.

As the next marketing insight box explains, sometimes PR must spearhead marketing communication efforts to help when a brand gets into trouble.

Furthermore, the more sincere the firm's response – public acknowledgement of the impact on consumers and willingness to take whatever steps are necessary to solve the crisis – the less likely it is that consumers will form negative views.

Marketing insight

Managing a brand crisis

Marketing managers must assume that, at some point in time, some kind of brand crisis will arise. Famous brands such as BP, Cadbury's, Nestlé and Perrier have all experienced a potentially crippling brand crisis. These may be particularly damaging if there are widespread repercussions: (1) a loss in sales; (2) reduced effectiveness of marketing activities; (3) an increased sensitivity to rival firms' marketing activities; and (4) reduced effectiveness of its marketing activities on the sales of competing, unaffected brands.

In general, the more strongly brand equity and corporate image have been established – especially corporate credibility and trustworthiness – the more likely it is that the firm can weather the storm. Careful preparation and a well-managed crisis management programme, however, are also critical. As with Perrier's mineral water contamination crisis, the key to managing a crisis is that consumers see the response by the firm as both *swift* and *sincere*. Customers must feel an immediate sense that the company truly cares. Listening is not enough.

The longer it takes a firm to respond, the more likely it is that consumers can form negative impressions from unfavourable media coverage or word of mouth. Perhaps worse, consumers may find they do not really like the brand after all and permanently switch brands or products.

In 1994 Perrier was forced to halt production worldwide and recall all existing product when traces of benzene, a known carcinogen, were found in excessive quantities in its bottled water The brand never recovered and eventually was taken over by Nestlé SA. More recently, British Airways had a difficult time minimising the damage to its reputation over the alleged price-fixing collusion with Virgin Atlantic. BP used PR techniques to damp down the damage it suffered after a large oil spillage off the Shetland Islands. Nestlé had to confront a worldwide PR crisis when it unwittingly supplied baby-formula to Aftrican mothers,

▶ Marketing insight *(continued)*

unaware that they would dilute the powder in local lakes that were often infested with dangerous bugs.

In 2006 Cadbury's was forced to suspend a key advertising contract on UK independent TV stations as it sought to keep a low profile in the wake of a salmonella scare. The company had to recall seven varieties of Cadbury's Dairy Milk chocolate items. The crisis damaged Cadbury's brand reputation and is estimated to have cost £30 million in profit. The company was also severely criticised by the UK government for seeking to disguise the salmonella outbreak for six months and by the UK Advisory Committee on the Microbiological Safety of Food for failing to keep up with modern risk assessment methods.

Sources: N. Klein and S. A. Greyser (2007) The Perrier recall: a source of trouble, Harvard Business School Case #9-590-104;

N. Klein and S. A. Greyser (2007) The Perrier relaunch, Harvard Business School Case #9-590-130; H. Van Heerde, K. Helsen and M. G. Dekimpe (2007) The impact of a product-harm crisis on marketing effectiveness, *Marketing Science*, 26, 230–45; M. L. Roehm and A. M. Tybout (2006) When will a brand scandal spill over and how should competitors respond?, *Journal of Marketing Research*, 43, 366–73; J. Klein and N. Dawar (2004) Corporate social responsibility and consumers' attributions and brand evaluations in a product-harm crisis, *International Journal of Research in Marketing*, 21(3), 203–17; R. Ahluwalia, R. E. Burnkrant and H. Rao Unnava (2000) Consumer response to negative publicity: the moderating role of commitment, *Journal of Marketing Research*, 37, 203–14; N. Dawar and M. M. Pillutla (2000) The impact of product-harm crises on brand equity: the moderating role of consumer expectations, *Journal of Marketing Research*, 37, 215–26; R. Alsop (1989) Enduring brands hold their allure by sticking close to their roots, *Wall Street Journal Centennial Edition*, 23 June; J. Wiggins (2006) Cadbury seeks a low profile after product recall, *Financial Times*, 9 July.

Marketing public relations

Many companies are turning to **marketing public relations** (MPR) to support corporate or market offering/product promotion and image making. MPR, like financial PR and community PR, serves a special constituency.

The old name for MPR was **publicity**, the task of securing editorial space – as opposed to paid space – in print and broadcast media to promote or 'hype' a product, service, idea, place, person or organisation. MPR goes beyond simple publicity and plays an important role in the following tasks:

- **Launching new products.** The amazing commercial success of toys such as Nintendo's DS and Wii owes a great deal to strong publicity.
- **Repositioning a mature product.** Glasgow had extremely bad press until the 'Glasgow – Smiles Better' campaign.
- **Building interest in a product category.** Companies and trade associations have used MPR to rebuild interest in declining commodities such as eggs, milk, beef and potatoes, and to expand consumption of such products as tea, pork and orange juice.
- **Influencing specific target groups.** Supermarkets throughout Europe sponsor special local events to build goodwill.
- **Defending products that have encountered public problems.** PR professionals must be adept at managing crises, such as the crisis suffered by Cadbury's in 2006 when one of its UK factories became contaminated.
- **Building the corporate image in a way that reflects favourably on its brand offerings.** Sir Richard Branson's activities have helped to create an innovative image for the Virgin Group.

As the power of mass advertising weakens, marketing managers are turning to MPR to build awareness and brand knowledge for both new and established lines. MPR is also effective in blanketing local communities and reaching specific groups, and can be more cost effective than advertising. Nevertheless, it must be planned jointly with advertising.[44] Marketing managers need to acquire more skill in using MPR resources.

Clearly, creative public relations can affect public awareness at a fraction of the cost of advertising. The company does not pay for media space or time, but only for staff to

Table 20.3 Major tools in marketing PR

Publications: Companies rely extensively on published materials to reach and influence their target markets. These include annual reports, brochures, articles, company newsletters and magazines, and audio-visual materials.

Events: Companies can draw attention to new products or other company activities by arranging special events such as news conferences, seminars, outings, trade shows, exhibits, contests and competitions, and anniversaries that will reach the target publics.

Sponsorships: Companies can promote their brands and corporate name by sponsoring sports and cultural events and highly regarded causes.

News: One of the major tasks of PR professionals is to find or create favourable news about the company, its products and its people, and to get the media to accept press releases and attend press conferences.

Speeches: Increasingly, company executives must field questions from the media or give talks at trade associations or sales meetings, and these appearances can build the company's image.

Public service activities: Companies can build goodwill by contributing money and time to good causes.

Identity media: Companies need a visual identity that the public immediately recognises. The visual identity is carried by company logos, stationery, brochures, signs, business forms, business cards, buildings, uniforms and dress codes.

---

develop and circulate the stories and manage certain events. An interesting story picked up by the media can be worth more than an advertising spend. Some experts say consumers are five times more likely to be influenced by editorial copy than by advertising.

Major decisions in marketing press relations

In considering when and how to use MPR, management must establish the marketing objectives, choose the PR messages and vehicles, implement the plan carefully and evaluate the results. The main tools of MPR are described in Table 20.3.[45]

Establishing objectives

MPR can build *awareness* by placing stories in the media to bring attention to a product, service, person, organisation or idea. It can build *credibility* by communicating the message in an editorial context. It can help boost sales force and dealer *enthusiasm* with stories about a new product before it is launched. It can hold down *promotion cost* because MPR costs less than direct mail and media advertising.

Breakthrough marketing

Virgin Group

Virgin, the brainchild of the UK's Richard Branson, vividly illustrates the power of strong traditional and non-traditional marketing communications. Branson emerged in the 1970s with his innovative Virgin Records. He signed unknown artists whom no one would touch and began a marathon of publicity that continues to this day. He has since sold Virgin Records (to Thorn-EMI for nearly US$1 billion in 1992) but created over 200 companies worldwide whose combined revenues exceed US$5 billion.

The Virgin name – the third most respected brand in Britain – and the Branson personality help to sell diverse products and services such as planes, trains, finance, soft drinks, music, mobile phones, cars, wine,

▶ Breakthrough marketing *(continued)*

publishing, even bridal wear. Clearly Branson can create interest in almost any business he wants by simply attaching the name 'Virgin' to it. Virgin Mobile exemplifies this strategy. Branson supplies the brand and a small initial investment and takes a majority control, and big-name partners come up with the cash.

Some marketing and financial critics argue that he is diluting the brand, that it covers too many businesses. Branson has had some fumbles: Virgin Cola, Virgin Cosmetics and Virgin Vodka have all but disappeared. But despite the diversity all the lines connote value for money, quality, innovation, fun and a sense of competitive challenge. The Virgin Group looks for new opportunities in markets with underserved, overcharged customers and complacent competition. Branson called these customer-hostile competitors 'big bad wolves'. 'Wherever we find them, there is a clear opportunity area for Virgin to do a much better job than the competition. We introduce trust, innovation, and customer friendliness where they don't exist,' Branson said. And once Virgin finds an opportunity, its vaunted marketing expertise kicks in.

A master of the strategic publicity stunt, Branson took on stodgy, overpriced British Airways by wearing

Canny marketing and public relations has helped Sir Richard Branson build an empire of successful brands under the Virgin name.
Source: Shawn Thew/epa/Corbis.

First World War era flying gear to announce the formation of Virgin Atlantic in 1984. The first Virgin flight took off laden with celebrities and media, and equipped with a brass band, waiters from Maxim's in white tie and tails, and free-flowing champagne. The airborne party enjoyed international press coverage and millions of dollars' worth of free publicity. Branson knew that photographers have a job to do and would turn up at his events if he gave them a good reason.

Although Branson eschews traditional market research, he stays in touch through constant customer contact. When he first set up Virgin Atlantic he called 50 customers every month to chat and get their feedback. He appeared in airports to rub elbows with customers, and if a plane was delayed he handed out gift certificates to a Virgin Megastore or discounts on future travel. Virgin's marketing campaigns include press and radio advertisements, direct mail and point-of-sale material. Virgin Mobile, for example, rolled out a postcard advertising campaign offering consumers discounts on new phones.

To identify where listeners to Virgin's web-based Virgin Radio reside, the company created a VIP club. Listeners join the club by giving their postcode, which then lets Virgin Radio target promotions and advertising to specific locations, just as a local radio station would. Once known as the 'hippie capitalist', Sir Richard Branson continues to look for new businesses and to generate publicity in his characteristic charismatic style. Remembering a friend's advice about publicity – 'If you don't give them a photograph that will get them on the front page, they won't turn up at your next event' – Branson always gives them a reason.

Sources: P. Elkind (2007) Branson gets grounded, *Fortune*, 5 February, 13–14; A. Deutschman (2006) The enlightenment of Richard Branson, *Fast Company*, September, 49; A. Serwer (2005) Do Branson's profits equal his joie de vivre?, *Fortune*, 17 October, 57; www.virgin.com; D. H. Silver and B. Austad (2004) Factors predicting the effectiveness of celebrity endorsement advertisements, *European Journal of Marketing*, 38(11/12), 1509–26; http://news.bbc.co.uk/1/hi/business/6936235.stm; news.bbc.co.uk/1/hi/business/7083517.stm; www.bbc.co.uk/consumer/tvandradio/watchdog/reports/services/services20071010.shtml.

Whereas PR practitioners reach their target publics through the mass media, MPR is increasingly borrowing the techniques and technology of direct-response marketing to reach target audience members one to one.

Choosing messages and vehicles

Suppose a relatively unknown college wants more visibility. The MPR practitioner will search for stories. Do any faculty members have unusual backgrounds, or are any working on unusual projects? Are any new and unusual courses being taught? Are any interesting events taking place on campus? If there are no interesting stories, the MPR practitioner should propose newsworthy events that the college could sponsor. Here the challenge is to create news. PR ideas include hosting major academic conventions, inviting expert or celebrity speakers, and promoting news conferences. Each event is an opportunity to develop a multitude of stories directed at different audiences. The following is a good example of reaching different audiences.

Vattenfall AB

From its humble roots as a local royal institution and Sweden's electrical company founded in 1909, Vattenfall has become an international brand with 33,000 employees and is now Europe's largest heating firm and fourth-largest electricity firm. This transformation was challenging because it meant mergers and acquisitions with local brands from Germany, Poland, Finland and Denmark, some as old as from the 1880s. Suspicion, lack of awareness and other obstacles required a number of marketing actions, but events and PR played a crucial role. Vattenfall's joint sponsorship and event strategy concentrated in three areas (with themes) – sports (outdoor life and teamwork), human care (life of future generations) and environment (sustainable development and wildlife). These sponsorships and events were set in local markets as well as across all markets. Broader sponsorship included the National Geographic Society and the World Childhood Foundation. Vattenfall garnered considerable publicity by also sponsoring a number of local events, such as Brandenburg Gate commemorations in Germany, heated bus stops in Poland, and the 2006 European Athletics (track and field) Championships in Gothenburg, Sweden. Through focused and highly integrated activities, Vattenfall was able to enjoy high public awareness, a competitive local image, top financial market performance and a huge increase in customer satisfaction.[46]

A wide variety of integrated promotions helped Sweden's Vattenfall, a large heating and electricity supplier, reach an equally broad spectrum of audiences and improve its financials.
Source: Lowe Brindfors AB.

Implementing the plan and evaluating results

MPR's contribution to the bottom line is difficult to measure because it is used along with other promotional tools.

The easiest measure of MPR effectiveness is the number of *exposures* carried by the media. Publicists supply the client with a clippings book showing all the media that carried news about the firm's items and a summary statement.

This measure is not very satisfactory because it contains no indication of how many people actually read, heard or recalled the message and what they thought afterwards; nor does it contain information about the net audience reached, because publications overlap in readership. Publicity's goal is reach, not frequency, so it would be more useful to know the number of unduplicated exposures.

A better measure is the *change in product awareness, comprehension or attitude* resulting from the MPR campaign (after allowing for the effect of other promotional tools). For example, how many people recall hearing the news item? How many told others about it (a measure of word of mouth)? How many changed their minds after hearing it?

Direct marketing

Setting objectives

Direct marketing is the use of consumer-direct (CD) channels to reach and market offerings to customers without using marketing middlemen. Direct marketers can use a number of channels to reach individual prospects and customers: direct mail, catalogue marketing, telemarketing, interactive TV, kiosks, websites and mobile devices. They often seek a measurable response, typically a customer order, through **direct-order marketing**.

Today, many direct marketers build long-term relationships with customers. Thirty-nine airlines, hotels and other businesses build strong customer relationships through frequency reward programmes and club programmes.[47]

Direct marketing has been a fast-growing mode for serving customers, partly in response to the high and increasing costs of reaching business markets through a sales force. Sales produced through traditional direct marketing channels (catalogues, direct mail and telemarketing) have been growing rapidly, along with direct mail sales, which include sales to the consumer markets, business-to-business, and fund-raising by charitable institutions.[48]

The benefits of direct marketing

Market demassification has resulted in an ever-increasing number of market niches. Time-poor consumers appreciate freephone numbers, websites available 24 hours a day and seven days a week, and direct marketers' commitment to customer service. The growth of next-day delivery by companies such as DHL has made ordering fast and easy. In addition, many chain stores have dropped slower-moving speciality items, creating an opportunity for direct marketers.

Sellers benefit as well. Direct marketers can buy a mailing list containing the names of almost any group. They can customise and personalise messages and build a continuous relationship with each customer.

Direct marketing[49] can reach prospects at the right moment and be read by more interested prospects. It lets marketers test alternative media and messages to find the most cost-effective or efficient approach. Direct marketing also makes the direct marketer's offer and strategy less visible to competitors. Finally, direct marketers can measure responses to their campaigns to gauge which have been the most profitable.

Direct marketing must be integrated with other marketing communications and distribution activities. Successful direct marketers ensure that customers can contact the company with questions and view a customer interaction as an opportunity. These marketers make sure they know enough about each customer to customise and personalise offers and messages, and develop a plan for lifetime marketing to each valuable customer, based on knowledge of life events and transitions. They also carefully integrate each element of their campaigns.

Guinness

The Direct Marketing Association's top Diamond ECHO award in 2006 went to Target Marketing for its multimedia/integrated media campaign, 'Guinness Relationship Marketing', on behalf of Diageo Ireland. A campaign was designed to maximise the value of the relationship between consumers and pub owners, build brand loyalty, and cross-sell cans of Draught Guinness to consumers who switched brands when drinking at home. Guinness sales representatives gave pub owners The Big Black Book, with information about the campaign. Pint vouchers brought consumers back to the pub. Western-themed posters asked, 'Are you one of the Guinness most wanted?' The campaign also tied in with football events, offering home kit boxes for consumers.[50]

Overview of the direct marketing mix

Here are some of the key issues that characterise different direct marketing channels.

Direct mail

Direct mail marketing means sending an offer, announcement, reminder or other item to an individual consumer. Using highly selective mailing lists, direct marketers send out millions of letters, flyers, foldouts, etc. each year. Some send CDs, DVDs and computer diskettes to prospects and customers.

Direct mail is a popular medium because it permits target market selectivity, can be personalised, is flexible, and allows early testing and response measurement. Although the cost per thousand people reached is higher than with mass media, the people reached are much better prospects. The success of direct mail, however, has also become its liability – so many marketers are sending out direct mail that consumers pay little attention to it. One of the biggest users of direct mail, the financial services industry, has seen its response rates from campaigns drop significantly in recent years.[51] In constructing an effective direct mail campaign, direct marketers must decide on their objectives, target markets and prospects; offer elements; means of testing the campaign; and measures of campaign success.

Objectives

Most direct marketers judge a campaign's success by the number of orders received. An order-response rate of 2 per cent is normally considered good, although this number varies with product category, price, and the nature of the offering. Direct mail can also produce prospect leads, strengthen customer relationships, inform and educate customers, remind customers of offers, and reinforce recent customer purchase decisions.

Target markets and prospects

Most direct marketers apply the RFM formula (recency, frequency, monetary amount). They select customers according to how much time has passed since their last purchase, how many times they have purchased, and how much they have spent since becoming a customer. Points are established for varying RFM levels; the more points, the more attractive the customer.

Marketers also identify prospects on the basis of age, sex, income, education, previous mail order purchases, and occasions. New students will buy laptop computers, backpacks and compact refrigerators; newlyweds look for housing, furniture, appliances and bank loans. Another useful variable is consumer lifestyle or 'passions' such as computers, cooking and the outdoors.

The company's best prospects are customers who have bought its products in the past. The direct marketer can also buy names from list brokers, but these often have problems, including name duplication, incomplete data and obsolete addresses. Better lists include overlays of demographic and psychographic information. Direct marketers typically buy and test a sample before buying more names from the same list. They can build their own lists by advertising a free offer and collecting responses.

Offer elements

The offer strategy has five elements – the *product*, the *offer*, the *medium*, the *distribution method* and the *creative strategy*.[52] Fortunately, all can be tested. The direct mail marketer needs to pay careful attention to five components of the mailing itself: the outside envelope, sales letter, circular, reply form and reply envelope.

1 The outside envelope should contain an illustration, preferably in colour, or an incentive to open it.
2 The sales letter, brief and on good-quality paper, should use a personal salutation and start with a headline in bold type. A computer-typed letter usually outperforms a printed letter, and a pithy PS increases response rate, as does the signature of someone whose title is important.
3 A colourful circular accompanying the letter usually increases the response rate by more than its cost.
4 Direct mailers should feature a freephone number and a website where recipients can print coupons.
5 A postage-free reply envelope will dramatically increase the response rate.

Direct mail should be followed up by an email, which is less expensive and less intrusive than a telemarketing call.

Testing elements

One of the great advantages of direct marketing is the ability to test, under real marketplace conditions, different elements of an offer strategy, such as products, product features, copy platform, mailer type, envelope, prices or mailing lists.

Response rates typically understate a campaign's long-term impact. Suppose only 2 per cent of the recipients who receive direct mail advertising Samsonite luggage place an order. A much larger percentage became aware of the product (direct mail has high readership), and some percentage may have formed an intention to buy at a later date (either by mail or at a retail outlet). Furthermore, some may mention luggage to others as a result of the direct mail piece. To better estimate a promotion's impact, some companies measure the impact of direct marketing on awareness, intention to buy and word of mouth.

Measuring campaign success: lifetime value

By totalling the planned campaign costs, the direct marketer can determine the needed breakeven response rate, which needs to be net of returned merchandise and bad debts.

Even when a specific campaign fails to break even in the short run, it can still be profitable in the long run if customer lifetime is factored in (see Chapter 7). Calculate the average customer longevity, average customer annual expenditure and average gross margin, minus the average cost of customer acquisition and maintenance (discounted for the opportunity cost of money).[53]

Catalogue marketing

In catalogue marketing, companies may send full-line merchandise, and speciality consumer and business catalogues, usually in print form but also sometimes in CDs, videos or online format. For example, Avon sells cosmetics, Coopers sells home interest items, IKEA sells furniture and Lakeland Ltd sells household products, crafts and food items through catalogues. Many direct marketers find combining catalogues and websites an effective way to sell. Thousands of small businesses also issue speciality catalogues. Large businesses send catalogues to business prospects and customers.

Catalogues generate a considerable amount of business. The success of a catalogue business depends on managing customer lists carefully to avoid duplication or bad debts, controlling inventory carefully, offering quality merchandise so returns are low, and projecting a distinctive image. Some companies add literary or information features, send swatches of materials, operate a special hotline to answer questions, send gifts to their best customers, and donate a percentage of profits to good causes.

Business marketers are making inroads as well. Putting their entire catalogue online provides better access to global consumers than ever before, saving printing and mailing costs.

Telemarketing

Telemarketing is the use of the telephone and call centres to attract prospects, sell to existing customers, and provide service by taking orders and answering questions. Telemarketing helps companies increase revenue, reduce selling costs and improve customer satisfaction. Companies use call centres for *inbound telemarketing* – receiving calls from customers – and *outbound telemarketing*: initiating calls to prospects and customers.

Although telemarketing is a major direct marketing tool, its sometimes intrusive nature led to legislation in many European countries that protects the right of consumers to refuse to receive direct marketing telephone calls. It is increasing in business-to-business marketing. Raleigh Bicycles, for example, uses telemarketing to reduce personal selling expense in contacting its dealers. Effective telemarketing depends on choosing the right telemarketers, training them well, and providing performance incentives.

Other media for direct response marketing

Direct marketers use all the major media. Newspapers and magazines carry abundant print advertisements offering books, articles of clothing, appliances, holidays, and other goods and services that individuals can order via freephone numbers. Radio advertisements present offers 24 hours a day. Some companies prepare 30- and 60-minute *infomercials* to combine the sell of television commercials with the draw of information and entertainment. Infomercials promote products that are complicated or technologically advanced, or which require a great deal of explanation (Mercedes, Microsoft, Philips Electronics, Universal Studios, and online financial and employment agencies).[54] Some at-home shopping channels are dedicated to selling goods and services on a freephone number for delivery within 48 hours.

Public and ethical issues in direct marketing

Direct marketers and their customers usually enjoy mutually rewarding relationships. Occasionally, however, a darker side emerges:

- **Irritation.** Many people are irritated by the large number of hard-sell, direct marketing solicitations. Especially annoying are calls at dinnertime or late at night, poorly trained callers and computerised calls by auto-dial recorded-message players.
- **Unfairness.** Some direct marketers take advantage of impulsive or less sophisticated buyers or prey on the vulnerable, especially the elderly.
- **Deception and fraud.** Some direct marketers design mailings and write copy intended to mislead. They may exaggerate product size, performance claims or the 'retail price'.
- **Invasion of privacy.** It seems that almost every time consumers order products by mail or telephone, apply for a credit card, or take out a magazine subscription, their names, addresses and purchasing behaviour may be added to several company databases. Critics worry that marketers may know too much about consumers' lives, and that they may use this knowledge to take unfair advantage.

People in the direct marketing industry are addressing the issues. They know that, left unattended, such problems will lead to increasingly negative consumer attitudes, lower response rates, and calls for greater regulation. In the final analysis, most direct marketers want the same thing consumers want: honest and well-designed marketing offers targeted only to those who appreciate hearing about the offer.

Interactive marketing

(See also Chapter 4.)

The newest channels for communicating and selling directly to customers are electronic. The internet provides marketers and consumers with opportunities for much greater *interaction* and *individualisation*. Few marketing programmes are considered complete without some type of prominent online component, which is gaining ground at the expense of traditional advertising agencies.

Interactive marketing offers unique benefits. Companies can send tailored messages that engage consumers by reflecting their special interests and behaviour. The internet is highly accountable and its effects can easily be traced. Online, advertisers can gauge response instantaneously by noting how many unique visitors or 'UVs' click on a page or advertisement, how long they spend with it, where they go afterwards and so on.[55]

The web offers the advantage of *contextual placement* and buying advertisements on sites that are related to the marketer's offerings. Marketers can also place advertising based on keywords from search engines, to reach people when they have actually started the buying process. Light consumers of other media, especially television, can be reached online. The web is especially effective at reaching people during the day.

Using the web also has disadvantages. Consumers can effectively screen out most messages. Marketers may think their advertisements are more effective than they are if bogus clicks are generated by software-powered websites. Advertisers lose some control over what consumers will do with their online messages. However, many feel the advantages outweigh the disadvantages, and the web is attracting marketers of all kinds.

To capitalise on advertisers' interest, firms are rushing online services and other support to marketers. Microsoft has invested in a broad range of businesses for placing advertisements on the web, videogames and mobile phones alongside internet search results. The breakthrough marketing box describes Yahoo!'s online efforts.

For marketers of cars, financial services, personal computers and telecommunications, marketing activities on the web have become crucial. However, others are quickly

Breakthrough marketing

Yahoo!

Since its foundation in 1994 Yahoo! has grown into a powerful force in internet media, attracting Microsoft to make a bid for it in 2007. Yahoo! has worked hard to be more than just a search engine. The company proudly proclaims it is 'the only place anyone needs to go to find anything, communicate with anyone, or buy anything'. Its wide range of web services includes email, news, weather, music, photos, games, shopping, auctions, travel and more.

Yahoo! sees one of its main advantages over rival Google as its vast array of original content. Yahoo! has alliances with hundreds of premier content providers to offer a personalisation option in My Yahoo!, which enables users to specify their favourite Yahoo! features and content to fit a single page. With a database of information about where its millions of registered users live and what their interests are, Yahoo! can present users with both more relevant search results and more

relevant advertising. Each month more than 475 million people worldwide visit one of its myriad sites, with billions of page views each day.

A large percentage of revenue comes from advertising, but the company continues to supplement its revenues through subscription sources such as online personal advertisements, premium email products and services for small businesses. In February 2007 Yahoo! launched a new search advertising system, Panama, to increase the quality of its search results as well the advertising revenue it generates from searches.

Sources: C. Holahan (2007) Yahoo!'s bid to think small, *BusinessWeek*, 26 February, 94; B. Elgin (2006) Yahoo!'s boulevard of broken dreams, *BusinessWeek*, 13 March, 76–7; J. Hibbard (2006) How Yahoo! gave itself a face-lift, *BusinessWeek*, 9 October, 74–7; K. J. Delaney (2006) As Yahoo! falters, executive's memo calls for overhaul, *Wall Street Journal*, 18 November; Yahoo!'s personality crisis, *The Economist*, 13 August, 49–50; F. Vogelstein (2005) Yahoo!'s brilliant solution, *Fortune*, 8 August, 42–55.

following. Although beauty pioneer Estée Lauder said she relied on three means of communication to build her cosmetics business – 'telephone, telegraph, and tell a woman' – she would now have to add the web, which helps to support Estée Lauder brands. Consumer packaged-goods giants such as Danone, Nestlé and Lindt are also significantly increasing their online budgets. Pepsi spent between 5 per cent and 10 per cent of its overall marketing communications budget online in 2006, compared to just 1 per cent in 2001, because of its cost effectiveness.[56]

Marketers must go where the customers are, and increasingly that's online. Customers define the rules of engagement, however, and insulate themselves with the help of agents and intermediaries if they so choose. Customers define what information they need, what offerings they are interested in, and what they are willing to pay (see Chapter 11). Online advertising was estimated at a little less than 6 per cent of global marketing communication spending in 2006, but is expected to jump to 10 per cent by 2010. Helping fuel that growth is the emergence of media advertisements that combine animation, video and sound with interactive features.

Placing advertisements and promotions online

A company chooses which forms of interactive marketing will be most cost effective in achieving communication and sales objectives.

Websites

Companies must design websites that embody or express their purpose, history, products and vision.[57] A key challenge is designing a site that is both attractive and interesting enough to encourage repeat visits.[58] Rayport and Jaworski propose that effective sites feature seven design elements they call the 7Cs (see Figure 20.5).[59] To encourage repeat visits, companies must pay special attention to context and content factors and embrace another 'C' – constant change.[60]

Visitors will judge a site's performance on ease of use and physical attractiveness. Ease of use has three attributes: (1) the site downloads quickly; (2) the first page is easy to understand; and (3) it is easy to navigate to other pages that open quickly. Physical attractiveness is determined by these factors: (1) individual pages are clean and not crammed with content; (2) typefaces and font sizes are very readable; and (3) the site makes good use of colour (and sound). Websites must also be sensitive to national characteristics,[61] security and privacy protection issues.

Microsites

A **microsite** is a limited area on the web managed and paid for by an external advertiser/company. Microsites are individual web pages or clusters of pages that function as

- **Context:** Layout and design
- **Content:** Text, pictures, sound and video the site contains
- **Community:** How the site enables user-to-user communication
- **Customisation:** Site's ability to tailor itself to different users or to allow users to personalise the site
- **Communication:** How the site enables site-to-user, user-to-site or two-way communication
- **Connection:** Degree that the site is linked to other sites
- **Commerce:** Site's capabilities to enable commercial transactions

Figure 20.5 Seven key design elements of an effective website
Source: J. F. Rayport and B. J. Jaworksi (2001) *e-commerce*, New York: McGraw-Hill, p. 116. Copyright © 2001 McGraw-Hill Companies.

supplements to a primary site. They are particularly relevant for companies selling low-interest products. People rarely visit an insurance company's website, but the company can create a microsite on used-car sites that offers advice for buyers of used cars and insurance at the same time. Some microsites have become huge online hits.

Search advertisements

A hot growth area in interactive marketing is **paid-search** or **pay-per-click advertisements**.[62] The search terms trigger relevant links to market offerings alongside search results from Google, MSN, Tiscali and Yahoo! Advertisers pay only if people click on the links. However, marketers believe consumers have already expressed an interest by clicking on the links and are good prospects.

Some believe the internet is moving from the era of search to the era of discovery, thanks to recommender sites and systems such as Amazon's 'getting to know you suggestions'. In February 2008 Brent Hoberman, who used to run Lastminute.com, launched Mydeco in the United Kingdom. The action centres on state-of-the-art technology that enables people to upload the dimensions of a room, add windows, doors and fireplaces and then choose from more than 20,000 items of furniture and accessories to see how they will look in the space. Once it is arranged, prospective customers can see a 3-D view of the room – and then buy it all over the Internet.

Display advertisements

Display advertisements or **banner ads** are small, rectangular boxes containing text and perhaps a picture that companies pay to place on relevant websites. The larger the audience, the more the placement costs. Some banners are accepted on a barter basis.[63]

Display advertisements still hold great promise compared to popular search advertisements. Given that internet users spend only 5 per cent of their time online actually searching for information, there are many opportunities to reach and influence consumers while they surf the web. However, advertisements need to be more attractive and influential, better targeted and more closely tracked.[64]

The emergence of behavioural targeting is allowing companies to track the online behaviour of target customers to find the best match between advertisement and prospect. For example, if a person clicks on three websites related to car insurance, then visits an unrelated site for sports or entertainment, car insurance advertisements may show up on that site, in addition to the car insurance sites. This practice ensures that advertisements are readily apparent for a potential customer likely to be in the market. Although critics worry about companies knowing too much about customers, Microsoft claims that behavioural targeting can increase the likelihood that a visitor clicks an advertisement by as much as 76 per cent.

Interstitials

Interstitials are advertisements, often with video or animation, that pop up between changes on a website. Many consumers find pop-up advertisements intrusive and distracting, so most ISPs now offer their subscribers a blocking option.

Internet-specific advertisements and videos

With user-generated content sites such as YouTube, MySpace Video and Google Video, consumers and advertisers can upload advertisements and videos to be shared virally by millions of people.

Sponsorships

Many companies appear on the internet by sponsoring special content on websites that carry news, financial information and so on. **Sponsorships** are best placed in well-targeted sites that offer relevant information or service. The sponsor pays for showing the content and in turn receives acknowledgement as the sponsor of that particular service on the site.

A popular vehicle for sponsorship is the *podcast*, digital media files created for playback on portable MP3 players, laptops or PCs. Although the costs are higher than for popular radio shows, podcasts are able to reach very specific market segments so analysts expect their popularity to grow.

Alliances

When one internet company works with another, they end up advertising each other through alliances and affiliate programmes. AOL has created many successful alliances. Amazon has almost 1 million affiliates that post their banners on its websites. Companies can also undertake guerrilla marketing actions to publicise their site and generate word of mouth.

Online communities

Many companies sponsor online communities whose members communicate through postings, instant messaging and chat discussions about special interests related to the company's products and brands. These communities can provide companies with useful, hard-to-get information. A key for success of online communities is to create individual and group activities that help form bonds among members.

Email

Email uses only a fraction of the cost of a 'd-mail', or direct mail, campaign. Consumers are besieged by emails, however, and many employ spam filters. Following are some important guidelines for productive email campaigns, which are followed by pioneering email marketers:[65]

- **Give the customer a reason to respond.** Offer powerful incentives for reading email pitches and online advertisements, such as email trivia games, scavenger hunts and instant-win sweepstakes.
- **Personalise the content of your emails.** IBM's iSource is distributed directly to customers' office email each week, delivering only 'the news they choose' in Announcements and Weekly Updates. Customers who agree to receive the newsletter select from topics listed on an interest profile.
- **Offer something the customer cannot get via direct mail.** Because email campaigns can be carried out quickly, they can offer time-sensitive information such as the availability of last-minute cheap airfares and holiday vacancies.
- **Make it easy for customers to 'unsubscribe'.** Online customers demand a positive exit experience. According to a Burston-Marsteller and Roper Starch Worldwide study, the top 10 per cent of web users who communicate much more often online typically share their views by email with 11 friends when satisfied, but contact 17 friends when dissatisfied.[66]

Mobile

(See also Chapters 17 and 18.)
Mobile is an emerging mode which is likely to benefit from the new generation of dual-mode phones that will make it increasingly easy to blend mobile phones with wireless internet service. The popularity of mobile phones is increasing marketers' interest in mobile marketing, especially as messages can be personalised. However, there is some doubt about how consumers will react to such advertisements.

Developing and managing the sales force

Setting objectives and strategy

The original and oldest form of direct marketing is the field sales call. Today most business-to-business companies rely heavily on a professional sales force to locate prospects, develop them into customers and grow the business, or they hire manufacturers' representatives and agents to carry out the direct selling task. In addition, many consumer companies such as Avon, Merrill Lynch, Anne Summers and Tupperware use a direct selling force. Hospitals and museums, for example, use fund-raisers to contact and solicit donations. For many firms, sales force performance is critical.

Although no one debates the importance of the sales force in marketing programmes, companies are sensitive to the high and rising costs of maintaining one. The term *sales representative* covers six positions, ranging from the least to the most creative types of selling:[67]

1 **Deliverer**: a salesperson whose major task is the delivery of a product (water, fuel, oil).
2 **Order taker**: an inside order taker (standing behind the counter) or outside order taker (calling on the supermarket manager).
3 **Missionary**: a salesperson not expected or permitted to take an order but rather to build goodwill or educate the actual or potential user (the medical 'detailer' representing an ethical pharmaceutical house).
4 **Technician**: a salesperson with a high level of technical knowledge (the engineering salesperson who is primarily a consultant to client companies).
5 **Demand creator**: a salesperson who relies on creative methods for selling tangible products (vacuum cleaners, cleaning brushes, household products) or intangibles (insurance, advertising services, education).
6 **Solution vendor**: a salesperson whose expertise is solving a customer's problem, often with a system of the company's products and services (for example, computer and communications systems).

In designing the sales force, the company must consider the development of sales force objectives, strategy, structure, size and compensation (see Figure 20.6).

Companies need to define specific sales force objectives. For example, a company might want its sales representatives to spend 80 per cent of their time with current customers and 20 per cent with prospects, and 85 per cent of their time on established market offerings and 15 per cent on new offerings. The specific allocation depends on the kind of offerings and customers. Irrespective of the context, salespeople will have one or more of the following specific tasks to perform:

- **prospecting**: searching for prospects, or leads;
- **targeting**: deciding how to allocate their time among prospects and customers;
- **communicating**: communicating information about the company's products and services;
- **selling**: approaching, presenting, answering questions, overcoming objections and closing sales;
- **servicing**: providing various services to the customers – consulting on problems, rendering technical assistance, arranging financing, expediting delivery;
- **information gathering**: conducting market research and doing intelligence work; and
- **allocating**: deciding which customers will get scarce products during product shortages.

Most companies are choosing a *leveraged sales force* that focuses representatives on selling the company's more complex and customised offerings to large accounts and uses inside salespeople and web ordering for small customers. Tasks such as lead generation, proposal writing, order fulfilment and after-sales support are assigned to others. Salespeople handle fewer accounts and are rewarded for key account growth. This is far different from expecting salespeople to sell to every possible account, the common weakness of geographically based sales forces.[68]

Companies must deploy sales forces strategically so they call on the right customers at the right time in the right way. Today's sales representatives act as 'account managers' who arrange fruitful contact between people in the buying and selling organisations.

Figure 20.6 Designing a sales force

Selling increasingly calls for teamwork and the support of others, such as *top management*, especially when national accounts or major sales are at stake; *technical people*, who supply information and service before, during or after product purchase; *customer service representatives*, who provide installation, maintenance and other services; and an *office staff*, consisting of sales analysts, order expediters and assistants, as they all have a vital part to play in the customer-perceived value offerings that companies bring to market.

To maintain a market focus, salespeople should know how to analyse sales data, measure market potential, gather market intelligence and develop marketing strategies and plans. Sales representatives, especially at the higher levels of sales management, need analytical marketing skills. Marketers believe sales forces are more effective in the long run if they understand that they are an integral part of the marketing team (see Chapter 22).[69]

Once the company chooses an approach, it can use a direct or a contractual sales force. A **direct (company) sales force** consists of full- or part-time paid employees who work exclusively for the company. Inside sales personnel conduct business from the office using the telephone and receive visits from prospective buyers, and field sales personnel travel to visit customers. A **contractual sales force** consists of manufacturers' representatives, sales agents and brokers, who earn a commission based on sales.

Sales force management issues

The sales force strategy has implications for its structure. A company that offers one product line offering to one end-using industry with customers in many locations would use a territorial structure. A company that sells many product offerings to many types of customer might need a product or market structure. Some companies need a more complex structure. Established companies need to revise their sales force structures as market and economic conditions change.

Figure 20.7 shows how a company must focus on different aspects of its sales force structure over the life cycle of the business. The marketing insight box discusses a specialised form of sales force structure, major account management.[70]

Figure 20.7 The four factors for a successful sales force
Source: Reprinted by permission of *Harvard Business Review*. From Match your sales-force structure to your business life cycle by Zolters, A., Sinha, P. and Lorimer, S.E., July–August 2006. Copyright © 2006 by the Harvard Business School Publishing Corporation; all rights reserved.

	Business life cycle stage			
	Start-Up	Growth	Maturity	Decline
	Emphasis			
Role of sales force and selling partners	⇨⇨⇨⇨	⇨⇨	⇨	⇨⇨⇨
Size of sales force	⇨⇨⇨	⇨⇨⇨⇨	⇨⇨	⇨⇨⇨⇨
Degree of specialisation	⇨	⇨⇨⇨⇨	⇨⇨⇨	⇨⇨
Sales force resource allocation	⇨⇨	⇨	⇨⇨⇨⇨	⇨
	Underlying customer strategy			
	Create awareness and generate quick product uptake	Penetrate deeper into existing segments and develop new ones	Focus on efficiently serving and retaining existing customers	Emphasise efficiency, protect critical customer relationships, exit unprofitable segments

Marketing insight

Major account management

Marketers usually pay special attention to major accounts (also called key, national, global or house accounts). A major account manager (MAM) usually reports to the national sales manager and supervises field representatives calling on customer plants within their territories. Large accounts are often handled by a strategic account management team with cross-functional personnel to cover all aspects of the customer relationship.

Some firms are creating cross-functional strategic account teams that integrate new product development, technical support, supply chain, marketing activities and multiple communication channels. Major account management is growing. As buyer concentration increases through mergers and acquisitions, fewer buyers account for a larger share of a company's sales. Many are centralising their purchases for certain items, which gives them more bargaining power. As market offerings become more complex, more groups in the buyer's organisation participate in the purchase process.

In selecting major accounts, companies look for those that purchase a high volume (especially of more profitable offerings), purchase centrally, require a high level of service in several geographic locations, may be price sensitive, and may want a long-term partnering relationship. Major account managers are responsible for delivering the required level of customer-perceived value offerings (see Chapter 11).

Many major accounts look for perceived added value more than a price advantage. They appreciate having a dedicated single point of contact; single billing; special warranties; EDI links; priority shipping; early information releases; customised products; and efficient maintenance, repair and upgraded service.

Sources: C. Doyle, B. McPhee and I. Harris (2005) Marketing, sales, and major account management: managing enterprise customers as a portfolio of opportunities, talk at the Marketing Science Institute's Marketing, Sales, and Customers conference, 7 December; S. Sherman, J. Sperry and S. Reese (2003) *The Seven Keys to Managing Strategic Accounts*, New York: McGraw-Hill; J. Neff (2003) Bentonville or bust, *Advertising Age*, 24 February; N. Capon (2001) *Key Account Management and Planning: The Comprehensive Handbook for Managing Your Company's Most Important Strategic Asset*, New York: Free Press. More information can be obtained from NAMA (National Account Management Association) at www.nasm.com.

Sales force size

Once the company establishes the number of customers it wants to reach, it can use a *workload approach* to establish sales force size. This method has five steps:

1 Group customers into size classes according to annual sales volume.
2 Establish desirable call frequencies (number of calls on an account per year) for each customer class.
3 Multiply the number of accounts in each size class by the corresponding call frequency to arrive at the total workload for the country, in sales calls per year.
4 Determine the average number of calls a sales representative can make per year.
5 Divide the total annual calls required by the average annual calls made by a sales representative, to arrive at the number of sales representatives needed.

Sales force compensation

To recruit top-quality sales representatives the company must develop an attractive compensation package. Several policies and procedures guide the firm in recruiting, selecting, training, supervising, motivating and evaluating sales representatives (see Figure 20.8).

Recruiting and selecting representatives

At the heart of any successful sales force is a means of selecting effective representatives.[71] Selection procedures can vary from a single informal interview to prolonged testing and interviewing. Although scores from formal tests are only one factor in a selection procedure, tests have been weighted quite heavily by IBM, Prudential and Procter & Gamble. Gillette claims that tests have reduced turnover and that scores correlated well with the progress of new representatives.

Managing the
sales force

Recruiting
and selecting
sales
representatives

Training
sales
representatives

Supervising
sales
representatives

Motivating
sales
representatives

Evaluating
sales
representatives

Figure 20.8 Managing the sales force

Training and supervising sales representatives

Today's customers expect salespeople to have a sound company and offer product knowledge, to add ideas to improve the customers' operations, and to be efficient and reliable. These demands have required companies to make a much higher investment in sales training.

Companies vary in how closely they supervise sales representatives. Representatives paid mostly on commission generally receive less supervision. Those who are salaried and must cover definite accounts are likely to receive substantial supervision. With multilevel selling, used by Endsleigh Insurance, Virgin and others, independent distributors are also in charge of their own sales force selling company products. These independent contractors or representatives are paid a commission not only on their own sales but also on the sales of people they recruit and train.

Norms for prospect calls

Companies often specify how much time representatives should spend prospecting for new accounts.

Using sales time efficiently

The best sales representatives manage their time both effectively and efficiently. Companies constantly try to improve sales force productivity. To cut costs, reduce time demands on their outside sales force, and take advantage of computer and telecommunications innovations, many have increased the size and responsibilities of their internal sales staff (technical support people, sales assistants and telemarketers).

One of the most valuable electronic tools for the sales representative are prospective companies' websites, which can provide much useful information. At the same time, the representative's own company website can provide an introduction to self-identified potential customers and might even receive the initial order. For more complex transactions, the site provides a way for the buyer to contact the seller. Selling over the internet supports relationship marketing by solving problems that do not require live intervention and thus allows more time to be spent on issues that are best addressed face to face.

Motivating sales representatives

The majority of sales representatives require encouragement and special incentives. Many companies set annual sales quotas (developed from the annual marketing plan) on sales revenue, unit volume, margin, selling effort or activity, or market offering/product type. Compensation is often tied to the degree of quota fulfilment.

Setting sales quotas can create problems. If the company underestimates and the sales representatives easily achieve their quotas, it has overpaid them. If the company overestimates sales potential, the salespeople will find it very hard to reach their quotas and be frustrated or leave. Another disadvantage is that quotas can drive representatives to get as much business as possible – often ignoring the ability of the company to deliver successfully the full customer-perceived value offering. The company then gains short-term results at the cost of long-term customer satisfaction.

Ford of Britain

As a sales incentive Ford ran a conference at the Palmeraie Golf Palace in Marrakesh for dealer sales managers to maintain sales momentum at the end of 2007. The location was specially selected as it echoed a product placement in the Bond film *Casino Royale*. The programme included film clips and captured the enthusiasm of the audience, who were well travelled and not always that easy to please[72].

Evaluating sales representatives

So far the *feed-forward* aspects of sales supervision – how management communicates what the sales representatives should be doing and motivates them to do it – has been discussed. However, good feed-forward requires good *feedback*, which means getting regular information from customers to assess the performance of the sales force.

Sources of information

The most important source of information about representatives is sales reports. Additional information comes through personal observation, salesperson self-reports, customer letters and complaints, customer surveys, and conversations with other sales representatives.

Formal evaluation

The sales force's reports along with other observations supply the raw materials for evaluation. If effective in producing sales, the representative may not be highly rated by customers. Success may come because competitors' salespeople are inferior, the representative's company market offer is better, or new customers are found to replace those who dislike the representative. Managers can gather customer opinions of their salespeople's performances by email and postal questionnaires or telephone calls.

Key principles of personal selling

Effective salespeople today have more than instinct; they are trained in methods of analysis and customer management. Companies train salespeople to transform them from passive order takers into active order winners. Representatives are taught methods such as the SPIN system to build long-term relationships with questions such as:[73]

1 **Situation questions.** These ask about facts or explore the buyer's present situation: for example, 'What system are you using to invoice your customers?'
2 **Problem questions.** These deal with problems, difficulties and dissatisfactions that the buyer is experiencing: for example, 'What parts of the system create errors?'
3 **Implication questions.** These ask about the consequences or effects of a buyer's problems, difficulties or dissatisfactions: for example, 'How does this problem affect your people's productivity?'
4 **Need-payoff questions.** These ask about the value or usefulness of a proposed solution: for example, 'How much would you save if our company could help reduce the errors by 80 per cent?'

Most sales training programmes agree on the major steps involved in any effective sales process and these are shown in Figure 20.9; their application to business-to-business selling is discussed below.[74]

The six steps of selling

1 **Prospecting and qualifying.** The first step in selling is to identify and qualify prospects.
2 **Pre-approach.** The salesperson needs to learn as much as possible about the prospect company (what it needs, who is involved in the purchase decision) and its buyers (personal characteristics and buying styles).
3 **Presentation and demonstration.** The salesperson tells the company/market offering 'story' to the buyer, using a *features, advantages, benefits* and *value* approach (FABV). Features describe physical characteristics of a market offering, such as chip-processing speeds or memory capacity. Advantages describe why the features provide an advantage to the customer. Benefits describe the economic, technical, service and social

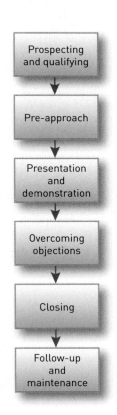

Figure 20.9 Major steps in effective selling

benefits delivered by the offering. Value explains the offering's worth in terms of CPV attributes (see Chapter 10). Salespeople often spend too much time on product features and not enough time stressing the prospective CPV of a market offering.

4 **Overcoming objections.** Customers typically pose objections. *Psychological resistance* includes resistance to interference, preference for established supply sources or brands, apathy, reluctance to give up something, unpleasant associations created by the sales representative, predetermined ideas, dislike of making decisions, and neurotic attitude towards money. *Logical resistance* might be objections to the price, delivery schedule, offering or company characteristics. To handle these objections, the salesperson should maintain a positive and professional approach and seek ways to satisfy the customer's perceived value requirements.

5 **Closing.** Closing signs from the buyer include physical actions, statements or comments, and questions. Representatives can ask for the order, recapitulate the points of agreement, offer to help write up the order, ask whether the buyer wants A or B, get the buyer to make minor choices such as colour or size, or indicate what the buyer will lose by not placing the order now. The salesperson might offer specific inducements to close, such as a special price, an extra quantity or a token gift.[75]

6 **Follow-up and maintenance.** Follow-up and maintenance are necessary to ensure customer satisfaction and repeat business. Immediately after closing, the salesperson should agree any necessary details about delivery time, purchase terms and other matters important to the customer. The salesperson should schedule a follow-up call after delivery to ensure proper installation, instruction and servicing and to detect any problems, assure the buyer of the salesperson's interest, and reduce any cognitive dissonance. Finally, the salesperson should develop an account maintenance and growth plan.

Relationship marketing (RM)

The principles of personal selling and negotiation are typically transaction oriented because their purpose is to close a specific sale. However, in today's buyers' markets, companies should be mindful of the need actively to seek and develop long-term supplier–customer relationships. The reason is simple: in buyers' markets (as opposed to sellers' markets), customers are in short supply. Furthermore, they will be keen to regard suppliers as being trusted members of their value chains. This is because, in highly competitive markets, wise companies are striving to gain a market edge by formulating and delivering customer-perceived value offerings that are superior to those of their competitors. So they prefer suppliers who can deliver a coordinated set of CPV offerings (comprised of core products and services) to many locations; who can quickly solve problems in different locations; and who can work closely with customer teams to improve CPV offerings and process issues.

When a relationship management programme is properly implemented, the organisation will focus on supplying what CPV offerings are wanted by its customers (market effectiveness in today's business environment) and on managing the development and supply of suitable CPV packages with due regard to its resources (efficiency) and which customers will respond profitably to relationship management. For further discussion of RM, see Chapter 21.

SUMMARY

1 Advertising is any paid form of non-personal presentation and promotion of ideas, goods or services by an identified sponsor. Advertisers include not only business firms but also charitable, non-profit and government agencies.

2 Developing an advertising programme is a five-step process: (1) set advertising objectives; (2) establish a budget; (3) choose the advertising message and creative strategy; (4) decide on the media; and (5) evaluate communication and sales effects.

3 Sales promotion consists of a diverse collection of incentive tools, mostly short term, designed to stimulate quicker or greater purchase of particular products or services by consumers or the trade. Sales promotion includes tools for consumer promotion, trade promotion, and business and sales force promotion (trade shows and conventions, contests for sales representatives and speciality advertising). In using sales promotion a company must establish its objectives, select the tools, develop the programme, pre-test the programme, implement and control it, and evaluate the results.

4 Events and experiences are a means to become part of special and more personally relevant moments in consumers' lives. Involvement with events can broaden and deepen the relationship of the sponsor with its target market, but only if managed properly.

5 Public relations (PR) involves a variety of programmes designed to promote or protect a company's image or its individual products. Many companies today use marketing public relations (MPR) to support the marketing department in corporate or product promotion and image making. MPR can affect public awareness at a fraction of the cost of advertising and is often much more credible. The main tools of PR are publications, events, news, speeches, public service activities and identity media.

6 Direct marketing is an interactive marketing system that uses one or more media to effect a measurable response or transaction at any location. Direct marketing, especially electronic marketing, is showing explosive growth.

7 Direct marketers plan campaigns by deciding on objectives, target markets and prospects, offers and prices. This is followed by testing and establishing measures to determine the campaign's success.

8 Major channels for direct marketing include face-to-face selling, direct mail, catalogue marketing, telemarketing, interactive TV, kiosks, websites and mobile devices.

9 Interactive marketing provides marketers with opportunities for much greater interaction and individualisation through well-designed websites, as well as online advertisements and promotions and other approaches.

10 Two notable forms of word-of-mouth marketing are buzz marketing, which seeks to get people talking about a brand by ensuring that a product or service or how it is marketed is out of the ordinary, and viral marketing, which encourages people to exchange information related one way or another to a product or service online.

11 Sales personnel serve as a company's link to its customers. The sales rep *is* the company to many of its customers, and it is the representative who brings back to the company much-needed information about the customer.

12 Designing the sales force requires decisions regarding objectives, strategy, structure, size and compensation. Objectives may include prospecting, targeting, communicating, selling, servicing, information gathering and allocating. Determining strategy requires choosing the most effective mix of selling approaches. Choosing the sales force structure entails dividing territories by geography, product or market (or some combination of these). Estimating how large the sales force needs to be involves estimating the total workload and how many sales hours (and hence salespeople) will be needed. Compensating the sales force entails determining what types of salaries, commissions, bonuses, expense accounts and benefits to give, and how much weight customer satisfaction should have in determining total compensation.

13 There are five steps involved in managing the sales force: (1) recruiting and selecting sales representatives; (2) training the representatives in sales techniques and in the company's products, policies and customer-satisfaction orientation; (3) supervising the sales force and helping representatives to use their time efficiently; (4) motivating the sales force and balancing quotas, monetary rewards and supplementary motivators; (5) evaluating individual and group sales performance.

14 Effective salespeople are trained in the methods of analysis and customer management, as well as the art of sales professionalism. No approach works best in all circumstances, but most trainers agree that selling is a six-step process: (1) prospecting and qualifying customers; (2) pre-approach; (3) presentation and demonstration; (4) overcoming objections; (5) closing; and (6) follow-up and maintenance.

APPLICATIONS

Marketing debates

Should marketers test advertising? Advertising creatives have long lamented advertisement pre-testing. They believe that it inhibits their creative process and results in much sameness in commercials. Marketers, on the other hand, believe that pre-testing provides necessary checks and balances as to whether an advertising campaign is being developed in a way that will connect with consumers and be well received in the marketplace.

Take a position: Advertisement pre-testing is often an unnecessary waste of marketing spend *versus* Advertisement pre-testing provides an important diagnostic function for marketers as to the likely success of an advertising campaign.

Are great salespeople born or made? One debate in sales is about the impact of training versus selection in developing an effective sales force. Some observers maintain the best salespeople are born that way and are effective due to their personalities and interpersonal skills, developed over a lifetime. Others contend that application of leading-edge sales techniques can make virtually anyone a sales star.

Take a position: The key to developing an effective sales force is selection *versus* The key to developing an effective sales force is training.

Marketing discussion

What are some of your favourite TV advertisements? Why? How effective are the message and creative strategies? How are they building brand equity?

References

[1]P. F. Nunes and J. Merrihue (2007) The continuing power of mass advertising, *Sloan Management Review*, Winter, 63–9.

[2]*Marketing*, 11 July 2007; *Marketing*, 7 November 2007; Andrex puppy voted tops, *Manchester Evening News*, 2 September 2007; Andrex puppy inducted into Madam Tussauds, *K9 Magazine*, 2 September 2007; www.andrexpuppy.co.uk.

[3]D. V. Thompson and R. W. Hamilton (2006) The effects of information processing on consumers' responses to comparative advertising, *Journal of Consumer Research*, 32 (March), 530–40; See also www.andrexpuppy.co.uk to view the new digital Andrex puppy.

[4]A popular saying attributed to John Wanamaker. See http://en.wikipedia.org/wiki/John_Wanamaker.

[5]See G. S. Low and J. J. Mohr (1998) Brand managers' perceptions of the marketing communications budget allocation process, Cambridge, MA: Marketing Science Institute, *Report*, No. 98-105, March; and their The advertising sales promotion trade-off: theory and practice, Cambridge, MA: Marketing Science Institute, *Report*, No. 92-127, October. Also see G. J. Beihal and D. A. Sheinen (1998) Managing the brand in a corporate advertising environment: a decision-making framework for brand managers, *Journal of Advertising*, 17(22), 99.

[6]D. Vakratsas, F. M. Feinberg, F. M. Bass and G. Kalyanaram (2004) The shape of advertising response functions revisited: a model of dynamic probabilistic thresholds, *Marketing Science*, 23(1), 109–19; M. Dossche, F. Heylen and D. Van den Poel (2010) The kinked demand curve and price rigidity: evidence from scanner data, *Scandinavian Journal of Economics*, 112(4), 723–52; Z. Yuqing, H. Kinnucan and H. Kaiser (2010) Measuring and testing advertising-induced rotation in the demand curve, *Applied Economics*, 42(13), 1601–14.

[7]L. M. Lodish, M. Abraham, S. Kalmenson, J. Livelsberger, B. Lubetkin, B. Richardson and M.-E. Stevens (1995) How TV advertising works: a meta-analysis of 389 real-world split cable TV advertising experiments, *Journal of Marketing Research*, 32 (May), 125–39.

[8]G. Allenby and D. Hanssens (2005) Advertising response, Marketing Science Institute, *Special Report*, No. 05-200; J. Neff (2004) TV doesn't sell package goods, *Advertising Age*, 24 May, 1, 30.

[9]N. Sandison (2008) *Brand Republic*, 4 March.

[10]www.stateofthenewsmedia.org/2007/narrative_newspapers_intro.asp?media=3.

[11]D. Ogilvy (1983) *Ogilvy on Advertising*, New York: Vintage Books. Also consider L. Percy, J. Rossiter and R. Elliott (2002) *Strategic Advertising Management*, Oxford: Oxford University Press; A. Hampp (2010) Who listens to radio these days, anyway? Doesn't everyone use their iPods and iPhones to hear music?, *Advertising Age*, 81(34), 50; M. Brassil, Radio advertising pros and cons, www.websitemarketingplan.com/small_business/radio.htm. See also article by M. P. Wachek at www.sideroad.com/Business_Communication/advantage-of-radio-advertising.html.

[12]K. B. Sheehan (2003) *Controversies in Contemporary Advertising*, Thousand Oaks, CA: Sage; MPs slam Google over gambling ads, *Campaign (UK)*, 13 February 2009, 2.

[13]P. Malaviya (2007) The moderating influence of advertising context on ad repetition effects: the role of amount and type of elaboration, *Journal of Consumer Research*, 34 (June), 32–40.

[14]F. M. Jukes (2009) Comparethemarket.com, *Revolution* (14605953), March, 68–69; From Russia with brand love, *Marketing Week* (01419285), 29 April 2010, 32; G. Everett, (2010) *Marketing Week* (01419285), 29 April, 32. The author explains the idea behind the use of a meerkat in advertisements for Comparethemarket.com in the UK.

[15]www.oaaa.org.

[16]B. Archer (2007) Outdoor media: digital formats – weblinks: airport advertising flies into the future, *Guardian*, 25 June, 2.

[17]M. A. Wiles and A. Danielova (2009) The worth of product placement in successful films: an event study analysis, *Journal of Marketing*, 73(4), 44–63; F. de Gregorio, Federico and Y. Sung (2010) Understanding attitudes toward and behaviors in response to product placement, *Journal of Advertising*, 39(1), 83–96; G. Guido, A. M. Peluso, P. Tedeschi, C. Nicole, C. Lauretti and A. Caciula (2010) Acceptance of product placement in Italy: effects of personality and product/consumer interactions, *International Journal of Marketing Studies*, 2(2), 34–46.

[18]W. Berger (2003) That's advertainment, *Business 2.0*, March, 91–5. See also the article *Inter Continental Hotels, Revolution* (14605953), July/August, 52: the article examines the advertorial-driven video advertising format used by InterContinental Hotels.

[19]For more on other media context effects, see J. Wang and B. J. Calder (2006) Media transportation and advertising, *Journal of Consumer Research*, 33 (September), 151–62; R. Pieters, M. Wedel and R. Batra (2010) The stopping power of advertising: Measures and effects of visual complexity, *Journal of Marketing*, 74(5), 48–60; A. C. Micu and J. T. Plummer (2010) Measurable emotions: how television ads really work, *Journal of Advertising Research*, 50(2), 137–53.

[20]J. L. C. M. Woltman Elpers, M. Wedel and R. G. M. Pieters (2003) Why do consumers stop viewing television commercials? Two experiments on the influence of moment-to-moment entertainment and information value, *Journal of Marketing Research*, 40 (November), 437–53; D. A. Truong, R. McColl and I. Descubes (2009) Testing US advertising belief and attitude measures in France, *Journal of Euromarketing*, 18(1), 35–46; D. A. Schweidel and R. J. Kent (2010) Predictors of the gap between program and commercial audiences: an investigation using live tuning data, *Journal of Marketing*, 74(3), 18–33.

[21]See, for example, A. G. Chessa and J. M. J. Murre (2007) A neurocognitive model of advertisement content and brand-name recall, *Marketing Science*, 26 (January–February), 130–41; T-H. Hsu, T-N Tsai and P-L. Chiang (2009) Selection of the optimum promotion mix by integrating a fuzzy linguistic decision model with genetic algorithms, *Information Sciences*, 179(1/2), 41–52.

[22]C. Clark, U. Doraszelski and M. Draganska (2009) The effect of advertising on brand awareness and perceived quality: an empirical investigation using panel data, *Quantitative Marketing and Economics*, 7(2), 207–36; J. Romaniuk and S. Wight (2009) The influence of brand usage on responses to advertising awareness measures, *International Journal of Market Research*, 51(2), 203–18; D. Zigmond and H. Stipp (2010) Assessing a new advertising effect, *Journal of Advertising Research*, 50(2), 162–8.

[23]N. Hollis (2004) The future of tracking studies, *Admap*, October, 151–3.

[24]L. Petrecca and T. Howard (2006) Nielsen wants to track who watches commercials, *USA Today*, 11 July.

[25]From R. C. Blattberg and S. A. Neslin, *Sales Promotion: Concepts, Methods, and Strategies*, Upper Saddle River, NJ: Prentice Hall. This text provides the most comprehensive and analytical treatment of sales promotion to date. An extremely up-to-date and comprehensive review of academic work on sales promotions can be found in S. Neslin (2002) Sales promotion, in B. Weitz and R. Wensley (eds), *Handbook of Marketing*, London: Sage, 310–38. Also consider J. Cummins and R. Mullin (2004) *Sales Promotion: How to Create, Implement and Integrate Campaigns that Really Work*, London: Kogan Page.

[26] K. L. Ailawadi, K. Gedenk, C. Lutzky and S. A. Neslin (2007) Decomposition of the sales impact of promotion-induced stockpiling, *Journal of Marketing Research*, 44 (August), 297–308;

E. T. Anderson and D. Simester (2004) The long-run effects of promotion depth on new versus established customers: three field studies, *Marketing Science*, 23(1), 4–20; L. Wathieu, A. V. Muthukrishnan and B. J. Bronnenberg (2004) The asymmetric effect of discount retraction on subsequent choice, *Journal of Consumer Research*, 31 (December), 652–65; Y. Liu and R. Yang (2009) Competing loyalty programs: impact of market saturation, market share, and category expandability, *Journal of Marketing*, 73(1), 93–108; MarketWatch: Tesco and Sainsbury: fighting for grocery market share through fuel discounts, *Global Round-up*, Aug 2010, 9(8), 159.

[27]S. Xuanming (2010) Intertemporal pricing and consumer stockpiling, *Operations Research*, 58(4), 1133–47.

[28]H. J. Van Heerde, S. Gupta and D. Wittink (2003) Is 75% of the sales promotion bump due to brand switching? No, only 33% is, *Journal of Marketing Research*, 40 (November), 481–91; H. J. Van Heerde, P. S. H. Leeflang and D. R. Wittink (2000) The estimation of pre- and postpromotion dips with store-level scanner data, *Journal of Marketing Research*, 37(3), 383–95.

[29]AutoVIBES (2004) *AutoBeat Daily*, 3 March, K. Lundegaard and S. Freeman (2004) Detroit's challenge: weaning buyers from years of deals, *Wall Street Journal*, 6 January.

[30]G. Jones (2008) ITV signs up Harveys to SMS voucher service, *Marketing*, 4 March (www.brandrepublic.com/News/787797/ITV-signs-Harveys-SMS-voucher-service).

[31]C. Foss (2007) Ford car maker targets sporty males, *Marketing Direct*, 2 October (www.brandrepublic.com/News/742978/Ford-car-maker-targets-sporty-males/)

[32]M. M. Abraham and L. M. Lodish (1990) Getting the most out of advertising and promotion, *Harvard Business Review*, May–June, 50–60. See also S. Srinivasan, K. Pauwels, D. Hanssens and M. Dekimpe (2004) Do promotions benefit manufacturers, retailers, or both?, *Management Science*, 50(5), 617–29.

[33]For a model for setting sales promotions objectives, see D. B. Jones (1994) Setting promotional goals: a communications relationship model, *Journal of Consumer Marketing*, 11(1), 38–49.

[34]K. L. Ailawadi, B. A. Harlam, J. Cesar and D. Trounce (2006) Promotion profitability for a retailer: the role of promotion, brand, category, and store characteristics, *Journal of Marketing Research*, 43 (November), 518–36; K. L. Ailawadi and B. A. Harlam (2009) Retailer promotion pass-through: a measure, its magnitude, and its determinants, *Marketing Science*, 28(4), 782–91; K. L. Ailawadi, J. P. Beauchamp, N. Donthu, D. K. Gauri and V. Shankar (2009) Communication and promotion decisions in retailing: a review and directions for future research, *Journal of Retailing*, 85(1), 42–55.

[35]K. L. Ailawadi and B. Harlam (2004) An empirical analysis of the determinants of retail margins: the role of store brand share, *Journal of Marketing*, 68 (January), 147–66; K. L. Ailawadi (2001) The retail power-performance conundrum: what have we learned?, *Journal of Retailing*, 77(3), 299–318; P. W. Farris and K. L. Ailawadi (1992) Retail power: monster or mouse?, *Journal of Retailing*, Winter, 351–69; K. Pauwels (in press), How retailer and competitor decisions drive the long-term effectiveness of manufacturer promotions, *Journal of Retailing*.

[36]A. Odoi (2008) *Marketing*, 3 March.

[37]C. J. Simmons and K. L. Becker-Olse (2006) Achieving marketing objectives through social sponsorships, *Journal of Marketing*, 70(4), 154–69; N. Clark (2005) Red Bull eyes sporting chance, *Marketing*, 27 July, 14–15; www.redbull.co.uk.

[38]P. Kotler (1973–4) Atmospherics as a marketing tool, *Journal of Retailing*, Winter, 48–64.

[39]B. Cornwell, M. S. Humphreys, A. M. Maguire, C. S. Weeks and C. Tellegen (2006) Sponsorship-linked marketing: the role of articulation in memory, *Journal of Consumer Research*, 33 (December), 312–21; A. M. Grey and K. Shildum-Reid (2003) *The Sponsorship Seeker's Toolkit*, Maidenhead: McGraw-Hill.

[40]A. G. Close, A. S. Krishen and M. S. Latour (2009) The event is me!, *Journal of Advertising* Research, 49(3), 271–84; K. Pasanen, H. Taskinen and J. Mikkonen (2009) Impacts of cultural events in eastern Finland: development of a Finnish event evaluation tool, *Scandinavian Journal of Hospitality and Tourism*, 9(2/3), 112–29.

[41]B. Schmitt (1999) *Experiential Marketing: How to Get Customers to Sense, Feel, Think, Act, Relate*, New York: Free Press.

[42]B. J. Pine and J. H. Gilmore (1999) *The Experience Economy: Work Is Theatre and Every Business a Stage*, Cambridge, MA: Harvard University Press; M. Morgan, J. Elbe and J. de Esteban Curiel (2009) Has the experience economy arrived? The views of destination managers in three visitor-dependent areas, *International Journal of Tourism Research*, 11(2), 201–16; D. E. Skold (2010) The other side of enjoyment: short-circuiting marketing and creativity in the experience economy, *Organization*, 17(3), 363–78.

[43]2006 experiential marketing study, www.jackmorton.com.

[44]Do we have a story for you! (2006) *The Economist*, 21 January, 57–8; A. Ries and L. Ries (2002) *The Fall of Advertising and the Rise of PR*, New York: HarperCollins; P. J. Stromback, M. A. Mitrook and S. Kiousis (2010) Bridging two schools of thought: applications of marketing theory to political marketing, *Journal of Political Marketing*, 9(1/2), 73–92.

[45]For further reading on cause-related marketing, see S. Youn and H. Kim (2008) Antecedents of consumer attitudes toward cause-related marketing, *Journal of Advertising Research*, 48(1), 123–37; G. Liu, C. Liston-Heyes and W-W Ko (2010) Employee participation in cause-related marketing strategies: a study of management perceptions from British consumer services industries, *Journal of Business Ethics*, 92(2), 195–210; S-u-R. Sheikh and R. Beise-Zee (2011) Corporate social responsibility or cause-related marketing? The role of cause specificity of CSR, *Journal of Consumer Marketing*, 28(1) 27–39; I. Papasolomou and P. J. Kitchen (2011) Cause-related marketing: developing a tripartite approach with BMW, *Corporate Reputation Review*, 14(1), 63–75.

[46]S. Nurpin (2007) From brand out of mind to brand in hand: brand unification by icons, totems, and titans, talk given at International Energy Group's 24th Annual Sponsorship Conference, 13 March.

[47]The terms *direct-order marketing* and *direct-relationship marketing* were suggested as subsets of direct marketing by Stan Rapp and Tom Collins (1990) in *The Great Marketing Turnaround*, Upper Saddle River, NJ: Prentice Hall. See also B. Thomas and M. Housden (2002) *Direct Marketing in Practice*, Oxford: Butterworth-Heinemann; R. Mullin (2003) *A Step-by-Step Guide to Effective Planning and Targeting* (Marketing in Action Series), London: Kogan Page; M. Stone, A. Band and E. Blake (2003) *The Definitive Guide to Direct and Interactive Marketing: How to Select, Reach and Retain the Right Customers*, London: Financial Times Prentice Hall.

[48]R. Kivetz and I. Simonson (2003) The idiosyncratic fit heuristic: effort advantage as a determinant of consumer response to loyalty programs, *Journal of Marketing Research*, 40 (November), 454–67; M. Faulkner and R. Kennedy (2008) A new tool for pre-testing direct mail, *International Journal of Market Research*, 50(4), 469–90. L. Jen, C. H. Chou and G. M. Allenby (2009) The importance of modeling temporal dependence of timing and quantity in direct marketing, *Journal of Marketing Research* (JMR), 46(4), 482–93.

[49]DMA's 2006 'Power of direct marketing' reports (2007) Direct Marketing Association, 5 June; Direct marketing's growth rate to cushion cooling US economy (2006) Direct Marketing Association, 17 October; C. Krol (2005) Direct hits it big, *BtoB*, 10 October, 29–31; M. Philips, D. T. McFadden and M. Sullins (2010) How effective is social networking for direct marketers?, *Journal of Food Distribution Research*, 41(1), 96–100.

[50]See www.the-dma.org.

[51]On the mat (2005) *The Economist*, 26 November, 78.

[52]E. L. Nash (2000) *Direct Marketing: Strategy, Planning, Execution*, 4th edn, New York: McGraw-Hill.

[53]The *average customer longevity* (N) is related to the *customer retention rate* (CR). Suppose the company retains 80 per cent of its customers each year. Then the average customer longevity is given by: $N = 1/(1 - CR) = 1/0.2 = 5$.

[54]J. Edwards (2001) The art of the infomercial, *Brandweek*, 3 September, 14–19.

[55]E. Steel (2007) Advertising's brave new world, *Wall Street Journal*, 25 May; J. L. Roberts (2006) How to count eyeballs, *Newsweek*, 27 November, 42; see also www.infomercials-reviwed.com.

[56]K. J. Delaney (2006) Once-wary industry giants embrace internet advertising, *Wall Street Journal*, 17 April.

[57]P. Kotler (2005) *According to Kotler*, New York: American Management Association.

[58]P. J. Danaher, G. W. Mullarkey and S. Essegaier (2006) Factors affecting web site visit duration: a cross-domain analysis, *Journal of Marketing Research*, 43 (May), 182–94; T. Zhou, L. Yaobin and W. Bin (2009) The relative importance of website design quality and service quality in determining consumers' online repurchasing behavior, *Information Systems Management*, 26(4), 327–37.

[59]J. F. Rayport and B. J. Jaworski (2001) *e-commerce*, New York: McGraw-Hill, 116.

[60]B. Tedeschi (2002) E-commerce report, *New York Times*, 24 June.

[61]J.-B. E. M. Steenkamp and I. Geyskens (2006) How country characteristics affect the perceived value of web sites, *Journal of Marketing*, 70 (July), 136–50.

[62]Prime clicking time (2003) *The Economist*, 31 May, 65; B. Elgin (2003) Search engines are picking up steam, *BusinessWeek*, 24 March, 86–7; see also the article, Make your website pay: Google AdSence, in *PC World*, January 2009, 26(1) 48.

[63]P. Manchanda, J.-P. Dubé, Khim Yong Goh and P. K. Chintagunta (2006) The effects of banner advertising on internet purchasing, *Journal of Marketing Research*, 43 (February), 98–108; Pay per sale (2005) *The Economist*, 1 October, 62; J. Möller and M. Eisend, (2010) A global investigation into the cultural and individual antecedents of banner advertising effectiveness, *Journal of International Marketing*, 18(2), 80–98.

[64]P. Sloan (2007) The quest for the perfect online ad, *Business 2.0*, March, 88–93; C. Holahan (2007) The promise of online display ads, *BusinessWeek*, 1 May.

[65]S. Godin (1999) *Permission Marketing: Turning Strangers into Friends and Friends into Customers*, New York: Simon & Schuster.

[66]C. R. Schoenberger (2002) Web? What web?, *Forbes*, 10 June, 132.

67Adapted from R. N. McMurry (1961) The mystique of super-salesmanship, *Harvard Business Review*, March–April, 114. Also see W. C. Moncrief III (1986) Selling activity and sales position taxonomies for industrial sales forces, *Journal of Marketing Research*, August, 261–70; T. J. Ryan (2009) The sales rep redefined, *SGB*, 14(4), 18–20.

68L. G. Friedman and T. R. Furey (1999) *The Channel Advantage: Going to Marketing with Multiple Sales Channels*, Oxford: Butterworth-Heinemann.

69P. Kotler, N. Rackham and S. Krishnaswamy (2006) Ending the war between sales and marketing, *Harvard Business Review*, July–August, 68–78; T. M. Smith, S. Gopalakrishna and R. Chaterjee (2006) A three-stage model of integrated marketing communications at the marketing–sales interface, *Journal of Marketing Research*, 43 (November), 546–79.

70M. Copeland (2004) Hits and misses, *Business 2.0*, April, 142.

71S. Albers (2002) Sales-force management: compensation, motivation, selection, and training, in B. Weitz and R. Wensley (eds), *Handbook of Marketing*, London: Sage, 248–66; D. Jobber and G. Lancaster (2000) *Selling and Sales Management*, Harlow: Prentice-Hall; I. A. Davies, L. J. Ryals and S. Holt (2010) Relationship management: a sales role? Or a state of mind?:

An investigation of functions and attitudes across a business-to-business sales force, *Industrial Marketing Management*, 39(7), 1049–62.

72Brandrepublic, 12 November 2007.

73N. Rackham (1988) *SPIN Selling*, New York: McGraw-Hill. Also see his *The SPIN Selling Fieldbook* (1996), New York: McGraw-Hill; J. Lardner (2002–3) Selling salesmanship, *Business 2.0*, December–January, 66; S. D. Morgen (1999) *Selling with Integrity: Reinventing Sales through Collaboration, Respect, and Serving*, New York: Berkeley Books; N. Rackham and J. De Vincentis (1996) *Rethinking the Sales Force*, New York: McGraw-Hill.

74Some of the following discussion is based on W. J. E. Crissy, W. H. Cunningham and I. C. M. Cunningham (1977) *Selling: The Personal Force in Marketing*, New York: John Wiley & Sons, 119–29.

75G. R. Franke and J.-E. Park (2006) Salesperson adaptive selling behaviour and customer orientation: a meta-analysis, *Journal of Marketing Research*, 43 (November), 693–702; R. G. McFarland, G. N. Challagalla and T. A. Shervani (2006) Influence tactics for effective adaptive selling, *Journal of Marketing*, 70 (October), 103–17.

Managing marketing implementation and control

Video documentary for Part 8

Go to **www.pearsoned.co.uk/ marketingmanagementeurope** to watch the video documentary that relates to Part 8 and consider the issues raised below.

In addition to their responsibilities to their companies to ensure that the marketing spend is measured and seen to be productive, marketing managers also have a number of challenges that are contextually and socially important.

Part 8: Managing marketing implementation and control explores two important themes:

1 selecting suitable marketing spends and monitoring their effectiveness; and
2 responding to broader contextual and social challenges.

Marketing expenditure, as with any other company activity, needs to be budgeted and result in a measurable return. Marketing activities are being professionally costed and attempts made to judge the effectiveness of different elements within the marketing budget.

However, the application of management accounting methods to assess the precise contribution of any specific marketing activity is difficult to achieve, as many of the sub-budgets within the responsibility of a marketing manager are attempting to meet revenue targets that are highly dynamic. Inevitably, marketing management is part intuition, part creative flare and part science, but nonetheless dependent crucially on the development and professional use of marketing metrics.

When watching the video documentary that accompanies Part 8, consider how the marketing managers being interviewed measure the effectiveness of their marketing spend, as well as rising to the challenge of ethical and social issues, including the implementation of environmentally sustainable practices.

Hear a variety of top marketing executives from a wide range of organisations offer their own interesting and varied perspectives on the key themes of Part 8 including: Henrik Otto, Senior Vice-President of Global Design, Electrolux (top); Julian Whitehead, Director of Sustainability and Social Responsibility, Land Rover (centre); and St Paul's Cathedral requires marketing support to raise the money needed to stay open (bottom).

Chapter 21

Implementing marketing management

IN THIS CHAPTER, WE WILL ADDRESS THE FOLLOWING QUESTIONS:

1 What are the important trends in marketing practices?

2 What are the keys to effective internal marketing?

3 How can a company build a creative marketing organisation?

4 How can companies be responsible social marketers?

5 What tools are available to help companies monitor and improve their marketing activities?

Sense and sensibility overcome pride and prejudice as a marketing executive from an underperforming company seeks advice from a marketing consultant.

Source: Serif.

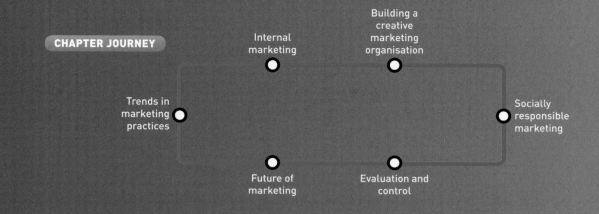

Trends in marketing practices

Internal marketing

Building a creative marketing organisation

Socially responsible marketing

Future of marketing

Evaluation and control

Healthy long-term growth for a brand requires that the marketing organisation be managed properly. Holistic marketers must engage in a host of carefully planned, interconnected marketing activities and satisfy an increasingly broad set of constituents. They must also consider the wider range of effects of their actions. Corporate social responsibility and sustainability have become a priority as organisations grapple with the short- and long-term effects of their marketing. Some firms have embraced this new vision of corporate enlightenment and made it the very core of what they do.

Consider Unilever and Reckitt Benckiser.

Imagine, for a second, that Unilever's latest turnaround plan does not work. Chief executive Patrick Cescau has slimmed down management, cut costs, shed some underperforming assets, and so far delivered three years of steady, if gradual, improvement in company performance. An expensive restructuring plan is designed to increase margins. But if the consumer goods giant trips up, perhaps on rising raw material prices, calls for more radical action will be heard. What might plan B look like?[1]

One option could be to try to import wholesale the culture from a smaller and more nimble rival. Reckitt Benckiser, which has been able to grow sales in developed markets where Unilever largely stagnates, leaps to mind. The UK household goods group was itself created in 1999 when the management of Benckiser effectively took control of the larger, but struggling, Reckitt & Colman. The combination of beer makers Interbrew and AmBev in 2004, where the latter's cost-cutting experts took the reins at the newly created InBev, offers a similar precedent.

Other brands such as Ben & Jerry's, Timberland and the Virgin Group have embraced similar philosophies and practices. Successful holistic marketing requires effective relationship marketing, integrated marketing, internal marketing and performance marketing. Preceding chapters addressed the first two topics and the strategy and tactics of marketing.[2] This chapter considers the latter two topics and how to conduct marketing responsibly. The discussion addresses how firms organise, implement, evaluate and control marketing activities and the increased importance of social responsibility. The chapter begins by examining changes in how companies conduct marketing today.

Trends in marketing practices

As a consequence of the paradigm change in the business environment from sellers' to buyers' markets, together with important changes in the marketing macroenvironment such as globalisation, deregulation and technological advances, many companies have or are in the process of restructuring their affairs by:

- **re-engineering**: appointing teams to manage customer-value-building processes and break down walls between departments;
- **outsourcing**: buying more goods and services from outside domestic or foreign vendors as they seek to convert traditional supply chains into value chains;
- **benchmarking**: studying 'best practice companies' to improve performance;
- **supplier partnering**: partnering with fewer but better value-adding suppliers;
- **customer partnering**: working more closely with customers to add value to their operations;
- **merging**: acquiring or merging with firms in the same or complementary industries to gain economies of scale and scope;
- **globalising**: increasing efforts to 'think global' and 'act local';
- **flattening**: reducing the number of organisational levels to get closer to the customer;
- **focusing**: determining the most profitable businesses and customers and focusing on them;
- **accelerating**: designing the organisation and setting up processes to respond more quickly to changes in the environment;
- **empowering**: encouraging and empowering personnel to produce more ideas and take more initiative.

The role of marketing in the organisation is also changing.[3] Traditionally, marketers have played the roles of middlemen, charged with understanding customer needs and transmitting the voice of the customer to various functional areas in the organisation. In today's markets, companies need to take a holistic view of the underlying philosophy of marketing, and bring to the marketplace customer-perceived value offerings that will satisfy and delight customers. Thus marketing needs to be regarded as more than a functional activity. A company's output is determined by both the corporate marketing philosophy and the result of the coordination of internal functions as well as those external ones that make up the value chain.

To find out why Paris-based L'Oréal, the world's biggest cosmetics group, acquired The Body Shop, the UK-based retailer of toiletries and cosmetics well known for its distinctive management approach, visit www.pearsoned.co.uk/marketingmanagementeurope

Internal marketing

The term *internal marketing* was first used in the 1970s and was initially associated with the marketing of services. However, over the years it has come to emphasise the importance in buyers' markets for a company to adopt a holistic attitude towards the concepts and goals of marketing and engage in choosing, providing and communicating customer-perceived value (see Chapter 11). The provision of CPV involves a coordinated effort spread across the whole company and is no longer seen as a strictly sales department responsibility.[4]

BenQ ready to signal its Siemens solution

When BenQ, the Taiwanese electronics maker with a brand created less than four years ago, announced in early June 2005 that it would take over the mobile handset business of Siemens, one of Europe's most traditional household names, many analysts reacted with scepticism.

The question most frequently asked was: 'How can two laggards become a leader by just joining together?' Siemens had been losing market share because of its 'uncool' handsets. BenQ was failing to sustain a forceful push up the global handset market rankings ▶

due to its lack of proprietary technology. Both were losing money. Chief marketing officer Jerry Wang is one of the Taiwanese executives who will help lead BenQ Mobile, the new company with headquarters in Munich. He identified Siemens' conservative, rigid group structure as the main reason why the German company's handset business was underperforming, and expressed confidence that joining BenQ would change its fortunes. 'The business is strangled by standards set in accordance with Siemens' mostly non-consumer operations,' he said. 'Products suffer from over-engineering, a lack of speed in response to market trends, and restrictions put on the brand image by the needs of other group businesses.' BenQ rolled out an internal marketing campaign to boost morale. 'Everybody has to embrace and love the brand,' said Wang.[5]

Marketing is about presenting a unified approach to the customer. If a brand's employees are not engaged by its marketing or, worse still, they do not understand it, any new sales targets will suffer. That is why internal marketing of brand strategy and activity can be one of the most powerful tools a marketing executive can employ. However, in general, internal marketing is underestimated and underutilised. Yet it theoretically has the potential to deliver many tangible benefits to both the company and the brand.

On a very basic level, it can help ease some of the frustrations that non-marketing people sometimes have with their marketing colleagues: 'Why do we have to have a brand campaign? Can't you just spend more of your unimaginably large budget on promoting our products?' Most marketers recognise this question and often become irritated at the inference that there is no relationship between brand and sales. However, the question around brand and market offering is valid, as is the answer. The most powerful brands are created when the external marketing reflects the internal culture. British Airways' 'World's Favourite Airline' proposition started life as an internal expression of identity for the airline's own staff.

Holding up a mirror to the organisation and then using the reflection to establish the brand proposition is one of the most effective and credible ways to market. 'This is who we are and this is what we stand for', as opposed to 'This is what we offer' gives consumers and staff alike a much greater insight into a company's brand.

Tesco, with 'Every little helps', and Apple Macintosh with 'Different' are two other brands whose *cri de cœur* works as well internally as it does externally. Indeed, these propositions simply could not work unless both audiences bought into them. Whichever direction a brand takes, if the internal community understands and owns the marketing, a bond is forged, spirits are high and advocates are created. If it does not, there is a pretty good chance that consumers won't either. The *Guardian* reported Sir Richard Branson as saying that 'the best internal marketing tool has been a desk calendar distributed to staff worldwide'. The CEO of Fortis, the Belgian/Dutch bank and insurance company, gave all its 56,000 employees a Rubik's cube style gadget inscribed with 14 imperatives such as 'Deliver results', 'Team spirit' and 'Develop results'. He wanted to encourage a common language and culture across his sprawling company.[6]

A company can have an excellent marketing department on paper, however, and fail to perform effectively. Much depends on how *other* company departments view customers. They must adopt the holistic view of marketing. Only when *all* employees realise their job is to create, serve and satisfy customers does the company become an effective marketer.[7] The marketing memo on page 864 presents a tool that evaluates which company departments are truly customer driven.[8]

Critique of internal marketing

Sceptics regard the concept of internal marketing as being based on a false premise that employees can be treated like external customers. In Europe there is little empirical evidence of its detailed and widespread company adoption. The concept is simple: use basic

Marketing memo

Characteristics of company departments that are truly customer driven

R & D
- They spend time meeting customers and listening to their problems.
- They welcome the involvement of marketing, manufacturing and other departments on each new project.
- They benchmark competitors' products and seek 'best of class' solutions.
- They solicit customer reactions and suggestions as the project progresses.
- They continuously improve and refine the product on the basis of market feedback.

Purchasing
- They proactively search for the best suppliers rather than choose only from those who solicit their business by offering the lowest prices.
- They build long-term relationships with fewer but more reliable high-quality suppliers, thereby developing a sustainable value chain.

Manufacturing
- They invite customers to visit and tour their plants.
- They visit customer factories to see how they use the company's products.
- They willingly work overtime when it is important to meet promised delivery schedules.
- They continuously search for ways to produce goods faster and/or at lower costs.
- They continuously improve product quality, aiming for zero defects.
- They meet customer requirements for 'customisation' where this can be done profitably.

Marketing
- They study customer needs and wants in well-defined market segments.
- They allocate marketing effort in relation to the long-run profit potential of the targeted segments.
- They develop winning offerings for each target segment.
- They measure company image and customer satisfaction on a continuous basis.
- They continuously gather and evaluate ideas for new products, product improvements and services to meet customers' needs.
- They influence all company departments and employees to be customer centred in their thinking and practice.

Sales
- They have specialised knowledge of the customer's industry.
- They strive to give the customer 'the best solution'.
- They make only promises they can keep.
- They feed back customers' needs and ideas to those in charge of product development.
- They serve the same customers for a long period of time.

Logistics
- They set a high standard for service delivery time and they meet this standard consistently.
- They operate a knowledgeable and friendly customer-service department that can answer questions, handle complaints and resolve problems in a satisfactory and timely manner.

Accounting
- They prepare periodic 'profitability' reports by product, market segment, geographic areas (regions, sales territories), order sizes and individual customers.
- They prepare invoices tailored to customer needs and answer customer queries courteously and quickly.

Finance
- They understand and support marketing expenditures (e.g. image advertising) that represent marketing investments which produce long-term customer preference and loyalty.
- They tailor the financial package to the customers' financial requirements.
- They make quick decisions on customer creditworthiness.

Public relations
- They disseminate favourable news about the company and they 'damage control' unfavourable news.
- They act as an internal customer and public advocate for better company policies and practices.

Other customer-contact personnel
- They are competent, courteous, cheerful, credible, reliable and responsive.

marketing approaches to communicate to employees in the same way that these methods can raise awareness, interest, intent and action with consumers.

The explanation for the revival of internal marketing is also simple. Marketing directors are increasingly delivering a range of internal communication tasks. The logic is that if an organisation is trying to deliver a differentiating customer experience, then who better to get employees lined up than the people responsible for defining the customer experience? The fact that the marketing function often has greater influence than do internal communications adds weight to the idea. With the importance and power of brand rising rapidly on the corporate agenda, the case is compelling. However, there is a basic problem with the whole idea. The nature of the employment relationship is essentially different from a consumer relationship. The psychological, emotional and rational processes at play in joining, working within and leaving a complex social system, where one spends at least one-third of one's adult life, are more complicated than the processes at play in considering even a significant investment such as a car or a home – let alone a snack, an Individual Savings Account (ISA), a mobile phone or a university education.

This is not to say that some of the methods, practices and tools that prove valuable in marketing do not have an important place in an effective internal communication effort. In fact, internal communication people can learn a lot from marketing approaches such as developing 'the big idea', defining the essence of a brand or value proposition, identifying, prioritising and segmenting stakeholders, and being more creative and inspirational in their overall approach. However, the internal marketing approach generally fails to consider important parts of the equation – for example, the human capital, organisational development and behaviour change elements. Probably most importantly, marketers have only recently realised the importance and power of interactivity and active listening in a world where consumer power is paramount.

Most marketing practice is based on crafting a message, packaging it and delivering it to an audience – and then gauging what happens and modifying the next round of activity accordingly. Internal communication, at its best, goes beyond so-called 'two-way' communication models, and creates an ongoing dialogue that both reflects and shapes the place where this conversation occurs. 'Internal marketers' can learn a lot from their internal communication, human resource and engagement colleagues. For example, internal communicators are now able to draw a line between their efforts, the effect of these efforts on the customer experience and the resulting financial impact. Their marketing colleagues have yet to make this link between their efforts and consumer behaviour.

While internal marketing may well be based on a false premise, the emerging truth is that no organisational silo – marketing, human resources, internal communications or IT – owns the whole solution. Best practice engagement is about making sure that these disciplines work together in a complementary manner to deliver the right result for the organisation.

At this point it is appropriate to look at how marketing departments are being organised, how they can work effectively with other departments, and how firms can foster a creative marketing culture within the entire organisation.

Organising the marketing department

Modern marketing departments can be organised in a number of different, sometimes overlapping ways:[9] functionally, geographically, by product or brand, by market, or in a matrix (see also Chapters 3 and 15).

Functional organisation

The most common form of marketing organisation, as adopted by Ford and General Motors, consists of functional specialists reporting to a senior marketing executive who coordinates their activities. Figure 21.1 shows five specialists. Additional specialists might include a customer service manager, a marketing planning manager, a market logistics manager, a direct marketing manager and a digital marketing manager.

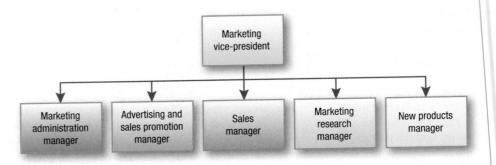

Figure 21.1 Functional organisation

The main advantage of a functional marketing organisation is its administrative simplicity, although it can be quite a challenge to develop smooth working relationships.[10] This form can also lose its effectiveness as the number of products and markets increases. For some retailers and fast-moving consumer goods companies such as Procter & Gamble, a functional organisation often leads to inadequate planning for specific products and markets. Then, each functional group competes with others for budget and status. The senior marketing executive constantly weighs the claims of competing functional specialists and faces a difficult coordination problem.

Geographic organisation

A company selling in a national market often organises its sales force (and sometimes other functions, including marketing) along geographic lines. Many food, beverage, car and pharmaceutical companies use this model of organisation. The national sales manager may supervise four regional sales managers, who each supervise six zone managers, who in turn supervise eight district sales managers, who each supervise ten sales people. If companies seek to market effectively in international markets then it is necessary to appoint *area market specialists* (e.g. EU states and non-EU states, the Middle East, etc.). Each country that is entered requires its own local specialist managers to advise headquarters staff of the variations in marketing mix that are required across regions and countries.

Product- or brand-management organisation

Companies producing a variety of market offerings and brands often establish a product- (or brand-) management organisation along the lines of the model originally developed by Procter & Gamble. It is important to realise that the traditional term 'product' should be interpreted as meaning a suitable customer-perceived market offering. The product-management organisation does not replace the functional organisation, but serves as another layer of management. A product manager supervises product category managers, who in turn supervise specific product and brand managers.

A product-management organisation makes sense if the company's products are quite different, or if the sheer number of products is beyond the ability of a functional organisation to handle. Kraft has used a product-management organisation in its Post division, with separate product category managers in charge of cereals, pet food and beverages. Within the cereal product group, Kraft has had a separate sub-category of managers for nutritional cereals, children's pre-sweetened cereals, family cereals and miscellaneous cereals.

Product and brand management is sometimes characterised as a **hub-and-spoke** system. The brand or product manager is figuratively at the centre, with spokes emanating out to various departments (see Figure 21.2). Some tasks that product or brand managers may perform include the following:

- developing a long-range and competitive strategy for the product;
- preparing an annual marketing plan and sales forecast;

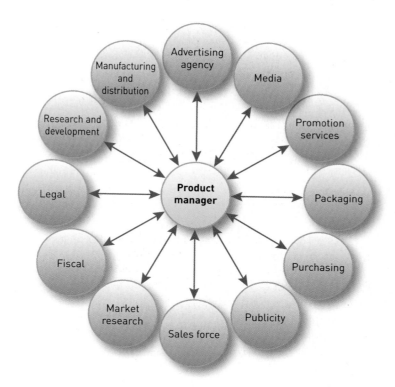

Figure 21.2 The product manager's interactions

- working with advertising and merchandising agencies to develop copy, programmes and campaigns;
- increasing support of the market offerings among the sales force and distributors;
- gathering continuous intelligence on the offer performance, customer and dealer attitudes, and new problems and opportunities;
- initiating offer improvements to meet changing market needs.

The product-management organisation lets the product manager concentrate on developing a cost-effective marketing mix and react more quickly to new products in the marketplace; it also gives the company's smaller brands a product advocate. However, this organisation also has disadvantages:

- Product and brand managers may lack sufficient authority to carry out their responsibilities.
- Product and brand managers become experts in their product area but rarely achieve functional expertise.
- The product-management system often turns out to be costly. One person is appointed to manage each major product or brand, and soon more are appointed to manage even minor products and brands.
- Brand managers normally manage a brand for only a short time. Short-term involvement leads to short-term planning and fails to build long-term strengths.
- The fragmentation of markets makes it harder to develop a national strategy. Brand managers must please regional and local sales groups, transferring power from marketing to sales.
- Product and brand managers focus the company on building market share rather than the customer relationship.

A second alternative in a product-management organisation is *product teams*. There are three types of structure: the vertical product team, triangular product team and horizontal product team (see Figure 21.3).

(a) Vertical product team

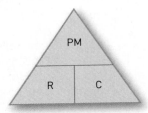

(b) Triangular product team

(c) Horizontal product team

PM = product manager
APM = associate product manager
PA = product assistant
R   = market researcher
C   = communication specialist
S   = sales manager
D   = distribution specialist
F   = finance/accounting specialist
E   = engineer

Figure 21.3 Three types of product team

The triangular and horizontal product-team approaches let each major brand be run by a **brand-asset management team** (BAMT) consisting of key representatives from functions that affect the brand's performance. The company is made up of several BAMTs that periodically report to a BAMT directors committee, which itself reports to a chief branding manager. This is quite different from the way brands have traditionally been handled.

A third alternative for a product-management organisation is to eliminate product manager positions for minor products and assign two or more products to each remaining manager. This is feasible where two or more products appeal to a similar set of needs. A cosmetics company has no need for product managers for each product because cosmetics serve one major need – beauty. A toiletries company needs different managers for headache remedies, toothpaste, soap and shampoo, because these products differ in use and appeal.

A fourth alternative is to introduce *category management*, in which a company focuses on product categories to manage its brands. Procter & Gamble, pioneers of the brand-management system, and several other leading firms including Colgate-Palmolive, Kraft and Unilever, made a significant shift to category management.[11] P&G cites a number of advantages. By fostering internal competition among brand managers, the traditional brand-management system created strong incentives to excel, but also much internal competition for resources and a lack of coordination. The new scheme was designed to ensure that all categories would be able to receive adequate resources.

Another rationale for category management is the increasing power of the trade. Because the retail trade has tended to think of profitability in terms of product categories, P&G felt it only made sense to deal along similar lines. Retailers and regional grocery chains such as ASDA and Carrefour, respectively, have embraced category management as a means to define a particular product category's strategic role within the store and address logistics, the role of private-label products and the trade-offs between product variety and inefficient duplication.

Category management is not a panacea. It is still a product-driven system. Colgate has moved from brand management (Colgate toothpaste) through category management (toothpaste category) to a new stage called 'customer-need management' (mouth care). This last step finally focuses the organisation on a basic customer need.[12]

Market-management organisation

Many companies operate in different markets. Canon sells fax machines to consumer, business and government markets. Corus markets steel to the railway, construction and public utility industries. When customers fall into different user groups with distinct buying preferences and practices, a **market-management organisation** is desirable. Market managers supervise several market-development managers, market specialists or industry specialists, and draw on functional services as needed. Market managers of important markets might even have functional specialists reporting to them.

Market managers are staff (not line) people, with duties similar to those of product managers. They develop long-range and annual plans for their markets. Their performance is judged by their market's growth and profitability. This system shares many advantages and disadvantages of product-management systems. Its strongest advantage is organising marketing activity to meet the needs of distinct customer groups rather than focusing on marketing functions, regions or products. Many companies are reorganising along market lines and becoming **market-centred organisations**. Xerox has converted from geographic selling to selling by industry, as have IBM and Hewlett-Packard.

In a **customer-management organisation**, companies can organise themselves to understand and deal with individual customers rather than with the mass market or even market segments.[13] When a close relationship is advantageous, such as when customers have diverse and complex requirements and buy an integrated bundle of products and services, customer-management organisations should prevail. IBM's Global Services are organised in this way because of their need to interact closely with customers. One study showed that companies organised by customer groups reported much higher accountability for the overall quality of relationships and employees' freedom to take actions to satisfy individual customers.[14]

Matrix-management organisation

Companies that produce many products for many markets may adopt a matrix organisation. This enables them to gain cost economies of scale and adapt their market offerings to suit local requirements. Some provide the context in which a matrix can thrive – flat, lean team organisations focused around business processes that cut horizontally across functions.[15] DuPont was a pioneer in developing the matrix structure (see Figure 21.4).

Market managers

	Menswear	Women's wear	Home furnishings	Industrial markets
Rayon				
Acetate				
Nylon				
Orlon				
Dacron				

Product managers

Figure 21.4 Product/management matrix system

DuPont

Before it was spun off, DuPont's textile fibres department consisted of separate product managers for Rayon, Acetate, Nylon, Orlon and Dacron; and separate market managers for menswear, women's wear, home furnishings and industrial markets. The product managers planned sales and profits for their respective fibres. They asked market managers to estimate how much of their fibre they could sell in each market at a proposed price. Market managers, however, were generally more interested in meeting their market's needs than pushing a particular fibre. In preparing their market plans, they asked each product manager about the fibre's planned prices and availabilities. The final sales forecast of the market managers and the product managers should have added up to the same grand total.

Companies such as DuPont and Courtaulds can go one step further and view the market managers as the main marketers, and their product managers as suppliers. The menswear market manager, for example, would be empowered to buy textile fibres from DuPont's product managers or, if DuPont's price is too high, from outside suppliers, forcing DuPont product managers to become more efficient. If a DuPont product manager was not able to match the '**arm's-length pricing**' levels of competitive suppliers, then perhaps DuPont should not produce that fibre.

A matrix organisation seems desirable in a multiproduct, multimarket company. The disadvantage is that it is costly and often creates conflicts. There is the cost of supporting all the managers, and questions about where authority and responsibility for marketing activities should reside – at headquarters or in the division? Some corporate marketing groups assist top management with overall opportunity evaluation, provide divisions with consulting assistance on request, help divisions that have little or no marketing, and promote the marketing concept throughout the company.

Getting it together

Matrix management is essentially a mindset first and an organisational form second. Many complex organisations, such as British Telecom and Citibank, benefit substantially from this management approach, which has caught the interest of many other organisations both large and small and is operating in both private and public enterprise businesses. Fortis, the dominant bank and insurer in Belgium and, since its formation in 1990 in one of Europe's first cross-border mergers, also a sizeable player in the Netherlands, has adopted a matrix approach to consolidate its business. Meanwhile, since 2005 in the Republic of Ireland, Enterprise Ireland, faced with the challenge of fostering innovation and market knowledge with a view to boosting small and medium-sized enterprises' export opportunities, has moved from a 'cellular structure' to a 'matrix structure'.

Relations with other departments

Under the marketing concept, all departments need to 'think customer' and work together to satisfy customer needs and expectations. The marketing department must drive this point home. The marketing director has two tasks: (1) to coordinate the company's internal marketing activities; and (2) to coordinate marketing with finance, operations and other company functions to serve the customer.

Yet there is little agreement on how much influence and authority marketing should have over other departments. Departments define company problems and goals from their viewpoint, so conflicts of interest and communication problems are unavoidable. Typically, the marketing director must work through persuasion rather than authority. To develop a balanced orientation in which marketing and other functions jointly determine what is in the company's best interests, companies can provide joint seminars to understand each other's viewpoints, joint committees and liaison personnel, personnel exchange programmes, and analytical methods to determine the most profitable course of action.[16]

Many companies now focus on key processes rather than departments, because departmental organisation can be a barrier to the smooth performance of fundamental business processes. They appoint process leaders, who manage cross-disciplinary teams that include marketing and salespeople. As a result, marketing personnel may have a solid-line responsibility to their teams and a dotted-line responsibility to the marketing department.

Building a creative marketing organisation

Many companies realise they are not yet really market and customer driven – they are product and sales driven. General Motors and Shell, for example, are attempting to transform themselves into true market-driven companies. This requires:

- developing a company-wide passion for customers;
- organising around customer segments instead of products; and
- understanding customers through qualitative and quantitative research.

The task is not easy; it is not simply a matter of the CEO making speeches and urging every employee to 'think customer'. However, the payoffs can be considerable.[17] See the marketing insight box on p. 872 for actions a CEO can take to improve marketing capabilities.

Persuading the company to embrace a customer-oriented philosophy is a *necessary* but not a *sufficient* condition for success. The organisation must also foster and sustain a creative culture. Companies today copy each other's advantages and strategies with increasing speed. Differentiation gets harder to achieve, let alone maintain, and margins fall when firms become more alike. The only answer is to build a capability in strategic innovation and idea generation to develop a succession of customer-perceived value offerings (see the marketing memo on p. 873). This capability comes from assembling tools, processes, skills and measures that let the firm generate more and better new ideas than its competitors.[18]

Taking the creative approach

There are two main applications to creativity. The first is to do what the company already does but in a 'better way'. This may mean doing it faster, at less cost, with less waste; raising customer-perceived quality standards or performing more cost effectively. All these options generally rely on – or at least benefit from – new ideas. The second use of creativity is to do better things. This entails coming up with new market offerings that have additional customer-perceived value. Best results, of course, are obtained when companies practise both approaches. Despite the best of intentions, some companies often fail to embrace fully the importance of the creative approach to marketing.

A common reason for this is a failure to understand what creativity is really all about. Essentially, creative thinking is a process that brings into being a new approach that can break through constraints imposed by habit and tradition, so making it possible to find new solutions to problems. Creative thinking can refer to all aspects of the marketing management domain. For example it can be used to:

- generate new ideas that customers will perceive as having value;
- develop innovative marketing communications;
- operate new forms of distribution; and
- come up with ingenious pricing initiatives.

Marketing insight

The marketing CEO

What steps can a CEO take to create a market- and customer-focused company?

1 **Convince senior management of the need to become customer focused.** The CEO personally exemplifies strong customer commitment and rewards those in the organisation who do likewise. For example, former CEOs Jack Welch of GE, Lou Gerstner of IBM and Sir John Harvey-Jones of ICI are said to have spent 100 days a year visiting customers, in spite of their many strategic, financial and administrative burdens; current Starbucks CEO Jim Donald visits 10–20 stores a week to go behind the counter and talk to store partners (employees) and customers.

2 **Appoint a senior marketing officer and marketing taskforce.** The marketing taskforce should include the CEO; the directors of sales, R & D, purchasing, manufacturing, finance and human resources; and other key individuals.

3 **Get outside help and guidance.** Consulting firms have considerable experience in helping companies move towards a marketing orientation.

4 **Change the company's reward measurement and system.** As long as purchasing and manufacturing are rewarded for keeping costs low, they will resist accepting some costs required to serve customers better. As long as finance focuses on short-term profit, it will oppose major investments designed to build satisfied, loyal customers.

5 **Hire strong marketing talent.** The company needs a strong marketing director who not only manages the marketing department but also gains respect from and influence with the other functional directors. A multidivisional company will benefit from establishing a strong corporate marketing department.

6 **Develop strong in-house marketing training programmes.** The company should design well-crafted marketing training programmes for corporate management, divisional general managers, marketing and sales personnel, manufacturing personnel, R & D personnel and others. Accenture, Bosch, Electrolux and VW run these programmes.

7 **Install a modern marketing planning system.** The planning format will require managers to think about the marketing environment, opportunities, competitive trends and other forces. These managers then prepare strategies and sales-and-profit forecasts for specific products and segments and are accountable for performance.

8 **Establish an annual marketing excellence recognition programme.** Business units that believe they have developed exemplary marketing plans should submit a description of their plans and results. Winning teams should be rewarded at a special ceremony and the plans disseminated to the other business units as 'models of marketing thinking'. The finance/insurance giant Accenture follows this strategy.

9 **Shift from a department focus to a process-outcome focus.** After defining the fundamental business processes that determine its success, the company should appoint process leaders and cross-disciplinary teams to re-engineer and implement these processes.

10 **Empower the employees.** Progressive companies encourage and reward their employees for coming up with new ideas and empower them to settle customer complaints to retain the customers' business. IBM, for example, lets its front-line employees spend up to US$5,000 to solve a customer problem on the spot.

Companies must watch trends and be ready to capitalise on them. Motorola was 18 months late in moving from analogue to digital mobile phones, giving Nokia and Ericsson a big lead. Nestlé was late seeing the trend towards coffee houses such as Starbucks. Coca-Cola was slow to pick up beverage trends towards fruit-flavoured drinks such as Snapple, energy drinks such as Red Bull, and designer mineral water brands. They were also slow to see the emerging market for large pack sizes for colas, thus presenting their rival Pepsi with a way to creatively challenge their hitherto accepted symbol of advantage – the hour-glass shaped bottle. Market leaders tend to miss trends when they are risk averse, obsessed about protecting their existing markets and physical resources, and more interested in efficiency than innovation.[19]

Marketing memo

Fuelling strategic innovation

Professor Stephen Brown of Ulster University has challenged a number of fundamental assumptions underlying the marketing concept. He thinks marketers make too much of researching and satisfying consumers, and they risk losing marketing imagination and significant consumer impact. How can companies build a capability for strategic innovation? Here are some approaches he advocates:

- Hire marketers who are unusually creative to counterbalance the majority who practise marketing by the textbook. These people may be unconventional – rule breaking, risk taking and even argumentative – but their ideas will at least present a challenge.

- Train employees in the use of creativity techniques, for groups (brainstorming, Synectics) and individuals (visualisation, attribute listing, forced relationships, morphological analysis, mind mapping).

- Note trends such as longer working hours, single parenting and new lifestyles, and tease out their implications for the firm.

- List unmet customer needs and imagine new offerings or solutions: how to help people lose weight, stop smoking, relieve stress, meet others.

- Run a 'best idea' competition once a month. Give a cash reward, extra holiday or travel awards to those who come up with the best ideas.

- Have senior managers take small sets of employees out to lunch or dinner once a week to discuss ideas for improving the business. Visit new settings, such as a football match or a shopping centre.

- Set up groups of employees to critique the company's and competitors' products and services. Let them critique the company's cherished beliefs and consider turning them upside down.

- Occasionally, hire creative resources from outside the firm. Many large advertising agencies, such as Leo Burnett, run a creativity service for clients.

Sources: For more on Brown's views, see S. Brown (2001) *Marketing: The Retro Revolution*, Thousand Oaks, CA: Sage. For more on creativity, see P. Fallon and F. Senn (2006) *Juicing the Orange: How to Turn Creativity Into a Powerful Business Advantage*, Boston, MA: Harvard Business School Press; B. Schmetterer (2003) *Leap: A Revolution in Creative Business Strategy*, Hoboken, NJ: John Wiley & Sons; J.-M. Dru (2002) *Beyond Disruption: Changing the Rules in the Marketplace*, Hoboken, NJ: John Wiley & Sons; M. Michalko (1998) *Cracking Creativity: The Secrets of Creative Genius*, Berkeley, CA: Ten Speed Press; J. M. Higgins (1994) *101 Creative Problem-Solving Techniques*, New York: New Management Publishing; and all the books by Edward DeBono.

Welcome to the meeting
Source: Serif

Building a creative culture

Creativity is a property of thought process that can be acquired and improved through instruction and practice. In this context, individual creativity mechanisms refer to activities undertaken by individual employees within an organisation to enhance their capability for developing something that is meaningful and novel within the work environment. Organisational creativity mechanisms refer to the extent to which the organisation has instituted formal approaches and tools, and provided resources to encourage meaningfully novel behaviours within the organisation. It is not enough for organisations to opt for a 'quick fix' by hiring creative people while making mainly cosmetic changes to their dominant modus operandi. Successful creative marketing requires both an organisational culture change and the training of existing and new staff. It is a TEAM approach. Football players are encouraged to work creatively as a unit and coaches frequently use the word 'team' as a mnemonic – Together Everyone Achieves More. The managers of successful football teams are acutely aware of the importance of both the intrinsic and extrinsic aspects of the creativity driver as they seek competitive success for their clubs.

Creativity – a mystical gift for some or something for all?

For the first time in history, creativity is largely understood. The logical basis of how the brain works is understood. From such an understanding it is possible to derive the deliberate tools of lateral thinking, of solving problems by circumventing traditional methods. These tools can be learned and used. As with any skill, some people will become more skilful than others but everyone can learn to be creative.[20] Most companies are confident to invest for the short term but many become more hesitant when faced with investing in the medium to longer term. Continuous creative marketing requires a long-term commitment because creativity and innovation are crucial elements in a competitive world. Something can be done about creativity; it is not just a magic talent. Businesses should take heart for they can always find new ways to add value.[21]

Gaining momentum – the 'Larreche prescription'

Professor Larreche, who holds the Heineken chair in marketing at INSEAD, maintains that *momentum* is something that can be created by companies and, once achieved, can be maintained by pursuing a creative marketing approach. He cites the examples of Toyota, Apple, Nintendo and Skype which have all entered the virtuous circle of continuous growth – 'the momentum effect'. Lasting competitive advantages are the result of getting certain fundamental aspects of business right. What Larreche terms 'value creation' – spotting what customers want and working hard to provide it – is where momentum starts to develop. A company 'that systematically places customers at the centre of its thinking and that strives to attain ambitious goals will be able to harness the power of the momentum and deliver the exceptional growth it provides'.

Professor Larreche takes a nuanced view of customers and argues that they are not always strictly rational. 'Their perception is their reality, and it may be quite different from the "rational" perspective of product-design engineers.' 'Momentum-deficient' businesses suffer from 'transaction myopia': failing to understand, for example, that the lifetime value of a customer is far more important than any short-term revenue 'hit'. Customer retention 'offers an extraordinary acceleration of profitable growth by exceptionally increasing average customer lifetime and, as a result, knowing customer acquisition costs'.

The concept of momentum does offer a big, unifying theory and the success stories referred to by Larreche do seem to share it. However, chance, the mistakes of competitors and sometimes sheer serendipity all play a part in highly competitive markets.[22]

Maintaining momentum

Delivering success is a team effort that extends to all management as they all have a contribution to make to the final offering that is presented to customers. The resulting coordinated corporate offering is much harder for a competitor to imitate than new technology and products. Professor Hamel, of the London Business School,[23] believes that for many companies real 'momentum' has slowed down because 'real innovation in management operations has slowed to a crawl'. Professor Hamel believes that, whereas previous advances in management focused on production processes, the management innovators of today must concentrate on people. Companies need to learn how to harness what he calls individual and group 'employee imagination'. In addition to the companies cited by Professor Larreche as good examples of his 'momentum effect', the Danish toymaker LEGO, according to Professor Torben Pedersen of the Copenhagen Business School, has expanded its creative and innovative team to include customers for years.

IBM provides proof that some of the biggest companies can innovate in search of 'momentum'. In January 2006, the company launched its 'Innovation Jam', posting dozens of white papers and internal documents online and inviting comment. 'Everyone got involved in discussing IBM's strategy,' according to Professor Hamel, and this included customers, suppliers, employees and family members of employees. The result was ten initiatives and hundreds of millions of US dollars of investment.

However, the majority of companies are failing to develop creative marketing approaches, as most managers are not taught to think of themselves as people whose job it is to be part of a team that aspires to create and invent.

Marketing implementation

Table 21.1 summarises the characteristics of a great marketing company, great not for 'what it is', but for 'what it does'. **Marketing implementation** is the process that turns marketing plans into action assignments and ensures they accomplish the plan's stated objectives.

A brilliant strategic marketing plan counts for little if it is not implemented properly. Strategy addresses the *what* and *why* of marketing activities; implementation addresses the *who, where, when* and *how*. They are closely related: one layer of strategy implies certain tactical implementation assignments at a lower level. For example, top management's strategic decision to 'harvest' a product must be translated into specific actions and assignments.

Table 21.1 Characteristics of a great marketing company

Percentage of 13–25 year olds who say they:	%
Feel personally responsible for making a difference in the world	61
Feel companies should join in the effort to make a difference in the world	75
Are likely to switch brands (given equal price and quality) to support a cause	89
Are more likely to pay attention to messages of companies deeply committed to a cause	74
Consider a company's social commitment when deciding where to shop	69
Consider a company's social commitment when recommending products	64

Source: Based on Cone Inc./AMP Insights survey of 1800 13–25-year-olds as reported in *BusinessWeek*, 6 November 2006, 13.

Companies today are striving to make their marketing operations more efficient and their return on marketing investment more measurable. Marketing costs can amount from 20 to 40 per cent of a company's total operating budget. Marketers need better templates for marketing processes, better management of marketing assets, and better allocation of marketing resources. Certain repetitive processes can be automated under such names as *marketing resource management* (MRM), *marketing investment management* (MIM), *enterprise marketing management* (EMM) and *marketing automation systems* (MAS).[24]

Marketing resource management software provides a set of web-based applications that automate and integrate such activities as project management, campaign management, budget management, asset management, brand management, customer relationship management and knowledge management. The knowledge management component consists of process templates, how-to wizards and best practices.

Software packages are web hosted and available to users with passwords. They add up to what some have called *desktop marketing* and give marketers whatever information and decision structures they need on computer screens. MRM software lets marketers improve spending and investment decisions, bring new products to market more quickly, and reduce decision time and costs.

Leadership

Ideas, however persuasive they may be in workplace discussion, need to be championed by a committed leader if they are to make a real difference to company performance in the marketplace. Effective and sustained creative marketing demands a subtle blending of the knowledge systems of leadership, creativity and innovation. A study completed by Manchester Business School identified nine themes that provide a revealing picture of the insights and skills of creative leaders.[25]

1 **Leadership, learning and knowledge systems.** Absorptive capacity resource-based models and cognitive framing are promising ways of integrating knowledge and leadership studies.
2 **Empowerment and delegated leadership.** Self-managed teams and distributed leadership systems are based on a facilitative or empowering leadership style. Cross-functional teams are necessary for required integration within projects. The collaborative paradigm within networks is also relevant.
3 **Creative problem-solving leadership.** Creative leadership (in and beyond formalised structures to stimulate creativity) is widely associated with a facilitative or process-oriented style. Person–environment fit (contingency) theories seem relevant too.
4 **Innovation and entrepreneurial leadership.** Roles in technological innovation are generally assumed to operate within a rational model of strategic change.
5 **Crisis leadership.** The theme concerns the concept of managing/leading in uncertain or turbulent environments.
6 **Change-centred leadership.** Change-centred leadership differentiates older and new leadership thinking.
7 **Creating the right environment for creativity to grow and flourish.** Ekvall and Amabile and their colleagues are regarded as key sources in climate and environment studies. Action research often seeks change by survey feedback of perceived blocks or barriers to change.
8 **Strategic planning leadership.** Resource-based theories help model global innovation.
9 **Evaluation of creativity.** This looks at the most appropriate ways to evaluate creativity (interpretative or social constructivist).

Methodology and madness – the importance of leaving room for creativity

Rigorous marketing training has traditionally been the preserve of companies such as Procter & Gamble and Unilever, which have long been acknowledged as excellent training grounds for marketers. However, now they are being joined by other companies that aspire to make marketing a more potent management activity. As companies strive to find that 'market edge', so there is an increasing need to think outside the traditional marketing toolbox. Creative approaches can bring spectacular success. The problem for many companies is that they can mean taking a risk and can run counter to the culture of traditional marketing methodology. Forward-thinking firms are beginning to lower their risk ceilings, back their creative thinking and not become too reliant on methodology as they seek to make a difference. They fully accept that being seen to be mad by their competitors can in fact make a difference!

Creative marketing

The creative approach to marketing makes a case that creativity in marketing theory is largely absent and that an alternative way forward for marketing is to apply a creative point of view. According to Ian Fillis (University of Stirling) and Ruth Rentschler (Deakin University),[26] creative marketing 'is used as an umbrella term to capture concepts from marketing and creativity'. Creativity writers in management and organisational studies include Teresa Amabile, Gareth Morgan, Howard Gardner and Richard Florida. Kotler's influence pervades marketing practice: on the bad side, he helped to establish the current marketing management mindset that critics view as prescriptive and formulaic; on the good side, he was an earlier advocate that the concept of marketing ought to be broadened. In this regard, creative marketing is part of the contemporary marketing landscape aligned with the 'critical' approach associated with Stephen Brown. Marketing is a broad church.

New approaches are certainly welcome. Fillis and Rentschler's core message is that

Inspiration for the creative marketing paradigm comes from the imagination of the entrepreneurial marketing practitioner, from both within the conventional notion of the business world and from the arts. It is drawn from the creative ability to bypass everyday thinking and make tangible the intangible. Insight into creative ideas can be gained by examining many aspects of the artistic realm.

As such, they draw from the experiences of artists such as Picasso and Diaghilev, present a definition of creativity based on 6Ps (place, people, property, process, practice and product), and conclude by proffering their creative marketing manifesto as 'a focal point for further discussion and theory construction'.

Is there a threat that creativity will be institutionalised as it serves the interests of marketers? Areas of interest include the nature of creativity; the differences between creativity and innovation and the relationship between the two; different models of the creative process; the conditions which stifle or stimulate creativity; the circumstances that lead from creativity to innovation; the role of risk in creativity and innovation; the value of creativity to business, the economy and society; and changes in how society understands creativity and values innovation in a knowledge economy.[27]

Much traditional (theoretical) marketing often seems to pass people by. If asked to name five TV commercials that they have viewed recently, surprisingly many people are

Unilever steps out and trusts market intuition

Observers believe that Unilever is benefiting from a more risk-taking marketing culture than its rival Procter & Gamble. It has been increasingly seeking new creative big ideas for its advertising campaigns. Top Unilever brands such as Dove, Persil and Lynx have all been associated with creativity, dynamism, innovation and energy in recent surveys, in contrast to the ratings of Procter & Gamble brands that are well known for their risk aversion. Nowhere has the new approach been more apparent than with the performance of Unilever's Dove brand, which is now a major contributor to the firm's profits.

Since early 2004 Dove's 'campaign for real beauty' has featured advertisements that have set out to challenge the stereotypical images of female glamour. Similar unorthodox creative marketing has benefited the performance of Persil with the strap line 'Dirt is good' and the creation of a fantasy female-staffed airline for male teenagers who buy Lynx cosmetics.[28]

Source: This section is based on a paper by T. Rickards and S. Morgan's (2006) Creative leaders: a decade of contributions from *Creativity and Innovation Management* journal, *Creativity and Innovation Management*, 15(1), 4–18.

unable to do so effortlessly. Perhaps TV commercials are becoming too much like innocuous wallpaper. Curiously enough, while creative marketing when apparent is recalled easily – for example, the Citroën Transformer commercials, the quirky Skoda cake, the mythical Guinness screenings – annoying advertisements such as Cillit Bang are the ones that people remember.

Socially responsible marketing

Effective marketing must be matched by a strong sense of ethics, values and social responsibility.[29] A number of forces are driving companies to practise a higher level of corporate social responsibility. These include rising customer expectations, evolving employee goals and ambitions, tighter government legislation and pressure, developing investor interest in social criteria, relentless media scrutiny, and changing business procurement practices.[30] The commercial success of ex-US Vice-President Al Gore's 2006 documentary, *An Inconvenient Truth*, shows how the general public has become more concerned about environmental issues.

Corporate social responsibility

The European Commission defines corporate social responsibility (CSR) as enterprises' contribution to sustainable development. Some companies, such as BP, British Telecom, McDonald's and Maersk, have responded positively to the CSR challenge. McDonald's, for example, with its Ronald McDonald House initiative in Norway, has sought to build a corporate brand reputation by means of community involvement.[31] Many others like to be regarded as 'talking the talk'.[32] However, the recent spate of corporate scandals, accounting frauds, allegations of executive greed and dubious business practices has led many to adopt mixed attitudes to CSR and regard it as a sham. Some observers have even dubbed it 'cynical social responsibility' and many have all but abandoned it for 'sustainability'.[33]

Raising the level of socially responsible marketing calls for making a three-pronged attack that relies on bona fide legal, ethical and social responsibilities.

Legal

Organisations must ensure that every employee knows and observes relevant laws. For example, salespeople's statements must legally match advertising claims. They should not offer bribes to purchasing agents or others influencing a business-to-business sale. They may not obtain or use competitors' technical or trade secrets through bribery or industrial espionage. Finally, they must not disparage competitors or their products by suggesting things that are not true. Every sales representative should know the law and act accordingly.[34]

Ethical

Business practices come under attack because commercial situations routinely pose tough ethical dilemmas. It is not easy to draw a clear line between normal marketing practice and that which is unethical. Some issues sharply divide critics. Though Walkers Crisps reacted quickly and positively and reduced the salt content of its snack items and Procter & Gamble reduced the sugar content of its orange drink Sunny Delight, some watch groups felt that was not enough.

At the same time, certain business practices are clearly unethical or illegal. These include bribery, theft of trade secrets, false and deceptive advertising, exclusive dealing and tying agreements, quality or safety defects, false warranties, inaccurate labelling, price fixing or undue discrimination, barriers to entry and predatory competition. Companies must adopt and disseminate a written code of ethics, build a company tradition of ethical behaviour, and hold people fully responsible for observing ethical and legal guidelines.[35] Companies that do not perform ethically or well are at greater risk of being exposed, thanks to the internet. In the past, a disgruntled customer might criticise a firm to 12 other people; today he or she can reach thousands. Microsoft, for example, has attracted scores of anti-Microsoft sites, including Hate Microsoft and Boycott Microsoft.

Striking a socially defensible balance between seeking to improve profits (efficiency) and marketing effectively in the light of the experienced environment can present companies with serious ethical dilemmas. Marketing ethics can be viewed as a continuum that stretches from *caveat emptor* (let the buyer beware) to *caveat venditor* (let the seller beware). Strictly speaking, the emphasis should be moving towards *caveat venditor* if the providers fully sign up to the underlying philosophy of the relationship marketing paradigm.[36] So why do food companies 'build bulk' by injecting water into meat? Why do supermarkets incur huge carbon footprints as they transport greengroceries across the oceans of the world? Why do some clothing companies import cheap merchandise from underdeveloped countries and turn a blind eye to the conditions which the workforces have to endure in these countries?

There are many questions surrounding the interpretation of ethical marketing that can result in corporations, divisions and individual brands finding their position on the *caveat emptor–caveat venditor* scale. The matter is not one of right or wrong or of white or black – real life is more complex than this – but it is a matter of conscience. So what does 'ethics' really mean in management activities? Is it a word full of promise but paradoxically also full of unfulfilled promises?[37] Most would agree that an ethical approach to marketing management is desirable in principle. So how can this opportunity be grasped?[38]

Smith proposes the maxims in the marketing memo to guide companies as to whether or not they are marketing ethically.

Social responsibility

Individual marketers must practise a 'social conscience' in specific dealings with customers and stakeholders. Increasingly, people want information about a company's record on social and environmental responsibility to help decide which companies to buy from, invest in, and work for.[39]

Deciding how to communicate corporate social responsibility can be difficult. Once a firm airs an environmental initiative, it can become a target for criticism. Many well-intentioned marketing initiatives attract unforeseen negative consequences. Palm oil was hailed as a renewable fuel for food companies looking to find a solution to a trans-fat ban, until its use was linked to the potential extinction of the orang-utan and the sun bear.

Corporate philanthropy also can pose problems as the motives of organisations can be misunderstood.[40]

Sustainability

Sustainability – the importance of meeting humanity's needs without harming future generations – has risen to the top of many corporate agendas. Major corporations now outline in great detail how they are trying to improve the long-term impact of their actions on communities and the environment. As one sustainability consultant put it, 'There is a triple bottom line – people, planet, and profit – and the people part of the equation must come first. Sustainability means more than being eco-friendly; it also means you are in it for the long haul.'[41]

Many CEOs believe that embracing sustainability can avoid the negative consequences of environmental disasters, political protests, and human rights or workplace abuses. Often a target of environmental criticism in the past, DuPont has moved through two phases of sustainability in the past 15 years: first, drastically reducing the emission of greenhouse gases, release of carcinogens and discharge of hazardous wastes; and second, embracing sustainability as a strategic goal via the introduction of alternative biofuels and energy-saving materials such as its new bio-PDO fibre.[42]

Investors are demanding ever more concrete information about what firms are doing to achieve sustainability. Sustainability ratings exist, although there is little agreement about what the appropriate metrics might be.[43]

Some feel companies that score well on sustainability factors typically exhibit high levels of management quality in that 'they tend to be more strategically nimble and better equipped to compete in the complex, high-velocity, global environment'.[44]

Marketing memo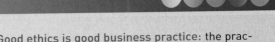

Key steps in assessing marketing ethics standards

- The golden rule: do unto others as you would be done by.
- The media test: would members of the marketing team be embarrassed in front of colleagues/family/friends, if marketing decisions were published in the media for all to see?
- The invoice test: are payments being requested that might not meet with the approval of internal and external auditors?

- Good ethics is good business practice: the practised belief that sellers should regard integrity as being in the best long-term interest of the business.
- The professional test: would marketing decisions be regarded as ethical by professional peers in other companies?
- When in doubt, reconsider proposed actions.

Source: Based on N. C. Smith (1999) Marketing ethics, in M. J. Bakers (ed.), *Encyclopaedia of Marketing*, London: International Thomson Business Press, 924.

Innovest

Founded in 1995, Innovest studies firms on 120 different factors, such as energy use, health and safety records, litigation, employee practices, regulatory history, and management systems for dealing with supplier problems. It uses these measures to assign 2,200 listed companies grades ranging from AAA to CCC, much like a bond rating. Companies scoring well include Nokia Corp. and Ericsson, which excel at tailoring products for developing nations, and banks such as HSBC Holdings and ABN-AMRO, which study the environmental impact of projects they help finance. Although Hewlett-Packard and Dell both rate AAA, Apple gets a middling BBB rating on the grounds of weaker oversight of offshore factories and lack of a 'clear environmental business strategy'.

Many companies in diverse industries beyond edible food products are embracing organic offerings that avoid the use of chemicals and pesticides to stress ecological preservation. Apparel and other non-food items make up the second-fastest growth category. Organic cotton grown by farmers who fight boll weevils with ladybirds, weed their crops by hand, and use manure for fertiliser has become a hot retail attraction. Sustainability is becoming more mainstream, and consumers are increasingly willing to pay more to support the environment.[45]

Levi's

Innovation delivers the first sustainable Levi's® jean launch in Europe.
Source: Ross Haily/Fort Worth Star Telegram/MCT/NewsCom.

Levi Strauss Europe launched its Levi's® eco jeans in October 2006. This was believed to be the first fully sustainable jean from a major denim brand, made using 100 per cent certified organic cotton, and sustainable product components and production processes. Levi Strauss Europe was granted an 'EKO sustainable textile' certification for the Levi® eco jeans from Control Union Certifications, a leading worldwide inspection and certification body for organic production and products. Even the garment tags and packaging are made of organic fabric or recycled paper and printed with soy-based ink.[46]

Many firms have decided to take a more active, strategic role with corporate responsibility. Even banana producer Chiquita, which once had a poor reputation for exploiting farm workers, contaminating water and destroying rain forest, has improved workers' conditions, significantly reduced pesticide use, reduced erosion and chemical run-off and even implemented a major recycling programme on its farms.[47]

Such a belief in the value of social responsibility has not been in evidence in the past. In 1776 the English economist Adam Smith proclaimed, 'I have never known much good done by those who profess to trade for the public good.' Legendary US economist Milton Friedman famously declared social initiatives 'fundamentally subversive' because he felt they undermined the profit-seeking purpose of public companies and wasted shareholders' money. Some critics worry that important business investment in areas such as research and development could suffer as a result of a focus on social responsibility.

These critics are in the minority. Many now believe that satisfying customers, employees and other stakeholders and achieving business success are closely tied to the adoption and implementation of high standards of business and marketing conduct. Firms are finding that one benefit of being seen as a socially responsible company is the ability to attract employees. The most admired – and increasingly most successful – companies in the world abide by a code of serving people's interests as well as their own.

Firms of Endearment

Researchers Sisodia, Wolfe and Sheth believe humanistic companies make great companies. They define 'Firms of Endearment' as those that have a culture of caring and serve the interests of their stakeholders. Stakeholders are defined in terms of the acronym SPICE: society, partners, investors, customers and employees. Firms of Endearment create a love affair with stakeholders. Their senior managers run an open-door policy and are passionate about customers, and their compensation is modest. They pay more to their employees, relate more closely to a smaller group of excellent suppliers, and give back to the communities in which they work. The researchers assert that Firms of Endearment actually spend less on marketing as a percentage but yet earn greater profits. It appears that the customers who love the company do most of the marketing. The authors see the twenty-first-century marketing paradigm as being essentially about firms creating value for all stakeholders and being recognised as socially responsible organisations.[48]

The breakthrough marketing box on pp. 883–4 describes the practices of Starbucks, a highly rated endearment firm. However, many smaller firms excel too.

Socially responsible business models

The future holds a wealth of opportunities.[49] Technological advances in solar energy, online networks, cable and satellite television, biotechnology and telecommunications promise to change the world as we know it. At the same time, forces in the socioeconomic, cultural and natural environments will impose new limits on marketing and business practices. Companies that innovate solutions and values in a socially responsible way are the most likely to succeed.[50]

Many companies, such as BASF, Bayer, Ben & Jerry's, Kwik-Fit, Marks & Spencer, Michelin and The Body Shop, are giving social responsibility a more prominent role. BASF has funded a research laboratory at Nottingham University in the United Kingdom after the company withdrew from chemical research in the city. Michelin is lending money to worthy manufacturing start-ups to give something back to the community.

Corporate philanthropy as a whole is on the increase. More firms are realising that corporate social responsibility in the form of cash donations, in-kind contributions, cause marketing and employee volunteer programmes is not just the 'right thing' but also the 'smart thing'[51] to do. Coutts, the London-based top-person's bank, is receiving more enquiries than ever from clients interested in setting up charitable trusts and foundations. The Marketing insight box on p. 884 offers two high-profile perspectives on how to make progress in that area.

Breakthrough marketing

Starbucks

Starbucks opened in Seattle in 1971 when coffee consumption in the United States had been declining for a decade. Rival coffee brands were also using cheaper coffee beans to compete on price. Starbucks' founders decided to experiment with a new concept: a store that would sell only the finest imported coffee beans and coffee-brewing equipment. The original store did not sell coffee by the cup, only beans.

Howard Schultz came to Starbucks in 1982. While in Milan on business, he walked into an Italian coffee bar and had a flash of inspiration with his espresso. 'There was nothing like this in America. It was an extension of people's front porch. It was an emotional experience,' he said. He knew right away that he wanted to take this concept to the United States. Schultz set about creating an environment for Starbucks coffee houses that would reflect Italian elegance melded with US informality. He envisioned Starbucks as a 'personal treat' for its customers, a 'Third Place' – a comfortable, sociable gathering spot bridging the workplace and the home.

From its launch in Seattle, Starbucks' expansion throughout the United States was carefully planned. The management team agreed that all stores would be owned and operated by the company, ensuring complete control to cultivate an unparalleled image of quality. Starbucks employed a 'hub' expansion strategy, in which coffee houses entered a new market in a clustered group. Although this deliberate saturation often cannibalised 30 per cent of one store's sales by introducing a store nearby, any drop in revenue was offset by efficiencies in marketing and distribution costs, and the enhanced image of convenience. A typical customer would stop by Starbucks in the United States as many as 18 times a month.

Part of the success of Starbucks undoubtedly lies in its market offerings, and its relentless commitment to providing customers with the richest possible sensory experiences. But another key is the enlightened sense of responsibility that manifests itself in a number of different ways.

Starbucks believes that by focusing and aligning the giving priorities of Starbucks Coffee Company with The Starbucks Foundation, a separate charitable organisation, its contributions will have greater impact and provide more benefit to communities around the world. The Starbucks Foundation celebrated its ten-year anniversary in 2007 with the announcement of Starbucks About Youth, a global philanthropic endeavour focused on supporting educational initiatives and youth leadership in Starbucks retail markets around the world.
Source: Starbucks Corporation.

Schultz believes that in order to exceed the expectations of customers it is first necessary to exceed the expectations of employees. As far back as 1990, Starbucks provided comprehensive health care to all employees, including part timers. Health insurance now costs Starbucks more each year than coffee. The firm also introduced a stock option plan called 'Bean Stock', which allows Starbucks' employees to participate in the company's financial success.

▶ Breakthrough marketing *(continued)*

The company donates large sums of money to charities via The Starbucks Foundation, created in 1997 with proceeds from the sale of Schultz's book. The mission of the foundation is to 'create hope, discovery, and opportunity in communities where Starbucks partners [employees] live and work'. The primary focus of the foundation has been on improving young people's lives by supporting literacy programmes for children and families. By 2007, the foundation had provided over US$12 million to more than 700 youth-focused organisations in the United States and Canada. Starbucks has also donated 5 cents of every sale of its Ethos bottled water to improving the quality of water in poor countries as part of a five-year US$10 million pledge.

Starbucks also promotes 'fair trade' export practices with third-world coffee bean producers and pays its producers in those countries an average of 23 per cent above market price. It took the company ten years of development to create the world's first recycled beverage cup, made from 10 per cent post-consumer fibre, conserving 5 million pounds of paper or approximately 78,000 trees a year.

Howard Schultz stepped down as CEO in 2000, and assumed the role of chairman and 'Chief Global Strategist'. Following a recent slide in the company's fortunes, Schultz has taken back the reins of the company. Starbucks currently has over 12,400 stores worldwide, with 115,000 employees and almost US$8 billion in revenue. The company hopes to expand to 40,000 outlets, cafés and kiosks worldwide, half of them outside the United States. No matter what the growth trajectory, Schultz believes Starbucks must retain a passion for coffee and a sense of humanity, to remain small even as it gets big, and always to treat workers as individuals.

Sources: H. Schultz (2006) Dare to be a social entrepreneur, *Business 2.0*, December, 87; E. Iwata (2006) Owner of small coffee shop takes on java titan starbucks, *USA Today*, 20 December; Staying pure: Howard Schultz's formula for Starbucks, *The Economist*, 25 February 2006, 72; D. Anderson (2006) Evolution of the eco cup, *Business 2.0*, June, 50; B. Horovitz (2006) Starbucks nation, *USA Today*, 19 May; T. Howard (2005) Starbucks takes up cause for safe drinking water, *USA Today*, 2 August; H. Schultz and D. Jones Yang (1997) *Pour Your Heart into It: How Starbucks Built a Company One Cup at a Time*, New York: Hyperion; see also www.starbucks.com.

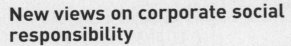

Marketing insight

New views on corporate social responsibility

Two of management's most renowned thinkers have turned their attention to corporate social responsibility, offering some unique perspectives that build on their past management research and thinking.

Michael Porter

Harvard's Michael Porter and Mark Kramer, managing director of FSG Social Impact Advisors, believe good corporate citizenship can be a source of opportunity, innovation and competitive advantage, as long as firms evaluate it using the same frameworks and concepts that guide their core business strategies. They feel corporate social responsibility must mesh with a firm's strengths, capabilities and positioning. They assert that *strategic corporate social responsibility* results when firms: (1) transform value chain activities to benefit society while reinforcing strategy; and (2) engage in strategic philanthropy that leverages capabilities to improve salient areas of competitive context.

According to the authors, firms should select causes that intersect their particular businesses to create shared value for the firm and society. For example, Toyota addressed public concerns about automotive emissions by creating a competitively strong and environmentally friendly hybrid vehicle, the Prius, and French banking giant Crédit Agricole differentiated itself through specialised environmentally friendly financial products.

Porter and Kramer note that

> By providing jobs, investing capital, purchasing goods, and doing business every day, corporations have a profound and positive influence on society. The most important thing a corporation can do for society, and for any community, is to contribute to a prosperous economy.

Although companies can address hundreds of social issues, only a handful offer the opportunity to build focused, proactive and integrated social initiatives that link with core business strategies to make a real difference to society and create a competitive advantage in the marketplace.

Clayton Christensen

Harvard's Clayton Christensen, along with his research colleagues, advocates *catalytic innovations* to address social sector problems. Like Christensen's disruptive innovations – which challenge industry incumbents by

Marketing insight *(continued)*

offering simpler, good enough alternatives to an under-served group of customers – catalytic innovations offer good enough solutions to inadequately addressed social problems. Catalytic innovators share five qualities:

1 They create systemic social change through scaling and replication.

2 They meet a need that is either overserved (because the existing solution is more complex than many people require) or not served at all.

3 They offer simpler, less costly products and services that may have a lower level of performance, but that users consider to be good enough.

4 They generate resources, such as donations, grants, volunteer manpower or intellectual capital, in ways that are initially unattractive to competitors.

5 They are often ignored, disparaged or even encouraged by existing players for whom the business model is unprofitable or otherwise unattractive, and who therefore avoid or retreat from the market segment.

To find organisations that are creating a catalytic innovation for investment or other purposes, Christensen and his colleagues offer some guidelines:

1 Look for signs of disruption in the process: Although not necessarily easily observed, pre-existing catalytic innovators may already be present in a market.

2 Identify specific catalytic innovations: Apply the five criteria listed.

3 Assess the business model: Determine whether the organisation can effectively introduce the innovation and scale it up and sustain it.

Sources: M. F. Porter and M. R. Kramer (2006) Strategy and society, *Harvard Business Review*, December, 78–82; C. M. Christensen, H. Baumann, R. Ruggles and T. M. Stadtler (2006) Disruption innovation for social change, *Harvard Business Review*, December, 94–101. See also: R. Steckel, E. Ford, C. Hilliard and T. Sanders (2004) *Cold Cash for Warm Hearts: 101 Best Social Marketing Initiatives*, Homewood, IL: High Tide Press.

Cause-related marketing

Many firms blend corporate social responsibility initiatives with marketing activities.[52] **Cause-related marketing** links the firm's contributions to a designated cause to customers' engaging directly or indirectly in revenue-producing transactions with the firm.[53] Cause marketing is part of *corporate societal marketing* (CSM), which Drumwright and Murphy define as marketing efforts 'that have at least one economic objective related to social welfare and use the resources of the company and/or of its partners'.[54] They also include other activities such as traditional and strategic philanthropy and volunteerism as part of CSM.

Tesco, a leading UK retailer, has created a 'Computers for Schools' programme: customers receive vouchers for every £10 spent, which they can donate to the school of their choice and the school can exchange the vouchers for new computer equipment. British Airways too has a particularly successful and highly visible programme.

British Airways

British Airways partnered with UNICEF and developed a cause-marketing campaign called 'Change for Good'. Passengers on British Airways flights are encouraged to donate left-over foreign currency from their travels. The scheme is simple: passengers deposit their surplus currency in envelopes provided by British Airways, which collects the deposits and donates them directly to UNICEF. British Airways advertises its programme during an in-flight video, on the backs of seat cards and with in-flight announcements. The company also developed a television advertisement that featured a child thanking British Airways for its contribution to UNICEF. Because 'Change for Good' can be directly targeted to passengers and can produce immediate results, it does not require extensive advertising or promotion and is highly cost efficient. Since 1994 it has distributed almost US$45 million around the world.[55]

Cause-marketing benefits and costs

A successful cause-marketing programme can improve social welfare; create differentiated brand positioning; build strong consumer bonds; enhance the company's public image with government officials and other decision makers; create a reservoir of goodwill; boost internal morale and galvanise employees; drive sales; and increase the market value of the firm.[56]

Customers may develop a strong, unique bond with the firm that transcends normal marketplace transactions.[57] Specifically, cause marketing can: (1) build brand awareness; (2) enhance brand image; (3) establish brand credibility; (4) evoke brand feelings; (5) create a sense of brand community; and (6) elicit brand engagement. Cause marketing has a particularly interested audience in civic-minded 13–25-year-old millennial customers.[58]

The danger, however, is that a cause-related marketing programme could misfire if customers question the link between the product and the cause and see the firm as self-serving and exploitative, as was the case with Cadbury Schweppes.[59]

Cadbury Schweppes plc

Cadbury's 'Sports for Schools' promotion offered sports and fitness equipment for schools in exchange for tokens. The problem was that the public and media saw a perverse incentive for children to eat more chocolate, a product associated with obesity. As Britain's Food Commission, a non-governmental organisation, said: 'Cadbury wants children to eat 2 million kilograms of fat – to get fit.' The commission estimated that to generate the 90 tokens to purchase a £5 netball would require spending £38 on Cadbury's confectionery and consuming more than 20,000 calories and over 1,000 grams of fat. The product and the cause seemed to be at war. Cadbury Schweppes quickly discontinued the token programme, but it continued its 'Get Active' campaign, offering teachers tips for sporty games in conjunction with the Youth Sport Trust and sponsored events such as Get Active Day with British sports stars. Putting a positive spin on the bad press, a Cadbury spokesperson insisted, 'The ensuing debate was very welcome. We have been trying to promote Get Active for two months. I don't think there can be anyone in the country who hasn't heard of it this week.'[60]

The knowledge, skills, resources and experiences of a top firm may be even more important to a non-profit or community group than funding, so they must be clear about what their goals are, communicate clearly what they hope to accomplish and have an organisational structure in place to work with different firms. Developing a long-term relationship with a firm can take a long time.

Firms must make a number of decisions in designing and implementing a cause-marketing programme, such as how many and which cause(s) to choose and how to brand the cause programme.

Choosing a cause

Some experts believe the positive impact of cause-related marketing is reduced by sporadic involvement with numerous causes. For example, Gillette's director of civic affairs states: 'When you're spreading out your giving in fifty-dollar to one-thousand-dollar increments, no one knows what you are doing . . . It doesn't make much of a splash.'[61] Many companies choose to focus on one or a few main causes to simplify execution and maximise impact. One such focused marketer is McDonald's. Ronald McDonald Houses in more than 27 countries offer more than 6,000 rooms each night to families needing support while their child is in hospital. The Ronald McDonald House programme has provided a 'home away from home' for nearly 10 million family members since its beginning in 1974.

Limiting support to a single cause, however, may limit the pool of consumers or other stakeholders who can transfer positive feelings from the cause to the firm. In addition, many popular causes already have numerous corporate sponsors. Over 300 companies, including Avon, Ford, Estée Lauder, Revlon, Lee Jeans, Polo Ralph Lauren, Yoplait, Saks, BMW and American Express, have associated themselves with breast cancer as a cause.[62] As a consequence, the brand may find itself 'lost in the shuffle'. Opportunities may be greater with 'orphan causes' – diseases that afflict fewer than 200,000 people[63] – or with overlooked diseases, such as pancreatic cancer. Most firms choose causes that fit their corporate or brand image and which matter to their employees and shareholders.

Social marketing

Cause-related marketing supports a cause. **Social marketing** has been defined by French and Blair-Stevens as 'the systematic application of marketing alongside other concepts and techniques, to achieve specific goals, for a social good', often by non-profit or government organisations. Typical campaigns encourage consumers to 'Say No to Drugs' or 'Exercise More and Eat Better'.[64] Social marketing goes back many years. In the 1950s, India started family planning campaigns. In the 1970s, Sweden ran social marketing campaigns to turn the country into a nation of non-smokers and non-drinkers; the Australian government ran 'Wear Your Seat Belt' campaigns; and the Canadian government launched campaigns to 'Say No to Drugs', 'Stop Smoking' and 'Exercise for Health'. In the 1980s, the World Bank, World Health Organization, and Centres for Disease Control and Prevention started to use the term and promote interest in social marketing. A number of different types of organisation conduct social marketing in most European countries.

Choosing the right goal or objective for a social marketing programme is critical. Should a family-planning campaign focus on abstinence or birth control? Should a campaign to fight air pollution focus on car sharing or public transport? Social marketing campaigns may have objectives related to changing people's cognitions, values or actions. The following examples illustrate the range of possible objectives:

Marketing memo

Key features of social marketing

The key features and concepts for understanding social marketing according to the UK's National Social Marketing Centre are:

- **Customer or consumer orientation:** a strong 'customer' orientation with importance attached to understanding where the customer is starting from, their knowledge, attitudes and beliefs, along with the social context in which they live and work.

- **Behaviour and behavioural goals:** clear focus on understanding existing behaviour and key influences on it, alongside developing clear behavioural goals, which can be divided into actionable and measurable steps or stages, phased over time.

- **'Intervention mix' and 'marketing mix':** using a range (or 'mix') of different interventions or methods to achieve a particular goal. When used at the strategic level, this is commonly referred to as the 'intervention mix', and when used operationally it is described as the 'marketing mix' or 'social marketing mix'.

- **Audience segmentation:** clarity of audience focus using 'audience segmentation' to target effectively.

- **'Exchange':** use and application of the 'exchange' concept – understanding what is being expected of 'the customer', the 'real cost to them'.

- **'Competition':** use and application of the 'competition' concept – understanding factors that impact on the customer and that compete for their attention and time.[65]

Cognitive campaigns

- Explain the nutritional value of different foods.
- Explain the importance of conservation.

Action campaigns

- Attract people for mass immunisation.
- Motivate people to vote 'yes' on a certain issue.
- Motivate people to donate blood.
- Motivate women to go for breast screening.

Social campaigns

- Discourage cigarette smoking.
- Discourage usage of hard drugs.
- Discourage excessive consumption of alcohol.

Value campaigns

- Alter ideas about abortion.
- Change attitudes of bigoted people.

Social marketing uses a number of different tactics to achieve its goals.[66] The planning process follows many of the same steps as for traditional products and services (see Table 21.2). Some key success factors in developing and implementing a social marketing programme include the following:

- Study the literature and previous campaigns.
- Choose target markets that are most ready to respond.
- Promote a single, do-able behaviour in clear, simple terms.
- Explain the benefits in compelling terms.
- Make it easy to adopt the behaviour.
- Develop attention-grabbing messages and media.
- Consider an education-entertainment approach.

Table 21.2 Social marketing planning process

Where are we?
- Determine programme focus.
- Identify campaign purpose.
- Conduct an analysis of strengths, weaknesses, opportunities and threats (SWOT).
- Review past and similar efforts.

Where do we want to go?
- Select target audiences.
- Set objectives and goals.
- Analyse target audiences and the competition.

How will we get there?
- Product: design the market offering.
- Price: manage costs of behaviour change.
- Distribution: make the product available.
- Communications: create messages and choose media.

How will we stay on course?
- Develop a plan for evaluation and monitoring.
- Establish budgets and find funding sources.
- Complete an implementation plan.

Social marketing programmes are complex; they take time and may require phased pro-grammes or actions. For example, recall the steps in discouraging smoking: raising taxes on cigarettes to pay for antismoking campaigns, cancer reports, labelling of cigarettes, banning cigarette advertising, education about secondary smoke effects, no smoking in aeroplanes and restaurants.

Social marketing organisations should evaluate programme success in terms of objec-tives. Criteria might include incidence of adoption, speed of adoption, continuance of adoption, low cost per unit of adoption, and absence of counterproductive consequences.[67]

Ethnic marketing

The ethnic minority population in some European countries, such as France, Germany and the United Kingdom, is sizeable and represents a viable and untapped market segment. In today's fragmented and increasingly turbulent markets, ethnic marketing offers a new strategic focus for market/offering (product/market) development and, in many respects, companies that ignore this do so at their own competitive peril. Companies wishing to do business with ethnic minority groups will fundamentally have to review the basic premises of their marketing plans to take account of the growing market pluralism and the emer-gent multiethnic reality of European countries.[68]

Marketing as a concept pays a great deal of attention to the individual market transac-tions, often ignoring the impact of marketing practices on society at a macro level. In multi-cultural marketplaces, marketers and consumers of different ethnic backgrounds coexist, interact and adapt to each other. In doing so, consumers act as skilled navigators who frequently engage in culture swapping to sample the many tastes, themes and sounds of different cultures and values. Marketing facilitates this culture swapping and contributes towards tolerance and acceptance of lifestyle among consumers. However, traditional racial or ethnic segmentation could become problematic due to the fact that consumers no longer conform either individually or as a group to any one specific segment or category.[69]

Green marketing

From the earliest of times, humankind has been aware of the importance of the environ-ment. Natural climatic and weather conditions have marked the passage of the seasons. Human activity such as political, population and profit pursuits have all interacted with the rhythm of the natural order but have essentially been subservient to it. In the early decades of the twenty-first century, there is mounting evidence that the environment is changing and that much of the cause of this change can be ascribed to human activity. As a result there is a growing concern about the natural changes that are occurring and those that are the direct result of the activity of humans.

As a consequence of these concerns, the term 'green marketing' came into prominence in the last two decades of the twentieth century. It has been defined by the American Mar-keting Association as 'the marketing of products that are presumed to be environmentally safe'. For marketers this has many implications. Market offerings will require modification so that their use does not damage the environment. Material extraction, preparation and production processes will need rethinking. Conventional packaging approaches will need re-evaluating. Many companies are using recycled materials but many are not. In the United Kingdom non-degradable plastic bags have suddenly been declared undesirable. Marketing communications will have to become less profligate in their use of resources.

Such is the complexity of the environmental challenge facing humankind that, while there is a general recognition of the existence of the problem, there is no commonly accepted creed. Hence the existence of terms such as 'environmental marketing' and 'ecological marketing' that all emphasise different aspects of the matter. Not surpris-ingly, there is little general agreement as to what private and public enterprise should do about it.

Stern Review on the economics of climate change

The most comprehensive review ever carried out on the economics of climate change was carried out by Sir Nicholas Stern, Head of the UK's Government Economic Service and former World Bank Chief Economist. The Review, published in October 2006, concludes that there is still time to avoid the worst impacts of climate change, if governments, businesses and individuals co-operate to respond to the challenge.

The first half of the Review focuses on the impacts and risks arising from uncontrolled climate change, and on the costs and opportunities associated with action to tackle it. The Review estimates that the dangers could be equivalent to 20 per cent of Gross Domestic Product (GDP) or more. In contrast, the costs of action to reduce greenhouse gas emissions to avoid the worst impacts of climate change can be limited to around 1 per cent of global GDP each year.

The second half of the Review examines the national and international policy challenges of moving to a low-carbon global economy. Three elements of policy are required for an effective response:

- Carbon pricing, through taxation, emissions trading or regulation, so that people are faced with the full social costs of their actions.

- Technology policy, to drive the development and deployment of a range of low-carbon and high-efficiency products.

- Action to remove barriers to energy efficiency, and to inform, educate and persuade individuals about what they can do to respond to climate change.

Effective action requires a global policy response, guided by a common international understanding of the long-term goals for climate policy and strong frameworks for co-operation. Key elements of future international frameworks should include:

- emissions trading
- technology co-operation
- action to reduce deforestation
- adaption.[70]

Source: Adapted from *Directgov* (http://www.direct.gov.uk/en/Nl1/Newsroom/DG_064854).

Approaching a green marketing response

The plurality of environmental beliefs hinders a concerted response to examining these beliefs and thus evaluating their impact on marketing activity. Peattie and Crane concluded that much of what has been commonly referred to as green marketing has not been underpinned by either a marketing or an environmental philosophy.[71] D'Souza et al.[72] suggested that green firms should pay particular regard to:

- the need to build a strong green and competitive advantage for their market offerings;
- the need to develop and project a green consumer profile based on demographic segmentation, targeting and positioning; and
- the need to meet customers' expectations by acting genuinely as well as being recognised as demonstrably environmentally responsible.

Practical advice on how to introduce a green philosophy and the functional activities needed to support it must, argues Grant,[73] be a central feature of company strategy. He stresses that it is not a matter of cosmetically 'green theming' and provides a road map to facilitate both the adoption and practical introduction of green marketing.

Existing firms

In many respects the task is harder for existing than for new firms. Cynics often argue that few companies pay more than lip-service to green marketing in terms of real acceptance and hence resource allocation but are quite happy to gain some PR advantage from time to time. This is, on the whole, a harsh view as companies such as IKEA, LEGO, Marks & Spencer, O2, SUT (Swedish broadcaster), Sky, Tesco, Toyota and the Virgin Group are

B&Q rebuilds its image to top the eco-friendly shoppers' chart

Following a 20 year journey, B&Q has taken a leadership position within the retail sector by committing to only buying 100 per cent responsibly-sourced wood. The home improvement and garden centre business was proud to announce in early 2011 that it could trace the timber in all its products back to well-managed sources.

The achievement was followed by the launch of its Forest Friendly programme- encouraging those concerned about deforestation to ask retailers about the sustainability credentials of their wooden products before they buy.

Two decades ago, when B&Q was challenged on the sourcing of its wooden products, there were no established processes for tracing the timber included in them from Forest to shop floor. During B&Q's journey to understanding its supply, the business

The UK do-it-yourself chain B&Q provides practical environmental advice and service.
Source: B&Q plc/ZPR London

helped to establish the Forestry Stewardship Council (FSC) – now widely recognised as the gold star of certification schemes. The retailer has steadily continued to improve its timber credentials and whilst it remains a founding member of the FSC it now also works with other certification schemes such as Programme for the Endorsement of Forest Certification (PEFC) and The Forest Trust (TFT) to encourage the sustainable management of more forests.

B&Q sells more than 16,000 products containing timber, which are all responsibly sourced. In a recent survey, 92 per cent of people said they would choose responsibly sourced wood every time if they knew there was no extra cost. B&Q is proud in the knowledge that after a 20 year journey this is exactly what it has delivered.

Source: www.diy.com/forestfriendly

all making progress. This is highly commendable and represents a real start, but the jury is still out as to whether this is a lasting commitment. The Body Shop and Ben & Jerry's were pioneers in green marketing and it is hoped that the Unilever Group will continue this tradition after acquiring these companies.

New firms

New firms have the advantage of being in a position to build in a green marketing approach from the start.

See the green light and go!

When Anya Pearson was forging a high-flying career working for high street clothing retailers, she noticed a lot of things about the fashion industry that she did not like. So two years ago she decided to take matters into her own hands and start a fashion label of her own, called Frank and Faith (Frankandfaith.com). Frank and Faith, which is based in Dorset, makes ethical clothing from sustainable sources for men, women and children, with all items made in Britain from organic cotton and prices similar to those on the high street.

'Over 20 years of working in the fashion industry I have seen a lot of sweatshops. I wanted to have everything made in Britain so I would know 100 per cent that nothing was made by children or abused workers,' she said. 'Being made in Britain means that our clothes are locally sourced and completely traceable.'

After much searching, Pearson found a specialist knitwear maker in Leicester, one of the last of its kind in Britain. It costs more than using a factory in China, but Pearson is happy with her choice. 'The only reason people are able to buy clothes at such low prices is because somebody else is losing out. It is the four-year-old Bangladeshi kid who should be in school who is losing out.' Instead of using sweatshop labour to keep costs down, Pearson has chosen to keep her prices competitive by reducing her own profit margins. As a result, business is booming and – something Pearson is pleased to note – not just from consciously green consumers:

The main core of shoppers is the people who can't afford ethical designer wear so this is my way of trying to get people in and trying to educate them in what it's all about. I want them to understand why clothing has become so cheap and throw-away in the past ten years. It is because of these hideous issues of sweatshop manufacturing and the complete disregard for the environment.

Pearson is one of a growing number of fledgling entrepreneurs who have decided that going green is not just something to be aware of, but is integral to the way they run their business. By incorporating sustainable, green ethics when they form their business, they create a strategy that places green values throughout the company. Furthermore larger companies, such as Marks & Spencer, were increasingly insisting that their small suppliers should become more sustainable in their operations. Many big companies want to move towards a green value chain.[74]

The key challenge for green marketers is to strengthen individuals' perception of the individual benefits to be gained from 'going green' by adding more and stronger emotional values to green brands. Future green market research should extend its analysis to the emotional values and benefits associated with environmentally responsible consumption behaviour.[75]

Companies are increasingly working with public interest groups to avoid perceptions of 'greenwashing' – insincere, phoney efforts to appear more environmentally sensitive than they really are. Alliances with environmentalists can achieve more satisfying solutions that both address public concerns and increase the firm's image and profits. DuPont once viewed Greenpeace as an enemy; the firm now uses Greenpeace's former head as a consultant. Greenpeace has also worked with McDonald's and others to stop farmers cutting down the Amazon rainforest to grow soybeans. When Greenpeace called out Coca-Cola on the eve of the 2000 Sydney Olympics for using a potent greenhouse gas in its nearly 10 million coolers and vending machines, Coca-Cola, along with PepsiCo, Unilever and McDonald's, invested US$30 million in a less damaging system that now displays a 'technology approved by Greenpeace' banner.[76]

Evaluation and control

In spite of the need to monitor and control marketing activities, many companies have inadequate control procedures. Table 21.3 lists four types of required marketing control: annual-plan control, profitability control, efficiency control and strategic control. We consider each.

Keeping a close eye on company progress
Source: Serif.

Table 21.3 Types of marketing control

Type of control	Prime responsibility	Purpose of control	Approaches
1 Annual-plan control	Top management Middle management	To examine whether the planned results are being achieved	<ul><li>Sales analysis</li><li>Market share analysis</li><li>Sales-to-expense ratios</li><li>Financial analysis</li><li>Market-based scorecard analysis</li></ul>
2 Profitability control	Marketing controller	To examine where the company is making and losing money	Profitability by:<ul><li>product</li><li>territory</li><li>customer</li><li>segment</li><li>trade channel</li><li>order size</li></ul>
3 Efficiency control	Line and staff management Marketing controller	To evaluate and improve the spending efficiency and impact of marketing expenditures	Efficiency of:<ul><li>sales force</li><li>advertising</li><li>sales promotion</li><li>distribution</li></ul>
4 Strategic control	Top management Marketing auditor	To examine whether the company is pursuing its best opportunities with respect to markets, products and channels	<ul><li>Marketing effectiveness rating instrument</li><li>Marketing audit</li><li>Marketing excellence review</li><li>Company ethical and social responsibility review</li></ul>

Annual-plan control

Annual-plan control ensures the company achieves its planned sales, profits and other goals. There are four steps (see Figure 21.5). First, management sets monthly or quarterly goals. Second, management monitors its performance in the marketplace. Third, management

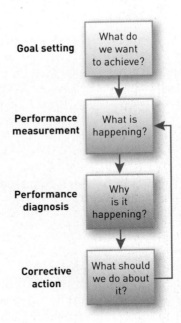

Figure 21.5 The control process

determines the causes of serious performance deviations. Fourth, management takes corrective action to close gaps between goals and performance.

This control model applies to all levels of the organisation. Top management sets annual sales and profit goals; each product manager, regional district manager, sales manager and sales representative is committed to attaining specified levels of sales and costs. Each period, top management reviews and interprets the results.

Marketers today have better marketing metrics for measuring the performance of marketing plans (see Table 22.1 on page 922 for some sample ones).[77] They can use four tools to check on plan performance: sales analysis, market share analysis, marketing expense-to-sales analysis and financial analysis.

Sales analysis

Sales analysis measures and evaluates actual sales in relationship to goals. Two specific tools make it work.

Sales-variance analysis measures the relative contribution of different factors to a gap in sales performance. Suppose the annual plan called for selling 4,000 widgets in the first quarter at €10 per widget, for total revenue of €40,000. At quarter's end, only 3,000 widgets were sold at €8 per widget, for total revenue of €24,000. How much of the sales performance gap is due to the price decline, and how much to the volume decline? This calculation answers the question:

$$\text{Variance due to price decline} = (€10 - €8)(3,000) = €\ 6,000 \quad 37.5\%$$
$$\text{Variance due to volume decline} = (€10)(4,000 - 3,000) = €10,000 \quad 62.5\%$$
$$\overline{€16,000} \quad 100.0\%$$

Almost two-thirds of the variance is due to failure to achieve the volume target. The company should look closely at why it failed to achieve expected sales volume.

Microsales analysis looks at specific products, territories and so forth that failed to produce expected sales. Suppose the company sells in three territories, and expected sales were 1,500 units, 500 units and 2,000 units, respectively. Actual volumes were 1,400 units, 525 units and 1,075 units, respectively. Thus territory 1 showed a 7 per cent shortfall in terms of expected sales; territory 2, a 5 per cent improvement over expectations; and territory 3, a 46 per cent shortfall. Territory 3 is causing most of the trouble. Maybe territory 3's sales representative is underperforming; a major competitor has entered this territory; or business is in a recession there.

Market share analysis

Company sales do not reveal how well the company is performing relative to competitors. For this purpose, management needs to track its market share in one of three ways.

Overall market share expresses the company's sales as a percentage of total market sales. **Served market share** is sales as a percentage of the total sales to the market. The **served market** is all the buyers able and willing to buy the product, and served market share is always larger than overall market share. A company could capture 100 per cent of its served market and yet have a relatively small share of the total market. **Relative market share** is market share in relationship to the largest competitor. A relative market share over 100 per cent indicates a market leader. A relative market share of exactly 100 per cent means the company is tied for the lead. A rise in relative market share means a company is gaining on its leading competitor.

Conclusions from market share analysis, however, are subject to certain qualifications:

- The assumption that outside forces affect all companies in the same way is often not true.
- The assumption that a company's performance should be judged against the average performance of all companies is not always valid.
- If a new firm enters the industry, every existing firm's market share might fall.
- Sometimes a market share decline is deliberately engineered to improve profits.
- Market share can fluctuate for many minor reasons.[78]

A useful way to analyse market share movements is in terms of four components:

$$\begin{array}{c}\text{Overall}\\\text{market share}\end{array} = \begin{array}{c}\text{Customer}\\\text{penetration}\end{array} \times \begin{array}{c}\text{Customer}\\\text{loyalty}\end{array} \times \begin{array}{c}\text{Customer}\\\text{selectivity}\end{array} \times \begin{array}{c}\text{Price}\\\text{selectivity}\end{array}$$

where:

Customer penetration	Percentage of all customers who buy from the company
Customer loyalty	Purchases from the company by its customers as a percentage of their total purchases from all suppliers of the same products
Customer selectivity	Size of the average customer purchase from the company as a percentage of the size of the average customer purchase from an average company
Price selectivity	Average price charged by the company as a percentage of the average price charged by all companies.

Now suppose the company's market share falls during the period. The overall market share equation provides four possible explanations: the company lost some customers (lower customer penetration); existing customers are buying less from the company (lower customer loyalty); the company's remaining customers are smaller in size (lower customer selectivity); or the company's price has slipped relative to competition (lower price selectivity).

Marketing expense-to-sales analysis

Annual-plan control requires making sure the company is not overspending to achieve sales goals. The key ratio to watch is *marketing expense-to-sales*. In one company, this ratio was 30 per cent and consisted of five component expense-to-sales ratios: sales force-to-sales (15 per cent); advertising-to-sales (5 per cent); sales promotion-to-sales (6 per cent); marketing research-to-sales (1 per cent); and sales administration-to-sales (3 per cent).

Fluctuations outside normal range are cause for concern. Management needs to monitor period-to-period fluctuations in each ratio on a *control chart* (see Figure 21.6). This chart shows that the advertising expense-to-sales ratio normally fluctuates between 8 per cent and 12 per cent, say 99 out of 100 times. In the 15th period, however, the ratio exceeded the upper control limit. One of two hypotheses can explain why: (1) the company still has good expense control, and this situation represents a rare chance event; (2) the company has lost control over this expense and should find the cause. If there is no investigation, the risk is that some real change might have occurred, and the company will fall behind. An investigation may also uncover nothing and be a waste of time and effort.

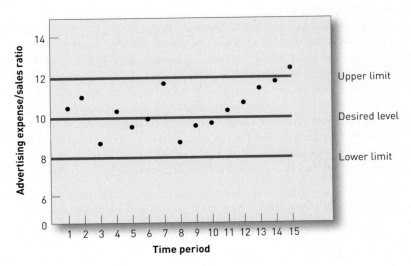

Figure 21.6 The control-chart model

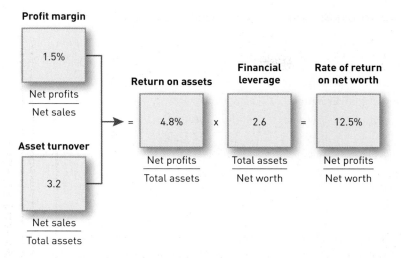

Figure 21.7 Financial model of return on net worth

Managers should watch the number of successive observations even within the upper and lower control limits. Note in Figure 21.6 that the level of the expense-to-sales ratio rose steadily from the 9th period onwards. The probability of encountering six successive increases in what should be independent events is only 1 in 64.[79] This unusual pattern should have led to an investigation some time before the 15th observation.

Financial analysis

Marketers should analyse the expense-to-sales ratios in an overall financial framework to determine how and where the company is making its money. They can, and increasingly are, using financial analysis to find profitable strategies beyond building sales.

Management uses financial analysis to identify factors that affect the company's *rate of return on net worth*.[80] The main factors are shown in Figure 21.7, along with illustrative numbers for a large chain-store retailer. The retailer is earning a 12.5 per cent return on net worth. The return on net worth is the product of two ratios, the company's *return on assets* and its *financial leverage*. To improve its return on net worth, the company must increase its ratio of net profits to assets, or increase the ratio of assets to net worth. The company should analyse the composition of its assets (cash, accounts receivable, inventory, and plant and equipment) and see whether it can improve its asset management.

The return on assets is the product of two ratios, the *profit margin* and the *asset turnover*. The profit margin in Figure 21.7 seems low, whereas the asset turnover is more normal for retailing. The marketing executive can seek to improve performance in two ways: (1) increase the profit margin by increasing sales or cutting costs; and (2) increase the asset turnover by increasing sales or reducing assets (inventory, receivables) held against a given level of sales.

Profitability control

Companies can benefit from deeper financial analysis and should measure the profitability of their products, territories, customer groups, segments, trade channels and order sizes. This information can help management determine whether to expand, reduce or eliminate any products or marketing activities.

Marketing profitability analysis

Consider the following example: the marketing director of a lawnmower company wants to determine the profitability of selling through three types of retail channel: hardware

Table 21.4 A simplified profit-and-loss statement

Sales		€60,000
Cost of goods sold		39,000
Gross margin		€21,000
Expenses		
Salaries	€9,300	
Rent	3,000	
Supplies	€3,500	
		15,800
Net profit		€5,200

stores, garden supply shops and department stores. The company's profit-and-loss statement is shown in Table 21.4.

Step 1: identifying functional expenses Assume the expenses listed in Table 21.4 are incurred to sell the product, advertise it, pack and deliver it, and bill and collect for it. The first task is to measure how much of each expense was incurred in each activity.

Suppose most of the salary expense went to sales representatives and the rest to an advertising manager, packing and delivery help, and an office accountant. Let the breakdown of the €9,300 be €5,100, €1,200, €1,400 and €1,600, respectively. Table 21.5 shows the allocation of the salary expense to these four activities.

Table 21.5 also shows the rent account of €3,000 allocated to the four activities. Because the sales reps work away from the office, none of the building's rent expense is assigned to selling. Most of the expenses for floor space and rented equipment are for packing and delivery. The supplies account covers promotional materials, packing materials, fuel purchases for delivery and home office stationery. The €3,500 in this account is reassigned to functional uses of the supplies.

Step 2: assigning functional expenses to marketing entities The next task is to measure how much functional expense was associated with selling through each type of channel. Consider the selling effort, indicated by the number of sales in each channel. This number is in the selling column of Table 21.6. Altogether, 275 sales calls were made during the period. Because the total selling expense amounted to €5,500 (see Table 21.6), the selling expense averaged €20 per call.

Advertising expense can be allocated according to the number of advertisements addressed to different channels. Because there were 100 advertisements altogether, the average advertising cost €31.

The packing and delivery expense is allocated according to the number of orders placed by each type of channel. This same basis was used for allocating invoicing and collection expense.

Table 21.5 Mapping natural expenses into functional expenses

Natural accounts	Total	Selling	Advertising	Packing and delivery	Invoicing and collecting
Salaries	€9,300	€5,100	€1,200	€ 1,400	€1,600
Rent	3,000	—	400	2,000	600
Supplies	3,500	400	1,500	1,400	200
	€15,800	€5,500	€3,100	€4,800	€2,400

Table 21.6 Bases for allocating functional expenses to channels

Channel type	Selling	Advertising	Packing and delivery	Invoicing and collecting
Hardware	200	50	50	50
Garden supply	65	20	21	21
Department stores	10	30	9	9
	275	100	80	80
Functional expense ÷	€5,500	€3,100	€4,800	€2,400
No. of units	275	100	80	80
Equals	€20	€31	€60	€30

Step 3: preparing a profit-and-loss statement for each marketing entity A profit-and-loss statement for each type of channel can now be prepared (see Table 21.7). Because hardware stores accounted for half of total sales (€30,000 out of €60,000), charge this channel with half the cost of goods sold (€19,500 out of €39,000). This leaves a gross margin from hardware stores of €10,500. From this we deduct the proportions of functional expenses hardware stores consumed. According to Table 21.6, hardware stores received 200 of 275 total sales calls. At an imputed value of €20 a call, hardware stores must bear a €4,000 selling expense. Table 21.6 also shows that hardware stores were the target of 50 advertisements. At €31 an advertisement, the hardware stores are charged with €1,550 of advertising. The same reasoning applies in computing the share of the other functional expenses. The result is that hardware stores gave rise to €10,050 of the total expenses (see Table 21.7). Subtracting this from gross margin, we find the profit of selling through hardware stores is only €450.

Repeat this analysis for the other channels. The company is losing money in selling through garden supply shops and makes virtually all its profits through department stores. Notice that gross sales is not a reliable indicator of the net profits for each channel.

Determining corrective action

It would be naive to conclude that the company should drop garden supply shops and possibly hardware stores so that it can concentrate on department stores. The following questions need to be answered first:

Table 21.7 Profit and loss account for channels

	Hardware	Garden supply	Department stores	Whole company
Sales	€30,000	€10,000	€20,000	€60,000
Cost of goods sold	19,500	6,500	13,000	39,000
Gross margin	€10,500	€3,500	€7,000	€21,000
Expenses				
Selling (€20 per call)	€4,000	€1,300	€200	€5,500
Advertising (€31 per advertisement)	1,550	620	930	3,100
Packing and delivery (€60 per order)	3,000	1,260	540	4,800
Invoicing (€30 per order)	1,500	630	270	2,400
Total expenses	€10,050	€3,810	€1,940	€15,800
Net profit or loss	€450	€(310)	€5,060	€5,200

- To what extent do consumers buy on the basis of type of retail outlet versus brand?
- What are the trends with respect to the importance of these three channels?
- How good are the company marketing strategies directed at the three channels?

On the basis of the answers, marketing management can evaluate five alternatives:

1 Establish a special charge for handling smaller orders.
2 Give more promotional aid to garden supply shops and hardware stores.
3 Reduce the number of sales calls and the amount of advertising going to garden supply shops and hardware stores.
4 Do not abandon any channel entirely, but only the weakest retail units in each channel.
5 Do nothing.

In general, marketing profitability analysis indicates the relative profitability of different channels, products, territories or other marketing entities. It does not prove that the best course of action is to drop the unprofitable marketing entities; nor does it capture the likely profit improvement if these marginal marketing entities are dropped.

Direct versus full costing

As with all information tools, marketing profitability analysis can lead or mislead marketing executives, depending on how well they understand its methods and limitations. The lawnmower company showed some arbitrariness in its choice of bases for allocating the functional expenses to its marketing entities. It used 'number of sales calls' to allocate selling expenses, generating less record keeping and computation, when in principle 'number of sales working hours' is a more accurate indicator of cost.

Far more serious is another judgemental element affecting profitability analysis – whether to allocate full costs or only direct and traceable costs in evaluating a marketing entity's performance. The lawnmower company sidestepped this problem by assuming that only simple costs that fit in with marketing activities; however, in the real world this would be unwise. Three types of cost can be distinguished:

1 Direct costs. These can be attributed directly to the proper marketing entities. Sales commissions are a direct cost in a profitability analysis of sales territories, sales representatives or customers. Advertising expenditures are a direct cost in a profitability analysis of products to the extent that each advertisement promotes only one product. Other direct costs for specific purposes are sales force salaries and travelling expenses.

2 Traceable common costs. Traceable common costs can only be assigned indirectly, but on a plausible basis, to the marketing entities. In the example, rent was charged this way.

3 Non-traceable common costs. Common costs whose allocation to the marketing entities is highly arbitrary are non-traceable common costs. To allocate 'corporate image' expenditures equally to all market offerings would be arbitrary because they do not all benefit equally. To allocate them proportionately to the sales of the various market offerings would be arbitrary because relative sales reflect many factors besides corporate image making. Other examples are top management salaries, taxes, interest and other overheads.

No one disputes the inclusion of direct costs in marketing cost analysis. There is some controversy about including traceable common costs, which consolidate costs that would and would not change with the scale of marketing activity. If the lawnmower company dropped garden supply shops, it would probably continue to pay the same rent. In this event, its profits would not rise immediately by the amount of the present loss in selling to garden supply shops (€310).

The major controversy is about whether to allocate the non-traceable common costs to the marketing entities. Such allocation is called the *full-cost approach*, and its advocates argue that all costs must ultimately be imputed in order to determine true profitability.

However, this argument confuses the use of accounting for financial reporting with its use for managerial decision making. Full costing has three major weaknesses:

1 The relative profitability of different marketing entities can shift radically when one arbitrary way to allocate non-traceable common costs is replaced by another.
2 The arbitrariness demoralises managers, who feel their performance is judged adversely.
3 The inclusion of no traceable common costs could weaken efforts at real cost control.

Operating management is most effective in controlling direct costs and traceable common costs. Arbitrary assignments of no traceable common costs can lead managers to spend their time fighting cost allocations instead of managing controllable costs well.

Companies show growing interest in using marketing profitability analysis, or its broader version, activity-based cost accounting, to quantify the true profitability of different activities.[81] Managers can then reduce the resources required to perform various activities, make the resources more productive, acquire them at lower cost or raise prices on products that consume heavy amounts of support resources. The contribution of ABC is to refocus management's attention away from using only or material standard costs to allocate full cost, and towards capturing the actual costs of supporting individual products, customers and other entities.

Efficiency control

Suppose a profitability analysis reveals that the company is earning poor profits in certain products, territories or markets. Are there more efficient ways to manage the sales force, advertising, sales promotion and distribution in connection with these marketing entities?

Some companies have established a *marketing controller* position to calculate work out of the controller's office and to specialise in improving marketing efficiency. Sophisticated companies such as Bosch, Danone and IKEA perform a sophisticated financial analysis of marketing expenditures and results. They examine adherence to profit plans, help prepare brand managers' budgets, measure the efficiency of promotions, analyse media production costs, evaluate customer and geographic profitability, and educate marketing personnel on the financial implications of marketing decisions.[82] They can examine the efficiency of the channel, sales force, advertising or any other form of marketing communication.

For example, in assessing channel efficiency, management needs to search for distribution economies in inventory control, warehouse locations and transportation modes. It should track such measures as:

- logistics costs as a percentage of sales;
- percentage of orders filled correctly;
- percentage of on-time deliveries; and
- number of invoicing errors.

Management should strive to reduce stocks while at the same time speeding up the order-to-delivery cycle. Dell Computers shows how to do both simultaneously.

Dell

A customer-customised computer ordered from Dell's website at 9 a.m. on Wednesday can be on the delivery van by 9 p.m. on Thursday. In that short period, Dell electronically orders the computer components from its suppliers' warehouses. Equally impressively, Dell gets paid electronically within 24 hours, whereas Compaq, supplying its computers to retailers, receives payment days later.

Strategic control

Each company should periodically reassess its strategic approach to the marketplace with a good marketing audit. Companies can also perform marketing excellence reviews and ethical/social responsibility reviews.

The marketing audit

In buyers' markets, companies can lose several of their customers in five years, several employees in four years, and many investors as the stock markets fluctuate. Wise companies carry out regular marketing audits.[83] A **marketing audit** is a comprehensive, systematic, independent and periodic examination of a company's or business unit's marketing environment, objectives, strategies and activities, with a view to determining problem areas and opportunities and recommending a plan of action to improve the company's marketing performance.

A marketing audit should be:

- **Comprehensive.** The marketing audit covers all the major marketing activities of a business, not just a few troublespots. It would be called a functional audit if it covered only the salesforce, pricing or some other marketing activity. Although functional audits are useful, they sometimes mislead management. Excessive sales force turnover, for example, could be a symptom not of poor sales force training or compensation but of weak company products and promotion. A comprehensive marketing audit is usually more effective in locating the real source of problems.
- **Systematic.** The marketing audit is an orderly examination of the organisation's macro- and micromarketing environments, marketing objectives and strategies, marketing systems and specific activities. The audit indicates the most-needed improvements, incorporating them into a corrective action plan with short- and long-run steps to improve overall effectiveness.
- **Independent.** Marketers can conduct a marketing audit in six ways: self-audit, audit from across, audit from above, company auditing office, company taskforce audit, and outsider audit. Self-audits, in which managers use a checklist to rate their own operations, lack objectivity and independence. Generally speaking, however, the best audits come from outside consultants who have the necessary objectivity, broad experience in a number of industries, some familiarity with the industry being audited, and undivided time and attention.
- **Periodic.** Typically, firms initiate marketing audits only after sales have turned down, sales force morale has fallen and other problems have occurred. Companies are thrown into a crisis partly because they failed to review their marketing operations during good times. A periodic marketing audit can benefit companies in good health as well as those in trouble.

A marketing audit starts with a meeting between the company officer(s) and the marketing auditor(s) to work out an agreement on the audit's objectives, coverage, depth, data sources, report format and time frame. It includes a detailed plan of who is to be interviewed, the questions to be asked, and where and when to minimise time and cost. The cardinal rule in marketing auditing is: do not rely solely on company managers for data and opinions. Ask customers, dealers and other outside groups. Many companies do not really know how their customers and dealers see them; nor do they fully understand customer needs.

The marketing audit examines six major components of the company's marketing situation. Table 21.8 lists the major questions.

Table 21.8 Components of a marketing audit

Part 1 Marketing environment audit

Macroenvironment

A. Demographic	What major demographic developments and trends pose opportunities or threats to this company? What actions has the company taken in response to these developments and trends?
B. Economic	What major developments in income, prices, savings and credit will affect the company? What actions has the company been taking in response to these developments and trends?
C. Environmental	What is the outlook for the cost and availability of natural resources and energy needed by the company? What concerns have been expressed about the company's role in pollution and conservation, and what steps has the company taken?
D. Technological	What major changes are occurring in product and process technology? What is the company's position in these technologies? What major generic substitutes might replace this product?
E. Political	What changes in laws and regulations might affect marketing strategy and tactics? What is happening in the areas of pollution control, equal employment opportunity, product safety, advertising, price control, and so forth, that affects marketing strategy?
F. Cultural	What is the public's attitude towards business and towards the company's products? What changes in customer lifestyles and values might affect the company?

Task environment

A. Markets	What is happening to market size, growth, geographical distribution and profits? What are the major market segments?
B. Customers	What are the customers' needs and buying processes? How do customers and prospects rate the company and its competitors on reputation, product quality, service, sales force and price? How do different customer segments make their buying decisions?
C. Competitors	Who are the major competitors? What are their objectives, strategies, strengths, weaknesses, sizes and market shares? What trends will affect future competition and substitutes for the company's products?
D. Distribution and dealers	What are the main trade channels for bringing products to customers? What are the efficiency levels and growth potentials of the different trade channels?
E. Suppliers	What is the outlook for the availability of key resources used in production? What trends are occurring among suppliers?
F. Facilitators and marketing firms	What is the cost and availability outlook for transportation services, warehousing facilities and financial resources? How effective are the company's advertising agencies and marketing research firms?
G. Publics	Which publics represent particular opportunities or problems for the company? What steps has the company taken to deal effectively with each public?

Part 2 Marketing strategy audit

A. Business mission	Is the business mission clearly stated in market-oriented terms? Is it feasible?
B. Marketing objectives and goals	Are the company and marketing objectives and goals stated clearly enough to guide marketing planning and performance measurement? Are the marketing objectives appropriate, given the company's competitive position, resources and opportunities?
C. Strategy	Has the management articulated a clear marketing strategy for achieving its marketing objectives? Is the strategy convincing? Is the strategy appropriate to the stage of the product life cycle, competitors' strategies and the state of the economy? Is the company using the best basis for market segmentation? Does it have clear criteria for rating the segments and choosing the best ones? Has it developed accurate profiles of each target segment? Has the company developed an effective positioning and marketing mix for each target segment? Are marketing resources allocated optimally to the major elements of the marketing mix? Are enough resources or too many resources budgeted to accomplish the marketing objectives?

(Continued)

Table 21.8 (*Continued*)

Part 3 Marketing organisation audit

A. Formal structure	Does the marketing vice-president have adequate authority and responsibility for company activities that affect customers' satisfaction? Are the marketing activities optimally structured along functional, product, segment, end user and geographical lines?
B. Functional efficiency	Are there good communication and working relationships between marketing and sales? Is the product management system working effectively? Are product managers able to plan profits or only sales volume? Are there any groups in marketing that need more training, motivation, supervision or evaluation?
C. Interface efficiency	Are there any problems between marketing and manufacturing, R & D, purchasing, finance, accounting and/or legal that need attention?

Part 4 Marketing systems audit

A. Marketing information system	Is the marketing intelligence system producing accurate, sufficient and timely information about marketplace developments with respect to customers, prospects, distributors and dealers, competitors, suppliers and various publics? Are company decision makers asking for enough marketing research, and are they using the results? Is the company employing the best methods for market measurement and sales forecasting?
B. Marketing planning system	Is the marketing planning system well conceived and effectively used? Do marketers have decision support systems available? Does the planning system result in acceptable sales targets and quotas?
C. Marketing control system	Are the control procedures adequate to ensure that the annual plan objectives are being achieved? Does management periodically analyse the profitability of products, markets, territories and channels of distribution? Are marketing costs and productivity periodically examined?
D. New product system	Is the company well organised to gather, generate and screen new product ideas? Does the development company do adequate concept research and business analysis before investing in new ideas? Does the company carry out adequate product and market testing before launching new products?

Part 5 Marketing productivity audit

A. Profitability analysis	What is the profitability of the company's different products, markets, territories and channels of distribution? Should the company enter, expand, contract or withdraw from any business segments?
B. Cost-effectiveness analysis	Do any marketing activities seem to have excessive costs? Can cost-reducing steps be taken?

Part 6 Marketing function audits

A. Products	What are the company's product line objectives? Are they sound? Is the current product line meeting the objectives? Should the product line be stretched or contracted upwards, downwards or both ways? Which products should be phased out? Which products should be added? What are the buyers' knowledge and attitudes towards the company's and competitors' product quality, features, styling, brand names and so on? What areas of product and brand strategy need improvement?
B. Price	What are the company's pricing objectives, policies, strategies and procedures? To what extent are prices set on cost, demand and competitive criteria? Do the customers see the company's prices as being in line with the value of its offer? What does management know about the price elasticity of demand, experience-curve effects and competitors' prices and pricing policies? To what extent are price policies compatible with the needs of distributors and dealers, suppliers and government regulation?

Table 21.8 (*Continued*)

C. Distribution	What are the company's distribution objectives and strategies? Is there adequate market coverage and service? How effective are distributors, dealers, manufacturers' representatives, brokers, agents and others? Should the company consider changing its distribution channels?
D. Marketing communications	What are the organisation's advertising objectives? Are they sound? Is the right amount being spent on advertising? Are the ad themes and copy effective? What do customers and the public think about the advertising? Are the advertising media well chosen? Is the internal advertising staff adequate? Is the sales promotion budget adequate? Is there effective and sufficient use of sales promotion tools such as samples, coupons, displays and sales contests? Is the public relations staff competent and creative? Is the company making enough use of direct, online and database marketing?
E. Sales force	What are the sales force's objectives? Is the sales force large enough to accomplish the company's objectives? Is the sales force organised along the proper principles of specialisation (territory, market, product)? Are there enough (or too many) sales managers to guide the field sales representatives? Do the sales compensation level and structure provide adequate incentive and reward? Does the sales force show high morale, ability and effort? Are the procedures adequate for setting quotas and evaluating performance? How does the company's sales force compare to competitors' sales forces?

The marketing excellence review

The three columns in Table 21.9 distinguish among poor, good and excellent business and marketing practices. Management can place a checkmark to indicate its perception of where the business stands. The profile that results from this marketing excellence review exposes weaknesses and strengths, highlighting where the company might make changes to become a truly outstanding player in the marketplace.

Table 21.9 The marketing excellence review: best practices

Poor	Good	Excellent
Product driven	Market driven	Market driving
Mass-market oriented	Segment oriented	Niche oriented and customer oriented
Product offer	Augmented product offer	Customer solutions offer
Average product quality	Better than average	Legendary
Average service quality	Better than average	Legendary
End-product oriented	Core-product oriented	Core-competency oriented
Function oriented	Process oriented	Outcome oriented
Reacting to competitors	Benchmarking competitors	Leapfrogging competitors
Supplier exploitation	Supplier preference	Supplier partnership
Dealer exploitation	Dealer support	Dealer partnership
Price driven	Quality driven	Value driven
Average speed	Better than average	Legendary
Hierarchy	Network	Teamwork
Vertically integrated	Flattened organisation	Strategic alliances
Stockholder driven	Stakeholder driven	Societally driven

As customers can usually choose from a number of companies in contemporary buyers' markets (see Chapter 10), effective marketing activity needs to be practised with appropriate sensitivity to society. The concluding section in this chapter highlights the important sensitivities that marketing management needs to take into account.

The future of marketing

The marketing manager's key tasks

The first two decades of the twenty-first century pose several exceptional challenges to marketers. Many markets in developed countries are oversupplied with most market offerings, leading to fierce competition that is of global proportions. The rapid rate of technological advance, increasingly sophisticated and demanding customers and new market regulations suggest that their functional activity will become of paramount importance to their companies. There are four key tasks for contemporary marketing managers, as outlined in the marketing memo.

Marketing memo

Key tasks of marketing managers

1   Develop a detailed and deep understanding of current and prospective customers. Much of this should come from regular direct contact with customers and from programmed ad hoc research to reveal new trends in customer preferences. Suitable customer-perceived value offerings should then be developed and introduced into the market as quickly as possible to gain or maintain a sustainable competitive advantage.

2   Develop a detailed and deep understanding of existing and emerging competitors by regarding

expenditure on suitable market research as an investment decision rather than a cost sign-off.

3   Develop a detailed and deep understanding of how markets are changing. This needs to be communicated clearly by regular briefing reports to all functional managers to facilitate a holistic approach to marketing in the company. Update topics might include the state of key markets (context), distribution and marketing communications issues.

4   Develop a strategic marketing approach to support corporate strategy. Seek to become a 'market driver' rather than be a company that is 'market-driven'.[84]

Keeping a close watch on the four leading marketing management issues
Source: Serif.

A holistic approach to marketing management

In January 2008 Deloitte & Touche LLP published a report on the role of marketing in driving business growth among European countries. The findings revealed the existence of a paradox. While 81 per cent of chief executives interviewed believed that marketing was a key factor for growth and 85 per cent said it was crucial to developing strategy, the report also suggested that not all CEOs felt that the involvement of senior marketers in the overall direction of the business was an assurance of growth for the organisation.[85] These findings reveal a disturbing picture of the current state of marketing management. Marketing thought and practice has evolved over the past 100 years from a philosophy of taking things to market to a philosophy of market(ing) to customers and, increasingly today, to a philosophy of market(ing) in social settings with customers.[86] So why has it lost its way? In view of the generally accepted value of marketing, it is alarming that relatively few marketers in the United Kingdom are acting CEOs.

The nature of marketing

To address this question it is useful to consider two important aspects of marketing. It is both a philosophical holistic concept and a functional activity. The Deloitte & Touche LLP report indicates that the connection between these aspects lacked some joined-up thinking. In theory, senior marketing executives should greatly assist the overall growth performance of organisations. Marketing is a word that in English ends in 'ing'. This implies that it is a doing word; skill and action within a social context are required to perform it. Another view of the malaise of marketing was dramatically exposed by Egan[87] when his researches found that marketing had, to all intents and purposes, been sidelined in many organisations.

Egan surveyed eight senior relationship-oriented marketing executives who were in top organisations representing business-to-business, conglomerate, energy, non-profit, service and technological companies. Regarding the holistic approach to marketing, it was felt that marketers appeared to have a non-structured view of business and so fitted poorly in the corporate world. They did not have a sufficient understanding of financial data and corporate metrics. Marketing tended to be seen as a cost and not as an investment that would generate income. Marketers took too many risks and were not sufficiently accountable for their expenditure. Marketers seemed to have little power to influence senior management. In the light of the fact that 70 per cent of the CEOs in the FTSE 100 listing in May 2007 were accountants, it is perhaps not surprising that marketers were considered to be lightweight and misunderstood.

As the slowing buyers' markets became evident, many companies started to question the role of marketers. There was a reluctance to sanction large expenditure on marketing with little indication of what and when the return on investment would result. CEOs and finance managers sought to reduce costs. Marketers seemed to have fallen from grace.

Marketing myopia

The world of business had become confused between the holistic and functional understanding of marketing. The shifting paradigm from sellers' to buyers' markets that is evident in developed economies focused interest on customers. They were now the scarce resource. How might they be attracted and retained in the face of mounting competition? Chapter 10 discussed the impact of the paradigm change and stressed the importance of the subtle transformation that occurred in the concept of value. In buyers' markets, value was a concept that was determined greatly by buyer perceptions. If the customer-centric philosophy of marketing was accepted, how could this new value concept be delivered? Some felt that it was a holistic matter and a concern of all, and others that it was a strictly functional issue for the marketers. Some theorists argued that non-customer relationship issues were outside the domain of marketing.

First things first

Many companies accept that in principle marketing makes sense as a philosophy. Many, too, are aware of the traditional functional tasks of marketers. A useful starting point in any attempt to indicate how marketing might be managed in the future is to address the issue of how a company thinks in the boardroom. Current buyers' markets place pressure on firms to promise and deliver the right market offering. This should be seen as a holistic response that will require the input of functional skills within the company and those of external parties such as the supply (or rather value) chain and interested stakeholders. Thus real teamwork is needed. The CEO must ensure that the task is fully understood and all players cooperate to provide the required customer-perceived value (see Chapter 11) offering for a targeted customer. In this sense the role of the CEO is similar to that of the conductor of an orchestra. The players in the respective sections, such as brass, percussion, strings and woodwind, are to apply their individual and group skills, in tune. This implies that they must have an appreciation of the nature of each other's functional skills.

Remember TEAM? Together everyone achieves more. This is the prime responsibility of the CEO. Next the CEO must answer the question: Who owns the customer? Is it the marketing department? The sales department? Or is it the accounts department? Worse still is the confusion evident here. The paradigm change from sellers' to buyers' markets has led loyal customers to become highly prized. Repeat business for the company's offerings signifies success is the essence of a good BRAND. The next section explores customer relationship activity.

Relationship activity

Relationship marketing

(See also Chapter 1.)

Relationship marketing (RM) was seen by many as the new way forward and has been very much 'in vogue' recently among both academics and practitioners. It became the 'hot topic' of marketing in the 1990s and was heralded as a breakthrough that would replace the traditional marketing mix model. In a world where premium paying customers were highly valued, all marketed offers should seek to build lasting relationships with customers and a good way to do this was to promise and deliver desirable CPV offerings.

The importance of greeting in building relationships
Source: Serif.

Despite the general adherence to the philosophy embedded in RM there is little evidence to reflect its success for companies that expressed interest in its execution in the opening decade of the twenty-first century. Few marketers rose to the CEO's chair. Mounting frustration at the perceived inability of functional marketers to deliver the RM promise resulted in mounting pressures to classify non-customer relationships as residing outside the marketing domain. The myopia here was the failure to appreciate that RM must translate into the promise and delivery of the right CPV packages. This requires coordinating company inputs rather than just independent functional contributions that are bundled together at the market gate.

Customer relationship marketing

The result was the birth of a new way forward that was termed *customer relationship marketing* (CRMk). A new resolve was born as many companies sought to talk to their suppliers and customers to create CPV packages. CRMk, it was claimed, was a distinct concept that was well suited to managing customer relationships in mass markets. It was under the control of general management and the marketing input was viewed as functional. With little real adoption of the TEAM requirement for holistic marketing, CRMk soon became dominated by general management's push for the most profit at the least cost with the least risk in the shortest period of time. Relationship building soon largely became confined to mechanised offers and sales promotions. Customer focus became subservient to the supplier or transactional marketing dyad. In many cases, customers became digits and were classified according to their present worth to the company. Furthermore, many firms were tempted to overuse technology and adopt too great a reliance on managing customer relations with digital methods such as CRMk software and internet programming. Cynics termed CRMk 'technology-enabled RM'. It was oversold and it seems to have failed to live up to expectations – a philosophic manifesto but without a suitable accompanying organisational toolkit. Overdigitisation – that is, the progressive loss of the human interface – flies in the face of the holistic approach to marketing. While programmed phones and internet 'help' pages have their place, they need to be carefully integrated into a people-friendly interface. Too much digital technology and consumers start to feel like numbers and robots. Successful relationships often seem to occur when companies carefully research what customers want, promise it and then successfully deliver it.

Customer-perceived value marketing

As more and more academics and practitioners have begun to realise the importance of customer-perceived value, of promising and delivering what customers want, so another concept – that of *customer-perceived value marketing* (CPVM) has appeared. This requires firms to develop an organisational structure that is top down, bottom up and side to side. The top management empowers TEAM players. Players at the customer interface are supported by top management. Marketers (or designated functional players) seek to co-create value with customers, the value chain and stakeholder interests. Figure 21.8 presents a matrix that charts the routes that companies are following and exploring to build a sustainable corporate advantage in the surplus microeconomic conditions of buyer's markets.

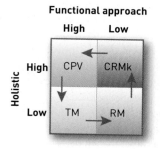

Figure 21.8 Key company market cultures
Source: M. R. V. Goodman, Durham University, UK.

For many the journey began with *transactional marketing* (TM), which was very much in evidence during the post-Second World War sellers' markets. The functional activity was focused around the traditional 4P (product, price, place and promotion) marketing mix. As the service industries assumed an ever-greater importance, so an additional 3Ps were added (*people, process and physical evidence*), as the original mix was felt by academics to be wanting. However, did these additional Ps really help?

Henry Ford of automotive fame was a major pioneer of mass production and once quipped that customers could 'have any colour they liked as long as it was black'. Clearly he had a *product* (the car); a *price* (the purchase cost); made his cars available (*place*); and communicated to interested parties (*promotion*).

Service marketers, on the other hand, were seen as being differentiated as their offerings were for *people*, involved *processes* and resulted in *physical evidence* that the service had been rendered. The ordinary man in the street might quip that Ford intended its cars for *people*, rolled out real cars from the end of the production line (*physical evidence*) and used a production *process* to build the cars.

The halcyon days of TM placed an emphasis on the supplier–customer dyad and in many cases relied heavily on the price and promotion tools of the marketing mix. When the roaring sellers' markets started to turn inexorably into today's buyers' markets from the late 1980s onwards, so companies began to focus on customer satisfaction and loyalty.

Enter, stage left, the new concept of relationship marketing (RM). This was greatly in fashion during the 1990s but failed to perform satisfactorily for several reasons, mainly from abundant confusions concerning the interaction between functional and holistic marketing. Also there was a tendency for academics to concentrate too much on the positive aspects of RM and to under-research customer dissatisfaction.[88] At the turn of the millennium, RM went through a process of metamorphism and customer relationship marketing emerged. For similar reasons to RM, CRMk has so far failed to live up to expectations.

The 1990s saw an awakening of interest in the concept of market-perceived value or, as Kotler terms it, customer-perceived value (see Chapter 11). This approach demands that to be effective in markets where customer choice is very much in evidence, companies should provide customers with what they want, not necessarily what companies would rather place on the market. It is a suitable philosophy on which to build an organisation that is well fitted to respond to the needs of the experience economy. However, it requires a deep and lasting commitment to managing organisational change.

As buyers' markets in the developed world start to lose their impetus, due to a complex factor set, including climate warming, increasing inflation in the leading nations of the underdeveloped world (primarily China and India), 'the credit crunch' and increased pressure on the world's material and energy resources, many markets will become very price sensitive. Add to this social problems caused by the failure of many poor economies to feed their people and the effects of the declining developed economies and the world is in turmoil. The effect of this could be increasingly to energise a new paradigm change away from CRM and CPV.

Many observers of the marketing scene are sensing that companies are consciously or unconsciously beginning to move away from the theories and concepts that have been formulated to assist in the management of customer relationships. The pressing requirement of many companies to return short-term profits places strong pressure on CEOs to favour the customer–supplier dyad: that is, return to TM at the expense of customer relationship concerns. This will make building a market-oriented value culture more difficult for all key players and greatly reduce the chances of the theory behind internal marketing being evident in practice. For marketers to achieve and hold down CEO status, they will need to challenge the underlying general management traditions and win the case for discovering, promising and delivering CPV offerings. The task in the twenty-first century is not easy for marketers and the challenge is real. The marketing profession has much to offer companies but it needs to become less intuitive and adopt a more scientific approach and adopt metrics that are a crucial part of the language of business.

Market research

Change is in the air and will remain so for the foreseeable future. Companies need to be sure that they are reading their operating environment effectively. This requires them to keep up to date with the latest developments and trends affecting their markets, customers, competitors, costs, channels and company response options. So expenditure on market research must be seen as an investment rather than an expenditure. As the developed economies seem to be lurching towards less affluent times, marketers need to be on their guard to detect a possible major paradigm shift back to sellers' market conditions. However, such a paradigm change is unlikely to happen overnight and will also occur at different rates in different markets.

New product development

Current buyers' market conditions encourage investment and rapid development of new products (meaning market offerings) as long as they mainly cater for previously researched customer needs (see Chapter 15). Jam today – and more, and juicier, jam tomorrow. Innovation promises sweet rewards, but there is no easy-to-follow recipe for developing market-leading products and services (offerings) that guarantee attractive profits. New product development is costly to sustain and often flies in the face of conventional general management thinking. It is by nature highly creative, qualitative and to many appears to rely on chance and serendipity. This is partially true, but companies that have achieved recognised success as innovators subscribe to Edison's dictum that 'genius is 1 per cent inspiration, 99 per cent perspiration'.

Marketing communications activity

Modern technological advances have already changed and will further change the traditional approach to marketing communications. TV advertising is likely to become highly interactive. More effort will be put into integrated marketing communications (IMC) to maximise customer reach, recall and capture. However, IMC should not be used to advance false messages and promises. Rather confusingly referred to as promotion in the traditional 4P marketing mix, marketing communications should not by default become the only live instrument of the traditional 4P toolbox.

Marketing morphs to greater focus on customer experience and engagement

Marketing managers operating in a highly competitive global marketplace in the age of the internet need to be vigilant to constantly track important developments affecting the delivery of marketing programmes that detect and meet the needs of customers. As a flyer to encourage readers to study Chapter 23 (available on the supportive website) an interesting trend to many practitioners is the call to refocus and redefine marketing in terms of an ever sharper focus on customer experience and engagement.[89] The case is compelling and emerges from a study of the following topics:

- responding to the change in traditional marketing practice from an essential transaction-focused approach to concentration on customer engagement;
- marketing is now an end in itself and must create customer-perceived value in its own right –
- 'ask not what your marketing can do for you, but what your marketing can do for your customer';
- the continual evolution from a tendency to concentrate on products to one that focuses on experiences;
- movement from unique selling points (USPs) to customer engagement points (CEPs);

- communicating to rather than shouting at customers;
- movement from a concentration on image to a quest to achieve, enhance and retain a sound customer reputation;
- understanding the need to explore collaborating both with other companies and customers to achieve attractive customer experiences.

Follow the argument further in Chapter 23.

Getting started

The mission of this text is to provide readers with the following:

- an understanding of marketing management;
- an appreciation of the main methods used by marketers to capture marketing insights;
- an overview of the ways in which marketers connect with customers;
- an insight into how marketing practitioners shape the market offering;
- an understanding of how marketers deliver value in global and local supply networks;
- an appreciation of the methods by which marketers communicate value;
- an overview of how marketers manage brands;
- an insight into how marketing management approaches issues of implementation and control.

Marketing memo

Getting to grips with the practice of marketing

1   Study the contextual factors that impact on the marketplace:

- Is the market domestic or international? (Each national market will need a separate application of this toolbox.)

- Political, economic, sociocultural and technological factors.

- Is the market a sellers' or a buyers' market?

- If a buyers' market, then the concept of CPV will be relevant.

2   Study the customer factors, such as:

- Segmentation, targeting and positioning.

- Product/market offering value circles (quality and price attributes).

- Branding activity.

- New product development.

- Branding.

3   Study the competition:

- Perceived product/market offering expertise.

- Breadth and width of product/market offering portfolio.

- NPD skills.

- Market share.

- Profitability.

4   Study the cash/cost matters:

- Invest in market research to make informed decisions on key market characteristics (context, customers, competition, channels).

- Pay careful attention to the development of revenue forecasts.

5   Study channel factors to achieve effective and efficient use of funds.

6   Examine the underlying company philosophy and practice:

- Is it mainly TM, RM, CRM or CVP?

Source: Based on K. Kashani and D. Turpin (1999) *Marketing Management: An International Perspective*, International Institute for Management Development (IMD), Lausanne, London: Macmillan Business, 3–15.

Additionally, readers are encouraged to try their hand at some 'hands-on' experience. Marketing is a discipline that requires know-what (knowledge) and is developed and fine tuned by practice (know-how). The marketing memo is offered as a guide to getting under way. For further guidance on developing a marketing plan, see Chapter 3, the Euromart sample marketing plan (p. 121).

SUMMARY

1 The modern marketing department has evolved through the years from a simple sales department into an organisational structure where marketing personnel work mainly on cross-disciplinary teams.

2 Modern marketing departments can be organised in a number of ways. Some companies are organised by functional specialisation, whereas others focus on geography and regionalisation. Still others emphasise product and brand management or market-segment management. Some companies establish a matrix organisation consisting of both product and market managers. Finally, some companies have strong corporate marketing, others have limited corporate marketing, and still others place marketing only in the divisions.

3 Effective modern marketing organisations are marked by a strong cooperation and customer focus among the company's departments: marketing, R & D, engineering, purchasing, manufacturing, operations, finance, accounting and credit.

4 A brilliant strategic marketing plan counts for little if it is not implemented properly. Implementing marketing plans calls for skills in recognising and diagnosing a problem, assessing the company level where the problem exists and evaluating results.

5 The marketing department must monitor and control marketing activities continuously. Marketing plan control involves analysis to ensure that the company achieves the sales, profits and other goals established in its annual plan. The main tools are sales analysis, market share analysis, marketing expense-to-sales analysis, and financial analysis of the marketing plan. Profitability control seeks to measure and control the profitability of various products, territories, customer groups, trade channels and order sizes. An important part of controlling for profitability is assigning costs and generating profit-and-loss statements. Efficiency control focuses on finding ways to increase the efficiency of the sales force, advertising, sales promotion and distribution. Strategic control entails a periodic reassessment of the company and its strategic approach to the marketplace using the tools of the marketing effectiveness and marketing excellence reviews, as well as the marketing audit.

6 Companies must practise social responsibility through their legal, ethical and social words and actions. Cause marketing can be a means for companies to link social responsibility productively to consumer marketing programmes. Social marketing is done by a non-profit or government organisation to address a social problem or cause directly.

7 Achieving marketing excellence in the future will require new challenges and opportunities. The resulting marketing imperatives will require a new set of skills and competencies.

APPLICATIONS

Marketing debate

Is marketing management an art or a science?
Some marketing observers maintain that good marketing is more of an art and does not lend itself to rigorous analysis and deliberation. Others strongly disagree and contend that marketing management is a highly disciplined enterprise that has much in common with other business disciplines.

Take a position: Marketing management is largely an artistic exercise and therefore highly subjective *versus* marketing management is largely a scientific exercise with well-established guidelines and criteria.

Marketing discussion

How does cause or corporate societal marketing affect your personal consumer behaviour? Do you ever buy or not buy products or services from a company because of its environmental policies or programmes? Why or why not?

REFERENCES

[1]Unilever and Reckett, *Financial Times*, 15 March 2008.

[2]For additional reading on academic thinking on marketing strategy and tactics, see D. Iacobucci and B. Calder (eds) (2003) *Kellogg on Integrated Marketing*, New York: John Wiley & Sons; and D. Iacobucci (ed.) (2001) *Kellogg on Marketing*, New York: John Wiley & Sons.

[3]F. E. Webster, Jr, A. J. Miller and S. Ganescan (2003) Can marketing regain its seat at the table?, *Marketing Science Institute Report* No. 03–113, Cambridge, MA: Marketing Science Institute.

[4]For a broad historical treatment of marketing thought, see D. G. B. Jones and E. H. Shaw (2002) A history of marketing thought, in B. A. Weitz and R. Wensley (eds.), *Handbook of Marketing*, London: Sage, 39–65; J. Pervaiz (2005) *Internal Marketing*, Oxford: Butterworth-Heinemann; for public sector setting, see also M. T. Ewing and A. Carvana (1999) An internal marketing approach to public sector management: the marketing and human resources interface, *Journal of Public Sector Management*, 12(1), 17–19. See also J. Wieseke, M. Ahearne, S. K. Lam and R. van Dick (2009) The role of leaders in internal marketing, *Journal of Marketing*, 73(2), 123–45; T. Proctor (2010) Internal marketing and its basis for sound customer relationship management, *Journal of Management and Marketing in Healthcare*, December, 3(4), 256–63.

[5]K. Hille (2005) BenQ ready to signal its Siemens solution, *Financial Times*, 19 September.

[6]S. Laitner and P. Thai Larsen (2006) Bid to rouse Belgium's sleeping beauty, *Financial Times*, 31 January; J. Chimhanzi (2002) The impact of marketing/HR interactions on marketing strategy implementation, *European Journal of Marketing*, 38(1/2), 73–98; S. N. Sheth and R. S. Sisodia (2006) *Does Marketing Need Reform? Fresh Perspectives on the Future*, New York: M. E. Sharp.

[7]H. Pringle and W. Gordon (2001) *Beyond Manners: How to Create the Self-Confident Organisation to Live the Brand*, Chichester: John Wiley & Sons. See also Special Issue 1999 of *Journal of Marketing Fundamental Issues and Directions for Marketing*; D. Ballantyne (2003) A relationship-mediated theory of internal marketing, *European Journal of Marketing*, 37(9), 1242–60; P. K. Ahmed and M. Rafiq (2003) Internal marketing issues and challenges, *European Journal of Marketing*, 37(9), 1177–86; M. Kelemen and I. Papasoloou (2007) Internal marketing: a qualitative study of culture change in the UK banking sector, *Journal of Marketing Management*, 23(7/8), 745–67.

[8]For an excellent account of how to convert a company into a market-driven organisation, see G. Day (1989) *The Market-Driven Organization: Aligning Culture, Capabilities, and Configuration to the Market*, New York: Free Press.

[9] Son K. Lam, F. Kraus and M. Ahearne (2010) The diffusion of market orientation throughout the organization: a social learning theory perspective, *Journal of Marketing*, 74(5), 61–79; C. Goswami and S. Goswami (2010) Role of organization structure in facilitating marketing, *Global Business and Marketing Management Research*, 2(2/3), 162–83.

[10]M. Sarkees, J. Hulland and J. Prescott (2010) Ambidextrous organizations and firm performance: the role of marketing function, *Journal of Strategic Marketing*, 18(2), 165–84.

[11]C-P. Wei, P. J-H. Hu and Y-H. Lee (2009) Preserving user preferences in automated document-category management: an evolution-based approach, *Journal of Management Information Systems*, 25(4), 109–43; J. M. Hall, P. K. Kopalle and A. Krishna (2010) Retailer dynamic pricing and ordering decisions: category management versus brand-by-brand approaches, *Journal of Retailing*, 86(2), 172–83.

[12]M. J. Zanor (1994) The profit benefits of category management, *Journal of Marketing Research*, May, 202–13. For business-to-business marketing implications, see A. Lindblom, R. Olkkonen, P. Ollila and S. Hyvönen (2009) Suppliers' roles in category management: a study of supplier–retailer relationships in Finland and Sweden, *Industrial Marketing Management*, 38(8), 1006–13.

[13]L. Selden and G. Colvin (2003) *Angel Customers & Demon Customers*, New York: Portfolio; P. Skålén (2009) Service marketing and subjectivity: the shaping of customer-oriented employees, *Journal of Marketing Management*, 25(7/8),795–809; B. Quancard (2010) DHL's global customer solutions organization, *Velocity*, 12(3/4), 43–7.

[14]For an in-depth discussion of issues around implementing a customer-based organisation, on which much of this paragraph is based, see G. S. Day (2006) Aligning the organization with the market, *MIT Sloan Management Review*, Fall, 41–9.

[15]R. E. Anderson (1994) Matrix redux, *Business Horizons*, November–December, 6–10. Also see the article: Design your governance model to make the matrix work, *People and Strategy*, 32(4), 16–25.

[16]B. P. Shapiro (1977) Can marketing and manufacturing coexist?, *Harvard Business Review*, September–October, 104–14; see also R. W. Ruekert and O. C. Walker, Jr (1987) Marketing's interaction with other functional units: a conceptual framework with other empirical evidence, *Journal of Marketing*, January, 1–19; R-T. Wang, Chien-Ta Bruc Ho and K. Oh (2010) Measuring production and marketing efficiency using grey relation analysis and data envelopment analysis, *International Journal of Production Research*, 48(1), 183–99; M. Brettel, F. Heinemann, A. Engelen and S. Neubauer (2011) Cross-functional integration of R & D, marketing, and manufacturing in radical and incremental product innovations and its effects on project effectiveness and efficiency, *Journal of Product Innovation Management*, 28(2), 251–69.

[17]E. Brynjolfsson and L. Hitt (1996) The customer counts, *InformationWeek*, 9 September.

[18]G. Hamel (2000) *Leading the Revolution*, Boston, MA: Harvard Business School Press; M. R. V. Goodman (2004) Managing in times of change: avoiding management myopia, in A. Ghobadian, N. O'Regan, D. Gallear and H. Viney (eds), *Strategy and Performance*, Basingstoke: Palgrave Macmillan, Chapter 9, 185–210; P. A. Titus (2007) Applied creativity: the creative marketing breakthrough model, *Journal of Marketing Education*, 29(3), 262–72.

[19]E. De Bono (2004) Creativity is an option for business, *Financial Times*, 6 July.

[20]J. N. Sheth (2007) *The Self-Destructive Habits of Good Companies . . . And How to Break Them*, Upper Saddle River, NJ: Wharton School Publishing.

[21]M. Witzel (2008) Managers who use a little imagination for big rewards, *Financial Times*, 6 May.

[22]J.-C. Larreche (2008) *The Momentum Effect: How to Ignite Exceptional Growth*, London: Financial Times Series; S. Stern (2008) An elusive concept for staying on a roll, *Financial Times*, 1 May.

[23]G. Hamel (2000) *Leading the Revolution*, Boston, MA: Harvard Business School Press.

[24]C. Marcus (2001) Marketing resource management: key components, *Gartner Research Note*, 22 August.

[25]W. M. Cohen and D. A. Levinthal (1990) Absorptive capacity: a new perspective on learning and innovation, *Administrative Science Quarterly*, 35, 28–52; D. K. Banner (1993) Self-managed work teams: an idea whose time has come?, *Creativity and Innovation Management*, 2(1), 27–36; C. C. Manz and H. P. Sims, Jr (1987) Leading workers to lead themselves: the external leadership of self-managing work teams, *Administrative Science Quarterly*, 32, 106–28; C. C. Manz and H. P. Sims, Jr (2001) *Superleadership: Leading Others to Lead Themselves*, Englewood Cliffs, NJ: Prentice Hall; M. B. Pinto, J. K. Pinto and J. E. Prescott (1993) Antecedents and consequences of project team cross-functional cooperation, *Management Science*, 39(10), 1281–97; S. J. Parnes (1997) *Sourcebook for Creative Problem-solving*, Buffalo, NY: Creative Education Foundation Press; M. R. V. Goodman (1995) *Creative Management*, Harlow: Pearson; J. Tidd, J. Bessant and K. Pavitt (2001) *Managing Innovation: Integrating Technological, Market, and Organizational Change*, 2nd edn, Chichester: John Wiley & Sons; S. Bharadwaj and A. Menon (2000) Making innovation happen in organizations: individual creativity mechanisms, organizational creativity mechanisms or both?, *Journal of Product Innovation Management*, 17(6), 424–34; E. C. Martins and F. Trerblanche (2003) Building organizational culture that stimulates creativity and innovation, *European Journal of Innovation Management*, 6(1), 64–74; K. M. Eisenhart (1989) Making fat strategic decisions, *Academy of Management Journal*, 32, 543–76; M. R. V. Goodman (2000) The frustration of talent: a study in scarlet, *Creativity and Innovation Management*, 9(1), 46–53; A. Bryman (1997) Leadership in organizations, in S. R. Clegg, C. Hardy and W. A. Nord (eds), *Handbook of Organization Studies*, London: Sage, 276–92; G. Ekvall (1993) Creativity in project work: a longitudinal study of a product development project, *Creativity and Innovation Management*, 2(1), 17–26; G. Ekvall (2000) Management and organizational philosophies and practices as stimulants or blocks to creative behaviour: a study of engineering, *Creativity and Innovation Management*, 9(2), 94–9; T. M. Amabile and R. Conti (1999) Changes in the work environment for creativity during downsizing, *Academy of Management Journal*, 42, 630–40; D. J. Teece, G. Pisano and A. Shuen (1997) Dynamic capabilities and strategic management, *Strategic Management Journal*, 18, 509–34; K. D. Elsbach and R. M. Kramer (2003) Assessing creativity in Hollywood pitch meetings: evidence for a dual-process model of creativity judgments, *Academy of Management Journal*, 46(3), 283–302.

[26]D. A. Pitta, V. R. Wood and F. J. Franzak (2008) Nurturing an effective creative culture within a marketing organization, *Journal of Consumer Marketing*, 25(3), 137–48; I. F. Fillis and R. Rentschler (2006) *Creative Marketing: An Extended Metaphor in a New Age*, Basingstoke: Palgrave Macmillan.

[27]A. O'Driscoll (2008) Exploring paradox in marketing: managing ambiguity towards synthesis, *Journal of Business and Industrial Marketing*, 23(2), 95–104.

[28]C. Grande (2007) Bearing rivals when it comes to risk-taking, *Financial Times*, 16 May.

[29]P. E. Murphy (2010) Business and marketing ethics: good news and bad news, *Business Ethics Quarterly*, October, 20(4), 751–3; P. H. Werhane (2010) Principles and practices for corporate responsibility, *Business Ethics Quarterly*, 20(4), 695–701; M. G. Luchs, R. W. Naylor, J. R. Irwin and R. Raghunathan (2010) The sustainability liability: potential negative effects of ethicality on product preference, *Journal of Marketing*, 74(5), 18–31; R. Lacey and P. Kennett-Hensel (2010) Longitudinal effects of corporate social responsibility on customer relationships, *Journal of Business Ethics*, 97(4), 581–97.

[30]J. Alsever (2006) Chiquita cleans up its act, *Business 2.0*, August, 56–8.

[31]P. S. Bronn (2006) Building corporate brands through community involvement: is it exportable? The case of the Ronald McDonald House in Norway, *Journal of Marketing Communications*, 2(4), 309–20.

[32]I. Carrasco (2007) Corporate social responsibility, values and cooperation, advances in economic research, 12(4), 454–60; B. Grow, S. Hamin and L. Lee (2005) The debate over doing good, *Business Week*, 5 August; C. Kamp (2008) Be seen to talk the talk: how national perception can influence a company's CSR strategy, *Strategic Direction*, 24(1), 25–7.

[33]M. Skapinker (2008) Corporate responsibility is not quite dead, *Financial Times*, 12 February.

[34]M. Fetscherin and M. Toncar (2009) Visual puffery in advertising, *International Journal of Market Research*, 51(2), 147–8; R. Mules (2010) The ethics of marketing sports drinks to youth market, *BusiDate*, 18(3), 2–5.

[35]M. Schultz, Y. M. Antorini and F. F. Csaba (2005) *Corporate Branding: Purpose, People and Process*, Koge, Denmark: Copenhagen Business School Press; R. J. Alsop (2004) *The 18 Immutable Laws of Corporate Reputation: Creating, Protecting, and Repairing Your Most Valuable Asset*, New York: Free Press; G. Svensson, G. Wood, J. Singh and M. Callaghan (2009) A cross-cultural construct of the ethos of the corporate codes of ethics: Australia, Canada and Sweden, *Business Ethics: A European Review*, 18(3), 253–67; G. Svensson, G. Wood and M. Callaghan (2009) A construct of the 'ethos of codes of ethics' (ECE): the case of private and public Sweden, *International Journal of Public Sector Management*, 22(6), 499–515.

[36]I. Harris, M. Mainelli and H. Jones (2008) Caveat emptor, caveat venditor: buyers and sellers beware the tender trap, *Strategic Change*, 17(1/2), 1–9.

[37]E. Baccarini (2008) What does ethical behaviour mean in management activities?, *TQM Journal*, 20(2), 154–65.

[38]T. Wagner, R. J. Lutz and B. A. Weitz (2009) Corporate hypocrisy: overcoming the threat of inconsistent corporate social responsibility perceptions, *Journal of Marketing*, 73(6), 77–91.

[39] S. Hiss (2009) From implicit to explicit corporate social responsibility: institutional change as a fight for myths, *Business Ethics Quarterly*, 19(3), 433–51; P. Shum and S. Yam, (2011) Ethics and law: guiding the invisible hand to correct corporate social responsibility externalities, *Journal of Business Ethics*, 98(4), 549–71.

[40]C. Spence and I. Thomson (2009) Resonance tropes in corporate philanthropy discourse, *Business Ethics: A European Review*, 18(4), 372–88; D. Koehn and J. Ueng (2010) Is philanthropy being used by corporate wrongdoers to buy good will?, *Journal of Management and Governance*, 14(1), 1–16.

[41]M. G. Luchs, R. W. Naylor, J. R. Irwin and R. Raghunathan (2010) The sustainability liability: potential negative effects of ethicality on product preference, *Journal of Marketing*, 74(5), 18–31; C. Cunha, A. Leoanardo and J. E. Fensterseifer (2011) Corporate sustainability measure from an integrated perspective: the corporate sustainability grid (CSG), *International Journal of Business Insights and Transformation*, January Special Issue, 3(3), 44–53.

[42]N. Varchaver (2007) Chemical reaction, *Fortune*, 2 April, 53–8.

[43]A. Scerri and P. James (2010) Accounting for sustainability: combining qualitative and quantitative research in developing 'indicators' of sustainability, *International Journal of Social Research Methodology*, 13(1), 41–53.

44 J. Sheth, N. Sethia and S. Shanthi (2011) Mindful consumption: a customer-centric approach to sustainability, *Journal of the Academy of Marketing Science*, 39(1), 21–39.

45 M. L. Costa (2010) Brands must put green into mainstream, *Marketing Week*, 33(40), 26–8.

46 Media Office, Levi Strauss Europe.

47 J. C. Long (2008) From Cocoa to CSR: Finding sustainability in a cup of hot chocolate. *Thunderbird International Business Review*, 50(5), 315–20; K. Byus, D. Deis and B. Ouyang (2010) Doing well by doing good: corporate social responsibility and profitability, *SAM Advanced Management Journal*, 75(1), 44–55.

48 R. Sisodia, D. B. Wolfe and J. Sheth (2007) *Firms of Endearment: How World-Class Companies Profit from Passion and Purpose*, Upper Saddle River, NJ: Wharton School Publishing.

49 See P. Kotler and N. Lee (2005) *Corporate Social Responsibility: Doing the Most Good for Your Company and Your Cause*, New York: John Wiley & Sons.

50 V. Vial (2008) How socially responsible engagement can change your business model: the radical experience of Armor Lux, *Global Business and Organizational Excellence*, 28(1), 24–34; R. Nidumolu, C. K. Prahalad and M. R. Rangaswami (2009) Why sustainability is now the key driver of innovation, *Harvard Business Review*, 87(9), 56–64.

51 W. Heli, C. Jaepil and L. Jiatao (2008) Too little or too much? Untangling the relationship between corporate philanthropy and firm financial performance, *Organization Science*, 19(1), 143–59; D. Campbell and R. Slack (2008) Corporate 'philanthropy strategy' and 'strategic philanthropy': some insights from voluntary disclosures in annual reports, *Business and Society*, 47(2), 187–212.

52 L. Chiagouris and I. Ray (2007) Saving the world with cause-related marketing, *Marketing Management*, July–August, 48–51; S. L. Grau and J. A. Garretson (2007) Cause related marketing (CRM), *Journal of Advertising*, 36(4), 19–33; C. Peters, J. Thomas and H. Tolson (2007) An exploratory study of cause-related retailing, *International Journal of Retail and Distribution Management*, 35(11), 895–911; M. Demetriou, I. Papasolomou and D. Vrontis (2010) Cause-related marketing: building the corporate image while supporting worthwhile causes, *Journal of Brand Management*, 17(4), 266–78; D. C. Moosmayer and A. Fuljahn (2010) Consumer perceptions of cause related marketing campaigns, *Journal of Consumer Marketing*, 27(6), 543–9.

53 For definition, see the Business Dictionary, www.businessdictionary.com/definition/cause-related-marketing.html.

54 M. Drumwright and P. E. Murphy (2001) Corporate societal marketing in P. N. Bloom and G. T. Gundlach (eds), *Handbook of Marketing and Society*, Thousand Oaks, CA: Sage, 162–83; see also M. Drumwright (1996) Company advertising with a social dimension: the role of noneconomic criteria, *Journal of Marketing*, 60 (October), 71–87.

55 See www.britishairways.com.

56 X. Luo and C. B. Bhattacharya (2006) Corporate social responsibility, customer satisfaction and market value, *Journal of Marketing*, 70 (October), 1–18; F. Farache, K. J. Perks, L. S. O. Wanderley and J. M. de Sousa Filho (2008) Cause related marketing: consumers' perceptions and benefits for profit and non-profit organizations, *Brazilian Administration Review* (BAR), 5(3), 210–24.

57 R. Chun (2007) Do happy staff make happy customers?, *International Commerce Review*, 7(1), 7; L. Mei-Lien and R. D. Green (2011) A mediating influence on customer loyalty: the role of perceived value, *Journal of Management and Marketing Research*, 7(March), 1–12.

58 P. N. Bloom, S. Hoeffler, K. L. Keller and C. E. Basurto (2006) How social-cause marketing affects consumer perceptions, *MIT Sloan Management Review*, Winter, 49–55; C. J. Simmons and K. L. Becker-Olsen (2006) Achieving marketing objectives through social sponsorships, *Journal of Marketing*, 70 (October), 154–69; G. Berens, C. B. M. van Riel and G. H. van Bruggen (2005) Corporate associations and consumer product responses: the moderating role of corporate brand dominance, *Journal of Marketing*, 69 (July), 35–48; S. Hoeffler and K. L. Keller (2002) Building brand equity through corporate societal marketing, *Journal of Public Policy and Marketing*, 21(1), 78–89. See also: 2003 Special issue: corporate responsibility, *Journal of Brand Management*, 10(2), 4–5.

59 M. R. Forehand and S. Grier (2003) When is honesty the best policy? The effect of stated company intent on consumer skepticism, *Journal of Consumer Psychology*, 12(3), 349–56; D. H. Dean (2002) Associating the corporation with a charitable event through sponsorship: measuring the effects on corporate community relations, *Journal of Advertising*, 31(4), 77–87.

60 N. C. Smith (2007) Out of left field, *Business Strategy Review*, 18(2), 55–9; A. Jones (2003) Choc horror over Cadbury tokens, *Financial Times*, 3 May, 14.

61 B. A. Lafferty (2009) Selecting the right cause partners for the right reasons: the role of importance and fit in cause–brand alliances, *Psychology and Marketing*, 26(4), 359–82.

62 S. Orestein (2003) The selling of breast cancer, *Business 2.0*, February, 88–94; H. Meyer (1999) When the cause is just, *Journal of Business Strategy*, November–December, 27–31.

63 C. Bittar (2002) Seeking cause and effect, *Brandweek*, 11 November, 18–24.

64 J. French and C. Blair-Stevens (2005) *Social Marketing Pocket Guide*, 2 edn, National Society Marketing Centre for Excellence (www.nsms.org.uk); P. Kotler, N. Roberto and N. Lee, (2002) *Social Marketing; Improving the Quality of Life*, Thousand Oaks, CA: Sage; K. Collins, A. Tapp and A. Pressley, (2010) Social marketing and social influences: Using social ecology as a theoretical framework, *Journal of Marketing Management*, 26(13/14), 1181–1200.

65 A fuller explanation of the key features and concepts is available from the National Social Marketing Centre in the UK (www.nsms.org.uk); L. Logie-MacIver and M.G. Piacentini (2011) Towards a richer understanding of consumers in social marketing contexts: revisiting the stage of change model, *Journal of Marketing Management*, 27(1/2), 60–76.

66 M. Katsiolondes, J. Grant and D. S. Mckechnie (2007) Social marketing: strengthening company–customer bonds, *Journal of Business Strategy*, 28(3), 55–64; J. DeGruchy and D. Coppel (2008) Listening to reason: a social marketing stop-smoking campaign in Nottingham, *Social Marketing Quarterly*, 14(1), 5–17; S. Bird and A. Tapp (2008) Social marketing and the meaning of cool, *Social Marketing Quarterly*, 14(1), 18–29; M. Stead, R. Gordon, K. Angus and L. McDermott (2007) A systematic review of social marketing effectiveness, *Health Education*, 107(2), 126–91.

67 G. Arulmari and A. Abdulla (2007) Capturing the ripples: addressing the sustainability of the impact of social marketing, *Social Marketing Quarterly*, 13(4), 84–107; C. Domegan (2007) The use of social marketing for science outreach activities in Ireland, *Irish Journal of Management*, 28(1), 103–25; C. T. Donegan (2008) Social marketing: implications for contemporary practices classification scheme, *Journal of Business and Industrial Marketing*, 2(2), 135–41; A. Thorpe, R. Merritt, D. McVey and A. Truss (2008) What next for social marketing: developing 'superman' or a sustainable system?, *Social Marketing Quarterly*, 14(1), 63–71.

[68]D. Burton (2002) Incorporating ethnicity into marketing intelligence and planning, *Marketing Intelligence and Planning*, 20(7), 442–57; K. Erdem and R. Ä. Schmidt (2008) Ethic marketing for Turks in Germany, *International Journal of Retail and Distribution Management*, 36(3), 212–23.

[69]A. Jamal (2003) Marketing in multicultural world: the interplay of marketing, ethnicity and consumption, *European Journal of Marketing*, 37(1/2), 1599–620.

[70]Directgov [http://www.direct.gov.uk/en/NI1/Newsroom/DG_064854].

[71]K. Peattie and A. Crane (2005) Green marketing: legend, myth or prophesy? *Qualitative Market Research: An International Journal*, 8(4), 357–70; J. Rivera-Comino (2007) Re-evaluating green marketing strategy: a stakeholder perspective, *European Journal of Marketing*, 41(11/12), 1328–58; L. J. Vermillion and P. Justin (2010) Allied Academies International Conference, *Proceedings of the Academy of Marketing Studies* (AMS), 15(1), 68–72.

[72]C. D'Souza, M. Taghian and R. Khosla (2007) Examination of environmental beliefs and its impact on the influence of price, quality and demographics with respect to green purchases, *Journal of Targeting Measurement and Analysis*, 15(2), 69–78.

[73]J. Grant (2007) *The Green Manifesto*, Chichester: John Wiley & Sons.

[74]R. Bridge (2008) Green means go for new firms, *The Sunday Times*, 9 March; The Carbon Trust, carbontrust.co.uk; Green Energy 360, greenenergy360.org.

[75]P. Hartmann and V. A. Ibanez (2006) Green value added, *Marketing Intelligence and Planning*, 24(7), 673–80; M. F. Junaedi and G. M. Shellyana (2007) The roles of consumer's knowledge and emotion in ecological issues, *International Journal of Business*, 9(1), 81–99.

[76]J. Pickard (2007) National news: property company 'green' group to be set up, *Financial Times*, 27 February.

[77]For other examples, see P. W. Ferris, N. T. Bendle, P. E. Pfeifer and D. J. Reibstein (2006) *Marketing Metrics: 501 Metrics Every Executive Should Master*, Upper Saddle River, NJ: Wharton School Publishing; M. Debruyne and K. Hubbard (2000) Marketing metrics, working paper series, Conference Summary, *Marketing Science Institute Report* No. 00–119.

[78]A. R. Oxenfeldt (1969) How to use market-share measurement, *Harvard Business Review*, January–February, 59–68.

[79]There is a one-half chance that successive observation will be higher or lower. Therefore, the probability of finding six successively higher values is given by (1/2) to the sixth, or 1/64.

[80]Alternatively, companies need to focus on factors affecting shareholder value. The goal of marketing planning is to increase shareholder value, which is the present value of the future income stream created by the company's present actions. Rate-of-return usually focuses on one year's results only. See A. Rapport (1997) *Creating Shareholder Value*, revised edn, New York: Free Press.

[81]For additional reading on financial analysis, see Chapter 22 of this text.

[82]R. C. Cooper and R. S. Kaplan (1991) Profit priorities from activity-based costing, *Harvard Business Review*, May–June, 130–5.

[83]S. R. Goodman (1982) *Increasing Corporate Profitability*, New York: Ronald Press, Chapter 1. See also: B. J. Jaworski, V. Stathakopoulos and S. Krishman (1993) Control combinations in marketing: conceptual framework and empirical evidence, *Journal of Marketing*, January, 57–69.

[84]M. R. V. Goodman (2001) Marketing quo vadis? *Eclectic: The Banking and Finance Faculty Magazine*, 5 (summer), 21–6.

[85]T. Ambler (2008) Marketing 2008: discipline in crisis, *Marketing*, 16 January, 26–8.

[86]R. Lusch (2007) Marketing's evolving identity: defining our future, *Journal of Public Policy and Marketing*, 2, 261–8.

[87]E. Gummesson (1987) The new marketing: developing long term interactive relationships, *Long Range Planning*, 20(4), 10–20; C. Gronroos (1994) From marketing mix to relationship marketing: towards a paradigm shift in marketing, *Management Decision*, 32(2), 4–20; J. Egan (2006) Sidelined? The future of marketing in the contemporary organisation, *Irish Journal of Management*, 27(2), 99–118.

[88]E. Kasabov (2007) Towards a contingent, empirically validated and power cognisant relationship marketing, *European Journal of Marketing*, 14(1/2), 94–120.

[89]G. Leonhard (2010) Five customer engagement predictions, www.youtube.com/watch?v=nvtQglauUjY.

Chapter 22

Managing marketing metrics

IN THIS CHAPTER, WE WILL ADDRESS THE FOLLOWING QUESTIONS:

1 What are marketing metrics?
2 What is the need for marketing metrics?
3 What are useful marketing metrics?
4 What are the key marketing metrics?
5 What metrics do companies use?
6 What is a marketing dashboard?

What you can't measure you can't manage – this is the true marketing metrics philosophy.

Source: Curt Pickens/iStockphoto.

CHAPTER JOURNEY

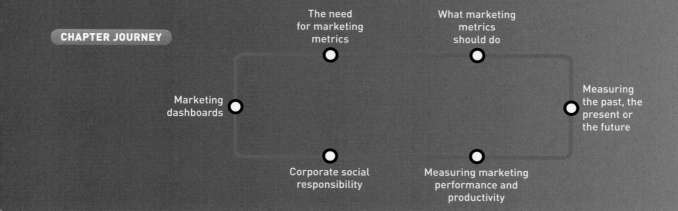

The need
for marketing
metrics

What marketing
metrics
should do

Marketing
dashboards

Measuring
the past, the
present or
the future

Corporate social
responsibility

Measuring marketing
performance and
productivity

To stay in business a company needs positive cash flows, which in turn are generated from the company's ability to create value. Since value is defined by customers, marketing makes a fundamental contribution to long-term business success. Recognising that evaluating marketing performance is a key task for management, marketing metrics are concerned with calculating the value of marketing activity in a company.

Brands spend large amounts of marketing money and the brand owners and their agencies need to be accountable for this money, and how it is spent. There is a constant need to create growth and thus prioritise spend behind campaigns, and media that are more effective, to get a 'bigger bang for our buck'. But you only know what is more effective if you measure and monitor the effect properly. BrandScience – a specialist unit within OmnicomMediaGroup – is a global network of econometric and marketing analysis experts specialising in delivering state-of-the-art, 100 per cent tailor-made brand, business and communication evaluation by quantifying and measuring properly what matters to businesses. Advanced statistical modelling methods are employed on hard data on the brand's sales, marketing and communications history, competitors and economic context in order to identify significant drivers of the businesses, separate the effects of different drivers and isolate and quantify the contribution from marketing both on a short-, medium- and long-term basis.[1]

Marketing managers are increasingly being held accountable for their investments and must be able to justify marketing expenditures to senior management.[2] Marketing metrics provide valuable data points against which the marketing organisation can track its progress, demonstrate accountability and allow marketers to better know, act upon and align efforts.[3] This chapter explores how companies can measure and improve their marketing performance by applying marketing metrics.

The need for marketing metrics

In the modern business environment, companies to an increasing degree derive substantial and sustained competitive advantage from intangible assets such as brand equity, knowledge, networks and innovative capability. Measuring the return on both tangible assets (fixed assets, e.g. land, buildings and machinery) and intangible assets (assets that have no physical substance, e.g. brand names, copyrights and patents, strong channel relationships, etc.) has therefore now become imperative for managers.[4] Without metrics to track performance, marketing and business plans are ineffective.

Marketing metrics are the set of measures that help firms to quantify, compare and interpret their marketing performance. In 2005 the American Marketing Association (AMA) established the following definition of marketing accountability: 'The responsibility for the systematic management of marketing resources and processes to achieve measurable gains in return on marketing investment and increased marketing efficiency, while maintaining quality and increasing the value of corporation.' The overall purpose of marketing metrics is twofold: (1) by increasing the accountability of marketing initiatives marketing metrics serve to justify spending valuable firm resources on marketing; and (2) to facilitate the identification of drivers of future customer and firm value.[5] Although we can easily quantify marketing expenses and investments as inputs in the short run, the resulting outputs such as broader brand awareness, enhanced brand image, greater customer loyalty and improved new product prospects may take months or even years to manifest themselves. Moreover, a whole host of internal changes within the organisation and external changes in the marketing environment may coincide with the marketing expenditures, making it hard to isolate the effects of any particular marketing activity.[6] Nevertheless, an important task of marketing research is to assess the efficiency and effectiveness of marketing activities. In one survey, 65 per cent of marketers indicated that return on marketing investment was a concern.[7] A recent survey of leading technology Chief Marketing Officers revealed that over 80 per cent of the companies surveyed expressed dissatisfaction with their ability to benchmark their marketing programme's business impact and value.[8]

A number of factors have elevated the importance of measuring marketing performance:[9]

- **Corporate trend for greater accountability of value added.** Companies that want to measure the return on marketing need to treat marketing expenditures as an investment instead of just a short-term expense. The investment perspective allows managers to compare marketing to other assets and thus enables companies to be financially accountable. Being financially accountable is also necessary when a company wants to be cost effective and/or wants to reduce costs. Moreover, marketing is generating a stream of revenue (through sales), and therefore it should be possible to pay for marketing activities by their results.[10]

- **Discontent with traditional metrics.** Conventional methods of productivity and return (e.g. balance sheets, income statements, gross margins) are often historical and say little about the future long-term performance of a company. In a competitive and highly dynamic company environment, past performance is a poor and almost useless predictor of future performance. In compliance with treating marketing as an investment, marketing metrics should be forward looking and should also involve a long-term performance perspective.

- **Availability of ICT and internet infrastructure.** The development of ICT and the internet has facilitated the development of new methods for marketing metrics. In addition, the prevalence of enterprise resource planning software, supply chain management software and customer relationship management software enables the use of more advanced and forward-looking marketing metrics.

- **Identification of new drivers of customer and firm value.** In recent years, still more customer characteristics – such as word of mouth and referral behaviour – have been linked to customer and firm value, which has led to an increase in the number of different types of marketing metrics.

Unfortunately, however, while many companies may be aware of the opportunities associated with marketing metrics, the reality is that many still rely on traditional historic metrics[11] such as balance sheets, gross margins and so on.

What marketing metrics should do

More than ever, marketers are being pressured to deliver hard data on how their efforts increased the company's bottom line. This trend seems to be global.[12] A focus on metrics can mean the difference between a marketing department that is considered highly valuable and one on the brink of extinction. For example, research giant IDC surveyed senior marketing executives in IT companies to determine their priorities for the coming year. Measuring and justifying their efforts and steering marketing initiatives towards tangible results were at the top of their lists.[13]

To find out more about how the Stockholm-based Ericsson Group, a world-leading telecommunications company, utilises a portfolio of metrics to monitor both operating efficiency and market effectiveness of their marketing activities, go to www.pearsoned.co.uk/marketingmanagementeurope.

Researchers Seggie, Cavusgil and Phelan[14] have formulated seven themes, or dimensions, that together define the capabilities of the 'ideal marketing metrics' – and at the same time also provide guidelines on how existing marketing metrics may be improved.

1 Marketing metrics should be financial. By speaking the same financial language as the rest of the company, senior management can obtain a greater understanding of marketing initiatives, intervene when necessary and take appropriate remedial action.

2 You cannot drive a car, or a company, by looking in the rearview mirror. Companies wanting to survive intense competition have to be at the forefront of environmental development and also need to be able to forecast the future results of actions taken today. In order to be forward, rather than backward looking, metrics should not just be projecting past results inflated by an uplift (an adjustment) factor.

3 Marketing actions may have both short- and long-term effects. By regarding marketing as an expense, the short-term perspective has been emphasised at the expense of the long-term perspective. However, the view of marketing as an investment introduces the long-term perspective necessary for the purpose of comparing the real benefits of marketing activities.

4 Looking only at aggregated, or average, tendencies among customers may mask important shifts among customer segments or even individual customers. Sufficient marketing metrics should therefore be capable of transforming data at the macro level into micro level data.

5 Independent metrics should be moved from separate measures to causal chains, thereby facilitating the direct measure of marketing activities as evaluated by their effect on the bottom line. Intermediate variables such as consumer attitudes and market share should be taken into account.

6 No company exists in a vacuum and value is most often reached in competition with company rivals. Reflecting this, marketing metrics should also be relative – not just absolute – to allow managers to contrast performance with that of the company's competitors.

7 Marketing metrics should be able to deliver objective data, which can be used for comparisons with other companies and with other company activities – and that can facilitate accountability.

Marketing researchers Rust, Ambler, Carpenter, Kumar and Srivastava[15] propose that there are three challenges to the measurement of marketing productivity. The first challenge is relating marketing activities to long-term effects. The second is the separation of individual marketing activities from other actions. Third, the use of purely financial methods has proved inadequate for justifying marketing investments.

Non-financial metrics are needed: for example, metrics that relate to innovations or employees. Since the late 1990s the economy has increasingly recognised that intangible (market-based) assets are the drivers of value.[16] A company's tangible or balance sheet assets (e.g. factories, raw materials, financial assets) have traditionally been seen as its most vital resource. However, in the modern market economy investors increasingly view intangible assets (e.g. brands, company knowledge, reputation, skills) as the key to superior business processess.[17]

London Business School's Tim Ambler suggests that if companies think they are already measuring marketing performance adequately, they should ask themselves five questions:[18]

1 Do you routinely research consumer behaviour (retention, acquisition, usage) and why consumers behave that way (awareness, satisfaction, perceived quality)?

2 Do you routinely report the results of this research to the board in a format integrated with financial marketing metrics?

3 In those reports, do you compare the results with the levels previously forecast in the business plans?

4 Do you also compare them with the levels achieved by your key competitor using the same indicators?

5 Do you adjust short-term performance according to the change in your marketing-based asset(s)?

Ambler believes that firms must give priority to measuring and reporting marketing performance through marketing metrics. He believes evaluation can be split into two parts: (1) short-term results; and (2) changes in brand equity. Short-term results often reflect profit-and-loss concerns as shown by sales turnover, shareholder value, or some combination of the two. Brand-equity measures could include customer awareness, attitudes and behaviours; market share; relative price premium; number of complaints; distribution and availability; total number of customers; perceived quality; and loyalty and retention.[19] DoubleClick, Inc., which places roughly 200 billion ads a month for clients, offers 50 different types of metrics, such as pauses, restarts, average view times and full screen views for video ads, to monitor campaigns.[20]

Companies can also monitor an extensive set of metrics internal to the company, such as innovation: for example, 3M tracks the proportion of sales resulting from its recent innovations. Ambler also recommends developing employee measures and metrics, arguing that 'end users are the ultimate customers, but your own staff are your first; you need

Table 22.1 Sample marketing metrics

1 External	**2 Internal**
Awareness	Awareness of goals
Market share (volume or value)	Commitment to goals
Relative price (market share value/volume)	Active innovation support
Number of complaints (level of dissatisfaction)	Resource adequacy
Consumer satisfaction	Staffing/skill levels
Distribution/availability	Desire to learn
Total number of customers	Willingness to change
Perceived quality/esteem	Freedom to fail
Loyalty/retention	Autonomy
Relative perceived quality	Relative employee satisfaction

Source: T. Ambler (2001) What does marketing success look like?, *Marketing Management*, Spring, 13–18. Reproduced with permission.

to measure the health of the internal market'. Table 22.1 summarises a list of popular internal and external marketing metrics from Ambler's survey in the United Kingdom.[21]

To date, marketing metrics results have been largely internal to the firm, although it has been argued that they should also be communicated to shareholders, subject to commercial confidentiality.[22]

The chain of marketing productivity

Regarding marketing as investment implies that the marketing assets in which the company invests should be identified. Also, it should be understood that these assets contribute to profits in the short run and provide potential for growth and sustained profits in the long run. Emphasis is not on underlying products, pricing or customer relationships, but on marketing expenditures such as marketing communications, promotions and other activities, and how these expenditures influence marketplace performance.[23] Marketing expenditures may influence, for example, customers' beliefs, attitudes, feelings and behaviour, which in turn may impact on the financial performance of the company, such as profit and shareholder value. Marketing actions both create and leverage market-based assets: for example, an advertising effort may improve, or build, brand equity. Brand equity may in turn be leveraged to improve short-term productivity – advertising in combination with stronger brands is usually more productive. Figure 22.1 illustrates 'the chain of marketing productivity'.[24]

Figure 22.1 The chain of marketing productivity
Source: Adapted from R. T. Rust, T. Ambler, G. S. Carpenter, V. Kumar and R. K. Srivastava (2004) Measuring marketing productivity: current knowledge and future directions, *Journal of Marketing*, 68, October, 77. Copyright © 2004 American Marketing Association. Reproduced with permission.

The chain of marketing productivity is concerned with marketing activities that require expenditures. Companies' strategies might include promotion strategy, product strategy, or any other marketing or company strategy. These strategies lead to tactical marketing actions taken by the firm, such as advertising campaigns, service improvement efforts, branding initiatives, loyalty programmes, or other specific initiatives designed to have a marketing impact. The tactical actions in turn impact customer satisfaction and attitude, and other customer-centred elements. Such customer-centred elements represent marketing assets to a company such as brand equity and customer equity. Customer behaviour influences may change market share and sales and thereby the market position of a company. The changes in market share, sales, etc. may have financial impact in terms of, for example, return on investment and economic value added (EVA): that is, net operating profit after taxes less the money cost of capital. Net operating profit after taxes (NOPAT) and cost of capital are considered in subsequent sections of this chapter. Return on investment (ROI) and EVA in turn influence the financial position of the company. The financial impacts have consequences for firm value in terms of market value added (MVA), which together with the financial position of the firm influences the value of the firm. The marketing insight box below provides some insight on what metrics are used by companies.

Effectiveness versus efficiency

The company should distinguish between the 'effectiveness' and the 'efficiency' of marketing actions.[25] For example, price cuts can be efficient in that they deliver short-term revenues and cash flows. However, to the extent that they invite competitive actions and destroy long-term profitability and brand equity, they may not be effective. Businesses also need to know which success factors require measuring, and they must understand the differences between measurements (the raw outcomes of quantification), metrics (ideal standards for measurement) and benchmarks (the standards by which all others are measured).[26]

Marketing insight

What metrics do companies use?

Marketing metrics include all internal and external measurements related to marketing and market position, which are believed to be linked to short- and long-term financial performance.[27] Barwise and Farley[28] have studied adoption of six metrics in the top five global markets: the United States, Japan, Germany, the United Kingdom and France. The six metrics were market share, perceived product or service quality, customer loyalty or retention, customer or segment profitability, relative price and actual or potential customer/segment lifetime value.

Most businesses in these five countries said that they now report one or more of the six metrics to the board, with market share (79 per cent) and perceived product/

service quality (77 per cent) the most used. Least used (40 per cent) was customer/segment lifetime value. Germany was above average for all six metrics, especially market share (97 per cent) and relative price (84 per cent). Japan was below average on all metrics. The US and UK samples were fairly close to average, while France was high on both market share and customer/segment lifetime value. No significant differences related to industry use of metrics were found. Some systematic firm-related differences were found in that multinational subsidiaries and larger firms tended to use more metrics.

Source: Based on P. Barwise and J. U. Farley (2004) Marketing metrics: status of six metrics in five countries, *European Management Journal*, 22(3), 257–62.

Measuring the past, the present or the future

Most customer metrics used by firms are rear-view mirrors reporting the past or dashboards reporting the present.[29] Such metrics are simply retrospective snapshots of the ways customers have evaluated the company, its employees, or its products and services in the past, including overall assessments, such as customer satisfaction, perceived quality, perceived value, loyalty, or attitudes toward the brand or organisation. While these easy-viewing metrics have several advantages – they help companies tracking performance over time, benchmarking against competitors, comparing performance across different parts of the company, and the like – they also have critical disadvantages. As noted by marketing professor Valarie A. Zeithaml and her colleagues, 'by the time we get the data from customer surveys, they represent yesterday rather than today. Perceptual measures also typically focus only on current customers, ignoring noncustomers whose perceptions are likely to be as important – or more important – than current customers.'[30] Moreover, rear-view mirrors have been shown to offer only limited ability to predict future customer behaviour and firm value.[31] For example, customer satisfaction and repeat purchase intentions have often only limited ability in explaining or predicting behaviour. As digital technology and CRM have evolved, companies have increasingly measured customers' observed behaviour. Attention has been devoted to 'real time' metrics such as number of acquired customers, traffic/visits, product returns, average order size and the like. The 'RFM' measure has become in particular popular. RFM reports the time since the customer's last purchase (*r*ecency), the customer's purchase frequency (*f*requency), and the average amount spend by the customer (*m*onetary value). RFM is often used for rank ordering existing customers based on their purchasing history, although it provides only little information concerning how much future profit each customer is likely to give.

Metrics reporting the past or the present should not be disregarded as they may be highly valuable to the company. For example, measuring customer satisfaction provides good feedback to employees and may be used by managers to determine relative performance and compensate the units responsible. However, in recognition that a company cannot survive solely on the basis of what it has earned yesterday, or what it earns today, marketing research has been increasingly interested in developing metrics that relate to future company performance. Examples of such attempts include assessments of customer lifetime value (CLV), which reflects the present value of the future net cash flows that are expected to be received over the lifetime of a customer, and customer referral value (CRV), which seeks to quantify the value of the referrals that each customer gives to the firm.[32] CLV and CRV, and other forward-looking metrics, will be addressed in detail later in this chapter.

Measuring marketing performance and productivity

Marketing performance and productivity is multidimensional and therefore different metrics should be seen as complements rather than substitutes.[33] Marketing has the main responsibility for achieving profitable revenue growth and this is done by finding, keeping and growing the value of profitable customers.[34] Taking this perspective, marketing metrics must relate to finding customers (customer acquisition), keeping customers (consumer retention) and growing customer value (monetisation). This approach[35] connects marketing to essential business outcomes, customer acquisition to market share, customer retention to lifetime value and monetisation to customer/brand equity and shareholder value. We divide these marketing metrics into three dimensions: (1) counting-based (or activity) metrics;

(2) accounting-based (or operational) metrics; and (3) outcome (or forward-looking) metrics. All three dimensions may comprise both external and internal company metrics.

Counting-based metrics

Counting-based metrics include, for example, number of complaints, sales, headcounts, number of customers, number of orders and new hires. In principle, any internal and external factor that can be counted may serve as a counting-based metric. Even though counting-based metrics are usually relatively simple to obtain, they still may provide invaluable information to the firm, as evidenced by the model that former COO Len Schlesinger used to revitalise The Limited's brick and mortar shopping centre stores. Figure 22.2 shows how The Limited broke down store sales to motivate store personnel.

Since retail prices were centrally determined and because traffic to the store was largely determined by shopping centre characteristics and the store's position in the shopping centre, incentives concentrated on focusing store personnel on conversion percentages and units purchased by transaction (the two mauve boxes in Figure 22.2). By focusing on two metrics that could be related directly to future store sales, Schlesinger created – in turn – a link to future firm profits and shareholder value.

Accounting-based metrics

ROI and ROA

Most marketing research on company performance has relied on accounting-based ratio measures, such as return of investment (ROI) and return on assets (ROA).[36] The formula for calculating ROI is:

$$ROI(\%) = \frac{\text{net income before tax} \times 100}{\text{investment}}$$

ROI is usually calculated for a specific activity or campaign at a specific point in time. Consider a company that invests €1,500,000 on marketing a new product where the company expects to earn a net profit of €200,000 the first year. ROI can then be calculated as:

$$ROI(\%) = \frac{200,000 \times 100}{€1,500,000} = 13.3\%$$

The investment profitability rate of 13.3 per cent is here reported before taxes – but sometimes it is reported after taxes in comparing geographical areas where taxes vary substantially.[37]

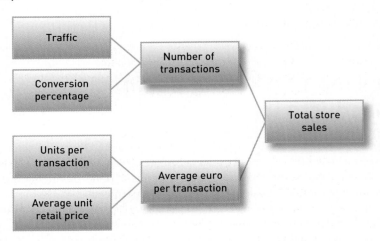

Figure 22.2 The Limited's model
Source: Adapted from J. A. Petersen, L. McAlister, D. J. Reibstein, R. S. Winer, V. Kumar, and G. Atkinson (2009) Choosing the right metrics to maximize profitability and shareholder value, *Journal of Retailing*, 85(1), 95–111.

The formula for calculating ROA is:

$$ROA(\%) = \frac{\text{net income before tax} \times 100}{\text{total assets}}$$

Total assets are the invested capital in the company, comprising both debt and equity. The major disadvantage of ROA is that the invested assets have multiple ways of being measured, including historical costs, book values, appraisal value market value and so on.[38] ROA tells how effectively the company converts invested capital into net income, usually before taxes. Thus if net income is €1,500,000 and assets are €10,000,000, the ROA(%) is 15 per cent. ROA can vary substantially across industries.

The ROI and ROA measures are both limited by two deficiencies.[39] First, the cost of capital is not considered. The company needs to set a standard for acceptable performance at a level above the company's cost of capital. If the cost of capital is 10 per cent, the estimated ROI or ROA must be higher to make the investment. Second, the measures may lead to potential dysfunctional decision making by unit managers. Some marketing managers acting in self-interest may choose to estimate ROI on the high side to get money for the project or on the low side to discourage undertaking a project.

Another limitation is that ROI and ROA do not fully measure impact. Studies by the advertising agency Young & Rubicam suggest that only one-third of a brand's impact is realised in current sales and operating earnings, while two-thirds of its influence is obtained via future financial performance. Thus, while ROI analyses may provide some insight into the short-term financial performance of marketing activities, they may capture only one-third of the total value creation of the marketing programme. Net present value (NPV) is a method that explicitly deals with the expected future cash flows as a result of company marketing activity.

NPV

Having €1000 in your hand today is better than having €1000 in five years from now. The reason is that over five years that €1000 that you have today would have a chance to grow by investing it. To calculate the net present value we discount the anticipated cash inflows with an acceptable discount rate.[40] NPV is the sum of all such discounted cash flows associated with a project.[41] NPV is calculated as:[42]

$$NPV = \sum_{t=0}^{n} \frac{C}{(1 + i)^t}$$

where

    t = the time of the cash flow
    n = the total time of the project
    i = the discount rate
    C_t = the net cash flow at time t

The discount rate is usually arrived at as a weighted average cost of capital. The company may also choose to use variable discount rates: for example, by using higher discount rates for riskier projects. Using an appropriate discount rate assures that the company only accepts projects where the expected cash flows add value to the company.

Outcome metrics

Marketing accountability also means that marketers must more precisely estimate the effects of different marketing investments. *Marketing-mix models* analyse data from a variety of sources, such as retailer scanner data, company shipment data, pricing, media and promotion spending data, to understand more precisely the effects of specific marketing activities.[43] To deepen understanding, marketers can conduct multivariate analyses to sort through how each marketing element influences marketing outcomes such as brand sales or market share.[44]

Advanced econometric modelling methods enable BrandScience to separate the effects of the different drivers and to isolate and quantify the contribution from marketing.

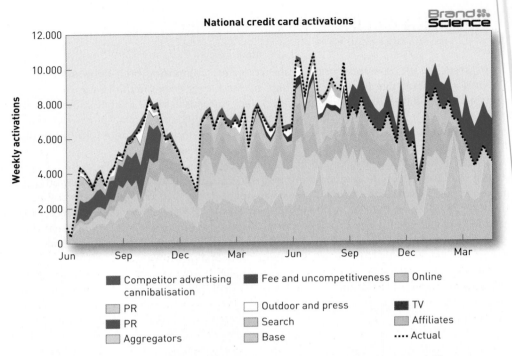

Figure 22.3 Sales decomposition – obtained through advanced econometric modelling
Source: Sales modelling carried out by BrandScience. Copyright © Omnicom Media Group. Reproduced with permission.

Figure 22.3 shows a sales decomposition conducted for a European financial services brand, where the weekly number of credit card activations has been modelled and the significant drivers and their changing influence over time identified.

The blue dotted line represents the actual number of activations that has been decomposed via econometric modelling. The light blue base is the 'worst case sales' if all marketing activities had not occurred. In the base the following effects have been aggregated in order to show the impact from marketing more clearly: the base line, seasonality, internal structural changes and increased brand awareness. At the end of the period, the uncompetitiveness (lack of competiveness) has prevented the company from realising the actual sales potential illustrated with the untapped dark blue area above the blue dotted *actual* line.

Seven outcome metrics – shareholder value, customer lifetime value, customer referral value, customer value added, brand equity measures and balanced scorecard are now described and discussed.

Shareholder value

Metric researcher Peter Doyle maintains that 'the real objective of marketing in the business enterprise is to develop and implement customer-led strategies that create shareholder value'.[45] **Shareholder value** is the value of the firm minus the future claims (future claims are also known as debts):

$$\text{Shareholder value} = \text{company value} - \text{debts}$$

where

$$\text{company value} = \text{present value of all future cash flows} + \text{value of non-operating assets}$$

Non-operating assets are assets that are not essential to the ongoing operations of a business, but may still generate income or provide a return on investment – for example, a company may own some property that generates a yearly income.[46] While the shareholder value can be used to estimate the value of the shareholders' stake in a company or business unit, it can also be used to formulate and evaluate marketing decisions.[47] Consider the following box.

Launching an advertising campaign for a French women's fragrance: the impact on shareholder value

The marketing department of a French producer of exclusive women's fragrances considers launching a €5 million advertising campaign in upmarket women's magazines such as *Elle* and *Vogue* in order to further promote its already popular series of fragrances.

The advertising campaign will run for five years with €1 million invested each year; the marketing department estimates that sales will increase by 5 per cent each year as a result. The company wants to estimate how the advertising campaign might affect the company's shareholder value. The calculations are shown in Table 22.2.

We assume an operating margin of 10 per cent. **Operating margin** is the ratio of operating profit divided by net sales. In year 1 the operating margin is obtained as: 10.5 (operating profits)/105 (sales) = 0.10. Since operating margin is 10 per cent, this means that operating costs are 90 per cent of sales – for example, in year 1: 94.5/105 = 0.90. Also, we assume that taxes are 25 per cent. Taxes are paid out of operating profits.

In Table 22.2 NOPAT is a company's after-tax operating profit. It is defined as follows:

$$NOPAT = \text{operating profits} \times (1 - \text{tax rate})$$

Following this definition, year 2 NOPAT is obtained as NOPAT = $11.0 \times (1 - 0.25) = 8.25$, which we round off to €8.3 million.

How will an advertising compaign for women's fragrance impact on shareholder value?
Source: Image courtesy of The Advertising Archives.

Table 22.2 Advertising campaign: calculating cash flow and shareholder value (€ million)

| | Year | | | | | |
	0	1	2	3	4	5
Sales	100.0	105.0	110.3	115.8	121.6	127.6
Operating costs	90.0	94.5	99.2	104.2	109.4	114.9
Operating profits	10.0	10.5	11.0	11.6	12.2	12.8
Tax (25%)	2.5	2.6	2.8	2.9	3.0	3.2
NOPAT	7.5	7.9	8.3	8.7	9.1	9.6
Advertising campaign		1.0	1.0	1.0	1.0	1.0
Cash flow		6.9	7.3	7.7	8.1	8.6
Discount factor (10%)		0.909	0.826	0.751	0.683	0.621
Net present value of cash flow		6.3	6.0	5.8	5.5	5.3
Cumulative net present value		6.3	12.3	18.1	23.6	28.9
Net present of value of cash flows after planning horizon						59.6
Value of company operation (including advertising campaign)						88.5
Initial shareholder value (before advertising campaign)						75.0
Shareholder value added from advertising campaign						13.5

The opportunity cost of capital is the return the capital could obtain if it was invested elsewhere in projects/activities of similar risk.[48] We estimate the opportunity cost of capital (the discount factor), i, to be 10 per cent. The *annual* discount factor is calculated as:

$$\text{Annual discount factor} = 1/(1+i)^t \quad \text{where } t = 1,2,\ldots \text{ is the year}$$

For example, the annual discount factor for year 3 ($t = 3$) is:

$$\text{Annual discount factor, year 3} = 1/(1+0.10)^3 = 0.751$$

By multiplying the year 3 cash flow, which is €7.7 million, by the year 3 annual discount factor, which is 0.751, we get €5.8 million (the net present value of cash flow in year 3). Similar calculations can be carried for years 1, 2, 4 and 5. NPV of cash flows during planning horizon is now obtained as the cumulative present value in year 5: €6.3 + €6.0 + €5.8 + €5.5 + €5.3 = €28.9 million.

In principle, cash flows for all future years beyond the planning period (year 6, year 7, year 8, etc.) should be estimated in a similar way in order for the value of the advertising campaign to be accurately determined. However, a short-cut approach is often used in practice.[49] Here the NPV of cash flows after the planning horizon is calculated by the standard perpetuity model, which is the year 5 NOPAT/i multiplied by the year 5 discount factor (= 0.621). Thus, the perpetuity method simply assumes that beyond the five-year planning period competition will drive down profits to a level such that new investments just earn the company's cost of capital.[50] The year 5 NOPAT is €9.6 million (Table 22.2) and the discount factor, i, is 10 per cent. Thus we can now calculate NPV of cash flows after planning horizon as 9.6/0.10 × 0.621 = €59.6 million.

Future cash flows have thus been divided into two time periods: those that occur during the planning horizon, and those that occur after the planning horizon. We add the cash flows from these two time periods and get the value of company operation: €28.9 + €59.6 = €88.5 million

The perpetuity method can also be used for calculating the initial shareholder value of the company. The company's initial shareholder value before the advertising campaign is €75 million. This is estimated by dividing the year 0 NOPAT (= €7.5 million) by the cost of capital: €7.5/0.10 = €75 million. The expected shareholder value added from the advertising campaign is then the 'value of company operation' (including advertising campaign) less the 'company's initial shareholder value': €88.5 − €75 = €13.5 million.

Taking a shareholder perspective may enhance the opportunity of making marketing recognised as a significant corporate value driver. Lukas, Whitwell and Doyle have emphasised five contributions of a shareholder value approach to marketing:[51]

1 **A shareholder value approach helps marketing properly define its objective.** To the extent that the governing business objective of a company is to maximise shareholder value, marketing should focus on contributing to this objective.

2 **A shareholder value approach provides the language for integrating marketing more effectively with the other functions of the company.** Shareholder value analysis is rooted in the discipline of finance, which is also the most common language in the boardroom. Unless marketing learns to speak this language, its influence will be limited.

3 **A shareholder value approach allows marketing to demonstrate the importance of its assets.** Many marketing assets are intangible (e.g. brand equity, customer loyalty). By relating these assets to shareholder value, marketing has the potential to increase its strategic influence in the company.

4 **A shareholder value approach protects marketing budgets from profit-maximisation policies.** Taking a shareholder value approach may prevent cuts in marketing budgets. Fundamentally, a shareholder approach is long term, with an explicit disdain for short-term solutions. Moreover, the shareholder approach emphasises that marketing assets should be considered as investments, which in turn emphasises that short-term, profit-driven marketing budgets may destroy rather than build company value.

5 **A shareholder value approach puts marketing in a pivotal role in the strategy formulation process.** Creating shareholder value is essential for creating a competitive advantage. Marketing provides the tools for creating such a competitive advantage.

The shareholder perspective should not be confused with the stakeholder perspective. The stakeholder perspective regards the purpose of a company as being to create value for all involved parties. Advocates say that this is even more likely to produce higher profits for the shareholders because the other parties will be more productive and better rewarded.

Customer lifetime value

As modern economies become predominantly service based, companies increasingly derive revenue from the creation and sustenance of long-term relationships with their customers. In such an environment, marketing serves the purpose of maximising customer lifetime value. The case for maximising long-term customer profitability is captured in the concept of customer lifetime value.[52] Customer lifetime value is rapidly gaining acceptance as a metric to acquire, grow and retain the 'right' customers in customer relationship management.[53]

ING Direct

The Dutch-owned global financial services group ING Direct appreciates that the customers are the most important asset to the business, along with its staff. ING Direct marketing intelligence function has a critical role in ensuring that product launches through to customer communications and customer service reflect what is known about those savers. 'It is an information-hungry business. There is a culture in which everyone from the CEO down is using information and doesn't make a decision without information to support it,' head of database marketing Ian Trudgett says. Understanding customer lifetime value is essential for ING Direct as it looks to extend its share of customers. Losing sight of the long-term customer value because of short-term opportunities is not something the company will be guilty of.[54]

The CLV approach assumes that customers who stay with a company for a long period generate more profits as compared with customers who only stay for a short period. It is more cost effective to deal with established customers whose needs and wants are known, and satisfied customers are also more likely to increase their purchases and to recommend the company to other customers. CLV can be seen as the series of transactions between a company and a customer over the period of time that the customer remains with the company.[55] CLV can be measured as the present value of the future net cash flows that are expected to be received over the lifetime of a customer, consisting of the revenue obtained from the customer less the cost of attracting, serving and satisfying the customer.[56] A key decision is what time horizon to use for estimating CLV. Typically, three to five years is reasonable.

The formula for estimating customer lifetime value is:

$$CLV = \sum_{t=0}^{T^*} \frac{(p_t - c_t)}{(1 + i)^t} - AC$$

where

p_t = price paid by a consumer at time t
c_t = direct cost of servicing the customer at time t
i = discount rate
t = expected lifetime of a customer
AC = acquisition cost

The formula can be applied for an individual customer and for segments of customers. CLV is a suitable metric for both business and consumer markets.

For example, a company may invest €10,000 in attracting a business customer. This acquisition cost (AC) consists of the costs associated with convincing a consumer to buy your product or service, including marketing, advertising costs, negotiating expenses in terms of human resources and travelling, conducting research and preparing various analyses on how to serve the customer in the best way, and so on. The customer stays with the company for three years, each year generating a €5,000 NOPAT to the company. The company estimates the opportunity cost of capital, i, to be 10 per cent. The annual discount factor for year 1 is calculated to be 0.909, for year 2 it is calculated to be 0.826, and for year 3 it is calculated to be 0.751. The lifetime value of the customer can now be calculated as

$$\text{CLV} = -10,000 + 5,000/1.10 + 5,000/1.10^2 + 5,000/1.10^3 = €2,434$$

We find the lifetime value of this customer to be €2,434. Since the lifetime value is larger than zero, this customer is expected to contribute positively to the value of the company.

It is useful for a company to find out what types of customer are the most profitable, how much it should spend on them and what product offerings should be made. The service and repair company Midas uses customer lifetime value as a tool for its direct marketing effort in several European countries. Midas tracks cars based on vehicle mileage and contacts customers to remind them of service and brake opportunities over the life of their vehicle.[57]

By comparing CLV with different types of customers, service activities and product offerings, the company can obtain highly useful knowledge and may also estimate **customer equity**. Customer equity (CE) is defined as the lifetime value of current and future customers.[58] CLV and CE focus on the long-term rather than the short-term profit or market share. Therefore, maximising CLV, and hence CE, is effectively maximising the long-term profitability and financial health of a company.[59]

Variations in customer lifetime value

Customers may vary dramatically in their overall value to a company. Niraj, Gupta and Narasimhan[60] studied the drivers of current customer profitability in a supply chain for a large distributor with a heterogeneous client base. They found that a small percentage of customers contribute to a large percentage of total profits, and that a substantial percentage (32 per cent of total) of customers are unprofitable.

An important question relating to CLV is whether shareholder value would benefit from changing the level of marketing investment in a certain customer. Spending too much on an individual customer, or a segment of customers, can have a damaging impact on shareholder value. Some bankers are known for lavish dinners or rounds of golf with VIPs, long-term customers who are probably unlikely to switch to another bank. On the other hand, insufficient spending can also decrease shareholder value because an underserved customer may defect to a competitor or reduce spending volume.[61]

Companies wanting to take advantage of the CLV measurement should build individual-level customer databases. Without such data, true longitudinal data analysis of customers' behavioural responses to marketing actions – and related costs – cannot be implemented.[62]

Customer referral value

Marketing researcher Frederick F. Reichheld proposes that the key to business growth lies in the positive word of mouth (WOM) of a firm's customers.[63] When a customer defects from a firm, the lost value stemming from that customer is not only a function of lost purchases, but also a function of the lost WOM the customer spread about the product, causing losses of potential future sales. Marketing research results even suggest that customers who are acquired via WOM are significantly more profitable in the long term than customers who are acquired via advertising and promotion.[64] For instance, it has been suggested that customers who are acquired using costly, but short-term marketing advertisements and promotions may provide fewer than half the future profits of customers acquired using cheap, but long-term investments in word-of-mouth marketing.[65] The emergence of social media, which facilitate WOM, underlines the importance of understanding customer referral value. Indeed, tracking approximately 10,000 customers of a leading German bank for almost three years, Schmitt, Skiera and Van den Bulte recently found that referred customers have a higher contribution margin, though this difference erodes over time; have a higher retention rate, and this difference persists over time; and are more valuable in both the short and the long run.[66] Notably, customers with a high CLV may not be the same as customers with a high customer referral value (CRV), making it especially important to know which customers are spreading word of mouth. Managers therefore need to have separate metrics to measure the value of their customers according to their referral behaviour (CRV) or their own transaction behaviour (CLV), although a positive relationship between the two measures is likely. High CLV customers are typically more attached to and involved with the firm than low CLV customers, and are therefore more likely to involve other customers actively when making referrals. Hence, prospects receiving referrals from high-CLV customers are more likely influenced by these referrals. In addition, highly satisfied customers have higher CLVs and also refer other customers more frequently.[67]

While several different measures of customer's CRV have been proposed (see V. Kumar and colleagues[68] for a review), we here illustrate with the following CRV-formula proposed by Cornelsen, which quantifies the annual referral value of customer X:[69]

$$RV_X = \left[\sum_{i=1}^{n} (Pj^* wj) \right]_X * OL_X * CS_X * RR_Z$$

where

RV_X = referral value of customer X
P_j = number of referral communications in social sphere j
W_j = weighting index of communication intensities within social sphere j
OL_X = opinion leader index of customer X
CS_X = customer satisfaction index of customer X
RR_Z = industry-specific referral volume (average purchase volume × net average referral rate)

The formula builds on the distinction between two main elements of referral value as displayed in Figure 22.4:

- an industry-specific average referral volume; and
- the individual customer's referral potential.

Consider a car-dealer in the upper price segment who wishes to determine CRV. In order to specify industry-specific referral volume RR_z the car-dealer needs to estimate both annual purchase volume per customer and net average referral rate. If we assume that customers on average purchase a new car every fifth year and that the average cost price is €35,000 then annual average purchase volume amounts to €7,000. Average net referral rate is calculated using a separate customer survey (see Chapter 6) that focuses on different information sources and their influence on the customer buying decision. For example, the car-dealer may discover that referrals explain 21 per cent of a purchase decision, meaning that the average referral rate is 21 per cent and that other information sources account for 79 per cent of the purchase decision. From the conducted survey, it is known that the annual average number of people a customer talks to concerning cars is 11. This means that a single

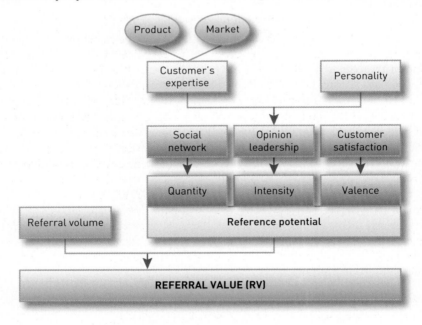

Figure 22.4 The determinant model of referral value
Source: Adapted from S. Helm (2003) Calculating the value of customers' referrals, *Managing Service Quality*, 13(2), 126.

referral influences 0.21/11 = 1.91 per cent of the decision to buy a new car. RR_z can now be calculated as €7,000 × 0.0191 = €133.70.

Opinion leadership (OL) for each of the car dealer's customers is also measured by the customer survey using each respondent's answers to a range of statements, which in turn is summarised into an index. For example, the following three statements can be used to measure opinion leadership concerning cars:[70] (1) my friends or neighbours often come to me for advice about cars; (2) I sometimes influence what car my friends buy; and (3) people come to me more often than I go to them for information about car brands. If a six-point Likert scale (1 = strongly disagree; 6 = strongly agree) is utilised for each of the statements, the maximum OL score would be 3 × 6 = 18. This means that if customer X has an OL score of 12 the OL-index for this customer results in 12/18 = 0.67.

P_j denotes the number of referral communications that customer X carries out in her/his social sphere per year. For customer X we assume that the total number of referral communications is 50, which for this customer divides into classes of social spheres in the following way: family members and relatives (25), friends (15) and work colleagues (10). Obviously, not all these communications may involve cars and therefore we multiply P_j by a weighting factor W_j, which we obtain in the survey by asking how often customer X's referral communications involve cars. For each of the three classes of social spheres, we use a five-point frequency scale ranging from 1 (= never) to 5 (= very often), where 'never' (= 1 on the scale) is given a weighting factor of 0, 'rarely (= 2 on the scale) is given weighting factor 0.25, 'sometimes' (= 3 on the scale) is given weighting factor 0.50, 'often' (= 4 on the scale) is given weighting factor 0.75, and 'very often' (= 5 on the scale) is given weighting factor 1.00. If customer X 'never' talks to work colleagues about cars, but talks about cars to family members and relatives 'sometimes' and to friends 'rarely', the total 'social network' index score (Σ (P_j × W_j)) would be (10 × 0 + 25 × 0.50 + 15 × 0.25) = 16.25.

In the survey, we measure the degree of customer satisfaction (CS) on a four-point scale (ranging from 1 = 'very satisfied' with weighting factor +2; to 2 = 'very dissatisfied' with weighting factor −2). We assume that customer X is 'satisfied', resulting in a weighting factor of +1. The annual referral value of customer X can now be calculated as:

$$CRV = 16.25 \times 0.67 \times 1 \times 133.70 = €1,455.66$$

We find the referral value of this customer to be €1,456. Since the customer referral value is larger than zero, the referrals of this customer are expected to contribute positively to the value of the company. The overall value of customer X is €8,456, meaning that the referral value represents about 17 per cent of the customer's total annual value. It should be noted that the CRV measurement reviewed here is only indicative of the referral value of a customer. First, in addition to the variables included in the CRV formula, other variables – such as involvement and perceived risk – may also influence customer referral value. Second, if a 'true' referral value were to be measured, the model would need to be more complicated. For example, the effects of customers' referrals should also take into account 'spin-off referrals' (i.e. referrals addressed to persons who do not consider buying a product themselves, but who refer to others). Third, the variables included in the formula may be subject to measurement errors. Fourth, managers should carefully consider the weighting of the variables. For example, in some cases dissatisfaction may be weighted more intense than satisfaction.[71] This being said, one of the clear strengths of the method is that it brings into the open one of marketing's most brilliant treasures: the value of positive customer WOM.

Customer value added

Metrics researchers Sexton, Sen and Cogitaas suggest that customer value added should be regarded as a key metric for indicating marketing financial performance. Customer value added (CVA®) is calculated as:

$$CVA® = \text{perceived value} - \text{incremental unit cost for a product or service}$$

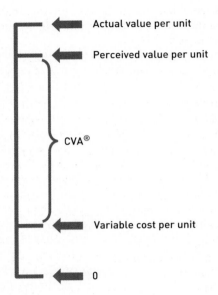

Figure 22.5 Customer value added
Source: Adapted from D. E. Sexton (2009) How Marketing Affects Shareholding Value, reprinted by permission of The Arrow Group Ltd, in the book *Value Above Cost*, Harlow: Pearson Education, 13.

where

perceived value = the maximum a customer is willing to pay for a product or service

When CVA® is high, the company is perceived to add a net value to society and will probably show strong financial performance. When CVA® is low, the perceived contribution to society and financial performance will be less strong. At the extreme, when CVA® is negative (perceived value is lower than the unit cost), the company can hardly sustain in the long term (Figure 22.5).

When calculating CVA®, costs need to be expressed as the incremental cost per unit, i.e. the variable cost. Because average costs take account of fixed costs, variable costs are typically lower than average costs. Since a customer rarely knows all the value a product or service provides, perceived customer value is usually lower than actual value. All marketing decisions, including design, targeting, communications, pricing and distribution, may influence consumers' perceived value.

While perceived value predicts revenue, CVA® predicts contribution. A large multinational FMCG detected strong associations between the perceived values and the future annual revenues of two major brands (toilet soaps and skin creams) in a key market.[72] Being calculated as the difference between perceived value per unit and cost per unit, CVA® rewards companies that successfully measure, monitor and manage both customer value and costs.

Brand equity and financial performance

Brand equity is probably the most prized measure for many companies of the value of the marketing asset.[73] We conceptualise brand equity as 'the added value endowed to products and services' by the brand name. This value may be reflected in how consumers think, feel and act with respect to the brand. Brand equity is an important intangible asset that has psychological and financial value to the company. Positive equity is likely to be associated with behaviour that benefits the brand through purchase frequency, brand loyalty, price insensitivity and willingness to recommend.[74]

There are two primary perspectives related to brand equity, one based on financial outcomes for the company and the other on softer, consumer-based perceptions of company performance. Most studies have focused on the consumer-based perspective. Also, much of the data necessary to test the financially based brand equity perspective are confidential and not available to marketing researchers.[75]

In the consumer-based brand equity (CBBE) perspective, the power of a brand lies in what customers have learned, thought, felt, seen and heard about the brand as a result of their experiences over time.[76]

There is a direct and an indirect approach to measure CBBE. The indirect approach requires measuring potential sources of brand equity by identifying and tracking consumer brand knowledge structures. The direct approach requires experiments in which one group of customers responds to an element in the marketing programme when it is attributed to the brand, and another group of customers responds to the same element when it is attributed to a fictitiously named or unnamed version of the product or service. 'Blind tests' constitute an example of the direct approach.[77] The indirect approach is concerned with detecting the causes of brand equity, whereas the direct approach is concerned with assessing the added value of the brand.

Examples of operationalising direct measures include price premiums for brand switching and purchase intention, while examples of indirect measures include unaided and aided recall (awareness), familiarity, brand image favourability and rating of beliefs of associations (brand image strength). No single concept or dimension can be applied for measuring CBBE since it is a multidimensional construct.

One view suggests that brand equity arises from the strength and favourability of the two components of consumer-based brand knowledge structures: brand awareness and brand image. Brand awareness relates to the strength of a brand in memory, and the likelihood and ease with which the brand will be recognised or recalled under various conditions. Brand image is defined as 'perceptions about the brand as reflected by the brand associations held in consumer memory'.[78] Netemeyer and his colleagues[79] found that in the fast-food industry the dimensions 'perceived brand quality' and 'perceived brand value for the cost' (these dimensions were collapsed into one dimension) and brand uniqueness are highly relevant in predicting customer-based brand equity.

Brand equity was operationalised (measured) as the willingness to pay a price premium for a brand. This operationalisation included four measurement items:

1 The price of (brand name) would have to go up quite a bit before I would switch to another brand of (product).

2 I am willing to pay a higher price for the (brand name) brand of (product) than for other brands of (product).

3 I am willing to pay X per cent more for the (brand name) brand over other brands of (product): 0 per cent, 5 per cent, 10 per cent, 15 per cent, 20 per cent, 25 per cent, 30 per cent, or more.

4 I am willing to pay a lot more for the (brand name) than for other brands of (product).

Items were measured on seven-point 'strongly disagree' to 'strongly agree' scales.

Higher levels of brand awareness and positive brand image are thought to increase the probability of brand choice, as well as produce greater customer loyalty and decrease vulnerability to marketing actions.[80] Some researchers have suggested that brand equity measures should also rely on market-based, objective measures because consumer attitude and preference measures are inherently subjective. Silverman, Sprott and Pascal[81] have explored the relationship between customer-based and financial/market-based brand equity measurements. They found only small, but positive, relationships between brand awareness – assessed by familiarity, usage and favourability – and market-based outcomes of brand value – measured by annual sales and Financial World brand ratings (see www.financialworld.co.uk).

Advertising agency Young & Rubicam has developed a model of brand equity called brand asset valuator (BAV), which can be accessed on its website : www.yrbav.com. BAV measures brand value by applying four broad factors:[82] (1) differentiation (the ability of a brand to stand apart from its competitors); (2) relevance (consumers' actual and perceived importance of the brand); (3) esteem (consumers' perceived brand quality together with their assessment of the popularity of the brand); and (4) knowledge (consumers' brand awareness together with their understanding of the brand's identity).

Young & Rubicam[83] has investigated to what extent BAV contributes to a company's financial performance.[84] Using unanticipated change in stock price as the dependent variable (i.e. financial measure), the relative contribution of individual brand components to changes in stock price was explored. The results revealed that energised brand strength (a combination of energy, differentiation and relevance) demonstrates a significant relationship with market value. BAV's energised brand strength was found to be 81 per cent as effective as sales growth in explaining changes in market value.

The balanced scorecard approach

Kaplan and Norton developed and advocated a balanced scorecard approach (BSC) on the grounds that purely financial metrics may tell the wrong story about a company. Consider the following racing car metaphor offered by Andra Gumbus.[85]

The need for both financial and non-financial metrics

Organisations that focus solely on financial measures can be compared to a racing car driver who only monitors his or her speed during a race. Suppose you are a driver in Formula 1 and are monitoring your car by looking at the RPM (revolutions [of the engine] per minute) gauge on your dashboard. You are not noticing the MPG (miles per gallon of fuel), nor the MPH (miles per hour, or speed your car is travelling), nor the temperature gauge. You might win the race, but you are putting yourself and your car at risk by not monitoring *all* the gauges while focusing exclusively on the RPM dial. You might run out of fuel, overheat the engine, crash into another car and make other errors in navigating the course.

Installing BSC in a company requires active participation from top management and sustaining the practice over time.[86] BSC provides a systematic tool that combines financial and non-financial performance metrics in one coherent measurement system. Metrics are constructed according to a predefined strategy, and the company's processes are aligned towards this strategy. BSC systematically measures the company in four areas:[87]

1 The *financial perspective* uses traditional accounting measures in order to evaluate a firm's short-term financial results. Metrics include ROI, cash-flow analyses and return on equity.

2 The *customer perspective* measures relate to customer satisfaction of identified target groups and is generally marketing focused. Metrics include delivery performance to customers, customer satisfaction rate and customer retention.

3 The *internal business process perspective* is based on the concept of the (firm-internal) value chain, including the process (or steps) needed to realise the intended product or service. Metrics include opportunity success rates, number of activities and defect rates.

4 The final dimension comprises the *innovation and learning perspective* that is inherent in a company by measuring various human resources-focused effects as well as learning systems support effectiveness. Metrics include illness rate, internal promotions in per cent and employee turnover.

By combining these four measures, Kaplan and Norton establish the BSC as a representation of a company's shared vision (see Figure 22.6).

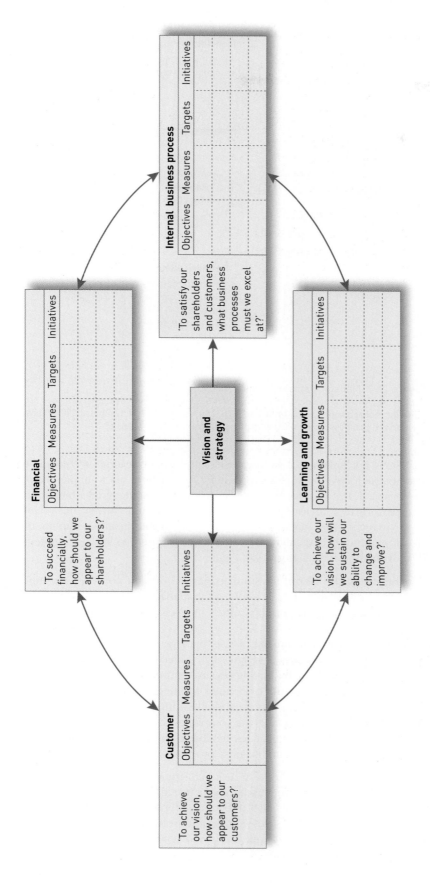

Figure 22.6 Translating vision and strategy: four perspectives

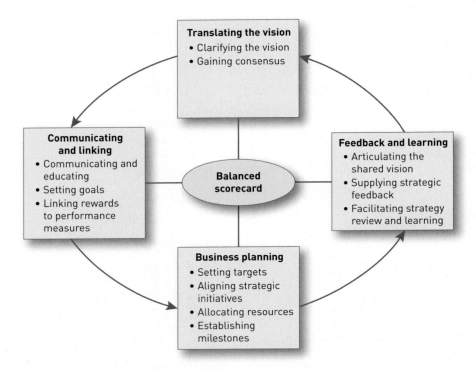

Figure 22.7 Managing strategy: four processes
Source: Reprinted by permission of *Harvard Business Review*. From Using the balanced scorecard as a strategic management system by Kaplan, R. S. and Norton, D. P., July–August 2007. Copyright © 2007 by the Harvard Business School Publishing Corporation; all rights reserved.

BSC is not only a tool for measurement, but also a tool for strategic management.[88] It has not been developed to serve strategy formulation, but to implement strategy. BSC can be regarded as a tool for translating a company's strategy into measurable goals, actions and performance measures. According to Kaplan and Norton, the set of measures gives top managers a fast but comprehensive view of the business. Kaplan and Norton[89] have developed four management processes that contribute to linking long-term strategic objectives with short-term actions (see Figure 22.7).

1 **Translating the vision**: assists managers to build a consensus around the company's vision and strategy. For example, a top management vision that the company wants to be the 'number-one supplier' offers by itself little guidance on how to operationalise that vision.
2 **Communicating and linking**: assists managers to communicate their strategy up and down the organisation and link it to objectives at the departmental and individual level – for example, by linking rewards to performance measures.
3 **Business planning**: assists companies to integrate their business and financial plans – for example, by setting targets and allocating sufficient resources.
4 **Feedback and learning**: enables companies to achieve strategic learning. The feedback and learning process facilitates feedback on all four perspectives (financial performance, customers, internal business processes, and learning and growth).

Accounting professor Erkki K. Laitinen argues that it is difficult to identify the relative importance of and the trade-offs between the suggested four perspectives of the approach.[90] Moreover, it is also difficult to identify the links between financial and non-financial performance measures. Kaplan and Norton acknowledge this criticism to a certain degree when stating that 'accumulating sufficient data to document significant correlations and causation among balanced scorecard measures can take a long time – months or years'.[91] Such data may enable a company to establish correlations between the various measures from the four perspectives.

Corporate social responsibility

As discussed in Chapter 21, although the meaning of **corporate social responsibility** (CSR) can be very broad, the concept can be described as enterprises' contribution to sustainable development. Companies may wish to report their CSR initiatives according to the global reporting framework issued by the Global Reporting Initiative (GRI).

The Global Reporting Initiative

CSR reporting measures an organisation's economic, social and environmental performance and impacts. The measurement of CSR's three dimensions is commonly called the triple bottom line (TBL).[92] The Global Reporting Initiative (GRI) is a network-based organisation that pioneered what is now the internationally accepted standard for TBL reporting. GRI's Reporting Framework is developed through a consensus-seeking, multi-stakeholder process. Participants are drawn from global business, civil society, labour, academic and professional institutions. The Sustainability Reporting Framework consists of the Sustainability Reporting Guidelines, Sector Supplements and the Technical Protocol – Applying the Report Content Principles. The framework is applicable to organisations of any size or type, from any sector or geographic region, and has been used by thousands of organisations worldwide as the basis for producing their sustainability reports.

A Swedish study reveals that CSR activities only have small direct effects on company profitability. However, the study also finds that while financial markets do not always react to *positive* CSR performance news, they react relatively strongly and negatively to *negative* news about companies' CSR efforts.[93] Consistent with this finding, many companies primarily use various CSR initiatives (such as reducing greenhouse gases, engaging in welfare work, and improving ethical regulations) to build and strengthen *relationships* with multiple stakeholder groups, including not only customers, suppliers, channel members and competitors, but also shareholders, employees, society, regulators, media and financial markets.[94] For instance, Puma CEO Jochen Zeitz points out that many shareholders are 'beginning to ask companies to behave in even more sustainable ways'.[95]

In that respect, marketing metric researchers Priya Raghubir, John Roberts, Katherine N. Lemon and Russell S. Winer have recently developed a stakeholder utility model, which is also useful in determining how stakeholders might evaluate the outcome of company CSR activity:

$$U_{ij} = \sum_k w_{ik} \times y_{ijk}$$

where
  y_{ijk} denotes how stakeholder i evaluates the outcome of CSR activity j on a range of relevant dimensions k
  w_{ik} denotes the weight that stakeholder i assign to each CSR dimension
  U_{ij} determines the utility (or disutility) to be gained from the activity from stakeholder i's perspective.

Time can also be incorporated into the calculation, since in the formula determining U_j, y_{ijk} may be calculated as:

$$y_{ijk} = \sum_1^T \frac{y_{ijkt}}{(1 + r_{ik})^t}$$

where r_{ik} is the discount rate (which may be specific to individual stakeholder i). This takes into account that net benefits (or net costs) of the outcome on dimension k may accrue over time. The impact on total public welfare, U_j, is given by the sum of each stakeholder's utility, weighted by the strength of the claim of that stakeholder (λ):

$$U_j = \sum_i \lambda_i \times U_{ij} = \sum_i \lambda_i \sum_k w_{ik} \times y_{ijk}$$

As can be seen, the model uses a standard multi-attribute utility calculation to determine stakeholder utility. The reader is referred to Chapter 7 for a further illustration and discussion of this type of model.

Marketing dashboards

Firms are also employing organisational processes and systems to make sure they maximise the value of all the different metrics. Management can assemble a summary set of relevant internal and external measures in a *marketing dashboard* for synthesis and interpretation. Marketing dashboards are like the instrument panel in a car or plane, visually displaying real-time indicators to ensure proper functioning. They are only as good as the information on which they are based, but sophisticated visualisation tools are helping bring data alive to improve understanding and analysis.[96]

Some companies are also appointing marketing controllers to review budget items and expenses. Increasingly, these controllers are using business intelligence software to create digital versions of marketing dashboards that aggregate data from disparate internal and external sources.

As input to the marketing dashboard, companies should include two key market-based scorecards that reflect performance and provide possible early warning signals.

1 A **customer-performance scorecard** records how well the company is doing year after year on such customer-based measures as those shown in Table 22.3. Management should set norms for each measure and take action when results get out of bounds.

2 A **stakeholder-performance scorecard** tracks the satisfaction of various constituencies who have a critical interest in and impact on the company's performance: employees, suppliers, banks, distributors, retailers and stockholders. Again, management should take action when one or more groups register increased or above-norm levels of dissatisfaction.[97]

Table 22.3 Sample customer-performance scorecard measures

- percentage of new customers to average number of customers;
- percentage of lost customers to average number of customers;
- percentage of win-back customers to average number of customers;
- percentage of customers falling into very dissatisfied, dissatisfied, neutral, satisfied and very satisfied categories;
- percentage of customers who say they would repurchase the product;
- percentage of customers who say they would recommend the product to others;
- percentage of target market customers who have brand awareness or recall;
- percentage of customers who say that the company's product is the most preferred in its category;
- percentage of customers who correctly identify the brand's intended positioning and differentiation;
- average perception of the company's product quality relative to chief competitor;
- average perception of the company's service quality relative to chief competitor.

Some executives worry that they will miss the big picture if they focus too much on a set of numbers on a dashboard. Others are concerned about privacy and the pressure that the technique places on employees. But most experts feel the rewards offset the risks.[98] The marketing insight box provides practical advice about the development of these marketing tools.

Marketing insight

Marketing dashboards to improve effectiveness and efficiency

Marketing consultant Pat LaPointe sees marketing dashboards as providing all the up-to-the-minute information necessary to run the business operations for a company – such as sales versus forecast, distribution channel effectiveness, brand equity evolution and human capital development. According to LaPointe, an effective dashboard will focus thinking, improve internal communications and reveal where marketing investments are paying off and where they are not.

LaPointe observes four common measurement 'pathways' that marketers are pursuing today (see Figure 22.8):

1 The customer metrics pathway looks at how prospects become customers, from awareness to preference to trial to repeat purchase. Many companies track progression through a 'hierarchy of effects' model to follow the evolution of broad market potential to specific revenue opportunities.

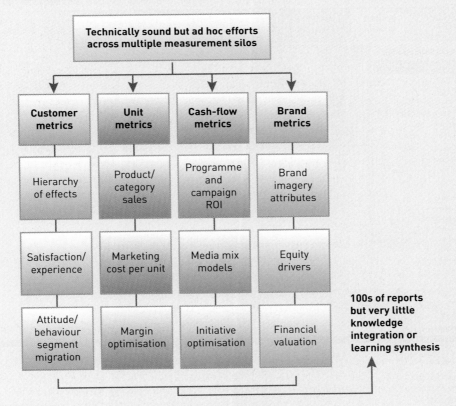

Figure 22.8 Marketing measurement pathways

Source: Adapted from D. Schultz (2005) Chapter 13 in P. Kotler and A. Tybout (ed.) *Kellog on Branding: The Marketing Faculty of the Kellog school of Management*, New York: John Wiley & Sons. Copyright © 2005 John Wiley & Sons, Inc. Reproduced with permission.

2 The unit metrics pathway reflects what marketers know about sales of product/service units – how much is sold by product line and/or by geography; the marketing cost per unit sold as an efficiency yardstick; and where and how margin is optimised in terms of characteristics of the product line or distribution channel.

3 The cash-flow metrics pathway focuses on how well marketing expenditures are achieving short-term returns. Programme and campaign ROI models measure the immediate impact or net present value of profits expected from a given investment.

4 The brand metrics pathway tracks the development of the longer-term impact of marketing through brand equity measures that assess both the perceptual health of the brand from customer and prospective customer perspectives as well as the overall financial health of the brand.

LaPointe emphasises that a marketing dashboard can present insights from all the pathways in a graphically related view that helps management see subtle links between them. A well-constructed dashboard can have a series of 'tabs' that allow the user to toggle easily between different 'families' of metrics organised by customer, product, brand, experience, channels, efficiency, organisational development and macroenvironmental factors. Each tab presents the three or four most insightful metrics, with data filtered by business unit, geography or customer segment based upon the user's needs (see Figure 22.9 for an example).

Ideally, the number of metrics presented in the marketing dashboard would be reduced to a handful of key drivers over time. Importantly, the process of developing and refining the marketing dashboard will undoubtedly raise and resolve many key questions about the business.

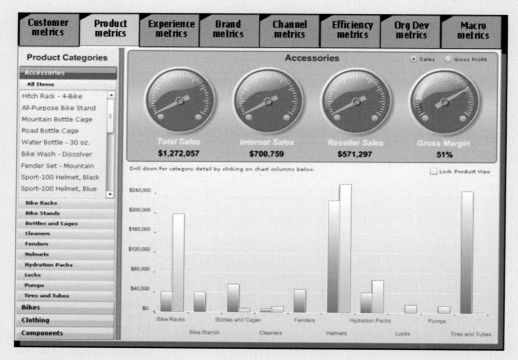

Figure 22.9 The marketing dashboard

Source: Adapted from P. LaPointe (2005) *Marketing by the Dashboard Light – How to Get More Insight, Foresight, and Accountability from Your Marketing Investments.* Copyright © 2005 Patrick LaPointe. Reproduced with permission.

SUMMARY

1 Marketers must be able to justify marketing expenditures to company management. Marketing metrics is the set of measures that helps firms to quantify, compare and interpret their marketing performance.

2 Good marketing metrics are financial, forward-looking and capture both short-term and long-term effects.

3 Marketing performance and productivity is multi-dimensional and therefore different metrics should be seen as complements rather than substitutes. Marketing has the main responsibility for achieving profitable revenue growth and this is done by finding, keeping and growing the value of profitable customers.

4 Marketing metrics are divided into three dimensions: (1) counting-based (or activity) metrics; (2) accounting-based (or operational) metrics; and (3) outcome metrics. All three dimensions comprise both external and internal metrics.

5 While ROI analyses may provide some insight into the financial performance of marketing activities, they may at the same time capture only one-third of the total value creation of the marketing programme. Net present value is a method that explicitly deals with the expected future cash flows as a result of company marketing activity.

6 Marketing should develop and implement customer-led strategies that create shareholder value. Taking a shareholder perspective enhances the opportunity of making marketing recognised as a significant corporate value driver.

7 Customer lifetime value is the net profit or loss to a company from a customer flowing from the lifetime of that customer's transactions with the company. CLV assumes that customers who stay with a company for a long period of time generate more profits than customers who stay for only a short period of time.

8 Customer referral value (CRV) seeks to quantify the value of the referrals that each customer gives to the firm.

9 Customer value added (CVA®) rewards companies that successfully measure, monitor and manage both customer value and costs. When CVA® is high, the company is perceived to add a net value to society and will probably show strong financial performance. When CVA® is low, the perceived contribution to society and financial performance will be less strong.

10 There are two primary perspectives related to brand equity, one based on financial outcomes for the company and one based on softer, consumer-based perceptions of company performance. Marketing performance during a period will be judged by whether brand equity has risen, is static, or has declined.

11 The balanced scorecard approach provides a systematic tool that combines financial and non-financial performance metrics in one coherent measurement system. Metrics are constructed according to a pre-defined strategy, and the company's processes are aligned towards this strategy. BSC systematically measures the company from four perspectives: the financial perspective, the customer perspective, the internal business process perspective, and the innovation and learning perspective.

12 CSR reporting measures an organisation's economic, social and environmental performance and impacts. The measurement of CSR's three dimensions is commonly called the triple bottom line (TBL).

13 A marketing dashboard provides up-to-the-minute information necessary to run the business operations for a company – such as sales versus forecast, distribution channel effectiveness, brand equity evolution and human capital development.

APPLICATIONS

Marketing debate

Take a position: For any marketing activity there should be an established link between the activity and its measurement in terms of cash flow, ROI, effect on shareholder value, and so on. Otherwise that activity should not be carried out *versus* Marketing activities are often based on feelings, experiences, and so on, which are difficult to quantify.

Therefore the outcome of a marketing activity need not be measurable for the marketing activity to be carried out.

Marketing discussion

What marketing activities need to be measured? Why? Which ones do not? What metrics should be used in relation to what companies and in relation to what activities?

REFERENCES

1 Based on dialogue with BrandScience; www.brandsciencenetwork.com.

2 J. McManus (2004) Stumbling into intelligence, *American Demographics*, April, 22–5.

3 L. Patterson (2007) MP 'classic truths': if you don't measure, you can't manage – the best metrics for managing marketing performance, *MarketingProfs*, 23 October.

4 S. H. Seggie, E. Cavusgil and S. E. Phelan (2007) Measurement of return on marketing investment: a conceptual framework and the future of marketing metrics, *Industrial Marketing Management*, 36, 834–41.

5 J. A. Petersen, L. McAlister, D. J. Reibstein, R. S. Winter, V. Kumar and G. Atkinson (2009) Choosing the right metrics to maximize profitability and shareholder value, *Journal of Retailing*, 85(1), 95–111.

6 K. V. Beaman, G. R. Guy and D. E. Sexton (2008) Managing and measuring return on marketing investment, Conference Board Research Report R-1435-08-RR.

7 Report: marketers place priority on nurturing existing customers, http://directmag.com/roi/0301-customer-satisfaction-retention.

8 www.factortg.com/ideas/CMO_MPM_Audit__cmo.pdf.

9 Seggie et al. (2007) op. cit.; Petersen et al. (2009) op. cit.

10 M. Uncles (2005) Marketing metrics: a can of worms or the path to enlightenment?, editorial to *Brand Management*, 12(6), 412–18.

11 T. Ambler, F. Kokkinaki and S. Puntoni (2004) Assessing marketing performance: reasons for metric selection, *Journal of Marketing Management*, 29(3/4), 475–98; P. Barwise and J. U. Farley (2004) Marketing metrics: status of six metrics in five countries, *European Management Journal*, 22(3), 257–62; Seggie et al. (2007) op. cit.

12 Barwise and Farley (2004) op. cit.

13 Marketing metrics: where to get them? Which ones work?, *Advertising and Marketing Review*, www.ad-mkt-review.com/public_html/docs/fs059.html.

14 Seggie et al. (2007) op. cit.

15 R. T. Rust, T. Ambler, G. S. Carpenter, V. Kumar and R. K. Srivastava (2004) Measuring marketing productivity: current knowledge and future directions, *Journal of Marketing*, 68 (October), 76–89.

16 AMI (2004) 'What value marketing? A position paper on marketing metrics in Australia', Australian Marketing Institute, Sydney, 1, available at www.ami.org.au.

17 P. Doyle (2001) Shareholder-value-based brand strategies, *Brand Management*, 9(1), 20–30.

18 T. Ambler (2003) *Marketing and the Bottom Line: The New Methods of Corporate Wealth*, 2nd edn, Harlow: Pearson Education.

19 K. L. Ailawadi, D. R. Lehmann and S. A. Neslin (2003) Revenue premium as an outcome measure of brand equity, *Journal of Marketing*, 67 (October), 1–17.

20 S. Baker (2006) Wiser about the web, *BusinessWeek*, 27 March, 53–7.

21 Ambler (2003) op. cit.

22 T. Ambler, P. Barwise and C. Higson (2001) *Market Metrics: What Should We Tell the Shareholders?*, Institute of Chartered Accountants in England and Wales, Centre for Business Performance, London; Barwise and Farley (2004) op. cit.

23 Rust et al. (2004) op. cit.

24 Ibid.

25 Ibid.

26 Patterson (2007) op. cit.

27 Ambler (2003) op. cit.

28 Barwise and Farley (2004) op. cit.

29 V. A. Zeithaml, R. N. Bolton, J. Deighton, T. L. Keiningham, K. N. Lemon and J. A. Petersen (2006) Forward-looking focus can firms have adaptive foresight?, *Journal of Service Research*, 9(2), 168–83.

30 Ibid.

31 Petersen et al. op. cit.

32 V. Kumar, J. A. Petersen and R. P. Leone (2010) Driving profitability by encouraging customer referrals: who, when, and how, *Journal of Marketing*, 74, 1–17.

33 Barwise and Farley (2004) op. cit.

34 P. Kotler (1999) *Kotler on Marketing: How to Create, Win, and Dominate Markets*, New York: Free Press.

35 L. Patterson (2007) Case study: taking on the metrics challenge, *Journal of Targeting, Measurement and Analysis for Marketing*, 15(4), 270–6.

36 E. W. Anderson, C. Fornell and S. K. Mazvancheryl (2004) Customer satisfaction and shareholder value, *Journal of Marketing*, 68, 172–85.

37 http://en.wikipedia.org/wiki/Return_on_investment.

38 R. D. Dillon and J. E. Owers (1997) EVA® as a financial metric: attributes, utilization, and relationship to NPV, *Financial Practice and Education*, Spring/Summer, 32–40.

39 Ibid.

40 http://moneyterms.co.uk/discount-rate/.

41 www.smartcapitalist.com/blog_36.shtml.

42 http://en.wikipedia.org/wiki/Net_present_value.

43 G. J. Tellis (2006) Modeling marketing mix, in R. Grover and M. Vriens (eds), *Handbook of Marketing Research*, Thousand Oaks, CA: Sage.

44 J. Neff (2004) P&G, Clorox rediscover modeling, *Advertising Age*, 29 March, 10.

45 P. Doyle (2000) Valuing marketing's contribution, *European Management Journal*, 18(3), 233–45.

46 www.investopedia.com/terms/n/nonoperatingasset.asp.

47 S. Cooper and M. Davies (2004) Measuring shareholder value: the metrics, in *Maximising Shareholder Value Achieving Clarity in Decision-making*, CIMA Technical Report, London: Chartered Institute of Management Accountants, November, 10–15.

48 Doyle (2000) op. cit.

49 Cooper and Davies (2004) op. cit.

50 Doyle (2000) op. cit.

51 B. A. Lukas, G. J. Whitwell and P. Doyle (2005) How can a shareholder value approach improve marketing's strategic influence?, *Journal of Business Research*, 58(4), 414–22.

52 S. Gupta, D. Hanssens, B. Hardie, W. Kahn, V. Kumar, N. Lin and N. R. S. Srinam (2006) Modeling customer lifetime value, *Journal of Service Research*, 19(2), 139–55.

53 R. Venkatesan and V. Kumar (2004) A customer lifetime value framework for customer selection and resource allocation strategy, *Journal of Marketing*, 68, 106–25.

54 Based on D. Reed (2011) Customers come first, especially when the time is right, *Marketing Week*, www.marketingweek.co.uk/

disciplines/data-strategy/customers-come-first-especially-when-the-time-is-right/3019370.article.

[55]D. Jain and S. S. Singh (2002) Customer lifetime value research in marketing: a review and future directions, *Journal of Interactive Research*, 16(4), 34–46.

[56]R. H. Chenhall and K. Langfield-Smith (2007) Multiple perspectives of performance measures, *European Management Journal*, 25(4), 266–82.

[57]R. Baran, C. Zerres and M. Zerres, Customer relationship management, free-learning summary in cooperation with www.ventus.dk; www.midas.com.

[58]S. Gupta and V. Zeithaml (2006) Customer metrics and their impact on financial performance, *Marketing Science*, 25(6), 718–39.

[59]Ibid.

[60]R. Niraj, M. Gupta and C. Narasimhan (2001) Customer profitability in a supply chain, *Journal of Marketing*, 65, July, 1–16.

[61]G. Cokins (2006) Measuring customer value: how BPM supports better marketing decisions, *Business Performance Management*, February, 13–18.

[62]Rust et al. (2004) op. cit.

[63]F. F. Reichheld (2003) The one number you need to grow, *Harvard Business Review*, 81 (12), 46–54.

[64]Petersen et al. (2009) op. cit.

[65]J. Villanueva, S. Yoo and D. M. Hanssens (2008) The impact of marketing-induced vs. word-of-mouth customer acquisition on customer equity growth, *Journal of Marketing Research*, 45(1), 48–59.

[66]P. Schmitt, B. Skiera and C. Van den Bulte (2011) Referral programs and customer value, *Journal of Marketing*, 75 (January), 46–59.

[67]V. Kumar, L. Aksoy, B. Donkers, R. Venkatesan, T. Wiesel and S. Tillmanns (2010) Undervalued or overvalued customers: capturing total customer engagement value, *Journal of Service Research*, 13(3), 297–310.

[68]Kumar et al. (2010) op. cit.

[69]Adapted from S. Helm (2003) Calculating the value of customers' referrals, *Managing Service Quality*, 13(2), 124–33.

[70]The three statements (i.e. OL measurement items) are based on W. D. Wells and D. Tigert (1971) Activities, interests, and opinions, *Journal of Advertising Research*, 11 (August), 27–35.

[71]Helm (2003), op. cit.

[72]D. E. Sexton (2009) *Value above Cost*, Harlow: Pearson Education; D. E. Sexton, K. Sen and V. M. Gorti (2010) Determining marketing accountability: applying economics and finance to marketing, *Journal of Marketing Trends*, October, 39–45.

[73]T. Ambler and Wang Xiucun (2003) Measures of marketing success: a comparison between China and the United Kingdom, *Asia Pacific Journal of Management*, 20, 267–81.

[74]T. J. Reynolds and C. B. Phillips (2005) In search of true brand equity metrics: all market share ain't created equal, *Journal of Advertising Research*, June, 171–86.

[75]S. A. Taylor, G. L. Hunter and D. L. Lindberg (2007) Understanding (customer-based) brand equity in financial services, *Journal of Services Marketing*, 21(4), 241–52; K. L. Keller (1993) Conceptualizing, measuring, and managing customer-based brand equity, *Journal of Marketing*, 57(1), 1–23.

[76]K. L. Keller (2003) *Strategic Brand Management: Building, Measuring and Managing Brand Equity*, 2nd edn, Englewood Cliffs, NJ: Prentice-Hall; E. Atilgan, S. Aksoy and S. Akinci (2005)

Determinants of the brand equity: a verification approach in the beverage industry in Turkey, *Marketing Intelligence and Planning*, 23(3), 237–48.

[77]Keller (1993) op. cit.; Hong-bumm Kim, Woo Gon Kim and Jeong A. An (2003) The effect of consumer-based brand equity on firms' financial performance, *Journal of Consumer Marketing*, 20(4), 335–51.

[78]Keller (1993) op. cit.

[79]R. G. Netemeyer, B. Krishnan, C. Pullig, G. Wang, M. Yagci, D. Dean, J. Ricks and F. Wirth (2004) Developing and validating measures of facets of customer-based brand equity, *Journal of Business Research*, 57, 209–24.

[80]Keller (1993) op. cit.

[81]S. N. Silverman, D. E. Sprott and V. J. Pascal (1999) Relating consumer-based sources of brand equity to market outcomes, *Advances in Consumer Research*, 26, 352–8.

[82]www.valuebasedmanagement.net/methods_brand_asset_valuator.html.

[83]In collaboration with Robert Jacobson from the University of Washington School of Business and Natalie Mizik from the Columbia Graduate School of Business.

[84]J. Gerzema (Young & Rubicam Brands), E. Lebar (BrandAsset® Valuator, Worldwide), M. Sussman (Y&R, North America) and J. Gaikowski (Young & Rubicam Brands) (2007) Energy: igniting brands to drive enterprise value, *International Journal of Market Research*, 49(1), 25–45.

[85]A. Gambus (2005) Introducing the balanced scorecard: creating metrics to measure performance, *Journal of Management Education*, 29(4), 617–30.

[86]Ibid.

[87]S. C. Voelpel, M. Leibold and R. A. Eckhoff (2006) The tyranny of the balanced scorecard in the innovation economy, *Journal of Intellectual Capital*, 7(1), 43–60; R. S. Kaplan and D. P. Norton (1992) The balanced scorecard: measures that drive performance, *Harvard Business Review*, 70(1), 71–85.

[88]Voelpel et al. (2006) op. cit.

[89]R. S. Kaplan and D. P. Norton (2007) Using the balanced scorecard as a strategic management system, *Harvard Business Review*, July–August, 150–61.

[90]E. K. Laitinen (2006) A constant growth model of the firm: empirical analysis of the balanced scorecard, *Review of Accounting and Finance*, 5(2), 140–73.

[91]Citation from Kaplan and Norton (2007) op. cit., 160.

[92]The balanced scorecard and corporate social responsibility: aligning values for profit, GreenBiz.com; www.globalreporting.org.

[93]C. Manescu (2010) Economic implications of corporate social responsibility and responsible investments, PhD thesis, University of Gothenburg, School of Business, Economics and Law.

[94]P. Raghubir, J. Roberts, K. N. Lemon and R. S. Winer (2010) Why, when, and how should the effect of marketing be measured? A stakeholder perspective for corporate social responsibility metrics, *Journal of Public Policy and Marketing*, 29(1), 66–77.

[95]B. Johnson (2011) Companies must think beyond CSR, thunders Puma CEO, *Marketing Week*, 17 March.

[96]J. Zabin (2006) Marketing dashboards: the visual display of marketing data, *Chief Marketer*, 26 June.

[97]R. S. Kaplan and D. P. Norton (1996) *The Balanced Scorecard*, Boston, MA: Harvard Business School Press.

[98]S. Ante (2006) Giving the boss the big picture, *BusinessWeek*, 13 February, 48–50.

Digitel marketing plan and exercises

The marketing plan: an introduction

As a marketing practitioner, you will need a good marketing plan to provide direction and focus for your brand, product or company. With a detailed plan, any business will be better prepared to launch an innovative new product or increase sales to current customers. Non-profit organisations also use a marketing plan to guide their fundraising and outreach activity. Even government agencies put together marketing plans for initiatives such as building public awareness of healthy eating and road safety.

The purpose and content of a marketing plan

A marketing plan has a more limited scope than a business plan which offers a broad overview of the entire organisation's vision, mission, objectives, strategy, and resource allocation. The marketing plan documents how the organisation's strategic objectives will be achieved through specific marketing strategies and tactics, with the customer as the starting point. It is also linked to the plans of other organisational departments. Suppose a marketing plan calls for selling 200,000 units annually. The production department must gear up to make that many units, finance must arrange funding to cover the expenses, human resources must be ready to hire and train staff, and so on. Without the appropriate level of organisational support and resources, no marketing plan can succeed.

Although the exact length and layout varies from company to company, a marketing plan usually adopts a similar approach to that described in Chapter 3 and Chapter 21. Smaller businesses may create shorter or less formal marketing plans, whereas corporations require highly structured marketing plans. To guide implementation effectively, every part of the plan must be described in considerable detail. Sometimes a company will post its marketing plan on an internal website so managers and employees in different locations can consult specific sections and collaborate on additions or changes.

The role of research

To develop innovative products, successful strategies, and action programmes, marketers need up-to-date information about the environment, the competition, and the selected market segments. Often, analysis of internal data is the starting point for assessing the

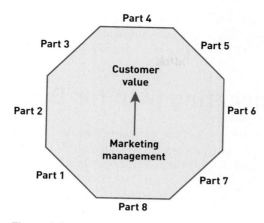

Figure A.1

current marketing situation, supplemented by marketing intelligence and research investigating the overall market, customers, the competition, cost and revenue implications, channel matters and company strategic issues. As the plan is implemented, marketers use research to monitor developments in their markets; to measure objectives and to identify areas for improvement if results fall short of expectations.

Finally, marketing research helps marketers learn more about their customers' requirements, expectations, perceptions, satisfaction, and loyalty. This deeper understanding provides a foundation for building competitive advantage through well-informed segmenting, targeting, and positioning decisions. Thus, the marketing plan should outline what marketing research will be conducted and when, as well as how the findings will be applied.

The role of relationships

Although the marketing plan shows how the company will establish and maintain profitable customer relationships, it also affects both internal and external relationships. First, it influences how marketing personnel work with each other and with other departments to deliver value and satisfy customers. Second, it affects how the company works with suppliers, distributors and partners to achieve the plan's objectives. Third, it influences the company's dealings with other stakeholders, including government regulators, the media, and the community at large. All these relationships are important to the organisation's success and must be considered when developing a marketing plan.

From marketing plan to marketing action

Most companies create yearly marketing plans, although some plans cover a longer period. Marketers start planning well in advance of the implementation date to allow time for marketing research, analysis, management review, and coordination between departments. Then, after each action programme begins, marketers monitor ongoing results, investigate any deviation from the projected outcome, and take corrective steps as needed. Some marketers also prepare contingency plans for implementation if certain conditions emerge. Because of inevitable and sometimes unpredictable environmental changes, marketers must be ready to update and adapt marketing plans at any time.

For effective implementation and control, the marketing plan should define how progress towards objectives will be measured. Managers typically use budget, schedules and marketing metrics for monitoring and evaluating results. With budgets, they can compare planned expenditures with actual expenditures for a given period. Schedules allow management to see when tasks were supposed to be completed and when they were actually completed. Marketing metrics track the actual outcomes of marketing programmes to see whether the company is moving forward towards its objectives.

Sample marketing plan for Digitel

This section takes you inside the sample marketing plan for Digitel, a hypothetical start-up company. The company's first product is the Digitel 1000, a multimedia, cellular/Wi-Fi-enabled personal digital assistant (PDA), also known as a handheld computer. Digitel will be competing with Palm, Hewlett-Packard, Motorola, Apple, and other well-established rivals in a crowded, fast-changing marketplace where smart phones and many other electronic devices have PDA functionality as well as entertainment capabilities. The annotations explain more about what each section of the plan should contain.

1. Executive summary

This section summarises market opportunities, marketing strategy, and marketing and financial objectives for senior managers who will read and approve the marketing plan.

Digitel is preparing to launch a new multimedia, dual-mode PDA product, the Digitel 1000, in a mature market. We can compete with both PDAs and smart phones because our product offers a unique combination of advanced features and functionality at a value-added price. We are targeting specific segments in the consumer and business markets, taking advantage of the growing interest in a single device with communication, organisation, and entertainment benefits.

The primary marketing objective is to achieve a first year European market share of 3 per cent with unit sales of 240,000. The primary financial objectives are to achieve first-year sales revenues of €60 million, keep first-year losses to less than €10 million, and break-even early in the second year.

2. Situation analysis

The situation analysis describes the market, the company's capability to serve targeted segments, and the competition.

Digitel, founded 18 months ago by two entrepreneurs with telecommunications experience, is about to enter the now mature PDA market. Multifunction cell phones, email devices and wireless communication devices are increasingly popular for both personal and professional use, with more than 5 million PDAs and 22 million smart phones sold worldwide each year. Competition is increasingly intense even as technology evolves, industry consolidation continues, and pricing pressures squeeze profitability. Palm, a PDA pioneer, is one of several key players having difficulty adapting to the smart-phone challenge. To gain market share in this dynamic environment, Digitel must carefully target specific segments with valued features and plan for a next-generation product to keep brand momentum going.

2.1 Market summary

Market summary includes size, needs, growth and trends. Describing the targeted segments in detail provides context for marketing strategies and programmes discussed later in the plan.

Digitel's market consists of customers and business users who prefer to use a single device for communication, information storage and exchange, organisation, and entertainment on the go. Specific segments being targeted during the first year include professionals, corporations, students, entrepreneurs, and medical users. Table A.1 shows how the Digitel 1000 addresses the needs of targeted customers and business segments.

Table A.1 Needs and corresponding features/benefits of Digitel PDA

Targeted segment	Customer need	Corresponding feature/benefit
Professionals	Stay in touch while on the go	Wireless email to conveniently send and receive messages from anywhere; cell phone capability for voice communication from anywhere
	Record information while on the go	Voice recognition for no-hands recording
Students	Perform many functions without carrying multiple gadgets	Compatible with numerous applications and peripherals for convenient, cost-effective functionality
	Express style and individuality	Case wardrobe of different colours and patterns allows users to make a fashion statement
Corporate users	Input and access critical data on the move	Compatible with widely available software
	Use for proprietary tasks	Customisable to fit diverse corporate tasks and networks
Entrepreneurs	Organise and access contacts, schedule details	No-hands, wireless access to calendar and address book to easily check appointments and connect with contacts
Medical users	Update, access and exchange medical records	No-hands, wireless recording and exchange of information to reduce paperwork and increase productivity

PDA purchasers can choose between models based on several different operating systems, including systems from Palm, Microsoft, and Symbian, plus Linux variations. Digitel licenses a Linux-based system because it is somewhat less vulnerable to attack by hackers and viruses. Storage capacity (hard drive or flash drive) is an expected feature for PDAs, so Digitel is equipping its first product with an ultra-fast 20-gigabyte drive that can be supplemented by extra storage. Technology costs are decreasing even as capabilities are increasing, which makes value-priced models more appealing to private customers and to business users with older PDAs who want to trade up to new, high-end multifunction units.

2.2 Strengths, weaknesses, opportunities and threat analysis

Digitel has several powerful strengths on which to build, but our major weakness is lack of brand awareness and image. The major opportunity is demand for multifunction communication, organisation, and entertainment devices that deliver a number of valued benefits. We also face the threat of ever-higher competition and downward pricing pressure.

Strengths Strengths are internal capabilities that can help the company reach its objectives. Digitel can build on three important strengths:

1 Innovative product: The Digitel 1000 offers a combination of features that would otherwise require customers to carry multiple devices, such as speedy, hands-free dual-mode cell/Wi-Fi telecommunications capabilities, and digital video/music/TV programme storage/playback.

2 **Security**: Our PDA uses a Linux-based operating system that is less vulnerable to hackers and other security threats that can result in stolen or corrupted data.

3 **Pricing**: Our product is priced lower than competing multifunction PDAs – none of which offer the same bundle of features – which gives us an edge with price-conscious customers.

Weaknesses Weaknesses are internal elements that may interfere with the company's ability to achieve its objectives. By waiting to enter the PDA market until considerable consolidation of competitors has occurred, Digitel has learned from the successes and mistakes of others. Nonetheless, we have two main weaknesses:

1 **Lack of brand awareness**: Digitel has no established brand or image, whereas Palm, Apple, and others have strong brand recognition. We will address this issue with a professional marketing communications plan.

2 **Heavier and thicker unit**: The Digitel 1000 is slightly heavier and thicker than most competing models because it incorporates many multimedia features and offers far more storage capacity than the average PDA. To counteract this weakness, we will emphasise our product's benefits and value-added pricing, two compelling competitive strengths.

Opportunities Opportunities are areas of buyer need or potential interest in which the company might perform profitably. Digitel can take advantage of two major opportunities:

1 **Increasing demand for multimedia devices with communication functions**: The market for multimedia, multifunction devices is growing much faster than the market for single-use devices. Growth is accelerating as dual-mode capabilities become mainstream, giving customers the flexibility to make phone calls over mobile phone or Internet connections. PDAs and smart phones are already commonplace in public, work, and educational settings; in fact, users who bought entry-level models are now trading up.

2 **Lower technology costs**: Better technology is now available at a lower cost than ever before. Thus, Digitel can incorporate advanced features at a value-added price that allows for reasonable profits.

Threats Threats are challenges posed by an unfavourable trend or development that could lead to lower sales and profits. We face three main threats at the introduction of the Digitel 1000:

1 **Increased competition**: More companies are offering devices with some but not all of the features and benefits provided by the Digitel 1000 PDA. Therefore, Digitel's marketing communications must stress our clear differentiation and value-added pricing.

2 **Downward pressure on pricing**: Increased competition and market share strategies are pushing PDA prices down. Still, our objective of seeking a 10 per cent profit on second-year sales of the original model is realistic, given the lower margins in the PDA market.

3 **Compressed product life-cycle**: PDAs have reached the maturity stage of their life-cycle more quickly than earlier technology products. Because of this compressed life-cycle, we plan to introduce a media-oriented second product during the year following the Digitel 1000's launch.

2.3 Competition

This section identifies key competitors, describes their market positions, and provides an overview of their strategies.

The emergence of new multifunction smart phones, including the Apple iPhone, has increased competitive pressure. Dell has already left the PDA market; the remaining competitors are continually adding features and sharpening price points. Competition from specialised devices for text and email messaging, such as Blackberry devices, is another major factor. Key competitors:

Palm: As the PDA market leader, with 34 per cent share, Palm has excellent distribution in multiple channels and alliances with a number of European telecommunications carriers. However, Palm's smart-phone share is well below that of Nokia and other handset marketers. Palm products use either the proprietary Palm operating system or Windows.

Hewlett-Packard: HP holds 22 per cent of the PDA market and targets business segments with its numerous iPAQ Pocket PC devices. Some of its PDAs can send documents to Bluetooth-equipped printers and prevent data loss if batteries run down. For extra security, one model allows access by fingerprint match as well as by password. HP enjoys widespread distribution and offers a full line of PDAs at various price points.

Motorola: Motorola sold 100 million of its RAZR clamshell phones worldwide in three years and now offers the RAZR2, smaller and lighter than earlier models and with two operating system options. The Motorola Q targets professionals and business users with PDA and email functions, a tiny keyboard, Bluetooth connections, multimedia capabilities, and more.

Apple: The iPhone, a smart phone with a 3.5 inch colour screen, has been designed with entertainment enthusiasts in mind. It's well equipped for music, video, and Web access, plus calendar and contact management functions. Apple initially partnered in the UK with O_2.

Samsung: Value, style, function: Samsung is a powerful competitor, offering a variety of smart phones and Ultra mobile PCs for consumer and business segments. Some of its smart phones are available for specific telecommunications carriers and some are 'unblocked', ready for any compatible telecommunications network.

Despite strong competition, Digitel can serve out a definite image and gain recognition among targeted segments. Our voice-recognition system for hands-off operation is a critical point of differentiation for competitive advantage. Our second product will have PDA functions but will be more media-oriented to appeal to segments where we will have strong brand recognition. Table A.2 shows a sample of competitive products and process.

Table A.2 Selected PDA products and pricing

Competitor	Model	Features	Price
PalmOne	Tungsten C	PDA functions, wireless capabilities colour screen, tiny keyboard, wireless capabilities	€499
PalmOne	M 130	PDA functions, colour screen expandable functionality	€199
Handspring	Treo 270	PDA and cell phone functions, colour screen, tiny keyboard, speakerphone capabilities; no expansion slot	€499
Samsung	i500	PDA functions, cell phone functions, mp3 player, colour screen, video capabilities	€599
Dell	Axim X5	PDA functions, colour screen, email, voice recorder, speaker, expandable	€199
Sony	Clie PEG-NX73V	PDA functions, digital camera, tiny keyboard, games, presentation software, MP3 player, voice recorder	€499

2.4 Product offerings

This section summarises the main features of the company's various products. The Digitel 1000 offers the following standard features:

- voice recognition for hands-free operation;
- organisation functions, including calendar, address book, synchronisation;
- built-in dual cell phone/Internet phone and instant calling facility;
- digital music/video/television recording, wireless downloading, and instant playback;
- wireless Web and email, text messaging, instant messaging;
- three-inch colour screen;
- ultra-fast 20-gigabyte drive and expansion slots;
- four megapixel camera with flash and photo editing/sharing tools.

First-year sales revenues are projected to be €60 million, based on sales of 240,000 of the Digitel 1000 model at a wholesale price of €250 each. Our second-year product will be the Digitel All Media 2000, stressing multimedia communication, networking, and entertainment functions with PDA capabilities as secondary features. The Digitel All Media 2000 will include Digitel 1000 features plus:

- built-in media beaming to share music, video, television files with other devices;
- web cam for instant capture and uploading to popular video websites;
- voice-command access to popular social networking websites;
- integrated eight megapixel camera, flash, and photo editing/sharing tools.

2.5 Distribution

Distribution explains each channel for the company's products and mentions new developments and trends.

Digitel-branded products will be distributed through a network of retailers in the top European markets. Among the most important channel partners being contacted are:

- office supply superstores;
- computer stores;
- electronics specialty stores;
- online retailers.

3. Marketing strategy

3.1 Objectives

Objectives should be defined in specific terms so management can measure progress and take corrective action to stay on track.

We have set aggressive but achievable objectives for the first and second years of market entry.

First-year objectives: We are aiming for a 3 per cent share of the European PDA market through a unit sales volume of 240,000

Second-year objectives: Our second-year objective is to achieve break-even on the Digitel 1000 and launch our second model.

3.2 Target markets

All marketing strategies start with segmentation, targeting and positioning. Digitel's strategy is based on a positioning of product differentiation. Our primary customer target for the Digitel 1000 is middle-to-upper-income professionals who need one device to coordinate their busy schedule, stay in touch with family and colleagues, and be entertained on the go. Our secondary customer target is senior school pupils and undergraduate and post graduate university students who want a multimedia, dual-mode device. This segment can be described demographically by age (16-39) and education status. Our Digitel All Media 2000 will be aimed at teens and twenty-somethings who want a device with features to support social networking and heavier entertainment media consumption.

The primary business target for the Digitel 1000 is mid- to large-sized companies that want to help their managers and employees stay in touch and input or access critical data when away from work. This segment consist of companies with more than €25 million annual sales and more than 100 employees. A secondary target is entrepreneurs and small business owners. Also we will target medical users who want to update or access patients' medical records.

Each of the marketing-mix strategies conveys Digitel's differentiation to these target market segments.

3.3 Positioning

Positioning strategy includes decisions about setting initial prices in response to opportunities and competitive challenges.

Using product differentiation, we are positioning the Digitel PDA as the most versatile, convenient, value-added model for personal and professional use. Our marketing will focus on the hands-free operation of multiple communication use, entertainment, and information capabilities differentiating the Digitel 1000.

3.4 Strategies

Product Product strategy includes decisions about product mix, lines, brands, packaging, labelling and warranties.

The Digitel 1000, including all the features described in the earlier Product Review section, will be sold with a one-year warranty. We will introduce the Digitel All Media 2000 during the following year, after we have established our Digitel brand. The brand and logo (Digitel's distinctive lightning streak) will be displayed on our products and packaging as well as in all marketing campaigns.

Pricing Pricing strategy covers decisions about setting initial prices and adapting processes in response to opportunities and competitive challenges.

The Digitel 1000 will be introduced at €250 wholesale/€350 estimated retail price per unit. We expect to lower the price of this model when we expand the product line by launching the Digitel All Media 2000, to be priced at €350 wholesale per unit. These prices reflect strategy of (1) attracting desirable channel partners and (2) taking market share from established competitors.

Distribution Distribution strategy includes selection and management of channel relationships to deliver value to customers.

Our distribution strategy is to be selective, marketing Digitel PDAs through well-known stores and online retailers. During the first year, we will add distribution partners until we have a coverage in all major European markets and the product is featured in the major electronics catalogues and websites. We will also investigate distribution through call-phone outlets maintained by major carriers. In support of distribution partners, we will provide demonstration products, detailed specification handouts, and full-colour photographs and displays featuring the product. Finally, we plan to arrange special payment terms for retailers that place volume orders.

Marketing communications Marketing communication strategy covers all efforts to communicate to target audiences and channel members.

By integrating all messages in all media, we will reinforce the brand name and the main points of product differentiation. Research about media consumption patterns will help our advertising agency choose appropriate media and timing to reach prospects before and during product introduction. Thereafter, advertising will appear on a pulsing basis to maintain brand awareness and communicate various differentiation messages. The agency will also coordinate public relations efforts to build the Digitel brand and support the differentiation message. To generate buzz, we will host a user-generated video contest on our website. To attract, retain, and motivate channel partners for a push strategy, we will use trade sales promotions and personal selling. Until the Digitel brand has been established, our communications will encourage purchases through channel partners rather than from our website.

3.5 Marketing mix

The Digitel 1000 will be introduced in February. Here are summaries of action programmes we will use during the first six months to achieve our stated objectives.

January We will launch a €200,000 trade sales promotion campaign and participate in major industry trade shows to educate dealers and generate distribution support for the product launch in February. Also, we will create buzz by providing samples to selected product reviewers, opinion leaders, influential bloggers, and celebrities. Our training staff will work with retail sales personnel at major chains to explain the Digitel 1000's features, benefits and advantages.

February We will start an integrated print/radio/internet campaign targeting professionals and private users. The campaign will show how many functions the Digitel PDA can perform and emphasise the convenience of a single, powerful handheld device. This multimedia campaign will be supported by point-of-sale signage as well as online-only advertisements and video tours.

March As the multimedia advertising campaign continues, we will add private user sales promotions such as a contest in which users post videos on our website, showing how they use the Digitel in creative and unusual ways. We will also distribute new point-of-purchase displays to support our retailers.

April We will hold a trade sales contest offering prizes for the salesperson and retail organisation that sells the most Digitel PDAs during the four week period.

May We plan to roll out a new national advertising campaign this month. The radio advertisements will feature celebrity voices telling their Digitel PDAs to perform functions such as initiating a phone call, sending an email, playing a song or video, and so on. The stylised print and online advertisements will feature these celebrities holding their Digitel PDAs. We plan to reprise this theme for next year's product launch.

June Our radio campaign will add a new voice-over tag line promoting the Digitel 1000 as a graduation gift. We will provide retailers with new competitive comparison handouts as a sales aid. In addition, we will analyse the results of customer satisfaction research for use in future campaigns and product development efforts.

3.6 Marketing research

This section shows how marketing research will support the development, implementation and evaluation of marketing strategies and programmes.

Using research, we will identify specific features and benefits our target market segments value. Feedback from market tests, surveys and focus groups will help us develop and fine-tune the Digitel All Media 2000. We are also measuring and analysing customers' attitudes toward competing brands and products. Brand awareness research will help us determine the effectiveness and efficiency of our messages and media. Finally, we will use customer satisfaction studies to gauge market reaction.

4. Financial matters

These include budgets and forecasts to plan for marketing expenditure, scheduling and operations.

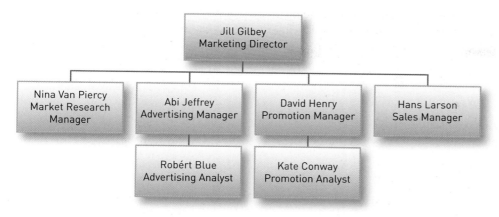

Figure A.2 Digitel's marketing department

Total first-year sales revenue for the Digitel 1000 is projected at €60 million, with an average wholesale price of €250 per unit and variable cost per unit of €150 for unit sales volume of 240,000. We anticipate a first-year loss of up to €10 million. Break-even calculations indicate that the Digitel will become profitable after the sales volume exceeds 267,500 during the product's second year. Our break-even analysis assumes per-unit wholesale revenue of €250 per unit, variable cost of €150 per unit, and estimated first-year fixed costs of €26,750,000.

5. Controls

Controls help management measure results and identify any problems or performance variations that need corrective action.

Controls are being established to cover implementation and the organisation of our marketing activities.

5.1 Implementation

We are planning tight control measures to closely monitor quality and customer service satisfaction. This will enable us to react very quickly in correcting any problems that may occur. Other early warning signals that will be monitored for signs of deviation from the plan include monthly sales (by segment and distribution outlet) and monthly expenses.

5.2 Marketing organisation

The marketing department may be organised by function, as in this sample, or by geography, product, customer, or some combination of these.

Digitel's marketing director, Jill Gilbey, holds overall responsibility for all of the company's marketing activities. Figure A.2 shows the structure of the seven person marketing department. Digitel has retained the Global Marketing agency to handle sales campaigns, trade and customer sales promotions and public relations activity.

Sample marketing plan chapter assignments

Chapter 3

As assistant to Jill Gilbey, Digitel's marketing director, you've been assigned to draft a mission statement for top management's review. This should cover the competitive spheres within which the firm will operate and your recommendation of an appropriate generic competitive strategy. Using your knowledge of marketing and the information you have about Digitel, answer the following questions.

- What should Digitel's mission be?
- In what markets (consumer and business) should Digitel operate?
- Which of Porter's generic competitive strategies would you recommend Digitel follow in formulating overall strategy?

As your instructor directs, enter your answers and supporting information in a written marketing plan. Follow the format given at the end of Chapter 3 or at the beginning of this Appendix.

Chapter 4

Your next task will require you to consult Nina Van Piercy, the Market Research Manager, Abi Jeffrey, the Advertising Manager and David Henry, the Promotion Manager. Jill has asked you to draft a memo to report on how Digitel could best use information communication technology (ICT) in their market research and marketing communications. She has asked you to address the following questions.

- How can Digitel best use ICT in its market research activity?
- How might Digitel use ICT to gain a competitive advantage in advertising activity?
- How can Digitel use ICT to boost its promotional activities?

Chapter 5

Jill Gilbey asks you to scan Digitel's external environment for early warning signals of new opportunities and emerging threats that could affect the success of the Digitel 1000 PDA.

Using the Internet or library sources, locate information to answer these questions about key areas of the macroenvironment.

- What demographic changes are likely to affect Digitel's targeted segments?
- What economic trends might influence buyer behaviour in Digitel's targeted segments?
- How might the rapid pace of technological change alter Digitel's competitive position?

Enter your answers about Digitel's environment in the appropriate sections of a written marketing plan.

Chapter 6

Your next task is to consider how marketing research can help Digitel support its marketing strategy. Jill Gilbey also asks you how Digitel can measure results after the marketing plan is implemented. She wants you to answer the following three questions.

- What surveys, focus groups, observation, behavioural data, or experiments will Digitel need to support its marketing strategy? Be specific about the questions or issues that Digitel needs to resolve using market research.
- Where can you find suitable secondary data about total demand for PDAs over the next two years? Identify at least two sources (online or offline), describe what you plan to draw from each source, and indicate how the data would be useful for Digitel's marketing planning.
- Recommend three specific marketing metrics for Digitel to apply in determining marketing effectiveness and efficiency.

Enter this information in the marketing plan you've been writing.

Chapter 7

You are responsible for researching and analysing the consumer market for Digitel's PDA product. Look again at the data you have already entered about the company's current situation and macroenvironment, especially the markets being targeted. Now answer these questions about the market and buyer behaviour.

- What cultural, social and personal factors are likely to most influence customer purchasing of PDAs? What research tools would help you better understand the effect on buyer attitudes and behaviour?
- Which aspects of customer behaviour should Digitel's marketing plan emphasise and why?
- What marketing activities should Digitel plan to coincide with each stage of the customer buying process?

After you have analysed these aspects of consumer behaviour, consider the implications for Digitel's marketing efforts to support the launch of its PDA. Finally, document your findings and conclusions in your written marketing plan.

Chapter 8

You have been learning more about the business market for Digetel's PDA. Jill Gilbey has defined this market as mid- to large-sized corporations that want their employees to stay in touch and be able to input or access data from any location. Respond to the following three questions based on your knowledge of Digitel's current situation and business-to-business marketing.

- What types of businesses appear to fit Gilbey's market definition? How can you research the number of employees and find other data about these types of businesses?
- What type of purchase would a Digitel PDA represent for these businesses? Who would participate in and influence this type of purchase?
- Would demand for PDAs among corporate buyers tend to be inelastic? What are the implications for Digitel's marketing plan?

Your answers to these questions will affect how Digitel plans marketing activities for the business segments to be targeted. Take a few minutes to note your ideas in a written marketing plan.

Chapter 9

Digitel is a new entrant in an established industry characterised by competitors with relatively high brand identity and strong market positions. Use research and your knowledge of how to deal with competitors to consider three issues that will affect the company's ability to introduce its first product successfully:

- What factors will you use to determine Digitel's strategic group?
- Should Digitel select a class of competitor to attack on the basis of strength versus weakness, closeness versus distance, or good versus bad? Why is this appropriate in the PDA market?
- As a start-up company, what competitive strategy would be most effective as Digitel introduces its first product?

Take time to analyse how Digitel's competitive strategy will affect its marketing strategy and tactics. Now summarise your ideas in a written marketing plan.

Chapter 10

Identifying suitable market segments and selecting targets are critical to the success of any marketing plan. As Jill Gilbey's assistant, you are responsible for market segmentation and targeting. Study the market information, buyer behaviour data, and competitive details and answer the following questions.

- Which variables should Digitel use to segment its consumer and business markets?
- How can Digitel evaluate the attractiveness of each identified segment? Should Digitel market to one consumer customer segment and one business consumer segment or target more than one in each market? Why?
- Should Digitel pursue full market coverage, market specialisation, product specialisation, selective specialisation, or single-segment concentration? Why?

Next consider how your decisions about segmentation and targeting will affect Digitel's marketing efforts. Depending on your instructor's directions summarise your conclusions in a written marketing plan.

Chapter 11

Digitel has decided to focus on total customer satisfaction as a way of encouraging brand loyalty in a highly competitive marketplace. With this in mind, you have been assigned to analyse three specific issues as you continue working on Digitel's marketing plan.

- How (and how often) should Digitel monitor customer satisfaction?
- To which customer touch points should Digitel pay particularly close attention, and why?

Consider your answers in the context of Digitel's current situation and the objectives it has set. Then enter your latest decisions in the written marketing plan.

Chapter 12

Digitel is a new brand with no prior brand associations, which presents a number of marketing opportunities and challenges. Jill Gilbey has given you responsibility for making recommendations about three brand equity issues that are important to Digitel's marketing plan.

- What brand elements would be most useful for differentiating the Digitel brand from competing brands?
- How can Digitel sum up its brand promise for the new PDA?
- Should Digitel add a brand for its second product or retain the Digitel name?

Be sure that your brand ideas are appropriate in the light of what you have learned about your targeted segments and the competition. Then add this information to your written marketing plan.

Chapter 13

As before, you are working with Jill Gilbey on Digitel's marketing plan for launching a new PDA. Now you are focusing on Digitel's positioning and product life-cycle strategies by answering three specific questions.

- In a sentence or two, what is an appropriate positioning statement for the Digitel 1000 PDA?
- Knowing the stage of Digitel's PDA in the product life-cycle, what are the implications for pricing, promotion, and distribution?

- In which stage of its evolution does the PDA market appear to be? What does this mean for Digitel's marketing plans?

Document your ideas in a written marketing plan. Note any additional research you may need to determine how to proceed after the Digitel 1000 has been launched.

Chapter 14

Introducing a new product entails a variety of decisions about product strategy, including differentiation, ingredient branding, packaging, labelling, warranty and guarantee. Your next task is to answer the following questions about Digitel's product strategy.

- Which aspect of product differentiation would be most valuable in setting Digitel apart from competitors, and why?
- Should Digitel use ingredient branding to tout the Linux-based operating system that it says makes its PDA more secure than PDAs based on some other operating systems?
- How can Digitel use packaging and labelling to support its brand image and help its channel partners sell the PDA product more effectively?

Once you have answered these questions, incorporate your idea into the marketing plan you have been writing.

Chapter 15

Knowing that the PDA market is not growing as quickly as the market for multimedia, multifunction communication devices, Jill Gilbey wants you to look ahead at how Digitel can develop new products outside the PDA market. Review the competitive situation and the market situation before you continue working on the Digitel marketing plan.

- List three new-product ideas that build Digitel's strengths and the needs of its various target segments. What criteria should Digitel use to screen these ideas?
- Develop the most promising idea into a product concept and explain how Digitel can test this concept. What particular dimensions must be tested?
- Assume that the most promising idea tests well. Now develop a marketing strategy for introducing it, including: a description of the target market; the product positioning; the marketing budget you will recommend for this new product introduction. If possible, estimate Digitel's costs and conduct a break-even analysis.

Document all the details of your new-product development ideas in the written marketing plan.

Chapter 16

You are in charge of pricing Digitel's product for its launch early next year. Review its strengths and weaknesses. Check on Digitel's competitive environment, targeting strategy and product positioning. Now continue working on your marketing plan by responding to the following questions.

- What should Digitel's primary pricing objective be? Explain your reasoning.
- Are PDA customers likely to be price sensitive? What are the implications for your pricing decisions?
- What price adaptations (such as discounts, allowances and promotional pricing) should Digitel include in its marketing plan?

Make notes about your answers to these questions and then document the information in a written plan.

Chapter 17

The next task you have been asked to tackle is to develop a suitable distribution channel model for the new Digitel 1000 PDA. On the basis of your knowledge of integrated distribution networks answer these questions.

- Jill Gilbey has intimated that she wants to move to an integrated demand driven network. Do you think that this would be wise? Explain your reasoning.
- The selection of distribution channel members should support each part of the value network (chain). How do you think Digitel can avoid conflicts in their selected distribution network?
- What technologies should be considered for the launch of the Digitel 1000 PDA?

Check that your distribution channel ideas support the product positioning and are consistent with the goals that Digitel have set. Record your responses in a written marketing plan.

Chapter 18

Imagine that you have been asked to plan the customer support services for Digitel's new PDA. Review what you know about your target market and its needs; also think about what Digitel's competitors are offering. Then respond to the questions about designing and managing a suitable services support.

- What service process design blueprint will customers need in support of the launch of Digitel's new PDA?
- How should Digitel manage staff and customers to support the service process?
- What role should technology play in the development and functioning of a successful service environment?

Think through how your service process design will support Digitel's overall marketing activity. Summarise your recommendations in a written marketing plan.

Chapter 19

Jill Gilbey has asked you to liaise with Abi Jeffrey, the Advertising Manager and David Henry, the Promotion Manager to formulate an integrated marketing communications plan for Digitel's new PDA. Review your written marketing plan so far before you answer the following questions.

- What communications objectives are required for Digitel's new PDA launch?
- How can Digitel use the eight major modes of the communications mix to best advantage?
- Which communication tools would you use to boost sales of the Digitel 1000 PDA six months after launch?

Check that your marketing communications plans are consistent with Digitel's overall marketing activities and record your work in a written marketing plan.

Chapter 20

The art/science of marketing communications lies in the subtle integration of affordable mass and personal communications vehicles. Jill Gilbey now wants you to further develop your communications mix ideas in detail with Abi Jeffrey and David Henry and to discuss them with Hans Larson, the Sales Manager. Then respond to the following questions to continue the process of developing Digitel's final marketing communications plan.

- What is the best way to thematically integrate Digitel's advertising and sales promotion activities?
- How can Digitel's exploit direct marketing and digital marketing activities such as viral marketing, mobile phone advertising and interactive TV advertising to boost sales?
- What decisions will need to be taken to ensure that the sales force is informed and managed effectively?

Document your ideas in your written marketing plan.

Chapter 21

As Jill Gilbey's assistant with the complete marketing plan now in place, you are now required to make recommendations as to how Digitel's marketing activities can be effectively and efficiently managed.

- What are the key trends in marketing practice? How should social responsibility feature in Digitel's marketing operations?
- How can Digitel build a creative marketing organisation to develop and sustain its reputation for developing and delivering highly valued offerings to its target customers?
- What general tools are available to help Digitel monitor and improve its marketing activities?

Chapter 22

Now that you have been a member of the Digitel marketing team and drafted an integrated marketing plan Jill Gilbey has invited you to a meeting of her department to discuss how the company can measure its performance as the plan is implemented. In addition to adopting a set of sales targets Jill has reminded you that it is vitally important to apply metrics to the cost side of the business. Before she finally drafts the agenda for the departmental meeting Jill has asked you to respond to the following questions.

- What do you understand by the term 'marketing metrics'?
- What are the key dimensions of marketing metrics?
- How can qualitative and quantitative factors be balanced to produce a sound marketing dashboard for Digitel?

To finish your work convey your responses to Jill and draft an executive summary of the plan's highlights to take to the meeting.

Glossary

A

accessibility the degree of ease with which the customer can get to or avail themselves of a service.

activity-based cost (ABC) accounting procedures that can quantify the true profitability of different activities by identifying their actual costs.

administered VMS coordinates successive stages of production and distribution through the size and power of one of the members.

adoption an individual's decision to become a regular user of a product or service.

advertising any paid form of non-personal presentation and promotion of ideas, goods or services by an identified sponsor.

advertising agency an organisation that specialises in providing specialist services such as media selection, creative work, production and campaign planning for clients.

advertising goal (or advertising objective) a communication targeted at a pre-selected audience at a specific time to stimulate increased sales.

advertising message the use of words, symbols and graphical illustrations to communicate with a targeted audience in a selected media mix.

advertorials print advertisements that offer editorial content reflecting favourably on the brand and which are difficult to distinguish from newspaper or magazine content.

agents companies who search for customers and may negotiate on the producer's behalf but do not take title to the goods.

ambient smell the smell that creates an ambience – like the smell of coffee beans in a coffee shop.

anchoring and adjustment heuristic when consumers arrive at an initial judgement and then make adjustments of their first impressions based on additional information.

arm's-length pricing the price charged by other competitors for the same or a similar product or service.

aspirational groups groups a person hopes or would like to join.

associative network memory model a conceptual representation that views memory as consisting of a set of nodes and interconnecting links, where nodes represent stored information or concepts and links represent the strength of association between this information or concepts.

atmosphere the creation of a sense or experience.

attitude a person's enduring favourable or unfavourable evaluation, emotional feeling, and action tendencies towards some object or idea.

attributes intangible or tangible components of a customer/market offering.

augmented product a product that includes features that go beyond consumer expectations and differentiate the product from competitors.

autocratic management style where the manager is fully responsible for making decisions.

availability heuristic when consumers base their predictions on the quickness and ease with which a particular example of an outcome comes to mind.

available market the set of consumers who have interest, income and access to a particular offer.

avatars graphical representations of animated characters that can act as online representatives or people or companies.

average cost the cost per unit at a given level of production; it is equal to total costs divided by production.

B

banner ads (internet) small, rectangular boxes containing text and perhaps a picture to support a brand.

basic product what specifically the actual product is.

behaviour skills how people interact with others: for example, are they good at helping others and deciding that others might need help?

belief a descriptive thought that a person holds about something.

benefits product or service characteristics that customers perceive as advantageous.

benefit segmentation the grouping of people based on different benefits they see from a market offering.

blog a mix of the word web and log, usually a type of personal online diary posted on the web in chronological order – the content of the blog does not have to be personal but can also be professional.

bounce rate the percentage visits in which the person left the website after they arrived on the entrance (landing) page.

brainstorming the technique where a group of people generate ideas without initial evaluation.

brand a name, term, sign, symbol or design, or a combination of them, intended to identify the goods or services of one company or group of companies and to differentiate them from those of competitors. To learn more about **corporate branding**, go to www.pearsoned.co.uk/marketingmanagementeurope for additional commentary from the authors.

brand advocate a powerful consumer who is willing to recommend a brand to their friends or advocate for the brand.

brand-asset management team consists of key representatives from functions that affect the brand's performance.

brand asset valuator provides comparative measures of the brand equity of thousands of brand, across hundreds of different categories. According to the BAV there are five key pillars of brand equity: differentiation, energy, relevance, esteem and knowledge.

brand associations all brand-related thoughts, feelings, perceptions, images, experiences, beliefs, attitudes and so on that become linked to the brand.

brand audit a consumer-focused exercise that involves a series of procedures to assess the health of the brand, uncover its sources of brand equity, and suggest ways to improve and leverage its equity.

brand awareness consumers' ability to identify the brand under different conditions, as reflected by their brand recognition or recall performance.

brand charter details in writing what the brand is and what it is not.

brand community a group of people who share their interest in a specific brand and create a parallel social universe with its own values, rituals, vocabulary and hierarchy.

brand contact any information-bearing experience a customer or prospect has with the brand, the product category, or the market that relates to the marketer's product or service.

brand culture the values and beliefs that people have about a brand in their hearts and minds.

brand development index the index of brand sales to category sales.

brand dilution when consumers no longer associate a brand with a specific product or highly similar products or start thinking less favourably about the brand.

branded variants specific brand lines uniquely supplied to different retailers or distribution channels.

brand elements those trademarkable devices that serve to identify and differentiate the brand such as a brand name, logo or character.

brand equity the added value endowed to products and services.

brand extension a company's use of an established brand to introduce a new product or service.

brand identity the way a company aims to identify or position itself or its product or service in the mind of the consumer.

brand image the perceptions and beliefs held by consumers, as reflected in the associations held in consumer memory.

branding endowing products and services with the power of a brand.

branding strategy the number and nature of common and distinctive brand elements and marketing programmes applied to the different products and services sold by the firm.

brand knowledge all the thoughts, feelings, images, experiences, beliefs and so on that become associated with the brand.

brand line all products, original as well as line and category extensions, sold under a particular brand name.

brand management uses the choice, design and implementation of marketing mix activities to build, measure and manage the brand value.

brand mantra an articulation of the heart and soul of the brand, closely related to other branding concepts like 'brand essence' and 'core brand promise.'

brand mix the set of all brand lines that a particular company makes available to buyers.

brand narrative branding based on deep metaphors that connect to people's memories, associations and stories.

brand personality the specific mix of human traits that may be attributed to a particular brand.

brand portfolio the set of all brands and brand lines a particular company offers for sale to buyers in a particular category.

brand promise the marketer's vision of what the brand must be and do for consumers.

brand reinforcing involves ensuring innovation in product design, manufacturing and merchandising, and ensuring relevance in user and usage imagery.

brand religion model describes the evolution of the role of brands in consumers' lives as a five-stage process and highlights the steps that customers can go through as they move forward in their beliefs about brands.

brand revitalisation requires either that lost sources of brand equity are recaptured or that new sources of brand equity are identified and established.

brand slogans sometimes called tag lines, sentences that are intended to convey something good about a brand or to remind consumers of a brand's attributes.

brand tracking studies collect quantitative data from consumers on a routine basis over time to provide marketers with consistent, baseline information about how their brands and marketing programmes are performing on key dimensions.

brand valuation an estimate of the total financial value of the brand.

brand value the intangible asset and goodwill that becomes part of the purchase price of a company when it is acquired.

brand value chain a structured approach to assessing the sources and outcomes of brand equity and the manner in which marketing activities create brand value.

brand vision a clear and consistent message about the value of the brand.

breakeven analysis a means by which management estimates how many units of the product the company would have to sell to break even with the given price and cost structure.

brick-and-click existing companies that have added an online site for information and/or e-commerce.

business database complete information about business customers' past purchases; past volumes, prices and profits.

business market all the organisations that acquire goods and services used in the production of other products or services that are sold, rented or supplied to others. To learn more about business markets, go to www.pearsoned.co.uk/marketingmanagementeurope for additional commentary from the authors.

business mission the organisation's purpose that sets out its competitive domain and core values that distinguish it from the competition.

buyers' market a market environment where the supply of goods exceeds the demand.

buzz a term used in word-of-mouth marketing (viral marketing) when a marketer conveys new relevant brand-related information through unexpected or even outrageous means to privileged trend setters, or to create a stir that will be spread by word or mouth.

C

capital items long-lasting goods that facilitate developing or managing the finished product.

captive products products that are necessary to the use of other products, such as razor blades or film.

cash cows brands which may be kept despite dwindling sales because they still manage to hold on to enough customers and maintain their profitability with virtually no resource outlay.

catalogue marketing the sale of market offerings through means of catalogues distributed to agents or directly to customers.

category extension using the parent brand to brand a new product or service outside the product category currently served by the parent brand.

category membership the products or sets of products with which a brand competes and which function as close substitutes.

cause-related marketing marketing that links a firm's contributions to a designated cause to customers engaging directly or indirectly in revenue-producing transactions with the firm.

celebrity branding where a celebrity uses his or her status in society to promote a product, service or charity.

channel conflict when one channel member's actions prevent the channel from achieving its goal.

channel coordination when channel members are brought together to advance the goals of the channel, as opposed to their own potentially incompatible goals.

channel power the ability to alter channel members' behaviour so that they take actions they would not have taken otherwise.

channel stewardship the ability of a given participant in a distribution channel – a steward – to create a go-to-market strategy that simultaneously addresses customers' best interests and drives profits for all channel partners.

club membership programme a tool used to attract and retain customers and to build long-term brand loyalty for their products or services.

clustered preferences result when natural market segments emerge from groups of customers with shared preferences.

co-branding (also called dual branding or brand bundling) when two or more well-known brands are combined into a joint market offering or marketed together in some fashion.

co-creation an open, ongoing collaboration between a company and its customers to define and create products, services, experiences, ideas and information together.

co-creation of value emphasises the generation and ongoing realisation of mutual firm–customer value. It views markets as forums for firms and active customers to share, combine and renew each other's resources and capabilities to create value for each party.

cohorts groups of individuals who are born during the same time period and travel through life together.

communication-effect research determining whether an advertisement is communicating effectively.

company demand the company's estimated share of market demand at alternative levels of company marketing effort in a given time period.

company sales forecast the expected level of company sales based on a chosen marketing plan and an assumed marketing environment.

company sales potential the sales limit approached by company demand as company marketing effort increases relative to that of competitors.

competitive advantage a company's ability to perform in one or more ways that competitors cannot or will not match.

conformance quality the degree to which all the produced units are identical and meet the promised specifications.

conjoint analysis a method for deriving the utility values that consumers attach to varying levels of a product's attributes.

conjunctive heuristic the consumer sets a minimum acceptable cutoff level for each attribute and chooses the first alternative that meets the minimum standard for all attributes.

consumer-based brand equity the differential effect that brand knowledge has on a consumer response to the marketing of that brand.

consumer behaviour the study of how individuals or groups buy, use and dispose of goods, services, ideas or experiences to satisfy their needs and wants.

consumer decision journey the stage the customer goes through from consider and evaluate to buy, enjoy and advocate.

consumer involvement the level of engagement and active processing undertaken by the consumer in responding to a marketing stimulus.

consumerist movement an organised movement of citizens and government to strengthen the rights and powers of buyers in relation to sellers.

consumer purchases generally made by individual decision makers or a decision-making unit, either for themselves or for others with whom they have relationships.

consumption system the way the user performs the tasks of getting and using products and services.

contractual sales force manufacturers' reps, sales agents and brokers, who are paid a commission based on sales.

contractual VMS consists of independent firms at different levels of production and distribution integrating their programmes on a contractual basis to obtain more economies or sales impact than they could alone.

controlling generally involves comparing actual performance to a predetermined standard.

convenience goods goods the consumer purchases frequently, immediately and with a minimum of effort.

convenience items item that sell in high volume but receive less promotion. These items can carry higher margins.

conventional marketing channel an independent producer, wholesaler(s) and retailer(s).

core benefit the service or benefit the customer is really buying.

core competency an attribute that (1) is a source of competitive advantage in that it makes a significant contribution to perceived customer benefits, (2) has applications in a wide variety of markets, (3) is difficult for competitors to imitate.

core product offering items that produce high sales volume and are heavily promoted but with low margins because they are viewed as undifferentiated commodities.

core values the belief systems that underlie consumer attitudes and behaviour, and that determine people's choices and desires over the long term.

corporate culture the shared experiences, stories, beliefs and norms that characterise an organisation.

corporate social responsibility the ethical principles that affect the interaction between an organisation and the environment and society.

corporate VMS combines successive stages of production and distribution under single ownership.

countertrade exchanging items that are paid for, in whole or part, with other items.

country branding aims to measure, build and manage the reputation of countries and places.

critical path scheduling a network-planning technique that calls for developing a master chart showing the simultaneous and sequential activities that must take place to launch a product or service.

cross-functional activities activities where individuals from different departments come together, managed by a preselected team leader.

cues stimuli that determine when, where and how a person responds.

culture the fundamental determinant of a person's wants and behaviour.

customer churn rate of customer defection.

customer consulting data, information systems and advice services that the seller offers to buyers.

customer database an organised collection of comprehensive information about individual customers or prospects that is current, accessible and actionable for marketing purposes.

customer equity the lifetime value of current and future customers.

customer experience all the experiences a customer has with a product or service, over the duration of their relationship with that company.

customerisation see **customisation**.

customer lifetime value the net present value of the stream of future profits expected over the customer's lifetime purchases.

customer mailing list a set of names, addresses and telephone numbers.

customer-management organisation where companies organise marketing activity to understand and deal with individual customers rather than with the mass market or even market segments.

customer-perceived value the difference between the prospective customer's evaluation of all the benefits and all the costs of an offering and the perceived alternatives.

customer-perceived value analysis a review of a company's strengths and weaknesses relative to those of various competitors.

customer-performance scorecard how well the company is doing year after year on particular customer-based measures.

customer profitability analysis a means of assessing and ranking customer profitability through accounting techniques such as activity-based costing (ABC).

Customer referral value the value that a customer creates through recommending the company to other people.

customer relationship management the process of carefully managing detailed information about individual customers and their encounters or interaction with the brand or product to maximise customer loyalty.

customer satisfaction the fulfilment of customers' perceived-value expectations.

customer-to-customer interactions/encounters direct or indirect, face-to-face or technology-mediated, active or passive interaction between two or more customers in the service setting or outside the service setting, which may or may not involve verbal communication.

customer training training the customer's employees to use the vendor's equipment properly and efficiently.

customer value added the maximum a customer is willing to pay for a product or service minus the incremental unit cost for a product or service.

customer value analysis report of the company's strengths and weaknesses relative to various competitors.

customer value hierarchy five product levels that must be addressed by marketers in planning a market offering.

customer value triad a combination of quality, service and price ('qsp').

customisation combination of operationally driven mass customisation with customised marketing in a way that empowers consumers to design the product and service offering of the choice.

D

dashboards on-screen easy-to-read summaries of key marketing metrics; a marketing dashboard is a personalised view of all marketing information relevant to a specific job and role.

database marketing the process of building, maintaining and using customer databases and other databases for the purpose of contacting, transacting and building customer relationships.

data mining the extracting of useful information about individuals, trends and segments from the mass of data.

data warehouse a collection of current data captured, organised, and stored electronically, designed to facilitate reporting and analysis.

delivery how well the product or service is delivered to the customer.

delivery channel the path or channel through which goods and services flow in one direction (from vendor to the consumer), and the payments generated by them flow in the opposite direction (from consumer to the vendor).

demand chain planning the process of designing the supply chain based on adopting a target market perspective and working backwards.

demand side management activities designed to stimulate consumer demand.

democratic management style where the manager usually delegates power to the subordinates and leave the decision making process to them.

department a higher-level division within companies, which encompasses many functions.

design a mix of features that affect how a market offering looks, feels and functions in terms of customer requirements.

developing country a country that has a relatively low standard of living, an undeveloped industrial base and a moderate to low Human Development Index (HDI) score and per capita income, but is in a phase of economic development.

developing markets nations with social or business activity in the process of rapid growth and industrialisation, as distinct from the developed markets which are countries that have achieved a level of economic growth and security.

differential advantage a clear, positive customer-verified performance differential over the competition.

differential marketing strategies market plans and marketing activities (mixes) that cover several targeted market segments.

diffused preferences exist when customers' preferences vary greatly in their requirements.

digital brand community also called online or virtual brand communities, are a social network of individuals who interact online, often across geographical boundaries in order to pursue mutual interest in a specific brand.

digital brand health an assessment of a how the brand is adhering to its strategic direction in the digital world.

digital branding the creation and management of brands through the use of all forms of digital technologies, many of which are controlled by the consumer.

digital marketing describes the management and execution of marketing using electronic or digital media such as the web, email, interactive TV, wireless media, mobile technology and self-service technology in conjunction with digital data from a range of databases and software applications about customers' characteristics and behaviour.

digital technology digitised information which is recorded in binary code of combinations of the digits 0 and 1, also called bits, which represent words and images. This enables immense amounts of information to be compressed on small storage devices that can be easily preserved and transported.

direct channel the manufacturer or service organisation going directly to the final consumer such as direct mail or use of internet advertising.

direct exporting occurs when a company managers their own exporting which can be through opening a branch or a subsidiary, their own sales force to hiring an agent.

direct marketing the use of consumer-direct (CD) channels to reach and deliver goods and services to customers without using marketing middlemen.

direct-order marketing marketing in which direct marketers seek a measurable response, typically a customer order.

direct product profitability a way of measuring a product's handling costs from the time it reaches the warehouse until a customer buys it in the retail store.

direct response advertising the use of mainstream media such as TV, radio, internet and press to stimulate customer interest.

direct (company) sales force full-or part-time paid employees who work exclusively for the company as sales representatives.

disclaimant groups groups to which a person belongs but whose values, norms or behaviour an individual seeks to avoid.

discrimination the process of recognising differences in sets of similar stimuli and adjusting responses accordingly.

disintermediation the elimination of channel inter-mediaries by product or service providers.

display advertisements (or banner advertisements) small, rectangular boxes containing text and perhaps a picture that companies pay to place on relevant websites or in other media.

dissociative groups those groups whose values or behaviour an individual rejects.

distribution channels sets of dependent or independent organisations involved in the process of making a product or service available for use or consumption.

distribution programming building a planned, professionally managed, vertical marketing sys-tem that meets the needs of both manufacturer and distributors.

drive a strong internal stimulus impelling action.

dual adaptation adapting both the product and the communications to the local market.

dumping a situation in which a company charges either less than its costs or less than it charges in its home market, in order to enter or win a market.

durability a measure of a product's expected operating life under natural or stressful conditions.

durable goods product offerings that have a longer use lifetime, e.g. refrigerators and machine tools.

E

earned media customer-created channels such as brand communities, which are not controlled by the company.

e-business the use of electronic means and platforms to conduct a company's business.

e-commerce a company or site offers to transact or facilitate the selling of products and services online.

effectiveness doing the right thing, making the right strategic decisions.

efficiency the wise stewardship of an organis-ation's resources in achieving its strategic and tacti-cal objectives – conventionally referred to as 'doing things right.'

elimination-by-aspects heuristic a situation in which the consumer compares brands on an attribute selected probabilistically, and brands are eliminated if they do not meet minimum acceptable cutoff levels.

email marketing sending a commercial message using electronic mail-email.

e-marketing a company's efforts to inform buyers, communicate, promote and sell its products and services over the Internet.

emotional branding engaging the consumer on the level of senses and emotions; forging a deep, last-ing, intimate emotional connection to the brand that transcends material satisfaction; it involves creating a holistic experience that delivers an emotional fulfilment so that the customer develops a special bond with and unique trust in the brand.

emotional intelligence (EI) the ability, skill or self-perceived ability to identify, assess and control the emotions of oneself, others and groups.

emotions mental and physiological states associated with a wide variety of feelings, thoughts and behaviour.

environmental threat a challenge posed by an unfavourable trend or development that would lead to lower sales or profit.

ethics the moral principles and values that underlie the actions and decisions of an individual or group.

events and experiences company-sponsored activities and programmes designed to create daily or special brand-related interactions.

everyday low pricing in retailing, a constant low price with few or no price promotions and special sales.

evoked set the set of brands the consumer will consider from the range of brands in the product or service category.

exchange the process of obtaining a desired product or service from someone by offering something in return. To learn more about **exchange**, go to www.pearsoned.co.uk/marketingmanagementeurope for additional commentary from the authors.

exclusive distribution severely limiting the number of intermediaries, in order to maintain control over the service level and outputs offered by resellers.

exhibition an event that brings potential buyers and sellers together in a commercial hall.

expectancy-value model consumers evaluate products and services by combining their brand beliefs – positive and negative – according to their weighted importance.

expected product a set of attributes and conditions that buyers normally expect when they purchase this product.

experience curve (learning curve) a decline in the average cost with accumulated production experience-as an individual or an organisation gets more experienced at a task, they usually become more efficient at it.

experience environment see **physical evidence**.

experimental research research designed to capture cause-and-effect relationships by eliminating competing explanations of the observed findings.

expert power occurs when the manufacturer has special knowledge or expertise that the intermediaries value.

F

facilitators assist in the distribution process but neither take title to goods nor negotiate purchases or sales.

fad a craze that is unpredictable, short-lived and intense.

family brand a situation in which the parent brand is already associated with multiple products through brand extensions.

family of orientation parents and siblings.

family of procreation spouse and children.

features things that enhance the basic function of a product.

financial value the monetary value of a company.

fixed (overhead) costs costs that do not vary with production or sales revenue.

flanker brands or 'fighter' brands are positioned with respect to competitors' brands so that more important (and more profitable) main or flagship brands can retain their desired positioning.

flexible market-perceived value offering (1) a naked solution containing the product and service elements that all segment members value, and (2) discretionary options that some segment members value.

focus group a gathering of six to ten people who are carefully selected based on certain demographic, psychographic or other considerations and brought together to discuss various topics of interest.

forecasting the art of anticipating what buyers are likely to do under a given set of conditions.

form the size, shape or physical structure of a product.

formal systems reflects the formal structure of the organisation and its activities including the formal systems for control, evaluation and reward.

forward invention creating a new product to meet a need in another country.

framing the manner in which choices are presented to and seen by a decision maker.

franchising a form of licensing where the franchisor offers a complete brand concept and operating system.

frequency programmes these are designed to provide rewards to customers who buy frequently and in substantial amounts.

functions a distinct group of staff who serve as specialists in achieving a set of given objectives and corresponding activities; they are usually permanent within organisations.

G

geodemographics the process of grouping households into geographic clusters on the basis of information such as accommodation type and location, occupation, number of children, interests and ethnic background.

global brand a brand that is available in many nations and where, though it may differ from country to country, the localised versions have a common goal and a similar identity.

global brand equity measurement system a set of research procedures designed to provide timely, accurate and actionable information for marketers on brands, so that they can make the best possible decisions in all relevant markets.

global community where people around the world view themselves as potential partners or even family members in a vast, increasingly interconnected human family.

global firm a firm that operates with multinational branches and captures R & D, production, logistical, marketing and financial advantages in its costs and reputation that are not available to purely domestic competitors.

global industry an industry in which the strategic positions of competitors in major geographic or national markets are fundamentally affected by their overall global positions.

globalisation the decoupling of space and time, emphasising that with instantaneous communications, knowledge and culture can be shared around the world simultaneously.

glocal marketing allows for local and global marketing activities to be optimised simultaneously.

glocal strategy standardises certain core elements and localises other elements it is a compromise between global and local (domestic) marketing strategies.

goal formulation the process of developing specific goals for the planning period.

goals/objectives the tangible measure of an achieved vision.

going-rate pricing pricing based largely on competitors' prices.

grey market branded products diverted from normal or authorised distributions channels in the country of product origin or across international borders. It is the trade of something legal through unofficial, unauthorised or unintended distribution channels.

guerrilla marketing an unconventional approach originally practised by small business to create targeted customer awareness in markets where the mainstream media is cluttered; it is increasingly being used by large business to achieve instant impact.

H

hedonic bias the phenomenon that people have a general tendency to attribute success to themselves and failure to external causes.

heuristics rules of thumb or mental shortcuts in the decision process.

high–low pricing charging higher prices on an everyday basis but then running frequent promotions and special sales.

holistic marketing a concept based on the development, design and implementation of marketing programmes, processes and activities that recognises their breadth and interdependencies.

homogeneous preferences when all customers have roughly the same preferences.

homogenisation the act of making something homogeneous, uniform or standardised in composition.

horizontal marketing system where two or more unrelated companies at the same level put together resources or programmes to exploit an emerging market opportunity.

house brand names the use of corporate, family or house brand name across a range of products or services.

hub-and-spoke system a system of marketing organisation where the brand or product manager is figuratively at the centre, with spokes emanating out to various departments.

hybrid channels use of multiple channels of distribution to reach customers in a defined market.

hygiene factors factors within the company that can cause dissatisfaction if missing but do not necessarily satisfy if increased.

I

iconic brands are those brands that customers 'regard with awe'.

image the set of beliefs, ideas and impressions that a person holds regarding an object.

indirect exporting companies typically start with export through independent intermediaries.

individual brand or generic brand name a brand name that does not identify with a named company.

industry a group of firms that offer a product or service or class of products or services that are close substitutes for one another.

informational appeal an appeal that elaborates on market offering quality and payment attributes or benefits.

information technologies all the technologies used to support information gathering, research, analysis, planning and monitoring.

ingredient branding a special case of co-branding that involves creating brand equity for materials, components or parts that are necessarily contained within other branded products.

innovation any good, service or idea that is perceived by someone as new.

innovation diffusion process the spread of a new idea from its source of invention or creation to its ultimate users or adopters.

installation the work done to make a product operational in its planned location.

institutional market schools, hospitals, nursing homes, prisons and other institutions that must provide goods and services to people in their care.

instrumental controls specific tangible costs and rewards designed to induce desired behaviour.

intangible product service attributes that are essential components of a successful brand in today's fiercely competitive buyers' market environment.

integrated marketing mixing and matching marketing activities to maximise their individual and collective efforts.

integrated marketing channel system where the strategies and tactics of selling through one channel reflect the strategies and tactics of selling through one or more other channels.

integrated marketing communications a concept of marketing communications planning that recognises the added value of a comprehensive plan in order to integrate and coordinate its message and media to deliver clear and reinforcing communication.

intensive distribution the manufacturer placing the goods or services in as many outlets as possible.

interaction technologies technologies which support communications, connections and collaborations with customers and businesses.

interactive marketing online and offline activities and programmes designed to engage customers or prospects and directly or indirectly raise awareness, improve image, or elicit sales of market offerings by moving from a transaction-based effort to a conversation or interaction with the customer.

interbrand model a method to evaluate the value of the firm from which the value of the brand will be measured. It uses three criteria – financial analysis, role of branding and brand strength.

intermediary any channel member that plays some role in bringing the product or service to market.

internal branding activities and processes that help to inform and inspire employees.

internal marketing the development and training of staff to ensure high levels of customer-experienced satisfaction.

internationalisation the process through which a firm moves from operating solely in the domestic or home marketplace to operating in international markets.

internet a ubiquitous, 24/7 communications technology which, through a low-cost, open standard, is available to individuals and companies to exchange products and services, money and information in an online setting.

interstitials advertisements, often with video or animation, that pop up between changes on a website.

J

joint venture a company in which multiple investors share ownership and control.

L

laissez-faire management style where the manager sets the tasks but then gives staff complete freedom to complete the task as they see fit.

leadership the process of influencing others to understand and agree about what needs to be done and how to do it, and the process of facilitating individual and collective efforts to accomplish shared objectives.

leading influencing others to achieve organisational objectives. It involves energising, directing, persuading others and creating a vision.

learning changes in an individual's behaviour arising from experience.

legitimate power where the manufacturer requests a behaviour that is warranted under the contract.

lexicographic heuristic consumers choosing the best brand on the basis of its perceived most important attribute.

licensed product or service one whose brand name has been licensed to other manufacturers which actually make the product, or to another service provider.

licensing where a licensor issues a license to a foreign company to use a manufacturing process, trademark, patent, trade secret, or other item of value for a fee or royalty.

life-cycle cost the product's purchase cost plus the discounted cost of maintenance and repair less the discounted salvage value.

lifestyle a person's pattern of living in the world as expressed in activities, interests and opinions.

lifestyle branding a focus on using the brand to symbolise the values and aspirations of a group or culture.

line extension where the parent brand is used to brand a new product or service that targets a new market segment within a product category currently served by the parent brand.

line stretching where a company lengthens its product or service line beyond its current range.

location-based services new forms of mobile service, which are delivered location dependent (it depends on where you are) and context sensitive (related to what you are doing or your particular needs), to mobile users.

logistics the flow of products from point of origin to end user.

long-term memory a permanent repository of information.

loyalty a commitment to rebuy or repatronise a preferred product or service.

M

maintenance and repair the service programme for helping customers keep purchased products in good working order.

management a process that involves the major functions of planning, organising, leading and controlling resources in order to achieve goals; management centres on trying to achieve objectives using the four major functions.

managers the people within the organisation charged with running the organisation on behalf of the owners.

managing the activity of trying to achieve a goal using resources of whatever kind.

market describes various groupings of customers who buy products or services.

market-buildup method identifying all the potential buyers in each market and estimating their potential purchases.

market-centred organisations where companies organise marketing activity to meet the needs of distinct customer groups rather than focusing on marketing functions, regions or products.

market demand the total volume of a product or service that would be bought by a defined customer group in a defined geographical area in a defined time period in a defined marketing environment under a defined marketing programme.

marketer someone who seeks a response (attention, purchase, vote, donation) from another party, called the prospect.

market forecast the market demand corresponding to the level of industry marketing expenditure.

marketing process of planning and executing the conception, pricing, promotion and distribution of ideas, goods and services to create exchanges that satisfy individual and organisational goals.

marketing audit a comprehensive, systematic, independent and periodic examination of a company's or business unit's marketing environment, objectives, strategies and activities.

marketing channels sets of interdependent organisations involved in the process of making a product or service available for use or consumption.

marketing channel system the particular set of marketing channels employed by a firm.

marketing communications the means by which firms attempt to inform, persuade and remind consumers – directly or indirectly – about products, services and brands that they sell.

marketing communications mix eight major modes of communication: advertising, sales promotion, events and experiences, public relations and publicity, direct marketing, interactive marketing, word-of-mouth marketing and personal selling.

marketing concept the organisation should strive to satisfy its customers' wants and needs while meeting the organisation's profit and other goals.

marketing dashboard see **dashboard**.

marketing decision support system a coordinated collection of data, systems, tools and techniques, with supporting software and hardware, by which an organisation gathers and interprets relevant information from business and the environment and turns it into a basis for marketing action.

marketing implementation the process that turns marketing plans into action assignments and ensures that such assignments are executed in a manner that accomplishes the plan's stated objectives.

marketing information system people, equipment and procedures to gather, sort, analyse, evaluate and distribute information to marketing decision makers.

marketing insights provide diagnostic information about how and why we observe certain effects in the marketplace, and what that means to marketers.

marketing intelligence system a set of procedures and sources that managers use to obtain everyday information about developments in the marketing environment.

marketing management the art and science of choosing target markets and getting, keeping and growing customers through creating, delivering and communicating superior customer value.

marketing metrics the set of measures that helps firms to quantify, compare and interpret their marketing performance.

marketing mix the marketing activities used to create, communicate and deliver value to the customer; there were originally four marketing mix variables expanded to seven to include the product/service, price, place, promotion, process, physical evidence and people.

marketing network the company and its supporting stakeholders, with whom it has built mutually profitable business relationships.

marketing opportunity an area of buyer need and interest in which there is a high probability that a company can profitably satisfy that need.

marketing philosophy see **marketing concept**.

marketing plan a written document that summarises what the marketer has learned about the marketplace, indicates how the firm plans to reach its marketing objectives, and helps direct and coordinate the marketing effort.

marketing public relations publicity and other activities that build corporate or brand image to facilitate marketing goals.

marketing research the systematic design, collection, analysis and reporting of data and findings relevant to a specific marketing situation facing the company.

market logistics planning the infrastructure to meet demand, then implementing and controlling the physical flows or materials and final goods from points of origin to points of use, to meet customer requirements at a profit.

market-management organisation where companies organise marketing activity to meet the needs of customers who fall into different user groups with distinct buying preferences and practices.

market mavens consumers possessing a broad expertise concerning many different products and decisions related to the marketplace.

market offering/product-mix pricing a set of prices that maximises profits on the total mix of products.

market opportunity analysis a system used to determine the attractiveness and probability of success.

market partitioning the process of investigating the hierarchy of attributes that consumers examine in choosing a brand if they use phased decision strategies.

market penetration index a comparison of the current level of market demand to the potential demand level.

market-penetration pricing a pricing strategy where prices start low to drive higher sales volume from price-sensitive customers and produce productivity gains.

marketplace a physical place of exchange, such as the shop you purchase in.

market potential the upper limit to market demand whereby increased marketing expenditures would not be expected to stimulate further demand.

market share the proportion of the available market that is being serviced by a company.

market-skimming pricing a pricing strategy where prices start high and are slowly lowered over time to maximise profits from less price-sensitive customers.

marketspace a digital place of exchange, such as when you buy online, conduct your banking online or use an ATM, or when you use a kiosk for booking, ordering or confirming.

market testing the limited and experiential trial of new market offerings prior to national or international roll-out.

mark-up pricing an item by adding a standard increase to the product's cost.

mass customisation the ability of a company to meet each customer's requirements – to prepare on a mass basis individually designed products, services, programmes and communications.

mass marketing when a seller engages in the mass production, distribution and promotion of one item for all buyers.

materials and parts goods that enter the manufacturer's product completely.

M-commerce allows people to connect to the Internet and place online orders through their mobile phones.

means–end chain a theory suggesting that products are not purchased for themselves or their characteristics, but rather for the meanings they engender in the mind of the consumer.

media selection finding the most cost-effective media to deliver the desired number and type of exposures to the target audience.

megamarketing the strategic coordination of economic, psychological, political and public relations skills, to gain the cooperation of a number of parties in order to enter or operate in a given market.

megatrends large social, economic, political and technological changes that are slow to form and, once in place, have an influence for seven to ten years or longer.

membership groups groups having a direct influence on a person.

memory encoding how and where information gets into memory.

memory retrieval how and from where information gets out of memory.

mental accounting the manner by which consumers code, categorise and evaluate financial outcomes of choices.

merchants intermediaries – such as wholesalers and retailers – who buy, take title to, and resell merchandise.

metamarket a cluster of complementary products and services that are closely related in the minds of consumers, but spread across a diverse set of industries.

metamediaries intermediaries that bring together collections of companies or people.

microsales analysis examination of specific products and territories that fail to produce expected sales.

microsite a limited area on the web managed and paid for by an external advertiser/company.

mission statements statements that organisations develop to share with managers, employees and (in many cases) customers.

mixed bundling the seller offers goods both individually and in bundles.

mobile commerce the use of the mobile phone to communicate with customers predominantly for service or purchases.

moment of truth an instance of contact or interaction between a customer and a company which gives the customer an opportunity to form or change their impression about the company.

motivator factors provide satisfaction and derive from the actual service or experience.

motive what drives consumers to act in order to reach a desired goal.

multibrand strategy involves having several brands in the same product category.

multichannel distribution systems occur when a single firm uses two or more marketing channels to reach customer segments. These are sometimes called hybrid channels.

multichannel strategy where the company has cross-channel benefits based on the management of multiple channels.

multi marketing channel strategy where the strategies and tactics of distribution and sales through one channel reflect the strategies and tactics of distribution and sales through other channels.

multiple channels strategy uses multiple channels but does not have a multichannel strategy across the channels.

multiplicity of channels the practice where customers seek information and products and service from an ever-increasing range of channels rather than just one.

multitasking doing two or more things at the same time. For instance, you may use a computer while listening to the radio.

N

net price analysis analysis that encompasses company list price, average discount, promotional spending and co-op advertising to arrive at net price.

network interlinks diverse members and each member has to reflect or be aware of other members and their needs.

network economy complex interacting sets of markets linked through exchange processes and driven by a dynamic and knowledge-rich technology-dominant environment.

network marketing aims to build mutually satisfying long-term relationships with key constituents in order to earn and retain their business.

non-compensatory models in consumer choice, when consumers do not simultaneously consider all positive and negative attribute considerations in making a decision.

non-durable goods offerings, usually termed fast-moving consumer goods (fmcgs), that are normally consumed in one or a few uses (e.g. beer and soap).

normative behaviour focuses on emotional rather than rational behaviour and involves shame, blame or pride; it uses peer pressure, norms of behaviour and other social influence to shape behaviour in the service environment.

O

online alliances and affiliate programs when one internet company works with another one and they advertise each other.

online branding digital or virtual world interactions supported by a variety of technologies; though the term is often used to refer to the internet, it includes any digital technology used.

online marketing uses a website to transact or facilitate the sale of products and services online.

open innovation where companies use external ideas as well as internal ideas, and internal and external paths to market.

operating margin the ratio of operating profit divided by net sales.

opinion leader the person in informal, product- or service-related communications who offers advice or information about a specific product or product category.

ordering ease how easy it is for the customer to place an order with the company.

organisation a company's structures, policies and corporate culture.

organisational buying the decision-making process by which formal organisations establish the need for purchased products and services, and identify, evaluate and choose among alternative brands and suppliers.

organisational context the way the organisation is structured and how it operates.

organisational design the process by which managers select and manage aspects of an organisation's structure and culture so that the organisation can control the activities necessary to achieve organisational goals.

organising the process of making sure the necessary human, physical, technological, financial and informational resources are available to carry out the plan which will achieve the organisational goals.

out-of-home advertising see **place advertising**.

outsourcing subcontracting a part of a company's operations such as product manufacturing, to a third-party company; the decision to outsource is often made in the interest of lowering costs as companies can often gain in effectiveness and efficiency by outsourcing to companies who can perform that task better and cheaper.

overall market share the company's sales expressed as a percentage of total market sales.

own-label brands brands that are created and owned by distributors and/or retailers.

P

packaging all the activities of designing and producing the container for a product or market offering.

paid-search advertisements (or pay-per-click advertisements) search terms that trigger relevant links to market offerings alongside search results from Google, MSN, Tiscali and Yahoo!. Advertisers pay only if people click on the links.

paradigm change a term used to describe the change from sellers' to a buyers' market environment experienced strongly by many business and organisations over the last two decades.

parent brand an existing brand that gives birth to a brand extension.

participative management style where the manager gives his staff and subordinates the chance to be involved in the decision making process.

partner relationship management activities the firm undertakes to build mutually satisfying long-term relations with key partners such as suppliers, distributors, ad agencies and marketing research suppliers.

pay-per-click advertisements see **paid-search advertisements**.

penetrated market the set of consumers who are buying a company's product or service.

people management the art of giving direction to people.

perceived value the value promised by the company's value proposition and perceived by the customer.

perception the process by which an individual selects, organises and interprets information inputs to create a meaningful picture of the world.

performance quality the level at which the product's or service's primary characteristics operate.

performance value the level at which the market offering's primary characteristic attributes operate.

personal communications channels two or more persons communicating directly face-to-face, person-to-audience, over the telephone, or through email.

personal influence the effect one person has on another's attitude or purchase probability.

personality a set of distinguishing human psychological traits that lead to relatively consistent responses to environmental stimuli.

personal selling face-to-face interaction with one or more prospective purchasers for the purpose of making presentations, answering questions and procuring orders.

physical evidence (the servicescape or experience environment) the surroundings where the service takes place – buildings, furnishing, layout, colour, packaging, signs, uniforms and products associated with the service, such as carrier bags, tickets, brochures and labels – which all combine to create the brand image desired.

place advertising (out-of-home advertising) ads that appear outside of home and where consumers work and play.

place branding see **country branding**.

planning the process of establishing goals and objectives and selecting a future course of action in order to achieve them; it involves figuring out how to achieve the overall goals.

point-of-purchase the location where a purchase is made, typically thought of in terms of a retail setting.

points-of-difference attributes or benefits that consumers strongly associate with a brand, positively evaluate, and believe they could not find to the same extent with a competing brand.

points-of-parity associations consumers make that are not unique to a brand and may be shared with other brands.

positioning the act of designing a company's customer/market offering and image to occupy a distinctive place in the minds of the target market.

potential market the set of consumers who profess a sufficient level of interest in a market offer.

potential product all the possible augmentations and transformations that the product or offering might undergo in the future.

price discrimination a company sells a product or service at two or more prices that do not reflect a proportional difference in costs.

price escalation an increase in the price of a product or service due to added costs of selling it in different countries.

primary groups groups with which a person interacts continuously and informally, such as family, friends, neighbours and co-workers.

principle of congruity a psychological mechanism that states that consumers like to see seemingly related objects as being as similar as possible in their favourability.

private label brand brands that retailers and wholesalers develop and market.

product anything that can be offered to a market to satisfy a want or need; it consists of a set of attributes, including physical goods, services, experiences, events, persons, places, properties, organisations, information and ideas.

product adaptation altering the product to meet local conditions or preferences.

product assortment the set of all products and items that a particular seller offers for sale.

product invention creating something new via product development or other means.

production concept the orientation within a company to focus on the product or service that the company makes or provides, rather than on a customer need.

production philosophy see **production concept**.

product map shows which competitors' items are competing against company X's items.

product mix see **product assortment**.

product penetration percentage the percentage of ownership or use of a product or service in a population.

product placement the deliberate placing of products and/or their logos in films and TV programmes, usually on a fee basis.

product portfolio the full range of products offered by a company.

product system a group of diverse but related items that function in a compatible manner.

profitable customer a person, household or company that over time yields a revenue stream that exceeds by an acceptable amount the company's cost stream of attracting, selling and servicing that customer.

prospecting searching for and seeking engagement with prospective customers.

prospect theory when consumers frame decision alternatives in terms of gains and losses according to a value function.

prosumers where the consumer moves from a passive role to an active role and becomes involved in the design and manufacture of products or services; the word is formed by linking the word 'producer' with the word 'consumer'.

psychographics the science of using psychology and demographics to better understand consumer market consumers.

public any group that has an actual or potential interest in or impact on a company's ability to achieve its objectives.

publicity the task of securing editorial space – as opposed to paid space – in print and broadcast media to promote something.

public relations a variety of programmes designed to promote or protect a company's image or its individual products or services.

pull strategy when the manufacturer uses advertising and promotion to persuade consumers to ask intermediaries for the product or service, thus inducing the intermediaries to order it.

purchase probability scale a scale to measure the probability of a buyer making a particular purchase.

pure bundling a firm only offers its products as a bundle.

pure-click companies that have launched a website without any previous existence as a firm.

push strategy when the manufacturer uses its sales force and trade promotion to induce intermediaries to carry, promote and sell the product and service to end users.

Q

QR code a matrix barcode (or two-dimensional code) that is readable by dedicated QR barcode readers, mobile phone cameras and, to a less common extent, computers with webcams; the QR code usually sends the user to a website.

questionnaire a set of questions that are presented to a number of respondents.

R

radio-frequency identification device a technology that uses radio waves to transfer data from an electronic tag, called an RFID tag or label, attached to an object, through a reader for the purpose of identifying and tracking the object.

reach the percentage of the target market exposed to an advertisement at least once during a specified period.

rebranding the changing of a brand or corporate name concept.

recession a general slowdown in economic activity over a sustained period of time, or a business cycle contraction.

reference groups all the groups that have a direct or indirect influence on a person's attitudes or behaviour.

reference prices pricing information that a consumer retains in memory which is used to interpret and evaluate a new price.

relational equity the cumulative value of the firm's network of relationships with its customers, partners, suppliers, employees and investors.

relationship marketing a form of marketing that places a strong emphasis on building a longer-term, more intimate bond between an organisation and its key customers.

relative market share market share in relation to a company's largest competitor.

reliability a measure of the probability that a product will not malfunction or will fail within a specified time period.

repairability a measure of the ease of fixing a product when it malfunctions or fails.

representativeness heuristic when consumers base their predictions on how representative or similar an outcome is to other examples.

results what have been accomplished, the actual outcome, the objective(s) attained.

retailer an intermediary that buys products either from manufactures or from wholesalers and resells them to consumers.

risk analysis a method by which possible rates of returns and their probabilities are calculated by obtaining estimates for uncertain variables affecting profitability.

role the activities a person is expected to perform.

S

sales analysis measuring and evaluating actual sales in relation to goals.

sales budget a conservative estimate of the expected volume of sales, used for making current purchasing, production and cash-flow decisions.

sales promotion a variety of short-term incentives to encourage trial or purchase of a product or service (market offering).

sales quota the sales goal set for a product or service, company division or sales representative.

sales-variance analysis a measure of the relative contribution of different factors to a gap in sales performance.

satisfaction a person's feelings of pleasure or disappointment resulting from comparing perceived performance or outcome in relation to his or her expectations.

scenario analysis developing plausible representations of a firm's possible future that make different assumptions about forces driving the market and include different uncertainties.

search engine optimisation attempts to discern patterns in search engine listings, and then to develop a methodology for improving rankings.

search-related ads advertisement in which search terms are used as a proxy for the consumer's consumption interests and relevant links to product or service offerings are listed alongside the search results.

secondary brand associations can create brand equity by linking the brand to other mental associations that convey meaning to consumers.

secondary groups groups which tend to be more formal and require less interaction than primary groups, such as religious, professional and trade union groups.

seeding the practice of purposely positioning a product or service within a blog.

selective attention the mental process of screening out certain stimuli while noticing others.

selective distortion the tendency to interpret information in a way that fits consumer perceptions.

selective distribution the use of more than a few but less than all of the intermediaries who are willing to carry a particular product or service.

selective retention the process of remembering only a small part of what a person is exposed to; people remember more accurately messages that are close to their interests, views and beliefs.

self-liquidating market offerings a form of merchandise based on sales promotion that invites the customer to part with cash and/or proof of purchase to obtain what appears to the customer to be a bargain buy, but which is also profitable to the provider.

self-service technologies provide customers with a technological interface which allows customers to produce services without direct service employee involvement.

sellers' market a market environment where the demand for goods (market offerings) is greater than the supply.

selling concept or philosophy a focus on making sales rather than really understanding customers. The selling concept suggests businesses have to persuade or force acustomers to buy the organisation's products or services.

served market all the buyers who are able and willing to buy a company's product or service.

served market share a company's sales expressed as a percentage of the total sales to its served market.

service any act or performance that one party can offer to another that is essentially intangible and is a process rather than a unit of output, focusing on dynamic resources such as skill or knowledge and an understanding of value as a collaborative process between providers and customers.

service blueprint a pictorial map of the essential components of the service performance.

service branding emphasises the integrative, reciprocal role of the brand that focuses on the value-adding processes.

service-level agreements formal service contracts (promise of service levels) normally agreed between companies.

service personnel any staff member that customers see or encounter, often called front-line staff.

service process the way in which the service system operates.

service process delivery by whom and how is the service to be delivered.

service process design describes and prescribes the procedures to be followed in service delivery.

service quality the perception the customer has of the level of service received; in general, the customer compares the perceived service with the expected service.

services traditionally viewed as intangible, inseparable, variable and perishable offerings, e.g. haircuts, legal advice and appliance repairs.

servicescape the impact on customer and employee behaviour of a service firm's physical surroundings or environment; it emphasises the importance of the physical environment in which a service process takes place.

shareholder value the value of the firm minus the future claims.

share penetration index a comparison of a company's current market share to its potential market share.

shopping goods goods that the consumer, in the process of selection and purchase, characteristically compares on such bases as suitability, quality, price and style.

short-term memory a temporary repository of information.

smartphone a mobile phone that offers more advanced computing ability and connectivity than a contemporary mobile phone and may be thought of as a handheld computer integrated with a mobile telephone.

social classes homogeneous and enduring divisions in a society, which are hierarchically ordered and whose members share similar values, interests and behaviour.

social marketing marketing done by a non-profit or government organisation to further a cause, such as 'say no to drugs'.

social media a group of internet-based applications that build on the ideological and technological foundations of Web 2.0 and that allow the creation and exchange of user-generated content.

social networking the grouping of individuals into specific groups, mostly carried out in its most popular form online.

social systems relates to the culture, shared norms and expectations within an organisation and also the use of power and influence. It can also reflect the informal networks or social relationships among organisational members.

spam the use of email to send unsolicited bulk messages indiscriminately.

specialities items with lower sales volume but which might be highly promoted or might generate income for services.

speciality goods goods that have unique characteristics or brand identification for which a sufficient number of buyers are willing to make a special purchasing effort.

sponsorships financial support of an event or activity in return for recognition and acknowledgement as the sponsor.

staffing dividing work into specific jobs and tasks, and specifying who has the authority to accomplish certain tasks.

stakeholder-performance scorecard a measure to track the satisfaction of various constituencies who have a critical interest in and impact on the company's performance.

standardisation means 'one size fits all' and helps keep costs low by using the same activities and reaching out to as many people as possible with the same marketing.

staples items with lower sales volume and no promotion that yield a somewhat higher margin.

status one's position within his or her own hierarchy or culture.

store image the positioning of a store in terms of its branding, merchandise offering, interior and exterior design, fixtures and fittings, lighting, etc.

straight extension introducing a product or service in a foreign market without any change in the product or service.

strategic brand management the design and implementation of marketing activities and programmes to build, measure and manage brands to maximise their value.

strategic business unit a single business or collection of related businesses that can be planned separately from the rest of the company, with its own set of competitors and a manager who is responsible for strategic planning and profit performance.

strategic group firms pursuing the same strategy directed to the same target market.

strategic marketing plan long-term decisions, such as the target markets, market position and value proposition that will be offered, based on analysis of the best market opportunities.

strategy a company's game plan for achieving its goals.

style a product's look and feel to the buyer.

sub-brand a new brand combined with an existing brand.

subculture subdivisions of a culture that provide more specific identification and socialisation, such as nationalities, religions, racial groups and geographical regions.

subliminal perception receiving and processing sub-conscious messages that affect behaviour.

supersegment a set of segments sharing some exploit-able similarity.

supplies and business services short-term goods and services that facilitate developing or managing the finished product.

supply chain set of three or more entities (organisations or individuals) directly involved in the upstream or downstream flows of product, service, finances and/or information from a source to a customer.

supply chain management procuring the right inputs (raw materials, components and capital equipment); converting them efficiently into finished products or services; and dispatching them to the final destinations.

supply network a system of partnerships and alliances that a firm creates to source, augment and deliver its offerings.

switchers consumers who are not loyal to any one brand within a market category.

T

tactical marketing plan related to the first year of the strategic plan, it is short term and gives specific actions. It is a highly detailed, heavily researched and well-written report that forces internally in order to understand fully the results of past marketing decisions; forces externally in order to understand fully the market in which it operates; sets future goals and provides direction for future marketing efforts that everyone within the organisation should understand and support. It is a key component in obtaining funding to pursue new initiatives.

talent management the skills of attracting highly skilled staff, integrating new staff, and developing and retaining current staff to meet current and future business objectives.

tangible product that part of a market offering that is composed of attributes that are permanent, including design, branding and product features; today's buyers' markets require the addition of intangible or service attributes to engage with and meet customers' expectations.

target costing deducting the desired profit margin from the price at which a market offering will sell, given its appeal and competitors' prices.

target market the part of the qualified available market that the company decides to pursue.

target-return pricing determining the price that would yield the firm's target rate of return on investment (ROI).

task competency having the skills required for a specific job/role.

team a group of people linked through a common purpose.

technology acceptance model a theory that regards an individual's psychological state with regard to his or her intended use of a particular technology.

technology management management concerned with exploring and understanding information technology as a corporate resource that determines both the strategic and operational capabilities of the firm in designing and developing products and services for maximum customer satisfaction, corporate productivity, profitability and competitiveness.

telemarketing the use of telephone and call centres to attract prospects, sell to existing customers, and provide service by taking orders and answering questions.

teleshopping a form of non-store retailing including shopping by telephone and via computer networks.

test marketing the restricted launch of a new market offering in a discrete area selected to be representative of the whole market.

theory of adaptation of innovation according to this theory the adaptation of an innovation depends on various factors such as, for instance, perceived capability and perceived relative advantage.

theory of planned behaviour a theory that regards a consumer's behaviour as determined by the consumer's behavioural intention, subjective norm and perceived behavioural control.

theory of reasoned action a theory that regards a consumer's behaviour as determined by the consumer's behavioural intention and subjective norm.

total costs the sum of the fixed and variable costs for any given level of production.

total customer benefit the perceived monetary value of the bundle of economic, functional and psychological benefits that customers expect from a given market offering because of the products, services, personnel and image involved.

total customer cost the bundle of costs that customers expect to incur in evaluating, obtaining, using and disposing of the given market offering, including monetary, time, energy and psychic costs.

total customer value the perceived monetary value of the bundle of economic, functional and psychological benefits that customers expect from a given market offering.

total market potential the maximum amount of sales that might be available to all the firms in an industry during a given period, under a given level of industry marketing effort and environmental conditions.

total quality management an organisation-wide approach to improving continuously the quality of all the organisation's processes, products and services.

touchpoints the many ways in which a customer comes into contact with the business.

tracking studies collecting information from consumers on a routine basis over time.

transaction a trade of values between two or more parties: A gives X to B and receives Y in return.

transaction costs include costs of obtaining relevant information, costs of evaluating relevant product, order costs, and the like.

transaction marketing attracting and satisfying potential buyers by managing the elements in the marketing mix, and actively managing communication 'to' buyers in the mass market in order to create discrete, arm's-length transactions.

transfer a gift, subsidy or charitable contribution: A gives X to B but does not receive anything tangible in return.

transfer price the price a company charges another unit in the company for goods it ships to foreign subsidiaries.

transformational appeal an appeal that elaborates on a non-market offering-related benefit or image.

trend a direction or sequence of events that has some momentum and durability.

two-part pricing a fixed fee plus a variable usage fee.

tying agreements agreement in which producers of strong brands sell their products to dealers only if dealers purchase related products or services, such as other products in the brand line.

U

undifferentiated marketing a market strategy where a company decides to ignore single market segments and seeks to develop a marketing mix for the whole market.

unsought goods those the consumer does not know about or does not normally think of buying, such as smoke detectors.

user-generated content any form of content such as video, blogs, discussion form posts, digital images, audio files and so on, created or posted by consumers or end-users and publicly available to other consumers and end-users.

V

value chain (value network) a company's supply of partnerships and alliances and how the company partners with specific suppliers, distributors, manufacturers and so on to source, create, augment and deliver products and services to the market; at each activity along the chain or within the network, the product or service gains either tangible or intangible value.

Value co-creation see co-creation.

value delivery system all the expectancies the customer will have on the way to obtaining and using the offering.

value network a system of partnerships and alliances that a firm creates to source, augment and deliver its offerings.

value pricing winning loyal customers by charging a fairly low price for a high-quality offering.

value proposition the whole cluster of benefits that the company promises to deliver.

variable costs costs that vary directly with the level of production.

venture team a cross-functional group charged with developing a specific product or business.

vertical integration a situation in which manufacturers try to control or own their suppliers, distributors or other intermediaries.

vertical marketing system producer, wholesaler(s) and retailer(s) acting as a unified system.

viral marketing any form of advertising and/or communication that spreads like a virus and is passed on from consumer to consumer and market to market; the use of the internet (particularly social networking sites) increases the speed and geographic coverage of these communications.

virtual world an online community that operates in an online simulated environment through which users can interact with one another using avatars.

W

warranties formal statements of expected product/market offering performance by the manufacturer.

weak theory of marketing communications a theory that assumes that marketing communications create an awareness of market offerings, but that attitudes and opinions are only created after a successful post-purchase experience.

Web 2.0 a collection of open-source, interactive and user-controlled online applications expanding the experiences, knowledge and market power of the users as participants in business and social processes.

Weber's law a rule saying that people are more likely to notice stimuli whose deviations are large in relationship to the normal size of the stimuli.

wholesaler an intermediary that buys in bulk from manufacturers with a view to reselling to customers, usually via retailers.

word-of-mouth marketing people-to-people oral, written or electronic communications that relate to the merits or experiences of purchasing and consuming market offerings.

Y

yield pricing a situation in which companies offer (1) discounted but limited early purchases, (2) higher-priced late purchases, and (3) the lowest rates on unsold inventory just before it expires.

Z

zero-level channel a manufacturer selling directly to the final customer.

zone of tolerance a range where a service dimension would be deemed satisfactory, anchored by the minimum level that consumers are willing to accept and the level they believe can and should be delivered.

Index

Organisation and brand index

Subject index

legal issues 724–5
levels 700–1
major alternatives 706–9
marketing *see* marketing channels
members 694, 708, 710–17
multiplicity 719–21
multipliers 495
partnerships 711–12
power 711, **966**
pricing 677
selection 789–90
service sector 701–3
service 15, 699
specialists 357
stewards 716
stewardship **966**
support 495
trade-offs 161, 162
charitable markets 19
charters, brands **965**
chatrooms 197, 225
checkouts 743
chief executive officers (CEO) 872,
907–9
children 251–2, 394–5, 743, 788
China 76, 532, 541–3
choice architecture 284
circulation, advertising 821
claims credibility, products 188–9
classical conditioning 265
classification of products 577–9
clickstreaming 225
clients becoming members 442
cliques 791
cloners 354
close competitors 339
closed questions 218–19
closing sales 852
club membership programmes
446, **966**
cluster samples 224
clustered preferences 368, **966**
clutter 777, 811, 814
CLV *see* customers: lifetime value
CMP (contemporary marketing
practice) 63–4
co-branding 477, 594–5, **966**
co-creation 11, 28, 450, 755–6, **966**
co-creators 701
coercive power 711
cognitive campaigns, social
marketing 888
cognitive resources 265–6
cognitive space 94
cognitive stages 781
cohorts 179–80, 381–3, **966**

collaborations 61–2, 134, 117
collection of data 54, 225–7
combo sites 198
comfortably well off consumers 25
commerce
mobile 155, **974**
sites 725
website design 844
commercial information
sources 271–2
commercialisation 639–41
common costs 900–1
commonality 803
communicability 402, 630, 644
communicating 847
communication-effect research
823–4, **966**
communications 134, 466
brand mantras 481
channels 15
co-branding based on **966**
corporate social responsibility 880
decoding 780
encoding 780
feedback 780
global 532
media 780
messages 780
model 781
noise 777, 780
receivers 780
responses 780
sales promotions 797
senders 789
skills 54
technologies 135
technology-based 697
website design 844
see also advertising; sales
promotions
communities 133
brands 520, 525–8, **965**
customers 726
digital brands 520, 525–8
engagement 522
global 529, **970**
online 757–8
website design 844
company costs 579
company demand 235, **966**
company-driven brand
communities 525
company environments 174, 177
company sales forecasts 235, **966**
company sales potential 235, **966**
comparative advertising 788

comparison websites 650
compatibility 162, 644
compensation 674, 723, 849
competencies 90–3, 94, 97–8, 753, 754
competent collaboration 61–2
competition 16, 23, 24, 330–1
analysis of competitors 336–41
balancing customer and competitor
orientations 357–9
definition 334
in economic downturns 359–60
five forces framework 332–3
identifying competitors 333–5
law, prices and 674
marketing channels 721–5
marketing plans 952–3
retailing 718
competitive advantage 90, 91–2, 142–4,
395, 409–10, 472, 755, **966**
competitive depositioning 275
competitive environments 532
competitive intelligence 196, 197, 197–8
competitive parity budgeting 794
competitive performance, improving
338–9
competitive points-of-parity 398–9
competitive strategies
customer analysis 339–40
frames of reference 397–8
increased product usage 344–5
market challengers 341, 350–3
market followers 341, 353–4
market leaders 341–3
market nichers 354–7
market share expansion 349–50
market share protection 345–9
new customer acquisition 343–4
total market expansion 343–5
see also niches
competitive superiority 495
competitor-centred companies 358
competitors 331–2
analysis 336–41
attacking 339, 350–3
competition orientation 357–9
costs 665
customers of, attracting 568
definition 333
global 532
identifying 333–5
marketing plans 952–3
objectives 336–7
offers 665
points-of-difference 398
prices 342–3, 665, 680–2
selecting 339